T0213384

Lecture Notes in Computer Science 10460

Commenced Publication in 1973
Founding and Former Series Editors:
Gerhard Goos, Juris Hartmanis, and Jan van Leeuwen

Luca Aceto · Giorgio Bacci
Giovanni Bacci · Anna Ingólfsdóttir
Axel Legay · Radu Mardare (Eds.)

Models, Algorithms, Logics and Tools

Essays Dedicated to Kim Guldstrand Larsen
on the Occasion of His 60th Birthday

 Springer

Editors

Luca Aceto
Reykjavik University
Reykjavik
Iceland

Anna Ingólfsdóttir
Reykjavík University
Reykjavik
Iceland

Giorgio Bacci (iD)
Aalborg University
Aalborg
Denmark

Axel Legay
Inria Campus Beaulieu
Rennes
France

Giovanni Bacci (iD)
Aalborg University
Aalborg
Denmark

Radu Mardare
Aalborg University
Aalborg
Denmark

ISSN 0302-9743   ISSN 1611-3349   (electronic)
Lecture Notes in Computer Science
ISBN 978-3-319-63120-2   ISBN 978-3-319-63121-9   (eBook)
DOI 10.1007/978-3-319-63121-9

Library of Congress Control Number: 2017946698

LNCS Sublibrary: SL1 – Theoretical Computer Science and General Issues

Cover illustration: The illustration appearing on the cover of this book represents the "Traffic Dilemma" problem originally stated by Bruyère et al. (Information and Computation, vol. 254(2), pp. 259–295) and encoded in UPPAAL Stratego by Marius Mikucionis. Used with permission.

Photograph on p. V: The photograph of the honoree was taken by Jiří Srba. Used with permission.

Printed on acid-free paper

This Springer imprint is published by Springer Nature
The registered company is Springer International Publishing AG
The registered company address is: Gewerbestrasse 11, 6330 Cham, Switzerland

Kim Guldstrand Larsen

One Step Ahead

It is with pleasure and pride that I congratulate Kim Guldstrand Larsen on his 60th birthday. I do so with pride because he represents my department and his achievements shed positive light on us all, and with pleasure because I have benefitted from his enthusiasm and insight since my own student days. In the early years of our university, there was a shortage of computer scientists and the concept of bootstrapping was illustrated in practice by letting the elder students teach the younger ones. This is where I first benefitted from Kim's insight and overview. The fundamentals of algorithms and data structures were described in an abstract, machine-independent language and were subsequently realized in Pascal. Nowadays this course is considered relatively difficult, but thanks to Kim it sharpened our interest for the core of our exciting field of science. Kim was one step ahead: not yet graduated, but already active in teaching the next generation.

Master level education was underway and our friends in mathematics played an important role in realizing the new studies. The major in computer science was introduced in the early 1980s, but Kim had already obtained his master's degree when it was formally approved. Hence, I can reveal that Kim is formally not a computer scientist, but a mathematician. One step ahead.

Computer science was consolidated in Denmark in those years and a number of Ph.D. stipends were granted to expand the field. It was discussed whether a stay abroad should be a requirement as part of a Ph.D. study and this is indeed the case today. I know that Kim approves of this decision, but he did not engage in the local discussion at the time. He was in Edinburgh doing his doctoral studies — one step ahead.

During the following three decades, the establishment of research activities became the focus area and, with the emergence of the UPPAAL tool and the formation of the Center for Embedded Software Systems, Kim became internationally recognized for useful and influential contributions. Since then, Kim has been heading numerous national and international projects that have impacted science and society. This is reflected in substantial recognitions, including two honorary doctorates, the CAV Award, the Grundfos Prize, and an advanced grant from the European Research Council. Kim is also Knight of the Order of the Dannebrog and member of national and international science academies. He is always on the move, always one step ahead.

Dear Kim. We congratulate you and salute you. And, should we lose sight of you, we know where to look — one step ahead.

May 2017

Kristian G. Olesen
Head of the Dept. of Computer Science, Aalborg University

Preface

Time flows by and many of us often have the feeling that its speed increases with every passing day. However, it is almost unbelievable that Kim Guldstrand Larsen will turn 60 this year. Indeed, despite the passing of time and his seemingly ever-increasing number of research projects to manage, research ideas to pursue, students to supervise, courses to give, invited talks to deliver, grant applications to write, and trips to make, Kim maintains the youthful enthusiasm, energy, and drive he had when he started as a young researcher about 30 years ago. Since then, he has built a truly remarkable research career and has offered a crucial contribution in making the Department of Computer Science at Aalborg University a very well respected center for research in concurrency theory, computer-aided verification, and the design and analysis of embedded software systems amongst others.

During the last three decades, Kim Guldstrand Larsen has made major contributions across a remarkably wide range of topics, including real-time, concurrent, and probabilistic models of computation, logic in computer science, and model checking. His work is characterized by a harmonious blend of theory, practice, and concern for industrial application, and it has been instrumental in making connections between different research areas and communities. For example, since 1995, he has been one of the prime movers behind the model-checking tool for real-time systems UPPAAL, for which he was a co-recipient of the CAV Award in 2013, and co-founder of the company UP4ALL International.

The influence of his work within the research community is witnessed, for instance, by the over 22,000 citations to his published papers and his h-index of 71, according to Google Scholar. Moreover, he was the recipient of the Danish Citation Laureates Award (Thomson Scientific) as the most cited Danish Computer Scientist in the period 1990–2004. Among his many seminal contributions, we recall the introduction of *Probabilistic Modal Logic* (PML) and a simple test language for checking the equivalence of probabilistic transition systems. In the same work from 1989, he contributed with the notion of *probabilistic bisimulation*, one of the most influential equivalences for reasoning about the behavior of probabilistic systems quantitatively. One year earlier, Kim introduced the very influential notion of *modal transition system*, a simple, yet powerful, specification formalism with a clear and elegant operational interpretation that allows for model refinement. Since its introduction, variations on the model of modal transition system have played a key rôle in a variety of fields including the study of interface theories and the synthesis of supervisory controllers. Other very significant research contributions by Kim include work on local model checking for the modal μ-calculus, compositional verification methodologies, symbolic model checking and, most recently, statistical model checking. By way of example, we mention the development of the so-called *compositional backward reachability technique* for the algorithmic analysis of models consisting of parallel compositions of hierarchical finite-state machines, which allowed for the verification of models with up to 1421 concurrent state machines and 10^{476} states.

The aforementioned contributions would be sufficient for several very successful research careers. However, most of Kim G. Larsen's work since 1995 can be related in some form or other to the development and application of UPPAAL, which is the foremost tool suite for the verification of real-time systems modeled as networks of timed automata.

UPPAAL has its roots in a tool originally developed in Uppsala and described in the conference paper *"Automatic Verification of Real-Time Communicating Systems by Constraint-Solving"* co-authored by Wang Yi, Paul Pettersson, and Mads Daniels (proceedings of FORTE 1994). Since then, UPPAAL has been jointly developed by Kim G. Larsen's research group at Aalborg University and by the group led by Wang Yi at Uppsala University. In this period, UPPAAL has become an industrial-strength tool for computer-aided verification of computing systems that has been applied to many case studies by several research groups in academia and industry. The efficiency of its computational engine has been improved greatly by theoretical and practical advances relying on highly non-trivial insights. Moreover, the tool now supports the analysis of quantitative extensions of timed automata, automatic model-based testing of real-time systems, and the synthesis of controllers in the context of timed games, amongst other things.

Overall, the UPPAAL tool is a real success story for the research community working on automated verification of computer systems. Like all long-term research and tool development efforts, the work on UPPAAL and its applications is due to many gifted researchers and their students. However, the creativity, vision, originality, important investment of time and effort, and the enormous drive and enthusiasm of Kim G. Larsen have played a crucial rôle in this success. Moreover, from the very beginning of the development of the tool, Kim applied UPPAAL to solve problems of relevance to industry, thus providing very successful examples of the holy grail for many computer science researchers, namely, the transfer of research results to industry. Indeed, UPPAAL has been applied to many industrial case studies. Here we limit ourselves to mentioning a few high-profile examples and invite the reader to consult the UPPAAL website for more recent ones.

- In 1996, the tool UPPAAL was used to carry out the automatic analysis of a version of the Philips Audio Control Protocol with two senders and bus collision handling. This case study was significantly larger than the real-time/hybrid systems previously analyzed using automatic tools. As written by Clarke and Wing in their article *"Formal Methods: State of the Art and Future Directions,"* this work completed "the quest of fully automating a human proof that as little as two years ago was considered far out of reach for algorithmic methods."
- In breakthrough work from 1997, Havelund, Larsen, and Skou used UPPAAL in the analysis of a protocol used by Bang & Olufsen to control the transmission of messages between audio/video components over a single bus. Although the protocol was known to be faulty, in that messages were lost occasionally, Bang & Olufsen were unable to detect the error using standard testing approaches. However, using UPPAAL, a shortest error trace consisting of 1998 basic transition steps was

automatically generated, and Larsen and his group were able to propose a corrected version of the protocol. This work is an elegant demonstration of the impact that UPPAAL has had on practical software development. The effort of modeling this protocol has, in addition, generated a number of suggestions for enriching the modeling language supported by UPPAAL. Hence, it is also an excellent example of the reverse impact.

- UPPAAL has been used to synthesize schedules for the SIDMAR steel production plant located at Ghent in Belgium and to analyze memory management for radars developed by Terma.
- In the European project Quasimodo (2008–2011), UPPAAL and its derivatives were applied to wireless sensor network protocols from Chess IT. Frits Vaandrager's group in Nijmegen discovered subtle timing issues in the MAC-layer protocols for certain network topologies by model checking with UPPAAL. These issues could be demonstrated on a real sensor network with the help of UPPAAL's automatic test generation tools.
- In the same project, Kim, with Jean-François Raskin et al., applied UPPAAL TiGa —based on Timed Games— to a plastic injection molding machine from Hydac GMBH, in order to synthesize a safe, robust, and optimal control for this hybrid system. They achieved 45% improvement in efficiency compared with a classic controller and a 33% gain with respect to Hydac's hand-made controller.

In addition, UPPAAL is being used in the teaching of various courses at several universities in the world and computer science students become acquainted with the tool even during their first year of study! For example, Roelof Hamberg and Frits Vaandrager have used the UPPAAL model checker in an introductory course on operating systems for first-year computer science students at the Radboud University Nijmegen. Using UPPAAL, their students have found mistakes in purported solutions to concurrency-control problems presented by Allen Downey in his popular textbook *The Little Book of Semaphores*. Moreover, Luca Aceto and Anna Ingólfsdóttir have successfully used the tool in a first-year, flipped-teaching course on modeling and verification at Reykjavik University. We believe that this pedagogical impact of the tool is important, as the use of UPPAAL may help current and future generations of computer science students develop an appreciation for computer-aided verification early on in their career.

The fact that Kim was one of the earliest precursors of Computer Science in Denmark makes his accomplishments even more impressive and provides yet another illustration of his quality as a researcher. We consider ourselves lucky to have had the pleasure to work with him at different stages of our research careers, as have many of the contributors to this volume. What better way to celebrate Kim's 60th birthday than this Festschrift with a large variety of papers dedicated to him and with a two-day workshop, the KiMfest, featuring a diverse range of speakers, held in Aalborg in his honor in August 2017.

We thank the authors for their contributions to this Festschrift and also for their help with the reviewing process. We are also thankful to the other external reviewers. We are grateful to Jiří Srba for providing us with the picture of Kim at the beginning of this volume. We also thank Alfred Hofmann for his support and help in producing this

Festschrift. Rikke W. Uhrenholt deserves our special thanks for helping in the organization of the KiMfest, the workshop in honor of Kim G. Larsen on the occasion of his 60th birthday. We also acknowledge the support we received from the Department of Computer Science at Aalborg University and the Technical Faculty of IT and Design.

May 2017

Luca Aceto
Giorgio Bacci
Giovanni Bacci
Anna Ingólfsdóttir
Axel Legay
Radu Mardare

Organization

Program Committee

Luca Aceto	Reykjavik University, Iceland
Giorgio Bacci	Aalborg University, Denmark
Giovanni Bacci	Aalborg University, Denmark
Anna Ingolfsdottir	Reykjavik University, Iceland
Axel Legay	IRISA/Inria Rennes, France
Radu Mardare	Aalborg University, Denmark

Additional Reviewers

Baig, Hasan
Basset, Nicolas
Benes, Nikola
Biondi, Fabrizio
Bouyer, Patricia
Caillaud, Benoît
Callia D'Iddio, Andrea
Cassel, Sofia
Decker, Normann
Della Monica, Dario
Dimovski, Aleksandar S.
Droste, Manfred
Enevoldsen, Søren
Fahrenberg, Uli
Falcone, Ylies
González De Aledo, Pablo
Götze, Doreen
Hahn, Ernst Moritz

Havelund, Klaus
Hennessy, Matthew
Huth, Michael
Jansen, Nils
Jensen, Peter Gjøl
Jéron, Thierry
Katoen, Joost-Pieter
Klaedtke, Felix
Klüppelholz, Sascha
Křetínský, Jan
Lamprecht, Anna-Lena
Maler, Oded
Mariegaard, Anders
Merro, Massimo
Morichetta, Andrea
Muniz, Marco
Nielson, Flemming
Norman, Gethin

Nyman, Ulrik
Olsen, Petur
Peressotti, Marco
Quilbeuf, Jean
Raskin, Jean-François
Sankur, Ocan
Schivo, Stefano
Steffen, Bernhard
Tesei, Luca
Traonouez, Louis-Marie
Tribastone, Mirco
Tschaikowski, Max
van Breugel, Franck
van de Pol, Jaco
Vandin, Andrea
Wasowski, Andrzej
Wunderlich, Sascha
Zhu, Huibiao

Contents

Real-Time and Distributed Systems

Modeling and Simulation

Formal Languages and Automata Theory

Information Flow for Timed Automata

Flemming Nielson$^{(\boxtimes)}$, Hanne Riis Nielson, and Panagiotis Vasilikos

Department of Applied Mathematics and Computer Science,
Technical University of Denmark, Kongens Lyngby, Denmark
{fnie,hrni,panva}@dtu.dk

Abstract. One of the key demands of cyberphysical systems is that they meet their safety goals. *Timed Automata* has established itself as a formalism for modelling and analysing the real-time safety aspects of cyberphysical systems. Increasingly it is also demanded that cyberphysical systems meet a number of security goals for confidentiality and integrity. *Information Flow Control* is an approach to ensuring that there are no flows of information that violate the stated security policy.

We develop a language based approach to the modelling and analysis of timed systems that allows to incorporate considerations of information flow control. We define a type system for information flow that takes account of the non-determinism and clocks of timed systems. The adequacy of the type system is ensured by means of a non-interference result.

1 Introduction

Motivation. Embedded systems are key components of cyberphysical systems and are often subject to stringent safety goals. Among the current approaches to the modelling and analysis of timed systems, the approach of *Timed Automata* [3] stands out as being a very successful approach with well-developed tool support – in particular the *UPPAAL* suite [16] of tools.

As cyberphysical systems become increasingly distributed and interconnected through wireless communication links it becomes even more important to ensure that they meet suitable security goals. This may involve safeguarding the confidentiality (or privacy) of sensor data or ensuring the integrity (or authenticity) of control commands; in both cases we need to limit the way information flows through the program. *Information Flow Control* [9,17] is a key approach to ensuring that software systems admit no flow of information that violate the stated security policy for confidentiality and/or integrity.

Contribution. It is therefore natural to extend the enforcement of safety properties of Timed Automata with the enforcement of appropriate Information Flow policies. It is immediate that the treatment of *clocks* will pose a challenge. It turns out that the *non-determinism* inherent in automata poses another challenge. More fundamentally there is the challenge that Timed Automata is an

© Springer International Publishing AG 2017
L. Aceto et al. (Eds.): Larsen Festschrift, LNCS 10460, pp. 3–21, 2017.
DOI: 10.1007/978-3-319-63121-9_1

automata based formalism whereas most approaches to Information Flow take a language based approach by developing type systems for programming languages or process calculi.

Consequently we take a language based approach to the study of timed systems. We adapt the Guarded Commands language of Dijkstra [10] to more closely correspond to the primitives of the Timed Automata formalism – resulting in the *Timed Command* language – and we show how to obtain Timed Automata from programs in Timed Commands. We then develop a type system for enforcing an Information Flow policy on programs in Timed Commands – the main novelty being our treatment of non-determinism. We demonstrate the adequacy of the type system by means of a non-interference result [17,18]. Throughout we demonstrate the development on a simple voting protocol.

Related Work. There are other papers dealing with Information Flow on systems with a notion of time. Discrete time is considered in [11] that develops a non-interference property based on bisimulations of processes from a discrete time process algebra. A somewhat different direction in taken in [2] where a transformational type system is used to remove discrete timing as a covert channel for deterministic programs. Our contribution focuses on the challenges of continuous time and guarded actions of Timed Automata.

Continuous time is considered in [6] and [7] that present a notion of a timed non-interference for timed automata, while the work of [13] defines a notion of timed non-interference based on bisimulations for probabilistic timed automata. Our contribution considers a model closer to the Timed Automata of UPPAAL [16] and the development of a type system. A somewhat different approach is taken in [12] that studies the synthesis of controllers. Our key contribution is to develop a type system that prevents unnecessary *label creep* (where the boolean conditions passed exercise information flow to all variables subsequently used) and that deals with *non-determinism*, *non-termination* and *continuous real-time*.

2 Timed Automata

A *Timed Automaton* [1,3] TA consists of a set of nodes Q, a set of annotated edges E, and a labelling function I on nodes. A node $q_\circ \in Q$ will be the initial node and a node $q_\bullet \in Q$ will be the final node; often $q_\bullet$ is intended not to be reachable. The mapping I maps each node in Q to a condition (to be introduced below) that will be imposed as an invariant at the node; we sometimes write dom(I) for Q and TA $= (E, I)$ or TA $= (E, I, q_\circ, q_\bullet)$.

The edges are annotated with actions and take the form $(q_s, g \rightarrow act\colon r, q_t)$ where *act* is given by

$$act\colon\colon = x := e \mid \text{publish } e$$

and $q_s \in Q$ is the source node and $q_t \in Q$ is the target node. The action $g \rightarrow x := e\colon r$ consists of a guard g that has to be satisfied in order for the multiple assignments $x := e$ to be performed and the clock variables r to be reset. We shall assume that the sequences x and e of program variables and

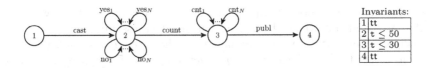

cast: $\rightarrow \mathbf{x}_1, ..., \mathbf{x}_N, \mathbf{y}_1, ..., \mathbf{y}_N, \mathbf{v}_1, ..., \mathbf{v}_N, \mathbf{c}:=0:$ t yes_i: $t < 50 \wedge \mathbf{x}_i = 0 \rightarrow \mathbf{x}_i, \mathbf{v}_i:=1, 1:$
count: $t = 50 \rightarrow : t$ no_i: $t < 50 \wedge \mathbf{x}_i = 0 \rightarrow \mathbf{x}_i, \mathbf{v}_i:=1, 0:$
publ: $t = 30 \rightarrow$ publish c: t cnt_i: $t < 30 \wedge \mathbf{x}_i = 1 \wedge \mathbf{y}_i = 0 \rightarrow \mathbf{y}_i, \mathbf{c}:=1, \mathbf{c} + \mathbf{v}_i:$

Fig. 1. The timed automaton VP (and the abbreviations used).

expressions, respectively, have the same length and that $\boldsymbol{x}$ does not contain any repetitions. To cater for special cases we shall allow to omit the assignments of $g \rightarrow \boldsymbol{x}:=\boldsymbol{e}$: $\boldsymbol{r}$ when $\boldsymbol{x}$ (and hence $\boldsymbol{e}$) is empty; also we shall allow to omit the guard g when it equals tt and to omit the clock resets when $\boldsymbol{r}$ is empty. The action $g \rightarrow$ publish $\boldsymbol{e}$: r is fairly similar, the main difference being that no assignments are performed – the role of this action will become clear later when we discuss the security policies.

It has already emerged that we distinguish between (program) variables x and clock variables (or simply clocks) r. We write R for the set of clocks. The expressions e, guards g and conditions c are defined as follows using boolean tests b:

$$e ::= e_1 \, \mathsf{op}_a \, e_2 \mid x \mid n$$
$$b ::= \mathsf{tt} \mid \mathsf{ff} \mid e_1 \, \mathsf{op}_r \, e_2 \mid \neg b \mid b_1 \wedge b_2$$
$$g ::= b \mid r \, \mathsf{op}_c \, n \mid (r_1 - r_2) \, \mathsf{op}_c \, n \mid g_1 \wedge g_2$$
$$c ::= b \mid r \, \mathsf{op}_d \, n \mid (r_1 - r_2) \, \mathsf{op}_d \, n \mid c_1 \wedge c_2$$

The arithmetic operators op_a and the relational operators op_r are as usual. For comparisons of clocks we use the operators $\mathsf{op}_c \in \{<, \leq, =\geq, >\}$ in guards and the less permissive set of operators $\mathsf{op}_d \in \{<, \leq, =\}$ in conditions.

Example 1. To illustrate our development we shall consider the voting protocol given by the timed automaton VP of Fig. 1. The protocol has N voters and three phases: casting (all edges leading to node number 2), counting (all edges leading to node number 3) and publishing (the edge leading to node number 4). For the casting phase a voter can choose to vote either yes ($\mathbf{v}_i = 1$) or no ($\mathbf{v}_i = 0$), or not to vote at all; $\mathbf{x}_i$ indicates whether or not the voter has voted. In the counting phase the votes are being counted using the variable c; here $\mathbf{y}_i$ indicates whether the vote has been counted or not. Finally at the end of the counting phase the result is published. The clock t bounds the duration of the different phases of the protocol as expressed by the invariants of the nodes.

To specify the semantics of timed automata let σ be a state mapping variables to values (which we take to be integers) and let δ be a clock assignment mapping clocks to non-negative reals. We then have total semantic functions $[\![\cdot]\!]$ for evaluating the expressions, boolean tests, guards and conditions; the values of the expressions and boolean expressions only depend on the states whereas that of guards and conditions also depend on the clock assignments.

The configurations of the timed automata have the form $\langle q, \sigma, \delta \rangle$ and we have transitions of two forms. Whenever $(q_s, g \rightarrow act\colon r, q_t)$ is in E we have the *instant* rule:

$$\langle q_s, \sigma, \delta \rangle \;\longrightarrow\; \langle q_t, \sigma', \delta' \rangle \text{ if } \begin{cases} [\![g]\!](\sigma, \delta) = \mathsf{tt}, \\ \sigma' = [\![act]\!]\sigma, \delta' = \delta[r \mapsto \mathbf{0}], \\ [\![\mathsf{I}(q_t)]\!](\sigma', \delta') = \mathsf{tt} \end{cases}$$

Whenever q is in Q we have a *delay* rule:

$$\langle q, \sigma, \delta \rangle \;\longrightarrow\; \langle q, \sigma, \delta' \rangle \text{ if } \begin{cases} \exists d > 0 : \delta' = \lambda r.\, \delta(r) + d, \\ [\![\mathsf{I}(q_s)]\!](\sigma, \delta') = \mathsf{tt} \end{cases}$$

The instant rule ensures that the guard is satisfied in the starting configuration and updates the mappings σ and δ and finally it ensures that the invariant is satisfied in the resulting configuration. Here the semantics of actions is given by $[\![x := e]\!]\sigma = \sigma[x \mapsto [\![e]\!]\sigma]$ (using the notation $\cdot[\cdot \mapsto \cdot]$) whereas $[\![\mathsf{publish}\ e]\!]\sigma = \sigma$. The delay rule only modifies the clock assignment with a delay d while ensuring that the invariant is satisfied in the resulting configuration. Initial configurations assume that all clocks are initialised to 0 and have the form $\langle q_\circ, \sigma, \lambda r.0 \rangle$ where $[\![\mathsf{I}(q_\circ)]\!](\sigma, \lambda r.0) = \mathsf{tt}$.

Trace Behaviour. We do not want to admit Zeno behaviours nor do we want to admit systems that delay forever. We therefore combine the instant and delay rules into a *joint* rule that effectively first performs a number of delay rules (possibly none) and then an instant rule. So whenever $(q_s, g \rightarrow act\colon r, q_t)$ is in E we have:

$$\langle q_s, \sigma, \delta \rangle \;\Longrightarrow\; \langle q_t, \sigma', \delta' \rangle \text{ if } \exists d \geq 0 : \begin{cases} [\![g]\!](\sigma, (\delta + d)) = \mathsf{tt}, \\ \sigma' = [\![act]\!]\sigma, \delta' = (\delta + d)[r \mapsto \mathbf{0}], \\ [\![\mathsf{I}(q_s)]\!](\sigma, \delta + d) = \mathsf{tt}, [\![\mathsf{I}(q_t)]\!](\sigma', \delta') = \mathsf{tt} \end{cases}$$

where $\delta + d$ abbreviates $\lambda r.\, \delta(r) + d$. Here we use that it suffices to test the condition at the beginning and at the end of the periods of delay, because a condition c satisfies that if $[\![c]\!](\sigma, \delta)$ and $[\![c]\!](\sigma, \delta + d + d')$ for $d, d' \geq 0$ then also $[\![c]\!](\sigma, \delta + d)$.

We define a *trace* from $\langle q_s, \sigma, \delta \rangle$ to q_t in a timed automaton TA to have one of three forms. It may be a finite "successful" sequence

$$\langle q_s, \sigma, \delta \rangle = \langle q_0', \sigma_0', \delta_0' \rangle \Longrightarrow \cdots \Longrightarrow \langle q_n', \sigma_n', \delta_n' \rangle$$
$$\text{such that } \{n\} = \{i \mid q_i' = q_t \wedge 0 < i \leq n\}.$$

in which case at least one step is performed. It may be a finite "unsuccessful" sequence

$$\langle q_s, \sigma, \delta \rangle = \langle q_0', \sigma_0', \delta_0' \rangle \Longrightarrow \cdots \Longrightarrow \langle q_n', \sigma_n', \delta_n' \rangle$$
$$\text{such that } \langle q_n', \sigma_n', \delta_n' \rangle \text{ is stuck and } q_t \notin \{q_1', \cdots, q_n'\}$$

where $\langle q'_n, \sigma'_n, \delta'_n \rangle$ is stuck when there is no joint action starting from $\langle q'_n, \sigma'_n, \delta'_n \rangle$. Finally, it may be an infinite "unsuccessful" sequence

$$\langle q_s, \sigma, \delta \rangle = \langle q'_0, \sigma'_0, \delta'_0 \rangle \Longrightarrow \cdots \Longrightarrow \langle q'_n, \sigma'_n, \delta'_n \rangle \Longrightarrow \cdots$$
$$\text{such that } q_t \notin \{q'_1, \cdots, q'_n, \cdots\}.$$

We may summarise the *trace behaviour* $[\![\text{TA} : q_s \mapsto q_t]\!](\sigma, \delta)$ of all traces from $\langle q_s, \sigma, \delta \rangle$ to q_t in the timed automaton TA by defining:

$[\![\text{TA} : q_s \mapsto q_t]\!](\sigma, \delta) =$
    $\{(\sigma', \delta') \mid$ a successful trace from $\langle q_s, \sigma, \delta \rangle$ to q_t in TA ends in $\langle q_t, \sigma', \delta' \rangle\}$
    $\cup \{\perp \mid$ there is an unsuccessful trace from $\langle q_s, \sigma, \delta \rangle$ to q_t in TA$\}$

The only behaviour not accounted for by this definition is the potential delay in q_t and the potential joint actions starting from q_t.

3 Information Flow

We envisage that there is a security lattice expressing the permissible flows [9]. Formally this is a complete lattice and the permitted flows go in the direction of the partial order. In our development it will contain just two elements, L (for low) and H (for high), and we set $L \sqsubseteq H$ so that only the flow from H to L is disallowed. For confidentiality one would take L to mean public and H to mean private and for integrity one would take L to mean trusted and H to mean dubious. A more general development might consider a richer security lattice encompassing the Decentralized Label Model [14].

Example 2. Returning to the voting protocol of Example 1 we shall assume that the variables x_i (indicating whether or not the i'th participant has voted) and y_i (indicating whether or not the vote of the i'th participant has been counted) are public whereas the variables v_i (the actual vote of the i'the participant) and c (the result of the voting) are private. We shall consider it natural to let the clock t be public as well.

A *security policy* is then expressed by a mapping $\mathcal{L}$ that assigns an element of the security lattice to each program variable, clock variable, and node (i.e. program point). An entity is called *high* if it is mapped to H by $\mathcal{L}$, and it is said to be *low* if it is mapped to L by $\mathcal{L}$.

Example 3. Returning to the voting protocol of Examples 1 and 2 we shall let the security policy $\mathcal{L}$ map the variables x_i and y_i and the clock t to the low security level (L), while it maps v_i and c to the high security level (H). Furthermore, $\mathcal{L}$ maps all nodes to the low security level (L).

To express adherence to the security policy we use the binary operation $\rightsquigarrow$ defined on sets χ and χ' (of variables, clocks and nodes):

$$\chi \rightsquigarrow \chi' \Leftrightarrow \forall u \in \chi : \forall u' \in \chi' : \mathcal{L}(u) \sqsubseteq \mathcal{L}(u')$$

This expresses that all the entities of χ may flow into those of χ'; note that if one of the entities of χ has a high security level then it must be the case that all the entities of χ' have high security level.

Information flow control enforces a security policy by imposing constraints of the form $\{y\} \rightsquigarrow \{x\}$ whenever the value of y may somehow influence (or flow into) that of x. Traditionally we distinguish between *explicit* and *implicit* flows as explained below.

As an example of an *explicit* flow consider a simple assignment of the form $x := e$. This gives rise to a condition $\mathsf{fv}(e) \rightsquigarrow \{x\}$ so as to indicate that the *explicit* flow from the variables of e to the variable x must adhere to the security policy: if e contains a variable with high security level then x also must have high security level.

For an example of an *implicit* flow consider a conditional assignment $g \rightarrow x := 0$ where x is assigned the constant value 0 in case g evaluates to true. This gives rise to a condition $\mathsf{fv}(g) \rightsquigarrow \{x\}$ so as to indicate that the *implicit* flow from the variables of g to the variable x must adhere to the security policy: if g contains a variable with high security level then x also must have high security level. (If used indiscriminately this gives rise to *label creep* where variables tend to have to be given the high security classification.)

In this paper we develop an approach to ensuring that the security policy is adhered to by the Timed Automaton of interest. The key idea is to ensure that $\{x\} \rightsquigarrow \{y\}$ whenever there is an *explicit* flow of information from x to y (as illustrated above) or an *implicit* flow from x to y; traditionally, implicit flows arise because of testing guards and conditions, but we shall see that the highly nondeterministic nature of Timed Automata provide yet another contribution. We shall say that we prevent information flows from high variables to low variables.

To overcome the vagueness of this explanation we need to define a semantic condition that encompasses our notion of permissible information flow. We begin by defining $(\sigma, \delta) \equiv (\sigma', \delta')$ to indicate that the two pairs are equal on low variables and low clocks:

$$(\sigma, \delta) \equiv (\sigma', \delta') \quad \text{iff} \quad \begin{aligned} &\forall x : \mathcal{L}(x) = L \Rightarrow \sigma(x) = \sigma'(x) \wedge \\ &\forall r : \mathcal{L}(r) = L \Rightarrow \delta(r) = \delta'(r) \end{aligned}$$

To cater for the $\perp$ behaviour produced by the trace behaviour we shall allow to write $\perp \equiv \perp$ and take it for granted that $\perp \not\equiv (\sigma, \delta)$ and $(\sigma, \delta) \not\equiv \perp$. It is immediate that this definition of $\equiv$ gives rise to an equivalence relation.

We next lift the operation $\equiv$ to work on sets:

$$\Gamma \equiv \Gamma' \quad \text{iff} \quad \begin{aligned} &\forall \gamma \in \Gamma : \exists \gamma' \in \Gamma' : \gamma \equiv \gamma' \wedge \\ &\forall \gamma' \in \Gamma' : \exists \gamma \in \Gamma : \gamma \equiv \gamma' \end{aligned}$$

Here γ ranges over pairs (σ, δ) as well as $\perp$, and it is immediate that this definition of $\equiv$ gives rise to an equivalence relation.

We can now express our semantic condition for when a Timed Automaton $\mathsf{TA} = (\mathsf{E},\mathsf{I})$ satisfies the Information Flow security policy by the condition:

$$(\sigma,\delta) \equiv (\sigma',\delta') \;\wedge\; [\![\mathsf{I}(q_\circ)]\!](\sigma,\delta) \;\wedge\; [\![\mathsf{I}(q_\circ)]\!](\sigma',\delta')$$
$$\Downarrow$$
$$[\![(\mathsf{E},\mathsf{I}) : q_\circ \mapsto q_\bullet]\!](\sigma,\delta) \equiv [\![(\mathsf{E},\mathsf{I}) : q_\circ \mapsto q_\bullet]\!](\sigma',\delta')$$

It says that if we consider two initial configurations that only differ on high variables and clocks then the final configurations are also only allowed to differ on high variabels and clocks; it is immediate that the final configurations (except $\bot$) also satisfy $\mathsf{I}(q_\bullet)$. In other words, there is no information flow from the initial values of high variables and clocks to the final values of low variables and clocks. The fact that the trace behaviour produces a set of configurations means that we take due care of non-determinism, and the fact that the trace behaviour may contain $\bot$ means that we take due care of non-termination (be it because of looping or because of getting stuck).

This semantic condition is more involved than in classical papers like [17] due to the highly non-deterministic nature of Timed Automata. As an example of the difficulties of treating non-determinism, the previous attempt of [5] is flawed because a command may terminate as well as loop – this was pointed out in [17, Sect. 7] which therefore performs a development for deterministic programs only. For another example, illustrating one of the problems solved by our type system, consider the program $y > 0 \rightarrow skip\ []\ \mathbf{tt} \rightarrow x := 0$ making a non-deterministic choice between two guarded actions. Writing $x \not\rightarrow y$ to indicate that y does not depend on x, the type system of [5] allows to establish

$$\vdash_1 \{x \not\rightarrow y, y \not\rightarrow x\}\, y > 0 \rightarrow skip\ []\ \mathbf{tt} \rightarrow x := 0\, \{y \not\rightarrow x\}$$

which is unsound. To see this note that for $\sigma_1 = [y \mapsto 1, x \mapsto 2]$ the final values of x can be 0 and 2, while for $\sigma_2 = [y \mapsto 0, x \mapsto 2]$, the final value of x can only be 0.

4   Timed Commands

The semantic condition for Information Flow is undecidable in general. To obtain a sound and decidable enforcement mechanism, the traditional approach is to develop a type system for a suitable programming language or process calculus. To this end we introduce the language TC of *Timed Commands*. It is strongly motivated by Dijkstra's language of Guarded Commands [10] but is designed so that it combines guards and assignments in the manner of Timed Automata. The syntax is given by:

$$
\begin{aligned}
TC &::= \mathbf{begin}^{[c_\circ]}\, C\ ^{[c_\bullet]}\mathbf{end} \\
C &::= g \rightarrow act\!:\ r \ \mid\ C_1;^{[c]}C_2 \ \mid\ \mathbf{do}\,T_1\,[]\,\cdots\,[]\,T_n\,\mathbf{od}\,[]\,T_{n+1}\,[]\,\cdots\,[]\,T_m \\
T &::= g \rightarrow act\!:\ r \ \mid\ T;^{[c]}C
\end{aligned}
$$

A timed command TC specifies a condition $c_\circ$ that must hold initially and a condition $c_\bullet$ that must hold if the command terminates. The command C itself can have one of three forms. One possibility is that it is an action of the form $g \to act\colon \boldsymbol{r}$. Another possibility is that it is a sequence of commands and then the condition c must be satisfied when moving from the first command to the second. The third possibility is that it is a looping construct with a number of branches $T_1, \cdots, T_n$ that will loop and a number of branches $T_{n+1}, \cdots, T_m$ that will terminate the looping behaviour. In case $n = 0$ and $m > 1$ we allow to dispense with the **do od**. Here T is a special form of command that starts with an action and potentially is followed by a number of commands. Conditions, guards and expressions are defined as in Sect. 2.

Example 4. Using the abbreviations of Fig. 1 the voting protocol of Example 1 is given by the following timed command:

$$\text{begin}^{[tt]}\ \text{cast};^{[t \le 50]}$$
$$(\text{do yes}_1\ []\ \cdots\ []\ \text{yes}_N\ []\ \text{no}_1\ []\ \cdots\ []\ \text{no}_N\ \text{od}\ []\ \text{count})\ ;^{[t \le 30]}$$
$$(\text{do cnt}_1\ []\ \cdots\ []\ \text{cnt}_N\ \text{od}\ []\ \text{publ})$$
$$^{[tt]}\text{end}$$

The first line performs the initialisation for the casting phase which happens in the second line; the third line expresses the counting of the votes and their publication. The timing constraints are expressed in the superscripts.

Transformational Semantics. We shall define the semantics of a timed command by mapping it into a timed automaton. Consider $\text{begin}^{[c_o]}\ C\ ^{[c_\bullet]}\text{end}$ and let q_o and $q_\bullet$ be two disctinct nodes; they will be the initial and final node of the resulting timed automaton and we shall ensure that $\mathsf{l}(q_o) = c_o$ and $\mathsf{l}(q_\bullet) = c_\bullet$. Additional nodes will be created during the construction using a judgement of the form:

$$\vdash^{qt}_{q_s} C : \mathsf{E}, \mathsf{l}$$

$$\vdash^{qt}_{q_s} g \to act\colon \boldsymbol{r} : \{(q_s, g \to act\colon \boldsymbol{r}, q_t)\}, [\,]$$

$$\frac{\vdash^{q}_{q_s} C_1 : \mathsf{E}_1, \mathsf{l}_1 \qquad \vdash^{qt}_{q} C_2 : \mathsf{E}_2, \mathsf{l}_2}{\vdash^{qt}_{q_s} C_1;^{[c]}C_2 : \mathsf{E}_1 \cup \mathsf{E}_2, \mathsf{l}_1 \cup \mathsf{l}_2 \cup [q \mapsto c]} \quad \text{where } q \text{ is fresh}$$

$$\frac{\bigwedge^{n}_{i=1} \vdash^{q_s}_{q_s} T_i : \mathsf{E}_i, \mathsf{l}_i \qquad\qquad \bigwedge^{m}_{i=n+1} \vdash^{qt}_{q_s} T_i : \mathsf{E}_i, \mathsf{l}_i}{\vdash^{qt}_{q_s} \text{do}\, T_1\, []\, \cdots\, []\, T_n\, \text{od}\, []\, T_{n+1}\, []\, \cdots\, []\, T_m : \bigcup_i \mathsf{E}_i, \bigcup_i \mathsf{l}_i}$$

$$\frac{\vdash^{q_\bullet}_{q_o} C : \mathsf{E}, \mathsf{l}}{\vdash \text{begin}^{[c_o]}\ C\ ^{[c_\bullet]}\text{end} : \mathsf{E}, \mathsf{l}', q_o, q_\bullet} \quad \text{where } \begin{cases} \mathsf{l}' = \mathsf{l}[q_o \mapsto c_o; q_\bullet \mapsto c_\bullet] \\ q_o, q_\bullet \text{ are fresh} \end{cases}$$

Fig. 2. From timed commands to timed automata.

Here C is a timed command, q_s and q_t are nodes, E is a set of edges, and the judgement will introduce additional nodes whose invariants are given by the labelling function I. This defines a timed automaton with initial node q_s, final node q_t, edges E, and labelling function I.

The judgement is specified by the axioms and rules of Fig. 2. In the axiom we simply create the edge $(q_s, g \to act: r, q_t)$ starting in q_s and ending in q_t and indicating the action to be performed; the resulting labelling function is empty as no new nodes are created in the construct.

In the first rule we create a *fresh* node q to be used to glue the timed automata for C_1 and C_2 together; the node q has the invariant c and is used as target node for C_1 as well as source node for C_2. The resulting set of edges is the union of the two sets; the two branches will create disjoint sets of nodes so the two mappings I_1 and I_2 will have disjoint domains and we write union for their combination.

In the rule for the looping construct we achieve the looping of the branches $T_1, \cdots, T_n$ by using q_s as source as well as target node, whereas for $T_{n+1}, \cdots, T_m$ we use q_t as target node. The overall set of edges are obtained as the union of the edges E_i and as in the previous case the domains of the mappings I_i will be disjoint so the mappings are easily combined.

Recall that T is a special form of timed command and hence timed automata can be constructed using the judgements of Fig. 2. The timed automata constructed from T always have exactly one edge leaving the initial node and do not contain any edge back to the initial node unless the initial and final nodes coincide. The timed automata constructed from C may have more than one edge leaving the initial node and may contain edges back to the initial node even when the initial and final nodes are distinct.

For the overall timed command $\mathbf{begin}^{[c_\circ]} C^{[c_\bullet]} \mathbf{end}$ we can now obtain a timed automaton with initial node $q_\circ$, final node $q_\bullet$, and edges E, and labelling function I' given by the last inference rule of Fig. 2.

Example 5. The transformation applied to the timed command of Example 4 gives rise to the timed automata of Fig. 1.

5   Type System

The information flow type system is specified using judgements of the form

$$\vdash_{[q_s:c_s]}^{[q_t:c_t]} C : \mathsf{E}, \mathsf{I} \,\& \,\chi$$

This is an extension of the judgements $\vdash_{q_s}^{q_t} C : \mathsf{E}, \mathsf{I}$ of the previous section for constructing timed automata from commands. The new judgements maintain information about the invariants c_s and c_t associated with the nodes q_s and q_t and a set χ of *latent variables and nodes* that influence the termination of the command; the influence of χ on q_t remains to be enforced. The type system is specified in Fig. 3 and explained below.

Assignment. Consider the first axiom of Fig. 3. The second line of the side condition expresses all the explicit flows from components of the vector of expressions

$$\vdash^{[q_t:c_t]}_{[q_s:c_s]} g \to \boldsymbol{x} := \boldsymbol{e} \colon \boldsymbol{r} : \{(q_s, g \to \boldsymbol{x} := \boldsymbol{e} \colon \boldsymbol{r}, q_t)\}, [\,] \,\&$$
$$\{q_s\} \cup \mathsf{fv}(c_s \wedge g \wedge c_t[\boldsymbol{e}/\boldsymbol{x}][\boldsymbol{0}/\boldsymbol{r}])$$

$$\text{if } \{q_s\} \rightsquigarrow \{q_t, \boldsymbol{x}, \boldsymbol{r}\}$$
$$\textstyle\bigwedge_i \mathsf{fv}(e_i) \rightsquigarrow \{x_i\}$$
$$\mathsf{fv}(c_s \wedge g \wedge c_t[\boldsymbol{e}/\boldsymbol{x}][\boldsymbol{0}/\boldsymbol{r}]) \rightsquigarrow \{\boldsymbol{x}, \boldsymbol{r}\}$$

$$\vdash^{[q_t:c_t]}_{[q_s:c_s]} g \to \mathbf{publish}\ e \colon \boldsymbol{r} : \{(q_s, g \to \mathbf{publish}\ e \colon \boldsymbol{r}, q_t)\}, [\,] \,\&$$
$$\{q_s\} \cup \mathsf{fv}(c_s \wedge g \wedge c_t[\boldsymbol{0}/\boldsymbol{r}])$$

$$\text{if } \{q_s\} \rightsquigarrow \{q_t, \boldsymbol{r}\}$$
$$\mathsf{fv}(c_s \wedge g \wedge c_t[\boldsymbol{0}/\boldsymbol{r}]) \rightsquigarrow \{\boldsymbol{r}\}$$

$$\dfrac{\vdash^{[q:c]}_{[q_s:c_s]} C_1 : \mathsf{E}_1, \mathsf{l}_1 \,\&\, \chi_1 \qquad \vdash^{[q_t:c_t]}_{[q:c]} C_2 : \mathsf{E}_2, \mathsf{l}_2 \,\&\, \chi_2}{\vdash^{[q_t:c_t]}_{[q_s:c_s]} C_1 ;^{[c]} C_2 : \mathsf{E}_1 \cup \mathsf{E}_2, \mathsf{l}_1 \cup \mathsf{l}_2 \cup [q \mapsto c] \,\&\, \chi_2}$$
$$\text{if } q \text{ is fresh}$$
$$\mathsf{fv}(c) \cup \{q\} \rightsquigarrow R \cup \{q\}$$
$$\chi_1 \rightsquigarrow \{q\}$$

$$\dfrac{\bigwedge^n_{i=1} \vdash^{[q_s:c_s]}_{[q_s:c_s]} T_i : \mathsf{E}_i, \mathsf{l}_i \,\&\, \chi_i \qquad\qquad \bigwedge^m_{i=n+1} \vdash^{[q_t:c_t]}_{[q_s:c_s]} T_i : \mathsf{E}_i, \mathsf{l}_i \,\&\, \chi_i}{\vdash^{[q_t:c_t]}_{[q_s:c_s]} \mathbf{do}\ T_1\ [\,]\ \cdots\ [\,]\ T_n\ \mathbf{od}\ [\,]\ T_{n+1}\ [\,]\ \cdots\ [\,]\ T_m : \bigcup_i \mathsf{E}_i, \bigcup_i \mathsf{l}_i \,\&\, \{q_t\}}$$
$$\text{if } \{q_s\} \rightsquigarrow \{q_t\}$$
$$\textstyle\bigwedge^n_{i=1} \chi_i \rightsquigarrow \{q_s\}$$
$$\varPhi^{T_1, \cdots, T_n}_{T_{n+1}, \cdots, T_m}[{}^{q_t:c_t}_{q_s:c_s}] \Rightarrow \bigwedge^m_{i=n+1} \chi_i \rightsquigarrow \{q_t\}$$
$$\textstyle\bigwedge_{i,j \mid i \neq j, \underline{\mathsf{sat}}(\mathsf{fst}^{\zeta_i}_{c_s}(T_i) \wedge \mathsf{fst}^{\zeta_j}_{c_s}(T_j))} \chi_i \rightsquigarrow \mathsf{ass}(T_j)$$
$$\text{where } \zeta_l \text{ is } c_s \text{ if } l \leq n \text{ and } \zeta_l \text{ is } c_t \text{ if } l > n$$
$$\textstyle\bigwedge^m_{i=n+1} \Big(\forall r \in \mathsf{fv}(\mathsf{fst}^{c_t}_{c_s}(T_i)) \cap R : \mathcal{L}(r) = L \,\wedge$$
$$\textstyle\bigwedge^m_{j=n+1} \overline{\mathsf{fst}^{c_t}_{c_s}(T_i)} \Leftrightarrow \overline{\mathsf{fst}^{c_t}_{c_s}(T_j)}\Big)$$

$$\dfrac{\vdash^{[q_\bullet : c_\bullet]}_{[q_0:c_0]} C : \mathsf{E}, \mathsf{l} \,\&\, \chi}{\vdash \mathbf{begin}^{[c_0]} C\ {}^{[c_\bullet]} \mathbf{end} : \mathsf{E}, \mathsf{l}', q_0, q_\bullet} \qquad \text{where}\ \begin{cases} \mathsf{l}' = \mathsf{l}[q_0 \mapsto c_0 ; q_\bullet \mapsto c_\bullet] \\ \mathsf{fv}(c_0) \cup \{q_0\} \rightsquigarrow R \cup \{q_0\} \\ \mathsf{fv}(c_\bullet) \cup \{q_\bullet\} \rightsquigarrow R \cup \{q_\bullet\} \\ \chi \rightsquigarrow \{q_\bullet\} \\ \mathcal{L}(q_\bullet) = L \\ q_0,\ q_\bullet \text{ are fresh} \end{cases}$$

Fig. 3. Type system for timed commands.

to corresponding components of the vector of variables. The first line of the side condition expresses that the modifications of variables and clocks as well as the termination relies on having started the action. The third line of the side condition expresses our knowledge that c_s holds and the implict flows arising from testing the guard g in the pre-state and the condition c_t in the post-state before performing the modifications of variables and clocks. (We are using the insight from Hoare logic [4] that evaluating c_t in the post-state is the same as evaluating $c_t[e/x][0/r]$ in the pre-state.) Rather than also expressing the implicit flow for termination (in the form of a side condition $\mathsf{fv}(c_s \wedge g \wedge c_t[e/x][0/r]) \rightsquigarrow \{q_t\}$) we produce the latent set of variables and nodes $\{q_s\} \cup \mathsf{fv}(c_s \wedge g \wedge c_t[e/x][0/r])$ as listed after the ampersand in the axiom. (We shall see the flexibiliity offered by this approach shortly.)

Example 6. Consider the action cnt_i of Fig. 1. It will be the case that $q_s = q_t = 3$ and $c_s = c_t = \mathsf{t} \leq 30$. The type system imposes the following constraints on the flows:

$$\{3\} \rightsquigarrow \{3, \mathsf{y}_i, \mathsf{c}\}, \quad \{\,\} \rightsquigarrow \{\mathsf{y}_i\}, \quad \{\mathsf{c}, \mathsf{v}_i\} \rightsquigarrow \{\mathsf{c}\}, \quad \{\mathsf{t}, \mathsf{x}_i, \mathsf{y}_i\} \rightsquigarrow \{\mathsf{y}_i, \mathsf{c}\}$$

It is easy to check that they are fulfilled for the security assignment of Example 3. The latent set of variables is $\{3, \mathsf{t}, \mathsf{x}_i, \mathsf{y}_i\}$.

Publish. The second axiom of Fig. 3 is a simplification of the first axiom in that the values computed are "published" but not recorded in the state. (The main purpose of this rule is to "bypass" the security policy in that we allow the publication of expressions even when they contain high variables.)

Example 7. For the action publ of Fig. 1 we have $q_s = 3$, $q_t = 4$, $c_s = \mathsf{t} \leq 30$ and $c_t = \mathsf{tt}$. The type system impose the contraints $\{3\} \rightsquigarrow \{4, \mathsf{t}\}$ and $\{\mathsf{t}\} \rightsquigarrow \{\mathsf{t}\}$ which clearly hold with the security assignment of Example 3.

Sequence. The first inference rule of Fig. 3 deals with the sequential composition of two commands. The second line of the side condition expresses the explicit flow possible due to the delay at the node q separating the two commands; here R is the set of all clock variables and it is included to mimick the effect of the potential delay. The third line of the side condition takes care of imposing the latent effect of the first command on the node q following immediately after it.

Example 8. Let us consider the sequencing construct $;^{[\mathsf{t} \leq 30]}$ between the two loops of the command of Example 4. The latent set of variables from the first loop will simply be $\{3\}$ and the two constraints will amount to $\{\mathsf{t}, 3\} \rightsquigarrow \{\mathsf{t}, 3\}$ and $\{3\} \rightsquigarrow \{3\}$ which are satisfied for the security assignment of Example 3.

Auxiliary Operations. Before approaching the last inference rule in Fig. 3 we shall introduce three auxiliary operations.

The auxiliary operation $\mathsf{ass}(C)$ overapproximates the set of variables and clocks modified by the command (ignoring any initial and final delays):

$$\mathsf{ass}(g \rightarrow x := e : r) = \{x, r\}$$
$$\mathsf{ass}(g \rightarrow \mathsf{publish}\ e : r) = \{r\}$$
$$\mathsf{ass}(C_1;^{[c]} C_2) = \mathsf{ass}(C_1) \cup \mathsf{ass}(C_2) \cup R$$
$$\mathsf{ass}\left(\begin{array}{c} \mathsf{do}\ T_1\ [] \ \cdots\ []\ T_n\ \mathsf{od} \\ []\ T_{n+1}\ []\ \cdots\ []\ T_m \end{array}\right) = \begin{cases} \mathsf{ass}(T_1) \cup \cdots \cup \mathsf{ass}(T_m) \cup R & \text{if } n > 0 \\ \mathsf{ass}(T_1) \cup \cdots \cup \mathsf{ass}(T_m) & \text{if } n = 0 \end{cases}$$

where R is the set of all clocks and it is included to mimick the effect of the potential (internal) delays of the loop.

Fact 1. If $\vdash_{q_s}^{q_t} C : \mathsf{E}, \mathsf{I}$ and if $(\sigma', \delta') \in [\![(\mathsf{E}, \mathsf{I}[q_s \mapsto c_s][q_t \mapsto c_t] : q_s \mapsto q_t]\!](\sigma, \delta)$ then $\exists d \geq 0 : \{x \mid \sigma(x) \neq \sigma'(x)\} \cup \{r \mid \delta(r) + d \neq \delta'(r)\} \subseteq \mathsf{ass}(C)$, where d corresponds to the initial delay.

The auxiliary operation $\mathsf{fst}_{c_s}^{c_t}(T)$ determines the initial guard and the condition immediately following it (in the manner of the rule for assignment):

$$\mathsf{fst}_{c_s}^{c_t}(g \rightarrow x := e\text{: } r) = c_s \wedge g \wedge c_t[e/x][0/r]$$
$$\mathsf{fst}_{c_s}^{c_t}(g \rightarrow \mathsf{publish}\ e\text{: } r) = c_s \wedge g \wedge c_t[0/r]$$
$$\mathsf{fst}_{c_s}^{c_t}(T;^{[c]}C) = \mathsf{fst}_{c_s}^{c}(T)$$

The inclusion of c_s is so as to get the strongest information for use in the rule for the looping construct in Fig. 3.

We shall need the auxiliary predicate $\Phi_{T_{n+1}, \cdots, T_m}^{T_1, \cdots, T_n}[{}_{q_s : c_s}^{q_t : c_t}]$ that must be true whenever it is possible that the construct $\mathsf{do}\,T_1\,[\!]\,\cdots\,[\!]\,T_n\,\mathsf{od}\,[\!]\,T_{n+1}\,[\!]\,\cdots\,[\!]\,T_m$ does *not* terminate from a state satisfying c_s; we return to this below.

Looping. We can now explain the inference rule in Fig. 3 for looping. The first line in the side condition expresses that the termination relies on having started the action as we saw in the axiom for assignment. The second line in the side condition takes care of imposing the latent effect χ_i of the looping commands on the loop header q_s.

The third line in the side condition takes care of imposing the latent effect of the terminating commands on the final node q_t. However, by using the predicate $\Phi_{T_{n+1}, \cdots, T_m}^{T_1, \cdots, T_n}[{}_{q_s : c_s}^{q_t : c_t}]$ we allow to dispense with imposing this latent effect in case termination of the looping construct is guaranteed. As an example this means that the type system will allow the following Timed Command

$$\big(\,(\mathsf{h} = 0 \rightarrow \mathsf{h} := \mathsf{h}\text{: }\,)\ [\!]\ (\mathsf{h} \neq 0 \rightarrow \mathsf{h} := \mathsf{h}\text{: }\,)\,\big)\text{;}^{[\mathsf{tt}]}\mathsf{tt} \rightarrow \mathsf{l} := \mathsf{l}\text{:}$$

that would otherwise be disallowed (assuming that h is a high variable and l is a low variable). Indeed it is in order to accomodate this kind of behaviour that the type system makes use of latent variables and nodes. This is essential for preventing unnecessary *label creep* where programs operating on high data too often end up in a high control point.

Using the notation of Fig. 3 we can now clarify our demands on the auxiliary notation $\Phi_{T_{n+1}, \cdots, T_m}^{T_1, \cdots, T_n}[{}_{q_s : c_s}^{q_t : c_t}]$ used in the third line:

$$\bot \in \bigcup\nolimits_{(\sigma, \delta) \mid [\![c_s]\!](\sigma, \delta)} [\![(\cup_i \mathsf{E}_i, \cup_i \mathsf{l}_i[q_s \mapsto c_s][q_t \mapsto c_t]) : q_s \mapsto q_t]\!](\sigma, \delta)$$
$$\Downarrow$$
$$\Phi_{T_{n+1}, \cdots, T_m}^{T_1, \cdots, T_n}[{}_{q_s : c_s}^{q_t : c_t}]$$

The subscript $(\sigma, \delta) \mid [\![c_s]\!](\sigma, \delta)$ is intended to let (σ, δ) range over all possibilities that satisfy $[\![c_s]\!](\sigma, \delta)$. Note that we do not require to capture non-termination precisely but will allow any over-approximation.

Before explaining the fourth line in the side condition it is helpful to establish the following property of the type system as stated in Fig. 3.

Lemma 1. *If* $\vdash^{[q_t:c_t]}_{[q_s:c_s]} C : \mathsf{E}, \mathsf{I} \,\&\, \chi$ *then we have that* $\{q_s\} \rightsquigarrow \mathsf{ass}(C) \cup \{q_t\}$ *and* $\forall \chi' : (\chi \rightsquigarrow \chi') \Rightarrow (\{q_s\} \rightsquigarrow \chi')$.

If $\vdash^{[q_t:c_t]}_{[q_s:c_s]} T : \mathsf{E}, \mathsf{I} \,\&\, \chi$ *then* $\forall \chi' : (\chi \rightsquigarrow \chi') \Rightarrow (\{q_s\} \cup \mathsf{fv}(\mathsf{fst}^{c_t}_{c_s}(T)) \rightsquigarrow \chi')$ *and* $\{q_s\} \cup \mathsf{fv}(\mathsf{fst}^{c_t}_{c_s}(T)) \rightsquigarrow \mathsf{ass}(T)$, *and* $\{q_s\} \rightsquigarrow \{q_t\}$.

(Note that the lack of reflexivity of $\rightsquigarrow$ means that we need to write slightly complex formulae like $\forall \chi' : (\chi \rightsquigarrow \chi') \Rightarrow ((\cdots) \rightsquigarrow \chi')$ because the formula $((\cdots) \rightsquigarrow \chi$ is in general incorrect.)

Proof. We prove the first statement by induction on $\vdash^{[q_t:c_t]}_{[q_s:c_s]} C : \mathsf{E}, \mathsf{I} \,\&\, \chi$ using that $\rightsquigarrow$ is transitive.

We prove the second statement by induction on $\vdash^{[q_t:c_t]}_{[q_s:c_s]} T : \mathsf{E}, \mathsf{I} \,\&\, \chi$. It is immediate for the two axioms for actions because $\{q_s\} \cup \mathsf{fv}(\mathsf{fst}^{c_t}_{c_s}(T)) = \chi$. In the rule for composition for $T;^{[c]}C$ observe that $\{q_s\} \cup \mathsf{fv}(\mathsf{fst}^{c_t}_{c_s}(T;^{[c]}C)) = \{q_s\} \cup \mathsf{fv}(\mathsf{fst}^{c}_{c_s}(T))$ and that the induction hypothesis gives that $\{q_s\} \cup \mathsf{fv}(\mathsf{fst}^{c}_{c_s}(T)) \rightsquigarrow \{q\}$ because $\chi_1 \rightsquigarrow \{q\}$. We have $\{q_s\} \cup \mathsf{fv}(\mathsf{fst}^{c}_{c_s}(T)) \rightsquigarrow \mathsf{ass}(T)$ from the induction hypothesis, $\{q\} \rightsquigarrow R$ from the rule, and $\{q\} \rightsquigarrow \mathsf{ass}(C)$ from the previous result, and then get $\{q_s\} \cup \mathsf{fv}(\mathsf{fst}^{c_t}_{c_s}(T;^{[c]}C)) \rightsquigarrow \mathsf{ass}(T;^{[c]}C)$. Next suppose $\chi = \chi_2 \rightsquigarrow \chi'$; from the previous result we have $\{q\} \rightsquigarrow \chi'$ and hence $\{q_s\} \cup \mathsf{fv}(\mathsf{fst}^{c_t}_{c_s}(T;^{[c]}C)) \rightsquigarrow \chi'$.

This lemma shows that we have already taken care of the so-called *block labels* of [9] and thereby take care of the implicit flows due to testing guards and conditions in the manner of [17]. However, the language considered in [17] is deterministic and the presence of non-determinism in Timed Commands poses a complication as illustrated by the following command:

$$\mathsf{tt} \to \mathsf{l}{:=}0: ;^{[\mathsf{tt}]} \left((\mathsf{h} = 0 \to \mathsf{h}{:=}\mathsf{h}:) \,[]\, (\mathsf{tt} \to \mathsf{l}{:=}1:) \right)$$

Here the final value of l will be 1 if $\mathsf{h} \neq 0$, but the final value of l may be either 0 or 1 if $\mathsf{h} = 0$. This presents a violation of our semantic conditions for adherence to the Information Flow security policy.

The purpose of the fourth line in the side condition is to take care of this possibility and this is a novel contribution with respect to [5,9,17] as discussed in Sect. 3. The notation $\underline{\mathsf{sat}}(\cdots)$ is intended to express the satisfiability of the $\cdots$ formula. We are considering all terminating branches in the looping construct and whenever there are two branches that are not mutually exclusive (that is, where $\underline{\mathsf{sat}}(\mathsf{fst}^{\zeta_i}_{c_s}(T_i) \wedge \mathsf{fst}^{\zeta_j}_{c_s}(T_j)))$ we make sure to record the information flow arising from *bypassing* the branch that would otherwise perform an assignment. This is essential for dealing with *non-determinism* and *non-termination*.

Before explaining the fifth condition let us consider the following command operating on a low clock l and a high clock h:

$$\mathsf{tt} \to \; : \mathsf{l};^{[\mathsf{tt}]} \left(\mathsf{do}\; \mathsf{od}\, []\, \mathsf{h} \geq 100 \to \; : \right)$$

Here we have that $(\sigma, \delta[\mathsf{h} \mapsto 110]) \equiv (\sigma, \delta[\mathsf{h} \mapsto 90])$ but running the command from $(\sigma, \delta[\mathsf{h} \mapsto 110])$ might produce $(\sigma, \delta[\mathsf{h} \mapsto 110])$ ifself whereas running the command from $(\sigma, \delta[\mathsf{h} \mapsto 90])$ can only produce $(\sigma, (\delta[\mathsf{h} \mapsto 90]) + d)$ for $d \geq 10$ in which case $(\sigma, \delta[\mathsf{h} \mapsto 110]) \not\equiv (\sigma, (\delta[\mathsf{h} \mapsto 90]) + d)$.

The purpose of the fifth line in the side condition is to take care of this possibility by enforcing that the terminating branches only test on low clocks and that the conditions on clocks are the same. To this end we define $\bar{g}$ as follows

$$\frac{\begin{array}{c} \bar{b} = \mathsf{tt} \\ \overline{r \ \mathsf{op}_c \ n} = r \ \mathsf{op}_c \ n \\ \overline{(r_1 - r_2) \ \mathsf{op}_c \ n} = (r_1 - r_2) \ \mathsf{op}_c \ n \end{array}}{\overline{g_1 \wedge g_2} = \overline{g_1} \wedge \overline{g_2}}$$

and we write $g \Leftrightarrow g'$ to express the equivalence of the guards g and g'. This is essential for the type system to deal correctly with the *continuous clocks*.

Example 9. Returning to Example 4 let us consider the looping command of the third line. Using the latent set of variables from Example 6 we obtain the following constraints from the first two lines of the condition:

$$\{3\} \rightsquigarrow \{4\}, \quad \{3, \mathsf{t}, x_1, \ldots, x_N, y_1, \ldots, y_N\} \rightsquigarrow \{3\}$$

We have no contribution from the third side condition of the rule since termination of the loop is guaranteed. From the fourth side condition we get

$$\bigcup_{i \neq j} \{3, \mathsf{t}, x_i, y_i\} \rightsquigarrow \{y_j, \mathsf{c}\}$$

and from the fifth line we get $\mathcal{L}(\mathsf{t}) = L$. It is easy to check that the above conditions are fulfilled with the security assignment of Example 3.

Timed Commands. Consider the last inference rule in Fig. 3. The first and last lines of the side condition are as in Fig. 2. The second and third lines of the side condition express the explicit flow possible due to the delay at the node $q_\circ$ and $q_\bullet$ and is analogous to our treatment of sequencing. The fourth line of the side condition takes care of imposing the latent effect of the command on the final node q_t and is analogous to our treatment of sequencing. The fifth line will allow us to invoke Theorem 1 of the next section.

6   Adequacy

To prove the adequacy of the type system we shall establish some terminology. A function like $[\![\mathsf{TA} : q_s \mapsto q_t]\!]$ mapping a pair of state and clock assignment to a set of pairs of states and clock assignments and possibly the symbol $\perp$ will be called a *semantic function*. Whenever F is a semantic function we define

$$F \models c_s \mapsto c_t \text{ iff } \forall (\sigma, \delta), (\sigma', \delta') : \quad (\sigma, \delta) \equiv_{c_s} (\sigma', \delta')$$
$$\Downarrow$$
$$F(\sigma, \delta) \equiv^{c_t} F(\sigma', \delta')$$

where (using $\equiv$ as defined in Sect. 3)

$(\sigma, \delta) \equiv_c (\sigma', \delta')$ abbreviates $(\sigma, \delta) \equiv (\sigma', \delta') \wedge [\![c]\!](\sigma, \delta) \wedge [\![c]\!](\sigma', \delta')$

$\Gamma \equiv^c \Gamma'$ abbreviates $\Gamma \equiv \Gamma' \wedge$
$$\forall (\sigma, \delta) \in \Gamma : [\![c]\!](\sigma, \delta) \wedge \forall (\sigma', \delta') \in \Gamma' : [\![c]\!](\sigma', \delta')$$

The semantic condition for when a Timed Automaton $\mathsf{TA} = (\mathsf{E}, \mathsf{I}, q_\circ, q_\bullet)$ satisfies the Information Flow security policy discussed in Sect. 3 then amounts to $[\![(\mathsf{E}, \mathsf{I}) : q_\circ \mapsto q_\bullet]\!] \models \mathsf{I}(q_\circ) \mapsto \mathsf{I}(q_\bullet)$. Finally, let us define the composition of two semantic functions F_1 and F_2 as follows:

$$F_1 \diamond F_2 = \lambda(\sigma_0, \delta_0). \, (F_1(\sigma_0, \delta_0) \cap \{\bot\}) \cup \bigcup_{(\sigma_1, \delta_1) \in F(\sigma_0, \delta_0) \backslash \{\bot\}} F_2(\sigma_1, \delta_1)$$

Fact 2. *If* $F_1 \models c_0 \mapsto c_1$ *and* $F_2 \models c_1 \mapsto c_2$ *then* $F_1 \diamond F_2 \models c_0 \mapsto c_2$.

We are then ready to state a non-interference result in the manner of [18]:

Theorem 1 (Adequacy of Commands). *If* $\vdash^{[q_t : c_t]}_{[q_s : c_s]} C : \mathsf{E}, \mathsf{I} \, \& \, \chi$ *and* $\chi \leadsto \{q_t\}$ *and* $\mathcal{L}(q_t) = L$ *and* $\mathsf{fv}(c_s) \leadsto \{q_s\}$ *then we have* $[\![(\mathsf{E}, \mathsf{I}[q_s \mapsto c_s][q_t \mapsto c_t]) : q_s \mapsto q_t]\!] \models c_s \mapsto c_t$.

Proof. We proceed by induction on $\vdash^{[q_t : c_t]}_{[q_s : c_s]} C : \mathsf{E}, \mathsf{I} \, \& \, \chi$.

Case: Assignment. Assume that $(\sigma_0, \delta_0) \equiv_{c_s} (\sigma_0', \delta_0')$ and that

$$\gamma \in [\![(\{(q_s, g \to \boldsymbol{x} := \boldsymbol{e} \colon \boldsymbol{r}, q_t)\}), [q_s \mapsto c_s][q_t \mapsto c_t]) : q_s \mapsto q_t]\!](\sigma_0, \delta_0)$$

In case $\gamma = (\sigma_1, \delta_1)$ it follows that there exists $d \geq 0$ such that $\sigma_1 = [\![\boldsymbol{x} := \boldsymbol{e}]\!]\sigma_0$ and $\delta_1 = (\delta_0 + d)[\boldsymbol{r} \mapsto \boldsymbol{0}]$, and such that $[\![g]\!](\sigma_0, (\delta_0 + d)) = \mathsf{tt}$, $[\![c_s]\!](\sigma_0, \delta_0 + d) = \mathsf{tt}$ and $[\![c_t]\!](\sigma_1, \delta_1) = \mathsf{tt}$. Defining $\gamma' = (\sigma_1', \delta_1') = ([\![\boldsymbol{x} := \boldsymbol{e}]\!]\sigma_0', (\delta_0' + d)[\boldsymbol{r} \mapsto \boldsymbol{0}])$ ensures that $[\![g]\!](\sigma_0', (\delta_0' + d)) = \mathsf{tt}$, $[\![c_s]\!](\sigma_0', \delta_0' + d) = \mathsf{tt}$ and $[\![c_t]\!](\sigma_1', \delta_1') = \mathsf{tt}$ because all variables and clocks tested are low and hence

$$\gamma \equiv_{c_t} \gamma' \in [\![(\{(q_s, g \to \boldsymbol{x} := \boldsymbol{e} \colon \boldsymbol{r}, q_t)\}), [q_s \mapsto c_s][q_t \mapsto c_t]) : q_s \mapsto q_t]\!](\sigma_0', \delta_0')$$

In case $\gamma = \bot$ it follows that there is no value of $d \geq 0$ such that $[\![g]\!](\sigma_0, (\delta_0 + d)) = \mathsf{tt}$, $[\![c_s]\!](\sigma_0, \delta_0 + d) = \mathsf{tt}$ and $[\![c_t]\!](\sigma_1, \delta_1) = \mathsf{tt}$. Then there also is no value of $d \geq 0$ such that $[\![g]\!](\sigma_0', (\delta_0' + d)) = \mathsf{tt}$, $[\![c_s]\!](\sigma_0', \delta_0' + d) = \mathsf{tt}$ and $[\![c_t]\!](\sigma_1', \delta_1') = \mathsf{tt}$ because all variables and clocks tested are low and hence setting $\gamma' = \bot$ establishes that

$$\gamma \equiv \gamma' \in [\![(\{(q_s, g \to \boldsymbol{x} := \boldsymbol{e} \colon \boldsymbol{r}, q_t)\}), [q_s \mapsto c_s][q_t \mapsto c_t]) : q_s \mapsto q_t]\!](\sigma_0', \delta_0')$$

The other direction is similar and this completes the assignment case.

Case: Publish. This case is analogous to the case for assignment.

Case: Sequence. We shall write

$$F = [\![(\mathsf{E}_1 \cup \mathsf{E}_2, \mathsf{I}_1 \cup \mathsf{I}_2[q_s \mapsto c_s][q \mapsto c][q_t \mapsto c_t]) : q_s \mapsto q_t]\!]$$
$$F_1 = [\![(\mathsf{E}_1, \mathsf{I}_1[q_s \mapsto c_s][q \mapsto c]) : q_s \mapsto q]\!]$$
$$F_2 = [\![(\mathsf{E}_2, \mathsf{I}_2[q \mapsto c][q_t \mapsto c_t]) : q \mapsto q_t]\!]$$

and observe that $F = F_1 \diamond F_2$. The result then follows from the induction hypotheses and Fact 2.

Case: Looping. We shall write

$$F = [\![(\bigcup_i E_i, \bigcup_i l_i[q_s \mapsto c_s][q_t \mapsto c_t]) : q_s \mapsto q_t]\!]$$

$$F_i = \begin{cases} [\![(E_i, l_i[q_s \mapsto c_s]) : q_s \mapsto q_s]\!] & \text{whenever } i \leq n \\ [\![(E_i, l_i[q_s \mapsto c_s][q_t \mapsto c_t]) : q_s \mapsto q_t]\!] & \text{whenever } i > n \end{cases}$$

and this gives rise to the equation

$$F = (\bigcup_{i=1}^{n} F_i \diamond F) \cup \bigcup_{i=n+1}^{m} F_i$$

We shall consider two subcases, one where the condition $\Phi_{T_{n+1},\cdots,T_m}^{T_1,\cdots,T_n}[{}^{q_t:c_t}_{q_s:c_s}]$ is true and one where it is false.

Subcase: Looping when $\Phi_{T_{n+1},\cdots,T_m}^{T_1,\cdots,T_n}[{}^{q_t:c_t}_{q_s:c_s}]$ is true. In this case (using the notation of Fig. 3) all the variables and clocks in $\bigcup_{i=1}^{m} \mathsf{fv}(\mathsf{fst}_{c_s}^{c_i}(T_i))$ are low. Assume that $(\sigma_0, \delta_0) \equiv_{c_s} (\sigma_0', \delta_0')$ and that $\gamma \in F(\sigma_0, \delta_0)$. This must be because of a trace as considered in Sect. 2.

If this trace visits q_s infinitely often we will be able to construct a sequence $k_1, k_2, \cdots, k_i, \cdots$ such that each $k_i \leq n$ and

$$\forall i > 0 : (\sigma_i, \delta_i) \in F_{k_i}(\sigma_{i-1}, \delta_{i-1})$$

and $\gamma = \bot$. By the induction hypothesis we can find (σ_i', δ_i') such that

$$\forall i > 0 : (\sigma_i, \delta_i) \equiv_{c_s} (\sigma_i', \delta_i') \in F_{k_i}(\sigma_{i-1}', \delta_{i-1}')$$

and this establishes that $\bot \in F(\sigma_0', \delta_0')$.

If the trace visits q_s only finitely often we will be able to construct a sequence $k_1, k_2, \cdots, k_j$ such that $\forall i < j : k_i \leq n$ and $k_j \leq m$ and

$$\forall i \in \{1, \cdots, j-1\} : (\sigma_i, \delta_i) \in F_{k_i}(\sigma_{i-1}, \delta_{i-1})$$
$$\gamma \in F_{k_j}(\sigma_{j-1}, \delta_{j-1})$$

By the induction hypothesis we can find (σ_i', δ_i') and γ' such that

$$\forall i \in \{1, \cdots, j-1\} : (\sigma_i, \delta_i) \equiv_{c_s} (\sigma_i', \delta_i') \in F_{k_i}(\sigma_{i-1}', \delta_{i-1}')$$
$$\gamma \equiv \gamma' \in F_{k_j}(\sigma_{j-1}', \delta_{j-1}')$$

and this establishes that $\gamma' \in F(\sigma_0', \delta_0')$.

The other direction is similar and this completes the subcase.

Subcase: Looping when $\Phi_{T_{n+1},\cdots,T_m}^{T_1,\cdots,T_n}[{}^{q_t:c_t}_{q_s:c_s}]$ is false. In this case all the variables and clocks in $\bigcup_{i=1}^{n+1} \mathsf{fv}(\mathsf{fst}_{c_s}^{c_i}(T_i))$ are low but this is not necessarily the case for those in $\bigcup_{i=n+1}^{m} \mathsf{fv}(\mathsf{fst}_{c_s}^{c_i}(T_i))$; however, we do know that $[\![c_s]\!](\sigma, \delta) \Rightarrow \bot \notin F(\sigma, \delta)$.

Assume that $(\sigma_0, \delta_0) \equiv_{c_s} (\sigma_0', \delta_0')$ and that $\gamma \in F(\sigma_0, \delta_0)$. The assumptions of the subcase ensure that $\gamma \neq \bot$.

We will be able to construct a sequence $k_1, k_2, \cdots, k_j$ such that $\forall i < j : k_i \leq n$ and $k_j > n$ and

$$\forall i \in \{1, \cdots, j-1\} : (\sigma_i, \delta_i) \in F_{k_i}(\sigma_{i-1}, \delta_{i-1})$$
$$\gamma \in F_{k_j}(\sigma_{j-1}, \delta_{j-1})$$

By the induction hypothesis we can find (σ_i', δ_i') such that

$$\forall i \in \{1, \cdots, j-1\} : (\sigma_i, \delta_i) \equiv_{c_s} (\sigma_i', \delta_i') \in F_{k_i}(\sigma_{i-1}', \delta_{i-1}')$$

There are now two scenarios for how to proceed.

Subcase scenario where all variables and clocks in $\mathsf{fv}(\mathsf{fst}_{C_s}^{C_t}(T_{k_j}))$ *are low.* In this case we can find $\gamma' \in F_{k_j}(\sigma_{j-1}', \delta_{j-1}')$ such that $\gamma \equiv \gamma'$.

Subcase scenario where at least one variable or clock in $\mathsf{fv}(\mathsf{fst}_{C_s}^{C_t}(T_{k_j}))$ *is high.* Then $\mathsf{ass}(T_{k_j})$ cannot contain any low variable or clock and hence there is $d \geq 0$ such that $\gamma \equiv (\sigma_{j-1}, \delta_{j-1} + d)$ where the addition of d takes care of the potential delay in q_s. Next we use that $\bot \notin F(\sigma_{j-1}', \delta_{j-1}')$ to obtain $k_j', \sigma_j', \delta_j'$ such that $(\sigma_j', \delta_j') \in F_{k_j'}(\sigma_{j-1}', \delta_{j-1}')$.

It cannot be the case that $k_j' \leq n$. To see this, assume by way of contradiction that $k_j' \leq n$. Then $(\sigma_{j-1}, \delta_{j-1})$ would be a witness for $\underline{\mathsf{sat}}(\mathsf{fst}_{C_s}^{C_t}(T_{k_j}) \wedge \mathsf{fst}_{C_s}^{C_s}(T_{k_j'}))$ ensuring that $\mathsf{fst}_{C_s}^{C_t}(T_{k_j}) \rightsquigarrow \mathsf{ass}(T_{k_j'})$ so that $\mathsf{ass}(T_{k_j'})$ could not contain a low variable or clock. It would follow that there would be $d' \geq 0$ such that $(\sigma_j', \delta_j') \equiv_{c_s} (\sigma_{j-1}, \delta_{j-1} + d')$ where the addition of d' is due to the possibility of delay in q_s. But then we would be able to construct an infinite sequence (σ_l', δ_l') for $l > j$ such that $(\sigma_l', \delta_l') \in F_{k_j'}(\sigma_{l-1}', \delta_{l-1}')$ and $(\sigma_l', \delta_l') \equiv_{c_s} (\sigma_{j-1}', \delta_{j-1}' + d')$ would hold for $l \geq j$. But this would contradict the fact that $\bot \notin F(\sigma_j', \delta_j')$.

We are left with the case where $k_j' > n$. We must have that $\mathsf{ass}(T_{k_j'})$ cannot contain any low variable or clock: either one variable or clock in $\mathsf{fst}_{C_s}^{C_t}(T_{k_j'})$ is high and it follows as in a case above, or all variables and clocks in $\mathsf{fst}_{C_s}^{C_t}(T_{k_j'})$ are low and it follows because $(\sigma_{j-1}, \delta_{j-1} + d)$ is a witness for $\underline{\mathsf{sat}}(\mathsf{fst}_{C_s}^{C_t}(T_{k_j}) \wedge \mathsf{fst}_{C_s}^{C_s}(T_{k_j'}))$ and we could proceed as in a case above. Hence $(\sigma_j', \delta_j') = (\sigma_{j-1}', \delta_{j-1}' + d')$ for some $d' \geq 0$.

It remains to show that d' can be chosen to be d. For this we use that all clocks in $\mathsf{fst}_{C_s}^{C_t}(T_{k_j})$ and $\mathsf{fst}_{C_s}^{C_s}(T_{k_j'})$ are low and that $\overline{\mathsf{fst}_{C_s}^{C_t}(T_{k_j})} = \overline{\mathsf{fst}_{C_s}^{C_s}(T_{k_j'})}$.

The other direction is similar and this completes the subcase.

We can now establish our main result that the type system enforces a sufficient condition for the absence of information flows violating the security policy.

Corollary 1 (Adequacy). *If* $\vdash \mathsf{begin}^{[c_\circ]} C \ ^{[c_\bullet]}\mathsf{end} : E, I, q_\circ, q_\bullet$ *then we have that* $[\![(E, I) : q_\circ \mapsto q_\bullet]\!] \models I(q_\circ) \mapsto I(q_\bullet)$.

7   Conclusion

We have shown how to successfully merge Timed Automata with Information Flow and Language Based Security through the introduction of the Timed Commands language patterned after Dijkstra's Guarded Commands. This has facilitated developing a type system that prevents unnecessary *label creep* and that deals with *non-determinism, non-termination* and *continuous real-time*. The type system has been proved adequate by means of a non-interference result (with observable non-determinism).

We are exploring how to automate the analysis and in particular how to implement (a sound approximation of) the $\Phi_{T_{n+1},\cdots,T_m}^{T_1,\cdots,T_n}$ predicate indicating the lack of termination of the looping construct. One possible way, is to use existing methodologies that deal with *time-lock* (deadlock) freedom checks for timed automata. The check of the predicate $\Phi_{T_{n+1},\cdots,T_m}^{T_1,\cdots,T_n}$ then amounts to check for *time-lock* freedom (infinite loops) or *time-locks* that do not occur at the final nodes (stack configurations) of the particular loop construct that the $\Phi_{T_{n+1},\cdots,T_m}^{T_1,\cdots,T_n}$ predicate refers too. The work of [8] presents a tool which is used in the conjuction with UPPAAL and is able to detect possible sources of deadlocks in timed-automata.

We are considering how to deal with more concepts from Timed Automata as for example urgents actions. Our treatment of **publish** e could be extended to a more general treatment of declassification and endorsement as permitted in the Decentralized Label Model [14]; our flow based security condition should suffice for expressing semantic correctness. To strengthen the security policies that can be expressed we are contemplating incorporating the content-dependent policies of [15].

A longer term goal is to allow policies to simultaneously dealing with safety and security properties of cyberphysical systems.

Acknowledgment. The authors are supported in part by the IDEA4CPS Reseearch Centre studying the Foundations for Cyber-Physical Systems and granted by the Danish Research Foundation for Basic Research (DNRF86-10). We would like to thank Ximeng Li for commenting upon a previous version.

References

1. Aceto, L., Ingolfsdottir, A., Larsen, K.G., Srba, J.: Reactive Systems: Modelling, Specification and Verification. Cambridge University Press, Cambridge (2007)
2. Agat, J.: Transforming out timing leaks. In: Proceedings of the POPL, pp. 40–53 (2000)
3. Alur, R., Dill, D.L.: A theory of timed automata. Theor. Comput. Sci. **126**(2), 183–235 (1994)
4. Apt, K.R.: Ten years of Hoare's logic: a survey - part 1. ACM Trans. Program. Lang. Syst. **3**(4), 431–483 (1981)
5. Banâtre, J.-P., Bryce, C., Métayer, D.: Compile-time detection of information flow in sequential programs. In: Gollmann, D. (ed.) ESORICS 1994. LNCS, vol. 875, pp. 55–73. Springer, Heidelberg (1994). doi:10.1007/3-540-58618-0_56

6. Barbuti, R., De Francesco, N., Santone, A., Tesei, L.: A notion of non-interference for timed automata. Fundam. Inform. **51**(1–2), 1–11 (2002)
7. Barbuti, R., Tesei, L.: A decidable notion of timed non-interference. Fundam. Inform. **54**(2–3), 137–150 (2003)
8. Bordbar, B., Okano, K.: Testing deadlock-freeness in real-time systems: a formal approach. In: Grabowski, J., Nielsen, B. (eds.) FATES 2004. LNCS, vol. 3395, pp. 95–109. Springer, Heidelberg (2005). doi:10.1007/978-3-540-31848-4_7
9. Denning, D.E., Denning, P.J.: Certification of programs for secure information flow. Commun. ACM **20**(7), 504–513 (1977)
10. Dijkstra, E.W.: Guarded commands, nondeterminacy and formal derivation of programs. Commun. ACM **18**(8), 453–457 (1975)
11. Focardi, R., Gorrieri, R., Martinelli, F.: Real-time information flow analysis. IEEE J. Sel. Areas Commun. **21**(1), 20–35 (2003)
12. Gardey, G., Mullins, J., Roux, O.H.: Non-interference control synthesis for security timed automata. Electr. Notes Theor. Comput. Sci. **180**(1), 35–53 (2007)
13. Lanotte, R., Maggiolo-Schettini, A., Troina, A.: Time and probability-based information flow analysis. IEEE Trans. Softw. Eng. **36**(5), 719–734 (2010)
14. Myers, A.C., Liskov, B.: A decentralized model for information flow control. In: ACM Symposium on Operating System Principles, SOSP 1997, pp. 129–142. ACM (1997)
15. Hanne Riis Nielson and Flemming Nielson: Content dependent information flow control. J. Log. Algebr. Meth. Program. **87**, 6–32 (2017)
16. UPPAAL. http://www.uppaal.com/index.php?sida=200&rubrik=95
17. Volpano, D.M., Smith, G., Irvine, C.E.: A sound type system for secure flow analysis. J. Comput. Secur. **4**(2/3), 167–188 (1996)
18. Zdancewic, S., Myers, A.C.: Observational determinism for concurrent program security. In: Proceedings of the CSFW, pp. 29–43 (2003)

A Nivat Theorem for Quantitative Automata on Unranked Trees

Manfred Droste and Doreen Götze[⊠]

Institut für Informatik, Universität Leipzig, 04109 Leipzig, Germany
{droste,goetze}@informatik.uni-leipzig.de

Abstract. We derive a Nivat theorem for weighted unranked tree automata which states that their behaviors are exactly the functions which can be constructed from recognizable unranked tree languages and behaviors of very simple weighted unranked tree automata by using operations like relabelings and intersections. Thereby we prove the robustness of the weighted unranked tree automata model introduced recently. Moreover, we derive a similar theorem for weighted ranked tree automata. The characterizations work for valuation monoids as weight structures; they include all semirings, bounded lattices, and computations of averages of weights.

Keywords: Weighted tree automata · Nivat classes · Valuation monoids · Nivat theorem

1 Introduction

In 1967, Thatcher [32] investigated the theory of finite pseudoterms (nowadays known as unranked trees) and pseudoautomata (or unranked tree automata). In contrast to ranked trees (see [9,22,23] for surveys), for unranked trees the number of children of a node is not determined by the label of that node. Since then, due to the development of the modern document language XML and the fact that (fully structured) XML-documents can be formalized as unranked trees, the theory of unranked tree automata and unranked tree languages has developed intensively, cf. e.g. [2,7,28–30,32] and Chap. 8 of [9].

Classical unranked tree automata (amongst others) provide the opportunity to cope with qualitative questions, like reachability. More recently, also quantitative aspects gained much attention in automata theory. For instance, weighted real-time automata were investigated in [27], weighted modal systems in [4], and axiomatizations of weighted transition systems in [25]. For ranked trees, weighted automata were introduced in [1,6]; for surveys we refer to [13,21]. Weighted automata for unranked trees over semirings were investigated in [20,26]. A weighted unranked tree automata model over tree valuation monoids was introduced in [12]. Tree valuation monoids provide a very general weight structure

The second author was partially supported by the DFG Graduiertenkolleg 1763 (QuantLA).

L. Aceto et al. (Eds.): Larsen Festschrift, LNCS 10460, pp. 22–35, 2017.
DOI: 10.1007/978-3-319-63121-9_2

including all semirings, bounded (possibly non-distributive) lattices, and in addition, computations of averages or discounting of weights.

Nivat-type results provide a close relationship between weighted and unweighted automata models. In 1968, Nivat [31] (see also [5], Theorem 4.1) proved the fundamental theorem which characterizes rational transductions, and thereby established a connection between rational transductions and rational languages. Droste and Kuske [14] extended Nivat's theorem to weighted word automata over semirings. They showed that recognizable word series are exactly those which can be constructed from recognizable languages and very particular recognizable series using operations like morphisms and intersections. Recently, other extensions followed. Nivat theorems were given in [17,18] for weighted timed automata and weighted timed pushdown automata over timed valuation monoids and thereby implicitly also for weighted word automata over valuation monoids, in [3] for weighted picture automata over picture valuation monoids, in [10] for weighted graph automata over semirings, and in [33,34] for probabilistic automata on finite and infinite words and ranked trees, respectively.

The goal of this paper is such a Nivat result for weighted unranked tree automata over tree valuation monoids. Such automata consist of a state set and a family of weighted word automata. The latter are used to calculate the local weight at a position of a tree by letting the weighted word automaton run on states at the children of the position. To define the behavior, we use extended runs which were already introduced in [20]. Additionally to the information of classical runs, extended runs also include runs of the weighted word automata called at positions of the input tree. Then the local weight of a position equals the weight of the transition taken for this position in the run of the position's parent. We use the valuation function of the tree valuation monoid to calculate the weights of an extended run in a global way, i.e. given a run we apply the valuation function to all local weights which appear along the extended run. We obtain the weight of the tree as the sum of the weights of all its extended runs. In [12] it was shown that this model of weighted unranked tree automata is expressively equivalent to a suitable weighted MSO logic for unranked trees.

The main result of this paper gives a Nivat-type result for weighted unranked tree automata. We show that the behaviors of weighted unranked tree automata are exactly the functions which can be constructed from recognizable tree languages and behaviors of very simple weighted unranked tree automata by using operations like relabelings and intersections. Indeed, it even suffices to take functions mapping tree labels to tree valuation monoid elements instead of the very simple weighted unranked tree automata. It is clear that these functions define simple, recognizable tree series. Together with the results of [12], our present main result shows that the weighted unranked tree automata model of [12] is robust. In comparison to the proofs of the Nivat theorem for words (cf. [14]), for unranked trees technical difficulties arise from the technically more complex extended runs. Moreover, we also give a Nivat theorem for weighted ranked tree automata over tree valuation monoids.

2   Preliminaries

Let $\mathbb{N} = \{1, 2, \ldots\}$ be the set of all natural numbers and $\mathbb{N}_0 = \mathbb{N} \cup \{0\}$. For a set H, we denote by $|H|$ the cardinality of H and by H^* the set of all finite words over H. The empty word is denoted by ε. For sets $H_1, \ldots, H_n$ and $x \in H_1 \times \ldots \times H_n$, x_i equals the i-th component of x.

2.1   Trees and Tree Valuation Monoids

A *tree domain* is a finite, non-empty subset $\mathcal{B}$ of $\mathbb{N}^*$ such that for all $u \in \mathbb{N}^*$ and $i \in \mathbb{N}$, if $u.i \in \mathcal{B}$, then $u, u.1, \ldots, u.(i-1) \in \mathcal{B}$. An *unranked tree* over a set H (of labels) is a mapping $t \colon \mathcal{B} \to H$ such that $\mathrm{dom}(t) = \mathcal{B}$ is a tree domain. The set of all unranked trees over H is denoted by U_H. For every $h \in H$, we denote also by h the particular tree defined by $t \colon \{\varepsilon\} \to H$ and $t(\varepsilon) = h$. Let $t \in U_H$. The elements of $\mathrm{dom}(t)$ are called *positions* of t. Let $u \in \mathrm{dom}(t)$. We call $t(u)$ the *label* of t at u. The *rank* $\mathrm{rk}_t(u)$ of u is defined to be $\max\{i \in \mathbb{N} \mid u.i \in \mathrm{dom}(t)\}$. If $\mathrm{rk}_t(u) = 0$, then u is also called a *leaf of t*. We denote by $\mathrm{leaf}(t)$ the set of all leaves of t.

A *tree valuation monoid* (*tv-monoid* for short) [11,15] is a quadruple $(D, +, \mathrm{Val}, \mathbb{0})$ such that $(D, +, \mathbb{0})$ is a commutative monoid and $\mathrm{Val} \colon U_D \to D$ is a function, called *(tree) valuation function*, which satisfies that $\mathrm{Val}(d) = d$ for every tree $d \in D$, and $\mathrm{Val}(t) = \mathbb{0}$ for every $t \in U_D$ with $\mathbb{0} \in \mathrm{im}(t)$.

Example 1. $\mathbb{Q}_{\max} = (\mathbb{Q} \cup \{-\infty\}, \max, \mathrm{avg}, -\infty)$ with $\mathrm{avg}(t) = \frac{\sum_{u \in \mathrm{dom}(t)} t(u)}{|\mathrm{dom}(t)|}$ for all $t \in U_{\mathbb{Q} \cup \{-\infty\}}$ is a tv-monoid. The valuation function of this tv-monoid calculates the average of all weights of a tree. The idea for the average calculation was already suggested in [8,16] for words and in [11] for trees.

2.2   Weighted Unranked Tree Automata

Here we recall the definition of the class of recognizable tree series which were introduced in connection with restricted weighted MSO logics, cf. [12]. Since weighted unranked tree automata use weighted word automata we first recall the definition of weighted word automata over tree valuation monoids.

Let $\mathbb{D}$ be a tv-momoid and Σ an *alphabet*, i.e. a non-empty, finite set. A *weighted word automaton* over Σ and $\mathbb{D}$ is a quadruple $\mathcal{A} = (P, I, \mu, F)$ where P is a non-empty, finite set of states, $I, F \subseteq P$ are the sets of initial and final states, respectively, and $\mu \colon P \times \Sigma \times P \to \mathbb{D}$. A *run* of $\mathcal{A}$ on $w = w_1 \ldots w_n$ with $w_1, \ldots, w_n \in \Sigma$ and $n \geq 0$ is a sequence $\pi = (p_{i-1}, w_i, p_i)_{1 \leq i \leq n}$ if $n > 0$, and a state $\pi = p_0$ if $n = 0$ where $p_0, \ldots, p_n \in P$. The run π is *successful* if $p_0 \in I$ and $p_n \in F$. In order to define the weight $\mathrm{wt}(\pi)$ of π using a tree valuation function Val, we define a tree t_π by letting $\mathrm{dom}(t_\pi) = \{1^i \mid 0 \leq i < n\}$ and $t_\pi(1^i) = \mu(p_{i-1}, w_i, p_i)$ $(0 \leq i < n)$ if $n > 0$, and $t_\pi(\varepsilon) = \mathbb{0}$ if $n = 0$. Then let $\mathrm{wt}(\pi) = \mathrm{Val}(t_\pi)$. The *behavior* of $\mathcal{A}$ is the function $\|\mathcal{A}\| \colon \Sigma^* \to \mathbb{D}$ with $\|\mathcal{A}\|(w) = \sum_{\pi \text{ successful run on } w} \mathrm{wt}(\pi)$ for $w \in \Sigma^*$.

A *weighted unranked tree automaton* (*WUTA* for short) over Σ and $\mathbb{D}$ is a triple $\mathcal{M} = (Q, \mathcal{A}, \gamma)$ where Q is a non-empty, finite set of states, $\mathcal{A} = (\mathcal{A}_{q,a} \mid q \in Q, a \in \Sigma)$ is a family of weighted word automata over Q as alphabet and $\mathbb{D}$, and $\gamma \colon Q \to \mathbb{D}$ is a *root weight function*. Let $\mathcal{A}_{q,a} = (P_{q,a}, I_{q,a}, \mu_{q,a}, F_{q,a})$ for all $q \in Q$, $a \in \Sigma$. We assume the sets $P_{q,a}$ to be pairwise disjoint and let $P_{\mathcal{A}} = \bigcup_{q \in Q, a \in \Sigma} P_{q,a}$. Moreover, let $\mu_{\mathcal{A}}$ be the union of the transition functions $\mu_{q,a}$.

Intuitively, an extended run assigns a state $q \in Q$ to each position u of a given tree $t \in U_{\Sigma}$ and then consists of one run of $\mathcal{A}_{q,t(u)}$ on $q_1 \ldots q_{\mathrm{rk}_t(u)}$ where q_i is the state assigned to the i-th child of u. Formally, an *extended run* of $\mathcal{M}$ on a tree t is a triple (q, s, l) such that

- $q \in Q$ is the *root state*;
- $s \colon \mathrm{dom}(t) \setminus \{\varepsilon\} \to P_{\mathcal{A}} \times Q \times P_{\mathcal{A}}$ is a function such that $s(1) \ldots s(\mathrm{rk}_t(\varepsilon))$ is a run of $\mathcal{A}_{q,t(\varepsilon)}$ and $s(u.1) \ldots s(u.\mathrm{rk}_t(u))$ is a run of $\mathcal{A}_{s(u)_2,t(u)}$ for every $u \in \mathrm{dom}(t) \setminus (\mathrm{leaf}(t) \cup \{\varepsilon\})$;
- $l \colon \mathrm{leaf}(t) \to P_{\mathcal{A}}$ is a function satisfying $l(\varepsilon) \in P_{q,t(\varepsilon)}$ if t only consists of the root, and if $u \neq \varepsilon$ is a leaf, then $l(u) \in P_{s(u)_2,t(u)}$.

An extended run (q, s, l) is *successful* if $s(u.1) \ldots s(u.\mathrm{rk}_t(u))$ is successful for all $u \in \mathrm{dom}(t) \setminus \mathrm{leaf}(t)$ and if $l(u)$ is successful for all $u \in \mathrm{leaf}(t)$ (i.e., $l(u)$ is an initial and final state of $\mathcal{A}_{s(u)_2,t(u)}$ if $u \neq \varepsilon$ respectively of $\mathcal{A}_{q,t(\varepsilon)}$ if $u = \varepsilon$). We let $\mathrm{succ}(\mathcal{M}, t)$ denote the set of all successful extended runs of $\mathcal{M}$ on t.

We will define the local weight of a position u by the weight of the transition taken for u in the run of the parent of u. This gives a tree $\mu(t, (q, s, l)) \in U_{\mathbb{D}}$ of weights with the same domain as t; then we apply Val to obtain the weight of the run (q, s, l) on t. Formally, we define a tree $\mu(t, (q, s, l)) \in U_{\mathbb{D}}$ where $\mathrm{dom}(\mu(t, (q, s, l))) = \mathrm{dom}(t)$ and

$$\mu(t, (q, s, l))(u) = \begin{cases} \gamma(q) & \text{if } u = \varepsilon, \\ \mu_{\mathcal{A}}(s(u)) & \text{otherwise} \end{cases}$$

for all $u \in \mathrm{dom}(t)$. We call $\mu(t, (q, s, l))(u)$ the *local weight* of u. Then $\mathrm{Val}(\mu(t, (q, s, l)))$ is the *weight* of (q, s, l) *on* t. The *behavior* of a WUTA $\mathcal{M}$ is the function $\|\mathcal{M}\| \colon U_{\Sigma} \to \mathbb{D}$ defined by

$$\|\mathcal{M}\|(t) = \sum_{(q,s,l) \in \mathrm{succ}(\mathcal{M},t)} \mathrm{Val}(\mu(t, (q, s, l)))$$

for all $t \in U_{\Sigma}$. If no successful extended run on t exists, we put $\|\mathcal{M}\|(t) = 0$.

Any mapping from U_{Σ} to $\mathbb{D}$ is called an *(unranked) tree series*. A tree series $S \colon U_{\Sigma} \to \mathbb{D}$ is called *recognizable* over $\mathbb{D}$ if there is a WUTA $\mathcal{M}$ over Σ and $\mathbb{D}$ with $\|\mathcal{M}\| = S$.

Remark: Every unranked tree automaton M (see [32] for a definition of unranked tree automata) over an alphabet Σ can be seen as a weighted unranked tree automaton over Σ and the boolean semiring $\mathbb{B} = (\{0, 1\}, \wedge, \vee, 0, 1)$. Let $M = (Q, A, \gamma)$ be an unranked tree automaton. In the following, we identify the weight functions γ and $\mu_{q,a}$ ($q \in Q, a \in \Sigma$) with their support sets. The language of M is defined as follows. We say that M recognizes $t \in U_\Sigma$ if there is a function $r\colon \operatorname{dom}(t) \to Q$ (which we call *successful run*) with $r(\epsilon) \in \gamma$ and such that there is a successful run of $A_{r(u),t(u)}$ on $r(u.1)\ldots r(u.\operatorname{rk}(t(u)))$ with $\operatorname{wt}(r(u.1)\ldots r(u.\operatorname{rk}(t(u)))) = 1$ for all $u \in \operatorname{dom}(t)$. The tree language recognized by M is defined by $L(M) = \{t \in U_\Sigma \mid M \text{ recognizes } t\}$. A tree language $L \subseteq U_\Sigma$ is *recognizable* if there is a unranked tree automaton M with $L(M) = L$. Note that this behavior definition is expressively equivalent to the earlier extended run behavior over the boolean semiring, nevertheless, we later use this behavior definition to avoid the syntactically more complex extended runs.

Example 2. Let $\mathbb{Q}_{\max}$ be the tv-monoid from Example 1 and Σ be an arbitrary, but fixed alphabet. In [12], a WUTA $\mathcal{M}$ which calculates the leaves-to-size ratio of a given input tree were given. The size of a tree is the number of all positions of the tree. For sake of completeness we include the definition of $\mathcal{M}$ and some considerations concerning $\mathcal{M}$'s behavior here. Let $\mathcal{M} = (\{c,n\}, \mathcal{A}, \gamma)$ over Σ with $\gamma(c) = 1$, $\gamma(n) = 0$, and

- $\mathcal{A}_{n,a} = (\{i,f\}, \{i\}, \mu_{n,a}, \{f\})$ where $\mu_{n,a}(i,n,f) = \mu_{n,a}(f,n,f) = 0$, $\mu_{n,a}(i,c,f) = \mu_{n,a}(f,c,f) = 1$ and $\mu_{n,a}(f,q,i) = \mu_{n,a}(i,q,i) = -\infty$
- $\mathcal{A}_{c,a} = (\{p\}, \{p\}, \mu_{c,a}, \{p\})$ where $\mu_{c,a}(p,q,p) = -\infty$

for all $q \in \{c,n\}$ and $a \in \Sigma$; for notational convenience, here we have dropped the condition on pairwise disjointness of the state sets. The sub-automata $\mathcal{A}_{n,a}$ and $\mathcal{A}_{c,a}$ depicted in Fig. 1 for some $a \in \Sigma$.

First, let us consider an example tree. For this, we choose $\Sigma = \{\alpha, \beta\}$ and the tree

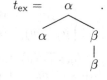

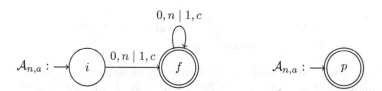

Fig. 1. Sub-automata of the example WUTA $\mathcal{M}$. Here, incoming arrows symbolize that a state is initial whereas a double border indicates that a state is final. An edge from one state p_1 to another state p_2 (p_1 and p_2 can be the same state) labeled with a, d stands for the transition (p_1, a, p_2) with weight d. Transitions with weight $-\infty$ are omitted.

Then (n, s, l) with $s =$ and $l=$

$$
\begin{array}{cc}
\overbrace{(i, c, f) \quad (f, n, f)} & \overbrace{\qquad\qquad} \\
\mid & p \qquad\qquad \mid \\
(i, c, f) & \qquad\qquad p
\end{array}
$$

is an extended run on t_{ex}. Note that the domain of s excludes ε. therefore, above, the position ε is unlabeled for s. Similarly, the function l has leaves of t_{ex} as domain; therefore, above, the positions ε and 1 are unlabeled for l.

Obviously (n, s, l) is successful, since the runs $s(1)s(2) = (i, c, f)(f, n, f)$ and $s(2.1) = (i, c, f)$ are successful in $\mathcal{A}_{n,\alpha}$ and $\mathcal{A}_{n,\beta}$, respectively, and the run p is successful in $\mathcal{A}_{c,\alpha}$ as well as in $\mathcal{A}_{c,\beta}$. The local weights of (n, s, l) are

$$
\mu(t_{\text{ex}}, (n, s, l)) = \qquad \gamma(n) \qquad = \qquad 0
$$

$$
\begin{array}{cc}
\overbrace{\mu_{\mathcal{A}}(i, c, f)\, \mu_{\mathcal{A}}(f, n, f)} & \overbrace{1 \qquad 0} \\
\mid & \mid \\
\mu_{\mathcal{A}}(i, c, f) & 1
\end{array}
$$

and thus the weight of (n, s, l) equals $\frac{1}{2}$.

Now let t be an arbitrary, but fixed tree. It is easy to see that for every successful extended run (q, s, l) on t, $l(u) = p$ for every leaf u of t. Assume that in addition (q, s, l) assigns the state n to each inner position of t. Let π_u be the unique run of $\mathcal{A}_{n,t(u)}$ for which t_{π_u} has no label equal to $-\infty$, thus, π_u leads directly from i to f and finally loops in f. If (q, s, l) consists for every inner position $u \neq \varepsilon$ of π_u, then (q, s, l) is the only successful extended run such that $\mu(t, (q, s, l))$ does not contain $-\infty$. Let π denote this unique extended run. For leaves u of t, $\mu(t, \pi)(u) = 1$ and for inner positions u', $\mu(t, \pi)(u') = 0$. Thus,

$$
\|\mathcal{M}\|(t) = \text{avg}(\mu(t, \pi)) = \frac{\sum_{u \in \text{dom}(t)} \mu(t, \pi)(u)}{|\text{dom}(t)|} = \frac{\text{"number of leaves of t"}}{\text{"size of t"}}.
$$

We will recall some properties of recognizable unranked tree series. Let $L \subseteq U_\Sigma$ and $S \colon U_\Sigma \to \mathbb{D}$. We define the *restriction of S on L* by the tree series $S \cap L \colon U_\Sigma \to \mathbb{D}$ by letting $(S \cap L)(t) = S(t)$ if $t \in L$ and $(S \cap L)(t) = \mathbb{0}$ if $t \notin L$.

Proposition 3 [12, **Lemma 3.4(2)**]. *Let $\mathbb{D}$ be a tv-monoid, $L \subseteq U_\Sigma$ and $S \colon U_\Sigma \to \mathbb{D}$ be recognizable. Then $S \cap L$ is also recognizable.*

Now we consider the closure under relabeling, similarly to [16,19]. Let Σ and Γ be two alphabets and $h \colon \Sigma \to 2^\Gamma$ be a mapping. Then h can be extended to a mapping $h' \colon U_\Sigma \to 2^{U_\Gamma}$ by letting $h'(t)$ be the set of all unranked trees t' over Γ such that $\text{dom}(t') = \text{dom}(t)$ and $t'(w) \in h(t(w))$ for each position $w \in \text{dom}(t)$. For every $S \colon U_\Sigma \to \mathbb{D}$ the tree series $h''(S) \colon U_\Gamma \to \mathbb{D}$ is defined by

$$
h''(S)(t') = \sum_{t \in U_\Sigma \,\wedge\, t' \in h'(t)} S(t)
$$

for all $t' \in U_\Gamma$. Clearly, the index set of the summation is finite. We denote h' and h'' also by h which we call a *relabeling*.

Proposition 4 [12, **Lemma 3.6**]. *Recognizable tree series are closed under relabeling.*

3   Nivat-Classes for Unranked Trees

Here we will define the set of all tree series which can be constructed from recognizable tree languages and behaviors of very simple weighted unranked tree automata by using operations like relabelings and intersections. Inspired by Weidner [35], we will call this set Nivat-class for unranked trees.

For the rest of this section let $\mathbb{D} = (D, +, \mathrm{Val}, \mathbb{0})$ be a tv-monoid, Γ be an alphabet and g: $\Gamma \to D$ be a function. The function g later assigns labels to valuation monoid elements. The extension g': $U_\Gamma \to U_D$ of g is defined by $g'(t)(u) = g(t(u))$ for all $t \in \mathcal{O}(\Gamma)$ and $u \in \mathrm{dom}(t)$. In the following we denote g' also by g. Then $\mathrm{Val} \circ g$ assigns to each tree $t \in U_\Gamma$ the weight $\mathrm{Val}(g(t))$.

Definition 5. *Let Σ be an alphabet, $\mathbb{D}$ be a tv-monoid. The* Nivat-class $\mathcal{N}_\mathbb{D}(U_\Sigma)$ *for unranked trees consists of all S: $U_\Sigma \to \mathbb{D}$ for which there are:*

- *an alphabet Γ,*
- *a recognizable tree language $L \subseteq U_\Gamma$,*
- *a relabeling h: $\Gamma \to \Sigma$,*
- *a function g: $\Gamma \to D$*

such that
$$S = h((\mathrm{Val} \circ g) \cap L).$$

Example 6. Let $\mathbb{Q}_{\max}$ be the tv-monoid of Example 1 and Σ be an arbitrary, but fixed alphabet. We will show that the tree series defined by the WUTA in Example 2, which calculates the leaves-to-size ratio of trees, is in $\mathcal{N}_{\mathbb{Q}_{\max}}(U_\Sigma)$. For this, let

- $\Gamma = \Sigma \times \{\mathrm{leaf}, \mathrm{noleaf}\}$,
- $L = \{t \in U_\Gamma \mid \forall u \in \mathrm{dom}(t) \setminus \mathrm{leaf}(t): t(u)_2 = \mathrm{noleaf}$
  $\wedge \forall u \in \mathrm{leaf}(t): t(u)_2 = \mathrm{leaf}\}$,
- $h(a) = a_1$ for all $a \in \Gamma$,
- $g(a, \mathrm{leaf}) = 1$ and $g(a, \mathrm{noleaf}) = 0$ for all $a \in \Sigma$.

It is easy to check that L is indeed recognizable and that

$$h((\mathrm{Val} \circ g) \cap L)(t) = \frac{\text{``number of leaves of}\, t\text{''}}{\text{``size of}\, t\text{''}}$$

for all $t \in U_\Sigma$.

Our main result will show that the Nivat-class for unranked trees and the set of all recognizable tree series are the same. For the proof of the inclusion of the

Nivat-class in the set of all recognizable tree series we first prove that $\mathrm{Val}(g)$ is recognizable by an especially simple weighted tree automaton $\mathcal{M}$. In particular, we can choose $\mathcal{M}$ with state set Γ and $\mathcal{A} = (A_{q,a} \mid q \in \Gamma, a \in \Gamma)$ where $\mathcal{A}_{q,a}$ has only one state.

Lemma 7. *Let Γ be an alphabet, $\mathbb{D} = (D, +, \mathrm{Val}, \mathbb{0})$ be a tv-monoid, and $g \colon \Gamma \to D$. Then $\mathrm{Val} \circ g$ is recognizable.*

Proof. We will build a WUTA $\mathcal{M}$ which recognizes $\mathrm{Val} \circ g$. Basically, $\mathcal{M}$ will have exactly one successful extended run per input tree $t \in U_\Gamma$. The local weight of this extended run at a position u shall be $g(t(u))$. For this we set the state set of $\mathcal{M}$ to Γ and let the root weight of state $a \in \Gamma$ be $g(a)$. Moreover, each subautomaton $\mathcal{A}_{a,a}$ $(a \in \Gamma)$ of $\mathcal{M}$ has only one state q which is initial and final (so that there is only one successful run), and each transition of $\mathcal{A}_{a,a}$ labeled with $b \in \Gamma$ has weight $g(b)$ (this generates the local weight which we would like to produce). All other subautomata do not produce any successful run. The latter secures that one only gets a successful extended run if for a-labeled positions $\mathcal{A}_{a,a}$ is called. Formally, let $\mathcal{M} = (\Gamma, \mathcal{A}, \gamma)$ with $\gamma(a) = g(a)$ for all $a \in \Gamma$ and $\mathcal{A} = (A_{q,a} \mid q \in \Gamma, a \in \Gamma)$ with $\mathcal{A}_{a,a} = (\{q\}, \{q\}, \mu_{a,a}, \{q\})$ with $\mu_{a,a}(b) = g(b)$ for all $b \in \Gamma$ and $\mathcal{A}_{c,a} = (\{q\}, \{q\}, \underline{\mathbb{0}}, \emptyset)$ for all $a, c \in \Gamma$ with $a \neq c$ where $\underline{\mathbb{0}}$ denotes a function which maps all triples to $\mathbb{0}$.

Using the intuition behind $\mathcal{M}$ given above, one can easily check that $\|\mathcal{M}\|(t) = \mathrm{Val}(g(t))$ for all $t \in U_\Gamma$. $\square$

Now we prove our main theorem.

Theorem 8. *Let Σ be an alphabet, $\mathbb{D}$ be a tv-monoid, and $S \colon U_\Sigma \to \mathbb{D}$ a tree series. Then S is recognizable iff $S \in \mathcal{N}_\mathbb{D}(U_\Sigma)$.*

Proof. We start with the proof of the "if"-implication. For this, let Γ be an alphabet, $L \subseteq U_\Gamma$ a recognizable tree language, $h \colon \Gamma \to \Sigma$ a relabeling, and $g \colon \Gamma \to D$ a function such that $S = h((\mathrm{Val} \circ g) \cap L)$. By Lemma 7, $\mathrm{Val} \circ g$ is recognizable, and thus, by Proposition 3, also $(\mathrm{Val} \circ g) \cap L$ is recognizable. Hence by Proposition 4, $S = h((\mathrm{Val} \circ g) \cap L)$ is recognizable.

For the converse, let S be recognizable and $\mathcal{M} = (Q, \mathcal{A}, \gamma)$ be a WUTA with $\|\mathcal{M}\| = S$. Moreover let $\mathcal{A}_{q,a} = (P_{q,a}, I_{q,a}, \mu_{q,a}, F_{q,a})$ for all $q \in Q$, $a \in \Sigma$. We assume the sets $P_{q,a}$ to be pairwise disjoint and let $P_\mathcal{A} = \bigcup_{q \in Q, a \in \Sigma} P_{q,a}$. Let $\mu_\mathcal{A}$ be the union of the transition functions $\mu_{q,a}$.

We will simulate the behavior of $\mathcal{M}$ by appropriately chosen Γ, L, h, and g. The main idea for the choice of Γ, L, h, and g is that L will be the set of successful extended runs of $\mathcal{M}$, g will determine the local weights of the extended runs in L, the valuation function Val will calculate the weights of the extended runs, and h will be a projection of the extended runs on their related trees (this results in the "sum over all trees" since h is a relabeling). Since L shall be a set of trees over an alphabet Γ, we have to encode (successful) extended runs by trees. As indicated in Example 2, each component q, s, and l, respectively, of an extended run (q, s, l) on a tree t can be viewed as a tree with possibly unlabeled positions over the tree domain $\mathrm{dom}(t)$. Then q has labels in $\Gamma_1 = Q$, s in $\Gamma_2 = P_A \times Q \times P_A$, and l in P_A whereby the root is the only labeled position in q and the only unlabeled position in s, respectively, and in l only leaves are labeled. We combine these three trees to one tree via building tuples from the labels of q, s, and l. The resulting tree then has labels in $\Gamma_1 \cup \Gamma_2 \cup \Gamma_3$ where $\Gamma_3 = ((P_A \times Q \times P_A) \times P_A)$. Thus we set $\Gamma = (\Gamma_1 \cup \Gamma_2 \cup \Gamma_3) \times \Sigma$. We built the Cartesian product with Σ, so that later h can extract the related tree. Let $t \in U_\Sigma$, (q, s, l) an extended run on t, and τ a tree over Γ. We say that τ encodes the pair $((q, s, l), t)$ if $\mathrm{dom}(t) = \mathrm{dom}(\tau)$ and $\tau(\varepsilon) = (q, t(\varepsilon))$, $\tau(u) = (s(u), t(u))$ for all $u \in \mathrm{dom}(t) \setminus (\{\varepsilon\} \cup \mathrm{leaf}(t))$, and $\tau(u) = ((s(u), l(u)), t(u))$ for all $u \in \mathrm{leaf}(t) \setminus \{\varepsilon\}$. From now on we identify a pair $((q, s, l), t)$ and its encoding $\tau \in U_\Gamma$.

Now we can define Γ, L, h, and g:

- $\Gamma = (\Gamma_1 \cup \Gamma_2 \cup \Gamma_3) \times \Sigma$
- $L = \{((q, s, l), t) \in U_\Gamma \mid (q, s, l) \in \mathrm{succ}(\mathcal{M}, t)\}$
- $h(q', a) = a$
- $g(q', a) = \begin{cases} \gamma(a) & \text{if } q' \in \Gamma_1 \\ \mu(p_1, q, p_2) & \text{if } q' = (p_1, q, p_2) \in \Gamma_2 \text{ or } q' = ((p_1, q, p_2), p) \in \Gamma_3 \end{cases}$

for $a \in \Sigma$ and $(q', a) \in \Gamma$.

We show that L is actually recognizable. For this, we construct an unranked tree automaton $\mathcal{M}_{\mathrm{runs}} = (Q_{\mathrm{runs}}, A, \gamma_{\mathrm{runs}})$ which has only τ as successful run on an input tree $\tau = ((q, s, l), t) \in U_\Gamma$ iff (q, s, l) is a successful extended run of $\mathcal{M}$ on t. Thus, the state set Q_{runs} of $\mathcal{M}_{\mathrm{runs}}$ will be Γ and only subautomata $A_{\alpha, \alpha}$ ($\alpha \in \Gamma$) actually accept a non-empty language. The subautomaton $A_{\alpha, \alpha}$ of $\mathcal{M}_{\mathrm{runs}}$ will be a version of the subautomaton $A_{q, a}$ (where q is the Q-component and a is the Σ-component, respectively, of α) of $\mathcal{M}$ without weights. Hence

- $\tau(1) \ldots \tau(\mathrm{rk}_\tau(\varepsilon)) \in L(\delta(\tau(\varepsilon), \tau(\varepsilon)))$ iff $s(1) \ldots s(\mathrm{rk}_t(u))$ is a successful run in $A_{q, t(\varepsilon)}$,
- $\tau(u.1) \ldots \tau(u. \mathrm{rk}_\tau(u)) \in L(\delta(\tau(u), \tau(u)))$ iff $s(u.1) \ldots s(u. \mathrm{rk}_t(u))$ is a successful run in $A_{s(u)_2, t(u)}$ for all $u \in \mathrm{dom}(t) \setminus (\{\varepsilon\} \cup \mathrm{leaf}(t))$,
- $\varepsilon \in L(\delta(\tau(u), \tau(u)))$ iff $l(u)$ is a successful run in $A_{s(u)_2, t(u)}$ for all leaves u

for all trees $\tau = ((q, s, l), t) \in U_\Gamma$. To guarantee that trees accepted by $\mathcal{M}_{\mathrm{runs}}$ have their root label in $\Gamma_1 \times \Sigma$, we let $\Gamma_1 \times \Sigma$ be the set of final states γ_{runs} of $\mathcal{M}_{\mathrm{runs}}$. Moreover, subautomata associated to a state in $\Gamma_2 \times \Sigma$ will not accept the empty word, hence, $\mathcal{M}_{\mathrm{runs}}$ does not allow runs where states in $\Gamma_2 \times \Sigma$ occur at leaf positions. Leaf positions shall be labeled with states in $\Gamma_3 \times \Sigma$. We achieve this by letting $A_{\alpha, \alpha}$ for $\alpha \in \Gamma_3 \times \Sigma$ be a word automaton which at most accepts the empty word.

Formally, let $\mathcal{M}_{\mathrm{runs}} = (\Gamma, A, Q \times \Sigma)$ with

- $A_{\alpha, \alpha} = (P_{q, a}, I_{q, a}, \mu_{q, a}, F_{q, a})$ for $\alpha = (q, a) \in (\Gamma_1 \times \Sigma)$ where $P_{q, a}, I_{q, a}, F_{q, a}$ are as in $A_{q, a}$ and

$$\mu_{q, a} = \{(p_1, (p_1, q', p_2), p_2) \mid p_1, p_2 \in P_{q, a}, q' \in Q\}$$
$$\cup \{(p_1, ((p_1, q', p_2), p), p_2) \mid p_1, p_2, p \in P_{q, a}, q' \in Q\}$$

– $A_{\alpha,\alpha} = (P_{q,a} \cup \overline{I_{q,a}}, \overline{I_{q,a}}, \mu'_{q,a}, F_{q,a})$ for $\alpha = ((p'_1, q, p'_2), a) \in (\Gamma_2 \times \Sigma)$ where $P_{q,a}, I_{q,a}, F_{q,a}$ are as in $\mathcal{A}_{q,a}$, $\overline{I_{q,a}}$ is a disjoint copy of $I_{q,a}$, and

$$\mu'_{q,a} = T_{q,a} \cup \{(\overline{i_1}, (i, q', p_2), p_2) \mid i \in I_{q,a}, p_2 \in P_{q,a}, q' \in Q\}$$
$$\cup \{(\overline{i}, ((i, q', p_2), p), p_2) \mid i \in I_{q,,a}, p_2, p \in P_{q,a}, q' \in Q\}$$

with

$$\mu_{q,a} = \{(p_1, (p_1, q', p_2), p_2) \mid p_1, p_2 \in P_{q,a}, q' \in Q\}$$
$$\cup \{(p_1, ((p_1, q', p_2), p), p_2) \mid p_1, p_2, p \in P_{q,a}, q' \in Q\}$$

– $A_{\alpha,\alpha} = (\{p_\alpha\}, \{p_\alpha\}, \emptyset, \{p_\alpha\})$ for $\alpha = (((p'_1, q, p'_2), p'), a) \in (\Gamma_3 \times \Sigma)$ with $p' \in I_{q,a} \cap F_{q,a}$ and $A_{\alpha,\alpha} = (\{p_\alpha\}, \{p_\alpha\}, \emptyset, \emptyset)$ for $\alpha = (((p'_1, q, p'_2), p'), a)$ with $p' \notin I_{q,a} \cap F_{q,a}$
– $A_{\alpha,\beta} = (\{p\}, \{p\}, \emptyset, \emptyset)$

for $\alpha, \beta \in \Gamma$ and $\alpha \neq \beta$. One can easily prove that $L(M_{\text{runs}}) = L$.

Now let $t \in U_\Sigma$. Then

$$h((\text{Val} \circ g) \cap L)(t) = \sum_{\tau \in U_\Gamma \wedge t \in h(\tau)} ((\text{Val} \circ g) \cap L)(\tau)$$

$$= \sum_{\tau = ((q,s,l),t) \wedge (q,s,l) \in \text{succ}(\mathcal{M},t)} \text{Val}(g(\tau))$$

$$= \sum_{\tau = ((q,s,l),t) \wedge (q,s,l) \in \text{succ}(\mathcal{M},t)} \text{Val}(\mu(t,(s,q,l)))$$

$$= \sum_{(q,s,l) \in \text{succ}(\mathcal{M},t)} \text{Val}(\mu(t,(s,q,l)))$$

$$= \|\mathcal{M}\|(t) \,.$$

□

4 The Ranked Tree Case

In this section we will show a version of Theorem 8 for ranked trees. For this, we briefly recall the definitions of ranked alphabets, ranked trees and weighted ranked tree automata over tv-monoids as well as some considerations on the relationship between weighted ranked tree automata and weighted unranked tree automata.

A *ranked alphabet* is a pair $(\Sigma, \text{rk}_\Sigma)$, where Σ is an alphabet and $\text{rk}_\Sigma \colon \Sigma \to \mathbb{N}_0$ is a mapping which assigns to each symbol of Σ its rank. We denote by $\Sigma^{(k)}$ the set of all symbols which have rank k and by $a^{(k)}$ that a is in $\Sigma^{(k)}$. Usually we drop rk_Σ and denote a ranked alphabet simply by Σ. In this paper we assume that $\Sigma^{(0)} \neq \emptyset$. We define $\max_\Sigma = \max\{\text{rk}_\Sigma(\sigma) \mid \sigma \in \Sigma\}$. A *ranked tree* over a ranked alphabet Σ is an unranked tree over the set Σ such that for all $u \in \text{dom}(t)$, $\text{rk}_t(u) = k$ whenever $t(u) \in \Sigma^{(k)}$. We denote the set of all ranked trees over Σ by T_Σ.

Let Σ be a ranked alphabet and $(D, +, \text{Val}, \mathbb{0})$ a tv-monoid. A *weighted ranked tree automaton* (*WRTA* for short) over Σ and D is a triple $\mathcal{M} = (Q, \mu, F)$ where Q is a non-empty finite set of states, $\mu = (\mu_m)_{0 \leq m \leq \max_\Sigma}$ is a family of transition mappings $\mu_m \colon Q^m \times \Sigma^{(m)} \times Q \to D$, and $F \subseteq Q$ is a set of final states.

A *run* r *of* $\mathcal{M}$ *on a tree* $t \in T_\Sigma$ is a mapping $r \colon \text{dom}(t) \to Q$. Since the domain of a run is a tree domain, each run r on t defines a tree $\mu(t, r) \in T_D$ where $\text{dom}(\mu(t, r)) = \text{dom}(t)$ and $\mu(t, r)(u) = \mu_m(r(u.1) \ldots r(u.m), t(u), r(u))$ with $t(u) \in \Sigma^{(m)}$ for all $u \in \text{dom}(t)$. We call r on t *successful* if $r(\varepsilon) \in F$. The *behavior* of a WRTA $\mathcal{M}$ is the function $\|\mathcal{M}\| \colon T_\Sigma \to D$ defined by

$$\|\mathcal{M}\|(t) = \sum \left(\text{Val}(\mu(t, r)) \mid r \text{ is successful run of } \mathcal{M} \text{ on } t \right)$$

for all $t \in T_\Sigma$. If no successful run on t exists, we put $\|\mathcal{M}\|(t) = \mathbb{0}$.

A *ranked tree series* is a mapping $S \colon T_\Sigma \to D$. A tree series S is called *recognizable* if $S = \|\mathcal{M}\|$ for some WRTA $\mathcal{M}$. As is well-known, a ranked tree automaton (cf. [9]) can be seen as a weighted ranked tree automaton over the boolean semiring, and conversely.

In passing, we note the following result. It shows that on ranked trees WRTA and WUTA have the same expressive power.

Proposition 9 [24, **Lemma 3.10 and Lemma 3.11**]. *Let Σ be a ranked alphabet.*

1. *For every WRTA $\mathcal{N}$ over Σ there exists a WUTA $\mathcal{M}$ such that $\|\mathcal{M}\|(t) = \|\mathcal{N}\|(t)$ for all $t \in T_\Sigma$ and $\|\mathcal{M}\|(t) = \mathbb{0}$ for all $t \in U_\Sigma \setminus T_\Sigma$.*
2. *For every WUTA $\mathcal{M}$ over Σ there exists a WRTA $\mathcal{N}$ such that $\|\mathcal{N}\|(t) = \|\mathcal{M}\|(t)$ for all $t \in T_\Sigma$.*

Now we define a Nivat-class for ranked trees. For this, we define for all $L \subseteq T_\Sigma$ and $S \colon T_\Sigma \to D$ the *restriction of S on L* analogously to the respective definition of the restriction of a tree series and an unranked tree language. Moreover, let Σ and Γ be two ranked alphabets and $h \colon \Sigma \to 2^\Gamma$ be a mapping with $\text{rk}_\Gamma(b) = \text{rk}_\Sigma(a)$ for all $b \in h(a)$. We extend h to a mapping h' from ranked trees over Σ to the power set of ranked trees over Γ, and afterwards to a mapping h'' from ranked tree series over Σ and $\mathbb{D}$ to ranked tree series over Γ and $\mathbb{D}$ analogously as we did in the unranked tree case. Again, we denote h' and h'' also by h which we call a *relabeling*. Let Γ be a ranked alphabet, $g \colon \Gamma \to D$ be a function, and the extension $g' \colon U_\Gamma \to U_D$ of g be defined by $g'(t)(u) = g(t(u))$ for all $t \in T_\Gamma$ and $u \in \text{dom}(t)$. In the following we denote g' also by g.

Definition 10. *The* Nivat-class $\mathcal{N}_\mathbb{D}(T_\Sigma)$ *for ranked trees consists of all $S \colon T_\Sigma \to \mathbb{D}$ for which there are:*

- *an alphabet Γ,*
- *a recognizable ranked tree language $L \subseteq T_\Gamma$,*
- *a relabeling $h \colon \Gamma \to \Sigma$,*
- *a function g$\colon \Gamma \to D$*

such that

$$S = h((\text{Val} \circ g) \cap L).$$

Example 11. Let Σ be a ranked alphabet. We will show that also the ranked tree series which calculates the leaves-to-size ratio of trees is in $\mathcal{N}_{\mathbb{Q}_{\max}}(T_\Sigma)$. We let $\Gamma = \Sigma$, $L = T_\Gamma$, $h(a) = a$ for all $a \in \Gamma$, and $g(a^{(0)}) = 1$ and $g(a^{(k)}) = 0$ for all $a \in \Sigma$ and $k > 0$. Obviously L is recognizable and $h((\text{Val} \circ g) \cap L)$ calculates the leaves-to-size ratio of ranked trees. A WRTA that recognizes $h((\text{Val} \circ g) \cap L)$ was given in [11].

Next we prove a Nivat theorem for ranked trees.

Theorem 12. *Let Σ be a ranked alphabet, $\mathbb{D}$ a tv-monoid, and $S \colon T_\Sigma \to \mathbb{D}$ a tree series. Then S is recognizable iff $S \in \mathcal{N}_\mathbb{D}(T_\Sigma)$.*

Proof. Let Γ be an alphabet, $L \subseteq T_\Gamma$ a recognizable ranked tree language, $h \colon \Gamma \to \Sigma$ a relabeling, and g$\colon \Gamma \to D$ a function such that $S = h((\text{Val} \circ g) \cap L)$. As is easy to see, $\text{Val} \circ g$ is accepted by a one state automaton $\mathcal{M}$. Indeed, $\mathcal{M} = (\{q\}, \mu, \{q\})$ with $\mu_m(q \ldots q, a, q) = g(a)$ for all $a \in \Gamma^{(m)}$ and $m \in \mathbb{N}$. By the versions of Proposition 3 and Proposition 4 for ranked trees (cf. [11]), $(\text{Val} \circ g) \cap L$ is recognizable, and thus, $S = h((\text{Val} \circ g) \cap L)$ is recognizable.

For the converse implication, let $S = \|\mathcal{M}\|$ for some WRTA $\mathcal{M} = (Q, \mu, F)$. Then let

- $\Gamma = \bigcup_{0 \leq m \leq \max_\Sigma} Q^m \times \Sigma^{(m)} \times Q$ with $\text{rk}(q_1 \ldots q_m, a, q) = \text{rk}(a)$ for all $q_1, \ldots, q_m, q \in Q$, $a \in \Sigma^{(m)}$ be the set of all transitions of $\mathcal{M}$,
- $L = \{t \in T_\Gamma \mid \forall u \in \text{dom}(t) \text{ with } t(u) \in \Gamma^{(m)} \colon t(u.i)_3 = (t(u)_1)_i \text{ for all } 1 \leq i \leq m \text{ and } t(\varepsilon)_3 \in F\}$ describing the set of all successful runs of $\mathcal{M}$,
- $h((q_1, \ldots, q_m), a, q) = a$,
- $g((q_1, \ldots, q_m), a, q) = \mu_m(q_1 \ldots q_m, a, q)$

for all $q_1, \ldots, q_m, q \in Q$, $a \in \Sigma^{(m)}$. One can check that L is recognizable and $h((\text{Val} \circ g) \cap L) = S$. $\square$

Conclusion

We proved two Nivat theorems for weighted unranked tree automata and for weighted ranked tree automata over tree valuation monoids.

In [17,33,34], the Nivat theorem was used to show the expressive equivalence of a suitable MSO logic and the respective automata model. We think that, similarly, Theorem 8 could be used to derive an alternative proof to the one in [12] showing that the weighted MSO logic defined there and weighted unranked tree automata over tree valuation monoids are expressively equivalent.

References

1. Alexandrakis, A., Bozapalidis, S.: Weighted grammars and Kleene's theorem. Inf. Process. Lett. **24**(1), 1–4 (1987)
2. Brüggemann-Klein, A., Wood, D.: Regular Tree Languages Over Non-Ranked Alphabets (1998)

3. Babari, P., Droste, M.: A Nivat theorem for weighted picture automata and weighted MSO logic. In: Dediu, A.-H., Formenti, E., Martín-Vide, C., Truthe, B. (eds.) LATA 2015. LNCS, vol. 8977, pp. 703–715. Springer, Cham (2015). doi:10.1007/978-3-319-15579-1_55

4. Bauer, S.S., Fahrenberg, U., Juhl, L., Larsen, K.G., Legay, A., Thrane, C.R.: Weighted modal transition systems. Form. Methods Syst. Des. **42**(2), 193–220 (2013)

5. Berstel, J.: Transductions and Context-Free Languages. Teubner Studienbücher: Informatik. Teubner, Leipzig (1979)

6. Berstel, J., Reutenauer, C.: Recognizable formal power series on trees. Theoret. Comput. Sci. **18**(2), 115–148 (1982)

7. Brüggemann-Klein, A., Murata, M., Wood, D.: Regular tree and regular hedge languages over unranked alphabets: version 1. Technical report HKUST-TCSC-2001-0, The Honkong University of Sience and Technologie (2001)

8. Chatterjee, K., Doyen, L., Henzinger, T.A.: Quantitative languages. In: Kaminski, M., Martini, S. (eds.) CSL 2008. LNCS, vol. 5213, pp. 385–400. Springer, Heidelberg (2008). doi:10.1007/978-3-540-87531-4_28

9. Comon, H., Dauchet, M., Gilleron, R., Löding, C., Jacquemard, F., Lugiez, D., Tison, S., Tommasi, M.: Tree automata techniques and applications (2007). http://www.grappa.univ-lille3.fr/tata. Release 12 October 2007

10. Droste, M., Dück, S.: Weighted automata and logics on graphs. In: Italiano, G.F., Pighizzini, G., Sannella, D.T. (eds.) MFCS 2015. LNCS, vol. 9234, pp. 192–204. Springer, Heidelberg (2015). doi:10.1007/978-3-662-48057-1_15

11. Droste, M., Götze, D., Märcker, S., Meinecke, I.: Weighted tree automata over valuation monoids and their characterization by weighted logics. In: Kuich, W., Rahonis, G. (eds.) Algebraic Foundations in Computer Science. LNCS, vol. 7020, pp. 30–55. Springer, Heidelberg (2011). doi:10.1007/978-3-642-24897-9_2

12. Droste, M., Heusel, D., Vogler, H.: Weighted unranked tree automata over tree valuation monoids and their characterization by weighted logics. In: Maletti, A. (ed.) CAI 2015. LNCS, vol. 9270, pp. 90–102. Springer, Cham (2015). doi:10.1007/978-3-319-23021-4_9

13. Droste, M., Kuich, W., Vogler, H. (eds.): Handbook of Weighted Automata. EATCS Monographs on Theoretical Computer Science. Springer, Heidelberg (2009)

14. Droste, M., Kuske, D.: Weighted automata. In: Pin, J.-E. (ed.) Automata: From Mathematics to Applications. European Mathematical Society (to appear)

15. Droste, M., Meinecke, I.: Describing average- and longtime-behavior by weighted MSO logics. In: Hliněný, P., Kučera, A. (eds.) MFCS 2010. LNCS, vol. 6281, pp. 537–548. Springer, Heidelberg (2010). doi:10.1007/978-3-642-15155-2_47

16. Droste, M., Meinecke, I.: Weighted automata and weighted MSO logics for average- and longtime-behaviors. Inf. Comput. **220–221**, 44–59 (2012)

17. Droste, M., Perevoshchikov, V.: A Nivat theorem for weighted timed automata and weighted relative distance logic. In: Esparza, J., Fraigniaud, P., Husfeldt, T., Koutsoupias, E. (eds.) ICALP 2014. LNCS, vol. 8573, pp. 171–182. Springer, Heidelberg (2014). doi:10.1007/978-3-662-43951-7_15

18. Droste, M., Perevoshchikov, V.: Logics for weighted timed pushdown automata. In: Beklemishev, L.D., Blass, A., Dershowitz, N., Finkbeiner, B., Schulte, W. (eds.) Fields of Logic and Computation II. LNCS, vol. 9300, pp. 153–173. Springer, Cham (2015). doi:10.1007/978-3-319-23534-9_9

19. Droste, M., Vogler, H.: Weighted tree automata and weighted logics. Theoret. Comput. Sci. **366**, 228–247 (2006)

20. Droste, M., Vogler, H.: Weighted logics for unranked tree automata. Theory Comput. Syst. **48**, 23–47 (2011)
21. Fülöp, Z., Vogler, H.: Weighted tree automata and tree transducers. In: Droste et al. [13], chap. 9, pp. 313–403
22. Gécseg, F., Steinby, M.: Tree Automata. Akadémiai Kiadó (1984). http://www.arxiv.org
23. Gécseg, F., Steinby, M.: Tree languages. In: Rozenberg, G., Salomaa, A. (eds.) Handbook of Formal Languages, vol. 3, pp. 1–68. Springer, Heidelberg (1997)
24. Götze, D.: Weighted unranked tree automata over tree valuation monoids (submitted)
25. Hansen, M., Larsen, K.G., Mardare, R., Pedersen, M.R., Xue, B.: A complete approximation theory for weighted transition systems. In: Fränzle, M., Kapur, D., Zhan, N. (eds.) SETTA 2016. LNCS, vol. 9984, pp. 213–228. Springer, Cham (2016). doi:10.1007/978-3-319-47677-3_14
26. Högberg, J., Maletti, A., Vogler, H.: Bisimulation minimisation of weighted automata on unranked trees. Fundamenta Informaticae **92**, 103–130 (2009)
27. Larsen, K., Behrmann, G., Brinksma, E., Fehnker, A., Hune, T., Pettersson, P., Romijn, J.: As cheap as possible: effcient cost-optimal reachability for priced timed automata. In: Berry, G., Comon, H., Finkel, A. (eds.) CAV 2001. LNCS, vol. 2102, pp. 493–505. Springer, Heidelberg (2001). doi:10.1007/3-540-44585-4_47
28. Libkin, L.: Logics for unranked trees: an overview. In: Caires, L., Italiano, G.F., Monteiro, L., Palamidessi, C., Yung, M. (eds.) ICALP 2005. LNCS, vol. 3580, pp. 35–50. Springer, Heidelberg (2005). doi:10.1007/11523468_4
29. Murata, M.: Forest-regular languages and tree-regular languages. Unpublished manuscript (1995)
30. Neven, F.: Automata, logic, and XML. In: Bradfield, J. (ed.) CSL 2002. LNCS, vol. 2471, pp. 2–26. Springer, Heidelberg (2002). doi:10.1007/3-540-45793-3_2
31. Nivat, M.: Transduction des langages de Chomsky. Ph.D. thesis, University of Paris (1968)
32. Thatcher, J.W.: Characterizing derivation trees of context-free grammars through a generalization of finite automata theory. J. Comput. Syst. Sci. **1**, 317–322 (1967)
33. Weidner, T.: Probabilistic automata and probabilistic logic. In: Rovan, B., Sassone, V., Widmayer, P. (eds.) MFCS 2012. LNCS, vol. 7464, pp. 813–824. Springer, Heidelberg (2012). doi:10.1007/978-3-642-32589-2_70
34. Weidner, T.: Probabilistic regular expressions and MSO logic on finite trees. In: Proceedings of FSTTCS 2015. LIPIcs, vol. 45, pp. 503–516. Schloss Dagstuhl - Leibniz-Zentrum fuer Informatik (2015)
35. Weidner, T.: Probabilistic Logic, Probabilistic Regular Expressions, and Constraint Temporal Logic. Ph.D. thesis, Universität Leipzig (2016)

30 Years of Modal Transition Systems: Survey of Extensions and Analysis

Jan Křetínský[(✉)]

Technical University of Munich, Munich, Germany
jan.kretinsky@in.tum.de

Abstract. We survey the specification formalism of modal transition systems (MTS). We discuss various extensions of MTS, their relationships and modelling capabilities. The extensions include more involved modalities, quantitative aspects, or infinite state spaces. Further, we discuss problems arising in verification and analysis of these systems. We cover refinement checking, model checking and synthesis, standard logical and structural operations as used in specification theories as well as the respective tool support.

1 Introduction

Correctness of complex systems can be ensured in various ways. The key idea of verification is to first *specify* a property the system under development should satisfy and then to *verify* that this is indeed the case. An alternative to verification is *refinement* of the original specification into an implementation, which is guaranteed to satisfy the specification, for the refinement is designed to preserve the properties of interest. The refinement can be done either in one step, where the implementation is *synthesized* from the specification, or in more steps in a process of *stepwise refinement*. The latter is particularly useful when some details of the requirements are not known at the beginning of the design process, or synthesis of the whole system is infeasible, or in the component-based design where other systems can be reused as parts of the new system.

The difference between verifying and refining systems is reflected in two fundamentally different approaches to specifications. Firstly, the *logical* approach, relying on model checking algorithms, makes use of specifications given as formulae of temporal or modal logics. Secondly, the *behavioural* approach, relying on refinement, requires specifications to be given in the same formalism as implementations, e.g. a kind of a machine with an operational interpretation. We focus on the latter.

Example 1. Consider the scenario of developing a piece of software illustrated in Fig. 1. We start with a viewpoint V_1 on the system, e.g. the client's view on the service functionality. This gets iteratively refined into a more concrete description V_m. Further, assume there is also another viewpoint W_1, e.g. a description of the service from the server point of view, which is refined in a similar fashion

© Springer International Publishing AG 2017
L. Aceto et al. (Eds.): Larsen Festschrift, LNCS 10460, pp. 36–74, 2017.
DOI: 10.1007/978-3-319-63121-9_3

resulting in W_n. After these viewpoints are precise enough (although still very underspecified), we merge them into one, say S, using an operation of *conjunction*. The complete description is now modelled by S, which is to be implemented. Suppose we have components C and D at our disposal, which perform subroutines needed in S. We put C and D together into a component T using an operation of *parallel composition*. What remains to be designed is a component X that we can compose with T in parallel so that the result conforms to the specification S. The most general such X is called the *quotient* of S by T. Once we have X we can further refine the underspecified behaviour in any desired way resulting in a specification Y. The final step is to automatically *synthesize* an implementation Z that, for instance, satisfies additional temporal *logic constraints* φ and/or is the *cheapest* implementation with respect to specified costs $\mathfrak{C}$. Specification theories [Lar90, BDH+12] are mathematical formalisms allowing for such development in a rigorous way.   △

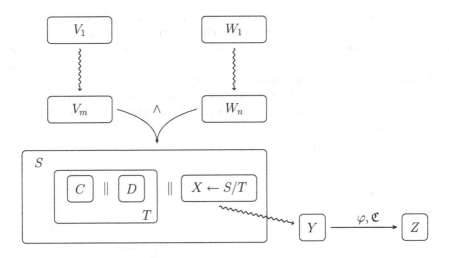

Fig. 1. An example of a component-based step-wise design scheme

A good specification theory should (i) allow for all the operations mentioned in the example and efficient algorithms to compute them. Moreover, it should (ii) be expressive enough to allow for convenient modelling. The behavioural formalism of *modal transition systems* (MTS) [LT88] provides a convenient basis for such a theory and has attracted a lot of attention. Unfortunately, it does not satisfy either of the two stipulations above completely. In this paper, we survey *extensions* of MTS that meet all these demands and efficient algorithms for their *analysis* such as the mentioned operations, refinements, verification and synthesis. Further, we discuss a link between the MTS extensions and logics, thus building a bridge between the behavioural and the logical world, allowing us to combine them, enjoying the best of both worlds.

1.1 History of Modal Transition Systems

Modal transition systems (MTS) were introduced by Larsen and Thomsen [LT88] three decades ago. The goal was to obtain an expressive specification formalism with operational interpretation, allowing for refinement. The main advantage of MTS is that they are a simple extension of labelled transition systems, which have proved appropriate for behavioural description of systems as well as their compositions.

MTS consist of a set of states and two transition relations. The *must* transitions prescribe what behaviour has to be present in every refinement of the system; the *may* transitions describe the behaviour that is allowed, but need not be realized in the refinements. This allows us to underspecify non-critical behaviour in the early stages of design, focusing on the main properties, verifying them and sorting out the details of the yet unimplemented non-critical behaviour later.

Example 2. An MTS specification of a coffee machine is displayed in Fig. 2 on the left. May transitions are depicted using dashed arrows, must transitions using solid arrows. In the left state, the machine can either start to clean or accept a coin. It may not always be possible to take the coin action, but if we do so the machine must offer coffee and possibly supplement the choice with tea. An implementation of this specification is displayed on the right. Here the clean is scheduled regularly after every two beverages. In addition, tea can always be chosen instead of coffee.   △

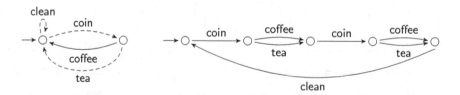

Fig. 2. An MTS specification and its implementation

The formalism of MTS has proven to be useful, most importantly in compositional reasoning and component-based design. Industrial applications are as old as [Bru97] where MTS have found use for an air-traffic system at Heathrow airport. Besides, MTS are advocated as an appropriate base for interface theories in [AHL+08a, RBB+09b, RBB+09a, RBB+11] and for product line theories in [LNW07a, Nym08, tBDG+15, tBFGM16, DSMB16]. Further, MTS-based software engineering methodology for design via merging partial descriptions of behaviour has been established in [UC04, BCU06, UBC07] and using residuation in [Rac07, Rac08, Ben08]. The theory found its applications also in testing [BDH+15, LML15]. MTS are used for program analysis using abstraction

[GHJ01, DGG97, Nam03, DN04, dAGJ04, NNN08, CGLT09, GNRT10]. MTS specificationformalismsaresupportedbyseveraltools[DFFU07, BML11, KS13a, VR14].

Over the years, many extensions of MTS have been proposed. While MTS can only specify whether or not a particular transition is required, some extensions equip MTS with more general abilities to describe what *combinations* of transitions are possible. For instance, disjunctive MTS (DMTS) [LX90] can specify that at least one of a given set of transitions is present. One-selecting MTS [FS08] specify that exactly one of them is present. Acceptance automata [Rac07] can even express any Boolean combination of transitions, but only for deterministic systems. In all the mentioned cases, every must transition is also automatically a may transition, modelling that whatever is required is also allowed. Sometimes this assumption is dropped and the two transition relations are given independently, giving rise to mixed transition systems (MixTS) [DGG97, AHL+08b].

These formalisms have also been studied under other names in different contexts. To some extent equivalent variations of MTS have been adapted for model-checking: Kripke modal transition systems (KMTS) [HJS01], partial Kripke structures [BG00], and 3-valued Kripke structures [CDEG03]. In the same manner MixTS correspond to Belnap transition systems [GWC06a]. Further, DMTS correspond to generalized KMTS [SG04] or abstract transition systems [dAGJ04]. While the variants of MTS and MixTS have been used in practical symbolic model-checkers (e.g. [CDEG03, GC06, GWC06b]), the "hypermust" transitions in DMTS are hard to encode efficiently into BDDs. A comparison of usability of these systems for symbolic model checking can be found in [WGC09]. Acceptance automata were also studied as acceptance trees [Hen85].

1.2   Outline of the Paper

Section 2 introduces modal transition systems formally, recalls several logics used later, and explains the stipulations on good specification formalisms. Section 3 discusses extensions of MTS with respect to specifying the combinations of present transitions. Section 4 discusses extensions of MTS with respect to the underlying graph structure of the MTS, focusing on weighted graphs and infinite graphs. In Sect. 5, results on refinements, operations, implementation synthesis, and the available tools are surveyed. Section 7 concludes and mentions several possible future directions.

1.3   Further Sources

This survey is an updated adaptation of the author's thesis [Kře14]. An excellent overview, however older, is provided in [AHL+08a]. Particular topics are explained in depth in several theses, e.g. applications to interface and product-line theories [Nym08], or extensions of MTS such as acceptance automata [Rac07], disjunctive MTS [Ben12], MTS under different semantics [Fis12], in quantitative settings [Juh13], with data [Bau12], or parameters and synchronization [Møl13].

2 Preliminaries

2.1 Modal Transition Systems

The original modal transition systems were introduced in [LT88] as follows, where Σ is an *action* alphabet.

Definition 1 (Modal transition system). *A* modal transition system (MTS) *is a triple* $(P, \dashrightarrow, \longrightarrow)$, *where P is a set of* processes *and* $\longrightarrow \subseteq \dashrightarrow \subseteq P \times \Sigma \times P$ *are* must *and* may *transition relations, respectively.*

The must and may transitions capture the required and allowed behaviour, as discussed in the introduction. The most fundamental notion of the theory of modal transition systems is the modal refinement. Intuitively, a process s refines a process t if s concretizes t (or in other words, t is more abstract than s). Since processes are meant to serve as specifications, this is defined by (i) only allowing in s what is already allowed in t and (ii) requiring in s what is already required in t.

Definition 2 (Modal refinement). *Let* $(P_1, \dashrightarrow_1, \longrightarrow_1)$, $(P_2, \dashrightarrow_2, \longrightarrow_2)$ *be MTS and* $s \in P_1, t \in P_2$ *be processes. We say that* s modally refines t, *written* $s \leq_m t$, *if there is a* refinement relation $R \subseteq P_1 \times P_2$ *satisfying* $(s,t) \in R$ *and for every* $(p,q) \in R$ *and every* $a \in \Sigma$:

1. *if* $p \dashrightarrow_1 p'$ *then there is a transition* $q \dashrightarrow_2 q'$ *such that* $(p',q') \in R$, *and*
2. *if* $q \overset{a}{\longrightarrow}_2 q'$ *then there is a transition* $p \overset{a}{\longrightarrow}_1 p'$ *such that* $(p',q') \in R$.

Example 3. In the course of the refinement process, must transitions are preserved, may transitions can turn into must transitions or disappear, and no new transitions are added. Note that refinement is a more complex notion than that of subgraph. Indeed, the same transition can be refined in different ways in different places as illustrated in Fig. 3.   △

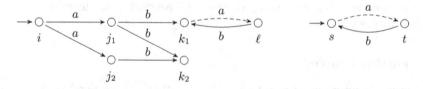

Fig. 3. The refinement $i \leq_m s$ is witnessed by the refinement relation $\{(i,s), (j_1,t), (j_2,t), (k_1,s), (k_2,s), (\ell,t)\}$. Note that whenever there is a must transition in an MTS, we do not depict its underlying may transitions. Moreover, when a designated process of an MTS is considered initial, it is depicted with an incoming arrow.

Whenever $s \leq_m t$, we call s a refinement of t and t an abstraction of s. We often consider MTS with a designated initial process; in such a case we say that an MTS refines another one if this is true of their initial processes.

One may refine MTS in a stepwise manner until $\dashrightarrow \; = \; \longrightarrow$ is obtained and no further refinement is possible. MTS with $\dashrightarrow \; = \; \longrightarrow$ are called *implementations* and can be considered as the standard labelled transition systems (LTS). Given a process s we denote by $[\![s]\!] = \{i \mid i$ is an implementation and $i \leq_m s\}$ the set of all implementations of s.[1] In the previous example, j_1 is not an implementation, while j_2 is considered an implementation since all reachable transitions satisfy the requirement. Further notice that $k_2 \in [\![s]\!]$.

Note that on implementations the refinement coincides with the strong bisimilarity, and on modal transition systems without any must transitions it corresponds to the simulation preorder. Further, the refinement has a respective game characterization [BKLS09b] similar to (bi)simulation games.

2.2 Logics

A set of implementations can be specified not only by a behavioural specification such as an MTS, but also by a formula of a logic. Here we briefly recall two logics: μ-calculus [Koz83] and LTL [Pnu77]. Let Ap be a set of atomic propositions.

μ-calculus is given by the syntax

$$\varphi ::= \mathbf{tt} \mid \mathbf{ff} \mid p \mid \neg p \mid \varphi \wedge \varphi \mid \varphi \vee \varphi \mid [a]\varphi \mid \langle a \rangle \varphi \mid \mu X.\varphi \mid \nu X.\varphi$$

where p ranges over Ap, a over Σ, and X over a set Var of variables. We call μ the least fixpoint and ν the greatest fixpoint.

Linear temporal logic (LTL) is given by the syntax

$$\varphi ::= \mathbf{tt} \mid \mathbf{ff} \mid p \mid \neg p \mid \varphi \wedge \varphi \mid \varphi \vee \varphi \mid \mathbf{X}\varphi \mid \mathbf{X}_a\varphi \mid \mathbf{F}\varphi \mid \mathbf{G}\varphi \mid \varphi \mathbf{U}\varphi$$

where p ranges over Ap and a over Σ. Given an implementation $(P, \longrightarrow)$ and a valuation $\nu : P \to 2^{Ap}$ over its state space, any run (maximal path in the directed graph of the LTS) induces a sequence from $(2^{Ap} \times \Sigma)^{\mathbb{N}}$ capturing the labelling of the visited processes and the actions taken there. The semantics here is a mixture of state-based and action-based properties:[2] given a sequence $\alpha_0 a_0 w$ we define $\alpha_0 a_0 w \models \mathbf{X}\varphi$ iff $w \models \varphi$; besides, $\alpha_0 a_0 w \models \mathbf{X}_a\varphi$ iff $w \models \varphi$ and $a = a_0$. The semantics of other operators is standard. An LTS satisfies φ if all runs from its initial process satisfy φ.

Example 4. Consider the LTS and its valuation depicted in Fig. 4. While it satisfies $\mathbf{G}p$ and $\nu X.p \wedge [a]X$, it does satisfy neither $\mathbf{F}q$ nor $\mu X.q \vee [a]X$ due to the run looping in s. $\triangle$

---

[1] The notation introduced in [BKLS09b] is adopted from semantics.

[2] In the context of MTS, [Ben12] elaborates on the differences of the two.

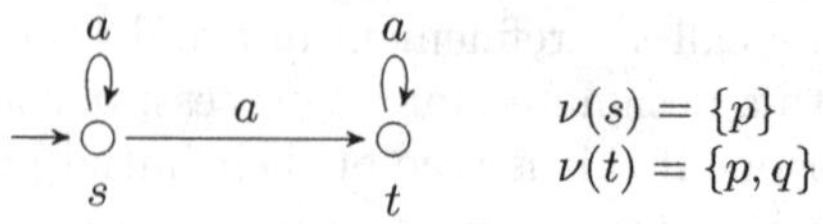

$$\nu(s) = \{p\}$$
$$\nu(t) = \{p, q\}$$

Fig. 4. An LTS with a valuation ν

2.3 Specification Theories

In order to support component based development, many specification theories have been designed. One usually requires existence and effective computability of several operations subject to various axioms. In the following, let s and t be processes, arguments of the operations.

Some operations are structural, stemming from the nature of behavioural descriptions, such as the operations of parallel composition and quotient. The *parallel composition* $\|$ should satisfy

(parallel) for any processes x and y, $x \parallel y \leq_m s \parallel t$ if $x \leq_m s$ and $y \leq_m t$,

called *independent implementability*. The *quotient* is an adjoint to parallel composition, hence the quotient s/t of s by t should satisfy

(quotient) for any process x, $x \leq_m s/t$ if and only if $t \parallel x \leq_m s$.

Given a specification s of the whole system and t of its component, the quotient s/t is thus a compact description of all systems that can be put in parallel with t to get a system complying with s.

Other operations are inherited from the logical view, such as Boolean operations. A *conjunction* of two systems is the most general refinement of the two systems. As the greatest lower bound with respect to $\leq_m$ it must satisfy

(conjunction) for any process x, $x \leq_m s \wedge t$ if and only if $x \leq_m s$ and $x \leq_m t$.

A bit weaker notion is that of *consistency* relation: a set of systems is consistent if they have a common implementation, i.e. if their conjunction has a non-empty set of implementations. Dually, one can define *disjunction* by requiring

(disjunction) for any process x, $s \vee t \leq_m x$ if and only if $s \leq_m x$ and $t \leq_m x$.

The remaining Boolean operation is that of *complement*:

(complement) for any process x, $x \leq_m \bar{s}$ if and only if $x \not\leq_m s$.

For the related notion of difference, see e.g. [SCU11].

It is often not possible to satisfy all axioms in this strong form. For instance, automata-based specification formalisms are sometimes too weak to express the complement, which is the case also for MTS. Besides, the "complete specification theories" of [BDH+12] only require **(parallel)** in the above-mentioned "if" form. The other desired direction cannot in general be achieved in MTS

[HL89, BKLS09b], see Fig. 5. Further, according to [BDH+12], existence of quotients and conjunctions is required if they have non-empty set of implementations. Here we presented a simpler version of the operator requirements, which is equivalent when MTS are enriched with the "inconsistent" specification with no implementations.

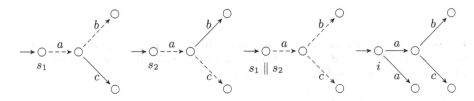

Fig. 5. $i \leq_m s_1 \parallel s_2$, but i cannot be written as $i_1 \parallel i_2$ for any $i_1 \leq_m s_1, i_2 \leq_m s_2$

3   Extensions of Modalities

Since the modelling capabilities of basic MTS are quite limited, many extensions have appeared in the literature. In this section, we focus on extensions of the may and must transition relations. Standard MTS have two transition relations $\longrightarrow, \dashrightarrow \subseteq P \times \Sigma \times P$ satisfying $\longrightarrow \subseteq \dashrightarrow$, which is called the syntactic consistency requirement. If this requirement is not imposed we obtain *mixed transition systems* as introduced in [DGG97].

Definition 3 (Mixed transition system). *A* mixed transition system (MixTS) *over an action alphabet* Σ *is a triple* $(P, \dashrightarrow, \longrightarrow)$, *where* P *is a set of* processes *and* $\longrightarrow, \dashrightarrow \subseteq P \times \Sigma \times P$ *are* must *and* may *transition relations, respectively.*

This extension allows us not only to have inconsistent specifications, but also a certain form of enforced non-deterministic choice:

Example 5. The specification of Fig. 6 requires an a transition followed by either only b's or only c's. Indeed, the must transition under a enforces a transition, but does not automatically allow it; only the two may transitions under a are allowed.   △

Nevertheless, even this feature is often insufficient to specify which *combinations* of transitions can be implemented.

Example 6. Figure 7 on the left depicts an MTS that specifies the following. A request from a client may arrive. Then we can process it directly on the server or make a query to a database where we are guaranteed an answer. In both cases we send a response.
    An MTS can be refined in two ways: a may transition is either implemented (and becomes a must transition) or omitted (and disappears as a transition).

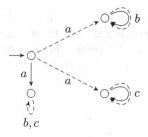

Fig. 6. A mixed transition system. Since must transitions are not necessarily also may transitions in MixTS, we depict may transitions explicitly for mixed systems here, even when there is a corresponding must transition.

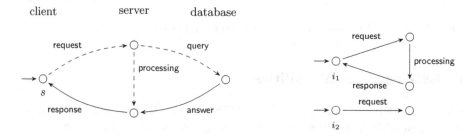

Fig. 7. A potentially deadlocking s and two of its implementations i_1, i_2

On the right of Fig. 7 there is an implementation i_1 of the system, where the processing branch is implemented and the database query branch is omitted. Similarly, there is also an implementation omitting the process branch and implementing only the query. However, there is also an undesirable implementation i_2 that does not implement any option and deadlocks as seen on the right of Fig. 7.   △

To avoid deadlocking, we want to specify that *either* processing *or* query will be implemented. This is possible in *disjunctive modal transition systems* [LX90]. They were actually introduced as natural means for solutions to process equations since they can express both conjunctions and disjunctions of properties.

Definition 4 (Disjunctive modal transition system). *A disjunctive modal transition system (DMTS) is a triple* $(P, \dashrightarrow, \longrightarrow)$, *where* P *is a set of processes and* $\dashrightarrow \subseteq P \times \Sigma \times P$ *is the may and* $\longrightarrow \subseteq P \times 2^{\Sigma \times P}$ *the must (or hyper-must) transition relation.*

Example 7. Intuitively, in DMTS we can enforce a choice between arbitrary transitions, not just with the same action as in Example 5. Instead of forcing a particular transition, a must transition in DMTS specifies a whole set of transitions at least one of which must be present in any refinement. In our example, it would be the set consisting of processing and query transitions, see Fig. 8.   △

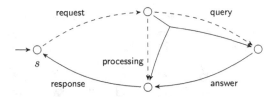

Fig. 8. A disjunctive modal transition system

Note that DMTS are capable of forcing any positive Boolean combination of transitions, simply by turning it into the conjunctive normal form. If the choice is supposed to be exclusive, we can use *one-selecting MTS (1MTS)* introduced in [FS08] with the property that *exactly* one transition from the set must be present. In 1MTS and also in *underspecified transition systems (UTS)* [FS05], both (hyper)must and (hyper)may transition relations are subsets of $P \times 2^{\Sigma \times P}$. For UTS, the syntactic consistency is required, i.e. the hyper-may is larger than the hyper-must.

Finally, explicit listing of all allowed combinations of outgoing transitions is used in *acceptance automata* [Rac08]. However, the language-theoretic definition is limited to deterministic systems.

Definition 5 (Acceptance automaton). *An* acceptance automaton *(AA) is a pair $(P, Possible\,TranSets)$, where P is a prefix-closed language over Σ and $Possible\,TranSets : P \to 2^{2^{\Sigma}} \setminus \emptyset$ satisfies the consistency condition: $wa \in P$ if and only if $a \in TranSet \in Possible\,TranSets(w)$ for some TranSet.*

Nevertheless, as the following example shows, convenient modelling requires even more features such as conditional or persistent choices.

Example 8. Consider a simple specification of a traffic light controller for several national variants for vehicles as well as for pedestrians, displayed on the right of Fig. 9. At any moment it is in one of the four states *red, green, yellow* or *yellowRed*. The intuitive requirements are: if *green* is on then the traffic light may either change to *red* or *yellow*, and if it turned *yellow* (as for vehicles) it must go to *red* afterwards; if *red* is on then it may either turn to *green* (as for pedestrians and also for vehicles in some countries) or *yellowRed*, and if it turns *yellowRed* it must go to *green* afterwards.

However, these requirements (expressible as MTS) allow for three different undesirable implementations: (i) the light is constantly *green*, (ii) the lights switch non-deterministically, (iii) the lights switch deterministically, but *yellow* is only displayed sometimes (e.g. every other time). While the first problem can be avoided using the choice in DMTS, the latter two cannot. To eliminate the second implementation, one needs an exclusive choice, as in 1MTS; for the third implementation to be removed, one needs a persistent choice. These can be modelled in *parametric MTS* [BKL+11, BKL+15] where a parameter describes whether and when the yellow light is used, making the choices permanent in the

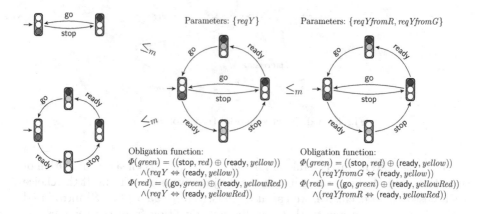

Fig. 9. Examples of PMTS and their modal refinement (Color figure online)

whole implementation. Additionally, the dependence on the parameter allows for modelling a conditional choice. Indeed, as illustrated in the middle of Fig. 9, depending on the value of another parameter, the yellow light can be consistently used or skipped in both phases. △

Definition 6 (Parametric modal transition system). *A* parametric MTS (PMTS) *is a tuple* $(P, \dashrightarrow, Par, \Phi)$ *where* P *is a set of* processes, $\dashrightarrow \subseteq P \times \Sigma \times P$ *is a* transition relation, Par *is a finite set of* parameters, *and* $\Phi : P \to BoolExp((\Sigma \times P) \cup Par)$ *is an* obligation function *assigning to each process a Boolean expression over outgoing transitions and parameters.*

These systems are "mixed"; a syntactic consistency $\forall s \in P : \forall (a, t) \in \Phi(s) :$ $s \overset{a}{\dashrightarrow} t$ may be additionally required, making them "pure". Intuitively, a set S of transitions from s is allowed if $\Phi(s)$ is true under the valuation induced by S and the fixed parameters; for an example see Fig. 9. A PMTS is

- *Boolean MTS (BMTS)* [BKL+11] if it is *parameter-free*, i.e. if $Par = \emptyset$,
- *transition system with obligation (OTS)* [BK10] if it is BMTS and only parameters can be negated,
- *DMTS* is an OTS with $\Phi(s)$ in the conjunctive normal form for all $s \in P$, DMTS is considered both mixed [LX90] and pure [BČK11],
- *MixTS* is a DMTS with $\Phi(s)$ being a conjunction of positive literals (transitions) for all $s \in P$ (and the syntactic consistency not required),
- *MTS* is a MixTS with the and the syntactic consistency required,
- *LTS* is an MTS with $\Phi(s) = \bigwedge T(s)$ for all $s \in P$, where $T(s) = \{(a, t) \mid s \overset{a}{\dashrightarrow} t\}$ is the set of all outgoing transitions of s.

The modal refinement over BMTS is an expected extension of that for MTS. Technically, let $\text{Tran}(s) = \{E \subseteq T(s) \mid E \models \Phi(s)\}$ be the set of all admissible sets of transitions from s and the refinement relation satisfies for every $(p, q) \in R$:

$$\forall M \in \mathrm{Tran}(p) : \exists N \in \mathrm{Tran}(q) : \quad \forall (a, p') \in M : \exists (a, q') \in N : (p', q') \in R \quad \wedge$$
$$\forall (a, q') \in N : \exists (a, p') \in M : (p', q') \in R.$$

For PMTS, intuitively, whatever parameters of the refining system we pick, the abstract system can emulate the same behaviour (by BMTS refinement) for some choice of its parameters. The original definition [BKL+11] requires a single refinement relation for all parameter choices. Later it was superseded by a more natural definition [BKL+15] where different relations are allowed for different parameter valuations; it is closer to the semantically defined notion of thorough refinement, see Definition 10, and keeps the same complexity.

Example 9. Consider the rightmost PMTS in Fig. 9. It has two parameters *reqYfromG* and *reqYfromR* whose values can be set independently and it can be refined by the system in the middle of the figure having only one parameter *reqY*. This single parameter binds the two original parameters to the same value. The PMTS in the middle can be further refined into the implementations where either *yellow* is always used in both cases, or never at all.   △

Expressive Power

Most of the formalisms have the same expressive power, as summarized in Fig. 10. However, they differ significantly in succinctness. In [KS13b], PMTS are transformed into exponentially larger BMTS and BMTS into exponentially larger DMTSm, see Fig. 10. Here *Cm* denotes a class *C* where systems are considered with more (but only finitely many) initial processes.

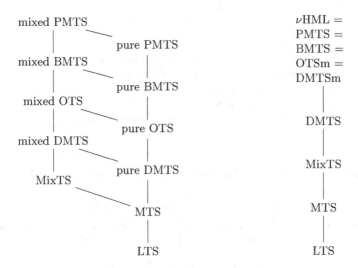

Fig. 10. The syntactic hierarchy of MTS extensions (on the left) and the semantic one, not considering empty specifications (on the right)

Except for the already discussed extra power of MixTS over MTS, mixed variants of systems can be transformed into pure, again at an exponential cost [BK10], up to the inconsistent specification, i.e. specifications with no implementations. Since this difference is not very important, we shall only deal with pure systems unless stated otherwise.

Each of the formalisms presented so far in this section was an automata-based behavioural formalism. These are often preferred as they are easier to read than, for instance, formulae of modal logics. The choice between logical and behavioural specifications is not only a question of preference. Automata-based specifications [Lar89, BG99] have a focus on compositional and incremental design in which logical specifications are somewhat lacking, with the trade-off of generally being less expressive than logics. Logical specification formalisms put a powerful logical language at the disposal of the user, and the logical approach to model checking [QS82, CE81] has seen a lot of success and tool implementations. Therefore, one would like to establish connections between behavioural and logical formalisms to exploit advantages of both at once. The relationship of MTS to logic was studied in [BL92, FP07]. It is established that MTS are equivalent to a fragment of μ-calculus where formulae are (1) consistent, (2) "prime", meaning the disjunction is allowed only in very special cases, and (3) do not contain the least fixpoint. Further, [BDF+13] proves that DMTSm (and thus BMTS and PMTS) are equivalent to ν-calculus (or Hennessy-Milner logic with greatest fixpoints, abbreviated νHML), which is a fragment of μ-calculus without the least fixpoint μ. Finally, the refinement corresponds to implication [FLT14], similarly to the refinement calculus for HML with recursion of [Hol89]. Moreover, both formalisms can be equipped with the desired operations coming from the other formalism, see Fig. 11, as further discussed in Sect. 5, bridging the gap between the two approaches.

$$
\begin{array}{rcl}
\text{logic} & & \text{MTS} \\
\text{model} & \sim & \text{implementation} \\
\text{implication/entailment} & \sim & \text{refinement} \\
\text{conjunction } \wedge & \sim & ? \\
\text{disjunction } \vee & \sim & ? \\
? & \sim & \text{parallel composition } \| \\
? & \sim & \text{quotient } /
\end{array}
$$

Fig. 11. Correspondences between the logical and the behavioural world

Example 10. Consider the following property: "at all time points after executing request, no idle nor further requests but only work is allowed until grant is executed". The property can be written in e.g. CTL [CE81] as

$$AG(\text{request} \Rightarrow AX(\text{work AW grant}))$$

Figure 12 shows an example of an equivalent νHML formula and a DMTS corresponding to this property.   △

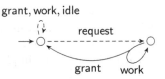

$$X = [\text{grant}, \text{idle}, \text{work}]X \wedge [\text{request}]Y$$
$$Y = (\langle\text{work}\rangle Y \vee \langle\text{grant}\rangle X) \wedge [\text{idle}, \text{request}]\mathbf{ff}$$

Fig. 12. Example of a νHML formula and an equivalent DMTS

Apart from the logical characterization, one can also describe processes using a process algebra and obtain the discussed subclasses mixed DMTS, pure DMTS, MixTS, MTS, LTS as syntactic subclasses [BK10].

4   Extensions of Transition Systems

The extensions discussed in the previous section focus on what *combinations* of transitions are possible. In this section, we discuss mainly extensions concerned with quantitative features or infinite memory/communication. Besides, to provide a better basis for interface theories, MTS have been also combined with I/O automata [GSSL94] and interface automata [dAH01] into *modal I/O transition systems* [LNW07a, RBB+09a, BHJ10, BMSH10, BHW10, BHB10, KM12, KDMU14] with input, output and internal actions, and its subset *modal interface automata* [LV13, LVF15, BFLV16, SH15]. Other MTS extensions feature specifically modified semantics, e.g., [BV15, BSV15, DSMB16].

4.1   Quantities

Here we discuss lifting the underlying transition systems to *quantitative settings* [LL12], with clear applications in the embedded systems design. This includes probabilistic specifications (see below) and various weighted specifications, where weights stand for various quantitative aspects (e.g. time, power or memory), which are highly relevant in the area of embedded systems. As far as the particular case of *timed* systems is concerned, the quantity of time can be refined in various ways. In the early work [CGL93, LSW95], the precise quantities are almost disregarded. More recently [JLS12, BPR09, BLPR09, DLL+10], the possible times are usually specified as time intervals, which can be narrowed down and thus made more specific. A more general option is to permit label refinement to anything smaller with respect to some *abstract ordering* of labels; [BJL+12a] provides the following conservative extension of MTS modal refinement along these lines:

Definition 7 (Modal refinement of MTS with structured labels). *Let the alphabet Σ be equipped with an ordering $\sqsubseteq$. Let $(P_1, \dashrightarrow_1, \longrightarrow_1), (P_2, \dashrightarrow_2, \longrightarrow_2)$ be MTS over Σ and $s \in P_1, t \in P_2$ be processes. We say that s modally refines t, written $s \leq_m t$, if there is a refinement relation $\mathcal{R} \subseteq P_1 \times P_2$ such that $(s,t) \in \mathcal{R}$ and for every $(p,q) \in R$ and every $a \in \Sigma$:*

1. if $p \overset{a}{\dashrightarrow}_1 p'$ then $q \overset{\bar{a}}{\dashrightarrow}_2 q'$ for some $a \sqsubseteq \bar{a}$ and $(p',q') \in R$, and
2. if $q \overset{\bar{a}}{\longrightarrow}_2 q'$ then $p \overset{a}{\longrightarrow}_1 p'$ for some $a \sqsubseteq \bar{a}$ and $(p',q') \in R$.

Example 11. Consider $\Sigma = L \times \mathfrak{I}$ where L is a finite set ordered by identity and $\mathfrak{I}$ is the set of intervals ordered by inclusion and Σ is ordered point-wise, standing for the action and the time required to perform it. A transition labelled by $(\ell, [a, b])$ can thus be implemented by a transition (ℓ, c) for any $c \in [a, b]$. $\triangle$

This definition generalizes also previously studied MTS with more weights at once [BJL+12b]. Moreover, one can also consider MTS with timed-automata clocks [BLPR12, FL12]. In all the quantitative settings, it is also natural to extend the qualitative notion of refinement into a quantitative notion of distance of systems [BFJ+11, BFLT12].

Another previously studied instantiation is the *modal transition systems with durations (MTSD)* [BKL+12]. It models time durations of transitions as controllable or uncontrollable intervals. Controllable intervals can be further refined into narrower intervals, whereas uncontrollable are considered under the control of an unpredictable environment and cannot be further narrowed down. Additionally, the actions are assigned running cost (or rewards) per time unit.

MTS have also been lifted to the *probabilistic* setting. In the classical setting, LTS is underspecified in that the presence of a certain transition is not specified. For Markov chains, one can underspecify the probability distributions on the outgoing transitions. *Interval Markov chains* [JL91] describe them with intervals of possible values. Additionally, we can consider 3-valued valuations of atomic propositions in processes (similarly to [HJS01, BG00, CDEG03], useful for abstractions), yielding *abstract Markov chains* [FLW06]. This approach is extensible also to continuous-time Markov chains [KKLW07, KKLW12]. Besides, *constraint Markov chains* [CDL+10] use richer constraints than intervals and usual operations on them have also been studied [DLL14]. Finally, *abstract probabilistic automata* [DKL+11a] combine this with the MTS may-must modality on transitions, allowing for abstractions of Markov decision processes. They have been studied with respect to the supported operations [DKL+11b, DFLL14], state space reduction [SK14], hidden actions (stutter steps) [DLL14], and there is a support by the tool APAC [DLL+11].

Moreover, probabilistic and timed-automata extensions are combined in *abstract probabilistic timed automata* [HKKG13]. Finally, *modal continuous-time automata* [HKK13] extend MTS with continuous time constraints on stochastic waiting times, allowing for specification of systems with stochastic continuous time.

Specification theories have been lifted to the quantitative settings and equipped with the notion of distance between systems [BFLT12, FL14, FKLT14, FLT14].

4.2   Infinite State Space

In this section, we consider *infinite-state* extensions of MTS. Several extensions have been proposed, such as systems with asynchronous communication based on FIFO [BHJ10] or Petri nets [EBHH10, HHM13]. Other extensions focus on input/output extensions of MTS with data constraints [BHB10, BHW10] or explicit representation of data [BLL+14].

A systematic exploration of infinite-state MTS is also possible. A convenient unifying framework for (non-modal) infinite-state systems is provided by process rewrite systems (PRS) [May00]. A PRS Δ is a finite set of rewriting rules, which model sequential and parallel computation. Depending on the syntactic restrictions imposed on the rules, we obtain many standard models such as pushdown automata (PDA) or Petri nets (PN), see Fig. 13. A finite PRS Δ thus induces possibly infinite LTS $\mathcal{LTS}(\Delta)$.

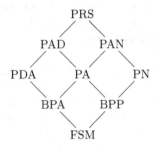

Fig. 13. PRS hierarchy

Example 12. A transition t of a Petri net with input places p, q and output places r, s can be described by the rule $p \parallel q \xrightarrow{t} r \parallel s$. A transition of a pushdown automaton in a state s with a top stack symbol X reading a letter a resulting in changing the state to r and pushing Y onto the stack can be written as $sX \xrightarrow{a} rYX$.

One can naturally lift PRS to the modal world [BK12] by having two sets of rules: may and must rules. The finite set of rules then generates a generally infinite MTS.

Definition 8 (Modal process rewrite system). *A modal process rewrite system (mPRS) is a tuple $\Delta = (\Delta_{\mathrm{may}}, \Delta_{\mathrm{must}})$ where $\Delta_{\mathrm{must}} \subseteq \Delta_{\mathrm{may}}$ are two PRS. The mPRS Δ induces an MTS $\mathcal{MTS}(\Delta) = (\mathcal{E}, \dashrightarrow, \longrightarrow)$ defined by $(\mathcal{E}, \dashrightarrow) = \mathcal{LTS}(\Delta_{\mathrm{may}})$ and $(\mathcal{E}, \longrightarrow) = \mathcal{LTS}(\Delta_{\mathrm{must}})$.*

Each subclass $\mathcal{C}$ of PRS has a corresponding modal extension m$\mathcal{C}$ containing all mPRS $(\Delta_{\mathrm{may}}, \Delta_{\mathrm{must}})$ with both Δ_{may} and Δ_{must} in $\mathcal{C}$. For instance, mFSM correspond to the standard finite MTS and mPN are modal Petri nets as introduced in [EBHH10].

Definition 9 (Modal refinement). *Given mPRS $\Delta_1 \in m\mathcal{C}_1, \Delta_2 \in m\mathcal{C}_2$ and process terms δ_1, δ_2, we say δ_1 refines δ_2, written $\delta_1 \leq_m \delta_2$, if $\delta_1 \leq_m \delta_2$ as processes of $MTS(\Delta_1)$ and $MTS(\Delta_2)$, respectively.*

What is the use of infinite MTS? Firstly, potentially infinite-state systems such as Petri nets are very popular for modelling whenever communication and/or synchronization between processes occurs. This is true even in cases where they are actually bounded and thus with a finite state space.

Example 13. Consider the following may rule (we use dashed arrows to denote may rules) generating a small Petri net.

$$\text{resource} \xrightarrow{\text{produce}} \text{money} \parallel \text{trash}$$

If this is the only rule with trash on the right side a safety property is guaranteed for all implementations of this system, namely that trash can only arise if there is at least one resource. On the other hand, it is not guaranteed that money can indeed be produced in such a situation. This is very useful as during the design process new requirements can arise, such as necessity of adding more participants to perform this transition. For instance,

$$\text{resource} \parallel \text{permit} \xrightarrow{\text{produce}} \text{money} \parallel \text{trash}$$

expresses an auxiliary condition required to produce trash, namely that a permit is available. Replacing the old rule with the new one is equivalent to adding an input place permit to the modal Petri net, see Fig. 14 in yellow. In the modal transition system view, the new system *refines* the old one. Indeed, the new system is only more specific about the allowed behaviour than the old one and does not permit any previously forbidden behaviour.

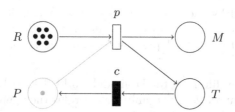

Fig. 14. A modal Petri net given by rules Resource $\parallel$ Permit $\xrightarrow{\text{produce}}$ Money $\parallel$ Trash and Trash $\xrightarrow{\text{clean}}$ Permit with may transitions drawn as empty boxes and must transitions as full boxes (Color figure online)

One can further refine the system into the one given by

$$\text{resource} \parallel \text{permit} \parallel \text{bribe} \xrightarrow{\text{produce}} \text{money} \parallel \text{trash}$$

where additional condition is imposed and now the money-producing transition has to be available (denoted by an unbroken arrow) whenever the left hand side condition is satisfied.   △

Further, infinitely many states are useful to capture unbounded memory. For instance, consider a specification where the total amount of permits is not explicitly limited. In an implementation, the number of permits might need to be remembered in the state of the system.

Example 14. Consider a basic process algebra (BPA) given by rules $X \xrightarrow{(} XX$ and $X \xrightarrow{)} \varepsilon$ for correctly parenthesized expressions with $X \dashrightarrow^{a} X$ for all other symbols a, i.e. with no restriction on the syntax of expressions. One can easily refine this system into a PDA that accepts correct arithmetic expressions by remembering in a control state whether the last symbol read was an operand or an operator. △

5 Analysis

In this section, we survey algorithms for and complexities of the most important problems on MTS and their extensions.

5.1 Refinements

Modal refinement is a syntactically defined notion extending both bisimulation and simulation. Similarly to bisimulation having a semantic counterpart in trace equivalence, here the semantic counterpart of modal refinement is the *thorough refinement*. As opposed to the syntactic definition using local notions, the semantic definition relates (by inclusion) the sets of implementations of the specifications. The definition is universal for all extensions of MTS as it only depends on the notion of implementation and not on syntax of the particular extension.

Definition 10 (Thorough refinement). *Given processes s and t, we say that s thoroughly refines t, written $s \leq_t t$, if $[\![s]\!] \subseteq [\![t]\!]$.*

Note that the two refinements are in general different as we illustrate in the following example due to [BKLS09b], simplifying [HL89]:

Example 15. Consider processes s and t of Fig. 15. On the one hand, the sets of implementations of s and t are the same, namely those that can perform either no action or one a or two a's or combine the latter two options. On the other hand, s does not modally refine t. Indeed, whenever $s \leq_m t$ then either $s' \leq_m t_1$ or $s' \leq_m t_2$. However, neither is true, as s' allows a transition while t_1 does not, and s' does not require any transition while t_2 does.

Although the two refinements differ, modal refinement is a sound under-approximation of the thorough refinement. Indeed, whenever we have $s \leq_m t$ and $i \in [\![s]\!]$ we also have $i \leq_m s$ and by transitivity of the modal refinement we obtain $i \leq_m t$.

Proposition 1. *Let s, t be processes. If $s \leq_m t$ then $s \leq_t t$.*

Moreover, [BKLS09b] shows the other direction holds whenever the refined system is deterministic. A process is *deterministic* if, for each process s of its underlying MTS and for each $a \in \Sigma$, there is at most one s' such that $s \dashrightarrow^{a} s'$.

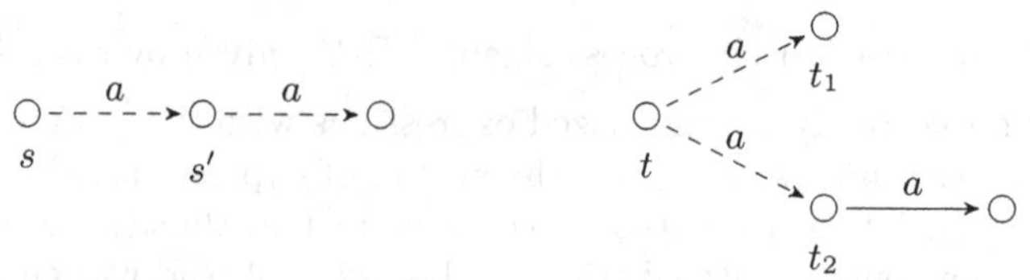

Fig. 15. $s \leq_t t$, but $s \not\leq_m t$

Proposition 2. *Let s, t be processes and t deterministic. If $s \leq_t t$ then $s \leq_m t$.*

In Table 1 we give an overview of the results related to deciding modal and thorough refinements for different combinations of processes on the left- and right-hand side (here D stands for deterministic processes and N for non-deterministic processes). Note that the co-inductive refinement relations are easy to compute using a fixed-point computation, although other methods are also possible, e.g. logical programming [AKRU11] or QBF solving [KS13b, BKL+15].

Table 1. MTS refinement complexity for various cases of (non)determinism

	Modal refinement $\leq_m$	Thorough refinement $\leq_t$
D≤D	NL-complete [BKLS09b]	NL-complete [BKLS09b]
N≤D	NL-complete [BKLS09b]	NL-complete [BKLS09b]
D≤N	∈ P [KS90, PT87]	∈ EXP [AHL+08b]
	P-hard [BKLS09b]	EXP-hard [BKLS12]
N≤N	∈ P [KS90, PT87]	∈ EXP [AHL+08b, BKLS09a]
	P-hard [BGS92]	EXP-hard [BKLS09a]

Since the thorough refinement is EXP-hard, it is much harder than the modal refinement. Therefore, we also investigate how the thorough refinement can be approximated by the modal refinement. While under-approximation is easy, as modal refinement implies thorough refinement, over-approximation is more diffi-cult. Here one can use the method of the *deterministic hull* for MTS [BKLS09b]. The deterministic hull $\mathcal{D}$ is a generalization of the powerset construction on finite automata and it is the *smallest* (w.r.t. modal refinement) deterministic system refined by the original system.

Proposition 3. *Let s be an arbitrary MTS process. Then $\mathcal{D}(s)$ is a determinis-tic MTS process such that $s \leq_m \mathcal{D}(s)$ and, for every deterministic MTS process t, if $s \leq_t t$ then $\mathcal{D}(s) \leq_m t$.*

Corollary 1. *For any processes s, t, if $s \not\leq_m \mathcal{D}(t)$ then $s \not\leq_t t$.*

There are also other notions of refinements of systems close to MTS, such as alternating refinements [AHKV98, AFdFE+11], branching refinement [FBU09], refinement preserving the termination possibility [CR12], or refinement for prod-uct lines [DSMB16].

Extensions. As to extensions of MTS with more complex modalities, the local conditions in modal refinement are more complex. Although various extensions have the same expressive power (see Fig. 10), the transformations are exponential and thus the extensions differ in succinctness. Therefore, the respective refinement problems are harder for the more succinct extensions. All the cases depending on the type of the left-hand and right-hand sides are discussed in [BKL+15]. In most cases without parameters, the refinement can be decided in P or NP, which is feasible using SAT solvers. For systems with parameters, the complexity is significantly higher, reaching up to Π_4^P. Since all the complexities are included in PSPACE, QBF solvers have been applied to this problem, improving scalability to systems with hundreds of states [KS13c,BKL+15]. The QBF approach basically eliminates the complexity threat of parameters, but is quite sensitive to the level of non-determinism.

Furthermore, the decision algorithm for thorough refinement checking over MTS [BKLS12,BKLS12] has been extended to the setting of DMTS [BČK10] and of BMTS and PMTS [KS13b], see Table 2. [KS13b] also generalizes the notion of the deterministic hull.

Table 2. Complexity of the thorough refinement and the relationship to the modal refinement

	MTS	DMTS	BMTS	PMTS
$N \leq_t N \in$	EXP	EXP	NEXP	2-EXP
for $N \leq D$	$\leq_m = \leq_t$	$\leq_m = \leq_t$	$\leq_m = \leq_t$	$\leq_m \neq \leq_t$

We now turn our attention to the refinement problems on other kinds of extensions of MTS. Assuming polynomial procedures for operations on structured labels, the complexity of the modal refinement stays the same as for the underlying MTS. As for infinite state systems, [BK12] shows that refinement between finite MTS and modal pushdown automaton and between modal visibly pushdown automata is decidable and EXP-complete, whereas between basic process algebras it is undecidable. When parallelism is involved, undecidability occurs very soon, already for finite MTS and basic parallel process. However, it is decidable for Petri nets when a weak form of determinism is imposed [EHH12,HHM13]. Finally, in the spirit of [AHKV98], a symmetric version of refinement resulting into a bisimulation notion over MTS is considered and shown decidable between a finite MTS and any modal process rewrite system, using the results of [KŘS05]. This allows us to check whether we can replace an infinite MTS with a particular finite one, which in turn may allow for checking further refinements.

5.2 Operations

Specification theories require the specification formalism to be closed under certain operations, as described in Sect. 2. However, not all classes of modal systems support all the operations. As an automata-based formalism, MTS automatically allow to compose systems structurally, whereas logical operations are either difficult to compute or cannot be expressed in the formalism at all. Therefore, most of the focus has been directed to the simple deterministic case, where some operations can be defined using local syntactic rules, even for the quantitative extensions [BFJ+13].

|| The *parallel composition* can often be lifted to the modal setting simply by applying the same SOS rules, e.g. for synchronous message passing, to both may and must transition functions. This holds for a wide class of operators as described in [BKLS09b] for MTS. Parallel composition can be extended to DMTS and other classes [BČK10,BDF+13]. Unfortunately, they inherit the incompleteness with respect to modal refinement from MTS, see [HL89,BKLS09b]. Therefore, the axiom (parallel) is only satisfied in one direction (the independent implementability), but not every implementation of the composition can actually be decomposed into a pair of implementations, see Fig. 5, and in general we have $[\![s]\!] \parallel [\![t]\!] \subset [\![s \parallel t]\!]$.

/ The *quotient* for deterministic MTS can be defined syntactically, using a few SOS rules [Rac07,Rac08]. For non-deterministic MTS, the problem is considerably more complex and the question was open for a long time. A construction for BMTS and DMTSm and an exponentially smaller one for MTS was given in [BDF+13]. Further related questions such as decomposition of a system into several components put in parallel [SUBK12] or quotient under reachability constraints [VR15] have also been investigated, but again only for deterministic systems.

∧ The situation is similar with *conjunction*. For deterministic MTS, we can again define it syntactically. For non-deterministic systems, there were several attempts. Unfortunately, the resulting MTS is not minimal (with respect to modal refinement) [UC04], or not finite even when claimed to be finite [FU08]: the "clone" operation may not terminate even in cases when it is supposed to, for example, for processes s_1, s_2 of Fig. 16 where the self-loops are redirected back to the initial processes. Actually, MTS are not closed under conjunction, see Fig. 16. However, a conjunction of two MTS has a unique greatest DMTS solution.

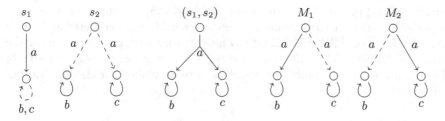

Fig. 16. MTS processes s_1, s_2, their greatest lower bound (s_1, s_2), and their two maximal MTS lower bounds M_1, M_2

Moreover, DMTS with one or more initial processes, and thus also BMTS and PMTS are closed under conjunction [BČK11]. The result of the construction is based on the synchronous product. Thus it is a system over tuples of processes where the length of the tuple is the number of input systems. This means that the conjunction (and thus also a common implementation) can be constructed in polynomial time, if n is fixed; and in exponential time, if n is a part of the input. Further, if deterministic MTS are input, the algorithm produces a deterministic MTS. Moreover, the conjunction is also the greatest lower bound with respect to the thorough refinement: $[\![s_1 \wedge s_2]\!] = [\![s_1]\!] \cap [\![s_2]\!]$ which is not achievable for the parallel composition. The conjunction construction was later extended to systems with different alphabets [BDCU13] and invisible actions [BCU16].

∨ *Disjunction* is easy to obtain for DMTSm, BMTS, and PMTS, again in the stronger form $[\![s_1 \vee s_2]\!] = [\![s_1]\!] \cup [\![s_2]\!]$. However, for MTS (deterministic or not) and DMTS with a single initial process this is not possible. Indeed, consider the MTS specifications in Fig. 17. While the disjunction can be described simply as a BMTS with obligation $\Omega(s_1 \vee s_2) = ((a, \bullet) \wedge (b, \bullet)) \vee (\neg(a, \bullet) \wedge \neg(b, \bullet))$, no DMTS can express this.

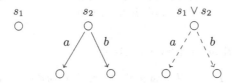

Fig. 17. MTS s_1 and s_2, and their MTS and BMTS least upper bounds $s_1 \vee s_2$

¬ While MTS are not closed under *complement* (not even deterministic ones), there have been attempts at characterizing symmetric difference [SCU11].

The results are summed up in the following statements and Table 3. With operations $\wedge$ and $\vee$, the set of BMTS (or DMTSm) processes forms a bounded distributive lattice up to $(\leq_m \cap \geq_m)$-equivalence. Moreover, with operations $\wedge, \vee, \|$ and $/$, the set of BMTS (or DMTSm) forms a commutative residuated lattice up to $(\leq_m \cap \geq_m)$-equivalence [BDF+13].

We are also interested in questions closely related to the discussed conjunction. The *common implementation* decision problem (CI) contains tuples of systems, such that there is an implementation refining each system of the tuple. For tuples of size two this is equivalent to non-emptiness of the conjunction, for one system (for instance a MixTS) this is equivalent to semantic consistency (or non-emptiness) [LNW07b], i.e. existence of implementation. Note that despite the lack of results on conjunction of non-deterministic systems the complexity was known long ago. The complexity improves when the input processes are deterministic (CI_D problem). Finally, rather surprisingly, the problem whether there is a deterministic common implementation (dCI) is hard. We display the

Table 3. Closure properties

	∧	∨	¬	‖	/
Deterministic MTS	✓	×	×	✓	✓
MTS	×	×	×	✓	?
MixTS	✓	×	×	✓	?
DMTS	✓	×	×	✓	?
DMTSm/BMTS/PMTS	✓	✓	×	✓	✓

Table 4. Complexity of the common implementation problems

	Single MTS	Single MixTS	Fixed # of systems	Arbitrary # of systems
CI	Trivial	EXP-c. [AHL+09]	P-c. [BGS92, HH08]	EXP-c. [AHL+09]
CI_D	Trivial	Trivial	NL-c. [BKLS09b]	PSPACE-c. [BKLS09b]
dCI	EXP-c. [BKLS09b]	EXP-c. [BKLS09b]	EXP-c. [BKLS09b]	EXP-c. [BKLS09b]

known results in Table 4 for several cases depending on whether the number of input processes is fixed or a part of the input. The results again indicate that several problems become more tractable if the given specifications are deterministic.

5.3   Model Checking and Synthesis

Given a valuation $\nu : P \to 2^{Ap}$ assigning to each process a set of atomic propositions valid in the process, one can check whether an MTS satisfies a CTL, LTL or μ-calculus formula φ over Ap. Since an MTS stands for a class of implementations, the question of satisfaction can be posed in two flavours:

($\models_\forall$-**problem**) Do all implementations satisfy φ?
($\models_\exists$-**problem**) Is there an implementation satisfying φ?

The problem of generalized model checking is to decide which of the three possible cases holds: whether all, only some, or no implementations satisfy φ. Further, if there exists a satisfying implementation it should also be automatically synthesized.

Generalized model checking of MTS was investigated with respect to a variant of safety [DDM10] as well as computation tree logic (CTL) [AHL+08a, GAW13], establishing it EXP-complete and providing a polynomial over- and under-approximation, similarly for μ-calculus. The EXP lower bound follows from the hardness of satisfiability of CTL and μ-calculus; the upper bound can be obtained through alternating tree automata [BG00].

In the rest, we focus on LTL. In [GP09] the generalized model checking of LTL over partial Kripke structures (PKS) is shown to be 2-EXP-hard. Further, [GJ03] describes a reduction from generalized model checking of μ-calculus over PKS to μ-calculus over MTS [Hut02, Hut99, GHJ01]. However, the hardness for

LTL does not follow since the encoding of an LTL formula into μ-calculus is exponential. There is thus no straightforward way to use the result of [GJ03] to establish the complexity for LTL.

On the one hand, answering the $\models_\forall$-problem is easy. Indeed, it is sufficient to perform standard model checking on the "greatest" implementation, i.e. such where all mays are turned into musts and thus all possible runs are present. On the other hand, the $\models_\exists$-problem is trickier. Similarly to the for $\models_\forall$-problem, we can take the minimal implementation of the MTS. However, whenever a deadlock occurs, the corresponding finite runs are ignored since LTL is usually interpreted over infinite words only. However, an undesirable consequence of this problem definition (call it ω, standing for infinite runs) is that all formulae are satisfied whenever there is an implementation without infinite runs, i.e. without a lasso of must transitions. There are several ways to avoid this vacuous satisfaction. Firstly, we can define LTL also on finite words [BČK11], which we denote by ∞ (for both finite and infinite runs). Secondly, we can consider only implementations without deadlocks, which we denote df. The deadlock-free approach has been studied in [UBC09] and the proposed solution was implemented in the tool MTSA [DFCU08]. It attempts to find a *deadlock-free* implementation of a given MTS that satisfies a given formula. However, the solution given in [UBC09] is incorrect in that the existence of a deadlock-free implementation satisfying a given formula is claimed even in some cases where no such implementation exists.

Example 16. The flaw can be seen on an example given in Fig. 18 [BČK11]. Clearly, s has no deadlock-free implementation with action a only, i.e. satisfying $\mathbf{GX}_a\mathbf{tt}$. Yet the method of [UBC09] as well as the tool [DFCU08] claim that such an implementation exists.   △

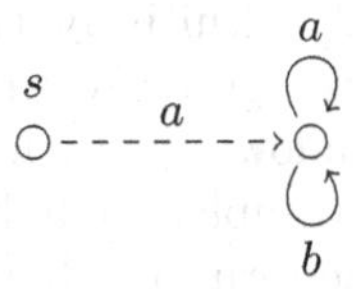

Fig. 18. No deadlock-free implementation of s satisfies $\mathbf{GX}_a\mathbf{tt}$

While the solution attempt of [UBC09] yields a PSPACE algorithm, the df-problem is actually 2-EXP-complete[BČK11]. Note that in this setting, there are no minimal implementations; non-trivial decisions have to be made which transitions to implement. For example, an MTS with only one may a-successor and one may b-successor cannot avoid deadlock in a unique way. Moreover, even if deadlocks are allowed, not implementing any choice may result in not satisfying $\mathbf{Xtt}$.

A solution to both df and ∞ as well as DMTS is provided in [BČK11]. It reduces the problem to a game where one player decides which transitions to implement in each step and another player chooses which of the implemented transitions is taken. Decisions of the players determine a run. The objective of the first player is to satisfy the formula on the run. He can always succeed irrespective of what the other player does if and only if there is an implementation satisfying the formula. Such LTL games are in general 2-EXP-complete [PR89]. The consequences are summarized in Table 5. Note that the winning strategy in the game yields a satisfying implementation, thus also solving the synthesis problem. This approach of reduction to an LTL game was also used to solve a similar problem of deciding whether all/some implementation can be pruned to satisfy a given LTL formula [DBPU12].

Table 5. Complexities of generalized LTL model checking (ω denoting finite runs are ignored, *df* denoting deadlock-free implementations are ignored, ∞ denoting no restriction)

	$\models_\forall$	$\models_\exists$
ω-MTS	PSPACE-complete	PSPACE-complete
df-MTS, ∞-MTS, DMTS	PSPACE-complete	2-EXP-complete

The best known time complexity bounds with respect to the size of system $|S|$ and the size of LTL formula $|\varphi|$ are the following. In all PSPACE-complete cases the time complexity is $\mathcal{O}(|S| \cdot 2^{|\varphi|})$; in all 2-EXP-complete cases the time complexity is $|S|^{2^{\mathcal{O}(|\varphi|)}} \cdot 2^{2^{\mathcal{O}(|\varphi|)}}$. The latter upper bound is achieved by translating the LTL formula into a deterministic (possibly generalized) Rabin automaton of size $2^{2^{\mathcal{O}(|\varphi|)}}$ with $2^{\mathcal{O}(|\varphi|)}$ accepting pairs, thus changing the LTL game into a Rabin game. For an efficient translation see e.g. [EK14,KK14]; for an algorithm solving Rabin games see [PP06,CGK13].

Another synthesis problem is the cheapest implementation, considered for (P)MTS with durations [BKL+12]. Intuitively, the constraint on the implementation here is to maximize the average reward per time unit while conforming to the specification and a budget allowing only for some combinations of actions implemented. The problem is NP-complete. Further, the problem of synthesizing a satisfying implementation in the form of a bounded Petri net was considered and shown undecidable [Sch16]. Finally, MTS themselves can be synthesized from constraints given as e.g. scenarios [SBUK13].

LTL model checking has also shed a better light on the problem of incompleteness of the parallel composition. Recall that there is a composition $s_1 \parallel s_2$ with an implementation i that does *not* arise as a composition $i_1 \parallel i_2$ of any two implementations $i_1 \leq_m s_1, i_2 \leq_m s_2$. Completeness can be achieved only under some restrictive conditions [BKLS09b]. [BČK11] shows that composition is sound and complete with respect to every logic of linear time: For DMTS and both ω and ∞,

$s_1 \parallel s_2 \models_\forall \varphi$ iff $i_1 \parallel i_2 \models \varphi$ for all implementations $i_1 \leq_m s_1, i_2 \leq_m s_2$

$s_1 \parallel s_2 \models_\exists \varphi$ iff $i_1 \parallel i_2 \models \varphi$ for some implementations $i_1 \leq_m s_1, i_2 \leq_m s_2$

Thus $\|$ is "LTL complete", i.e. preserves and reflects all LTL properties. Therefore, the only spurious implementations are sums of legal implementations.

6   Tools

The tool support is quite extensive; we focus our attention to the support for the operations required for complete specification theories [BDH+12] and several further problems. This includes modal refinement checking, parallel composition, quotient, conjunction (merge) and the related consistency checking and maximal implementation generation, deterministic hull and generalized LTL model checking. The comparison of the functionality of the available tools is depicted in Table 6. Apart from no longer maintained TAV [BLS95], the currently available tools are the following:

MTSA (Modal Transition System Analyzer) [DFFU07]

- is a tool for MTS,
- supports modal refinement, parallel composition and consistency using the cloning operation, which may not terminate; it also offers a model checking procedure, which is, unfortunately, flawed as discussed in Example 16.

MIO (Modal Input Output Workbench) [BML11,BMSH10]

- is a tool for modal I/O automata (MIOA) [LNW07a,RBB+11], which combine MTS and interface automata based on I/O automata; although MIOA have three types of may and must transitions (input, output, and internal), if we restrict to say only input transitions, the refinement works the same as for MTS, and some other operations, too,
- supports modal refinement, the MIOA parallel composition, conjunction for deterministic systems, and quotient for deterministic systems.

$\longrightarrow \Longrightarrow \dashrightarrow$
MoTraS (Modal Transition Systems) [KS13a]

- is a tool for MTS and DMTS, with partial support for BMTS and PMTS,
- supports full functionality for MTS as well as more general DMTS and in all cases also for *non-deterministic* systems; in particular, the algorithms for conjunction and quotient are considerably more complex than for the deterministic case; further, it features QBF-based algorithms for BMTS and PMTS refinement; finally, it also provides the deterministic hull, which enables us to both over- and under-approximate the very hard thorough refinement using the fast modal refinement.

MAccS (Marked Acceptance Specifications) [VR14]

- is a tool for acceptance automata (deterministic BMTS) with accepting states,
- features all the operations for acceptance automata, hence also for *deterministic* MTS.

Table 6. Functionality of the available tools. Here "det." denotes a functionality limited to deterministic systems.

Operation	MTS			DMTS	B/PMTS	det.AA
Parallel composition	MTSA	MIO	MoTraS	MoTraS		MAccS
Consistency	MTSA(of 2 systems)	MIO(det.)	MoTraS	MoTraS		MAccS
Conjunction		MIO(det.)	MoTraS	MoTraS		MAccS
Quotient (det.)		MIO	MoTraS			MAccS
Generalized LTL	MTSA(incorrect)		MoTraS	MoTraS		
Det. hull			MoTraS	MoTraS	MoTraS	
Refinement	MTSA	MIO	MoTraS	MoTraS	MoTraS	MAccS

Note that both MTSA and MIO can only handle modal systems, not their disjunctive extension. MoTraS supports DMTS, which have more expressive power. In contrast to (non-deterministic) MTS, DMTS are rich enough to express solutions to process equations [LX90] (hence a specification of a missing component in a system can be computed) and are closed under all operations, particularly conjunction. MAccS is similar in that AA are equally expressive and it supports all the operations, however, only for deterministic systems.

In order to make the tools easily extensible, a file format *xmts* was designed [MTS], which facilitates textual representation of different extensions of modal transition systems.

Besides, there are the following tools for related formalisms:
ECDAR (Environment for Compositional Design and Analysis of Real Time Systems) [DLL+10]

– is a tool for timed I/O automata (with no modalities);
– supports refinement, conjunction, composition and quotient, but all for only deterministic systems, as can be expected in the timed setting.

APAC (Abstract Probabilistic Automata Checker) [DLL+11]

– is a tool for abstract probabilistic automata;
– supports refinement, abstraction, conjunction, and composition.

7   Conclusion and Some Directions for Future Work

Firstly, we have surveyed MTS and its many extensions, including more involved modalities (combined, exclusive, persistent or conditional choices), quantitative models, or infinite-state systems. The comparison of various classes leads us to identifying a robust class of DMTS with more initial states, equivalent to several other formalisms, including the modal ν-calculus. This unifies the behavioural and logical approach to specification and verification and enables us to mix the two.

Secondly, we have surveyed solutions to problems arising in system design via MTS, such as logical and structural operations, refinement (modal, thorough, approximations using the deterministic hull) and synthesis of implementations based on temporal or reward constraints. We have also discussed the tool support for these problems.

As for future work, we mention several open issues. Firstly, although the *complexity* of many problems has been established, there are still several complexity gaps left open, for instance, the complexity of thorough refinement for BMTS and PMTS, the quotient construction (we conjecture the exponential blow-up is in general unavoidable), whether MTS, MixTS and DMTS are closed under quotient (we conjecture the opposite), or conditions on decidability of refinement over infinite systems, e.g. determinism as in [BKLS09b, EBHH10, HHM13].

Secondly, one may also extend the *model checking and synthesis* algorithms to more complex settings such as the cheapest implementation with an additional requirement that the partial sums stay within given bounds as done in [BFL+08], or cheapest implementation satisfying a temporal property as suggested in [CdAHS03, CD10], model checking metric temporal logic (LTL with time durations) [Koy90], model checking infinite-state MTS similarly to PDA in [Wal96], or cheapest implementation of mPDA using methods like [CV12].

Thirdly, on the *practical* side, all the tools only offer a limited support. In particular, the quotient of non-deterministic systems is very important for practical design and has not yet been implemented. Refinement algorithms do not scale too well on MTS extensions. Apart from multi-threading for all algorithms, one could use a combined modal refinement checker, which uses the standard modal refinement checker to prune the initial relation before the QBF-based checker is called. Altogether, the topic is still lively and subject to further practical developments, e.g. the currently prepared update of MoTraS features faster model checking due to integrating a better LTL-to-automata translator **Rabinizer 3** [KK14] and the cheapest implementation synthesizer [BKL+12, Man13].

Finally, the practical usability of MTS could be greatly improved by providing a higher-level *language*, possibly tailored to particular domains, which has MTS semantics, but a friendlier appearance to the domain-specific engineering practice.

Acknowledgement. I would like to thank Kim G. Larsen for introducing me to the topic of MTS and research in general, the pleasant collaboration during my Erasmus stay as a Master student at AAU a decade ago and ever since then. Arriving to Aalborg right after the paper *20 Years of Modal and Mixed Specifications* [AHL+08a] was published, my first paper with Kim [BKLS09b] was on MTS as a part of the Festschrift to Mogens Nielsen's 60th birthday [CSV09]. It is a pleasure and an honour to contribute today to Kim's Festschrift.

References

[AFdFE+11] Aceto, L., Fábregas, I., Frutos Escrig, D., Ingólfsdóttir, A., Palomino, M.: Relating modal refinements, covariant-contravariant simulations and partial bisimulations. In: Arbab, F., Sirjani, M. (eds.) FSEN 2011. LNCS, vol. 7141, pp. 268–283. Springer, Heidelberg (2012). doi:10.1007/978-3-642-29320-7_18

64   J. Křetínský

[AHKV98] Alur, R., Henzinger, T.A., Kupferman, O., Vardi, M.Y.: Alternating refinement relations. In: Sangiorgi, D., Simone, R. (eds.) CONCUR 1998. LNCS, vol. 1466, pp. 163–178. Springer, Heidelberg (1998). doi:10.1007/BFb0055622

[AHL+08a] Antonik, A., Huth, M., Larsen, K.G., Nyman, U., Wasowski, A.: 20 years of modal and mixed specifications. Bull. EATCS **95**, 94–129 (2008)

[AHL+08b] Antonik, A., Huth, M., Larsen, K.G., Nyman, U., Wąsowski, A.: Complexity of decision problems for mixed and modal specifications. In: Amadio, R. (ed.) FoSSaCS 2008. LNCS, vol. 4962, pp. 112–126. Springer, Heidelberg (2008). doi:10.1007/978-3-540-78499-9_9

[AHL+09] Antonik, A., Huth, M., Larsen, K.G., Nyman, U., Wasowski, A.: EXPTIME-complete decision problems for modal and mixed specifications. Electron. Notes Theor. Comput. Sci. **242**(1), 19–33 (2009)

[AKRU11] Alrajeh, D., Kramer, J., Russo, A., Uchitel, S.: An inductive approach for modal transition system refinement. In: Gallagher, J.P., Gelfond, M. (eds) ICLP (Technical Communications). LIPIcs, vol. 11, pp. 106–116. Schloss Dagstuhl - Leibniz-Zentrum fuer Informatik (2011)

[Bau12]   Bauer, S.S:. Modal specification theories for component-based design. Ph.D. thesis, Ludwig Maximilians University Munich (2012)

[BČK10]   Beneš, N., Černá, I., Křetínský, J.: Disjunctive modal transition systems and generalized LTL model checking. Technical report FIMU-RS-2010-12, Faculty of Informatics, Masaryk University, Brno (2010)

[BČK11]   Beneš, N., Černá, I., Křetínský, J.: Modal transition systems: composition and LTL model checking. In: Bultan, T., Hsiung, P.-A. (eds.) ATVA 2011. LNCS, vol. 6996, pp. 228–242. Springer, Heidelberg (2011). doi:10.1007/978-3-642-24372-1_17

[BCU06]   Brunet, G., Chechik, M., Uchitel, S.: Properties of behavioural model merging. In: Misra, J., Nipkow, T., Sekerinski, E. (eds.) FM 2006. LNCS, vol. 4085, pp. 98–114. Springer, Heidelberg (2006). doi:10.1007/11813040_8

[BCU16]   Ben-David, S., Chechik, M., Uchitel, S.: Observational refinement and merge for disjunctive MTSs. In: Artho, C., Legay, A., Peled, D. (eds.) ATVA 2016. LNCS, vol. 9938, pp. 287–303. Springer, Cham (2016). doi:10.1007/978-3-319-46520-3_19

[BDCU13] Ben-David, S., Chechik, M., Uchitel, S.: Merging partial behaviour models with different vocabularies. In: D'Argenio, P.R., Melgratti, H. (eds.) CONCUR 2013. LNCS, vol. 8052, pp. 91–105. Springer, Heidelberg (2013). doi:10.1007/978-3-642-40184-8_8

[BDF+13] Beneš, N., Delahaye, B., Fahrenberg, U., Křetínský, J., Legay, A.: Hennessy-milner logic with greatest fixed points as a complete behavioural specification theory. In: D'Argenio, P.R., Melgratti, H. (eds.) CONCUR 2013. LNCS, vol. 8052, pp. 76–90. Springer, Heidelberg (2013). doi:10.1007/978-3-642-40184-8_7

[BDH+12] Bauer, S.S., David, A., Hennicker, R., Guldstrand Larsen, K., Legay, A., Nyman, U., Wąsowski, A.: Moving from specifications to contracts in component-based design. In: Lara, J., Zisman, A. (eds.) FASE 2012. LNCS, vol. 7212, pp. 43–58. Springer, Heidelberg (2012). doi:10.1007/978-3-642-28872-2_3

[BDH+15] Beneš, N., Daca, P., Henzinger, T.A., Křetínský, J., Nickovic, D.: Complete composition operators for IOCO-testing theory. In: Kruchten, P., Becker, S., Schneider, J.-G. (eds.) Proceedings of the 18th International ACM SIGSOFT Symposium on Component-Based Software Engineering, CBSE 2015, Montreal, QC, Canada, 4–8 May 2015, pp. 101–110. ACM (2015)

[Ben08] Benveniste, A.: Multiple viewpoint contracts and residuation. In: 2nd International Workshop on Foundations of Interface Technologies (FIT) (2008)

[Ben12] Beneš, N.: Disjunctive modal transition systems. Ph.D. thesis, Masaryk University (2012)

[BFJ+11] Bauer, S.S., Fahrenberg, U., Juhl, L., Larsen, K.G., Legay, A., Thrane, C.: Quantitative refinement for weighted modal transition systems. In: Murlak, F., Sankowski, P. (eds.) MFCS 2011. LNCS, vol. 6907, pp. 60–71. Springer, Heidelberg (2011). doi:10.1007/978-3-642-22993-0_9

[BFJ+13] Bauer, S.S., Fahrenberg, U., Juhl, L., Larsen, K.G., Legay, A., Thrane, C.R.: Weighted modal transition systems. Formal Methods Syst. Des. 42(2), 193–220 (2013)

[BFL+08] Bouyer, P., Fahrenberg, U., Larsen, K.G., Markey, N., Srba, J.: Infinite runs in weighted timed automata with energy constraints. In: Cassez, F., Jard, C. (eds.) FORMATS 2008. LNCS, vol. 5215, pp. 33–47. Springer, Heidelberg (2008). doi:10.1007/978-3-540-85778-5_4

[BFLT12] Bauer, S.S., Fahrenberg, U., Legay, A., Thrane, C.: General quantitative specification theories with modalities. In: Hirsch, E.A., Karhumäki, J., Lepistö, A., Prilutskii, M. (eds.) CSR 2012. LNCS, vol. 7353, pp. 18–30. Springer, Heidelberg (2012). doi:10.1007/978-3-642-30642-6_3

[BFLV16] Bujtor, F., Fendrich, S., Lüttgen, G., Vogler, W.: Nondeterministic modal interfaces. Theor. Comput. Sci. 642, 24–53 (2016)

[BG99] Bruns, G., Godefroid, P.: Model checking partial state spaces with 3-valued temporal logics. In: Halbwachs, N., Peled, D. (eds.) CAV 1999. LNCS, vol. 1633, pp. 274–287. Springer, Heidelberg (1999). doi:10.1007/3-540-48683-6_25

[BG00] Bruns, G., Godefroid, P.: Generalized model checking: reasoning about partial state spaces. In: Palamidessi, C. (ed.) CONCUR 2000. LNCS, vol. 1877, pp. 168–182. Springer, Heidelberg (2000). doi:10.1007/3-540-44618-4_14

[BGS92] Balcázar, J.L., Gabarró, J., Santha, M.: Deciding bisimilarity is p-complete. Formal Asp. Comput. 4(6A), 638–648 (1992)

[BH11] Bultan, T., Hsiung, P.-A. (eds.): ATVA 2011. LNCS, vol. 6996. Springer, Heidelberg (2011). doi:10.1007/978-3-642-24372-1

[BHB10] Bauer, S.S., Hennicker, R., Bidoit, M.: A modal interface theory with data constraints. In: Davies, J., Silva, L., Simao, A. (eds.) SBMF 2010. LNCS, vol. 6527, pp. 80–95. Springer, Heidelberg (2011). doi:10.1007/978-3-642-19829-8_6

[BHJ10] Bauer, B.B., Hennicker, R., Janisch, S.: Interface theories for (a)synchronously communicating modal I/O-transition systems. In: Legay, A., Caillaud, B. (eds.) FIT. EPTCS, vol. 46, pp. 1–8 (2010)

[BHW10] Bauer, S.S., Hennicker, R., Wirsing, M.: Building a modal interface theory for concurrency and data. In: Mossakowski, T., Kreowski, H.-J. (eds.) WADT 2010. LNCS, vol. 7137, pp. 1–12. Springer, Heidelberg (2012). doi:10.1007/978-3-642-28412-0_1

66   J. Křetínský

[BJL+12a] Bauer, S.S., Juhl, L., Larsen, K.G., Legay, A., Srba, J.: Extending modal
           transition systems with structured labels. Math. Struct. Comput. Sci.
           22(4), 581–617 (2012)
[BJL+12b] Bauer, S.S., Juhl, L., Larsen, K.G., Srba, J., Legay, A.: A logic for
           accumulated-weight reasoning on multiweighted modal automata. In:
           Margaria, T., Qiu, Z., Yang, H. (eds.) TASE, pp. 77–84. IEEE (2012)
  [BK10]   Beneš, N., Křetínský, J.: Process algebra for modal transition system-
           ses. In: Matyska, L., Kozubek, M., Vojnar, T., Zemcik, P., Antos, D.
           (eds.) MEMICS. OASICS, vol. 16, pp. 9–18. Schloss Dagstuhl - Leibniz-
           Zentrum fuer Informatik, Germany (2010)
  [BK12]   Beneš, N., Křetínský, J.: Modal process rewrite systems. In: Roychoud-
           hury, A., D'Souza, M. (eds.) [RD12], pp. 120–135
[BKL+11]   Beneš, N., Křetínský, J., Larsen, K.G., Møller, M.H., Srba, J.: Parametric
           modal transition systems. In: Bultan, T., Hsiung, P.-A. (eds.) ATVA
           2011. LNCS, vol. 6996, pp. 275–289. Springer, Heidelberg (2011). doi:10.
           1007/978-3-642-24372-1_20
[BKL+12]   Beneš, N., Křetínský, J., Guldstrand Larsen, K., Møller, M.H., Srba, J.:
           Dual-priced modal transition systems with time durations. In: Bjørner,
           N., Voronkov, A. (eds.) LPAR 2012. LNCS, vol. 7180, pp. 122–137.
           Springer, Heidelberg (2012). doi:10.1007/978-3-642-28717-6_12
[BKL+15]   Beneš, N., Křetínský, J., Larsen, K.G., Møller, M.H., Sickert, S., Srba,
           J.: Refinement checking on parametric modal transition systems. Acta
           Inf. **52**(2–3), 269–297 (2015)
[BKLS09a] Beneš, N., Křetínský, J., Larsen, K.G., Srba, J.: Checking thorough
           refinement on modal transition systems is EXPTIME-complete. In:
           Leucker, M., Morgan, C. (eds.) [LM09], pp. 112–126
[BKLS09b] Beneš, N., Křetínský, J., Larsen, K.G., Srba, J.: On determinism in
           modal transition systems. Theor. Comput. Sci. **410**(41), 4026–4043
           (2009)
[BKLS12]   Beneš, N., Křetínský, J., Larsen, K.G., Srba, J.: EXPTIME-completeness
           of thorough refinement on modal transition systems. Inf. Comput. **218**,
           54–68 (2012)
  [BL92]   Boudol, G., Larsen, K.G.: Graphical versus logical specifications. Theor.
           Comput. Sci. **106**(1), 3–20 (1992)
[BLL+14]   Bauer, S.S., Larsen, K.G., Legay, A., Nyman, U., Wasowski, A.: A modal
           specification theory for components with data. Sci. Comput. Program.
           83, 106–128 (2014)
[BLPR09]   Bertrand, N., Legay, A., Pinchinat, S., Raclet, J.-B.: A compositional
           approach on modal specifications for timed systems. In: Breitman, K.,
           Cavalcanti, A. (eds.) ICFEM 2009. LNCS, vol. 5885, pp. 679–697.
           Springer, Heidelberg (2009). doi:10.1007/978-3-642-10373-5_35
[BLPR12]   Bertrand, N., Legay, A., Pinchinat, S., Raclet, J.-B.: Modal event-clock
           specifications for timed component-based design. Sci. Comput. Program.
           77(12), 1212–1234 (2012)
  [BLS95] Børjesson, A., Larsen, K.G., Skou, A.: Generality in design and composi-
           tional verification using TAV. Formal Methods Syst. Des. **6**(3), 239–258
           (1995)
  [BML11] Bauer, S.S., Mayer, P., Legay, A.: MIO workbench: a tool for composi-
           tional design with modal input/output interfaces. In: Bultan, T., Hsiung,
           P.-A. (eds.) ATVA 2011. LNCS, vol. 6996, pp. 418–421. Springer, Hei-
           delberg (2011). doi:10.1007/978-3-642-24372-1_30

[BMSH10] Bauer, S.S., Mayer, P., Schroeder, A., Hennicker, R.: On weak modal compatibility, refinement, and the MIO workbench. In: Esparza, J., Majumdar, R. (eds.) TACAS 2010. LNCS, vol. 6015, pp. 175–189. Springer, Heidelberg (2010). doi:10.1007/978-3-642-12002-2_15

[BPR09] Bertrand, N., Pinchinat, S., Raclet, J.-B.: Refinement and consistency of timed modal specifications. In: Dediu, A.H., Ionescu, A.M., Martín-Vide, C. (eds.) LATA 2009. LNCS, vol. 5457, pp. 152–163. Springer, Heidelberg (2009). doi:10.1007/978-3-642-00982-2_13

[Bru97] Bruns, G.: An industrial application of modal process logic. Sci. Comput. Program. 29(1–2), 3–22 (1997)

[BSV15] Bujtor, F., Sorokin, L., Vogler, W.: Testing preorders for DMTS: deadlock- and the new deadlock/divergence-testing. In: 15th International Conference on Application of Concurrency to System Design, ACSD 2015, Brussels, Belgium, 21–26 June 2015, pp. 60–69. IEEE Computer Society (2015)

[BV15] Bujtor, F., Vogler, W.: Failure semantics for modal transition systems. ACM Trans. Embed. Comput. Syst. 14(4), 67:1–67:30 (2015)

[CD10] Chatterjee, K., Doyen, L.: Energy parity games. In: Abramsky, S., Gavoille, C., Kirchner, C., Meyer auf der Heide, F., Spirakis, P.G. (eds.) ICALP 2010. LNCS, vol. 6199, pp. 599–610. Springer, Heidelberg (2010). doi:10.1007/978-3-642-14162-1_50

[CdAHS03] Chakrabarti, A., Alfaro, L., Henzinger, T.A., Stoelinga, M.: Resource interfaces. In: Alur, R., Lee, I. (eds.) EMSOFT 2003. LNCS, vol. 2855, pp. 117–133. Springer, Heidelberg (2003). doi:10.1007/978-3-540-45212-6_9

[CDEG03] Chechik, M., Devereux, B., Easterbrook, S.M., Gurfinkel, A.: Multi-valued symbolic model-checking. ACM Trans. Softw. Eng. Methodol. 12(4), 371–408 (2003)

[CDL+10] Caillaud, B., Delahaye, B., Larsen, K.G., Legay, A., Pedersen, M.L., Wasowski, A.: Compositional design methodology with constraint Markov chains. In: QEST, pp. 123–132. IEEE Computer Society (2010)

[CE81] Clarke, E.M., Emerson, E.A.: Design and synthesis of synchronization skeletons using branching time temporal logic. In: Kozen, D. (ed.) Logic of Programs 1981. LNCS, vol. 131, pp. 52–71. Springer, Heidelberg (1982). doi:10.1007/BFb0025774

[CGK13] Chatterjee, K., Gaiser, A., Křetínský, J.: Automata with generalized rabin pairs for probabilistic model checking and LTL synthesis. In: Sharygina, N., Veith, H. (eds.) CAV 2013. LNCS, vol. 8044, pp. 559–575. Springer, Heidelberg (2013). doi:10.1007/978-3-642-39799-8_37

[CGL93] Čerāns, K., Godskesen, J.C., Larsen, K.G.: Timed modal specification—theory and tools. In: Courcoubetis, C. (ed.) CAV 1993. LNCS, vol. 697, pp. 253–267. Springer, Heidelberg (1993). doi:10.1007/3-540-56922-7_21

[CGLT09] Campetelli, A., Gruler, A., Leucker, M., Thoma, D.: Don't know for multi-valued systems. In: Liu, Z., Ravn, A.P. (eds.) ATVA 2009. LNCS, vol. 5799, pp. 289–305. Springer, Heidelberg (2009). doi:10.1007/978-3-642-04761-9_22

[CR12] Caillaud, B., Raclet, J.-B.: Ensuring reachability by design. In: Roychoudhury, A., D'Souza, M. (eds.) [RD12], pp. 213–227

[CSV09] Carbone, M., Sobocinski, P., Valencia, F.D.: Foreword: Festschrift for mogens nielsen's 60th birthday. Theor. Comput. Sci. 410(41), 4001–4005 (2009)

[CV12]   Chatterjee, K., Velner, Y.: Mean-payoff pushdown games. In: LICS, pp. 195–204. IEEE (2012)

[dAGJ04]   de Alfaro, L., Godefroid, P., Jagadeesan, R.: Three-valued abstractions of games: uncertainty, but with precision. In: LICS04 [LIC04], pp. 170–179

[dAH01]   de Alfaro, L., Henzinger, T.A.: Interface automata. In: ESEC/SIGSOFT FSE, pp. 109–120. ACM (2001)

[DBPU12]   D'Ippolito, N., Braberman, V.A., Piterman, N., Uchitel, S.: The modal transition system control problem. In: Giannakopoulou, D., Méry, D. (eds.) [GM12], pp. 155–170

[DDM10]   Darondeau, P., Dubreil, J., Marchand, H.: Supervisory control for modal specifications of services. In: WODES, pp. 428–435 (2010)

[DFCU08]   D'Ippolito, N., Fischbein, D., Chechik, M., Uchitel, S.: MTSA: the modal transition system analyser. In: ASE, pp. 475–476. IEEE (2008)

[DFFU07]   D'Ippolito, N., Fischbein, D., Foster, H., Uchitel, S.: MTSA: eclipse support for modal transition systems construction, analysis and elaboration. In: Cheng, L.-T., Orso, A., Robillard, M.P. (eds.) ETX, pp. 6–10. ACM (2007)

[DFLL14]   Delahaye, B., Fahrenberg, U., Larsen, K.G., Legay, A.: Refinement and difference for probabilistic automata. Log. Methods Comput. Sci. 10(3) (2014)

[DGG97]   Dams, D., Gerth, R., Grumberg, O.: Abstract interpretation of reactive systems. ACM Trans. Program. Lang. Syst. 19(2), 253–291 (1997)

[DKL+11a]   Delahaye, B., Katoen, J.-P., Larsen, K.G., Legay, A., Pedersen, M.L., Sher, F., Wąsowski, A.: Abstract probabilistic automata. In: Jhala, R., Schmidt, D. (eds.) VMCAI 2011. LNCS, vol. 6538, pp. 324–339. Springer, Heidelberg (2011). doi:10.1007/978-3-642-18275-4_23

[DKL+11b]   Delahaye, B., Katoen, J.-P., Larsen, K.G., Legay, A., Pedersen, M.L., Sher, F., Wasowski, A.: New results on abstract probabilistic automata. In: Caillaud, B., Carmona, J., Hiraishi, K. (eds.) 11th International Conference on Application of Concurrency to System Design, ACSD 2011, Newcastle Upon Tyne, UK, 20–24 June 2011, pp. 118–127. IEEE Computer Society (2011)

[DLL+10]   David, A., Larsen, K.G., Legay, A., Nyman, U., Wąsowski, A.: ECDAR: an environment for compositional design and analysis of real time systems. In: Bouajjani, A., Chin, W.-N. (eds.) ATVA 2010. LNCS, vol. 6252, pp. 365–370. Springer, Heidelberg (2010). doi:10.1007/978-3-642-15643-4_29

[DLL+11]   Delahaye, B., Larsen, K.G., Legay, A., Pedersen, M.L., Wasowski, A.: APAC: a tool for reasoning about abstract probabilistic automata. In: Eighth International Conference on Quantitative Evaluation of Systems, QEST 2011, Aachen, Germany, 5–8 September 2011, pp. 151–152. IEEE Computer Society (2011)

[DLL14]   Delahaye, B., Larsen, K.G., Legay, A.: Stuttering for abstract probabilistic automata. J. Log. Algebr. Program. 83(1), 1–19 (2014)

[DM13]   D'Argenio, P.R., Melgratti, H. (eds.): CONCUR 2013. LNCS, vol. 8052. Springer, Heidelberg (2013). doi:10.1007/978-3-642-40184-8

[DN04]   Dams, D., Namjoshi, K.S.: The existence of finite abstractions for branching time model checking. In: LICS04 [LIC04], pp. 335–344

[DSMB16]   Diskin, Z., Safilian, A., Maibaum, T., Ben-David, S.: Faithful modeling of product lines with kripke structures and modal logic. Sci. Ann. Comput. Sci. 26(1), 69–122 (2016)

[EBHH10] Elhog-Benzina, D., Haddad, S., Hennicker, R.: Process refinement and asynchronous composition with modalities. In: Donatelli, S., Kleijn, J., Machado, R.J., Fernandes, J.M. (eds.) ACSD/Petri Nets Workshops. CEUR Workshop Proceedings, vol. 827, pp. 385–401. CEUR-WS.org (2010)

[EHH12] Elhog-Benzina, D., Haddad, S., Hennicker, R.: Refinement and asynchronous composition of modal petri nets. Trans. Petri Nets Other Models Concurr. **5**, 96–120 (2012)

[EK14] Esparza, J., Křetínský, J.: From LTL to deterministic automata: a safraless compositional approach. In: Biere, A., Bloem, R. (eds.) CAV 2014. LNCS, vol. 8559, pp. 192–208. Springer, Cham (2014). doi:10.1007/978-3-319-08867-9_13

[FBU09] Fischbein, D., Braberman, V.A., Uchitel, S.: A sound observational semantics for modal transition systems. In: Leucker, M., Morgan, C. (eds.) [LM09], pp. 215–230

[Fis12] Fischbein, D.: Foundations for behavioural model elaboration using modal transition systems. Ph.D. thesis, Imperial College London, UK, (2012)

[FKLT14] Fahrenberg, U., Křetínský, J., Legay, A., Traonouez, L.-M.: Compositionality for quantitative specifications. In: Lanese, I., Madelaine, E. (eds.) [LM15], pp. 306–324

[FL12] Fahrenberg, U., Legay, A.: A robust specification theory for modal eventclock automata. In: Bauer, S.S., Raclet, J.-B. (eds) FIT. EPTCS, vol. 87, pp. 5–16 (2012)

[FL14] Fahrenberg, U., Legay, A.: General quantitative specification theories with modal transition systems. Acta Inf. **51**(5), 261–295 (2014)

[FLT14] Fahrenberg, U., Legay, A., Traonouez, L.-M.: Structural refinement for the modal nu-Calculus. In: Ciobanu, G., Méry, D. (eds.) ICTAC 2014. LNCS, vol. 8687, pp. 169–187. Springer, Cham (2014). doi:10.1007/978-3-319-10882-7_11

[FLW06] Fecher, H., Leucker, M., Wolf, V.: *Don't know* in probabilistic systems. In: Valmari, A. (ed.) SPIN 2006. LNCS, vol. 3925, pp. 71–88. Springer, Heidelberg (2006). doi:10.1007/11691617_5

[FP07] Feuillade, G., Pinchinat, S.: Modal specifications for the control theory of discrete event systems. Discret. Event Dyn. Syst. **17**(2), 211–232 (2007)

[FS05] Fecher, H., Steffen, M.: Characteristic μ-calculus formulas for underspecified transition systems. Electr. Notes Theor. Comput. Sci. **128**(2), 103–116 (2005)

[FS08] Fecher, H., Schmidt, H.: Comparing disjunctive modal transition systems with an one-selecting variant. J. Log. Algebr. Program. **77**(1–2), 20–39 (2008)

[FU08] Fischbein, D., Uchitel, S.: On correct and complete strong merging of partial behaviour models. In: Harrold, M.J., Murphy, G.C. (eds.) SIGSOFT FSE, pp. 297–307. ACM (2008)

[GAW13] Guerra, P.T., Andrade, A., Wassermann, R.: Toward the revision of CTL models through Kripke modal transition systems. In: Iyoda, J., Moura, L. (eds.) SBMF 2013. LNCS, vol. 8195, pp. 115–130. Springer, Heidelberg (2013). doi:10.1007/978-3-642-41071-0_9

[GC06] Gurfinkel, A., Chechik, M.: Why waste a perfectly good abstraction? In: Hermanns, H., Palsberg, J. (eds.) TACAS 2006. LNCS, vol. 3920, pp. 212–226. Springer, Heidelberg (2006). doi:10.1007/11691372_14

[GHJ01]   Godefroid, P., Huth, M., Jagadeesan, R.: Abstraction-based model check-
          ing using modal transition systems. In: Larsen, K.G., Nielsen, M. (eds.)
          CONCUR 2001. LNCS, vol. 2154, pp. 426–440. Springer, Heidelberg
          (2001). doi:10.1007/3-540-44685-0_29
[GJ03]   Godefroid, P., Jagadeesan, R.: On the expressiveness of 3-valued models.
          In: Zuck, L.D., Attie, P.C., Cortesi, A., Mukhopadhyay, S. (eds.) VMCAI
          2003. LNCS, vol. 2575, pp. 206–222. Springer, Heidelberg (2003). doi:10.
          1007/3-540-36384-X_18
[GM12]   Giannakopoulou, D., Méry, D. (eds.): FM 2012. LNCS, vol. 7436.
          Springer, Heidelberg (2012). doi:10.1007/978-3-642-32759-9
[GNRT10] Godefroid, P., Nori, A.V., Rajamani, S.K., Tetali, S.: Compositional
          may-must program analysis: unleashing the power of alternation. In:
          Hermenegildo, M.V., Palsberg, J. (eds.) POPL, pp. 43–56. ACM (2010)
[GP09]   Godefroid, P., Piterman, N.: LTL generalized model checking revisited.
          In: Jones, N.D., Müller-Olm, M. (eds.) [JMO09], pp. 89–104
[GSSL94] Gawlick, R., Segala, R., Søgaard-Andersen, J., Lynch, N.: Liveness in
          timed and untimed systems. In: Abiteboul, S., Shamir, E. (eds.) ICALP
          1994. LNCS, vol. 820, pp. 166–177. Springer, Heidelberg (1994). doi:10.
          1007/3-540-58201-0_66
[GWC06a] Gurfinkel, A., Wei, O., Chechik, M.: Systematic construction of abstrac-
          tions for model-checking. In: Emerson, E.A., Namjoshi, K.S. (eds.)
          VMCAI 2006. LNCS, vol. 3855, pp. 381–397. Springer, Heidelberg
          (2005). doi:10.1007/11609773_25
[GWC06b] Gurfinkel, A., Wei, O., Chechik, M.: YASM: a software model-checker for
          verification and refutation. In: Ball, T., Jones, R.B. (eds.) CAV 2006.
          LNCS, vol. 4144, pp. 170–174. Springer, Heidelberg (2006). doi:10.1007/
          11817963_18
[Hen85]   Hennessy, M.: Acceptance trees. J. ACM 32(4), 896–928 (1985)
[HH08]   Hussain, A., Huth, M.: On model checking multiple hybrid views. Theor.
          Comput. Sci. 404(3), 186–201 (2008)
[HHM13]   Haddad, S., Hennicker, R., Møller, M.H.: Specification of asynchronous
          component systems with modal I/O-petri nets. In: Abadi, M., Lluch
          Lafuente, A. (eds.) TGC 2013. LNCS, vol. 8358, pp. 219–234. Springer,
          Cham (2014). doi:10.1007/978-3-319-05119-2_13
[HJS01]   Huth, M., Jagadeesan, R., Schmidt, D.: Modal transition systems: a foun-
          dation for three-valued program analysis. In: Sands, D. (ed.) ESOP 2001.
          LNCS, vol. 2028, pp. 155–169. Springer, Heidelberg (2001). doi:10.1007/
          3-540-45309-1_11
[HKK13]   Hermanns, H., Krčál, J., Křetínský, J.: Compositional verification and
          optimization of interactive Markov chains. In: D'Argenio, P.R., Mel-
          gratti, H.C. (eds.) [DM13], pp. 364–379
[HKKG13] Han, T., Krause, C., Kwiatkowska, M.Z., Giese, H.: Modal specifications
          for probabilistic timed systems. In: Bortolussi, L., Wiklicky, H. (eds.)
          QAPL. EPTCS, vol. 117, pp. 66–80 (2013)
[HL89]   Hüttel, H., Larsen, K.G.: The use of static constructs in a model
          process logic. In: Meyer, A.R., Taitslin, M.A. (eds.) Logic at Botik 1989.
          LNCS, vol. 363, pp. 163–180. Springer, Heidelberg (1989). doi:10.1007/
          3-540-51237-3_14
[Hol89]   Holmström, S.: A refinement calculus for specifications in Hennessy-
          Milner logic with recursion. Formal Asp. Comput. 1(3), 242–272 (1989)

[Hut99]   Huth, M.: A unifying framework for model checking labeled kripke structures, modal transition systems, and interval transition systems. In: Rangan, C.P., Raman, V., Ramanujam, R. (eds.) FSTTCS 1999. LNCS, vol. 1738, pp. 369–380. Springer, Heidelberg (1999). doi:10.1007/3-540-46691-6_30

[Hut02]   Huth, M.: Model checking modal transition systems using Kripke structures. In: Cortesi, A. (ed.) VMCAI 2002. LNCS, vol. 2294, pp. 302–316. Springer, Heidelberg (2002). doi:10.1007/3-540-47813-2_21

[JL91]   Jonsson, B., Larsen, K.G.: Specification and refinement of probabilistic processes. In: LICS, pp. 266–277. IEEE Computer Society (1991)

[JLS12]   Juhl, L., Larsen, K.G., Srba, J.: Modal transition systems with weight intervals. J. Log. Algebr. Program. **81**(4), 408–421 (2012)

[JMO09]   Jones, N.D., Müller-Olm, M. (eds.): VMCAI 2009. LNCS, vol. 5403. Springer, Heidelberg (2009). doi:10.1007/978-3-540-93900-9

[Juh13]   Juhl, L.: Quantities in games and modal transition systems. Ph.D. thesis, Department of Computer Science, Aalborg University (2013)

[KDMU14]   Krka, I., D'Ippolito, N., Medvidović, N., Uchitel, S.: Revisiting compatibility of input-output modal transition systems. In: Jones, C., Pihlajasaari, P., Sun, J. (eds.) FM 2014. LNCS, vol. 8442, pp. 367–381. Springer, Cham (2014). doi:10.1007/978-3-319-06410-9_26

[KK14]   Komárková, Z., Křetínský, J.: Rabinizer 3: safraless translation of LTL to small deterministic automata. In: Cassez, F., Raskin, J.-F. (eds.) ATVA 2014. LNCS, vol. 8837, pp. 235–241. Springer, Cham (2014). doi:10.1007/978-3-319-11936-6_17

[KKLW07]   Katoen, J.-P., Klink, D., Leucker, M., Wolf, V.: Three-valued abstraction for continuous-time Markov chains. In: Damm, W., Hermanns, H. (eds.) CAV 2007. LNCS, vol. 4590, pp. 311–324. Springer, Heidelberg (2007). doi:10.1007/978-3-540-73368-3_37

[KKLW12]   Katoen, J.-P., Klink, D., Leucker, M., Wolf, V.: Three-valued abstraction for probabilistic systems. J. Log. Algebr. Program. **81**(4), 356–389 (2012)

[KM12]   Krka I., Medvidovic, N.: Revisiting modal interface automata. In: Gnesi, S., Gruner, S., Plat, N., Rumpe, B. (eds.) Proceedings of the First International Workshop on Formal Methods in Software Engineering - Rigorous and Agile Approaches, FormSERA 2012, Zurich, Switzerland, 2 June 2012, pp. 30–36. IEEE (2012)

[Koy90]   Koymans, R.: Specifying real-time properties with metric temporal logic. Real-Time Syst. **2**(4), 255–299 (1990)

[Koz83]   Kozen, D.: Results on the propositional μ-calculus. Theor. Comput. Sci. **27**, 333–354 (1983)

[Kře14]   Křetínský, J.: Modal transition systems: extensions and analysis. Ph.D. thesis, Masaryk University, Brno, Department of Computer Science (2014)

[KŘS05]   Křetínský, M., Řehák, V., Strejček, J.: Reachability of Hennessy-Milner properties for weakly extended PRS. In: Sarukkai, S., Sen, S. (eds.) FSTTCS 2005. LNCS, vol. 3821, pp. 213–224. Springer, Heidelberg (2005). doi:10.1007/11590156_17

[KS90]   Kanellakis, P.C., Smolka, S.A.: CCS expressions, finite state processes, and three problems of equivalence. Inf. Comput. **86**(1), 43–68 (1990)

[KS13a]   Křetínský, J., Sickert, S.: MoTraS: a tool for modal transition systems and their extensions. In: Hung, D., Ogawa, M. (eds.) ATVA 2013. LNCS, vol. 8172, pp. 487–491. Springer, Cham (2013). doi:10.1007/978-3-319-02444-8_41

[KS13b] Křetínský, J., Sickert, S.: On refinements of Boolean and parametric modal transition systems. In: Liu, Z., Woodcock, J., Zhu, H. (eds.) ICTAC 2013. LNCS, vol. 8049, pp. 213–230. Springer, Heidelberg (2013). doi:10.1007/978-3-642-39718-9_13

[KS13c] Křetínský, J., Sickert, S.: On refinements of Boolean and parametric modal transition systems. Technical report abs/1304.5278, arXiv.org (2013)

[Lar89] Larsen, K.G.: Modal specifications. In: Sifakis, J. (ed.) CAV 1989. LNCS, vol. 407, pp. 232–246. Springer, Heidelberg (1990). doi:10.1007/3-540-52148-8_19

[Lar90] Guldstrand Larsen, K.: Ideal specification formalism = expressivity + compositionality + decidability + testability +. In: Baeten, J.C.M., Klop, J.W. (eds.) CONCUR 1990. LNCS, vol. 458, pp. 33–56. Springer, Heidelberg (1990). doi:10.1007/BFb0039050

[LIC04] 19th IEEE Symposium on Logic in Computer Science (LICS 2004), 14–17 July 2004, Turku, Finland, Proceedings. IEEE Computer Society (2004)

[LL12] Larsen, K.G., Legay, A.: Quantitative modal transition systems. In: Martí-Oliet, N., Palomino, M. (eds.) WADT 2012. LNCS, vol. 7841, pp. 50–58. Springer, Heidelberg (2013). doi:10.1007/978-3-642-37635-1_3

[LM09] Leucker, M., Morgan, C. (eds.): ICTAC 2009. LNCS, vol. 5684. Springer, Heidelberg (2009). doi:10.1007/978-3-642-03466-4

[LM15] Lanese, I., Madelaine, E. (eds.): FACS 2014. LNCS, vol. 8997. Springer, Cham (2015). doi:10.1007/978-3-319-15317-9

[LML15] Luthmann, L., Mennicke, S., Lochau, M.: Towards an I/O conformance testing theory for software product lines based on modal interface automata. In: Atlee, J.M., Gnesi, S. (eds.) Proceedings 6th Workshop on Formal Methods and Analysis in SPL Engineering, FMSPLE@ETAPS 2015, London, UK, 11 April 2015. EPTCS, vol. 182, pp. 1–13 (2015)

[LNW07a] Larsen, K.G., Nyman, U., Wąsowski, A.: Modal I/O automata for interface and product line theories. In: Nicola, R. (ed.) ESOP 2007. LNCS, vol. 4421, pp. 64–79. Springer, Heidelberg (2007). doi:10.1007/978-3-540-71316-6_6

[LNW07b] Larsen, K.G., Nyman, U., Wąsowski, A.: On modal refinement and consistency. In: Caires, L., Vasconcelos, V.T. (eds.) CONCUR 2007. LNCS, vol. 4703, pp. 105–119. Springer, Heidelberg (2007). doi:10.1007/978-3-540-74407-8_8

[LSW95] Larsen, K.G., Steffen, B., Weise, C.: Fischer's protocol revisited: a simple proof using modal constraints. In: Alur, R., Henzinger, T.A., Sontag, E.D. (eds.) HS 1995. LNCS, vol. 1066, pp. 604–615. Springer, Heidelberg (1996). doi:10.1007/BFb0020979

[LT88] Larsen, K.G., Thomsen, B.: A modal process logic. In: LICS, pp. 203–210. IEEE Computer Society (1988)

[LV13] Lüttgen, G., Vogler, W.: Modal interface automata. Log. Methods Comput. Sci. 9(3) (2013)

[LVF15] Lüttgen, G., Vogler, W., Fendrich, S.: Richer interface automata with optimistic and pessimistic compatibility. Acta Inf. 52(4–5), 305–336 (2015)

[LX90] Larsen, K.G., Xinxin, L.: Equation solving using modal transition systems. In: LICS, pp. 108–117. IEEE Computer Society (1990)

[Man13] Manta, A.: Implementation of algorithms for modal transition systems with durations. Bachelor's thesis, Technische Universität München (2013)

[May00] Mayr, R.: Process rewrite systems. Inf. Comput. **156**(1–2), 264–286 (2000)

[Møl13] Møller, M.H.: Modal and component-based system specifications. Ph.D. thesis, Department of Computer Science, Aalborg University (2013)

[MTS]   Motras. http://www7.in.tum.de/kretinsk/motras.html

[Nam03] Namjoshi, K.S.: Abstraction for branching time properties. In: Hunt, W.A., Somenzi, F. (eds.) CAV 2003. LNCS, vol. 2725, pp. 288–300. Springer, Heidelberg (2003). doi:10.1007/978-3-540-45069-6_29

[NNN08] Nanz, S., Nielson, F., Riis Nielson, H.: Modal abstractions of concurrent behaviour. In: Alpuente, M., Vidal, G. (eds.) SAS 2008. LNCS, vol. 5079, pp. 159–173. Springer, Heidelberg (2008). doi:10.1007/978-3-540-69166-2_11

[Nym08] Nyman, U.: Modal transition systems as the basis for interface theories and product lines. Ph.D. thesis, Aalborg Universitet (2008)

[Pnu77] Pnueli, A. The temporal logic of programs. In: FOCS, pp. 46–57. IEEE Computer Society (1977)

[PP06]   Piterman, N., Pnueli, A.: Faster solutions of Rabin and Streett games. In: LICS, pp. 275–284. IEEE Computer Society (2006)

[PR89]   Pnueli, A., Rosner, R.: On the synthesis of a reactive module. In: POPL, pp. 179–190. ACM Press (1989)

[PT87]   Paige, R., Tarjan, R.E.: Three partition refinement algorithms. SIAM J. Comput. **16**(6), 973–989 (1987)

[QS82]   Queille, J.P., Sifakis, J.: Specification and verification of concurrent systems in CESAR. In: Dezani-Ciancaglini, M., Montanari, U. (eds.) Programming 1982. LNCS, vol. 137, pp. 337–351. Springer, Heidelberg (1982). doi:10.1007/3-540-11494-7_22

[Rac07] Raclet, J.-B.: Quotient de spécifications pour la réutilisation de composants. Ph.D. thesis, Université de Rennes I (2007). (In French)

[Rac08] Raclet, J.-B.: Residual for component specifications. Electr. Notes Theor. Comput. Sci. **215**, 93–110 (2008)

[RBB+09a] Raclet, J.-B., Badouel, E., Benveniste, A., Caillaud, B., Legay, A., Passerone, R.: Modal interfaces: unifying interface automata and modal specifications. In:Chakraborty, S., Halbwachs, N., (eds.) EMSOFT, pp. 87–96. ACM (2009)

[RBB+09b] Raclet, J.-B., Badouel, E., Benveniste, A., Caillaud, B., Passerone, R.: Why are modalities good for interface theories? In: ACSD, pp. 119–127. IEEE Computer Society (2009)

[RBB+11] Raclet, J.-B., Badouel, E., Benveniste, A., Caillaud, B., Legay, A., Passerone, R.: A modal interface theory for component-based design. Fundam. Inform. **108**(1–2), 119–149 (2011)

[RD12]   Roychoudhury, A., D'Souza, M. (eds.): ICTAC 2012. LNCS, vol. 7521. Springer, Heidelberg (2012). doi:10.1007/978-3-642-32943-2

[SBUK13] Sibay, G.E., Braberman, V.A., Uchitel, S., Kramer, J.: Synthesizing modal transition systems from triggered scenarios. IEEE Trans. Softw. Eng. **39**(7), 975–1001 (2013)

[Sch16] Schlachter, U.: Bounded petri net synthesis from modal transition systems is undecidable. In: Desharnais, J., Jagadeesan, R. (eds.), 27th International Conference on Concurrency Theory, CONCUR 2016, Québec City, Canada, 23–26 August 2016. LIPIcs, vol. 59, pp. 15:1–15:14. Schloss Dagstuhl - Leibniz-Zentrum fuer Informatik (2016)

[SCU11] Sassolas, M., Chechik, M., Uchitel, S.: Exploring inconsistencies between modal transition systems. Softw. Syst. Model. 10(1), 117–142 (2011)

[SG04] Shoham, S., Grumberg, O.: Monotonic abstraction-refinement for CTL. In: Jensen, K., Podelski, A. (eds.) TACAS 2004. LNCS, vol. 2988, pp. 546–560. Springer, Heidelberg (2004). doi:10.1007/978-3-540-24730-2_40

[SH15] Siirtola, A., Heljanko, K.: Parametrised modal interface automata. ACM Trans. Embed. Comput. Syst. 14(4), 65:1–65:25 (2015)

[SK14] Sharma, A., Katoen, J.-P.: Layered reduction for abstract probabilistic automata. In: 14th International Conference on Application of Concurrency to System Design, ACSD 2014, Tunis La Marsa, Tunisia, 23–27 June 2014, pp. 21–31. IEEE Computer Society (2014)

[SUBK12] Sibay, G.E., Uchitel, S., Braberman, V.A., Kramer, J.: Distribution of modal transition systems. In: Giannakopoulou, D., Méry, D. (eds.) [GM12], pp. 403–417

[tBDG+15] Beek, M.H., Damiani, F., Gnesi, S., Mazzanti, F., Paolini, L.: From featured transition systems to modal transition systems with variability constraints. In: Calinescu, R., Rumpe, B. (eds.) SEFM 2015. LNCS, vol. 9276, pp. 344–359. Springer, Cham (2015). doi:10.1007/978-3-319-22969-0_24

[tBFGM16] ter Beek, M.H., Fantechi, A., Gnesi, S., Mazzanti, F.: Modelling and analysing variability in product families: model checking of modal transition systems with variability constraints. J. Log. Algebr. Meth. Program. 85(2), 287–315 (2016)

[UBC07] Uchitel, S., Brunet, G., Chechik, M.: Behaviour model synthesis from properties and scenarios. In: ICSE, pp. 34–43. IEEE Computer Society (2007)

[UBC09] Uchitel, S., Brunet, G., Chechik, M.: Synthesis of partial behavior models from properties and scenarios. IEEE Trans. Softw. Eng. 35(3), 384–406 (2009)

[UC04] Uchitel, S., Chechik, M.: Merging partial behavioural models. In: Taylor, R.N., Dwyer, M.B. (eds.) SIGSOFT FSE, pp. 43–52. ACM (2004)

[VR14] Verdier, G., Raclet, J.-B.: Maccs: a tool for reachability by design. In: Lanese, I., Madelaine, E. (eds.) [LM15], pp. 191–197

[VR15] Verdier, G., Raclet, J.-B.: Quotient of acceptance specifications under reachability constraints. In: Dediu, A.-H., Formenti, E., Martín-Vide, C., Truthe, B. (eds.) LATA 2015. LNCS, vol. 8977, pp. 299–311. Springer, Cham (2015). doi:10.1007/978-3-319-15579-1_23

[Wal96] Walukiewicz, I.: Pushdown processes: games and model checking. In: Alur, R., Henzinger, T.A. (eds.) CAV 1996. LNCS, vol. 1102, pp. 62–74. Springer, Heidelberg (1996). doi:10.1007/3-540-61474-5_58

[WGC09] Wei, O., Gurfinkel, A., Chechik, M.: Mixed transition systems revisited. In: Jones, N.D., Müller-Olm, M. (eds.) [JMO09], pp. 349–365

Derivatives of Quantitative Regular Expressions

Rajeev Alur[1], Konstantinos Mamouras[1(✉)], and Dogan Ulus[2]

[1] University of Pennsylvania, Philadelphia, PA, USA
mamouras@seas.upenn.edu
[2] Verimag, Université Grenoble-Alpes, Grenoble, France

Abstract. Quantitative regular expressions (QREs) have been recently proposed as a high-level declarative language for specifying complex numerical queries over data streams in a modular way. QREs have appealing theoretical properties, and each QRE can be compiled into an efficient streaming algorithm for its evaluation. In this paper, we generalize the notion of Brzozowski derivatives for classical regular expressions to QREs. Such derivatives immediately lead to an algorithm for incremental evaluation of QREs. While this algorithm does not have better time or space complexity than the previously known evaluation technique, it has the benefit of being simpler to explain and easier to prove correct.

1   Introduction

There are numerous applications that require the real-time processing of data generated at high rates such as: analyzing stock market data, monitoring production and manufacturing using sensors, network traffic monitoring, and click-stream analysis on the web. A core computational problem that is relevant to all such applications is the incremental aggregation of a stream of data items into numerical values that are useful for real-time decision making. Due to the enormous volume of data, these applications have hard constraints regarding space usage and the time required to process each newly arriving element.

There is a large body of prior research on stream processing which focuses on algorithmic techniques, often involving approximation and randomization, for computing efficiently specific numerical quantities such as the median [18], the number of distinct elements [17], the frequency moments [2], and aggregates over sliding windows [15]. There have also been several proposals for languages and systems that integrate stream processing with the data processing capabilities of traditional relational database systems [1,8,9].

The formalism of Quantitative Regular Expressions (QREs) was recently introduced in [5] with the orthogonal goal of providing convenient high-level programming abstractions for specifying complex queries over data streams in a modular way. QREs extend regular expressions, a well-established formalism for imparting hierarchical structure to sequences of symbols, with numerical operations such as sum, difference, min, max, average, and median. A QRE thus

© Springer International Publishing AG 2017
L. Aceto et al. (Eds.): Larsen Festschrift, LNCS 10460, pp. 75–95, 2017.
DOI: 10.1007/978-3-319-63121-9_4

describes both the regular parsing of the stream prefix seen so far and the hierarchical calculation of a quantitative aggregate that reflects the structure of the parse tree. This combination gives rise to a powerful declarative language, which can express conveniently many useful queries and is amenable to space- and time-efficient evaluation in the streaming model of computation. An implementation of QREs extended with extra features for processing realistic workloads is reported in [21]. The expressiveness of QREs coincides with the class of regular functions, which can be characterized with the model of Cost Register Automata (CRAs) [4] or, equivalently, with the MSO-definable graph transformations [14].

The main computational problem for QREs is their evaluation in the streaming model of computation. An efficient algorithm has already been described in [5] and implemented in [21], but it is not based on automata-theoretic techniques, and the question remains of whether there exists a simple model of automata for the streaming evaluation of QREs. In the simpler setting of classical regular expressions, the translation into a Nondeterministic Finite Automaton (NFA) gives rise to a very efficient streaming evaluation algorithm: the state of the algorithm consists of the active states of the NFA, and upon the arrival of a new symbol the state is updated by performing all possible transitions. Another approach for the evaluation problem is based on a technique proposed by Brzozowski in 1964 [11], where he introduced the notion of *derivation* for regular expressions extended with arbitrary Boolean operations. The *derivative* of an expression e with respect to a symbol a, typically denoted as $D_a(e)$, is an expression given by a simple recursive definition on the structure of e. The crucial property of these derivatives is that a string of the form aw (starting with the symbol a) matches an expression e iff the suffix w matches the derivative $D_a(e)$. This suggests a streaming evaluation algorithm for regular expressions: the state is an expression, and upon arrival of a new symbol a the state is replaced by its derivative with respect to a. A refinement of Brzozowski's ideas was proposed by Antimirov [7] under the name of *partial derivatives*. He described a representation of derivatives as sets of partial derivatives, which correponds closely to the construction of a NFA from an expression.

Given the success of automata-based techniques for the evaluation of plain regular expressions, it is worthwhile investigating whether similar ideas can be used for QRE evaluation. The well-studied model of weighted automata over semirings (see the monograph [16] for a broad survey) seems relevant, but unfortunately it is not expressive enough to handle the complex nesting of several different quantitative operations found in QREs. In particular, by the Kleene-Schützenberger theorem [22], weighted regular expressions can be easily translated into equivalent weighted automata and evaluated efficiently. On the other hand, QREs can be translated into the model of deterministic CRAs [4], but this translation incurs a doubly exponential blowup and is therefore not conducive to efficient evaluation. A hierarchical automaton model for the streaming computation of an interesting class of quantitative queries is introduced in [6], but its precise relationship to QREs and other automata formalisms remains to be clarified. A conclusively appropriate notion of automaton for the efficient evaluation of general quantitative queries has not been proposed yet, therefore a meaningful

Table 1. Complexity results under syntactic and semantic restrictions

Query language	Time-per-element and space complexity
Unrestricted, multiset semantics	Exponential in stream/query
Unrestricted, unambiguous semantics	Constant in stream, exponential in query
Strongly typed	Constant in stream, polynomial in query

investigation is the development of a notion of derivative. Indeed, in the present paper, we extend the notion of Brzozowski derivatives to QREs, and we show that there is a representation of QRE derivatives that gives rise to an efficient evaluation algorithm. This result offers a simple and clean alternative proof of why QREs can be efficiently evaluated, and it strongly suggests the possibility of an automata-based formulation of the evaluation algorithm. We should note here that derivatives have already been studied in the weighted setting [20], but the case of QREs is substantially different. See also [10] for an investigation of how Brzozowski derivatives can be extended to various algebraic structures.

Outline of Paper. In Sect. 2 we present the syntax and meaning of QREs. We consider two different natural semantics: (1) The *multiset semantics* allows for several output values for a given stream prefix, each of which corresponds to a different parse tree. (2) The *unambiguous semantics*, on the other hand, specifies the output to be undefined when the input stream can be parsed in more than one way. Thus, the unambiguous semantics ensures a single output value for each input sequence. In Sect. 3 we define derivatives of QREs by generalizing the classical notion of Brzozowski derivatives of regular expressions, and we propose an incremental evaluation algorithm based on derivatives. We also consider in Sect. 4 a representation of QRE derivatives that is analogous to Antimirov's partial derivatives [7]. In the presence of intersection the number of distinct Antimirov derivatives (for plain regular expressions) is exponentially bounded by the size of the expression. We show how to obtain a similar bound for QRE evaluation using the unambiguous semantics. Finally, we consider in Sect. 5 a syntatic restriction for QREs [5] that guarantees unambiguous parsing. Our complexity results for the streaming evaluation problem are summarized in Table 1. Although the proposed derivative-based algorithm has the same time and space complexity as the previously known method [5], our approach here is cleaner and the analysis of the algorithm much simpler. We conclude in Sect. 6 with a summary of our results and directions for future work.

2 Quantitative Regular Expressions

The formalism of Quantitative Regular Expressions offers a declarative language for describing complex hierarchical computations on streams of data values. As an illustrative example, consider the application of patient monitoring, where the data stream is a time series of timestamped measurements produced by a

sensor attached to a patient. We want to analyze the data stream by first identifying regions of interest which we call "episodes". These are maximal intervals where the measurements are above a fixed threshold value. Every episode
is summarized by recording the average measurement, the maximum measurement, and the duration of the episode. The top-level query is an aggregation over
the last 30 days (e.g., by calculating the average) of the episode statistics. This
query imparts a hierarchical structure on the data stream by splitting it into
episodes, bucketing episodes into days, and considering the last 30 days every
time the aggregate statistics are computed. To describe this computation we
need a language that supports regular constructs such as iteration (to express,
e.g., that an episode is a sequence of measurements exceeding the threshold)
and concatenation (to express, e.g., that an episode is followed by a sequence
of measurements below the threshold), extended with quantitative operations
for computing numerical aggregates (e.g., the maximum measurement of the
sequence of measurements that constitute an episode).

In this section we present the syntax and semantics of Quantitative Regular
Expressions. A QRE is interpreted over a stream of data values, and specifies
for each finite prefix of the stream an output value. We consider two different
semantics: the multiset semantics which records several different output possibilities, and the unambiguous semantics which only allows the output to be defined
when it is uniquely determined. Since we are interested in computing well-defined
functions on data streams, the multiset semantics is not satisfactory. We consider it here, however, because it is a natural semantics from a mathematical
perspective, and it is useful for formulating and proving our results regarding
efficient evaluation. The unambiguous semantics is simply a projection of the
multiset semantics, and therefore several results w.r.t. to the multiset semantics
transfer essentially unchanged to the unambiguous semantics.

To define QREs, we first choose a typed signature which describes the basic
data types and operations for manipulating them. We fix a collection of *basic
types*, and we write $A, B, \ldots$ to range over them, as well as a collection of *basic
operations* on them, e.g. $op : A_1 \times \cdots \times A_k \to B$. The identity function on
D is written $id_D : D \to D$. For every basic type D, assume that we have
fixed a collection of *atomic predicates*, so that the satisfiability of their Boolean
combinations is decidable. We write $\phi : D \to \mathbb{B}$ to indicate that ϕ is a predicate
on D, and $true_D : D \to \mathbb{B}$ for the predicate that is always true. The *unit type*,
with unique inhabitant def, is $\mathbb{U}$ and $!_D : D \to \mathbb{U}$ is the unique function from
D to $\mathbb{U}$. We also write $\pi_1 : A \times B \to A$ and $\pi_2 : A \times B \to B$ for the left and
right projection respectively. We assume that the collection of basic operations
contains all identities and projections, and is closed under pairing and function
composition. For example, if $op : A \times B \to C$ and $a \in A$ are basic operations,
then so is $(op\, a) = \lambda b.op(a, b) : B \to C$.

Every QRE is defined on a regular subset of stream prefixes, so we first
introduce a variant of regular expressions with unary predicates to describe the
domains of definition of QREs. For a basic type D, we define *(Symbolic) Regular
Expressions (REs)* over D with the grammar $r ::= \bot \mid \varepsilon \mid \phi \mid r \sqcup r \mid r \cdot r \mid r^* \mid r \sqcap r$,
where $\phi : D \to \mathbb{B}$. The expression r^n is abbreviation for $r \cdot r \cdots r$ with r repeated

$$\frac{}{\bot : \mathsf{QRE}\langle D, C\rangle} \text{ (bottom)} \qquad \frac{c \in C}{\mathsf{eps}(c) : \mathsf{QRE}\langle D, C\rangle} \text{ (empty)}$$

$$\frac{\text{satisfiable } \phi : D \to \mathbb{B} \qquad op : D \to C}{\mathsf{atom}(\phi, op) : \mathsf{QRE}\langle D, C\rangle} \text{ (single item)} \qquad \frac{\mathsf{f}, \mathsf{g} : \mathsf{QRE}\langle D, C\rangle}{\mathsf{f} \sqcup \mathsf{g} : \mathsf{QRE}\langle D, C\rangle} \text{ (choice)}$$

$$\frac{\mathsf{f} : \mathsf{QRE}\langle D, A\rangle \qquad \mathsf{g} : \mathsf{QRE}\langle D, B\rangle \qquad op : A \times B \to C}{\mathsf{split}(\mathsf{f}, \mathsf{g}, op) : \mathsf{QRE}\langle D, C\rangle} \text{ (split)}$$

$$\frac{\mathsf{init} : \mathsf{QRE}\langle D, B\rangle \quad \mathsf{body} : \mathsf{QRE}\langle D, A\rangle \quad \mathcal{E}(\mathsf{body}) = \emptyset \quad op : B \times A \to B}{\mathsf{iter}(\mathsf{init}, \mathsf{body}, op) : \mathsf{QRE}\langle D, B\rangle} \text{ (iteration)}$$

$$\frac{\mathsf{f} : \mathsf{QRE}\langle D, A\rangle \qquad op : A \to B}{op(\mathsf{f}) : \mathsf{QRE}\langle D, B\rangle} \text{ (application)}$$

$$\frac{\mathsf{f} : \mathsf{QRE}\langle D, A\rangle \qquad \mathsf{g} : \mathsf{QRE}\langle D, B\rangle \qquad op : A \times B \to C}{op(\mathsf{f}, \mathsf{g}) : \mathsf{QRE}\langle D, C\rangle} \text{ (combination)}$$

$$\mathcal{E}(\bot) = \emptyset \qquad\qquad \mathcal{E}(\mathsf{f} \sqcup \mathsf{g}) = \mathcal{E}(\mathsf{f}) \uplus \mathcal{E}(\mathsf{g})$$
$$\mathcal{E}(\mathsf{eps}(c)) = \{c\} \qquad\qquad \mathcal{E}(\mathsf{split}(\mathsf{f}, \mathsf{g}, op)) = \mathsf{M}(op)(\mathcal{E}(\mathsf{f}), \mathcal{E}(\mathsf{g}))$$
$$\mathcal{E}(\mathsf{atom}(\phi, op)) = \emptyset \qquad\qquad \mathcal{E}(\mathsf{iter}(\mathsf{f}, \mathsf{g}, op)) = \mathcal{E}(\mathsf{f})$$
$$\mathcal{E}(op(\mathsf{f})) = \mathsf{M}(op)(\mathcal{E}(\mathsf{f})) \qquad\qquad \mathcal{E}(op(\mathsf{f}, \mathsf{g})) = \mathsf{M}(op)(\mathcal{E}(\mathsf{f}), \mathcal{E}(\mathsf{g}))$$

Fig. 1. Syntax of Quantitative Regular Expressions (QREs) without ε-cycles.

n times. We write $r : \mathsf{RE}\langle D\rangle$ to indicate that r is a regular expression over D. We define $[\![r]\!] : D^* \to \mathbb{N}$ to be the weighted semantics of regular expressions without ε-cycles (i.e., no ε-cycles in the corresponding ε-NFA [19]) that counts the number of different parse trees.

$$[\![\bot]\!]\, w = 0 \qquad [\![\varepsilon]\!]\, w = 0 \ (w \neq \varepsilon) \qquad [\![r_1 \sqcup r_2]\!]\, w = ([\![r_1]\!]\, w) + ([\![r_2]\!]\, w)$$
$$[\![\varepsilon]\!]\, \varepsilon = 1 \qquad [\![\phi]\!]\, d = 1 \ (d \models \phi) \qquad [\![r_1 \cdot r_2]\!]\, w = \textstyle\sum_{w=uv}([\![r_1]\!]\, u) \cdot ([\![r_2]\!]\, v)$$
$$[\![\phi]\!]\, d = 0 \ (d \not\models \phi) \qquad [\![r^*]\!]\, w = \textstyle\sum_{w=u_1\cdots u_n}([\![r]\!]\, u_1) \cdots ([\![r]\!]\, u_n)$$
$$[\![\phi]\!]\, w = 0 \ (w \notin D) \qquad [\![r_1 \sqcap r_2]\!]\, w = ([\![r_1]\!]\, w) \cdot ([\![r_2]\!]\, w)$$

This semantics corresponds to standard operations for formal power series [16].

In Fig. 1 we define *Quantitative Regular Expressions (QREs)*, which we also call *queries*. The queries are typed, and we write $\mathsf{f} : \mathsf{QRE}\langle D, C\rangle$ to indicate that the query f has *input type* D and *output type* C. The original definition of QREs in [5] was more general in that it involved an extra sort of typed parameters, and the outputs were essentially algebraic terms built from the parameters and the operations of the signature. The definition of [5] was motivated by expressiveness considerations, i.e. so that QREs capture exactly the class of regular functions over the same signature [3,4,14]. We consider here a simpler language, where the outputs are just values. This simplification makes QREs significantly more usable for practical queries and obviates the need for a *term simplification* procedure (see Sect. 3.2 of [5]) that depends on the nature of the data types and operations of the signature.

The language of Fig. 1 has eight core constructs: (1) $\bot$ is undefined for every input sequence; (2) $\texttt{eps}(c)$ maps the empty stream to the output value c; (3) $\texttt{atom}(\phi, op)$ maps an input stream consisting of a single item satisfying the predicate ϕ to an output computed by applying the operation op; (4) $\texttt{f} \sqcup \texttt{g}$ nondeterministically chooses either $\texttt{f}$ or $\texttt{g}$ to apply; (5) $\texttt{split}(\texttt{f}, \texttt{g}, op)$ splits the input stream into two parts, applies the queries $\texttt{f}$ and $\texttt{g}$ to the left and right parts respectively, and combines their results using the operation op; (6) $\texttt{iter}(\texttt{init}, \texttt{body}, op)$ splits the input into multiple parts $uv_1v_2\ldots v_n$, applies $\texttt{init}$ to u (which gives b) and $\texttt{body}$ to each v_i (which gives a_i), and combines the sequence of values $a_1a_2\ldots a_n$ using the initial value b and the binary aggregation operation op in the style of the *fold combinator* used in functional programming; (7) $op(\texttt{f})$ applies the query $\texttt{f}$ and transforms its output using the operation op; (8) $op(\texttt{f}, \texttt{g})$ applies both $\texttt{f}, \texttt{g}$ and combines their results using the operation op.

The definition of queries is by mutual induction with the function $\mathcal{E}$, which sends a query of type $\mathsf{QRE}\langle D, C\rangle$ to a finite multiset over its output type C. The $\mathcal{E}$ function is meant to give the output of a query on the empty sequence, and it is used for the assumption $\mathcal{E}(\texttt{body}) = \emptyset$ for the iteration query $\texttt{iter}(\texttt{init}, \texttt{body}, op)$. It is necessary to define the syntax of queries simultaneously with $\mathcal{E}$ in order to eliminate queries with ε-cycles, that is, queries where the body $\texttt{g}$ of the iteration query $\texttt{iter}(\texttt{f}, \texttt{g}, op)$ matches the empty sequence ε. When the semantics is defined later, we will see that ε-cycles result in having an infinity of output values. This complication of ε-cycles appears also in the context of weighted automata and expressions [16]. The operation $\uplus$ in Fig. 1 is multiset union. For a set X, we write $\mathsf{M}(X)$ to denote the set of all finite multisets over X. For a unary operation $op : A \to B$, we define the lifting $\mathsf{M}(op) : \mathsf{M}(A) \to \mathsf{M}(B)$ by $\mathsf{M}(op)(X) = \{op(a) \mid a \in X\}$. Similarly, for an operation $op : A \times B \to C$, we define the lifting $\mathsf{M}(op) : \mathsf{M}(A) \times \mathsf{M}(B) \to \mathsf{M}(C)$ by $\mathsf{M}(op)(X, Y) = \{op(a, b) \mid a \in X \text{ and } b \in Y\}$.

Multiset Semantics. We give a denotational semantics of queries in terms of functions of type $D^* \to \mathsf{M}(C)$. We call this the *multiset semantics* of queries. The *domain* of f is the set of sequences for which the value of f is nonempty, i.e. $\mathrm{dom}(f) = \{w \in D^* \mid f(w) \neq \emptyset\}$. The denotation of a query $\texttt{f} : \mathsf{QRE}\langle D, C\rangle$ is the function $[\![\texttt{f}]\!] : D^* \to \mathsf{M}(C)$, where $[\![\cdot]\!]$ is called the interpretation function and is defined by induction on the structure of queries as shown in Fig. 2. To reduce the notational clutter we sometimes write $[\![\texttt{f}]\!]\, w$ instead of $[\![\texttt{f}]\!](w)$. The semantics of iteration involves the *multiset fold* combinator mfold, which is a generalization of the familiar fold combinator to multisets of values. The definitions of mfold and fold are by recursion on the length of the sequence. For example, $\mathrm{fold}(s, op, a_1a_2) = op(op(s, a_1), a_2))$ and

$$\mathrm{mfold}(\{b_1, b_2\}, op, \{a_1\}\{a_2, a_3\}) =$$
$$\{op(op(b_1, a_1), a_2), op(op(b_1, a_1), a_3), op(op(b_2, a_1), a_2), op(op(b_2, a_1), a_3)\}.$$

For an iteration query $\texttt{h} = \texttt{iter}(\texttt{f}, \texttt{g}, op)$, the typing restriction $\mathcal{E}(\texttt{g}) = \emptyset$ implies that $[\![g]\!]\,\varepsilon = \emptyset$ (formally proved later in Theorem 5). So, to calculate the value

$$\llbracket \bot \rrbracket\, w = \emptyset \qquad\qquad \llbracket \mathtt{f} \sqcup \mathtt{g} \rrbracket\, w = \llbracket \mathtt{f} \rrbracket\, w \uplus \llbracket \mathtt{g} \rrbracket\, w$$

$$\llbracket \mathtt{eps}(c) \rrbracket\, \varepsilon = \{c\} \qquad\qquad \llbracket \mathtt{split}(\mathtt{f}, \mathtt{g}, op) \rrbracket\, w = \biguplus_{w=uv} \mathsf{M}(op)(\llbracket \mathtt{f} \rrbracket\, u, \llbracket \mathtt{g} \rrbracket\, v)$$

$$\llbracket \mathtt{atom}(\phi, op) \rrbracket\, d = \{op(d)\},\ \text{if } d \models \phi \qquad \llbracket op(\mathtt{f}) \rrbracket\, w = \mathsf{M}(op)(\llbracket \mathtt{f} \rrbracket\, w)$$

$$\llbracket \mathtt{atom}(\phi, op) \rrbracket\, d = \emptyset,\ \text{if } d \not\models \phi \qquad \llbracket op(\mathtt{f}, \mathtt{g}) \rrbracket\, w = \mathsf{M}(op)(\llbracket \mathtt{f} \rrbracket\, w, \llbracket \mathtt{g} \rrbracket\, w)$$

$$\llbracket \mathtt{iter}(\mathtt{f}, \mathtt{g}, op) \rrbracket\, w = \biguplus_{w=uv_1\cdots v_n} \mathsf{mfold}(\llbracket \mathtt{f} \rrbracket\, u, op, \llbracket \mathtt{g} \rrbracket\, v_1 \cdots \llbracket \mathtt{g} \rrbracket\, v_n)$$

$$\mathsf{fold} : B \times (B \times A \to B) \times A^* \to B \quad \mathsf{mfold} : \mathsf{M}(B) \times (B \times A \to B) \times \mathsf{M}(A)^* \to \mathsf{M}(B)$$

$$\mathsf{fold}(s, op, \varepsilon) = s \qquad\qquad \mathsf{mfold}(S, op, \varepsilon) = S$$

$$\mathsf{fold}(s, op, wa) = op(\mathsf{fold}(s, op, w), a) \quad \mathsf{mfold}(S, op, WX) = \mathsf{M}(op)(\mathsf{mfold}(S, op, W), X)$$

Fig. 2. Finite multiset semantics of Quantitative Regular Expressions without ε-cycles.

$\llbracket \mathtt{h} \rrbracket\, w$ (see Fig. 2) we only need to consider the splittings $w = uv_1 \ldots v_n$ of w where $n \geq 0$ and $v_i \neq \varepsilon$ for every $i = 1, \ldots, n$.

For every input sequence w, the value $\llbracket \mathtt{f} \rrbracket\, w$ is a finite multiset whose size is at most exponential in the size of w. More precisely, (size of $\llbracket \mathtt{f} \rrbracket\, w) \leq 2^{|\mathtt{f}| \cdot |w|}$ for every query $\mathtt{f} : \mathsf{QRE}\langle D, C \rangle$ and every sequence $w \in D^*$.

The multiset semantics of queries induces an equivalence relation on them, written as $\equiv$. Two queries are equivalent if their denotations are equal. We can then write equations such as $\mathtt{split}(\mathtt{f}, \mathtt{eps}(b), op) \equiv op_b(\mathtt{f})$, where op_b is the unary operation given by $op_b(x) = op(x, b)$ for all x.

Example 1. The query $\mathtt{f} = \mathtt{atom}(true_\mathbb{N}, id_\mathbb{N}) : \mathsf{QRE}\langle \mathbb{N}, \mathbb{N} \rangle$ matches a single number and returns it. Using it as the body of an iteration, we write the query $\mathtt{g} = \mathtt{iter}(\mathtt{f}, \mathtt{f}, +)$ which processes a nonempty sequence of numbers and returns their sum. Now, the query $\mathtt{g}' = \mathtt{iter}(\mathtt{f}', \mathtt{f}', +)$, where $\mathtt{f}' = \mathtt{atom}(true_\mathbb{N}, \lambda x.1)$, processes a nonempty sequence and returns its length. If $\mathsf{div} : \mathbb{N} \times \mathbb{N} \to \mathbb{Q}$ and $\mathsf{div}(x, y)$ is the result of dividing x by y, the query $\mathtt{h} = \mathsf{div}(\mathtt{g}, \mathtt{g}') : \mathsf{QRE}\langle \mathbb{N}, \mathbb{Q} \rangle$ calculates the average of a nonempty sequence of natural numbers.

Rates. The *rate* of a query is a symbolic regular expression that denotes its domain. It is defined by induction:

$$\mathsf{rate}(\bot) = \bot \qquad\qquad \mathsf{rate}(\mathtt{f} \sqcup \mathtt{g}) = \mathsf{rate}(\mathtt{f}) \sqcup \mathsf{rate}(\mathtt{g})$$

$$\mathsf{rate}(\mathtt{eps}(c)) = \varepsilon \qquad\qquad \mathsf{rate}(\mathtt{split}(\mathtt{f}, \mathtt{g}, op)) = \mathsf{rate}(\mathtt{f}) \cdot \mathsf{rate}(\mathtt{g})$$

$$\mathsf{rate}(\mathtt{atom}(\phi, op)) = \phi \qquad\qquad \mathsf{rate}(\mathtt{iter}(\mathtt{f}, \mathtt{g}, op)) = \mathsf{rate}(\mathtt{f}) \cdot \mathsf{rate}(\mathtt{g})^*$$

$$\mathsf{rate}(op(\mathtt{f})) = \mathsf{rate}(\mathtt{f}) \qquad\qquad \mathsf{rate}(op(\mathtt{f}, \mathtt{g})) = \mathsf{rate}(\mathtt{f}) \sqcap \mathsf{rate}(\mathtt{g})$$

Notice that the value of rate is always an expression without ε-cycles.

Unambiguous Semantics. We defined previously the multiset semantics of queries, which allows a query to have several (finitely many) outputs for a given input sequence. Now, we take the viewpoint that a query should specify a unique output value (or be undefined) for a given input sequence. This means that we want to ignore output multisets of cardinality greater than one, which we do by setting the output to be undefined. This is the *unambiguous semantics* for queries. For a query $f : \mathsf{QRE}\langle D, C \rangle$, this is given formally as follows:

$$\langle\!\langle f \rangle\!\rangle\, w = \theta([\![f]\!]\, w), \text{ where } \theta(X) = X \text{ if } |X| = 1 \text{ and } \theta(X) = \emptyset \text{ otherwise}$$

So, $\langle\!\langle f \rangle\!\rangle$ is a function $D^* \to M(C)$ so that each output multiset is of cardinality at most one, which we call an *unambiguous function*. This means that $\langle\!\langle f \rangle\!\rangle$ can be also represented as a partial function $D^* \rightharpoonup C$. We say that a query f is *unambiguous* when the multiset meaning $[\![f]\!]$ is an unambiguous function. This is equivalent to $[\![f]\!] = \langle\!\langle f \rangle\!\rangle$, which says that the multiset and unambiguous semantics coincide. See the papers [12,13] for recent surveys of unambiguity in traditional automata theory.

It is necessary that the $[\![-]\!]$ semantics records the multiplicity of each output value, otherwise $\langle\!\langle - \rangle\!\rangle$ cannot be defined as a projection or $[\![-]\!]$. Indeed, we see in the example below that we can write queries that return exactly one output value of multiplicity greater than one.

Example 2. The query $f = \mathsf{iter}(\mathsf{eps}(0), \mathsf{atom}(true_\mathbb{N}, id_\mathbb{N}), +) : \mathsf{QRE}\langle \mathbb{N}, \mathbb{N} \rangle$, which processes a sequence of natural numbers and returns their sum, is unambiguous. The query $g = \mathsf{iter}(\mathsf{eps}(\mathsf{def}), \mathsf{atom}(true_\mathbb{N}, !_\mathbb{N}), !_{\mathbb{N} \times \mathbb{N}}) : \mathsf{QRE}\langle \mathbb{N}, \mathbb{U} \rangle$, which matches a sequence of natural numbers and returns nothing, is also unambiguous. The query $\mathsf{split}(g, f, \pi_2) : \mathsf{QRE}\langle \mathbb{N}, \mathbb{N} \rangle$, which matches a sequence of natural numbers and returns the sum of every suffix of the sequence, is ambiguous because every sequence of length ℓ can be parsed in $\ell + 1$ different ways. The query that matches sequences of length at least two and returns the sum of the last two elements is $\mathsf{split}(g, \mathsf{split}(\mathsf{atom}(true_\mathbb{N}, id_\mathbb{N}), \mathsf{atom}(true_\mathbb{N}, id_\mathbb{N}), +), \pi_2) : \mathsf{QRE}\langle \mathbb{N}, \mathbb{N} \rangle$ and is unambiguous. The query $\mathsf{split}(f, f, +) : \mathsf{QRE}\langle \mathbb{N}, \mathbb{N} \rangle$ is ambiguous but single-valued: for a sequence of length ℓ, it returns the sum of its elements with multiplicity equal to $\ell + 1$.

The unambiguous semantics of queries induces an equivalence relation on them, written as $\approx$. Two queries f and g are $\approx$-equivalent if their denotations $\langle\!\langle f \rangle\!\rangle$ and $\langle\!\langle g \rangle\!\rangle$ are equal. We observe that the equivalence relation $\approx$ is strictly coarser than $\equiv$, that is, $f \equiv g$ implies $f \approx g$ and there exist queries that are $\approx$-equivalent but $\equiv$-inequivalent.

Observation 3. A finite multiset Q of queries of the same type can also be thought of as a query, namely the finite choice over the queries of Q. We now want to find some sufficient conditions for reducing the cardinality of Q, while preserving its meaning under the unambiguous semantics. This will turn out to be useful later in Sect. 4, where an evaluation algorithm for QREs using Antimirov derivatives is presented (Fig. 3 and Theorem 9).

Suppose Q contains the queries $f_1, f_2, \ldots, f_k$ with $k \geq 2$ that have the same rate, that is $r = \mathsf{rate}(f_i)$ for every i, and there is no other query in Q that has this rate. The condition on the rates implies that all functions $[\![f_i]\!]$ have the same domain $D_1 = \mathrm{dom}([\![f_i]\!])$, and moreover all functions $\langle\!\langle f_i \rangle\!\rangle$ have the same domain $D_2 = \mathrm{dom}(\langle\!\langle f_i \rangle\!\rangle) \subseteq D_1$.

(1) Remove all of $f_1, \ldots, f_k$ (*wrong*): We claim that $Q' = Q \setminus \{f_1, \ldots, f_k\}$ is not necessarily equivalent to Q. Suppose that $Q = \{f_1, \ldots, f_k, g\}$, the queries of Q are all unambiguous, and the domains $\text{dom}(\llbracket g \rrbracket) = \text{dom}(\langle\!\langle g \rangle\!\rangle)$ and $D_1 = D_2$ intersect. So, all queries of Q are defined on some sequence w. Then, $\langle\!\langle Q \rangle\!\rangle$ is not defined on w because the cardinality of $\llbracket Q \rrbracket\, w$ is greater than one, but $\langle\!\langle Q' \rangle\!\rangle$ is defined on w and equal to $\langle\!\langle g \rangle\!\rangle\, w$. So, $Q \not\approx Q'$.

(2) If $k \geq 3$ then remove $f_3, \ldots, f_k$ and keep f_1, f_2 (*correct*): Define the multiset $Q' = Q \setminus \{f_3, \ldots, f_k\}$. We claim that $Q \approx Q'$. Let w be an arbitrary sequence. If w belongs to the domain of the functions $\llbracket f_i \rrbracket$, then both $\langle\!\langle Q \rangle\!\rangle$ and $\langle\!\langle Q' \rangle\!\rangle$ are undefined on w, because the cardinalities of $\llbracket Q \rrbracket\, w$ and $\llbracket Q' \rrbracket\, w$ are greater than one. Suppose now that w does not belong to the domain of the functions $\llbracket f_i \rrbracket$. Then, $\llbracket Q \rrbracket\, w = \llbracket Q \setminus \{f_i \mid i\} \rrbracket\, w = \llbracket Q' \rrbracket\, w$ and hence $\langle\!\langle Q \rangle\!\rangle\, w = \langle\!\langle Q' \rangle\!\rangle\, w$.

This means that we can always reduce Q so that it has at most two queries with the same rate, while preserving its unambiguous semantics.

3   Brzozowski Derivative

We introduce in this section the *Brzozowski derivative* [11] of Quantitative Regular Expressions, which is a straightforward adaption of derivatives for classical regular expressions. The main property of these derivatives is that their semantic counterpart agrees with the syntactic counterpart. This agreement property gives as a corollary the existence of an incremental algorithm for evaluating QREs on streams of data items.

Example 4. The Brzozowski derivative $\mathcal{D}_a^B(r)$ of a regular expression r w.r.t. the letter a denotes the language that results from the language of r by removing the starting a letter from those words that start with a. For example, $r = (a \sqcup b)^* bb$ denotes the language of all strings over $\Sigma = \{a, b\}$ that end in bb, $\mathcal{D}_a^B(r) = (a \sqcup b)^* bb = r$, $\mathcal{D}_{ab}^B(r) = \mathcal{D}_b^B(\mathcal{D}_a^B(r)) = \mathcal{D}_b^B(r) = r \sqcup b$ and $\mathcal{D}_{abb}^B(r) = \mathcal{D}_b^B(\mathcal{D}_{ab}^B(r)) = \mathcal{D}_b^B(r \sqcup b) = r \sqcup b \sqcup \varepsilon$. The string abb matches r because the empty string ε matches the derivative $\mathcal{D}_{abb}^B(r)$.

A query of type $\mathsf{QRE}\langle \mathbb{N}, \mathbb{N} \rangle$ that is similar in form to the regex r is $k = \text{split}$ $(g, h, \max)$, where $g = \text{iter}(\text{eps}(0), f_e \sqcup f_o, +)$, $f_e = \text{atom}(even_{\mathbb{N}}, id_{\mathbb{N}})$, $f_o = \text{atom}(odd_{\mathbb{N}}, id_{\mathbb{N}})$, and $h = \text{split}(f_o, f_o, +)$. The unambiguous query k matches sequences that end with two odd numbers and returns the maximum of x, y where y is the sum of the last two numbers and x is the sum of the rest of the numbers. The extension of derivatives to QREs should give rise to the following calculations:

$$\mathcal{D}_4^B(k) = \text{split}(\text{iter}((\lambda x.0 + x)(\text{eps}(4)), f_e \sqcup f_o, +), h, \max)$$

$$\mathcal{D}_{43}^B(k) = \text{split}(\text{iter}((\lambda x.4 + x)(\text{eps}(3)), f_e \sqcup f_o, +), h, \max) \sqcup$$
$$(\lambda x. \max(4, x))((\lambda x.3 + x)(f_o))$$

$$\mathcal{D}_{435}^B(k) = \text{split}(\text{iter}((\lambda x.7 + x)(\text{eps}(5)), f_e \sqcup f_o, +), h, \max) \sqcup$$
$$(\lambda x. \max(7, x))((\lambda x.5 + x)(f_o)) \sqcup$$
$$(\lambda x. \max(4, x))((\lambda x.3 + x)(\text{eps}(5)))$$

$$\mathcal{D}^{\text{B}}_{4351}(\text{k}) = \text{split}(\text{iter}((\lambda x.12 + x)(\text{eps}(1)), \text{f}_e \sqcup \text{f}_o, +), \text{h}, \max) \sqcup$$
$$(\lambda x. \max(12, x))((\lambda x.1 + x)(\text{f}_o)) \sqcup$$
$$(\lambda x. \max(7, x))((\lambda x.5 + x)(\text{eps}(1)))$$

From the above we notice that ε matches $\mathcal{D}^{\text{B}}_{435}(\text{k})$ with value $\max(4, 3+5) = 8$, and it also matches $\mathcal{D}^{\text{B}}_{4351}(\text{k})$ with value $\max(7, 5+1) = 7$.

A simple streaming algorithm that implements the computation described by h can be given by maintaining the following state: the sum of all elements so far except for the last two, and the two most recent elements. The reader can observe that the derivatives calculated earlier record this information, and it can be found inside the queries that are constructed. For example, in the derivative $\mathcal{D}^{\text{B}}_{4351}(\text{k})$ we see (last line) the sum 7 and the elements 5, 1. The structure of the derivative also encodes how these three numbers should be combined to produce the output $max(7, 5+1) = 7$. □

For a function $f : D^* \to \text{M}(C)$, we define the *semantic derivative* $\mathcal{D}_u(f) : D^* \to \text{M}(C)$ with respect to the sequence $u \in D^*$ of data items as

$$\mathcal{D}_u(f) w = f(uw) \text{ for all } w \in D^*.$$

An immediate consequence is that $\mathcal{D}_v(\mathcal{D}_u(f)) = \mathcal{D}_{uv}(f)$ for all sequences u and v in D^*. Moreover, $f(u) = \mathcal{D}_u(f)(\varepsilon)$ for every sequence $u \in D^*$. For a query f of type $\text{QRE}\langle D, C \rangle$ and a data item $d \in D$, the *(syntactic) Brzozowski derivative* $\mathcal{D}^{\text{B}}_d(\text{f})$ of f w.r.t. d is also a query of type $\text{QRE}\langle D, C \rangle$.

$$\mathcal{D}^{\text{B}}_d(\text{eps}(c)) = \mathcal{D}^{\text{B}}_d(\bot) = \bot \qquad\qquad \mathcal{D}^{\text{B}}_d(\text{f} \sqcup \text{g}) = \mathcal{D}^{\text{B}}_d(\text{f}) \sqcup \mathcal{D}^{\text{B}}_d(\text{g})$$
$$\mathcal{D}^{\text{B}}_d(\text{atom}(\phi, op)) = \bot, \text{ if } d \not\models \phi \qquad\qquad \mathcal{D}^{\text{B}}_d(op(\text{f})) = op(\mathcal{D}^{\text{B}}_d(\text{f}))$$
$$\mathcal{D}^{\text{B}}_d(\text{atom}(\phi, op)) = \text{eps}(op(d)), \text{ if } d \models \phi \qquad \mathcal{D}^{\text{B}}_d(op(\text{f}, \text{g})) = op(\mathcal{D}^{\text{B}}_d(\text{f}), \mathcal{D}^{\text{B}}_d(\text{g}))$$
$$\mathcal{D}^{\text{B}}_d(\text{split}(\text{f}, \text{g}, op)) = \text{split}(\mathcal{D}^{\text{B}}_d(\text{f}), \text{g}, op) \sqcup \bigsqcup_{a \in \mathcal{E}(\text{f})}(op\ a)(\mathcal{D}^{\text{B}}_d(\text{g}))$$
$$\mathcal{D}^{\text{B}}_d(\text{iter}(\text{f}, \text{g}, op)) = \text{iter}(\mathcal{D}^{\text{B}}_d(\text{f}), \text{g}, op) \sqcup \bigsqcup_{b \in \mathcal{E}(\text{f})}\text{iter}((op\ b)(\mathcal{D}^{\text{B}}_d(\text{g})), \text{g}, op)$$

The derivative $\mathcal{D}^{\text{B}}_w(\text{f})$ w.r.t. a sequence $w \in D^*$ is defined by induction on w: $\mathcal{D}^{\text{B}}_\varepsilon(\text{f}) = \text{f}$ and $\mathcal{D}^{\text{B}}_{dw}(\text{f}) = \mathcal{D}^{\text{B}}_w(\mathcal{D}^{\text{B}}_d(\text{f}))$. A crucial result is the correpondence between semantic and syntactic derivatives:

Theorem 5 (Derivative Agreement). For every query f of type $\text{QRE}\langle D, C \rangle$ and every data item $d \in D$, we have that $\mathcal{E}(\text{f}) = [\![\text{f}]\!] \varepsilon$ and $\mathcal{D}_d([\![\text{f}]\!]) = [\![\mathcal{D}^{\text{B}}_d(\text{f})]\!]$.

Theorem 5 suggests immediately an algorithm for evaluating queries. Given a sequence $w = d_1 d_2 \ldots d_n$ and a query f, we notice that $[\![\text{f}]\!] w$ is equal to

$$\mathcal{D}_w([\![\text{f}]\!]) \varepsilon = \mathcal{D}_{d_n} \cdots \mathcal{D}_{d_1}([\![\text{f}]\!]) \varepsilon = [\![\mathcal{D}^{\text{B}}_{d_n} \cdots \mathcal{D}^{\text{B}}_{d_1}(\text{f})]\!] \varepsilon = \mathcal{E}(\mathcal{D}^{\text{B}}_{d_n} \cdots \mathcal{D}^{\text{B}}_{d_1}(\text{f})).$$

So, to compute the value of a query on a given input, we iteratively calculate the derivative of the query w.r.t. each input item, and finally apply the $\mathcal{E}$ function. We suggest an optimization of this evaluation procedure by incorporating *query rewriting* to eliminate subqueries that cannot contribute to the result. The equations $op(\bot) \equiv \bot$ and

$$\bot \sqcup f \equiv f \quad \mathtt{split}(\bot, f, op) \equiv \bot \quad op(\bot, f) \equiv \bot \quad \mathtt{iter}(\bot, f, op) \equiv \bot$$
$$f \sqcup \bot \equiv f \quad \mathtt{split}(f, \bot, op) \equiv \bot \quad op(f, \bot) \equiv \bot \quad \mathtt{iter}(f, \bot, op) \equiv f$$

are all valid, that is, they are true for every query f. If we orient these equations from left to right, then we get a rewrite system for simplifying queries. We will assume that our Brzozowski derivative-based evaluation procedure simplifies all intermediate queries as much as possible (according to this rewrite system).

Example 6. Consider the always-true predicate $true_\mathbb{N} : \mathbb{N} \to \mathbb{B}$, the identity function $id_\mathbb{N} : \mathbb{N} \to \mathbb{N}$, the constant zero function $\lambda x.0 : \mathbb{N} \to \mathbb{N}$, and the binary sum $+ : \mathbb{N} \times \mathbb{N} \to \mathbb{N}$. Using these operations we write the queries

$$f = \mathtt{atom}(true_\mathbb{N}, id_\mathbb{N}) \quad g = \mathtt{atom}(true_\mathbb{N}, \lambda x.0) \quad h = \mathtt{iter}(\mathtt{eps}(0), f \sqcup g, +)$$

of type $\mathrm{QRE}\langle \mathbb{N}, \mathbb{N} \rangle$. The top-level query is h, which maps an input sequence of natural numbers into the multiset of all possible partial sums over those numbers. First, notice that the derivatives of f and g w.r.t. the number $d \in \mathbb{N}$ are $\mathcal{D}_d^\mathtt{B}(f) = \mathtt{eps}(d)$ and $\mathcal{D}_d^\mathtt{B}(g) = \mathtt{eps}(0)$ respectively. Moreover, $\mathcal{E}(\mathtt{eps}(0)) = \{0\}$. We will use the derivative-based evaluation algorithm to find the value of the query h on the input sequence $abc \in \mathbb{N}^*$. This amounts to calculating $\mathcal{E}(\mathcal{D}_c^\mathtt{B}(\mathcal{D}_b^\mathtt{B}(\mathcal{D}_a^\mathtt{B}(h))))$, since Theorem 5 implies that it equals $[\![h]\!]\, abc$. The steps of this calculation are:

$$\mathcal{D}_a^\mathtt{B}(h) = \mathtt{iter}(\mathtt{eps}(a) \sqcup \mathtt{eps}(0), f \sqcup g, +)$$
$$\mathcal{E}(\mathcal{D}_a^\mathtt{B}(h)) = \{a, 0\}$$
$$\mathcal{D}_b^\mathtt{B}(\mathcal{D}_a^\mathtt{B}(h)) = \mathtt{iter}((\lambda x.a + x)(\mathtt{eps}(b) \sqcup \mathtt{eps}(0)), f \sqcup g, +) \sqcup$$
$$\mathtt{iter}((\lambda x.0 + x)(\mathtt{eps}(b) \sqcup \mathtt{eps}(0)), f \sqcup g, +)$$
$$\mathcal{E}(\mathcal{D}_b^\mathtt{B}(\mathcal{D}_a^\mathtt{B}(h))) = \{a + b, a, b, 0\}$$
$$\mathcal{D}_c^\mathtt{B}(\mathcal{D}_b^\mathtt{B}(\mathcal{D}_a^\mathtt{B}(h))) = \mathtt{iter}((\lambda x.(a + b) + x)(\mathtt{eps}(c) \sqcup \mathtt{eps}(0)), f \sqcup g, +) \sqcup$$
$$\mathtt{iter}((\lambda x.a + x)(\mathtt{eps}(c) \sqcup \mathtt{eps}(0)), f \sqcup g, +) \sqcup$$
$$\mathtt{iter}((\lambda x.b + x)(\mathtt{eps}(c) \sqcup \mathtt{eps}(0)), f \sqcup g, +) \sqcup$$
$$\mathtt{iter}((\lambda x.0 + x)(\mathtt{eps}(c) \sqcup \mathtt{eps}(0)), f \sqcup g, +)$$
$$\mathcal{E}(\mathcal{D}_c^\mathtt{B}(\mathcal{D}_b^\mathtt{B}(\mathcal{D}_a^\mathtt{B}(h)))) = \{a + b + c, a + b, a + c, a, b + c, b, c, 0\}$$

We have used implicitly the rewrite rules for eliminating $\bot$ as much as possible.

The previous example shows that there are queries whose evaluation requires an enormous amount of computational resources. Given that the size of the output can be exponential in the size of the input sequence and the size of the query, we have exponential time and space requirements for every evaluation algorithm.

4   Antimirov Derivative

The evaluation of the general QREs of Fig. 1 w.r.t. the multiset semantics is inherently expensive, since the output itself can be of size exponential in the size of the query and the input sequence. So, we focus here on the evaluation of QREs w.r.t. the unambiguous semantics, and our goal is to describe a streaming algorithm that uses resources that are independent of the size of the input stream. Using a variant of the partial derivatives of Antimirov [7], we show that this is indeed possible. We obtain a streaming algorithm for evaluation that uses space and time-per-element exponential in the size of the query and independent of the stream length. The crucial idea for this algorithm is that we can prune the Antimirov derivative to contain only a couple of QREs with the same rate without changing its unambiguous meaning. Antimirov-style derivatives are preferable for the results of this section, because the representation itself encodes many valid equations on queries that are useful for proving the result. This is similar to classical regular expressions where the Antimirov derivatives encode the ACI rules (associativity, commutativity and idempotence) by virtue of the set-based representation.

Example 7. We continue with Example 4 to consider Antimirov derivatives. Recall that $r = (a \sqcup b)^*bb$, and that Antimirov derivatives are a set-based representation of Brzozowski derivatives. That is, $\mathcal{D}_a^A(r) = \{r\}$, $\mathcal{D}_{ab}^A(r) = \mathcal{D}_b^A(\{r\}) = \{r, b\}$ and $\mathcal{D}_{abb}^A(r) = \mathcal{D}_b^A(\{r, b\}) = \{r, b, \varepsilon\}$. For the query k of Example 4 we calculate using Antimirov-style derivatives:

$$\mathcal{D}_4^A(\mathbf{k}) = \{\mathtt{split}(\mathtt{iter}((\lambda x.0 + x)(\mathtt{eps}(4)), \mathbf{f}_e \sqcup \mathbf{f}_o, +), \mathbf{h}, \max)\}$$

$$\mathcal{D}_{43}^A(\mathbf{k}) = \{\mathtt{split}(\mathtt{iter}((\lambda x.4 + x)(\mathtt{eps}(3)), \mathbf{f}_e \sqcup \mathbf{f}_o, +), \mathbf{h}, \max),$$
$$(\lambda x. \max(4, x))((\lambda x.3 + x)(\mathbf{f}_o))\}$$

$$\mathcal{D}_{435}^A(\mathbf{k}) = \{\mathtt{split}(\mathtt{iter}((\lambda x.7 + x)(\mathtt{eps}(5)), \mathbf{f}_e \sqcup \mathbf{f}_o, +), \mathbf{h}, \max),$$
$$(\lambda x. \max(7, x))((\lambda x.5 + x)(\mathbf{f}_o)),$$
$$(\lambda x. \max(4, x))((\lambda x.3 + x)(\mathtt{eps}(5)))\}$$

Since the choice operation $\sqcup$ for queries is not idempotent, we need multisets for the representation of QRE Antimirov derivatives.   □

For a regular expression $r : \mathsf{RE}\langle D \rangle$ we define $\mathcal{E}(r) \in \{0, 1\}$ (the two-element Boolean algebra with join operation $+$ and meet operation $\cdot$) and the *Antimirov derivative* $\mathcal{D}_d^A(r)$ w.r.t. $d \in D$, which is a set of regular expressions of type $\mathsf{RE}\langle D \rangle$:

$$\mathcal{E}(\bot) = 0 \qquad\qquad \mathcal{D}_d^A(\varepsilon) = \mathcal{D}_d^A(\bot) = \emptyset$$

$$\mathcal{E}(\varepsilon) = 1 \qquad\qquad \mathcal{D}_d^A(\phi) = \emptyset, \text{ if } d \not\models \phi$$

$$\mathcal{E}(\phi) = 0 \qquad\qquad \mathcal{D}_d^A(\phi) = \{\varepsilon\}, \text{ if } d \models \phi$$

$$\mathcal{E}(r_1 \sqcup r_2) = \mathcal{E}(r_1) + \mathcal{E}(r_2) \qquad \mathcal{D}_d^A(r_1 \sqcup r_2) = \mathcal{D}_d^A(r_1) \cup \mathcal{D}_d^A(r_2)$$

$$\mathcal{E}(r_1 \sqcap r_2) = \mathcal{E}(r_1) \cdot \mathcal{E}(r_2) \qquad \mathcal{D}_d^A(r_1 \sqcap r_2) = \mathcal{D}_d^A(r_1) \sqcap \mathcal{D}_d^A(r_2)$$

$$\mathcal{E}(r_1 \cdot r_2) = \mathcal{E}(r_1) \cdot \mathcal{E}(r_2) \qquad \mathcal{D}_d^A(r_1 \cdot r_2) = \mathcal{D}_d^A(r_1) \cdot r_2 \cup \mathcal{E}(r_1) \cdot \mathcal{D}_d^A(r_2)$$

$$\mathcal{E}(r^*) = 1 \qquad\qquad \mathcal{D}_d^A(r^*) = \mathcal{D}_d^A(r) \cdot r^*$$

State : Finite multiset S of queries of type $\mathsf{QRE}\langle D, C \rangle$.

Initialization() : Set the state S to the singleton multiset $\{\mathbf{f}\}$.

Update(d) : Compute the Antimirov derivative $S' = \mathcal{D}_d^{\mathsf{A}}(S) = \biguplus \{\mathcal{D}_d^{\mathsf{A}}(\mathbf{g}) \mid \mathbf{g} \in S\}$. Now, iterate the following conditional modification until no further changes can be made: if S' contains at least three queries that have the same rate, keep only two of them and remove the rest. Finally, set S to be equal to S'.

Output() : If $\mathcal{E}(S) = \biguplus \{\mathcal{E}(\mathbf{g}) \mid \mathbf{g} \in S\}$ is the singleton multiset $\{c\}$, then return the value c. Otherwise, the output is undefined.

Fig. 3. Streaming evaluation algorithm for an arbitrary query $\mathbf{f} : \mathsf{QRE}\langle D, C \rangle$, with respect to the unambiguous semantics of QREs.

For subsets X, Y of expressions we have used in the definition the abbreviations: $X \sqcap Y = \{r \sqcap s \mid r \in X, s \in Y\}$, $X \cdot s = \{r \cdot s \mid r \in X\}$, $0 \cdot X = \emptyset$ and $1 \cdot X = X$.

Lemma 8. For every regular expression r, the set $\bigcup_{w \in D^*} \mathcal{D}_w^{\mathsf{A}}(r)$ of all derivatives of r is of size exponential in r.

For a query $\mathbf{f}$ of type $\mathsf{QRE}\langle D, C \rangle$ and a data item $d \in D$, the *Antimirov derivative* $\mathcal{D}_d^{\mathsf{A}}(\mathbf{f})$ of $\mathbf{f}$ w.r.t. d is a finite **multiset** of queries of type $\mathsf{QRE}\langle D, C \rangle$.

$$\mathcal{D}_d^{\mathsf{A}}(\mathtt{eps}(c)) = \mathcal{D}_d^{\mathsf{A}}(\bot) = \emptyset \qquad\qquad \mathcal{D}_d^{\mathsf{A}}(\mathbf{f} \sqcup \mathbf{g}) = \mathcal{D}_d^{\mathsf{A}}(\mathbf{f}) \uplus \mathcal{D}_d^{\mathsf{A}}(\mathbf{g})$$

$$\mathcal{D}_d^{\mathsf{A}}(\mathtt{atom}(\phi, op)) = \emptyset, \text{ if } d \not\models \phi \qquad\qquad \mathcal{D}_d^{\mathsf{A}}(op(\mathbf{f})) = op(\mathcal{D}_d^{\mathsf{A}}(\mathbf{f}))$$

$$\mathcal{D}_d^{\mathsf{A}}(\mathtt{atom}(\phi, op)) = \{\mathtt{eps}(op(d))\}, \text{ if } d \models \phi \qquad \mathcal{D}_d^{\mathsf{A}}(op(\mathbf{f}, \mathbf{g})) = op(\mathcal{D}_d^{\mathsf{A}}(\mathbf{f}), \mathcal{D}_d^{\mathsf{A}}(\mathbf{g}))$$

$$\mathcal{D}_d^{\mathsf{A}}(\mathtt{split}(\mathbf{f}, \mathbf{g}, op)) = \mathtt{split}(\mathcal{D}_d^{\mathsf{A}}(\mathbf{f}), \mathbf{g}, op) \uplus \biguplus_{a \in \mathcal{E}(\mathbf{f})}(op\, a)(\mathcal{D}_d^{\mathsf{A}}(\mathbf{g}))$$

$$\mathcal{D}_d^{\mathsf{A}}(\mathtt{iter}(\mathbf{f}, \mathbf{g}, op)) = \mathtt{iter}(\mathcal{D}_d^{\mathsf{A}}(\mathbf{f}), \mathbf{g}, op) \uplus \biguplus_{b \in \mathcal{E}(\mathbf{f})}\mathtt{iter}((op\, b)(\mathcal{D}_d^{\mathsf{A}}(\mathbf{g})), \mathbf{g}, op)$$

We have used above convenient abbreviations like $op(X) = \{op(\mathbf{f}) \mid \mathbf{f} \in X\}$. The derivative $\mathcal{D}_w^{\mathsf{A}}(\mathbf{f})$ w.r.t. a sequence $w \in D^*$ is defined by induction on w: $\mathcal{D}_\varepsilon^{\mathsf{A}}(\mathbf{f}) = \{\mathbf{f}\}$ and $\mathcal{D}_{dw}^{\mathsf{A}}(\mathbf{f}) = \bigcup \{\mathcal{D}_w^{\mathsf{A}}(\mathbf{g}) \mid \mathbf{g} \in \mathcal{D}_d^{\mathsf{A}}(\mathbf{f})\}$.

Theorem 9. The algorithm of Fig. 3 solves the evaluation problem for QREs w.r.t. the unambiguous semantics. It requires space and time-per-element that are constant in the length of the stream, and exponential in the size of the query.

Proof. To prove that the algorithm of Fig. 3 is correct, we observe that it satisfies the following crucial invariant: after consuming the input $w \in D^*$, the multiset S is $\approx$-equivalent to the derivative $\mathcal{D}_w^{\mathsf{A}}(\mathbf{f})$. This is because the removal step of the **Update** procedure preserves the unambiguous meaning of S (recall Observation 3). It remains to see that the Antimirov derivative is a streamlined representation of the Brzozowski derivative. That is, for every query $\mathbf{f} : \mathsf{QRE}\langle D, C \rangle$ and every data item $d \in D$, it holds that $\mathcal{D}_d^{\mathsf{B}}(\mathbf{f}) \equiv \bigsqcup \mathcal{D}_d^{\mathsf{A}}(\mathbf{f})$. The equivalences

$$\mathbf{f} \sqcup \mathbf{g} \equiv \mathbf{g} \sqcup \mathbf{f} \qquad\qquad op(\mathbf{f} \sqcup \mathbf{g}, \mathbf{h}) \equiv op(\mathbf{f}, \mathbf{h}) \sqcup op(\mathbf{g}, \mathbf{h})$$
$$op(\mathbf{f} \sqcup \mathbf{g}) \equiv op(\mathbf{f}) \sqcup op(\mathbf{g}) \quad op(\mathbf{f}, \mathbf{g} \sqcup \mathbf{h}) \equiv op(\mathbf{f}, \mathbf{g}) \sqcup op(\mathbf{f}, \mathbf{h})$$
$$\mathtt{split}(\mathbf{f} \sqcup \mathbf{g}, \mathbf{h}) \equiv \mathtt{split}(\mathbf{f}, \mathbf{h}) \sqcup \mathtt{split}(\mathbf{g}, \mathbf{h})$$
$$\mathtt{iter}(\mathbf{f} \sqcup \mathbf{g}, \mathbf{h}, op) \equiv \mathtt{iter}(\mathbf{f}, \mathbf{h}, op) \sqcup \mathtt{iter}(\mathbf{g}, \mathbf{h}, op)$$

are used in the proof of this claim. Essentially, the above equations are encoded in the derivatives by way of their representation as multisets of queries. The output procedure returns $\langle\!\langle S \rangle\!\rangle \, \varepsilon = \langle\!\langle \mathcal{D}_w^A(\mathbf{f}) \rangle\!\rangle \, \varepsilon = \theta(\llbracket \mathcal{D}_w^B(\mathbf{f}) \rrbracket \, \varepsilon) = \theta(\llbracket \mathbf{f} \rrbracket \, w) = \langle\!\langle \mathbf{f} \rangle\!\rangle \, w$.

The Antimirov derivatives on QREs correspond closely to the Antimirov derivatives on regular expressions. For every query $\mathbf{g} \in \mathcal{D}_d^A(\mathbf{f})$, it holds that $\mathsf{rate}(\mathbf{g}) \in \mathcal{D}_d^A(\mathsf{rate}(\mathbf{f}))$. Because of the pruning step, the state S contains at most two queries for every possible rate of the derivatives. Since there are at most exponentially many derivatives of $\mathsf{rate}(\mathbf{f})$ by Lemma 8, the cardinality of S is also at most exponential in $\mathbf{f}$ and independent of the size of the input sequence. The time to process each element is also exponential in $|\mathbf{f}|$. $\qquad\square$

Example 10. The query $\mathbf{f} = \mathtt{atom}(true_{\mathbb{N}}, id_{\mathbb{N}})$ is of type $\mathsf{QRE}\langle \mathbb{N}, \mathbb{N} \rangle$ and it maps a single natural number to itself. The query $\mathbf{g} = \mathtt{iter}(\mathtt{eps}(0), \mathbf{f}, +)$ maps any sequence of natural numbers to their sum. We calculate the derivative of $\mathbf{g}$:

$$\mathcal{E}(\mathtt{eps}(0)) = \{0\} \quad \mathcal{D}_d^A(\mathbf{f}) = \{\mathtt{eps}(d)\} \quad \mathcal{D}_d^A(\mathtt{eps}(0)) = \emptyset$$
$$\mathcal{D}_d^A(\mathbf{g}) = \mathtt{iter}(\mathcal{D}_d^A(\mathtt{eps}(0)), \mathbf{f}, +) \uplus \mathtt{iter}((\lambda x.0 + x)(\mathcal{D}_d^A(\mathbf{f})), \mathbf{f}, +)$$
$$= \{\mathtt{iter}((\lambda x.0 + x)(\mathtt{eps}(d)), \mathbf{f}, +)\}$$

For $x, y \in \mathbb{N}$ define $\mathbf{g}_{xy} = \mathtt{iter}((\lambda z.x + z)(\mathtt{eps}(y)), \mathbf{f}, +)$. The derivative of $\mathbf{g}_{xy}$ is:

$$\mathcal{D}_d^A(\mathbf{g}_{xy}) = \mathtt{iter}(\mathcal{D}_d^A((\lambda z.x + z)(\mathtt{eps}(y))), \mathbf{f}, +) \uplus$$
$$\mathtt{iter}((\lambda z.(x + y) + z)(\mathcal{D}_d^A(\mathbf{f})), \mathbf{f}, +)$$
$$= \{\mathtt{iter}((\lambda z.(x + y) + z)(\mathtt{eps}(d)), \mathbf{f}, +)\} = \mathbf{g}_{x+y, d}$$

because $\mathcal{E}((\lambda z.x + z)(\mathtt{eps}(y))) = \{x + y\}$ and $\mathcal{D}_d^A((\lambda z.x + z)(\mathtt{eps}(y))) = \emptyset$. $\qquad\square$

5   Strongly Typed Queries and Hierarchical Derivatives

Following [5], we consider a syntactic restriction of QREs that ensures unambiguity of parsing. This means that the multiset and unambiguous semantics coincide, thus this subclass of QREs inherently describes well-defined functions on data streams. Together with an additional restriction that demands in expressions of the form $op(\mathbf{f}, \mathbf{g})$ the subqueries $\mathbf{f}$ and $\mathbf{g}$ to have the same domain, it can be ensured that the evaluation of QREs can be performed efficiently, that is, using space and time-per-element that is polynomial in the size of the query and independent of the stream. Such an algorithm is proposed in [5] and implemented in [21], but it is hard to describe and even harder to analyze. We consider here an alternative approach based on derivatives, which gives rise to an evaluation algorithm of the same complexity that is much easier to describe and prove correct. The main technical tool is a novel representation of derivatives, which we call *hierarchical derivatives*. This is a very space-efficient representation and is crucial for obtaining our complexity bounds.

Before defining the subclass of strongly typed queries, we introduce some definitions that will be used for formalizing the idea of uniqueness of parsing. The languages L_1, L_2 are said to be *unambiguously concatenable* if for every word $w \in L_1 \cdot L_2$ there are unique $w_1 \in L_1$, $w_2 \in L_2$ with $w = w_1 w_2$. The language L is said to be *unambiguously iterable* if for every word $w \in L^*$ there is a unique integer $n \geq 0$ and unique $w_i \in L$ with $w = w_1 \cdots w_n$. These definitions extend to regular expressions in the obvious way.

We say that a query is *strongly typed* if the following hold: (1) for every subquery $\mathtt{f} \sqcup \mathtt{g}$ the rates $\mathsf{rate}(\mathtt{f})$ and $\mathsf{rate}(\mathtt{g})$ are disjoint, (2) for every subquery $\mathtt{split}(\mathtt{f}, \mathtt{g}, op)$ the rates $\mathsf{rate}(\mathtt{f})$ and $\mathsf{rate}(\mathtt{g})$ are unambiguously concatenable. (3) for every subquery $\mathtt{iter}(\mathtt{f}, \mathtt{g}, op)$ the rate $\mathsf{rate}(\mathtt{g})$ is unambiguously iterable and $\mathsf{rate}(\mathtt{f})$, $\mathsf{rate}(\mathtt{g})^*$ are unambiguously concatenable, and (4) for every subquery $op(\mathtt{f}, \mathtt{g})$ the rates $\mathsf{rate}(\mathtt{f})$ and $\mathsf{rate}(\mathtt{g})$ are equivalent. It is shown in [5] that checking whether a query is strongly typed can be done in polynomial-time.

Lemma 11. *If the query* $\mathtt{f}$ *is strongly typed, then* $[\![\mathtt{f}]\!]$ *is an unambiguous function. So, the multiset and unambiguous semantics coincide, i.e.* $[\![\mathtt{f}]\!] = \langle\!\langle \mathtt{f} \rangle\!\rangle$.

The main problem with the Antimirov derivative of Sect. 4 is the treatment of $op(\mathtt{f}, \mathtt{g})$, where $\mathcal{D}_d^{\mathtt{A}}(op(\mathtt{f}, \mathtt{g})) = \{ op(\mathtt{f}', \mathtt{g}') \mid \mathtt{f}' \in \mathcal{D}_d^{\mathtt{A}}(\mathtt{f}), \mathtt{g}' \in \mathcal{D}_d^{\mathtt{A}}(\mathtt{g}) \}$. This definitions corresponds to a cartesian product of derivatives, thus causing a quadratic blowup in the number of possible derivatives. As we will see later in Example 14, this blowup can materialize even in the context of strongly typed queries. Since the output combination operation can nest with other regular constructs, the Antimirov representation can result in an exponenial blowup, which is avoidable in the strongly typed case. In order to prove this, we need a new representation that avoids this "cartesian product" problem of the Antimirov derivative by allowing sets of queries to be used as subexpressions.

We thus generalize the syntax of strongly typed queries to allow finite sets of queries as subexpressions. Intuitively, these finite sets of queries extend the choice operation $\sqcup$ to a finite number of arguments. Since the subqueries of $\mathtt{f} \sqcup \mathtt{g}$ must have disjoint domains, the $\sqcup$ constructor is associative and commutative, which means that we can represent $(\mathtt{f} \sqcup \mathtt{g}) \sqcup \mathtt{h}$ as $\{\mathtt{f}, \mathtt{g}, \mathtt{h}\}$. This finite choice constructor can be nested arbitrarily with the other query constructors. In Fig. 4 we see the formal definition, where queries and *q-sets* (finite sets of queries) are defined by mutual induction. To reduce the notational clutter, we sometimes write the query $\mathtt{f}$ instead of the q-set $\{\mathtt{f}\}$, for example $\mathtt{iter}\langle \mathtt{f}, \mathtt{g}, op \rangle$ instead of $\mathtt{iter}\langle \{\mathtt{f}\}, \{\mathtt{g}\}, op \rangle$. The rate of a generalized query is defined in the usual way, the only difference being $\mathsf{rate}(\{\mathtt{f}_1, \ldots, \mathtt{f}_k\}) = \mathsf{rate}(\mathtt{f}_1) \sqcup \cdots \sqcup \mathsf{rate}(\mathtt{f}_k)$.

For the expressions of Fig. 4 we define in Fig. 5 a new kind of derivative, called the *(syntactic) hierarchical derivative* $\mathcal{D}_d^{\mathtt{H}}(\cdot)$, which maps a query of type

$$\frac{c \in C}{\mathtt{eps}(c) : \mathsf{QRE}\langle D, C\rangle} \qquad \frac{\text{satisfiable } \phi : D \to \mathbb{B} \qquad op : D \to C}{\mathtt{atom}(\phi, op) : \mathsf{QRE}\langle D, C\rangle}$$

$$\frac{\mathtt{F} : \mathsf{QSET}\langle D, A\rangle \qquad \mathtt{G} : \mathsf{QSET}\langle D, B\rangle \qquad op : A \times B \to C}{\mathtt{F}, \mathtt{G} \neq \emptyset \qquad \mathtt{rate}(\mathtt{F}), \mathtt{rate}(\mathtt{G}) \text{ unambiguously concatenable}}{\mathtt{split}\langle \mathtt{F}, \mathtt{G}, op\rangle : \mathsf{QRE}\langle D, C\rangle}$$

$$\frac{op : B \times A \to B \quad \mathtt{F} : \mathsf{QSET}\langle D, B\rangle \quad \mathtt{rate}(\mathtt{F}), \mathtt{rate}(\mathtt{G})^* \text{ unambiguously concatenable}}{\mathtt{F}, \mathtt{G} \neq \emptyset \qquad \mathtt{G} : \mathsf{QSET}\langle D, A\rangle \quad \mathtt{rate}(\mathtt{G}) \text{ unambiguously iterable}}{\mathtt{iter}\langle \mathtt{F}, \mathtt{G}, op\rangle : \mathsf{QRE}\langle D, B\rangle}$$

$$\frac{\mathtt{F} \neq \emptyset : \mathsf{QSET}\langle D, A\rangle}{op : A \to B}{op\langle \mathtt{F}\rangle : \mathsf{QRE}\langle D, C\rangle} \qquad \frac{\mathtt{F} : \mathsf{QSET}\langle D, A\rangle \qquad \mathtt{G} : \mathsf{QSET}\langle D, B\rangle \qquad op : A \times B \to C}{\mathtt{F}, \mathtt{G} \neq \emptyset \qquad \mathtt{rate}(\mathtt{F}) \text{ and } \mathtt{rate}(\mathtt{G}) \text{ are equivalent}}{op\langle \mathtt{F}, \mathtt{G}\rangle : \mathsf{QRE}\langle D, C\rangle}$$

$$\frac{\mathtt{f}_1, \ldots, \mathtt{f}_k : \mathsf{QRE}\langle D, C\rangle \qquad \mathtt{rate}(\mathtt{f}_1), \ldots, \mathtt{rate}(\mathtt{f}_k) \text{ pairwise disjoint}}{\{\mathtt{f}_1, \ldots, \mathtt{f}_k\} : \mathsf{QSET}\langle D, C\rangle}$$

Fig. 4. Generalized syntax for strongly typed QREs.

$$\mathcal{D}_d^{\mathsf{H}}(\{\mathtt{f}_i \mid i \in I\}) = \bigcup_{i \in I} \mathcal{D}_d^{\mathsf{H}}(\mathtt{f}_i) \qquad \mathcal{D}_d^{\mathsf{H}}(\mathtt{atom}(\phi, op)) = \emptyset, \text{ if } d \not\models \phi$$

$$\mathcal{D}_d^{\mathsf{H}}(\mathtt{eps}(c)) = \emptyset \qquad \mathcal{D}_d^{\mathsf{H}}(\mathtt{atom}(\phi, op)) = \{\mathtt{eps}(op(d))\}, \text{ if } d \models \phi$$

$$\mathcal{D}_d^{\mathsf{H}}(op\langle \mathtt{F}\rangle) = \{op\langle \mathcal{D}_d^{\mathsf{H}}(\mathtt{F})\rangle\} \qquad \mathcal{D}_d^{\mathsf{H}}(op\langle \mathtt{F}, \mathtt{G}\rangle) = \{op\langle \mathcal{D}_d^{\mathsf{H}}(\mathtt{F}), \mathcal{D}_d^{\mathsf{H}}(\mathtt{G})\rangle\}$$

$$\mathcal{D}_d^{\mathsf{H}}(\mathtt{split}\langle \mathtt{F}, \mathtt{G}, op\rangle) = \{\mathtt{split}\langle \mathcal{D}_d^{\mathsf{H}}(\mathtt{F}), \mathtt{G}, op\rangle\} \cup \{(op\, a)\langle \mathcal{D}_d^{\mathsf{H}}(\mathtt{G})\rangle \mid a \in \mathcal{E}(\mathtt{f})\}$$

$$\mathcal{D}_d^{\mathsf{H}}(\mathtt{iter}\langle \mathtt{F}, \mathtt{G}, op\rangle) = \{\mathtt{iter}\langle \mathcal{D}_d^{\mathsf{H}}(\mathtt{F}), \mathtt{G}, op\rangle\} \cup \{\mathtt{iter}\langle (op\, b)\langle \mathcal{D}_d^{\mathsf{H}}(\mathtt{G})\rangle, \mathtt{G}, op\rangle \mid b \in \mathcal{E}(\mathtt{F})\}$$

$$\mathcal{E}(\mathtt{eps}(c)) = \{c\} \qquad \mathcal{E}(op\langle \mathtt{F}\rangle) = \mathsf{M}(op)(\mathcal{E}(\mathtt{F}))$$

$$\mathcal{E}(\mathtt{atom}(\phi, op)) = \emptyset \qquad \mathcal{E}(op\langle \mathtt{F}, \mathtt{G}\rangle) = \mathsf{M}(op)(\mathcal{E}(\mathtt{F}), \mathcal{E}(\mathtt{G}))$$

$$\mathcal{E}(\{\mathtt{f}_i\}_i) = \bigcup_i \mathcal{E}(\mathtt{f}_i) \qquad \mathcal{E}(\mathtt{split}\langle \mathtt{F}, \mathtt{G}, op\rangle) = \mathsf{M}(op)(\mathcal{E}(\mathtt{F}), \mathcal{E}(\mathtt{G}))$$

$$\mathcal{E}(\mathtt{iter}\langle \mathtt{F}, \mathtt{G}, op\rangle) = \mathcal{E}(\mathtt{F})$$

Fig. 5. Hierarchical derivatives for generalized QREs.

$\mathsf{QRE}\langle D, C\rangle$ or a q-set of type $\mathsf{QSET}\langle D, C\rangle$ to a q-set of type $\mathsf{QSET}\langle D, C\rangle$. The hierarchical derivative $\mathcal{D}_w^{\mathsf{H}}(\mathtt{F})$ w.r.t. a sequence $w \in D^*$ is defined by induction on w: $\mathcal{D}_\varepsilon^{\mathsf{H}}(\mathtt{F}) = \mathtt{F}$ and $\mathcal{D}_{dw}^{\mathsf{H}}(\mathtt{F}) = \mathcal{D}_w^{\mathsf{H}}(\mathcal{D}_d^{\mathsf{H}}(\mathtt{F}))$. For every sequence $u \in D^*$, the derivative $\mathcal{D}_u^{\mathsf{H}}(\mathtt{split}\langle \mathtt{F}, \mathtt{G}, op\rangle)$ is of the form:

$$\{\mathtt{split}\langle \mathcal{D}_u^{\mathsf{H}}(\mathtt{F}), \mathtt{G}, op\rangle, op\langle a_1, \mathcal{D}_{v_1}^{\mathsf{H}}(\mathtt{G})\rangle, \ldots, op\langle a_n, \mathcal{D}_{v_n}^{\mathsf{H}}(\mathtt{G})\rangle\}$$

for some $a_i \in A$ and sequences $v_i \in D^*$. Because of unambiguity, the rates of the derivatives $\mathcal{D}_{v_1}^{\mathsf{H}}(\mathtt{G}), \ldots, \mathcal{D}_{v_n}^{\mathsf{H}}(\mathtt{G})$ are pairwise disjoint. Similarly, for every sequence $u \in D^*$, the derivative $\mathcal{D}_u^{\mathsf{H}}(\mathtt{iter}\langle \mathtt{F}, \mathtt{G}, op\rangle)$ is of the form:

$$\{\mathtt{iter}\langle \mathcal{D}_u^{\mathsf{H}}(\mathtt{F}), \mathtt{G}, op\rangle, \mathtt{iter}\langle op\langle b_1, \mathcal{D}_{v_1}^{\mathsf{H}}(\mathtt{G})\rangle, \mathtt{G}, op\rangle, \ldots, \mathtt{iter}\langle op\langle b_n, \mathcal{D}_{v_n}^{\mathsf{H}}(\mathtt{G})\rangle, \mathtt{G}, op\rangle\}$$

for some $b_i \in B$ and sequences $v_i \in D^*$. Again, because of unambiguity, the rates of the derivatives $\mathcal{D}_u^H(F)$, $\mathcal{D}_{v_1}^H(G)$, ..., $\mathcal{D}_{v_n}^H(G)$ are pairwise disjoint. A key technical lemma to obtain an efficient evaluation algorithm is that the derivatives of strongly typed queries are of polynomial size. To show this, first we define a reasonable notion of size of queries:

$$\text{size}(\{f_i\}_i) = \sum_i \text{size}(f_i) \qquad\qquad \text{size}(op\langle F\rangle) = 1 + \text{size}(F)$$
$$\text{size}(\text{eps}(c)) = 1 \qquad\qquad \text{size}(op\langle F, G\rangle) = 1 + \text{size}(F) + \text{size}(G)$$
$$\text{size}(\text{atom}(\phi, op)) = 2 \qquad \text{size}(\text{split}\langle F, G, op\rangle) = 1 + \text{size}(F) + \text{size}(G)$$
$$\text{size}(\text{iter}\langle F, G, op\rangle) = 1 + \text{size}(F) + \text{size}(G)$$

In order to obtain the desired lemma, the claim has to be strengthened:

Lemma 12. Let F be a q-set in $\mathsf{QSET}\langle D, C\rangle$ and $u_1, \ldots, u_n$ be sequences over D such that the rates of $\mathcal{D}_{u_1}^H(F)$, ..., $\mathcal{D}_{u_n}^H(F)$ are pairwise disjoint. Then:

(1) At most $\text{size}(F)$ of the sets $\mathcal{D}_{u_1}^H(F)$, ..., $\mathcal{D}_{u_n}^H(F)$ are nonempty.
(2) The space needed to represent $\mathcal{D}_{u_1}^H(F) \cup \cdots \cup \mathcal{D}_{u_n}^H(F)$ is bounded by $\text{size}(F)^2$.

Proof. To prove the lemma, we must extend the same claim to queries as well. The proof then proceeds by induction on the structure of queries and q-sets. The base cases $\text{eps}(c)$ and $\text{atom}(\phi, op)$ and the step case $op\langle F\rangle$ are easy.

For the case of a q-set $F = \{f_1, \ldots, f_m\}$ we first notice for an arbitrary j in $\{1, \ldots, m\}$ that: $\mathsf{rate}(f_j) \subseteq \mathsf{rate}(F)$ and therefore $\mathsf{rate}(\mathcal{D}_v^H(f_j)) \subseteq \mathsf{rate}(\mathcal{D}_v^H(F))$ for every $v \in D^*$. It follows that the rates of the derivatives $\mathcal{D}_{u_1}^H(f_j)$, ..., $\mathcal{D}_{u_n}^H(f_j)$ are pairwise disjoint. To show part (1), we observe that

$$\{i \mid \mathcal{D}_{u_i}^H(F) \neq \emptyset\} = \{i \mid \mathcal{D}_{u_i}^H(f_1) \cup \cdots \cup \mathcal{D}_{u_i}^H(f_m) \neq \emptyset\} = \bigcup_{j=1}^m \{i \mid \mathcal{D}_{u_i}^H(f_j) \neq \emptyset\}.$$

By the induction hypothesis, the size of this set is bounded by $\sum_{j=1}^m \text{size}(f_j) = \text{size}(F)$. Now,

$$\text{space}(\bigcup_{i=1}^n \mathcal{D}_{u_i}^H(F)) = \text{space}(\bigcup_{i=1}^n \bigcup_{j=1}^n \mathcal{D}_{u_i}^H(f_j))$$
$$= \sum_{j=1}^n \text{space}(\bigcup_{i=1}^n \mathcal{D}_{u_i}^H(f_j))$$
$$\leq \sum_{j=1}^n \text{size}(f_j)^2,$$

which is less than $(\text{size}(f_1) + \cdots + \text{size}(f_m))^2 = \text{size}(F)^2$.

For the case of the query $h = op\langle F, G\rangle$, we first recall that $\mathsf{rate}(h) = \mathsf{rate}(F) \equiv \mathsf{rate}(G)$. So, the hypotheses of the lemma hold for both F and G. This means that at most $\min(\text{size}(F), \text{size}(G)) \leq \text{size}(h)$ of the sets $\mathcal{D}_{u_1}^H(h)$, ..., $\mathcal{D}_{u_n}^H(h)$ are nonempty. For part (2), we have that

$$\text{space}(\bigcup_{i=1}^n \mathcal{D}_{u_i}^H(h)) = \text{space}(\{op\langle \mathcal{D}_{u_i}^H(F), \mathcal{D}_{u_i}^H(G)\rangle \mid i = 1, \ldots, n\})$$
$$\leq \text{size}(F) + \left(\sum_{i=1}^n \text{space}(\mathcal{D}_{u_i}^H(F))\right) + \left(\sum_{i=1}^n \text{space}(\mathcal{D}_{u_i}^H(G))\right)$$
$$\leq \text{size}(F) + \text{size}(F)^2 + \text{size}(G)^2,$$

which is less than $(1 + \text{size}(F) + \text{size}(G))^2 = \text{size}(op\langle F, G\rangle)^2$.

State : Q-set H of type $\mathsf{QSET}\langle D, C \rangle$.

Initialization() : Set the state H to the singleton q-set $\{\mathsf{f}\}$.

Update(d) : Replace H by its hierarchical derivative $\mathcal{D}_d^{\mathsf{H}}(\mathsf{H})$.

Output() : If $\mathcal{E}(\mathsf{H})$ is the singleton multiset $\{c\}$, then return the value c. Otherwise, the output is undefined.

Fig. 6. Streaming evaluation algorithm for a strongly typed query $\mathsf{f} : \mathsf{QRE}\langle D, C \rangle$.

We handle now the case $\mathsf{h} = \mathtt{split}\langle \mathsf{F}, \mathsf{G}, op \rangle$. As discussed previously, the union $\mathcal{D}_{u_1}^{\mathsf{H}}(\mathsf{h}) \cup \cdots \cup \mathcal{D}_{u_n}^{\mathsf{H}}(\mathsf{h})$ of the derivatives is of the form

$$\mathsf{H} = \{\mathtt{split}\langle \mathcal{D}_{u_1}^{\mathsf{H}}(\mathsf{F}), \mathsf{G}, op \rangle, \ldots, \mathtt{split}\langle \mathcal{D}_{u_n}^{\mathsf{H}}(\mathsf{F}), \mathsf{G}, op \rangle,$$
$$op\langle a_1, \mathcal{D}_{v_1}^{\mathsf{H}}(\mathsf{G}) \rangle, \ldots, op\langle a_n, \mathcal{D}_{v_m}^{\mathsf{H}}(\mathsf{G}) \rangle \}$$

for some $a_1, \ldots, a_m \in A$ and $v_1, \ldots, v_m \in D^*$. Now, H is unambiguous and therefore the q-sets $\mathcal{D}_{u_1}^{\mathsf{H}}(\mathsf{F})$, $\ldots$, $\mathcal{D}_{u_n}^{\mathsf{H}}(\mathsf{F})$ are pairwise disjoint, and similarly the q-sets $\mathcal{D}_{v_1}^{\mathsf{H}}(\mathsf{G})$, $\ldots$, $\mathcal{D}_{v_m}^{\mathsf{H}}(\mathsf{G})$ are pairwise disjoint. From the induction hypothesis (part 1) for F and G, we get that H is of size $\leq \mathrm{size}(\mathsf{F}) + \mathrm{size}(\mathsf{G})$, which implies part (1) for h. To measure the space needed to represent H, we first observe that the subquery G is shared by several queries in H and therefore we can replace every G occurrence with a pointer to a representation of G. Total space:

$$\mathsf{space}(\mathsf{H}) \leq \mathrm{size}(\mathsf{F})^2 + 2 \cdot \mathrm{size}(\mathsf{F}) + \mathrm{size}(\mathsf{G})^2 + \mathrm{size}(\mathsf{G}),$$

which is less than $(1 + \mathrm{size}(\mathsf{F}) + \mathrm{size}(\mathsf{G}))^2 = \mathrm{size}(\mathsf{h})^2$.

Finally, we consider the case $\mathsf{h} = \mathtt{iter}\langle \mathsf{F}, \mathsf{G}, op \rangle$ of iteration. As discussed previously, the union $\mathcal{D}_{u_1}^{\mathsf{H}}(\mathsf{h}) \cup \cdots \cup \mathcal{D}_{u_n}^{\mathsf{H}}(\mathsf{h})$ of the derivatives is of the form

$$\mathsf{H} = \{\mathtt{iter}\langle \mathcal{D}_{u_1}^{\mathsf{H}}(\mathsf{F}), \mathsf{G}, op \rangle, \ldots, \mathtt{iter}\langle \mathcal{D}_{u_n}^{\mathsf{H}}(\mathsf{F}), \mathsf{G}, op \rangle,$$
$$\mathtt{iter}\langle op\langle b_1, \mathcal{D}_{v_1}^{\mathsf{H}}(\mathsf{G}) \rangle, \mathsf{G}, op \rangle, \ldots, \mathtt{iter}\langle op\langle b_n, \mathcal{D}_{v_m}^{\mathsf{H}}(\mathsf{G}) \rangle, \mathsf{G}, op \rangle \}$$

for some $b_1, \ldots, b_m \in B$ and $v_1, \ldots, v_m \in D^*$. The total space requirements are:

$$\mathsf{space}(\mathsf{H}) \leq \mathrm{size}(\mathsf{F})^2 + 2 \cdot \mathrm{size}(\mathsf{F}) + \mathrm{size}(\mathsf{G})^2 + 3 \cdot \mathrm{size}(\mathsf{G}),$$

which is less than $(1 + \mathrm{size}(\mathsf{F}) + \mathrm{size}(\mathsf{G}))^2 = \mathrm{size}(\mathsf{h})^2$. $\qquad\square$

Lemma 12 establishes, in particular, that the hierarchical derivative of any strongly typed q-set F w.r.t. any sequence is of size at most quadratic in the size of F. Using this fact, we can prove the main theorem of this paper:

Theorem 13. The algorithm of Fig. 6 solves the evaluation problem for strongly typed QREs. It requires space and time-per-element that are constant in the length of the stream, and polynomial in the size of the query.

Proof. First, we observe that the hierarchial derivative is simply a different representation of the Brzozowski derivative, which is streamlined for space efficiency. This implies that $\mathcal{D}_d^{\mathsf{B}}(\mathsf{f})$, $\mathcal{D}_d^{\mathsf{A}}(\mathsf{f})$ and $\mathcal{D}_d^{\mathsf{H}}(\mathsf{f})$ are all $\equiv$-equivalent when

f : $\mathsf{QRE}\langle D, C \rangle$ is strongly typed. The algorithm of Fig. 6 satisfies the invariant: after consuming input $w \in D^*$, the q-set H is equal to the hierarchical derivative $\mathcal{D}_w^{\mathsf{H}}(f)$. The correctness of the algorithm then follows immediately from the semantic agreement of the hierarchical derivative with the Brzozowski derivative. At every step of the computation the state H is of the form $\mathcal{D}_w^{\mathsf{H}}(f)$, where w is the input sequence seen so far. Lemma 12 give us immediately that H can be represented using space that is quadratic in the size of the input query. It follows that the time to process each element is also quadratic in the query. □

Example 14. The queries h_1, h_2 below calculate the maximum and minimum respectively of two consecutive natural numbers, where $f = \mathsf{atom}(true_{\mathbb{N}}, id_{\mathbb{N}})$. The top-level query k shown below is strongly typed, and it calculates the average of the maximum and minimum of the last two elements of the stream.

$$h_1 = \mathsf{split}(f, f, \max) \qquad\qquad k_1 = \mathsf{split}(g, h_1, \pi_2)$$
$$h_2 = \mathsf{split}(f, f, \min) \qquad\qquad k_2 = \mathsf{split}(g, h_2, \pi_2)$$
$$g = \mathsf{iter}(\mathsf{eps}(0), \mathsf{atom}(true_{\mathbb{N}}, \lambda x.0), \pi_2) \qquad k = \mathsf{avg}(k_1, k_2)$$

The Antimirov and hierarchical derivatives of g are the following:

$$\{g'\} = \mathcal{D}_w^{\mathsf{A}}(g) = \{\mathsf{iter}((\lambda x.\pi_2(0, x))(\mathsf{eps}(0)), \mathsf{atom}(true_{\mathbb{N}}, \lambda x.0), \pi_2)\}$$
$$g'' = \mathcal{D}_w^{\mathsf{H}}(g) = \{\mathsf{iter}\langle(\lambda x.\pi_2(0, x))\langle\mathsf{eps}(0)\rangle, \mathsf{atom}(true_{\mathbb{N}}, \lambda x.0), \pi_2\rangle\}$$

for every $w \neq \varepsilon$. For the Antimirov derivative of k w.r.t. 3 we calculate:

$$\mathcal{D}_3^{\mathsf{A}}(k_1) = \{\mathsf{split}(g', h_1, \pi_2), (\lambda x.\pi_2(0, x))((\lambda x.\max(3, x))(f))\}$$
$$\mathcal{D}_3^{\mathsf{A}}(k_2) = \{\mathsf{split}(g', h_2, \pi_2), (\lambda x.\pi_2(0, x))((\lambda x.\min(3, x))(f))\}$$
$$\mathcal{D}_3^{\mathsf{A}}(k) = \{\mathsf{avg}(\mathsf{split}(g', h_1, \pi_2), \mathsf{split}(g', h_2, \pi_2)),$$
$$\mathsf{avg}(\mathsf{split}(g', h_1, \pi_2), (\lambda x.\pi_2(0, x))((\lambda x.\min(3, x))(f))),$$
$$\mathsf{avg}((\lambda x.\pi_2(0, x))((\lambda x.\max(3, x))(f)), \mathsf{split}(g', h_2, \pi_2)),$$
$$\mathsf{avg}((\lambda x.\pi_2(0, x))((\lambda x.\max(3, x))(f)),$$
$$(\lambda x.\pi_2(0, x))((\lambda x.\min(3, x))(f)))\}$$

and then the Antimirov derivative $\mathcal{D}_{35}^{\mathsf{A}}(k)$ contains $3 \cdot 3 = 9$ queries. For the hierarchical derivative of k w.r.t. 3 we calculate:

$$\mathcal{D}_3^{\mathsf{H}}(k_1) = \{\mathsf{split}\langle g'', h_1, \pi_2\rangle, (\lambda x.\pi_2(0, x))\langle(\lambda x.\max(3, x))\langle f\rangle\rangle\}$$
$$\mathcal{D}_3^{\mathsf{H}}(k_2) = \{\mathsf{split}\langle g'', h_2, \pi_2\rangle, (\lambda x.\pi_2(0, x))\langle(\lambda x.\min(3, x))\langle f\rangle\rangle\}$$
$$\mathcal{D}_3^{\mathsf{A}}(k) = \{\mathsf{avg}\langle\mathcal{D}_3^{\mathsf{H}}(k_1), \mathcal{D}_3^{\mathsf{H}}(k_2)\rangle\}$$

In the hierarchical derivative $\mathcal{D}_{35}^{\mathsf{H}}(k)$, on the other hand, the subexpressions $\mathcal{D}_{35}^{\mathsf{H}}(k_1)$ and $\mathcal{D}_{35}^{\mathsf{H}}(k_2)$ contain a total of $3 + 3 = 6$ queries. This example illustrates the quadratic blowup for Antimirov derivatives, which is avoided using hierarchical derivatives.

6   Conclusion

This paper introduces syntactic derivatives for the Quantitative Regular Expressions (QREs) of [5]. The most natural generalization of the classical Brzozowski derivative to QREs is appropriate for the so-called multiset semantics of QREs, which records the possibility of several (finitely many) outputs. Since QREs are meant to describe well-defined functions on streams, we consider a projection of the multiset semantics into the so-called *unambiguous semantics*. Using a representation of derivatives that is inspired from Antimirov's variant of classical derivatives, we obtain an evaluation algorithm for QREs with streaming space and time complexity that is constant in the stream and exponential in the query. We then restrict attention to the strongly-typed QREs, also considered in [5], which admit more efficient streaming evaluation. We devise a novel representation of derivatives on QREs, which we call *hierarchical derivatives*, and we obtain an evaluation algorithm that streaming space and time complexity that is polynomial in the query. This matches the bounds of [5,21], but the algorithm presented here is much easier to describe, prove correct, and analyze.

The treatment of QRE evaluation using derivatives is a significant step towards developing automata models for QREs that play the same role as NFAs do for plain regular exressions. The definition of the space-efficient hierarchical derivatives of Sect. 5 suggests that the *parallel evaluation* of f, g in subqueries of the form $op(f, g)$ and some form of *hierarchical nesting* are essential features of a model that can support efficient evaluation of QREs. A hierarchical automaton model for the streaming computation of quantitative queries is described in [6], but its precise relationship to the QREs of [5] remains to be clarified. Finding the appropriate model of automata for QREs is an important direction for future work, since it would also open the door for query optimization by applying equivalence preserving transformations on the automata.

References

1. Abadi, D.J., Carney, D., Cetintemel, U., Cherniack, M., Convey, C., Lee, S., Stonebraker, M., Tatbul, N., Zdonik, S.: Aurora: a new model and architecture for data stream management. VLDB J. **12**(2), 120–139 (2003)
2. Alon, N., Matias, Y., Szegedy, M.: The space complexity of approximating the frequency moments. J. Comput. Syst. Sci. **58**(1), 137–147 (1999)
3. Alur, R., D'Antoni, L.: Streaming tree transducers. In: Czumaj, A., Mehlhorn, K., Pitts, A., Wattenhofer, R. (eds.) ICALP 2012. LNCS, vol. 7392, pp. 42–53. Springer, Heidelberg (2012). doi:10.1007/978-3-642-31585-5_8
4. Alur, R., D'Antoni, L., Deshmukh, J., Raghothaman, M., Yuan, Y.: Regular functions and cost register automata. In: Proceedings of the 28th Annual ACM/IEEE Symposium on Logic in Computer Science (LICS 2013), pp. 13–22 (2013)
5. Alur, R., Fisman, D., Raghothaman, M.: Regular programming for quantitative properties of data streams. In: Thiemann, P. (ed.) ESOP 2016. LNCS, vol. 9632, pp. 15–40. Springer, Heidelberg (2016). doi:10.1007/978-3-662-49498-1_2
6. Alur, R., Mamouras, K., Stanford, C.: Automata-based stream processing. In: ICALP 2017 (2017, to appear)

7. Antimirov, V.: Partial derivatives of regular expressions and finite automaton constructions. Theoret. Comput. Sci. **155**(2), 291–319 (1996)
8. Arasu, A., Babu, S., Widom, J.: The CQL continuous query language: Semantic foundations and query execution. VLDB J. **15**(2), 121–142 (2006)
9. Babu, S., Widom, J.: Continuous queries over data streams. ACM Sigmod Rec. **30**(3), 109–120 (2001)
10. Bonchi, F., Bonsangue, M.M., Hansen, H.H., Panangaden, P., Rutten, J., Silva, A.: Algebra-coalgebra duality in Brzozowski's minimization algorithm. ACM Trans. Comput. Log. (TOCL) **15**(1), 3:1–3:29 (2014)
11. Brzozowski, J.A.: Derivatives of regular expressions. J. ACM **11**(4), 481–494 (1964)
12. Colcombet, T.: Forms of determinism for automata (invited talk). In: Proceedings of the 29th International Symposium on Theoretical Aspects of Computer Science (STACS 2012). Leibniz International Proceedings in Informatics (LIPIcs), vol. 14, pp. 1–23 (2012)
13. Colcombet, T.: Unambiguity in automata theory. In: Shallit, J., Okhotin, A. (eds.) DCFS 2015. LNCS, vol. 9118, pp. 3–18. Springer, Cham (2015). doi:10.1007/978-3-319-19225-3_1
14. Courcelle, B.: Monadic second-order definable graph transductions: a survey. Theoret. Comput. Sci. **126**(1), 53–75 (1994)
15. Datar, M., Gionis, A., Indyk, P., Motwani, R.: Maintaining stream statistics over sliding windows. SIAM J. Comput. **31**(6), 1794–1813 (2002)
16. Droste, M., Kuich, W., Vogler, H. (eds.): Handbook of Weighted Automata. Springer, Heidelberg (2009)
17. Flajolet, P., Martin, G.N.: Probabilistic counting algorithms for data base applications. J. Comput. Syst. Sci. **31**(2), 182–209 (1985)
18. Greenwald, M., Khanna, S.: Quantiles and equidepth histograms over streams. In: Garofalakis, M., Gehrke, J., Rastogi, R. (eds.) Data Stream Management: Processing High-Speed Data Streams. Data-Centric Systems and Applications, pp. 45–86. Springer, Heidelberg (2016). doi:10.1007/978-3-540-28608-0_3
19. Hopcroft, J.E., Motwani, R., Ullman, J.D.: Introduction to Automata Theory, Languages, and Computation, 3rd edn. Pearson Education, Upper Saddle River (2006)
20. Lombardy, S., Sakarovitch, J.: Derivatives of rational expressions with multiplicity. Theoret. Comput. Sci. **332**(1), 141–177 (2005)
21. Mamouras, K., Raghothaman, M., Alur, R., Ives, Z.G., Khanna, S.: StreamQRE: modular specification and efficient evaluation of quantitative queries over streaming data. In: PLDI 2017 (2017, to appear)
22. Schützenberger, M.P.: On the definition of a family of automata. Inf. Control **4**(2), 245–270 (1961)

Improving the Timed Automata Approach to Biological Pathway Dynamics

Rom Langerak[⊠], Jaco van de Pol, Janine N. Post, and Stefano Schivo

University of Twente, Enschede, The Netherlands
r.langerak@utwente.nl

Abstract. Biological systems such as regulatory or gene networks can be seen as a particular type of distributed systems, and for this reason they can be modeled within the Timed Automata paradigm, which was developed in the computer science context. However, tools designed to model distributed systems often require a computer science background, making their use less attractive for biologists. ANIMO (Analysis of Networks with Interactive MOdeling) was built with the aim to provide biologists with access to the powerful modeling formalism of Timed Automata in a user friendly way. Continuous dynamics is handled by discrete approximations.

In this paper we introduce an improved modeling approach that allows us to considerably increase ANIMO's performances, opening the way for the analysis of bigger models. Moreover, this improvement makes the introduction of model checking in ANIMO a realistic feature, allowing for reduced computation times. The user interface of ANIMO allows to rapidly build non-trivial models and check them against properties formulated in a human-readable language, making modeling a powerful support for biological research.

1 Introduction

To understand the possible causes of a disease and design effective cures it is necessary to closely study the behavior exhibited by biological cells under particular conditions. A *signaling pathway* describes the chain of interactions occurring between the reception of a *signal* and the response with which the cell reacts to such signal. A signal is typically represented by a substance which can bind to specific receptors on the cell surface, activating them. *Active* molecules relay the signal inside the cell by activating other molecules until a target is reached. The target of a signaling pathway is usually a transcription factor, a molecule with the task of controlling the production of some protein. Such regulation is considered to be the response of the cell to the received signal.

The current knowledge on signaling pathways (mostly organized in databases such as KEGG [11] or PhosphoSite [10]) suggests that the interactions involved in a cellular response assume more often the shape of a network than that of a simple chain of signal relays. Such networks are typically highly connected, involving feedback loops and crosstalk between multiple pathways, making it

© Springer International Publishing AG 2017
L. Aceto et al. (Eds.): Larsen Festschrift, LNCS 10460, pp. 96–111, 2017.
DOI: 10.1007/978-3-319-63121-9_5

difficult to grasp their dynamic behavior. For this reason, computational support is required when studying non-trivial biological networks.

A number of software tools are available for modeling complex networks of biochemical interactions [3,8,9,14,24]. These tools significantly contribute to the process of formalizing the knowledge on biological processes, rendering them amenable to computational analysis. However, a lack of familiarity with the formalisms underlying many available tools hampers their direct application by biology experts. ANIMO (Analysis of Networks with Interactive Modeling, [2,18,19,22]) is a software tool based on the formalism of Timed Automata [1] that supports the modeling of biological signaling pathways by adding a dynamic component to traditional static representations of signaling networks. ANIMO allows to compare the behavior of a model with wet-lab data, and to explore such behavior in a user-friendly way. In order to achieve a good level of user-friendliness for a public of biologists, the complexity of Timed Automata is hidden *under the hood*, presenting ANIMO as an app for Cytoscape [12], a tool specifically developed for visualizing and elaborating biological networks. Additionally, a web interface for ANIMO has been developed [23], that allows to access the tool from any web browser without the need to install any software. Students in biology and bio-medical courses have been using ANIMO to learn about signaling networks, explain existing data and plan experiments. Thanks to the students' feedback the features of ANIMO have been constantly improving. Moreover, the tool is currently being applied in biological research to gain insight on cell differentiation. Models are built and managed by biologists independently, and provide a useful and visually appealing way to represent the key interactions under investigation.

Previously, ANIMO supported only interactive exploration of network dynamics based on simulation runs. Model checking queries could be answered through the UPPAAL tool [13], but the required knowledge of temporal logic together with the usually long response times slowed down the investigation process. In order to encourage the use of model checking on non-trivial models of signaling networks, we updated ANIMO with a new way of modeling reactions. This marks a relevant improvement in terms of performance with respect to the model previously used in ANIMO. Moreover, consistently with the intents of our tool, we implemented also a user interface for the definition of model checking queries in ANIMO. This allows a user to interrogate an ANIMO model without requiring previous experience in temporal logics. These new features are available in the latest version of ANIMO, which was recently reimplemented as a Cytoscape 3 app [4]: this lets users profit from the additional analysis features made available by the other apps in the Cytoscape environment.

The paper continues as follows. After introducing the basic concepts in Sect. 2, we illustrate in Sect. 3 a new way of using Timed Automata in ANIMO. In Sect. 4 we present a comparison between the new modeling approach and the one previously used in ANIMO, focusing on model analysis performances. In Sect. 5 we describe how model checking was made accessible to ANIMO users. We conclude the paper with Sect. 6, discussing future work.

2   Preliminaries

2.1   Signaling Pathways in Biology

A signaling pathway is an abstract representation of the reactions occurring inside a biological cell when, e.g., a signaling substance comes in contact with the cell surface receptors. In this setting, a reaction is the interaction between two components: the upstream enzyme (the molecule holding the active role in the reaction) and the downstream substrate (the passive molecule). The enzyme can be for example a kinase, which attaches a phosphate group to its substrate, performing a phosphorylation: this determines a change in the shape of the substrate and consequently a new function (Fig. 1). The new state reached by the substrate is often called *active*: if the substrate of the reaction is itself a kinase, it can then proceed in passing on the signal by activating its own target molecule, continuing a chain of reactions leading to the target of the signaling chain. Such target is usually a transcription factor, i.e. a molecule that influences the genetic response of the cell, for example promoting the production of a particular protein.

Pathways are traditionally represented in a nodes-edges form (see Fig. 1a), with nodes representing molecular species and edges standing for reactions, where → represents activation and ⊣ represents inhibition (i.e. inactivation).

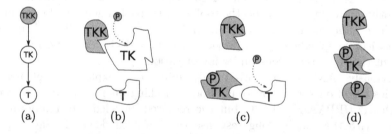

Fig. 1. A kinase signaling network represented in the nodes-edges form **(a)** and its evolution represented by abstract molecular interactions **(b–d)**. T is the target of the signaling pathway, TK is the kinase that activates T, and TKK is the kinase that activates TK. **(b)** An already active (yellow) TKK can bind to an inactive (empty) TK, catalyzing its phosphorylation (i.e. binding of a phosphate group, P). This causes a change in the shape of TK, activating its enzymatic function **(c)**. The active TK can in turn activate its target T, enabling it to carry out its function **(d)**. (Color figure online).

The current knowledge on signaling pathways [10,11] evidences the fact that signaling interactions are rarely a simple chain of activations as represented in Fig. 1a. More often, they assume the shape of a network with multiple feedback loops and crosstalk from different signaling sources. This complexity is an added difficulty for the study of such networks, reducing the possibilities to deduce the dynamic behavior of a signaling network by inspecting its static representation. For this reason, efficient computational support is essential when representing and analyzing the behavior of complex signaling networks.

2.2   Timed Automata

Timed Automata (TA) are finite-state automata enriched with real-valued clocks and synchronization channels. All clocks in a TA system advance with the same rate, and transitions between the locations of an automaton depend on conditions on clocks. In particular, a *guard* defines when a transition may be taken, while an *invariant* is the condition for permanence in a location. A transition can also allow two automata to *synchronize*, with each participant performing one of two complementary actions (*input* and *output*) on a synchronization channel. A set of clocks may also be reset by a transition, causing them to restart from 0.

The models we will present here were implemented using the software tool UPPAAL [13], which adds a number of features to the basic definition of TA. Some of these extensions include: support for integer variables in addition to clocks, broadcast synchronization channels (one sender, many receivers), definition of C-like functions to perform more operations besides clock resets. UPPAAL also allows for a special type of locations, named *committed* (marked with a C in the graphical representation). As long as an automaton is in a committed location, time is not allowed to flow. This feature can be used for example to perform immediate updates to local variables before letting the computation proceed. Examples of the listed features are found in the TA model in Sect. 3.2.

2.3   Activity-Based Models in ANIMO

ANIMO allows the definition of *activity-based* models. This means that we assume each signaling molecule in a cell to be at any time in one of two states: active or inactive. Active molecules can take an active role in reactions, changing the state of other molecules, activating inactive molecules or inhibiting (i.e. deactivating) active molecules. In a kinase-based signaling network an activation process can be a phosphorylation, and it is usually countered by the corresponding dephosphorylation. However, our models are not limited to kinase networks: other features like different post-translational modifications or gene promotion can be likewise represented, as long as their role has immediate effects on the ability of a target to perform its task.

As ANIMO is a Cytoscape app, models are defined through the Cytoscape user interface (see Fig. 2), where the user inserts a node for each molecular species and an edge for each reaction, with → indicating activation and ⊣ indicating inhibition similarly to traditional representations of signaling networks (Fig. 1a).

We consider a *molecular species* (also called *reactant*) to include all the molecules of the same substance in both their active and inactive state inside the cell. In order to distinguish between the two activity states in which each molecule can be, we define the *activity level* to represent the percentage of active molecules over an entire molecular species. In an ANIMO model, this value is discretized on a given integer interval. The user can choose the granularity for each molecular species separately, on a scale between 2 (the reactant is seen as either completely

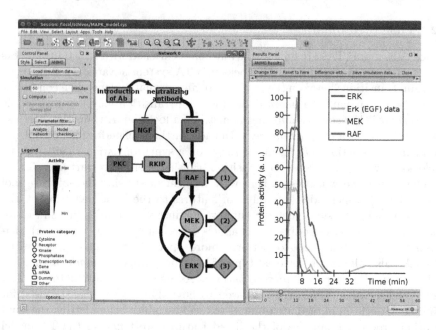

Fig. 2. The Cytoscape 3 user interface running the new ANIMO app (model from [19]). The *Network* panel in the center contains the nodes-edges model of the cross-talking signaling pathways of growth factors NGF and EGF, with colors indicating node activity levels and shapes representing different protein categories (see the *Legend* on the left). The *Results Panel* on the right contains a graph plotting activity levels of selected nodes during the first hour of evolution of the model. The slider under the graph allows the user to select the time instant (marked as a vertical red line in the graph) on which the colors of the nodes in the *Network* are based. The edge thickness is used to give an idea of the reactions' speed at the selected time instant. The series Erk (EGF) data in the graph is the experimental data from [16] for the 100 ng/ml EGF treatment. (Color figure online)

inactive or completely active) and 101 levels (allowing to represent activity as $0, 1\%, 2\% \ldots 100\%$). The activity level of a molecular species is represented in the ANIMO network by coloring the corresponding node according to the scale shown in the Activity legend in Fig. 2, where the minimum indicates that all molecules of the given species are inactive.

The occurrence of a *reaction* modifies by one discrete step the activity level of its target reactant, making it increase or decrease depending on whether the reaction is defined, respectively, as activating or inhibiting. The rate with which a reaction occurs depends on a formula selected by the user. Choosing one of three available scenarios allows the user to make the reaction rate depend on the activity of one or two reactants. The rate of each reaction can be scaled by modifying the value of one kinetic constant k, possibly using a qualitative measure from a predefined set (very slow, slow, medium, fast, very fast). The approximation allows us to reduce the dependence of a model from often unavailable quantitative parameters for biochemical reaction kinetics, while keeping a precision level that is still high enough to be useful. For a more precise explanation on how reaction rates are computed in ANIMO, we recommend [19], where the previously used TA model is presented. The reader interested in the current methods for parameter setting in ANIMO can refer to [17].

3   A New Way of Modeling Signaling Pathways with TA

We present here a novel model to represent signaling pathways with TA in ANIMO. We define the model previously used in ANIMO to be *reaction-centered*, as for each reaction in the network an instance of a TA template is generated to mimic the occurrences of that reaction. Observing that signaling networks tend to be highly connected, containing noticeably more reactions than reactants, we shift the focus on reactants instead, achieving what we call a *reactant-centered* model. This change of view is inspired by the classical way in which biological events are modeled with ordinary differential equations (ODEs) [5].

3.1   The Reactant-Centered Approach

The reactant-centered model presented here is based on the concept of *net effect* of a set of reactions on a reactant: instead of considering each reaction in isolation, we consider their combined influence on each reactant. As an example, consider a reactant A activated by reactions R_1 and R_2, and inhibited by reaction R_3 (see Fig. 3a). The net effect of these three reactions on A defines the *net reaction* $R_A = R_1 + R_2 - R_3$. Applying a concept similar to the definition of an ODE, where the rate of change of each reactant depends on the rate of the reactions influencing it, the rate of R_A is computed as the sum of the rates of the reactions influencing A:

$$r_A = r_1 + r_2 - r_3$$

where r_i is the rate of reaction R_i and is defined as follows. Consider R_1 to be the reaction $B \rightarrow A$ with kinetic constant k_1. Suppose the settings in the ANIMO network for R_1 make its rate depend only on the activity level of B. Then we compute the rate of R_1 as $r_1 = [B] \times k_1$, with $[B]$ the current activity level of B.

If r_A is positive, the activity level of A will increase; otherwise, A will decrease its activity level. The absolute value of r_A determines the speed with which such change happens. The value of the reaction rate is thus translated into a time value to be used as time bound in the TA representing R_A (see Fig. 3b) by computing

$$T_A = \frac{1}{\text{abs}(r_A)}$$

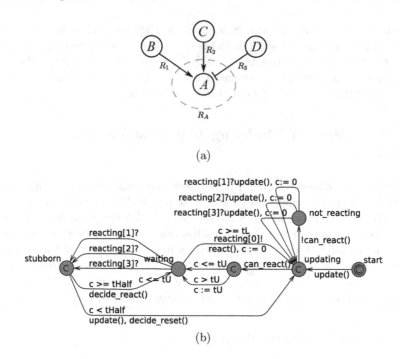

(a)

(b)

Fig. 3. (a) A signaling network where one node is influenced by three distinct reactions. The (virtual) reaction R_A is defined in the reactant-centered model as the algebraic sum of the reactions influencing A. **(b)** TA template generated by ANIMO for the reactant-centered model of the network in **(a)**. The template has been edited to increase readability. All the functions used in **(b)** are described in Sect. 3.2.

with $abs(r_A)$ the absolute value of r_A. In order to represent a natural uncertainty or variability in reaction timing, we relax the exact value of T_A by defining bounds of $\pm 5\%$ (which can be changed by the user):

$$\text{tL} = T_A \times 0.95 \qquad \text{tU} = T_A \times 1.05$$

Analogously to the reaction-centered model of [19], we will call tL the *lower time bound* and tU the *upper time bound*. So we replace an exact reaction time by an interval of possible reaction times, implicitly assuming a uniform distribution over this interval.

3.2   The New Timed Automata Model

The TA model we propose uses one TA template to represent each reactant: in Fig. 3b we show the automaton that models how the activity level of reactant A is changed by the (virtual) reaction R_A. Note that automata for B, C and D are not needed in our example, as no reactions influence them. We will now explain how the TA template for R_A works and how its discrete behavior approximates a continuous model.

The proposed TA template fulfils two main tasks:

- Perform the reaction, changing the activity level of the modelled reactant A
- Update the time bounds tL and tU in response to changes in the network.

The occurrence of the reaction is modelled with the central location waiting, where the automaton waits for the internal clock c to reach the time interval [tL, tU]; when the condition tL $\leq$ c $\leq$ tU is verified, the reaction can occur. This takes the automaton to location updating and simultaneously changes the activity level of A (react() in the transition). Together with all the remaining locations, updating is used to update the time bounds tL and tU to reflect the new state of the network and to determine how the reaction R_A will continue.

Note that all locations apart from waiting and not_reacting are declared as committed (C inside the location's circle): we use them to perform *instant* updates to the automaton and its variables. In UPPAAL, no clock advances as long as an automaton is in a committed location, and transitions exiting from committed locations have the precedence over other transitions.

Location updating: **Decide Whether** A **Can Change.** All transitions entering location updating call the function update() (a call to update() is performed inside react() before returning), which performs the computations described in Sect. 3.1 and thus determines the new values of r_A, tL and tU. At this point, one of the following conditions is true:

1. The newly computed reaction rate r_A is 0
2. A has reached its maximum activity level and $r_A > 0$
3. A has reached the activity level 0 and $r_A < 0$
4. The boundaries for A's activity level have not been reached and $r_A \neq 0$.

In the first three cases, the function can_react() will return false, meaning that the activity level of A cannot be updated further in the current conditions. This enables the transition to not_reacting, as the guard !can_react() is true.

In the case 4, the reaction R_A can still occur (can_react() evaluates to true), so the automaton returns to the waiting location to perform a new step of the reaction. The passage through the interposed committed location allows us to ensure that the invariant c $\leq$ tU of location waiting is always respected. In fact, it is possible that c has not been reset upon entering location updating (transition from stubborn, explained later on).

Channel reacting[]: **Adapt to Changes in the Environment.** When the reaction R_A occurs, A is updated to its new activity level (call to react() when exiting from waiting) and a synchronization is performed, using reacting[0]! to indicate that the activity level of A has changed. reacting[] is an array of broadcast channels, each one associated to a reactant in the network: in the example network, the channel with index 0 corresponds to A, 1 to B, and so on. The reception of a communication along one of those channels indicates that the corresponding reactant has changed its activity level. The automaton representing R_A can receive communications on the channels associated to the three reactants influencing A (see the transitions exiting from not_reacting and those entering stubborn). Note that in UPPAAL synchronizations along broadcast channels allow output (!) actions to be performed even if no receiver is present. However, whenever an automaton performs an output action, any other automaton currently in a location where the corresponding input (?) action is enabled will necessarily synchronize with the sender. In our example, this means that A is able to perform the output action reacting[0]! even if no other automaton is present in the network, and would be able to react to any changes in B, C or D if automata representing those reactants were added to the model.

Location stubborn: **Reduce the Approximation Error.** The transitions entering location stubborn after a synchronization on a reacting[] channel allow to respond to a change in the environment while R_A is occurring. In this event, one of the following conditions is true:

1. At least half of the current reaction step has been performed
2. Less than half of the current reaction step has been performed.

In case 1 ($c \geq$ tHalf $= \frac{T_A}{2}$, transition to waiting), the current reaction step will be completed immediately if the effect of the changes occurred in the reactants influencing A is *dramatic*. We define a change to be dramatic if it causes the new value of r_A to be at least twice the old value, or if it changes the direction of the reaction (r_A changes sign). The comparison between the possible values of r_A, together with the actions to immediately enable[1] R_A, are taken in the function decide_react(). From this behavior comes the name of location stubborn.

In case 2 ($c <$ tHalf, transition to updating), the new status of the system is immediately acknowledged (call to function update()) without performing the reaction first. Here, a decision is taken on whether to reset clock c, i.e. whether to throw away the "job already done" or not. Again, the decision depends on the change: a dramatic change causes clock c to be reset, while a non-dramatic change implies that the work will proceed at a slightly different speed instead of being restarted. This allows to avoid starvation for R_A in case of a series of changes with minor effects. Note that in some conditions we could have c > tU: this means that with the new configuration the reaction should already have occurred. Thanks to the committed location leading to location waiting we make sure that the reaction occurs as soon as possible without violating the invariant.

Locations not_reacting **and** start. While the automaton cannot perform any change to A's activity level, it waits in location not_reacting for changes in the reactants from which A depends. In the event of any such changes, location updating is reached to check on the feasibility of R_A.

Location start is used to perform the first step of the model, which is to initialize the parameters of the automaton.

3.3 Computations on the Fly

Reaction rates are all computed at run-time by the function update(), and are based on the user-chosen scenarios, their kinetic constant k and the activity level

---

[1]   In practice, we set tL = tU = c = 0.

of the involved reactants. As such computations require floating-point precision but UPPAAL only provides integer variables and operators, we use a significand-and-exponent notation with 4 significant figures, which allows for an error in the order of 0.1% while avoiding integer overflow in UPPAAL's engine. For example, the floating point number $a = 1.23456$ will be represented as the pair $\langle 1235, -3 \rangle$, which is translated back as $a = 1235 \times 10^{-3} = 1.235$. The interested reader can find the UPPAAL definitions and functions needed to compute rate and time values for the TA templates, together with all other functions such as update() and react(), inside any UPPAAL model file generated by ANIMO with a reactant-centered model type[2].

4   Reaction-Centered vs Reactant-Centered

We will now apply some basic model checking queries to the case study presented in [19], measuring the performances of the two modeling approaches. This will allow us to evaluate the benefit brought by the shift in perspective from a reaction- to a reactant-centered model.

All experiments were carried out on an Intel®Core™ i7 CPU at 2.80 GHz equipped with 12 Gb RAM and running Ubuntu GNU/Linux 16.04 64 bit. UPPAAL version 4.1.19 64 bit was used to compute the result of the queries, asking for "some trace" with random depth-first search order when an execution trace was expected to be produced. For the simulation queries using the statistical model checking engine, we left all options at their default values.

The case study we use as a testbed is the network model shown in the *Network* panel in Fig. 2, which represents signaling events downstream of growth factors EGF (epidermal growth factor) and NGF (nerve growth factor) in PC12 cells (a cell line used to study neuronal differentiation). The model topology proposed in [16] was analyzed with an ANIMO model based on the reaction-centered approach, reproducing the experimentally observed ERK (extracellular signal-regulated kinase) activity changes [19].[3] In particular, a 10 min stimulation with EGF resulted in transient behavior (i.e. peak-shaped, see also the graph in Fig. 2), while NGF stimulation led to sustained activity (data not shown).

4.1   Simulation Cost

We start by evaluating the cost of simulation with the two different models. This is a particularly important aspect to consider, as during the model building phase a user may need to perform a large number of simulations, continuously adapting the topology or quantitative parameters of a network model. In order to make the modeling approach in ANIMO as interactive as possible, it is desirable to decrease waiting times, and this translates into reducing the computational cost

---

[2] Models generated by ANIMO are saved in the system's temporary directory. Further details are available in the ANIMO manual at http://fmt.cs.utwente.nl/tools/animo/content/Manual.pdf.

[3] Model available at http://fmt.cs.utwente.nl/tools/animo/models.html.

of model analysis as much as possible. In this experiment, we query UPPAAL for simulation runs on the models generated by ANIMO applying the reaction- and reactant-centered modeling approaches to the case study. To define the initial state of the model, we consider the starting condition to be the treatment with 50 ng/ml NGF, which translates into setting the activity level of node NGF to 15/15, while changing EGF to be at 0/15 activity. This configuration was chosen as it generates a more interesting behavior from the biological point of view, also w.r.t. the model checking queries in Sect. 4.2; the treatment with 100 ng/ml EGF was also tested and gave similar performance results. Table 1 illustrates the computation time and memory usage when performing 100 simulation runs on each of the two considered models. Computing the simulation runs took about 91% less time with the reactant-centered model, using 97% less memory. This decrease in computation time for long simulation runs brings the approach nearer to the idea of interactive exploration of a network.

Table 1. UPPAAL processor time and memory usage for reaction- and reactant-centered modeling approaches when computing the query `simulate 100 [36000]` { R1, R2, ..., R11 } on the model from [19] with starting condition NGF = 15/15, EGF = 0/15, corresponding to a treatment with 50 ng/ml NGF. The query asks for 100 time series of the activity levels of all reactants in the model over the first 60 min of execution.

Model type	Time (s)	Memory (peak KB)
Reaction-centered	30.72	291 576
Reactant-centered	2.86	9 768

The scalability of the reactant-centered model was further tested performing 100 simulation runs on a much larger network, consisting of 93 nodes and 297 edges [20,21]. The network represents the main signaling and transcription events involved in osteoarthritis in human chondrocytes (cells involved in the production and maintainance of cartilage). In the test, we analyzed a particularly complex scenario, which models a possible path from healthy to osteoarthritic chondrocyte. Using the reactant-centered approach required 757.14 s of CPU time and 128 840 KBs of memory, while the analysis of the reaction-centered did not terminate after several hours.

4.2 Model Checking Performances

Next, we set out to test the model checking performances on the two versions of the TA model, comparing the execution times and memory requirements for a number of interesting queries:

– (1) and (2): A[] `not deadlock`. The model continues to execute indefinitely (A refers to all possible paths in the transition system of the model, and [] asks the property to always hold along a path).

- (3): RKIP < 10 $--->$ ERK >= 40. After RKIP (Raf kinase inhibitory protein) activity has been lowered, ERK activity increases. As in the model RKIP has 20 levels of granularity and ERK has 100 levels, RKIP < 10 means that RKIP is less than half active, and ERK >= 40 means that ERK activity is at least 40%.
- (4): E <> RKIP < 10. Find a point when RKIP is low (E asks for the existence of at least one path for which the property holds, while <> requires the property to hold at least once in a given path). This query is expected to generate a trace, the last point of which will be used as initial configuration for model checking queries (5) and (6).
- (5): A[]ERK < 70 and (6): A[]ERK > 35. Once RKIP activity has significantly decreased, ERK activity is sustained at an intermediate level.

The initial conditions are:

- (1): EGF = 15/15 and NGF = 0/15, all others as the original configuration, corresponding to the treatment condition with 100 ng/ml EGF.
- (2) – (4): EGF = 0/15, NGF = 15/15, all others as the original configuration, corresponding to the treatment condition with 50 ng/ml NGF[4].
- (5) and (6): all activities as in the last state of the trace computed from query (4).

We note that performing model checking means dealing with state space explosion problems, and model reduction is recommendable in order to obtain any result within adequate time limits. One of the most user-accessible ways available in ANIMO to reduce the size of a model is setting the "natural uncertainty" defined in Sect. 3.1 to 0 before performing model checking queries. In order to still consider some biological variability, the user can manually perform multiple model checking queries with changed interaction parameters. The tests performed in this section have an uncertainty level set to 0, instead of the 5% recommended for simulation-based experiments, to make model checking feasible within seconds.

The queries were used with both the reaction- and reactant-centered TA models, and returned the same results as expected: in particular, query (1) returned false and all other queries returned true. From the biological point of view, the answer to query (1) confirms that under EGF treatment no other activity is observed in the model after the initial peak, while query (2) confirms that with NGF activity continues indefinitely. Moreover, queries (3)–(6) confirm the result of the simulations shown in [19], with NGF treatment leading to sustained ERK activity.

The results of the model checking performance test are shown in Table 2.

---

[4] In the laboratory experimental setting, NGF is used at a lower concentration than EGF, but it is still enough to saturate all NGF receptors, which are rarer than EGF receptors.

Table 2. UPPAAL processor time and memory usage for reaction- and reactant-centered modeling approaches when computing the given queries on the case study from [19].

Query	Reaction-centered		Reactant-centered		Improvement	
	Computation time (s)	Memory usage (peak KB)	Computation time (s)	Memory usage (peak KB)	Time (n-fold)	Memory (n-fold)
(1)	126.56	523 448	1.04	9 236	122	57
(2)	159.29	436 496	1.73	11 480	92	38
(3)	146.09	439 484	1.04	10 384	140	42
(4)	0.74	293 508	0.06	7 484	12	39
(5)	581.79	448 764	6.86	16 880	85	27
(6)	561.01	449 248	6.42	15 852	87	28

4.3   Analysis of the Results

Requesting a full inspection of the state space as we do when using a query of the type $A[]\phi$ returning true in cases (5) and (6), allows us to indirectly compare the state space size of the two model versions. As the computation time improvements in Table 2 show, the reactant-centered model produces indeed a noticeably smaller state space, allowing for a higher level of interactivity also when performing non-trivial model checking. Moreover, our experiments point out that the reactant-centered approach considerably lowers the memory requirements for the model. This is not only due to the absence of possibly large precomputed time tables, which can contain thousands of elements each. Indeed, this point was further investigated by implementing a reaction-centered model which avoids the use of tables and instead makes on-the-fly computations of the time bounds with the same number representation as in the reactant-centered model. This resulted in improved performances in the cases of reachability and simulation-based queries, with memory requirements closer to the ones for the reactant-centered model (0.69 s and 24 796 KB for query (4)). However, in all other cases a much larger amount of memory (around 2 Gb) was used with respect to the table-based implementation of the same model, without leading to appreciable benefits in terms of execution time: in some cases performances were noticeably deteriorated (600–800 s for queries (1)–(3)). These findings seem to support the idea that reactant-centered models have a smaller state space.

5   Model Checking in ANIMO

In order to allow a non-expert user to profit from the power of model checking, we have implemented a template-based user interface to define queries directly inside the ANIMO Cytoscape App: Fig. 4 shows the interface for composing a model checking query in ANIMO. The mappings between user interface templates and actual model checking queries were inspired by the ones proposed in [15], and are shown in Table 3.

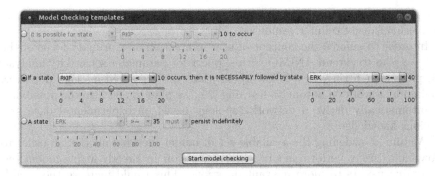

Fig. 4. The interface used in ANIMO to compose a model checking query. The settings on the three lines correspond, from top to bottom, to queries (4), (3) and (6).

Table 3. Mapping between queries as presented in ANIMO user interface and the corresponding model checking queries in UPPAAL syntax. State formulas indicated by ϕ and ψ are all in the form $R \bowtie n$, with R the identifier of a reactant in the model, $\bowtie \in \{<, \leq, =, \geq, >\}$ and $n \in [0, g(R)]$ a valid activity level value between 0 and the granularity (number of discrete levels) of R.

ANIMO template	UPPAAL formula
It is possible for state ϕ to occur	$E <> \phi$
State ϕ never occurs	$A[] \ !(\phi)$
If a state ϕ occurs, then it is necessarily followed by a state ψ	$\phi --> \psi$
A state ϕ can persist indefinitely	$E[] \ \phi$
A state ϕ must persist indefinitely	$A[] \ \phi$

If the answer to a model checking query contains a (counter-) example trace, the trace is automatically parsed by ANIMO and presented to the user in form of a graph of activity levels, in the same fashion as is normally done with simulation runs. Finally, a button positioned near the time slider under a simulation graph allows the user to easily change the initial activity levels of the whole network by setting them as in the currently selected time instant. This feature was used after executing query (4) to set the initial conditions for queries (5)–(6). Such an addition makes it easier to inspect the behavior of a network by using a sequence of model checking interrogations.

6 Conclusions and Future Work

We have presented here how the ANIMO tool was improved to provide a more interactive modeling process. Thanks to the increased performances of the new reactant-centered modeling approach, we are able to obtain answers to model checking queries in a matter of seconds. The features of model checking are made accessible without the need to directly deal with TA models. In this way, ANIMO acts as an intermediary between the biologist and a formal representation of biological signaling pathways, letting the experts concentrate on investigating the mechanisms of cellular responses.

In order to enforce the concept of user interaction as a primary focus of the tool, we plan to extend ANIMO with support for parameter sensitivity analysis and parameter fitting, as a follow-up to what was presented in [17]. Moreover, inspired by a work on automata learning [25], we plan to add also the possibility to automatically derive a network topology based on experimental data and previous knowledge.

We aim at widening the available set of model checking queries, in order to allow biologists to perform in silico experiments on an already fitting model and to obtain answers to more relevant questions. This would increase the usefulness of a model as a help to drive wet-lab investigation. In order to allow for meaningful in silico experiments, we plan to purposefully introduce user-defined non-deterministic parts in our models, which would allow for drug dosage investigations through model checking. This can be done e.g. through the definition of intervals for the values of some reaction kinetic constants, adding considerable uncertainty in the timing of those reactions. Interesting work has been done on statistical model checking using UPPAAL SMC on models created via ANIMO [7]. Finally, in order to further improve performances, the extension of ANIMO with support for a multi-core model checking approach based on the work by Dalsgaard et al. [6] is under study.

References

1. Alur, R., Dill, D.L.: A theory of timed automata. Theor. Comput. Sci. **126**, 183–235 (1994)
2. ANIMO. http://fmt.cs.utwente.nl/tools/animo
3. Ciocchetta, F., Hillston, J.: Bio-PEPA: a framework for the modelling and analysis of biological systems. Theor. Comput. Sci. **410**, 3065–3084 (2009)
4. Cytoscape 3 ANIMO app. http://apps.cytoscape.org/apps/animo
5. Daigle, B.J., Srinivasan, B.S., Flannick, J.A., Novak, A.F., Batzoglou, S.: Current progress in static and dynamic modeling of biological networks. In: Choi, S. (ed.) Systems Biology for Signaling Networks. Systems Biology, vol. 1, pp. 13–73. Springer, New York (2010)
6. Dalsgaard, A.E., Laarman, A., Larsen, K.G., Olesen, M.C., van de Pol, J.: Multicore reachability for timed automata. In: Jurdziński, M., Ničković, D. (eds.) FORMATS 2012. LNCS, vol. 7595, pp. 91–106. Springer, Heidelberg (2012). doi:10.1007/978-3-642-33365-1_8
7. David, A., Larsen, K.G., Legay, A., Mikučionis, M., Poulsen, D.B., Sedwards, S.: Statistical model checking for biological systems. Int. J. Softw. Tools Technol. Transfer **17**(3), 351–367 (2015)
8. de Jong, H., Geiselmann, J., Hernandez, C., Page, M.: Genetic network analyzer: qualitative simulation of genetic regulatory networks. Bioinformatics **19**(3), 336–344 (2003)
9. Dematté, L., Priami, C., Romanel, A.: Modelling and simulation of biological processes in BlenX. SIGMETRICS Perform. Eval. Rev. **35**, 32–39 (2008)
10. Hornbeck, P.V., Chabra, I., Kornhauser, J.M., Skrzypek, E., Zhang, B.: PhosphoSite: a bioinformatics resource dedicated to physiological protein phosphorylation. Proteomics **4**(6), 1551–1561 (2004)

11. Kanehisa, M., Goto, S.: KEGG: kyoto encyclopedia of genes and genomes. Nucleic Acids Res. **28**(1), 27–30 (2000)
12. Killcoyne, S., Carter, G.W., Smith, J., Boyle, J.: Cytoscape: a community-based framework for network modeling. Methods Mol. Biol. (Clifton, N.J.) **563**, 219–239 (2009)
13. Larsen, K.G., Pettersson, P., Yi, W.: UPPAAL in a Nutshell. Int. J. Softw. Tools Technol. Transf. (STTT) **1**, 134–152 (1997)
14. Mendes, P., Hoops, S., Sahle, S., Gauges, R., Dada, J., Kummer, U.: Computational modeling of biochemical networks using COPASI systems biology. vol. 500 of Methods in Molecular Biology, chapter 2, pp. 17–59. Humana Press, Totowa, NJ (2009)
15. Monteiro, P.T., Ropers, D., Mateescu, R., Freitas, A.T., de Jong, H.: Temporal logic patterns for querying dynamic models of cellular interaction networks. Bioinformatics **24**(16), i227–i233 (2008)
16. Santos, S.D.M., Verveer, P.J., Bastiaens, P.I.H.: Growth factor-induced MAPK network topology shapes Erk response determining PC-12 cell fate. Nat. Cell Biol. **9**(3), 324–330 (2007)
17. Schivo, S., Scholma, J., Karperien, H.B.J., Post, J.N., van de Pol, J.C., Langerak, R.: Setting parameters for biological models with ANIMO. In: André, E., Frehse, G. (ed) Proceedings 1st International Workshop on Synthesis of Continuous Parameters, Grenoble, France, vol. 145 of Electronic Proceedings in Theoretical Computer Science, pp. 35–47. Open Publishing Association, April 2014
18. Schivo, S., Scholma, J., van der Vet, P.E., Karperien, M., Post, J.N., van de Pol, J., Langerak, R.: Modelling with ANIMO: between fuzzy logic and differential equations. BMC Syst. Biol. **10**(1), 56 (2016)
19. Schivo, S., Scholma, J., Wanders, B., Urquidi Camacho, R.A., van der Vet, P., Karperien, M., Langerak, R., van de Pol, J., Post, J.: Modelling biological pathway dynamics with timed automata. IEEE J. Biomed. Health Inf. **18**(3), 832–839 (2013)
20. Scholma, J., Kerkhofs, J., Schivo, S., Langerak, R., van der Vet, P.E., Karperien, H.B.J., van de Pol, J.C., Geris, L., Post, J.N.: Mathematical modeling of signaling pathways in osteoarthritis. In: Lohmander, S. (ed.) 2013 Osteoarthritis Research Society International (OARSI) World Congress. Philadelphia, USA, vol. 21, Supplement, pp. S123–S123. Elsevier, Amsterdam (2013)
21. Scholma, J., Schivo, S., Kerkhofs, J., Langerak, R., Karperien, H.B.J., van de Pol, J.C., Geris, L., Post, J.N.: ECHO: the executable chondrocyte. In: Tissue Engineering & Regenerative Medicine International Society, European Chapter Meeting, Genova, Italy, vol. 8, pp. 54–54, Malden, June 2014 (Wiley)
22. Scholma, J., Schivo, S., Urquidi Camacho, R.A., van de Pol, J., Karperien, M., Post, J.: Biological networks 101: Computational modeling for molecular biologists. Gene **533**(1), 379–384 (2014)
23. Siers, W., Bakker, M., Rubbens, B., Haasjes, R., Brandt, J., Schivo, S.: webANIMO: Improving the accessibility of ANIMO [version 1; referees: 3 approved with reservations]. F1000Research, **5**(1714) (2016)
24. Tomita, M., Hashimoto, K., Takahashi, K., Shimizu, T.S., Matsuzaki, Y., Miyoshi, F., Saito, K., Tanida, S., Yugi, K., Venter, J.C., Hutchison III, C.A.: E-CELL: software environment for whole-cell simulation. Bioinformatics **15**(1), 72–84 (1999)
25. Tretmans, J.: Model-based testing and some steps towards test-based modelling. In: Bernardo, M., Issarny, V. (eds.) Formal Methods for Eternal Networked Software Systems. LNCS, vol. 6659, pp. 297–326. Springer, Heidelberg (2011)

Bicategories of Markov Processes

Florence Clerc, Harrison Humphrey, and Prakash Panangaden[✉]

School of Computer Science, McGill University, Montreal, Canada
prakash@cs.mcgill.ca

Abstract. We construct bicategories of Markov processes where the objects are input and output sets, the morphisms (one-cells) are Markov processes and the two-cells are simulations. This builds on the work of Baez, Fong and Pollard, who showed that a certain kind of finite-space continuous-time Markov chain (CTMC) can be viewed as morphisms in a category. This view allows a compositional description of their CTMCs. Our contribution is to develop a notion of simulation between processes and construct a bicategory where the two-cells are simulation morphisms. Our version is for processes that are essentially probabilistic transition systems with discrete time steps and which do not satisfy a detailed balance condition. We have also extended the theory to continuous space processes.

1 Introduction

A recent paper by Baez et al. [1] develops a compositional framework for Markov processes. More precisely, they work with finite-state processes with a population associated with each state. Transitions are governed by *rates* and are memoryless. Thus, they are working with continuous-time Markov chains (see *e.g.* [8]). The important innovation in their work is to define "open" Markov chains with inputs and outputs. This allows them to connect Markov chains together and build more complex ones from simpler ones.

Our work is inspired by their treatment but differs in two significant ways. First, we work with Markov processes viewed operationally. That is, the states represent states of a transition system and the system moves between states according to a probabilistic law: thus they are closer in spirit to probabilistic automata. We do not impose a detailed balance condition; it would not make any sense in the scenario we are examining. Importantly we allow continuous state spaces; which forces us into some measure-theoretic considerations. The crucial idea that we borrow from Baez et al. [1] is the use of *open* processes that can be composed. Though the details are different from [1] essentially the mathematics is inspired by their work and the work of Fong [3] on decorated cospans.

The second significant difference is the development of a bicategorical picture. The idea here is to have two-cells that capture *simulation*. The concepts of simulation and bisimulation have played a central role in the development of

© Springer International Publishing AG 2017
L. Aceto et al. (Eds.): Larsen Festschrift, LNCS 10460, pp. 112–124, 2017.
DOI: 10.1007/978-3-319-63121-9_6

process algebra [5,6,10] and the probabilistic version has been similarly important [4,9]. We have used simulation morphisms similar in spirit to those used by Desharnais et al. [2,9].

Dedication

It is a pleasure for the third author to dedicate this paper to Kim Larsen. Kim's fundamental work on probabilistic bisimulation nearly 30 years ago was a breakthrough and the inspiration for his own work [2] on the subject. Ever since then he has been infected with the probability bug and has maintained ties with Kim and his research group. This paper also deals with exactly those topics and we hope that Kim will accept this as a tribute to his remarkable career and achievements.

2 Discrete Markov Processes

We begin by developing the theory on finite state spaces so that we can postpone the measure theory issues until later. It is pleasing that the measure theory and the category theory can be more or less "factored" into separate sections.

Definition 1. *Given a finite set M, a Markov kernel on M is a map $\tau : M \times M \to [0,1]$ such that for all $m \in M$, $\tau(m,.)$ is a subprobability measure on M. A labelled Markov process on M is a collection (τ_a) of Markov kernels on M that is indexed by a set of actions Act.*

Markov processes are the standard model of memoryless probabilistic dynamical systems like a probabilistic program executing or particles moving over time subject to random influences. Let us fix a set of actions *Act* throughout this paper. These actions correspond to interactions between the process and the environment; for instance, a user performing control actions on a stochastic system.

Note that here we are only requiring subprobability measures. This is because it might be the case that the process does not terminate and some of the probability mass might be lost. We also want to have some cases where the transition probabilities are zero which subprobability distributions allow us to accommodate.

As in [1], we can view our labelled Markov processes as morphisms between input and output sets.

Definition 2. *Given two finite sets X, Y, a discrete labelled Markov process (DLMP) from X to Y is a tuple $(M, (\tau_a)_{a \in Act}, i, o)$ consisting of a finite set M, a labelled Markov process $(\tau_a)_{a \in Act}$ on M, and two injective morphisms $i : X \to M$ and $o : Y \to M$ called input and output.*
We also require that for $a \in Act$, $y \in Y$ and $m \in M$, $\tau_a(o(y), m) = 0$.

The last condition says that when the process reaches a state corresponding to the output it stops there. When we compose processes, these will become inputs to the next process and will be subject to a new dynamics. Note that a state can be input and output: this means that if the system is started in this state it will just stay there. We will also write $\tau_a(m, A)$, where $A \subseteq M$, to mean $\sum_{x \in A} \tau_a(m, x)$.

The key difference between the standard definition of finite labelled Markóv process and this definition of DLMP is the use of input and output sets that allows us to specify the state in which the system is at the start and the state when the experiment stops.

An outside observer is allowed to influence the system using the actions in *Act*, which result in a probabilistic response by the system; the response to performing the action a at state m is given by the final state (sub)distribution $\tau_a(m, \cdot)$. Particles flow through the Markov process, beginning at inputs, according to the kernels τ_a, until they reach an output state. When a system hits an output state it stops. Later we will describe how composed systems behave; essentially the output states become the input states of the next system.

Let us illustrate this definition using the example of a pinball machine. The position of the ball represents the state of the process. The ball is introduced when the player starts the game; this is the input state. The ball then moves around (this is the process) with the player using flippers (actions) to act on its trajectory. The game ends when the ball reaches the drain (output).

Note that the requirement on the Markov kernels is not symmetric between inputs and outputs. This is a direct consequence of the fact that input and output correspond respectively to start and end of observation or experiment. In that setting, a start state can lead to another start state whereas once the experiment is over, it cannot evolve anymore.

2.1   Viewing DLMPs as Morphisms

Viewing Markov processes as processes from inputs to outputs makes it tempting to construct a category **DLMP**. However, we will see that there is a problem with the composition being associative only up to isomorphism. The objects are finite sets and the morphisms $X \to Y$ are DLMPs from X to Y.

Let us first give an intuition for this composition: this corresponds to cascading the Markov processes one after the other by identifying states that were outputs in the first DLMP with inputs in the second DLMP. Consider three finite sets X, Y, Z and two DLMPs

$$\mathcal{M} := (M, (\tau_a^M)_{a \in Act}, i_M, o_M) : X \to Y$$

and

$$\mathcal{N} := (N, (\tau_a^N)_{a \in Act}, i_N, o_N) : Y \to Z$$

The category of finite sets and functions between them has pushouts. Let us denote $M +_Y N$ the pushout of M and N along i_N and o_M, and let j_N and j_M be the inclusion maps.

$$Y \xrightarrow{\ o_M\ } M$$

with vertical arrows i_N (left, $Y \to N$) and j_M (right, $M \to M +_Y N$), and

$$N \xrightarrow{\ j_N\ } M +_Y N$$

The pushout $M +_Y N$ can be expressed as $M +_Y N := (M \uplus N)/\sim$ where $\sim$ denotes the smallest equivalence relation on $M + N$ such that for all $y \in Y$, $j_M(o_M(y)) \sim j_N(i_N(y))$.

The composition of $\mathcal{M}$ and $\mathcal{N}$ denoted $\mathcal{N} * \mathcal{M}$ is the DLMP with input X and output Z defined as follows.

$$\mathcal{N} * \mathcal{M} := (M +_Y N, (\tau'_a)_{a \in Act}, j_M \circ i_M, j_N \circ o_N)$$

where, for $m, n \in M +_Y N$

$$\tau'_a(m,n) = \begin{cases} \tau^N_a(m,n) & \text{if } m, n \in j_N(N) \\ \tau^M_a(m,n) & \text{if } m, n \notin j_N(N) \text{ and } m, n \in j_M(M) \\ 0 & \text{otherwise} \end{cases}$$

Note that if m and n are both outputs of the first DLMP and inputs of the second one, we use τ^N.

The universal property of the pushout in **FinSet** ensures that composition is associative only up to isomorphism. This will be explained in more detail in the coming section; but note that it prevents us from constructing a category of DLMPs. Given any finite set X, the identity 1_X is the DLMP $(X, (\tau_a)_{a \in Act}, id_X, id_X)$, where for all $a \in Act$, and for all $x, y \in X$, $\tau_a(x,y) = 0$. Note that it is only an identity up to isomorphism.

2.2   Simulations as Morphisms Between DLMPs

Given two Markov processes with the same input and output sets, it is natural to ask whether they are related in some way or not. To this end, we first introduce the notion of simulation, and then show how it provides a natural framework for extending the previous construction to a bicategory.

Definition 3. *Given two DLMPs $\mathcal{N} = (N, (\tau^N_a)_{a \in Act}, i_N, o_N)$ and $\mathcal{M} = (M, (\tau^M_a)_{a \in Act}, i_M, o_M)$ defined with the same input and output sets, a simulation of $\mathcal{N}$ by $\mathcal{M}$ is a function $f : N \to M$ on the state spaces satisfying the following conditions:*

- *$f \circ i_N = i_M$ and $f \circ o_N = o_M$, and*
- *for all $a \in Act$, $n \in N$ and $m \in M$, $\tau^M_a(f(n), m) \geq \tau^N_a(n, f^{-1}(m))$.*

where $f^{-1}(m)$ stands for $f^{-1}(\{m\})$. In such a case, we say that $\mathcal{M}$ simulates $\mathcal{N}$ and write $f : \mathcal{N} \Rightarrow \mathcal{M}$.

Given two finite sets X and Y, we have the "hom-set" $\mathbf{DLMP}(X, Y)$ of the previously defined "category $\mathbf{DLMP}$." The quotation marks signify that we don't really have a category. However, it is possible to extend the set $\mathbf{DLMP}(X, Y)$ to a category with objects the DLMPs from X to Y and as morphisms simulations between such DLMPs in such a way that we obtain a bicategory. We carry this out in the next subsection.

The composition of two simulations with the same input and output sets is given by standard function composition; it is denoted $\circ$. The standard composition is associative which ensures that $\circ$ is also associative.

Proof. Let us now check that the composition of two simulations is a simulation. Consider two simulations $f : \mathcal{M}_1 \Rightarrow \mathcal{M}_2$ and $g : \mathcal{M}_2 \rightarrow \mathcal{M}_3$ with $\mathcal{M}_k = (M_k, (\tau_a^k)_{a \in Act}, i_k, o_k) : X \rightarrow Y$. Note that for any m in M_1 and n in M_3:

$$\tau_a^3(g \circ f(m), n) \geq \tau_a^2(f(m), g^{-1}(n)) \geq \tau_a^1(m, (g \circ f)^{-1}(n))$$

using the fact that g and f are both simulations. Finally note that $(g \circ f) \circ i_1 = g \circ i_2 = i_3$ and similarly for the output map. This proves that the composition of two simulations is a simulation.

Given a DLMP $\mathcal{M} = (M, (\tau_a^M)_{a \in Act}, i_M, o_M)$, the identity $\mathrm{id}_\mathcal{M}$ is the identity on the underlying set id_M. It is indeed an identity for the composition we have just defined.

2.3 The Bicategory DLMP

We had started with trying to construct a category $\mathbf{DLMP}$ with finite sets as objects and DLMPs as morphisms. We have constructed a categorical structure on the hom-set $\mathbf{DLMP}(X, Y)$ for all finite sets X, Y. It is natural to further extend it in order to make $\mathbf{DLMP}$ into a bicategory.

One of the things missing from our construction is a horizontal composition, namely for every triple of finite sets X, Y and Z a functor.

$$c_{XYZ} : \mathbf{DLMP}(Y, Z) \times \mathbf{DLMP}(X, Y) \rightarrow \mathbf{DLMP}(X, Z)$$

Given two DLMPs $\mathcal{M} : X \rightarrow Y$ and $\mathcal{N} : Y \rightarrow Z$, $c_{XYZ}(\mathcal{N}, \mathcal{M})$ is their composition $\mathcal{N} * \mathcal{M}$ defined in Sect. 2.1.

Let us now define the functor c_{XYZ} acting on the simulations. Let us consider four DLMPs (with $k = 1, 2$):

$$\mathcal{M}_k = (M_k, (\tau_a^{M,k})_{a \in Act}, i_{M,k}, o_{M,k}) : X \rightarrow Y$$

and

$$\mathcal{N}_k = (N_k, (\tau_a^{N,k})_{a \in Act}, i_{N,k}, o_{N,k}) : Y \rightarrow Z$$

as well as two simulations

$$f : \mathcal{M}_1 \Rightarrow \mathcal{M}_2 \quad \text{and} \quad g : \mathcal{N}_1 \Rightarrow \mathcal{N}_2$$

Let us denote $j_{N,k} : N_k \rightarrow M_k +_Y N_k$ and $j_{M,k} : M_k \rightarrow M_k +_Y N_k$ the pushout maps obtained by performing the horizontal composition $\mathcal{N}_k * \mathcal{M}_k$.

We are now ready to define their horizontal composition $c_{XYZ}(g,f) : \mathcal{N}_1 * \mathcal{M}_1 \Rightarrow \mathcal{N}_2 * \mathcal{M}_2$ as follows. For $m \in M_1 +_Y N_1$,

$$(g * f)(m) = \begin{cases} j_{N,2} \circ g(n') & \text{if } \exists n' \in N_1 \text{ such that } m = j_{N,1}(n') \\ j_{M,2} \circ f(m') & \text{if } \exists m' \in M_1 \text{ such that } m = j_{M,1}(m') \end{cases}$$

We denote $c_{XYZ}(g,f)$ by $g * f$.

Note that $g * f(m)$ is well defined.

Proof. Assume that there exists n' in N_1 and $m' \in M_1$ such that $m = j_{N,1}(n') = j_{M,1}(m')$. By definition of the pushout, there exists y in Y such that $m' = o_{M,1}(y)$ and $n' = i_{N_1}(y)$.

$$\begin{aligned} (j_{M,2} \circ f)(m') &= (j_{M,2} \circ f \circ o_{M,1})(y) \\ &= (j_{M,2} \circ o_{M,2})(y) \quad \text{as } f \text{ is a simulation} \\ &= (j_{N,2} \circ i_{N,2})(y) \quad \text{using the pushout} \\ &= (j_{N,2} \circ g \circ i_{N,1})(y) \quad \text{as } g \text{ is a simulation} \\ &= (j_{N,2} \circ g)(n') \end{aligned}$$

The case where there would be n_1 and n_2 in N_1 (resp. m_1 and m_2 in M_1) satisfying both the first (resp. second) condition is prevented by the injectivity of $i_{N,1}$ (resp. $o_{M,1}$).

Lemma 1. *The horizontal composition $g * f$ is a simulation.*

Proof. Diagrammatically, the situation is the following:

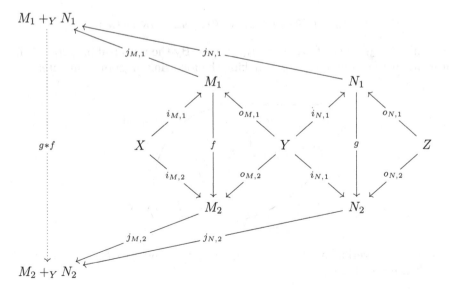

In order to prove that it is indeed a simulation, we have first to prove that $(g*f)\circ j_{M,1}\circ i_{M,1} = j_{M,2}\circ i_{M,2}$. Let x in X, note that $i_{M,1}(x) \in M_1$, therefore by definition of $g*f$, $(g*f)\circ j_{M,1}\circ i_{M,1}(x) = j_{M,2}\circ f(i_{M,1}(x))$. But f is a simulation, hence $f(i_{M,1}(x)) = i_{M,2}(x)$ proving the desired equality. The corresponding equality with output maps is proven similarly.

Let us denote $(\tau_a^k)_{a\in Act}$ the Markov process corresponding to the composition $\mathcal{N}_k * \mathcal{M}_k$. There remains to prove that for all $a \in Act$, $m_1 \in M_1 +_Y N_1$ and $m_2 \in M_2 +_Y N_2$, $\tau_a^2((g*f)(m_1), m_2) \geq \tau_a^1(m_1, (g*f)^{-1}(m_2))$. There are many cases that correspond to the different cases for $g*f$, τ_a^1 and τ_a^2. The proof is straightforward but tedious.

Lemma 2. *The exchange law holds. Namely, let* $\mathcal{M}_k, \mathcal{N}_k$ *with* $k = 1,2,3$ *be DLMPs with* $\mathcal{M}_k : X \to Y$ *and* $\mathcal{N}_k : Y \to Z$ *and let us consider simulations* $f_1 : \mathcal{M}_1 \Rightarrow \mathcal{M}_2$, $f_2 : \mathcal{M}_2 \Rightarrow \mathcal{M}_3$, $g_1 : \mathcal{N}_1 \Rightarrow \mathcal{N}_2$ *and* $g_2 : \mathcal{N}_2 \Rightarrow \mathcal{N}_3$ *corresponding to*

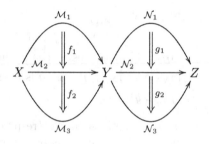

then $(g_2 \circ g_1) * (f_2 \circ f_1) = (g_2 * f_2) \circ (g_1 * f_1)$.

Proof. Let us denote as usual $j_{M,k} : M_k \to M_k +_Y N_k$ and $j_{N,k} : N_k \to M_k +_Y N_k$ for $k = 1,2,3$ the corresponding pushout maps. As g_1 and g_2 are simulations, we know that

$$j_{N,3} \circ g_2 \circ g_1 \circ i_{N,1} = j_{N,3} \circ g_2 \circ i_{N,2} = j_{N,3} \circ i_{N,3}$$

and similarly $j_{M,3} \circ f_2 \circ f_1 \circ o_{M,1} = j_{M,3} \circ o_{M,3}$. By the universal property of the pushout, there is a unique map h making the following diagram commute:

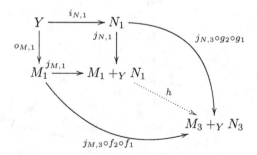

It can be easily verified that both $(g_2 \circ g_1) * (f_2 \circ f_1)$ and $(g_2 * f_2) \circ (g_1 * f_1)$ work for h, hence they are equal.

Lemma 3. *The horizontal composition is associative up to isomorphisms, i.e. for any finite sets X, Y, Z and W, we have natural isomorphisms called the associators.*

$$\alpha_{WXYZ} : c_{WYZ} \circ (id, c_{WXY}) \to c_{WXZ} \circ (c_{XYZ}, id)$$

Proof. Let us consider three DLMPs $\mathcal{M} = (M, (\tau_a^M), i_M, o_M) : W \to X$, $\mathcal{N} = (N, (\tau_a^N), i_N, o_N) : X \to Y$ and $\mathcal{P} = (P, (\tau_a^P), i_P, o_P) : Y \to Z$. Let us construct the associator $\alpha_{\mathcal{MNP}} : \mathcal{P} * (\mathcal{N} * \mathcal{M}) \Rightarrow (\mathcal{P} * \mathcal{N}) * \mathcal{M}$, i.e. a simulation map.

$$\alpha_{\mathcal{MNP}} : (M +_X N) +_Y P \to M +_X (N +_Y P)$$

We will denote the pushout maps $j_M^{M+_Y N} : M \to M +_Y N$ etc.

First note that $X \xrightarrow{i_N} N \xrightarrow{j_N^{N+_Y P}} N +_Y P$ is the input map of the DLMP $\mathcal{N} * \mathcal{P}$, making the outer diagram commute:

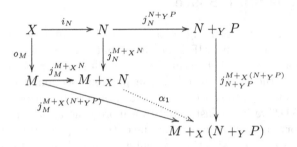

By the universal property of the pushout $M +_X (N +_Y P)$, there exists a unique map $\alpha_1 : M +_X N \to M +_X (N +_Y P)$ making the above diagram commute.

To show that the outer diagram commutes, we calculate as follows:

$$\alpha_1 \circ j_N^{M+_Y N} \circ o_N = j_{N+_Y P}^{M+_X(N+_Y P)} \circ j_N^{N+_Y P} \circ o_N \quad \text{using the definition of } \alpha_1$$

$$= j_{N+_Y P}^{M+_X(N+_Y P)} \circ j_P^{N+_Y P} \circ i_P \quad \text{using the pushout square of } N +_Y P$$

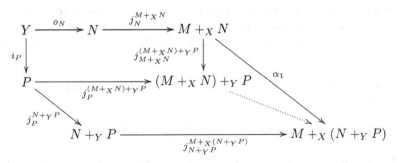

By universal property of the pushout $(M +_X N) +_Y P$, there exists a unique map $(M +_X N) +_Y P \to M +_X (N +_Y P)$ making this diagram commute. We call this map $\alpha_{\mathcal{MNP}}$. Note that we could have constructed the associator from the explicit definition of the pushout given in Sect. 2.1.

Naturality and isomorphism of the associator follow from similar constructions and the fact that all pushout maps are injective as the input and output maps are injective.

Remember that we had defined identity DLMP $1_X = (X, (0)_{a \in Act}, id_X, id_X)$. Similar constructions using pushouts give us two natural isomorphisms corresponding to the unitors: for all $\mathcal{M} : X \to Y$ a DLMP, we have

$$\lambda_{\mathcal{M}} : \mathcal{M} * 1_X \to \mathcal{M} \quad \text{and} \quad \rho_{\mathcal{M}} : \mathcal{M} \to 1_Y * \mathcal{M}$$

Pentagon identities and triangle identities are proven using similar computations. This proves the following result: the main goal of this section.

Theorem 4. DLMP *is a bicategory.*

3 Continuous State Space

While the finite case is interesting to start with, in many cases of interest the underlying state space of an LMP is not finite but an arbitrary measurable set or perhaps a more restricted structure like a Polish space or an analytic space. However, most of the work we did in the previous section does not rely on LMPs having a finite state space and it becomes very tempting to extend the bicategory **DLMP** we just constructed to a more general notion of LMP. It is not as straightforward as it may seem as the output map is more complicated in the continuous case. The restriction to analytic spaces is important for proving the logical characterization of bisimulation or simulation. Since we are not doing that here we will consider general measurable spaces.

3.1 LMP and Simulation in the Continuous Case

Definition 5. *Given a measurable space (M, Σ) a Markov kernel is a function $\tau : M \times \Sigma \to [0, 1]$ where for each $m \in M$ the function $\tau(m, \cdot)$ is a subprobability measure on (M, Σ) and for each measurable set $B \in \Sigma$ the function $\tau(\cdot, B) :$ $M \to [0, 1]$ is measurable where $[0, 1]$ is equipped with the standard Borel-algebra. A labelled Markov process is a collection (τ_a) of Markov kernels on (M, Σ) that is indexed by a set of actions Act.*

Let us now extend our previous definition of DLMPs to deal with the continuous case.

Definition 6. *Given two finite sets X and Y, a continuous labelled Markov process (CLMP) from X to Y is a tuple $(M, \Sigma, (\tau_a)_{a \in Act}, i, o)$ consisting of (M, Σ) a measurable space, a labelled Markov Process $(\tau_a)_{a \in Act}$, an injective function $i : X \to M$ and a function $o : Y \to \Sigma$ such that for all y_1 and y_2 in Y $o(y_1) \cap o(y_2) = \emptyset$, satisfying the following additional condition for all $a \in A$:*

$$\text{for all } y \in Y, \ m \in o(y) \text{ and } B \in \Sigma \quad \tau_a(m, B) = 0$$

Note that here we have an input point but a (measurable) output *set*. To avoid painfully long notations, we will also write $o(Y)$ for the set $\bigcup_{y \in Y} o(y) \in \Sigma$.

We now adapt the definition of simulation to this setting.

Definition 7. *Given two CLMPs* $\mathcal{N} = (N, \Lambda, (\tau_a^N)_{a \in Act}, i_N, o_N)$ *and* $\mathcal{M} = (M, \Sigma, (\tau_a^M)_{a \in Act}, i_M, o_M)$ *defined with the same input and output sets, a simulation of* $\mathcal{N}$ *by* $\mathcal{M}$ *is a measurable function* $f : N \to M$ *on the state spaces satisfying the following conditions:*

- $f \circ i_N = i_M$ *and* $o_N = f^{-1} \circ o_M$, *and*
- *for all* $a \in Act$, $n \in N$ *and* $B \in \Sigma$, $\tau_a^M(f(n), B) \geq \tau_a^N(n, f^{-1}(B))$.

In such a case, we say that $\mathcal{M}$ *simulates* $\mathcal{N}$ *and write* $f : \mathcal{N} \Rightarrow \mathcal{M}$.

3.2 The Bicategory CLMP

We now extend what was done in the finite case to the continuous case in order to construct the bicategory **CLMP**.

Given two finite sets X, Y, there is a category **CLMP**(X, Y) which has as objects the CLMPs $X \to Y$ and as morphisms the simulations between them. Composition is given by the standard composition on their underlying sets and the identities are the standard identities on the underlying state spaces.

The next order of business is to define the horizontal composition both on the CLMPs and the simulations. Let us start with the CLMPs.

Given three finite sets X, Y and Z and two CLMPs $\mathcal{M} = (M, \Sigma, i_M, o_M, \tau^M)$: $X \to Y$ and $\mathcal{N} = (N, \Lambda, i_N, o_N, \tau^N)$: $Y \to Z$, there are two inclusion maps $j_N : N \to M + N$ and $j_M : M \to M + N$. We then define the relation $\sim$ on $M + N$ as the smallest equivalence such that

$$\forall y \in Y \; \forall m \in o_M(y) \; j_M(m) \sim j_N(i_N(y))$$

We then define the quotient map q between measurable spaces $q : (M + N, \Sigma + \Lambda) \to ((M + N)/ \sim, (\Sigma + \Lambda)/ \sim)$ where $(\Sigma + \Lambda)/ \sim$ is the smallest σ-algebra such that q is measurable.

Note that here we are mimicking the explicit construction of the pushout given in the finite case. We will therefore also denote $(N + M)/ \sim$ as $N +_Y M$ and $(\Sigma + \Lambda)/ \sim$ as $\Sigma +_Y \Lambda$. We define the horizontal composition of $\mathcal{M}$ and $\mathcal{N}$ as:

$$\mathcal{N} * \mathcal{M} = (M +_Y N, \Sigma +_Y \Lambda, q \circ j_M \circ i_M, q \circ j_N \circ o_N, \tau')$$

where the LMP is defined for $m \in M +_Y N$ and $B \in \Sigma +_Y \Lambda$ as

$$\tau_a'(m, B) = \begin{cases} \tau_a^M(m', j_M^{-1}q^{-1}(B)) \text{ if } \exists m' \in M \setminus o_M(Y) \; m = q \circ j_M(m') \\ \tau_a^N(n', j_N^{-1}q^{-1}(B)) \text{ if } \exists n' \in N \; m = q \circ j_M(n') \\ 0 \text{ otherwise} \end{cases}$$

Note here how the condition on the input and output maps is used: remember that the input map is injective and that the output maps gives sets that are pairwise disjoint. This ensures that if $m_1 \sim m_2$ with m_1 and m_2 in M then there exists y in Y such that m_1 and m_2 are in $o_M(y)$ and if $n_1 \sim n_2$ with n_1 and n_2 in N then $n_1 = n_2$. This guarantees that τ'_a is well-defined.

The identity is the same as the one we have defined in the discrete case: let X be a finite set and let Σ be the discrete σ-algebra on X, then the identity is

$$1_X = (X, \Sigma, (\tau_a), \mathrm{id}_X, o_X)$$

where $\tau_a(x, B) = 0$ for all $x \in X$ and $B \in \Sigma$ and $o_X(x) = \{x\}$.

For every triple of finite sets X, Y and Z, we define the horizontal composition on the simulations. Consider $f : \mathcal{M}_1 \Rightarrow \mathcal{M}_2 : X \to Y$ and $g : \mathcal{N}_1 \Rightarrow \mathcal{N}_2 : Y \to Z$ where $\mathcal{M}_k = (M_k, \Sigma_k, \tau^{M,k}, i_{M,k}, o_{M,k})$ and $\mathcal{N}_k = (N_k, \Lambda_k, \tau^{N_k}, i_{N,k}, o_{N,k})$ ($k = 1, 2$). We use similar notations as for the composition of CLMPs but index them by 1 or 2 (see following diagram).

We define their horizontal composition as

$$g * f : M_1 +_Y N_1 \to M_2 +_Y N_2$$

$$n \mapsto q_2 \circ j_N^2 \circ g(n') \text{ if } \exists n' \in N_1 \; n = q_1 \circ j_N^1(n')$$

$$m \mapsto q_2 \circ j_M^2 \circ f(m') \text{ if } \exists m' \in M_1 \; m = q_1 \circ j_M^1(m')$$

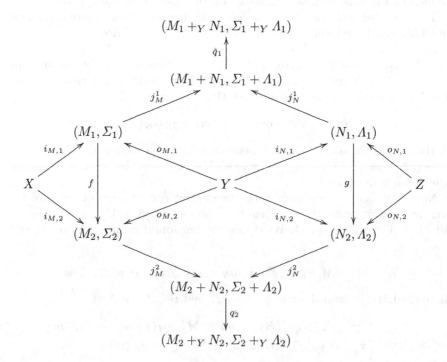

This is again mimicking what happens in the finite case. Note that the remark used previously to show that the horizontal composition of DLMPs is well-defined is used here to prove that the horizontal composition of the CLMPs is well-defined. The proofs with the associators and the unitors are similar to the finite case except that they rely on the universal property of the quotient instead of the universal property of the pushout.

We can now state the main result of this paper.

Theorem 8. CLMP *is a bicategory.*

4   Conclusions

We have developed a notion of bicategory of Markov processes where the two-cells capture the notion of simulation. The original paper of Baez, Fong and Pollard developed a compositional theory of a certain class of CTMCs. We have developed an analogous theory for Markov processes in both discrete and continuous state-space versions. By adding the two-cells we have incorporated one of the most powerful and widely used tools for reasoning about the behaviour of Markov processes and this opens the way for compositional reasoning.

Of course, this paper is just a start. There are many interesting directions to explore. Perhaps the most pressing is to understand how feedback can be incorporated via a trace structure. Certain categories of probabilistic relations do have a traced monoidal structure; it remains to be seen how to incorporate that here in a manner consistent with the two-cell structure. We are also working on using more general coalgebras as the morphisms instead of just Markov processes.

In earlier work [9] logical formalisms (modal logics) for reasoning about bisimulation have been developed. Here we have the framework where one can think about compositional logical reasoning. In a paper about a decade ago Mislove et al. [7] have studied duality for Markov processes (our CLMPs) and also developed a notion of composing Markov processes. We have not yet worked out the relations between that framework and ours but clearly it is an interesting topic to be examined.

Acknowledgements. We are very grateful to Brendan Fong for helpful discussions. We thank the reviewers for their detailed comments and feedback. This research has been supported by a research grant from NSERC.

References

1. Baez, J.C., Fong, B., Pollard, B.S.: A compositional framework for Markov processes, September 2015. arXiv:1508.06448
2. Desharnais, J., Edalat, A., Panangaden, P.: Bisimulation for labeled Markov processes. Inf. Comput. **179**(2), 163–193 (2002)
3. Fong, B.: Decorated cospans. Theory Appl. Categ. **30**, 1096–1120 (2015)
4. Larsen, K.G., Skou, A.: Bisimulation through probablistic testing. Inf. Comput. **94**, 1–28 (1991)
5. Milner, R. (ed.): A Calculus of Communicating Systems. LNCS, vol. 92. Springer, Heidelberg (1980)
6. Milner, R.: Communication and Concurrency. Prentice-Hall, Upper Saddle River (1989)

7. Mislove, M., Ouaknine, J., Pavlovic, D., Worrell, J.: Duality for labelled Markov processes. In: Walukiewicz, I. (ed.) FoSSaCS 2004. LNCS, vol. 2987, pp. 393–407. Springer, Heidelberg (2004). doi:10.1007/978-3-540-24727-2_28
8. Norris, J.R.: Markov Chains. Cambridge Series in Statistical and Probabilistic Mathematics. Cambridge University Press, Cambridge (1997)
9. Panangaden, P.: Labelled Markov Processes. Imperial College Press, London (2009)
10. Park, D.: Concurrency and automata on infinite sequences. In: Deussen, P. (ed.) GI-TCS 1981. LNCS, vol. 104, pp. 167–183. Springer, Heidelberg (1981). doi:10.1007/BFb0017309

Property-Preserving Parallel Decomposition

Bernhard Steffen[(✉)] and Marc Jasper

TU Dortmund University, 44221 Dortmund, Germany
{steffen,marc.jasper}@cs.tu-dortmund.de

Abstract. We propose a systematic approach to generate highly parallel benchmark systems with guaranteed temporal properties. Key to our approach is the iterative property-preserving parallel decomposition of an initial Modal Transition System, which is based on lightweight assumption commitment. Property preservation is guaranteed on the basis of *Modal Contracts* that permit a refinement into a component and its context while supporting the chaining of dependencies that are vital for the validity of considered properties. We illustrate our approach, which can be regarded as a simplicity-oriented variant of correctness by construction, by means of an accompanying example.

1 Introduction

Today's software verification and analysis tools are increasingly complex and often comprise diverse technologies like SMT solving, data and process mining, statistical methods or even runtime analysis. This hybrid tool structure makes traditional verification of verification tools almost intractable and asks for alternative validation support. Bottleneck of experimental evaluation approaches, in particular for analysis and verification tools for distributed systems, is the shortage of adequate benchmark problems [22,23] which are of challenging size and structure, and guaranteed to exhibit/violate interesting (temporal) properties. 'Realistic' benchmark systems come with the risk that it is unknown whether the considered property holds [22]. In such cases, the presumed solution is often chosen by some kind of majority vote which is, of course, no guarantee for correctness. On the other hand, manual benchmark design typically does not scale and therefore does not provide truly challenging verification scenarios. Work on the systematic construction of benchmark systems, like [12,19,38], is still very limited for distributed systems.

In this paper, we systematically enhance the approach sketched in [12] by proposing an incremental process to expand a given benchmark scenario $B(M, \Phi)$ that consists of a Modal Transition System (MTS) [29] specification M for some concurrent implementation of controllable size[1] together with a set of properties

---

[1] What we mean here is that M can be conveniently model checked with state-of-the-art technology.

© Springer International Publishing AG 2017
L. Aceto et al. (Eds.): Larsen Festschrift, LNCS 10460, pp. 125–145, 2017.
DOI: 10.1007/978-3-319-63121-9_7

Φ that is guaranteed to be correct for M^2. This expansion results in a system with an arbitrary degree of parallelism, where all parallel components need to be considered for validation.

Key to our approach is the property-preserving parallel decomposition in a light-weight assumption commitment style. Property preservation is guaranteed on the basis of *Modal Contracts* (MCs) that permit a (weak) refinement into a component and its context while supporting the propagation of dependencies that are vital for the validity of considered properties. More technically, our development is based on the weak refinement [20] of convergent systems which preserves an interesting class of temporal properties. In the following, we will not discuss sufficient conditions for this kind of preservation, but simply assume that properties are preserved by weak refinement of convergent systems, be they branching time, linear time, safety or liveness properties.

Even though we eventually aim at parallel compositions of Labeled Transition Systems (LTSs) for our benchmark problems, we will mainly focus on MTSs in the following, as the missing part is just a straightforward (randomized) refinement process (see Fig. 1).

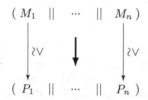

Fig. 1. Obtaining a parallel composition of LTSs $(P_1 \mid\mid ... \mid\mid P_n)$ by refinement.

We present our approach in two parts, one explaining our MC-based parallel decomposition and the other concerning a subsequent alphabet expansion which is in particular required for scalability.

Figure 2 sketches the first part that consists of two phases. It starts with an existing benchmark scenario $B(M, \Phi)$. In this figure, M_s and M_c are the result of the decomposition on the basis of an MC I. $\mathcal{U}_\Sigma$ is an MTS that semantically reflects the effect of abstracting from structure imposed by the corresponding component with its alphabet Σ (cf. Definition 5).

Part two of our presentation concerns how the first part can be enhanced to achieve scalability and to guarantee a certain hardness of the constructed benchmark problems. This is realized by allowing each of the indicated decomposition steps to be enhanced by alphabet expansion as described in Sect. 7.

---

[2] Our exposition focuses on the preservation of validity. It should be noted that our MTS-based approach also maintains the existence of counterexamples, which is something different for linear time temporal formulas.

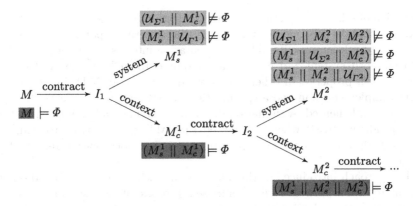

Fig. 2. Our iterative destroy and repair process. (Parallel compositions below the flow-chart are colored green, those above red.) (Color figure online)

Characteristic of our overall approach is a repetitive destroy (M_s does no longer satisfy the envisioned property) and repair (parallel composition with M_c reinforces the validity of the envisioned property) pattern which essentially works as follows[3]:

Phase I: Starting with $B(M, \Phi)$ a contract in terms of an MC I is constructed from M by

- choosing a sub-alphabet Γ of M's alphabet Σ,
- marking must transitions with labels from Γ by coloring them green, and
- (randomly) adding red transitions with labels from Γ in a way that they do not conflict with existing may transitions.

The intuition here is that the to be constructed context component M_c must guarantee to provide communication partners for green transitions, while it has to make sure that red transitions will never find a communication partner.

Phase II: Decomposing I into a system component M_s that will be maintained in the following and a context component M_c which may be further decomposed. Important here is that both components are vital for the validity of Φ: Neither M_s nor M_c alone suffice to guarantee Φ, but their parallel composition does.

This way, our approach harnesses the power of correctness by construction [24] where the essential dependencies are designed and therefore known during the iterative decomposition process. Revealing them afterwards during a-posteriori verification is a very different challenge, similar in flavor to the difference between proof checking and proof construction.

In the last almost three decades, variants and applications of MTSs have been proposed to serve as light-weight versions of temporal specifications [7,34], primarily with the goal of establishing a specification/implementation relation

---

[3] The following sketch omits some details which are however elaborated on in the corresponding sections of this paper.

via a notion of refinement [4, 10, 25–28, 31, 41]. In this paper, we specifically follow the idea of context dependency: Given a certain (internally parallel) process, we express how to decompose its MTS representation into a system and its context such that both system and context are required to make the overall system satisfy a given property. In other words, we decompose an MTS by generating a partial implementation and a specification of external commitments that still need to be implemented. A similar question was systematically analyzed by Kim Larsen et al. in [21, 31] where he showed that MTSs, in contrast to temporal logics [3, 9, 30], are not enough to provide a complete specification relative to a context.

The approach introduced in this paper is somewhat dual. It is based on the following question: How can we decompose a process into a system and its context such that the behavior of the corresponding parallel composition which is relevant to the considered properties depends on both components? Moreover, as our goal is only to construct valid benchmarks, completeness of the arising specifications is not an issue. For our goal, it is sufficient to iteratively establish dependencies between components and their contexts without which the benchmark verification problem cannot be solved. In other words, we construct benchmark scenarios that feature highly parallel systems whose corresponding verification problem cannot be solved without considering all parallel components.

Our MC, an extension of MTSs following and generalizing the ideas of [8], is specifically designed to manage the system/context relationship in a way so that the system can be iteratively decomposed into arbitrarily many parallel components while propagating dependencies throughout the entire system.

An MC is a contract according to the definition in [5]. Even though MCs induce a related refinement, they do, however, not implement the meta-theory proposed in [5] because similar to regular MTS refinement, a greatest lower bound of two specifications typically does not exist.

In contrast to classical assumption commitment [1, 16, 35] and approaches like the ones presented in [14, 15], the iterative decomposition based on MCs scales very well. However, admittedly, to achieve a different kind of goal because we do not require completeness and can therefore focus on a simplistic approach [32]. This scalability, which intuitively exists due to the difference between a-posteriori verification and correctness by construction, can be regarded as the essence of our benchmark generation approach [12, 19, 38].

After introducing relevant preliminaries in Sect. 2, Sect. 3 presents our notion of parallel composition that requires synchronization whenever the alphabets of components overlap, and Sect. 4 our notion of a parallel verification benchmark scenario. Subsequently, Sect. 5 introduces our notion of Modal Contracts, the basis for our corresponding decomposition process, before the construction of an adequate context MTS M_c is described in Sect. 6. Finally, Sect. 7 sketches how the decomposition described in Sect. 5 can be enhanced to guarantee scalability as well as a notion of benchmark hardness, before Sect. 8 concludes this paper and presents some directions to future work.

2   Preliminaries

The Modal Contracts (MCs) proposed in this paper are an extension of Modal Transition Systems (MTSs). This section introduces fundamental definitions that are important for understanding the remainder of this paper. We assume that the reader is familiar with regular languages and related automata. Knowledge of linear temporal logic (LTL) and (action-based) computational tree logic (CTL) might help to better understand Example 2.

Definition 1 (Modal Transition Systems). *Let S be a set of states and Σ an alphabet of action symbols. $M = (S, s_0, \Sigma, \diamond, \Box)$ is called a **(rooted) Modal Transition System (MTS)** with root s_0 if the following condition holds:*

$$\Box \subseteq \diamond \subseteq (S \times \Sigma \times S)$$

Elements of $\diamond$ are called may transitions, those of $\Box$ must transitions. We sometimes call the set $(\diamond \setminus \Box)$ may-only transitions. Throughout this paper, the domain of all possible MTSs is referred to as $\mathcal{M}$.

We further define the following operators:

$$states(M) =_{def} S$$
$$alph(M) =_{def} \Sigma$$
$$may(M) =_{def} \diamond$$
$$must(M) =_{def} \Box$$

For any $t = (p, \sigma, q) \in \diamond$, we call $sym(t) =_{def} \sigma$ the symbol or label of t. Operator $sym(\cdot)$ extends naturally to transition relations, $sym(T) =_{def} \bigcup_{t \in T}(\{sym(t)\})$ for any $T \subseteq (S \times \Sigma \times S)$.

An MTS can be seen as an extension of a traditional (rooted) Labeled Transition System (LTS), which allows the following definition.

Definition 2 (Labeled Transition Systems). *A **Labeled Transition System (LTS)** is an MTS $M = (S, s_0, \Sigma, \diamond, \Box)$ with*

$$\diamond = \Box.$$

*The **language $\mathcal{L}(M)$** of M is defined as the language of the related prefix-closed non-deterministic finite automaton (NFA) that results from marking all states in S as accepting.*

Intuitively speaking, a may transition in an MTS stands for an underspecification and indicates a transition that may or may not be present in an actual implementation. An MTS therefore specifies a set of LTSs. These LTSs can be retrieved by refinement according to the following definition [29].

Definition 3 (MTS Refinement). *Let* $M_p = (S_p, s_0^p, \Sigma_p, \diamond_p, \Box_p)$, $M_q = (S_q, s_0^q, \Sigma_q, \diamond_q, \Box_q) \in \mathcal{M}$ *be two MTSs. A relation* $\lesssim \subseteq (S_p \times S_q)$ *is called a* **refinement** *if the following hold for all* $(p, q) \in \lesssim$:

$$1. \ \forall (p, \sigma, p') \in \diamond_p, \ \exists (q, \sigma, q') \in \diamond_q : (p', q') \in \lesssim$$
$$2. \ \forall (q, \sigma, q') \in \Box_q, \ \exists (p, \sigma, p') \in \Box_p : (p', q') \in \lesssim$$

M_p *refines* M_q, *written as* $M_p \lesssim M_q$, *if there exists a refinement* $\lesssim$ *with* $(s_0^p, s_0^q) \in \lesssim$. *In addition, we call* M_p *a strict refinement of* M_q, *denoted as* $M_p \underset{\not\sim}{\lesssim} M_q$, *if* $M_p \lesssim M_q$ *and* $M_q \not\lesssim M_p$.

For the construction of adequate contexts, the maximal language defined by an MTS is important.

Definition 4 (Largest Language of an MTS). *Let* $M = (S, s_0, \Sigma, \diamond, \Box)$ *be an MTS. We call the language*

$$\mathcal{L}_\top(M) =_{def} \mathcal{L}((S, s_0, \Sigma, \diamond, \diamond))$$

the **largest language of** M.

Parallel components might need to be considered during verification if they cannot be abstracted away according to the following notion of a weakest specification [30].

Definition 5 (Weakest Modal Specification). *Let* Σ *be an alphabet. We call the one-state MTS* $\mathcal{U}_\Sigma$ *that always features an enabled may-only transition for every* $\sigma \in \Sigma$ *the* **weakest modal** Σ-**specification**:

$$\mathcal{U}_\Sigma =_{def} (\{s\}, s, \Sigma, (\{s\} \times \Sigma \times \{s\}), \emptyset).$$

3 Parallel MTS Composition

Our parallel composition operator for MTSs is reminiscent of CSP [18] with synchronization of components on their common alphabets:

Definition 6 (Parallel MTS Composition). *Let* $M_p = (S_p, s_0^p, \Sigma_p, \diamond_p, \Box_p)$, $M_q = (S_q, s_0^q, \Sigma_q, \diamond_q, \Box_q) \in \mathcal{M}$ *be two MTSs, and let* $T \in \{\diamond, \Box\}$ *identify the type of transition. The* **parallel composition**

$$(M_p \parallel M_q) =_{def} (S_p \times S_q, (s_0^p, s_0^q), \Sigma_p \cup \Sigma_q, \diamond, \Box)$$

is then defined as a commutative and associative operation satisfying the following operational rules with $p, p' \in S_p$ *and* $q, q' \in S_q$:[4]

$$\frac{p \xrightarrow{\sigma}_T p' \quad q \xrightarrow{\sigma}_T q'}{(p, q) \xrightarrow{\sigma}_T (p', q')} \qquad \frac{p \xrightarrow{\sigma}_T p' \quad \sigma \notin \Sigma_q}{(p, q) \xrightarrow{\sigma}_T (p', q)}$$

---

[4] This definition depends on the fact that each must transition is also a may transition.

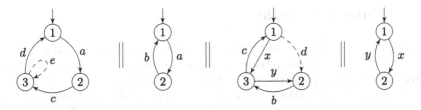

Fig. 3. A parallel composition $(M_1 \parallel M_2 \parallel M_3 \parallel M_4)$ of four MTSs. Transitions with the same label have to synchronize (see Definition 6). Dashed transitions are may-only transitions and therefore represent uncertain behavior.

Example 1 (Parallel MTS Composition). Figure 3 illustrates four MTSs that are components in a parallel composition $M = (M_1 \parallel M_2 \parallel M_3 \parallel M_4)$. The expanded MTS that represents the semantics of this parallel composition is depicted in Fig. 4.

It is straightforward to establish that $\parallel$ preserves refinement for both operands.

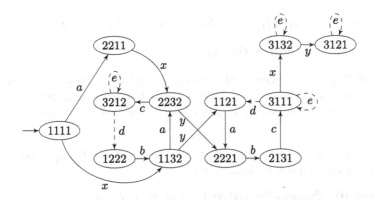

Fig. 4. Expanded MTS $M = (M_1 \parallel M_2 \parallel M_3 \parallel M_4)$ that represents the semantics of the parallel composition illustrated in Fig. 3.

Proposition 1 (Refinement Monotonicity). *Let $M, M', M'' \in \mathcal{M}$ be three arbitrary MTSs. Refining a component of a parallel composition also refines the composition:*

$$(M \lesssim M') \implies ((M \parallel M'') \lesssim (M' \parallel M'')).$$

Note that due to the commutativity of operator $\parallel$, this monotonicity holds for both components of a composition.

4 Benchmark Scenario

Throughout this paper, we are interested in the generation of complex benchmark scenarios that provide intricate challenges to state-of-the-art model checking tools. This section is dedicated to the development of a notion of hardness for parallel verification benchmarks based on the possibility to abstract from entire components. We therefore first of all define our notion of a benchmark scenario.[5]

Definition 7 (Benchmark Scenario). *Let* $M = (M_1 \parallel ... \parallel M_n)$ *be the parallel composition of* n *MTSs and* Φ *a set of properties. Then we call* $\boldsymbol{B(M, \Phi)}$ *a **benchmark scenario** if each property* $\phi \in \Phi$ *is either satisfied or violated by* M.

The following four definitions are required to establish our notion of benchmark hardness.

Definition 8 (Component Abstraction). *Let* $M = (M_1 \parallel ... \parallel M_n)$ *be a parallel MTS composition,* $alph(M_i) = \Sigma_i$ *be the alphabet of the* i-*th component of* M, *and* $\mathcal{U}_{\Sigma_i}$ *be the weakest modal* Σ_i-*specification (see Definition 5). Then we call the parallel MTS composition*

$$\alpha(M, i) =_{def} (M_1 \parallel ... \parallel M_{i-1} \parallel \mathcal{U}_{\Sigma_i} \parallel M_{i+1} \parallel ... \parallel M_n)$$

the i-*th component abstraction of* M.

Definition 9 (ϕ-Lossy Generalization). *Let* $M \in \mathcal{M}$ *be an MTS and* ϕ *be a temporal property. We call any MTS* M' *a* $\boldsymbol{\phi}$-***lossy generalization** of* M *if and only if* ϕ *can be verified or disproved for* M, *but yields an indecisive result for* M'.

Now we can state what it means for a set of temporal properties Φ to be sensitive to a parallel composition M.

Definition 10 (System-Sensitive Properties). *Let* $M = (M_1 \parallel ... \parallel M_n)$ *be a parallel MTS composition and* ϕ *be a temporal property. We call* ϕ $\boldsymbol{M}$-***sensitive** if the following holds:*

$$\forall i \in \mathbb{N}_{\leq n} : \alpha(M, i) \text{ is a } \phi\text{-lossy generalization of } M$$

Furthermore, a set Φ *of temporal properties is called* M-*sensitive if the following holds*

$$\forall i \in \mathbb{N}_{\leq n}, \exists \phi \in \Phi : \alpha(M, i) \text{ is a } \phi\text{-lossy generalization}$$

---

[5] As stated in Sect. 1, we focus on a parallel composition M of MTSs because a later refinement can yield a concrete implementation (see Fig. 1).

Note that due to the monotonicity of $\parallel$ w.r.t. refinement, the fact that ϕ is M-sensitive means that no subset of the components in M can be reduced without losing the ability to successfully analyze ϕ for M.

Definition 11 (Benchmark Hardness). *Let $B(M, \Phi)$ be a benchmark scenario with $M = (M_1 \parallel \dots \parallel M_n)$ and let $r \in \mathbb{N}_{\leq n}$. We call $B(M, \Phi)$ $(\boldsymbol{n, r})$-hard if the following three conditions are met:*

1. *Φ is M-sensitive*
2. *Φ only considers symbols from the alphabets of r different MTSs*
3. *The expanded MTS M consists of at least 2^n distinct states*

The following Section defines Modal Contracts as a basis to automatically generate arbitrarily hard benchmarks.

5   Modal Contracts

This section establishes our notion of a Modal Contract which is designed to support the property-preserving decomposition of its argument MTS into two components that both need to be considered for verification.

Definition 12 (Label Projection). *Let T be a transition relation with $sym(T) = \Sigma$. Let $\Gamma \subseteq \Sigma$ be a subset of Σ. We call the transition relation*

$$\alpha_\Gamma(T) =_{def} \{(p, \gamma, q) \in T \mid \gamma \in \Gamma\}$$

the (label) projection of T onto Γ.

Definition 13 (Modal Contract (MC)). *Let $M = (S, s_0, \Sigma, \diamond, \Box)$ be an MTS and $\Gamma \subseteq \Sigma$. A Modal Contract (MC) of M with communication alphabet $\Gamma(I) =_{def} \Gamma$ is a tuple*

$$I = (S, s_0, \Sigma, \diamond, \Box, G, R)$$

where

- *$G =_{def} \alpha_\Gamma(\Box)$, and*
- *R is a set of transitions over the alphabet Γ that do not exist in $\diamond$ and such that they are not in conflict with G, meaning there do not exist two paths of may transitions in M with the same label sequence such that one ends with a transition in G and the other with one in R.[6]*

Moreover $G(I) =_{def} G$ and $R(I) =_{def} R$, and we color transitions of $G(I)$ green and transitions of $R(I)$ red.

---

[6] Such a conflict can easily be detected via the determinization of the may automaton of I.

Definition 14 (Meaning of an MC). *Let* $I = (S, s_0, \Sigma, \diamond, \square, G, R)$ *be an MC.*
Let

$$R' =_{def} \{(p, \sigma, r) \mid q \in S : (p, \sigma, q) \in R\}$$

be a redirection of transitions in R to a new (sink) state $r \notin S$ *and let*

$$R^* =_{def} R' \cup \{(r, \sigma, r) \mid \sigma \in \Sigma\}$$

denote the extension of R with arbitrary subsequent behavior.
   I defines a so called **system MTS**

$$M_s(I) =_{def} ((S \uplus \{r\}), s_0, \Sigma, (\diamond \cup R^*), \square)$$

and a set of corresponding **context MTSs**

$$\mathcal{M}_C(I) =_{def} \{M_c(I) \mid (M_s(I) \parallel M_c(I)) \lesssim M\}$$

An MTS $M_c(I) \in \mathcal{M}_C(I)$ *is called a* **correct context** *of I.*

Intuitively speaking, an MC specifies an assume-guarantee contract [1,5,16, 35] based on an MTS M such that the parallel composition of the system MTS and a corresponding context MTS is guaranteed to refine M.

Our initial setting illustrated in Fig. 2 is an MTS M for which a set of properties Φ is guaranteed to hold. The following definition expresses in which situation none of the components of an MC-based decomposition can be ignored for verification:

Definition 15 (Property-Sensitive Decomposition). *Let* ϕ *be a temporal property,* $M \in \mathcal{M}$ *be an MTS with* $alph(M) = \Sigma$ *such that* $M \models \phi$, *and* I *be an MC of M. We call* I *a* **ϕ-sensitive decomposition** *of M if the following hold for all correct contexts* $M_c(I) \in \mathcal{M}_C(I)$:

$$1.\ (M_s(I) \parallel \mathcal{U}_{\Gamma(I)}) \not\models \phi$$
$$2.\ (\mathcal{U}_\Sigma \parallel M_c(I)) \not\models \phi$$

We further call an MC I *a* Φ-*sensitive decomposition for a given set of properties* Φ *if* I *is a* ϕ-*sensitive decomposition for some* $\phi \in \Phi$.

We are now going to start with an example that illustrates the generation of a $(3, 2)$-hard benchmark based on the initial MTS M that is illustrated in Fig. 4 (see also Fig. 2). This implies that there exists a property $\phi \in \Phi$ that cannot be analyzed successfully when abstracting from one or more of these three components entirely (see Definition 11).

Example 2 (Property-Sensitive Decomposition). Let M be the MTS illustrated in Fig. 4. According to our initial setting depicted in Fig. 2, we know that M satisfies a given set of temporal properties Φ. Let $\Phi = \{\phi_1, \phi_2, \phi_3\}$ consist of the following three properties:

ϕ_1 (LTL, safety): $\mathbf{G}(c \implies (\neg b \, \mathbf{W} \mathbf{U} \, d))$

"Whenever c is observed, b does not occur before d"

ϕ_2 (LTL, safety): $\mathbf{G}(y \implies \mathbf{X}(x \, \mathbf{R} \, \neg y))$

"Whenever y is observed, y is only allowed once released by a preceding x"

ϕ_3 (CTL, bounded liveness): $\mathbf{EF}(< y > (\mathbf{EF} < y > true))$

"There exists a path where y is observed twice"

As an initial step, we define an MC I_1 of M with $\Gamma(I_1) = \{x, y\}$ which means that I_1 is a Φ-sensitive decomposition[7]. This MC I_1 is illustrated in Fig. 5. Note that subsets of $\Gamma(I_1)$ might suffice to guarantee a Φ-sensitive decomposition: The green transitions in Fig. 5 for example yield a ϕ_3-sensitive decomposition, however the alternative choice $\Gamma(I') = \{y\}$ that results in the set $G(I') =_{def} \alpha_{\{y\}}(must(M))$ would suffice to ensure the ϕ_3-sensitive decomposition. The unique system MTS $M_s(I_1)$ corresponding to the MC I_1 is illustrated in Fig. 6.

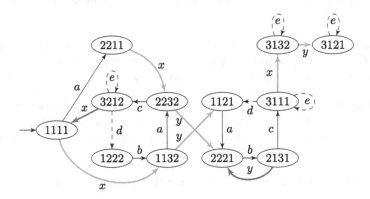

Fig. 5. MC I_1 based on the initial composition $M = (M_1 \parallel M_2 \parallel M_3 \parallel M_4)$ illustrated in Fig. 4. (Transitions $(3212, x, 1111)$ and $(2131, y, 2221)$ are colored red, all others labeled x or y are colored green.) (Color figure online)

Given an MTS M and a corresponding Modal Contract I, the corresponding system MTS is uniquely determined. The next section discusses how to obtain a matching context MTS.

6 Green/Red-Based Context Generation

Given an MC I, we now define a specific MTS $M_c^*(I)$, called the green/red context of I, such that $M_c^*(I)$ is correct with regards to I. Our goal is to specify an $M_c^*(I)$ with little must behavior in order to have many possible choices in the actual implementation of this context. We first define the green-only context

---

[7] Note that within this example, I_1 is also a ϕ-sensitive decomposition for all $\phi \in \Phi$.

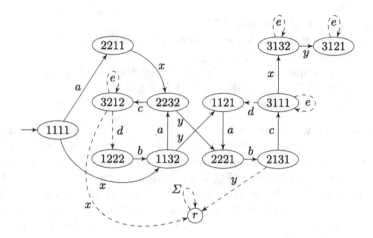

Fig. 6. System MTS $M_s(I_1)$ of the MC I_1 that is depicted in Fig. 5. The transition labeled Σ represents a set of transitions, one for each symbol of $\Sigma = \{a, b, c, d, e, x, y\}$.

$M_c^g(I)$ and the red-only context $M_c^r(I)$ of I separately. They are correct if $R(I) = \emptyset$ and if $G(I) = \emptyset$ respectively. Afterwards, we introduce the green/red context $M_c^*(I)$ through a notion of MTS conjunction.

Definition 16 (Language Projection). *Let Σ, Γ be two alphabets with $\Gamma \subseteq \Sigma$. For any word $w = (\sigma_1, ..., \sigma_n) \in \Sigma^*$, the **projection** $\alpha_\Gamma(w)$ of w onto Γ results from skipping symbols $\sigma_i \notin \Gamma$. This projection extends naturally to languages.*

Using this projection, we can now define the green-only context.

Definition 17 (Green-Only Context $M_c^g(I)$). *Let $M \in \mathcal{M}$ be an MTS and let I be an MC of M (Definition 13) and F_d be the minimal DFA that describes the prefix-closed language $\alpha_{\Gamma(I)}(\mathcal{L}_\top(M))$.*

*We define the **green-only context** $M_c^g(I)$ as the MTS that is the result of the following transformation based on F_d:*

1. *Consider all incoming and outgoing transitions of the unique non-accepting sink state as may-only transitions.*
2. *Consider all other transitions as must transitions.*
3. *Disregard the property of accepting/non-accepting states.*

Note that a correct green-only context that is coarser than $M_c^g(I)$ in terms of MTS refinement can be realized based on the notion of weak refinement and a definition of MTS determinization. For the sake of simplicity, we focus on the presented heuristic $M_c^g(I)$ in this section.

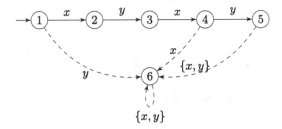

Fig. 7. Green-red correct context $M_c^*(I_1)$ based on the MC I_1 of Fig. 5. It would be the green-only context $M_c^g(I_1)$ if there existed may-only transitions $(2, x, 6)$ and $(3, y, 6)$.

Example 3 (Green-Only Context). Let us consider the MC I_1 of Fig. 5. Let us have a look at the MTS illustrated in Fig. 7. If we add a x-labeled may-only transitions from state 2 to state 6 and a y-labeled may-only transitions from state 3 to state 6, then the resulting MTS is the green-only context $M_c^g(I_1)$.

The following lemma states the correctness of the green-only context.

Lemma 1 (Correctness of Green-Only Context). *Let $M \in \mathcal{M}$ be an MTS. Let I^g be an MC of M (Definition 13) with $R(I^g) = \emptyset$ and $M_c^g(I^g)$ be the corresponding green-only context according to Definition 17. Then the following holds:*

$$(M_s(I^g) \parallel M_c^g(I^g)) \lesssim M$$

In order to fully harness the potential of context-based assumptions that can be expressed by an MC, we would like to generate a correct context $M_c^*(I)$ for an MC I with both green and red transitions. We now first define the red-only context $M_c^r(I)$ which we afterwards try to combine with the green-only context $M_c^g(I)$ in order to retrieve $M_c^*(I)$.

Definition 18 (Red-Only Context $M_c^r(I)$). *Let I (Definition 13) be an MC. Let $\mathcal{L}_R$ be the language of words for which a path in I exists that contains a red transition $t \in R$. Let F_d be the minimal DFA that describes the prefix-closed language $(\Gamma(I)^* \setminus \alpha_{\Gamma(I)}(\mathcal{L}_R))$ (see also Definition 16).*

*We define the **red-only context MTS $M_c^r(I)$** as the MTS that results from the following transformations of F_d:*

1. *Remove all incoming and outgoing transitions of the unique non-accepting sink state together with this sink state itself.*
2. *Consider all remaining transitions as may-only transitions.*
3. *Disregard the property of accepting/non-accepting states.*

Example 4 (Red-Only Context). Consider again the MC I_1 of Fig. 5. Figure 8 illustrates the corresponding red-only context $M_c^r(I_1)$.

The following lemma states the correctness of a red-only context.

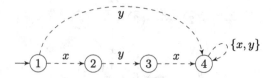

Fig. 8. Red-only context $M_c^r(I_1)$ based on the MC I_1 of Fig. 5.

Lemma 2 (Correctness of Red-Only Context). *Let $M \in \mathcal{M}$ be an MTS, I^r be an MC of M (Definition 13) with $G(I^r) = \emptyset$, and $M_c^r(I^r)$ be the red-only context according to Definition 18. Then the following holds:*

$$(M_s(I^r) \parallel M_c^r(I^r)) \lesssim M$$

Having defined both the green-only and red-only context, we now specify our notion of MTS conjunction in a fashion similar to Definition 6 and as a preparation for defining the green/red context.

Definition 19 (MTS Conjunction). *Let $M_p = (S_p, s_0^p, \Sigma, \diamond_p, \square_p), M_q = (S_q, s_0^q, \Sigma, \diamond_q, \square_q) \in \mathcal{M}$ be two MTSs. The **conjunction***

$$(M_p \wedge M_q) =_{def} (S_p \times S_q, (s_0^p, s_0^q), \Sigma, \diamond, \square)$$

of M_p and M_q is then defined as a commutative and associative operation satisfying the following operational rules with $p, p' \in S_p$ and $q, q' \in S_q$.[8]

$$\frac{p \xrightarrow{\sigma}_{\square_p} p' \quad q \xrightarrow{\sigma}_{\diamond_q} q'}{(p,q) \xrightarrow{\sigma}_{\square} (p',q')} \qquad \frac{p \xrightarrow{\sigma}_{\diamond_p} p' \quad q \xrightarrow{\sigma}_{\diamond_q} q'}{(p,q) \xrightarrow{\sigma}_{\diamond} (p',q')} \qquad \frac{p \xrightarrow{\sigma}_{\square_p} p' \quad q \xarrownot\to_{\diamond_q}}{(p,q) \xrightarrow{\sigma} error}$$

Whenever an error occurs, the conjunction of M_p and M_q is undefined.

The MTS conjunction of Definition 19 guarantees that a refining MTS refines both components:

Proposition 2 (Conjunction of Refinement Constraints). *Let $M, M_p, M_q \in \mathcal{M}$ be three MTSs. If $(M_p \wedge M_q)$ is defined, then the following holds:*

$$(M \lesssim (M_p \wedge M_q)) \iff (M \lesssim M_p \wedge M \lesssim M_q)$$

Based on the just defined conjunction of two MTSs, we can now realize our green/red context $M_c^*(I)$:

Definition 20 (Green/Red Context $M_c^*(I)$). *Let I be an MC with green-only context $M_c^g(I)$ (Definition 17) and red-only context $M_c^r(I)$ (Definition 18). Then the corresponding **green/red context** $M_c^*(I)$ is defined as follows:*

$$M_c^*(I) =_{def} (M_c^r(I) \wedge M_c^g(I))$$

---

[8] This definition again depends on the fact that each must transition is also a may transition.

Example 5 (Green/Red Context). Figure 7 illustrates the green/red context MTS $M_c^*(I_1)$ based on the MC I_1 of Fig. 5.

As green and red transitions are guaranteed to be non-conflicting (see Definition 13), the following theorem follows straightforwardly from Lemmas 1 and 2, as well as Proposition 2.

Theorem 1 (Correctness of Green/Red Context). *Let $M \in \mathcal{M}$ be an MTS. Let I be an MC of M (Definition 13) with its green/red context $M_c^*(I)$ according to Definition 20. Then $M_c^*(I)$ is well-defined and the following holds:*

$$(M_s(I) \parallel M_c^*(I)) \lesssim M$$

7 Hardness and Scalability

Is is easy to see that green/red-based modal decomposition guarantees the first hardness property, but is insufficient to achieve the second hardness property and scalability:

– The globally reachable state space does not grow, and
– the decomposition potential is limited by the alphabet of the original system.

Both problems can be overcome if we constrain the considered properties, allow dynamic alphabet extension and base our development on weak refinement, which requires the following definitions:

Definition 21 (Label Hiding). *Let $M = (S, s_0, \Sigma, \diamond, \Box) \in \mathcal{M}$ be an MTS. Let $\Gamma \subseteq \Sigma$ be a sub-alphabet. The Γ-hiding*

$$hid_\Gamma(M) =_{def} (S, s_0, ((\Sigma \setminus \Gamma) \cup \{\tau\}), hid(\diamond), hid(\Box))$$

of M relabels all transitions t of M such that $sym(t) \in \Gamma$ with the special symbol τ and therefore features the following transition relations for all $T \in \{\diamond, \Box\}$:

$$hid(T) = \{(p, \tau, q) \mid \exists \gamma \in \Gamma : (p, \gamma, q) \in T\} \cup \{(p, \sigma, q) \in T \mid \sigma \in (\Sigma \setminus \Gamma)\}$$

In order to prepare the (standard) definition of weak MTS refinement, we define the usual observational relation of a transition relation.

Definition 22 (Observational Relation). *Let $(\Sigma \cup \{\tau\})$ be an alphabet with τ and let $T \subseteq (S \times (\Sigma \cup \{\tau\}) \times S)$ be a transition relation between states in S. Let $p, p', q, q' \in S$. We define the observational relation $obs(T)$ of T as follows.*

Let $p \xrightarrow{\sigma} p'$ denote a feasible transition $(p, \sigma, p') \in T$ and $p \xLongrightarrow{\sigma} p'$ a feasible transition $(p, \sigma, p') \in obs(T)$. The transition relation $obs(T)$ results from an exhaustive application of the following three rules for all $\sigma \in \Sigma$:

$$p \xLongrightarrow{\epsilon} p \qquad \frac{p \xrightarrow{\tau} p' \quad p' \xLongrightarrow{\epsilon} q}{p \xLongrightarrow{\epsilon} q} \qquad \frac{p \xLongrightarrow{\epsilon} p' \quad p' \xrightarrow{\sigma} q' \quad q' \xLongrightarrow{\epsilon} q}{p \xLongrightarrow{\sigma} q}$$

The observational MTS is now simply defined by replacing the original transition relations by their observable counterparts.

Definition 23 (Observational MTS). *Let* $M = (S, s_0, \Sigma, \diamond, \Box) \in \mathcal{M}$ *be an MTS. The* **observational MTS** $\omega(M)$ *of* M *is based on the observational expansion of its transition relations (Definition 22):*

$$\omega(M) =_{def} (S, s_0, ((\Sigma \setminus \{\tau\}) \cup \{\epsilon\}), obs(\diamond), obs(\Box))$$

This is sufficient to introduce weak MTS refinement [20].

Definition 24 (Weak MTS Refinement). *Let* $M, M' \in MTS$ *be two MTSs.* **Weak refinement** $\precsim$ *is defined as follows:*

$$(M \precsim M') \Longleftrightarrow (\omega(M) \precsim \omega(M'))$$

Weak refinement is insensitive to *divergence*, i.e. the possibility that the system engages in an infinite τ sequence, and therefore does not preserve liveness properties. In order to partially repair this drawback we will reduce our attention to convergent systems.

Definition 25 (Convergent MTS). *An MTS is called* **convergent** *if every allowed τ-sequence is finite.*

Weak refinement of convergent systems preserves an interesting class of temporal properties. We will therefore restrict our attention to properties of this class, be they branching time, linear time, safety or liveness properties.

Definition 26 (Σ_E Context Extension). *Let* $M \in \mathcal{M}$ *be an MTS and let* I *be an MC of* M. *Let* Σ_E *be a new alphabet, i.e.* $(\Sigma_E \cap alph(M)) = \emptyset$.

1. *An MTS* M_E *is called* Σ_E **context extension** *of* $\Gamma(I)$ *if it results from the following three-step construction.*
   - *Choose an arbitrary MTS* M' *over* Σ_E *with the following two properties:*
     - M' *restricted to its must transitions is deadlock free*
     - *Each state of* M' *is reachable via must transitions*
   - *Select a set* S *of transitions with the property that every infinite trace in* M' *visits a state in* S *infinitely often.*[9]
   - *Replace each transition of* S *by a set of must transitions, one for each symbol in* $\Gamma(I)$.
2. *Let* $M_c^*(I)$ *be the green/red context of* I *(Definition 20) and let* M_E *be a* Σ_E *context extension of* $\Gamma(I)$. *An MTS*

$$M_c^*(I, M_E) =_{def} (M_c^*(I) \parallel M_E)$$

is called a Σ_E-**extended context** *of* I.

We have:

---

[9] This definition is similar to the notion of cut points in Floyd's inductive assertion method.

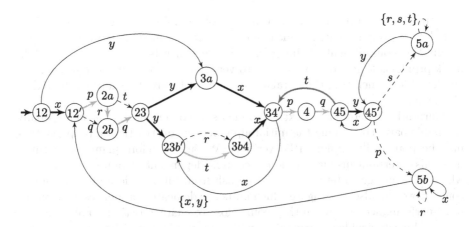

Fig. 9. MC I_2 based on an Σ_E-extended context $M_c^*(I_1, M_E)$ (see Example 6). Transition $(45, t, 34')$ is colored red. Transitions $(12', p, 2a)$, $(2a, r, 2b)$, $(2b, q, 23)$, $(23b', t, 3b4)$, $(34', p, 4)$, and $(4, q, 45)$ are colored green. (Color figure online)

Theorem 2 (Correctness of Σ_E-Extended Context). *Let $M \in \mathcal{M}$ be an MTS, let I be an MC of M (Definition 13), and let M_E be a Σ_E context extension of $\Gamma(I)$. Then we have:*

1. $hid_{\Sigma_E}(M_s(I) \parallel M_c^*(I, M_E)) \gtrapprox M$
2. $hid_{\Sigma_E}(M_s(I) \parallel M_c^*(I, M_E))$ *is convergent.*

Without going into detail here, it should be (intuitively) clear that, based on Σ_E-extended contexts, it is possible to iteratively generate benchmark systems of exponentially growing size, and that there is no limit to this process when successively extending the alphabet. A concrete strategy pattern for generating such benchmark systems is presented in [39]. This strategy underlies the generation of the parallel benchmark problems for future iterations of the RERS Challenge.

Example 6 (New MC Based on a Σ_E-Extended Context). Note that none of the three temporal properties of Example 2 require that a system performs an action in the next time step or at any time that lies a fixed number of steps in the future. Let $\Sigma_E = \{p, q, r, s, t\}$ be a new alphabet. We can choose a Σ_E-extended context $M_c^*(I_1, M_E)$ and define a second MC I_2 based on this extended context. One possible I_2 that still preserves all properties of Example 2 is illustrated in Fig. 9.

8   Conclusion

In this paper, we have proposed a systematic approach to generate highly parallel benchmark systems with guaranteed temporal properties. Key to our approach is the iterative property-preserving parallel decomposition in a light-weight

assumption commitment style on the basis of Modal Contracts. We have illustrated how design choices, which may well be automated, steer the applied
assumption-commitment chaining in order to generate highly parallel benchmark problems that are very difficult to verify. The described procedure will be
employed for generating the parallel problems of future iterations of the RERS
Challenge.

Currently, generated context components are deterministic on their globally
reachable parts concerning the initial alphabet by construction, a property that
may be potentially exploited by verifiers. We are therefore planning to eliminate this determinisms via a notion of context-dependent semantic determinism,
which we envisage to be hard to distinguish from full non-determinism. In this
context, we will also investigate which influence dedicated properties have on the
tools performance, e.g. when they come close to characteristic formulae [36,37].

Benchmark problems generated with our method can be guaranteed to
explode in size [39]. It has to be seen whether our notion of hardness is stable in the context of advanced reduction/verification techniques such as (lazy)
CEGAR [6,17] and partial order reduction [11,13,33,40]. The planned investigation of the corresponding interplay between the introduction and reduction of
difficulty is envisioned to boost the progress of system verification.

Another line of future research is to include data and arithmetic in the modeling language [2], for example in the fashion proposed for sequential benchmarks
in [38]. In particular when allowing shared memory between the components this
imposes new challenges both for the generation process and, even more so, for
the solution of resulting benchmark problems.

We plan to make our generation tool available open source in order to invite
users to enhance the generation potential and to contribute to a library of classifi-
able benchmarks. Ideally, this will help to establish an accepted quality standard.

Acknowledgement. We are very grateful to Axel Legay and Maximilian Fecke for
their suggestions and remarks regarding this paper.

References

1. Bauer, S.S., David, A., Hennicker, R., Guldstrand Larsen, K., Legay, A., Nyman,
   U., Wąsowski, A.: Moving from specifications to contracts in component-based
   design. In: Lara, J., Zisman, A. (eds.) FASE 2012. LNCS, vol. 7212, pp. 43–58.
   Springer, Heidelberg (2012). doi:10.1007/978-3-642-28872-2_3
2. Bauer, S.S., Larsen, K.G., Legay, A., Nyman, U., Wasowski, A.: A modal specification theory for components with data. Sci. Comput. Program. **83**, 106–128
   (2014)
3. Beneš, N., Delahaye, B., Fahrenberg, U., Křetínský, J., Legay, A.: Hennessy-Milner
   logic with greatest fixed points as a complete behavioural specification theory. In:
   D'Argenio, P.R., Melgratti, H. (eds.) CONCUR 2013. LNCS, vol. 8052, pp. 76–90.
   Springer, Heidelberg (2013). doi:10.1007/978-3-642-40184-8_7
4. Beneš, N., Křetínský, J., Larsen, K.G., Møller, M.H., Srba, J.: Parametric modal
   transition systems. In: Bultan, T., Hsiung, P.-A. (eds.) ATVA 2011. LNCS, vol.
   6996, pp. 275–289. Springer, Heidelberg (2011). doi:10.1007/978-3-642-24372-1_20

5. Benveniste, A., Caillaud, B.: Synchronous interfaces and assume/guarantee contracts. In: Aceto, L., Bacci, G., Bacci, G., Ingólfsdóttir, A., Legay, A., Mardare, R. (eds.) Larsen Festschrift. LNCS, vol. 10460, pp. 233–248. Springer, Cham (2017)
6. Clarke, E., Grumberg, O., Jha, S., Lu, Y., Veith, H.: Counterexample-guided abstraction refinement. In: Emerson, E.A., Sistla, A.P. (eds.) CAV 2000. LNCS, vol. 1855, pp. 154–169. Springer, Heidelberg (2000). doi:10.1007/10722167_15
7. Clarke, E.M., Emerson, E.A.: Design and synthesis of synchronization skeletons using branching time temporal logic. In: Kozen, D. (ed.) Logic of Programs 1981. LNCS, vol. 131, pp. 52–71. Springer, Heidelberg (1982). doi:10.1007/BFb0025774
8. Cleaveland, R., Steffen, B.: A preorder for partial process specifications. In: Baeten, J.C.M., Klop, J.W. (eds.) CONCUR 1990. LNCS, vol. 458, pp. 141–151. Springer, Heidelberg (1990). doi:10.1007/BFb0039057
9. Fahrenberg, U., Legay, A.: A linear-time–branching-time spectrum of behavioral specification theories. In: Steffen, B., Baier, C., Brand, M., Eder, J., Hinchey, M., Margaria, T. (eds.) SOFSEM 2017. LNCS, vol. 10139, pp. 49–61. Springer, Cham (2017). doi:10.1007/978-3-319-51963-0_5
10. Fecher, H., Schmidt, H.: Comparing disjunctive modal transition systems with an one-selecting variant. J. Logic Algebraic Program. **77**(1–2), 20–39 (2008)
11. Flanagan, C., Godefroid, P.: Dynamic partial-order reduction for model checking software. ACM SIGPLAN Not. **40**, 110–121 (2005)
12. Geske, M., Jasper, M., Steffen, B., Howar, F., Schordan, M., Pol, J.: RERS 2016: parallel and sequential benchmarks with focus on LTL verification. In: Margaria, T., Steffen, B. (eds.) ISoLA 2016. LNCS, vol. 9953, pp. 787–803. Springer, Cham (2016). doi:10.1007/978-3-319-47169-3_59
13. Godefroid, P. (ed.): Partial-Order Methods for the Verification of Concurrent Systems. LNCS, vol. 1032. Springer, Heidelberg (1996). doi:10.1007/3-540-60761-7
14. Graf, S., Steffen, B.: Compositional minimization of finite state processes. Comput.-Aided Verification **90**, 57–73 (1990)
15. Graf, S., Steffen, B., Lüttgen, G.: Compositional minimisation of finite state systems using interface specifications. Form. Asp. Comput. **8**(5), 607–616 (1996)
16. Grumberg, O., Long, D.E.: Model checking and modular verification. ACM Trans. Program. Lang. Syst. (TOPLAS) **16**(3), 843–871 (1994)
17. Henzinger, T.A., Jhala, R., Majumdar, R., Sutre, G.: Lazy abstraction. ACM SIGPLAN Not. **37**(1), 58–70 (2002)
18. Hoare, C.A.R.: Communicating sequential processes. In: Hansen, P.B. (ed.) The Origin of Concurrent Programming, pp. 413–443. Springer, Heidelberg (1978). doi:10.1007/978-1-4757-3472-0_16
19. Howar, F., Isberner, M., Merten, M., Steffen, B., Beyer, D.: The RERS greybox challenge 2012: analysis of event-condition-action systems. In: Margaria, T., Steffen, B. (eds.) ISoLA 2012. LNCS, vol. 7609, pp. 608–614. Springer, Heidelberg (2012). doi:10.1007/978-3-642-34026-0_45
20. Hüttel, H., Larsen, K.G.: The use of static constructs in a model process logic. In: Meyer, A.R., Taitslin, M.A. (eds.) Logic at Botik 1989. LNCS, vol. 363, pp. 163–180. Springer, Heidelberg (1989). doi:10.1007/3-540-51237-3_14
21. Jonsson, B., Larsen, K.G.: On the complexity of equation solving in process algebra. In: Abramsky, S., Maibaum, T.S.E. (eds.) CAAP 1991. LNCS, vol. 493, pp. 381–396. Springer, Heidelberg (1991). doi:10.1007/3-540-53982-4_21
22. Kordon, F., Garavel, H., Hillah, L.M., Hulin-Hubard, F., Chiardo, G., Hamez, A.,Jezequel, L., Miner, A., Meijer, J., Paviot-Adet, E., Racordon, D., Rodriguez, C., Rohr, C., Srba, J., Thierry-Mieg, Y., Tri.nh, G., Wolf, K.: Complete Results for the 2016 Edition of the Model Checking Contest, June 2016. http://mcc.lip6.fr/2016/results.php

23. Kordon, F., et al.: Report on the model checking contest at petri nets 2011. In: Jensen, K., Aalst, W.M., Ajmone Marsan, M., Franceschinis, G., Kleijn, J., Kristensen, L.M. (eds.) Transactions on Petri Nets and Other Models of Concurrency VI. LNCS, vol. 7400, pp. 169–196. Springer, Heidelberg (2012). doi:10.1007/978-3-642-35179-2_8

24. Kourie, D.G., Watson, B.W.: The Correctness-by-Construction Approach to Programming. Springer Science & Business Media, Berlin (2012). doi:10.1007/978-3-642-27919-5

25. Křetínský, J.: Modal transition systems: extensions and analysis. Ph.D. thesis, Masarykova univerzita, Fakulta informatiky (2014)

26. Larsen, K.G., Steffen, B., Weise, C.: A constraint oriented proof methodology based on modal transition systems. In: Brinksma, E., Cleaveland, W.R., Larsen, K.G., Margaria, T., Steffen, B. (eds.) TACAS 1995. LNCS, vol. 1019, pp. 17–40. Springer, Heidelberg (1995). doi:10.1007/3-540-60630-0_2

27. Larsen, K.G., Steffen, B., Weise, C.: The methodology of modal constraints. In: Broy, M., Merz, S., Spies, K. (eds.) Formal Systems Specification. LNCS, vol. 1169, pp. 405–435. Springer, Heidelberg (1996). doi:10.1007/BFb0024437

28. Larsen, K.G., Thomsen, B.: Partial specifications and compositional verification. Theoret. Comput. Sci. **88**(1), 15–32 (1991)

29. Larsen, K.G.: Modal specifications. In: Sifakis, J. (ed.) CAV 1989. LNCS, vol. 407, pp. 232–246. Springer, Heidelberg (1990). doi:10.1007/3-540-52148-8_19

30. Guldstrand Larsen, K.: Ideal specification formalism = expressivity + compositionality + decidability + testability +. In: Baeten, J.C.M., Klop, J.W. (eds.) CONCUR 1990. LNCS, vol. 458, pp. 33–56. Springer, Heidelberg (1990). doi:10.1007/BFb0039050

31. Larsen, K.G., Xinxin, L.: Equation solving using modal transition systems. In: Proceedings of the Fifth Annual IEEE Symposium on Logic in Computer Science, LICS 1990, pp. 108–117. IEEE (1990)

32. Margaria, T., Steffen, B.: Simplicity as a driver for agile innovation. Computer **43**(6), 90–92 (2010)

33. Peled, D.: All from one, one for all: on model checking using representatives. In: Courcoubetis, C. (ed.) CAV 1993. LNCS, vol. 697, pp. 409–423. Springer, Heidelberg (1993). doi:10.1007/3-540-56922-7_34

34. Pnueli, A.: The temporal logic of programs. In: 18th Annual Symposium on Foundations of Computer Science, pp. 46–57. IEEE (1977)

35. Raclet, J.B., Badouel, E., Benveniste, A., Caillaud, B., Legay, A., Passerone, R.: A modal interface theory for component-based design. Fundamenta Informaticae **108**(1–2), 119–149 (2011)

36. Steffen, B.: Characteristic formulae. In: Ausiello, G., Dezani-Ciancaglini, M., Rocca, S.R. (eds.) ICALP 1989. LNCS, vol. 372, pp. 723–732. Springer, Heidelberg (1989). doi:10.1007/BFb0035794

37. Steffen, B., Ingólfsdóttir, A.: Characteristic formulas for processes with divergence. Inf. Comput. **110**(1), 149–163 (1994)

38. Steffen, B., Isberner, M., Naujokat, S., Margaria, T., Geske, M.: Property-driven benchmark generation: synthesizing programs of realistic structure. Int. J. Softw. Tools Technol. Transfer **16**(5), 465–479 (2014)

39. Steffen, B., Jasper, M., van de Pol, J., Meijer, J.: Property-preserving generation of tailored benchmark petri nets. In: Proceedings of ACSD 2017. IEEE Computer Society (2017, to appear)

40. Valmari, A.: Stubborn sets for reduced state space generation. In: Rozenberg, G. (ed.) ICATPN 1989. LNCS, vol. 483, pp. 491–515. Springer, Heidelberg (1991). doi:10.1007/3-540-53863-1_36

41. Wei, O., Gurfinkel, A., Chechik, M.: Mixed transition systems revisited. In: Jones, N.D., Müller-Olm, M. (eds.) VMCAI 2009. LNCS, vol. 5403, pp. 349–365. Springer, Heidelberg (2008). doi:10.1007/978-3-540-93900-9_28

A Generic Algorithm for Learning Symbolic Automata from Membership Queries

Oded Maler and Irini-Eleftheria Mens$^{(\boxtimes)}$

VERIMAG, CNRS, University of Grenoble-Alpes, Grenoble, France
{oded.maler,irini-eleftheria.mens}@univ-grenoble-alpes.fr

Abstract. We present a generic algorithmic scheme for learning languages defined over large or infinite alphabets such as bounded subsets of $\mathbb{N}$ and $\mathbb{R}$, or Boolean vectors of high dimension. These languages are accepted by deterministic *symbolic automata* that use predicates to label transitions, forming a finite partition of the alphabet for every state. Our learning algorithm, an adaptation of Angluin's L^*, combines standard automaton learning by state characterization, with the learning of the static predicates that define the alphabet partitions. We do not assume a helpful teacher who provides minimal counter-examples when the conjectured automaton is incorrect. Instead we use random sampling to obtain PAC (probably approximately correct) learnability. We have implemented the algorithm for numerical and Boolean alphabets and the preliminary performance results show that languages over large or infinite alphabets can be learned under more realistic assumptions.

Keywords: Symbolic automata · Automata learning · Infinite alphabets

1 Introduction

The (classical) theory of regular languages and automata [14,19,27] deals mainly with alphabets that are small and "flat", that is, sets without any additional structure. In many applications, however, alphabets are large and structured. In hardware verification, for example, behaviors are sequences of states and inputs ranging over valuations of Boolean state variables that give rise to exponentially large alphabets, treated symbolically using BDDs and other logical formalisms. As another motivation, consider the verification of continuous and hybrid systems against specifications written in formalisms such as *signal temporal logic* (STL) [20,21]. Automata over *numerical alphabets*, admitting an order or partial-order relation, can define the semantics of such requirements.

In recent years, *symbolic automata* [31] have been studied extensively as a generic framework for recognizing regular languages over large alphabets. In such automata the number of states and transitions is typically small and the transitions are labeled by predicates from a corresponding theory, denoting subsets of

---

Dedicated with friendship to Kim Larsen, 60 years old but time-invariant.

© Springer International Publishing AG 2017
L. Aceto et al. (Eds.): Larsen Festschrift, LNCS 10460, pp. 146–169, 2017.
DOI: 10.1007/978-3-319-63121-9_8

the alphabet. The extension of classical results of automata theory to symbolic automata has become an active area of research, including fundamental issues such as minimization [10] or effective closure under various operations [30,32,33] as well as the adaptation of learning algorithms [6,17,23]. The comparison with other related work is postponed to the conclusion section, after the technical issues are explained in the body of the paper.

In [23] Angluin's L^* algorithm [1] for learning automata from queries and counter-examples has been extended to learn languages over an alphabet Σ which is a high-cardinality bounded subset of $\mathbb{N}$ or $\mathbb{R}$. Such languages are represented by symbolic automata where transitions are labeled by symbolic letters, such that the concrete semantics $[\![a]\!]$ of a symbolic letter a is a sub-interval of Σ. Determinism is maintained by letting the semantics at each state form a partition of Σ. The learning algorithm uses symbolic observation tables with symbolic words in the rows to provide access sequences s to discovered states. To determine the transitions outgoing from state s, one needs, in principle, to ask membership queries concerning $s \cdot a \cdot e$ for every $s \in [\![s]\!]$, $a \in \Sigma$ and $e \in E$ where E is a set of distinguishing suffixes. To avoid a large or infinite number of queries, the characterization of states is based on partial information: a small set $\mu(a)$ of concrete letters, called the *evidence* for a, is associated with every symbol a. This notion is lifted to symbolic words and membership queries are asked only for the words in $\mu(s) \cdot \mu(a) \cdot E$.

In this framework, the learning procedure is decomposed into a vertical/temporal component, consisting of discovering new states as in the original L^* algorithm, and a horizontal/spatial component where the boundaries of the alphabet partitions in every state are learned and modified. The advantage of this decomposition is that the first part is generic, invariant under alphabet change, while the second part has some alphabet specific features. To take a concrete example, alphabet partitions over a totally-ordered alphabet such as $\mathbb{R}$ are made using intervals with endpoints that can be shifted as new evidence accumulates. On the other hand, for an alphabet like $\mathbb{B}^n$, the partitions are represented by decision trees which are modified by restructuring.

A major weakness of [23], partly inherited from L^*, is that in addition to membership queries, it also uses *equivalence* queries: each time an automaton is conjectured, an oracle EQ either confirms the conjecture or provides a counter-example which is also minimal in the lexicographic order on Σ^*. Counter-examples of this type facilitate significantly the discovery of new states and the detection of the alphabet partition boundaries but such a helpful teacher is unrealistic in most real-life situations. In this paper we develop an algorithm that uses only membership queries. Some of those are used to fill the observation table in order to characterize states, while others, posed for randomly selected words, are used to test conjectures. Consequently, we have to replace certain and exact learnability by a weaker notion, in the spirit of Valiant's PAC (probably approximately correct) learning [29]: the algorithm converges with high probability to a language close to the target language.

Adapting the algorithm to this more challenging and less pedagogical setting of random sampling involves several modifications relative to [23]. First, when a new state q is discovered, we sample the alphabet at several points rather than only at the minimal elements. The sampled letters are used in queries to characterize the successors of q. In order to avoid an exponential growth in the number of membership queries, we refine the notion of evidence for symbolic words and ask queries only for the successors of *representative* evidences. Secondly, to determine whether a given counter-example leads to the discovery of a new state, to the introduction of a new transition or just to a modification of the partition boundaries associated with some existing transitions, we use an extended version of the breakpoint method of [26] which also appears in [16] in a similar form. This method identifies an erroneous position in the counter-example, classifies its nature and reacts accordingly.

We thus obtain an efficient algorithm for learning languages over large alphabets under much more realistic assumptions concerning the information available to the learner. We use one-dimensional numerical alphabets, partitioned into a bounded number of intervals, to illustrate the principles of the algorithm. The algorithmic scheme can be easily adapted to other domains provided that alphabet partitions are not too complex and consist of a small number of simple blocks. We demonstrate this fact by adapting the algorithm to Boolean alphabets partitioned into finitely many unions of sub-cubes.

The rest of the paper is organized as follows. In Sects. 2 and 3 we define, respectively, symbolic automata and symbolic observation tables while explaining their role in learning. The symbolic learning algorithm is described in detail in Sect. 4 for one-dimensional numerical domains, followed by its extension to Boolean alphabets in Sect. 5. Section 6 provide some theoretical and empirical evaluation of the algorithm performance. In Sect. 7 we summarize our results, compare with other work on learning over large alphabets and suggest directions for future work.

The paper assumes some familiarity with automaton learning and the reader is invited to read more detailed explanations of concrete learning algorithms in [5] and of the framework underlying this paper in [23]. Likewise, some basic acquaintance with decision trees is assumed that can be obtained by consulting [8].

2   Preliminaries

Let Σ be an alphabet, and let Σ^* be the set of all finite sequences (words) over Σ. With a language $L \subseteq \Sigma^*$ we associate a *characteristic function* $f : \Sigma^* \to \{+, -\}$, where $f(w) = +$ if $w \in L$ and $f(w) = -$, otherwise. With every $s \in \Sigma^*$ we associate a *residual characteristic function* defined as $f_s(w) = f(s{\cdot}w)$. Two sequences s and r are Nerode equivalent [24] with respect to L, denoted by $s \sim_L r$, if $f_s = f_r$. The relation $\sim_L$ is a right congruence satisfying $s \sim_L r \to s \cdot a \sim_L r \cdot a$ and its equivalence classes correspond to the states of the minimal automaton that accepts L. The identification of these classes underlies minimization procedures as well as most automaton learning algorithms since [13].

A *symbolic automaton* over a *concrete alphabet* Σ is an automaton whose transitions are labeled by *symbolic letters* or *symbols*, taken from a *symbolic alphabet* $\boldsymbol{\Sigma}$, that denote subsets of Σ. We assume $\boldsymbol{\Sigma}$ to be a disjoint union of finite alphabets of the form $\boldsymbol{\Sigma}_q$, each associated with a state of the automaton. Concrete letters are mapped to symbols through a mapping $\psi : \Sigma \to \boldsymbol{\Sigma}$, decomposable into state-specific mappings $\psi_q : \Sigma \to \boldsymbol{\Sigma}_q$. The Σ-*semantics* of a symbol $\boldsymbol{a} \in \boldsymbol{\Sigma}_q$ is the inverse of ψ_q, that is, $[\![\boldsymbol{a}]\!] = \{a \in \Sigma : \psi_q(a) = \boldsymbol{a}\}$. The Σ-semantics is extended to symbolic words of the form $\boldsymbol{w} = \boldsymbol{a}_1 \cdots \boldsymbol{a}_{|\boldsymbol{w}|} \in \boldsymbol{\Sigma}^*$ as the concatenation of the concrete one-letter languages associated with the respective symbolic letters or, recursively speaking, by letting $[\![\varepsilon]\!] = \{\varepsilon\}$ and $[\![\boldsymbol{w} \cdot \boldsymbol{a}]\!] = [\![\boldsymbol{w}]\!] \cdot [\![\boldsymbol{a}]\!]$ for $\boldsymbol{w} \in \boldsymbol{\Sigma}^*$, $\boldsymbol{a} \in \boldsymbol{\Sigma}$.

A symbolic automaton is *complete* and *deterministic* over Σ when for each state q the set $\{[\![\boldsymbol{a}]\!] : \boldsymbol{a} \in \boldsymbol{\Sigma}_q\}$ forms a partition of Σ. For this, we always let ψ_q be a total function. Moreover, by letting ψ to be surjective we avoid symbols with empty semantics. We often omit ψ and ψ_q from the notation and use $[\![\boldsymbol{a}]\!]$ when ψ, which is always present, is clear from the context.

Definition 1 (Symbolic Automaton). *A deterministic symbolic automaton is a tuple $\boldsymbol{\mathcal{A}} = (\Sigma, \boldsymbol{\Sigma}, \psi, Q, \boldsymbol{\delta}, q_0, F)$, where Σ is the input alphabet, $\boldsymbol{\Sigma}$ is a finite alphabet, decomposable into $\boldsymbol{\Sigma} = \biguplus_{q \in Q} \boldsymbol{\Sigma}_q$, $\psi = \{\psi_q : q \in Q\}$ is a family of total surjective functions $\psi_q : \Sigma \to \boldsymbol{\Sigma}_q$, Q is a finite set of states, q_0 is the initial state and F is the set of accepting states, $\boldsymbol{\delta} : Q \times \boldsymbol{\Sigma} \to Q$ is a partial transition function decomposable into a family of total functions $\boldsymbol{\delta}_q : \{q\} \times \boldsymbol{\Sigma}_q \to Q$.*

The transition function is extended to words as in the concrete case. The symbolic automaton can be viewed as an acceptor of a concrete language, that is, when at q and reading a concrete letter a, the automaton takes the transition $\boldsymbol{\delta}(q, \psi(a))$. Hence, the language $L(\boldsymbol{\mathcal{A}})$ consists of all concrete words whose run leads from q_0 to a state in F. A language $L \subseteq \Sigma^*$ is *symbolic recognizable* if there exists a symbolic automaton $\boldsymbol{\mathcal{A}}$ such that $L = L(\boldsymbol{\mathcal{A}})$.

3   Symbolic Observation Tables

The present algorithm relaxes the strong assumption of a helpful teacher [1,23]. Such a teacher responds positively to an equivalence query EQ($\boldsymbol{\mathcal{A}}$), where $\boldsymbol{\mathcal{A}}$ is an automaton conjectured by the learning algorithm, only if $L(\boldsymbol{\mathcal{A}})$ is indeed equivalent to the target language; otherwise, it returns a minimal counter-example which helps the learner to localize the modification site. In the new relaxed setting, equivalence queries are approximated by *testing queries*: a call to EQ yields membership queries for a set of randomly selected words; when all of them agree with the hypothesis, the algorithm terminates with a non-zero probability of misclassification; otherwise, we have a counter-example to process. The number of such queries may depend on what we assume about the distribution over Σ^* and what we want to prove about the algorithm, for example PAC learnability as in [1], which is further discussed in Sect. 6.

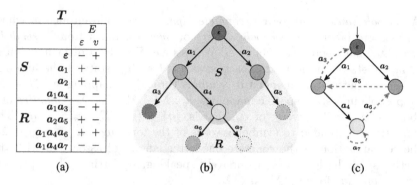

Fig. 1. (a) A symbolic observation table, (b) its balanced symbolic Σ-tree, and (c) the conjectured automaton.

Counter-examples obtained via testing queries need not be minimal neither in length nor lexicographically and hence partition boundaries are determined with some possible approximation error. Unlike [23], the present algorithm requires the use of multiple evidences for each symbol. To avoid an undesirable growth in the number of queries one of the evidences is chosen as a *representative* and certain queries during subsequent stages of the learning process are restricted to words with a representative prefix.

As an underlying data-structure for identifying states based on examples we use symbolic observation tables [23], slightly modified to accommodate for representative and non-representative evidences. The rows of the table correspond to symbolic words (access sequences to states) while the columns are concrete words. Readers unfamiliar with L^* [1] can find in [23] more detailed intuitive explanations of observation tables and their adaptation to the symbolic setting.

Let Σ and $\boldsymbol{\Sigma}$ be two alphabets, let $\boldsymbol{S} \uplus \boldsymbol{R}$ be a prefix-closed subset of $\boldsymbol{\Sigma}^*$ and let $\psi = \{\psi_s\}_{s \in S}$ be a family of total surjective functions of the form $\psi_s :$ $\Sigma \to \boldsymbol{\Sigma}_s$, where $\biguplus_{s \in S} \boldsymbol{\Sigma}_s = \boldsymbol{\Sigma}$. A *balanced symbolic Σ-tree* is a tuple $(\boldsymbol{\Sigma}, \boldsymbol{S}, \boldsymbol{R}, \psi)$, where for every $s \in \boldsymbol{S}$ and $a \in \boldsymbol{\Sigma}_s$, $s \cdot a \in \boldsymbol{S} \cup \boldsymbol{R}$, and for any $r \in \boldsymbol{R}$ and $a \in \boldsymbol{\Sigma}$, $r \cdot a \notin \boldsymbol{S} \cup \boldsymbol{R}$. Elements of $\boldsymbol{R}$ are called *boundary elements* of the tree.

The structure of a balanced tree appears in Fig. 1-(b) together with its corresponding automaton at Fig. 1-(c). The underlying intuition is that elements of $\boldsymbol{S}$, also known as access sequences, correspond to a spanning tree of the transition graph of the automaton to be learned, while elements of the boundary $\boldsymbol{R}$ correspond to back- and cross-edges relative to this spanning tree.

Definition 2 (Symbolic Observation Table). *A symbolic observation table is a tuple $\boldsymbol{T} = (\Sigma, \boldsymbol{\Sigma}, \boldsymbol{S}, \boldsymbol{R}, \psi, E, \boldsymbol{f}, \mu, \hat{\mu})$ such that*

- *Σ is an alphabet,*
- *$(\boldsymbol{\Sigma}, \boldsymbol{S}, \boldsymbol{R}, \psi)$ is a balanced symbolic Σ-tree,*
- *$E \subseteq \Sigma^*$ is a set of distinguishing words,*
- *$\boldsymbol{f} : (\boldsymbol{S} \cup \boldsymbol{R}) \cdot E \to \{-, +\}$ is the symbolic classification function,*
- *$\mu : \boldsymbol{\Sigma} \to 2^{\Sigma} - \{\emptyset\}$ is the evidence function, where $\mu(\boldsymbol{a}) \subseteq \llbracket \boldsymbol{a} \rrbracket$ for all $\boldsymbol{a} \in \boldsymbol{\Sigma}$,*
- *$\hat{\mu} : \boldsymbol{\Sigma} \to \Sigma$ is the representative function, where $\hat{\mu}(\boldsymbol{a}) \in \mu(\boldsymbol{a})$ for all $\boldsymbol{a} \in \boldsymbol{\Sigma}$.*

The evidence and representative functions are extended to symbolic words in $S \cup R$ as follows:

$$\begin{aligned} \mu(\varepsilon) &= \{\varepsilon\} & \hat{\mu}(\varepsilon) &= \varepsilon \\ \mu(s \cdot a) &= \hat{\mu}(s) \cdot \mu(a) & \hat{\mu}(s \cdot a) &= \hat{\mu}(s) \cdot \hat{\mu}(a). \end{aligned} \qquad (1)$$

The symbolic characteristic function values are based on the representative of the symbolic prefix rather than the set of all evidences, i.e., to fill the (s, e) entry in the table we let $\boldsymbol{f}(\boldsymbol{s}, e) = f(\hat{\mu}(\boldsymbol{s}) \cdot e)$, where f is the characteristic function of the target language. With every $\boldsymbol{s} \in \boldsymbol{S} \cup \boldsymbol{R}$ we associate a *residual classification function* defined as $\boldsymbol{f_s}(e) = \boldsymbol{f}(\boldsymbol{s}, e)$. The symbolic sample associated with $\boldsymbol{T}$ is the set $M_{\boldsymbol{T}} = (\boldsymbol{S} \cup \boldsymbol{R}) \cdot E$ and the concrete sample is $M_T = \mu(\boldsymbol{S} \cup \boldsymbol{R}) \cdot E$.

Handling multiple evidences to determine partition boundaries is the major novel feature in learning symbolic automata. Evidences of the same symbol should behave the same and when this is not the case, that is, when two concrete letters in the evidence of a symbol lead to different residual functions, we call this a manifestation of *evidence incompatibility*. The rigorous detection and resolution of evidence incompatibility is a major contribution of the algorithm presented in this work. The topic has also been addressed in [17] but in an unsatisfactory manner, leaving the transition function undefined outside the evidence. Evidence incompatibility can be characterized and measured as follows.

Definition 3 (Incompatibility Instance). *Let $\mu_{\boldsymbol{s}} = \bigcup_{a \in \Sigma_s} \mu(a)$ be the set of all evidences for state $\boldsymbol{s}$. A state $\boldsymbol{s} \in \boldsymbol{S}$ has an* incompatibility instance *at evidence $a \in \mu_{\boldsymbol{s}}$ when $\boldsymbol{f}_{\hat{\mu}(\boldsymbol{s}) \cdot a} \neq \boldsymbol{f}_{\hat{\mu}(\boldsymbol{s}) \cdot \hat{\mu}(\psi_{\boldsymbol{s}}(a))}$, and this fact is denoted $\mathrm{INC}(\boldsymbol{s}, a)$. The* evidence incompatibility degree *associated with $\boldsymbol{s}$ is $M(\boldsymbol{s}) = |\{a \in \mu_{\boldsymbol{s}} : \mathrm{INC}(\boldsymbol{s}, a)\}|$.*

Definition 4 (Table Properties). *A table $\boldsymbol{T} = (\Sigma, \boldsymbol{\Sigma}, \boldsymbol{S}, \boldsymbol{R}, \psi, E, \boldsymbol{f}, \mu, \hat{\mu})$ is*

- Closed *if $\forall r \in \boldsymbol{R}, \exists s \in \boldsymbol{S}, \boldsymbol{f_r} = \boldsymbol{f_s}$,*
- Reduced *if $\forall s, s' \in \boldsymbol{S}, \boldsymbol{f_s} \neq \boldsymbol{f_{s'}}$, and*
- Evidence compatible *if $M(\boldsymbol{s}) = 0, \forall \boldsymbol{s} \in \boldsymbol{S}$.*

The following result [23] is the natural generalization of the derivation of an automaton from an observation table [1] to the symbolic setting.

Theorem 1 (Automaton from Table). *From a closed, reduced and evidence compatible table one can construct a deterministic symbolic automaton compatible with the concrete sample.*

Proof. The proof is similar to the concrete case. Let $\boldsymbol{T} = (\Sigma, \boldsymbol{\Sigma}, \boldsymbol{S}, \boldsymbol{R}, \psi, E, \boldsymbol{f}, \mu, \hat{\mu})$ be such a table, which is reduced and closed and thus a function $g : \boldsymbol{R} \to \boldsymbol{S}$, such that $g(\boldsymbol{r}) = \boldsymbol{s}$ iff $\boldsymbol{f_r} = \boldsymbol{f_s}$, is well defined. The automaton derived from the table is then $\mathcal{A}_{\boldsymbol{T}} = (\Sigma, \boldsymbol{\Sigma}, \psi, Q, \boldsymbol{\delta}, q_0, F)$, where $Q = \boldsymbol{S}$, $q_0 = \varepsilon$, $F = \{\boldsymbol{s} \in \boldsymbol{S} : \boldsymbol{f_s}(\varepsilon) = +\}$, and $\boldsymbol{\delta} : Q \times \boldsymbol{\Sigma} \to Q$ is defined as

$$\boldsymbol{\delta}(\boldsymbol{s}, a) = \begin{cases} \boldsymbol{s} \cdot a & \text{when } \boldsymbol{s} \cdot a \in \boldsymbol{S} \\ g(\boldsymbol{s} \cdot a) & \text{when } \boldsymbol{s} \cdot a \in \boldsymbol{R} \end{cases}$$

By construction and like the L^* algorithm, $\mathcal{A}_T$ classifies correctly via f the symbolic sample and, due to evidence compatibility, this classification agrees with the characteristic function f on the concrete sample. $\square$

4   The Symbolic Learning Algorithm

In this section we present the symbolic learning algorithm using a high-cardinality bounded subset of $\mathbb{N}$ or $\mathbb{R}$ as an input alphabet. The concrete semantics of each symbolic letter is a sub-interval of the alphabet. We disallow disconnected partition blocks, for example, two subsets of even and odd numbers, respectively. Thus, if two disconnected intervals take the same transition, two symbolic letters will be considered. In this setting, the endpoints of an interval associated with a symbolic letter are such that all evidence points between them have the same residual function, while the nearest points outside the interval have different residuals. The algorithm adapts easily to other alphabet types as we will show in Sect. 5.

The symbolic learning algorithm (Algorithm 1) alternates between two phases. In the first phase it attempts to make the table closed and evidence compatible so as to construct a symbolic automaton. In the second phase, after formulating an equivalence query (EQ), it processes the provided counter-example which renders the table not closed or evidence incompatible. These phases alternate until no counter-example is found. Note that the table, by construction, is always kept reduced. We use MQ as a shorthand for membership queries.

Table Initialization (Procedure 2). The algorithm builds an initial observation table T, with $\Sigma_\varepsilon = \{a\}$, $S = \{\varepsilon\}$, $R = \{a\}$, $E = \{\varepsilon\}$. The newly introduced symbol a is initialized with concrete semantics, evidence and a representative,

---

Algorithm 1. A sampling-based symbolic learning algorithm

1: *learned* = *false*
2: INITTABLE(T)
3: **repeat**
4:      **while** T is not closed **or** not evidence compatible **do**
5:          CLOSE
6:          EVCOMP
7:      **end while**
8:      **if** EQ($\mathcal{A}_T$) **then**   ▷ check hypothesis $\mathcal{A}_T$
9:          *learned* = *true*
10:     **else**   ▷ a counter-example w is provided
11:         COUNTEREX($\mathcal{A}_T, w$)   ▷ process counter-example
12:     **end if**
13: **until** *learned*

Procedure 2. Initialize the table

1: **procedure** INITTABLE(T)
2:   $\Sigma_\varepsilon = \{a\}$; $S = \{\varepsilon\}$; $R = \{a\}$; $E = \{\varepsilon\}$ ▷ a is a new symbol
3:     INITSYMBOL(a)
4:     Ask MQ(u) for all $u \in \mu(a) \cup \{\varepsilon\}$
5:     $f(\varepsilon) = f(\varepsilon)$; $f(a) = f(\hat{\mu}(a))$
6:     $T = (\Sigma, \boldsymbol{\Sigma}, S, R, \psi, E, f, \mu, \hat{\mu})$
7: **end procedure**

Procedure 3. Initialize new symbol a

1: **procedure** INITSYMBOL(a)
2:   $[\![a]\!] = \Sigma$
3:   $\mu(a) = sample(\Sigma, k)$
4:   $\hat{\mu}(a) = select(\mu(a))$
5: **end procedure**

---

via the procedure INITSYMBOL which is invoked each time a new state is introduced. Then membership queries are posed to update f and fill the table.

Symbol Initialization (Procedure 3). For a new symbolic letter a we let $[\![a]\!] = \Sigma$ and as an evidence $\mu(a)$ we take a set of k concrete letters, denoted by $sample(\Sigma, k)$. This set can be selected randomly or be the result of a more adaptive process that may depend on the outcome of membership queries. One element of the evidence, denoted by $select(\mu(a))$, is chosen as a representative and will be used to fill table entries for all rows in which a appears. Already at this stage, some elements of $\mu(a)$ may behave differently from the representative and this will flag an evidence incompatibility condition to be treated subsequently.

Table Closing (Procedure 4). A table is not closed when there exists some $r \in R$ without any equivalent element $s \in S$ such that $f_r = f_s$. To render the table closed r should be considered as a new state. To this end, r is moved from R to S with alphabet $\Sigma_r = \{a\}$, where a is a new symbol which is initialized. To balance the table a new word $r \cdot a$ is added to R, its evidence $\mu(r \cdot a)$ and representative $\hat{\mu}(r \cdot a)$ are computed following (1) and membership queries are posed to update f and fill the table.

Fixing Evidence Incompatibility (Procedure 5). A table is not evidence compatible when the incompatibility degree of a state in S is greater than zero. Evidence incompatibility appears either after the initialization of a symbol, or after a counter-example treatment. It is resolved by consecutive calls to EVCOMP where each call reduces $M(s)$ until the total incompatibility degree of the observation table becomes zero.

Procedure 4. Close the table

1: **procedure** CLOSE
2:    **Given** $r \in R$ such that $\forall s \in S$, $f_r \neq f_s$
3:    $S = S \cup \{r\}$ ▷ declare r a new state
4:    $\Sigma_r = \{a\}$ ▷ introduce a new symbol a
5:    INITSYMBOL(a)
6:    $R = (R - \{r\}) \cup \{r \cdot a\}$ ▷ add new boundary element
7:    Ask MQ(u) for all $u \in \mu(r \cdot a) \cdot E$
8:    $f_{r \cdot a} = f_{\hat\mu(r \cdot a)}$
9: **end procedure**

For a state s, an incompatibility instance at a indicates either that the partition boundary is imprecise or that a transition (and its corresponding symbol) is missing. In the first case, the incompatible evidence a appears next to the boundary of the interval and its classification matches the classification of a neighboring symbol a'. In this situation, modifying the boundary so that a is moved to $[\![a']\!]$ resolves the incompatibility. On the the other hand, when the evidence a is in the interior of an interval, or does not behave like a neighboring symbol, the incompatibility is resolved by adding a new symbol and refining the existing partition. These two cases are illustrated in Figs. 2-(a) and (b), respectively.

Formally, let $s \in S$ be a state with positive incompatibility degree $M(s) > 0$, and let $\mu_s = \{a^1, \ldots, a^k\} \subset S$ be the set of evidences, ordered such that $a^{i-1} < a^i$ for all i. To simplify notation, f^i denotes the residual $f_{\hat\mu(s) \cdot a^i}$ when state s is understood from the context. Moreover, let a^j and a^{j+1} denote symbols in Σ_s with adjacent semantics, that is, given any three letters $a, b, c \in \Sigma$, with $a < b < c$, then $a \in [\![a^j]\!] \wedge c \in [\![a^{j+1}]\!]$ implies $b \in [\![a^j]\!] \cup [\![a^{j+1}]\!]$.

Let $a^{i-1}, a^i \in \mu_s$ be two evidences from the same interval that behave differently, $f^{i-1} \neq f^i$, and let $a^j \in \Sigma_s$ be the symbol such that $a^{i-1}, a^i \in \mu(a^j)$ where $[\![a^j]\!] = [c, c')$. Procedure $p = split(a^{i-1}, a^i)$ returns a point $p \in (a^{i-1}, a^i)$ between them. We let $split$ return the middle point, $split(a, a') = (a + a')/2$. One can think of more sophisticated methods, based on binary search, that can be applied instead.

Procedure 5 fixes the incompatibility by separating a^{i-1} and a^i and mapping them to different symbols. The way this separation is realized, with or without introducing a new symbol, depends on the positions of a^{i-1} and a^i in the set of evidences and the residual functions of their neighboring intervals.

1. *Boundary modification.* Suppose the incompatibility instance is at $a^i \in \mu(a^j)$ and that all other evidences $\mu(a^j)$ to the right of a^i behave like $\min \mu(a^{j+1})$. By changing the partition boundaries and moving a^i from $[\![a^j]\!]$ to $[\![a^{j+1}]\!]$, the incompatibility instance at a^i is eliminated. The new boundary between these two intervals is set to p, see Fig. 2-(a). The symmetric case, where the

---

Procedure 5. Make evidence compatible

1: **procedure** EvComp
2:     Let $s \in S$, for which $M(s) > 0$, where
3:     $\mu_s = \{a^1, \ldots, a^k\}$ such that $a^{i-1} < a^i, \forall i = 2, \ldots, k$
4:     Let $a^j \in \Sigma_s$, $[\![a^j]\!] = [c, c')$, such that $\exists i : f^{i-1} \neq f^i$ for $a^{i-1}, a^i \in \mu(a^j)$
5:     $p = split(a^{i-1}, a^i)$ ▷ new partitioning point
6:     **if** $f^i = f^{i+1} = \cdots = f^{i+l+1}$ where $a^i, \ldots, a^{i+l} \in \mu(a^j), a^{i+l+1} \in \mu(a^{j+1})$ **then**
7:         $[\![a^j]\!] = [c, p)$; $[\![a^{j+1}]\!] = [p, c') \cup [\![a^{j+1}]\!]$ ▷ change right frontier
8:         $\mu(a^{j+1}) = (\mu(a^{j+1}) \cup \mu(a^j)) \cap [\![a^{j+1}]\!]$
9:         $\mu(a^j) = \mu(a^j) \cap [\![a^j]\!]$
10:     **else if** $f^{i-1} = \cdots = f^{i-l}$ where $a^{i-1}, \ldots, a^{i-l+1} \in \mu(a^j), a^{i-l} \in \mu(a^{j-1})$ **then**
11:         $[\![a^{j-1}]\!] = [\![a^{j-1}]\!] \cup [c, p)$; $[\![a^j]\!] = [p, c')$ ▷ change left frontier
12:         $\mu(a^{j-1}) = (\mu(a^{j-1}) \cup \mu(a^j)) \cap [\![a^{j-1}]\!]$
13:         $\mu(a^j) = \mu(a^j) \cap [\![a^j]\!]$
14:     **else**
15:         $\Sigma_s = \Sigma_s \cup \{b\}$ ▷ introduce a new symbol b
16:         $R = R \cup \{s \cdot b\}$
17:         **if** $\hat{\mu}(a^j) \leq p$ **then**
18:             $[\![a^j]\!] = [c, p)$; $[\![b]\!] = [p, c')$
19:         **else**
20:             $[\![b]\!] = [c, p)$; $[\![a^j]\!] = [p, c')$
21:         **end if**
22:         $\mu(b) = \mu(a^j) \cap [\![b]\!]$; $\mu(a^j) = \mu(a^j) \cap [\![a^j]\!]$
23:         $\hat{\mu}(b) = select(\mu(b))$
24:         $f_{s \cdot b} = f_{\hat{\mu}(s \cdot b)}$
25:     **end if**
26: **end procedure**

---

incompatibility occurs at $a^{i-1} \in a^j$ with all other evidences of $\mu(a^j)$ on its left behaving like $\max \mu(a^{j-1})$, is treated similarly.

2. *Symbol introduction.* When the above condition does not hold and boundary modification cannot be applied, the incompatibility is solved by refining the partition. The semantics $[\![a^j]\!]$ is split into two intervals $[c, p)$ and $[p, c')$, a new symbol b is introduced and the interval not containing $\hat{\mu}(a^j)$ is moved from $[\![a^j]\!]$ to $[\![b]\!]$ along with the evidences it contains, see Fig. 2-(b).

Processing Counter-Examples (Procedure 6). A counter-example is a word w misclassified by the current hypothesis. The automaton should be modified to classify w correctly while remaining compatible with the evidence accumulated so far. These modifications can be of two major types that we call *vertical* and *horizontal*. The first type, which is the only possible modification in concrete learning, involves the discovery of a new state $s \cdot a$. A counter-example which demonstrates that some letter a took a wrong transition $\delta(s, a)$ has a horizontal effect that fixes a transition or adds a new one without creating a new state. The procedure described in the sequel reacts to the counter-example by adding a to the evidence of s and thus modifying the table, which should then be made closed and evidence compatible before we continue with a new hypothesis.

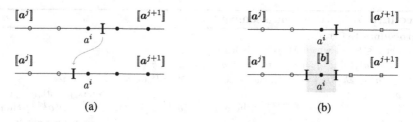

Fig. 2. Evidence incompatibility solved either by (a) boundary modification, or by (b) introducing a new symbol. This depends on the position of the incompatibility instance inside the partition.

The same counter-example is tested again and when it is correctly classified, we proceed by posing a new equivalence query. We treat counter-examples using a symbolic variant of the breakpoint method introduced in [26]. A similar method has been proposed in [16].

Let $\mathcal{A}_T$ be a symbolic automaton derived from a symbolic table T, and let $w = a_1 \cdots a_{|w|}$ be a counter-example whose symbolic image is $\boldsymbol{a}_1 \cdots \boldsymbol{a}_{|w|}$. An *i-factorization* of w is $w = u_i \cdot a_i \cdot v_i$ such that $u_i = a_1 \cdots a_{i-1}$ and $v_i = a_{i+1} \cdots a_{|w|}$. For every *i*-factorization of w, we let $\boldsymbol{u}_i$ be the symbolic image of u_i, and $\boldsymbol{s}_i = \delta(\varepsilon, \boldsymbol{u}_i \cdot \boldsymbol{a}_i)$ be the symbolic state (an element of $\boldsymbol{S}$) reached in $\mathcal{A}_T$ after reading $\boldsymbol{u}_i \cdot \boldsymbol{a}_i$.

Proposition 1 (Symbolic Breakpoint). *If w is a counter-example to $\mathcal{A}_T$ then there exists an i-factorization of w such that either*

$$f(\hat{\mu}(\boldsymbol{s}_{i-1}) \cdot a_i \cdot v_i) \neq f(\hat{\mu}(\boldsymbol{s}_{i-1}) \cdot \hat{\mu}(\boldsymbol{a}_i) \cdot v_i) \tag{2}$$

or

$$f(\hat{\mu}(\boldsymbol{s}_{i-1} \cdot \boldsymbol{a}_i) \cdot v_i) \neq f(\hat{\mu}(\boldsymbol{s}_i) \cdot v_i) \tag{3}$$

Proof. Condition (2) states that a_i is not well represented by $\hat{\mu}(\boldsymbol{a}_i)$ while Condition (3) implies $\boldsymbol{s}_{i-1} \cdot \boldsymbol{a}_i$ is a new state different from $\boldsymbol{s}_i$, see Fig. 3. We prove the proposition assuming that none of the above inequalities holds for any *i*-factorization of w. By using alternatively the negations of (2) and (3) for all values of i, we conclude that $f(\hat{\mu}(\boldsymbol{s}_0) \cdot a_1 \cdot v_1) = f(\hat{\mu}(\boldsymbol{s}_{|w|}))$, where $\hat{\mu}(\boldsymbol{s}_0) \cdot a_1 \cdot v_1$ is the counter-example and $\boldsymbol{s}_{|w|}$ is the state reached in $\mathcal{A}_T$ after reading w. Thus w cannot be a counter-example. □

Procedure 6 iterates over i values and checks whether one of the conditions (2) and (3) holds for some i. We let i take values in a monotonically descending order and keep the suffixes as short as possible. In this case, it suffices to compare $f(\hat{\mu}(\boldsymbol{s}_{i-1} \cdot \boldsymbol{a}_i) \cdot v_i)$ and $f(\hat{\mu}(\boldsymbol{s}_{i-1}) \cdot a_i \cdot v_i)$ with the classification of the counter-example, which is kept in a flag variable. In line 5, Condition (3) is checked and if it holds, adding v_i to E will distinguish between states $\boldsymbol{s}_{i-1} \cdot \boldsymbol{a}_i$ and $\boldsymbol{s}_i$, resulting in a table which is not closed. Otherwise, if Condition (2) holds,

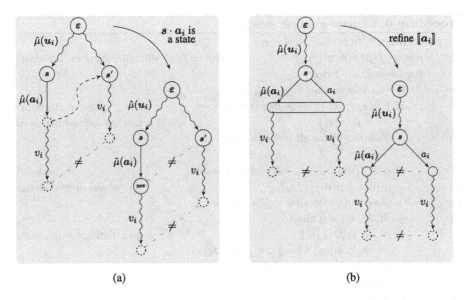

(a)   (b)

Fig. 3. A counter-example expands a hypothesis either (a) vertically, discovering a new state; or (b) horizontally, modifying the alphabet partition in a state.

which is checked in line 9, the letter a_i is added to the evidence of a_i and new membership queries are posed. These queries will render the table evidence incompatible and will lead to refining $[\![a_i]\!]$. The suffix v_i is added to E in case it is the only witness for the incompatibility. Note that checking the conditions involves supplementary membership queries, based on the suffix of the counter-example w, where the prefix u_i of w is replaced by $\hat{\mu}(s_{i-1})$, the representative of its shortest equivalent symbolic word in the table. Both cases will lead to a new conjectured automaton which might still not classify w correctly. In that case, the procedure should be invoked with the same counter-example and the new hypothesis until $\mathcal{A}_T$ classifies w correctly.

Example 1. We demonstrate the working of the algorithm in learning a target language L over the alphabet $\Sigma = [0, 100) \subseteq \mathbb{R}$. The observation tables, semantic functions and hypotheses used in this example are shown in Figs. 4 and 5.

The table is initialized with $S = \{\varepsilon\}$ and $E = \{\varepsilon\}$. To determine the alphabet partition at the initial state ε, the learner asks membership queries for the randomly selected one-letter words $\{13, 42, 68, 78, 92\}$. All words in this set except 13 are rejected. Consequently, there are at least two distinct intervals that we take $split(13, 42) = 27$ as their boundary. Each interval is represented by a symbolic letter resulting in $\Sigma_\varepsilon = \{a_1, a_2\}$, $\mu(a_1) = \{13\}$, $\hat{\mu}(a_1) = 13$, $\mu(a_2) = \{42, 68, 78, 92\}$, and $\hat{\mu}(a_2) = 68$. The representatives are randomly chosen from the set of evidences. The semantics, ψ maps all letters smaller than 27 to a_1, and maps the rest to a_2, that is, $[\![a_1]\!] = [0, 27)$ and $[\![a_2]\!] = [27, 100)$. The table boundary updates to $R = \{a_1, a_2\}$ and the observation table is T_0, shown in Fig. 4.

Procedure 6. Counter-example treatment

```
 1: procedure COUNTEREX(𝒜_T, w)
 2:     flag = f(μ̂(δ(ε, w)))                              ▷ flag = f(w) when iterating on 1,…,|w|
 3:     for i = |w|,…, 1 do
 4:         For an i-factorization w = u_i · a_i · v_i
 5:         if f(μ̂(s_{i-1} · a_i) · v_i) ≠ flag then                        ▷ check (3)
 6:             E = E ∪ {v_i}                            ▷ add a new distinguishing word
 7:             Ask MQ(u) for all u ∈ μ(S ∪ R) · v_i
 8:             break
 9:         else if f(μ̂(s_{i-1}) · a_i · v_i) ≠ flag then                    ▷ check (2)
10:             μ(a_i) = μ(a_i) ∪ {a_i}                          ▷ add new evidence
11:             Ask MQ(u) for all u ∈ μ̂(s_{i-1}) · a_i · E
12:             if M(s_i) = 0 then
13:                 E = E ∪ {v_i}                        ▷ add distinguishing word
14:                 Ask MQ(u) for all u ∈ μ(S ∪ R) · v_i
15:             end if
16:             break
17:         end if
18:     end for
19: end procedure
```

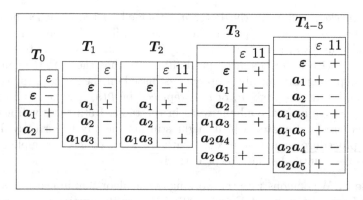

Fig. 4. Observation tables used in Example 1.

Table T_0 is not closed and in order to fix this, the learner moves a_1 to the set of states S. To find the possible partitions of Σ at this new state a_1, the learner randomly chooses a sample $\{2, 18, 26, 46, 54\}$ of letters and asks membership queries concerning the words in $\{13 \cdot 2, 13 \cdot 18, 13 \cdot 26, 13 \cdot 46, 13 \cdot 54\}$. Note that the prefix used here is the representative of a_1. The teacher classifies all words as rejected. The new table is T_1 with $\Sigma_{a_1} = \{a_3\}$, $\mu(a_3) = \{2, 18, 26, 46, 54\}$, $\hat{\mu}(a_3) = 18$, and $[\![a_3]\!] = [0, 100)$. The new table is closed and the first hypothesis $\mathcal{A}_1$ is conjectured.

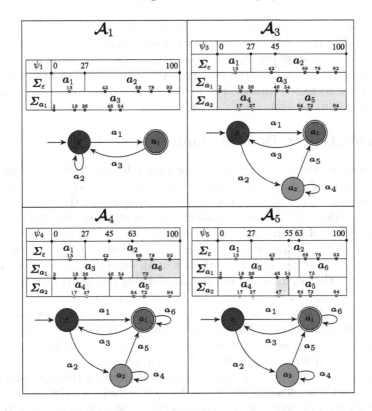

Fig. 5. Symbolic automata and semantics function learned in Example 1.

The hypothesis is tested on a set of words, randomly chosen from some distribution, typically unknown to the learner. After some successful tests, a word $35 \cdot 52 \cdot 11$ is found, which is accepted by $\mathcal{A}_1$ but is outside the target language. The learner takes this word as a counter-example and analyzes it using the symbolic breakpoint method. At iteration $i = 2$ of Procedure 6, condition (3) is violated, in particular $\text{MQ}(\hat{\mu}(\varepsilon \cdot a_2) \cdot 11) = \text{MQ}(68 \cdot 11) \neq \mathit{flag} = +$. Thus, the suffix 11 is added as a distinguishing word to E. The observation table T_2 obtained after adding the new suffix is, as expected, not closed. The table is made closed by letting a_2 be a new state, resulting in table T_3, where $\Sigma_{a_2} = \{a_4, a_5\}$, $\mu(a_4) = \{17, 27\}$, $\hat{\mu}(a_4) = 17$, $[\![a_4]\!] = [0, 45)$, $\mu(a_5) = \{64, 72, 94\}$, $\hat{\mu}(a_5) = 72$ and $[\![a_5]\!] = [45, 100)$. The corresponding new conjecture is $\mathcal{A}_3$.

Automaton $\mathcal{A}_3$ is tested and a counter-example $12 \cdot 73 \cdot 4$ is provided. The breakpoint method discovers that condition (2) is violated, because letter 73 is not part of the semantics of a_3. This letter is added as a new evidence to $\mu(a_3)$. The evidence inconsistency is solved by splitting the existing partition into two subintervals. A new symbol a_6 is added to Σ_{a_1}, such that $\mu(a_6) = \{73\}$ and $[\![a_6]\!] = [63, 100)$. The new observation table and hypothesis automaton are T_4 and $\mathcal{A}_4$, respectively.

The next counter-example $52 \cdot 47$, also adds a new evidence, this time to symbol a_5. The classification of the new evidence matches the classification of a_4, which is a neighboring symbol. The boundary between $[\![a_4]\!]$ and $[\![a_5]\!]$ is moved from 45 to 55, thus resolving the evidence incompatibility. The new hypothesis $\mathcal{A}_5$ is successfully tested without discovering any other counter-example and the algorithm terminates while returning $\mathcal{A}_5$ as an answer.   □

5   Adaptation to Boolean Alphabets

We demonstrate the versatility of the algorithm by adapting it to languages over the alphabet $\Sigma = \mathbb{B}^n$ of Boolean vectors accessed by variables $\{x_1, \ldots, x_n\}$. All components of the algorithm remain the same except the construction of alphabet partitions and their modification due to evidence incompatibility. These should be adapted to the particular nature of the Boolean hyper-cube. The concrete semantics of the symbolic letters in a state q will be defined by a function $\psi_q : \mathbb{B}^n \to \Sigma_q$. Let μ_s be the set of all evidences for state s. At any given moment, the raw data for inducing the alphabet partition at s is the sample $\{(a^i, f^i) : a^i \in \mu_s\}$ where for every a^i, $f^i = f_{\hat{\mu}(s) \cdot a^i}$ is the residual associated with a^i. Let $\mathcal{F}_s$ denote the set of all observed distinct residuals associated with the one-letter successors of s. On our way to construct ψ_q, we first derive another function $\psi_s : \mathbb{B}^n \to \mathcal{F}_s$ associated with any $s \in S$. The function ψ_s is compatible with the sample if it agrees with it on the elements of μ_s.

We represent both ψ_s and ψ_q by isomorphic decision trees [8] whose leaf nodes are labeled by elements of $\mathcal{F}_s$ and Σ_q, respectively. By abuse of notation, we use ψ for the functions and for their associated decision trees. We first build ψ_s as a decision tree where all evidences mapped to the same leaf node agree on their residual function. Hence, learning alphabet partitions is an instance of learning decision trees using algorithms such as CART [8], ID3 [25], or ID5 [28] that construct a tree compatible with a labeled sample.

These algorithms work roughly as follows. They start with a tree consisting of a single root node, with which all sample points are associated. A node is said to be *pure* if all its sample points have the same label. For each impure node, two descendants are created and the sample is split among them based on the value of some selected variable x_i. The variable is chosen according to some purity measure, such as information gain, that characterizes the quality of the split based on each variable. The selection is greedy and the algorithm terminates when the tree becomes sample compatible and sends each sample point to a pure leaf node.

Evidence incompatibility in a state s appears when the decision tree ψ_s is not compatible with the sample. This may happen in three occasions during the execution of the algorithm, the first being symbol initialization. Recall that when a new state s is introduced, we create a new symbol a and collect evidences for it, which may have different residuals while being associated with the same single root node. The second occasion occurs when new evidence is added to a symbol, making a leaf node in the tree impure. Finally, when some new suffix is added to E, the set $\mathcal{F}_s$ of distinct residuals (rows in the table) may increase and the labels of existing evidences may change.

Procedure 7. Make evidence compatible (Boolean alphabets)

1: **procedure** EvComp
2:      Let $s \in S$ be a state for which $M(s) > 0$
3:      Update(ψ_s) ▷ build a tree consistent with sample
4:      **for all** $h \in \mathcal{F}_s$ **do**   ▷ for all existing residuals
5:          **if** $\exists a \in \Sigma_s$ s.t. $h = f_{\hat{\mu}(s) \cdot \hat{\mu}(a)}$ **then**
6:                       ▷ h is already associated with an existing symbol a
7:              $\mu(a) = \{a^i \in \mu_s : f^i = h\}$ ▷ update evidence
8:              $[\![a]\!] = \bigcup\{[\![t]\!] : t \in leaves(\psi_s)$ and $label(t) = h\}$ ▷ update semantics
9:          **else**   ▷ h does not match any pre-existing residual
10:              $\Sigma_s = \Sigma_s \cup \{b\}$ ▷ introduce a new symbol
11:              $R = R \cup \{s \cdot b\}$ ▷ and a new candidate state
12:              $\mu(b) = \{a^i \in \mu_s : f^i = h\}$ ▷ define evidence
13:              $\hat{\mu}(b) = select(\mu(b))$ ▷ select representative
14:              $[\![b]\!] = \bigcup\{[\![t]\!] : t \in leaves(\psi_s)$ and $label(t) = h\}$ ▷ update semantics
15:          **end if**
16:      **end for**
17: **end procedure**

The simplest way to fix a decision tree is to split impure leaf nodes until purification. However, this may lead to very deep trees and it is preferable to reconstruct the tree each time the sample is updated in a way that leads to incompatibility. In the simple (second) case where a new evidence is added, we can use an incremental algorithm such as ID5 [28], which restructures only parts of the tree that need to be modified, leaving the rest of the tree intact. This algorithm produces the same tree as a non-incremental algorithm would, while performing less computation. In the third case, we build the tree from scratch and this is also what we do after initialization where the incremental and non-incremental algorithms coincide.

Once a tree ψ_s is made compatible with the sample, the semantics of the symbolic alphabet, expressed via ψ_s, is updated. This is nothing but mapping the leaves of ψ_s to Σ_q. Had we wanted to follow the "convex" partition approach that we used for numerical alphabets, we should have associated a fresh symbol with each leaf node of the tree, thus letting $[\![a]\!]$ be a cube/term for every $a \in \Sigma_q$. We prefer, however, to associate the same symbol with multiple leaf nodes that share the same label, allowing the semantics of a symbol to be a finite union of cubes. This way $|\Sigma_s| = |\mathcal{F}_s|$ and there is at most one symbol that labels a transition between any pair of states.

Each time ψ_s is restructured, we modify ψ_q as follows. First, with each symbol a that already exists, we re-associate the leaves that agree with the labels of its representative (note that the representative of an existing symbol never changes). Then, in the case where the set $\mathcal{F}_s$ of distinct residuals has increased, we introduce a new symbolic letter for each new residual and select its representative. The whole process is described in Procedure 7. We use $[\![t]\!]$ to denote all evidences associated with a leaf node t and $label(t)$ to denote its residual.

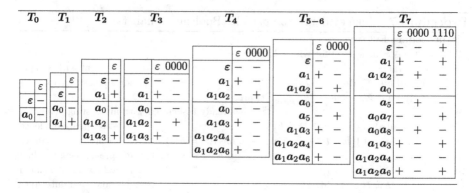

Fig. 6. Observation tables generated during the execution of the algorithm on Example 2.

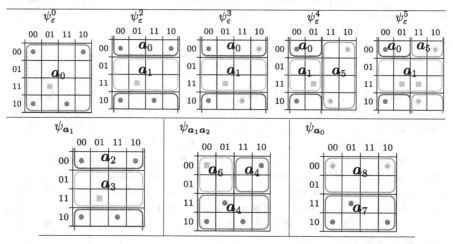

Fig. 7. Semantics functions used in Example 2. We show the evolution of ψ_ε over time, while for the other states we show only the final partition. We use symbols such as $\{\bullet, \blacksquare, \blacklozenge\}$ to indicate different residuals.

Example 2. We show how the algorithm learns a target language over $\Sigma = \mathbb{B}^4$. All tables encountered during the execution of the algorithm are shown in Fig. 6 and the decision trees appear in Fig. 7 in the form of Karnaugh maps. The learner starts by initializing the observation table. Like any new state, initial state ε admits one outgoing transition that represents all concrete letters, that is $\Sigma_\varepsilon = \{a_0\}$ and $[\![a_0]\!] = \Sigma$. A set of concrete letters is sampled and is used as the evidence for the new symbol, $\mu(a_0) = \{(0000), (0010), (1011), (1000), (1101)\}$, while $\hat{\mu}(a_0) = (0000)$ is chosen as a representative. At this point, the observation table is T_0 and the decision tree is ψ_ε^0, consisting of a single node.

The observation table is not evidence compatible because evidence $(1101) \in \mu(a_0)$ behaves differently, and thus the partition needs refinement. The tree

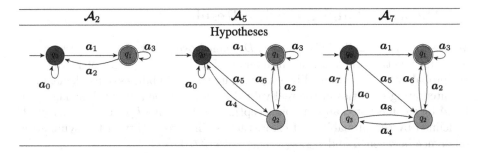

Fig. 8. Intermediate and final conjectured automata for Example 2.

induction algorithm CART, which is used throughout this example, finds that Σ is best split into two blocks based on the values of variable x_2. That is, all letters for which $x_2 = 0$ are mapped to a_0 while the others are mapped to a new symbol a_1, added to Σ_ε (see ψ_ε^2). The resulting observation table T_1 is made closed by letting a_1 be a state. The evidence for the new state/symbol is sampled and, after resolving evidence incompatibility for it, we obtain the table T_2 with $\psi = \{\psi_\varepsilon^2, \psi_{a_1}\}$.

The first conjectured automaton A_2, shown in Fig. 8, is tested. A counter-example $w = (1010) \cdot (0000)$ is found and the learner applies the breakpoint method which adds the distinguishing word (0000) to E. The table is filled in by posing MQ's, resulting in T_3 which is neither closed nor evidence compatible.

The table is made closed with $a_1 a_2$ becoming a state. The outgoing transitions are defined as before, resulting in table T_4 and $\psi_{a_1 a_2}$. The added suffix (0000) causes an evidence incompatibility at ε by changing the residual functions of the evidence, see ψ_ε^3. The decision tree is reconstructed from scratch to become compatible with the updated sample. Then the symbols are rearranged so as to match the residuals of their representatives and a new symbol a_5 is added. The partition is updated to the evidence compatible ψ_ε^4 and the corresponding observation table is T_5.

The new hypothesis A_5 is tested for equivalence, providing the counter-example (1111). The breakpoint method adds (1111) to $\mu(a_5)$ as a new evidence, causing once more an incompatibility at the initial state, which is fixed by updating the tree ψ_ε into ψ_ε^5. Since this incompatibility is due to a new evidence, the tree is updated using an incremental algorithm. Observe that this last counter-example only fixes the partition by rearranging the sub-cubes of $\mathbb{B}^4$ without adding any new transition.

A counter-example to the next hypothesis A_6 is $w = (1000) \cdot (1000) \cdot (0000) \cdot (0000) \cdot (1110)$, which adds the new suffix (1110) to E. The prefix a_0 is now identified as a state and after refining ψ_{a_0} to become evidence compatible, the observation table T_7 is obtained. The new and last hypothesis A_7 is tested on 855 words with no counter-example. We can conclude (see next section) with 95% confidence that A_7 is correct with a maximum error of 1%.   □

6   Theoretical and Empirical Results

We assume a probability distribution D defined over Σ^* which is expressed via a density function when Σ is a sub-interval of $\mathbb{R}$. For any $L \subseteq \Sigma^*$ let $Pr_D(L)$ be the probability of L, obtained by summing up the probabilities of its elements or by integrating densities in the real-valued case. Let L be a target language and let $\mathcal{A}$ be a conjectured automaton accepting the language $L_{\mathcal{A}}$. The quality of $\mathcal{A}$ is defined by the probability of error, that is, the probability of the symmetric difference between L and $L_{\mathcal{A}}$: $d(L, L_{\mathcal{A}}) = Pr_D(L \oplus L_{\mathcal{A}})$.

Definition 5 (PAC Learning [29]**).** *A learning algorithm learns a language L in a probably-approximately correct (PAC) manner with probability parameters ϵ (accuracy) and δ (confidence) if its output $\mathcal{A}$ satisfies $Pr(d(L, L_{\mathcal{A}}) \leq \epsilon) \geq 1 - \delta$.*

Given that our algorithm implements equivalence checks by comparing membership in L and in $L_{\mathcal{A}}$ for words randomly selected according to D, the following result from [1] applies in a straightforward way to the symbolic case.

Proposition 2. *The symbolic learning algorithm PAC-learns a language L if the i-th equivalence query tests $r_i = \frac{1}{\epsilon}(\ln \frac{1}{\delta} + (i + 1) \ln 2)$ random words without finding a counter-example.*

A class of functions or sets is *efficiently* PAC learnable if there is an algorithm that PAC learns it in time (and number of queries) polynomial in $1/\epsilon$, $1/\delta$, and in the size parameters of the learned object. For a target language $L \subset \Sigma^*$, the size is based on the minimal symbolic automaton $\mathcal{A}$ recognizing L which is assumed to have n states and at most m outgoing transitions from every state.

Concerning the size of the observation table and the sample used to learn L, the set of prefixes S is monotonically increasing and reaches the size of at most n elements. Since the table, by construction, is always kept reduced, the elements in S represent exactly the states of the automaton. The size of the boundary is always smaller than the total number of transitions in the automaton, that is, $mn - n + 1$. The number of suffixes in E, that play a distinguishing role for the states of the automaton, range between $\log_2 n$ and n. The size of the table ranges between $(n + m) \log_2 n$ and $n(mn + 1)$. The size of the symbolic sample follows the size of prefixes and boundary which is at most $\mathcal{O}(mn^2)$, while the concrete sample depends on the number of evidences used in the table and its size is $\sum_{s \in S} |\mu_s| \cdot |E|$.

A counter-example improves a hypothesis either by expanding the automaton, discovering a new state or transition, or by modifying the boundaries of already existing transitions. At most $n - 1$ counter-examples discover new states and at most $n(m - 1)$ introduce new transitions, resulting in at most $\mathcal{O}(mn)$ equivalence queries and counter-examples of this kind. The number of counter-examples that only change the boundaries in a partition is bounded in a probabilistic setting of approximate learning. The probability of finding a non-expansive counter-example ultimately decreases converging to zero. Hence, there exists a hypothesis i for which after r_i tests no counter-example is returned.

From this we can conclude that our algorithm terminates, resulting in a symbolic automaton which is a PAC representation of the target language L.

Proposition 3. *The symbolic learning algorithm terminates with probability 1 returning a symbolic automaton that is a PAC acceptor of the target language L.*

Algorithm 1 and all procedures that appear in the present paper have been implemented in Python. In particular, methods $sample(\Sigma, k)$ in Procedure 3 returns a sample of size k chosen uniformly from Σ. Likewise, method $select(\cdot)$ uses a uniform distribution over the set of evidences to choose one representative. The *split* method, used in Procedure 5, returns the middle point of the interval. For the case of Boolean alphabets the UPDATE method in Procedure 7 uses the CART algorithm [8] with information gain as the purity measure.

For theoretical results, it is sufficient that the same distribution is assumed for the random queries and the error estimation. For the implementation of random queries and for the empirical evaluation we have to be more concrete. The distribution D that we use is a composition of two distributions: a log-normal distribution, used to select the length of the word, and a uniform distribution over the alphabet, used to choose a letter at each position in the word. The log-normal distribution is chosen so that shorter words are preferred over longer ones.

Once an automaton $\mathcal{A}$ has been learned by our algorithm, its quality can be evaluated as follows. When we have an explicit description of the automaton for the target language L, we can build its product with $\mathcal{A}$ to accept the symmetric difference $L' = L \oplus L_{\mathcal{A}}$. Then for any given k, using techniques similar to the volume computation applied by [2] to timed automata, we can compute the relative volume $|L' \cap \Sigma^k|/|\Sigma|^k$ which gives the probability of error over words of length k. Since the probability becomes negligible beyond some k, this is sufficient to obtain a good approximation of the error. Note that we can use volume because we assume a uniform distribution over Σ. Other distributions can be handled by more complex integration. It is worth mentioning the result of [11] concerning the influence of noise on automata which states that for certain types of automata, even a very small difference in the transition probabilities between a pair of automata may lead to a divergence in their long run behavior as $k \to \infty$. The use of a log-normal distributions protects our evaluation from this effect. An alternative way to evaluate the quality of the approximation, which can be applied also when the target language is represented as a black box, is just to draw words according to D and compare their classification by the target and learned languages.

We have compared our algorithm with three non-symbolic algorithms due to [1,22,26] using the same oracle for membership and equivalence queries. All algorithms were tested on the same target languages defined over a numerical input alphabet Σ, intersected with $\mathbb{N}$ to allow the concrete enumerative algorithms to run as well. We evaluated the behavior of the algorithm in two ways. The first was to keep the structure of the automaton fixed while increasing the size of the alphabet. The second kept the alphabet size fixed and varied the number of states in the (randomly generated) target automaton. Naturally, the symbolic algorithm admits the most modest growth in the total number of membership queries including queries used for testing, in both evaluation scenarios. Not surprisingly, it generates more hypotheses and testing queries, and obtains more counter-examples. Similar results were observed in a case study where the target languages were sets of valid passwords. Here too, the symbolic algorithm required less MQ's on average than any other method in all types of passwords, and the difference increases as the passwords rules become more complicated and the automata require more states and transitions. It is remarkable, however, that the symbolic algorithm managed to discover more states in general. More experimental results will be reported elsewhere.

7   Conclusions and Future Work

We presented an algorithmic scheme for learning languages over large alphabets. The algorithm targets languages acceptable by symbolic automata with a modest number of states and transitions, guarded by simple constraints on the alphabet, which can be arbitrarily large. The new algorithm replaces the helpful teacher of the L^* algorithm by random testing and is thus applicable to more realistic settings. The price of this modification is in the probabilistic relaxation of the correctness criterion and in a more general procedure for handling counter-examples and refining the alphabet partitions. This generality pays off as attested by the easy adaptation of the algorithm to the Boolean domain.

Concerning *related work*, ideas similar to ours have been suggested and explored in a series of papers [4,16,17] that also adapt automaton learning to large alphabets. While some design decisions are similar, for example, to use distinct symbolic alphabets at every state [17], our approach is more rigorous in the way it treats evidence incompatibility and the modification of partition boundaries. We do not consider each modification as a partition refinement, but rather try first just to modify the boundaries without adding a new symbol. As a result, we have the following property whenever we conclude the treatment of evidence incompatibility: the mapping of concrete letters to symbols is always sample-compatible and is well-defined for the whole alphabet, which does not seem to be the case for the scheme presented in [4], which has the potential of generating new symbols indefinitely, or the case in [16,17], which results in a partially-defined hypothesis. Recently, new results presented in [12] in the context of learning symbolic automata give a more general justification for a learning scheme like ours by proving that learnability is closed under product and disjoint union.

Our work on abstract automata should not be confused with work dealing with register automata, another extension of automata to infinite alphabets [3, 15,18]. These are automata augmented with additional variables that can store some input letters and newly-read letters. Newly-read letters can be compared with the registers but typically not with constants in the domain. Such automata can express, for example, the requirement that the password at login is the same as the password at sign-up. In the most recent work on learning register automata

[9], a strong *tree oracle* is used. Given a concrete prefix and a symbolic prefix, the teacher returns a special type of a register automaton that has a tree structure. This fills in the entries of the observation table and provides the information about the registers and guards in the automaton. This algorithm is efficient only in the presence of shortest counter-examples and, in addition, when applied on a theory of inequalities and extended to use constants, these constants should be known in advance.

We believe that our comprehensive framework for learning languages over large alphabets is unique in employing *all* the following features:

1. It is based on a clean and general definition of the relation between the concrete and symbolic alphabets;
2. It can work without a helpful teacher and replace its counter-examples by random sampling, resulting in counter-examples which are not assumed to be minimal (neither in length nor in lexicographic order);
3. It employs an adaptation of the breakpoint method to analyze in an efficient way the information provided by counter-examples;
4. It treats the modification of alphabet partitions in a rigorous way which guarantees that no superfluous symbols are introduced;
5. It is modular, separating the general aspects from those that are alphabet specific, thus providing for a relatively easy adaptation to new alphabets.

A natural future extension of the algorithm is to consider alphabets which are subsets of $\mathbb{N}^n$ and $\mathbb{R}^n$. Preliminary work in this direction has been reported in [23] but used a very restricted type of monotone partitions in order to keep the notion of a minimal counter-example meaningful. Now that we are not restricted to such counter-examples we can use more general partitions, represented by regression trees, a generalization of decision trees to numerical domains.

We are currently conducting more experiments to assess the scalability of our algorithms, mostly in the Boolean domain. These are mostly synthetic examples which are intended to confirm the sensitivity of the algorithm to the complexity of the partitions (the number of blocks and the number of variables that are involved on their definition, rather on the total number of variables which determines the alphabet size. Once the scalability issue is resolved, it remains to find a convincing class of real-world applications that benefits from such algorithms. In the numerical domain we are rather convinced in the existence of mechanisms, say, in cellular information processing in Biology [7] where discrete transitions are taken based on threshold crossings of continuous variables without remembering their values. Likewise, in the Boolean domain, we have to find applications in the specification of large complex systems with many components (digital circuit, distributed multi-agent systems). Hopefully such specifications could be expressible by symbolic automata where the complexity can be confined to the alphabet partitions and need not proliferate into states and cause explosion.

References

1. Angluin, D.: Learning regular sets from queries and counterexamples. Inf. Comput. **75**(2), 87–106 (1987)
2. Asarin, E., Basset, N., Degorre, A.: Entropy of regular timed languages. Inf. Comput. **241**, 142–176 (2015)
3. Benedikt, M., Ley, C., Puppis, G.: What you must remember when processing data words. In: AMW. CEUR Workshop Proceedings, vol. 619 (2010)
4. Berg, T., Jonsson, B., Raffelt, H.: Regular inference for state machines with parameters. In: Baresi, L., Heckel, R. (eds.) FASE 2006. LNCS, vol. 3922, pp. 107–121. Springer, Heidelberg (2006). doi:10.1007/11693017_10
5. Berg, T., Raffelt, H.: 19 model checking. In: Broy, M., Jonsson, B., Katoen, J.-P., Leucker, M., Pretschner, A. (eds.) Model-Based Testing of Reactive Systems. LNCS, vol. 3472, pp. 557–603. Springer, Heidelberg (2005). doi:10.1007/11498490_25
6. Botinčan, M., Babić, D.: Sigma*: symbolic learning of input-output specifications. In: POPL, pp. 443–456. ACM (2013)
7. Bray, D.: Wetware: A Computer in Every Living Cell. Yale University Press, New Haven (2009)
8. Breiman, L., Friedman, J., Stone, C.J., Olshen, R.A.: Classification and Regression Trees. CRC Press, Boca Raton (1984)
9. Cassel, S., Howar, F., Jonsson, B., Steffen, B.: Active learning for extended finite state machines. Formal Aspects Comput. **28**(2), 233–263 (2016)
10. D'Antoni, L., Veanes, M.: Minimization of symbolic automata. In: POPL, pp. 541–554. ACM (2014)
11. Delyon, B., Maler, O.: On the effects of noise and speed on computations. Theoret. Comput. Sci. **129**(2), 279–291 (1994)
12. Drews, S., D'Antoni, L.: Learning symbolic automata. In: Legay, A., Margaria, T. (eds.) TACAS 2017. LNCS, vol. 10205, pp. 173–189. Springer, Heidelberg (2017). doi:10.1007/978-3-662-54577-5_10
13. Mark Gold, E.: System identification via state characterization. Automatica **8**(5), 621–636 (1972)
14. Hopcroft, J.E., Motwani, R., Ullman, J.D.: Introduction to Automata Theory, Languages, and Computation, 3rd edn. Addison-Wesley Longman Publishing Co. Inc., Boston (2006)
15. Howar, F., Steffen, B., Jonsson, B., Cassel, S.: Inferring canonical register automata. In: Kuncak, V., Rybalchenko, A. (eds.) VMCAI 2012. LNCS, vol. 7148, pp. 251–266. Springer, Heidelberg (2012). doi:10.1007/978-3-642-27940-9_17
16. Howar, F., Steffen, B., Merten, M.: Automata learning with automated alphabet abstraction refinement. In: Jhala, R., Schmidt, D. (eds.) VMCAI 2011. LNCS, vol. 6538, pp. 263–277. Springer, Heidelberg (2011). doi:10.1007/978-3-642-18275-4_19
17. Isberner, M., Howar, F., Steffen, B.: Inferring automata with state-local alphabet abstractions. In: Brat, G., Rungta, N., Venet, A. (eds.) NFM 2013. LNCS, vol. 7871, pp. 124–138. Springer, Heidelberg (2013). doi:10.1007/978-3-642-38088-4_9
18. Kaminski, M., Francez, N.: Finite-memory automata. Theoret. Comput. Sci. **134**(2), 329–363 (1994)
19. Lewis, H.R., Papadimitriou, C.H.: Elements of the Theory of Computation. Prentice Hall PTR, Upper Saddle River (1997)
20. Maler, O., Nickovic, D.: Monitoring temporal properties of continuous signals. In: Lakhnech, Y., Yovine, S. (eds.) FORMATS/FTRTFT -2004. LNCS, vol. 3253, pp. 152–166. Springer, Heidelberg (2004). doi:10.1007/978-3-540-30206-3_12

21. Maler, O., Nickovic, D., Pnueli, A.: Checking temporal properties of discrete, timed and continuous behaviors. In: Avron, A., Dershowitz, N., Rabinovich, A. (eds.) Pillars of Computer Science. LNCS, vol. 4800, pp. 475–505. Springer, Heidelberg (2008). doi:10.1007/978-3-540-78127-1_26

22. Maler, O., Pnueli, A.: On the learnability of infinitary regular sets. Inf. Comput. **118**(2), 316–326 (1995)

23. Mens, I.-E., Maler, O.: Learning regular languages over large ordered alphabets. Log. Methods Comput. Sci. (LMCS) **11**(3:13), 1–22 (2015)

24. Nerode, A.: Linear automaton transformations. Proc. Am. Math. Soc. **9**(4), 541–544 (1958)

25. Quinlan, J.R.: Induction of decision trees. Mach. Learn. **1**(1), 81–106 (1986)

26. Rivest, R.L., Schapire, R.E.: Inference of finite automata using homing sequences. Inf. Comput. **103**(2), 299–347 (1993)

27. Sipser, M.: Introduction to the Theory of Computation. PWS, Boston (1997)

28. Utgoff, E.P.: Incremental induction of decision trees. Mach. Learn. **4**(2), 161–186 (1989)

29. Valiant, L.G.: A theory of the learnable. Commun. ACM **27**(11), 1134–1142 (1984)

30. Van Noord, G., Gerdemann, D.: Finite state transducers with predicates and identities. Grammars **4**(3), 263–286 (2001)

31. Veanes, M.: Applications of symbolic finite automata. In: Konstantinidis, S. (ed.) CIAA 2013. LNCS, vol. 7982, pp. 16–23. Springer, Heidelberg (2013). doi:10.1007/978-3-642-39274-0_3

32. Veanes, M., Bjørner, N., De Moura, L.: Symbolic automata constraint solving. In: Fermüller, C.G., Voronkov, A. (eds.) LPAR 2010. LNCS, vol. 6397, pp. 640–654. Springer, Heidelberg (2010). doi:10.1007/978-3-642-16242-8_45

33. Veanes, M., Hooimeijer, P., Livshits, B., Molnar, D., Bjørner, N.: Symbolic finite state transducers: algorithms and applications. In: POPL, pp. 137–150. ACM (2012)

Teaching Academic Concurrency
to Amazing Students

Sebastian Biewer[1,2], Felix Freiberger[1,2], Pascal Leo Held[1],
and Holger Hermanns[1(✉)]

[1] Saarland University, Saarland Informatics Campus, Saarbrücken, Germany
`hermanns@cs.uni-saarland.de`
[2] Saarbrücken Graduate School of Computer Science, Saarbrücken, Germany

Abstract. Milner's CCS is a cornerstone of concurrency theory. This
paper presents CCS as a cornerstone of concurrency practice. CCS is the
semantic footing of PSEUCO, an academic programming language designed
to teach concurrent programming. The language features a heavily simplified Java-like look and feel. It supports shared-memory as well as
message-passing concurrent programming primitives, the latter being
inspired by the Go programming language. The behaviour of PSEUCO programs is described by a formal translational semantics mapping on value-
passing CCS and made executable using compilation to Java. PSEUCO is
not only a language but an interactive experience: PSEUCO.COM provides
access to a web application designed for first hands-on experiences with
CCS and with concurrent programming patterns, supported by a rich and
growing toolset. It provides an environment for students to experiment
with and understand the mechanics of the fundamental building blocks
of concurrency theory and concurrent programming based on a complete
model of the program behaviour. Altogether this implements the TACAS
(Teaching Academic Concurrency to Amazing Students) vision.

1 Introduction

In our times, *concurrency* is a topic that affects computing more than ever
before. The *Calculus of Communicating Systems*, CCS, is a foundational pillar
of concurrency theory, developed by Robin Milner in Edinburgh [21,22] in the
80ies of the last century. In this period, Kim Larsen was working towards his
PhD thesis under the guidance of Milner [17]. And Rance Cleaveland, Joachim
Parrow, and Bernhard Steffen were working on a verification tool for CCS, the
Concurrency Workbench [6,7].

The Concurrency Workbench is an automated tool to cater for the analysis
of networks of finite-state processes expressed in Milner's Calculus of Communicating Systems. It was part of a first wave of initiatives providing tool support for process algebraic principles. Other initiatives at that time included the
AUTO/AUTOGRAPH project by Robert de Simone and Didier Vergamini [3]
in Sophia Antipolis, the tool VENUS [26] by Amelia Soriano, as well as

L. Aceto et al. (Eds.): Larsen Festschrift, LNCS 10460, pp. 170–195, 2017.
DOI: 10.1007/978-3-319-63121-9_9

the Caesar/Aldebaran tools developed by Hubert Garavel and coworkers in Grenoble [10]. The latter focussed on LOTOS, an ISO standard developed by a committee around Ed Brinksma [2,16] from Twente. In turn, AUTOGRAPH pioneered graph visualisation and animation using early versions of tcl/tk. All three initiatives provided inspirations, in one way or another, to Kim Larsen in his early efforts to pioneer tool support for real-time system verification [18], the topic for which he would later become world famous [4]. And Bernhard, Ed, Kim, and Rance later joined forces to found TACAS, a scientific conference that is considered the flagship of European verification research by many.

In subsequent years, further tools emerged, such as the FDR toolset [24] supporting Hoare's CSP approach to concurrency theory, or the PAC tool [5] that aimed at providing a front-end for different process algebras via instantiation of the individual operational semantics. Also, the principles behind the Concurrency Workbench were further developed by Rance Cleaveland in North Carolina [8]. Lately, an Aalborg edition of the workbench has been announced [1] for the purpose of teaching concurrency theory with CCS [19].

At the turn of the millennium, Jeff Kramer and Jeff Magee proposed a new level of tool support for process calculi as part of their textbook on "Concurrency – state models and Java programs" [20]. This book came with an easy-to-install and ready-to-use tool LTSA supporting their language FSP, a CSP-inspired process calculus. The (to our opinion) most remarkable aspect of this toolset was the deep integration of process-algebraic thinking into a lecture concept introducing concurrency practice: To develop a thorough understanding of concurrent programming principles and pitfalls, informal descriptions and concrete Java examples were paired with abstract FSP models, readily supported by the LTSA tool.

The present paper follows this very line of work by presenting an even deeper integration of concurrency theory into concurrency practice for the purpose of teaching concurrent programming. It revolves around a programming language called PSEUCO. The language features a heavily simplified Java-like look and feel. It supports shared-memory as well as message-passing concurrent programming primitives, the latter being inspired by the Go programming language. The behaviour of PSEUCO programs is described by a formal translational semantics mapping on value-passing CCS and made executable using compilation to Java. PSEUCO is not only a language, it is an interactive experience: PSEUCO.COM provides access to a web application designed for first hands-on experiences with CCS and with concurrent programming patterns, supported by a rich and growing toolset. It provides an environment for students to experiment with and understand the mechanics of the fundamental building blocks of concurrency theory and concurrent programming based on a complete model of the program behaviour. This platform provides access to the tools targeting PSEUCO, most notably: the PSEUCO-to-Java compiler, the translation of PSEUCO programs to CCS, the CCS semantics in terms of LTS, and more.

2   The Concepts Behind PSEUCO

This section describes the context, features, and semantic embedding of PSEUCO.

2.1   Context

A profound understanding of concurrency has to be part of the basic repertoire of every computer scientist. Concurrency phenomena are omnipresent in databases, communication networks, and operating systems, in multi-core computing, and massively parallel graphics systems, as well as in emerging fields such as computational biology. Nowadays, software developers are confronted with concurrency problems on a daily basis, problems which are notoriously difficult to handle. Therefore, competence in this field is a must for every computer scientist. Unlike sequential systems, even non-critical applications can no longer be adequately tested for functional correctness. Therefore, it is indispensable that formal verification procedures are known, at least conceptually, to every undergraduate computer science student we educate. A solid theoretical underpinning of the matter and its interrelation with the practice of concurrent programming is a necessary prerequisite.

A Lecture on Concurrent Programming. For this purpose, the lecture "Concurrent Programming" at Saarland University develops these competences starting off with a solid explanation of concurrency theory and then lifts and intertwines them with practical aspects of concurrent programming. The lecture is a mandatory module worth 6 ECTS points in the Bachelor education of computer science and related fields and is currently in its tenth edition. It is scheduled at the end of the second year but we encourage talented students to already enrol into it at the end of their first year. It received the 2013 award for innovations in teaching from the *Fakultätentag Informatik*, the association of German computer science faculties.

After an extensive motivation which stresses the relevance of the matter, the students embark into the basics of CCS including syntax, labelled transition systems, operational semantics, trace equivalence, strong bisimulation, and observational congruence, and finally value-passing CCS. At various places along the lecture, the understanding is supported by the CCS view of pseuCo.com shown in Fig. 3.

At this point, the main innovation of our approach gradually enters the stage: PSEUCO. Contrary to CCS, PSEUCO is a real programming language. It supports both the shared-memory and message-passing programming paradigms. In order to connect concurrency theory and concurrency practice, PSEUCO has a translational semantics mapping on value-passing CCS.

Listing 1.1: Distortion-tolerant transmission protocol in CCS

```
1  range Dig := 0..9 // defining a finite range of values
2
3  Sender := put?x. send!x. Sending[x]      // take the value,
   ↳ send it out, remember it
4  Sending[x] := ack?. Sender              // forget value if ok
5             + nAck?. send!x. Sending[x] // resend if not ok
6
7  Medium[snd] := snd?x:Dig. (receive!x.1 + i. garbled!.1);
   ↳ Medium[snd]
8
9  Receiver[n] := receive?x:0..9. get!x. ack!. Receiver[n+1]
10            + garbled?. nAck!. Receiver[n]
11            + when (n==4) println!"succ"^"ess".0
12
13 Protocol := (Sender | (Receiver[0]) | Medium[send]) \ {send,
   ↳ receive,ack,nAck,garbled}
14
15 (Protocol | put!2. put!4. put!2. put!8) \ {put}
```

CCS with Value-Passing. We will base the discussion of our pragmatic extension of CCS on the example shown in Listing 1.1. It describes a simple distortion-tolerant transmission protocol between a sender and a receiver. While the data is transmitted over a medium that may distort messages, for simplicity, acknowledgements are assumed to travel directly from receiver to sender.

The first line defines a finite range of values to be used later. In line 3, we see the defining equation of the Sender process. It receives a value x and continues by sending out that value with the action send. It then turns into the process Sending defined in line 4 which is parametric in the value x so as to make it possible to remember the value in case retransmissions are needed. This demonstrates that process definitions can be parametrised by data values. Our CCS dialect allows Booleans, integers or strings as process parameters. The Sending process waits for either a positive acknowledgement and then returns to being a Sender or for a negative acknowledgement which triggers a retransmission of the value.

Line 7 defines the Medium over which Sender and Receiver communicate data. First, the Medium receives a value that was sent with the action snd!. After having received a value in the range defined before, the Medium decides nondeterministically to either pass it on or to instead transmit a (distorted) garbled! message. In both cases, this part of the process ends as the special process 1 indicating successful termination. This allows the sequence operator ; to continue to a fresh Medium which waits for the next transmission. Sequencing is usually not part of CCS but since it increases specification convenience and is semantically well understood [2,22], it is included in our CCS dialect. The operator is present in this line of our example for the sole purpose of demonstrating its use, and the same holds true for the action snd appearing as a process parameter of the

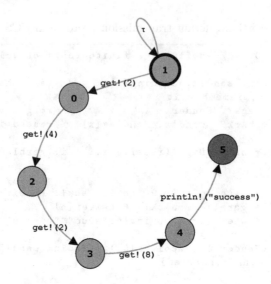

Fig. 1. Behaviour of the process shown in Listing 1.1

Medium process. Using actions as process parameters enables emulating restricted forms of action relabelling. Other than this, no explicit relabelling operator is supported in our dialect of CCS.

Line 9 contains the definition of the Receiver process. It offers up to three behaviours: (a) If a value x is received that lies in the integer range from 0 to 9, that value is passed on with the get! action and acknowledged; (b) if a garbled? message is received, a negative acknowledgement is sent; or (c) if 4 digits have been received, "success" (formed via string concatenation) is printed and the receiver stops. For the latter, the process uses a data parameter and simple arithmetic to count the digits that have been received. A when guard disables the "success" message until this counter reaches 4. Such guards form the expectable link between data values and behaviour.

Line 13 composes Sender, Receiver and Medium (appropriately parametrised) running parallel to form a single Protocol process. The restriction operator \ enforces synchronisation between the processes where appropriate. Finally, line 15 defines the overall process consisting of the Protocol and a user requesting the values 2, 4, 2 and 8 to be sent. The resulting behaviour (more precisely the quotient transition system under observational congruence) of this example is depicted in Fig. 1.

2.2   The Language PSEUCO

Nowadays, mainstream programming is carried out in imperative programming languages. PSEUCO is an imperative language featuring a heavily simplified Java-like look and feel paired with language concepts inspired by the Go programming language. It also has similarities with Holzmann's Promela language [15]. A first, very simplistic pseuCo example is depicted in Listing 1.2.

Listing 1.2. Shared memory concurrent counting in PSEUCO

```
1  int n = 10;
2  lock guard_n;
3
4  void countdown() {
5      for (int i = 5; i >= 1; i--) {
6          lock(guard_n);
7          n--;
8          unlock(guard_n);
9      }
10 }
11
12 mainAgent {
13     agent a = start(countdown());
14     countdown();
15     join(a);
16     println("The value is "+ n);
17 }
```

This program implements concurrent counting. A shared integer, n, is initialised to 10. The procedure countdown() decrements this counter five times. The mainAgent, which is run when the program is started, starts a second agent that runs countdown() before calling countdown() itself. After both agents have executed this procedure, the mainAgent prints the final value of n. To ensure mutually exclusive access to the shared variable, a globally defined lock named guard_n is used within the countdown() procedure.

An alternative (and usually recommended) way to perform safe computations in the presence of concurrency and shared-memory is to encapsulate critical sections within a monitor [12,14]. This concept is indeed supported in PSEUCO. For the example above, this would mean to wrap the shared variable in a monitor AtomicInteger, offering procedures to read and to modify its value without interference by others.

We demonstrate the PSEUCO support for monitors by an implementation of a semaphore [9]. Semaphores provide means of controlling access to common resources, similar to locks, but are more general: they manage a pool of an initially provided, limited number of resources (allocated by init(v)). Any agent can request one of the resources by calling down(). When the agent does not need the resource anymore, it can hand it back to the semaphore by calling up(). Listing 1.3 presents the implementation of a semaphore providing the three procedures init, down, and up as a monitor in PSEUCO. An instance sem of such a monitor is obtained by declaring Semaphore sem. For these instances, no explicit locking is necessary because the data structure is declared as a monitor as opposed to a simple struct. This means that each instance has an implicit, built-in lock. This lock is automatically locked at the entrance of any procedure declared in the monitor and unlocked on its exit.

Listing 1.3. A monitor in PSEUCO implementing a semaphore

```
1  monitor Semaphore {
2      int value ;
3      condition valueNonZero with (!( value ==0));
4
5      void init (int v) {
6          value = v;
7      }
8      void down () {
9          waitForCondition(valueNonZero);
10         value-- ;
11     }
12     void up () {
13         value++ ;
14         signalAll (valueNonZero);
15     }
16 }
```

As in the example, monitors can be equipped with conditions and condition synchronisation in a way that very closely follows the original proposal [13]. For the semaphore example, an agent has to wait in case it is requesting a resource but finds the pool of resources to be empty. This non-emptiness condition (a predicate on variables guarded by the monitor) is declared in line 3. It is checked in line 9. The semantics of waitForCondition is exactly as described above: If the condition is satisfied, the procedure continues. If it is not, the implicit lock of the monitor is released and the agent needs to wait. In order to wake up the agent and let it re-check the condition, the waiting agents are signaled in line 14 after a resource has been handed back (which makes the condition satisfied). While signalAll wakes up all agents waiting for the specific condition, signal would nondeterministically pick a single waiting agent to wake up.

Message-passing concurrency is arguably less difficult to handle than shared-memory concurrency. PSEUCO provides native support for message-passing concurrency, and indeed, this is explained to the students before discussing the latter. An example is presented in Listing 1.4. An agent running the procedure concat interacts via three different channels with the mainAgent. In a nutshell, concat builds up a string s by prefixing it with parts received from channel arg. Empty parts make it report an error on channel err while otherwise the updated value of s is reported on channel res. This channel is declared globally in line 1, the others are parameters of concat and declared in lines 16 and 17. Two of them are channels that can hold strings (res and parts), one can hold Booleans (err). Channel parts is a FIFO buffer which can hold up to 2 elements, the others are unbuffered, meaning that they induce a handshake between the agents sending to (via <!) and receiving from (via <?) them. After starting the agent, the mainAgent feeds three strings into the channel parts (one of them empty)

Listing 1.4. Message-passing concurrency in PSEUCO

```
1  stringchan res;
2
3  void concat (stringchan arg, boolchan emp) {
4      string s = "";
5      while (true) {
6          string pref = <? arg;
7          if (pref == "") emp <! true;
8          else {
9              s = pref + s;
10             res <! s;
11         }
12     }
13 }
14
15 mainAgent {
16     stringchan2 parts;
17     boolchan err;
18
19     start(concat(parts, err));
20     parts <! "strand";
21     parts <! "";
22     parts <! "Guld";
23
24     string r;
25     while (true) {
26         select {
27             case r = <? res: {
28                 println(r);
29             }
30             case <? err: {
31                 println("Empty string reported!");
32             }
33         }
34     }
35 }
```

and then waits for results sent back to him. These may arrive on two different channels (`err` and `res`) and therefore a `select-case` statement is used to specify dedicated reactions. In case an `error` is reported, this is reported to the user in a `println`. Otherwise, the results received on channel `res` are printed out. PSEUCO has borrowed the `select-case` concept from Go [11]. A `select` statements consist of several `cases`. Except for default cases, each case has a guard and a statement. The guard contains exactly one send (`<!`) or receive operation (`<?`). At runtime, a case can be selected only if the message-passing operation of the guard is possible, i.e. if the channel can be read or be written to, respectively. One of those

cases is selected nondeterministically and its guard and statement are processed. A default case can always be selected. If there are multiple cases that can be selected, one of them is selected non-deterministically.

These examples give an impression of the features provided by PSEUCO, all of which are given semantics by translation to CCS.

2.3 Translational Semantics

Several of the peculiarities of imperative programming languages do not have a direct counterpart in process calculi like CCS. The most challenging ones include jumping and branching, buffers, memory and dynamic object referencing, buffered channels, reentrant locks, monitors, and condition synchronisation. In the following sections, we give an intuition of how PSEUCO programs are given semantics in terms of CCS. We cover each part of the PSEUCO language and explain the non-trivial parts in particular detail.

Program Structure. In Listings 1.2 and 1.4, we have seen that concurrency is supported in PSEUCO by the possibility of wrapping procedures into *agents* which run concurrently to the remainder of the program. Similar to the Go language [11], any procedure can be started as an agent by using the start primitive in front of the procedure call (lines 13 and 19). On the CCS level, each agent corresponds to a process that runs in parallel to the others. In addition, further parallel processes implement the necessary bookkeeping and coordination.

The translational semantics of PSEUCO to CCS is of compositional nature and best explained by looking at the abstract syntax tree of a PSEUCO program. Roughly speaking, the closer nodes are to the root of the tree, the more they determine the top-level structure by influencing whether processes are composed in parallel or sequentially. Nodes that are lowest in the syntax tree map PSEUCO terms to CCS terms. When passed to their parent nodes, these are usually composed sequentially or as nondeterministic alternatives such that the control flow of the PSEUCO program is respected. The topmost nodes compose global variables, locks, conditions, arrays, and channels (and the bookkeeping needed to support those) as processes running in parallel to the execution of the main agent. Moreover, for each procedure that is wrapped as an agent, there is a process responsible for starting it, also running in parallel to the other processes. On the outermost level, we hide all actions of the resulting model that are not println! or exception!.

Whereas composing everything in parallel is very intuitive, finding appropriate CCS terms and coordinating them in a control-flow-preserving way requires some interesting concepts. In the remainder of this section, we provide a description of the main ideas and concepts structured along the different language features of PSEUCO.

Expressions and Assignments. PSEUCO supports arithmetic and Boolean expressions, constants, and variables. For now, we only consider variables local to an agent. Global variables are discussed later. Local variables in PSEUCO are mapped to process parameters on the CCS level. However, assignments to variables are not supported there. Instead, an assignment triggers that on the CCS level, all occurrences of that variable are substituted by the expression on the right side of the assignment. For each arithmetic and Boolean operator in PSEUCO there is a counterpart operator in CCS. For instance, the following program is compiled into the single CCS action `println!3+(2*3)+(2*3)`:

```
1  int x = 3;
2  int y = 2 * x;
3  x = x + y;
4  println(x + y);
```

Memory. While local variables in a PSEUCO program can be cast into process parametrisation on the CCS level, we need to proceed differently for non-local PSEUCO variables. This applies especially to shared variables in shared-variable concurrency. In order to represent such variables on the CCS level, we need to represent memory in CCS. A common abstraction of memory is a set of memory cells. A cell is independent of the representation of values (e.g. bits), its only purpose is to store a particular value. In CCS, a memory `Cell` can be modelled as a parallel process that provides actions for getting the currently stored value `cur` and for setting it to a **new** value:

```
1  Cell_x[cur] := get_x!cur.  Cell_x[cur]
2                + set_x?new.  Cell_x[new]
```

When a process reads or writes the value of a cell, it needs to perform a handshake synchronisation with the action provided by the cell as in the following CCS snippet:

```
1  (get_x?x.  println!x.  0  |  Cell_x[-3])  \{get_x}
```

Object References. Imperative programming languages use references in order to access objects in memory. In PSEUCO, structs and monitors are accessed by references, but also locks, arrays and channels are accessed this way. Consequently, there can be arbitrarily many objects. Hence, memory cells of an object must store the reference to the object they represent. Therefore, the cell definitions for a member of a structure or monitor `A` need an additional argument `i` for the reference as in `Env_class_A[i, x]`. For example, the process for the monitor `Semaphore` in Listing 1.3 has the name `Env_class_Semaphore[i, g, value]` because it holds a reference to its implicit lock `g` and it stores the `value` for its variable.

Anyhow, the actions for accessing variable `x`, `get_x` and `set_x`, would still be shared across all memory cells for `x` of the struct (or the `monitor`), so using `get_x` (for example) would cause an `x`-value from any `struct` instance to be read. In order to make access to `struct` and `monitor` instances unique, each cell needs unique actions for accessing it. Since there may be arbitrarily many instances, making actions unique is not trivial. With the intention of keeping the resulting CCS code readable and intuitive, we have added the possibility of parametrising action names to our CCS dialect. This parametrisation effectively extends the expressiveness of our dialect to that of the π-calculus [23] since the parameters can be passed around as values. However, we restrict this mechanism to integer parameters and allow integer arithmetic on those. The PSEUCO semantics uses this for integer references to memory cells and other objects. The definition of such cells is to be adjusted as follows, where the (i) is the parametrisation occurring in the action name:

```
1  Env_class_A[i, x] :=
2    env_class_A_get_x(i)!x. Env_class_A[i, x]    +
3    env_class_A_set_x(i)?v. Env_class_A[i, v]
```

Another example of objects that are accessed by reference are arrays. Arrays are modelled as simple CCS processes that have as many process parameters as there are elements in the array (plus one reference i for identifying the object, as explained above). In order to access a specific array element, the user must first communicate the element index and can then choose between reading or writing. For each array capacity occurring in the PSEUCO program, there must be a dedicated CCS process. Below we present one for capacity 3:

```
1  Array3[i, v0, v1, v2] := array_access(i)?idx. (
2    when (idx == 0) (
3      array_get(i)!v0. Array3[i, v0, v1, v2]    +
4      array_set(i)?v. Array3[i, v, v1, v2]
5    ) + when (idx == 1) (
6      ...
7    ) + when (idx == 2) (
8      ...
9  )
```

As it is the case for real memory, it must be possible to *allocate* a memory cell. For example, in Listing 1.3, there is an allocation of a lock in line 2. Hence, each type of cell has a constructor that manages the references and adds a new memory process in parallel to the program processes whenever necessary. The following listing shows the constructor for a struct A containing a single variable x. The process `Env_class_A` is as shown above.

```
1  Env_class_A_cons[i] := class_A_create!(i).
2    (Env_class_A[i, 0] | Env_class_A_cons[i+1])
```

Some types of objects are supported by several constructors. Arrays, for example, have a distinct constructor for every array size. Still, all arrays must share the same reference space. There is one process that manages the references (using integer arithmetic on references) for arrays and each array constructor requests a free reference for the next instance it is supposed to initialise.

```
1 ArrayManager[i] := array_new!(i). ArrayManager[i+1]
```

Below is how the constructor of arrays of size 3 uses the array manager. The constructor itself acts independent of the type of the elements so it is necessary for initialisation to provide the constructor with a default value for the cells (i.e. `Array3_cons` can be used for bool, int, or string arrays so the default value is false, zero, or the empty string).

```
1 Array3_cons := array_new?i. array3_create!(i).
2   array_setDefault(i)?d. (Array3_cons | Array3[i, d, d, d])
```

The necessary communication with the array manager introduces some superfluous interleavings because the next array reference can be requested at any time. This can be avoided at the price of a more involved encoding.

Procedures and Jumping. In CCS, the base "execution" order is linear, i.e. its semantics executes one prefix after the other. There is no built-in history that enables going back to a previous point in execution. In PSEUCO (and other languages), however, it is possible to call procedures. After the procedure has been executed, the execution of the program jumps back to the point where the procedure was called. Hence, procedure calls can not be defined within CCS directly, but they can be tackled by means of sequencing (;). With sequencing, it is indeed straightforward to embed procedures in CCS processes. When a procedure is called, the process' name appears in front of the sequence operator.

For non-void procedures, it is necessary to return a value to the caller, but a direct handshake is not possible (since they run sequentially, not in parallel). In our encoding, we use a dedicated parallel process which collects and delivers the values to return. With that, a procedure can return a value by sending it to the dedicated process, and the caller can receive it from there as part of a sequence operator.

Control Flow. Most imperative programs need conditional branching. For example, the `for` loop in Listing 1.2 must jump from the end of its body either to the beginning of the loop or behind the loop, and the `if-then-else` in Listing 1.4 determines the control flow according to its condition. In CCS, jumping and branching is not supported directly. However, processes can be given names (appearing on the left hand side of defining equations). Similarly to what has been discussed for procedures, we accommodate conditional branching by splitting into several named sub-processes. Each sub-process name is the equivalent of a jump label, and branching to a sub-process boils down to using the name of the sub-process. The following listing shows a simple loop:

```
1 while(a > 0) {
2   println("loop");
3   a = a-1;
4 }
5 println("a is zero");
```

Its semantics is the CCS code below:

```
1 P[a]  := when (a <= 0) Q[a]
2       + when (a > 0) println!"loop". P[a-1]
3 Q[a]  := println!"a is zero". 0
```

The presented pattern can be used for the other branching statements as well.

Mutual Exclusion and Locks. PSEUCO supports locks, monitors, and conditions. In its basic form, a lock is encoded as a process occupying one out of two states, locked and unlocked. Only one parallel process can perform the locking at a time:

```
1 Lock[i]  := lock(i)?. unlock(i)!. Lock[i]
```

As we have seen previously, the parameter i is a reference to allow uniquely identifying a specific lock. The actions lock and unlock can then be used to lock and unlock the lock, respectively, as demonstrated in the example Lock[i] | lock(i)!. println!"CriticalSection". unlock(i)?. 0.

An advanced variant of locks are reentrant locks where a single agent, the lock owner, is allowed to take the lock multiple times. The lock is released to other potential owners only if the owner has unlocked it the same number of times it has been locked. Modelling this in CCS is more intricate than single-entrant locks. The lock process needs two additional arguments: one that holds the agent identity owning the lock and one that keeps a count of the number of locks still to be unlocked. The process allows anyone to become owner by acquiring the lock provided nobody else already owns it. If an agent a owns the lock, then the process ensures that further locks are only made possible for a. It throws an exception if an unlock is requested by a non-owner:

```
1 Lock[i, c, a]  :=
2   when (c==0) lock(i)?a. Lock[i, 1, a] +
3   when (c>0) (
4     lock(i)?(a). Lock[i, c+1, a] +
5     unlock(i)?a2. (
6       when (a==a2) Lock[i, c-1, a] +
7       when (a!=a2) exception!("Exception").0))
```

In this fragment, there is a peculiar difference between the `lock` actions in lines 2 and 4. In line 4, there are additional parentheses around a. This forces the current value of the expression a to be evaluated (instead of overriding it) and therefore ensures that `lock(i)!e` (effectuated by some agent referenced as e who may not be the owner) and `lock(i)?(a)` can handshake if and only if e and a evaluate to the same value (a concept called value matching in some calculi). This is how we ensure that re-entrances are only granted to the agent that already owns the lock.

Agents. For each procedure that is used as an agent, there is an agent process in parallel to existing agents. It is responsible for starting the agent, similar to a constructor. The following listing shows the agent process `Agent_f` that is responsible for starting a procedure f with one argument x:

```
1  Agent_f := get_free_ref?a. start_f!a. set_arg_x?v.
2                           (Agent_f | Proc_f[a, v]; 0)
```

As we have seen already for arrays, agents share a common reference space, so `Agent_f` first gets an unused reference from a management process. It then offers to send this reference with `start_f!a`. As soon as an agent wants to start f as a new agent, it begins by receiving this message `start_f?a` to get the reference for the new agent. If f needs arguments to be called, as in the example above, then the starting agent has to send values for each of the arguments. Afterwards, `Agent_f` calls the procedure f with the arguments it has received in parallel with a fresh copy of itself.

Other agents can choose to wait for this new agent's termination before they continue their own execution. In PSEUCO, this is done by calling the primitive join. Hence, we augment the CCS representation so that after termination of the agent, the process continues with a process that offers an unlimited number of `join(a)!` actions. The translational semantics of the join primitive is the complementary action `join(a)?`. Due to the unlimited offers of individual `join(.)!`-transitions provided by each agent upon termination, any attempt to `join(.)?` an already terminated agent will not block.

```
1  AgentJoins[a] := join(a)!. AgentJoins[a]
2  Agent_f := get_free_ref?a. start_f!a. set_arg_x?v.
3                  (Agent_f | Proc_f[a, v] ; AgentJoins[a])
```

Message Passing via Channels. As shown in Listing 1.4, PSEUCO supports message-passing communication via unbuffered and via (FIFO) buffered channels of fixed capacity (as in lines 17 and 16). CCS, on the other hand, provides unbuffered communication via handshaking of complementary actions with value-passing. Hence, PSEUCO's unbuffered channels can be encoded directly. For buffered channels, we need the ability to store the buffer state which is comprised of the items to be buffered and their order. Basically, a buffered channel behaves similarly to an array of memory cells, however it has restricted actions for access (namely only pushing and popping). A straightforward encoding is as follows:

```
1  Buffer_n[i, c, v_1 , ... , v_n]  :=
2    when (c==0) put(i)?v_1. Buffer_n[i, c, v_1 , ... , v_n] +
3    ... +
4    when (c==n-1) put(i)?v_n. Buffer_n[i, c, v_1 , ... , v_n] +
5    when (c>0) chan(i)!v_0. Buffer_n[i, c-1, v_2 , ... , v_n ,0]
```

Here, n is the capacity of the buffer, c is the number of items that are currently buffered and v_j are the cells of the buffer (i is the buffer reference as usual). The channel allows sending values to it provided $c < n$. Due to the dedicated when-statements guarding each put, the value received over action put is stored in the next free cell. Values can be received from the channel provided $c > 0$. The channel sends the value contained in v_0 over action chan, decreases the item counter by one and shifts all buffered values to the left.

The type system of PSEUCO needs to accommodate for the fact that channels can be referred to without specifying whether they are buffered or unbuffered. For example, in Listing 1.4, the type of the parameter arg of concat is stringchan although the main agent passes a stringchan2 to it. Once such a channel is used for sending, it is necessary to determine the buffer type dynamically because unbuffered channels are used with action chan(i)! and buffered channels are filled with action put(i)!. We overcome this problem by using negative numbers as references for unbuffered channels and positive numbers for buffered ones. The following listing shows the CCS code corresponding to sending a value v over a channel with reference i for which the buffer type is not known in advance.

```
1  when (i < 0) chan(i)!v. 1   +   when (i > 0) put(i)!v. 1
```

Select Statement. The select statement introduces nondeterministic choice to PSEUCO. For example, in Listing 1.4, the main agent can nondeterministically choose to either process a result or an error sent by concat. There is a direct counterpart in CCS, namely the nondeterministic choice operator +. In the encoding, it is important to assure that on the CCS level, the leftmost prefix of each resulting nondeterministic alternative corresponds to the channel appearing in the respective case to ensure that the selection is made based on the correct external stimulus.

Monitors and Conditions. As already shown in Listing 1.3, PSEUCO supports monitors in the form of a struct that has an implicit, built-in lock. We have seen that monitors can be enhanced with conditions so as to support condition synchronisation. The Semaphore in Listing 1.3 employs a condition to make agents wait until a resource becomes available. A waiting agent does not perform any work. In particular, it does not run in a loop that tries to enter and exit the monitor over and over until the condition is found to be satisfied (a so-called *busy-wait*). Instead, the classical monitor concept comes with a notification mechanism where waiting agents wait until they are notified. PSEUCO supports this via the two primitives `signal` and `signalAll` that need to be used actively by some agents. The `Semaphore` example in Listing 1.3 uses `signalAll` in line 14 once a resource has been handed back.

We illustrate the behaviour of a condition as agents that rest inside a waiting room until they are notified that a change they are waiting for happened. This metaphor emphasizes that agents actually stop working and do not have to do anything actively until they receive a signal. In the semaphore example, an agent that finds the pool of resources empty goes to the waiting room and stays there until a resource is handed back and thus `signalAll` is called. PSEUCO's conditions are only available inside monitors so there is always the implicit monitor lock that the condition is related to.

In CCS, we adapt the waiting room metaphor and use two processes: one for the waiting room and one that broadcasts the signal to waiting agents.

```
1  WaitRoom[i, c]  :=
2    signal(i)?.(
3      when (c==0) WaitRoom[i, c] +
4      when (c>0) wait(i)?.WaitRoom[i, c-1] )  +
5    add(i)?.WaitRoom[i, c+1]  +
6    signal_all(i)?.WaitDistributor[i, c] ; WaitRoom[i, 0]
7
8  WaitDistributor[i, c] :=
9    when (c<=0) 1 +
10   when (c>0) wait(i)?.WaitDistributor[i, c-1]
```

The waiting room counts the number of waiting agents and supports the following four operations:

– If an agent wants to use a condition, it must perform two steps. First, it must add itself to the waiting room (using `add`) while still holding the monitor lock.
– After an `unlock`, the agent synchronises over channel `wait`. However, the waiting room joins the synchronisation only when the agent is supposed to continue its work.
– Working agents use the action `signal` in order to notify one of the waiting agents that the condition may have changed. When a signal is received, the waiting room either ignores it if no agent is waiting or it offers a single `wait` for synchronisation to the waiting agents. Which of the waiting agents synchronises with the waiting room is non-deterministic.
– Similarly, `signal_all` is used to notify all waiting agents. This task is delegated to the process `WaitDistributor`. The wait distributor gets the number of waiting agents and then offers each of them a `wait` action for synchronisation.

The resulting CCS encoding of some program using conditions may look as follows:

```
1 WaitAgt[m, c] := lock(m)!. getB?b.
2   when (b) println!"Condition␣holds". unlock(m)!. 1  +
3   when (!b) add(c)!. unlock(m)!. wait(c)!. WaitAgt[m, c]
4 WorkAgt[m, c] := lock(m)!.
5   setB!true. signal_all(c)!.
6   unlock(m)!. 1
7
8 WaitAgt[m, c] | WorkAgt[m, c] | Lock[m] | WaitRoom[c, 0]
```

3 PSEUCO.COM – A Web Platform for Learning PSEUCO

To propel the use of PSEUCO in academic teaching, we have developed a web application available on https://pseuco.com/. It serves as an interactive platform for students learning CCS and PSEUCO as part of our concurrent programming lecture and provides the user with access to the translational semantics of PSEUCO described in Sect. 2.3. The following section provides a detailed description of PSEUCO.COM.

LTS Viewing. PSEUCO.COM users will often find themselves looking at an LTS – either one that was generated by the semantics of a CCS expression that they entered or that was generated by the PSEUCO compiler, or one that was sent to them. In all cases, PSEUCO.COM uses the same approach to display them:

In the beginning, only the initial state of the LTS is shown. Clicking or, for touch-enabled devices, tapping it reveals the initial state's successors. The user can continue expanding states step by step, either by continuing to click states they are interested in, or by using the [Expand all] button which will reveal the successors of all *visible* states. Expanded states can also be collapsed by another click on them which hides all successor nodes that no longer have a path to the initial state. Figure 2 demonstrates this behaviour in a small LTS.

This behaviour and the absence of support for infinitely branching transition systems ensure that PSEUCO.COM never tries to display an infinite number of states. The LTS itself can be infinite. In that case, the users will never be able to fully expand the system. Still, he is free to explore any part of the graph he can reach from the initial state.

Because of this interactive approach, we have certain requirements for our graph layout algorithm:

1. Graph layout must be *continuous*: When the graph changes (for example because a node has been expanded), the existing nodes should not move far, and this move should be animated so users can easily keep track of the states.
2. Graph layout must be *interactive*: Users need to be able to move nodes as they see fit, and the graph layout should pay respect to the user-given node placement while still optimising overall readability.

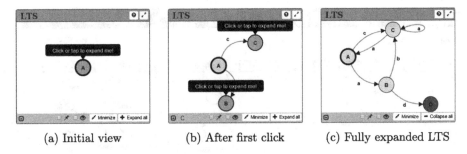

(a) Initial view   (b) After first click   (c) Fully expanded LTS

Fig. 2. A labelled transition system as shown in PSEUCO.COM. The user has to click on a state to reveal its successors. This is explained to first-time users by a floating hint shown until two states have been expanded.

3. Graph layout must *feel natural* so users are not confused by the visual changes they cause by moving nodes.

To fulfil these requirements, we use a force-based approach to graph layout: The visible part of the LTS behaves like a physical simulation where nodes are inert masses that carry an electrical charge, connected by springs, with a gravitational pull towards the middle of the graph. The inertia ensures a smooth, continuous movement of all nodes. The electrical charge ensures that nodes repel each other, avoiding overlap and keeping a reasonable distance from other nodes. The springs can push or pull on nodes to achieve consistent spacing between nodes. Finally, the gravitational pull centres the whole system within the allocated space.

Because transitions are labelled by actions and multiple transitions may exist between the same pair of states, both states *and transitions* correspond to nodes in the simulation. The nodes for states directly correspond to the position where the state is rendered. For transitions, the corresponding nodes (which have a weaker simulated electrical charge than states) correspond to the position where the transition's label is drawn. Therefore, the electrical charge of these nodes automatically optimises for overlap-free rendering of the labels. The transition is rendered as a Bézier curve between the two states with the transition node's position serving as the control point. This ensures that multiple transitions between the same states are rendered correctly as demonstrated in Fig. 2c by the transitions $A \xrightarrow{c} C$ and $C \xrightarrow{a} A$. It also allows self-loops to automatically rotate away from other transitions or states.

If the user wants to layout parts of the graph himself, he can drag and drop nodes at any time using the mouse or touch. In the latter case, we also support simultaneous dragging of multiple nodes. The remaining nodes continue to be affected by the forces, and after the user stops dragging a node, it returns to normal behaviour. This allows the user to get the graph into another stable state that he prefers.

To gain even more control over the placement of nodes, the user can check ⭐ Pin dragged nodes . If this setting is enabled, after the user lets go of a node,

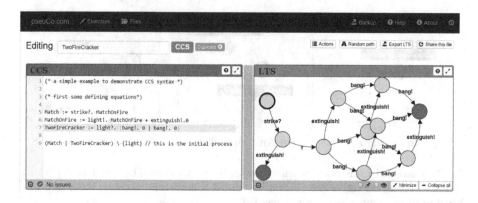

Fig. 3. A screenshot of the CCS editing interface

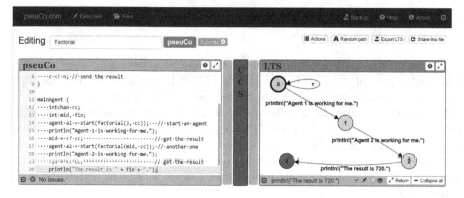

Fig. 4. A screenshot of the PSEUCO editing interface

it will seize all movement and will no longer be affected by the forces. This allows the user to layout any part of the graph manually without interference from the automatic layout while the remaining part of the graph will still be arranged automatically.

CCS Editing. While editing a CCS file, the user sees two windows as demonstrated in Fig. 3. The first one contains a text editor with his CCS code while the second one contains the LTS editor described in Sect. 3. The user can drag the grey separator bar to freely distribute the horizontal space between both windows or use a ⬚ Maximize ⬚ button in the title bar to allocate all horizontal space to that window. In that case, the other window will be reduced to a thin vertical strip.

During editing, the CCS expression is parsed continuously so the LTS shown to the right is never stale.

PSEUCO *Editing.* When editing a PSEUCO file, the user is shown the PSEUCO code, the CCS code produced by the PSEUCO compiler, and the corresponding LTS, as demonstrated in Fig. 4. As with CCS editing, the input is evaluated

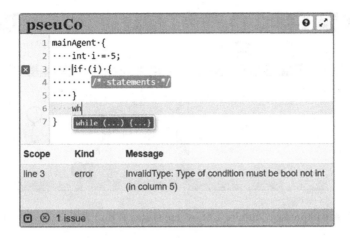

Fig. 5. A screenshot of the PSEUCO text editor

automatically, and the user can freely divide the horizontal space between the windows. While the CCS code is read-only (as it is generated by the compiler), the user can experiment with it: A [Fork ☑] button in the title bar of the CCS window opens the generated CCS code as a new file to allow the user to edit it. Of course, the user can always go [Back] to his original PSEUCO file.

The PSEUCO editor provides the support typical of a basic IDE including snippet completion and in-line highlighting of compiler error messages as demonstrated in Fig. 5.

File Management and Sharing. PSEUCO.COM allows users to store and manage files in a virtual file system stored locally by their web browser. Files are always saved automatically and kept until they are deleted assuming that the user has entered a file name. Even unnamed files are saved temporarily to allow recovering lost data but they expire after one week.

To encourage students to discuss their findings, PSEUCO.COM features a file sharing facility. At any time during editing, users can select [☑ Share this file] to upload a copy of their current file to our server. In return, they receive a sharing link containing a random identifier for them to share, for example https://pseuco.com/#/edit/remote/50xshwwyuza86w4pjtke. Anyone opening this link in a modern browser will immediately be presented with a read-only view of this file.

PSEUCO.COM also allows users to export transition systems as TRA-, AUT-, and DOT-files (in addition to its own JSON-based format) for processing with external tools. It can also import AUT[1]-files.

Tracing Support. The application provides a way to compute random traces through an LTS which can by shown including or omitting τ-steps.

---

[1] http://cadp.inria.fr/man/aut.html.

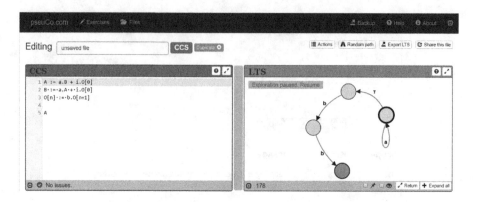

Fig. 6. A compressed, infinite LTS where states A and B have been merged

In addition to allowing random tracing, PSEUCO.COM also collects a list of (non-τ) actions found within an LTS (which can be shown by clicking ☰ Actions) and can compute traces leading to these actions by backchaining. For example, this can be used to check whether a PSEUCO program can produce an unexpected output and to synthesise an interleaving explaining this output.

Minimization. To aid in analysing large LTS, PSEUCO.COM implements minimization under observational congruence [22]. This feature can be invoked by the ⚟ Minimize button in the LTS toolbar.

Whenever an LTS is displayed, a background thread is dispatched to precompute all its states. When minimization is invoked, it only considers states that have been found up to this point. If minimization is started before all states have been explored, the result is not guaranteed to be minimal – it is only minimal with respect to the already explored part of the system. While exploration is running, the minimization button is labelled ⚟ Compress to emphasize this fact.

This behaviour allows compression of systems that are infinite or too large to be explored in a reasonable time frame. Figure 6 shows an example of this.

Offline Use. PSEUCO.COM is a pure, JavaScript-based web application. While this provides many benefits, most importantly the ability to run without any installation or bootstrapping, this opens up the question of whether the application can be used without an internet connection. Indeed, PSEUCO.COM provides full support for offline use using the HTML5 Application Cache APIs. Upon the first visit of PSEUCO.COM, all major modern web browsers automatically download the full web application and store it in a permanent cache. Afterwards, network connectivity is only needed to download application or template updates and to upload and download shared files.

All computation, including PSEUCO-to-Java compilation and the CCS semantics, is always performed directly in the user's browser.

Modes, Exercises, and Use in Teaching. While PSEUCO.COM can be used by any-one as a tool for exploring CCS and PSEUCO semantics, it is specifically tailored to educational usage. The needs of students learning concurrent programming differ from those of an expert looking for a tool. By our experience, providing features like CCS semantics or LTS minimization to students that have not yet understood the corresponding concepts *impedes* learning because it takes away an incentive to explore and apply these concepts by hand.

To accommodate these different needs, PSEUCO.COM can be operated in two different modes. In *tool mode*, all features are available without restriction. In *teaching mode*, users are prevented from creating files initially, only allowing them to view (but not edit) files that were shared with them. Instead, they get access to a set of *exercises*.

These exercises are meant to accompany a lecture or book teaching concur-rent programming and provide milestones that unlock PSEUCO.COM features. For example, users need to demonstrate their ability to infer transitions of CCS terms by the SOS rules and to write small CCS terms with predetermined character-istics to unlock the ability to create and edit CCS files including the automatic creation of the corresponding LTS.

Upon first use, PSEUCO.COM will normally ask the user to select a mode. When providing links to students as part of the lecture notes, we use special links that cause PSEUCO.COM to default to teaching mode.

PSEUCO.COM has been introduced in the *Concurrent Programming* lecture at Saarland University in the summer term 2014.

4   Analysis Support

In our concurrent programming lecture, we sensitise our students to problems related to concurrency. We explicate that data races (race conditions), deadlocks and such are considered program errors and must be avoided at all costs. To further aid our students, we want to have tool support to detect, investigate, and possibly fix such errors.

This requires sophisticated and often computationally intensive program analyses. This is where the PSEUCO.COM platform – and its JavaScript basis – reaches its limits. To circumvent this issue and to complement the capabilities of the PSEUCO.COM platform we have started exploring new ways of giving students access to enhanced tools and analyses.

The first tool developed under this premise is able to statically detect data races on a subset of the language facilities of PSEUCO. It is implemented in C++.

Next, we describe the major ideas that underlie this analysis based on the example in Listing 1.2 from Sect. 2.2.

Static Data Race Detection. In PSEUCO, a data race occurs if two or more agents can access the same global variable simultaneously and at least one of these accesses is writing. In this respect, the example presented in Listing 1.2 is free of data races. However, the statement in line 7 is an access to the global variable n.

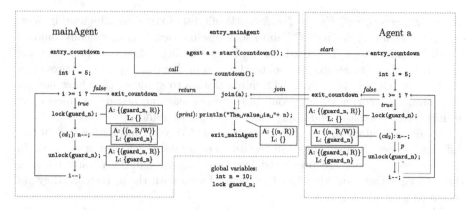

Fig. 7. Annotated control flow graph. A: accesses to global variables (R: read, W: write, R/W: read and write), L: locks guaranteed to be held. Nodes without annotation default to A: {} and L: {}

Without the `lock` and `unlock` statements in lines 6 and 8, respectively, this program would have a data race due to the concurrent, i.e. potentially simultaneous accesses to n. How can we infer this automatically without running the program?

To do so, we use a static program analysis that computes an overapproximation of all possible program behaviours and then tries to find unguarded concurrent memory accesses to global variables. This is done in three steps:

1. Compute a graph that holds all control flow information.
2. Annotate this graph with information relevant to identifying data races: accesses to global variables and which regions are guarded by locks.
3. Perform a graph search to find pairs of memory accesses.
4. Check each of these pairs for a potential data race.

Figure 7 shows the relevant part of the annotated graph for the example program. Deriving it is mostly straightforward[2].

The graph search is a basic reachability analysis and applied to pairs of memory accesses. First, all candidate memory accesses are collected (i.e. accesses to global variables) and grouped by the accessed variables. Then, for each such access group a list containing all the individual access pairs is constructed[3].

The characteristics differentiating potentially harmful from harmless access pairs are more interesting:

1. Do both accesses happen in the same agent?
2. Are both accesses read-only?

---

[2] There are some corner cases requiring careful analysis. We omit them due to scope and space constraints.

[3] Reflexive and symmetric pairs are omitted directly for precision (by construction a memory access cannot race with itself) and efficiency reasons.

3. Do these accesses share common locks, i.e. is there at least one lock that is held during both of the accesses?
4. Using the graph search, is it possible to construct a causality path between the two accesses?

If at least one of these indicators is satisfied, the affected pair is no longer considered to be a data race candidate. Otherwise, the access pair is considered a *potential* data race. This does not imply that an actual data race materialises but warns the user that the program may need more thought and reasoning. This imprecision is rooted in our decision to overapproximate program behaviour and to underapproximate locking information, if necessary. An argument showing the absence of a data race in a program that exhibits more behaviour and has weaker locking information than the real program (and its semantics) also extends to that original program while the converse does not.

Continuing with our example, there are three memory accesses to n: cd_1, cd_2 and *print*. This yields the following data race candidates: (cd_1, cd_2), $(cd_1, print)$, and $(cd_2, print)$. The first candidate is covered by the third indicator since guard_n is a common lock held during both accesses. Candidate two is not considered a data race as both accesses happen in the same agent and thus satisfy indicator one. As illustrated in Fig. 7, there is a causality path p (indicated in red) connecting cd_2 to *print*. Hence, the last candidate satisfies the fourth indicator and is no data race either.

Without lines 6 and 8, the pair (cd_1, cd_2) would not satisfy any of the indicators and would be returned by the analysis as a potential data race.

5 Conclusion

This paper has introduced the PSEUCO approach to teaching concurrent programming. We have presented an overview of the language features and presented details of a translational semantics that maps any PSEUCO program to the variant of CCS we presented. That semantics is implemented as part of an interactive web platform, PSEUCO.COM. This platform provides access to the tools targeting PSEUCO, most notably: the translation of PSEUCO programs to CCS, the CCS semantics in terms of LTS, the PSEUCO-to-Java compiler, and more. Due to space constraints, we have not covered the compilation of PSEUCO to Java which makes it possible to execute any PSEUCO program, and we have only sketched our efforts to enable deep semantic analyses for PSEUCO, especially for flagging data race problems in shared-memory concurrency. We will continue to work on the TACAS (Teaching Academic Concurrency to Amazing Students) vision.

Acknowledgments. This work is supported by the ERC Advanced Investigators Grant 695614 (POWVER) and by the CDZ project CAP (GZ 1023).

References

1. Andersen, J.R., Andersen, N., Enevoldsen, S., Hansen, M.M., Larsen, K.G., Olesen, S.R., Srba, J., Wortmann, J.K.: CAAL: concurrency workbench, aalborg edition. In: Leucker, M., Rueda, C., Valencia, F.D. (eds.) ICTAC 2015. LNCS, vol. 9399, pp. 573–582. Springer, Cham (2015). doi:10.1007/978-3-319-25150-9_33

2. Bolognesi, T., Brinksma, E.: Introduction to the ISO specification language LOTOS. Comput. Netw. **14**, 25–59 (1987)

3. Boudol, G., Roy, V., de Simone, R., Vergamini, D.: Process calculi, from theory to practice: verification tools. In: Sifakis [25], pp. 1–10

4. CAV award (2013). http://i-cav.org/cav-award

5. Cleaveland, R., Madelaine, E., Sims, S.: A front-end generator for verification tools. In: Brinksma, E., Cleaveland, W.R., Larsen, K.G., Margaria, T., Steffen, B. (eds.) TACAS 1995. LNCS, vol. 1019, pp. 153–173. Springer, Heidelberg (1995). doi:10.1007/3-540-60630-0_8

6. Cleaveland, R., Parrow, J., Steffen, B.: The concurrency workbench. In: Sifakis [25], pp. 24–37

7. Cleaveland, R., Parrow, J., Steffen, B.: The concurrency workbench: a semantics-based tool for the verification of concurrent systems. ACM Trans. Program. Lang. Syst. **15**(1), 36–72 (1993)

8. Cleaveland, R., Sims, S.: The NCSU concurrency workbench. In: Alur, R., Henzinger, T.A. (eds.) CAV 1996. LNCS, vol. 1102, pp. 394–397. Springer, Heidelberg (1996). doi:10.1007/3-540-61474-5_87

9. Dijkstra, E.W.: Over seinpalen. Circulated privately, n.d

10. Garavel, H.: Compilation et vérification de programmes LOTOS. Ph.D. thesis, Joseph Fourier University, Grenoble, France (1989)

11. The Go programming language specification. http://golang.org/ref/spec

12. Hansen, P.B.: Shared classes. In: Operating System Principles. Prentice-Hall Series in Automatic Computation, pp. 226–232. Prentice-Hall (1973)

13. Hansen, P.B.: Monitors and concurrent pascal: a personal history. In: Lee, J.A.N., Sammet, J.E. (eds.) History of Programming Languages Conference (HOPL-II), Preprints, Cambridge, Massachusetts, USA, 20–23 April 1993, pp. 1–35. ACM (1993)

14. Hoare, C.A.R.: Monitors: an operating system structuring concept. Commun. ACM **17**(10), 549–557 (1974)

15. Holzmann, G.: The Spin Model Checker - Primer and Reference Manual, 1st edn. Addison-Wesley Professional, Boston (2003)

16. ISO. Information processing systems - Open Systems Interconnection - LOTOS - a formal description technique based on the temporal ordering of observational behaviour. ISO ISO 8807:1989, International Organization for Standardization, Geneva, Switzerland (1989)

17. Larsen, K.: Context-dependent bisimulation between processes. Ph.D. thesis, University of Edinburgh, Mayfield Road, Edinburgh, Scotland (1986)

18. Larsen, K.G., Pettersson, P., Yi, W.: UPPAAL in a nutshell. STTT **1**(1–2), 134–152 (1997)

19. Aceto, L., Ingólfsdóttir, A., Larsen, K.G., Srba, J.: Reactive Systems: Modelling, Specification and Verification. Cambridge University Press, Cambridge (2007)

20. Magee, J., Kramer, J.: Concurrency - State Models and Java Programs. Wiley, Hoboken (1999)

21. Milner, R. (ed.): A Calculus of Communicating Systems. LNCS, vol. 92. Springer, Heidelberg (1980)
22. Milner, R.: Communication and Concurrency. PHI Series in Computer Science. Prentice Hall, Upper Saddle River (1989)
23. Milner, R.: Communicating and Mobile Systems - The Pi-calculus. Cambridge University Press, Cambridge (1999)
24. Roscoe, A.W.: Modelling and verifying key-exchange protocols using CSP and FDR. In: The Eighth IEEE Computer Security Foundations Workshop (CSFW 1995), 13–15 March 1995, Kenmare, County Kerry, Ireland, pp. 98–107. IEEE Computer Society (1995)
25. Sifakis, J. (ed.): CAV 1989. LNCS, vol. 407. Springer, Heidelberg (1990)
26. Soriano, A.: Prototype de venus: un outil d'aide á la verification de systemes communicantes. In: Cori, R., Wirsing, M. (eds.) STACS 1988. LNCS, vol. 294, pp. 401–402. Springer, Heidelberg (1988). doi:10.1007/BFb0035867

Logic

Negative Results on Decidability and Small Model Property of Process Equations

Xinxin Liu$^{(\boxtimes)}$

State Key Laboratory of Computer Science, Institute of Software,
Chinese Academy of Sciences, Beijing, China
xinxin@ios.ac.cn

Abstract. This paper studies the *decidability* and *small model property* of process equations of the form

$$(P|\Pi_{i=1}^n C_i(X_i))\backslash L \equiv (Q|\Pi_{j=1}^m D_j(Y_j))\backslash K$$

where P, Q are finite state processes, X_i, Y_j are process variables, and $C_i(X_i)$, $D_j(Y_j)$ are process expressions *linear* in X_i and Y_j respectively. It shows that, when $n + m > 1$, the equation problem is not decidable and does not have small model property for any equivalence relation $\equiv$ which is at least as strong as complete trace equivalence but not stronger than strong bisimilarity.

1 Introduction

This paper examines *small model property* and *decidability* of equations in process algebras [Mil89, Hoa85, BK85]. In general, process equations have the following form

$$C(X_1, \ldots, X_n) \equiv D(Y_1, \ldots, Y_m) \tag{1}$$

where C, D are process contexts, $X_1, \ldots, X_n$ and $Y_1, \ldots, Y_m$ are process variables, $\equiv$ is some equivalence relation on processes. Some well studied equivalence relations on processes are strong and weak bisimilarities $\sim$ and $\approx$ [Mil89], branching bisimilarity $\approx_b$ [vGW96], testing equivalence [NH84], failure equivalence [BHR84], GSOS trace congruence or $\frac{2}{3}$-bisimilarity [BIM95, LS91], and 2-nested simulation equivalence [GV89]. Equation (1) is said to be solved by processes $P_1, \ldots, P_n$ and $Q_1, \ldots, Q_m$ if the following equality holds

$$C(P_1, \ldots, P_n) \equiv D(Q_1, \ldots, Q_m).$$

In this case we say that (1) is *solvable*. A type of equation is said to be *decidable* if the solvability of that type of equation is decidable. A type of equation is said to have *small model property* if whenever an equation of that type is solvable then it can be solved by finite-state processes. We are interested in these two properties because decidability indicates that the possibility of solving the problem by automatic tools and small model property often suggests some simple method of finding solutions.

© Springer International Publishing AG 2017
L. Aceto et al. (Eds.): Larsen Festschrift, LNCS 10460, pp. 199–210, 2017.
DOI: 10.1007/978-3-319-63121-9_10

Throughout the paper it is assumed that the reader is familiar with Milner's CCS [Mil82, Mil89]. We study the decidability and small model property of a class of process equations which take the following form

$$(P|\Pi_{i=1}^{n}C_i(X_i))\backslash L \equiv (Q|\Pi_{j=1}^{m}D_j(Y_j))\backslash K \tag{2}$$

where P, Q are finite state processes, $|$ and Π are the parallel operator and the parallel product of CCS, $\backslash L$ and $\backslash K$ are restriction operators of CCS with L, K being sets of actions, $\equiv$ is some equivalence relation, $C_i(X_i)$ and $D_j(Y_j)$ are CCS expressions *linear* in X_i and Y_j respectively. An expression $C(X)$ is said to be linear in X if the only variables in it are X (if any) and no two occurrences of X are subexpressions of two processes in parallel position, for example $a.X + b.X$ is linear in X while $a.X|b.X$ is not. More precisely, for a given variable X, the set $LE(X)$ of the expressions linear in X is the smallest set such that $X \in LE(X), P \in LE(X)$, if $C(X), D(X) \in LE(X)$ then $C(X)+D(X) \in LE(X)$, and if $C(X)$ is in $LE(X)$ then so are $a.C(X), C(X)|P, P|C(X), C(X)\backslash L, C(X)[f]$, where a is any action, P is any finite state process expression not containing any free variables, f is any rename function, and L is any set of labels. The variables X_i's and Y_j's in Eq. (2) are not necessarily all distinct, i.e. some parallel components (even from different sides of the equation) may share the same variable, thus the total number of variables in Eq. (2) can be less than $m + n$. For convenience we will call equations of form (2) which satisfy these restrictions k-ary $n \equiv m$ equations, where k is the total number of variables in the equation. Note that only when the contexts C_i's and D_j's are restricted to linear contexts, the classification using m, n can be made meaning full (otherwise the equation $(a.X + P)|(b.X + Q)\backslash L \equiv R$ can be an unary $2 \equiv 0$ equation as well as an unary $1 \equiv 0$ equation).

Many $1 \equiv 0$ equations (unary of cause) have already been studied in the literature. In [Shi89, Par89, QL90], some subclasses of $1 \approx 0$ equations of the form $(P|X)\backslash L \approx Q$ are studied with various restrictions on P, L, and Q. The results show that these subclasses are all decidable with small model property. Results in [LX90b] show that the whole $1 \sim 0$ class is decidable with small model property. Later in [Liu92], the whole $1 \approx 0$ class and $1 \approx_b 0$ class are shown to be decidable with small model property.

The above mentioned works mainly concentrate on how to actually find a solution whenever solutions exist, rather than simply to decide whether the equation is solvable. In fact, from the decidability and small model property of the modal μ-calculus [Koz82, KP83, SE89] one can also conclude the decidability and small model property of many $1 \equiv 0$ type equation problems. To see this, consider the following equation where Q is a finite state process and $C(X)$ is linear in X:

$$C(X) \equiv Q \tag{3}$$

Results in [ZIG87, SI94, Liu92] show that, for many equivalence relations $\equiv$ (including $\sim, \approx$, and $\approx_b$), Q has a *Characteristic formula* $F_Q^{\equiv}$ in the modal μ-calculus such that, for any process P, $C(P) \equiv Q$ if and only if $C(P)$ satisfies $F_Q^{\equiv}$. According to [LX90a], a formula $\mathcal{W}(C, F_Q^{\equiv})$ can be effectively constructed such that $C(P)$ satisfies $F_{\overline{Q}}^{\equiv}$ just in case P satisfies $\mathcal{W}(C, F_{\overline{Q}}^{\equiv})$. Thus the solutions to Eq. (3) are exactly those processes satisfying $\mathcal{W}(C, F_{\overline{Q}}^{\equiv})$. It is obvious that any $1 \equiv 0$ equation has form (3), so the decidability and small model property of these $1 \equiv 0$ equations are guaranteed by the fact that the satisfiability of modal μ-calculus formula is decidable and that if such a formula is satisfiable then it is satisfiable by a finite state process.

Now it is tempting to try to obtain similar results for equation problems with more variables. In [JJLL93], the problem of constructing processes $P_1, \ldots, P_n$ such that $C(P_1, \ldots, P_n)$ satisfies F is considered, where C is an arbitrary context described as action transducer and F is a formula of modal μ-calculus with pure maximal fixed-point operators. In that paper, a procedure for constructing models was proposed. If this procedure terminates successfully then a finite state model can be constructed while if it terminates unsuccessfully it is guaranteed that no model exists. It is conjectured in [JJLL93] that the method guarantees termination in all circumstances. This conjecture implies that n-ary $n \sim 0$ equation problem is decidable and has small model property. This is because for any n-ary $n \sim 0$ equation $(P|\Pi_{i=1}^n C_i(X_i))\backslash L \sim Q$, the left hand side can be expressed as $C(X_1, \ldots, X_n)$ where C is a context described as an action transducer, and the characteristic formula $F_{\widetilde{Q}}$ is a formula with pure maximal fixed-point operator.

In summary, the picture as we see it at the moment is that, $1 \equiv 0$ equation problems are decidable with small model property for many useful equivalence relations and the cases for k-ary $n \equiv m$ equations such that $n + m > 1$ are not clear. In this paper, we show that the unary and binary $1 \equiv 1$ equation problems, and the unary and binary $2 \equiv 0$ equation problems are already undecidable and do not have small model property for those equivalence relations. Then, since by a simple reduction these problems are special cases of the more general problem, we know that for most of the interesting equivalence relations including those mentioned earlier, the more general case of k-ary $n \equiv m$ equation problem is not decidable and does not have small model property when $n + m > 1$. This gives a negative answer to the conjecture put forward in [JJLL93].

2   Some Useful CCS Processes and Contexts

A standard way to show undecidability is to demonstrate an effective reduction from some known undecidability problem. The first undecidable problem to come into one's mind would probably be the halting problem of Turing machines. We will show this kind of reduction to prove the undecidability of equation problems in the next section. For this purpose, in this section we construct some useful CCS processes and contexts and show some of their properties.

First we construct a process T which imitates the blank tape of a Turing machine. A Turing machine tape can be seen as a row of cells, each holding a letter of a finite alphabet A or holding the bland symbol b. Each cell must be in one of the following states according to its relative position to the read and write head and the letter it holds:

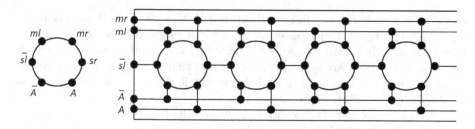

Fig. 1. A cell and the tape

1. It holds x with the head pointing to it. We write $W(x)$ for this state and say that the cell is awake.
2. It holds x with the head on its left. We write $S_l(x)$ for this state and say that the cell is asleep and waiting to be awakened from the left.
3. It holds x with the head on its right. We write $S_r(x)$ for this state and say that the cell is asleep and waiting to be awakened from the right.

When a cell is in the state $W(x)$, that is awake and holding x, the following actions and only the following actions can happen to it. The environment can read out its contents by synchronizing on the port $\overline{x}$. The environment can also change its content by synchronizing on the port y and thereby changing its state to $W(y)$. On receiving a signal on the port ml (moving to the left), the cell will wake its left side neighbor by signaling on the port $\overline{sl}$ (signal left) and then enter the state $S_l(x)$. Likewise, on receiving a signal on the port mr (moving to the right), the cell will wake its right side neighbor by signaling on the port $\overline{sr}$ (signal right) and then enter the state $S_r(x)$. When a cell is asleep in $S_l(x)$ ($S_r(x)$), the only possible action for it is to receive a signal on the port $\overline{sl}$ (sr) and enter the state $W(x)$. The precise behavior is expressed by the following CCS expressions:

$$W(x) \overset{d}{=} \overline{x}.W(x) + \Sigma_{y \in A} y.W(y) + ml.\overline{sl}.S_l(x) + mr.\overline{sr}.S_r(x),$$
$$S_l(x) \overset{d}{=} \overline{sl}.W(x),$$
$$S_r(x) \overset{d}{=} sr.W(x).$$

Now, the blank tape in its initial state is just a row of cells in state $S_l(b)$. The following recursive definition gives the blank tape T:

$$T \overset{d}{=} (S_l(b)[link/sr]|T[link/sl]) \backslash link.$$

The construction is pictured in Fig. 1, where A and $\overline{A}$ are in fact two sets of ports named by the letters and barred letters in the alphabet of the Turing machine.

A Turing machine tape can also be described by the following infinite set of equations about $B(s_1, s_2)$, where $s_1 \in (A \cup \{b\})^*$ is the contents of the tape between the end of the tape and the current position of the read/write head,

$s_2 \in (A \cup \{b\})^* b^\omega$ is the contents of the rest of the tape, $\mathtt{hd}, \mathtt{tl}$, and $\hat{\ }$ are the usual head, tail and concatenation functions on strings.

$$B(s_1, s_2) \stackrel{d}{=} \overline{\mathtt{hd}(s_1)}.B(s_1, s_2) + \Sigma_{y \in A} y.B(y \hat{\ } \mathtt{tl}(s_1), s_2)$$
$$+ ml.\tau.B(\mathtt{tl}(s_1), \mathtt{hd}(s_1) \hat{\ } s_2) + mr.\tau.B(\mathtt{hd}(s_2) \hat{\ } s_1, \mathtt{tl}(s_2)), \quad (s_1 \neq \epsilon)$$
$$B(\epsilon, s_2) \stackrel{d}{=} \overline{sl}.I(s_2),$$
$$I(s_2) \stackrel{d}{=} \overline{sl}.B(\mathtt{hd}(s_2), \mathtt{tl}(s_2)).$$

We can take $I(b^\omega)$ to be a blank tape in its initial state.

It is not difficult to check that both $I(b^\omega)$ and T solve the following equation when $\equiv$ is $\sim$ (strong bisimilarity)

$$X \equiv \overline{sl}.(W(b)[link/sr] | X[link/sl]) \backslash link \tag{4}$$

(note that the τ actions in the definition of $I(b^\omega)$ are not necessary apart from making $I(b^\omega)$ into a solution to that equation in terms of $\sim$). Because this equation is weakly guarded, it has unique solution modulo $\sim$ (Proposition 14, page 103 of [Mil89]). Thus $T \sim I(b^\omega)$, which is a formal justification that T indeed simulates a blank tape of Turing machine. We will talk more about this equation later, and in the rest of the paper we will write $D(X)$ for $\overline{sl}.(W(b)[link/sr] | X[link/sl]) \backslash link$, hence Eq. (4) above is $X \equiv D(X)$.

At this point we clarify some notations. The reader is referred to [Mil89] for a full account of the operational semantics of CCS processes. Following [Mil89] we write $P \stackrel{a}{\longrightarrow} Q$ to mean that the process P (in this state) can perform action a and change its state to Q, $P \stackrel{a}{\not\longrightarrow}$ to mean that P is not capable of any a action. Let $a_1, \ldots, a_n$ be a sequence of visible actions (not τ), then $P \stackrel{a_1 \ldots a_n}{\Longrightarrow} Q$ means that P can reach Q by performing action sequence $a_1, \ldots, a_n$ with finitely many τ's interleaved.

Definition 1. *A finite sequence of visible actions s is a* trace *of P if $P \stackrel{s}{\Longrightarrow} P'$ for some P'. A finite sequence of visible actions s is a* complete trace *of P if $P \stackrel{s}{\Longrightarrow} P'$ for some P' with $P' \stackrel{a}{\not\longrightarrow}$ for any a. Let $Tr(P)$ denotes the set of traces of P and $CTr(P)$ the set of complete traces of P, two processes P and Q are said to be* trace equivalent, *written $P \approx_t Q$, if $Tr(P) = Tr(Q)$, and two processes P and Q are said to be* complete trace equivalent, *written $P \approx_{ct} Q$, if $Tr(P) = Tr(Q)$ and $CTr(P) = CTr(Q)$.*

Note that, with this definition $CTr(P)$ contains only finite complete traces (those ending with a dead locked state) but not infinite traces.

Lemma 1. *When $\equiv$ is $\approx_t$, Eq. (4) has unique solution modulo $\approx_t$.*

Proof. For any process P, lets write $D^n(P)$ for $D(D^{n-1}(P))$ when $n > 0$ and $D^0(P)$ for P. Notice that if $D^n(P) \stackrel{s}{\Longrightarrow} R$ and the number of mr's in s is less than n, then the transitions must be independent of P. More precisely, in this case R has the form $H\{P/X\}$ for some expression H such that for any process $Q, D^n(Q) \stackrel{s}{\Longrightarrow} H\{Q/X\}$. Now suppose P and Q are two solutions and $P \stackrel{s}{\Longrightarrow} P'$

for some P'. We can choose a sufficiently large n such that the number of mr's in s is less than n. By the congruence property of $\approx_t$ (Proposition 2, page 204 of [Mil89]), $P \approx_t D(P)$ implies $P \approx_t D^n(P)$. Thus $D^n(P) \xrightarrow{s} R$ for some R. By the above analysis, there exists an expression H such that $D^n(Q) \xrightarrow{s} H\{Q/X\}$. So $Q \xrightarrow{s} Q'$ for some Q' because $Q \approx_t D(Q)$ implies $Q \approx_t D^n(Q)$. Thus $Tr(P) \subseteq Tr(Q)$. We can show $Tr(Q) \subseteq Tr(P)$ in the same way, so $P \approx_t Q$. It is interesting to observe that Eq. (4) is not sequential, thus does not satisfy the sufficient condition for having unique solution (Proposition 13, page 158 of [Mil89]). □

Lemma 2. *If $P \approx_t I(b^\omega)$ then P is an infinite state process.*

Proof. Assume that P has a finite state space, then $Tr(P)$ is a regular set because by treating each state of P as acceptance state and each τ move as empty move we obtain a finite automaton which accepts $Tr(P)$. Since we start from $P \approx_t I(b^\omega)$, this implies that $Tr(b^\omega)$ is a regular set which further implies that $Tr(I(b^\omega)) \cap \overline{sl}(ml+mr)^*\overline{sl}$ is also regular. However the latter is not regular for the following reason. By the construction, $I(b^\omega)$ starts with an $\overline{sl}$ action, and from then on before the second $\overline{sl}$ action, the number of ml's is exactly one more than the number of mr's, and they are balanced like left and right parenthesis (intuitively, after the signal $\overline{sl}$, the read-write head of the tape is at the starting of the tape, so when $\overline{sl}$ is enabled the second time the head has just returned to the starting position for the first time). Thus $Tr(I(b^\omega)) \cap \overline{sl}(ml + mr)^*\overline{sl}$ is not regular because it consists of strings of the form $\overline{sl}\hat{s}\hat{ml}\hat{sl}$ where s is a sequence of mr's and ml's balanced like left and right parenthesis. Thus P must have infinite states. □

Next, we construct a dyadic context C which acts as a coordinator between the sub-processes in this context such that it will deadlock if one of the sub-process cannot follow the actions of the other. Let $L = A \cup \overline{A} \cup \{ml, mr, \overline{sl}\}$, where A is the finite alphabet of the Turing machine. It is obvious that all possible visible actions of T are contained in L. Let L_1, L_2 be two disjoint sets of actions such that they are both isomorphic to L with f_1, f_2 being the corresponding isomorphic maps (that is f_i is one and onto and $f_i(\overline{a}) = \overline{f_i(a)}$ for $a \in L$). Let syn, err (for synchronizing and error) be two labels not in $L_1 \cup L_2$. Then f_1, f_2 can be extended to rename functions by defining $f_1(a) = f_2(a) = err$ for any $a \notin L$. Now define

$$R \overset{d}{=} \Sigma_{a \in L - \{\overline{ml}, \overline{mr}\}} f_1(a).Q_a + f_1(\overline{ml}).f_2(\overline{ml}).syn.R + f_1(\overline{mr}).f_2(\overline{mr}).syn.R,$$

$$Q_a \overset{d}{=} f_2(a).Q_1 + \tau.f_2(a).Q_2, \qquad\qquad (a \in L - \{\overline{ml}, \overline{mr}\})$$

$$Q_1 \overset{d}{=} syn.\tau.\tau.R + \tau.Q_2,$$

$$Q_2 \overset{d}{=} syn.\tau.R + \tau.syn.R.$$

R is to be used in a context $C(\_,\_)$ in which R will monitor the coordination of two processes P, Q such that $C(P, Q)$ will indicate everything is fine by only performing syn^ω, and $C(P,Q)$ will produce err action or deadlock otherwise. This definition of R is slightly complicated by the insertion of τ's in various places. Basically, R could be defined as $R \stackrel{d}{=} \Sigma_{a \in L} f_1(a).f_2(a).syn.R$, which may still give a better idea how R actually works. However, these τ's are necessary in order to satisfy the equation in the first part of Lemma 3 below which enables us to derive more general conclusions. Otherwise, using the simpler definition, we can only show a weaker version of the equation with $\approx$ in place of $\sim$. From now on we will write $C(X,Y)$ for $(X[f_1]|R|Y[f_2])\backslash L_1 \cup L_2$. It is not difficult to see that a necessary condition for $C(P,Q)$ to be always capable of doing syn and nothing else (no err) is that whatever visible action P may perform, Q must be able to follow. This and some other useful properties of C are stated in the following lemma. In the lemma, as well as the rest of the paper, T_0 is a finite state process defined by $T_0 \stackrel{d}{=} sl.T_0 + \overline{mr}.\tau.T_0$.

Lemma 3. *For C, T, and T_0 constructed as above, the following hold:*

1. $C(T,T) \sim C(T_0,T_0)$;
2. $CTr(C(P,Q)) \subseteq CTr(C(T_0,T_0))$ *and* $Tr(C(P,Q)) \subseteq Tr(C(T_0,T_0))$ *implies* $Tr(P) \subseteq Tr(Q)$.

Proof. Let $Dir(I(b^\omega)) = \{P | \exists s \in L^*.I(b^\omega) \stackrel{s}{\Longrightarrow} P\}$, i.e. the set of derivatives of $I(b^\omega)$. It is not difficult to see that the following is a strong bisimulation relation containing $(C(I(b^\omega), I(b^\omega)), C(T_0, T_0))$:

$$\{((P[f_1]|Q|P[f_2])\backslash L_1 \cup L_2, (T_0[f_1]|Q|T_0[f_2])\backslash L_1 \cup L_2) \,|$$
$$P \in Dir(I(b^\omega)), P \not\stackrel{\tau}{\longrightarrow}, Q \in \{R, \tau.R, \tau.\tau.R, syn.R, Q_1, Q_2\}\}\cup$$
$$((P'[f_1]|Q_a|P[f_2])\backslash L_1 \cup L_2, (T_0[f_1]|Q_{sl}|T_0[f_2])\backslash L_1 \cup L_2) \,|$$
$$P \in Dir(I(b^\omega)), a \in L - \{ml, \overline{mr}\}, P \stackrel{a}{\longrightarrow} P'\}\cup$$
$$((P'[f_1]|f_2(a).Q_2|P[f_2])\backslash L_1 \cup L_2, (T_0[f_1]|f_2(sl).Q_2|T_0[f_2])\backslash L_1 \cup L_2) \,|$$
$$P \in Dir(I(b^\omega)), a \in L - \{ml, \overline{mr}\}, P \stackrel{a}{\longrightarrow} P'\}\cup$$
$$((P'[f_1]|f_2(a).syn.R|P[f_2])\backslash L_1 \cup L_2, (\tau.T_0[f_1]|f_2(\overline{mr}).syn.R|T_0[f_2])\backslash L_1 \cup L_2) \,|$$
$$P \in Dir(I(b^\omega)), a \in \{\overline{ml}, \overline{mr}\}, P \stackrel{a}{\longrightarrow} P'\}\cup$$
$$((P'[f_1]|f_2(a).syn.R|P[f_2])\backslash L_1 \cup L_2, (T_0[f_1]|f_2(\overline{mr}).syn.R|T_0[f_2])\backslash L_1 \cup L_2) \,|$$
$$P \in Dir(I(b^\omega)), a \in \{\overline{ml}, \overline{mr}\}, \exists P''.P \stackrel{a}{\longrightarrow} P'', P'' \stackrel{\tau}{\longrightarrow} P'\}\cup$$
$$((P[f_1]|Q|\tau.P[f_2])\backslash L_1 \cup L_2, (T_0[f_1]|Q|\tau.T_0[f_2])\backslash L_1 \cup L_2) \,|$$
$$P \in Dir(I(b^\omega)), P \not\stackrel{\tau}{\longrightarrow}, Q \in \{R, syn.R\}\}.$$

Hence $C(I(b^\omega), I(b^\omega)) \sim C(T_0, T_0)$ and $C(T,T) \sim C(T_0, T_0)$.

Note that $C(T_0, T_0) \approx_{ct} syn^\omega$, where syn^ω is the process which performs syn forever. Moreover according to Definition 1, $CTr(syn^\omega) = \emptyset$ because syn^ω does not have any finite complete trace. So to prove 2 it is equivalent to prove $CTr(C(P,Q)) = \emptyset$ and $Tr(C(P,Q)) \subseteq Tr(sync^\omega)$ implies $Tr(P) \subseteq Tr(Q)$. Suppose $CTr(C(P,Q)) = \emptyset$ and $Tr(C(P,Q)) \subseteq Tr(syn^\omega)$. Now if $P \stackrel{a}{\Longrightarrow} P'$ for some action $a \neq \tau$, then $a \in L$ (otherwise, $f_1(a) = err$ and $C(P,Q) \stackrel{err}{\Longrightarrow} C(P',Q)$, contradict to the assumption that $Tr(C(P,Q)) \subseteq Tr(C(T_0, T_0))$).

And moreover $Q \stackrel{a}{\Longrightarrow} Q'$ for some Q' (otherwise $C(P,Q)$ would deadlock, contradict to the fact that $C(P,Q)$ does not have finite complete trace). Now we have $C(P,Q) \stackrel{syc}{\Longrightarrow} C(P',Q')$, thus $CTr(C(P',Q')) \subseteq CTr(P,Q) = \emptyset$ and $Tr(C(P',Q')) \subseteq Tr(P,Q) \subseteq Tr(syn^\omega)$. Then it is easy to see that for any finite visible action sequence s, if $P \stackrel{s}{\Longrightarrow} P'$ then $Q \stackrel{s}{\Longrightarrow} Q'$, that is $Tr(P) \subseteq Tr(Q)$. In fact, here we have outlined a proof that $CTr(C(P,Q)) = \emptyset$ and $Tr(C(P,Q)) \subseteq Tr(syn^\omega)$ implies that (P,Q) is contained in a *weak simulation* relation, which would guarantee that $Tr(P) \subseteq Tr(Q)$. However since we did not formally state the definition and properties of weak simulations, we should stay within trace based relations.   □

The processes T, T_0, R, contexts C, D, and label sets L, L_1, L_2 with rename functions f_1, f_2 defined here are referred in the proofs of the main results in the next section.

3   Main Results

With the preparation in the last section, we are now ready to show the main results of the paper, namely that many equation problems are undecidable and do not have small model property.

Theorem 1. *For any $\equiv$ such that $\sim \subseteq \equiv \subseteq \approx_t$, both the unary $1 \equiv 1$ equation problem and the binary $1 \equiv 1$ equation problem are not decidable and do not have small model property.*

Proof. It is sufficient to construct some effective reduction from the divergence problem of Turing machines, which is well known to be not even semi-decidable. There is a systematic way of constructing a finite state process M_i which simulates the finite-state control mechanism of the i-th Turing machine for each i. Thus $(M_i|T)\backslash L$ will simulate the i-th Turing machine such that $(M_i|T)\backslash L \sim \tau^\omega$ if and only if the i-th Turing machine does not holt on a blank tape, and also that $(M_i|T)\backslash L \stackrel{a}{\Longrightarrow} P$ for some P if and only if the i-th Turing machine halts, where τ^ω is the process which only performs internal actions forever.

Now we can show that the i-th Turing machine diverges if and only if the following unary $1 \equiv 1$ equation is solvable when $\sim \subseteq \equiv \subseteq \approx_t$ and $a \neq b$.

$$a.(M_i|X)\backslash L + b.X \equiv a.\tau^\omega + b.D(X). \tag{5}$$

For one direction, suppose the i-th Turing machine diverges, that is to say $(M_i|T)\backslash L \sim \tau^\omega$. Since $T \sim D(T)$, and $\sim \subseteq \equiv$, T solves Eq. (5).

For the converse direction, suppose T' solves Eq. (5). Because $\equiv \subseteq \approx_t$ and $a \neq b$, in this case $(M_i|T')\backslash L \approx_t \tau^\omega$ and $T' \approx_t D(T')$. By Lemma 1 $T' \approx_t T$, thus $(M_i|T)\backslash L \approx_t (M_i|T')\backslash L \approx_t \tau^\omega$, and the i-th Turing machine diverges on a blank tape (otherwise there must exist a visible action a and P such that $(M_i|T)\backslash L \stackrel{a}{\Longrightarrow} P$).

Similarly, it is easy to work out that the i-th Turing machine diverges if and only if the following binary $1 \equiv 1$ equation is solvable when $\sim \subseteq \equiv \subseteq \approx_t$ and a, b, c are three different actions.

$$a.(M_i | X) \backslash L + b.X + c.D(X) \equiv a.\tau^\omega + b.Y + c.Y \tag{6}$$

Thus we showed effective reductions from the divergence problem of Turing machines to the unary and binary $1 \equiv 1$ equation problems. So the unary $1 \equiv 1$ equation problem and the binary $1 \equiv 1$ equation problem are not even semi-decidable and thus not decidable.

In order to prove that a type of equations does not have small model property, we only need to find a solvable equation of that type and show that any solution to the equation has infinite states. It is easy to see from Lemmas 1 and 2 that, when $\equiv \subseteq \approx_t$, Eq. (4) is a solvable unary $1 \equiv 1$ equation which only has infinite state solutions. Also for the same reason, when $\equiv \subseteq \approx_t$ and $a \neq b$, the following is a solvable binary $1 \equiv 1$ equation which only has infinite state solutions

$$a.X + b.D(X) \equiv a.Y + b.Y.$$

Thus both unary and binary $1 \equiv 1$ equation problems do not have small model property. $\square$

Theorem 2. *For any $\equiv$ such that $\sim \subseteq \equiv \subseteq \approx_{ct}$, both unary $2 \equiv 0$ equation problem and binary $2 \equiv 0$ equation problem are not decidable and do not have small model property.*

Proof. Again we will construct some effective reduction from the divergence problem of Turing machines. Lets say that M_i is a finite state process which simulates the finite-state control mechanism of the i-th Turing machine. Thus $(M_i | T) \backslash L$ will simulate the i-th Turing machine such that $(M_i | T) \backslash L \sim \tau^\omega$ if and only if the i-th Turing machine does not halt on blank tape, and if and only if $Tr((M_i | T) \backslash L) = \{\epsilon\}$ and $CTr((M_i | T) \backslash L) = \emptyset$, that is $Tr((M_i | T) \backslash L)$ does not have any trace other than the empty trace and $CTr((M_i | T) \backslash L)$ does not contain any finite complete trace. We will show that, when $\sim \subseteq \equiv \subseteq \approx_{ct}$, the i-th Turing machine diverges if and only if the following equation is solvable

$$\tau.(M_i[f_2] | X[f_2]) \backslash L_1 \cup L_2 + \tau.C(D(X), X) + \tau.C(X, D(X)) \equiv \tau^\omega + \tau.C(T_0, T_0) \tag{7}$$

which has the exact solution set as the following unary $2 \equiv 0$ equation where $a, b \in L_1 \cup L_2$ and $a \neq b$

$$((a.M_i[f_2] + a.(D(X)[f_1] | R) + b.X[f_1])$$
$$| (\bar{a}.X[f_2] + \bar{b}.(R | D(X)[f_2]))) \backslash L_1 \cup L_2 \equiv \tau^\omega + \tau.C(T_0, T_0).$$

The reason that the above two equations have the same set of solution follows is that, by the expansion law (Proposition 9, page 96 of [Mil89]), the left hand sides of the equations are equal under strong bisimilarity.

For one direction, suppose the i-th Turing machine diverges, that is to say $(M_i|T)\backslash L \sim \tau^\omega$ and therefor $(M_i[f_2]|T[f_2])\backslash L_1 \cup L_2 \sim ((M_i|T)\backslash L)[f_2]\backslash L_1 \sim \tau^\omega$. Since $T \sim D(T)$ and by Lemma 3 $C(T,T) \sim C(T_0,T_0)$, thus T solves Eq. (7) since $\sim \subseteq \equiv$.

For the converse direction, suppose Eq. (7) is solvable with solution T'. Because $\equiv \subseteq \approx_{ct}$, this implies that $(M_i[f_2|T'[f_2]])\backslash L_1 \cup L_2$ has no complete trace, and that $CTr(C(T',D(T')))$ and $CTr(C(D(T'),T'))$ are both subsets of $CTr(C(T_0,T_0))$. By Lemma 3, $T' \approx_t D(T')$, and by Lemma 1 $T' \approx_t T$. Thus $(M_i[f_2|T[f_2]])\backslash L_1 \cup L_2$ has no complete trace, nor has $((M_i|T)\backslash L)[f_2]\backslash L_1$ nor $(M_i|T)\backslash L$. So the i-th Turing machine diverges on a blank tape.

In a similar way, we can work out that the i-th Turing machine diverges if and only if the following binary $2 \equiv 0$ equation is solvable with $\sim \subseteq \equiv \subseteq \approx_{ct}$ and $a, b \in L_1 \cup L_2, a \neq b$:

$$((a.M_i[f_2] + a.(X[f_1]|R) + a.(D(X)[f_1]|R) + b.X[f_2]$$
$$+b.D(X)[f_2])|(\overline{a}.Y[f_2] + \overline{b}.(Y[f_1]|R))\backslash L_1 \cup L_2 \equiv \tau^\omega + \tau.C(T_0,T_0).$$

Thus we showed effective reductions from the divergence problem of Turing machine to the unary and binary $2 \equiv 0$ equation problems. So the unary $2 \equiv 0$ and binary $2 \equiv 0$ equation problems are not even semi-decidable, and thus not decidable.

Now, let $a, b \in L_1 \cup L_2, a \neq b$. With Lemmas 1 and 3, the Turing machine tape T is a solution for X in the following unary $2 \equiv 0$ equation when $\equiv \subseteq \approx_{ct}$

$$((a.((D(X)[f_1])|R) + b.(X[f_1]|R))|(\overline{a}.X[f_2] + \overline{b}.D(X)[f_2]))\backslash L_1 \cup L_2 \equiv \tau.C(T_0,T_0),$$

and T is also a solution for both X and Y in the following binary $2 \equiv 0$ equation when $\equiv \subseteq \approx_{ct}$

$$((a.X[f_1] + a.D(X)[f_1] + b.X[f_2] + b.D(X)[f_2])$$
$$|(\overline{a}.(R|Y[f_2]) + \overline{b}.(Y[f_1]|R)))\backslash L_1 \cup L_2 \equiv \tau.C(T_0,T_0).$$

And moreover, by Lemmas 1 and 2, the above equations do not have finite-state solutions. Thus both unary and binary $2 \equiv 0$ equation problems do not have small model property.   □

In the last section we showed that four types of $n \equiv m$ equation problems are not decidable and do not have small model property for any equivalence relation which is at least as strong as complete trace equivalence (this can be relaxed to trace equivalence in the case of $1 \equiv 1$) but not stronger than strong bisimilarity. These four types of equation problems are the unary and binary $1 \equiv 1$ equation problems and the unary and binary $2 \equiv 0$ equation problems. Undecidability of $1 \equiv 1$ is somewhat expected because recursion can be coded into such an equation problem, but undecidability of $2 \equiv 0$ equation problems is rather unexpected. In a sense this shows the computation power of communication.

The negative results about these four basic type of equation problems have very general implications. Because any k-ary $n \equiv m$ equation problem with

$m + n > 1$ would have one of these basic problems as special case, such k-ary $n \equiv m$ equation problem is surely undecidable and does not have small model property if $\equiv$ is at least as strong as complete trace equivalence but not stronger than strong bisimilarity. Also the range of equivalence relations from complete trace equivalence to strong bisimilarity covers the most interesting equivalence relations in the study of concurrency, including all the equivalence relations mentioned in the beginning of the Introduction. Indeed, one would expect a reasonable equivalence relation of concurrent system to be in this range. Although the constructions are specific for CCS, similar reductions could be constructed to show similar results within other process algebras.

Undecidability results show the limitation of automatic tools for solving process equations. Lack of small model property means the need for more insight in order to construct solutions for these equations. Thus machine assisted semi-automatic tool such as the one proposed in [JJLL93] and techniques of constructing infinite state solutions seem to be necessary.

Acknowledgments. The results reported in this work were obtained more than twenty years ago, from the time when I was a PhD student under the supervision of Kim G. Larsen, to sometime not long after I finished my thesis. To this day I still remember many detailed discussions with Kim about this research, which had given me great inspirations as well as immense pleasure. Kim encouraged me to write a paper about the results and submit it for publication, but somehow the process never got finished. I am very happy that now I can contribute with it to the Festschrift in his honor.

References

[BHR84] Brookes, S.D., Hoare, C.A.R., Roscoe, A.W.: A theory of communicating sequential processes. J. ACM **31**(3), 560–599 (1984)

[BIM95] Bloom, B., Istrail, S., Meyer, A.R.: Bisimulation can't be traced. J. ACM **42**(1), 232–268 (1995)

[BK85] Bergstra, J.A., Klop, J.W.: Algebra of communicating processes with abstraction. Theoret. Comput. Sci. **37**, 77–121 (1985)

[GV89] Groote, J.F., Vaandrager, F.: Structured operational semantics and bisimulation as a congruence. In: Ausiello, G., Dezani-Ciancaglini, M., Rocca, S.R. (eds.) ICALP 1989. LNCS, vol. 372, pp. 423–438. Springer, Heidelberg (1989). doi:10.1007/BFb0035774

[Hoa85] Hoare, C.A.R.: Communicating Sequential Processes. Prentice Hall International Series in Computer Science. Prentice Hall, Upper Saddle River (1985)

[JJLL93] Jensen, O.H., Jeppesen, C., Lang, J.T., Larsen, K.G.: Model construction for implicit specifications in modal logic. In: Best, E. (ed.) CONCUR 1993. LNCS, vol. 715, pp. 247–261. Springer, Heidelberg (1993). doi:10.1007/3-540-57208-2_18

[Koz82] Kozen, D.: Results on the propositional μ-calculus. In: Nielsen, M., Schmidt, E.M. (eds.) ICALP 1982. LNCS, vol. 140, pp. 348–359. Springer, Heidelberg (1982). doi:10.1007/BFb0012782

[KP83] Kozen, D., Parikh, R.: A decision procedure for the propositional μ-calculus. In: Clarke, E., Kozen, D. (eds.) Logic of Programs 1983. LNCS, vol. 164, pp. 313–325. Springer, Heidelberg (1984). doi:10.1007/3-540-12896-4_370

[Liu92] Liu, X.: Specification and decomposition in concurrency. Ph.D. thesis, University of Aalborg, Fredrik Bajers Vej 7, DK 9220 Aalborg ø, Denmark (1992)

[LS91] Larsen, K.G., Skou, A.: Bisimulation through probabilistic testing. Inf. Comput. **94**(1), 1–28 (1991)

[LX90a] Larsen, K.G., Xinxin, L.: Compositionality through an operational semantics of contexts. In: Paterson, M.S. (ed.) ICALP 1990. LNCS, vol. 443, pp. 526–539. Springer, Heidelberg (1990). doi:10.1007/BFb0032056

[LX90b] Larsen, K.G., Xinxin, L.: Equation solving using modal transition systems. In: Proceedings of the Fifth Annual Symposium on Logic in Computer Science (LICS 1990), Philadelphia, Pennsylvania, USA, 4–7 June 1990, pp. 108–117. IEEE Computer Society (1990)

[Mil82] Milner, R. (ed.): A Calculus of Communicating Systems. LNCS, vol. 92. Springer, Heidelberg (1980)

[Mil89] Milner, R.: Communication and Concurrency. Prentice-Hall International Series in Computer Science. Prentice Hall, Upper Saddle River (1989)

[NH84] De Nicola, R., Hennessy, M.: Testing equivalence for processes. Theoret. Comput. Sci. **34**(1), 83–133 (1984)

[Par89] Parrow, J.: Submodule construction as equation solving in CCS. Theoret. Comput. Sci. **68**(2), 175–202 (1989)

[QL90] Qin, H., Lewis, P.: Factorization of finite state machines under observational equivalence. In: Baeten, J.C.M., Klop, J.W. (eds.) CONCUR 1990. LNCS, vol. 458, pp. 427–441. Springer, Heidelberg (1990). doi:10.1007/BFb0039075

[SE89] Streett, R.S., Emerson, E.A.: An automata theoretic decision procedure for the propositional mu-calculus. Inf. Comput. **81**(3), 249–264 (1989)

[Shi89] Shields, M.W.: A note on the simple interface equation. Technical report, University of Kent at Canterbury (1989)

[SI94] Steffen, B., Ingolfsdottir, A.: Characteristic formulas for processes with divergence. Inf. Comput. **110**(1), 149–163 (1994)

[vGW96] van Glabbeek, R.J., Weijland, W.P.: Branching time and abstraction in bisimulation semantics. J. ACM **43**(3), 555–600 (1996)

[ZIG87] Zeeberg, M., Ingolfsdottir, A., Godskesen, J.C.: Fra Hennessy-Milner logik til CCS-processer. Master's thesis, Aalborg University (1987)

Timed Temporal Logics

Patricia Bouyer[1]($\boxtimes$), François Laroussinie[2], Nicolas Markey[3],
Joël Ouaknine[4,5], and James Worrell[5]

[1] LSV, CNRS & ENS Paris-Saclay, Cachan, France
bouyer@lsv.fr
[2] IRIF, CNRS & Université Paris Diderot, Paris, France
[3] IRISA, CNRS & INRIA & Université Rennes 1, Rennes, France
[4] Max Planck Institute for Software Systems, Saarbrücken, Germany
[5] Department of Computer Science, Oxford University, Oxford, UK

Abstract. Since the early 1990's, classical temporal logics have been extended with timing constraints. While temporal logics only express contraints on the order of events, their timed extensions can add quantitative constraints on delays between those events. We survey expressiveness and algorithmic results on those logics, and discuss semantic choices that may look unimportant but do have an impact on the questions we consider.

1 Introduction

Timed automata [6] are a well-established model for real-time systems. One of their most fundamental properties is that reachability properties can be decided. This has given rise to multiple works, both on theoretical aspects and on more algorithmic and practical aspects. Several tools have even been developed for automatically verifying timed automata, for instance HyTech [28], Kronos [21] or Uppaal [12,41]. Among the success stories of that model, one can cite the verification and the correction of the Bang & Olufsen audio/video protocol [27] made using the tool Uppaal.

Timed automata are adequate to represent systems, but not that much for representing properties of systems. If $\mathcal{A}$ is a timed automaton representing the system, and $\mathcal{P}$ a timed automaton representing the property, verifying that $\mathcal{A}$ satisfies the property $\mathcal{P}$ corresponds to checking that all behaviours of $\mathcal{A}$ are also behaviours of $\mathcal{P}$. This is a language-inclusion question, which turns out to be undecidable for timed automata [6].

In order to circumvent this difficulty, following the development of temporal logics in model-checking [20,50], timed temporal logics have been proposed, which extend classical untimed temporal logics with timing constraints. There are several ways of expressing such constraints, a standard one consists in constraining temporal modalities. For instance, one can write a formula such as

$$\mathbf{G}(\mathsf{problem} \to \mathbf{F}_{\leq 5\,\mathrm{min}}\mathsf{repair})$$

© Springer International Publishing AG 2017
L. Aceto et al. (Eds.): Larsen Festschrift, LNCS 10460, pp. 211–230, 2017.
DOI: 10.1007/978-3-319-63121-9_11

to express the *quantitative* property that any problem must be followed by a repair action within 5 min. This kind of properties cannot be expressed using standard temporal logics, as those logics can only refer to the relative order of events, not to their relative distance (in time).

Several timed extensions of CTL [20] and LTL [50] have been proposed. In this paper, we focus on some of those extensions that have been studied for the purpose of model-checking real-time systems. We start with the definition of timed automata, and we discuss several possible semantics for this model (Sect. 2). While the choice of semantics is harmless for many issues, it is crucial here in the context of timed temporal logics. We then turn to branching-time logics, and present TCTL as well as timed extensions of modal logics (Sect. 3). We end with linear-time logics, which are strongly related to first-order logics over the reals (Sect. 4). We end up with some conclusions and with further research directions (Sect. 5).

2   Continuous vs. Pointwise Semantics

Timed automata [6] are extensions of standard finite automata with finitely many clock variables. These variables, which take their values in a time domain, aim at constraining delays between events. The choice of the time domain has been discussed from the early definition of the model (see e.g. [4]); there has been a clear partition between papers considering dense-time domains such as the set $\mathbb{Q}_{\geq 0}$ of nonnegative rationals, or the set $\mathbb{R}_{\geq 0}$ of nonnegative reals, and papers considering a discrete-time domain like the set $\mathbb{Z}_{\geq 0}$ of nonnegative integers. In this paper, we assume that the time domain is $\mathbb{R}_{\geq 0}$.

In the setting of dense time, there is another distinction, which has been less clearly identified in the framework of timed automata: it is related to the nature of runs in a timed automaton. Indeed, the observation of the system can be considered continuous (executions are then viewed as *signals*), or it can be discrete (executions are then viewed as *timed words*) [4,52]. This distinction will be important in the context of logics, as we will see in this article. We begin with discussing this issue.

2.1   Timed Automata

Timed automata extend finite-state automata with a finite set C of clocks, which measure delays between events that occur in the automaton. A configuration of a timed automaton is thus given by a pair (s, v) where s is a state of the automaton and $v \colon C \to \mathbb{R}_{\geq 0}$ is a clock valuation. For $d \in \mathbb{R}_{\geq 0}$, we let $v' = v + d$ be the clock valuation such that $v'(c) = v(c) + d$ for each clock, corresponding to letting d time units elapse. For a subset $R \subseteq C$, we let $v' = v[R]$ be the valuation such that $v'(c) = 0$ when $c \in R$, and $v'(c) = v(c)$ when $c \in C \setminus R$. This corresponds to resetting clocks in R.

A clock constraint is a conjunction of atomic constraints of the form $c \in J$, where $c \in C$ and J is an interval of $\mathbb{R}_{\geq 0}$ with bounds in $\mathbb{Z}_{\geq 0} \cup \{+\infty\}$. Whether a clock valuation satisfies a clock constraint is defined in the natural way. We write $\mathcal{G}(\mathsf{C})$ for the set of clock constraints on C, and $\mathcal{G}_M(\mathsf{C})$ for the set of all clock constraints on C using integer constants less than or equal to integer M.

Definition 1. *Let AP be a finite set of atomic propositions. A timed automaton $\mathcal{A} = \langle S, C, E, \ell \rangle$ over AP is made of a finite set S of states, a finite set C of clocks, a finite set of edges $E \subseteq S \times \mathcal{G}(C) \times 2^C \times S$, and a labelling function $\ell \colon S \to 2^{AP}$.*

The operational semantics of a timed automaton is defined through an infinite-state transition system, whose states are all the configurations $(s, v) \in S \times \mathbb{R}_{\geq 0}^C$, with transitions from configuration (s, v) to configuration (s', v') when one of the following two conditions is fulfilled:

- $s = s'$ and there exists a delay $d \in \mathbb{R}_{\geq 0}$ such that $v' = v + d$;[1]
- there exists an edge $e = (s, g, R, s') \in E$ such that $v \models g$ and $v' = v[R]$.

This transition system mixes discrete changes (given by the second rule) with continuous changes due to time elapsing (given by the first rule). In particular, since delays are taken in $\mathbb{R}_{\geq 0}$, the underlying graph has infinite branching.

2.2   Semantics for Temporal Logics over Timed Automata

We assume the reader is reasonably familiar with standard untimed temporal logics like LTL [50] and CTL [19,51]. While these untimed logics can well be interpreted over timed automata, extensions with quantitative constraints over delays are very much relevant in this setting. To define such constraints, one can either decorate the modalities with intervals specifying time delays that are allowed to satisfy the properties, or explicitly use clock variables in the formulas, in pretty much the same way as they are used in automata. These considerations will be discussed specifically in the sections over branching-time logics and linear-time logics.

There is a second important issue with interpreting temporal logics over timed automata, which is semantical. We need indeed to make precise which part of the behaviour of the timed automaton $\mathcal{A} = \langle S, C, E, \ell \rangle$ is observed. We illustrate the possible choices using the *constrained until* formula. Intuitively, $\phi_1 \mathbf{U}_J \phi_2$ (where J is an interval of $\mathbb{R}_{\geq 0}$ with bounds in $\mathbb{Q}_{\geq 0} \cup \{+\infty\}$) holds along an execution of $\mathcal{A}$ if it is the case that ϕ_2 eventually holds, within a delay that belongs to interval J, and that ϕ_1 holds at all intermediary points in time. We will see that the choice of the semantics (more precisely, which *intermediary points in time* we consider) is crucial.

Discrete-Observation Semantics. A natural way to observe the system is to see paths in the transition system of the timed automaton as sequences of configurations reached when the automaton performs discrete transitions.

---

[1] Zero-delay transitions are not allowed here, but could be included without affecting the presented results.

Formally, a path is a (finite or infinite) sequence $\pi = (s_i, v_i)_{i < L}$ of configurations, such that there is a delay transition between (s_i, v_i) and $(s_i, v_i + d_i)$, and a discrete transition between $(s_i, v_i + d_i)$ and (s_{i+1}, v_{i+1}). Notice that we do not require time divergence here, even for paths of infinite length.

For convenience, we assume that our timed automata include a special clock, named t hereafter, that is never reset and never used in any timing constraint.

The discrete-observation semantics (also called the pointwise semantics in the literature) of the constrained-until modality along a path $\pi = (s_i, v_i)_{i < L}$ in $\mathcal{A}$ can be defined as follows:

$$\mathcal{A}, \pi \models_{\mathsf{disc}} \phi_1 \mathbf{U}_J \phi_2 \quad \Leftrightarrow \quad \exists n > 0.\ \mathcal{A}, \pi_{\geq n} \models_{\mathsf{disc}} \phi_2 \text{ and } v_n(t) - v_0(t) \in J$$
$$\text{and } \forall 0 < m < n.\ \mathcal{A}, \pi_{\geq m} \models_{\mathsf{disc}} \phi_1 \quad (1)$$

where $\pi_{\geq k}$ is the path $(s_i, v_i)_{k \leq i < L}$. We see here that satisfaction of subformulas is checked *only* at discrete time points, precisely when there is a transition taken in the timed automaton, and not while delaying in the timed automaton. Notice that we consider the strict version of the until modality, imposing no constraint in the present time point. This is an arbitrary choice, which makes the logic slightly more expressive.

Continuous-Observation Semantics. It is also natural to consider continuous observations of the evolution of the automaton: let $\pi = (s_i, v_i)_{< L}$ be a path as formerly defined, with an additional global clock t. We associate with π a signal ϖ which maps every nonnegative real number to the configuration of the system at that time: for every $r \in \mathbb{R}_{\geq 0}$, $\varpi(r) = (s_i, v)$ where i is the largest index such that $v_i(t) \leq r$, and $v = v_i + r - v_i(t)$. This can be interpreted intuitively as follows: the system is observed continuously, hence when time elapses, increasing values of clocks are observed. So, at time $v_i(t)$, state s_i is entered, and then, while delaying, all clocks increase. We made the arbitrary choice to assume that at time $v_i(t)$, the system is already in state s_i. In order to avoid arbitrary switches between states, it is often required that ϖ has finite variability, that is, its set of discontinuities has no limit points.

The continuous-observation semantics of the constrained-until modality along a path π (or equivalently, along its associated signal ϖ) in $\mathcal{A}$ can then be defined as follows:

$$\mathcal{A}, \varpi \models_{\mathsf{cont}} \phi_1 \mathbf{U}_J \phi_2 \quad \Leftrightarrow \quad \exists r > 0.\ \mathcal{A}, \varpi_{\geq r} \models_{\mathsf{cont}} \phi_2 \text{ and } r \in J$$
$$\text{and } \forall 0 < r' < r.\ \mathcal{A}, \varpi_{\geq r'} \models_{\mathsf{cont}} \phi_1 \quad (2)$$

where $\varpi_{\geq r}$ is the signal which associates to $r' \in \mathbb{R}_{\geq 0}$ the value $\varpi(r' + r)$. We also write $\mathcal{A}, \pi \models_{\mathsf{cont}} \phi$ when $\mathcal{A}, \varpi \models_{\mathsf{cont}} \phi$.

Example 1. Consider the timed automaton depicted on Fig. 1. A path in that timed automaton is $\pi = (a, 0)(c, 3.2)$. The corresponding signal is ϖ which associates to every $r < 3.2$ the configuration (a, r) and to every $r \geq 3.2$ the configuration (c, r).

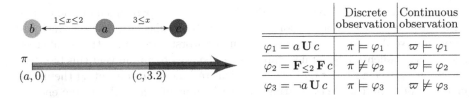

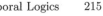

	Discrete observation	Continuous observation
$\varphi_1 = a\,\mathbf{U}\,c$	$\pi \models \varphi_1$	$\varpi \models \varphi_1$
$\varphi_2 = \mathbf{F}_{\leq 2}\,\mathbf{F}\,c$	$\pi \not\models \varphi_2$	$\varpi \models \varphi_2$
$\varphi_3 = \neg a\,\mathbf{U}\,c$	$\pi \models \varphi_3$	$\varpi \not\models \varphi_3$

Fig. 1. A run π of a timed automaton, and its value against some formulas

Interestingly, we get different satisfaction relations, depending on the particular choice of the semantics. Classically, the modality $\mathbf{F}_J\phi$ stands for $\mathtt{true}\,\mathbf{U}_J\phi$. Formula φ_2 in Fig. 1 requires the existence of an intermediary point along the execution where the subformula $\mathbf{F}c$ holds. This is the case in the continuous-observation setting, but not in the discrete-observation setting. On the other hand, φ_3 holds on π since there is no point in time where $\neg a$ has to be tested, whereas φ_3 does not hold on ϖ.

3   Branching-Time Temporal Logics with Timing Constraints

In this section, we present some of the main results about the branching-time framework.

3.1   Timed CTL

Let us begin with the simpler case of plain CTL, with no constraints on *until* modalities. The main ingredient for model checking CTL, which already gives its lower-bound, is the original algorithm for reachability in timed automata:

Theorem 1 [6]. *Reachability in timed automata is* PSPACE-*complete.*

Let $\mathcal{A} = \langle \mathsf{S}, \mathsf{C}, \mathsf{E}, \ell \rangle$ be a timed automaton, and let M be the maximal constant appearing in a clock constraint of $\mathcal{A}$. The above result is proved by quotienting the infinite state space of timed automata into finitely many *regions*: a region for a timed automaton $\mathcal{A}$ is made of a state of $\mathcal{A}$ and of sets of valuations defined by equivalence classes of the *region equivalence* $\equiv_M$. This relation is defined by $v \equiv_M v'$ whenever: for every $x \in \mathsf{C}$, (i) $v(x) > M$ iff $v'(x) > M$, (ii) if $v(x) \leq M$, then the integral parts of $v(x)$ and $v'(x)$ coincide; and for every $x, y \in \mathsf{C}$ such that $v(x), v(y) \leq M$, $\{v(x)\} \leq \{v(y)\}$ iff $\{v'(x)\} \leq \{v'(y)\}$ ($\{\cdot\}$ denotes the fractional part). The main property of region equivalence is that it defines a time-abstract bisimulation, and a finite automaton called the *region automaton* can be constructed based on this equivalence, which represents in an abstract manner the behaviour of $\mathcal{A}$.

A second ingredient for CTL model checking is that any two configurations whose clock valuations belong to the same region satisfy the same CTL formulas.

As a consequence, standard CTL model checking can be performed on the region automaton by labelling all regions with the subformulas they satisfy. Such an algorithm would take exponential time in the worst case, since the number of regions is exponential. Several techniques can be used to circumvent this blowup, e.g. by using tree automata, or space-efficient techniques recomputing the information on-demand while evaluating the truth value of a formula. In the end:

Theorem 2. *CTL model checking is* PSPACE-*complete over timed automata.*

Remark 1. It must be noted that there are CTL formulas that take different truth values in a given region, depending on the (discrete-observation or continuous-observation) semantics. Consider formula $\mathbf{E}(\neg\mathbf{EF}c)\mathbf{U}\,b$. This formula expresses the existence of a path eventually reaching a b-state, without l visiting intermediary states from which c would be reachable. In the automaton depicted at Fig. 1, this formula holds true in the discrete-observation semantics, as witnessed by the path $(a, 0)(b, 3)$: along this path, the latter condition holds vacuously. Obviously, in the continuous-observation semantics, the formula fails to hold.

This can be reflected in the algorithm by considering different constructions for the region automaton: for the discrete-observation semantics, we would merge a delay and an action transition into a single transition of the region automaton (as performed e.g. in [6]). For the continuous-observation semantics we would have delay transitions to the immediate time-successor region only, and action transitions directly translated in the region automaton (as e.g. in [5]).

We now focus on TCTL. Two versions of this logic have been considered in the literature, either using decorated modalities or with formula clocks. We only consider the latter logic here, as it has more expressive power while having very similar algorithmic properties. Syntactically, the logic is defined as

$$\mathsf{TCTL} \ni \phi ::= \top \mid p \mid x \in J \mid \neg\phi \mid \phi \wedge \phi \mid \mathbf{E}\phi\mathbf{U}_\phi \mid \mathbf{A}\phi\mathbf{U}_\phi \mid x \cdot \phi$$

where p ranges over the set of atomic propositions AP, x ranges over a finite set of formula clocks C_F (these are *not* the clocks appearing in the automaton), J ranges over the set of intervals of $\mathbb{R}_{\geq 0}$ with integral bounds[2].

The two semantics discussed in Sect. 2.2 for the Until modality can be applied to TCTL. The semantics of $\top$ (always true) and of Boolean operators is omitted. Given a configuration (s, v) of $\mathcal{A}$, and a valuation u for the formula clocks, the satisfaction relation is defined as:

$$\begin{aligned}
\mathcal{A}, (s, v, u) &\models p &&\Leftrightarrow p \in \ell(s) \\
\mathcal{A}, (s, v, u) &\models x \in J &&\Leftrightarrow u(x) \in J \\
\mathcal{A}, (s, v, u) &\models x \cdot \phi &&\Leftrightarrow \mathcal{A}, (s, v, u[\{x\}]) \models \phi \\
\mathcal{A}, (s, v, u) &\models \mathbf{E}\phi_1\mathbf{U}_{\phi_2} &&\Leftrightarrow \text{there is a path } \pi \text{ (resp. signal } \varpi) \text{ from } (s, v, u) \text{ s.t.} \\
& && \qquad \mathcal{A}, \pi \models \phi_1\mathbf{U}_{\phi_2} \text{ (resp. } \mathcal{A}, \varpi \models \phi_1\mathbf{U}_{\phi_2}) \\
\mathcal{A}, (s, v, u) &\models \mathbf{A}\phi_1\mathbf{U}_{\phi_2} &&\Leftrightarrow \text{for every path } \pi \text{ (resp. signal } \varpi) \text{ from } (s, v, u), \\
& && \qquad \mathcal{A}, \pi \models \phi_1\mathbf{U}_{\phi_2} \text{ (resp. } \mathcal{A}, \varpi \models \phi_1\mathbf{U}_{\phi_2})
\end{aligned}$$

---

[2] Rational bounds could be considered at the expense of scaling all constants by an appropriate factor.

Formula clocks are integrated to the paths and signals (without being reset by the timed automaton).

Example 2. The constrained-until formula $\mathbf{E}\phi_1 \mathbf{U}_J \phi_2$ can be written as:

$$x \cdot \mathbf{E}\phi_1 \mathbf{U}(\phi_2 \wedge x \in J)$$

It is not difficult to extend the CTL model-checking algorithm above to TCTL: one easily shows that again two valuations in the same region satisfy the same TCTL formulas. This can be shown by induction on the structure of the formula, taking formula clocks into account in the definition of region equivalence. Then the algorithm is similar to the algorithm for CTL, again taking care of the considered semantics.

Theorem 3 [5]. *TCTL model checking is PSPACE-complete over timed automata (regardless of the semantics choice).*

Note that the syntax of the specification language used in Uppaal is inspired from TCTL, but basically all properties can be reduced to some kind of reachability properties. See Remark 2 later for more details.

As is the case for CTL, TCTL cannot express fairness properties. In particular, it cannot rule out Zeno runs, which are infinite runs along which time converges. Following the untimed approach, one may consider TCTL*, in which Until modalities can be freely nested (without inserting path quantifications). This logic then embeds MTL, the extension of LTL with timing constraints, for which model checking is undecidable (see Sect. 4). An intermediary fragment is defined in [17], with the following syntax:

$$\mathsf{TCTL}_{\mathsf{LTL}} \ni \phi_s ::= \top \mid p \mid x \in J \mid \neg\phi_s \mid \phi_s \wedge \phi_s \mid \mathbf{E}\phi_p \mid x \cdot \phi_s$$
$$\phi_p ::= \phi_s \mid \neg\phi_p \mid \phi_p \wedge \phi_p \mid \phi_p \mathbf{U} \phi_p.$$

Notice that in this fragment, formula clocks may only be reset at the level of state formulas. This allows us to recover decidability of model checking (in exponential space) [17], while being able to express fairness properties.

We conclude this section with a few words on the satisfiability problem for TCTL. We only deal here with *finite satisfiability* [5], asking whether there exists a finite-state timed automaton in which a given TCTL formula holds true. This problem is undecidable, which can be derived from the undecidability of satisfiability for MTL (see Sect. 4) by pairing each temporal modality with a universal path quantifier: such a formula is satisfiable if, and only if, the original MTL formula is. It is proven in [37] that forbidding equality constraints in TCTL makes finite satisfiability decidable; this is to be compared with what happens for MITL in the setting of linear-time logics (see Theorem 9).

3.2 Timed Modal Logics

In this section, we consider timed modal logics. The development of these logics is related to the attempt to extend different frameworks to the timed setting, such as Milner's work on process algebra CCS, the HML logic [44], and the framework of modal specifications [40]. Here we only consider the logic part, and we interpret formulas over timed automata (see [54] for a contribution on timed CCS, [18] for the timed modal specifications and [26] for a presentation of the tool Epsilon for timed modal specifications).

Let Σ be a finite alphabet of *actions*. We assume that every edge of a timed automaton is labelled with an action $a \in \Sigma$, in addition to the guard and the set of clocks to be reset; thus we now assume $\mathsf{E} \subseteq \mathsf{S} \times \mathcal{G}(\mathsf{C}) \times \Sigma \times 2^{\mathsf{C}} \times \mathsf{S}$. Since modal logics are appropriate for compositional analysis, we also consider parallel compositions of timed automata $(\mathcal{A}_1 \mid \ldots \mid \mathcal{A}_n)_f$, where f is an n-ary synchronization function over Σ with renaming. We refer to [3, Sect. 4] for a formal definition, but the intuition is that f specifies how the various automata should synchronize on labels over transitions; for instance, f can force processes $\mathcal{A}_1$ and $\mathcal{A}_2$ to synchronize on action a while producing a b, by defining $f(a, a, \bullet, \ldots, \bullet) = b$; here labels $\bullet$ indicate that the corresponding processes do not take part in the synchronization. Such a parallel composition does not add expressive power (i.e., the parallel composition of several automata is equivalent to a single automaton) but it is a convenient way to describe complex systems. We will see that the modal logics we consider enjoy interesting expressiveness and compositionality properties over such parallel compositions.

HML is a modal logic interpreted over labelled transition systems: in addition to Boolean operators, there are two modalities: the existential and the universal quantification over actions (which we denote $\langle a \rangle$ and $[a]$, respectively). For example, formula $[a] \langle b \rangle \top$ specifies that after any a-transition, a b-transition is enabled.

Timed extensions of HML use the same syntax and, moreover, allow one to quantify over delay transitions: for delay transitions, instead of using explicit values (representing the delays) as labels, we consider a symbolic label δ to represent any delay; $\langle \delta \rangle$ (resp. $[\delta]$) stands for the existential (resp. universal) quantification over delay transitions. The formula $[a] [\delta] \langle b \rangle \top$ specifies that after any a-transition and any delay, a b-transition is enabled, while the formula $[a] \langle \delta \rangle \langle b \rangle \top$ specifies that after any a-transition, a b-transition will be enabled after some delay. To complete these modalities, we use formula clocks (as in TCTL): a formula clock x can be reset before evaluating φ (written $x \cdot \varphi$), and it can be used in constraints of the form $x \in J$, where J is an interval of $\mathbb{R}_{\geq 0}$ with bounds in $\mathbb{Q}_{\geq 0} \cup \{+\infty\}$. We use C_F to denote the set of formula clocks. Note that this logic has been mostly studied using the discrete-observation paradigm, even though one could extend it to a continuous-observation setting. In this section, we focus on the former semantics.

As for HML, we can add maximal or minimal fixpoint operators to specify properties over executions based on unbounded sequences of actions: for example $\min(X, \varphi \vee \bigvee_{a \in \Sigma} \langle a \rangle X \vee \langle \delta \rangle X)$ holds for a state when it is possible to reach a state satisfying φ. The dual formula $\max(X, \varphi \wedge \bigwedge_{a \in \Sigma} [a] X \wedge [\delta] X)$ specifies that φ holds for every reachable state. We use *Var* to denote the set of variables.

We can define several logics depending on which of the above operators are allowed. Here we just introduce the logic L_ν [39] whose syntax is given by the following grammar:

$$L_\nu \ni \varphi, \psi ::= \top \mid \bot \mid x \sim c \mid x \cdot \varphi \mid \varphi \wedge \psi \mid \varphi \vee \psi \mid \langle \ell \rangle \varphi \mid [\ell] \varphi \mid \max(X, \varphi) \mid X$$

where $\ell \in \Sigma \cup \{\delta\}$, $x \in C_F$, $\sim \in \{<, >\}$, $c \in \mathbb{N}$, and $X \in Var$. An L_ν formula φ is interpreted over a configuration (s, v) of a timed automaton $\mathcal{A}$ (or over a configuration $(\bar{s}, \bar{v})$ of a parallel composition $(\mathcal{A}_1 \mid \ldots \mid \mathcal{A}_n)_f$) with a valuation u for the formula clocks. We omit the formal semantics, which can be derived from the previous discussion.

L_ν benefits from the same decidability properties as TCTL: two (extended) states in the same region satisfy the same L_ν formulas.

Theorem 4 [3]. *L_ν model checking is* EXPTIME-*complete over (parallel compositions of) timed automata.*

The EXPTIME membership can be obtained by applying standard model-checking algorithms over the region automaton corresponding to the system (note that adding minimal fixpoints would not change the complexity). The EXPTIME-hardness proof uses the same encoding of linear-bounded Turing machines we use to show PSPACE-hardness of reachability in timed automata, extended to simulate *alternating* Turing machine with the existential and universal modalities in L_ν.

Remark 2. The tool Uppaal mostly analyzes reachability-like properties. It was therefore natural, early in the process of development of the tool, to properly understand which properties can be expressed and verified using the tool. To that aim, a fragment of L_ν has been investigated [1], which fully characterizes properties that can be expressed through a reachability query via *test automata*. A test automaton for a property $\varphi \in L_\nu$ is a timed automaton $\mathcal{A}_\varphi$ such that for every timed automaton $\mathcal{A}$, it holds $\mathcal{A} \models \varphi$ if, and only if, some designated target set of states in the composition $(\mathcal{A} \mid \mathcal{A}_\varphi)_{f_s}$ where f_s enforces the synchronization of actions of the automata, is not reachable. The resulting fragment of L_ν has a PSPACE-complete model-checking problem.

L_ν is very expressive as a specification language. For example, it is easy to observe that timed bisimilarity can be expressed in L_ν: two timed automata over the same alphabet Σ $\mathcal{A}_1$ and $\mathcal{A}_2$ are *strongly timed bisimilar* (denoted $\mathcal{A}_1 \sim \mathcal{A}_2$) if, and only if, their parallel composition $(\mathcal{A}_1 \mid \mathcal{A}_2)_{f_{\mathrm{inter}}}$, where f_{inter} is an interleaving synchronization with a renaming[3] of every action $a \in \Sigma$ of $\mathcal{A}_i$ by action a_i, satisfies the following L_ν formula:

$$\Psi_{\mathrm{bisim}} = \max\left(Z, \bigwedge_{a \in \Sigma} ([a_1] \langle a_2 \rangle Z \wedge [a_2] \langle a_1 \rangle Z) \wedge [\delta] Z\right).$$

---

[3] That is, for every $a \in \Sigma$, $f_{\mathrm{inter}}(a, \bullet) = a_1$ and $f_{\mathrm{inter}}(\bullet, a) = a_2$.

This ability to deal with single action transitions of an automaton is very useful and allows a *compositional algorithm* for model-checking (as for the classical modal μ-calculus [11]). Given a specification φ, an automaton $\mathcal{A}$ and a synchronization function f describing its interaction with another component $\mathcal{B}$, one can build a *quotient formula* $\varphi/_f\mathcal{A}$ such that $(\mathcal{A} \mid \mathcal{B})_f \models \varphi$ if, and only if, $\mathcal{B} \models (\varphi/_f\mathcal{A})$. Note that the clocks of the quotiented automaton $\mathcal{A}$ become formula clocks in $\varphi/_f\mathcal{A}$: any behaviour of $\mathcal{A}$ that is relevant w.r.t. φ is encoded in the formula and this includes all timing informations.

By iterating this quotienting, one can reduce a model-checking instance $(\mathcal{A}_1 \mid \ldots \mid \mathcal{A}_n)_f \models \varphi$ to some question $\texttt{nil} \models \varphi'$ where φ' is the quotient formula $\varphi/\mathcal{A}_1/\mathcal{A}_2/\ldots/\mathcal{A}_n$, and $\texttt{nil}$ is a process letting time elapse without performing any action. Of course, in this approach, the size of the formula grows exponentially with quotienting (the state-space explosion problem is translated from the model to the formula), but this approach still provides an alternative way of performing model-checking [38], and it gives also many interesting results for such logics.

From the previous properties, it is easy to deduce the construction of *characteristic formulas* for timed automata: the quotient formula $\Psi_{\text{bisim}}/_{f_{\text{inter}}}\mathcal{A}_1$ holds true for some automaton $\mathcal{A}_2$ if, and only if, $\mathcal{A}_1 \sim \mathcal{A}_2$. The formula $\Psi_{\text{bisim}}/_{f_{\text{inter}}}\mathcal{A}_1$ is the characteristic formula of $\mathcal{A}_1$, it describes the precise behaviour of $\mathcal{A}_1$ up to timed bisimulation. See [2] for more results on characteristic formulas for timed automata.

Finally, quotienting is also useful for the control synthesis problem. The problem is defined as follows: given a system $\mathcal{S}$ to be controlled and a global specification Φ that has to be satisfied by the complete system, one aims at synthesizing a controller $\mathcal{C}$ such that $(\mathcal{S} \mid \mathcal{C})_f \models \Phi$. The quotient construction allows us to build a specification for the controller with $\Phi/_f\mathcal{S}$. Notice however that the satisfiability for L_ν is undecidable (actually even for its non-recursive fragment) [33], and only a strong bounded-resources version of the problem has been shown decidable [39].

4   Linear-Time Temporal Logics with Timing Constraints

In this section we survey some of the main results concerning expressiveness and decidability of linear-time temporal logics in the metric setting. In general, a linear-time specification determines a set of runs of a given system: a collection of signals in the continuous semantics and a collection of timed words in the pointwise semantics. In this section we will mostly focus on the continuous semantics when talking about expressiveness (because the theory is cleaner), but we consider decidability issues with respect to both semantics.

The results surveyed in this section should be read in the context of two classical theorems about linear temporal logic in the non-metric setting. The first, a celebrated result of Kamp [34], is that the linear-time temporal logic (LTL) is expressively complete for monadic first-order logic over both the ordered integers $(\mathbb{Z}, <)$ and ordered reals $(\mathbb{R}, <)$. The second result, due to Wolper et al. [53], is that the model checking problem for LTL formulas on Kripke structures is PSPACE-complete (Note that, notwithstanding the equivalent expressiveness of LTL and monadic first-order logic, the model checking problem for monadic first-order logic is non-elementary).

4.1 Monadic First-Order Logic

A natural approach to specifying properties of signals is to use first-order logic. Consider a first-order language L_{MET} over a signature with a binary relation symbol $<$, an infinite collection of unary predicate symbols $AP = \{P_1, P_2, \ldots\}$, and an infinite family of unary function symbols $+q$, $q \in \mathbb{Q}$.

Formulas of L_{MET} can naturally be interpreted over signals $\varpi \colon \mathbb{R} \to 2^{AP}$. Such a signal determines a first-order structure in which the universe is $\mathbb{R}$, the relation symbol $<$ and function symbols $+q$, $q \in \mathbb{Q}$, are interpreted by the standard order relation and addition function on $\mathbb{R}$, and where each unary predicate symbol P_i is interpreted as $\{r \in \mathbb{R} \mid P_i \in \varpi(r)\}$. For example, the formula

$$\varphi(x) := \exists y \, \exists z \, ((x < y < z < x + 1) \wedge P(y) \wedge P(z)) \tag{3}$$

holds at a point $r \in \mathbb{R}$ in a signal if P is true at least twice in the open interval $(r, r+1)$.

The satisfiability problem for L_{MET} asks whether a given sentence is satisfied by some signal. The model-checking problem asks whether a given sentence is satisfied by all signals in the language of a given timed automaton.

Theorem 5. *The satisfiability and model checking problems for L_{MET} are undecidable.*

Proof (Sketch). Let P be a monadic predicate symbol and consider the following two properties of a signal:

- for all $r \in \mathbb{R}$, P is true at r if and only if it is true at $r + 1$;
- the set of $r \in \mathbb{R}$ at which P holds has no accumulation point.

These two properties can easily be expressed in L_{MET}, using only the order relation $<$ and $+1$ function. Moreover any signal satisfying these properties embeds a grid of dimensions $\mathbb{Z} \times \{0, \ldots, N\}$, for some $N \in \mathbb{N}$, where the (i, j)-th cell in the grid maps to the j-th P-position within the open interval $(i, i+1)$. We can use the relation $<$ and function $+1$ to navigate horizontally and vertically through such a grid and thereby reduce the halting problem for Turing machines to the satisfiability problem for L_{MET}.

Undecidability of model checking follows immediately from undecidability of satisfiability.   □

4.2 Metric Temporal Logic

The above-mentioned result of Kamp [34] on the expressiveness of LTL motivates the search for an expressively complete temporal logic for L_{MET}. A natural candidate is *Metric Temporal Logic (MTL)* [35], a popular and widely studied temporal logic that augments LTL with time-constrained versions of the *Until* and *Since* modalities (*Since* is symmetric to *Until*: $\varphi_1 \mathbf{S} \varphi_2$ requires that φ_2 holds at some position in the past, and that φ_1 holds in all intermediary positions).

Given a set AP of atomic propositions, the formulas of MTL are given by the following grammar

$$\mathsf{MTL} \ni \varphi ::= \top \mid p \mid \varphi \wedge \varphi \mid \neg \varphi \mid \varphi \mathbf{U}_I \varphi \mid \varphi \mathbf{S}_I \varphi,$$

where $p \in \mathsf{AP}$ and $I \subseteq (0, \infty)$ is an interval with endpoints in $\mathbb{Q}_{\geq 0} \cup \{\infty\}$. We also use derived boolean operators such as $\varphi_1 \rightarrow \varphi_2 = \neg\varphi_1 \vee \varphi_2$ and $\varphi_1 \leftrightarrow \varphi_2 = (\varphi_1 \rightarrow \varphi_2) \wedge (\varphi_2 \rightarrow \varphi_1)$, and derived temporal connectives like $\mathbf{F}_I \varphi = \top \mathbf{U}_I \varphi$ and $\mathbf{P}_I \varphi = \top \mathbf{S}_I \varphi$.

Note that we consider signals whose domain is the set $\mathbb{R}$ of all real numbers. Below we will also consider the future fragment of MTL on signals over the non-negative real numbers $\mathbb{R}_{\geq 0}$.

4.3   Expressive Completeness

At first glance MTL seems to have weak expressive power. For example, consider the formula (3) expressing that there will be at least two p-states in the next time unit. MTL cannot naturally express both the consecution of two events and a timing constraint on the *second* event. This led to the conjecture that such constraints cannot be expressed in MTL (try to express (3) before reading further!); cf. [9,10]. However, as shown in [14], this formula can indeed be expressed in MTL:

Example 3. We give an MTL formula $\varphi^\dagger$ that is equivalent to the $\mathsf{L}_{\mathrm{MET}}$ formula $\varphi(x)$ in (3) in the sense that for every signal ϖ and $r \in \mathbb{R}$, $\varpi \models \varphi[r]$ if and only if $\varpi, r \models \varphi^\dagger$. The key is to use fractional constants in the definition of $\varphi^\dagger$. We define the formula as a disjunction of three overlapping cases according to position of the two times at which p holds that witness the truth of φ.

$$\varphi^\dagger := \mathbf{F}_{(0,\frac{1}{2})}(p \wedge \mathbf{F}_{(0,\frac{1}{2})}p) \vee \mathbf{F}_{(0,\frac{1}{2})}(\mathbf{F}_{(0,\frac{1}{2})}p \wedge \mathbf{F}_{\{\frac{1}{2}\}}p) \vee (\mathbf{F}_{(0,\frac{1}{2})}p \wedge \mathbf{F}_{(\frac{1}{2},1)}p).$$

The "trick" in the previous example of using fractional constants to boost the expressiveness of MTL turns out to be very powerful:

Theorem 6 [32]. *For every* $\mathsf{L}_{\mathrm{MET}}$ *formula* $\varphi(x)$ *there is an equivalent MTL formula* $\varphi^\dagger$.

Let us briefly discuss two key ideas underlying the proof of Theorem 6: namely *boundedness* and *separation*. Given $N \in \mathbb{N}$, an $\mathsf{L}_{\mathrm{MET}}$ formula $\varphi(x)$ is N-bounded if all quantifiers are relativised to the interval $(x-N, x+N)$. Exploiting a normal form for $\mathsf{FO}(<)$ [25], we show how to translate bounded $\mathsf{L}_{\mathrm{MET}}$ formulas into MTL. Extending this translation to arbitrary $\mathsf{L}_{\mathrm{MET}}$ formulas requires an appropriate analog of Gabbay's notion of *separation* [24].

Gabbay [24] shows that every LTL formula can be equivalently rewritten as a Boolean combination of formulas, each of which depends only on the past, present, or future. This property underlies an inductive translation from first-order logic over $(\mathbb{R}, <)$ to LTL. The proof of Theorem 6 relies on an analogous result for MTL:

Lemma 1 (Separation Lemma). *Every MTL formula can be equivalently rewritten as a Boolean combination of MTL formulas, each of which has one of the following three forms:*

- Bounded: *the interval I in every temporal operator $\mathbf{U}_I$ and $\mathbf{S}_I$ is bounded;*
- Distant Future: *has the form $\mathbf{F}_{(1,\infty)}\varphi$, for φ a formula with no past connectives;*
- Distant Past: *has the form $\mathbf{P}_{(1,\infty)}\varphi$, for φ a formula with no future connectives.*

Gabbay's separation result for LTL is an ingredient of the proof of the Separation Lemma for MTL. As we have said, the latter result can be used to give an inductive translation from $\mathsf{L}_{\mathrm{MET}}$ to MTL. A key difference to the purely order-theoretic case is that in the metric setting the different types of formulas in the Separation Lemma may talk about overlapping parts of the signal. For this reason it is crucial that we already have a separate translation of bounded $\mathsf{L}_{\mathrm{MET}}$ formulas to MTL.

Integer Constants. Having rational constants plays a crucial role in the proof of Theorem 6. Indeed, as illustrated in Example 3, the translation from $\mathsf{L}_{\mathrm{MET}}$ to MTL does not preserve the granularity of timing constraints. Pursuing this issue, define $\mathsf{L}_{\mathrm{MET}}^{(1)}$ to be the fragment of $\mathsf{L}_{\mathrm{MET}}$ in which the family of unary addition function symbols $+q$, $q \in \mathbb{Q}$, is replaced by a single unary function symbol $+1$. It was shown by Hirshfeld and Rabinovich [29] that MTL with integer constants is not expressively complete for $\mathsf{L}_{\mathrm{MET}}^{(1)}$. Indeed [29] proves a much stronger impossibility result: no temporal logic whose modalities are definable by a set of formulas of $\mathsf{L}_{\mathrm{MET}}^{(1)}$ of bounded quantifier depth can be expressively complete for $\mathsf{L}_{\mathrm{MET}}^{(1)}$. Later, and again based on the Separation Lemma, Hunter [31] gave an expressively complete temporal logic for $\mathsf{L}_{\mathrm{MET}}^{(1)}$ by taking the fragment of MTL with integer constants and augmenting it with an infinite family of unary *counting modalities* $\mathbf{C}_n$ (first considered in [29]).

Given a positive integer n, the semantics of the counting modality $\mathbf{C}_n$ is defined as follows:

- $\varpi, r \models \mathbf{C}_n(\varphi)$ if there exist $r < r_1 < \ldots < r_n < r+1$ such that $\varpi, r_i \models \varphi$ for $i = 1, \ldots, n$.

Notice that the $\mathsf{L}_{\mathrm{MET}}^{(1)}$-formula in (3) is equivalent to $\mathbf{C}_2(p)$. Notice also that the the natural way to render $\mathbf{C}_n(p)$ as an $\mathsf{L}_{\mathrm{MET}}$ formula requires quantifier depth n, consistent with the above-referenced "impossibility result" of [29].

Theorem 7 [31]. *For every* $L_{MET}^{(1)}$ *formula* $\varphi(x)$ *there is an equivalent formula* $\varphi^\dagger$ *in MTL augmented with the unary counting modalities* $\mathbf{C}_n$, $n \in \mathbb{N}$, *such that* $\varphi^\dagger$ *mentions only integer constants.*

Future Modalities. Another crucial feature of MTL for obtaining expressive completeness is the presence of past connectives. Recall in this regard that for any sentence φ of monadic first-order logic over the structure $(\mathbb{R}_{\geq 0}, <)$, there is an equivalent LTL formula $\varphi^\dagger$ that uses only future connectives. Here equivalence is considered with respect to the initial semantics and over finitely variable signals. More precisely we have that for any finitely variable signal $\varpi \colon \mathbb{R}_{\geq 0} \to 2^{AP}$, (i.e., one with finitely many discontinuities in any bounded interval) one has $\varpi \models \varphi$ if, and only if, $\varpi, 0 \models \varphi^\dagger$.[4] The following result, which follows immediately from [14, Proposition 4], shows that the analogous expressive completeness fails for MTL.

Theorem 8. *Over the initial semantics the* L_{MET} *sentence*

$$\varphi = \exists x \exists y \forall z \, (x < y < x + 1 \wedge p(y) \wedge (y < z < x + 1 \to q(z)))$$

cannot be expressed in MTL using only $\mathbf{U}_I$.

4.4   Satisfiability and Model Checking

The satisfiability and model checking problems for MTL are formulated in a similar manner to the corresponding problems for L_{MET}.

Since the translation from L_{MET} to MTL in Theorem 6 is effective, it follows that satisfiability and model checking for MTL are undecidable. Alternatively, one can give a direct proof along the same lines of Theorem 5 (see, e.g., [10]). However a number of expressive and decidable fragments of MTL have been identified. The best-known such fragment, called *Metric Interval Temporal Logic* (MITL), arises by restricting the interval I in the modalities $\mathbf{U}_I$ and $\mathbf{S}_I$ to be non-singular. In particular, the formula

$$\mathbf{G}_{(0,\infty)}(p \leftrightarrow \mathbf{F}_{\{1\}}p) \,,$$

which features in the undecidability proof of MTL cannot be expressed in MITL.

Both the satisfiability and model checking problems for MITL were shown to be decidable in [7] via an exponential translation of MITL formulas to equivalent timed automata. Combined with the fact that language emptiness for timed automata is in PSPACE one obtains:

Theorem 9 [7]. *The model checking problem for MITL is* EXPSPACE-*complete.*

Another decidable fragment of MTL, called Bounded MTL, arises by restricting the interval I in the modalities $\mathbf{U}_I$ and $\mathbf{S}_I$ to be bounded. While Bounded

---

[4] As shown in [30] this property fails without the assumption of finite variability.

MTL can express punctual properties, it obviously can only express time-bounded properties. A common extension of MITL and Bounded MTL with an EXPSPACE-complete model checking problem is identified in [15].

The proof that satisfiability and model checking for MTL are undecidable works similarly in the pointwise semantics as in the continuous semantics. However, if one restricts to the future fragment of MTL (that is, keeping $\mathbf{U}_I$ but omitting $\mathbf{S}_I$) then the situation becomes more delicate. While both problems are again undecidable, the proof becomes substantially different.

Consider the formula $\mathbf{G}_{(0,\infty)}(p \leftrightarrow \mathbf{F}_{\{1\}}p)$, which is instrumental in the proof of undecidability of MTL. A timed word satisfies this formula if every p-event is followed by a p-event exactly one time unit later. However, the formula does not require that every p-event be preceded by a p-event one time unit earlier (indeed, one cannot enforce that there be *any* event one time unit earlier). For this reason, a direct encoding of the computations of a Turing machine or 2-counter machine into a language of timed words (as in the undecidability proofs in [6] and [10]) fails for MTL. However one can encode computations of channel machines (finite automata, equipped with an unbounded FIFO memory) with *insertion errors*, that is, channel machines under a semantics in which extra letters may non-deterministically be inserted anywhere in the channel during each transition. Using this idea, [47] shows undecidability of satisfiability for the future fragment of MTL in the pointwise semantics by reduction from the recurrence problem for channel machines with insertion errors, that is, the problem of whether a given channel machine has a computation that visits an accepting control state infinitely often. Naturally, the ability of MTL to express the recurrence property $\mathbf{GF}p$ plays a key role in this proof.

The undecidability result of [47] only works over infinite words. Indeed, it was shown in [46] that both satisfiability and model checking are decidable for the future fragment of MTL over finite timed words. The decision procedure in [46] involves translating an MTL formula into an equivalent alternating timed automaton. Crucially such an automaton requires only a single clock. The main technical result of [46] was to show that the language emptiness problem for one-clock alternating timed automata is decidable. This was done by a method analogous to the region-automaton construction for ordinary timed automata. However in the case of alternating automata this construction does not yield a finite quotient, and [46] relies on the existence of a well-quasi-order (established using Higman's Lemma) on the set of configurations of a given one-clock alternating timed automaton to prove termination of the algorithm for deciding language emptiness.

Theorem 10 [46]. *The satisfiability and model checking problems for (the future fragment of) MTL over finite timed words are non-primitive recursive.*

Over infinite words, using similar methods, one can identify a safety fragment of MTL for which model checking is decidable [48].

4.5   Timed Propositional Temporal Logic

The logic TPTL [8] is another extension of LTL to the metric setting, this time using so-called *formula clocks*. The formulas of TPTL are given by the following grammar:

$$\varphi ::= p \mid x \sim c \mid \neg\varphi \mid \varphi \wedge \varphi \mid x \cdot \varphi \mid \varphi \mathbf{U}_\varphi \mid \varphi \mathbf{S}\varphi$$

where $p \in \mathsf{AP}$, x is a formula clock, $\sim \in \{<, >\}$ and $c \in \mathbb{Q}_{\geq 0}$.

Example 4. As for the case of branching-time, one easily expresses decorated modalities using formula clocks: formula $p\mathbf{U}_I q$ translates as $x \cdot p\mathbf{U}(q \wedge x \in I)$, which is in TPTL since I is required to have rational endpoints.

It is easy to see that for every MTL formula there is an equivalent TPTL formula, and for every TPTL formula there is an equivalent $\mathsf{L}_{\mathrm{MET}}$ formula. It immediately follows from Theorem 6 that TPTL with rational constants is expressively complete for $\mathsf{L}_{\mathrm{MET}}$. Similarly, it follows from Theorem 7 that TPTL with integer constants is expressively complete for $\mathsf{L}_{\mathrm{MET}}^{(1)}$. Finally, if we disallow the past operator $\mathbf{S}_I$ in both MTL and TPTL, then the latter is strictly more expressive, since it can express the property of Theorem 8.

5   Conclusion

Timed temporal logics have been defined to express quantitative constraints over delays between events. For instance, one can express the property that any request is answered within some fixed delay. We have first discussed semantic choices: formulas of (linear-time) timed temporal logics can either be interpreted using a discrete-observation setting (only actions are observed), or using a continuous-observation setting (time elapsing in states and changes of states are both observed). While this may seem harmless (though one can easily exhibit examples distinguishing the two semantics), it actually impacts the complexity of model-checking.

In a second part, we have focused on branching-time temporal logics. We have both discussed extensions of CTL and of modal logics. We have explained that the model-checking problem of TCTL over timed automata can be done using a simple extension of standard technics for reachability analysis. We have then turned to timed extensions of HML and have discussed the model-checking problem as well as other properties like compositionality.

In the last part of the paper, we have focused on linear-time, and we have explained the expressive completeness of MTL with respect to the natural metric extension of first-order logic over the reals. We have then discussed the model-checking and the satisfiability problems for (fragments of) MTL, and finished the section with a short discussion on a timed extension of LTL with explicit clock variables.

A short survey cannot be exhaustive on such a wide topic, and there are a number of related results that we could not mention in this paper. We refer e.g. to [13,22,23,36,45,49,52, to cite only a few] for more results on the very topic developed in this paper. (Linear-time) timed temporal logics have also been used in other domains, e.g. in the prolific domains of monitoring and run-time verification for real-time systems [43]. We refer to [42] for a recent discussion on this problematic.

While timed temporal logics are rather well-understood now, several important questions are still to be investigated. In particular, the satisfiability (or synthesis) problem for timed logics is not fully (or satisfactorily) understood yet. For instance, the synthesis problem for TCTL and L_ν is undecidable, and only a strong assumption on the resources leads to decidability [39]. Similar resource restrictions have to be made [16] to be able to solve the so-called reactive-synthesis problem for MITL (while without restrictions it is shown to be undecidable). Therefore, designing (efficient) algorithms for the synthesis of real-time systems is a real challenge!

References

1. Aceto, L., Bouyer, P., Burgueño, A., Larsen, K.G.: The power of reachability testing for timed automata. Theoret. Comput. Sci. **300**(1–3), 411–475 (2003). http://dx.doi.org/10.1016/S0304-3975(02)00334-1
2. Aceto, L., Ingólfsdóttir, A., Pedersen, M.L., Poulsen, J.: Characteristic formulae for timed automata. RAIRO - Theoret. Inf. Appl. **34**(6), 565–584 (2000). http://dx.doi.org/10.1051/ita:2000131
3. Aceto, L., Laroussinie, F.: Is your model checker on time? J. Log. Algebr. Program. **52**(53), 3–51 (2002). http://dx.doi.org/10.1016/S1567-8326(02)00022-X
4. Alur, R.: Techniques for automatic verification of real-time systems. Ph.D. thesis, Stanford University, Palo Alto, California, USA (1991)
5. Alur, R., Courcoubetis, C., Dill, D.L.: Model-checking in dense real-time. Inf. Comp. **104**(1), 2–34 (1993). http://dx.doi.org/10.1006/inco.1993.1024
6. Alur, R., Dill, D.L.: A theory of timed automata. Theoret. Comput. Sci. **126**(2), 183–235 (1994). http://dx.doi.org/10.1016/0304-3975(94)90010-8
7. Alur, R., Feder, T., Henzinger, T.A.: The benefits of relaxing punctuality. J. ACM **43**(1), 116–146 (1996). http://dx.doi.org/10.1145/227595.227602
8. Alur, R., Henzinger, T.A.: A really temporal logic. In: FOCS 1989, pp. 164–169. IEEE Computer Society Press (1989). http://dx.doi.org/10.1109/SFCS.1989.63473
9. Alur, R., Henzinger, T.A.: Logics and models of real time: a survey. In: Bakker, J.W., Huizing, C., Roever, W.P., Rozenberg, G. (eds.) REX 1991. LNCS, vol. 600, pp. 74–106. Springer, Heidelberg (1992). doi:10.1007/BFb0031988
10. Alur, R., Henzinger, T.A.: Real-time logics: complexity and expressiveness. Inf. Comp. **104**(1), 35–77 (1993). http://dx.doi.org/10.1006/inco.1993.1025
11. Andersen, H.R.: Partial model-checking (extended abstract). In: LICS 1995, pp. 398–407. IEEE Computer Society Press (1995). http://dx.doi.org/10.1109/LICS.1995.523274
12. Behrmann, G., David, A., Larsen, K.G., Håkansson, J., Pettersson, P., Yi, W., Hendriks, M.: Uppaal 4.0. In: QEST 2006, pp. 125–126. IEEE Computer Society Press (2006). http://dx.doi.org/10.1109/QEST.2006.59
13. Bersani, M.M., Rossi, M., Pietro, P.S.: Deciding the satisfiability of MITL specifications. In: GandALF 2013, EPTCS, vol. 119, pp. 64–78 (2013). http://dx.doi.org/10.4204/EPTCS.119.8

14. Bouyer, P., Chevalier, F., Markey, N.: On the expressiveness of TPTL and MTL. In: Sarukkai, S., Sen, S. (eds.) FSTTCS 2005. LNCS, vol. 3821, pp. 432–443. Springer, Heidelberg (2005). doi:10.1007/11590156_35

15. Bouyer, P., Markey, N., Ouaknine, J., Worrell, J.: The cost of punctuality. In: LICS 2007, pp. 109–118. IEEE Computer Society Press (2007). http://dx.doi.org/10.1109/LICS.2007.49

16. Brihaye, T., Estiévenart, M., Geeraerts, G., Ho, H.-M., Monmege, B., Sznajder, N.: Real-time synthesis is hard!. In: Fränzle, M., Markey, N. (eds.) FORMATS 2016. LNCS, vol. 9884, pp. 105–120. Springer, Cham (2016). doi:10.1007/978-3-319-44878-7_7

17. Brihaye, T., Laroussinie, F., Markey, N., Oreiby, G.: Timed concurrent game structures. In: Caires, L., Vasconcelos, V.T. (eds.) CONCUR 2007. LNCS, vol. 4703, pp. 445–459. Springer, Heidelberg (2007). doi:10.1007/978-3-540-74407-8_30

18. Čerāns, K., Godskesen, J.C., Larsen, K.G.: Timed modal specification — theory and tools. In: Courcoubetis, C. (ed.) CAV 1993. LNCS, vol. 697, pp. 253–267. Springer, Heidelberg (1993). doi:10.1007/3-540-56922-7_21

19. Clarke, E.M., Emerson, E.A.: Design and synthesis of synchronization skeletons using branching time temporal logic. In: Kozen, D. (ed.) Logic of Programs 1981. LNCS, vol. 131, pp. 52–71. Springer, Heidelberg (1982). doi:10.1007/BFb0025774

20. Clarke, E.M., Emerson, E.A., Sistla, A.P.: Automatic verification of finite-state concurrent systems using temporal logic specifications. ACM Trans. Program. Lang. Syst. 8(2), 244–263 (1986). http://dx.doi.org/10.1145/5397.5399

21. Daws, C., Olivero, A., Tripakis, S., Yovine, S.: The tool KRONOS. In: Alur, R., Henzinger, T.A., Sontag, E.D. (eds.) HS 1995. LNCS, vol. 1066, pp. 208–219. Springer, Heidelberg (1996). doi:10.1007/BFb0020947

22. D'Souza, D., Prabhakar, P.: On the expressiveness of MTL in the pointwise and continuous semantics. Int. J. Softw. Tools Technol. Transf. 9(1), 1–4 (2007). http://dx.doi.org/10.1007/s10009-005-0214-9

23. Furia, C.A., Rossi, M.: On the expressiveness of MTL variants over dense time. In: Raskin, J.-F., Thiagarajan, P.S. (eds.) FORMATS 2007. LNCS, vol. 4763, pp. 163–178. Springer, Heidelberg (2007). doi:10.1007/978-3-540-75454-1_13

24. Gabbay, D.M.: Expressive functional completeness in tense logic (preliminary report). In: Mönnich, U. (ed.) SYLI, vol. 147, pp. 91–117. Springer, Heidelberg (1981). doi:10.1007/978-94-009-8384-7_4

25. Gabbay, D.M., Pnueli, A., Shelah, S., Stavi, J.: On the temporal analysis of fairness. In: POPL 1980, pp. 163–173. ACM Press (1980). http://dx.doi.org/10.1145/567446.567462

26. Godskesen, J.C., Larsen, K.G., Skou, A.: Automatic verification of real-time systems using epsilon. In: IFIP Conference Proceedings on PSTV 1994, vol. 1, pp. 323–330. Chapman & Hall (1995)

27. Havelund, K., Skou, A., Larsen, K.G., Lund, K.: Formal modelling and analysis of an audio/video protocol: an industrial case study using Uppaal. In: RTSS 1997, pp. 2–13. IEEE Computer Society Press (1997). http://dx.doi.org/10.1109/REAL.1997.641264

28. Henzinger, T.A., Ho, P.-H., Wong-Toi, H.: HyTech: a model-checker for hybrid systems. Int. J. Softw. Tools Technol. Transf. 1(1–2), 110–122 (1997). http://dx.doi.org/10.1007/s100090050008

29. Hirshfeld, Y., Rabinovich, A.: Expressiveness of metric modalities for continuous time. Log. Methods Comput. Sci. 3(1:3), 1–11 (2007). http://dx.doi.org/10.2168/LMCS-3(1:3)2007

30. Hirshfeld, Y., Rabinovich, A.M.: Future temporal logic needs infinitely many modalities. Inf. Comp. **187**(2), 196–208 (2003). http://dx.doi.org/10.1016/S0890-5401(03)00163-9
31. Hunter, P.: When is metric temporal logic expressively complete? In: CSL 2013, LIPIcs, vol. 23, pp. 380–394. Leibniz-Zentrum für Informatik (2013). http://dx.doi.org/10.4230/LIPIcs.CSL.2013.380
32. Hunter, P., Ouaknine, J., Worrell, J.: Expressive completeness for metric temporal logic. In: LICS 2013, pp. 349–357. IEEE Computer Society Press (2013). http://dx.doi.org/10.1109/LICS.2013.41
33. Jaziri, S., Larsen, K.G., Mardare, R., Xue, B.: Adequacy and complete axiomatization for timed modal logic. In: Proceedings of the 30th Conference on Mathematical Foundations of Programming Semantics (MFPS 2014), ENTCS, vol. 308, pp. 183–210. Elsevier Science Publishers (2014)
34. Kamp, J.A.W.: Tense logic and the theory of linear order. Ph.D. thesis, Computer Science Department, University of California at Los Angeles, USA (1968)
35. Koymans, R.: Specifying real-time properties with metric temporal logic. Real-Time Syst. **2**(4), 255–299 (1990). http://dx.doi.org/10.1007/BF01995674
36. Krishna, S.N., Madnani, K., Pandya, P.K.: Metric temporal logic with counting. In: Jacobs, B., Löding, C. (eds.) FoSSaCS 2016. LNCS, vol. 9634, pp. 335–352. Springer, Heidelberg (2016). doi:10.1007/978-3-662-49630-5_20
37. Torre, S.L., Napoli, M.: A decidable dense branching-time temporal logic. In: Kapoor, S., Prasad, S. (eds.) FSTTCS 2000. LNCS, vol. 1974, pp. 139–150. Springer, Heidelberg (2000). doi:10.1007/3-540-44450-5_11
38. Laroussinie, F., Larsen, K.G.: CMC: a tool for compositional model-checking of real-time systems. In: IFIP Conference Proceedings on FORTE/PSTV 1998, vol. 135, pp. 439–456. Kluwer Academic (1998)
39. Laroussinie, F., Larsen, K.G., Weise, C.: From timed automata to logic — and back. In: Wiedermann, J., Hájek, P. (eds.) MFCS 1995. LNCS, vol. 969, pp. 529–539. Springer, Heidelberg (1995). doi:10.1007/3-540-60246-1_158
40. Larsen, K.G.: Modal specifications. In: Sifakis, J. (ed.) CAV 1989. LNCS, vol. 407, pp. 232–246. Springer, Heidelberg (1990). doi:10.1007/3-540-52148-8_19
41. Larsen, K.G., Pettersson, P., Yi, W.: Uppaal in a nutshell. Int. J. Softw. Tools Technol. Transf. **1**(1–2), 134–152 (1997). http://dx.doi.org/10.1007/s100090050010
42. Maler, O.: Some thoughts on runtime verification. In: Falcone, Y., Sánchez, C. (eds.) RV 2016. LNCS, vol. 10012, pp. 3–14. Springer, Cham (2016). doi:10.1007/978-3-319-46982-9_1
43. Maler, O., Nickovic, D.: Monitoring temporal properties of continuous signals. In: Lakhnech, Y., Yovine, S. (eds.) FORMATS/FTRTFT -2004. LNCS, vol. 3253, pp. 152–166. Springer, Heidelberg (2004). doi:10.1007/978-3-540-30206-3_12
44. Milner, R.: Communication and Concurrency, Prentice Hall International Series in Computer Science. Prentice Hall Int., Upper Saddle River (1989)
45. Ouaknine, J., Rabinovich, A., Worrell, J.: Time-bounded verification. In: Bravetti, M., Zavattaro, G. (eds.) CONCUR 2009. LNCS, vol. 5710, pp. 496–510. Springer, Heidelberg (2009). doi:10.1007/978-3-642-04081-8_33
46. Ouaknine, J., Worrell, J.: On the decidability of metric temporal logic. In: LICS 2005, pp. 188–197. IEEE Computer Society Press (2005). http://dx.doi.org/10.1109/LICS.2005.33
47. Ouaknine, J., Worrell, J.: On metric temporal logic and faulty turing machines. In: Aceto, L., Ingólfsdóttir, A. (eds.) FoSSaCS 2006. LNCS, vol. 3921, pp. 217–230. Springer, Heidelberg (2006). doi:10.1007/11690634_15

48. Ouaknine, J., Worrell, J.: Safety metric temporal logic is fully decidable. In: Hermanns, H., Palsberg, J. (eds.) TACAS 2006. LNCS, vol. 3920, pp. 411–425. Springer, Heidelberg (2006). doi:10.1007/11691372_27

49. Pandya, P.K., Shah, S.S.: On expressive powers of timed logics: comparing boundedness, non-punctuality, and deterministic freezing. In: Katoen, J.-P., König, B. (eds.) CONCUR 2011. LNCS, vol. 6901, pp. 60–75. Springer, Heidelberg (2011). doi:10.1007/978-3-642-23217-6_5

50. Pnueli, A.: The temporal logic of programs. In: FOCS 1977, pp. 46–57. IEEE Computer Society Press (1977). http://dx.doi.org/10.1109/SFCS.1977.32

51. Queille, J.P., Sifakis, J.: Specification and verification of concurrent systems in CESAR. In: Dezani-Ciancaglini, M., Montanari, U. (eds.) Programming 1982. LNCS, vol. 137, pp. 337–351. Springer, Heidelberg (1982). doi:10.1007/3-540-11494-7_22

52. Raskin, J.-F.: Logics, automata and classical theories for deciding real time. Thèse de doctorat, FUNDP, Namur, Belgium (1999)

53. Wolper, P., Vardi, M.Y., Sistla, A.P.: Reasoning about infinite computation paths. In: FOCS 1983, pp. 185–194. IEEE Computer Society Press (1983). http://dx.doi.org/10.1109/SFCS.1983.51

54. Yi, W.: CCS + time = an interleaving model for real time systems. In: Albert, J.L., Monien, B., Artalejo, M.R. (eds.) ICALP 1991. LNCS, vol. 510, pp. 217–228. Springer, Heidelberg (1991). doi:10.1007/3-540-54233-7_136

Verification, Model Checking and Testing

Synchronous Interfaces
and Assume/Guarantee Contracts

Albert Benveniste[(✉)] and Benoît Caillaud

Inria, Campus de Beaulieu, 35042 Rennes cedex, France
{albert.benveniste,benoit.caillaud}@inria.fr

Abstract. In this short note, we establish a link between the theory of Moore Interfaces proposed in 2002 by Chakraborty et al. as a specification framework for synchronous transition systems, and the Assume/Guarantee contracts as proposed in 2007 by Benveniste et al. as a simple and flexible contract framework. As our main result we show that the operation of *saturation* of A/G contracts (namely the mapping $(A, G) \mapsto (A, G \vee \neg A)$), which was considered a drawback of this theory, is indeed implemented by the *Moore Game* of Chakraborty et al. We further develop this link and come up with some remarks on Moore Interfaces.

Keywords: Assume/Guarantee contract · Moore interface · Synchronous interface · Compositional design

1 Introduction

Since the early 2000 and the pioneering paper [22], the community of formal verification started to address component based design in a new, game based, way. The idea is to support a process, by which different actors would contribute to developing a system by designing sub-systems independently, for subsequent integration by the system designer. Each sub-system is developed with some abstract specification of what the system should do, as well as its contexts of use. And the goal is, of course, that, after integration, the resulting system shall work as expected.

Hej Kim!: It is both a pleasure and an honor to write a tribute to Kim. Kim was *preincarnated* a "contractor": in his previous life, by inventing modal specifications he contributed to contracts way before the concept ever existed. But there was a long way to the grail: getting to the point where Modal Interfaces have become comprehensive and solid occurred only recently. While joining the aristocracy of formal methods, Modal Interfaces have become terribly sophisticated. Tom (Hallo Tom!) kept telling us: "those asynchronous interfaces are too complex, look for the synchronous ones". We offer this trial to Kim as a gift. Is it really simple? We let you judge.

The authors apologize for having used sometimes set theoretic operations {union, intersection} and in other places logical operations {or, and}. The reader will easily correct this.

© Springer International Publishing AG 2017
L. Aceto et al. (Eds.): Larsen Festschrift, LNCS 10460, pp. 233–248, 2017.
DOI: 10.1007/978-3-319-63121-9_12

Specification [1–3,6–9], *Interface* [15–17,19,22,23,25–27], and *Contract* [9,10, 14,20,21,24] theories were proposed with this common objective in mind. The models are numerous and vary in many respects: automata or state machines, transition systems, dataflow systems are considered as an underlying paradigm; assumptions and guarantees may be explicitly manipulated, or they may be folded into a single entity called the "interface"; in all cases, however, a notion of environment is considered. The area is rich in technicalities. As a result, the reader may get confused when searching for the essence of the subject beyond its general objectives.

For these reasons a group of hard workers has proposed a *meta-theory of contracts* [12] as an attempt to capture the essence of all the different frameworks. This meta-theory supports the cooperative development of systems from sub-systems and/or components, all of them generically referred to as *components* in the meta-theory. Regarding the components, we assume a composition $\times$ for them that is commutative and associative. The meta-theory defines the semantics of a contract as a pair of two sets of components: a set of legal *environments* (or contexts of use), and a set of *implementations*: $\mathbf{Sem}(\mathscr{C}) = (\mathcal{E}, \mathcal{M})$. To rephrase this, a component E is a legal environment for $\mathscr{C}$ (written $E \models^{E} \mathscr{C}$) if $E \in \mathcal{E}$ and a component M is a legal implementation for $\mathscr{C}$ (written $M \models^{M} \mathscr{C}$) if $M \in \mathcal{M}$. To account for the fact that some syntax must exist for contracts to be finitely described, not all pairs of sets of components define contracts. We thus assume some underlying abstract class $\mathbb{C}$ of contracts, whose semantics are pairs $(\mathcal{E}, \mathcal{M})$. To capture substitutability, we say that $\mathscr{C}'$ *refines* $\mathscr{C}$, written $\mathscr{C}' \preceq \mathscr{C}$, if $\mathcal{E}' \supseteq \mathcal{E}$ and $\mathcal{M}' \subseteq \mathcal{M}$, which immediately defines the *conjunction* as the Greatest Lower Bound (GLB) $\mathscr{C}_1 \wedge \mathscr{C}_2$. Most interesting is then the definition of the contract composition $\mathscr{C}_1 \otimes \mathscr{C}_2$ in the meta-theory: it is the *min* of the set of all contracts $\mathscr{C}$ such that: (*i*) $M_1 \models^{M} \mathscr{C}_1$ and $M_2 \models^{M} \mathscr{C}_2$ imply $M_1 \times M_2 \models^{M} \mathscr{C}$, and (*ii*) $E \models^{E} \mathscr{C}$ and $M_2 \models^{M} \mathscr{C}_2$ imply $E \times M_2 \models^{E} \mathscr{C}_1$. Parallel composition is shown to be monotonic with respect to refinement. We regard as axioms the existence of the above invoked GLB and min. To summarize, it is shown in [12] that the meta-theory by itself supports substitutability and other properties that are useful for systems design in an OEM/supplier context.

In [12], it was also shown that, by instantiating the framework of components in various ways, the meta-theory instantiates as existing theories of interfaces or contracts, thus capturing the very essence of them. Among them, *Assume/Guarantee contracts* (A/G contracts) are simple and elegant [10,12]. An A/G contract is a pair (A, G) of *assumption* and *guarantee*, consisting of predicates over the sets of behaviors of a tuple of variables. The pairs $(\mathcal{E}, \mathcal{M})$ of the meta-theory follow directly via the association $\mathcal{E} \leftrightarrow A$ (legal environments are those satisfying A) and $\mathcal{M} \leftrightarrow [A \Rightarrow G]$, where $\Rightarrow$ denotes implication (legal implementations are those satisfying the entailment $A \Rightarrow G$). The latter association reflects that implementations must meet the guarantees only if put in a legal context. The need for manipulating the so-called *saturation* operation $(A, G) \mapsto [A \Rightarrow G] = [A \vee \neg G]$, which seemingly requires computing disjunctions and complements, has been considered a drawback of A/G contracts — even if G

Table 1. Two verbatims from [19]

In the study of compatibility, game-based approaches quantify inputs existentially, and outputs universally. When two interfaces $\mathscr{C}_1$ and $\mathscr{C}_2$ are composed, their composition may have illegal states, where one component emits outputs that are illegal inputs for the other one. Yet, $\mathscr{C}_1$ and $\mathscr{C}_2$ are considered compatible as long as there is some input behavior that ensures that, for all output behaviors, the illegal states are avoided: in other words, $\mathscr{C}_1$ and $\mathscr{C}_2$ are compatible if there is some environment in which they can be used correctly together. In turn, the input behaviors that ensure compatibility constitute the legal behaviors for the composition $\mathscr{C}_1 \otimes \mathscr{C}_2$: when composing component models, both the possible output behaviors, and the legal input behaviors, are composed

---

The game view leads to an *alternating* view of refinement: a more detailed interface $\mathscr{C}_2$ refines an abstract interface $\mathscr{C}_1$ if all legal inputs for $\mathscr{C}_1$ are also legal for $\mathscr{C}_2$, and if, when $\mathscr{C}_1$ and $\mathscr{C}_2$ are subject to the same legal inputs, $\mathscr{C}_2$ generates output behaviors that are a subset of those of $\mathscr{C}_1$. This definition ensures that, whenever $\mathscr{C}_2 \preceq \mathscr{C}_1$, we can substitute $\mathscr{C}_2$ for $\mathscr{C}_1$ in every design without creating any incompatibility: in the game view, substitutivity of refinement holds

---

is a finite state automaton, computing its complement is computationally costly as soon as G is nondeterministic.

In a landmark paper [19], *Synchronous Interfaces* with the special case of *Moore Interfaces*, were introduced. Two verbatims from [19] (modulo notations) are reproduced in Table 1. These requirements for an interface theory stated in [19] suggest that synchronous interfaces should obey the meta-theory. While reading the above reference in an attempt to properly discussing it in our paper [12], we observed that the game associated to the composition of Moore interfaces seemed to solve the *saturation* operation on A/G contracts: $(A, G) \mapsto (A, G \vee \neg A)$, see (6). We thought that this observation was worth further investigations, which lead to this paper in which we show that this guess was indeed correct. The contributions of this paper are the following:

1. We show that the *Moore Game* of [19] yields an effective algorithm for performing the *saturation* operation $(A, G) \mapsto (A, G \vee \neg A)$.
2. We clarify the correspondence between A/G contracts and Moore Interfaces. It turns out to be almost perfect. The only missing feature of the alternating refinement of Moore Interfaces is the proper consideration of legal environments, which has consequences for the parallel composition of Moore Interfaces as well.
3. We propose a slight adjustment of the Moore Interfaces that match A/G contracts (and thus the meta-theory).

2 Background on Synchronous Assume/Guarantee Contracts

In Assume/Guarantee contracts (A/G contracts), Assumptions characterize the valid environments for the considered component, whereas the Guarantees specify the commitments of the component itself, when put in interaction with a valid environment. We develop here A/G contracts for synchronous frameworks in which behaviors are sequences of successive reactions assigning values to the set of variables of the considered system. To simplify the exposure, we focus on the simplest case of a *fixed* alphabet of variables. The extension to the general case relies on a standard mechanism of alphabet extension, for which the reader is referred to [12].

We consider a finite alphabet V of variables possessing identical domain D. Synchronous assertions, which constitute the basis of synchronous A/G-components and contracts, are introduced next. A *reaction* assigns to each variable of V a value from its domain: $s \in D^V$. By adding a distinguished symbol $\perp \notin D$ to model the *absence* of an actual variable in the considered reaction, we get the multiple-clocked synchronous model used by synchronous languages [13]. Denote by $\varepsilon = \perp^V$ the *silent reaction*, assigning $\perp$ to every variable. A *synchronous behavior* σ is a finite or infinite sequence of reactions. A *synchronous assertion* P is a set of synchronous behaviors:

$$P \subseteq (V \mapsto (D \cup \{\perp\}))^\omega. \tag{1}$$

Say that P is *stuttering invariant* [11] if: (1) it is closed under the transformations

$$\sigma = s_1, \ldots, s_k, s_{k+1}, \ldots \quad \mapsto \quad stretch_k(\sigma) = s_1, \ldots, s_k, \perp^V, s_{k+1}, \ldots \tag{2}$$

where k is an arbitrary integer — inserting at any time k a silent reaction in a behavior of P still yields a behavior of P —, and (2) P is a closed set when $(V \mapsto (D \cup \{\perp\}))^\omega$ is equipped with the product discrete topology. In particular, if P is stuttering invariant, then by using condition (1) of stuttering invariance, it contains behaviors beginning with the silent behavior ε^k with an arbitrary length k. By condition (2) of stuttering invariance, the behavior ε^ω having only silent reactions, which is the limit with respect to the product topology of a sequence of behaviors beginning by ε^k, also belongs to P. Stuttering invariance is a desirable property for an open system, since it may be subsequently put in an environment that is acting when the considered system is sleeping. From now on and until otherwise mentioned, we omit the term "synchronous". Assertions are equipped with the set algebra $\cap, \cup, \neg$, where $\neg$ denotes set complement.

Definition 1. *A component is any stuttering invariant assertion.*

Thus, it is always allowed for a component to do nothing. The class of components is stable under intersection. Two components are always composable and we define component composition by the intersection of their respective assertions:

$$P_1 \times P_2 = P_1 \cap P_2 \tag{3}$$

Formulas (1) and (3) define a framework of synchronous components. It coincides with the framework used in [11].

Definition 2. *A contract is a pair* $\mathscr{C} = (A, G)$ *of assertions, called the* assumptions *and the* guarantees. *The set* $\mathcal{E}_\mathscr{C}$ *of the legal environments for* $\mathscr{C}$ *collects all components E such that $E \subseteq A$. The set* $\mathcal{M}_\mathscr{C}$ *of all components implementing* $\mathscr{C}$ *is defined by $A \times M \subseteq G$.*

Observe that we are not requiring any particular condition on the sets A and G. In particular, they may not be stuttering invariant — for instance the guarantee G may request that every reaction shall be non-silent, which is a progress condition. A or G may even be empty. For this section, the underlying set $\mathbb{C}$ of contracts is the set of all pairs (A, G) of assumptions and guarantees as defined above. By Definition 1,

contract $\mathscr{C} = (A, G)$ is *compatible* if and only if $\varepsilon^\omega \in A$, and in this case

$$E_\mathscr{C} = A \text{ is the maximal (for set inclusion) environment of } \mathscr{C}. \tag{4}$$

Denoting by $\neg A$ the complement of set A, any component M such that $M \subseteq G \cup \neg A$ is an implementation of $\mathscr{C}$. Thus,

contract $\mathscr{C} = (A, G)$ is *consistent* if and only $\varepsilon^\omega \in G \cup \neg A$, and in this case

$$M_\mathscr{C} = G \cup \neg A \text{ is the maximal (for set inclusion) implementation of } \mathscr{C}. \tag{5}$$

Observe that two contracts $\mathscr{C}$ and $\mathscr{C}'$ with identical alphabets of variables, identical assumptions $A' = A$, and such that $G' \cup \neg A' = G \cup \neg A$, possess identical sets of implementations: $\mathcal{M}_{\mathscr{C}'} = \mathcal{M}_\mathscr{C}$. According to our meta-theory, such two contracts are equivalent. Say that contract

$$\mathscr{C} = (A, G) \text{ is } saturated \text{ if } G = G \cup \neg A, \text{ or, equivalently, if } G \cup A = \Omega, \tag{6}$$

where $\Omega =_{\text{def}} (V \mapsto D)^* \cup (V \mapsto D)^\omega$ is the trivial assertion collecting all behaviors. Contract $\mathscr{C} = (A, G)$ is equivalent to its saturated form $(A, G \cup \neg A)$. Refinement, conjunction, and parallel composition are defined as follows, for A/G contracts in saturated form:

Definition 3. *Let $\mathscr{C}_1$ and $\mathscr{C}_2$ be two saturated contracts with identical alphabets of variables.*

1. *Say that $\mathscr{C}_2$ refines $\mathscr{C}_1$, written $\mathscr{C}_2 \preceq \mathscr{C}_1$, iff $A_2 \supseteq A_1$ and $G_2 \subseteq G_1$;*
2. *The conjunction of $\mathscr{C}_1$ and $\mathscr{C}_2$ is defined as being the corresponding GLB:* $\mathscr{C}_1 \wedge \mathscr{C}_2 =_{\text{def}} (A_1 \cup A_2, G_1 \cap G_2)$;
3. *The parallel composition of $\mathscr{C}_1$ and $\mathscr{C}_2$, denoted by $\mathscr{C}_1 \otimes \mathscr{C}_2$, is defined as being the pair (A, G) such that $G = G_1 \cap G_2$ and $A = (A_1 \cap A_2) \cup \neg(G_1 \cap G_2)$.*

Comment 1 (Regarding saturated contracts). As the reader has noticed, getting saturated contracts is important in A/G contracts. This seems to require computing unions and complements of assertions. In fact, we only need to be able to compute the operation $(A, G) \mapsto G \cup \neg A$, which we like to interpret as the entailment $A \Rightarrow G$. As we shall see in Sect. 4, it turns out that the *Moore Interfaces*, the simplest form of *Synchronous Component Interfaces* proposed by Chakrabarti et al. [19], provide a way of computing this entailment, for a restricted class of A/G contracts.

3 An Illustration Example for Moore Interfaces

To give the intuition behind Moore Interfaces, we reproduce the following example, borrowed verbatim from the thesis of Arindam Chakrabarti [18]. It is shown in Fig. 1.

The guarded-command syntax used in this figure is derived from the one of reactive modules [4] and Mocha [5]; input atoms describe the input assumptions, and the output atoms describe the output behavior. When more than one guard is true, the command is selected nondeterministically. Input variables not mentioned by the command are updated nondeterministically.

We illustrate the features of Moore interfaces by modeling a simple example: a ± 1 adder driven by a binary counter. The adder $\mathtt{Adder}$ has two control inputs q_0 and q_1, data inputs $i_7, \ldots, i_0$, and data outputs $o_7, \ldots, o_0$. When $q_0 = q_1 = 1$, the adder leaves the input unchanged: the next value of $o_7, \ldots, o_0$ is equal to $i_7, \ldots, i_0$. When $q_0 = 0$ and $q_1 = 1$, the next outputs are given by $[o'_7, \ldots, o'_0] = [i_7, \ldots, i_0] + 1 \mod 2^8$, where primed variables denote the values at the next clock cycle, and $[o'_7, \ldots, o'_0]$ is the integer encoded in binary by $o'_7, \ldots, o'_0$. Similarly, when $q_1 = 0$ and $q_0 = 1$, we have $[o'_7, \ldots, o'_0] = [i_7, \ldots, i_0] - 1 \mod 2^8$.

The adder is designed with the assumption that q_0 and q_1 are not both 0: hence, the input transition relation of $\mathtt{Adder}$ states that $q'_0 q'_1 \neq 00$. In order to cycle between adding $0, +1, -1$, the control inputs q_0 and q_1 are connected to the outputs q_1 and q_0 of a two-bit count-to-zero counter $\mathtt{Counter}$. The counter has only one input, cl: when $cl = 0$, then $q'_0 q'_1 = 11$; otherwise, $[q'_1 q'_0] = [q_1 q_0] - 1 \mod 4$.

When the counter is connected to the adder, the joint system can take a transition to a state where $q_1 q_0 = 00$, violating the adder's input assumptions. In spite of this, the counter and the adder are compatible, since there is a way to use them together: to avoid the incompatible transition, it suffices to assert $cl = 0$ early enough in the count-to-zero cycle of the counter. To reflect

```
interface Counter                        interface Adder
  output q0, q1: bool;                      input q0, q1: bool; di: [0..7];
  input cl: bool;                           output do: [0..7];
  input atom                                input atom
    init                                      init
      [] true -> cl :=nondet                    [] true -> q0:=1
    update                                       [] true -> q1:=1
      [] true -> cl:=nondet                   update
  endatom                                       [] true -> q0:=1
  output atom                                   [] true -> q1:=1
    init                                    endatom
      [] true -> q0:=1; q1:=1;            output atom
    update                                    init
      [] cl -> q1:=1; q0:=1                      [] true -> do:=nondet
      [] ~cl & q1 & q0 -> q1:=1; q0:=0        update
      [] ~cl & q1 & ~q0 -> q1:=0; q0:=1          [] q0 & q1 -> do:=di
      [] ~cl & ~q1 & q0 -> q1:=0; q0:=0          [] ~q0 & q1 -> do:=di+1
      [] ~cl & ~q1 & ~q0 -> q1:=1; q0:=1         [] q0 & ~q1 -> do:=di-1
  endatom                                    endatom
end interface                            end interface
```

Fig. 1. A counter (left) and an adder (right) modeled as Moore interfaces.

this, when we compose Counter and Adder, we synthesize for their composition Counter × Adder a new input assumption, that ensures that the input assumptions of both Counter and Adder are satisfied.

To determine the new input assumption, we solve a game between Input, which chooses the next values of cl and $i_7, \ldots, i_0$, and Output, which chooses the next values of q_0, q_1, and $o_7, \ldots, o_0$. The goal of Input is to avoid a transition to $q_1q_0 = 00$. At the states where $q_1q_0 = 01$, Input can win if $cl = 0$, since at the next clock cycle we will have $q'_0q'_1 = 11$; but Input cannot win if $cl = 1$. By choosing $cl' = 0$, Input can also win from the states where $q_1q_0 = 10$. Finally, Input can always win from the states where $q_1q_0 = 11$, for all cl'. Thus, we associate with Counter × Adder a new input assumption encoded by the transition relation requiring that whenever $q_1q_0 = 10$, then $cl' = 0$. The input requirement $q_1q_0 = 00$ of the adder gives rise, in the composite system, to the requirement that the reset-to-1 occurs early in the count-to-zero cycle of the counter.

So far this was verbatim quote from [18]. This text illustrates the intuition for how composition works for Moore Interfaces. Can we relate this to the composition of A/G contracts?

Item 3 of Definition 3 states that, in the composition of A/G contracts, the overall assumption A is discharged from what is already mutually guaranteed by the two contracts — this corresponds to the term $\cup \neg (G_1 \cap G_2)$. To parallel this with the discussion of the game associated with Moore Interfaces, the Input only checks what, in the raw product of the two machines, may lead to violating input assumptions of one interface. This expresses that the job of the game is to complement what is already natively offered by each interface.

Considering again the composition of A/G contracts, the remaining duty of the overall assumption A is to ensure that input assumptions of both interfaces remain satisfied in the composition — referring to Item 3 of Definition 3, this corresponds to the term $A_1 \cap A_2$. But this is exactly what the game associated with Moore Interfaces finds, namely: "whenever $q_1q_0 = 10$, then $cl' = 0$" is the missing global property that inputs must satisfy in the composition of the two Moore interfaces.

This parallel suggests that there should be a tight relation between Moore Interfaces and A/G contracts. Formalizing this relation is the subject of this paper.

4   Implementing Contract Saturation Using Moore Interfaces [19]

In this section we develop the results announced in Comment 1 regarding contract saturation. We specialize our previous trace- or behavior-based framework of A/G contracts to a sub-case where the saturation operation can be made effective by using the Moore Interfaces.

4.1 Moore Interfaces and Associated A/G Contracts

We now assume that assertions A and G are defined via transition relations having a specific structure. We are given a disjoint copy V' of the set V of variables and call it the set of *next variables*. For $x \in V$, its counterpart in V' is x'. For P a predicate on V, we denote by P' the predicate obtained by replacing in P every $x \in V$ by $x' \in V'$. We next assume that each variable from V has finite domain $D \cup \{\bot\}$ and a decomposition of V is given into *input* and *output* variables: $V = V^{\text{in}} \uplus V^{\text{out}}$. We finally assume

$$\begin{aligned} &\text{a predicate } I_A \text{ on } V^{\text{in}} \quad \text{and a predicate } T_A \text{ on } V \cup (V^{\text{in}})'; \\ &\text{a predicate } I_G \text{ on } V^{\text{out}} \text{ and a predicate } T_G \text{ on } V \cup (V^{\text{out}})'. \end{aligned} \qquad (7)$$

Thus, predicates I_A and T_A control input variables, whereas predicates I_G and T_G control output variables.[1] Call *Moore Interface* [19] the tuple

$$\mathscr{C} = (V, I_A, I_G, T_A, T_G).$$

Each Moore Interface defines an A/G contract (A, G) where the two synchronous assertions A (assumption) and G (guarantee) are given by

$$\begin{aligned} A &= \{ \sigma \mid \sigma(0) \models I_A \text{ and } \forall k. (\sigma(k), \sigma(k+1)) \models T_A \} \\ G &= \{ \sigma \mid \sigma(0) \models I_G \text{ and } \forall k. (\sigma(k), \sigma(k+1)) \models T_G \} \end{aligned} \qquad (8)$$

where, as usual, symbol $\models$ means "satisfies". We now need to define what the components are, for this contract framework.

4.2 Components for Moore Interfaces

Throughout this section we use the concepts introduced in Sect. 4.1 and develop what the right notion of component is, for A/G contracts defined by Moore Interfaces. Since assumptions A and guarantees G are both specified as transition systems, it is natural to require that the underlying class $\mathbb{M}$ of components consists of all transitions systems on V of the form

$$M = (V_M^{\text{in}}, V_M^{\text{out}}, I_M, T_M),$$

where $V = V_M^{\text{in}} \uplus V_M^{\text{out}}$ is a decomposition of V into *input* and *output* variables, the *initial condition* I_M is a predicate over V^{out}, and the *transition relation* T_M is a predicate over $V \cup (V^{\text{out}})'$. We assume the following conditions on predicates I_M and T_M, where $[V/\bot]$ denotes the assignment of the value $\bot$ to every variable belonging to V and similarly for $[V'^{\text{out}}/\bot]$:

$$\begin{aligned} &[V/\bot] \text{ satisfies } I_M; \text{ and} &(a) \\ &\forall V. T_M [V'^{\text{out}}/\bot] \text{ holds,} &(b) \end{aligned} \qquad (9)$$

---

[1] In addition, [19] assumes some kind of satisfiability condition for these four predicates. We do not consider this assumption in our development.

which means that M is stuttering invariant. Note that, for an arbitrary pair (I_M, T_M), the transformation

$$(I_M, T_M) \quad \mapsto \quad (I_M \lor [\forall v \in V : v = \bot], T_M \lor [\forall v' \in V'^{out} : v' = \bot]) \qquad (10)$$

returns a pair satisfying (9). It is, however, a weakening of the original pair.

Two components M_1 and M_2 are *composable* if $V_{M_1}^{out} \cap V_{M_2}^{out} = \emptyset$. The composition $M = M_1 \times M_2$ is given by

- $V_M^{out} = V_{M_1}^{out} \cup V_{M_2}^{out}$, $V_M^{in} = V \setminus V_M^{out}$,
- $I_M = I_{M_1} \land I_{M_2}$, and $T_M = T_{M_1} \land T_{M_2}$.

Observe that the so defined pair (I_M, T_M) satisfies (9). The composition $\times$ is associative and commutative.

4.3   Computing the Maximal Environment and the Maximal Implementation

The authors of [19] associate, to a pair of Moore Interfaces, a certain two-player game and use it to define the parallel composition and compatibility condition. In our development, we reuse a variation of this game to compute the most liberal environment and the most liberal implementation.

More precisely, to $\mathscr{C}$ a Moore Interface as above, we associate the two-player "Moore game" $\Gamma_{\mathscr{C}}$ introduced next. Playing $\Gamma_{\mathscr{C}}$ results in the construction of a certain behavior σ through its successive reactions. Each round of the game extends the current behavior by one more reaction. We borrow the description of the game $\Gamma_{\mathscr{C}}$ from [19], while exchanging the roles of players *in* and *out*:

Definition 4 (Moore Game $\Gamma_{\mathscr{C}}$ [19])

- At each round of the game, player *in* chooses new values for the input variables V^{in} according to I_A at the first round, and then according to T_A;
- Simultaneously and independently, player *out* chooses unconstrained new values for the output variables V^{out};
- Player *out* wins if the resulting behavior σ belongs to G defined in (8).

The Moore game $\Gamma_{\mathscr{C}}$ is an adaptation of the game introduced in [19] — the original game will be reintroduced in our context in Sect. 4.4, when discussing the compatibility between Moore Interfaces and their parallel composition. We closely adapt from [19] an iterative algorithm for computing, if it exists, the most liberal winning strategy for player *out*. This algorithm approximates iteratively

- the predicate C characterizing the set of states from which the player *out* can win the game, and
- the most liberal winning transition relation.

Set $C_0 = \top$ and, for $k \geq 0$:

$$\begin{aligned}
T_{k+1} &= \forall (V^{in})'.\, [T_A \Rightarrow (T_G \land C_k')] \\
C_{k+1} &= C_k \land \exists (V^{out})'.\, T_{k+1}
\end{aligned} \qquad (11)$$

Note that T_{k+1} is a predicate on $V \cup (V^{\mathrm{out}})'$ and C_{k+1} is a predicate on V. The sequences of predicates C_k and T_k are non-increasing. Since all variables possess a finite domain, the convergence of C_k and T_k to their limits C_∞ and T_∞ arises in finitely many steps and we have

$$
\begin{aligned}
C_\infty &= \exists (V^{\mathrm{out}})'.\forall (V^{\mathrm{in}})'. [T_A \Rightarrow (T_G \wedge C'_\infty)] \\
T_\infty &= \qquad \forall (V^{\mathrm{in}})'. [T_A \Rightarrow (T_G \wedge C'_\infty)]
\end{aligned}
\tag{12}
$$

which expresses that C_∞ represents the set of states from which player *out* can win the game when setting the initial condition of G to true. Hence,

- $I_\star =_{\mathrm{def}} [I_A \Rightarrow I_G] \wedge C_\infty$ is the weakest initial condition that player *out* must select;
- $T_\star =_{\mathrm{def}} [C_\infty \Rightarrow T_\infty]$ is the most liberal transition relation for *out* to win the game.

The following result is immediate:

Lemma 1. *If T_G satisfies condition (9-b), then the pair (C_∞, T_∞) satisfies (9). If, in addition, I_G satisfies condition (9-a), then the pair $(I_\star, T_\star)$ also satisfies (9).*

Reference [19] contains detailed implementation considerations regarding algorithm (11). If (I_A, T_A) satisfies (9), then $\mathscr{C}$ is compatible and we can consider the component $E_\mathscr{C} =_{\mathrm{def}} (V^{\mathrm{out}}, V^{\mathrm{in}}, I_A, T_A)$. If player *out* can win, i.e., $I_\star$ is satisfiable, and if $(I_\star, T_\star)$ satisfies (9), then $\mathscr{C}$ is consistent and we can consider the component $M_\mathscr{C} =_{\mathrm{def}} (V^{\mathrm{in}}, V^{\mathrm{out}}, I_\star, T_\star)$.

Theorem 1

1. When seeing $\mathscr{C}$ as an A/G contract, $E_\mathscr{C}$ is the maximal environment for $\mathscr{C}$, and $M_\mathscr{C}$ is the maximal implementation of $\mathscr{C}$, see (5).
2. The map $(T_A, T_A \Rightarrow T_G) \mapsto M_\mathscr{C}$ is nondecreasing, when predicates are equipped with the order inherited from $\mathrm{F} \leq \mathrm{T}$ and components are ordered by inclusion.

Proof. Statement 1 holds by the very definition of the Moore game. We thus focus on Statement 2. To prove it, it is enough to prove by induction that

$$
\text{the map } (T_A, T_A \Rightarrow T_G) \quad \mapsto \quad (C_k, T_{k+1}, T_A \Rightarrow C'_k) \text{ is nondecreasing.} \tag{13}
$$

Property (13) holds for $k = 0$ by construction, since $C_0 = \mathrm{T}$ and $T_1 = \forall (V^{\mathrm{in}})'. [T_A \Rightarrow T_G]$. Assume that (13) holds until $k - 1$ and consider two pairs (T_{A_1}, T_{G_1}) and (T_{A_2}, T_{G_2}) s.t.

$$
T_{A_1} \leq T_{A_2} \text{ and } [T_{A_1} \Rightarrow T_{G_1}] \leq [T_{A_2} \Rightarrow T_{G_2}]
$$

By the induction assumption we have

$$
C^1_{k-1} \leq C^2_{k-1} \text{ and } T^1_k \leq T^2_k \text{ and } [T_{A_1} \Rightarrow C^{1'}_k] \leq [T_{A_2} \Rightarrow C^{2'}_k]
$$

Using (11) we get, on the one hand,

$$C_k^1 = C_{k-1}^1 \wedge \exists (V^{\text{out}})'.T_k^1 \leq C_{k-1}^2 \wedge \exists (V^{\text{out}})'.T_k^2 = C_k^2$$

which implies, since $T_{A_1} \leq T_{A_2}$

$$[T_A^1 \Rightarrow C_k^{1'}] \leq [T_A^2 \Rightarrow C_k^{2'}]$$

On the other hand, we have:

$$
\begin{aligned}
T_{k+1}^1 &= \forall (V^{\text{in}})'. \left[T_A^1 \Rightarrow (T_G^1 \wedge C_k^{1'}) \right] \\
&= \forall (V^{\text{in}})'. \left[(T_A^1 \Rightarrow T_G^1) \wedge (T_A^1 \Rightarrow C_k^{1'}) \right] \\
&\leq \forall (V^{\text{in}})'. \left[(T_A^2 \Rightarrow T_G^2) \wedge (T_A^2 \Rightarrow C_k^{2'}) \right] \\
&\leq T_{k+1}^2
\end{aligned}
$$

which finishes the proof of Statement 2. □

4.4 Moore Interfaces, Seen as A/G Contracts

The Parallel Composition: We continue our development of the link between Moore Interfaces and A/G contracts by considering the parallel composition. The parallel composition and associated compatibility property were the motivation for the authors of [19] to introduce Moore Interfaces and their associated game. Two Moore Interfaces $\mathscr{C}_1$ and $\mathscr{C}_2$ are *composable* if $V_1^{\text{out}} \cap V_2^{\text{out}} = \emptyset$ and their parallel composition should then coincide with the composition $\mathscr{C}_1 \otimes \mathscr{C}_2$ where $\mathscr{C}_1$ and $\mathscr{C}_2$ are seen as A/G contracts.

Returning to A/G contracts, if $\mathscr{C}_1$ and $\mathscr{C}_2$ are two A/G contracts in saturated form, then we have seen that their parallel composition is given by the assume/guarantee pair

$$\mathscr{C}_1 \otimes \mathscr{C}_2 = \left([A_1 \wedge A_2] \vee \neg[G_1 \wedge G_2], \, G_1 \wedge G_2 \right). \tag{14}$$

We immediately see that the computation of this parallel composition can be performed as follows:

1. Introduce the dual contract $\widetilde{\mathscr{C}} = (G_1 \wedge G_2, \, A_1 \wedge A_2)$;
2. Compute its saturated form $\left(G_1 \wedge G_2, \, [A_1 \wedge A_2] \vee \neg[G_1 \wedge G_2] \right)$; (15)
3. Take the dual of the result.

The key point is that step 2 of (15) can be performed by computing the winning strategy of the game associated to $\widetilde{\mathscr{C}}$, seen as a Moore Interface. This indeed yields the algorithm originally presented in equation (1) of [19] for checking compatibility:

$$
\begin{aligned}
T_{k+1} &= \forall (V^{\text{out}})'. [(T_{G_1} \wedge T_{G_2}) \Rightarrow (T_{A_1} \wedge T_{A_2} \wedge C_k')] \\
C_{k+1} &= C_k \wedge \exists (V^{\text{in}})'.T_{k+1}
\end{aligned}
\tag{16}
$$

This is summarized in the following result:

Theorem 2. *Computing the parallel composition of two saturated contracts $\mathscr{C}_1 \otimes \mathscr{C}_2$, as defined in (14), is achieved by computing the fixpoint of the algorithm originally presented in equation (1) of [19] for checking compatibility.*

Refinement: We now compare the refinement relation $\mathscr{C}_2 \preceq \mathscr{C}_1$ stated in Definition 3 for saturated contracts, with the *alternating simulation* of the game $\Gamma_{\mathscr{C}_2}$ by the game $\Gamma_{\mathscr{C}_1}$, as proposed in [19]. The phrasing from [19] reproduced in Table 1 suggests that this alternating refinement should coincide with the refinement for A/G contracts. We now investigate this question.

Let $\mathscr{C}_i = (V_i^{\text{in}} \uplus V_i^{\text{out}}, I_{A_i}, I_{G_i}, T_{A_i}, T_{G_i}), i = 1, 2$, be two Moore Interfaces and denote by (A_i, G_i) their associated A/G contracts. Following Definition 3 of Sect. 2, we have

$$(A_2, G_2) \preceq (A_1, G_1) \text{ iff } \begin{cases} E_{\mathscr{C}_2} \supseteq E_{\mathscr{C}_1} & (a) \\ M_{\mathscr{C}_2} \subseteq M_{\mathscr{C}_1} & (b) \end{cases} \tag{17}$$

By Statement 2 of Theorem 1, a sufficient condition for the right hand side of (17) to hold is

$$\begin{cases} I_{A_1} \Rightarrow I_{A_2} \text{ and } T_{A_1} \Rightarrow T_{A_2} & (a) \\ [I_{A_2} \Rightarrow I_{G_2}] \Rightarrow [I_{A_1} \Rightarrow I_{G_1}] \text{ and } [T_{A_2} \Rightarrow T_{G_2}] \Rightarrow [T_{A_1} \Rightarrow T_{G_1}] & (b) \end{cases} \tag{18}$$

Following Definition 5 of [19] with appropriate change of notations and taking into account the fact that the alphabet of actions V is fixed, we have $\mathscr{C}_2 \preceq \mathscr{C}_1$ iff $V_2^{\text{in}} = V_1^{\text{in}}$ and the following formulas are valid:

$$[I_{A_1} \wedge I_{G_2} \Rightarrow I_{A_2} \wedge I_{G_1}] \text{ and } [T_{A_1} \wedge T_{G_2} \Rightarrow T_{A_2} \wedge T_{G_1}] \tag{19}$$

Setting $Q = I_A$ or T_A and $P = I_G$ or T_G, we wish to check the following:

$$[Q_2 \Rightarrow P_2] \Rightarrow [Q_1 \Rightarrow P_1] \overset{?}{=} [Q_1 \wedge P_2 \Rightarrow Q_2 \wedge P_1]$$

On the one hand we have:

$$[Q_1 \wedge P_2 \Rightarrow Q_2 \wedge P_1] = [Q_2 \wedge P_1] \vee \neg [Q_1 \wedge P_2]$$
$$= [Q_2 \wedge P_1] \vee \neg Q_1 \vee \neg P_2$$
$$= [Q_2 \vee \neg Q_1 \vee \neg P_2] \wedge [P_1 \vee \neg Q_1 \vee \neg P_2]$$

On the other hand, we have:

$$[Q_2 \Rightarrow P_2] \Rightarrow [Q_1 \Rightarrow P_1] = [P_2 \vee \neg Q_2] \Rightarrow [P_1 \vee \neg Q_1]$$
$$= P_1 \vee \neg Q_1 \vee [\neg P_2 \wedge Q_2]$$
$$= [P_1 \vee \neg Q_1 \vee \neg P_2] \wedge [P_1 \vee \neg Q_1 \vee Q_2]$$
$$= [Q_2 \vee \neg Q_1 \vee P_1] \wedge [P_1 \vee \neg Q_1 \vee \neg P_2]$$

The two expressions differ by the two terms in red. Now, taking (18-*a*) into account, i.e., $Q_1 \Rightarrow Q_2$, the substitution $P_1 \leftrightarrow \neg P_2$ is absorbed by the tautology $Q_2 \vee \neg Q_1$. Thus,

assuming condition $(18 - a)$, conditions $(18 - b)$ and (19) become equivalent. (20)

Hence, we can state:

Theorem 3. *Augmenting the alternating refinement* (19) with condition (18−a) makes it stronger than A/G contract refinement.

The possible gap between alternating refinement and A/G contract refinement lies in the fact that (18) is only sufficient for A/G contract refinement. Having (18) *restricted to the set of reachable states* is necessary and sufficient.

The bottom line is that the refinement developed in [19] seems to ignore the condition regarding assumptions. Interestingly enough, the authors were able to relate refinement to parallel composition as expected: parallel composition is monotonic w.r.t. refinement, thus supporting independent development. The following question arises then:

> Is there really any added value in paying attention to both implementations *and environments* as we did in A/G contracts (and in the meta-theory)?

So, what are we missing for sure if we do not handle environments as first class citizens? The answer lies in the meta-theory. One property is lost by Moore Interfaces à la Chakrabarti, namely:

> If E is a legal environment for the composition $\mathscr{C}_1 \otimes \mathscr{C}_2$, and M_1 is an implementation of $\mathscr{C}_1$, then $E \times M_1$ is a legal environment for $\mathscr{C}_2$.

This is a missing property in Moore Interfaces — even in the mind of the authors, see the quotes from [19] reproduced in Table 1 — and we believe its lack weakens somehow Moore Interfaces as a support for independent development.

5   Conclusion

One can say that our contribution in this paper is to mildly modify the Moore Interfaces to make them equivalent to A/G contracts and thus meta-theory compliant, with the advantage of being computationally effective.

We think that the term "interface" used by the authors of [19] is in disagreement with our terminology — we nevertheless kept this term for our exposure. Indeed the "synchronous interfaces" are not an interface model, in which environments and implementations are folded into a single entity: the "interface". In Moore Interfaces, we rather have two entities T_A and T_G, although both act on the same underlying set of variables. The tight link between Moore Interfaces and A/G contracts — they are nearly identical — that we have just established, further justifies this standpoint. We believe that this link is beneficial both for the A/G contracts and the Moore Interfaces. For A/G contracts, it provides a solution to the embarrassing issue of contract saturation. For Moore Interfaces it points out a (seemingly) missing condition in the alternating refinement.

Reference [19] also generalizes the Moore Interfaces to *Bidirectional Interfaces*. Bidirectional Interfaces offer a dynamic definition of the i/o profile and initial and transition predicates, in that the decomposition $V = V^{\text{in}}(q) \uplus V^{\text{out}}(q)$ and predicates $I_A(q), I_G(q)$ and $T_A(q), T_G(q)$ depend on some *location* $q \in Q$, where the location q evolves according to a deterministic transition system whose transitions are guarded by predicates over the variables of V. This additional flexibility preserves the possibility of considering the game $\Gamma_{\mathscr{C}}$. The follow-up paper [23] studies the conjunction of such interfaces, under the term of *shared refinement*.

As a final observation, Moore Interfaces require finite domains for their variables. Clearly, contract frameworks allowing for any type of data are needed. By only manipulating abstract assertions (sets of behaviors), A/G contracts offer this possibility [12]. In this case, of course, the contract algebra is no longer effective, hence, in [12] we proposed semi-decision procedures based either on *observers* (a kind of test) or on *abstractions*. It may be worth exploring how to extend the Moore Interfaces to this situation. Can Moore Games still be defined? Can we propose semi-decision procedures based on Moore Games? Is this any superior to the existing approaches?

Hej Kim, what do you think?

References

1. Abadi, M., Lamport, L.: Composing specifications. ACM Trans. Program. Lang. Syst. **15**(1), 73–132 (1993)
2. Abadi, M., Lamport, L., Wolper, P.: Realizable and unrealizable specifications of reactive systems. In: Ausiello, G., Dezani-Ciancaglini, M., Rocca, S.R. (eds.) ICALP 1989. LNCS, vol. 372, pp. 1–17. Springer, Heidelberg (1989). doi:10.1007/BFb0035748
3. Abarbanel, Y., Beer, I., Gluhovsky, L., Keidar, S., Wolfsthal, Y.: FoCs – automatic generation of simulation checkers from formal specifications. In: Emerson, E.A., Sistla, A.P. (eds.) CAV 2000. LNCS, vol. 1855, pp. 538–542. Springer, Heidelberg (2000). doi:10.1007/10722167_40
4. Alur, R., Henzinger, T.A.: Reactive modules. Form. Methods Syst. Des. **15**(1), 7–48 (1999)
5. Alur, R., Henzinger, T.A., Mang, F.Y.C., Qadeer, S., Rajamani, S.K., Tasiran, S.: MOCHA: modularity in model checking. In: Hu, A.J., Vardi, M.Y. (eds.) CAV 1998. LNCS, vol. 1427, pp. 521–525. Springer, Heidelberg (1998). doi:10.1007/BFb0028774
6. Antonik, A., Huth, M., Larsen, K.G., Nyman, U., Wąsowski, A.: Complexity of decision problems for mixed and modal specifications. In: Amadio, R. (ed.) FoSSaCS 2008. LNCS, vol. 4962, pp. 112–126. Springer, Heidelberg (2008). doi:10.1007/978-3-540-78499-9_9
7. Balarin, F., Passerone, R.: Functional verification methodology based on formal interface specification and transactor generation. In: Proceedings of the Conference on Design, Automation and Test in Europe (DATE 2006), pp. 1013–1018, Munich, Germany, 6–10 March 2006. European Design and Automation Association, 3001 Leuven, Belgium (2006)
8. Balarin, F., Passerone, R.: Specification, synthesis and simulation of transactor processes. IEEE Trans. Comput.-Aided Des. Integr. Circuits Syst. **26**(10), 1749–1762 (2007)
9. Bauer, S.S., David, A., Hennicker, R., Guldstrand Larsen, K., Legay, A., Nyman, U., Wąsowski, A.: Moving from specifications to contracts in component-based design. In: Lara, J., Zisman, A. (eds.) FASE 2012. LNCS, vol. 7212, pp. 43–58. Springer, Heidelberg (2012). doi:10.1007/978-3-642-28872-2_3

10. Benveniste, A., Caillaud, B., Ferrari, A., Mangeruca, L., Passerone, R., Sofronis, C.: Multiple viewpoint contract-based specification and design. In: Boer, F.S., Bonsangue, M.M., Graf, S., Roever, W.-P. (eds.) FMCO 2007. LNCS, vol. 5382, pp. 200–225. Springer, Heidelberg (2008). doi:10.1007/978-3-540-92188-2_9

11. Benveniste, A., Caillaud, B., Le Guernic, P.: Compositionality in dataflow synchronous languages: specification and distributed code generation. Inf. Comput. **163**(1), 125–171 (2000)

12. Benveniste, A., Caillaud, B., Nickovic, D., Passerone, R., Raclet, J.-B., Reinkemeier, P., Sangiovanni-Vincentelli, A., Damm, W., Henzinger, T., Larsen, K.: Contracts for system design. Monograph to appear in Found. Trends Electron. Des. Autom. **XX**(XX), 1–259 (2017)

13. Benveniste, A., Caspi, P., Edwards, S.A., Halbwachs, N., Le Guernic, P., de Simone, R.: The synchronous languages 12 years later. Proc. IEEE **91**(1), 64–83 (2003)

14. Benvenuti, L., Ferrari, A., Mangeruca, L., Mazzi, E., Passerone, R., Sofronis, C.: A contract-based formalism for the specification of heterogeneous systems. In: Proceedings of the Forum on Specification, Verification and Design Languages (FDL 2008), pp. 142–147, Stuttgart, Germany, 23–25 September 2008

15. Bujtor, F., Fendrich, S., Lüttgen, G., Vogler, W.: Nondeterministic modal interfaces. Theoret. Comput. Sci. **642**, 24–53 (2016)

16. Bujtor, F., Vogler, W.: Error-pruning in interface automata. In: Geffert, V., Preneel, B., Rovan, B., Štuller, J., Tjoa, A.M. (eds.) SOFSEM 2014. LNCS, vol. 8327, pp. 162–173. Springer, Cham (2014). doi:10.1007/978-3-319-04298-5_15

17. Bujtor, F., Vogler, W.: Error-pruning in interface automata. Theoret. Comput. Sci. **597**, 18–39 (2015)

18. Chakrabarti, A.: A framework for compositional design and analysis of systems. Ph.D. thesis, Electrical Engineering and Computer Sciences University of California at Berkeley, December 2007. http://www.eecs.berkeley.edu/Pubs/TechRpts/2007EECS-2007-174.html

19. Chakrabarti, A., Alfaro, L., Henzinger, T.A., Mang, F.Y.C.: Synchronous and bidirectional component interfaces. In: Brinksma, E., Larsen, K.G. (eds.) CAV 2002. LNCS, vol. 2404, pp. 414–427. Springer, Heidelberg (2002). doi:10.1007/3-540-45657-0_34

20. Chilton, C., Jonsson, B., Kwiatkowska, M.Z.: Compositional assume-guarantee reasoning for input/output component theories. Sci. Comput. Program. **91**, 115–137 (2014)

21. Damm, W., Thaden, E., Stierand, I., Peikenkamp, T., Hungar, H.: Using contract-based component specifications for virtual integration and architecture design. In: Proceedings of the 2011 Design, Automation and Test in Europe (DATE 2011), March 2011. To appear

22. de Alfaro, L., Henzinger, T.A.: Interface automata. In: Proceedings of the 9th ACM SIGSOFT International Symposium on Foundations of Software Engineering (FSE 2001), pp. 109–120. ACM Press (2001)

23. Doyen, L., Henzinger, T.A., Jobstmann, B., Petrov, T.: Interface theories with component reuse. In: Proceedings of the 8th ACM & IEEE International conference on Embedded software, EMSOFT 2008, pp. 79–88 (2008)

24. Graf, S., Passerone, R., Quinton, S.: Contract-based reasoning for component systems with rich interactions. In: Sangiovanni-Vincentelli, A., Zeng, H., Di Natale, M., Marwedel, P. (eds.) Embedded Systems Development: From Functional Models to Implementations. Embedded Systems, vol. 20, pp. 139–154. Springer, New York (2014). doi:10.1007/978-1-4614-3879-3_8

25. Larsen, K.G., Nyman, U., Wąsowski, A.: Modal I/O automata for interface and product line theories. In: Nicola, R. (ed.) ESOP 2007. LNCS, vol. 4421, pp. 64–79. Springer, Heidelberg (2007). doi:10.1007/978-3-540-71316-6_6

26. Raclet, J.-B., Badouel, E., Benveniste, A., Caillaud, B., Legay, A., Passerone, R.: Modal interfaces: unifying interface automata and modal specifications. In: Proceedings of the Ninth International Conference on Embedded Software (EMSOFT 2009), pp. 87–96, Grenoble, France, 12–16 October 2009

27. Raclet, J.-B., Badouel, E., Benveniste, A., Caillaud, B., Legay, A., Passerone, R.: A modal interface theory for component-based design. Fundam. Inform. **108**(1–2), 119–149 (2011)

From Transition Systems to Variability Models and from Lifted Model Checking Back to **UPPAAL**

Aleksandar S. Dimovski[(✉)] and Andrzej Wąsowski

Computer Science, IT University of Copenhagen, Copenhagen, Denmark
adim@itu.dk

Abstract. Variational systems (system families) allow effective building of many custom system variants for various configurations. Lifted (family-based) verification is capable of verifying all variants of the family simultaneously, in a single run, by exploiting the similarities between the variants. These algorithms scale much better than the simple enumerative "brute-force" way. Still, the design of family-based verification algorithms greatly depends on the existence of compact variability models (state representations). Moreover, developing the corresponding family-based tools for each particular analysis is often tedious and labor intensive.

In this work, we make two contributions. First, we survey the history of development of variability models of computation that compactly represent behavior of variational systems. Second, we introduce variability abstractions that simplify variability away to achieve efficient lifted (family-based) model checking for real-time variability models. This reduces the cost of maintaining specialized family-based real-time model checkers. Real-time variability models can be model checked using the standard **UPPAAL**. We have implemented abstractions as syntactic source-to-source transformations on **UPPAAL** input files, and we illustrate the practicality of this method on a real-time case study.

1 Introduction

The strong trend for customization in modern economy leads to construction of many highly-configurable systems. Efficient methods to achieve customization, such as *Software Product Line Engineering* (SPLE), use features, or a similar concept, to mark the variable functionality. Family members, called *variants* of a *variational system*, are derived by switching features on and off. The reuse of code common to many variants is maximized. The SPLE method is very popular in the embedded systems domain. Moreover, many of the variational systems, such as device drivers, controllers, and communication protocols are time-critical. A rigorous verification and validation of their timing properties is important. *Model checking* [3] is an automatic technique often used to check for temporal properties of their designs.

Both authors are supported by The Danish Council for Independent Research under a Sapere Aude project, VARIETE.

© Springer International Publishing AG 2017
L. Aceto et al. (Eds.): Larsen Festschrift, LNCS 10460, pp. 249–268, 2017.
DOI: 10.1007/978-3-319-63121-9_13

Variability and SPLE are major enablers, but also a source of complexity. Analyzing variational systems is challenging. From only a few configuration options, exponentially many variants can be derived. Thus, a simple brute-force application of single-system model checking to each variant is infeasible for realistic systems. In essence, the same behaviour is checked multiple times, whenever it is shared by many variants. To address this problem, we need compact structures exploiting the similarity within the family, on which specialized lifted (family-based) verification algorithms can operate. The quest for obtaining such compact models of computation, underpins a great deal of SPLE research. Many of the efforts are inspired by seminal works of Kim Larsen in concurrency theory, originally conceived with an entirely different goal (abstraction in system modeling and verification). We now survey the history of these efforts.

One of the earliest related models is the *Modal Transition System* (MTS) introduced by Larsen and Thomsen in 1988 [30]. It inspired Larsen et al. who proposed to use MTSs as a framework for describing behavioral variational systems 20 years later [27]. In the first part of this work, we survey the history of development of various variability models, largely inspired by the seminal work of Kim and Bent cited above. Ultimately, we arrive at the popular *Featured Transition Systems* (FTSs) introduced by Classen et al. [10,11] and widely accepted as the model essentially sufficient for most purposes of family-based model checking of variational systems.

Then we turn our attention to the corresponding models with a real-time flavor, an area where Kim Larsen was particularly prolific throughout his research career. Here, a similar story of inspiration leading from his early works on *Timed Automata* and UPPAAL [29] to the ultimate *Featured Timed Automata* (FTAs) [13] can be traced—achieving model-checking capability for a wide class of real-time variational systems. Both for FTSs and FTAs specifically designed family-based model checking algorithms exist, which check common execution behaviour only once across variants that are able to produce it. The algorithms are implemented in the ProVeLines family-based model checker [12].

Unfortunately, maintaining specialized family-based model-checkers is expensive, and these tools do not benefit from continuous improvements introduced by research in the classic (non family-based) model checking. Moreover, their performance *still* heavily depends on the size and complexity of the configuration space of the analyzed system. In the second part of this work, we introduce a range of variability abstractions for real-time variational systems. The abstractions are applied at the variability level and aim to reduce the exponential blow-up of the number of variants (configurations) to be more tractable. These new variability abstractions are applied to a FTA, producing an "abstract FTA" which is smaller than the input one, while having at least the same universal Timed CTL properties. We can use the variability abstractions to obtain an abstract FTA (with a low number of variants), which can then be model checked in the brute-force fashion using the (single-system) UPPAAL model-checker. In the extreme case, all variability can be abstracted away, and the classic UPPAAL can be used to show universal properties for the entire system family. We illustrate this method on a simple real-time example, and show that it is still considerably faster than the brute-force enumeration.

2   Superimposition-Based Behavioral Variability Models

We now survey the historical development of several modeling formalisms that have either directly, or indirectly contributed to development of behavioral variability models. We begin with standard (discrete-time) models, and then discuss the parallel line of the related real-time models. The presentation uses a simple example of a mine pump system adapted from models by Cordy et al. [13].

2.1   From Transition Systems to FTSs

Transition systems [3,32] have for long been used to model the behavior of systems. A *transition system* $(S, Act, trans, I, AP, L)$ comprises a set of states S; a set of initial states $I \subseteq S$, a transition relation *trans* relating source and target states from S with action labels from Act; and a labelling function L determining which atomic propositions from a set AP hold at which state. An execution (behavior) of a transition system is a sequence of transitions starting from an initial state. We take the semantics of a transition system to be the set of all its executions.

Figure 1a shows a transition system modeling behavior of a basic mine pump, using the familiar concrete syntax. States are shown as circle nodes. Initial states are pointed to by dangling arrows (a single one in this example, labelled by off). The transition relation is represented by arrows between states: each triple in the relation consists of the source state of the arrow, target state of the arrow and the action label placed on the arc. Finally, the L function is shown by listing the names of propositions that hold in each state. In our example, off holds in the left state, and on holds in the right state. We will use similar notation in further examples, only explaining significant differences from now on. The atomic proposition indicates the pump's current status: on or off. Initially, the

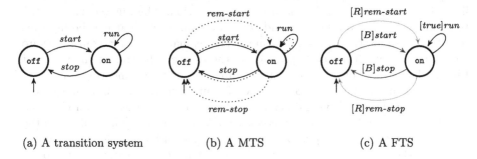

(a) A transition system   (b) A MTS   (c) A FTS

Fig. 1. From single-system models to variability models.

pump is in the off state. Transitions *start* and *stop* model switching between states, while the transition *run* indicates that the pump is still working in the state on.

In his PhD dissertation [26], Larsen developed the notion of contextual equivalence between CCS processes known as *relativized bisimulation*. Roughly speaking, two processes S and T (represented by their transition systems) are equivalent in the context process E, written $S \sim_E T$, iff the context process cannot observe any difference in their behavior. Twenty years later, this notion inspired one of the authors to create an early behavioral variability model, the *colour-blind transition systems* (CBTSs) [28]. In this model, the behavior of many variants in a family is captured in a single transition system, as the union of all behaviors, a kind of *superimposition of all variants* [14]. Variant selection is done by modeling contexts representing different users. Given a family model F and a variant context model V one can obtain a variant product model P by bisimulation minimization against the criterion $P \sim_V F$. CBTSs allowed natural modeling of variability in the input alphabet of a system. For instance, one variant model allows the users less interaction modes with the machine than another, blocking availability of a given feature. It was however cumbersome to model different reactions of variants to the same environment interaction.

Modal Transition Systems (MTSs), also known as *modal specifications*, are a generalization of transition systems that allows describing not just a sum of all behavior of a system but also an over- and under-approximation of the behavior. MTSs were introduced about thirty years ago by Larsen and Thomsen [30]. A MTS is a transition system equipped with two transition relations: *must* and *may*. The former (must) is used to specify the required behavior of a system, while the latter (may) is used to specify the allowed behavior of a system. Now an implementation of a MTS is a standard transition system that realizes all the required (must) behavior, and adds some (possibly none) of the allowed (may) behavior. We take the semantics of a MTS to be the set of all the transition systems that implement the MTS. In this sense, a MTS can be seen as a superimposition of many transition systems, each representing a single system variant. This inspired the idea of using modalities to represent variability in behavior [27].

Figure 1b shows an example of a MTS that models a (minuscule) family of pumps. Must transitions are denoted by solid lines, may transitions by dotted lines. Each must transition is also a may transition. The allowed part of the behavior includes the *rem-start* and *rem-stop* transitions that can be used for remotely changing the state of the pump. The regular *stop/start* transitions are modeling the switch placed physically on the device. The transition system of Fig. 1a, discussed above, is one of the possible variants implementing this MTS.

In fact, the example MTS describes infinitely many variants, due to co-inductive semantics, allowing different implementation choices at each visit to a specification state. For instance *rem-start* might become available only from the second power cycle of the pump. This co-inductive variation was an advantage of MTSs when used for abstracting behaviors, but less so in variability modeling, where one would expect a single variant to behave consistently whenever it visits the same specification state (*rem-start* should be always available in `off`, not only sometimes). Furthermore, there is not easy way in MTSs to represent dependency between variations—for instance, it is not easy to say that if *rem-start* is available in state `off` then *rem-stop* should be available in state `on`. These problems have ultimately led to development of feature transition systems and similar models.

Featured transition systems (FTSs) [10,11] are a compact representation of the behavior of all instances of a variational system, similar to MTSs but relying on a syntactic notion of implementation (subgraph projection) and allowing to constrain which transitions must, or must not, co-occur in implementation variants. To formally define FTSs, assume a finite set $\mathbb{F} = \{A_1, \ldots, A_n\}$ of Boolean variables representing features. A specific set of features $k \subseteq \mathbb{F}$, known as *configuration*, specifies a variant of a variational system. The *set of all valid configurations* is a subset $\mathbb{K} \subseteq 2^{\mathbb{F}}$ (equivalently represented using a Boolean formula). Each configuration $k \in \mathbb{K}$ can be represented by a term formula: $k(A_1) \wedge \ldots \wedge k(A_n)$, where $k(A_i) = A_i$ if $A_i \in k$, and $k(A_i) = \neg A_i$ if $A_i \notin k$ for $1 \leq i \leq n$. FTSs are an extension of transition systems, where transitions are guarded (labeled) with feature expressions, known as *presence conditions*. Presence conditions are propositional formulae over $\mathbb{F}$: $\psi ::= true \mid A \in \mathbb{F} \mid \neg \psi \mid \psi_1 \wedge \psi_2$. We use *FeatExp*$(\mathbb{F})$ to denote the set of all feature expressions. The presence condition ψ labelling a transition indicates for which variants the corresponding transition is enabled. We write $[\![\psi]\!]$ to denote the set of variants $k \in \mathbb{K}$ that satisfy the presence condition ψ, i.e. $k \in [\![\psi]\!]$ iff $k \models \psi$.

Definition 1. *A featured transition system is a tuple $\mathcal{F} = (S, Act, trans, I, AP, L, \mathbb{F}, \mathbb{K}, \delta)$, where $(S, Act, trans, I, AP, L)$ is a transition system; $\mathbb{F}$ is the set of available features, $\mathbb{K}$ is a set of valid configurations, and $\delta : trans \rightarrow FeatExp(\mathbb{F})$ is a total function labelling transitions with presence conditions.*

The *projection* of an FTS $\mathcal{F}$ to a variant $k \in \mathbb{K}$, denoted $\pi_k(\mathcal{F})$, is the transition system $(S, Act, trans', I, AP, L)$, where $trans' = \{t \in trans \mid k \models \delta(t)\}$. The *semantics* of a FTS $\mathcal{F}$, denoted $[\![\mathcal{F}]\!]_{FTS}$, is the union of behaviors of the projections on all variants $k \in \mathbb{K}$, i.e. $[\![\mathcal{F}]\!]_{FTS} = \cup_{k \in \mathbb{K}}[\![\pi_k(\mathcal{F})]\!]_{TS}$, where $[\![\mathcal{T}]\!]_{TS}$ denotes the semantics of the transition system $\mathcal{T}$.

Figure 1c presents a FTS describing the behavior of a variational pump. It contains two features: `Button` (denoted by B) for turning `on`/`off` the pump manually using a button; and `Remote` (denoted by R) for turning `on`/`off` the pump using a remote control. The presence condition of a transition is shown next to its action label, placed in square brackets. For ease of reading the transitions enabled by the same feature are colored in the same way. For example, $[B]start$ means that the transition *start* is enabled only for variants satisfying B. Figure 1a shows the basic variant of the pump that can be operated only manually using a button. This variant is selected by configuration $\{B\}$ (or $B \wedge \neg R$). It can be obtained by projecting the FTS of Fig. 1c onto the configuration $\{B\}$. The set of all valid configurations of the variational pump can be obtained by combining the available features $\mathbb{F} = \{B, R\}$. The pump has four variants: $\mathbb{K} = \{\{B, R\}, \{B\}, \{R\}, \emptyset\}$, or written as the formula: $\mathbb{K} = (B \wedge R) \vee (B \wedge \neg R) \vee (\neg B \wedge R) \vee (\neg B \wedge \neg R)$.

Summary. Figure 2 summarizes the history of development of variability models. The left side is concerned with models discussed above. All points in the figure representing variability modeling contributions are typeset with a bold font. The papers introducing foundational models of computation that influenced the later variability models, are typeset with a regular font.

MTSs generalize transition systems with mandatory (must) transitions and optional (may) transitions, with the main applications originally being under-specification and abstraction. Their semantics superimposes multiple variants. It took however almost 20 years until the first works using MTSs for variability modeling appeared around 2006. Although, MTSs are suitable for representing optional behavior using may transitions, there is no explicit notion of variability in MTSs and so they cannot associate behaviors with the exact set of variants able to execute them. To overcome this limitation, FTSs rely on presence con-ditions guarding transitions that determine in which variants the transitions appear. Therefore, the presence of a transition may depend on the transitions taken before as well. FTSs are closely related to parametric MTSs (PMTSs) introduced by Benes et al. [5]. PMTSs extend considerably the expressiveness of MTSs, thus overcoming many of their limitations. A PMTS is equipped with a finite set of parameters (which are Boolean variables) that have fixed values for any implementation. Fixing a priori the parameters makes the instantiation of the (may) transitions permanent (uniform) in the whole implementation. How-ever, no model checking tool that works on PMTS have been implemented so far, which was the main limitation for their wider application. So far they were mostly studied from theoretical points of view.

2.2 From Timed Automata to FTA

Alur and Dill have introduced *timed automata* (TA) [2] as a modelling formal-ism for time-critical systems. Timed automata are an application of transition systems (more precisely, program graphs [3]) in which real-valued clock variables

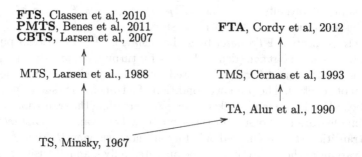

Fig. 2. The history of development of variability models (left part) and real-time vari-ability models (right part). Bold labels indicate variability models, while the regular font labels denote the basic models of computation that laid the foundation and inspired the variability models.

(or clocks for short) are made part of the state and used to measure the elapse of time. The real-time assumptions on system behavior are specified using *clock constraints*, which are conditions that depend on the values of clocks.

A *timed automaton* $(Loc, Act, C, trans, I, Inv, AP, L)$ consist of a set of locations $l \in Loc$ each equipped with an invariant, $Inv(l)$, which is a constraint over clocks in the set C. The constraint $Inv(l)$ limits the amount of time that may be spent in the location l. A set $I \subseteq Loc$ defines the locations active in the initial state of any execution. A transition relation *trans* comprises guarded transitions between locations. Guards are (again) clock constraints that specify when the transition may be taken. Each transition also has an action label $\lambda \in Act$; and a subset of clocks C which are reset to zero upon the firing of the transition. A labelling function L specifies which atomic propositions from AP hold at what locations. As any program graph, a timed automaton can be unfolded into an (infinite-state) transition system [3]. The semantics of a timed automaton is determined by the semantics of the underlying transition system obtained from unfolding, where only time-divergent executions are considered (infinite executions in which the time progress is unbounded).

Figure 3a shows an example of a timed automaton that models the basic behavior of a pump. Like in the transition system in Fig. 1a, the pump has two locations on and off, and transitions *start*, *stop*, and *run* that describe how the locations can evolve. In addition to these constructs, the timed automaton has a clock x to characterize time passing. Initially, the clock x has the value 0. Invariants are shown inside locations and are omitted when they are *true*. Thus, the system can remain in off only when the value of clock x is less than 9. Similarly, it can move from location off to on when the value of x is greater than 6. Overall, this means that the system remains in off between 6 and 9 time units. Upon execution of *start* and *stop* transitions, the value of x is reset to 0. We often omit to write true guards and empty sets of clocks to reset.

Cernas et al. [8] have introduced *timed modal specifications* (TMSs), which represent timed automata equipped with may (allowed) and must (required) transitions. We observe that a family of timed automata can be derived as

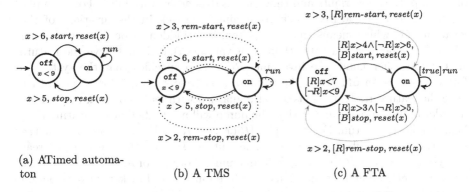

(a) ATimed automaton

(b) A TMS

(c) A FTA

Fig. 3. From timed single-system to timed variability models.

implementations of a specification given as a TMS. We show one example of a TMS in Fig. 3b, such that the timed automaton in Fig. 3a represents an implementation of it.

Like for the MTSs, the timed modal specifications have been generalized to *featured timed automata* (FTA) by Cordy et al. [12], where different variants (implementations) are derived by feature selection. A *featured clock constraint* over a set $\mathbb{F}$ of features and a set C of clocks is a formula of the form:

$$g ::= true \mid [\chi](c < n) \mid [\chi](c \le n) \mid [\chi](c > n) \mid [\chi](c \ge n) \mid g_1 \wedge g_2 \ ,$$

where $c \in C$, $n \in \mathbb{N}$, $\chi \in FeatExp(\mathbb{F})$. We denote the set of featured clock constraints over C and $\mathbb{F}$ by $FCC(C, \mathbb{F})$. We can now define FTA for modelling behavior of real-time variational systems.

Definition 2. *A featured timed automaton is a tuple* $\mathcal{FTA} = (Loc, Act, C, trans, I, Inv, AP, L, \mathbb{F}, \mathbb{K}, \delta)$, *where* $Loc, Act, I, AP, L, \mathbb{F}, \mathbb{K}$, *and* δ *are defined as in FTSs; trans* $\subseteq Loc \times FCC(C, \mathbb{F}) \times Act \times C \times Loc$ *is a finite set of transitions,* $Inv : Loc \to FCC(C, \mathbb{F})$ *is an invariant function that associates featured clock constraints (called invariants) to locations.*

The *projection* of a featured timed automaton $\mathcal{FTA}$ to a variant $k \in \mathbb{K}$, denoted $\pi_k(\mathcal{FTA})$, is the timed automaton $(Loc, Act, C, trans', I, Inv', AP, L)$, with $Inv'(l) = Inv(l)_{|k}$ and $trans' = \{t = (l, g_{|k}, \lambda, R, l') \mid t \in trans \wedge k \models \delta(t)\}$, where the projection of a featured clock constraint g to a variant k is defined inductively:

$$g_{|k} = \begin{cases} (g_1)_{|k} \wedge (g_2)_{|k} & \text{if } g = g_1 \wedge g_2 \\ g' & \text{if } g = [\chi]g' \wedge k \models \chi \\ true & \text{otherwise} \end{cases} \tag{1}$$

The *semantics* of an FTA $\mathcal{FTA}$, denoted $[\![\mathcal{FTA}]\!]_{FTA}$, is the union of behaviors of the projections on all variants $k \in \mathbb{K}$, that is $[\![\mathcal{FTA}]\!]_{FTA} = \cup_{k \in \mathbb{K}} [\![\pi_k(\mathcal{FTA})]\!]_{TA}$, where $[\![\mathcal{TA}]\!]_{TA}$ denotes the semantics of the timed automaton $\mathcal{TA}$.

Figure 3c presents an FTA describing the timed behavior of several variants of a pump. Both invariants and time guards depend on variability. For example, $[\neg R](x < 9)$ is a featured clock constraint occurring in the invariant of the location off, which means that the system is forbidden to be in that location when the value of x is greater than 9 for variants that do not have the feature R. On the other hand, the invariant $[R](x < 7)$ specifies that the system is forbidden to be in off when the value of x is greater than 7 for variants that have the feature R. Transitions are also guarded with featured clock constraints in order to model requirement that the pump will need different preheating time before it begins to run. For example, $[R](x > 4) \wedge [\neg R](x > 6)$ means that the transition *start* can be taken after 4 time units for systems that have R, whereas for systems without R this delay is 6 time units. For ease of reading the presence conditions $\delta(t)$ labelling transitions are placed in square brackets next to action labels. The timed automaton shown in Fig. 3a is obtained by projection of the FTA of Fig. 3c to the variant $\{B\}$ (that is, $B \wedge \neg R$).

Summary. The right side of Fig. 2 summarizes the history of development of the real-time variability models. Timed automata were introduced as a concise syntax for a class of infinite transition systems. The timed modal specifications generalized timed automata by adding may and must modality to transitions. Finally, the featured timed automata were developed as generalizations of the timed modal specifications, arriving at an expressive formalism for modeling real-time behavior in variational system models.

3 Variability Abstractions

In this section, first we show how FTA can be transformed into FTA that contain only clock constraints and presence condition (feature expression) labels on transitions. Then, we define variability abstractions [18,19] for decreasing the size of such transformed FTA. Finally, we show that the obtained abstract FTA preserve the universal fragment of Timed CTL properties.

3.1 Transforming FTA

It has been shown [12] that any FTA can be transformed into an equivalent FTA without featured clock constraints. In particular, any featured clock constraint $g \in FCC(C, \mathbb{F})$ can be replaced with a combination of classical clock constraints and presence conditions. For each g, we create a partitionings $\mathbb{K}_1, \ldots, \mathbb{K}_n$ of $\mathbb{K}$ such that any two variants k and k' from the same partitioning $\mathbb{K}_j$ ($1 \leq j \leq n$) have the same projections $g_{|k}$ and $g_{|k'}$. Those projections are classical clock constraints, and we denote them $c_1, \ldots, c_n$, respectively. Let $t = (l, g, \lambda, R, l')$ be a transition and g be a featured clock constraint. We create a copy of t, denoted t_j (that is, (l, c_j, λ, R, l')), for each partitioning $\mathbb{K}_j$ where the guard is c_j and the presence condition is $\delta(t_j) = \delta(t) \wedge \mathbb{K}_j$. We add all transitions t_j in the transformed FTA, but we remove t from it. Let l be a location and $Inv(l)$ be a featured clock constraint. We create a copy of l, denoted l_j, for each partitioning $\mathbb{K}_j$ such that $Inv(l_j)$ is c_j. We copy all outgoing transitions t of l to be outgoing of any l_j, and all incoming transitions t to l to be incoming to any l_j with the corresponding presence condition $\delta(t) \wedge \mathbb{K}_j$. If l is an initial location, we create a new initial location with all clocks set to zero and add transitions to all l_j labelled with presence condition $\mathbb{K}_j$, (silent) action label τ, and time guard *true*. Finally, we remove l and all associated transitions from the transformed FTA. We show in Fig. 4 the result of transforming the FTA in Fig. 3c. Note that for ease of reading presence conditions are placed in square brackets before the labelling of a transition (which is a triple: time guard, action label, and set of resettable clocks). Both FTA have the same semantics, but the transformed one uses only classical clock constraints and presence conditions. From now on, we only consider such transformed FTA.

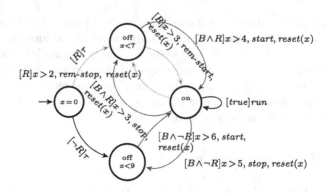

Fig. 4. An FTA with classical clock constraints and presence condition labels.

3.2 Abstracting FTA

Sometimes the computational task on a *concrete* complete lattice (domain) may be too costly or even uncomputable and this motivates replacing it with a simpler *abstract* lattice. A *Galois connection* is a pair of total functions, $\alpha : L \to M$ and $\gamma : M \to L$ (respectively known as the *abstraction* and *concretization* functions), connecting two complete lattices, $\langle L, \leqslant_L \rangle$ and $\langle M, \leqslant_M \rangle$ (often called the *concrete* and *abstract* domain, respectively), such that: $\alpha(l) \leqslant_M m \iff l \leqslant_L \gamma(m)$ for all $l \in L, m \in M$, which is often typeset as: $\langle L, \leqslant_L \rangle \xrightleftharpoons[\alpha]{\gamma} \langle M, \leqslant_M \rangle$. Here $\leqslant_L$ and $\leqslant_M$ are the partial-order relations for L and M, respectively.

The aim of variability abstractions is to weaken feature expressions, effectively making transitions of an FTS present in more variants. In the following, we define variability abstractions as Galois connections for reducing the Boolean complete lattice of feature expressions (propositional formulae over $\mathbb{F}$): $(FeatExp(\mathbb{F})_{/\equiv}, \models, \vee, \wedge, true, false)$. Elements of $FeatExp(\mathbb{F})_{/\equiv}$ are equivalence classes of propositional formulae $\psi \in FeatExp(\mathbb{F})$ obtained by quotienting by the semantic equivalence $\equiv$. The partial-order relation $\models$ is defined as the satisfaction relation from propositional logic, whereas the least upper bound operator is $\vee$ and the greatest lower bound operator is $\wedge$. Furthermore, the least element is *false*, and the greatest element is *true*. Subsequently, we will lift the definition of variability abstractions to FTA.

The *join abstraction*, α^{join}, merges the control-flow of all variants, obtaining a single variant that includes all executions occurring in any variant. The information about which transitions are associated with which variants is lost. Each feature expression ψ defined over $\mathbb{F}$ is replaced with *true* if there exists at least one configuration from $\mathbb{K}$ that satisfies ψ. The new abstract set of features is empty: $\alpha^{\text{join}}(\mathbb{F}) = \emptyset$, and the abstract set of valid configurations is a singleton: $\alpha^{\text{join}}(\mathbb{K}) = \{true\}$ if $\mathbb{K} \neq \emptyset$. The abstraction $\alpha^{\text{join}} : FeatExp(\mathbb{F}) \to FeatExp(\emptyset)$ and concretization functions $\gamma^{\text{join}} : FeatExp(\emptyset) \to FeatExp(\mathbb{F})$ are:

$$\alpha^{\text{join}}(\psi) = \begin{cases} true & \text{if } \exists k \in \mathbb{K}.k \models \psi \\ false & \text{otherwise} \end{cases} \qquad \begin{array}{l} \gamma^{\text{join}}(true) = true \\ \gamma^{\text{join}}(false) = \bigvee_{k \in 2^{\mathbb{F}} \setminus \mathbb{K}} k \end{array}$$

The proposed abstraction-concretization pair is a Galois connection [18,19].

The *feature ignore abstraction*, $\boldsymbol{\alpha}_A^{\text{fignore}}$, ignores a single feature $A \in \mathbb{F}$ by merging the control flow paths that only differ with regard to A, but keeps the precision with respect to control flow paths that do not depend on A. Let ψ be a formula in negation normal form (NNF). We write $\psi[l_A \mapsto true]$ to denote the formula ψ where the literal of A, that is A or $\neg A$, is replaced with *true*. The abstract sets of features and configurations are: $\boldsymbol{\alpha}_A^{\text{fignore}}(\mathbb{F}) = \mathbb{F} \backslash \{A\}$, and $\boldsymbol{\alpha}_A^{\text{fignore}}(\mathbb{K}) = \{k[l_A \mapsto true] \mid k \in \mathbb{K}\}$. The abstraction and concretization functions between $FeatExp(\mathbb{F})$ and $FeatExp(\boldsymbol{\alpha}_A^{\text{fignore}}(\mathbb{F}))$, which form a Galois connection [18,19], are defined as:

$$\boldsymbol{\alpha}_A^{\text{fignore}}(\psi) = \psi[l_A \mapsto true] \qquad \boldsymbol{\gamma}_A^{\text{fignore}}(\psi') = (\psi' \wedge A) \vee (\psi' \wedge \neg A)$$

where ψ and ψ' are in NNF.

The composition $\alpha_2 \circ \alpha_1$ runs two abstractions α_1 and α_2 in sequence (see [18,19] for precise definition). In the following, we will simply write (α, γ) for any Galois connection $\langle FeatExp(\mathbb{F})_{/\equiv}, \models \rangle \xrightarrow[\alpha]{\gamma} \langle FeatExp(\alpha(\mathbb{F}))_{/\equiv}, \models \rangle$ constructed using the operators presented in this section.

Given a Galois connection (α, γ) defined on the level of feature expressions, we now induce a notion of abstraction between (transformed) FTA.

Definition 3. *Let* $\mathcal{FTA} = (Loc, Act, C, trans, I, Inv, AP, L, \mathbb{F}, \mathbb{K}, \delta)$ *be an FTA, and* (α, γ) *be a Galois connection. We define the abstract FTA* $\alpha(\mathcal{FTA})$ *as the tuple* $(Loc, Act, C, trans, I, Inv, AP, L, \alpha(\mathbb{F}), \alpha(\mathbb{K}), \alpha(\delta))$, *where* $\alpha(\delta) : trans \to FeatExp(\alpha(\mathbb{F}))$ *is defined as:* $\alpha(\delta)(t) = \alpha(\delta(t))$.

We also define the *projection* of an (transformed) FTA with classical clock constraints $\mathcal{FTA}$ to a set of variants $\mathbb{K}' \subseteq \mathbb{K}$, denoted as $\pi_{\mathbb{K}'}(\mathcal{FTA})$, as the FTA $(Loc, Act, C, trans', I, Inv, AP, L, \mathbb{F}, \mathbb{K}', \delta)$, where $trans' = \{t \in trans \mid \exists k \in \mathbb{K}'.k \models \delta(t)\}$. We observe that we can combine variability abstractions with various projections on FTA, thus obtaining interesting (featured) timed automata that can be used for verification of the concrete FTA.

Example 1. Consider $\mathcal{FTA}$ in Fig. 4 with the set of valid configurations $\mathbb{K} = \{\{B\}, \{R\}, \{B, R\}, \emptyset\}$. We show $\boldsymbol{\alpha}^{\text{join}}(\pi_{[\![R]\!]}(\mathcal{FTA}))$, $\boldsymbol{\alpha}^{\text{join}}(\pi_{[\![\neg R]\!]}(\mathcal{FTA}))$, and $\boldsymbol{\alpha}_R^{\text{fignore}}(\mathcal{FTA})$ in Fig. 5. We do not show transitions labelled with the feature expression *false* and unreachable locations. Note that both $\boldsymbol{\alpha}^{\text{join}}(\pi_{[\![R]\!]}(\mathcal{FTA}))$ and $\boldsymbol{\alpha}^{\text{join}}(\pi_{[\![\neg R]\!]}(\mathcal{FTA}))$ are ordinary timed automata, since all transitions are labelled with the feature expression *true*. For $\boldsymbol{\alpha}^{\text{join}}(\pi_{[\![R]\!]}(\mathcal{FTA}))$ in Fig. 5a, we have $\mathbb{K} \cap [\![R]\!] = \{\{R\}, \{B, R\}\}$ so transitions annotated with $\neg R$ are removed. For $\boldsymbol{\alpha}^{\text{join}}(\pi_{[\![\neg R]\!]}(\mathcal{FTA}))$ in Fig. 5b, we have $\mathbb{K} \cap [\![\neg R]\!] = \{\{B\}, \emptyset\}$, so transitions annotated with R are removed. Note that $\boldsymbol{\alpha}_R^{\text{fignore}}(\mathcal{FTA})$ in Fig. 5c is an FTA with the singleton set of features $\{B\}$ and two valid configurations $\{B\}$ and $\emptyset$ (that is, B and $\neg B$ respectively). $\qquad \square$

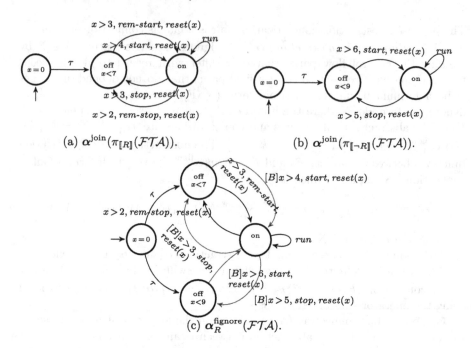

Fig. 5. Some abstractions of the real-time variability pump.

3.3   TCTL Properties and Their Preservation

We consider the universal fragment of the Timed CTL (TCTL) [1]. TCTL is a timed variant of CTL used to express properties of timed automata. An universal TCTL formula is defined inductively as:

$$\Phi ::= true \mid a \in AP \mid \neg a \mid g \in CC(C) \mid \Phi_1 \wedge \Phi_2 \mid \forall(\Phi_1 \, U^J \, \Phi_2) \mid \forall \Diamond^J \Phi \mid \forall \Box^J \Phi$$

where the formulae are in negation normal form ($\neg$ is applied only to atomic propositions), $CC(C)$ is a set of classical clock constraints over the set of clocks C, and $J \subseteq \mathbb{R}^+$ is a subinterval of $[0, \infty)$. The quantifier $\forall$ means that all time-divergent executions that start in a state satisfy the following temporal operator. Intuitively, $\forall(\Phi_1 \, U^J \, \Phi_2)$ means that for all (time-divergent) executions whenever at some point in J, a state is reached satisfying Φ_2 then at all previous time instants $\Phi_1 \vee \Phi_2$ holds. $\forall \Diamond^J \Phi = \forall(true \, U^J \, \Phi)$ means that for all (time-divergent) executions a state satisfying Φ can be reached during the interval J; whereas $\forall \Box^J \Phi$ asserts that for all (time-divergent) executions during the interval J the formula Φ always holds.

We show that abstract FTA have some interesting preservation properties. In particular, we show that an universal TCTL formula satisfied by an abstract FTA is also satisfied by the corresponding concrete FTA. First, we use a helping lemma shown in [18,19], which states that for any valid variant $k \in \mathbb{K}$ that can execute a behaviour guarded by feature expressions $\psi_0, \psi_1, \ldots$, there exists an abstract variant $k' \in \alpha(\mathbb{K})$ that can execute the same behaviour.

Lemma 1. *Let $\psi_0, \psi_1, \ldots \in FeatExp(\mathbb{F})$, $\mathbb{K}$ be a set of configurations over $\mathbb{F}$, and (α, γ) be a Galois connection. Let $k \in \mathbb{K}$, such that $k \models \psi_i$ for all $i \geq 0$. Then there exists $k' \in \alpha(\mathbb{K})$, such that $k' \models \alpha(\psi_i)$ for all $i \geq 0$.*

By using Lemma 1, we can prove the following result.

Theorem 1 (Soundness). *Let (α, γ) be a Galois connection. We have that $\alpha(\mathcal{FTA}) \models \Phi \implies \mathcal{FTA} \models \Phi$.*

Proof. We proceed by contraposition. Assume $\mathcal{FTA} \not\models \Phi$. Then, there exist a configuration $k \in \mathbb{K}$ and an (time-divergent) execution $\rho = s_0 \lambda_1 s_1 \lambda_2 \ldots \in [\![\pi_k(\mathcal{FTA})]\!]_{TA}$ such that $\rho \not\models \Phi$, i.e. $\rho \models \neg\Phi$. Note that ρ is an execution of the underlying transition system obtained by unfolding $\pi_k(\mathcal{FTA})$. This means that for all transitions in ρ, $t_i = s_i \xrightarrow{\lambda_{i+1}} s_{i+1}$ for $i = 0, 1, \ldots$, we have that $k \models \delta(t_i)$ for all $i \geq 0$. By Lemma 1, we have that there exists $k' \in \alpha(\mathbb{K})$, such that $k' \models \alpha(\delta(t_i))$ for all $i \geq 0$. Hence, the execution ρ is realizable for $\alpha(\mathcal{FTA})$, i.e. $\rho \in [\![\pi_{k'}(\alpha(\mathcal{FTA}))]\!]_{TA}$ and $\rho \models \neg\Phi$. It follows that $\alpha(\mathcal{FTA}) \not\models \Phi$.   □

The family-based model checking problem, $\mathcal{FTA} \models \Phi$, can be reduced to a number of smaller problems by partitioning the set of valid configurations $\mathbb{K}$.

Proposition 1. *Let the subsets $\mathbb{K}_1, \mathbb{K}_2, \ldots, \mathbb{K}_n$ form a partition of the set $\mathbb{K}$. Then: $\mathcal{FTA} \models \Phi$, if and only if, $\pi_{\mathbb{K}_1}(\mathcal{FTA}) \models \Phi \wedge \ldots \wedge \pi_{\mathbb{K}_n}(\mathcal{FTA}) \models \Phi$.*

Corollary 1. *Let $\mathbb{K}_1, \mathbb{K}_2, \ldots, \mathbb{K}_n$ form a partition of $\mathbb{K}$, and $(\alpha_1, \gamma_1), \ldots, (\alpha_n, \gamma_n)$ be Galois conn. If $\alpha_1(\pi_{\mathbb{K}_1}(\mathcal{FTA})) \models \Phi, \ldots, \alpha_n(\pi_{\mathbb{K}_n}(\mathcal{F})) \models \Phi$, then $\mathcal{FTA} \models \Phi$.*

The soundness results (Theorem 1 and Corollary 1) mean that the correctness of abstract FTA implies correctness of the concrete FTA. Note that verification of the abstract FTA can be drastically (even exponentially) faster. However, if the abstract FTA invalidate a property then the concrete FTA may still satisfy the property, i.e. the found counterexample in the abstract FTA may be *spurious* (introduced due to the abstraction) for some variants.

Example 2. Consider the property: "the pump will move from state off to on within 7 time unit", which is expressed by the universal TCTL formula $\Phi = \forall\Box(\text{off} \implies \forall\Diamond^7 \text{on})$. We also consider timed automata $\alpha^{\mathrm{join}}(\pi_{[\![R]\!]}(\mathcal{FTA}))$ and $\alpha^{\mathrm{join}}(\pi_{[\![\neg R]\!]}(\mathcal{FTA}))$ shown in Fig. 5. First, we can successfully verify that $\alpha^{\mathrm{join}}(\pi_{[\![R]\!]}(\mathcal{FTA})) \models \Phi$, which implies that all valid variants from $\mathbb{K}$ that contain the feature R satisfy the property Φ. On the other hand, we have $\alpha^{\mathrm{join}}(\pi_{[\![\neg R]\!]}(\mathcal{FTA})) \not\models \Phi$ with the counterexample where the system remains in off more than 7 time units and afterwards (e.g. at 8.5 time unit) it goes to on. This counterexample is genuine for the variants from $\mathbb{K}$ that do not contain the feature R. In this way, the problem of verifying $\mathcal{FTA}$ against Φ can be reduced to verifying whether two timed automata, $\alpha^{\mathrm{join}}(\pi_{[\![\neg R]\!]}(\mathcal{FTA}))$ and $\alpha^{\mathrm{join}}(\pi_{[\![R]\!]}(\mathcal{FTA}))$, satisfy Φ.   □

4   A Case Study: The Train-Gate System

The train-gate example comes with the installation of UPPAAL. It represents a railway control system which automatically controls access to a bridge for several trains, such that the bridge may be accessed only by one train at a time. The system should safely guide trains from several tracks crossing the bridge. First, we describe the basic version of the train-gate system [4,34]. Then, we add variability into it thus creating a variational version of the system. Finally, we evaluate the verification of several interesting universal properties of the variational system using variability abstractions and UPPAAL.

4.1   Basic System

The basic system is modelled as a network of n trains and a controller in parallel. The model of a train, $Train_i$, is shown in Fig. 6a. It has five locations: Safe, Appr, Stop, Start, and Cross. The initial location is Safe, which corresponds to a train not approaching the bridge yet. When a train is approaching the bridge, it sends the signal $appr_i$ to the controller and goes to location Appr. This location has the invariant $x_i \leq 20$ (written next to the location), so it must be left within 20 time units. If the bridge is occupied the controller sends a $stop_i$ signal to prevent the train from entering the bridge by going to the location Stop. Otherwise, if $Train_i$ does not receive a $stop_i$ signal within 10 time units, it will start to cross the bridge by going to location Cross. The crossing train is assumed to leave the bridge within 3 to 5 time units by sending the signal $leave_i$. A stopped train waits for a go_i signal sent from the controller to the first train in the waiting list to restart. A restarted train from Start location reaches the crossing section between 7 and 15 time units non-deterministically.

The model of a gate controller, which synchronizes with trains, is shown in Fig. 6b. It uses a list L to keep record of the trains waiting to cross the bridge and

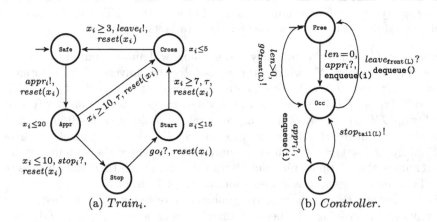

(a) $Train_i$.   (b) $Controller$.

Fig. 6. The basic train-gate system.

an integer variable *len* for the length of L. The controller starts in the location `Free`, where the bridge is free and checks whether the list L is empty. If L is empty and a train is approaching, then this train is added at the back of L with `enqueue()` operation. If L is not empty, then $Train_i$ at the front of L is restarted with the go_i signal. In the `Occ` location, the train at the front of L, $Train_i$, is crossing the bridge. When the crossing train leaves the bridge, the controller receives a *leave*$_i$ signal and removes it from the list L with `dequeue()` operation. If another $Train_i$ is approaching the bridge in `Occ` location, that train is added at the back of L and stopped with the *stop*$_i$ signal. Note that the location C represents a committed location which avoids any time delay in it [4].

4.2   Variational System

We now extend the basic train-gate system given in Fig. 6, to construct a variational system that describes the behaviours of a family of train-gate systems. Figure 7 shows all additional transitions in the variational system that do not occur in the basic system in Fig. 6. They are labelled with presence conditions, which denote whether a transition is included (present) in a given variant. We assume that all transitions in the basic system in Fig. 6, which are shown in bold in Fig. 7, are enabled in all variants, i.e. their presence condition is *true*. The variational train-gate system has four optional features, which are assigned an identifying letter and a color. The feature `Fast` (denoted by F, in red) is used for denoting fast approaching trains, which are placed at the front of the waiting list L thus having higher priority than the others. When a fast approaching $Train_i$ comes to the bridge it sends the *fast*$_i$ signal to the controller. If the bridge is occupied, the train is stopped and added at the second position of L just after the crossing train using `secqueue(i)` operation. The second feature `Capacity` (denoted by C, in green) is used for a controller that allows $\frac{2}{3}n$ trains to be able

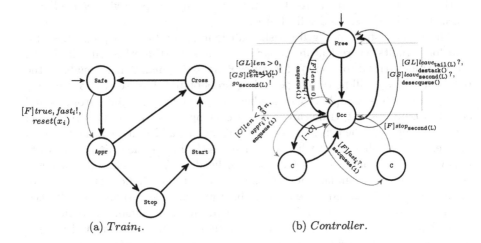

(a) $Train_i$.   (b) *Controller*.

Fig. 7. The variational train-gate system. (Color figure online)

to approach the bridge. When the feature `Capacity` is enabled, the controller will ignore any approach signal if the number of approaching and crossing trains is greater or equal than $\frac{2}{3}n$. The feature `GoSecond` (denoted by GS, in brown) is used for controller to allow the second train in the waiting list L to restart instead of the first one, after a crossing train has left the bridge. The transitions enabled by `GoSecond` use the operations: `second()` to retrieve the second element of L, and `desecqueue()` to remove the second element of L. The feature `GoLast` (denoted by GL, in blue) is used for controller to allow the last train in the waiting list L to restart after a crossing train has left the bridge. The operations are: `tail()` to retrieve the last element of L, and `destack()` to remove the last element of L.

4.3   Verification

Implementation. Inputs to UPPAAL represent XML files where all locations and transitions are described in separate tags. To describe variational systems, we use the color attribute of the transition tag to encode the presence condition that labels a transition. The sets of available features and valid configurations are defined using TVL files [9]. We have implemented variability abstractions as source-to-source transformations of XML files that represent variational systems.

Properties. We check several interesting universal properties to check on the variational train-gate system. The property "$\phi_1 = \forall\square$ forall $(i : int[0, n{-}1])$ forall $(j : int[0, n-1])$ $(Train_i.Cross \land Train_j.Cross \implies i == j)$" states that there is never more than one train crossing the bridge at any time instance. The property "$\phi_2 = \forall\square\,(Gate.L[n] == 0)$" states that there can never be n elements in the waiting list, thus the list L will not overflow. The property "$\phi_3 = \forall\square\,(Train_0.Appr \implies \forall\lozenge\,Train_0.Cross)$" states that whenever the train 0 approaches the bridge, it will eventually cross. Similar properties can be written for the other trains from 1 to $n-1$. Finally, the property "$\phi_4 = \forall\square\,not\,deadlock$" checks that the system is deadlock-free.

The basic system in Fig. 6 satisfies all four properties. All properties also hold for variants where feature `Capacity` is enabled (the others are disabled). For variants with all (or some) of features `Fast`, `GoSecond`, `GoLast` enabled, the properties ϕ_1, ϕ_2 still hold, but ϕ_3 and ϕ_4 are violated. In case of `Fast` enabled and ϕ_3, a counter-example is shown where an approaching train is stopped and added to L but all next trains are fast approaching, so the (no fast) approaching one can never cross the bridge. In case of `GoSecond` enabled and ϕ_3, the reported counter-example shows that when a train leaves the bridge the train that restarts is never the first one, so this train at the head of L is stuck and can never cross the bridge. A similar counter-example is obtained if `GoLast` is enabled. In case of both `Fast` and `GoSecond` enabled and ϕ_4, the system is deadlocked when it chooses the second train in L to restart with *go* signal, but then a fast approaching train is added to L using *fast* signal. Thus, the restarted train is not able to leave the bridge since it is now on the third place in L and the first two trains in L are both stopped.

The variational train-gate system has $2^4 = 16$ variants in total. We use two approaches to check the above four properties. First, the brute-force approach consists of verifying a property by calling UPPAAL to check it for each individual variant (thus we have 16 UPPAAL calls). Second, the approach based on variability abstractions consists of applying an abstraction on the variational system and then verifying the corresponding property on the obtained abstract system. The properties ϕ_1 and ϕ_2 (satisfied by all variants) can be checked by applying α^{join}, on the variational system and then calling UPPAAL once to verify the obtained abstract system. The property ϕ_3 is violated by variants that satisfy Fast ∨ GoSecond ∨ GoLast (14 in total). We use UPPAAL to verify satisfaction of ϕ_3 against four models obtained by applying α^{join}, on the following projections of the variational train-gate system: $\pi_{[\![Fast]\!]}$, $\pi_{[\![GoSecond]\!]}$, $\pi_{[\![GoLast]\!]}$, and $\pi_{[\![\neg Fast \wedge \neg GoSecond \wedge \neg GoLast]\!]}$. Using four calls to UPPAAL we obtain that ϕ_3 is violated by the first three abstracted projections, and is satisfied by the last abstracted projection. The property ϕ_4 is violated by variants that satisfy (Fast∧GoSecond)∨GoLast (10 in total). In this case, we verify ϕ_4 against four models obtained by applying α^{join}, on the following projections: $\pi_{[\![\neg Fast \wedge \neg GoLast]\!]}$, $\pi_{[\![\neg GoSecond \wedge \neg GoLast]\!]}$, $\pi_{[\![Fast \wedge GoSecond]\!]}$, and $\pi_{[\![GoLast]\!]}$. The first two abstract models satisfy ϕ_4, but the last two models do not satisfy ϕ_4.

Results. All experiments are executed on a 64-bit Intel®Core^{TM} i5 CPU with 8 GB memory. All times are reported as averages over five runs with the highest and lowest number removed. Figure 8 compares the performance of our approach based on variability abstractions with the brute-force approach to verify the above four properties for the system with $n = 6$ trains. For each experiment, we report: the number of calls to UPPAAL, the total verification time (TIME) and the total number of explored states (SPACE). TIME (resp., SPACE) is the sum of verification times (resp., the number of explored states) of all individual UPPAAL calls taken in verifying each property. We can see that our abstraction-based approach achieves improvements in both TIME and SPACE for all properties.

prop.	brute-force			abstraction-based		
	CALLS	TIME	SPACE	CALLS	TIME	SPACE
ϕ_1	16	18.5	347,920	1	1.4	42,145
ϕ_2	16	19.2	347,920	1	1.1	42,145
ϕ_3	16	15.1	16,232	4	3.7	3,244
ϕ_4	16	18.9	275,596	4	4.8	83863

Fig. 8. Performances of the brute-force vs. abstraction-based approaches for the variational train-gate system with $n = 6$. TIME in seconds.

5   Related Work

Recently, various family-based techniques have been proposed which lift existing single-program verification techniques to work on the level of program families. This includes family-based syntax checking [22,25], family-based type checking

[24], family-based static analysis [6,7,31], family-based verification by rewriting variability [23,33], etc. TYPECHEF [25] and SUPERC [22] are variability-aware parsers, which can parse C language with preprocessor annotations; whereas family-based type checking for Featherweight Java was presented in [24]. Brabrand et al. [7] show how to lift any single-program dataflow analysis from the monotone framework to work on the level of program families; whereas Midtgaard et al. [31] show the lifting for any static analysis from the abstract interpretation framework. The obtained family-based analyses are much faster than ones based on the naive brute-force approach that generates and analyzes all variants one by one. In order to speed-up such family-based static analyses, variability abstractions have been introduced in [15,20]. They aim to abstract (reduce) the configuration space of the given family. Each abstraction expresses a compromise between precision and speed in the induced abstract family-based analyses [15]. However, the number of possible abstractions is intractably large with most abstractions being too imprecise or too costly to show the analysis's ultimate goal. The work in [20] proposes a technique to efficiently find a suitable variability abstraction for a family-based static analysis to establish a given query. Another efficient implementation of family-based analysis formulated within the IFDS framework for inter-procedural distributive environments has been proposed in SPL^{LIFT} [6]. The works [23,33] are based on using transformations to generate a single program which simulates the behaviour of all variants in a family. This is achieved by replacing compile-time variability with run-time variability (non-determinism). Then, existing single-system analyzers are used to analyze the generated simulator. An approach for family-based software model checking using game semantics has been introduced in [17]. It verifies safety of #ifdef-based second-order program families containing undefined components, which are compactly represented using symbolic game semantics models [16].

6   Conclusion

We have proposed variability abstractions to derive abstract model checking for real-time variational systems. By exploiting the knowledge of a variability model and property, we may carefully devise variability abstractions that are able to verify interesting properties in only a few calls to UPPAAL. As a future work, we want to automate our verification approach by developing an abstraction refinement procedure, similarly to the context of SPIN and FPromela [21]. The abstraction refinement procedure will use spurious counterexample to iteratively refine abstract variational models until either a genuine counter-example is found or the property satisfaction is shown for all variants in the family.

References

1. Alur, R., Courcoubetis, C., Dill, D.L.: Model-checking in dense real-time. Inf. Comput. **104**(1), 2–34 (1993). http://dx.doi.org/10.1006/inco.1993.1024
2. Alur, R., Dill, D.L.: A theory of timed automata. Theor. Comput. Sci. **126**(2), 183–235 (1994). http://dx.doi.org/10.1016/0304-3975(94)90010-8

3. Baier, C., Katoen, J.: Principles of Model Checking. MIT Press, Cambridge (2008)
4. Behrmann, G., David, A., Larsen, K.G.: A tutorial on UPPAAL. In: Bernardo, M., Corradini, F. (eds.) SFM-RT 2004. LNCS, vol. 3185, pp. 200–236. Springer, Heidelberg (2004). doi:10.1007/978-3-540-30080-9_7
5. Beneš, N., Křetínský, J., Larsen, K.G., Møller, M.H., Srba, J.: Parametric modal transition systems. In: Bultan, T., Hsiung, P.-A. (eds.) ATVA 2011. LNCS, vol. 6996, pp. 275–289. Springer, Heidelberg (2011). doi:10.1007/978-3-642-24372-1_20
6. Bodden, E., Tolêdo, T., Ribeiro, M., Brabrand, C., Borba, P., Mezini, M.: SPLLIFT: statically analyzing software product lines in minutes instead of years. In: ACM SIGPLAN Conference on PLDI 2013, pp. 355–364 (2013)
7. Brabrand, C., Ribeiro, M., Tolêdo, T., Winther, J., Borba, P.: Intraprocedural dataflow analysis for software product lines. In: Leavens, G.T., Chiba, S., Tanter, É. (eds.) Transactions on Aspect-Oriented Software Development X. LNCS, vol. 7800, pp. 73–108. Springer, Heidelberg (2013). doi:10.1007/978-3-642-36964-3_3
8. Čerāns, K., Godskesen, J.C., Larsen, K.G.: Timed modal specification - Theory and tools. In: Courcoubetis, C. (ed.) CAV 1993. LNCS, vol. 697, pp. 253–267. Springer, Heidelberg (1993). doi:10.1007/3-540-56922-7_21
9. Classen, A., Boucher, Q., Heymans, P.: A text-based approach to feature modelling: syntax and semantics of TVL. Sci. Comput. Program. 76(12), 1130–1143 (2011). http://dx.doi.org/10.1016/j.scico.2010.10.005
10. Classen, A., Cordy, M., Heymans, P., Legay, A., Schobbens, P.: Model checking software product lines with SNIP. STTT 14(5), 589–612 (2012). http://dx.doi.org/10.1007/s10009-012-0234-1
11. Classen, A., Cordy, M., Schobbens, P., Heymans, P., Legay, A., Raskin, J.: Featured transition systems: foundations for verifying variability-intensive systems and their application to LTL model checking. IEEE Trans. Softw. Eng. 39(8), 1069–1089 (2013). http://doi.ieeecomputersociety.org/10.1109/TSE.2012.86
12. Cordy, M., Classen, A., Heymans, P., Schobbens, P., Legay, A.: Provelines: a product line of verifiers for software product lines. In: 17th International Software Product Line Conference Co-located Workshops, SPLC 2013 Workshops, pp. 141–146. ACM (2013). http://doi.acm.org/10.1145/2499777.2499781
13. Cordy, M., Schobbens, P., Heymans, P., Legay, A.: Behavioural modelling and verification of real-time software product lines. In: 16th International Software Product Line Conference, SPLC 2012, vol. 1, pp. 66–75. ACM (2012). http://doi.acm.org/10.1145/2362536.2362549
14. Czarnecki, K., Antkiewicz, M.: Mapping features to models: a template approach based on superimposed variants. In: Glück, R., Lowry, M. (eds.) GPCE 2005. LNCS, vol. 3676, pp. 422–437. Springer, Heidelberg (2005). doi:10.1007/11561347_28
15. Dimovski, A., Brabrand, C., Wąsowski, A.: Variability abstractions: trading precision for speed in family-based analyses. In: 29th European Conference on Object-Oriented Programming ECOOP 2015. LIPIcs, vol. 37, pp. 247–270. Schloss Dagstuhl - Leibniz-Zentrum fuer Informatik (2015)
16. Dimovski, A.S.: Program verification using symbolic game semantics. Theor. Comput. Sci. 560, 364–379 (2014). http://dx.doi.org/10.1016/j.tcs.2014.01.016
17. Dimovski, A.S.: Symbolic game semantics for model checking program families. In: Bošnački, D., Wijs, A. (eds.) SPIN 2016. LNCS, vol. 9641, pp. 19–37. Springer, Cham (2016). doi:10.1007/978-3-319-32582-8_2
18. Dimovski, A.S., Al-Sibahi, A.S., Brabrand, C., Wąsowski, A.: Family-based model checking without a family-based model checker. In: Fischer, B., Geldenhuys, J. (eds.) SPIN 2015. LNCS, vol. 9232, pp. 282–299. Springer, Cham (2015). doi:10.1007/978-3-319-23404-5_18

19. Dimovski, A.S., Al-Sibahi, A.S., Brabrand, C., Wasowski, A.: Efficient family-based model checking via variability abstractions. In: STTT, pp. 1–19 (2016)
20. Dimovski, A.S., Brabrand, C., Wąsowski, A.: Finding suitable variability abstractions for family-based analysis. In: Fitzgerald, J., Heitmeyer, C., Gnesi, S., Philippou, A. (eds.) FM 2016. LNCS, vol. 9995, pp. 217–234. Springer, Cham (2016). doi:10.1007/978-3-319-48989-6_14
21. Dimovski, A.S., Wąsowski, A.: Variability-specific abstraction refinement for family-based model checking. In: Huisman, M., Rubin, J. (eds.) FASE 2017. LNCS, vol. 10202, pp. 406–423. Springer, Heidelberg (2017). doi:10.1007/978-3-662-54494-5_24
22. Gazzillo, P., Grimm, R.: SuperC: parsing all of C by taming the preprocessor. In: ACM SIGPLAN Conference on Programming Language Design and Implementation, PLDI 2012, pp. 323–334. ACM (2012). http://doi.acm.org/10.1145/2254064.2254103
23. Iosif-Lazar, A.F., Melo, J., Dimovski, A.S., Brabrand, C., Wasowski, A.: Effective analysis of C programs by rewriting variability. In: The Art, Science, and Engineering of Programming, Programming 2017, vol. 1, no. 1, pp. 1–25 (2017)
24. Kästner, C., Apel, S., Thüm, T., Saake, G.: Type checking annotation-based product lines. ACM Trans. Softw. Eng. Methodol. 21(3), 14 (2012)
25. Kästner, C., Giarrusso, P.G., Rendel, T., Erdweg, S., Ostermann, K., Berger, T.: Variability-aware parsing in the presence of lexical macros and conditional compilation. In: OOPSLA 2011, pp. 805–824. ACM, Portland (2011)
26. Larsen, K.G.: Context-dependent bisimulation between processes. Ph.D. thesis, University of Edinburgh, UK, May 1986
27. Larsen, K.G., Nyman, U., Wąsowski, A.: Modal I/O automata for interface and product line theories. In: Nicola, R. (ed.) ESOP 2007. LNCS, vol. 4421, pp. 64–79. Springer, Heidelberg (2007). doi:10.1007/978-3-540-71316-6_6
28. Larsen, K.G., Nyman, U., Wasowski, A.: Modeling software product lines using color-blind transition systems. STTT 9(5–6), 471–487 (2007)
29. Larsen, K.G., Pettersson, P., Yi, W.: UPPAAL in a nutshell. STTT 1(1–2), 134–152 (1997). http://dx.doi.org/10.1007/s100090050010
30. Larsen, K.G., Thomsen, B.: A modal process logic. In: Proceedings of the Third Annual Symposium on Logic in Computer Science (LICS 1988), pp. 203–210. IEEE Computer Society (1988). http://dx.doi.org/10.1109/LICS.1988.5119
31. Midtgaard, J., Dimovski, A.S., Brabrand, C., Wąsowski, A.: Systematic derivation of correct variability-aware program analyses. Sci. Comput. Program. 105, 145–170 (2015). http://dx.doi.org/10.1016/j.scico.2015.04.005
32. Minsky, M.: Computation: Finite and Infinite Machines. Prentice Hall, Princeton (1967)
33. von Rhein, A., Thüm, T., Schaefer, I., Liebig, J., Apel, S.: Variability encoding: from compile-time to load-time variability. J. Log. Algebr. Meth. Program. 85(1), 125–145 (2016)
34. Yi, W., Pettersson, P., Daniels, M.: Automatic verification of real-time communicating systems by constraint-solving. In: Formal Description Techniques VII, Proceedings of the 7th IFIP WG6.1 International Conference on Formal Description Techniques, IFIP Conference Proceedings, vol. 6, pp. 243–258. Chapman & Hall (1994)

Firm Deadline Checking of Safety-Critical Java Applications with Statistical Model Checking

Anders P. Ravn[1(✉)], Bent Thomsen[1], Kasper Søe Luckow[2], Lone Leth[1], and Thomas Bøgholm[1]

[1] Department of Computer Science, Aalborg University, Aalborg, Denmark
apr@cs.aau.dk
[2] Carnegie Mellon University, Silicon Valley, NASA Ames,
Mountain View, USA

Abstract. In cyber-physical applications many programs have hard real-time constraints that have to be stringently validated. In some applications, there are programs that have hard deadlines, which must not be violated. Other programs have soft deadlines where the value of the response decreases when the deadline is passed although it is still a valid response. In between, there are programs with firm deadlines. Here the response may be occasionally delayed; but this should not happen too often or with too large an overshoot. This paper presents an extension to an existing approach and tool for checking hard deadline constraints to the case of firm deadlines for application programs written in Safety-Critical Java (SCJ). The existing approach uses models and model checking with the Uppaal toolset; the extension uses the statistical model checking features of Uppaal-smc to provide a hold on firm deadlines and performance in the case of soft deadlines. The extended approach is illustrated with examples from applications.

1 Introduction

Real-time programs are typically embedded in cyber-physical systems, and consist of a number of logically concurrently executing tasks. Each task is typically released periodically or when certain external or internal events occur. The result of the computation during each release typically ends up in updating directly or indirectly the state of the cyber-physical system through actuators. For a popular illustration, just consider the software of an autonomous vehicle. It is evident that the system as a whole may enter undesirable physical states if the internally computed state deviates too much from the external system state. For the physical state it is very reasonable to assume that it changes little within a short time period, thus the correspondence of the internal state can be assured when computations are completed within a specified time. This is realised by computations having *deadlines* for each release. Clearly, the deadlines vary for different tasks. Think of an ABS-brake versus a cruise-control, they operate at different time scales.

© Springer International Publishing AG 2017
L. Aceto et al. (Eds.): Larsen Festschrift, LNCS 10460, pp. 269–288, 2017.
DOI: 10.1007/978-3-319-63121-9_14

For any real-time application it is crucial to check that deadlines for the various tasks are satisfied. Thus the topic *schedulability analysis* has been investigated for decades, and many important results have emerged. The primary focus has been on *hard deadlines*, where the aim is to guarantee that the deadlines are met under all circumstances. Established techniques, see e.g. [8], separate the analysis into determining a Worst Case Execution Time (*WCET*) for each task, and then analyse, for a collection of tasks, their *schedulability* under a given scheduling regime. WCET analysis has to be conservative, for instance use upper bounds for loops, and expect cache and pipeline flows to be interrupted during execution. Also, schedulability analysis relies on over-approximations of control flow, for instance in inter-task synchronisation and for multi-core systems, known techniques do not readily apply [14].

For real-time systems developed in Java, the mentioned conservatism can be even higher. This is partly due to the fact that Java is object-oriented, but also due to the fact that Java usually is implemented via a translation to Java Bytecode, which is then either interpreted by a Java Virtual Machine (JVM) or further translated to native code. This level of indirection complicates formal analysis as both program and JVM implementation have to be taken into account for a given hardware platform.

To accommodate these issues, we have developed an open-source tool called TETASARTS[1]. It was introduced at the Workshop on Java Technologies for Real-time and Embedded Systems 2013 (JTRES'13) [28]. It analyses real-time programs that conform to the upcoming Safety-Critical Java profile (*SCJ*) [26]. In the tool, the tasks are modelled with exact release patterns, interleavings, and synchronisation. Also, the tool has a pluggable platform model with details of caching and pipelining. Thus less pessimistic schedulability analysis can be conducted.

The tool uses a model-based approach inspired by the TIMES [1], SARTS [6] and TetaJ [16] tools. TETASARTS can be viewed as an optimising compiler that produces a model of the system amenable to model checking using UPPAAL [3,22], given the program source as input. The model is constructed such that model checking simulates an abstract execution of the real-time tasks, taking into account the exact execution environment and scheduling policy.

However, hard deadlines are often too strict a requirement in practice. For many control applications, transient violations of their deadlines are acceptable; they can be interpreted as the usual disturbances that occur due to ignored physical impacts in the control laws. Thus the concept of a *firm deadline* arises. It is a deadline which should be satisfied most of the time. In order to make this operational, a stochastic formulation is useful. A firm deadline is satisfied when the deadline can be assumed to be satisfied for some proportion of releases, see for instance the paper by Liu [25] for more details. As a simple example, if the deadline is satisfied for 95% of the releases and the variation in execution time occurs independently for each release, then the probability of violation for more than a succession of 10 releases is in the order of 10^{-6} which is an acceptable failure rate for many systems. Thus, there are good reasons to study such applications.

---

[1] The tool can be obtained at http://people.cs.aau.dk/~boegholm/tetasarts/.

Since the developed tool is using the UPPAAL toolset with engines for Statistical Model Checking UPPAAL-SMC [11,12], we have extended it to analyse features like firm deadlines as well as other quality of service or performance properties related to the *expected* (timing) behaviour of the analysed system. These are expressed in terms of probabilistic quantitative guarantees that may be useful for *soft deadlines*, where the deadline is essentially a decreasing value function of the execution time.

This paper presents this result as follows: in Sect. 2, we present related work followed by Sect. 3, which discusses our overall SCJ related framework. Section 4 is a discussion of the merits of the model checking approach compared to traditional approaches for schedulability analysis. The design of the TETASARTS tool is summarised in Sect. 5. Section 6 introduces the new extension to TETASARTS that uses statistical model checking. Section 7 presents the evaluation of the extended TETASARTS showing its applicability for the use of statistical techniques to gather refined performance properties for systems understanding and for finding concrete counter examples that disprove schedulability. Section 8 presents the conclusion.

2   Related Work

For analysing timing properties of systems, the traditional methods for schedulability analysis include response time analysis [8]: For each task, the response time is calculated, and the system is schedulable if the response times for the tasks are less than their respective deadlines. Tools and techniques based on the traditional method tend to be rather conservative. In general, response time analysis is based on a coarse, control-flow insensitive model. Hence, it cannot account for the release patterns of sporadic tasks which are regarded as periodic with a period set to the minimum inter-arrival time. Yet, it is a mature method, as an example, the RapidRMA [19] tool can be used for conducting response time analysis.

Also, the required WCET analysis is difficult, when it has to include detailed information about the underlying hardware, such as caching and pipelines. Even if the WCET analysis takes into account the state of the cache during the execution of a task, the improved WCET result may not be useful for response time analysis, since the result of the WCET analysis assumes the analysed code to be executed in isolation, i.e. without being interrupted, and thereby have its cache state invalidated by other tasks. That benefits can be had by tighter modelling of a platform is evident, an influential early example is by Zhang et al. [37]. For a survey of results and challenges, many of which remain, see [35].

The TIMES [1] tool presents a model-based, control-flow sensitive technique for schedulability analysis in which a specification for the real-time system is built as a set of tasks modeling their timing properties e.g. cost, dependencies, and deadlines. Supplementary code can be provided. This results in an NTA model which is checked using the UPPAAL [3] model checker. TIMES does not perform timing analysis of the code associated with the tasks, which must be performed using external WCET analysis tools such as aiT [15], METAMOC [10], WCET Analyzer (WCA) [33] or TetaJ [16]. The aiT and METAMOC tools are targeted at timing analysis of C-programs and use respectively a combination of abstract interpretation and integer linear programming, and model checking. For Java, either WCA or TetaJ can be used. WCA makes available two techniques for timing analysis; model checking and Implicit Path Enumeration [24]. WCA, however, is targeted at the JOP [30], a JVM implementation in hardware. For dedicated schedulability analysis of Java programs, SARTS [6] can be used which also employs a model-based technique itself inspired from TIMES.

Firm deadlines have been studied less intensively, although the paper by Bernat et al. [4] gives a firm foundation. It is however extending classical scheduling analysis, so WCET is still needed. A stochastic approach to WCET analysis using extreme value statistical theory is demonstrated by Hansen et al. [17]. Yet, it turns out that a purely statistical approach, where measurements are collected from executing the task on a given platform, shows little promise of success, because a huge amount of measurements have to be used. This is probably due to the fact that the system under observation is regarded as a black box, so internal structure cannot be used to constrain the search. First with Statistical Model Checking (SMC)[20, 23, 34, 36], where modelling and statistical analysis come together, there may be a way forward. It is interesting to note that in more recent work, SMC is used for the even more intricate problem of distributed real-time systems [21].

3   Real-Time Programming Model

Safety-critical applications have different complexity levels. To cater for this the SCJ programming model is based on tasks grouped in missions, where a mission encapsulates a specific functionality or phase in the lifetime of the real-time system as a set of schedulable entities. The SCJ specification lets developers tailor the capabilities of the platform to the needs of the application through three compliance levels. Level 0, provides a simple, frame-based cyclic executive model which is single threaded with a single mission. Level 1 extends this model with multi-threading via periodic and aperiodic event handlers, multiple missions, and a fixed-priority preemptive scheduler (FPS). Level 2 lifts restrictions on threads and supports nested missions. The development of SCJ applications at Level 0 is well described in [32]. We will focus on Level 1 and review some important areas and concepts of the SCJ programming model that are particularly relevant to our work.

Missions. A mission is used for capturing a phase during the lifetime of the system: Each phase contains a set of schedulable entities that collectively fulfills the tasks of the phase. A schedulable entity encapsulates a specific functionality, and has assigned certain temporal parameters, notably the temporal scope describing its release time and deadline. In addition, a release pattern is also attached which can be either periodic or aperiodic.

The classic example for illustrating the mission concept, is that of flight-control system: during the lifetime of such a system it goes through states corresponding to when the aircraft is taking off, cruising, and landing. Each of states are encapsulated in their own dedicated mission. A mission encapsulates a specific functionality or phase in the lifetime of the real-time system as a set of schedulable entities. For instance, a flight-control system may be composed of take-off, cruising, and landing each of which can be assigned a dedicated mission.

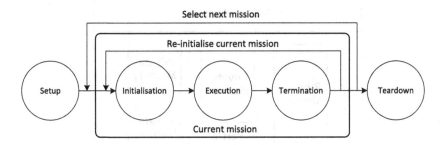

Fig. 1. Overview of the concept of missions [27].

The concept of missions is illustrated in Fig. 1; it contains five phases:

Setup. In this phase, mission objects are allocated when the system starts. Tasks of this phase are not time-critical.

Initialisation. Here all object allocations that pertain to the operations of the mission (or the application) are performed. This phase is time-critical in applications with mode changes consisting of a sequence of missions.

Execution. This is the phase in which the entire application logic is executed and schedulable entities are set for execution governed by a pre-emptive priority scheduler. This phase is considered time-critical.

Termination. This phase will be entered if the mission terminates and will be used for completing execution the schedulable entities of the mission. In addition, this phase is used for executing logic pertaining to the cleanup of the mission. When this phase completes, the mission may either be restarted, a new mission is selected, or the final phase, Teardown, is entered. This phase is time-critical in applications with mode changes consisting of a sequence of missions.

Teardown. This is the final phase of the application and is used for performing proper cleanup of objects, locks etc. For example, certain application-wide objects are deallocated at this point. This phase is not time-critical.

To govern the order with which missions are selected, a *mission sequencer* is used.

Memory Model. The memory model of SCJ is based on the concept of *scoped memory* from RTSJ [7]. It is a memory model that avoids the use of a (garbage collected) heap which eases the task of verifying temporal properties of SCJ applications. An overview of the SCJ memory model is shown in Fig. 2, which has three levels of memories;

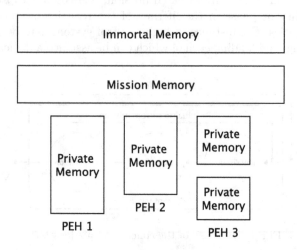

Fig. 2. The memory model in SCJ [27].

Private memory which is associated with each real-time event handler. The private memory exists for the entire duration of the handler. Upon task finish, the memory area is reset.

Mission memory is associated with every mission of the system and manages the memories of all real-time handlers part of the mission as well as objects that are shared among the handlers. When the mission completes execution, the mission memory is reset.

Immortal memory is the memory area that exists for the lifetime of the system.

Dynamic class loading is not part of the SCJ specification, which would greatly complicate timing analysis if classes were to, e.g., be loaded over a network connection. Furthermore, the SCJ specification prescribes that finalizers will not be executed.

We make the reasonable assumption that Java Bytecode verification is done before a time-critical phase. Finalizers can however be accommodated; not by SCJ, but the Predictable Java profile [5] (a Java profile for hard real-time systems) has support for finalizers. As shown in [9] timing analysis is possible when finalizers are used with this profile.

4   Merits of Model-Checking Approach

The primary functionality of TETASARTS is schedulability analysis, which takes into account the scheduling policy and task interactions. In this section we illustrate how the presented model-checking approach may give tighter results than traditional Response-time analyses based on plain WCET and blocking times. We consider two examples:

- Branching involving sporadic tasks.
- Blocking involving access to shared resources.

These examples are indeed very simple in nature, but the effect illustrated could be significant in larger systems involving multiple tasks. To illustrate the difference between the methods, we use the timeline notation in Fig. 3. In our illustrations execution time is expressed as *time units* as opposed to actual execution times in clock cycles or similar, and we assume fixed-priority preemptive scheduling with priority ceiling protocol. We will compare our results to the traditional approaches, and begin this by a short introduction to the traditional response time analysis method [8].

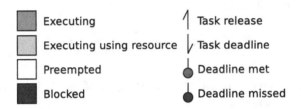

Fig. 3. Timeline notation used for task-illustration.

4.1 Response-Time Analysis

In the response time analysis, the response time is calculated for each task in the system, and the system is schedulable if the response time for each task is less than its respective deadline. Sporadic tasks can be included as periodic tasks with period set to the minimum inter-arrival time. The blocking time is calculated based on priority inversion avoidance protocols, priority inheritance or priority ceiling. In our example, only the priority ceiling protocol is considered.

For a set of tasks, $\{task_1, \ldots, task_n\}$, each with static priority according to deadline monotonic priority assignment[2] the response time analysis of $task_i$, R_i is given by the equation:

$$R_i = C_i + B_i + I_i \tag{1}$$

where

- C_i is the execution time of $task_i$,
- B_i is the maximum blocking time of $task_i$. This is dependent on the protocol used for priority inversion avoidance.

---

[2] In case of identical deadlines, one can safely arbitrarily assign different priorities, as long as these do not violate the priority of other tasks.

- The maximum blocking time for $task_i$ using the priority ceiling protocol is given by:

$$B_i = \max_{r \in R} (usage(i,r)WCET_r) \qquad (2)$$

where R is a set of resources, $WCET_r$ is the WCET of the critical sections involving resource r, and $usage(i,r)$ evaluates to 1 if resource r is used by a task with lower priority than $task_i$ and used by a task with priority higher than or equal to the priority of $task_i$; 0 otherwise,
- and I_i is the maximum interruption time of $task_i$ by tasks of higher priority, given by the equation

$$I_i = \sum_{j \in hp(i)} \left\lceil \frac{R_i}{T_j} \right\rceil C_j \qquad (3)$$

where $hp(i)$ is the set of tasks of higher priority than task i and T_i is the period of $task_i$.

This gives the recursion:

$$R_i^{n+1} = C_i + B_i + \sum_{j \in hp(i)} \left\lceil \frac{R_i^n}{T_j} \right\rceil C_j \qquad (4)$$

for which a fixed-point solution, $R_i^{n+1} = R_i^n$ with $R_i^0 = C_i$, is guaranteed if the utilization is less than 1 [2].

4.2   Conditional Sporadic-Release

In this example, we illustrate how two sporadic tasks running mutually exclusive are analysed in our approach and the traditional approach. Consider the periodic task, $PTask$ with

- Total cost: 4
- Period: 10
- Deadline: 5

and the implementation given by:

```
protected boolean run(){
    // read sensors/compute
    if(<condition>){
        sporadic1.fire();
    } else {
        sporadic2.fire();
    }
    return true;
}
```

And two sporadic tasks, $Spo.\ 1$ and $Spo.\ 2$, with identical characteristics, except for deadlines which are 6 and 7 for the respectively:

- Total cost: 2

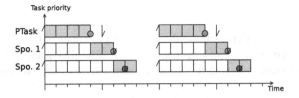

Fig. 4. Timeline considered in the response time analysis.

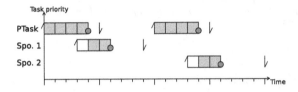

Fig. 5. Real timeline as expressed by the system

- Min. inter-arrival time: 10
- Deadline: 6 and 7

and trivial implementations.

Using the traditional response time analysis, the system is deemed not-schedulable, as the response time of task *Spo. 2* is 8, which exceeds the deadline, which for this task is 7:

$$(PTask)\ R_1^0 = 4 \quad R_1^1 = 4 \quad R_1^2 = 4 \quad = 4$$

$$(Spo.1)\ R_2^0 = 2 \quad R_2^1 = 2 + \underbrace{\left\lceil \frac{2}{10} \right\rceil 4}_{4} \quad R_2^2 = 2 + \underbrace{\left\lceil \frac{6}{10} \right\rceil 4}_{4} \quad = 6$$

$$(Spo.2)\ R_3^0 = 2 \quad R_3^1 = 2 + \underbrace{\left\lceil \frac{2}{10} \right\rceil 4}_{4} + \underbrace{\left\lceil \frac{2}{10} \right\rceil 2}_{2} \quad R_3^2 = 2 + \underbrace{\left\lceil \frac{8}{10} \right\rceil 4}_{4} + \underbrace{\left\lceil \frac{8}{10} \right\rceil 2}_{2} \quad = 8$$

The system execution considered in the response time analysis could be illustrated by the timeline in Fig. 4, in which the utilization is seemingly 80%. It is clear, however, that this does not correspond to an actual execution of the system since the two sporadic tasks are mutually exclusive.

In any execution of the tasks, the utilization would be only 60%, as seen in Fig. 5, and additionally, it is clear from the figure, that the system is indeed schedulable. The strength of the presented approach is, that in this case, it is the actual execution displayed in Fig. 5, which is analysed. The more precise analysis would yield the utilization of 60% and possibly allow the addition of extra tasks or even to use a cheaper or more energy efficient(and slower) CPU. By manually inspecting the system, one could adjust their analysis according to such patterns. However, as this requires manual work and intricate knowledge about the system, one might end up with an unsafe result, especially in later development cycles.

4.3   Blocking

In this example, we illustrate how blocking is handled in our approach and how it compares to the traditional approach to schedulability analysis. We consider a system of two tasks, sharing a common resource, given by the code:

```
// Task1
// Period   : 9
// Deadline: 4
protected boolean run(){
    calc();      // one time unit
    critical(); // two time units, using shared resource
    return true;
}

// Task2
// Period: 18
// Deadline: 17
protected boolean run(){
    if(<condition>)  // one time unit
      extra_calc();  // seven time units
    critical();      // two time units, using shared resource
    calc();          // one time unit
    return true;
}
```

In this example, using the response time analysis we would determine this system as *not schedulable*, since *Task1* might be blocked for up to two time units, completing execution five time units after its release, missing its deadline. The calculated response time is as follows:

The worst case blocking times experienced by the tasks B_1 and B_2 are, calculated using the method described above, as follows:

$$B_1 = 1 * 2 = 2$$
$$B_2 = 0 * 2 = 0$$

And then the response time calculations are as follows:

$$R_1^0 = \quad 3 \quad R_1^1 \quad = 3 + 2 \qquad\qquad R_1^2 = \qquad\qquad 3 + 2 = \quad 5$$
$$R_2^0 = \quad 11 \quad R_2^1 \quad = 11 + 0 + \underbrace{\left\lceil \frac{11}{9} \right\rceil 3}_{6} \qquad R_2^2 = \quad 11 + 0 + \underbrace{\left\lceil \frac{17}{9} \right\rceil 3}_{6} = \quad 17$$

Using the response-time analysis, the system is *not schedulable*, which is illustrated graphically in Fig. 6. The illustration depicts the time-line from the *critical instant*, from a classical response-time analysis perspective. $Task_1$ is blocked for 2 units and then needs to execute for 3 units, missing its deadline. $Task_2$ is pre-empted for 6 time units, and then needs 11 time units of execution time, before it meets its deadline.

The actual execution pattern for the tasks, and the execution pattern also considered using the presented approach, is illustrated in Fig. 7. It is clear from the time line, that the system is actually schedulable because of the actual interaction with the shared resource.

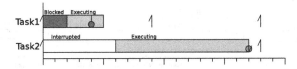

Fig. 6. Illustration of time-line for $Task_1$ and $Task_2$, as considered in the response time analysis; a depiction of the analysis rather than the actual execution pattern.

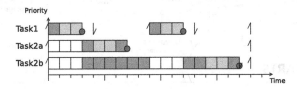

Fig. 7. Actual time-line for $Task_1$ and $Task_2$. Here, **Task2a** and **Task2b** illustrates the two different execution patterns of $Task_2$ caused its branch.

5   TETASARTS Architecture

TETASARTS employs a model checking approach for its timing analyses. In this approach, both the application classes constituting the real-time systems as well as the underlying JVM implementation are transformed into individual Networks of Timed Automata (NTA); the modeling formalism of UPPAAL. These models, capturing the timing behavior of their respective component, are then combined with proper models of the underlying hardware of the system. The composition of these models is then used for checking properties with UPPAAL.

TETASARTS performs the translation of the application classes and the JVM into NTAs in an automated way. A benefit of this approach is that the produced models have a tight correspondence with the actual code that is run by the system. We note that the translation process is fairly fast—usually taking less than a minute—hence being applicable for, e.g., an agile development process where timing properties are analyzed frequently to test how changes affect them.

Figure 8 shows an overview of the architecture of TETASARTS.

TETASARTS takes as input the class files (i.e., Java Bytecode) of the real-time system, and transforms the tasks into an TETASARTS Intermediate Representation (TIR), a CFG-based representation annotated with additional details. TIR is used for performing various static analyses like loop identification analysis which is used for retrieving loop bounds. Loop bounds are currently specified manually using annotations in the source code. TETASARTS will extract the bounds, and annotate the corresponding loops in TIR with this information.

TETASARTS currently disallows recursion, despite being permitted by the current version of the SCJ specification. However, we note that usually, recursion is avoided in real-time systems, since it complicates memory analysis [26].

After generating TIR, TETASARTS proceeds to the next phase where a high-level translation to NTA is performed from the TIR. We refer to the resulting

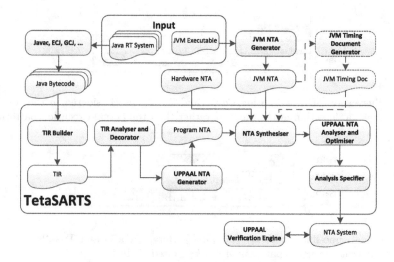

Fig. 8. The components of TETASARTS.

NTA as the *Program NTA*. Provided a hardware model (referred to as the *Hardware NTA* and information about the temporal behavior of the JVM (see below), the two NTAs are synthesised into a single NTA that is amenable to model checking of temporal properties such as schedulability.

The temporal behavior of the JVM can be provided in two ways: either a precise model of the JVM in the form of an NTA (similar to the *Program NTA*) that captures the control-flow of the individual bytecode instructions; or from a so-called *JVM Timing Doc* that draws similarities with VMTMs [18]. A *JVM Timing Doc* captures the Best Case Execution Time (BCET) and WCET of the Java Bytecode implementations as obtained by an auxiliary tool: *JVM Timing Document Generator* that for each Java Bytecode implementation, generates an NTA (similar to how the *Program NTA* is constructed) and then checks for properties that yield the BCET and WCET.

Thus, the *JVM Timing Doc* is the less precise alternative to using the explicit model of the *JVM NTA* at the benefit that the state space is significantly reduced. The reader is referred to [16,28,29] for more information about the *JVM NTA*.

6   Performance Analysis

In this section, we introduce the extension to TETASARTS that allows analysing performance properties of the SCJ system as well as for finding concrete traces for, e.g., *disproving* schedulability. Our approach is inspired by the work of [13,31] with the difference that our approach applies to a model generated from the actual source code of the system thus having a tight correspondence with the evolving development process as opposed to a manually encoded architecture and design of the system. The enabling technology is Statistical Model Checking, a technique that relies on monitoring a series of randomly generated runs and applying statistical algorithms on the results for estimating property satisfaction. An SMC engine, UPPAAL-SMC, has recently been integrated into the toolset of UPPAAL, which analyses NPTAs [11] (a generalization of NTA where clocks can evolve with different rates in different locations) under a stochastic semantics, which, informally, is defined by associating to each location a delay density function and an output probability function. The former will be either a uniform distribution or an exponential distribution (with an additional distribution rate component) depending on whether the delay is bounded or not. The output probability function will be the uniform distribution over the possible outputs in that location.

UPPAAL-SMC generates random runs corresponding to the stochastic semantics up to a certain bound (thus we are considering finite runs), which may be defined, e.g., in terms of discrete steps or a clock value of a specified clock present in the model. In this work, we assume that data-dependent choices as generated by, e.g., the conditional instructions, are resolved according to a uniform distribution. However, a refined system model that takes into account domain/expert knowledge of the data-choices can be embedded in the model as well by adding weights i.e. probabilities (a feature of UPPAAL-SMC) to the choices accordingly.

While generating the run, UPPAAL-SMC monitors the checked properties, and based on the results applies a statistical algorithm. These permit to answer questions of the type:

- Qualitative: is the probability of satisfying a property (within the specified bound) greater or equal to a certain threshold? This problem is formulated as a hypothesis testing problem and solved using Wald's sequential hypothesis test.
- Quantitative: what is the probability for satisfying the property? In this case, the algorithm, based on the Chernoff-Hoeffding bound, computes the number of runs required to produce an interval, $[p-\epsilon, p+\epsilon]$, for satisfying the property with probability p with confidence $1 - \alpha$.
- Comparative: is the probability of satisfying a property greater or equal to the probability of satisfying another property? This check relies on an extension to the sequential hypothesis test that compares the probabilities without computing them.

Furthermore, UPPAAL-SMC supports evaluating the expected values of the minimum and maximum of, e.g., clock variables.

Naturally, SMC cannot be used for providing hard guarantees of correctness, but it can be seen as a complementary technique because it can be used for disproving schedulability, since it relies on analysing concrete traces. SMC can be seen as the dual of symbolic model checking, which can provide hard guarantees on schedulability but may possibly be inconclusive in disproving schedulability as a consequence of over-approximation.

Enabling the NTA model to be used for statistical model checking requires only minor modifications. We use stop-watch expressions in all locations of the Program NTA to capture pre-emption thus, from a static point of view, the delay is unbounded meaning that the delay density function is defined by an exponential distribution with rate component, $R(l)$ for location l. Essentially it means that a delay will be picked from an exponential distribution and added *after* an outgoing edge of a location becomes enabled.

This is clearly not what we want; instead we want the edge to be immediately taken when it is enabled. We can obtain this behaviour by using a sufficiently high rate component which will be defined as a constant and used throughout the entire model. In the limit of $R(l)$, the delay will become zero, thus giving us the desired behaviour.

7 Evaluation

We will demonstrate the uses of the performance analysis extension of TETASARTS using the Real-Time Sorting Machine (RTSM) [6] example.

As an initial result, we harness the *simulate* query extension to the UPPAAL specification language. These can be used to visualise the value of an expression as a function of time (or discrete steps) and we will use this feature to visualise the behaviour of the tasks by plotting their state as function of time thus resembling the conventional time-line notation [8]. Figure 9 shows the states of the four tasks of the RTSM with the clock frequency set at 100 MHz. The query used here is

$$simulate\ 1\ [\# <= 150]\{running[PT_1] - 2 * blocked[PT_1],$$
$$running[PT_2] - 2 * blocked[PT_2] + 2,$$
$$running[ST_1] - 2 * blocked[ST_1] + 4,$$
$$running[ST_2] - 2 * blocked[ST_2] + 6\}$$

$PT_\#$ and $ST_\#$ where $\# \in \{1, 2\}$ denote the ID of respectively the periodic tasks and sporadic tasks of the RTSM. Peaks represent that the respective task is running. The example also demonstrates that in the particular run, none of the tasks were blocked.

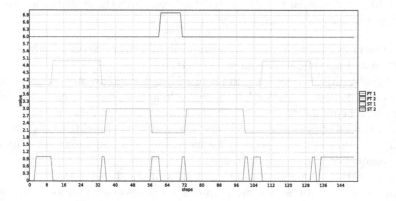

Fig. 9. Task behaviour over time for the RTSM at 60 MHz.

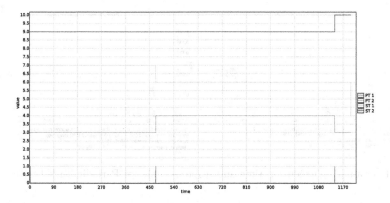

Fig. 10. Task behaviour over time for the RTSM at 1 MHz. Sporadic Task 1 is released, but misses its deadline.

Using simulate queries, we also get the possibility of providing concrete witnesses to non-schedulability; a feature that is not possible with regular, symbolic model checking due to over-approximation. To demonstrate this, let us revisit the RTSM on the JOP with clock frequency set to 1 MHz and VTA used for devirtualisation for which symbolic model checking was inconclusive as to the schedulability of the system [28]. Using simulate queries, it turns out, that in fact schedules exist for which the system *is* schedulable and we will therefore expand our query to keep sampling possible behaviours and return a counter example to schedulability (in case it exists). Our new query is:

$$simulate\ 1000\ [<=4000]\{running[PT_1] - 2 * error[PT_1],$$
$$running[PT_2] - 2 * error[PT_2] + 2,$$
$$running[ST_1] - 2 * error[ST_1] + 4,$$
$$running[ST_2] - 2 * error[ST_2] + 6\}$$
$$:\ 1\ :\ error[PT_1]\ ||\ error[PT_2]\ ||\ error[ST_1]\ ||\ error[ST_2]$$

The new query uses a filter to filter out a single run for which at least one of the error flags of the tasks have been set (signalling deadline violation). After 12 simulations of system behaviours (which takes a couple of seconds), UPPAAL returns the example shown in Fig. 10 which disproves that the RTSM at 1 MHz (using VTA for devirtualisation) is schedulable because Sporadic Task 1 misses its deadline.

Another feature of the combination of SMC and our timing model, is that we can estimate performance properties of the system as well as estimating the likelihood of timing events. Having shown that the RTSM at 1 MHz is not schedulable, we can now try to quantify the likelihood of this event happening, thus giving us refined information about system behaviour. The probability estimation extension to the query language allows us to answer these questions and we will formulate this property as

$$Pr[<= 5000]\ (<> error[ST_1])$$

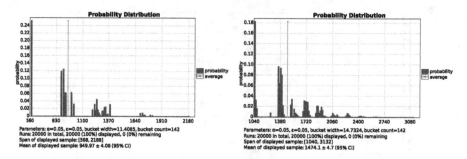

Fig. 11. Evaluating execution time and response time for Periodic Task 1 with 20.000 samples.

i.e. we are asking what the probability is for a run to reach a state where the error[ST₁] flag is set within 5000 time units (note that the task misses its deadline much earlier according to Fig. 10). UPPAAL settles this query after 287 runs (taking a second to perform) and the result is [0.1794, 0.2793] with the confidence parameter set to 95%. Note that UPPAAL returns an interval which is a consequence of the approximation procedure. Also note that the lower bound is strictly greater than zero, thus again confirming that the system is not schedulable.

Let us now focus on the second use of statistical model checking to estimate the expected performance of the system. UPPAAL allows us to estimate the maximum value of expressions including clocks. Thus, estimating the maximum value of the wcrt clock gives an estimate on the overall responsiveness of the respective task. Also, we could estimate the maximum value of the wcet clock which estimates the distribution of the execution times of the task. The query can be formulated as

$$E[<= bound; samples]\ (max : clock)$$

As an example, we estimate execution and response times of Periodic Task 1 of the RTSM on the JOP at 60 MHz for making a comparison with the exact analysis presented in [28]. For all results, we set a bound on the wcrt corresponding to their exact values obtained previously and we are interested in results for the 95% confidence interval. Furthermore, as an initial experiment, we ran the estimation procedure with 20.000 samples. In all cases the analysis times ranged from 16–17 s with a modest memory consumption of approximately 200 MB.

The results of this analysis are shown in Fig. 11.

Note that time is represented as clock cycles. Interestingly for Periodic Task 1, we exercise the behaviour of the system that yields the WCET (2.188 clock cycles corresponds to 36.5 μs) of the task whereas the maximum response time is found to be 52.2 μs (which is a 19% deviation from the exact result). The expected average execution time and response time for the 95% confidence interval are calculated to be 15.8 ± 0.068 μs and 24.6 ± 0.08 μs.

We can also get results more rapidly by decreasing the number of samples at the expense of loss of precision. Figure 12 shows the distributions of execution time and response time when decreasing the sample size to 1.000. The analyses

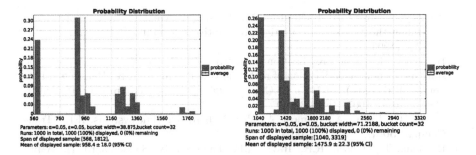

Fig. 12. Evaluating execution time and response time for Periodic Task 1 with 1000 samples.

take less than a second. The results for expected execution time and response time for the 95% confidence interval are $16.0 \pm 0.3\,\mu s$ and $24.6 \pm 0.4\,\mu s$.

8   Conclusion

This paper presented an extension of the TETASARTS schedulability analysis tool with Statistical Model Checking (SMC) facilities. The original tool focused on giving hard guarantees for Safety-Critical Java programs on specified platforms. The primary purpose of that tool is schedulability analysis, but it also facilitates processor utilisation and idle time analysis, Worst Case Execution Time analysis, Worst Case Blocking Time analysis, and Worst Case Response Time analysis taking into account any pre-emption and blocking. The extended tool provides probabilistic estimates of expected behaviour with user specified confidence levels. This addresses needs for analyzing real-time systems with firm or soft deadlines, or even mixed-criticality requirements. Expected behaviour is provided as distributions of the analysed property resulting from a sample-based approach. We envision this to be particularly useful for comprehending the dynamics of a system as well as for profiling and performance analysis.

We have shown on realistic real-time systems that such information can be obtained in a few seconds, thus TETASARTS is an efficient tool *during* real-time systems development. The combination of the timing analyses facilitates multiple development approaches; if a system is not schedulable, the other analyses can be used for debugging timing properties, e.g., revealing unusually high blocking times or WCET of real-time tasks. The statistical approach embedded in TETASARTS can find concrete witnesses disproving schedulability. The tool can even produce a timeline notation of task behaviour especially useful for understanding systems behaviour leading to a deadline violation.

References

1. Amnell, T., Fersman, E., Mokrushin, L., Pettersson, P., Yi, W.: TIMES: a tool for schedulability analysis and code generation of real-time systems. In: Larsen, K.G., Niebert, P. (eds.) FORMATS 2003. LNCS, vol. 2791, pp. 60–72. Springer, Heidelberg (2004). doi:10.1007/978-3-540-40903-8_6

2. Audsley, N., Burns, A., Richardson, M., Tindell, K., Wellings, A.J.: Applying new scheduling theory to static priority pre-emptive scheduling. Softw. Eng. J. 8(5), 284–292 (1993)
3. Bengtsson, J., Larsen, K., Larsson, F., Pettersson, P., Yi, W.: UPPAAL — a tool suite for automatic verification of real-time systems. In: Alur, R., Henzinger, T.A., Sontag, E.D. (eds.) HS 1995. LNCS, vol. 1066, pp. 232–243. Springer, Heidelberg (1996). doi:10.1007/BFb0020949
4. Bernat, G., Burns, A., Llamosí, A.: Weakly hard real-time systems. IEEE Trans. Comput. 50(4), 308–321 (2001)
5. Bøgholm, T., Hansen, R.R., Ravn, A.P., Thomsen, B., Søndergaard, H.: A predictable Java profile - rationale and implementations. In: Proceedings of the 7th International Workshop on Java Technologies for Real-Time and Embedded Systems, JTRES 2009, pp. 150–159 (2009)
6. Bøgholm, T., Kragh-Hansen, H., Olsen, P., Thomsen, B., Larsen, K.G.: Model-based schedulability analysis of safety critical hard real-time Java programs. In: Proceedings of the 6th International Workshop on Java Technologies for Real-time and Embedded Systems, JTRES 2008, pp. 106–114 (2008)
7. Bollella, G.: The Real-time Specification for Java. Addison-Wesley Java Series. Addison-Wesley, Boston (2000)
8. Burns, A., Wellings, A.: Real-Time Systems and Programming Languages: ADA 95, Real-Time Java, and Real-Time POSIX, 4th edn. Addison-Wesley Educational Publishers Inc., Boston (2009)
9. Bøgholm, T., Hansen, R.R., Ravn, A.P., Thomsen, B., Søndergaard, H.: Schedulability analysis for Java finalizers. In: Proceedings of the 8th International Workshop on Java Technologies for Real-Time and Embedded Systems, JTRES 2010, pp. 1–7. ACM, New York (2010)
10. Dalsgaard, A.E., Olesen, M.C., Toft, M., Hansen, R.R., Larsen, K.G.: META-MOC: modular execution time analysis using model checking. In: 10th International Workshop on Worst-Case Execution Time Analysis (2010)
11. David, A., Larsen, K.G., Legay, A., Mikučionis, M., Poulsen, D.B., Vliet, J., Wang, Z.: Statistical model checking for networks of priced timed automata. In: Fahrenberg, U., Tripakis, S. (eds.) FORMATS 2011. LNCS, vol. 6919, pp. 80–96. Springer, Heidelberg (2011). doi:10.1007/978-3-642-24310-3_7
12. David, A., Larsen, K.G., Legay, A., Mikučionis, M., Wang, Z.: Time for statistical model checking of real-time systems. In: Gopalakrishnan, G., Qadeer, S. (eds.) CAV 2011. LNCS, vol. 6806, pp. 349–355. Springer, Heidelberg (2011). doi:10.1007/978-3-642-22110-1_27
13. David, A., Larsen, K.G., Legay, A., Mikučionis, M.: Schedulability of herschel-planck revisited using statistical model checking. In: Margaria, T., Steffen, B. (eds.) ISoLA 2012. LNCS, vol. 7610, pp. 293–307. Springer, Heidelberg (2012). doi:10.1007/978-3-642-34032-1_28
14. Davis, R.I., Burns, A.: A survey of hard real-time scheduling for multiprocessor systems. ACM Comput. Surv. 43(4), 35:1–35:44 (2011)
15. Ferdinand, C.: Worst case execution time prediction by static program analysis. In: Proceedings of the 18th International Parallel and Distributed Processing Symposium, p. 125. IEEE (2004)
16. Frost, C., Jensen, C.S., Luckow, K.S., Thomsen, B.: WCET analysis of Java bytecode featuring common execution environments. In: 9th International Workshop on Java Technologies for Real-Time and Embedded Systems (2011)

17. Hansen, J.P., Hissam, S.A., Moreno, G.A.: Statistical-based WCET estimation and validation. In: 9th International Workshop on Worst-Case Execution Time Analysis, WCET 2009, Dublin, Ireland, 1–3 July 2009 (2009)

18. Hu, E.Y.-S., Wellings, A., Bernat, G.: XRTJ: an extensible distributed high-integrity real-time Java environment. In: Chen, J., Hong, S. (eds.) RTCSA 2003. LNCS, vol. 2968, pp. 208–228. Springer, Heidelberg (2004). doi:10.1007/978-3-540-24686-2_13

19. Tri-Pacific Software Inc.: RAPID RMA (2013). http://www.tripac.com/rapid-rma

20. Katoen, J.-P., Zapreev, I.S., Hahn, E.M., Hermanns, H., Jansen, D.N.: The ins and outs of the probabilistic model checker MRMC. Perform. Eval. **68**(2), 90–104 (2011)

21. Kyle, D., Hansen, J., Chaki, S.: Statistical model checking of distributed adaptive real-time software. In: Bartocci, E., Majumdar, R. (eds.) RV 2015. LNCS, vol. 9333, pp. 269–274. Springer, Cham (2015). doi:10.1007/978-3-319-23820-3_17

22. Larsen, K.G., Pettersson, P., Yi, W.: Uppaal in a nutshell. Int. J. Softw. Tools Technol. Transf. (1997)

23. Legay, A., Delahaye, B., Bensalem, S.: Statistical model checking: an overview. In: Barringer, H., Falcone, Y., Finkbeiner, B., Havelund, K., Lee, I., Pace, G., Roşu, G., Sokolsky, O., Tillmann, N. (eds.) RV 2010. LNCS, vol. 6418, pp. 122–135. Springer, Heidelberg (2010). doi:10.1007/978-3-642-16612-9_11

24. Li, Y.-T.S., Malik, S.: Performance analysis of embedded software using implicit path enumeration. In: Proceedings of the 32nd Annual ACM/IEEE Design Automation Conference, DAC 1995, pp. 456–461. ACM, New York (1995)

25. Liu, D., Hu, X.S., Lemmon, M.D., Ling, Q.: Firm real-time system scheduling based on a novel QoS constraint. IEEE Trans. Computers **55**(3), 320–333 (2006)

26. Locke, D., Andersen, B.S., Brosgol, B., Fulton, M., Henties, T., Hunt, J.J., Nielsen, J.O., Nilsen, K., Schoeberl, M., Tokar, J., Vitek, J., Wellings, A.: Safety-Critical Java Technology Specification, Public draft (2013)

27. Luckow, K.S., Thomsen, B., Korsholm, S.E.: HVM-TP: a time predictable and portable Java virtual machine for hard real-time embedded systems. In: 12th International Workshop on Java Technologies for Real-Time and Embedded Systems (2014, to appear)

28. Luckow, K.S., Bøgholm, T., Thomsen, B., Larsen, K.G.: TetaSARTS: a tool for modular timing analysis of safety critical Java systems. In: Proceedings of the 11th International Workshop on Java Technologies for Real-Time and Embedded Systems, JTRES 2013, pp. 11–20 (2013)

29. Luckow, K.S., Thomsen, B., Korsholm, S.E.: HVMTP: a time predictable and portable java virtual machine for hard real-time embedded systems. Concurr. Comput.: Pract. Exp. (2016). cpe.3828

30. Schoeberl, M.: JOP: A Java Optimized Processor for Embedded Real-Time Systems. VDM Verlag Dr. Müller, Saarbrücken (2008). ISBN 978-3-8364-8086-4

31. Mikučionis, M., Larsen, K.G., Rasmussen, J.I., Nielsen, B., Skou, A., Palm, S.U., Pedersen, J.S., Hougaard, P.: Schedulability analysis using Uppaal: Herschel-Planck case study. In: Margaria, T., Steffen, B. (eds.) ISoLA 2010. LNCS, vol. 6416, pp. 175–190. Springer, Heidelberg (2010). doi:10.1007/978-3-642-16561-0_21

32. Plsek, A., Zhao, L., Sahin, V.H., Tang, D., Kalibera, T., Vitek, J.: Developing safety critical Java applications with oSCJ/L0. In: Proceedings of the 8th International Workshop on Java Technologies for Real-Time and Embedded Systems, JTRES 2010, pp. 95–101. ACM, New York (2010)

33. Schoeberl, M., Puffitsch, W., Pedersen, R.U., Huber, B.: Worst-case execution time analysis for a Java processor. Softw.: Pract. Exp. **40**(6), 507–542 (2010)

34. Sen, K., Viswanathan, M., Agha, G.: Statistical model checking of black-box prob-abilistic systems. In: Alur, R., Peled, D.A. (eds.) CAV 2004. LNCS, vol. 3114, pp. 202–215. Springer, Heidelberg (2004). doi:10.1007/978-3-540-27813-9_16
35. Wilhelm, R., Engblom, J., Ermedahl, A., Holsti, N., Thesing, S., Whalley, D., Bernat, G., Ferdinand, C., Heckmann, R., Mitra, T., Mueller, F., Puaut, I., Puschner, P., Staschulat, J., Stenström, P.: The worst-case execution-time problem–overview of methods and survey of tools. ACM Trans. Embed. Comput. Syst. **7**(3), 36:1–36:53 (2008)
36. Younes, H.L.S., Reid, G.: Simmons. Statistical probabilistic model checking with a focus on time-bounded properties. Inf. Comput. **204**(9), 1368–1409 (2006)
37. Zhang, N., Burns, A., Nicholson, M.: Pipelined processors and worst case execution times. Real-Time Syst. **5**(4), 319–343 (1993)

Symbolic Verification and Strategy Synthesis for Linearly-Priced Probabilistic Timed Automata

Marta Kwiatkowska[1], Gethin Norman[2(✉)], and David Parker[3]

[1] Department of Computer Science, University of Oxford, Oxford, UK
[2] School of Computing Science, University of Glasgow, Glasgow, UK
gethin.norman@glasgow.ac.uk
[3] School of Computer Science, University of Birmingham, Birmingham, UK

Abstract. Probabilistic timed automata are a formalism for modelling systems whose dynamics includes probabilistic, nondeterministic and timed aspects including real-time systems. A variety of techniques have been proposed for the analysis of this formalism and successfully employed to analyse, for example, wireless communication protocols and computer security systems. Augmenting the model with prices (or, equivalently, costs or rewards) provides a means to verify more complex quantitative properties, such as the expected energy usage of a device or the expected number of messages sent during a protocol's execution. However, the analysis of these properties on probabilistic timed automata currently relies on a technique based on integer discretisation of real-valued clocks, which can be expensive in some cases. In this paper, we propose symbolic techniques for verification and optimal strategy synthesis for priced probabilistic timed automata which avoid this discretisation. We build upon recent work for the special case of expected time properties, using value iteration over a zone-based abstraction of the model.

1 Introduction

Real-time systems are at the heart of application domains such as communication protocols, embedded systems, hardware circuits, autonomous transport, robotics and manufacturing. The presence of hard real-time constraints within a distributed, reactive environment means that their correct functioning depends on the timing pattern of the interaction of the system with its environment, making correctness guarantees difficult.

Timed automata [2] are a powerful formalism for modelling and verification of real-time systems. They are finite-state automata equipped with real-valued clocks which measure the passage of time, and whose transitions are annotated with guards that specify the time constraints that have to be satisfied for the transition to be taken. Since timed automata allow the modelling of dense real-time, the decidability of model checking depends on a number of assumptions.

Several verification approaches have been introduced, see e.g. [1,21,22,32], of which the symbolic *zone-based* approach enables greater scalability compared to

© Springer International Publishing AG 2017
L. Aceto et al. (Eds.): Larsen Festschrift, LNCS 10460, pp. 289–309, 2017.
DOI: 10.1007/978-3-319-63121-9_15

the digital clocks method, which assumes an integral model of time as opposed to a dense model of time. Timed automata have been widely used for modelling and analysis of real-world systems; in particular, they are supported by the UPPAAL [31] model checker, the gold standard in computer-aided verification for real-time systems.

When modelling and analysing real-time systems, it is often necessary to consider quantities other than time, for example energy consumption, network bandwidth or number of packets lost. The model of *(linearly) priced timed automata* [3,7] extends timed automata with *prices* (weights) annotating the locations and transitions, thus enabling reasoning about costs or rewards accumulated over time as the execution progresses. This model has good decidability properties and several algorithms have been proposed for its analysis, based on an extension of regions or zones with prices. Priced timed automata are also supported by UPPAAL, and have been used for timing analysis of a range of embedded real-time systems, with several flaws discovered and corrected.

However, many distributed real-time systems also employ *randomisation*, for example random back-off in wireless network protocols. A natural model for such systems is a probabilistic extension of (priced) timed automata called *probabilistic timed automata* (PTAs) [6,19,29]. They can be viewed as timed automata whose transitions are probability distributions over the set of edges, where each such edge specifies a successor location and a set of clocks to reset.

A key property studied here is *expected reachability*, namely the expected time/price until some event occurs. This problem has been found unsuitable for symbolic zone-based methods, including priced zones, since accumulated prices are unbounded. Recently, [24,25] introduced a zone-based symbolic method to compute *minimum and maximum expected time* for PTAs and to synthesise a corresponding strategy. Prior to this, expected reachability properties of PTAs could only be verified using the digital clocks method [28] that can suffer from state-space explosion.

Probabilistic timed automata are supported by the PRISM [27] model checker via the zone-based and digital clocks abstractions (though not yet the method of [25]) and have used been for the analysis of a broad range of real-world protocols, see for example [18,28]. A second tool supporting PTAs is mcpta [20], which applies the digital clocks abstraction to translate a subset of the modelling language Modest [15] directly into the PRISM modelling language. The related problem of price-bounded probabilistic reachability [10] (known to be undecidable [9]) can be analysed via a semi-decision procedure using priced zones, implemented in FORTUNA [11].

In this paper we study the computation of the *minimum/maximum expected price* for linearly-priced probabilistic timed automata, for which, to the best of our knowledge, no zone-based method exists at present. More specifically, we extend [25], where only the restricted case of expected time is considered. The minimum expected price problem for a related model of priced timed games in stochastic environments was tackled in [16] using *statistical model checking* with UPPAAL-SMC. Since this approach is based on simulation, rather than numerical model checking, it gives approximate results with probabilistic guarantees.

As in [24,25], our method relies on an interpretation of the PTA as an uncountable-state Markov decision process (MDP) and employs a representation in terms of an extension of the 'simple' and 'nice' functions of [4]. The optimal prices are computed via a Bellman equation using value iteration, which gives guaranteed eventual convergence to the correct values. Moreover, an ε-optimal strategy can be extracted by stepping backwards and retrieving the locally optimal choices once some convergence criterion has been satisfied. For minimum expected time, it is always optimal to let as little time pass as possible. However, for minimum price, it turns out that this is not always the case, and it can be optimal to let time pass now and accumulate a lower price, as opposed to waiting and accumulating a higher price later. The case of maximum time/price is dual.

Paper Structure. In Sect. 2 we summarise the relevant background, mainly concerning uncountable MDPs and the computation of optimal reward. Section 3 defines the priced extension of probabilistic timed automata (PTAs) and their interpretation as an uncountable MDP under appropriate assumptions. In Sect. 4, we introduce a representation of the value functions that generalise the simple and nice functions of [4], and present our algorithms for computing optimal expected price and synthesis of an ε-optimal strategy using the backwards zone graph of a PTA.

2 Background

Let $\mathbb{R}$ denote the non-negative reals, $\mathbb{N}$ natural numbers, $\mathbb{Q}$ rationals and $\mathbb{Q}_+$ non-negative rationals. A *discrete probability distribution* over a (possibly uncountable) set S is a function $\mu : S \rightarrow [0,1]$ such that $\sum_{s \in S} \mu(s) = 1$ and the set $\{s \in S \mid \mu(s) > 0\}$ is finite. Let $\mathrm{dist}(S)$ denote the set of distributions over S. A distribution $\mu \in \mathrm{dist}(S)$ is a *point distribution* if $\mu(s) = 1$ for some $s \in S$.

In preparation for the sections that follow, we present some background material and known results for the model of Markov decision processes (MDPs).

Definition 1. *An MDP is a tuple* $\mathsf{M} = (S, s_0, A, Prob_\mathsf{M}, Price_\mathsf{M})$, *where:*

- S *is a (possibly uncountable) set of states and* $s_0 \in S$ *is an initial state;*
- A *is a (possibly uncountable) set of actions;*
- $Prob_\mathsf{M} : S \times A \rightarrow \mathrm{dist}(S)$ *is a (partial) probabilistic transition function;*
- $Price_\mathsf{M} : S \times A \rightarrow \mathbb{R}$ *is a price function.*

In each state s of an MDP M, there is a set of enabled actions, denoted by $A(s)$, containing those actions a for which $Prob_\mathsf{M}(s, a)$ is defined. In state s, a transition corresponds to first nondeterministically choosing an available action and, assuming action $a \in A(s)$ is chosen, then selecting a successor state randomly according to the distribution $Prob_\mathsf{M}(s, a)$. Taking an a-labelled transition from state s incurs a *price* of $Price_\mathsf{M}(s, a)$. We use the terminology "price" for consistency with the model of priced probabilistic timed automata used later, but these are commonly also referred to as *costs* or, dually, *rewards* for MDPs.

A *path* of an MDP M is given by a finite or infinite sequence of transitions $\omega = s_0 \xrightarrow{a_0} s_1 \xrightarrow{a_1} s_2 \xrightarrow{a_2} \cdots$ with $Prob_{\mathsf{M}}(s_i, a_i)(s_{i+1}) > 0$ for all $i \geq 0$. The $(i+1)$th state of a path ω and action associated with the $(i+1)$th transition are denoted by $\omega(i)$ and $\omega[i]$ respectively. The set of infinite (finite) paths is denoted by $IPaths_{\mathsf{M}}$ ($FPaths_{\mathsf{M}}$) and the last state of a finite path ω by $last(\omega)$.

A *strategy* (also called an adversary, scheduler or policy) of an MDP M represents one resolution of the nondeterminism in M.

Definition 2. *A strategy of an MDP* M *is a function* $\sigma : FPaths_{\mathsf{M}} \rightarrow \mathrm{dist}(A)$ *such that* $\sigma(\omega)(a) > 0$ *only if* $a \in A(last(\omega))$.

For a given strategy σ and state s of an MDP M, we can construct a probability measure $\mathcal{P}_s^{\sigma}$ over the set of infinite paths starting in s [26]. A strategy σ is *memoryless* if its choices only depend on the current state, and *deterministic* if $\sigma(\omega)$ is a point distribution for all $\omega \in FPaths_{\mathsf{M}}$. The set of all strategies of MDP M is denoted Σ_{M}.

Key quantitative properties for MDPs are the probability of reaching a target and the expected price incurred before doing so. We will refer to these as *probabilistic reachability* and *expected reachability*, respectively. For a strategy σ, state s and set of target states $F \subseteq S$ of an MDP M, these values are given by:

$$\mathbb{P}_{\mathsf{M}}^{\sigma}(s, F) \stackrel{\text{def}}{=} \mathcal{P}_s^{\sigma}\{\omega \in IPaths_{\mathsf{M}} \mid \exists k \in \mathbb{N}.\, \omega(k) \in F\}$$

$$\mathbb{E}_{\mathsf{M}}^{\sigma}(s, F) \stackrel{\text{def}}{=} \int_{\omega \in IPaths_{\mathsf{M}}} price(\omega, F)\, \mathrm{d}\mathcal{P}_s^{\sigma}$$

where for any infinite path ω:

$$price(\omega, F) \stackrel{\text{def}}{=} \sum_{i=0}^{k_F} Price_{\mathsf{M}}(\omega(i), \omega[i])$$

and $k_F = \min\{k - 1 \mid \omega(k) \in F\}$ if there exists $k \in \mathbb{N}$ such that $\omega(k) \in F$ and $k_F = \infty$ otherwise. As usual we consider the optimal values of these properties, i.e. the minimum and maximum values over all strategies:

$$\mathbb{P}_{\mathsf{M}}^{\min}(s, F) \stackrel{\text{def}}{=} \inf_{\sigma \in \Sigma_{\mathsf{M}}} \mathbb{P}_{\mathsf{M}}^{\sigma}(s, F) \qquad \mathbb{P}_{\mathsf{M}}^{\max}(s, F) \stackrel{\text{def}}{=} \sup_{\sigma \in \Sigma_{\mathsf{M}}} \mathbb{P}_{\mathsf{M}}^{\sigma}(s, F)$$
$$\mathbb{E}_{\mathsf{M}}^{\min}(s, F) \stackrel{\text{def}}{=} \inf_{\sigma \in \Sigma_{\mathsf{M}}} \mathbb{E}_{\mathsf{M}}^{\sigma}(s, F) \qquad \mathbb{E}_{\mathsf{M}}^{\max}(s, F) \stackrel{\text{def}}{=} \sup_{\sigma \in \Sigma_{\mathsf{M}}} \mathbb{E}_{\mathsf{M}}^{\sigma}(s, F)$$

One approach to computing these optimal values is through *Bellman operators* [8] using either *value iteration* or *policy iteration* [12,13]. In the case of expected reachability, the Bellman operators have the following form.

Definition 3. *Let* M *be an MDP with state space* S, $F \subseteq S$ *be a target set, and let* $\mathrm{opt} \in \{\min, \max\}$. *The Bellman operator* $T_{\mathsf{M}}^{\mathrm{opt}} : (S \rightarrow \mathbb{R}) \rightarrow (S \rightarrow \mathbb{R})$ *for optimal expected reachability is defined as follows. For any function* $f : S \rightarrow \mathbb{R}$ *and state* $s \in S$:

$$T_{\mathsf{M}}^{\mathrm{opt}}(f)(s) = \begin{cases} 0 & \text{if } s \in F \\ \mathrm{opt}_{a \in A(s)}^{\star} \left\{ Price_{\mathsf{M}}(s, a) + \sum_{s' \in S} Prob_{\mathsf{M}}(s, a)(s') \cdot f(s') \right\} & \text{if } s \notin F \end{cases}$$

where $\min^{\star} = \inf$ *and* $\max^{\star} = \sup$.

Value iteration works by starting with an initial approximation $f_0 : S \to \mathbb{R}$ and repeatedly applying $T_{\mathsf{M}}^{\mathrm{opt}}$ until it converges to the optimal expected reachability value. In practice, an approximate result is obtained by terminating the computation once some convergence criterion is satisfied, for example, by checking that the maximum pointwise difference between $(T_{\mathsf{M}}^{\mathrm{opt}})^n(f_0)$ and $(T_{\mathsf{M}}^{\mathrm{opt}})^{n+1}(f_0)$ is below some threshold $\varepsilon \in \mathbb{R}$. The process also yields an (approximately) optimal strategy for either minimising or maximising expected reachability. Policy iteration starts from a (deterministic and memoryless) strategy, and repeatedly attempts to find an improved (deterministic and memoryless) strategy by computing the expected reachability values for the current strategy and trying to update action choices to optimise expected reachability values.

Below, we state some known results from [23] regarding MDPs and value iteration, which are needed later in the paper (and which were adapted for the case of PTAs in [25]). This requires us to make the following assumptions.

Assumption 1. *For any MDP* $\mathsf{M} = (S, s_0, A, Prob_{\mathsf{M}}, Price_{\mathsf{M}})$ *and target set* F:

(a) $A(s)$ *is compact for all* $s \in S$;
(b) $Price_{\mathsf{M}}$ *is bounded and* $a \mapsto Price_{\mathsf{M}}(s, a)$ *is continuous for all* $s \in S$;
(c) *if* σ *is a memoryless, deterministic strategy which is not proper, then* $\mathbb{E}_{\mathsf{M}}^{\sigma}(s, F)$ *is unbounded for some* $s \in S$;
(d) *there exists a proper, memoryless, deterministic strategy;*

where a strategy σ *is called proper if* $\mathbb{P}_{\mathsf{M}}^{\sigma}(s, F) = 1$ *for all* $s \in S$.

Theorem 1 [23]. *If* M *and* F *are an MDP and target set for which Assumption 1 holds, and the minimum expected price values are bounded below, then:*

- *there exists a memoryless, deterministic strategy that achieves the minimum expected price of reaching* F;
- *the minimum expected price values are the unique solutions to* $T_{\mathsf{M}}^{\mathrm{min}}$;
- *value iteration over* $T_{\mathsf{M}}^{\mathrm{min}}$ *converges to the minimum expected price values when starting from any bounded function;*
- *policy iteration converges to the minimum expected price values when starting from any proper, memoryless, deterministic strategy.*

Corollary 1. *If* M *and* F *are an MDP and target set for which Assumption 1 holds and the maximum expected price values are bounded above, then:*

- *there exists a memoryless, deterministic strategy that achieves the maximum expected price of reaching* F;
- *the maximum expected price values are the unique solutions to* $T_{\mathsf{M}}^{\mathrm{max}}$;
- *value iteration over* $T_{\mathsf{M}}^{\mathrm{max}}$ *converges to the maximum expected price values when starting from any bounded function;*
- *policy iteration converges to the maximum expected price values when starting from any proper, memoryless, deterministic strategy.*

3   Priced Probabilistic Timed Automata

In this section we introduce *probabilistic timed automata* (PTAs) [6,19,29], a formalism for modelling systems whose dynamics includes probabilistic, nondeterministic and timed aspects, and the extended model of *linearly-priced PTAs* [28], which augment PTAs with prices. We will commonly refer to the latter simply as PTAs.

Clocks, Clock Valuations and Zones. We assume we have a finite set $\mathcal{X}$ of real-valued variables called *clocks* which increase at the same, constant rate. A clock valuation is a function $v : \mathcal{X} \rightarrow \mathbb{R}$ and let $\mathbb{R}^{\mathcal{X}}$ be the set of all clock valuations. We denote by $\mathbf{0}$ the clock valuation that assigns 0 to all clocks. For any subset of clocks R, non-negative real value t and clock valuation v, $v[R]$ is the clock valuation where $v[R](x) = 0$ if $x \in R$ and $v[R](x) = v(x)$ if $x \in \mathcal{X} \backslash R$, and $v + t$ is the clock valuation where $(v + t)(x) = v(x) + t$ for all $x \in \mathcal{X}$. The set of *zones* over $\mathcal{X}$, written $Zones(\mathcal{X})$, is defined by the syntax:

$$\zeta ::= \mathsf{true} \mid x \leq d \mid c \leq x \mid x + c \leq y + d \mid \neg\zeta \mid \zeta \wedge \zeta$$

where $x, y \in \mathcal{X}$ and $c, d \in \mathbb{N}$. We can restrict the syntax to *convex* zones by removing negation. For a clock valuation v and zone ζ, we say v satisfies ζ, denoted $v \models \zeta$, if ζ is true after substituting each occurrence of each clock x with $v(x)$. The semantics of a zone ζ is the set of clock valuations satisfying it. We require the following zone operations [33], for zone ζ and subset of clocks R:

- $\nearrow\zeta = \{v \in \mathbb{R}^{\mathcal{X}} \mid \exists t \in \mathbb{R}.\, v + t \models \zeta\}$;
- $\zeta[R] = \{v[R] \mid v \models \zeta\}$;
- $[R]\zeta = \{v \in \mathbb{R}^{\mathcal{X}} \mid v[R] \models \zeta\}$.

Syntax and Semantics of PTAs. We now present the formal syntax and semantics of linearly-priced PTAs.

Definition 4. *A linearly-priced probabilistic timed automaton (PTA)* P *is a tuple* $(L, l_0, \mathcal{X}, Act, \mathsf{enab}, \mathsf{prob}, \mathsf{inv}, \mathsf{price})$ *where:*

- *L is a finite set of locations and $l_0 \in L$ is an initial location;*
- *$\mathcal{X}$ is a finite set of clocks;*
- *Act is a finite set of actions;*
- *$\mathsf{enab} : L \times Act \rightarrow Zones(\mathcal{X})$ is an enabling condition;*
- *$\mathsf{prob} : L \times Act \rightarrow \mathsf{dist}(2^{\mathcal{X}} \times L)$ is a probabilistic transition function;*
- *$\mathsf{inv} : L \rightarrow Zones(\mathcal{X})$ is an invariant condition;*
- *$\mathsf{price} = (\mathsf{price}_L, \mathsf{price}_{Act})$ is a price structure where $\mathsf{price}_L : L \rightarrow \mathbb{Q}_+$ is a location price function and $\mathsf{price}_{Act} : L \times Act \rightarrow \mathbb{Q}_+$ an action price function.*

The underlying semantics of PTA P is an MDP with an infinite set of both states and actions. The states are location-valuation pairs (l, v) such that v satisfies the invariant $\mathsf{inv}(l)$ and the initial state is the initial location with all clocks set to 0. The available actions in state (l, v) are the time-action pairs (t, a) such the invariant $\mathsf{inv}(l)$ remains true while letting t time units pass, after this time the enabling condition $\mathsf{enab}(l, a)$ is satisfied, and the successor location and the clocks that are reset are then chosen according to the distribution $\mathsf{prob}(l, v)$. Furthermore, a price is incurred at rate $\mathsf{price}_L(l)$ while letting the t time units pass and a price $\mathsf{price}_{Act}(l, a)$ is incurred when performing the action a.

Definition 5. *For a PTA* $\mathsf{P} = (L, l_0, \mathcal{X}, Act, \mathsf{enab}, \mathsf{prob}, \mathsf{inv}, \mathsf{price})$ *the semantics of* P *is given by the MDP* $[\![\mathsf{P}]\!] = (S, s_0, \mathbb{R} \times Act, Prob_{[\![\mathsf{P}]\!]}, Price_{[\![\mathsf{P}]\!]})$ *where:*

- $S = \{(l, v) \in L \times \mathbb{R}^{\mathcal{X}} \mid v \models \mathsf{inv}(l)\}$ *and* $s_0 = (l_0, \mathbf{0})$;
- *if* $(l, v) \in S$ *and* $(t, a) \in \mathbb{R} \times Act$, *then* $Prob_{[\![\mathsf{P}]\!]}((l, v), (t, a)) = \mu$ *if and only if* $v + t' \models \mathsf{inv}(l)$ *for* $0 \leq t' \leq t$, $v + t \models \mathsf{enab}(l, a)$ *and for any* $(l', v') \in S$:

$$\mu(l', v') = \textstyle\sum_{R \subseteq \mathcal{X} \wedge v' = (v+t)[R]} \mathsf{prob}(l, a)(R, l')$$

- $Price_{[\![\mathsf{P}]\!]}((l, v), (t, a)) = \mathsf{price}_L(l) \cdot t + \mathsf{price}_{Act}(l, a)$ *for all* $(l, v) \in S$ *and* $(t, a) \in \mathbb{R} \times Act$.

Expected Prices. The property of PTAs on which we focus in this paper is the optimal (minimum or maximum) expected price incurred before reaching a target, which is defined along the same lines as the equivalent property for MDPs defined in Sect. 2. The differences are that, firstly, the target is now defined as a set $F \subseteq L$ of locations and, secondly, prices are incurred both when time elapses in a location, and when an action is performed. Since the semantics of a PTA is an (infinite-state) MDP, the expected price for a PTA is defined in straightforward fashion in terms of the MDP. For PTA P, target locations F, state (l, v) and $opt \in \{\min, \max\}$, we have:

$$\mathbb{E}_{\mathsf{P}}^{opt}((l, v), F) \stackrel{\text{def}}{=} \mathbb{E}_{[\![\mathsf{P}]\!]}^{opt}((l, v), S_F) \text{ where } S_F \stackrel{\text{def}}{=} \{(l, v) \mid l \in F \wedge v \models \mathsf{inv}(l)\}.$$

When computing these values, we make several assumptions about PTAs, similar to those imposed in [25]. Firstly, this will ensure that Assumption 1 holds for the underlying MDP, which allows us to apply Theorem 1 and Corollary 1. Secondly, it makes sure that unrealistic behaviours are discarded.

Assumption 2. *For any PTA* P, *we have:*

(a) *all invariants of* P *are bounded;*
(b) *only non-strict inequalities are allowed in clock constraints, i.e.,* P *is closed;*
(c) *all invariant and enabling conditions of* P *are convex;*
(d) *all location prices of* P *are positive;*
(e) P *is structurally non-zeno [34] (this can be identified syntactically and in a compositional fashion [35] and guarantees time-divergent behaviour).*

The reasons for these assumptions are similar to those given in [25]. The main difference is that, in order to ensure that Assumption 1(c) holds, we require that all location prices are positive (Assumption 2(d)), in addition to the structural non-zeno assumption. More precisely, for any PTA satisfying Assumption 2(d) and (e), if, from some state and under some strategy a target is not reached with probability 1, then from this state and under this strategy the expected price of reaching the target is infinite. Expected time (as in [25]) is a special case of expected price where all action prices are 0 and all location prices are 1, and therefore Assumption 1(d) will always hold in this case.

4 Optimal Expected Price Algorithms for PTAs

In this section, we present our symbolic approach for computing optimal expected reachability prices and for synthesising a corresponding optimal strategy. We first extend the approach of [25] for computing optimal expected times, a key building block of which is an initial backwards exploration of the state space, using the techniques from [30]. Computing expected rewards can then be performed using value iteration over the zone graph constructed during backwards exploration. This process is described in Sect. 4.1. Next, in Sect. 4.2, we discuss the use of *rational k-simple functions* and *rational (r, k)-nice functions* to represent the prices stored during value iteration. Finally, Sect. 4.3 presents an example of the process.

To simplify the presentation, for the remainder of this section we will fix a PTA $P = (L, l_0, \mathcal{X}, Act, \mathsf{enab}, \mathsf{prob}, \mathsf{inv}, \mathsf{price})$, target set of locations $F \subseteq L$ and let $[\![P]\!] = (S, s_0, \mathbb{R} \times Act, Prob_{[\![P]\!]}, Price_{[\![P]\!]})$.

4.1 Computation of Expected Prices and Optimal Strategies

The first step is the construction of a *zone graph* $G = (Z, E)$, whose vertices Z are *symbolic states*. A symbolic state of P is a location-zone pair (l, ζ) and represents the set of states $\{(l, v) \mid v \in \mathbb{R}^{\mathcal{X}} \wedge v \models \zeta \wedge \mathsf{inv}(l)\}$ of $[\![P]\!]$. If $z = (l, \zeta)$ and $z' = (l, \zeta')$ are symbolic states, then let $z \wedge z' = (l, \zeta \wedge \zeta'), z \subseteq z'$ when $\zeta \subseteq \zeta'$ and $z = \varnothing$ if and only if $\zeta = \mathsf{false}$. For any symbolic state $z = (l, \zeta)$, locations l' and l'', action a and set of clocks R we will use the following time and discrete predecessor operations:

$$\mathsf{tpre}(z) \overset{\text{def}}{=} (l, \mathsf{inv}(l) \wedge \swarrow \zeta)$$

$$\mathsf{dpre}(l', a, (R, l''))(z) \overset{\text{def}}{=} \begin{cases} (l', \mathsf{false}) & \text{if } l \neq l'' \\ (l', \mathsf{enab}(l', a) \wedge [R]\zeta) & \text{otherwise.} \end{cases}$$

As in [25], we use the backwards reachability algorithm of [30] (adding action labels to the edge tuples) to build a zone graph, shown in Fig. 1.

Given a zone graph $G = (Z, E)$, for any $(l, \zeta) \in Z$ let $E(l, \zeta) \subseteq 2^E$ represent the following sets of edges: $E \in E(l, \zeta)$ if and only if there exists $a \in Act$ such that $\mathsf{edges}(l, a) = \{(R_1, l_1), \ldots, (R_n, l_n)\}$ and:

$$E = \{(z, a, (R_1, l_1), z_1), \ldots, (z, a, (R_n, l_n), z_n)\}$$

for some $z_1, \ldots, z_n \in Z$.

BackwardsReach(P, F)

```
1   Z := ∅
2   E := ∅
3   Y := {(l, inv(l)) | l ∈ F}
4   while (Y ≠ ∅)
5     choose (y ∈ Y)
6     Y := Y\{y}
7     Z := Z ∪ {y}
8     for ((l, a) ∈ (L\F)×Act) and ((R, l') ∈ edges(l, a))
9       z := dpre(l, a, R, l')(tpre(y))
10      if (z ≠ ∅)
11        if (z ∉ Z)
12          Y := Y ∪ {z}
13        E := E ∪ {(z, a, (R, l'), y)}
14        for ((z̃, a, (R̃, l̃'), ỹ) ∈ E) such that ((R̃, l̃') ≠ (R, l'))
15          if ((z∧z̃ ≠ ∅) ∧ (z∧z̃ ∉ Z))
16            Y := Y ∪ {z∧z̃}
17  for (z ∈ Z) and ((z', a, (R, l'), z'') ∈ E)
18    if (z ⊆ z')
19      E := {(z, a, (R, l'), z'')} ∪ E
20  return G := (Z, E)
```

Fig. 1. Backwards reachability algorithm [30]

After building the zone graph, the next step is to find and restrict $[\![P]\!]$ and G to include only those states for which the optimal expected price to reach the target is finite, i.e., states for which the maximum probability of reaching the target is 1 in the case of minimum expected prices and for which the minimum probability of reaching the target is 1 in the case of maximum expected prices.

Symbolic (zone-based) algorithms for performing this restriction, which extend the algorithms developed for MDPs [14,17], can be found in [25]. For the remainder of the section we suppose that $S_{\min}$ and $S_{\max}$ are the states of $[\![P]\!]$ for which the minimum and maximum reachability probability is 1, and $[\![P]\!]_{\min}$ and $[\![P]\!]_{\max}$ are the sub-MDPs restricted to these sets of states. We will also assume that $G_{\min} = (Z_{\min}, E_{\min})$ and $G_{\max} = (Z_{\max}, E_{\max})$ are the restrictions of the zone graph $G = (Z, E)$ to these sets of states.

It follows that the restricted MDPs $[\![P]\!]_{\min}$ and $[\![P]\!]_{\max}$ satisfy Assumption 1, and we can therefore use Theorem 1 in the case of minimum expected pices and Corollary 1 in the case of maximum expected prices. In particular, we can use the fact that value iteration for the Bellman operators $T^{\min}_{[\![P]\!]_{\min}}$ and $T^{\max}_{[\![P]\!]_{\max}}$ (see Definition 3) for the target set S_F converges to the minimum and maximum expected prices, respectively, when starting from any bounded function.

Next, we present a value iteration method over the restricted zone graphs $G_{\min}$ and $G_{\max}$, based on the function $T^{\mathrm{opt}}_{G_{\mathrm{opt}}}$, which has a direct correspondence with value iteration over the sub-MDPs $[\![P]\!]_{\min}$ and $[\![P]\!]_{\max}$.

Definition 6. *The operator* $T_{\mathsf{G}_{opt}}^{opt} : (\mathsf{Z}_{opt} \rightarrow (\mathsf{S}_{opt} \rightarrow \mathbb{R})) \rightarrow (\mathsf{Z}_{opt} \rightarrow (\mathsf{S}_{opt} \rightarrow \mathbb{R}))$ *on the zone graph* G_{opt} *is such that for* $g : \mathsf{Z}_{opt} \rightarrow (\mathsf{S}_{opt} \rightarrow \mathbb{R}), \mathbf{z} = (l, \zeta) \in \mathsf{Z}_{opt}$ *and* $s = (l, v) \in \mathsf{S}_{opt}$ *where* $s \in \mathsf{tpre}(\mathbf{z})$ *we have* $T_{\mathsf{G}_{opt}}^{opt}(g)(\mathbf{z})(s)$ *equals 0 if* $l \in F$ *and otherwise equals:*

$$\underset{\substack{t \in \mathbb{R} \wedge \\ v+t \in \zeta}}{opt^{\star}} \underset{E \in \mathsf{E}(\mathbf{z})}{opt} \left\{ \mathsf{price}_L(l) \cdot t + \mathsf{price}_{Act}(l, a) \right.$$

$$\left. + \sum_{(\mathbf{z}, a, (R, l'), \mathbf{z}') \in E} \mathsf{prob}(l, a)(R, l') \cdot g(\mathbf{z}')(l', (v + t)[R]) \right\}.$$

for $opt \in \{\min, \max\}$*, and where* $\min^{\star} = \inf$ *and* $\max^{\star} = \sup$.

The proof of the following proposition follows directly from the proofs presented in [25] for optimal expected time computation.

Proposition 1. *For* $opt \in \{\min, \max\}$*, if* $f : \mathsf{S}_{opt} \rightarrow \mathbb{R}$ *and* $g : \mathsf{Z}_{opt} \rightarrow (\mathsf{S}_{opt} \rightarrow \mathbb{R})$ *are functions such that* $f(s) = g(\mathbf{z})(s)$ *for all* $s \in \mathsf{S}_{opt}$ *and* $\mathbf{z} \in \mathsf{Z}_{opt}$ *such that* $s \in \mathsf{tpre}(\mathbf{z})$*, then for any* $s \in \mathsf{S}_{opt}$ *and* $n \in \mathbb{N}$ *we have:*

$$(T_{\llbracket \mathsf{P} \rrbracket_{opt}}^{opt})^n(f)(s) = opt\{ (T_{\mathsf{G}_{opt}}^{opt})^n(g)(\mathbf{z})(s) \mid \mathbf{z} \in \mathsf{Z}_{opt} \wedge s \in \mathsf{tpre}(\mathbf{z}) \}.$$

Consequently, value iteration, using function $T_{\mathsf{G}_{opt}}^{opt}$, converges to the optimal expected reachability price for the original PTA, a result that follows from Theorem 1, Corollary 1 and Proposition 1. The final step is then to synthesise an ε-optimal deterministic, memoryless strategy for expected reachability on the PTA. This can be done by stepping through the backwards graph and selecting the time-action pairs that achieve the results returned by value iteration in each state of the zone graph.

Unlike traditional value iteration for MDPs, which iterates over real-valued vectors over states, the value iteration process for PTAs outlined above uses state vectors whose values are themselves real-valued functions. In the following section, we will show how this can be achieved using classes of functions called rational k-simple functions and rational (r, k)-nice functions.

4.2 Rational Simple Functions and Rational Nice Functions

To simplify the presentation we will assume that $\mathcal{X} = \{x_1, \ldots, x_n\}$ and $k \in \mathbb{N}$ is the maximum constant appearing in P. Since P satisfies Assumption 2(a), it is bounded, and therefore all clock values appearing in $\llbracket \mathsf{P} \rrbracket$ are bounded by k. We first define polyhedra with rational time bounds.

Definition 7. *A (convex)* k*-polyhedron* $C \subseteq \{v \in \mathbb{R}^{\mathcal{X}} \mid v(x) \leq k \text{ for } x \in \mathcal{X}\}$ *is defined by finitely many linear inequalities; formally, it is of the form:*

$$C = \{v \in \mathbb{R}^{\mathcal{X}} \mid \textstyle\sum_{i=1}^{n} q_{ij} \cdot v(x_i) \leq f_j \text{ for } 1 \leq j \leq M\}$$

where $q_{ij}, f_j \in \mathbb{Q}$ *and* $f_j \leq k$ *for all* $1 \leq i \leq n$ *and* $1 \leq j \leq M$ *for some* $M \in \mathbb{N}$.
Furthermore, a k-*bipolyhedron is a set of the form* $\{(v,t) \mid v \in C \wedge v + t \in D\}$
where C *and* D *are* k-*polyhedra.*

For the case of expected price reachability computation, [25] introduced the notions of *rational* k-*simple* and k-*nice* functions to represent the functions encountered during value iteration.

Definition 8. *For zone* ζ, *a function* $f : \zeta \rightarrow \mathbb{R}$ *is rational* k-*simple if and only if it can be represented as:*

$$f(v) = \begin{cases} c_j & \text{if } v \in C_j \\ d_l - \sum_{i=1}^{n} p_{il} \cdot v(x_i) & \text{if } v \in D_l \end{cases}$$

where $c_j, d_l, p_{il} \in \mathbb{Q}_+$ *such that* $\sum_{i=1}^{n} p_{il} \leq 1$ *and* C_j, D_l *are* k-*polyhedra for all*
$1 \leq i \leq n, 1 \leq j \leq M$ *and* $1 \leq l \leq N$ *for some* $M, N \in \mathbb{N}$.
Furthermore, a function $f : Z \rightarrow (S \rightarrow \mathbb{R})$ *is rational* k-*simple if the function*
$f(l, \zeta)(l, \cdot) : \diagup \zeta \rightarrow \mathbb{R}$ *is rational* k-*simple for all* $(l, \zeta) \in Z$.

Definition 9. *For a zone* ζ, *a function* $g : (\zeta \times \mathbb{R}) \rightarrow \mathbb{R}$ *is rational* k-*nice if and only if it can be represented as:*

$$g(v,t) = \begin{cases} c_j + t & \text{if } (v,t) \in F_j \\ d_l - \sum_{i=1}^{n} p_{il} \cdot v(x_i) + (1 - \sum_{i=1}^{n} p_{il}) \cdot t & \text{if } (v,t) \in G_l \end{cases}$$

where $c_j, d_l, p_{il} \in \mathbb{Q}_+$ *such that* $\sum_{i=1}^{n} p_{il} \leq 1$ *and* F_j, G_l *are rational* k-*bipolyhedra for all* $1 \leq i \leq n, 1 \leq j \leq M$ *and* $1 \leq l \leq N$ *for some* $M, N \in \mathbb{N}$.

* We now extend these definitions to allow the representation of the value functions encountered when computing optimal expected price reachability using value iteration and either $T_{\mathsf{G}_{\min}}^{\min}$ or $T_{\mathsf{G}_{\max}}^{\max}$ (see Definition 6). We first extend the definition of rational k-simple functions and then consider the different operations performed by $T_{\mathsf{G}_{\min}}^{\min}$ and $T_{\mathsf{G}_{\max}}^{\max}$ and analyse their effect on the extended definition of rational k-simple functions.

Definition 10. *For zone* ζ, *a function* $f : \zeta \rightarrow \mathbb{R}$ *is rational* k-*simple if and only if it can be represented as:*

$$f(v) = \begin{cases} c_j & \text{if } v \in C_j \\ d_l - \sum_{i=1}^{n} p_{il} \cdot v(x_i) & \text{if } v \in D_l \end{cases}$$

where $c_j, d_l, p_{il} \in \mathbb{Q}$ *and* C_j, D_l *are* k-*polyhedra for all* $1 \leq i \leq n, 1 \leq j \leq M$
and $1 \leq l \leq N$ *for some* $M, N \in \mathbb{N}$.

Furthermore, a function $f : Z \rightarrow (S \rightarrow \mathbb{R})$ *is rational* k-*simple if the function*
$f(l, \zeta)(l, \cdot) : \diagup \zeta \rightarrow \mathbb{R}$ *is rational* k-*simple for all* $(l, \zeta) \in Z$.

The above definition extends the k-simple functions of [25] (see Definition 8) by allowing any linear combination of clock values and allowing negative as well as non-negative rational constants. The first operation we consider for rational k-simple functions is the resetting of clocks.

Definition 11. *If $f : \zeta \to \mathbb{R}$ is a rational k-simple function and $R \subseteq \mathcal{X}$, let $f[R] : [R]\zeta \to \mathbb{R}$ be the function where $f[R](v) = f(v[R])$ for all $v \in \zeta$.*

The following lemma demonstrates that resetting clocks preserves rational simplicity.

Lemma 1. *If $f : \zeta \to \mathbb{R}$ is rational k-simple and $R \subseteq \mathcal{X}$, then $f[R] : [R]\zeta \to \mathbb{R}$ is rational k-simple.*

Proof. For any k-polyhedron C and $R \subseteq \mathcal{X}$, let $[R]C$ be the k-polyhedron $\{v \in \mathbb{R}^{\mathcal{X}} \mid v[R] \in C \wedge v(x) \leq k$ for $x \in \mathcal{X}\}$. Now consider any $R \subseteq \mathcal{X}$ and rational k-simple function $f : \zeta \to \mathbb{R}$ such that for any $v \in \zeta$:

$$f(v) = \begin{cases} c_j & \text{if } v \in C_j \\ d_l - \sum_{i=1}^n p_{il} \cdot v(x_i) & \text{if } v \in D_l \end{cases} \tag{1}$$

where $c_j, d_l, p_{il} \in \mathbb{Q}$ and C_j, D_l are k-polyhedra for all $1 \leq i \leq n, 1 \leq j \leq M$ and $1 \leq l \leq N$ for some $M, N \in \mathbb{N}$. By Definition 11, for any $v \in [R]\zeta$ we have:

$$f[R](v) = f(v[R])$$

$$= \begin{cases} c_j & \text{if } v[R] \in C_j \\ d_l - \sum_{i=1}^n p_{il} \cdot v[R](x_i) & \text{if } v[R] \in D_l \end{cases} \qquad \text{(by (1))}$$

$$= \begin{cases} c_j & \text{if } v \in [R]C_j \\ d_l - \sum_{i=1}^n p_{il} \cdot v[R](x_i) & \text{if } v \in [R]D_l \end{cases} \qquad \text{(by definition of } [R]C)$$

$$= \begin{cases} c_j & \text{if } v \in [R]C_j \\ d_l - \sum_{i=1}^n p'_{il} \cdot v(x_i) & \text{if } v \in [R]D_l \end{cases}$$

where $p'_{il} = 0$ if $x_i \in R$ and $p'_{il} = p_{il}$ otherwise. It therefore follows that $f[R]$ is rational k-simple as required. □

The next operation performed by $T_{G_{\min}}^{\min}$ and $T_{G_{\max}}^{\max}$ builds function of the form $v \mapsto p \cdot t + p' + f(l, \zeta)(l, v + t)$. This motivates first demonstrating that adding constants (corresponding to the accumulation of action prices) preserves k-simplicity.

Lemma 2. *If $f : \zeta \to \mathbb{R}$ is rational k-simple and $p' \in \mathbb{Q}_+$, then $f + p' : \zeta \to \mathbb{R}$ is also rational k-simple.*

Proof. The proof follows from the definition of k-simple functions (see Definition 10). □

We now extend rational k-nice functions of [25] (see Definition 9) to (p, k)-nice functions, where the additional parameter p corresponds to the current rate at which prices are accumulated as time passes.

Definition 12. *For $p \in \mathbb{Q}_+$ and zone ζ, a function $g : (\zeta \times \mathbb{R}) \to \mathbb{R}$ is rational (p, k)-nice if and only if it can be represented as:*

$$g(v, t) = \begin{cases} c_j + p \cdot t & \text{if } (v, t) \in F_j \\ d_l - \sum_{i=1}^{n} p_{il} \cdot v(x_i) + (p - \sum_{i=1}^{n} p_{il}) \cdot t & \text{if } (v, t) \in G_l \end{cases}$$

where $c_j, d_l, p_{il} \in \mathbb{Q}$ and F_j, G_l are rational k-bipolyhedra for all $1 \leq i \leq n, 1 \leq j \leq M$ and $1 \leq l \leq N$ for some $M, N \in \mathbb{N}$.

Next we show that rational k-nicety is preserved under taking convex combinations of functions of the form $v \mapsto p \cdot t + f(l, \zeta)(l, v + t)$.

Lemma 3. *A convex combination of rational (p, k)-nice functions is rational (p, k)-nice.*

Proof. It is sufficient to consider a binary convex combination, as any other convex combination can be rewritten as a sequence of binary convex combinations. Therefore, consider any zone ζ, rationals $\lambda, \lambda' \in \mathbb{Q}_+$ and rational (p, k)-nice functions $g, g' : (\zeta \times \mathbb{R}) \to \mathbb{R}$ such that $\lambda + \lambda' = 1$ and for any $v \in \zeta$:

$$g(v, t) = \begin{cases} c_j + p \cdot t & \text{if } (v, t) \in F_j \\ d_l - \sum_{i=1}^{n} p_{il} \cdot v(x_i) + (p - \sum_{i=1}^{n} p_{il}) \cdot t & \text{if } (v, t) \in G_l \end{cases}$$

$$g'(v, t) = \begin{cases} c'_{j'} + p \cdot t & \text{if } (v, t) \in F'_{j'} \\ d'_{l'} - \sum_{i=1}^{n} p'_{il'} \cdot v(x_i) + (p - \sum_{i=1}^{n} p'_{il'}) \cdot t & \text{if } (v, t) \in G'_{l'} \end{cases}$$

where $c_j, d_l, p_{il}, c'_{j'}, d'_{l'}, p'_{il'} \in \mathbb{Q}$ and $C_j, D_l, C'_{j'}, D'_{l'}$ are k-polyhedra for all $1 \leq i \leq n, 1 \leq j \leq M, 1 \leq l \leq N, 1 \leq j' \leq M'$ and $1 \leq l' \leq N'$ for some $M, M', N, N' \in \mathbb{N}$. Let $h : (\zeta \times \mathbb{R}) \to \mathbb{R}$ be the function such that $h(v, t) = \lambda \cdot g(v, t) + \lambda' \cdot g'(v, t)$ for all $(v, t) \in \zeta \times \mathbb{R}$. Taking any $(v, t) \in \zeta \times \mathbb{R}$, we have the following four cases to consider.

- If $(v, t) \in F_j \cap F'_{j'}$ for some j and j', then

$$h(v, t) = \lambda \cdot (c_j + p \cdot t) + \lambda' \cdot (c'_{j'} + p \cdot t) = (\lambda \cdot c_j + \lambda' \cdot c'_{j'}) + p \cdot t$$

since $\lambda + \lambda' = 1$.
- If $(v, t) \in F_j \cap G'_{l'}$ for some j and l', then

$$h(v, t) = \lambda \cdot (c_j + p \cdot t) + \lambda' \cdot \left(d'_{l'} - \sum_{i=1}^{n} p'_{il'} \cdot v(x_i) + (p - \sum_{i=1}^{n} p'_{il'}) \cdot t \right)$$

$$= (\lambda \cdot c_j + \lambda' \cdot d'_{l'}) - \sum_{i=1}^{n} (\lambda' \cdot p'_{il'}) \cdot v(x_i) + \left(\lambda \cdot p + \lambda' \cdot p - \sum_{i=1}^{n} (\lambda' \cdot p'_{il'}) \right) \cdot t$$
$$\text{(rearranging)}$$

$$= (\lambda \cdot c_j + \lambda' \cdot d'_{l'}) - \sum_{i=1}^{n} (\lambda' \cdot p'_{il'}) \cdot v(x_i) + (p - \sum_{i=1}^{n} (\lambda' \cdot p'_{il'})) \cdot t$$

since $\lambda + \lambda' = 1$.

– If $(v,t) \in G_l \cap F'_{j'}$ for some l and j', then similarly to the above:

$$h(v,t) = \lambda \cdot \left(d_l - \sum_{i=1}^{n} p_{il} \cdot v(x_i) + (p - \sum_{i=1}^{n} p_{il}) \cdot t \right) + \lambda' \cdot (c'_{j'} + t)$$

$$= (\lambda \cdot d_l + \lambda' \cdot c'_{j'}) - \sum_{i=1}^{n}(\lambda \cdot p_{il}) \cdot v(x_i) + (p - \sum_{i=1}^{n}(\lambda \cdot p_{il})) \cdot t.$$

– If $(v,t) \in G_l \cap G'_{l'}$ for some l and l', then using fact $\lambda + \lambda' = 1$ we have:

$$h(v,t) = \lambda \cdot \left(d_l - \sum_{i=1}^{n} p_{il} \cdot v(x_i) + (p - \sum_{i=1}^{n} p_{il}) \cdot t \right)$$

$$+\lambda' \cdot \left(d'_{l'} - \sum_{i=1}^{n} p'_{il'} \cdot v(x_i) + (p - \sum_{i=1}^{n} p'_{il'}) \cdot t \right)$$

$$= (\lambda \cdot d_l + \lambda' \cdot d'_{l'}) + \sum_{i=1}^{n}(\lambda \cdot p_{il} + \lambda' \cdot p'_{il'}) \cdot v(x_i) + (r - \sum_{i=1}^{n}(\lambda \cdot p_{il} + \lambda' \cdot p'_{il'})) \cdot t.$$

As these are all the cases to consider and the intersection of k-polyhedra is a k-polyhedron, it follows that h is a rational (p,k)-nice function as required. □

After the convex combination, $T^{\min}_{G_{\min}}$ and $T^{\max}_{G_{\max}}$ take a minimum or maximum value respectively, and therefore we show that these operations also preserve (p,k)-nicety.

Lemma 4. *The minimum and maximum of rational (p,k)-nice functions are rational (p,k)-nice.*

Proof. We prove the case for the minimum of rational (p,k)-nice functions; the case for maximum follows similarly. Given rational (p,k)-nice functions g, g' : $(\zeta \times \mathbb{R}) \rightarrow \mathbb{R}$ such that for any $(v,t) \in \zeta \times \mathbb{R}$:

$$g(v,t) = \begin{cases} c_j + p \cdot t & \text{if } (v,t) \in F_j \\ d_l - \sum_{i=1}^{n} p_{il} \cdot v(x_i) + (p - \sum_{i=1}^{n} p_{il}) \cdot t & \text{if } (v,t) \in G_l \end{cases}$$

$$g'(v,t) = \begin{cases} c_{j'} + p \cdot t & \text{if } (v,t) \in F'_{j'} \\ d'_{l'} - \sum_{i=1}^{n} p'_{il'} \cdot v(x_i) + (p - \sum_{i=1}^{n} p'_{il'}) \cdot t & \text{if } (v,t) \in G'_{l'} \end{cases}$$

where $c_j, d_l, p_{il}, c'_{j'}, d'_{l'}, p'_{il'} \in \mathbb{Q}$ and $C_j, D_l, C'_{j'}, D'_{l'}$ are k-polyhedra for all $1 \leq i \leq n, 1 \leq j \leq M, 1 \leq l \leq N, 1 \leq j' \leq M'$ and $1 \leq l' \leq N'$ for some $M, M'N, N' \in \mathbb{N}$. Letting $h = \min\{g, g'\}$ and considering $h(v,t)$ for any $(v,t) \in \zeta \times \mathbb{R}$, we have the following four cases to consider.

– If $(v,t) \in F_j \cap F'_{j'}$ for some j and j', then

$$h(v,t) = \begin{cases} c_j + p \cdot t & \text{if } (v,t) \in F_j \cap H \\ c_{j'} + p \cdot t & \text{if } (v,t) \in F'_{j'} \cap H' \end{cases}$$

where $H = \{(v,t) \in \zeta \times \mathbb{R} \mid c_j + p \cdot t \leq c'_{j'} + p \cdot t\} = \{(v,t) \in \zeta \times \mathbb{R} \mid c_j \leq c'_{j'}\}$ and similarly $H' = \{(v,t) \in \zeta \times \mathbb{R} \mid c'_{j'} \leq c_j\}$.

– If $(v,t) \in F_j \cap G'_{l'}$ for some j and l', then

$$h(v,t) = \begin{cases} c_j + p \cdot t & \text{if } (v,t) \in F_j \cap H \\ d'_{l'} - \sum_{i=1}^{n} p'_{il'} \cdot v(x_i) + (p - \sum_{i=1}^{n} p'_{il'}) \cdot t & \text{if } (v,t) \in G'_{l'} \cap H' \end{cases}$$

where

$$H = \{(v,t) \in \zeta \times \mathbb{R} \mid c_j + p \cdot t \le d'_{l'} - \sum_{i=1}^{n} p'_{il'} \cdot v(x_i) + (p - \sum_{i=1}^{n} p'_{il'}) \cdot t\}$$
$$= \{(v,t) \in \zeta \times \mathbb{R} \mid \sum_{i=1}^{n} p'_{il'} \cdot (v(x_i) + t) \le d'_{l'} - c_j\} \qquad \text{(rearranging)}$$
$$= \{(v,t) \in \zeta \times \mathbb{R} \mid \sum_{i=1}^{n} p'_{il'} \cdot (v+t)(x_i) \le d'_{l'} - c_j\} \quad \text{(by definition of } v+t)$$

and similarly $H' = \{(v,t) \in \zeta \times \mathbb{R} \mid \sum_{i=1}^{n} -p'_{il'} \cdot (v+t)(x_i) \le c_j - d'_{l'}\}$.

- If $(v,t) \in G_l \cap F'_{j'}$ for some l and j', then

$$h(v,t) = \begin{cases} d_l - \sum_{i=1}^{n} p_{il} \cdot v(x_i) + (p - \sum_{i=1}^{n} p_{il}) \cdot t & \text{if } (v,t) \in G_l \cap H \\ c_{j'} + t & \text{if } (v,t) \in F'_{j'} \cap H' \end{cases}$$

and by a similar reduction to the case above we have:

$$H = \{(v,t) \in \zeta \times \mathbb{R} \mid \sum_{i=1}^{n} -p_{il} \cdot (v+t)(x_i) \le c_{j'} - d_l\}$$
$$H' = \{(v,t) \in \zeta \times \mathbb{R} \mid \sum_{i=1}^{n} p_{il} \cdot (v+t)(x_i) \le d_l - c_{j'}\}.$$

- If $(v,t) \in G_l \cap G'_{l'}$ for some l and l', then

$$h(v,t) = \begin{cases} d_l - \sum_{i=1}^{n} p_{il} \cdot v(x_i) + (p - \sum_{i=1}^{n} p_{il}) \cdot t & \text{if } (v,t) \in G_l \cap H \\ d'_{l'} - \sum_{i=1}^{n} p'_{il'} \cdot v(x_i) + (p - \sum_{i=1}^{n} p'_{il'}) \cdot t & \text{if } (v,t) \in G'_{l'} \cap H' \end{cases}$$

where

$$H = \{(v,t) \in \zeta \times \mathbb{R} \mid d_l - \sum_{i=1}^{n} p_{il} \cdot v(x_i) + (p - \sum_{i=1}^{n} p_{il}) \cdot t$$
$$\le d'_{l'} - \sum_{i=1}^{n} p'_{il'} \cdot v(x_i) + (p - \sum_{i=1}^{n} p'_{il'}) \cdot t\}$$
$$= \{(v,t) \in \zeta \times \mathbb{R} \mid \sum_{i=1}^{n} (p'_{il'} - p_{il}) \cdot v(x_i) + \sum_{i=1}^{n} (p'_{il'} - p_{il}) \cdot t \le d'_{l'} - d_l\}$$
$$\text{(rearranging)}$$
$$= \{(v,t) \in \zeta \times \mathbb{R} \mid -\sum_{i=1}^{n} (p'_{il'} - p_{il}) \cdot (v(x_i) + t) \le d'_{l'} - d_l\}$$
$$\text{(rearranging again)}$$
$$= \{(v,t) \in \zeta \times \mathbb{R} \mid -\sum_{i=1}^{n} (p'_{il'} - p_{il}) \cdot (v+t)(x_i) \le d'_{l'} - d_l\}$$

by definition of $v+t$ and similarly we have:

$$H' = \{(v,t) \in \zeta \times \mathbb{R} \mid -\sum_{i=1}^{n} (p_{il} - p'_{il'}) \cdot (v+t)(x_i) \le d_l - d'_{l'}\}.$$

Since in each case H and H' are k-bipolyhedra, if follows from Definition 12 that the lemma holds. $\qquad \square$

The final operations performed by $T_{G_{\min}}^{\min}$ and $T_{G_{\max}}^{\max}$ concern taking the infimum or supremum over t of a function of the form $v \mapsto p \cdot t + f(l, \zeta)(l, v+t)$. Hence, we now show that performing either of these operations on a rational (p, k)-nice function returns a rational k-simple function.

Lemma 5. *For any zone ζ, if $g : (\zeta \times \mathbb{R}) \to \mathbb{R}$ is rational (p, k)-nice, then the functions $f_1 : \zeta \to \mathbb{R}$ and $f_2 : \zeta \to \mathbb{R}$ where $f_1(v) = \inf_{t \in \mathbb{R}} g(v, t)$ and $f_2(v) = \sup_{t \in \mathbb{R}} g(v, t)$ for $v \in \zeta$ are rational k-simple.*

Proof. We prove the case for f_1; the case for f_2 follows similarly (swapping Δ^- and Δ^+). Consider any zone ζ and rational (p, k)-nice function $g : (\zeta \times \mathbb{R}) \to \mathbb{R}$. By Definition 12, for any $(v, t) \in \zeta \times \mathbb{R}$, we have:

$$g(v, t) = \begin{cases} c_j + p \cdot t & \text{if } (v, t) \in F_j \\ d_l - \sum_{i=1}^n p_{il} \cdot v(x_i) + (p - \sum_{i=1}^n p_{il}) \cdot t & \text{if } (v, t) \in G_l \end{cases}$$

where $c_j, d_l, p_{il} \in \mathbb{Q}$ and

$$F_j = \{(v, t) \mid v \in C_j \wedge v + t \in C'_j\} \quad \text{and} \quad G_l = \{(v, t) \mid v \in D_l \wedge v + t \in D'_l\}$$

for some k-polyhedra C_j, C'_j, D_l and D'_l for all $1 \leq i \leq n, 1 \leq j \leq M$ and $1 \leq l \leq N$ for some $M, N \in \mathbb{N}$.

For any k-polyhedron C, let

$$\Delta^-(v, C) \overset{\text{def}}{=} \inf\{t \mid v + t \in C\} \quad \text{and} \quad \Delta^+(v, C) \overset{\text{def}}{=} \sup\{t \mid v + t \in C\}.$$

Following the arguments of [4], it follows that the functions $\Delta^-(\cdot, C) : \zeta \to \mathbb{R}$ and $\Delta^+(\cdot, C) : \zeta \to \mathbb{R}$ are both k-simple over k-polyhedra. If $f_1(v) = \inf_{t \in \mathbb{R}} g(v, t)$, for any $v \in \zeta$ we have $f_1(v)$ equals:

$$\begin{cases} c_j & \text{if } v \in C_j \cap C'_j \\ c_j + p \cdot \Delta^-(v, C'_j) & \text{if } v \in C_j \setminus C'_j \\ d_l - \sum_{i=1}^n p_{il} \cdot v(x_i) & \text{if } v \in D_l \cap D'_l \text{ and } p - \sum_{i=1}^n p_{il} \geq 0 \\ d_l - \sum_{i=1}^n p_{il} \cdot v(x_i) + (p - \sum_{i=1}^n p_{il}) \cdot \Delta^-(v, D'_l) & \text{if } v \in D_l \setminus D'_l \text{ and } p - \sum_{i=1}^n p_{il} \geq 0 \\ d_l - \sum_{i=1}^n p_{il} \cdot v(x_i) + (p - \sum_{i=1}^n p_{il}) \cdot \Delta^+(v, D'_l) & \text{if } v \in D_l \text{ and } p - \sum_{i=1}^n p_{il} < 0 \end{cases}$$

In all except the final two cases, since $\Delta^-(\cdot, C) : \zeta \to \mathbb{R}$ is k-simple, it follows that f_1 is rational k-simple. Considering the penultimate case, by definition of k-simple functions we have the following two cases to consider.

– if $\Delta^-(v, D'_l) = d'_l$ for some $d'_l \in \mathbb{Q}_+$, then for any $v \in D_l \setminus D'_l$:

$$f_1(v) = d_l - \sum_{i=1}^n p_{il} \cdot v(x_i) + (p - \sum_{i=1}^n p_{il}) \cdot \Delta^-(v, D'_l)$$
$$= \left(d_l + (p - \sum_{i=1}^n p_{il}) \cdot d'_l\right) - \sum_{i=1}^n p_{il} \cdot v(x_i) \qquad \text{(rearranging)}$$

which is rational k-simple, since g is rational (p, k)-nice.
– if $\Delta^-(v, D'_l) = d'_l - v(x_{i'_l})$ for some $d'_l \in \mathbb{Q}_+$ and $1 \leq i'_l \leq n$, then for any $v \in D_l \setminus D'_l$:

$$f_1(v) = d_l - \sum_{i=1}^n p_{il} \cdot v(x_i) + (p - \sum_{i=1}^n p_{il}) \cdot \Delta^-(v, D'_l)$$
$$= d_l - \sum_{i=1}^n p_{il} \cdot v(x_i) + (p - \sum_{i=1}^n p_{il}) \cdot (d'_l - v(x_{i'_l})) \qquad \text{(rearranging)}$$
$$= \left(d_l + (p - \sum_{i=1}^n p_{il}) \cdot d'_l\right) - \sum_{i=1}^n p'_{il} \cdot v(x_i)$$

where $p'_{il} = p_{il} + (p - \sum_{i=1}^n p_{il})$ if $i = i'_l$ and $p'_{il} = p_{il}$ otherwise.

The final case follows similarly to the penultimate using the fact $\Delta^+(v, D'_l)$ is a k-simple function. Therefore, we can conclude that f_1 is rational k-simple as required. $\qquad \square$

In the related proof of [25] we see that, for minimum expected time computation, it is always optimal to let as little time pass as possible in the current polyhedron and, for maximum expected time computation, it is always optimal to let as much time pass as possible. However, for prices, we see that this is not always the case, e.g., $\Delta^+(v, C)$ is used in the computation of minimum expected prices. This is due to the fact that price rates in locations reached at a later stage can be higher, and in such cases it can be optimal to let time pass now and accumulate a lower price, as opposed to waiting and accumulating a higher price later.

We now combine the above results and show that rational k-simple functions are a suitable representation for value functions when computing optimal expected time using value iteration and either $T_{G_{\min}}^{\min}$ or $T_{G_{\max}}^{\max}$.

Proposition 2. *For* opt $\in$ {min, max}, *if* $f : Z_{\text{opt}} \to (S_{\text{opt}} \to \mathbb{R})$ *is a rational k-simple function, then* $T_{G_{\text{opt}}}^{\text{opt}}(f)$ *is rational k-simple.*

Proof. We only the consider when opt = min, the case when opt = max follows similarly. Consider any rational k-simple function, $\mathbf{z} = (l, \zeta) \in Z_{\min}$ and $E \in$ $E(\mathbf{z})$. For any $v \in \mathbb{R}^{\mathcal{X}}$ and $t \in \mathbb{R}$ and letting $r = \text{price}_L(l)$ and $p' = \text{price}_{Act}(l, a)$:

$$p \cdot t + p' + \sum_{(\mathbf{z}, a, (R, l')), \mathbf{z}_{(R, l')}) \in E} \text{prob}(l, a)(R, l') \cdot f(\mathbf{z}_{(R, l')})(l', (v + t)[R])$$

$$= p \cdot t + p' + \sum_{(\mathbf{z}, a, (R, l')), \mathbf{z}_{(R, l')}) \in E} \text{prob}(l, a)(R, l') \cdot f[R](\mathbf{z}_{(R, l')})(l', v + t)$$

$$\text{(by Definition 11)}$$

$$= \sum_{(\mathbf{z}, a, (R, l')), \mathbf{z}_{(R, l')}) \in E} \text{prob}(l, a)(R, l') \cdot \left(p \cdot t + p' + f[R](\mathbf{z}_{(R, l')})(l', v + t)\right)$$

$$(2)$$

since $\text{prob}(l, a)$ is a distribution. By construction, f is rational k-simple, and hence for any $(\mathbf{z}, a, (R, l'), \mathbf{z}_{(R, l')}) \in E$ using Lemmas 1 and 2 we have that $p' + f[R]$ is also rational k-simple. Using Definition 12 it follows that:

$$(v, t) \mapsto p \cdot t + p' + f[R](\mathbf{z}_{(R, l')})(l', v + t)$$

is rational (p, k)-nice. Thus, since $(\mathbf{z}, a, (R, l'), \mathbf{z}_{(R, l')}) \in E$ was arbitrary, using Lemma 3 and (2) we have that:

$$(v, t) \mapsto p \cdot t + p' + \sum_{(\mathbf{z}, a, (R, l')), \mathbf{z}_{(R, l')}) \in E} \text{prob}(l, a)(R, l') \cdot f(\mathbf{z}_{(R, l')})(l', (v + t)[R])$$

is also rational (p, k)-nice. Since $E \in E(\mathbf{z})$ was arbitrary and $E(\mathbf{z})$ is finite, Lemma 4 tells us:

$$(v, t) \mapsto \min_{E \in E(\mathbf{z})} \left\{ p \cdot t + p' + \sum_{(\mathbf{z}, a, (R, l')), \mathbf{z}_{(R, l')}) \in E} \text{prob}(l, a)(R, l') \cdot f(\mathbf{z}_{(R, l')})(l', (v + t)[R]) \right\}$$

is again rational (p, k)-nice. Finally, using Definition 6 and Lemma 5, it follows that $T_G(f)(\mathbf{z})$ is rational k-simple as required. □

Proposition 2 tells us that value iteration over a zone graph to compute expected prices, as specified in Definition 6, can be performed using rational k-simple functions (and rational (p, k)-nice functions).

4.3 Example

Figure 2 shows an example of a linearly-priced PTA. Location prices are indicated next to each location; all action prices are zero so they are omitted from the figure. For this example, we consider the target set $F = \{l_2\}$ and compute both the minimum and maximum expected price of reaching F. For this PTA, all states reach the target with minimum (and maximum) probability 1, and therefore the zone graphs used for minimum and maximum expected price computation are the same and equal that constructed using the algorithm presented in Fig. 1. This zone graph is shown in Fig. 3.

In the case of the minimum expected price, performing value iteration over the zone graph G of Fig. 3 gives, for $n \geq 3$:

$$(T_{\mathsf{G}}^{\min})^n (f_0)(z_0)(l_0, v) = \left(2 + 0.5 \cdot \left(3 + \sum_{i=0}^{n-3} 0.25^i\right)\right) - v(x)$$

$$(T_{\mathsf{G}}^{\min})^n (f_0)(z_1)(l_1, v) = \begin{cases} 9 - 3 \cdot v(x) & \text{if } v(x) \leq 3 \\ 0 & \text{if } 3 \leq v(x) \leq 4 \end{cases}$$

$$(T_{\mathsf{G}}^{\min})^n (f_0)(z_2)(l_2, v) = \sum_{i=0}^{n-2} 0.25^i - v(x)$$

$$(T_{\mathsf{G}}^{\min})^n (f_0)(z_3)(l_3, v) = 0$$

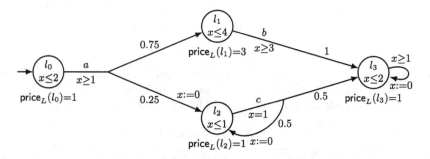

Fig. 2. Example PTA P

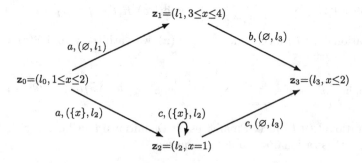

Fig. 3. Backwards zone graph G for PTA of Fig. 2 and target set $\{l_3\}$

It then follows that the minimum expected price to reach the target from the initial state equals 4.166667. On the other hand, for the maximum expected price, performing value iteration yields for $n \geq 3$:

$$(T_G^{\max})^n(f_0)(z_0)(l_0, v) = \begin{cases} \left(1 + 0.5 \cdot \left(9 + \sum_{i=0}^{n-3} 0.25^i\right)\right) - v(x) & \text{if } x \leq 1 \\ 0.5 \cdot \left(12 + \sum_{i=0}^{n-3} 0.25^i\right) - 3 \cdot v(x) & \text{if } 1 \leq x \leq 2 \end{cases}$$

$$(T_G^{\max})^n(f_0)(z_1)(l_1, v) = 12 - 3 \cdot v(x)$$
$$(T_G^{\max})^n(f_0)(z_2)(l_2, v) = \sum_{i=0}^{n-2} 0.25^i - v(x)$$
$$(T_G^{\max})^n(f_0)(z_3)(l_3, v) = 0$$

and hence the maximum expected price for the initial state is 6.166667.

The optimal strategy for the minimum expected price is to always perform an action as soon as it is enabled. The choices of the optimal strategy for the maximum expected price are to leave l_0 as soon as the action a is enabled, as this allows it to remain longer in l_1, yielding a higher overall expected price.

5   Conclusions

We have extended the techniques of [25] for the symbolic computation of optimal expected time and strategy synthesis to expected prices for linearly-priced probabilistic timed automata. The approach involves building the backwards zone graph of the PTA under study and then performing value iteration over this graph. We have demonstrated that an extension of simple and nice functions over rational valued polyhedra provide an effective representation of the value functions required for this computation. One restriction that we impose on the linearly-priced PTAs we consider is that all location prices are positive. We note that it should be possible to remove this restriction by extending the algorithms of [17] for removing zero-priced end components for finite state MDPs to linearly-priced PTAs.

As already mentioned in [25], an important next step is to perform a rigorous investigation into the advantages and disadvantages of our approach in comparison with the digital clocks method [28]. This will require implementing the algorithms introduced here, for example using the Parma Polyhedra Library [5], which includes efficient ways of manipulating convex polyhedra and has already been used effectively to implement a number of real-time verification algorithms. Finally, we also plan to investigate policy iteration since it converges to optimal expected prices (see Theorem 1 and Corollary 1).

Acknowledgments. This work was partly supported by the EPSRC Mobile Autonomy Programme Grant EP/M019918/1 and the PRINCESS project, funded by the DARPA BRASS programme.

References

1. Alur, R., Courcoubetis, C., Dill, D.: Model checking in dense real time. Inf. Comput. **104**(1), 2–34 (1993)
2. Alur, R., Dill, D.: A theory of timed automata. Theor. Comput. Sci. **126**, 183–235 (1994)
3. Alur, R., Torre, S., Pappas, G.J.: Optimal paths in weighted timed automata. In: Di Benedetto, M.D., Sangiovanni-Vincentelli, A. (eds.) HSCC 2001. LNCS, vol. 2034, pp. 49–62. Springer, Heidelberg (2001). doi:10.1007/3-540-45351-2_8
4. Asarin, E., Maler, O.: As soon as possible: time optimal control for timed automata. In: Vaandrager, F.W., van Schuppen, J.H. (eds.) HSCC 1999. LNCS, vol. 1569, pp. 19–30. Springer, Heidelberg (1999). doi:10.1007/3-540-48983-5_6
5. Bagnara, R., Hill, P., Zaffanella, E.: The Parma Polyhedra Library: toward a complete set of numerical abstractions for the analysis and verification of hardware and software systems. Sci. Comput. Program. **72**(1–2), 3–21 (2008)
6. Beauquier, D.: On probabilistic timed automata. Theor. Comput. Sci. **292**(1), 65–84 (2003)
7. Behrmann, G., Fehnker, A., Hune, T., Larsen, K., Pettersson, P., Romijn, J., Vaandrager, F.: Minimum-cost reachability for priced time automata. In: Di Benedetto, M.D., Sangiovanni-Vincentelli, A. (eds.) HSCC 2001. LNCS, vol. 2034, pp. 147–161. Springer, Heidelberg (2001). doi:10.1007/3-540-45351-2_15
8. Bellman, R.: Dynamic Programming. Princeton University Press, Princeton (1957)
9. Berendsen, J., Chen, T., Jansen, D.N.: Undecidability of cost-bounded reachability in priced probabilistic timed automata. In: Chen, J., Cooper, S.B. (eds.) TAMC 2009. LNCS, vol. 5532, pp. 128–137. Springer, Heidelberg (2009). doi:10.1007/978-3-642-02017-9_16
10. Berendsen, J., Jansen, D., Katoen, J.-P.: Probably on time and within budget - on reachability in priced probabilistic timed automata. In: Proceedings of the 3rd International Conference Quantitative Evaluation of Systems (QEST 2006), pp. 311–322. IEEE Press (2006)
11. Berendsen, J., Jansen, D., Vaandrager, F.: Fortuna: model checking priced probabilistic timed automata. In: Proceedings of the 7th International Conference Quantitative Evaluation of Systems (QEST 2010), pp. 273–281. IEEE Press (2010)
12. Bertsekas, D.: Dynamic Programming and Optimal Control, vol. 1 and 2. Athena Scientific, Belmont (1995)
13. Bertsekas, D., Tsitsiklis, J.: An analysis of stochastic shortest path problems. Math. Oper. Res. **16**(3), 580–595 (1991)
14. Bianco, A., de Alfaro, L.: Model checking of probabilistic and nondeterministic systems. In: Thiagarajan, P.S. (ed.) FSTTCS 1995. LNCS, vol. 1026, pp. 499–513. Springer, Heidelberg (1995). doi:10.1007/3-540-60692-0_70
15. Bohnenkamp, H., D'Argenio, P., Hermanns, H., Katoen, J.-P.: Modest: a compositional modeling formalism for hard and softly timed systems. IEEE Trans. Softw. Eng. **32**(10), 812–830 (2006)
16. David, A., Jensen, P.G., Larsen, K.G., Legay, A., Lime, D., Sørensen, M.G., Taankvist, J.H.: On time with minimal expected cost!. In: Cassez, F., Raskin, J.-F. (eds.) ATVA 2014. LNCS, vol. 8837, pp. 129–145. Springer, Cham (2014). doi:10.1007/978-3-319-11936-6_10
17. de Alfaro, L.: Computing minimum and maximum reachability times in probabilistic systems. In: Baeten, J.C.M., Mauw, S. (eds.) CONCUR 1999. LNCS, vol. 1664, pp. 66–81. Springer, Heidelberg (1999). doi:10.1007/3-540-48320-9_7

18. Duflot, M., Kwiatkowska, M., Norman, G., Parker, D.: A formal analysis of Bluetooth device discovery. Int. J. Softw. Tools Technol. Transf. **8**(6), 621–632 (2006)

19. Gregersen, H., Jensen, H.: Formal design of reliable real time systems. Master's thesis, Department of Mathematics and Computer Science, Aalborg University (1995)

20. Hartmanns, A., Hermanns, H.: A modest approach to checking probabilistic timed automata. In: Proceedings of the 6th International Conference on Quantitative Evaluation of Systems (QEST 2009), pp. 187–196. IEEE Press (2009)

21. Henzinger, T.A., Manna, Z., Pnueli, A.: What good are digital clocks? In: Kuich, W. (ed.) ICALP 1992. LNCS, vol. 623, pp. 545–558. Springer, Heidelberg (1992). doi:10.1007/3-540-55719-9_103

22. Henzinger, T., Nicollin, X., Sifakis, J., Yovine, S.: Symbolic model checking for real-time systems. Inf. Comput. **111**(2), 193–244 (1994)

23. James, H., Collins, E.: An analysis of transient Markov decision processes. J. Appl. Probab. **43**(3), 603–621 (2006)

24. Jovanović, A., Kwiatkowska, M., Norman, G.: Symbolic minimum expected time controller synthesis for probabilistic timed automata. In: Sankaranarayanan, S., Vicario, E. (eds.) FORMATS 2015. LNCS, vol. 9268, pp. 140–155. Springer, Cham (2015). doi:10.1007/978-3-319-22975-1_10

25. Jovanovic, A., Kwiatkowska, M., Norman, G., Peyras, Q.: Symbolic optimal expected time reachability computation and controller synthesis for probabilistic timed automata. Theoret. Comput. Sci. **669**, 1–21 (2017)

26. Kemeny, J., Snell, J., Knapp, A.: Denumerable Markov Chains. Springer, New York (1976)

27. Kwiatkowska, M., Norman, G., Parker, D.: PRISM 4.0: verification of probabilistic real-time systems. In: Gopalakrishnan, G., Qadeer, S. (eds.) CAV 2011. LNCS, vol. 6806, pp. 585–591. Springer, Heidelberg (2011). doi:10.1007/978-3-642-22110-1_47

28. Kwiatkowska, M., Norman, G., Parker, D., Sproston, J.: Performance analysis of probabilistic timed automata using digital clocks. Formal Methods Syst. Des. **29**, 33–78 (2006)

29. Kwiatkowska, M., Norman, G., Segala, R., Sproston, J.: Automatic verification of real-time systems with discrete probability distributions. Theoret. Comput. Sci. **282**, 101–150 (2002)

30. Kwiatkowska, M., Norman, G., Sproston, J., Wang, F.: Symbolic model checking for probabilistic timed automata. Inf. Comput. **205**(7), 1027–1077 (2007)

31. Larsen, K., Pettersson, P., Yi, W.: Uppaal in a nutshell. Int. J. Softw. Tools Technol. Transf. **1**, 134–152 (1997)

32. Larsen, K.G., Pettersson, P., Yi, W.: Model-checking for real-time systems. In: Reichel, H. (ed.) FCT 1995. LNCS, vol. 965, pp. 62–88. Springer, Heidelberg (1995). doi:10.1007/3-540-60249-6_41

33. Tripakis, S.: The analysis of timed systems in practice. Ph.D. thesis, Université Joseph Fourier, Grenoble (1998)

34. Tripakis, S.: Verifying progress in timed systems. In: Katoen, J.-P. (ed.) ARTS 1999. LNCS, vol. 1601, pp. 299–314. Springer, Heidelberg (1999). doi:10.1007/3-540-48778-6_18

35. Tripakis, S., Yovine, S., Bouajjani, A.: Checking timed Büchi automata emptiness efficiently. Formal Methods Syst. Des. **26**(3), 267–292 (2005)

Runtime Verification Logics
A Language Design Perspective

Klaus Havelund[1]([⊠]) and Giles Reger[2]

[1] Jet Propulsion Laboratory, California Institute of Technology, Pasadena, USA
klaus.havelund@jpl.nasa.gov
[2] University of Manchester, Manchester, UK

Abstract. Runtime Verification is a light-weight approach to systems verification, where actual executions of a system are processed and analyzed using rigorous techniques. In this paper we shall narrow the term's definition to represent the commonly studied variant consisting of verifying that a single system execution conforms to a specification written in a formal specification language. Runtime verification (in this sense) can be used for writing test oracles during testing when the system is too complex for full formal verification, or it can be used during deployment of the system as part of a fault protection strategy, where corrective actions may be taken in case the specification is violated. Specification languages for runtime verification appear to differ from for example temporal logics applied in model checking, in part due to the focus on monitoring of events that carry data, and specifically due to the desire to relate data values existing at different time points, resulting in new challenges in both the complexity of the monitoring approach and the expressiveness of languages. Over the recent years, numerous runtime verification specification languages have emerged, each with its different features and levels of expressiveness and usability. This paper presents an overview and a discussion of this design space.

1 Introduction

Runtime Verification (RV) [31,48] is narrowly viewed[1] as the process of monitoring and checking the runtime behavior of a system, from here on referred to as the System Being Monitored (SBM), against a formal specification. RV can be applied for safety, security, and comprehension purposes. The SBM must emit an event stream (via instrumentation or otherwise), the execution trace,

---

K. Havelund—The research performed by this author was carried out at Jet Propulsion Laboratory, California Institute of Technology, under a contract with the National Aeronautics and Space Administration.

G. Reger—The work of this author is related to COST Action ARVI IC1402, supported by COST (European Cooperation in Science and Technology).

[1] RV more broadly includes such topics as checking traces with algorithms, learning specifications including statistical information from traces, trace visualization, program instrumentation, and fault protection.

L. Aceto et al. (Eds.): Larsen Festschrift, LNCS 10460, pp. 310–338, 2017.
DOI: 10.1007/978-3-319-63121-9_16

which is then consumed by a monitor, which as a secondary input takes a formal specification. RV can be applied in online mode, where the monitor executes at the same time as the SBM, tracking its moves step by step, or it can be applied in offline mode to a log produced by the SBM. Orthogonally, RV can be applied before deployment of the software, for example as part of the testing process, or after deployment, for example as part of a fault protection strategy, where the monitor can influence the behavior of the SBM. In this case, the monitor will usually be run in online mode. The monitor in the simplest case will produce a true/false verdict, but can be more informative, and produce richer information about the trace seen so far.

To be effective, a runtime verification method requires an *expressive specification language* to capture properties of interest, an *elegant specification language* allowing specifications to be succinct and easy to write and read, and an *efficient monitoring algorithm* to ensure that monitoring does not impede the running of the monitored system. In this paper we shall focus on the former two (although efficiency will be discussed as it does indeed influence the design space), and investigate what we consider the most common variations of specification languages for RV. Numerous such specification languages have been developed in recent time. These are usually based on well known concepts such as e.g. state machines, regular expressions, temporal logics (past time as well as future time), timed logics, context free grammars, variations of the μ-calculus, rule-based systems, stream processing, and process algebras.

A big emphasis over the last decade has been on data parameterized logics, suited for monitoring sequences of events carrying data parameters (named records). Temporal logics applied in model checking (MC) [39] have to some extent allowed data as well. However, state of the art RV logics tend to support relating data across time points in a manner not as commonly supported in temporal logics for MC (although instances exist, e.g. [1]). To illustrate this, assume that we analyze finite traces (logs), and that we operate with a variant of LTL [53] with a finite trace semantics. Consider the following classical MC formula: $\Box(p \rightarrow \Diamond q)$, meaning if p is true in a position in the trace, then q must be true at a later point in that finite trace. In a system such as SPIN, it is possible to associate expressions over the state to the propositions p and q, for example $p = x \geq 0$ and $q = y \geq 0$. Expanding these names in the formula, we get the formula: $\Box(x \geq 0 \rightarrow \Diamond y \geq 0)$. This formula refers to data. However, to monitor such a formula (on a finite trace) requires a memory of only 1 bit, raised iff. $x \geq 0$ has been observed true and $y \geq 0$ has not yet been observed true when analyzing the trace from left to right. Consider now a different formula, expressing that whenever $x \geq 0$ and has a value k then y should eventually obtain that value: $\forall k \ \Box((x \geq 0 \land x = k) \rightarrow \Diamond y = k)$. This property can be very costly to monitor since the monitor from any point where $x \geq 0$ will have to remember the value k of x until y catches up.

Due to the nature of RV where only a single trace is examined, it is considered possible to allow very expressive specification languages, in contrast to static analysis, where expressiveness of the specification language normally is considered in conflict with degree of automation achievable. It is this perceived freedom to explore richer logics that have caused RV logics to incorporate data on a larger scale. It is, however, not the case that RV logics need to be so different from for example MC logics. RV logics can fundamentally focus on finite traces (safety properties), whereas MC logics must handle infinite traces (safety and liveness properties). But beyond this point, the two classes of logics could in principle have a very large intersection. Runtime verification can be seen as exploring new branches of logics also potentially useful for model checking.

This paper presents a discussion of some of the design space for state-of-the-art RV logics, that we have found of general interest. The presentation is split into a discussion of core temporal constructs without considering data (although data occur), followed by considerations of how to deal with data. The discussion is in part based on property examples and their specifications produced by participants of two recent runtime verification competitions, CRV (Competition on Runtime Verification) 2014 [8] and CRV 2015 [32]. Participants used their favorite specification language to specify a set of shared properties proposed by the participants. In this study we inspected properties submitted by the developers of MARQ [55], LOGFIRE [37], Larva [22], JAVAMOP [51], JUnitRV [24], Monpoly [10], and Solist [17]. The paper focuses due to lack of space specifically on state machines, regular expressions and temporal logics, since these are the most commonly seen. This leaves out RV systems for such formalisms as context free grammars [51], variations of the μ-calculus [4], rule-based systems [6,37], stream processing [23], and process algebras [7], all of which are quite interesting alternatives. As the focus of this paper is on the usability of specification languages, we will often make use of ASCII representations of specifications in different formalisms. However, where the focus is not on usability, but on some other feature of the language, we will use more convenient formalisms such as graphical automata and mathematical formula.

The paper is organized as follows. We begin with a brief summary of the main elements considered of importance in runtime verification (Sect. 2). We then present parts of the design space for propositional logics ignoring data (Sect. 3) and then with data (Sect. 4). We conclude with a summary of our findings (Sect. 5).

2   Fundamentals of Runtime Verification

To set the scene we briefly recall what we mean by runtime verification (RV) in this paper and, therefore, what a specification language for RV involves. In runtime verification we *abstract* an executing system being monitored (SBM) as a sequence of discrete observations, also referred to as a *trace*. We call these observations *events*. Commonly events are either propositional names or named data records i.e. a pair of a name and a list of data values. Events can be produced directly by the system, or extracted by code instrumentation: special code pieces inserted in the executing code, either manually or using some form of automated code instrumentation software, for example aspect-oriented programming technology [41]. In the case of offline monitoring, the trace will be finite. In the case of online monitoring, the executing system may be theoretically non-terminating. However, even in this case any monitor will at any time have to rely only on a finite set of observations - a finite *prefix* of the theoretically infinite execution.

We shall refer to a desired behavior of a system to be monitored as a *property*. Let Γ denote the set of all possible traces. A property is abstractly seen as a subset $\mathcal{P} \subseteq \Gamma$ of traces, namely the traces that we say satisfy (belong to) the property. We shall usually describe properties in informal English, and then formalize them in a specification language. A specification language allows us to formally define $\mathcal{P}$ via a textual specification φ. The property (set of traces) represented by a specification φ is denoted by $\mathcal{P}(\varphi)$. The monitoring problem is then to check whether a particular trace τ belongs to this set i.e. to check $\tau \in \mathcal{P}(\varphi)$. This is often referred to as *matching* the trace against the property. Note that specifications can be provided in negative form as discussed below. For this reason we need to distinguish between the language $\mathcal{L}(\varphi)$ denoted by a specification, which is a very straight forward definition, and the property $\mathcal{P}(\varphi)$ denoted by the specification, defined in terms of $\mathcal{L}(\varphi)$. This will be clarified in the following. A number of concerns must be addressed in any RV system, as discussed below.

Polarity. A specification φ may specify the *good* (desired) behavior or the *bad* (undesired) behavior. In the positive case $\mathcal{P}(\varphi) = \mathcal{L}(\varphi)$. In the negative case $\mathcal{P}(\varphi) = \Gamma \setminus \mathcal{L}(\varphi)$. In the former case matching represents *validation* and in the latter it represents *violation* of the property. This choice can have an impact on the readability of a specification. For example, consider the following *UnsafeMapIterator* property about JAVA collection objects.

Property 1 (UnsafeMapIterator). Given a map object m, collection object c, and iterator object i, if c is created from m (c is for example the set of m's key values), and i is created from c, and later m is updated, then i should not be used any further. We use the event `create(x, y)` to indicate that object y is created from object x, `use(i)` to indicate that iterator i is used for iteration, and `update(m)` to indicate that map m is updated.

A positive formulation of this property using a data parameterized regular expression[2] (note that the main emphasis is not on data here) could be:

$$\Lambda m, c, i : \texttt{create}(m, c).\texttt{update}(m)^*.\texttt{create}(c, i).\texttt{use}(i)^*.\texttt{update}(m)^* \quad (1)$$

This property states the sequence of events that are allowed (for a map m, collection c and iterator i). Most notably, this sequence disallows an use event occurring after a map update. The positive formulation needs to capture all acceptable behaviors. A negative formulation could be:

$$\exists m, c, i : \texttt{create}(m, c).\texttt{create}(c, i).\texttt{update}(m).\texttt{use}(i) \quad (2)$$

---

[2] Here $\Lambda m, c, i$ is related to trace-slicing (see Sect. 4.4) and has the meaning that the property should hold *for all* subtraces projected on possible values for m, c, i.

Where we take a non-standard *skip* semantics (see Sect. 3.1) that skips any event that does not match the next expected event. In the negative formulation it suffices to describe the sequence of events required to lead to failure, which in some cases can be simpler. Therefore, there is an argument for allowing for both positive and negative formulations even if the underlying language is closed under negation.

Where to Match. In the previous example we matched the total trace against the formulas, that is checking $\tau \in \mathcal{L}(\varphi)$ in the positive case and $\tau \in \Gamma \setminus \mathcal{L}(\varphi)$ in the negative case. This is referred to as *total* matching, and is the most common approach. An alternative is to perform *suffix* matching, first proposed in [2], where a trace belongs to the property denoted by the specification if a suffix of the trace belongs to the language of the specification. That is: $\mathcal{P}(\varphi) = \{\sigma.\tau \mid \tau \in \mathcal{L}(\varphi), \sigma \in \Gamma\}$. To see how this can improve readability consider the following property, also about JAVA objects.

Property 2 (HasNextIterator). For every iterator object i, a call to `next` must be preceded by a call to `hasNext` returning `true`, without any other `next` calls occurring in between.

The following two specifications of this property are negative (the undesired case). One (left) uses total-matching on the whole trace, and the other (right) uses suffix-matching.

$$\Lambda i : (\mathtt{hasNext}(i, \mathtt{true})^+.\mathtt{next}(i))^*.\mathtt{next}(i) \qquad \Lambda i : (\epsilon \mid \mathtt{next}(i)).\mathtt{next}(i)$$

Where ϵ denotes the start of the trace. Suffix-matching also allows us to write the slightly more concise $\Lambda i : \mathtt{next}(i).\mathtt{next}(i)$, which is not quite equivalent as it misses the case where the trace begins with $\mathtt{next}(i)$. Suffix matching is typically combined with negatively formulated regular expressions.

Finite versus Infinite Traces. When monitoring a trace produced by a system, at any point in time the trace observed so far will be finite. This means that the semantics of runtime verification logics should deal with finite traces. Finite state machines and regular expressions are typically defined over *finite* traces. However, traditionally, temporal logics applied in, for example, model checking, are defined over infinite traces, and such temporal logics must be adapted to the finite trace scenario, re-defining their semantics, when applied in a runtime verification context. One such approach, which for example is applicable to off-line log file analysis, is to handle obligations such as $\Diamond p$ as false on a finite trace where p never occurs. Hence the result of evaluating a temporal formula on a trace is either true or false, as in the case of finite state machines and regular expressions (language membership). A different approach, applicable to online monitoring, consists of viewing a finite trace as a prefix of some infinite trace. At each time point the current verdict depends on whether the finite trace observed so far potentially can be extended to a satisfying (finite or infinite) trace. This naturally leads one to go beyond the true and false verdicts, and introduce additional verdicts, such as "so far true" and "so far false", for cases where there are both satisfying and violating extensions. The reader is invited to consult [14,31] for further discussions.

Safety and Co-safety Properties. A *safety* property intuitively captures the notion that nothing bad happens [44]. The languages of such properties are prefix-closed since if a trace is safe then all of its prefixes must be safe. A consequence of this is that safety properties can be falsified by a finite prefix of a trace i.e. there can be a point before the end of the trace where it is known that the property has been falsified. Conversely, *co-safety* properties capture the notion that something good happens, are extension-closed[3], and can be *validated* by a finite prefix. Properties may be neither safety or co-safety properties but may share qualities with both classes. A *response* property of the form *"whenever A happens B should eventually happen"* is an example of a property that is neither, and can not be decided by a prefix of a trace. One may therefore deem such a property non-monitorable. However, in the case of offline monitoring, where one checks a finite trace that is not extended, it is possible to give a very precise true/false semantics to such a formula. Classes of monitorable properties are discussed further in [15,30].

Beyond Language Inclusion. So far we have mostly discussed logics for checking Boolean satisfaction in the form of: $\tau \in \mathcal{P}(\varphi)$. We have, however, briefly mentioned extending the Boolean verdict domain $\{true, false\}$ with values such as "so far true" and "so far false" [14,15], in some work unified into a "so far unknown" ?-result [51]. The full generalization of the Boolean result domain is any data domain D considered useful. For example, a logic could be designed for computing statistical information as to how well the trace satisfies a property, or even producing user-defined computations over the trace. Collecting statistical information as a query is described in [33]. The LOLA system [23] produces streams of data. Statistical model checking [46,47] is an approach where executions of the systems are monitored until an algorithm from statistics can produce an estimate for the system to satisfy a given property.

3 The Choice of Base Language

The first, and most important, choice when designing an RV logic is that of the base language. Here we consider the most classical choices of state machines and regular expressions [58], as well as temporal logic [49].

3.1 State Machines

One of the most fundamental formalisms for specifying orderings of events is state machines. We begin by introducing a property well-suited to state machines, concerned with the allocation of resources to tasks.

---

[3] A language is extension closed if whenever τ is in the language then so is $\tau.\sigma$ for any σ.

Property 3 (Resource Lifecycle). For every task t and resource r there is a life-cycle of allowed actions. Initially the task does not own the resource and from this state it can request the resource. This request can be denied or granted. If denied it returns to the unowned state, if granted it moves to an owned state. In an owned state the task can be asked to rescind the resource (hand it back), in which case it stays in this state, or the task can cancel its ownership, in which case it returns to the unowned state. A granted resource must eventually be canceled. No other action orderings are allowed.

If we ignore the data part (task and resource identities), this property can be specified as a state machine as follows, where only states 1 and 2 are acceptance states, meaning that a granted resource must be eventually canceled. We give both a graphical and textual representation of the state machine.

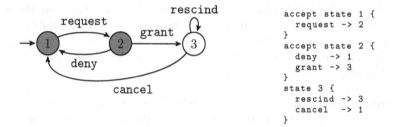

```
accept state 1 {
    request -> 2
}
accept state 2 {
    deny   -> 1
    grant  -> 3
}
state 3 {
    rescind -> 3
    cancel  -> 1
}
```

The Semantics of Missing Transitions. In the above state machine the transition relation is not complete (closed) i.e. we do not have a next target state for each combination of source state and event. For example, there is no transition with the label +deny+ leaving state 1. The implicit understanding is that the transition relation is closed to an implicit *failure* state: all missing transitions lead to the *failure* state. We will call this approach a *next semantics* as it requires each next event to cause a transition. The alternative is a *skip semantics* where observed events may be skipped if there is no transition for them. Note that the standard interpretation of finite state machines (in theoretical computer science) is a next semantics. In contrast, UML statecharts [27,52] are often given a skip semantics. See [3,5] for RV systems allowing a mix of next and skip semantics.

To illustrate the difference, let us return to Property 1 (UnsafeMapIterator) where we gave a positive (formula (1) page 4) and negative (formula (2) page 4) formulation of the property as regular expressions. We can turn these regular expressions into state machines[4] as follows. Graphically we represent states with

---

[4] As before, the focus is not on the data part. Here we use the same operators as before, which are like universal and existential quantification for the positive and negative formulations respectively. The way we add parameters to state machines is covered extensively in Sect. 4.

a next and skip semantics as circles and squares respectively[5]. The positive state machine formulation is:

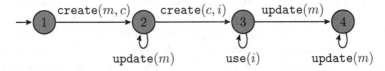

The negative state machine formulation of this property is:

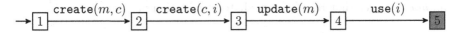

Traditionally regular expressions are translated to finite state machines with next-states. We observe that the positive formulation uses next-states whilst the negative uses skip-states. It is quite common to use a next semantics with positive formulations and a skip semantics with negative formulations. We would, however, want to allow a mixture of such states within one specification, allowing a fine-grained control over the closure. As a simple example demonstrating this desire, consider a property over an alphabet of events $\{e_1, \ldots, e_n, \text{quiet}, \text{loud}\}$ stating that no other events should occur between quiet and loud. Below we demonstrate three different state machines capturing this property. The first uses implicit next states, the second uses implicit skip states, and the third uses a mixture. Using a mixture of states allows us to specify the property more concisely. Whilst this is a simple example, the general idea extends to more complex properties.

```
accept state 1 {
    e1 -> 1
    ...
    en -> 1
    quiet -> 2
}
accept state 2 {
    loud -> 2
}
```

```
accept state 1 {
    quiet -> 2
}
accept state 2 {
    e1 -> error
    ...
    en -> error
    loud -> 2
}
```

```
accept skip state 1 {
    quiet -> 2
}
accept next state 2 {
    loud -> 2
}
```

Alphabets. In the case where next-states are used, as in the first positive formulation above, where each observed incoming event must match a transition, it is crucial that only *events of concern* are matched against the transitions. Otherwise any trace with additional events might easily fail to conform. To avoid this problem, such a specification must be associated with an alphabet: the events of concern. A trace that contains events not in the alphabet must first be projected to remove such. Often the alphabet is the set of events mentioned in the specification, but that is not always the case.

---

[5] We note that this graphical presentation has been reversed compared to some previous work [3,55]. We have chosen this presentation here as a next semantics is more typical for state machines as is a circle being used to represent a state, and states in state charts, which usually have skip semantics, normally are drawn as boxes, although typically with rounded corners.

Fine-Grained Acceptance. An advantage of state machines is that they allow for a fine-grained notion of acceptance. This is demonstrated in the above state machine for Property 3 (Resource Lifecycle) where state 3 is non-final whilst states 1 and 2 are final. This is key for any language wanting to capture properties which are not purely safety properties. An extension of this fine-grained acceptance is the ability to attach different kinds of failures to different states. This has particular use in runtime monitoring where different correction actions may be required for different forms of failure, as i.e. supported in [51]. Indeed, it would allow a specification to separate *soft* failures that only require reporting and *hard* failures that require immediate termination or intervention.

Anonymous States. One reason that temporal logics and regular expressions often yield more succinct specifications than state machines is that all intermediate states need to be explicitly named in the state machine. A simple syntactic layer of syntax on top of state machines can, however, allow *anonymous states* [5], making state machines more succinct. Below left we merge states 1 and 2 of the Resource Lifecycle property by turning state 2 into an anonymous acceptance state (state 3, which is not shown, is the same as before). Ignoring the rescind event, below right is shown how an event with a single outgoing transition can be treated even more concisely (here states are accepting by default and there is a next-semantics).

```
accept state 1 {                    state 1 {
  request -> accept {                 request -> {
    deny  -> 1                          deny  -> 1
    grant -> 3                          grant -> cancel -> 1
  }                                   }
}                                   }
```

Generally, one has to capture these assumptions (acceptance state or not, next-state or skip-state) with an additional annotations in the non-default cases.

3.2   Regular Expressions

Anonymous states are carried to the extreme in regular expressions i.e. there are no named states. State machines and regular expressions have the same expressive power in the propositional case. Regular expressions are more succinct than their corresponding state machines since intermediate states are not mentioned by name, only transitions are mentioned.

Standard Operators. We have already seen several examples of regular expressions and how they related to state machines, including how next-states and skip-states can be used to model their semantics. The basic form of a regular expression is a letter, such as for example: a, representing the language $\{a\}$. The operators apply semantically to languages and produce new languages. Given two regular expressions E_1 and E_2, the basic operators are union: $E_1|E_2$ (the union of the languages denoted by E_1 and E_2, sometimes written, although not here, as $E_1 + E_2$); concatenation: $E_1 E_2$ (the set of words, each of the form $l_1 l_2$ where l_i is a word in the language denoted by E_i); and finally closure: E^* (set of words each obtained by concatenating any number of words denoted by E). Additional operators are usually defined for convenience, but provide no additional expressive power. These include the dot: '.' (representing any letter, the union of all letters in the alphabet); plus: E^+ (meaning one or more, equivalent to EE^*); optional: $E?$ (meaning $E|\epsilon$ where ϵ accepts the empty string); and repetition: E^n (for some number n, meaning n copies of E, and variants of this operator indicating minimum and maximum number of occurrences). Negation is also commonly seen but most typically on letters. A common approach is to write unions of many letters: $a_1|a_2|\ldots|a_n$, as a list: $[a_1, a_2, \ldots, a_n]$, and negation of all these letters is then written as $[^\wedge a_1, a_2, \ldots, a_n]$. Negation of entire regular expressions, as in $\neg E$, is also semantically possible, but usually avoided due to complexity in generating the corresponding state machine.

Safety Properties. The standard interpretation of the regular expression concatenation operator (that $E_1 E_2$ denotes the set of words $l_1 l_2$ where l_i is in the language denoted by E_i) makes it inconvenient to express certain safety properties. Consider for example the language denoted by the following state machine:

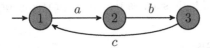

The main observation here is that all states are acceptance states, hence the language includes strings such as a, ab, abc, $abca$, etc. Representing this language as a regular expression with the standard semantics, however, becomes slightly inconvenient and error prone to write:

$$(a\, b\, c)^*(\epsilon \,|\, a \,|\, a\, b)$$

It would instead be desirable just to write:

$$(a\, b\, c)^*$$

However, this formula denotes the following automaton with the standard interpretation of regular expressions:

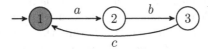

If we want the former interpretation, but the latter formulation of the regular expression, we need to provide a closure operation that closes a language to include all its prefixes. That is, given a regular expression E with the standard interpretation one can form the closure $closure(E)$ of this to include the language denoted by E as well as all its prefixes. Our property would then become $closure((a\, b\, c)^*)$.

Limitations of Regular Expressions. While regular expressions generally are very succinct and useful, in some cases the regular expression formulation of e.g. a state machine can become so convoluted that an ordinary user will be challenged in creating it, as well as in reading it. To illustrate this let us revisit Property 3 (ResourceLifecycle). Recall that the state machine was pretty straightforward to create. A regular expression version of this property is the following:

$$((request\ deny)^*\ request\ grant\ rescind^*\ cancel)^*\ request?$$

This regular expression is not completely obvious to create, in part due to the fact that some of the states in the state machine are acceptance states and some are not. In fact, we got this regular expression wrong in the first attempt. It is easy to see that if the state machine gets much more complicated, the regular expression becomes overly complex to write and even read. Furthermore, updatable data variables, which are straightforward to support in state machines, are not straightforward to introduce in regular expressions, this will be discussed in the subsequent section. Consequently, one may want to pursue a formalism that supports state machines (or a similar concept such as rule systems or variants of the μ-calculus [43], which in common have that states can be named and used in loops) in addition to a logic such as regular expressions or/and temporal logic.

3.3   Temporal Logic

In Sect. 3.1 it was discussed how states in a state machine can be anonymous, mixing anonymous states and named states in one notation. Regular expressions go to the extreme and eliminate the notion of named state all together. Likewise, temporal logic eliminates the notion of named states. It was generally clear from the competition benchmarks that temporal logic provided the most elegant formulation of many properties. The difference was rather remarkable in several cases.

Standard Operators. Introducing temporal logic in its many variations is beyond the scope of this paper. However, we will discuss the standard operators of future time Linear Temporal Logic (LTL) [53], the most common temporal logic used in runtime verification[6], and their past time counterparts. Future time LTL can be described as propositional logic plus the temporal operators $\bigcirc$ (*next*) and $\mathcal{U}$ (*until*). Their semantics are that $\bigcirc\varphi$ holds if φ holds at the next time point, and $\varphi_1\,\mathcal{U}\,\varphi_2$ holds if φ_2 holds at some future time point and φ_1 holds at all time points from the current until and including the one before that future time point. The operators $\Diamond$ (*eventually*), $\Box$ (*always*), and $\mathcal{W}$ (*weak until*) can then be defined as follows: $\Diamond\varphi = true\,\mathcal{U}\,\varphi$, $\Box\varphi = \neg\Diamond\neg\varphi$, and $\varphi_1\,\mathcal{W}\,\varphi_2 = \Box\varphi_1\vee(\varphi_1\,\mathcal{U}\,\varphi_2)$. Similarly, past time operators include $\bullet$ (*previous*, the dual of $\bigcirc$) and $\mathcal{S}$ (*since*, the dual of $\mathcal{U}$). Their semantics are that $\bullet\varphi$ holds if φ holds at the previous

---

[6] CTL (Computation Tree Logic) [21] is a logic on execution path trees, and has therefore not been popular in runtime verification. However, one can imagine a CTL-like logic being used for analyzing a set of traces, merged into a tree.

time point, and $\varphi_1 \, \mathcal{S} \, \varphi_2$ holds if φ_2 holds at some past time point and φ_1 holds at all time points since then to the current. The operators ◆ (*sometime in the past*) and ■ (*always in the past*) can then be defined as follows: ◆$\varphi = true \, \mathcal{S} \, \varphi$, ■$\varphi = \neg$◆$\neg\varphi$. A convenient logic is likely one that includes past time as well as future time operators.

The symbols just introduced look mathematically elegant, but they are not in ASCII format. Therefore it is typical to replace these logical symbols by text. For example □ may be written as the word `always`, or as the symbol `[]`. We will use a mix of the logical and textual word presentations here.

Illustrating Strength of Temporal Logic. With the following property we shall illustrate the advantage of a temporal logic over a state machine.

Property 4 (ResourceConflictManagement). This property represents the management of conflicts between resources as managed by a planetary rover's internal resource management system - or any resource management system in general. It is assumed that conflicts between resources are declared at the beginning of operation. After this point resources that are in conflict with each other cannot be granted at the same time. A conflict between resources r_1 and r_2 is captured by the event `conflict`(r_1, r_2) and a conflict is symmetrical. Resources are granted and canceled using `grant`(r) and `cancel`(r) respectively.

The specification of this property as a state machine in textual format becomes somewhat verbose (note that here we write properties in ASCII format for better illustrating how they would be written down in practice):

```
For all r1,r2
accept skip state start {
  conflict(r1,r2) -> free
  conflict(r2,r1) -> free
}
accept skip state free {
  grant(r1) -> granted
}
accept skip state granted {
  cancel(r1) -> free
  grant(r2)  -> failure
}
```

Alternatively, this property can be stated as a more concise temporal logic formula, for example as the following future time temporal logic formula:

```
forall r1,r2
  always ((conflict(r1,r2) or conflict(r2,r1)) =>
    (always (grant(r1) =>
      ((not grant(r2)) weakuntil cancel(r1))))))
```

That is, it is always the case that if a conflict is declared between two resources r_1 and r_2, then it is always the case that if r_1 is granted then r_2 is not thereafter granted unless r_1 is canceled first. In both formulations, to capture the symmetric conflict event, we need to match against either `conflict`(r_1, r_2) or `conflict`(r_2, r_1).

We can express this as a negative (a match is an error) regular expression as follows:

```
forall r1,r2
  (conflict(r1,r2)|conflict(r2,r1)).* grant(r1) (!cancel(r1))* grant(r2)
```

When working in temporal logic one usually formulates properties positively: what is desired to hold, whereas when formulating the same properties as regular expressions they appear easier to write in negative form. When formalizing requirements, however, it may appear somewhat inconvenient to have to negate the properties. Another example is the property $\Box(a \Rightarrow \Diamond b)$, which as a regular expression may be stated as a suffix matching negative expression $a.(\neg b)^*$. A positive regular expression formulation gets rather convoluted: $((\neg a)^*(a.^*b)?)^*$. Hence if a positive formulation of requirements is desired, as e.g. in project requirement documents, temporal logic may in some scenarios be more attractive than regular expressions.

The Convenience of Past Time Operators. The same property can also be stated as a past time formula, as follows.

$$(\forall r_1, r_2)\Box\left(\left(\mathbf{grant}(r_1) \wedge \blacklozenge\begin{pmatrix}\mathtt{conflict}(r_1, r_2)\\ \vee \\ \mathtt{conflict}(r_2, r_1)\end{pmatrix}\right) \Rightarrow \neg\bullet\begin{pmatrix}\neg\mathtt{cancel}(r_2)\\ \mathcal{S} \\ \mathbf{grant}(r_2)\end{pmatrix}\right)$$

However, this past time logic formula is not convincingly easier to read than the future time version. Especially as there are multiple references to different points in the past. There are, however, cases where past time is more convenient, as also pointed out in [45]. Consider the hasNextIterator Property 2 again. The property states that every call of next on an iterator should be preceded by a call of hasNext (which returns true). If we should state this property as a future time property, it would become:

$$(\forall i)\left(\begin{array}{l}(\neg\mathbf{next}(i) \ \mathcal{W} \ \mathbf{hasNext}(i, \mathit{true}))\wedge \\ \Box(\mathbf{next}(i) \Rightarrow \bigcirc(\neg\mathbf{next}(i) \ \mathcal{W} \ \mathbf{hasNext}(i, \mathit{true})))\end{array}\right)$$

This property seems overly complicated. This is caused by the necessity to separate two scenarios: (i) the first occurring **next** in the trace, and (ii) subsequent **next** events, appearing after previous **next** events. The property becomes slightly more concise, and thus more readable, when formulated in past time logic:

$$(\forall i) \ \Box(\mathbf{next}(i) \to \bullet(\neg\mathbf{next}(i) \ \mathcal{S} \ \mathbf{hasNext}(i, \mathit{true})))$$

Adding Convenient Operators. Temporal logic is often attributed being difficult to use, and it is occasionally claimed that even state machines are easier to use by practitioners. The specification of the competition exercises, however, shows to us that temporal logic makes specification substantially easier in quite many cases. A logic like LTL, however, appears to have some flaws from a usability point of view, including: binary operators that are tricky to remember the semantics of (such as *weak until* versus *until*, *since*, etc.), formulas tend to get nested, requiring use of parentheses for grouping sub-expressions for even the simplest formulas, and cumbersome handing of sequencing. We briefly recall how some of these problems can be alleviated with convenient alternative syntax.

Consider the previous past time formulation of the HasNextIterator property, that contains the subterm: $\neg$next(i) S hasNext$(i, true)$, meaning: hasNext $(i, true)$ has occurred in the past and since then no next(i) has occurred. This is not a very readable formulation of this property. An example of a more convenient operator is the temporal operator $[P, Q)$ from MaC [42], meaning P has been true in the past and since then Q has not. Using this operator the subterm becomes: $[$hasNext$(i, true),$ next$(i))$, which visually better illustrates the temporal order of events. The property now becomes:

$$(\forall i)\ \Box(\text{next}(i) \rightarrow \bullet[\text{hasNext}(i, true), \text{next}(i)))$$

Consider further that in such implications usually the right-hand temporal expression is meant to be true in the previous state (hence the use of the $\bullet$-operator). One could fold the $\rightarrow$-operator and $\bullet$-operator into one operator $\stackrel{\bullet}{\rightarrow}$, assume all variables quantified, and a $\Box$ in front of all properties, and write the property as follows:

$$\text{next}(i) \stackrel{\bullet}{\rightarrow} [\text{hasNext}(i, true), \text{next}(i))$$

Similarly one can imagine a $P \stackrel{\bigcirc}{\rightarrow} Q = P \rightarrow \bigcirc Q$ operator for future time logic. Another classical convenient operator is *never P* being equivalent to $\Box\neg P$.

Limitations of Temporal Logic. As shown in [61], LTL cannot express all regular properties (it is only star-free regular), for example it cannot express the property: *"p holds at every other moment"*, which can easily be expressed as a state machine or a regular expression as follows: $(.\,p)^*$. LTL is furthermore also at times inconvenient as a notation. We shall consider two examples here, a state machine, and a temporal formula conditioned on a sequence of events. First the *state machine*. The temporal logic formulation of Property 3 (ResourceLifecycle), ignoring the data element, can be given as follows:

$$\text{stop} \vee (\text{request} \wedge \Box \begin{pmatrix} \text{request} \rightarrow \bigcirc(\text{deny} \vee \text{grant} \vee \text{stop}) \\ \text{deny} \rightarrow \bigcirc(\text{request} \vee \text{stop}) \\ \text{grant} \rightarrow \bigcirc(\text{rescind}\ \mathcal{U}\ \text{cancel}) \\ \text{cancel} \rightarrow \bigcirc(\text{request} \vee \text{stop}) \end{pmatrix}$$

where $\text{stop} = \Box\neg(\text{request} \vee \text{deny} \vee \text{grant} \vee \text{rescind} \vee \text{cancel})$, and is used to indicate that no further events are required. These rules exactly mirror the state transitions of the state machine. In this case, temporal logic, specifically LTL, is arguably less elegant than state machines. Note that without introducing the name `stop` the formula would become even more complicated.

As our second example, let us consider *a temporal formula conditioned on a sequence of events*. To do this we will use Property 1 (UnsafeMapIterator). Suppose we wanted to express this property in temporal logic. A possible formulation would be the following rather unreadable formula:

$$\Lambda m, c, i : \Box \neg \left((\mathtt{create}(m, c) \wedge \left(\begin{array}{c} \neg\mathtt{create}(c, i) \; \mathcal{U} \; (\mathtt{create}(c, i) \wedge \\ (\neg\mathtt{update}(m) \; \mathcal{U} \; (\mathtt{update}(m) \wedge \Diamond\mathtt{use}(i)))) \end{array} \right) \right)$$

A more readable temporal logic formula is the following, which, however, does not say quite the same thing (since the second and third $\Box$-operator occurrences each quantify over all future events), although it seems in this case to be usable.

$$\Lambda m, c, i : \Box(\mathtt{create}(m, c) \Rightarrow \Box(\mathtt{create}(c, i) \Rightarrow \Box(\mathtt{update}(m) \Rightarrow \Box\neg\mathtt{use}(i))))$$

To obtain a more readable formula, we could instead combine regular expressions and temporal logic and write it as follows, using a regular expression on the left-hand side of the implication and an LTL formula on the right-hand side:

$$\Lambda m, c, i : \mathtt{create}(m, c).\mathtt{create}(c, i).\mathtt{update}(m) \Rightarrow \Box\neg\mathtt{use}(i)$$

The temporal logic PSL [28] adds an operator to LTL named *suffix implication*, and denoted $r \mapsto \psi$, for a regular expression r and a temporal logic formula ψ, which holds on a word w if for every prefix of w recognized by r, the suffix of w starting at the letter on which that prefix ends, satisfies ψ. This addition to LTL results in a logic with an expressive power corresponding to ω-regular languages (PSL is a logic intended for model checking, where infinite words are considered). Similar ideas are also seen in dynamic logic, see for example [34]. PSL generally contains several operators, which make modeling easier. These include beyond the suffix implication also: repetition $r * n$ (repeat a regular expression n times); intersection $r_1 \cap r_2$; a past time operator $ended(r)$ that turns a regular expression r to hold on the past trace; strong $r!$ and weak regular expressions r, where strong is the normal interpretation of a regular expression, and a weak regular expression denotes the language of the strong regular expression augmented with all prefixes (what on page 10 was referred to as the closure of a regular expression and denoted by $closure(r)$).

4   Handling Data

The previous section ignored the details of how each of the languages could be extended to deal with data. Here we review the main approaches. We shall first outline what we mean by data. Subsequently, the handling of data is discussed in the contexts of state machines, regular expressions and temporal logics. However, the discussion of data for one base language usually carries over to other base languages.

4.1 Where Do Data Occur?

Data can come from three sources.

Variables in the SBM. The monitor may be able to directly observe the internal state of the executing program. For example, if the monitor code is embedded (as code snippets) into the SBM. Program assertions, as supported by most programming languages, form an example of this. Alternatively, a transition of a state machine may be guarded by $x > 4$ where x is a program variable. This introduces a tight coupling between the specification and system being monitored. This form of data is not discussed here.

Event Parameters. Events transmitted from the SBM to the monitor can carry data as parameters. That is, an event consist of a name and a list of data values. An example is the event $login(u, t)$ representing the logging in by user u at time t. Within the runtime verification community such events are often called *parametric events*, as the data values are seen as parameters, and traces of these events are called *parametric traces*. Parametric events are the main source of data in this presentation.

Variables in the Monitor. The monitor itself can declare, update and read variables local to the monitor. This is seen in solutions where monitors are given as state machines or written in a programming language. This approach will also be discussed below.

4.2 Extended Finite State Machines

Conventional finite state machines have a finite number of control states and transitions are labelled with atomic letters over a finite alphabet. Extended finite state machines (EFSM) [19,40] extend finite state machines by allowing the declaration of a set of mutable variables, which can be read in transition guards, and updated in transition actions, where an action is a sequence of assignment statements assigning values to the variables. The standard transition relation is lifted to configurations, i.e. pairs of (control) states and variable valuations. Turing machines and pushdown automata (with the expressive power of context free languages) [58] are examples of EFSMs, so this is a powerful model. However, as we shall see, EFSMs are not convenient for our purposes in their original form. We use the following property to illustrate EFSMS.

Property 5 (Reconciling Account). The administrator must reconcile an account every 1000 attempted external money transfers or an aggregate total of one million dollars. The `reconcile` event is recorded when accounts are reconciled and the event `transfer(a)` records a transfer of a dollars.

Note that the `transfer(a)` event in this property carries data (the amount a transferred). EFSMs traditionally do not operate on such parameterized events but on atomic events. We shall, however, make this extension here in our first example, moving from evaluating input over a finite alphabet to input over an infinite alphabet. The EFSM for this property is shown in the following.

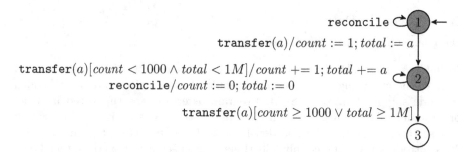

Two variables are introduced. The variables *count* and *total* hold the number of transfers respectively the sum of amounts transferred since the last reconciliation. Transitions are now written as **event**[*guard*]/*assignment*. Event **transfer**(*a*) on a transition is used to *match* a concrete event in the trace and bind the value in that event to the variable *a*. Each new transfer in the trace causes *a* to be bound to a new value, it is essentially just a variable just like *count* and *total*. Typically variables are used to hold data of primitive types (integers, reals, Booleans, etc.), but they could be used to hold more complex data structures. It is worth observing that UML state charts effectively are a form of extended state machines, with added concepts such as hierarchical states.

4.3 Typestates

Extended state machines with parameterized events as described above, where parameters are mutable variables, however, are still not convenient for specification purposes. We need an event parameter concept where parameters once bound stay constant, and we have a copy of the state machine for each parameter value. In other words, we need to quantify over parameters. To demonstrate a case where this may be required let us consider a further extension of the account reconciliation example.

Property 6 (Reconciling Accounts). The administrator must reconcile every account x every 1000 attempted external money transfers or an aggregate total of one million dollars. The **reconcile** event is recorded when accounts are reconciled and the event **transfer**(x, a) records a transfer of a dollars for account x.

This can be specified in the same way as before but this time adding a quantification over account x.

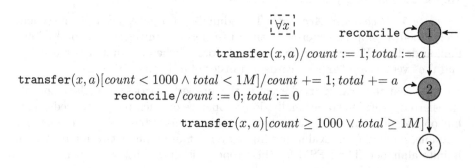

There will be an instance spawned of this state machine for each account x being monitored. This notion of quantification corresponds to what is also referred to as a *typestate* property [60], a programming language concept for static typing, which extends the notion of type with a (safety) state machine over the methods of that type. This state machine is quantified over all objects of the given type. Consider the account as a type with the methods $\texttt{transfer}(a)$ and $\texttt{reconcile}()$. A typestate is a refinement of such a type where a constraint is defined on the order in which these methods can be called. A typestate monitor can very simply be implemented by adding the EFSM monitor to each object of the type (state). This approach can also be used for Property 2 (HasNextIterator).

As noted, there are now two kinds of variables in the state machine, those that are quantified (x) and constant once bound, and those that are continuously mutable (a, *count*, *total*), referred to as *free* variables. In this formulation we want each instance of the state machine to have its own copies of the free variables. Therefore, we can view these variables as having *local scope* i.e. they are local to each particular instantiation of quantified variables. In extended finite state machines variables are often thought of us *global*, but it is clear that in this case we want locality. There is, however, a case to be made for variables with *global scope* where all instances of the extended finite state machine read from and write to such. This would be needed i.e. if reconciliation frequency depended on the total number of transfers for all accounts.

4.4   Parametric Trace Slicing

Typestates, implemented as extended state machines, although pleasantly simple, are not sufficiently convenient for commonly occurring monitoring scenarios due to the restriction of only quantifying over one variable. Consider for example Property 3 (Resource Lifecycle). We here need to deal with tasks as well as resource objects. We want to specify the appropriate behavior *for each pair* of tasks and resources. Similarly for Property 1 (UnsafeMapIterator). A generalization of the typestate approach is the concept of *parametric trace slicing*, first introduced in Tracematches [2] to work for regular expressions, and then generalized in JavaMOP [18,51] for adding parametric trace slicing to any propositional temporal language, that can be defined as a "plugin". Quantified Event Automata (QEA) [3,54] are a further generalization adding existential quantification and free variables (see below). Consider for example the following property (not taken from the competitions).

Property 7 (Simple ResourceManagement). A resource can only be granted once to a task until the task cancels the resource (granting and canceling a resource wrt. a particular task must alternate). A resource r is granted to a task t using the event $\texttt{grant}(t, r)$ and canceled using $\texttt{cancel}(t, r)$.

This property can be formalized as follows using a trace slicing approach.

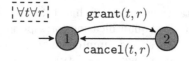

The parametric trace slicing approach considers *collections* of instantiations of quantified variables. In the original formulation of this idea, each collection is associated with a propositional monitor for that combination of parameter values. In this case the propositional monitor is a standard state machine. The trace is then *projected* into slices: one for each instantiation (combination of parameter values), so that only events relevant to the instantiation are included in the monitoring wrt. these particular values. This view of quantification requires domains for the quantified variables (the sets of values they quantify over). A typical choice is to let these domains consist of the values occurring in the trace. Given the above state machine, the following (satisfying) trace results in the domain for the variable t to be $\{A\}$ and the domain for the variable r to be $\{R_1, R_2\}$:

$$\texttt{grant}(A, R_1).\texttt{cancel}(A, R_1).\texttt{grant}(A, R_2).\texttt{cancel}(A, R_2)$$

4.5   Parametric Trace Slicing with Free Variables

In parametric trace slicing each instantiation of quantified variables encountered in the trace is associated with a propositional monitor, and only events concerned with that instantiation are mapped to the monitor. Things, however, become more complex when free variables are introduced, which is necessary to increase expressiveness (see [3] for how parametric trace slicing is extended with free variables). To illustrate this, we introduce a more complex version of Property 7 (SimpleResourceManagement).

Property 8 (ResourceManagement). In addition to Property 7 (i.e. granting and canceling a resource wrt. a particular task must alternate), a resource can only be held by at most one task at a time. Recall that a resource r is granted to a task t using the event $\texttt{grant}(t, r)$ and canceled using $\texttt{cancel}(t, r)$.

The previous specification for Property 7 does not capture this property. Consider the trace $\texttt{grant}(A, R).\texttt{grant}(B, R)$, violating the property. This generates two variable valuations: $[t = A, r = R]$ and $[t = B, r = R]$. The event $\texttt{grant}(B, R)$ is not relevant for the instance $[t = A, r = R]$, it is only relevant for the instance $[t = B, r = R]$, and vice versa. The trace is unfortunately consequently sliced into two independent subtraces: $\texttt{grant}(A, R)$ and $\texttt{grant}(B, R)$, with no connection between them. Therefore this formulation will not detect a violation in this trace.

To detect a violation we need to detect the existence of a violating task, i.e. the one that tries to take the resource r whilst it is held by task t. We could attempt to do this using a free variable t_{free} to capture the violating task as follows.

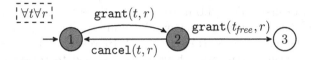

It turns out that we need to re-define the notion of projection to handle such free variables. Assume again the quantification instance $[t = A, r = R]$. Clearly, events that only mention A and R are relevant as before. But also **grant** events mentioning R and some other task are also relevant as they could match **grant**(t_{free}, r). This would mean that **grant**(B, R) would be relevant to the instance $[t = A, r = R]$. But now we can see a further issue. Consider the safe trace **grant**(B, R).**cancel**(B, R).**grant**(A, R). The projection to $[t = A, r = R]$ will be **grant**(B, R).**grant**(A, R), since **grant**(B, R) is considered relevant for the reason mentioned above, and since **cancel**(B, R) is not since $A \neq B$. This trace will therefore be rejected as the monitor cannot make a transition on the first event **grant**(B, R).

This highlights the subtleties that occur when dealing with free variables and projection. Once an event with a free variable has been added to the alphabet the user should consider how this affects the events that could be relevant at other states. This leads to a final correct, but less attractive, formulation:

$$\boxed{\forall t \forall r} \quad \downarrow \quad \text{grant}(t, r)$$

$$\text{grant}(t_{free}, r)[t \neq t_{free}] \quad \overset{\frown}{\underset{\text{cancel}(t, r)}{\bigcirc\!\!\!\!1}} \quad \overset{\text{grant}(t_{free}, r)}{\underset{2}{\longrightarrow}} \quad 3$$

This extends the state machine with a looping transition to skip grants of the resource to other tasks when the current task t does not hold the resource. An alternative solution would have been to existentially quantify t_{free}. However, this has implications related to the efficiency of the associated monitoring algorithm, which we do not discuss here [54].

4.6   Quantification in Temporal Logics

First-Order Quantification. The standard way of dealing with data in logic via *quantification* is relevant to temporal logic, and is based on the notion of evaluating a formula with respect to a first-order temporal structure. The standard approach is to add a formula expression such as $\forall x.\varphi$ to the syntax of the logic and include a case similar to the following in the trace semantics [10]

$$\mathcal{T}, i, \sigma \models \forall x.\varphi \quad \textit{iff for every } d \in \mathcal{D}(x) \quad \textit{we have} \quad \mathcal{T}, i, \sigma[x \mapsto d] \models \varphi$$

where the temporal structure $\mathcal{T}$ captures the trace, i.e. it is a finite sequence of structures where each structure describes which events are present in that time point. This usually follows the standard logical approach of modeling events as *predicates* and defining an *interpretation* evaluating events occurring at that time point to true and all other events to false. The temporal structure also defines the domain function $\mathcal{D}$ but the way in which it does this differs between approaches, as described below.

The notion of first-order LTL introduced by Emerson [29] follows this approach, although assumes predicates have global interpretation, which is not suitable here but the extension is straightforward. However, for pragmatic reasons, languages for runtime verification have been designed to consider alternative first-order extensions of LTL. The rest of this section discusses these alternative design decisions.

Different Notions of Quantification. There are two main approaches to defining the domain function $\mathcal{D}$ above. Simply, either $\mathcal{D}$ is local to the current time point (as in [13,36]), or it is constant throughout the temporal structure (as in [10] and the original work of Emerson). If the domain function is local then it is typically derived from the events occurring in that time point. If the domain function is constant then it typically consists of (a superset of) values appearing in the trace. The idea of the first approach is to restrict quantification so that it is only used to create future obligations about events occurring at the current point in time. For this to work it is necessary to syntactically restrict the occurrence of quantification so that the values it is quantifying over occur at the current time point e.g. the first of the following two (normally) equivalent formulas would break this rule.

$$(\forall f)\Box(\texttt{open}(f) \to \Diamond\texttt{close}(f)) \qquad \Box(\forall f)(\texttt{open}(f) \to \Diamond\texttt{close}(f))$$

The second formula has the same interpretation in the two models of quantification (where we assume that the domain in the current time point is a subset of the constant domain) as the right-side of the implication will only be true for values in the current time point. This demonstrates that, under certain syntactic restrictions, the two models of quantification coincide. This can be advantageous as monitoring algorithms dealing with the first model of quantification will generally be more straightforward as decisions about quantification can be local. To see that the two models are different, note that the formula

$$\Box(\exists x)(\neg p(x))$$

is unsatisfiable in general for the first model of quantification as the domain of x is given exactly by the values such that $p(x)$ is true at the current time point. But in the second model of quantification this becomes a reasonable statement.

Note that the first model is dependent on *where* quantification happens and as a result cannot express some formulas. For example, this formula cannot be expressed in this model as the values being quantified over cannot be present in the current time point:

$$(\forall f)\Box(\texttt{open}(f) \to \exists u : (\Diamond\texttt{read}(f, u) \lor \Diamond\texttt{write}(f, u)))$$

In either setting it is possible for domains to be *infinite* (in theory) as long as formulas are *domain independent*, which is a semantic notion ensuring that only a finite subset of the domain is required for trace-checking (see [11,20]). As an example, $(\forall x)\Diamond p(x)$ is not domain independent, but $(\forall x)\Box p(x) \to \Diamond q(x)$ is domain independent as checking this formula only requires checking the finite subset of values v such that $p(v)$ appears in the trace. Note that determining whether a formula is domain independent is undecidable and practically this is checked via conservative syntactic restrictions.

The Difference with Parametric Trace Slicing. It is at this point appropriate to point out, that the standard logic interpretation of quantification presented above is different from the parametric slicing approach, resulting in subtly different interpretations of formulas. Consider Property 3 (Resource Lifecycle). Previously (page 14) we gave a propositional temporal logic formulation (no data) that included the sub-formula:

$$\Box(\mathtt{request} \rightarrow \bigcirc(\mathtt{deny} \vee \mathtt{grant} \vee \mathtt{stop}))$$

When we add first-order quantification this becomes:

$$(\forall r)\Box(\mathtt{request}(r) \rightarrow \bigcirc(\mathtt{deny}(r) \vee \mathtt{grant}(r) \vee \mathtt{stop}(r)))$$

This formula, however, no longer means what we want it to. Consider e.g. the trace:

$$\mathtt{request}(A).\mathtt{request}(B).\mathtt{deny}(A).\mathtt{deny}(B)$$

This is expected to be a correct trace, but it does not satisfy the quantified formula since in the first state $\mathtt{request}(A)$ is true but none of $\mathtt{deny}(A)$, $\mathtt{grant}(A)$, nor $\mathtt{stop}(A)$ are true in the next (second) state. However, with parametric trace slicing, the formula (note the use of Λ instead of $\forall$).

$$\Lambda r.\; \Box(\mathtt{request}(r) \rightarrow \bigcirc(\mathtt{deny}(r) \vee \mathtt{grant}(r) \vee \mathtt{stop}(r)))$$

has the intended interpretation (accepting the trace), as parametric trace slicing *projects* the trace to a slice only including events relevant for r. As outlined in [57], the main difference is the treatment of the notion of *next*.

Everything is Quantification. We have previously seen the need for introducing free variables in state machines in combination with parametric trace slicing. Free variables are not needed in temporal logic, where quantification is sufficient. Consider for example Property 8 (ResourceManagement) and the corresponding state machine on page 19, which uses a free task variable t_{free} in addition to the quantified t. The property can alternatively be formulated in temporal logic only using quantification as follows:

$$(\forall t, r)\Box(\mathtt{grant}(t, r) \Rightarrow \bigcirc((\neg(\exists t')\, \mathtt{grant}(t', r))\; \mathcal{W}\; \mathtt{cancel}(t, r)))$$

The approach is to allow quantification inside the formula, and not only at the outermost level. In first-order temporal logic it is generally possible to write the quantifiers at arbitrary points of the specification. It is important to understand that quantification is to be evaluated at the point in the trace that it is met. For example,

$$(\forall x)\Diamond \mathtt{f}(x) \not\equiv \Diamond(\forall x)\mathtt{f}(x)$$

as the first property says that for every x the event $\mathtt{f}(x)$ eventually happens, but for different values for x this could happen at different points, whereas the second property requires that these all happen at the same point. However, in some cases quantification inside a temporal operator can be lifted outside, the standard identities are the following:

$$(\forall x)\Box\varphi \equiv \Box(\forall x)\varphi \qquad (\exists x)\Diamond\varphi \equiv \Diamond(\exists x)\varphi$$

The main reason why quantification is enough in temporal logic is due to the fact that temporal logic has a notion of sub-formula, and a quantification is over some sub-formula. In state machines we usually do not operate with a notion of sub-machine (except in state charts), and it therefore becomes difficult to define the scope of a quantifier. One can imagine embedded quantifiers in regular expressions, however, just as one can imagine free variables in regular expressions.

Section 4.3 discussed the concept of free variables with global scope. A similar notion in temporal logic could correspond to the usage of so-called *counting quantifiers*. Suppose for example that we wanted to state that each task t can at most hold N resources at a time. This can be captured as the property:

$$\Box(\forall t)(\exists^{\leq N}r)(\neg\mathtt{cancel}(t,r)\ S\ \mathtt{grant}(t,r))$$

This can be read as: *it is always the case that for all tasks, there exist at most N resources r, that have not been canceled by t since they were granted to t.* Counting quantifiers typically preserve the expressiveness of the language, assuming that the language includes predicates.

Some properties of interest to runtime verification go beyond the expressiveness of first-order temporal logic. A simple extension is the usage of so-called *percentage counting quantifiers* [50] of the form $\mathbf{A}_{\geq P}x : p(x) \Rightarrow \phi$ which capture the property that for at least $P\%$ of the values d in the domain of x such that $p(d)$ holds, the statement ϕ holds. This allows for the expression of properties such as

$$\mathbf{A}_{\geq 0.95}s : \mathtt{socket}(s) \Rightarrow (\Box\mathtt{receive}(s) \Rightarrow \Diamond\mathtt{respond}(s))$$

stating that at least 95% of open sockets are eventually closed.

Another property of interest corresponding to *second-order* quantification is that of *deadlock avoidance*. As described in [16], if a graph is constructed where directed edges between locks indicate a lock ordering, then a cycle in this graph indicates a potential deadlock. Cycle detection is a reachability property, which is inherently second-order i.e. it relates to the second-order temporal property

$$\neg\exists\{l_1,\ldots l_n\}\left(\mathtt{lock}(l_{n+1},l_1) \wedge \bigwedge_{i=0}^{i=n-1} \mathtt{lock}(l_i,l_{i+1})\right)$$

i.e. there does not exist a set of locks containing a cycle.

The Past is Not Simpler. Concerning monitoring algorithms, future time logic with data lends itself to a very simple syntax-oriented tableaux-like procedure, as in [4,5,12,36]. Past time logics interestingly require a different more elaborate approach, i.e. dynamic programming, as described in [10,38].

Events and the Signature. Typically in first-order logic one has *predicates* and *functions*. As mentioned previously, it is normal for first-order extensions of LTL for runtime verification to model events as predicates interpreted as either true or false in the current time point. This easily supports the notion of multiple events occurring in a single time point. Indeed, if one were to restrict this to a single event then this notion becomes an implicit axiom of the logic, changing the semantics i.e. the formula $(\forall x, y)\Diamond(\mathbf{f}(x) \wedge \mathbf{g}(y))$ becomes unsatisfiable.

Some extensions also allow other non-event predicates and functions to appear in the signature. In this case the temporal structure should provide an interpretation for these symbols. This can support the calling of external functions. It would be usual for these interpretations to be constant throughout the trace. A specific case of this is when those predicates and functions are taken from a particular *theory* as described next.

Modulo Theories. There has been a lot of recent interest in automated reasoning in first-order logic, also referred to as *Satisfiability Modulo Theories* (SMT). The general idea is to extend first order logic with theories for particular subdomains (i.e. arithmetic, arrays, datatypes, etc.), and build decision procedures specific to those domains. The same concept can be extended to reasoning in first-order temporal logic. SMT can specifically be applied in runtime verification, as described in [25], which presents an approach for *monitoring modulo theories*, which relies on an SMT solver to discharge the data related obligations in each state.

4.7 Register Automata and Freeze Quantification

Register automata [40] and freeze quantifiers in temporal logic [26] are systems based on the notion of *registers*, in which data observed in the trace can be stored, and later read and compared with other data in the trace. A register automaton [40] has in addition to the traditional control states also a finite set of registers. Data observed in the trace can be stored in registers when encountered, and can later be read for comparison with other data. Register automata form a subclass of extended finite state machines where the registers play the role of the variables. Similarly, *freeze quantifiers* [26] are used in temporal logic to capture "storing" of values. The formula $\downarrow_r \varphi$ stores the data value at the current position in the trace in register r (actually it stores an equivalence class denoting all those positions having an equivalent value), and evaluates the formula with that register assignment. The unfreeze formula $\uparrow_r$ checks whether the data value at the current position is equivalent to that in register r. As an example, the following temporal property using quantification:

$$(\forall f)\Box(\mathtt{open}(f) \rightarrow \Diamond\mathtt{close}(f))$$

can instead be formulated as follows using a freeze quantifier:

$$\Box(\texttt{open} \rightarrow \downarrow_r \Diamond(\texttt{close} \land \uparrow_r))$$

Such registers here can be seen as the equivalent of the pattern matching solutions found in systems such as JLO [59] and TraceContract [5], and correspond to quantification over the current time point (see page 20). Register-based systems are typically studied for their theoretical properties, and are usually somewhat limited. For example is it usually only possible to compare data for equality. Register automata have been used within runtime verification [35].

5   Conclusion

Our discussion has centered around state machines, regular expressions, and temporal logics, and how data can be integrated in such. Important systems have due to lack of space been left out of this discussion, including context free grammars, variations of the μ-calculus, rule-based systems, stream processing, and process algebras. We have, however, hopefully succeeded in illustrating important parts of the design space for runtime verification logics. It has been pointed out that formulas in a logic can be used to identify good traces (positive formulations) or bad traces (negative formulations), and that the succinctness of specifications can depend on this choice. Furthermore, such formulas can be matched against the entire trace, or just against a suffix of the trace. Negative formulations usually go with suffix matching. The useful distinction between next-states and skip-states in state machines has also been pointed out. For writing formalized requirements for a project, the positive formulation over total traces is probably to be preferred, whereas negative formulations over suffixes can be more succinct in some cases. It has been illustrated how different base logics appear advantageous for particular examples, a fact that is not too surprising. How to (whether to) handle data is a crucial problem in the design of a runtime verification logic, and alternative approaches have been promoted in the literature. Parametric trace slicing has so far shown the most efficient [9,56], although initially causing limited expressiveness.

If we allow ourselves to dangerously imagine an ideal runtime verification logic, it would be a combination of regular expressions (allowing to conveniently express sequencing) and future and past time temporal logic (often resulting in succinct specifications). However, the notion of states, as found in state machines and rule systems is important as well. The ability to distinguish between next-states and skip-states seems useful, in state machines as well as in regular expressions. It is interesting that state machines with anonymous states (where intermediate states are not named) is a formalism very related to future time temporal logic. It would be useful if convenient shorthands for formulas and aggregation operators could be user-defined. A logic should support time, scopes, and should allow for modularizing specifications. The Eagle logic [4], based on a linear μ-calculus with future and past time operators as well as a sequencing operator, was an attempt to support many of these ideas. Eagle allowed for user defined temporal operators, including the standard Linear Temporal Logic operators.

Working with engineers has shown that current practice to write trace checkers consists of programming in high-level scripting/programming languages, such as for example Python. Observing the kind of checks performed on such traces suggests that a monitoring logic needs to be rather expressive, and probably Turing complete for practical purposes, allowing for example advanced string processing features and arithmetic computations. Some specification logics have been developed as APIs in programming languages, in the realization of these observations. The distinction between formal specification in a domain-specific logic on the one hand, and programming in a general purpose programming language on the other hand, might get blurred in the field of runtime verification due to the practical needs of monitoring systems. We also expect to see more systems that compute data from traces rather than just produce Boolean-like verdicts.

References

1. XTL Manual. http://cadp.inria.fr/man/xtl.html
2. Allan, C., Avgustinov, P., Christensen, A.S., Hendren, L., Kuzins, S., Lhoták, O., de Moor, O., Sereni, D., Sittampalam, G., Tibble, J.: Adding trace matching with free variables to AspectJ. SIGPLAN Not. **40**, 345–364 (2005)
3. Barringer, H., Falcone, Y., Havelund, K., Reger, G., Rydeheard, D.: Quantified event automata: towards expressive and efficient runtime monitors. In: Giannakopoulou, D., Méry, D. (eds.) FM 2012. LNCS, vol. 7436, pp. 68–84. Springer, Heidelberg (2012). doi:10.1007/978-3-642-32759-9_9
4. Barringer, H., Goldberg, A., Havelund, K., Sen, K.: Rule-based runtime verification. In: Steffen, B., Levi, G. (eds.) VMCAI 2004. LNCS, vol. 2937, pp. 44–57. Springer, Heidelberg (2004). doi:10.1007/978-3-540-24622-0_5
5. Barringer, H., Havelund, K.: TRACECONTRACT: a scala DSL for trace analysis. In: Butler, M., Schulte, W. (eds.) FM 2011. LNCS, vol. 6664, pp. 57–72. Springer, Heidelberg (2011). doi:10.1007/978-3-642-21437-0_7
6. Barringer, H., Rydeheard, D., Havelund, K.: Rule systems for run-time monitoring: from Eagle to RuleR. J. Log. Comput. **20**(3), 675–706 (2010)
7. Bartetzko, D., Fischer, C., Möller, M., Wehrheim, H.: Jass - Java with assertions. In: Proceedings of the 1st International Workshop on Runtime Verification (RV 2001), Paris, France, ENTCS, vol. 55, no. 2, pp. 103–117. Elsevier, July 2001. http://citeseerx.ist.psu.edu/viewdoc/download?doi=10.1.1.92.144&rep=rep1&type=pdf
8. Bartocci, E., Bonakdarpour, B., Falcone, Y.: First international competition on software for runtime verification. In: Proceedings of the Runtime Verification - 5th International Conference, RV 2014, Toronto, ON, Canada, 22–25 September 2014, pp. 1–9 (2014)
9. Bartocci, E., Falcone, Y., Bonakdarpour, B., Colombo, C., Decker, N., Havelund, K., Joshi, Y., Klaedtke, F., Milewicz, R., Reger, G., Rosu, G., Signoles, J., Thoma, D., Zalinescu, E., Zhang, Y.: First international competition on runtime verification: rules, benchmarks, tools, and final results of CRV 2014. Int. J. Softw. Tools Technol. Transf. 1–40 (2017). https://link.springer.com/article/10.1007%2Fs10009-017-0454-5

10. Basin, D., Klaedtke, F., Marinovic, S., Zălinescu, E.: Monitoring of temporal first-order properties with aggregations. Formal Methods Syst. Des. **46**, 262–285 (2015)
11. Basin, D., Klaedtke, F., Müller, S., Pfitzmann, B.: Runtime monitoring of metric first-order temporal properties. In: Proceedings of the 28th IARCS Annual Conference on Foundations of Software Technology and Theoretical Computer Science. Leibniz International Proceedings in Informatics (LIPIcs), vol. 2, pp. 49–60. Schloss Dagstuhl - Leibniz Center for Informatics (2008)
12. Bauer, A., Goré, R., Tiu, A.: A first-order policy language for history-based transaction monitoring. In: Leucker, M., Morgan, C. (eds.) ICTAC 2009. LNCS, vol. 5684, pp. 96–111. Springer, Heidelberg (2009). doi:10.1007/978-3-642-03466-4_6
13. Bauer, A., Küster, J., Vegliach, G.: The ins and outs of first-order runtime verification. Formal Methods Syst. Des. **46**(3), 286–316 (2015)
14. Bauer, A., Leucker, M., Schallhart, C.: The good, the bad, and the ugly, but how ugly is ugly? In: Sokolsky, O., Taşıran, S. (eds.) RV 2007. LNCS, vol. 4839, pp. 126–138. Springer, Heidelberg (2007). doi:10.1007/978-3-540-77395-5_11
15. Bauer, A., Leucker, M., Schallhart, C.: Runtime verification for LTL and TLTL. ACM Trans. Softw. Eng. Methodol. **20**(4), 14:1–14:64 (2011)
16. Bensalem, S., Havelund, K.: Dynamic deadlock analysis of multi-threaded programs. In: Ur, S., Bin, E., Wolfsthal, Y. (eds.) HVC 2005. LNCS, vol. 3875, pp. 208–223. Springer, Heidelberg (2006). doi:10.1007/11678779_15
17. Bianculli, D., Ghezzi, C., San Pietro, P.: The tale of SOLOIST: a specification language for service compositions interactions. In: Păsăreanu, C.S., Salaün, G. (eds.) FACS 2012. LNCS, vol. 7684, pp. 55–72. Springer, Heidelberg (2013). doi:10.1007/978-3-642-35861-6_4
18. Chen, F., Roşu, G.: MOP: an efficient and generic runtime verification framework. In: Object-Oriented Programming, Systems, Languages and Applications (OOPSLA 2007), pp. 569–588. ACM Press (2007)
19. Cheng, K.T., Krishnakumar, A.S.: Automatic functional test generation using the extended finite state machine model. In: Proceedings of the 30th International Design Automation Conference, DAC 1993, pp. 86–91. ACM, New York (1993)
20. Chomicki, J., Toman, D., Böhlen, M.H.: Querying ATSQL databases with temporal logic. ACM Trans. Database Syst. **26**(2), 145–178 (2001)
21. Clarke, E.M., Emerson, E.A.: Design and synthesis of synchronization skeletons using branching time temporal logic. In: Kozen, D. (ed.) Logic of Programs 1981. LNCS, vol. 131, pp. 52–71. Springer, Heidelberg (1982). doi:10.1007/BFb0025774
22. Colombo, C., Pace, G.J., Schneider, G.: LARVA – safer monitoring of real-time Java programs (tool paper). In: Proceedings of the 2009 Seventh IEEE International Conference on Software Engineering and Formal Methods, SEFM 2009, pp. 33–37. IEEE Computer Society, Washington, DC (2009)
23. D'Angelo, B., Sankaranarayanan, S., Sánchez, C., Robinson, W., Finkbeiner, B., Sipma, H.B., Mehrotra, S., Manna, Z.: LOLA: runtime monitoring of synchronous systems. In: Proceedings of the 12th International Symposium on Temporal Representation and Reasoning, pp. 166–174. IEEE Computer Society (2005)
24. Decker, N., Leucker, M., Thoma, D.: jUnit^{RV}–adding runtime verification to jUnit. In: Brat, G., Rungta, N., Venet, A. (eds.) NFM 2013. LNCS, vol. 7871, pp. 459–464. Springer, Heidelberg (2013). doi:10.1007/978-3-642-38088-4_34
25. Decker, N., Leucker, M., Thoma, D.: Monitoring modulo theories. Int. J. Softw. Tools Technol. Transf. **18**, 1–21 (2015)
26. Demri, S., Lazić, R.: LTL with the freeze quantifier and register automata. ACM Trans. Comput. Log. **10**(3), 16:1–16:30 (2009)

27. Drusinsky, D.: Modeling and Verification using UML Statecharts, 400 p. Elsevier, Amsterdam (2006). ISBN-13: 978-0-7506-7949-7
28. Eisner, C., Fisman, D.: Temporal logic made practical. In: Handbook of Model Checking (2014, to appear). http://www.cis.upenn.edu/~fisman/publications.html
29. Emerson, E.A.: Temporal and modal logic. In: Handbook of Theoretical Computer Science, vol. B, pp. 995–1072. MIT Press, Cambridge (1990)
30. Falcone, Y., Fernandez, J.-C., Mounier, L.: Runtime verification of safety-progress properties. In: Bensalem, S., Peled, D.A. (eds.) RV 2009. LNCS, vol. 5779, pp. 40–59. Springer, Heidelberg (2009). doi:10.1007/978-3-642-04694-0_4
31. Falcone, Y., Havelund, K., Reger, G.: A tutorial on runtime verification. Eng. Dependable Softw. Syst. **34**, 141–175 (2013)
32. Falcone, Y., Ničković, D., Reger, G., Thoma, D.: Second international competition on runtime verification. In: Bartocci, E., Majumdar, R. (eds.) RV 2015. LNCS, vol. 9333, pp. 405–422. Springer, Cham (2015). doi:10.1007/978-3-319-23820-3_27
33. Finkbeiner, B., Sankaranarayanan, S., Sipma, H.: Collecting statistics over runtime executions. Formal Methods Syst. Des. **27**(3), 253–274 (2005)
34. Fischer, M.J., Ladner, R.E.: Propositional dynamic logic of regular programs. J. Comput. Syst. Sci. **18**, 194–211 (1979)
35. Grigore, R., Distefano, D., Petersen, R.L., Tzevelekos, N.: Runtime verification based on register automata. In: Piterman, N., Smolka, S.A. (eds.) TACAS 2013. LNCS, vol. 7795, pp. 260–276. Springer, Heidelberg (2013). doi:10.1007/978-3-642-36742-7_19
36. Hallé, S., Villemaire, R.: Runtime enforcement of web service message contracts with data. IEEE Trans. Serv. Comput. **5**(2), 192–206 (2012)
37. Havelund, K.: Rule-based runtime verification revisited. Int. J. Softw. Tools Technol. Transf. **17**(2), 143–170 (2015)
38. Havelund, K., Roşu, G.: Efficient monitoring of safety properties. Int. J. Softw. Tools Technol. Transf. **6**(2), 158–173 (2004)
39. Holzmann, G.: The SPIN Model Checker. Addison-Wesley, Boston (2004)
40. Kaminski, M., Francez, N.: Finite-memory automata. Theoret. Comput. Sci. **134**(2), 329–363 (1994)
41. Kiczales, G., Hilsdale, E., Hugunin, J., Kersten, M., Palm, J., Griswold, W.G.: An overview of AspectJ. In: Knudsen, J.L. (ed.) ECOOP 2001. LNCS, vol. 2072, pp. 327–354. Springer, Heidelberg (2001). doi:10.1007/3-540-45337-7_18
42. Kim, M., Viswanathan, M., Kannan, S., Lee, I., Sokolsky, O.: Java-MaC: a runtime assurance approach for Java programs. Formal Methods Syst. Des. **24**(2), 129–155 (2004)
43. Kozen, D.: Results on the propositional μ-calculus. Theoret. Comput. Sci. **27**(3), 333–354 (1983)
44. Kupferman, O., Vardi, M.Y.: Model checking of safety properties. Formal Methods Syst. Des. **19**(3), 291–314 (2001)
45. Laroussinie, F., Markey, N., Schnoebelen, P.: Temporal logic with forgettable past. In: Proceedings of the 17th Annual IEEE Symposium on Logic in Computer Science, LICS 2002, pp. 383–392. IEEE Computer Society, Washington, DC (2002)
46. Larsen, K.G., Legay, A.: Statistical model checking: past, present, and future. In: Margaria, T., Steffen, B. (eds.) ISoLA 2016. LNCS, vol. 9952, pp. 3–15. Springer, Cham (2016). doi:10.1007/978-3-319-47166-2_1
47. Legay, A., Delahaye, B., Bensalem, S.: Statistical model checking: an overview. In: Barringer, H., et al. (eds.) RV 2010. LNCS, vol. 6418, pp. 122–135. Springer, Heidelberg (2010). doi:10.1007/978-3-642-16612-9_11

48. Leucker, M., Schallhart, C.: A brief account of runtime verification. J. Log. Algebr. Program. **78**(5), 293–303 (2009)

49. Manna, Z., Pnueli, A.: Temporal Verification of Reactive Systems: Safety. Springer, New York Inc. (1995)

50. Medhat, R., Bonakdarpour, B., Fischmeister, S., Joshi, Y.: Accelerated runtime verification of LTL specifications with counting semantics. In: Falcone, Y., Sánchez, C. (eds.) RV 2016. LNCS, vol. 10012, pp. 251–267. Springer, Cham (2016). doi:10.1007/978-3-319-46982-9_16

51. Meredith, P.O., Jin, D., Griffith, D., Chen, F., Roşu, G.: An overview of the MOP runtime verification framework. J. Softw. Tools Technol. Transf. **14**, 1–41 (2011)

52. OMG. OMG Unified Modeling Language (OMG UML), Superstructure, Version 2.4.1, August 2011

53. Pnueli, A.: The temporal logic of programs. In: Proceedings of the 18th Annual Symposium on Foundations of Computer Science, SFCS 1977, pp. 46–57. IEEE Computer Society, Washington, DC (1977)

54. Reger, G.: Automata based monitoring and mining of execution traces. Ph.D. thesis, University of Manchester (2014)

55. Reger, G., Cruz, H.C., Rydeheard, D.: MarQ: monitoring at runtime with QEA. In: Proceedings of the 21st International Conference on Tools and Algorithms for the Construction and Analysis of Systems (TACAS 2015) (2015)

56. Reger, G., Hallé, S., Falcone, Y.: Third international competition on runtime verification CRV 2016. In: Proceedings of the Runtime Verification - 16th International Conference, RV 2016 (2016)

57. Reger, G., Rydeheard, D.: From first-order temporal logic to parametric trace slicing. In: Bartocci, E., Majumdar, R. (eds.) RV 2015. LNCS, vol. 9333, pp. 216–232. Springer, Cham (2015). doi:10.1007/978-3-319-23820-3_14

58. Sipser, M.: Introduction to the Theory of Computation, 3rd edn. Cengage Learning, Boston (2013)

59. Stolz, V., Bodden, E.: Temporal assertions using AspectJ. In: Proceedings of the 5th International Workshop on Runtime Verification (RV 2005), ENTCS, vol. 144, no. 4, pp. 109–124. Elsevier (2006)

60. Strom, R.E., Yemini, S.: Typestate: a programming language concept for enhancing software reliability. IEEE Trans. Softw. Eng. **12**(1), 157–171 (1986)

61. Vardi, M.Y.: From church and prior to PSL. In: Grumberg, O., Veith, H. (eds.) 25 Years of Model Checking. LNCS, vol. 5000, pp. 150–171. Springer, Heidelberg (2008). doi:10.1007/978-3-540-69850-0_10

Testing Divergent Transition Systems

Ed Brinksma, Mariëlle I.A. Stoelinga, and Mark Timmer(⊠)

Formal Methods and Tools, Faculty of EEMCS, University of Twente,
Enschede, The Netherlands
{h.brinksma,m.i.a.stoelinga,m.timmer}@utwente.nl

Abstract. We revisit model-based testing for labelled transition systems in the context of specifications that may contain divergent behaviour, i.e., infinite paths of internal computations. The standard approach based on the theory of input-output conformance, known as the ioco-framework, cannot deal with divergences directly, as it restricts specifications to strongly convergent transition systems. Using the model of Quiescent Input Output Transition Systems (QIOTSs), we can handle divergence successfully in the context of quiescence. Quiescence is a fundamental notion that represents the situation that a system is not capable of producing any output, if no prior input is provided, representing lack of productive progress. The correct treatment of this situation is the cornerstone of the success of testing in the context of systems that are input-enabled, i.e., systems that accept all input actions in any state. Our revised treatment of quiescence also allows it to be preserved under determinization of a QIOTS. This last feature allows us to reformulate the standard ioco-based testing theory and algorithms in terms of classical trace-based automata theory, including finite state divergent computations.

1 Introduction

Quiescence is a fundamental notion that represents the situation that a system is not capable of producing any output, if no prior input is provided, representing lack of productive progress. The correct treatment of this situation is the cornerstone of the success of testing in the context of systems that are input-enabled, i.e., systems that accept all input actions in any state. The standard approach to model-based testing of labelled transition systems, based on the theory of input-output conformance, known as the ioco-framework, is based on the explicit treatment of quiescence as an observable property of a system under test, by treating inaction with respect to output as a special kind of null action.

The proper treatment of quiescence is complicated by the phenomenon of divergence. Transition systems are said to be divergent if their computation

---

This research has been partially funded by NWO under grants 612.063.817 (SYRUP), Dn 63-257 (ROCKS) and 12238 (ArRangeer), and by the EU under grant 318490 (SENSATION).

L. Aceto et al. (Eds.): Larsen Festschrift, LNCS 10460, pp. 339–366, 2017.
DOI: 10.1007/978-3-319-63121-9_17

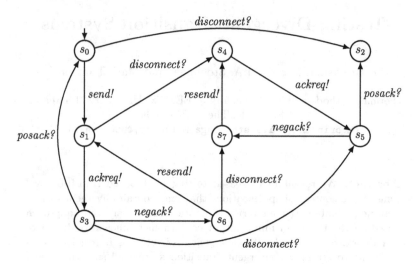

Fig. 1. A simple communication system with acknowledgements.

traces include infinite sequences of internal steps, i.e., steps that are not observable as part of the communication of the system with its environment. The possibility of such infinite internal computations can be a source of quiescence. The ioco-framework cannot deal with divergent behaviour in specifications directly: it requires specifications to be strongly convergent, i.e., they must contain only finite sequences of internal actions in computations [1]. Divergence, however, does often occur in practice.

Example 1.1. Consider for instance the simple communication system with acknowledgements and retransmissions shown in Fig. 1. When hiding all actions related to retransmissions (*ackreq, negack, posack,* and *resend*) by renaming them to the internal action τ, we obtain a specification in which infinite cycles of internal actions are possible in the two 'triangles' of the system, cycling through s_1, s_3, s_6, and s_4, s_5, s_7, respectively.   □

We use this example to show that there are differences between divergences that matter in the context of testing. It would be too simple, for example, to create observations of quiescence for every τ-loop. In the example, the infinite execution of the loops of the triangles can be considered unfair, in the sense that they would ignore the transitions of the (hidden) *posack* action. Our approach will be that such unfair divergences cannot occur, expecting internal or output actions to never be delayed infinitely many times. This means that the triangle s_1, s_3, s_6 will ultimately enable a *send* action in state s_0, and will not cause quiescence, whereas the control cycling through s_4, s_5, s_7 will eventually reach s_2, which is quiescent. Of course, some τ-loops can occur fairly. If we turn the above example into an input-enabled system, which will be the typical case in the context of this theory, then self-loops with missing input actions will be added to states. In particular, state s_2 will get three extra transitions to itself, labelled

with *posack?*, *negack?* and *disconnect?*. Upon hiding, the first two become
τ-loops, and cycling continuously through both of them is a fair execution of
divergence, as this does not compete with other locally controlled actions such
as other outgoing τ-actions or outputs. The theory that we wish to develop must
deal with this variety in divergences and all the subtleties involved.

A way forward has been proposed in [2] in the form of the model of Divergent
Quiescent Transition Systems (DQTSs). This model is formulated using input-
output automata (IOA), introduced by Lynch and Tuttle [3], and improves the
existing theory in three respects. Firstly, it removes the restriction to strongly
convergent specifications; secondly, it deals correctly with the notion of quiescence in the presence of divergence, i.e., it distinguishes between infinite computations that can block output from occurring (and therefore should signal
quiescence) vs. those that do not; and thirdly, it revises the definition of quiescence so that it is preserved under determinization, allowing the reformulation of
ioco-based testing theory including divergence and the related test generation
algorithms in terms of classical trace-based automata theory.

Our purpose in this paper is also threefold. First, we want to obtain a simplified version of the model that does not need the full works of the IOA framework,
such as the possibility to name internal actions and to specify fairness constraints
in great generality using task partitions. Instead, and this is our second goal,
when dealing with divergences it should use the notion of fair execution that
is implicitly behind most labelled transition system modelling involving just a
single anonymous internal step τ, as for example captured by Milner's weak
bisimulation equivalence [4]. Finally, we want to connect this theory to the standard ioco-algorithms for test generation [5], which is only suggested by the work
in [2], but has not yet been carried out. In doing so, this paper is nicely representative of the work on model-based testing at the University of Twente during
the long period of collaboration that we have had with Kim Larsen.

Origins. The notion of quiescence was first introduced by Vaandrager [6] to
obtain a natural extension of blocking states: if a system is input-enabled (i.e.,
always ready to receive inputs), then no states are blocking, since each state
has outgoing input transitions. Quiescence models the fact that a state is blocking when considering only the internal and output actions. In the context of
model-based testing, Tretmans introduced *repetitive quiescence* [1,7]. This notion
emerged from the need to continue testing, even in a quiescent state. To accommodate this, Tretmans introduced the *Suspension Automaton* (SA) as an auxiliary concept [8]. An SA is obtained from an Input-Output Transition System
(IOTS) by first adding to each quiescent state a self-loop labelled by the quiescence label δ and by subsequently determinizing the model. As stated above, SAs
cannot cope with divergence, since divergence leads to new quiescent states. In
an attempt to remedy this situation, the TGV framework [9] handles divergence
by adding δ-labelled self-loops to such states. However, this treatment is not
satisfactory in our opinion: quiescence due to divergence can in [9] be followed
by an output action, which we find counterintuitive.

Overview of the Paper. The rest of the paper is organized as follows. Section 2 introduces the QIOTS model, and Sect. 3 provides operations and properties for them. Sections 4, 5 and 6 present the notions of test cases for QIOTSs, an overview of testing with respect to `ioco` and algorithms for generating test cases, respectively. Conclusions and future work are presented in Sect. 7.

This paper simplifies and unites the concepts from [2] and [5] (partly by the same authors); parts of this paper overlap with these works.

2 Quiescent Input Output Transition Systems

Preliminaries. Given a set L, we use L^* to denote the set of all *finite sequences* $\sigma = a_1 a_2 \ldots a_n$ over L. We write $|\sigma| = n$ for the *length* of σ, and ϵ for the *empty sequence*, and let $L^+ = L^* \setminus \{\epsilon\}$. We let L^ω denote the set of all *infinite sequences* over L, and use $L^\infty = L^* \cup L^\omega$. Given two sequences $\rho \in L^*$ and $\upsilon \in L^\infty$, we denote the *concatenation* of ρ and υ by $\rho \upsilon$. The *projection of an element* $a \in L$ on $L' \subseteq L$, denoted $a \upharpoonright L'$, is a if $a \in L'$ and ϵ otherwise. The projection of a sequence $\sigma = a \sigma'$ is defined inductively by $(a \sigma') \upharpoonright L' = (a \upharpoonright L')(\sigma' \upharpoonright L')$, and the projection of a set of sequences Z is defined as the set of projections.

If $\sigma, \rho \in L^*$, then σ is a *prefix* of ρ (denoted by $\sigma \sqsubseteq \rho$) if there is a $\sigma' \in L^*$ such that $\sigma \sigma' = \rho$. If $\sigma' \in L^+$, then σ is a *proper prefix* of ρ (denoted by $\sigma \sqsubset \rho$). We use $\wp(L)$ to denote the *power set* of L. Finally, we use the notation $\exists^\infty$ for 'there exist infinitely many'.

2.1 Basic Model and Definitions

Quiescent Input Output Transition Systems (QIOTSs) are labelled transition systems that model quiescence, i.e., the absence of outputs or internal transitions, via a special δ-action. Internal actions, in turn, are all represented by the special τ-action. Thus, QIOTSs are a variety of Input Output Transition Systems of the `ioco`-framework, and an adaptation of the DQTS model of [2], which, in turn, is based on the well-known model of Input-Output Automata [3,10].

Definition 2.1 (Quiescent Input Output Transition Systems). *A* Quiescent Input Output Transition System *(QIOTS) is a tuple* $\mathcal{A} = \langle S, s^0, L^I, L^O, \rightarrow \rangle$, *where* S *is a set of states;* $s^0 \in S$ *is its initial state;* L^I *and* L^O *are disjoint sets of input and output labels, respectively; and* $\rightarrow \subseteq S \times L \times S$ *is the transition relation, where* $L = L^I \cup L^O \cup \{\tau, \delta\}$. *We assume* $\delta, \tau \notin (L^I \cup L^O)$ *and* $\delta \neq \tau$, *and use* $L^O_\delta = L^O \cup \{\delta\}$. *We refer to* (L^I, L^O_δ) *as the* action signature *of* $\mathcal{A}$.

The following two requirements apply:

1. *A QIOTS must be* input-enabled, *i.e., for each* $s \in S$ *and* $a \in L^I$, *there exists an* $s' \in S$ *such that* $(s, a, s') \in \rightarrow$.
2. *A QIOTS must be* well-formed. *Well-formedness requires technical preparation and is defined in Sect. 2.3.*

We write $\mathcal{QIOTS}(L^I, L^O_\delta)$ *for the set of all possible QIOTSs over the action signature* (L^I, L^O_δ).

Semantically, QIOTSs assume progress. That is, QIOTSs are not allowed to remain idle forever when output or internal actions are enabled. Without this assumption, each state would be potentially quiescent. All sets in the definition of QIOTSs can potentially be uncountable.

Given a QIOTS $\mathcal{A}$, we denote its components by $S_\mathcal{A}, s^0_\mathcal{A}, L^I_\mathcal{A}, L^O_\mathcal{A}, \rightarrow_\mathcal{A}$. We omit the subscript when it is clear from the context.

Actions. We use the terms label and action interchangeably. We often suffix a question mark (?) to input labels and an exclamation mark (!) to output labels. These are, however, not part of the label. The label τ represents an internal action. Output and internal actions are called *locally controlled*, because their occurrence is under the control of the QIOTS. The special label δ is used to denote the occurrence of quiescence.

We use the standard notations for transitions.

Definition 2.2 (Transitional notations). *Let $\mathcal{A}$ be a QIOTS with $s, s' \in S, a, a_i \in L, b, b_i \in L \setminus \{\tau\}$, and $\sigma \in (L \setminus \{\tau\})^+$, then:*

$$
\begin{aligned}
s \xrightarrow{a} s' \quad &=_{\text{def}} \quad (s, a, s') \in \rightarrow \\
s \xrightarrow{a} \quad &=_{\text{def}} \quad \exists s'' \in S . s \xrightarrow{a} s'' \\
s \not\xrightarrow{a} \quad &=_{\text{def}} \quad \nexists s'' \in S . s \xrightarrow{a} s'' \\
s \xrightarrow{a_1 \cdots a_n} s' \quad &=_{\text{def}} \quad \exists s_0, \ldots, s_n \in S . s = s_0 \xrightarrow{a_1} \cdots \xrightarrow{a_n} s_n = s' \\
s \xRightarrow{\epsilon} s' \quad &=_{\text{def}} \quad s = s' \text{ or } s \xrightarrow{\tau \cdots \tau} s' \\
s \xRightarrow{b} s' \quad &=_{\text{def}} \quad \exists s_0, s_1 \in S . s \xRightarrow{\epsilon} s_0 \xrightarrow{b} s_1 \xRightarrow{\epsilon} s' \\
s \xRightarrow{b_1 \cdots b_n} s' \quad &=_{\text{def}} \quad \exists s_0, \ldots, s_n \in S . s = s_0 \xRightarrow{b_1} \cdots \xRightarrow{b_n} s_n = s'
\end{aligned}
$$

If $s \xrightarrow{a}$, we say that a is enabled in s. We use $L(s)$ to denote the set of all actions $a \in L$ that are enabled in state $s \in S$, i.e., $L(s) = \{ a \in L \mid s \xrightarrow{a} \}$. The notions are lifted to infinite traces in the obvious way.

We use the following language notations for QIOTSs and their behaviour.

Definition 2.3 (Language notations). *Let $\mathcal{A}$ be a QIOTS, then:*

- *A finite path in $\mathcal{A}$ is a sequence $\pi = s_0 a_1 s_1 a_2 s_2 \ldots s_n$ such that $s_{i-1} \xrightarrow{a_i} s_i$ for all $1 \le i \le n$. Infinite paths are defined analogously. The set of all paths in $\mathcal{A}$ is denoted $paths(\mathcal{A})$.*
- *Given any path, we write $first(\pi) = s_0$. Also, we denote by $states(\pi)$ the set of states that occur on π, and by ω-$states(\pi)$ the set of states that occur infinitely often. That is, ω-$states(\pi) = \{ s \in states(\pi) \mid \exists^\infty j . s_j = s \}$.*
- *We define $trace(\pi) = \pi \restriction (L \setminus \{\tau\})$, and say that $trace(\pi)$ is the trace of π. For every $s \in S, traces(s)$ is the set of all traces corresponding to paths that start in s, i.e., $traces(s) = \{ trace(\pi) \mid \pi \in paths(\mathcal{A}) \wedge first(\pi) = s \}$. We define $traces(\mathcal{A}) = traces(s^0)$, and say that two QIOTSs $\mathcal{B}$ and $\mathcal{C}$ are trace-equivalent, denoted $\mathcal{B} \approx_{\text{tr}} \mathcal{C}$, if $traces(\mathcal{B}) = traces(\mathcal{C})$.*
- *For a finite trace σ and state $s \in S, reach(s, \sigma)$ denotes the set of states in $\mathcal{A}$ that can be reached from s via σ, i.e., $reach(s, \sigma) = \{ s' \in S \mid s \xRightarrow{\sigma} s' \}$. For a set of states $S' \subseteq S$, we define $reach(S', \sigma) = \bigcup_{s \in S'} reach(s, \sigma)$.*

When needed, we add subscripts to indicate the QIOTS these notions refer to.

Definition 2.4 (Determinism). *A QIOTS $\mathcal{A}$ is deterministic if $s \xrightarrow{a} s'$ and $s \xrightarrow{a} s''$ imply $a \neq \tau$ and $s' = s''$, for all $s, s', s'' \in S$ and $a \in L$. Otherwise, $\mathcal{A}$ is nondeterministic.*

Each QIOTS has an obviously trace-equivalent deterministic QIOTS. Determinization is carried out using the well-known subset construction procedure. This construction yields a system in which every state has a unique target state per action, and internal transitions are not present anymore.

Definition 2.5 (Determinization). *The determinization of a QIOTS $\mathcal{A} = \langle S, s^0, L^{\mathrm{I}}, L^{\mathrm{O}}, \rightarrow \rangle$ is the QIOTS $det(\mathcal{A}) = \langle \wp(S)^+, \{s^0\}, L^{\mathrm{I}}, L^{\mathrm{O}}, \rightarrow_{\mathrm{D}} \rangle$, with $\wp(S)^+ = \wp(S) \setminus \varnothing$ and $\rightarrow_{\mathrm{D}} = \{(U, a, V) \in \wp(S)^+ \times L \times \wp(S)^+ \mid V = reach_{\mathcal{A}}(U, a) \wedge V \neq \varnothing\}$.*

Example 2.1. The (not yet well-formed) QIOTS $\mathcal{A}$ in Fig. 2(a) is nondeterministic; its determinization $det(\mathcal{A})$ is shown in Fig. 2(b).   □

2.2   Quiescence, Fairness and Divergence

Definition 2.6 (Quiescent state). *Let $\mathcal{A}$ be a QIOTS. A state $s \in S$ is quiescent, denoted $q(s)$, if it has no locally-controlled actions enabled, i.e. $q(s)$ if $s \not\xrightarrow{a}$ for all $a \in L^{\mathrm{O}} \cup \{\tau\}$. The set of all quiescent states of $\mathcal{A}$ is denoted $q(\mathcal{A})$.*

Example 2.2. States s_0, s_5 and s_6 of the QIOTS in Fig. 2(a) are quiescent.   □

As we have already discussed in the introduction, the notion of fairness plays a crucial role in the treatment of divergences in QIOTSs. As announced, we take the solution proposed in [2] for DQTSs—which in turn uses a notion of fairness that stems from [3,10,11]—and simplify it for our purposes. Restricted to QIOTSs, fairness states that every locally controlled action enabled from a state that is visited infinitely often, must also be executed infinitely often. Note that finite paths are fair by default.

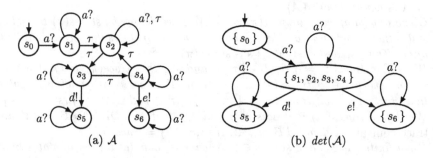

(a) $\mathcal{A}$ (b) $det(\mathcal{A})$

Fig. 2. Visual representations of the (not yet well-formed) QIOTSs $\mathcal{A}$ and $det(\mathcal{A})$.

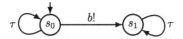

Fig. 3. A simple transition system with two types of divergence.

Definition 2.7 (Fair path). *Let $\mathcal{A}$ be a QIOTS and $\pi = s_0\, a_1\, s_1\, a_2\, s_2 \ldots$ a path of $\mathcal{A}$. Then, π is fair if for all $s \in \omega\text{-states}(\pi)$ and $s \xrightarrow{a} s'$ with $a \in (L^O \cup \{\tau\})$ the transition $s\, a\, s'$ occurs infinitely often in π.*

The set of all fair paths of a QIOTS $\mathcal{A}$ is denoted fpaths($\mathcal{A}$), and the set of corresponding traces is denoted ftraces($\mathcal{A}$).

Unfair paths are considered not to occur, so from now on we only consider *fpaths*($\mathcal{A}$) and *ftraces*($\mathcal{A}$) for the behaviour of $\mathcal{A}$.

Example 2.3. Consider the QIOTS in Fig. 3. The infinite path given by $\pi = s_0\, \tau\, s_0\, \tau\, s_0 \ldots$ is not fair as the b-output is ignored forever.   □

We can now formally introduce divergence as fair infinite internal behaviour.

Definition 2.8 (Divergent path). *Let $\mathcal{A}$ be a QIOTS, then a path π is divergent if $\pi \in$ fpaths($\mathcal{A}$) and it contains only transitions labelled with the internal action τ. The set of all divergent paths of $\mathcal{A}$ is denoted dpaths($\mathcal{A}$).*

Example 2.4. Consider the QIOTS in Fig. 3 again. The infinite path given by $\pi = s_1\, \tau\, s_1\, \tau\, s_1 \ldots$ is divergent. Note that divergent traces are not preserved by determinization.   □

We are now all set to allow divergent paths to occur in QIOTSs. For computability reasons, however, we assume that each divergent path in a QIOTS contains only a finite number of states.

Definition 2.9 (State-finite path). *Let $\mathcal{A}$ be a QIOTS and let $\pi \in$ fpaths($\mathcal{A}$) be an infinite path. If $|\text{states}(\pi)| < \infty$, then π is state-finite.*

When the system is on a state-finite divergent path, it continuously loops through a finite number of states on this path. We call these states divergent.

Definition 2.10 (Divergent state). *Let $\mathcal{A}$ be a QIOTS. A state $s \in S$ is divergent, denoted d(s), if there is a (state-finite and fair) divergent path on which s occurs infinitely often, i.e., if there is a path $\pi \in$ dpaths($\mathcal{A}$) such that $s \in \omega\text{-states}(\pi)$. The set of all divergent states of $\mathcal{A}$ is denoted d($\mathcal{A}$).*

Divergent paths in QIOTSs may cause the observation of quiescence in states that are not necessarily quiescent themselves. As already illustrated in Fig. 3, state s_1 is not quiescent, since it enables the internal action τ. Still, output is never observed on the divergent path $\pi = s_1\, \tau\, s_1\, \tau \ldots$, so that quiescence is observed from a non-quiescent state. Note that the assumption of strong convergence of [1] does not allow such behaviour.

2.3   Well-Formedness

In Definition 2.1 we have already stipulated that, for QIOTS to be meaningful, they have to adhere to some well-formedness conditions ensuring the consistency of the representation of quiescence and divergence. Technically speaking, these conditions ensure that our QIOTSs are particular instances of the DQTS model of [2], so that we may profit from the proven properties of the more elaborate model from [2]. We first introduce the DQTS model.

Definition 2.11 (Divergent Quiescent Transition System). *A* Divergent Quiescent Transition System *(DQTS) is a tuple* $\mathcal{A} = \langle S, S^0, L^I, L^O, L^H, P, \rightarrow \rangle$, *where S is a set of states; $S^0 \subseteq S$ is a non-empty set of initial states; L^I, L^O and L^H are disjoint sets of input, output and internal labels, respectively; P is a partition of $L^O \cup L^H$; and $\rightarrow \; \subseteq S \times L \times S$ is the transition relation, where $L = L^I \cup L^O \cup L^H \cup \{\delta\}$. We assume $\delta \notin (L^I \cup L^O \cup L^H)$.*

1. *A DQTS $\mathcal{A}$ must be* input-enabled, *i.e. for each $s \in S$ and $a \in L^I$, there exists an $s' \in S$ such that $(s, a, s') \in \rightarrow$.*
2. *A DQTS must be* well-formed, *i.e. it fulfils Rules R1, R2, R3, and R4 stipulated below.*

We use the notions $q(s)$ and $d(s)$, defined earlier for QIOTSs, for DQTSs as well in the obvious way.

Definition 2.12 (Well-formedness). *A DQTS (or a QIOTS) $\mathcal{A}$ is* well-formed *if it satisfies the following rules for all $s, s', s'' \in S$ and $a \in L^I$:*

Rule R1 (Quiescence is observable)**:** *if $q(s)$ or $d(s)$, then $s \xrightarrow{\delta}$.*

Rule R2 (Quiescence follows quiescence)**:** *if $s \xrightarrow{\delta} s'$, then $q(s')$.*

We require the observation of quiescence to result in a quiescent state. This makes sure that no outputs are observed following a quiescence observation. We could have been a bit more liberal for QIOTSs, replacing this rule by "if $s \xrightarrow{\delta} s'$, then $q(s') \lor d(s')$". After all, divergent states can never invisibly reach any output transitions under our current fairness assumption. However, we chose to be more strict here, requiring traditional quiescence (the absence of any locally controlled actions) following a δ-transition. That way, these rules still work in the presence of a more liberal fairness assumption that also allows output actions to be enabled from divergent states (as in [2]).

Rule R3 (Quiescence enables no new behaviour)**:** *if $s \xrightarrow{\delta} s'$, then $traces(s') \subseteq traces(s)$.*

The observation of quiescence must not lead to actions that were not enabled before its observation. As the observation of quiescence may be the result of an earlier nondeterministic choice, its observation may lead to a state with fewer enabled actions.

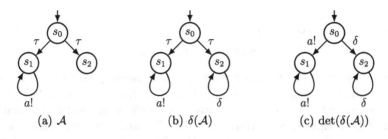

Fig. 4. Illustration of Rule R3.

Rule R4 (Repeated quiescence preserves behaviour): if $s \xrightarrow{\delta} s'$ and $s' \xrightarrow{\delta} s''$, then $traces(s'') = traces(s')$.

The potential reduction of enabled actions of the previous clause only manifests itself in the first observation of quiescence; its continued observation adds no new information.

For finite DQTSs/QIOTSs the validity of all rules is computable. Further below we will discuss the computation of $d(s)$.

Example 2.5. To illustrate the necessity of using $\subseteq$ instead of $=$ in Rule R3, observe the (not yet well-formed) nondeterministic system in Fig. 4(a). To make it follow Rule R1, we added a δ-transition to state s_2, as shown in Fig. 4(b). Then, we determinized the system, obtaining the QIOTS shown in Fig. 4(c). All rules are satisfied. Indeed, as allowed by Rule R3, $traces(s_2)$ is a proper subset of $traces(s_0)$. $\square$

2.4 QIOTSs versus DQTSs

Looking at the definition of DQTSs we observe a few differences with QIOTSs. As the definition of DQTSs is based on the Input-Output Automata model of Lynch and Tuttle [3], the three differences are that there is a set of initial states, rather than a single state; that there is a set of named internal actions, rather than just τ; and that a partition P of $L^O \cup L^H$ is part of the model. Concerning the first two differences, the QIOTS model is just a straightforward special case of the DQTS model. The partition P represents the fairness conditions that apply to the model, which can be tuned as part of the model. The definition of a fair path for a DQTS is as follows: a path $\pi = s_0\, a_1\, s_1\, a_2\, s_2\, \ldots$ is fair if for every $A \in P$ such that $\exists^\infty j \,.\, L(s_j) \cap A \neq \varnothing$, we have $\exists^\infty j \,.\, a_j \in A$. As for QIOTSs, state-finite divergence is assumed. The definition below shows which DQTSs correspond to QIOTSs.

Definition 2.13 (Associated DQTS). *Let* $\mathcal{A} = \langle\, S, s^0, L^I, L^O, \rightarrow \,\rangle$ *be a QIOTS, then its associated Divergent Quiescent Transition System* $DQTS(\mathcal{A})$ *is defined by the tuple* $\langle\, S, \{\, s^0\, \}, L^I, L^O, L^H, P, \rightarrow' \,\rangle$ *with*

1. $L^H = \{ \tau_{(s,s')} \mid s \xrightarrow{\tau} s' \in \rightarrow \}$;
2. $P = \{ \{a\} \mid a \in L^O \cup L^H \}$;
3. $\rightarrow' = \rightarrow \setminus \{ (s, \tau, s') \mid (s, \tau, s') \in \rightarrow \} \cup \{ (s, \tau_{(s,s')}, s') \mid (s, \tau, s') \in \rightarrow \}$.

It is straightforward to check that this association preserves the intended fairness condition for QIOTSs. In [2] it is proven that well-formed DQTSs and SAs are equivalent in terms of expressible observable behaviour: it is shown that for every DQTS there exists a trace equivalent SA, and vice versa. Hence, except for divergences, their expressivity coincides. This result carries over to QIOTSs, as their restriction with respect to DQTSs does not affect the observable traces.

3   Operations and Properties

3.1   Deltafication: From IOTS to QIOTS

Usually, specifications are not modelled as QIOTSs directly, but rather in a formalism whose operational semantics can be expressed in terms of IOTSs. Hence, we need a way to convert an IOTS to a (well-formed) QIOTS that captures all possible observations of it, including quiescence. This conversion is called *deltafication*. As for QIOTSs, we require all IOTSs to be input-enabled for deltafication.

To satisfy rule R1, every state in which quiescence may be observed (i.e., all quiescent and divergent states) must have an outgoing δ-transition. Hence, to go from an IOTS to a QIOTS, the deltafication operator adds a δ-labelled self-loop to each quiescent state. Also, a new *quiescence observation state* qos_s is introduced for each divergent state $s \in S$: When quiescence is observed in s, a δ-transition will lead to qos_s. To preserve the original behaviour, inputs from qos_s must lead to the same states that the corresponding input transitions from s led to. All these considerations together lead to the following definition for the deltafication procedure for IOTSs.

As mentioned before, the SA construction that adds δ-labelled self-loops to all quiescent states does not work for divergent states, since divergent states must have at least one outgoing internal transition (and possibly even output transitions when taking a more lenient fairness assumption, as in [2]). So, a δ-labelled self-loop added to a divergent state would contradict rule R2.

Definition 3.1 (Deltafication). *Let* $\mathcal{A} = \langle S_A, s^0, L^I, L^O, \rightarrow_A \rangle$ *be an IOTS with* $\delta \notin L$. *The* deltafication *of* $\mathcal{A}$ *is* $\delta(\mathcal{A}) = \langle S_\delta, s^0, L^I, L^O, \rightarrow_\delta \rangle$. *We define* $S_\delta = S_A \cup \{ qos_s \mid s \in d(\mathcal{A}) \}$, *i.e.,* S_δ *contains a new state* $qos_s \notin S_A$ *for every divergent state* $s \in S_A$ *of* $\mathcal{A}$. *The transition relation* $\rightarrow_\delta$ *is as follows:*

$$
\begin{aligned}
\rightarrow_\delta = \rightarrow_A \ &\cup \{ (s, \delta, s) & \mid s \in q(\mathcal{A}) \} \\
&\cup \{ (s, \delta, qos_s) & \mid s \in d(\mathcal{A}) \} \cup \{ (qos_s, \delta, qos_s) \mid s \in d(\mathcal{A}) \} \\
&\cup \{ (qos_s, a?, s') \mid s \in d(\mathcal{A}) \wedge a? \in L^I \wedge s \xrightarrow{a?}_A s' \}
\end{aligned}
$$

Note that computing $q(\mathcal{A})$ is trivial: simply identify all states without outgoing output or internal transitions. Determining $d(\mathcal{A})$ is discussed further below.

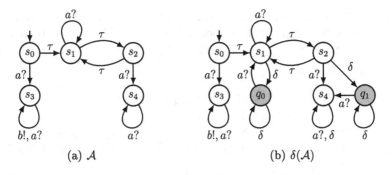

Fig. 5. An IOTS $\mathcal{A}$ and its deltafication $\delta(\mathcal{A})$. Newly introduced states are grey.

Example 3.1. See Fig. 5 for IOTS $\mathcal{A}$ and its deltafication. States s_1 and s_2 are divergent, and q_0 and q_1 quiescence observation states. Note that s_0 has an outgoing divergent path, while in accordance to rule R1 it is not given an outgoing δ-transition. The reason is that, when observing quiescence due to divergence, rule R4 prescribes that the system can only reside in s_1 or s_2. The states reachable from a given state via unobservable paths assume a similar role as the *stable* states (not having outgoing τ-transitions) in [1], which does not deal with divergence. So, quiescence cannot be observed from s_0, and therefore also the a-transition to s_3 should not be enabled anymore after observation of quiescence. This is now taken care of by not having a direct δ-transition from s_0. Because of this, no trace first having δ and then the $b!$ output is present. □

The results from [2] imply directly that the deltafication $\delta(\mathcal{A})$ indeed yields a well-formed QIOTS for every IOTS $\mathcal{A}$.

In order to compute the set of divergent states $d(\mathcal{A})$ in a QIOTS $\mathcal{A}$, we proceed as follows. First, we mark all states that enable an output action; say we colour those states red. Then, we consider the directed graph G that we obtain from $\mathcal{A}$ by keeping only the τ transitions, and removing all transitions labelled by an input or output action. Thus, $G = (S, E)$ with $E = \{(s, s') \mid s \xrightarrow{\tau} s'\}$. In G, we compute, using Tarjan's algorithm [12], the set of all bottom strongly connected components. Now, a state is divergent if and only if it is contained in a bottom strongly connected component that contains no red state and has at least one τ-transition.

3.2 Composition of QIOTSs

Parallel composition is an important standard operation on well-formed QIOTSs, and again is a straightforward specialization of the corresponding definition for DQTSs in [2]. To apply the parallel composition operator we require every output action to be under the control of at most one component [3].

Definition 3.2 (Compatibility). *Two QIOTSs $\mathcal{A}$ and $\mathcal{B}$ are compatible if* $L_{\mathcal{A}}^O \cap L_{\mathcal{B}}^O = \varnothing$.

Definition 3.3 (Parallel composition). *Given two well-formed compatible QIOTSs $\mathcal{A}$ and $\mathcal{B}$, the* parallel composition *of $\mathcal{A}$ and $\mathcal{B}$ is the QIOTS $\mathcal{A} \parallel \mathcal{B}$, with $S_{\mathcal{A} \parallel \mathcal{B}} = S_{\mathcal{A}} \times S_{\mathcal{B}}, s^0_{\mathcal{A} \parallel \mathcal{B}} = (s^0_{\mathcal{A}}, s^0_{\mathcal{B}}), L^I_{\mathcal{A} \parallel \mathcal{B}} = (L^I_{\mathcal{A}} \cup L^I_{\mathcal{B}}) \setminus (L^O_{\mathcal{A}} \cup L^O_{\mathcal{B}}),$ $L^O_{\mathcal{A} \parallel \mathcal{B}} = L^O_{\mathcal{A}} \cup L^O_{\mathcal{B}}, and$*

$$
\begin{aligned}
\rightarrow_{\mathcal{A} \parallel \mathcal{B}} = \{\, ((s,t), a, (s',t')) \in S_{\mathcal{A} \parallel \mathcal{B}} \times ((L_{\mathcal{A}} \cap L_{\mathcal{B}}) \setminus \{\tau\}) \times S_{\mathcal{A} \parallel \mathcal{B}} \mid \\
s \xrightarrow{a}_{\mathcal{A}} s' \wedge t \xrightarrow{a}_{\mathcal{B}} t' \,\} \\
\cup \{\, ((s,t), a, (s',t)) \in S_{\mathcal{A} \parallel \mathcal{B}} \times (L_{\mathcal{A}} \setminus (L_{\mathcal{B}} \setminus \{\tau\})) \times S_{\mathcal{A} \parallel \mathcal{B}} \mid s \xrightarrow{a}_{\mathcal{A}} s' \,\} \\
\cup \{\, ((s,t), a, (s,t')) \in S_{\mathcal{A} \parallel \mathcal{B}} \times (L_{\mathcal{B}} \setminus (L_{\mathcal{A}} \setminus \{\tau\})) \times S_{\mathcal{A} \parallel \mathcal{B}} \mid t \xrightarrow{a}_{\mathcal{B}} t' \,\}
\end{aligned}
$$

We have $L_{\mathcal{A} \parallel \mathcal{B}} = L^I_{\mathcal{A} \parallel \mathcal{B}} \cup L^O_{\mathcal{A} \parallel \mathcal{B}} \cup \{\tau\} = L_{\mathcal{A}} \cup L_{\mathcal{B}}.$

In essence this is the usual process algebraic definition of parallel composition with synchronization on shared labels (first set of transitions in the definition of $\rightarrow_{\mathcal{A} \parallel \mathcal{B}}$) and interleaving on independent labels (second and third sets of transitions in the definition of $\rightarrow_{\mathcal{A} \parallel \mathcal{B}}$). Note that δ is a shared label that must synchronize, and that τ never synchronizes.

3.3 Preservation Properties

In [2] it is shown that well-formed DQTSs are preserved under parallel composition and determinization. These results carry over directly to QIOTSs. This is only possible because of the refined treatment of the definition of quiescence.

With the representation of quiescence by simple δ-loops, as it is done in the SA model, preservation under determinization fails. It requires that δ-loops can be unwound, because of the need to preserve Rule R2 under determinization.

Another crucial operation (on IOTSs) is deltafication. A pleasing result is that deltafication and parallel composition commute [2]. That is, given two compatible IOTSs $\mathcal{A}, \mathcal{B}$, such that $\delta \notin L_{\mathcal{A}} \cup L_{\mathcal{B}}$, we have $\delta(\mathcal{A} \parallel \mathcal{B}) \approx_{\mathrm{tr}} \delta(\mathcal{A}) \parallel \delta(\mathcal{B})$.

With deltafication and determinization the situation is more involved. This is a direct consequence of the fact that determinization does not preserve quiescence. Of course, determinization removes divergences by construction, but this is not the only source of problems, as the example in Fig. 6 shows (omitting some self-loops needed for input-enabledness, for presentation purposes).

It follows that when transforming a nondeterministic IOTS $\mathcal{A}$ to a deterministic, well-formed QIOTS, one should always first derive $\delta(\mathcal{A})$ and only then obtain a determinized version. As demonstrated in Fig. 6(e), self-loops labelled δ may turn into regular transitions, motivating once more our choice of moving away from Suspension Automata (that were not closed under determinization) to a more general framework in which δ-transitions are treated as first-class citizens.

3.4 Conformance for QIOTSs

The core of the ioco-framework is its *conformance relation*, relating specifications to implementations if and only if the latter is 'correct' with respect to

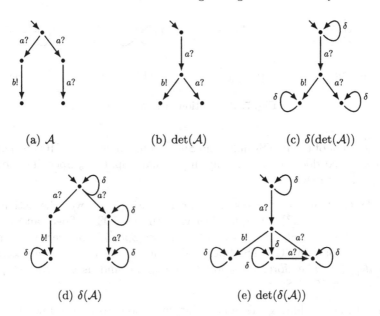

(a) $\mathcal{A}$ (b) $\det(\mathcal{A})$ (c) $\delta(\det(\mathcal{A}))$

(d) $\delta(\mathcal{A})$ (e) $\det(\delta(\mathcal{A}))$

Fig. 6. Determinization and deltafication.

the former. For ioco, this means that the implementation never provides an unexpected output (including quiescence) when it is only fed inputs that are allowed by the specification. Traditionally, this was formalized based on the SAs corresponding to the implementation and the specification. Now, we can apply well-formed QIOTSs, as they already model the expected absence of outputs by explicit δ-transitions. As QIOTSs support divergence, using them also allows ioco to be applied in the presence of (finite state) divergence.

Definition 3.4 (ioco). *Let* Impl, Spec *be well-formed QIOTSs over the same alphabet. Then,* Impl $\sqsubseteq_{ioco}$ Spec *if and only if*

$$\forall\,\sigma \in \mathit{traces}(\mathsf{Spec}) \,.\, \mathit{out}_{\mathsf{Impl}}(\sigma) \subseteq \mathit{out}_{\mathsf{Spec}}(\sigma),$$

where $\mathit{out}_{\mathcal{A}}(\sigma) = \{a \in L^O_\delta \mid \sigma a \in \mathit{traces}(\mathcal{A})\}$.

This new notion of ioco-conformance can be applied to extend the testing frameworks in [5,8], using the same basic schema: during testing, continuously choose to either try and provide an input, observe the behaviour of the system or stop testing. As long as the trace obtained this way, including the δ actions as the result of either quiescence or divergence, is also a trace of the specification, the implementation is correct.

Since all QIOTSs are required to be input-enabled, it is easy to see that ioco-conformance precisely corresponds to traditional trace inclusion over well-formed QIOTSs (and hence, $\sqsubseteq_{ioco}$ is transitive). Note that this only holds because the specification Spec and implementation Impl are already represented as QIOTSs;

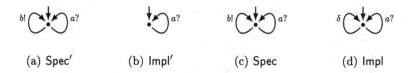

(a) Spec′   (b) Impl′   (c) Spec   (d) Impl

Fig. 7. Illustration of Example 3.2.

trace inclusion of the IOTSs Impl′ and Spec′ from which these QIOTSs may have been generated does not necessarily imply that Impl $\sqsubseteq_{\mathtt{ioco}}$ Spec. The following example illustrates this.

Example 3.2. Consider the systems shown in Fig. 7, all over the action signature $(L^I, L_\delta^O) = (\{a?\}, \{b!, \delta\})$. Clearly, both the IOTSs Spec′ and Impl′ are input-enabled, and also $traces(\text{Impl}') \subseteq traces(\text{Spec}')$. However, when looking at the corresponding QIOTSs Spec and Impl, we see that $\delta \in out_{\text{Impl}}(\epsilon)$, but $\delta \notin out_{\text{Spec}}(\epsilon)$. Therefore, $out_{\text{Impl}}(\epsilon) \not\subseteq out_{\text{Spec}}(\epsilon)$, and as $\epsilon \in traces(\text{Spec})$ by definition Impl $\not\sqsubseteq_{\mathtt{ioco}}$ Spec.   □

Clearly, action hiding—renaming output actions to τ—does not necessarily preserve $\sqsubseteq_{\mathtt{ioco}}$. After all, it may introduce quiescence where that is not allowed by the specification. (Note also that δ-transitions may need to be added after hiding. We refer to [2] for a detailed exposition of the hiding operator on DQTSs.)

4   Test Cases and Test Suites

We present part of the testing framework introduced in [5], applying it to QIOTSs instead of the more basic QTSs used there. Whether the δ-transitions in QIOTSs were introduced because of traditional quiescence or divergence does not influence their behaviour, so all results from [5] still hold and the proofs are not all repeated here.

4.1   Tests over an Action Signature

We apply model-based testing in a *black-box* manner: to execute a test case on a system, one only needs an executable of the implementation. Hence, test cases and test suites can be defined solely based on the so-called *action signature* (L^I, L_δ^O), also called *interface*, of the implementation.

A test case describes the behaviour of a tester. At each moment in time the tester either stops, or waits for the system to do something, or tries to provide an input. This is represented for each trace (a *history*) σ in the test case having either (1) no other traces of which σ is a prefix, (2) several traces $\sigma b!$ that extend σ with all output actions from L_δ^O, or (3) a single trace $\sigma a?$ extending σ with an input action $a? \in L^I$. In the third case, there should also be traces $\sigma b!$ for all actions $b! \in L^O$ (excluding δ), as the implementation may be faster than the tester. A test case contains all behaviour that *may* occur during testing—during an actual test, however, only one complete trace of the test will be observed.

Definition 4.1 (Test case). *A test case (or shortly a* test*) over an action signature* (L^I, L^O_δ) *is a set of traces* $t \subseteq (L^I \cup L^O_\delta)^*$ *such that*

- *t is prefix-closed;*
- *t does not contain an infinite increasing sequence $\sigma_0 \sqsubset \sigma_1 \sqsubset \sigma_2 \sqsubset \ldots$ [1];*
- *For every trace $\sigma \in t$, we have either*
  1. *$\{a \in L^I \cup L^O_\delta \mid \sigma a \in t\} = \varnothing$, or*
  2. *$\{a \in L^I \cup L^O_\delta \mid \sigma a \in t\} = L^O_\delta$, or*
  3. *$\{a \in L^I \cup L^O_\delta \mid \sigma a \in t\} = \{a?\} \cup L^O$ for some $a? \in L^I$.*

Test cases should not contain an infinite trace $aaa\ldots$ (taken care of by using $(L^I \cup L^O_\delta)^*$ instead of $(L^I \cup L^O_\delta)^\infty$) or an infinite increasing sequence $a, aa, aaa, \ldots$ (taken care of by the second condition), since we want the test process to end at some point. By requiring them to adhere to the observations made above on the type of traces that they contain, they necessarily represent a deterministic tester (i.e., they never nondeterministically choose between different input actions).

We note that test cases can be represented as directed acyclic graphs (DAGs) as well.

Definition 4.2 (Test case notations). *Given an action signature (L^I, L^O_δ),*

- *we use $\mathcal{T}(L^I, L^O_\delta)$ to denote the set of all tests over (L^I, L^O_δ).*
- *we define a* test suite *over (L^I, L^O_δ) to be a set of tests over (L^I, L^O_δ). We denote the set of all test suites over (L^I, L^O_δ) by $\mathcal{TS}(L^I, L^O_\delta)$.*

Given a test case t over (L^I, L^O_δ),

- *we say that the* length *of t is the supremum of the lengths of the traces in t, i.e., $\sup\{|\sigma| \mid \sigma \in t\}$. Note that this length is an element of $\mathbb{N} \cup \{\infty\}$.*
- *we say that t is* linear *if there exists a trace $\sigma \in t$ such that every non-empty trace $\rho \in t$ can be written as $\sigma' a$, where $\sigma' \sqsubseteq \sigma$ and $a \in L^I \cup L^O_\delta$. The trace σ is called the* main trace *of t.*
- *we use ctraces(t) to denote the* complete traces *of t, i.e., all traces $\sigma \in t$ for which there is no $\rho \in t$ such that $\sigma \sqsubset \rho$.*

Example 4.1. The restriction that a test case cannot contain an infinite increasing sequence makes sure that every test process will eventually terminate. However, it does not mean that the length of a test case is necessarily finite.

To see this, observe the two tests shown in Fig. 8 (represented as DAGs, and for presentation purposes not showing all transitions). The DAG shown in Fig. 8(a) is not allowed, as it contains the infinite path $b! \, b! \, b! \, b! \ldots$. Therefore, a test process based on this DAG may never end. The DAG shown in Fig. 8(b), however, is a valid test. Although it has infinite length (after all, there is no boundary below which the length of every path stays), there does not exist an infinite path; every path begins with an action a_i and then continues with $i - 1 < \infty$ actions.

Note that every test that can be obtained by cutting off Fig. 8(a) at a certain depth is linear, whereas the test in Fig. 8(b) is not.   □

---

[1] If $L^I \cup L^O_\delta$ is finite, we can replace this requirement by asking that t is finite.

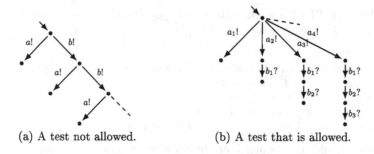

(a) A test not allowed.   (b) A test that is allowed.

Fig. 8. Infinite tests.

Definition 4.3 (Tests for a specification). *Let* Spec $= \langle S, s^0, L^I, L^O, \rightarrow \rangle$ *be a specification (i.e., a QIOTS), then a test for* Spec *is a test over* (L^I, L^O_δ). *We denote the universe of tests and test suites for* Spec *by* $\mathcal{T}$(Spec) *and* $\mathcal{TS}$(Spec), *respectively.*

4.2 Test Annotations, Executions and Verdicts

Before testing a system, we obviously need to define which outcomes of a test case are considered correct (the system *passes*), and which are considered incorrect (the system *fails*). For this purpose we introduce *annotations*.

Definition 4.4 (Annotations). *Let t be a test case, then an* annotation *of t is a function* $a : ctraces(t) \rightarrow \{pass, fail\}$. *A pair* $\hat{t} = (t, a)$ *consisting of a test case together with an annotation for it is called an* annotated test case, *and a set of such pairs* $\widehat{T} = \{(t_i, a_i)\}$ *is called an* annotated test suite.

When representing a test case as DAG, we depict the annotation function by means of labels on its leaves (see Fig. 9(b)).

Running a test case can basically be considered as the parallel composition of the test and the implementation, after first mirroring the action labels of the test for synchronisation to take place (changing inputs into outputs and the other way around)[2]. Note that the test and the implementation synchronise on all visible actions, that the implementation cannot block any inputs and that the test cannot block any outputs (except at the end). Therefore, it can easily be seen that the set of possible traces arising from this parallel composition is just the intersection of the trace sets of the test and the implementation. We are mainly interested in the complete traces of this intersection, as they contain the most information. Also, we prefer to exclude the empty trace, as it cannot be observed during testing anyway (rather, it could be observed by means of a δ-transition).

---

[2] Technically, parallel composition was only defined for QIOTSs, and test cases are no QIOTSs. However, the idea can easily be lifted. Moreover, the actual formal definition of the execution of a test case below circumvents this issue by directly defining the results of the parallel composition.

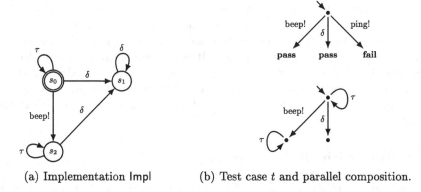

(a) Implementation Impl   (b) Test case t and parallel composition.

Fig. 9. An implementation, test case and their parallel composition.

To accommodate this, we directly define the set of possible *executions* of a test case t given an implementation Impl as follows.

Definition 4.5 (Executions). *Let* (L^I, L^O_δ) *be an action signature, t a test case over* (L^I, L^O_δ), *and* Impl *an QIOTS over* (L^I, L^O_δ). *Then,*

$$exec_t(\mathsf{Impl}) = traces(\mathsf{Impl}) \cap ctraces(t)$$

are the executions *of t given* Impl.

Example 4.2. Consider the implementation in Fig. 9(a) and the corresponding test case in Fig. 9(b). Figure 9(b) additionally shows their parallel composition (after first mirroring the test case). Note that it is immediately clear from this parallel composition that the erroneous output *ping!* is not present in the implementation. By definition, the executions of this test case t given the implemention Impl are $exec_t(\mathsf{Impl}) = \{\text{beep!}, \delta\}$. □

Based on an annotated test case (or test suite) we assign a verdict to implementations; the verdict *pass* is given when the test case can never find any erroneous behaviour (i.e., there is no trace in the implementation that is also in *ctraces(t)* and was annotated by *fail*), and the verdict *fail* is given otherwise.

Definition 4.6 (Verdict functions). *Let* (L^I, L^O_δ) *be an action signature and* $\hat{t} = (t, a)$ *an annotated test case over* (L^I, L^O_δ). *The* verdict function *for $\hat{t}$ is the function*

$$v_{\hat{t}} \colon \mathcal{QIOTS}(L^I, L^O_\delta) \to \{pass, fail\},$$

given for any QIOTS Impl *by*

$$v_{\hat{t}}(\mathsf{Impl}) = \begin{cases} pass \; if \; \forall \, \sigma \in exec_t(\mathsf{Impl}) \, . \, a(\sigma) = pass; \\ fail \;\; otherwise. \end{cases}$$

We extend $v_{\hat{t}}$ *to a function* $v_{\hat{T}} \colon \mathcal{QIOTS}(L^I, L^O_\delta) \to \{pass, fail\}$ *assigning a verdict to implementations based on a test suite, by putting* $v_{\hat{T}}(\mathsf{Impl}) = pass$ *if* $v_{\hat{t}}(\mathsf{Impl}) = pass$ *for all* $\hat{t} \in \hat{T}$, *and* $v_{\hat{T}}(\mathsf{Impl}) = fail$ *otherwise.*

Remark 4.1. Note that during (and after) testing we only have a partial view of the set $exec_t(\mathsf{Impl})$, and hence of Impl: each time we run a test case on an implementation, we see only one single trace in the test case. Additionally, we are not in control of which traces we see. It is the implementation that decides which branch is selected. Hence, each test case should be executed a number of times to cover all behaviour. This implies that testing is inherently incomplete; even though no failure has been observed, there still may be faults left in the system.   □

5   Testing with Respect to $\sqsubseteq_{ioco}$

The conformance relation $\sqsubseteq_{ioco}$ is of vital importance in the test process, as it captures precisely which behaviour is considered valid and which is considered invalid. Based on Definition 3.4, it induces the following annotation function:

Definition 5.1 (ioco-annotation). *Let t be an (unannotated) test case for a specification* Spec. *The annotation function* $a^{ioco}_{\mathsf{Spec},t}: ctraces(t) \rightarrow \{pass, fail\}$ *for t is given by*

$$a^{ioco}_{\mathsf{Spec},t}(\sigma) = \begin{cases} fail \;\; if\, \exists\, \sigma_1 \in traces(\mathsf{Spec}), a! \in L^O_\delta \, . \\ \qquad \sigma \sqsupseteq \sigma_1 a! \wedge \sigma_1 a! \notin traces(\mathsf{Spec}); \\ pass \; otherwise. \end{cases}$$

The basic idea is that we generally assign a *fail* verdict only to sequences σ that can be written as $\sigma = \sigma_1 a! \sigma_2$ such that $\sigma_1 \in traces(\mathsf{Spec})$ and $\sigma_1 a! \notin traces(\mathsf{Spec})$; that is, when there is an output action that leads us out of the traces of Spec. Note that if we can write $\sigma = \sigma_1 b? \sigma_2$ such that $\sigma_1 \in traces(\mathsf{Spec})$ and $\sigma_1 b? \notin traces(\mathsf{Spec})$, then we assign a *pass*, because in this case an unexpected input $b? \in L^I$ was provided by the test case. Hence, any behaviour that comes after this input is ioco-conforming.

Remark 5.1. In our setting of input-enabled specifications, the scenario in which $\sigma = \sigma_1 b? \sigma_2$ such that $\sigma_1 \in traces(\mathsf{Spec})$ and $\sigma_1 b? \notin traces(\mathsf{Spec})$, cannot occur. The definition reduces to $a^{ioco}_{\mathsf{Spec},t}(\sigma) = pass$ if and only if $\sigma \in traces(\mathsf{Spec})$.   □

Example 5.1. In Fig. 10, test case t_3 is annotated according to $a^{ioco}_{\mathsf{Spec},t_3}$. Test case t_1 is not, though, since it should allow the trace $a!$ and not the trace $b!$ (since $\epsilon \in traces(\mathsf{Spec}), b! \in L^O_\delta$ and $b! \notin traces(\mathsf{Spec})$). Test case t_2 is also not annotated according to $a^{ioco}_{\mathsf{Spec},t_3}$, since it erroneously allows δ.   □

Given a specification Spec, any test case t annotated according to $a^{ioco}_{\mathsf{Spec},t}$ is *sound* for Spec with respect to $\sqsubseteq_{ioco}$. Intuitively, a sound test case never rejects a correct implementation. That is, for all implementations $\mathsf{Impl} \in \mathcal{QIOTS}(L^I, L^O_\delta)$ it holds that $v_{\hat{t}}(\mathsf{Impl}) = fail$ implies $\mathsf{Impl} \not\sqsubseteq_{ioco} \mathsf{Spec}$. It is easy to see that, as $\sqsubseteq_{ioco}$ coincides with trace inclusion due to input-enabledness, a test case is sound if $\forall\, \sigma \in ctraces(t)\, .\, \sigma \in traces(\mathsf{Spec}) \implies a(\sigma) = pass$.

The fact that $a^{ioco}_{\mathsf{Spec},t}$ yields sound test cases follows directly from the above observation and Remark 5.1.

Proposition 5.1. *Let* Spec *be a specification, then the annotated test suite* $\widehat{T} = \{(t, a_{\text{Spec},t}^{\text{ioco}}) \mid t \in \mathcal{T}(\text{Spec})\}$ *is sound for* Spec *with respect to* $\sqsubseteq_{\text{ioco}}$.

To also state a completeness property we first introduce a canonical form for sequences, based on the idea that it is never needed to test for quiescence multiple times consecutively.

Definition 5.2 (Canonical traces). *Let* σ *be a sequence over a label set* L *with* $\delta \in L$, *then its canonical form* $canon(\sigma)$ *is the sequence obtained by replacing every occurrence of two or more consecutive* δ *actions by* δ, *and, when* σ *ends in one or more* δ *actions, removing all those. The canonical form of a set of sequences* $S \subseteq L^*$ *is the set*

$$canon(S) = \{ canon(\sigma) \mid \sigma \in S \}.$$

The following proposition precisely characterises the requirement for a test suite to be complete with respect to $\sqsubseteq_{\text{ioco}}$. Intuitively, a complete test suite never accepts an incorrect implementation. That is, $\widehat{T}$ is *complete* for Spec with respect to $\sqsubseteq_{\text{ioco}}$ if for all implementations Impl $\in \mathcal{QIOTS}(L^I, L_\delta^O)$ it holds that Impl $\not\sqsubseteq_{\text{ioco}}$ Spec $\implies v_{\widehat{T}}(\text{Impl}) = \textit{fail}$.

Proposition 5.2. *Given a specification* Spec *and a test suite* $\widehat{T} \subseteq \{(t, a_{\text{Spec},t}^{\text{ioco}}) \mid t \in \mathcal{T}(\text{Spec})\}, \widehat{T}$ *is complete for* Spec *with respect to* $\sqsubseteq_{\text{ioco}}$ *if and only if*

$$\forall \, \sigma \in canon(traces(\text{Spec})) \,.$$
$$(out_{\text{Spec}}(\sigma) \neq L_\delta^O \implies \exists (t, a) \in \widehat{T} \,.\, \sigma\delta \in t)$$

Proof (sketch). This proposition states that a complete test suite should be able to observe the implementation's behaviour following every canonical trace of the specification (except when all behaviour is allowed). Hence, no possible unexpected (erroneous) outputs are impossible to detect, and indeed every incorrect implementation can be caught. The fact that we can restrict to canonical traces stems from well-formedness rules R2 and R4, which make sure that it is never necessary to directly observe again after observing quiescence. $\qquad\square$

Example 5.2. Consider the specification, implementation and test cases shown in Fig. 10, all assuming $L^O = \{a!, b!\}$ and $L^I = \varnothing$. Note that Impl $\not\sqsubseteq_{\text{ioco}}$ Spec due to the unexpected $b!$ output.

Test case t_1 is not sound for Spec with respect to $\sqsubseteq_{\text{ioco}}$, since it fails the correct implementation Spec. Test case t_2 is sound, though, as it only rejects implementations that start with an unexpected $b!$ (as not allowed by $\sqsubseteq_{\text{ioco}}$). Although t_2 is sound, it is not complete; it does not detect Impl to be erroneous, since it stops testing after the first transition.

Using the characterisation of completeness, we can now easily show that each test suite containing the test case t_3 is complete for Spec with respect to $\sqsubseteq_{\text{ioco}}$. After all, $canon(traces(\text{Spec})) = \{\epsilon, a!\}$, and indeed $\delta \in t_3$ and $a!\delta \in t_3$. Note that we can indeed stop testing after the δ observation, since the well-formedness rules of QIOTSs do not allow any outputs after a δ transition. $\qquad\square$

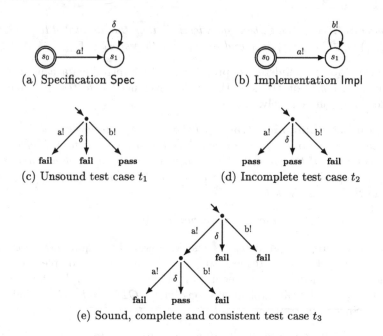

(a) Specification Spec

(b) Implementation Impl

(c) Unsound test case t_1

(d) Incomplete test case t_2

(e) Sound, complete and consistent test case t_3

Fig. 10. A specification, implementation and test cases.

Soundness is a necessary, but not a sufficient property for an annotated test case to be useful. Indeed, a test case annotated with only pass verdicts is always sound. Therefore, we prefer a test case to give a fail verdict whenever it should, i.e., whenever its execution with an implementation produces a trace that is not allowed by the specification. Of course, completeness of a test suite makes sure that such traces are failed by at least one test case in the suite, but that is not necessarily efficient, and moreover, full completeness is rarely achievable. In practice, there are two reasons why testing is always incomplete: first, a complete test suite typically has infinitely many test cases, whereas we can execute only finitely many of them. Second, as observed in Remark 4.1, executing one test case yields only a partial view of the implementation, as each test execution reveals a single trace from the test. Therefore, we propose the more local notion of consistency, extending soundness by requiring that implementations should not pass a test case that observes behaviour that is not allowed by the specification.

Definition 5.3 (Consistency). *Let* Spec *be a specification over an action signature* (L^I, L_δ^O), *and* $\hat{t} = (t, a)$ *an annotated test case for* Spec. *Then,* $\hat{t}$ *is consistent for* Spec *with respect to* $\sqsubseteq_{ioco}$ *if it is sound, and for every trace* $\sigma \in ctraces(t)$ *it holds that* $a(\sigma) = pass$ *implies that* σ *is indeed allowed by the specification, i.e.,*

$$\forall \sigma \in ctraces(t) . a(\sigma) = pass \implies \sigma \in traces(\mathsf{Spec})$$

An annotated test suite is consistent with respect to $\sqsubseteq_{ioco}$ *if all its test cases are.*

As soundness requires that $\sigma \in \mathit{traces}(\mathsf{Spec})$ implies $a(\sigma) = \mathit{pass}$ for every $\sigma \in \mathit{ctraces}(t)$, and consistency additionally requires that $a(\sigma) = \mathit{pass}$ implies $\sigma \in \mathit{traces}(\mathsf{Spec})$, together they require

$$\forall\, \sigma \in \mathit{ctraces}(t)\, .\, a(\sigma) = \mathit{pass} \iff \sigma \in \mathit{traces}(\mathsf{Spec})$$

Clearly, if a consistent (and hence sound) test suite contains all traces of the specification, it is complete.

Example 5.3. In Example 5.2, the test case t_2 is not consistent, since it allows quiescence in the initial state. The specification does not allow this behaviour, though. Test case t_3 is sound, complete *and* consistent.   □

Besides being sound and possibly complete, the test cases annotated according to $a^{\mathtt{ioco}}$ are also consistent. Hence, whenever they detect behaviour that could not occur in any correct implementation, they assign a *fail* verdict. This follows directly from Remark 5.1 and the definition of consistency.

Proposition 5.3. *Let* Spec *be a specification, then the annotated test suite* $\widehat{T} = \{(t, a^{\mathtt{ioco}}_{\mathsf{Spec},t}) \mid t \in \mathcal{T}(\mathsf{Spec})\}$ *is consistent for* Spec *with respect to* $\sqsubseteq_{\mathtt{ioco}}$.

Obviously, for all practical purposes test suites definitely should be sound, and preferably complete (although the latter can never be achieved for any nontrivial specification due to an infinite amount of possible traces). Moreover, inconsistent test suites should be avoided as they ignore erroneous behaviour.

Note that, as already mentioned in Remark 4.1, not the whole possible range of traces that Impl may exhibit will in general be observed during a single test execution. Moreover, although our fairness assumption implies that all traces of Impl will eventually be seen, many executions may be necessary to indeed detect all erroneous behaviour.

5.1   Optimisation: Fail-Fast and Input-Minimal Tests

The tests from Tretmans' ioco-theory [8] are required to be *fail-fast* (i.e., they stop testing after the first observation of an error) and *input-minimal* (i.e., they do not apply input actions that are unexpected according to the specification).

Definition 5.4 (Optimisations). *Let* Spec *be a specification over an action signature* $(L^{\mathrm{I}}, L^{\mathrm{O}}_\delta)$, *then*

- *a test* t *is* fail-fast *with respect to* Spec *if* $\sigma \notin \mathit{traces}(\mathsf{Spec})$ *implies that* $\forall a \in L\,.\,\sigma a \notin t$;
- *a test* t *is* input-minimal *with respect to* Spec *if for all* $\sigma a? \in t$ *with* $a? \in L^{\mathrm{I}}$ *it holds that* $\sigma \in \mathit{traces}(\mathsf{Spec})$ *implies* $\sigma a? \in \mathit{traces}(\mathsf{Spec})$.

The reason for restricting to fail-fast test cases is that ioco defines implementations to be nonconforming if they have at least one nonconforming trace. Hence, once such a trace is observed, the verdict can be given and no further testing is needed. The reason for restricting to input-minimal test cases is that ioco allows any behaviour after a trace $\sigma \notin \mathit{traces}(\mathsf{Spec})$ anyway, invalidating the need to test for such behaviour. We note that, in our context of input-enabled specifications, all tests are input-minimal.

Note that for a test case t that is both fail-fast and input-minimal $\sigma a? \in t$ implies $\sigma a? \in \mathit{traces}(\mathsf{Spec})$.

6   Algorithms for Test Case Derivation

So far, we defined a framework in which specifications can be modelled as QIOTSs and test cases for them can be specified, annotated and executed. Moreover, we presented the conformance relation ioco, and provided a way to annotate test cases according to ioco in a sound manner. Finally, we discussed that we can restrict test suites to only contain fail-fast and input-minimal test cases.

The one thing still missing is a procedure to automatically generate test cases from a specification. We describe two algorithms for test case generation: batch testing, or offline testing, that generates a set of test cases first, and then executes these; and on-the-fly or online test case generation, which generates test inputs while executing the system-under-test.

6.1   Batch Test Case Derivation

Algorithm 1 describes batchGen, which generates a set of test cases. The input of this function is a specification Spec and a history $\sigma \in \mathit{traces}(\mathsf{Spec})$. The output then is a test case that can be applied *after* the history σ has taken place. The idea is to call the function initially with history ϵ, obtaining a test case that can be applied without any start-up phase.

For each call to batchGen, a nondeterministic choice is made. Either the empty test case is returned (used for termination), or a test case is generated that starts by observation, or a test case is generated that starts by stimulation. The fair execution of these alternatives will guarantee eventually the selection of the first alternative, and with that, termination.

In case stimulation of some input action $a?$ is chosen, this results in the test case containing the empty trace ϵ (to stay prefix-closed), a number of traces of the form $a?\sigma'$ where σ' is a trace from a test case starting with history $\sigma a?$, and, for every possible output action $b! \in L^O$ (so $b! \neq \delta$), a number of traces of the form $b!\sigma'$, where σ' is a trace from a test case starting with history $\sigma b!$. No traces of the form $b!\sigma'$ (with $\sigma' \neq \epsilon$) are added when the output $b!$ is erroneous; this makes sure that the resulting test case will be fail-fast.

If observation is chosen, this results in the test case containing the empty trace ϵ (again, to stay prefix-closed) and, for every possible output action $b! \in L_\delta^O$, some traces of the form $b!\sigma'$, where σ' is a trace from a test case starting with history $\sigma a?$. Again, we stop instantly after an erroneous output.

Algorithm 1. Batch test case generation for ioco.

Input: A specification Spec and history $\sigma \in traces(\mathsf{Spec})$
Output: A test case t for Spec such that t is input-minimal and fail-fast

---

procedure batchGen(Spec, σ)
1   [**true**] $\rightarrow$
2   **return** $\{\epsilon\}$
3   [**true**] $\rightarrow$
4   result := $\{\epsilon\}$
5   **forall** $b! \in L_\delta^O$ **do**
6   **if** $\sigma b! \in traces(\mathsf{Spec})$ **then**
7   result := result $\cup \{b!\sigma' \mid \sigma' \in$ batchGen(Spec, $\sigma b!)\}$
            else
8   result := result $\cup \{b!\}$
            end
        end
9   **return** result
10   [$a? \in L^I$] $\rightarrow$
11   result := $\{\epsilon\} \cup \{a?\sigma' \mid \sigma' \in$ batchGen(Spec, $\sigma a?)\}$
12   **forall** $b! \in L^O$ **do**
13   **if** $\sigma b! \in traces(\mathsf{Spec})$ **then**
14   result := result $\cup \{b!\sigma' \mid \sigma' \in$ batchGen(Spec, $\sigma b!)\}$
            else
15   result := result $\cup \{b!\}$
            end
        end
16   **return** result

Remark 6.1. Note that, for efficiency reasons, the algorithm could be changed to remember the states in which the system might be after history σ. Then, the parameters of batchGen would become (Spec, σ, S'), the conditions in line 6 and 16 would become $\exists s \in S' . b! \in L_{\mathsf{Spec}}(s)$, the recursive calls in line 7 and 14 would add a third parameter $reach_{\mathsf{Spec}}(S', b!)$, and the recursive call in line 14 would add a third parameter $reach_{\mathsf{Spec}}(S', a?)$. $\square$

Remark 6.2. Clearly, it is impossible to explicitly store any nontrivial test case for a specification over an infinite number of output actions, as for such systems a single observation already leads to an infinite test case. In that case, the algorithm should be considered a pseudo-algorithm. The algorithm for on-the-fly test case derivation, presented in the next section, will still be feasible. $\square$

Theorem 6.1. *Let* Spec *be a specification, and* $t =$ batchGen(Spec, ϵ). *Then,* t *is a fail-fast and input-minimal test case for* Spec.

Proof (sketch). We need to show that the conditions of Definition 4.1 are satisfied. Prefix-closedness can be shown using induction over the length of a trace, as every step of the algorithm suffixes at most one action and also returns ϵ. Furthermore, as every iteration of the algorithm increases the length of the test case by one, a test case obtained by running the algorithm (a finite amount of time) can never have an infinite increasing sequence. Finally, the required structure of the traces precisely corresponds to what's happening in the three nondeterministic choices: either suffixing nothing, suffixing all outputs including δ, or suffixing an input and all output actions excluding δ. □

Note that Propositions 5.1 and 5.3 imply that $\hat{t} = (t, a_{\mathsf{Spec},t}^{\text{ioco}})$ is sound and consistent for Spec with respect to $\sqsubseteq_{\texttt{ioco}}$.

The next theorem states that, in principle, every possible fault can be discovered by a test case generated using Algorithm 1. More specifically even, it can always be found by a *linear* one.

Theorem 6.2. *Let* Spec *be a specification, and* T *the set of all linear test cases that can be generated using Algorithm 1. Then, the annotated test suite* $\hat{T} = \{(t, a_{\mathsf{Spec},t}^{\text{ioco}}) \mid t \in T\}$ *is complete for* Spec *with respect to* $\sqsubseteq_{\texttt{ioco}}$.

Proof. By Proposition 5.2 we know that $\hat{T}$ is complete for Spec with respect to $\sqsubseteq_{\texttt{ioco}}$ if for all $\sigma \in canon(traces(\mathsf{Spec}))$ either the specification allows all outputs (including quiescence) after σ, or there exists an annotated test case $(t, a) \in \hat{T}$ such that $\sigma\delta \in t$.

Let $\sigma = a_1 a_2 \ldots a_n \in canon(traces(\mathsf{Spec}))$. We now show that indeed there exists a linear test case $t \in T$ such that $\sigma\delta \in t$ by constructing this test case. We will construct it in such a way that σ will be the main trace of t.

In the first iteration, we resolve the nondeterminism based on the action a_1. If $a_1 \in L^I$, then we choose to stimulate a_1. This results in several recursive calls; one for the history $a?$ and one for every $b! \in L^O$. For all the outputs $b!$ the next choice should be to return ϵ; that way, t remains linear as all traces only deviate one action from the main trace σ. If $a_1 \in L_\delta^O$, then we choose to observe. This results again in several recursive calls; one for every $b! \in L_\delta^O$. Now, for all outputs $b! \neq a_1$ the recursive call should return ϵ for t to remain linear.

In the second iteration, caused by the recursive call with history a_1, the same strategy should be applied. Finally, at the $(n+1)^{\text{th}}$ iteration, having history σ, choose to observe. This causes $\sigma\delta$ to be added to t. Now return ϵ in all remaining recursive calls to terminate the algorithm. □

Clearly, this implies that the set of all (not necessarily linear) test cases that can be generated using Algorithm 1 is complete. Still, some issues need to be taken into consideration.

First, as mentioned before, almost every system needs an infinite test suite to be tested completely, which of course is not achievable in practice. In case of a countable number of actions and states this test suite can at least be provided by the algorithm in the limit to infinitely many recursive steps, but for uncountable specifications this would not even be the case anymore (because in infinitely many steps the algorithm is only able to provide a countable set of test cases).

Second, although the set of all test cases derivable using the algorithm is in theory complete, this does not necessarily mean that every erroneous implementation is detected by running all of these tests once. After all, because of nondeterminism, faulty behaviour might not show during testing, even though it may turn up afterwards. Only if all possible outcomes of every nondeterministic choice are guaranteed to be taken at least once during testing, a complete test suite can indeed observe all possible erroneous traces of an implementation. We refer to [13] for more details on expected test coverage (including probabilistic computations).

Despite these restrictions, the completeness theorem provides important information about the test derivation algorithm: it has no 'blind spots'. That is, for every possible erroneous implementation there exists a test case that can be generated using Algorithm 1 and can detect the erroneous behaviour. So, in principle every fault can be detected.

6.2   On-the-Fly Test Case Derivation

Instead of executing predefined test cases, it is also possible to derive test cases on-the-fly. A procedure to do this in a sound manner is depicted in Algorithm 2. We note that the efficiency considerations of Remark 6.1 also apply to this algorithm.

The input of the algorithm consists of a specification Spec and a concrete implementation Impl. The algorithm contains one local variable, σ, which represents the trace obtained thus far; it is therefore initialised with the empty trace ϵ. Then, the while loop is executed a nondeterministic number of times.

For every test step there is a nondeterministic choice between ending the test, observing, or stimulating the implementation by any of the input actions. In case observation is chosen, the output provided by the implementation (either a real output action or δ) is appended to σ. Also, the correctness of this output is verified by checking if the trace obtained thus far is contained in $traces(\text{Spec})$. If not, the verdict *fail* can be given, otherwise we continue. In case stimulation is chosen, the implementation is stimulated with one of the inputs that are allowed by the specification, and the history is updated. By definition of ioco no *fail* verdict can immediately follow from stimulation, so we continue with the next iteration. As the implementation might provide an output action before we are able to stimulate, a try-catch block is positioned around the stimulation to be able to handle an incoming output action. Moreover, the stimulation and the update of σ are put in an atomic block, preventing the scenario where an output that occurs directly after a stimulation prevents σ from being updated properly.

Theorem 6.3. *Algorithm 2 is sound and consistent with respect to $\sqsubseteq_{\texttt{ioco}}$.*

Proof. We first prove soundness. Note that σ keeps track of the trace exhibited by the implementation thus far. The only way for the algorithm to return *fail* is when $\sigma \notin traces(\text{Spec})$ after an observation. In that case, indeed we found that $traces(\text{Impl}) \not\subseteq traces(\text{Spec})$ and hence $\text{Impl} \not\sqsubseteq_{\texttt{ioco}} \text{Spec}$.

Algorithm 2. On-the-fly test case derivation for `ioco`.

Input: A specification Spec, a concrete implementation Impl.
Output: The verdict *pass* when the observed behaviour of Impl was
            ioco-conform Spec, and the verdict *fail* when a nonconforming trace
            was observed during the test.

```
1  σ := ε
2  while true do
3      [true] →
4              return pass
5      [true] →
6              observe Impl's next output b! (possibly δ)
7              σ := σb!
8              if σ ∉ traces(Spec) then return fail
9      [a? ∈ L^I] →
10             try
11                 atomic
12                     stimulate Impl with a?
13                     σ := σa?
                   end
14             catch an output b! occurs before a? could be provided
15                 σ := σb!
16                 if σ ∉ traces(Spec) then return fail
               end
       end
17 return pass
```

For consistency, note that the only way for the algorithm to return *pass* is when $\sigma \in traces(\mathsf{Spec})$ by the end of the last iteration. As the on-the-fly algorithm basically is a test case with only one complete trace, this directly satisfies the definition of consistency.   □

The algorithm is obviously not complete when run only once. However, it is easy to see that, just like for the batch test case generation algorithm, there is no erroneous implementation that cannot be caught in principle. The more often it is run, the more likely that erroneous transitions are detected.

7   Conclusions and Future Work

This paper has revisited the ioco-theory for model-based testing so that it can handle divergences, i.e., τ-loops. Divergences are common in practice, for instance as a result of action hiding. Hence, our results extend model-based testing techniques to an important class of new models.

We have phrased ioco-theory in a trace-based setting, using only standard concepts from labelled transition systems. Technically, our treatment of divergence proceeds via the QIOTS model, where quiescence is modelled as a special output action. QIOTSs constitute a clean modelling framework, closed under parallel composition, action hiding and determinization. This paves the way to further study compositionality results; compositionality is widely recognized as one of the most crucial techniques to handle the complexity of today's systems. Further, testers can be oblivious of the QIOTS model, since any input/output transition system can be transformed into a QIOTS via a deltafication operator.

This work spawns two directions for future research. First, our setting requires that τ-loops contain finitely many states only. This restriction is needed to ensure well-formedness of the deltification operator. Second, as mentioned, it is interesting to study compositionality results for systems with divergences.

Acknowledgements. We would like to thank the reviewers for their thorough comments that really helped improve this paper. We thank Gerjan Stokkink for his large contributions to work that provides important ingredients for this paper [2,14–16].

Since this paper is a part of the Festschrift at the occasion of the 60th birthday of Kim Guldstrand Larsen, we like to thank Kim for the many exciting and fruitful discussions we have had, and still have, over all these years in project meetings, at conferences and many other occasions—Kim was never quiescent.

References

1. Tretmans, J.: Test generation with inputs outputs and repetitive quiescence. Softw. – Concepts Tools **17**(3), 103–120 (1996)
2. Stokkink, W.G.J., Timmer, M., Stoelinga, M.I.A.: Divergent quiescent transition systems. In: Veanes, M., Viganò, L. (eds.) TAP 2013. LNCS, vol. 7942, pp. 214–231. Springer, Heidelberg (2013). doi:10.1007/978-3-642-38916-0_13
3. Lynch, N.A., Tuttle, M.R.: An introduction to input/output automata. CWI Q. **2**, 219–246 (1989)
4. Milner, R.: Communication and Concurrency. Prentice Hall, Upper Saddle River (1989)
5. Timmer, M., Brinksma, E., Stoelinga, M.I.A.: Model-based testing. In: Software and Systems Safety: Specification and Verification. NATO Science for Peace and Security Series D, vol. 30, pp. 1–32. IOS Press, Amsterdam (2011)
6. Vaandrager, F.W.: On the relationship between process algebra and input/output automata (extended abstract). In: Proceedings of the 6th Annual Symposium on Logic in Computer Science (LICS), pp. 387–398. IEEE Computer Society (1991)
7. Tretmans, J.: Test generation with inputs, outputs, and quiescence. In: Margaria, T., Steffen, B. (eds.) TACAS 1996. LNCS, vol. 1055, pp. 127–146. Springer, Heidelberg (1996). doi:10.1007/3-540-61042-1_42
8. Tretmans, J.: Model based testing with labelled transition systems. In: Hierons, R.M., Bowen, J.P., Harman, M. (eds.) Formal Methods and Testing. LNCS, vol. 4949, pp. 1–38. Springer, Heidelberg (2008). doi:10.1007/978-3-540-78917-8_1
9. Jard, C., Jéron, T.: TGV: theory, principles and algorithms. Int. J. Softw. Tools Technol. Transf. **7**(4), 297–315 (2005)
10. Lynch, N.A., Tuttle, M.R.: Hierarchical correctness proofs for distributed algorithms. In: Proceedings of the 6th Annual ACM Symposium on Principles of Distributed Computing (PODC), pp. 137–151. ACM (1987)
11. De Nicola, R., Segala, R.: A process algebraic view of input/output automata. Theor. Comput. Sci. **138**, 391–423 (1995)

12. Tarjan, R.E.: Depth-first search and linear graph algorithms (working paper). In: Proceedings of the 12th Annual Symposium on Switching and Automata Theory (SWAT), pp. 114–121. IEEE Computer Society (1971)
13. Stoelinga, M., Timmer, M.: Interpreting a successful testing process: risk and actual coverage. In: Proceedings of the 3rd IEEE International Symposium on Theoretical Aspects of Software Engineering (TASE), pp. 251–258. IEEE Computer Society (2009)
14. Stokkink, W.G.J., Timmer, M., Stoelinga, M.I.A.: Talking quiescence: a rigorous theory that supports parallel composition, action hiding and determinisation. In: Proceedings of the 7th Workshop on Model-Based Testing (MBT). EPTCS, vol. 80, pp. 73–87 (2012)
15. Stokkink, W.G.J., Timmer, M., Stoelinga, M.I.A.: Talking quiescence: a rigorous theory that supports parallel composition, action hiding and determinisation (extended version). Technical report TR-CTIT-12-05, University of Twente (2012)
16. Stokkink, G.: Quiescent transition systems. Master's thesis, University of Twente (2012)

The Cost of Exactness
in Quantitative Reachability

Krishnendu Chatterjee[1], Laurent Doyen[2]([✉]), and Thomas A. Henzinger[1]

[1] IST Austria, Klosterneuburg, Austria
[2] CNRS & LSV, ENS Paris-Saclay, Cachan, France
doyen@lsv.fr

Abstract. In the analysis of reactive systems a quantitative objective assigns a real value to every trace of the system. The value decision problem for a quantitative objective requires a trace whose value is at least a given threshold, and the exact value decision problem requires a trace whose value is exactly the threshold. We compare the computational complexity of the value and exact value decision problems for classical quantitative objectives, such as sum, discounted sum, energy, and mean-payoff for two standard models of reactive systems, namely, graphs and graph games.

1 Introduction

The formal analysis of reactive systems is a fundamental problem in computer science. Traditionally the analysis focuses on correctness properties, where a Boolean objective classifies the traces of the reactive system as either correct or incorrect. Recently there has been significant interest in the performance analysis of reactive systems as well as the analysis of reactive systems in resource-constrained environments such as embedded systems. In such scenarios quantitative objectives are necessary. A quantitative objective assigns a real value to every trace of the system which measures how desirable the trace is.

Given a reactive system and a quantitative objective, we consider two variants of the decision problem. First, the value decision problem for a quantitative objective requires a trace whose value is at least a given threshold. Second, the exact value decision problem requires a trace whose value is exactly the threshold.

Based on the length of the traces to be analyzed, quantitative objectives can be classified into three categories as follows: (a) infinite-horizon objectives where traces of infinite length are considered; (b) finite-horizon objectives where traces of a given bounded length are considered; (c) indefinite-horizon objectives

This research was supported in part by the Austrian Science Fund (FWF) under grants S11402-N23 and S11407-N23 (RiSE/SHiNE), and Z211-N23 (Wittgenstein Award), ERC Start grant (279307: Graph Games), Vienna Science and Technology Fund (WWTF) through project ICT15-003.

L. Aceto et al. (Eds.): Larsen Festschrift, LNCS 10460, pp. 367–381, 2017.
DOI: 10.1007/978-3-319-63121-9_18

where, given source and target vertices of the system, traces starting at the source and ending at the target are considered. While infinite-horizon and finite-horizon objectives have been traditionally studied, indefinite-horizon objectives are natural in many applications, such as robotics, where the robot must reach a goal state while optimizing the cost of the path [4].

In this work, we focus on two finite-state models of reactive systems, namely, graphs and graph games. Every transition of the system is assigned an integer-valued weight representing a reward (or cost). We consider three classical quantitative objectives, which are variants of the sum of the weights: (i) the standard sum of the weights, (ii) the discounted sum of the weights, and (iii) the energy objective, which is the sum but requires that all partial sums along the trace are non-negative. We study the computational complexity of the value and exact-value decision problems for the indefinite-horizon case of the above three quantitative objectives, both for graphs and games. We also distinguish whether the numbers are represented in unary and binary. We show how to extend and adapt existing results from the literature to obtain a comprehensive picture about the computational complexity of the problems we study. The results are summarized in Table 1 for graphs and Table 2 for graph games.

Related Works. The value decision problem for quantitative objectives has been extensively studied for graphs and games. For the finite-horizon case the standard solution is the value iteration (or dynamic programming) approach [17,27]. For the infinite-horizon case there is a rich literature: for mean-payoff objectives in graphs [25] and games [8,16,19,30], for energy objectives in graphs and games [5, 8,9], for discounted-sum objectives in graphs [1] and games [21,30]. The exact value decision problem represents an important special case of the problem where there are multiple objectives. The multiple objectives problem has been studied for mean-payoff and energy objectives [14,24,29]. For discounted-sum objectives the problem has been studied in other contexts (such as for randomized selection of paths) [12,13]. The special case of multiple objectives defined using a single quantitative function leads to interval objectives [23]. While finite-horizon and infinite-horizon problems have been studied for graphs and games, the indefinite-horizon problem has been studied mainly in artificial intelligence and robotics for different models (such as partially-observable MDPs) [4,10,11]. In this work we present a comprehensive study for indefinite-horizon objectives in graphs and games.

2   Preliminaries

A *weighted graph* $G = \langle V, E, w \rangle$ consists of a finite set V of vertices, a set $E \subseteq V \times V$ of edges, and a function $w : E \to \mathbb{Z}$ that assigns an integer weight to each edge of the graph. In the sequel, we consider weights encoded in unary, as well as in binary.

A *path* in G is a sequence $\rho = v_0 v_1 \ldots v_k$ such that $(v_i, v_{i+1}) \in E$ for all $0 \leq i < k$. We say that ρ is a path from v_0 to v_k. Given two vertices $s, t \in V$, we denote by $\mathsf{Paths}(s, t)$ the set of all paths from s to t in G (we assume that

Table 1. The complexity of the quantitative (s, t)-reachability problem for graphs, for threshold and exact value, with weights encoded in unary or in binary.

	≥ 0		$= 0$	
	Unary	Binary	Unary	Binary
Sum	PTIME		PTIME	NP-c
Disc_λ	PTIME		Decidability is open; finite-path hard	
Energy	PTIME		PTIME	NP-c

the graph G is clear from the context). A *prefix* of ρ is a sequence $\rho[0 \ldots j] = v_0 v_1 \ldots v_j$ where $j \leq k$. We denote by $\mathsf{Pref}(\rho)$ the set of all prefixes of ρ.

The total weight of ρ is defined by $\mathsf{Sum}(\rho) = \sum_{i=0}^{k-1} w(v_i, v_{i+1})$, and given a discount factor $0 < \lambda < 1$, the discounted sum of ρ is $\mathsf{Disc}_\lambda(\rho) = \sum_{i=0}^{k-1} \lambda^i \cdot w(v_i, v_{i+1})$. Note that for $\lambda = 1$, we have $\mathsf{Disc}_1(\rho) = \mathsf{Sum}(\rho)$. In the sequel, we consider a rational discount factor represented by two integers encoded like the weights in the graph (in unary or in binary). A winning condition is a set of paths. We consider the following winning conditions, which contain paths from s to t satisfying quantitative constraints. For $\sim \, \in \{=, \geq\}$, define

- $\mathsf{Sum}^{\sim 0}(s, t) = \{\rho \in \mathsf{Paths}(s, t) \mid \mathsf{Sum}(\rho) \sim 0\}$,
- $\mathsf{Disc}_\lambda^{\sim 0}(s, t) = \{\rho \in \mathsf{Paths}(s, t) \mid \mathsf{Disc}_\lambda(\rho) \sim 0\}$,
- $\mathsf{Energy}^{\sim 0}(s, t) = \{\rho \in \mathsf{Sum}^{\sim 0}(s, t) \mid \mathsf{Sum}(\rho') \geq 0 \text{ for all } \rho' \in \mathsf{Pref}(\rho)\}$.

Note that the energy condition is a variant of the sum requiring that all partial sums are nonnegative. For example, $\mathsf{Sum}^{=0}(s, t)$ is the set of all paths from s to t with a total weight equal to 0, and $\mathsf{Energy}^{=0}(s, t)$ are all such paths that maintain the total weight nonnegative along all their prefixes. Note that the energy condition is the same as the requirement that counters remain nonnegative used in VASS (Vector Addition Systems with States) and counter automata [2].

Definition 1 (Quantitative (s, t)-reachability problem for graphs). *The quantitative (s, t)-reachability problem for graphs asks, given a graph G and a winning condition $\varphi \in \{\mathsf{Sum}^{\sim 0}, \mathsf{Disc}_\lambda^{\sim 0}, \mathsf{Energy}^{\sim 0}\}$, whether the set $\varphi(s, t)$ is nonempty.*

3 Graphs

In this section we assume without loss of generality that there is no incoming edge in vertex s, and no outgoing edge from vertex t. We discuss the details of the complexity results for graphs.

Theorem 1. *The complexity bounds for the quantitative (s, t)-reachability problem for graphs are shown in Table 1.*

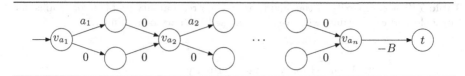

Fig. 1. Reduction from the subset-sum problem with $A = \{a_1, \ldots, a_n\}$ for the NP-hardness result of $\mathsf{Sum}^{=0}$ in graphs ($s = v_{a_1}$).

3.1   Results for Sum

Results for Sum$^{\geq 0}$. The problem asks whether there exists a path from s to t of total weight at least 0. We can compute the longest path between s and t using Bellman-Ford algorithm, which detects positive cycles (the algorithm is the same as for finding a shortest path with opposite sign of the weights). Hence the problem is in PTIME for weights encoded in binary (and thus for weights encoded in unary as well).

Results for Sum$^{=0}$. The problem asks whether there exists a path from s to t of total weight exactly 0. A pseudo-polynomial algorithm is known for this problem [26, Theorem 6]. Therefore, the problem is in PTIME for weights encoded in unary. It is also known that the problem is NP-complete for weights encoded in binary [26, Theorem 1, Theorem 9]. The NP upper bound is obtained by a reduction to integer linear programming (ILP) over variables x_e ($e \in E$) that represent the number of times edge e is used in a path from s to t, and where the ILP constraints require that for every vertex v, the number of incoming edges in v is equal to the number of outgoing edges from v (except for the source and target nodes s and t). The solution of the ILP should form a strongly connected component when a back-edge is added from t to s, which can be checked in polynomial time. The NP lower bound is obtained by a reduction from the subset sum problem, which asks, given a finite set $A \subseteq \mathbb{N}$ and a number $B \in \mathbb{N}$, whether there exists a subset $Z \subseteq A$ such that $\Sigma_{z \in Z} z = B$ (the sum of the elements of Z is B). The reduction, illustrated in Fig. 1, consists in constructing a graph in which there is a vertex v_a for each $a \in A$, and from v_a there are two outgoing edges, one with weight a, the other with weight 0. The two edges lead to intermediate vertices from which there is one edge with weight 0 to the vertex $v_{a'}$ (where a' is the successor of a in some total order over A). From the last vertex v_a, there is an edge to t with weight $-B$. The answer to the subset sum problem is Yes if and only if there is a path of total weight 0 from the first vertex v_a to t.

3.2   Results for Disc$_\lambda$

Results for Disc$_\lambda^{\geq 0}$. We present a polynomial-time algorithm for weights and discount factor encoded in binary (thus also for weights and discount factor encoded in unary). First we compute the co-reachable vertices in the graph, namely the set $\mathsf{coReach}(t) = \{v \in V \mid \mathsf{Paths}(v, t) \neq \varnothing\}$ of vertices from which there exists a path to t, and we consider the graph $G' = \langle V \cap \mathsf{coReach}(t), E \cap (\mathsf{coReach}(t) \times \mathsf{coReach}(t)) \rangle$ in which the vertex t has a self-loop with weight 0.

Then, we compute for each vertex $v \in \mathsf{coReach}(t)$, the largest value of the discounted sum of an infinite path from v in G'. The discounted sum of an infinite path $v_0 v_1 \cdots \in V^\omega$ is $\sum_{i=0}^{\infty} \lambda^i \cdot w(v_i, v_{i+1})$. Note that the series converges because $\lambda < 1$ and the weights are bounded. The largest discounted sum of a path from a given vertex can be computed in polynomial time using linear programming [1, Section 3.1].

We consider the following cases:

- If the value $val(s)$ in the source vertex s is strictly greater than 0, then the answer to the (s,t)-reachability problem is Yes. Indeed, consider a prefix ρ' of length n of an optimal path ρ from s, where n is such that $\frac{2\lambda^n}{1-\lambda} \cdot W < val(s)$ (where W is the largest weight of G' in absolute value). Then it is easy to show that ρ' can be continued to a path that reaches t with positive weight.
- If $val(s) < 0$ then the answer to the (s,t)-reachability problem is No, as all finite paths from s to t have negative value (otherwise, there would be an infinite path with value at least 0, by prolonging the path through the self-loop on t).
- If $val(s) = 0$ then consider the graph G'' obtained from G' by keeping only the optimal edges, where an edge $e = (v, v')$ is *optimal* if $val(v) = w(v, v') + \lambda \cdot val(v')$. The answer to the (s,t)-reachability problem is Yes if and only if there is a path from s to t in G'', which can be computed in polynomial time. Indeed, if there exists a path from s to t with discounted sum equal to 0, then this path is optimal for the infinite-path problem since $val(s) = 0$, and therefore it uses only optimal edges. Moreover, if an infinite path from s uses only optimal edges, then it has value $val(s) = 0$, thus if such a path reaches t, then it gives a solution to the problem since from t the only outgoing edge is a self-loop with weight 0.

Results for $\mathsf{Disc}_\lambda^{=0}$. The decidability of the problem is open. Note that the decidability of the problem of finding an infinite path with exact discounted sum 0 is also open [3].

3.3   Results for Energy

Results for $\mathsf{Energy}^{\geq 0}$. The problem asks whether there exists a path from s to t that maintains the total weight (of all its prefixes) at least 0. We present a polynomial-time algorithm for weights encoded in binary (thus also for weights encoded in unary).

The algorithm relies on the fact that if there exists a path from s to t, then either the path is acyclic, or it contains a cycle, and that cycle needs to be positive (otherwise, we can remove the cycle and get an equally good path). Accordingly, the algorithm has two steps. First, we compute for each vertex $v \in V$ the largest total weight of a path from s to v (where the path must have all its prefixes nonnegative). To do that, we start from a function $\mu_0 : V \to \mathbb{N} \cup \{-\infty\}$ such that $\mu_0(s) = 0$ and $\mu_0(v) = -\infty$ for all $v \in V \setminus \{s\}$ and we iterate the operator Post : $(V \to \mathbb{N} \cup \{-\infty\}) \to (V \to \mathbb{N} \cup \{-\infty\})$ defined as follows:

$$\mathsf{Post}(\mu)(v) = \max\{\mu(u) + w(u, v) \mid (u, v) \in E \wedge \mu(u) + w(u, v) \geq 0\} \cup \{\mu(v)\}$$

where $\max \varnothing = -\infty$. Consider $\mathsf{Post}^n(\mu_0)$, the nth iterate of Post on μ_0 where $n = |V|$. Intuitively, the value $\mathsf{Post}^n(\mu_0)(v)$ is the largest credit of energy (i.e., total weight) with which it is possible to reach v from s with a path of length at most n while maintaining the energy always nonnegative along the way. If $\mathsf{Post}^n(\mu_0)(t) \geq 0$, then the answer to the (s, t)-reachability problem is Yes. Otherwise, it means that there is no acyclic path from s to t that satisfies the energy constraint, and thus a positive cycle is necessary to reach t.

The second step of the algorithm is to check, for each vertex v with initial energy $\tilde{\mu}_0$ defined by $\tilde{\mu}_0(v) = \mathsf{Post}^n(\mu_0)(v)$ and $\tilde{\mu}_0(v') = -\infty$ for all $v' \neq v$, whether a positive cycle can be executed from v, that is whether $\mathsf{Post}^n(\tilde{\mu}_0)(v) > \tilde{\mu}_0(v)$. Note that only the vertices v such that $\mathsf{Post}^n(\mu_0)(v) \neq -\infty$ need to be considered. If there exists such a vertex from which t is reachable (without any constraint on the path from v to t), then the answer to the (s, t)-reachability problem is Yes. Otherwise, the answer to the problem is No because if there existed a path from s to t satisfying the energy constraint, it could not be an acyclic path (by the result of the first step of the algorithm), and it could not contain a cycle because (i) there is no positive cycle that can be reached from s and executed (by the result of the second step of the algorithm), and (ii) all negative cycles can be removed from the path to obtain a simpler, eventually acyclic, path that satisfies the energy constraint, which is impossible, as shown above. It is easy to see that the above computation can be done in polynomial time.

Consider the weighted graph with five vertices in Fig. 2. The graph has two cycles around v_2, both are positive. The vertex t is reachable from s, but in order to maintain the energy level nonnegative, we need to go through a cycle around v_2 which increases the energy level and allows to take the transition from v_2 to t with weight -15.

The algorithm first computes for each vertex the largest energy level that can be obtained by a path of length 5 from s (while maintaining the energy level always nonnegative). The result is shown in Fig. 2 as $\mu_5 = \mathsf{Post}^5(\mu_0)$. Note that $\mu_5(t) = -\infty$, thus there is no acyclic path from s to t with nonnegative energy level. The second step of the algorithm is a positive cycle detection, from each vertex of the graph. The computation from v_2 is illustrated in Fig. 2. Since the value at v_2 has strictly increased, a positive cycle is detected, and since t is reachable from v_2 (even if it is by a negative path), we can reach t from s (through v_2) with energy always at least 0.

Results for Energy$^{=0}$. The problem is in PTIME for weights encoded in unary, as this a reachability problem in VASS (Vector Addition Systems with States) of dimension one, which is known to be NL-complete [2, Section 1]. The problem is NP-complete for weights encoded in binary, as this is exactly the reachability problem for one-counter automata, which is NP-complete [20, Proposition 1,

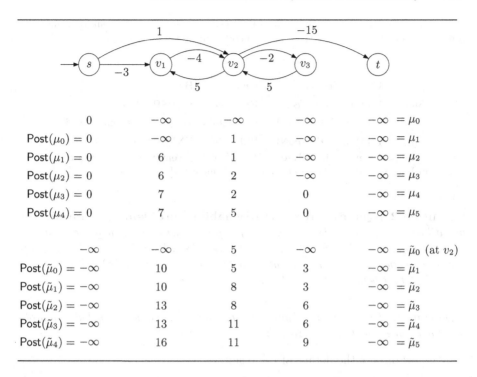

Fig. 2. Sample of the fixpoint iterations to decide if there exists a path from s to t with energy (sum of weights) always at least 0.

Theorem 1]. The NP upper bound follows since one-counter automata allow zero-tests along the execution, and the NP lower bound holds even without zero-tests using a reduction from the subset-sum problem (see also Fig. 1).

4   Games

A *game* consists of a weighted graph $G = \langle V, E, w \rangle$ where V is partitioned into the sets V_1 of player-1 vertices, and the set V_2 of player-2 vertices. We assume that player-1 vertices and player-2 vertices alternate, i.e., $E \subseteq (V_1 \times V_2) \cup (V_2 \times V_1)$. This incurs no loss of generality as we can insert intermediate vertices along every transition that does not 'alternate'. We also assume that every vertex has a successor, that is for all $v \in V$ there exists $v' \in V$ such that $(v, v') \in E$.

A *strategy* of player 1 is a function $\sigma : V^* V_1 \to V$ such that $(v, \sigma(\rho \cdot v)) \in E$ for all $\rho \in V^*$ and all $v \in V_1$. A strategy σ is *memoryless* if it depends on the last vertex only, that is $\sigma(\rho \cdot v) = \sigma(\rho' \cdot v)$ for all $\rho, \rho' \in V^*$ and all $v \in V_1$. Given an initial vertex v, and a strategy σ of player 1, we say that an infinite path $\rho = v_0 v_1 \ldots$ is an *outcome* of σ from v if $v_0 = v$ and $\sigma(v_0 \ldots v_j) = v_{j+1}$ for all $j \geq 0$ such that $v_j \in V_1$. We denote by $\mathsf{Outcome}_v^\omega(\sigma)$ the set of all outcomes of strategy σ from vertex v.

Table 2. The complexity of the quantitative (s,t)-reachability problem for games, for threshold and exact value, with weights encoded in unary or in binary.

	≥ 0		$= 0$	
	Unary	Binary	Unary	Binary
Sum	PTIME	NP $\cap$ coNP	PSPACE-c	EXPSPACE-c
Disc_λ	PTIME	NP $\cap$ coNP[a]	Decidability is open; finite-path hard	
Energy	PTIME	NP $\cap$ coNP	PSPACE-c	EXPSPACE-c

[a]The problem can be solved in PTIME if the weights in the graph are in binary, and the discount factor is in unary [21]

Definition 2 (Quantitative (s,t)-reachability problem for games). *The quantitative (s,t)-reachability problem for games asks, given a game G and a winning condition $\varphi \in \{\text{Sum}^{\sim 0}, \text{Disc}_\lambda^{\sim 0}, \text{Energy}^{\sim 0}\}$, whether there exists a strategy σ of player 1 such that for all outcomes $\rho \in \text{Outcome}_s^\omega(\sigma)$ there exists a prefix of ρ that belongs to the set $\varphi(s,t)$.*

Theorem 2. *The complexity bounds for the quantitative (s,t)-reachability problem for games are shown in Table 2.*

We now discuss the details of the results.

4.1   Results for Sum

Results for Sum$^{\geq 0}$. The game problem for Sum$^{\geq 0}$ is also known as the max-cost reachability problem. The problem is in NP $\cap$ coNP for weights encoded in binary [18, Theorem 5.2]. The result of [18, Theorem 5.2] holds for the winning conditions defined as a strict threshold, namely Sum$^{>0}(s,t) = \{\rho \in \text{Paths}(s,t) \mid \text{Sum}(\rho) > 0\}$, and the same proof idea works for non-strict threshold. The result is obtained by a reduction to mean-payoff games [16,30], which can be viewed as games where one player 1 wins if he can ensure that all cycles formed along a play are positive. Such games can be solved in NP $\cap$ coNP. The reduction constructs a mean-payoff game as a copy of the original game over the set of states from which player 1 can ensure to reach t, and adds an edge from t back to s with weight 0. Then player 1 can ensure a positive cycle if and only if he can ensure the objective Sum$^{>0}(s,t)$: either he can reach t and loop through it (with a positive total weight), or he can ensure positive cycles that can be repeated until the total weight is sufficiently high to let him reach t while the total weight remains positive. Conversely, if he can reach t with positive total weight, then he can win the mean-payoff game by repeatedly reaching t. Note that memoryless strategies are sufficient for player 2, but not for player 1 as he may need to accumulate weights along positive cycles before switching to the strategy that ensures reaching t.

It is not known whether mean-payoff games can be solved in polynomial time. The game problem for Sum$^{\geq 0}$ is at least as hard as mean-payoff games, thus in the same status as mean-payoff games. This result is analogous to [7, Theorem 1(2)]. The idea of the reduction is, given a mean-payoff game G with initial vertex v, to construct a game G' from G by adding a transition with weight $-nW - 1$ from every player-1 vertex to a new vertex t where n is the number of vertices in G and W is the largest absolute weight in G. The reduction works because player-1 vertices and player-2 vertices alternate. The reduction is correct because if player 1 wins the mean-payoff game (with strict threshold), then he has a memoryless strategy to ensure that all reachable cycles are positive. Then, in G' player 1 can play the mean-payoff winning strategy long enough to accumulate total weight $nW+1$, and then use the transition with weight $-nW-1$ to reach t, and thus win in G'. In the other direction, if player 1 does not win the mean-payoff game, then player 2 can fix a memoryless strategy to ensure that all cycles are non-positive. Hence, the total weight of all finite prefixes of all outcomes is at most nW (the largest possible weight of an acyclic path), which is not sufficient to reach t, thus player 2 wins in G'.

For weights encoded in unary, the game problem for $\mathsf{Sum}^{\geq 0}$ can be solved in polynomial time using the algorithm of [7, Theorem 1(4)], a fixpoint iteration that relies on backward induction to compute the optimal cost for $i + 1$ rounds of the game, knowing the optimal cost for i rounds, similar to the pseudo-polynomial algorithm for solving mean-payoff games [8,30]. The fixpoint iteration stops when the cost stabilizes to a finite value, or exceeds nW indicating that an arbitrary large cost can be achieved.

Results for $\mathsf{Sum}^{=0}$. The game problem for $\mathsf{Sum}^{=0}$ is a reachability problem where the target consists in both the vertex and the weight value. The problem was shown to be PSPACE-complete for weights encoded in unary [28, Theorem 5], and EXPSPACE-complete for weights encoded in binary [22, Theorem 1].

4.2   Results for Disc_λ

Results for $\mathsf{Disc}_\lambda^{\geq 0}$. The game problem for $\mathsf{Disc}_\lambda^{\geq 0}$ is in NP ∩ coNP for weights encoded in binary, by an argument similar to [18, Theorem 5.2] which shows the result for strict threshold (where the winning condition is the set of paths ρ from s to t such that $\mathsf{Disc}_\lambda(\rho) > 0$). The solution for strict threshold can be modified for non-strict threshold along the same idea as for the graph problem, thus by a reduction to infinite-horizon discounted sum games, which are solvable in NP ∩ coNP [30], and even in PTIME for unary encoding of the discount factor (even if the weights are encoded in binary) [21].

It is not known whether discounted sum games can be solved in polynomial time, and we show that discounted sum games reduce to the (s,t)-reachability problem for $\mathsf{Disc}_\lambda^{\geq 0}$. Given an infinite-horizon discounted sum game G, consider the game G' obtained from G by adding a vertex t, and edges (v,t) for all vertices v of player 1 in G (with weight 0). The reduction works because player-1 vertices and player-2 vertices alternate. Given the rational threshold ν for the game G, due to the separation of values in discounted sum games (which means that the optimal value in discounted sum games is the value of a play consisting of an acyclic prefix followed by a simple cycle, thus a rational number with denominator bounded by b^n, where b is the denominator of the discount factor λ, and n is the number of vertices in G) we can construct a number $\nu' < \nu$ such that if the optimal value in G is smaller than ν, then it is also smaller than ν'. The reduction produces the game G' with vertices s, t and threshold ν' (which can be replaced by threshold 0, by subtracting $(1 - \lambda) \cdot \nu'$ to all weights). It is easy to see that (i) if player 1 can ensure discounted sum at least ν from an initial vertex s in G, then by playing sufficient long the optimal strategy from s, player 1 can ensure a value sufficiently close to ν to ensure reaching t with value at least ν'. Conversely, (ii) if player 1 does not win the discounted sum game G from s with threshold ν, then player 1 cannot win for threshold ν' and thus he cannot win in G' for (s, t)-reachability, which establishes the correctness of the reduction.

Results for Disc$_\lambda^{=0}$. For Disc$_\lambda^{=0}$, the decidability of the problem is open, as it is already open for graphs.

4.3 Results for Energy

Results for Energy$^{\geq 0}$. For Energy$^{\geq 0}$, the problem is inter-reducible with energy games: we consider infinite-horizon energy games where the winning condition for player 1 requires to maintain the total payoff (i.e., the energy) at least 0 along all prefixes of the (infinite) play, starting with initial energy 0. Memoryless strategies are sufficient for player 1 in energy games, and after fixing a memoryless strategy, all finite outcomes have nonnegative total weight thus all reachable simple cycles are nonnegative.

The reductions follow the same general ideas as between Sum$^{\geq 0}$ and mean-payoff games, with some additional care. While nonnegative cycles are sufficient for player 1 in energy games, the reduction works only for the slightly stronger winning condition that asks player 1 to form only strictly positive cycles (while maintaining the energy condition on all acyclic outcomes as well). This stronger winning condition is equivalent to an energy condition in a modified graph where the weights are decreased by a value $\epsilon > 0$ where ϵ is sufficiently small to ensure that negative simple cycles remain negative (thus $n\epsilon < 1$). Moreover, since the initial energy 0 may now no longer be sufficient to survive the acyclic paths, we need to give a slightly positive initial energy value (by an initial transition of weight $n\epsilon$). Note that this initial energy does not allow player 1 to survive a negative finite prefix as $n\epsilon < 1$. We can take $\epsilon = \frac{1}{n+1}$ and scale up the weights by a factor $n + 1$ to get integer weights. From this game graph with modified weights, we can use the same reductions as between Sum$^{=0}$ and mean-payoff games.

It follows that the problem has the same status as energy games with fixed initial credit, namely it is in NP $\cap$ coNP for weights encoded in binary, and in PTIME for weights encoded in unary [5, Proposition 12, Theorem 13].

Results for Energy$^{=0}$. For Energy$^{=0}$, the game problem is PSPACE-complete for weights encoded in unary [6, Theorem 11], and EXPSPACE-complete for weights encoded in binary [22, Theorem 1].

5   Survey of Infinite-Horizon Quantitative Objectives

We present a survey of the computational complexity for the problem of satisfying a quantitative objective over an infinite duration, that requires an infinite trace with value either at least, or exactly a given threshold.

We consider winning conditions defined by the following quantitative measures over infinite paths (we denote by Paths$^\omega$ the set of all infinite paths in the graph G, where G is clear from the context), for $\sim \in \{=, \geq\}$:

- $\text{Disc}_\lambda^{\sim 0} = \{\rho \in \text{Paths}^\omega \mid \text{Disc}_\lambda(\rho) \sim 0\}$,
- $\overline{\text{MP}}^{\sim 0} = \{\rho \in \text{Paths}^\omega \mid \limsup_{n\to\infty} \frac{1}{n} \cdot \text{Sum}(\rho[0\ldots n]) \sim 0\}$,
- $\underline{\text{MP}}^{\sim 0} = \{\rho \in \text{Paths}^\omega \mid \liminf_{n\to\infty} \frac{1}{n} \cdot \text{Sum}(\rho[0\ldots n]) \sim 0\}$.

The discounted sum is well defined for infinite paths (the infinite sum always exists). The $\overline{\text{MP}}$ and $\underline{\text{MP}}$ conditions are the mean-payoff objectives (see also Sect. 4.1), which are well defined as the limsup and liminf always exist, although the limit itself may not exist.

5.1   Results for Graphs

We consider the infinite-horizon quantitative problem for graphs, which is to decide, given a graph G and a winning condition $\varphi \in \{\text{Disc}^{\sim 0}, \overline{\text{MP}}^{\sim 0}, \underline{\text{MP}}^{\sim 0}\}$, whether the set φ is nonempty.

Theorem 3. *The complexity bounds for the infinite-horizon quantitative problem for graphs are shown in Table 3.*

The results of Table 3 for discounted sum follow from the linear programming approach for computing the largest discounted sum of an infinite path [1, Section 3.1], and the decidability of the exact-value problem is open [3].

For mean-payoff, the infinite-horizon quantitative problem can be solved in polynomial time using Karp's algorithm to compute the reachable cycle with

Table 3. The complexity of the infinite-horizon quantitative problem for graphs, for threshold and exact value, with weights encoded in unary or in binary.

	≥ 0		$= 0$	
	Unary	Binary	Unary	Binary
Disc_λ	PTIME		Decidability is open; infinite-path hard	
$\overline{\text{MP}}, \underline{\text{MP}}$	PTIME		PTIME	

Table 4. The complexity of the infinite-horizon quantitative problem for games, for threshold and exact value, with weights encoded in unary or in binary.

	≥ 0		$= 0$	
	Unary	Binary	Unary	Binary
Disc_λ	PTIME	NP ∩ coNP[a]	Decidability is open	
			Infinite-path hard	
$\overline{\mathsf{MP}}$, $\underline{\mathsf{MP}}$	PTIME	NP ∩ coNP	PTIME	NP ∩ coNP

[a] The problem can be solved in PTIME if the weights in the graph are in binary, and the discount factor is in unary [21]

largest mean value, which runs in polynomial time [25]. For the exact-value problem, it is easy to see that the answer is **Yes** if and only if there exists a strongly connected component (scc) that contains both a nonnegative cycle and a nonpositive cycle. The path that reaches such an scc and then alternates between the two cycles (essentially repeating the nonnegative cycle until the partial sum of weights becomes positive, then switching to the nonpositive cycle until the partial sum of weights becomes negative, and so on) has mean-payoff value 0 (for both limsup and liminf) because the partial sum of the acyclic parts of the path (obtained by removing all cycles) is bounded by nW, where n is the number of vertices in G and W is the largest absolute weight in G. The scc decomposition and cycle with largest (resp., least) mean value can be computed in polynomial time.

5.2   Results for Games

We consider the infinite-horizon quantitative problem for games, which is to decide, given a graph G, an initial vertex v, and a winning condition $\varphi \in \{\mathsf{Disc}^{\sim 0}, \overline{\mathsf{MP}}^{\sim 0}, \underline{\mathsf{MP}}^{\sim 0}\}$, whether there exists a strategy σ of player 1 such that $\mathsf{Outcome}_v^\omega(\sigma) \subseteq \varphi$.

Theorem 4. *The complexity bounds for the infinite-horizon quantitative problem for games are shown in Table 4.*

The results of Table 4 for discounted sum follow from the results of [3,21,30] (see also Sect. 4.2).

For mean-payoff, the results for the threshold problem follow from [16,30] in particular there is a pseudo-polynomial algorithm for solving mean-payoff games [8,30]. The NP ∩ coNP result for the exact-value problem follows from [23, Corollary 6], and the set Z of initial vertices from which player 1 has a winning strategy has the following characterization: from every vertex in Z, player 1 has a strategy to ensure nonnegative mean-payoff value, and player 1 has a (possibly different) strategy to ensure nonpositive mean-payoff value. Moreover if from some vertex player 1 does not have a strategy to ensure nonnegative (or nonpositive) mean-payoff value, then player 1 does not have a winning strategy from that vertex for the exact-value objective. By an argument analogous to the case of graphs, we can show that player 1 wins from every vertex in Z by switching between the strategies to ensure nonpositive and nonnegative mean-payoff value, because the partial sums will remain bounded by nW, thus the mean-payoff value is 0 (both for limsup and liminf).

We can compute the set Z by removing from the set V of vertices the vertices that are losing for player 1, iteratively as follows, until a fixpoint is obtained: at each iteration, remove the vertices where player 1 does not win either the nonpositive or the nonnegative mean-payoff objective, and remove the vertices from which player 2 can ensure to reach an already removed vertex (this amounts to solving a reachability game, thus in polynomial time). The number of iterations is at most n, thus the algorithm is polynomial for weights in unary. Note that player 2 has a memoryless strategy from all removed vertices, to ensure that the mean-payoff value is not 0.

It follows that for weights in binary, the exact-value problem can be solved in NP by guessing the set Z and checking that from every vertex in Z player 1 wins the nonpositive mean-payoff objective as well as the nonnegative mean-payoff objective (possibly with a different strategy), and in coNP by guessing a memoryless winning strategy for player 2 in $V \setminus Z$ and solving in PTIME the exact-value problem for mean-payoff in graphs.

Note that the exact-value problem can be reduced to a two-dimensional mean-payoff objective, which is known to be solvable in NP ∩ coNP for $\overline{\mathsf{MP}}$, but only in coNP for $\underline{\mathsf{MP}}$ [29]. In contrast, the exact-value problem is solvable in NP as well for $\underline{\mathsf{MP}}$.

6   Conclusion

In this work we studied the complexity of the value decision problem and the exact-value decision problem for sum, discounted sum, and energy objectives for the indefinite-horizon case. We studied them for graphs and graph games, and also distinguished the representation of numbers in unary and binary. In several cases the exact decision problem is computationally harder as compared to the non-exact counterpart. An interesting direction of future work is to consider the problems we studied in other related models, such as stochastic games (extending the work of [15]), Markov decision processes, timed games, etc.

References

1. Andersson, D.: An improved algorithm for discounted payoff games. In: Proceedings of 11th ESSLLI Student Session, pp. 91–98 (2006)
2. Blondin, M., Finkel, A., Göller, S., Haase, C., McKenzie, P.: Reachability in two-dimensional vector addition systems with states is PSPACE-complete. In: Proceedings of LICS: Symposium on Logic in Computer Science, pp. 32–43. IEEE Computer Society (2015)

3. Boker, U., Henzinger, T.A., Otop, J.: The target discounted-sum problem. In: Proceeings of LICS: Symposium on Logic in Computer Science, pp. 750–761. IEEE Computer Society (2015)

4. Bonet, B., Geffner, H.: Solving POMDPs: RTDP-Bel vs. point-based algorithms. In: Proceedings of IJCAI: International Joint Conference on Artificial Intelligence, pp. 1641–1646 (2009)

5. Bouyer, P., Fahrenberg, U., Larsen, K.G., Markey, N., Srba, J.: Infinite runs in weighted timed automata with energy constraints. In: Cassez, F., Jard, C. (eds.) FORMATS 2008. LNCS, vol. 5215, pp. 33–47. Springer, Heidelberg (2008). doi:10. 1007/978-3-540-85778-5_4

6. Brázdil, T., Jančar, P., Kučera, A.: Reachability games on extended vector addition systems with states. In: Abramsky, S., Gavoille, C., Kirchner, C., Meyer auf der Heide, F., Spirakis, P.G. (eds.) ICALP 2010. LNCS, vol. 6199, pp. 478–489. Springer, Heidelberg (2010). doi:10.1007/978-3-642-14162-1_40

7. Brihaye, T., Geeraerts, G., Haddad, A., Monmege, B.: To reach or not to reach? efficient algorithms for total-payoff games. In: Proceedings of CONCUR: Concurrency Theory. LIPIcs, vol. 42, pp. 297–310. Schloss Dagstuhl - Leibniz-Zentrum fuer Informatik (2015)

8. Brim, L., Chaloupka, J., Doyen, L., Gentilini, R., Raskin, J.-F.: Faster algorithms for mean-payoff games. Formal Methods Syst. Des. **38**(2), 97–118 (2011)

9. Chakrabarti, A., de Alfaro, L., Henzinger, T.A., Stoelinga, M.: Resource interfaces. In: Alur, R., Lee, I. (eds.) EMSOFT 2003. LNCS, vol. 2855, pp. 117–133. Springer, Heidelberg (2003). doi:10.1007/978-3-540-45212-6_9

10. Chatterjee, K., Chmelik, M.: Indefinite-horizon reachability in Goal-DEC-POMDPs. In: Proceedings of ICAPS: International Conference on Automated Planning and Scheduling, pp. 88–96. AAAI Press (2016)

11. Chatterjee, K., Chmelik, M., Gupta, R., Kanodia, A.: Optimal cost almost-sure reachability in POMDPs. Artif. Intell. **234**, 26–48 (2016)

12. Chatterjee, K., Forejt, V., Wojtczak, D.: Multi-objective discounted reward verification in graphs and MDPs. In: McMillan, K., Middeldorp, A., Voronkov, A. (eds.) LPAR 2013. LNCS, vol. 8312, pp. 228–242. Springer, Heidelberg (2013). doi:10.1007/978-3-642-45221-5_17

13. Chatterjee, K., Majumdar, R., Henzinger, T.A.: Markov decision processes with multiple objectives. In: Durand, B., Thomas, W. (eds.) STACS 2006. LNCS, vol. 3884, pp. 325–336. Springer, Heidelberg (2006). doi:10.1007/11672142_26

14. Chatterjee, K., Velner, Y.: Hyperplane Separation technique for multidimensional mean-payoff games. In: D'Argenio, P.R., Melgratti, H. (eds.) CONCUR 2013. LNCS, vol. 8052, pp. 500–515. Springer, Heidelberg (2013). doi:10.1007/978-3-642-40184-8_35

15. Chen, T., Forejt, V., Kwiatkowska, M., Simaitis, A., Trivedi, A., Ummels, M.: Playing stochastic games precisely. In: Koutny, M., Ulidowski, I. (eds.) CONCUR 2012. LNCS, vol. 7454, pp. 348–363. Springer, Heidelberg (2012). doi:10.1007/978-3-642-32940-1_25

16. Ehrenfeucht, A., Mycielski, J.: Positional strategies for mean payoff games. Int. J. Game Theory **8**(2), 109–113 (1979)

17. Filar, J., Vrieze, K.: Competitive Markov Decision Processes. Springer-Verlag, Heidelberg (1997)

18. Filiot, E., Gentilini, R., Raskin, J.-F.: Quantitative languages defined by functional automata. Logical Methods Comput. Sci. **11**(3) (2015)

19. Gurvich, V.A., Karzanov, A.V., Khachiyan, L.G.: Cyclic games and an algorithm to find minimax cycle means in directed graphs. USSR Comput. Math. Math. Phy. **28**(5), 85–91 (1988)

20. Haase, C., Kreutzer, S., Ouaknine, J., Worrell, J.: Reachability in succinct and parametric one-counter automata. In: Bravetti, M., Zavattaro, G. (eds.) CONCUR 2009. LNCS, vol. 5710, pp. 369–383. Springer, Heidelberg (2009). doi:10.1007/978-3-642-04081-8_25

21. Hansen, T.D., Miltersen, P.B., Zwick, U.: Strategy iteration is strongly polynomial for 2-player turn-based stochastic games with a constant discount factor. J. ACM **60**(1), 1:1–1:16 (2013)

22. Hunter, P.: Reachability in succinct one-counter games. In: Bojańczyk, M., Lasota, S., Potapov, I. (eds.) RP 2015. LNCS, vol. 9328, pp. 37–49. Springer, Cham (2015). doi:10.1007/978-3-319-24537-9_5

23. Hunter, P., Raskin, J.-F.: Quantitative games with interval objectives. In: Proceedings of FSTTCS, vol. 29 of LIPIcs, pp. 365–377. Schloss Dagstuhl - Leibniz-Zentrum fuer Informatik (2014)

24. Jurdziński, M., Lazić, R., Schmitz, S.: Fixed-dimensional energy games are in pseudo-polynomial time. In: Halldórsson, M.M., Iwama, K., Kobayashi, N., Speckmann, B. (eds.) ICALP 2015. LNCS, vol. 9135, pp. 260–272. Springer, Heidelberg (2015). doi:10.1007/978-3-662-47666-6_21

25. Karp, R.M.: A characterization of the minimum cycle mean in a digraph. Discrete Math. **23**, 309–311 (1978)

26. Nykänen, M., Ukkonen, E.: The exact path length problem. J. Algorithms **42**(1), 41–53 (2002)

27. Puterman, M.L.: Markov Decision Processes. Wiley, Hoboken (1994)

28. Reichert, J.: On the complexity of counter reachability games. In: Abdulla, P.A., Potapov, I. (eds.) RP 2013. LNCS, vol. 8169, pp. 196–208. Springer, Heidelberg (2013). doi:10.1007/978-3-642-41036-9_18

29. Velner, Y., Chatterjee, K., Doyen, L., Henzinger, T.A., Rabinovich, A.M., Raskin, J.-F.: The complexity of multi-mean-payoff and multi-energy games. Inf. Comput. **241**, 177–196 (2015)

30. Zwick, U., Paterson, M.: The complexity of mean payoff games on graphs. Theor. Comput. Sci. **158**(1&2), 343–359 (1996)

Towards Automated Variant Selection for Heterogeneous Tiled Architectures

Christel Baier[✉], Sascha Klüppelholz[✉], and Sascha Wunderlich[✉]

Institute of Theoretical Computer Science, Technische Universität Dresden,
01062 Dresden, Germany
{christel.baier,sascha.klueppelholz,sascha.wunderlich}@tu-dresden.de

Abstract. Heterogeneous hardware/software systems that include many components with different characteristics offer great potential for high performance and energy-efficient computing. To exploit this potential, adaptive allocation and scheduling algorithms are needed for selecting software variants and mapping them to processing elements that attempt to achieve a good balance between resource-awareness and performance. The evaluation is typically carried out using simulation techniques. However, the space spanned by the possible combinations of hardware/software variants and management strategies is huge, which makes it nearly impossible to find an optimum using simulation-based methods. The purpose of the paper is to illustrate the general feasibility of an alternative approach using probabilistic model checking for families of systems that are obtained by varying, e.g., the hardware-software combinations or the resource management strategies. More precisely, we consider heterogeneous multi-processor systems based on tiled architectures and provide a tool chain that yields a flexible and comfortable way to specify families of concrete systems and to analyze them using the probabilistic model checker PRISM and PROFEAT as a front end. We illustrate how the family-based approach can be used to analyze the potential of heterogeneous hardware elements, software variants and adaptive resource management and scheduling strategies by applying our framework to a simplified model of the multi-processor Tomahawk platform that has been designed for integrating heterogeneous devices.

1 Introduction

Tiled architectures are designed to exploit massive quantities of resources, including computing elements and storage elements. For this, processing elements and memory components are equipped with a switch to create modular elements which are called tiles. Tiles are connected via their switch to a communication network [15], e.g., a mesh network based network on chip (NoC), that allows

---

S. Wunderlich—The authors are supported by the DFG through the collaborative research centre HAEC (SFB 912), the Excellence Initiative by the German Federal and State Governments (cluster of excellence cfAED), the Research Training Groups QuantLA (GRK 1763) and the DFG-project BA-1679/11-1.

© Springer International Publishing AG 2017
L. Aceto et al. (Eds.): Larsen Festschrift, LNCS 10460, pp. 382–399, 2017.
DOI: 10.1007/978-3-319-63121-9_19

for sending and receiving messages as well as for exchanging data between tiles. The major advantage of tiled architectures is that they are scalable (both, in performance and energy) due to vast amount of resources available for different types of parallel computing, including instruction-level parallelism, task and data parallelism, as well as stream parallelism. Tile-based computing platforms often provide special instruction sets that allow software to take advantage of the available resources for parallel applications and hence for further improvements in performance and efficiency. Prominent examples of tiled system architectures are the Raw processor [23], the TILE64, TILEPro, TILE-Gx and Stratton platforms by Tilera [4] and Intel's Single-Chip Cloud Computer [16].

Heterogeneous tile-based multi-processor systems (such as the Chameleon architecture [22] or the Tomahawk platform [1]) yield additional options on how to take advantage of the flexibility provided by the computing platform. These kinds of platforms combine different types of tiles, such as special purpose processing elements that are optimized for specific types of computational tasks. Heterogeneous hardware enables additional flexibility on the software level as software could be made available in different variants. For example, one parallel implementation that can be executed on general purpose processing elements and another implementation for special purpose processing elements. The flexibility of such hardware/software system comes at the price that programming and the design of low-level protocols become a highly non-trivial task (see e.g. [11,19,28,30,31]). One major challenge is how to construct, manage and use heterogeneous tile-based multi-processor systems efficiently, not only in terms of performance, but also by means of energy consumption. This task includes finding a beneficial hardware architecture (e.g., by identifying advantageous mixtures of tiles), but also the development of heuristics for selecting among software variants and mapping them to the compatible tiles at run time. Additionally, the task of resource allocation, configuration and reallocation becomes more complex and goes beyond what is classically being done by operating systems. Optimal usage of such systems requires a global view on the system, including the hardware characteristics, the current system configuration and its state, as well as knowledge about the applications, algorithms, the current load situation and user requirements.

As the number of possible combinations arising by selecting concrete instances of hardware tiles, software variants and resource management strategies grows exponentially, an exhaustive comparison using simulation techniques is nearly impossible. Nevertheless, the simulation-based analysis for a few selected combinations is the de-facto standard in the design of tile architectures. The purpose of this paper is to propose an alternative approach that relies on a family-based analysis and probabilistic model checking.

Contribution. The paper provides a first step towards supporting the design of tiled architectures and resource management strategies by means of formal methods for the quantitative evaluation. For this, we introduce a tool chain that provides a flexible approach for the analysis of families $\mathcal{C} = (C_i)_{i \in I}$ of concrete systems C_i using the probabilistic model checker PRISM [17,20,21].

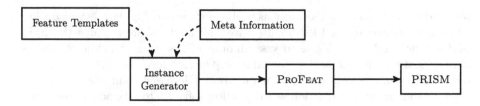

Fig. 1. The tool chain.

The family members C_i rely on a common tiled architecture, but differ, e.g., in the resource management or the variant selection strategies. This family is modeled by a (single) Markov decision process (MDP) $\mathcal{M}_C$ with one initial state for each system C_i. Probabilistic behaviour is given by stochastic assumptions on the execution times of tasks in the resource profiles (see below).

With PRISM's (symbolic) analysis engines for MDPs one can, e.g., compute the expected energy requirements of all systems C_i in the family. This, for instance, yields a simple way to compare different strategies with a single analysis. If all decisions of the strategies are modelled nondeterministically, the analysis with PRISM can be used to synthesize a strategy where the expected energy requirements are minimal.

The tool chain as depicted in Fig. 1 takes as input a series of feature templates specifying tiles, software variants and resource management strategies together with some meta information (e.g., number and type of tiles and jobs, resource profiles) required for the instantiation. The instance generator of the tool chain then automatically translates the feature templates into feature modules in the syntax of the tool PROFEAT [7], which yields a feature-oriented specification of system family $(C_i)_{i\in I}$. PROFEAT then translates the feature modules into PRISM's syntax, which yields a feature-less PRISM specification for a combined system C that contains each family member C_i as a subsystem.

The template-based approach offers a comfortable way to analyze different system families by modifying the meta information, e.g., by adding new tile types, increasing the number of tiles or changing the energy characteristics in the resource profiles. The meta information can also contain analysis-specific elements, such as additional fairness constraints to exclude nonsensical behaviour or counters that only serve to compute certain performance measures, but do not affect the operational behavior of the hardware tiles or software components. As such counters can lead to a drastic blow up of the MDP size, it is desirable to include them only in case of need. Thus, the template-based approach also provides a simple way to choose the granularity of the models for (families of) concrete systems, depending on the evaluation criteria.

To illustrate the feasibility of our approach, we provide a template-based specification of a heterogeneous tile architecture that can be viewed as a simplification of the Tomahawk platform [1]. Its tiles are general purpose RISC computing elements or computing elements designed for digital signal processing (DSP). Apart from the tiles, the Tomahawk platform contains a logically decoupled piece of hardware, called core manager, responsible for the allocation and configuration of processing elements as well as for task scheduling and the data transfer from the global memory. Using the tool chain, we consider several system families and employ PRISM's symbolic MDP engines to demonstrate the benefit of heterogeneous structures over homogeneous ones and to study the impact of power and scaling strategies on the energy requirements.

Related Work. To the best of our knowledge, family-based approaches for the formal analysis of tile architectures and to determine optimal hardware-software combinations using probabilistic model checking have not been addressed before. Several authors have studied formal verification techniques to establish functional properties of heterogeneous multiprocessor systems (see, e.g., [6,13,29]). Research on the use of model checking for the quantitative analysis of heterogeneous multiprocessor systems has mainly concentrated on statistical model checking (see, e.g., [3]). An exception is [18] where probabilistic model checking has been used to analyze dynamic power management strategies for multicore systems.

Family-based approaches for (software) product lines have been studied by several authors. This includes the work on feature transition systems and symbolic model checking techniques [8,9] as well as other formal analysis techniques for product lines [5,10,24,26,27]. The formal quantitative analysis of product lines using Markovian models has been addressed only recently in combination with probabilistic model checking [7,14] or statistical model checking [12,25]. As stated before, our tool chain uses the tool PROFEAT of [7] for translating feature-oriented specifications into PRISM's input language.

2   The Tool Chain

In this section we present the tool chain for automated model generation and the (family-based) quantitative analysis of heterogeneous tiled multi-processor architectures in detail[1]. Apart from the details considered below, additional aspects could naturally be added as part of future work. (See Sect. 4 for a discussion on possible extensions.)

The heterogeneous tiled system as supported by the tool chain consists of a pool of processing elements called tiles with different types and with different resource characteristics. Additionally, there is a core manager providing the interface to the tiles, allowing for frequency scaling, job scheduling, and for powering up and down tiles. For the moment we not consider the NoC communication and fully abstract from the topology of the system. Our simplified assumption here is, that the NoC communication between arbitrary tiles is (equally) fast and negligible compared to the computation time of jobs. Jobs are characterized by their type and a weight that stands for their expected number of atomic steps. Jobs can be scheduled completely in parallel, but only on compatible tiles suited

---

[1] The implementation and examples are available for download at https://wwwtcs. inf.tu-dresden.de/ALGI/PUB/KimFest17/.

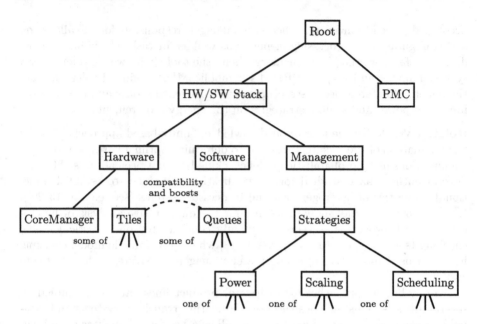

Fig. 2. Feature diagram of the output of the instance generator, a hierarchical feature model. Left out are leaves of varying number, of which either *some* or *one* can be active at the same time.

for the respective job type. Furthermore, we consider the jobs to be compute intensive and independent in terms of order and communication. The concrete execution time and energy consumption depend on the tile type on which the jobs are scheduled.

2.1   Instance Generator

The starting point for our tool chain is the instance generator, which takes as input a set of component feature templates, meta information and a family declaration and generates a hierarchical feature model as shown in Fig. 2.

At the top of the feature diagram is the Root feature which has the a feature for the system's hardware/software stack one with information for probabilistic model checking (PMC) as children. The stack contains all hardware and software components whereas the PMC feature contains the analysis specific components. One can see that the hardware part consists of the core manager and a set of tiles whereas the software is characterized by a set of queues for the different job types. There are additional constrains on the compatibility of tiles and job types as well as information on the boost factor a given job has for each type of tile. On the management side we have the resource management strategies which split into the different domains for power management, scaling and scheduling. A combination of such strategies yields a combined strategy, restricting and potentially resolving the nondeterministic choices in the MDP model. Leaving

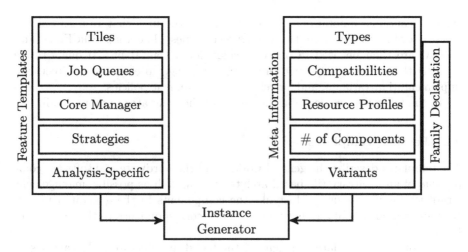

Fig. 3. The instance generator and its inputs.

one or more parts of this combined strategy underspecified leads again to an MDP model where we can ask for best (or worst) possible schedulers resolving the nondeterministic choices. In the experiment section (cf. Sect. 3) we leave the scheduling nondeterministic and compare the best (and worst) possible scheduling for different variants of hardware/software/strategy variants. Together with the meta information on the variant space to be considered, a family model with the above structure is being created.

Figure 3 shows the details of the instance generator. The first part of the input are the feature templates that capture the general operational behavior of all relevant components. These feature templates are used as building blocks within the instantiation. This set includes feature templates for (1) the parts of the architecture (e.g., the operational behavior of a tile and a core manager), (2) describing the characteristic behavior of running applications (e.g., the classification of different job types), (3) declaring the characteristic behavior of resource management strategies, and (4) a few analysis-specific components, which will be instantiated whenever needed in the later analysis.

The second part of the input is meta information about the concrete instance that should be generated. This meta information is provided in configuration files and includes (a) type declarations of tiles and jobs, (b) compatibility information regarding jobs and tiles, (c) resource profiles for tiles and jobs, (d) global resource profiles, and (e) variable values on how many tiles should be instantiated.

The third part of the input is a family declaration, i.e., the variants for which a family model will be created and hence which alternative designs should be considered in the later comparative analysis.

The output of the instance generator is formalized in the PROFEAT input language. The semantics of the family model created by the instance generator is given in terms of a weighted MDP. This MDP for the family of hardware/software systems contains annotations for cost/reward structures that result from the meta information given in the configuration files. The tools PROFEAT and PRISM are then be used in our tool chain for a (family-based) quantitative analysis that allows evaluating and comparing, e.g., alternative architectures, implementation variants, and/or resource management policies.

In the following, we describe the inputs of the generator in more detail.

2.2   Feature Templates

The templates describe the general workings of the hardware and software components of an arbitrary tile-based architecture, as well as possible management strategies for its resources. Just like the components in the generated model, they are compositional and have a one-to-one correspondence to the diagram in Fig. 2.

To reuse the templates for general tile-based architectures, abstractions in the form of parametrizations are necessary. While the main characteristics of heterogeneous systems are encoded in the templates, the specific characteristics of a platform are left out, so they can be defined in the meta information.

Tiles. The atomic hardware components of a tile-based architecture are tiles. They are processing elements that can be turned on or off during run time. They exhibit characteristic cost and performance measures due to their substrate material, purpose, architecture and quality. The corresponding templates need to be parametrized by their type, their possible scaling multipliers (i.e., processing speeds) and the corresponding power consumption. It is also possible to modify the probability distribution governing their task completion probabilities.

Tiles can be in one of two modes, idle or working mode, and react to three actions: setting their power state, their current multiplier, and scheduling a job on them. While the first two are simple state changes, scheduling a job causes the tile to go into working mode. Then, it is impossible to turn it off or to schedule another job onto it until it is idle again. The completion of jobs is governed by a geometric distribution, i.e., jobs are completed with a certain probability p in each step. p depends on the mean execution time of the job, the current multiplier of the tile and the boost the job may receive because of advantageous hardware properties. The exact recipe for the composition of p can be given in the meta information.

Job Queues. To leverage specialized hardware components, it is necessary to generate specialized code for the tasks to be done. Therefore, we introduce multiple typed job queues with specific mean running times for their jobs. While the job queues are assumed to have infinite capacity in the most general case, job counters can be added to them via an analysis-specific component.

Core Manager. We assume a global controlling component for the system runtime, the *core manager*. The core manager can turn idle tiles on or off, set their scaling factor and schedules tasks on them according to their compatibility.

```
<%def name="performance()">
feature StrategyScale_performance
  modules strategy_scale_performance_impl;
endfeature

module strategy_scale_performance_impl
  // Set all the multipliers that are NOT maximal to false
  % for nr,tile in enumerate(c.tiles):
    % for i,mult in enumerate(c.tiles[nr].mults):
      % if mult!=max(c.tiles[nr].mults):
        [mult_${nr}_${mult}] false -> true;
      % endif
    % endfor
  % endfor
endmodule
</%def>
```

Fig. 4. Definition of the performance scaling strategy. Lines with % and $ symbols denote template macros which are sensitive to meta information.

In general, we make no assumptions on its behaviour or timing. It can however only schedule jobs onto compatible tiles. The core manager is also responsible for the system clocking: it splits the run time into turns, called *ticks*, during which each of the components can choose its actions in an ordered fashion.

Strategies. While the core manager has total control over the tiles and scheduling in general, we allow restrictions on its behaviour. For this, we identify three kinds of *management strategies*, depending on what they restrict or control: power, scaling and scheduling strategies. They can influence the behaviour during initialization as well as during run time.

Power strategies control the power toggling actions of the core manager. They restrict the powering or unpowering of tiles. We only provide one such strategy: the *alwayson* strategy, which forces the core manager to turn on all tiles during initialization and subsequently forbids their switching off.

To restrict and control the setting of scaling multipliers, scaling strategies are used. They are orthogonal to power strategies since they do not control a tiles' power state directly. One prominent example here is the *powersave* strategy, which locks all multipliers to their lowest setting. Its opposite is the *performance* strategy, locking them to their highest setting.

To decide which job is scheduled on which tile, a scheduling strategy is used. We only provide a simple *probabilistic* scheduling strategy here, that assigns jobs to compatible tiles according to a probability distribution. In our case the distribution is uniform, but it can easily be replaced by a more realistic distribution derived from simulations or measurements.

Since strategies are compositional like the rest of the model, it is possible to introduce new strategies by adding new templates for them in a straightforward fashion. As an example, consider the listing for the performance scaling strategy in Fig. 4.

Analysis-Specific Components. We provide modules to add on-demand tracking to the model and disable corner-case behaviour. This is sometimes necessary to obtain proper results. However, it may also change the model size significantly. To enable quotas on the job queues, we give the *JobCounter* module, adding a counter to each queue. The *TimeStop* module reduces all transitions to self-loops after all job counters reach zero. The *FairSchedule* module forbids scheduling jobs from queues that reached their quota as long as uncompleted queues are still available. As long as valid scheduling mappings are available, the *ForceSchedule* module forces the core manager to schedule something.

2.3   Meta Information

The meta information given to the generator contains the specific information about the given architecture. It consists of a set of configuration files, using a domain specific language for the creation of tiles and queues, the expression of compatibilities and speed boosts and the concise description of resource profiles and the number of used components.

Type Descriptions. Concrete types and their associated characteristics are given to the tiles and queues. To define a tile type, we assign a name, a set of possible scaling multipliers and an associated energy consumption profile. For example, to configure a RISC tile with possible scaling multipliers 1, 2 and 4 and a DSP tile with multipliers 1 and 2 with a corresponding quadratic increase in power consumption (in the chosen multiplier) for both, we write

```
% Tile(type, multipliers, energy_profile)
tileRISC = Tile("RISC", [1,2,4], quadratic)
tileDSP = Tile("DSP", [1,2], quadratic)
```

Similarly, job queue types are defined by a name and a mean execution time for the job. This way, it is possible to represent non-atomic jobs that need multiple processing steps to complete. For example, to define a queue for DEFAULT jobs with a mean runtime of four steps, and a SIGNALPROC queue with the same average, we write

```
% JobQueue(type, mean_execution_time)
queueDefault = JobQueue("Default", 4)
queueSignalProc = JobQueue("SignalProc", 4)
```

Compatibilities and Resource Profiles. One important aspect of heterogeneous systems is the speed up of certain hardware-software combinations, achieved by leveraging different kinds of processors and instruction sets. In our model, we consider types of job queues to be *compatible* with types of tiles. Additionally, we allow speed *boosts* for certain advantageous combinations. Both are encoded into a simple array (see below). For example, a SIGNALPROC job can be worked by a general purpose RISC processor, but receives an two-fold boost when scheduled on a specialized DSP tile. Conversely, a generic DEFAULT computation can be done by the RISC tile but not the DSP one:

```
% speed[jobtype] = {tiletype: boost, ...}
speed["Default"] = {"RISC": 1}
speed["SignalProc"] = {"RISC": 1, "DSP": 2}
```

The **speed** mapping signifies compatibilities and boosts at the same time: non-existent tile type entries stand for incompatible tiles.

Number of Components. With the declared types of tiles and queues, we can now give the concrete sets of components necessary to define a platform. The enabled job queues are given by a list, for example, to have a DEFAULT and a SIGNALPROC queue as defined above:

```
queues = [queueDefault, queueSignalProc]
```

Sets of tiles are given in the form of tile configurations, given each occurring tile type and its cardinality. It is possible to define multiple configurations. For example, to give a platform which can be either homogeneous with four RISC tiles or heterogeneous with two RISC and two DSP tiles:

```
% TileConfig(name, tile_multiset)
tcHomogeneous = TileConfig("Homogeneous", {tileRISC: 8})
tcHeterogeneous = TileConfig("Heterogeneous", {tileRISC: 4, tileDSP: 4})
tileConfigs = [tcHomogeneous, tcHeterogeneous]
```

2.4 Family Declaration and Variants

Depending on the possible configurations given above, the instance generator produces a family model. Besides generating a family member for each entry in the `tileConfigs` array, there are more options to automatically generate variants. By giving possible active strategies, a family member is generated for each entry. For example, to have all the choices of the strategies described in the previous section as well as no strategy in each category:

```
strategies_power = ["alwayson","none"]
strategies_scale = ["powersave","performance","none"]
strategies_schedule = ["none"]
```

This alone would generate $2 \cdot 3 \cdot 1 = 6$ individual members.

It is also possible to generate variants by varying the job counters. For example, to generate all possibilities of distributing eight jobs among the job queues:

```
max_job_count = 8;
jobs_are_even = False; % jobs are not evenly distributed
```

If `jobs_are_even` is set to True, only one variant with, e.g., four jobs in each of the two queues, is generated.

3 Experiments

We now describe our experimental results for a model instance representing the second iteration of the Tomahawk architecture. We therefore used the meta information as exemplified in Sect. 2.3 within the instance generation. To recall: the Tomahawk contains two different types of tiles, general purpose RISC tiles and DSP tiles for digital signal processing jobs. Jobs can either be of type SIG-NALPROC for signal processing jobs or of type DEFAULT. Jobs of type DEFAULT can only be executed on RISC tiles, whereas SIGNALPROC jobs can be executed more efficiently on DSP tiles (SIGNALPROC jobs enjoy a speed-up of two). For the experiments we fix the number of tiles to four which are either of the type RISC or DSP. For the different jobs we introduce two queues, one for DEFAULT jobs and one for SIGNALPROC jobs. At the end of this section we address the scalability considering larger numbers of tiles and jobs. Analysis-specific components for job counting and fair and forced scheduling are enabled.

In the given setting, the comparative studies focus on three different aspects. In the first family-based analysis we compare a homogeneous architecture (four RISC tiles) with a heterogeneous architecture (two RISC and two DSP tiles). The second family-analysis focuses on the influence of specialized software variants on a heterogeneous architecture, whereas in the third part of the experiments the focus is on comparing variants of resource management strategies, again for the a heterogeneous architecture. In all three parts of the experiments we compute expected run times and the expected energy consumption for finishing certain number of jobs (quota for each job queue), and the minimum energy needed to finish this number of jobs with significantly high probability. The comparison is made on the basis of the best (and worst) possible scheduling of jobs in the given setting. This corresponds to computing minimal and maximal probabilities and expectations as well as quantiles [2] in the MDP of the respective family. The used reward functions "ticks" and "energy" are defined as expected: a *tick* is a turn in the core manager, and *energy* is used by tiles during power-up, idling and working.

All experiments were carried out on a machine with two Intel Xeon E5-2680 4-core CPUs at 2.13 GHz and 192 GB RAM, running Linux. Turbo-Boost was enabled. The tool chain used PROFEAT version 0.108.0.0 and PRISM version 4.3.1.dev with custom patches supporting among other things the symbolic computation of quantile values. The experimental setting and full tool chain are available for download at https://wwwtcs.inf.tu-dresden.de/ALGI/PUB/KimFest17/.

3.1 Homogeneous vs. Heterogeneous Architectures

This experiment compares performance, energy and the tradeoff between energy and performance for the homogeneous architecture with four general purpose RISC tiles and a heterogeneous architecture with two RISC tiles and two DSP tiles. We assume that the given job quota is evenly distributed among the two queue for DEFAULT and the SIGNALPROC. As no strategies are set, the minimal (and maximal) expectation corresponds to the best (and worst) possible choices available to the worst core manager. An overview of the results can be seen in Table 1. Clearly, the heterogeneous system outperforms the homogeneous system in terms of energy consumption, in the worst as well as in the best case. At the

Table 1. Maximal and minimal expected energy and time consumption to fulfill the job quota for a homogeneous and a heterogeneous tile configuration.

Job quota	Architecture	Ex_{energy}^{min}	Ex_{energy}^{max}	Ex_{ticks}^{min}	Ex_{ticks}^{max}
(3, 3)	Homogeneous	72.915	280.741	5.691	40.589
	Heterogeneous	51.808	264.705	5.738	38.147
(4, 4)	Homogeneous	96.868	356.227	7.623	52.521
	Heterogeneous	68.359	339.523	7.709	50.096
(5, 5)	Homogeneous	120.812	430.930	9.576	64.436
	Heterogeneous	84.899	414.356	9.693	62.029
(6, 6)	Homogeneous	144.737	505.595	11.548	76.338
	Heterogeneous	101.436	489.204	11.682	73.953
(8, 8)	Homogeneous	192.567	654.967	15.522	100.069
	Heterogeneous	134.504	638.676	15.672	97.732

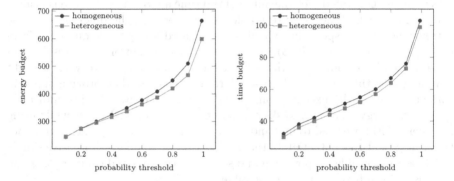

Fig. 5. The minimal necessary energy (left) and time (right) budget to fulfill the job quota with a probability threshold, for the homogeneous and heterogeneous model with four tiles and eight jobs.

same time, the best case run times are better and the worst case ones almost the same. This yields a strong indication that heterogeneous architecture provide large potential for energy-efficient computing.

While the expected optimal values give an indication on the average behaviour of a model, hard guarantees are also interesting. We investigated two quantiles: the minimal energy and run time budget necessary to complete the job quota with a certain probability threshold. As can be seen in Fig. 5 the heterogeneous model is better for every threshold.

As the results for the heterogeneous architecture seem to be very promising we will now focus on this architecture and consider software variants and strategy variants in the following. The goal is to quantify the additional potential of considering software variants and strategy variants.

3.2   Software Variants

While the generated jobs were evenly spread among the job queues before, we now consider the case of varying ratios between the queues in the heterogeneous model from before. A total amount of eight jobs is distributed among two job queues in varying ratios.

The interpretation is that an incoming task can be solved using different algorithmic approaches or by using alternative variants a compiler has generated for the same piece of code. The different software variants lead to different numbers of jobs for each job type to be scheduled on the system, i.e., to different quotas for the job queues. In the given example we only consider the balance between SIGNALPROC jobs and DEFAULT jobs as characteristic for alternative software variants of, e.g., a Fourier transform task.

The results can be seen in Table 2. A clear trend towards specialized jobs for a better minimal energy consumption can be seen. The maximal energy consumption behaves similarly, but becomes slightly better again if no specialized jobs at all are generated. For the minimal run time almost no difference is visible. The maximal run time is quite stable as well, with slight differences at the extreme ends of the spectrum. We also investigated the quantile questions from above for the cases of a $(0, 8), (4, 4)$ and $(8, 0)$ distribution. The results can be seen in Fig. 6, indicating the same close results from above with a slight advantage for the mixed $(4, 4)$ case. Here, one can see that proving software variants suited to be executed on special purpose hardware yields additional benefit in energy efficiency. Tasks can potentially be finished faster while using less energy. Still, we need to find and implement resource management strategies that can exploit this potential. In the next section we compare alternative simple heuristics responsible for powering and scaling of the tiles and compare them on the basis of the best (and worst) possible scheduling.

3.3   Influence of Strategies

The impact of given power and scaling strategies can be seen in Table 3. For this experiment, no scheduling strategy has been given, but the power and scaling strategies have been present. Recall that the alwayson strategy forces all tiles to be powered at all times and the powersave and performance strategies lock their scaling multiplier to their lowest or highest value respectively. The fully nondeterministic case (i.e., no power and no scaling strategy) served as a baseline for the comparison, as there can not exist any better heuristics. In Table 3 these cases are marked with "none".

In the given setting, it can be seen that the powersave scaling strategy is optimal for minimizing the expected energy consumption. An optimal value can however not be reached if all tiles are always powered. Interestingly, when comparing the maximum expected energy for the case where all tiles are always on is lower than in the nondeterministic power management case. This is due to the fact that powering tiles requires additional energy. Regarding the expected run time, the performance and the alwayson strategies are optimal within their

Table 2. Maximal and minimal expected energy and time consumption for a heterogeneous system a varying distribution of DEFAULT (d) and SIGNALPROC (s) jobs.

d	s	$\mathrm{Ex}_{energy}^{min}$	$\mathrm{Ex}_{energy}^{max}$	$\mathrm{Ex}_{ticks}^{min}$	$\mathrm{Ex}_{ticks}^{max}$
0	8	37.571	238.585	7.462	30.974
1	7	42.249	247.239	7.462	32.250
2	6	45.678	247.591	7.462	32.248
3	5	49.106	247.857	7.462	32.248
4	4	52.534	248.153	7.463	32.248
5	3	55.960	248.442	7.464	32.248
6	2	59.338	248.741	7.470	32.248
7	1	62.552	248.614	7.504	32.250
8	0	64.949	240.432	7.707	30.974

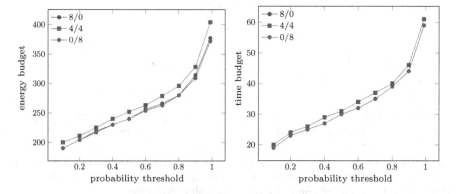

Fig. 6. The minimal necessary energy (left) and time (right) budget to fulfill the job quota with a probability threshold for the heterogeneous model with four tiles and eight jobs of which 0, 4 or 8 are of DEFAULT type and the rest of SIGNALPROC type.

domain. Combining the two strategies alwayson and performance yields the best result for the worst case expected execution time. The results for the quantile questions can be seen in Fig. 7. The minimal energy budget is smallest for the powersave strategy. It has better guarantees then no scaling strategy, since the worst-case behaviour of the latter allows to use more energy. Interestingly, the alwayson strategy allows for better guarantees as no strategy as well. The minimal time budget is best for the alwayson strategy, since it disallows delaying computations by disabling tiles.

In the remainder of this section we address the scalability and present the sizes of the created MDP models for an increasing number of tiles and increased quotas for the jobs.

Table 3. Maximal and minimal expected energy and time consumption to finish eight jobs for differing power and scaling strategies. The lowest numbers in each column are printed in bold.

Power	Scaling	Ex_{energy}^{min}	Ex_{energy}^{max}	Ex_{ticks}^{min}	Ex_{ticks}^{max}
Alwayson	Powersave	87.232	**146.664**	11.626	20.807
Alwayson	Performance	169.541	315.603	**7.709**	**9.180**
Alwayson	None	87.232	317.065	**7.709**	20.807
None	Powersave	**68.350**	198.419	11.626	50.096
None	Performance	69.350	339.865	**7.709**	50.095
None	None	**68.350**	339.924	**7.709**	50.096

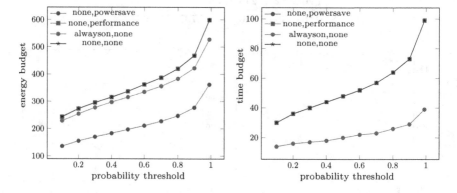

Fig. 7. The minimal necessary energy (left) and time (right) budget to fulfill the job quota with a probability threshold for the heterogeneous model with four tiles and eight jobs with a choice of enabled power and scaling strategies.

3.4   Scalability

The growth in the model size depending on the length of the job queues can be seen in Table 4 and depending on the number of tiles in Table 5. We list the number of reachable states and the number of transition in the MDP along with the number of nodes in the binary decision diagram (BDD) that PRISM used to store the MDP model symbolically. It can be seen that the model scales well in the number of jobs, but not so well in the number of tiles. Even for six tiles results can hardly be expected, as the number of reachable states is too large.

Besides handling the family members one-by-one in separate models instead of as a single larger model for all of them, one possibility to reduce the model sizes is to enable deterministic or probabilistic strategies. For example, by enabling all three kinds of the management strategies described above, the size of the eight-tile model can be brought down to 27.902.368.740 states, i.e., by a factor of 200. This allows the evaluation of pre-generated strategies even for otherwise too large models.

Table 4. Model sizes for the homogeneous-heterogeneous comparison for an architecture with four tiles and varying job quotas.

Jobs	States	Transitions	BDD nodes
6	45.182.997	166.721.618	143.394
8	77.520.707	284.561.823	145.098
10	118.177.353	432.630.772	145.364
12	167.103.823	610.795.529	145.428
16	289.766.235	1.057.412.467	146.502

Table 5. Model sizes for the homogeneous-heterogeneous comparison for a system with a quota of eight jobs and varying number of tiles.

Tiles	States	Transitions	BDD nodes
4	77.520.707	284.561.823	145.098
6	63.785.055.348	344.857.398.616	431.427
8	59.336.342.091.105	425.950.823.937.621	988.555

4   Conclusion

In this paper we presented a tool chain for the automated generation and quantitative analysis of families of system models for heterogeneous multi-processor systems based on tiled architectures. The families are obtained by varying, e.g., the hardware-software combinations and/or the resource management strategies and analyzed by means of probabilistic model checking using PROFEAT and PRISM. We illustrated how the family-based analysis can be used to quantify the potential of heterogeneous hardware elements, software variants and adaptive resource management and scheduling strategies. For this we applied our tool chain to a simplified model of the multi-processor Tomahawk platform that has been designed for integrating heterogeneous devices. The presented approach is rather flexible and can in principle be easily extended in various ways. New tile types and job types can simply be characterized by providing the meta information that characterize a new tile, job type and the corresponding compatibility. Additional resource management strategies can simply be provided by defining a new feature template that can then be used in the automated instance generator. In the same way new feature templates can be added that provide additional functionality, e.g., a more detailed view on the applications would require a component that creates concrete jobs/tasks according to some probability distribution. Also in this case the instance generator must be extended accordingly. Similarly, adding new characteristics, e.g., cost/reward parameters demands for extending existing feature templates with the respective information and adding their treatment to the instance generator. Additional aspects that are not yet considered, e.g., dependencies between jobs, can also be added, but require more involved modifications in particular to the instance generator.

References

1. Arnold, O., Matus, E., Noethen, B., Winter, M., Limberg, T., Fettweis, G.: Tomahawk: parallelism and heterogeneity in communications signal processing MPSoCs. ACM Trans. Embed. Comput. Syst. **13**(3s), 107:1–107:24 (2014)

2. Baier, C., Daum, M., Dubslaff, C., Klein, J., Klüppelholz, S.: Energy-utility quantiles. In: Badger, J.M., Rozier, K.Y. (eds.) NFM 2014. LNCS, vol. 8430, pp. 285–299. Springer, Cham (2014). doi:10.1007/978-3-319-06200-6_24

3. Basu, A., Bensalem, S., Bozga, M., Delahaye, B., Legay, A.: Statistical abstraction and model-checking of large heterogeneous systems. STTT **14**(1), 53–72 (2012)

4. Bell, S., Edwards, B., Amann, J., Conlin, R., Joyce, K., Leung, V., MacKay, J., Reif, M., Bao, L., Brown III, J.F., Mattina, M., Miao, C.-C., Ramey, C., Wentzlaff, D., Anderson, W., Berger, E., Fairbanks, N., Khan, D., Montenegro, F., Stickney, J., Zook, J.: TILE64 - processor: a 64-core soc with mesh interconnect. In: 2008 IEEE International Solid-State Circuits Conference, ISSCC 2008, Digest of Technical Papers, San Francisco, CA, USA, 3–7 February 2008, pp. 88–89. IEEE (2008)

5. Bodden, E., Tolêdo, T., Ribeiro, M., Brabrand, C., Borba, P., Mezini, M.: Spl^{lift}: statically analyzing software product lines in minutes instead of years. In: ACM SIGPLAN Conference on Programming Language Design and Implementation (PLDI), pp. 355–364. ACM (2013)

6. Brekling, A.W., Hansen, M.R., Madsen, J.: Models and formal verification of multiprocessor system-on-chips. J. Logic Algebraic Program. **77**(1–2), 1–19 (2008)

7. Chrszon, P., Dubslaff, C., Klüppelholz, S., Baier, C.: Family-based modeling and analysis for probabilistic systems – featuring PROFEAT. In: Stevens, P., Wąsowski, A. (eds.) FASE 2016. LNCS, vol. 9633, pp. 287–304. Springer, Heidelberg (2016). doi:10.1007/978-3-662-49665-7_17

8. Classen, A., Cordy, M., Schobbens, P., Heymans, P., Legay, A., Raskin, J.: Featured transition systems: foundations for verifying variability-intensive systems and their application to LTL model checking. IEEE Trans. Softw. Eng. **39**(8), 1069–1089 (2013)

9. Cordy, M., Classen, A., Heymans, P., Schobbens, P., Legay, A.: ProVeLines: a product line of verifiers for software product lines. In: 17th International Software Product Line Conference Co-located workshops (SPLC), pp. 141–146. ACM (2013)

10. Damiani, F., Schaefer, I.: Family-based analysis of type safety for delta-oriented software product lines. In: Margaria, T., Steffen, B. (eds.) ISoLA 2012. LNCS, vol. 7609, pp. 193–207. Springer, Heidelberg (2012). doi:10.1007/978-3-642-34026-0_15

11. Dastgeer, U., Kessler, C.W.: Performance-aware composition framework for GPU-based systems. J. Supercomput. **71**(12), 4646–4662 (2015)

12. Devroey, X., Perrouin, G., Cordy, M., Samih, H., Legay, A., Schobbens, P., Heymans, P.: Statistical prioritization for software product line testing: an experience report. Softw. Syst. Model. **16**(1), 153–171 (2017)

13. Donaldson, A.F., Kroening, D., Rümmer, P.: Automatic analysis of scratch-pad memory code for heterogeneous multicore processors. In: Esparza, J., Majumdar, R. (eds.) TACAS 2010. LNCS, vol. 6015, pp. 280–295. Springer, Heidelberg (2010). doi:10.1007/978-3-642-12002-2_24

14. Dubslaff, C., Baier, C., Klüppelholz, S.: Probabilistic model checking for feature-oriented systems. Trans. Asp.-Oriented Softw. Dev. **12**, 180–220 (2015)

15. Wentzlaff, D., Griffin, P., Hoffmann, H., Bao, L., Edwards, B., Ramey, C., Mattina, M., Miao, C.-C., Brown III, J.F., Agarwal, A.: On-chip interconnection architecture of the tile processor. IEEE Micro **27**, 15–31 (2007)

16. Gries, M., Hoffmann, U., Konow, M., Riepen, M.: SCC: a flexible architecture for many-core platform research. Comput. Sci. Eng. **13**(6), 79–83 (2011)
17. Kwiatkowska, M., Norman, G., Parker, D.: PRISM 4.0: verification of probabilistic real-time systems. In: Gopalakrishnan, G., Qadeer, S. (eds.) CAV 2011. LNCS, vol. 6806, pp. 585–591. Springer, Heidelberg (2011). doi:10.1007/978-3-642-22110-1_47
18. Lungu, A., Bose, P., Sorin, D.J., German, S., Janssen, G.: Multicore power management: ensuring robustness via early-stage formal verification. In: 7th ACM/IEEE International Conference on Formal Methods and Models for Codesign (MEMOCODE), pp. 78–87. IEEE (2009)
19. Paolucci, P.S., Jerraya, A.A., Leupers, R., Thiele, L., Vicini, P.: SHAPES: a tiled scalable software hardware architecture platform for embedded systems. In: 4th International Conference on Hardware/Software Codesign and System Synthesis (CODES+ISSS), pp. 167–172. ACM (2006)
20. Parker, D.: Implementation of symbolic model checking for probabilistic systems. Ph.D. thesis, University of Birmingham (2002)
21. PRISM model checker. http://www.prismmodelchecker.org/
22. Smit, G.J.M., Kokkeler, A.B.J., Wolkotte, P.T., Hölzenspies, P.K.F., van de Burgwal, M.D., Heysters, P.M.: The chameleon architecture for streaming DSP applications. EURASIP J. Embed. Syst. **2007** (2007). Article ID 078082
23. Taylor, M.B., Kim, J., Miller, J., Wentzlaff, D., Ghodrat, F., Greenwald, B., Hoffman, H., Johnson, P., Lee, J.-W., Lee, W., Ma, A., Saraf, A., Seneski, M., Shnidman, N., Strumpen, V., Frank, M., Amarasinghe, S., Agarwal, A.: The raw microprocessor: a computational fabric for software circuits and general-purpose programs. IEEE Micro **22**(2), 25–35 (2002)
24. ter Beek, M.H., Fantechi, A., Gnesi, S., Mazzanti, F.: Using FMC for family-based analysis of software product lines. In: 19th International Conference on Software Product Line (SPLC), pp. 432–439. ACM (2015)
25. ter Beek, M.H., Legay, A., Lluch Lafuente, A., Vandin, A.: Statistical model checking for product lines. In: Margaria, T., Steffen, B. (eds.) ISoLA 2016. LNCS, vol. 9952, pp. 114–133. Springer, Cham (2016). doi:10.1007/978-3-319-47166-2_8
26. Thüm, T.: Product-line specification and verification with feature-oriented contracts. Ph.D. thesis, Otto von Guericke University Magdeburg (2015)
27. Thüm, T., Schaefer, I., Hentschel, M., Apel, S.: Family-based deductive verification of software product lines. In: Generative Programming and Component Engineering (GPCE), pp. 11–20. ACM (2012)
28. Vajda, A.: Programming Many-Core Chips. Springer, New York (2011)
29. Velev, M.N., Gao, P.: Formal verification of safety of polymorphic heterogeneous multi-core architectures. In: 15th International Symposium on Quality Electronic Design (ISQED), pp. 611–617. IEEE (2014)
30. Völp, M., Klüppelholz, S., Castrillon, J., Härtig, H., Asmussen, N., Aßmann, U., Baader, F., Baier, C., Fettweis, G., Fröhlich, J., Goens, A., Haas, S., Habich, D., Hasler, M., Huismann, I., Karnagel, T., Karol, S., Lehner, W., Leuschner, L., Lieber, M., Ling, S., Märcker, S., Mey, J., Nagel, W., Nöthen, B., Penaloza, R., Raitza, M., Stiller, J., Ungethüm, A., Voigt, A.: The orchestration stack: the impossible task of designing software for unknown future post-CMOS hardware. In: Proceedings of the 1st Workshop on Post-Moore's Era Supercomputing (PMES) (2016, accepted for publication)
31. Wilhelm, R., Reineke, J.: Embedded systems: many cores - many problems. In: 7th IEEE International Symposium on Industrial Embedded Systems (SIES), pp. 176–180. IEEE (2012)

Algorithmic Game Theory and Mechanism Design

Admissible Strategies in Timed Games

Nicolas Basset[1], Jean-François Raskin[1], and Ocan Sankur[2(✉)]

[1] Université libre de Bruxelles, Brussels, Belgium
{nbasset,jraskin}@ulb.ac.be
[2] CNRS, IRISA, Rennes, France
ocan.sankur@irisa.fr

Abstract. In this paper, we study the notion of admissibility in timed games. First, we show that admissible strategies may not exist in timed games with a continuous semantics of time, even for safety objectives. Second, we show that the discrete time semantics of timed games is better behaved w.r.t. admissibility: the existence of admissible strategies is guaranteed in that semantics. Third, we provide symbolic algorithms to solve the model-checking problem under admissibility and the assume-admissible synthesis problem for real-time non-zero sum n-player games for safety objectives.

1 Introduction

An embedded controller is a reactive system that maintains a continuous interaction with its environment and has the objective to enforce outcomes, from this interaction, that satisfy some good properties. As the actions taken by the environment in this interaction are out of the direct control of the controller, those actions should be considered as adversarial. Indeed, a controller should be correct no matter how the environment in which it operates behaves. As reactive systems most often exhibit characteristics, like real-time constraints, concurrency, or parallelism, etc., which make them difficult to develop correctly, formal techniques have been advocated to help to their systematic design. One well-studied formal technique is model checking [3] which compares a model of a system with its specification. Model-checking either provides a proof of correctness of the model of the controller within its environment or provides a counter-example that can be used to improve the design.

A scientifically more challenging technique is *synthesis* that uses algorithms that transform the specification of a reactive system and a model of its environment into a correct system, i.e., a system that enforces the specification no matter how the environment behaves. Synthesis can take different forms: from computing optimal values of parameters to the full-blown automatic synthesis

This work was partially supported by the ERC Starting grant 279499 (inVEST), the ARC project "Non-Zero Sum Game Graphs: Applications to Reactive Synthesis and Beyond" (Fédération Wallonie-Bruxelles, J.-F. Raskin is Professeur Francqui de Recherche.

© Springer International Publishing AG 2017
L. Aceto et al. (Eds.): Larsen Festschrift, LNCS 10460, pp. 403–425, 2017.
DOI: 10.1007/978-3-319-63121-9_20

of a model of the system's components. Albeit this diversity, one mathematical model has emerged to perform synthesis for reactive systems: two-player zero-sum games played on graphs; and the main solution concept for those games is the notion of winning strategy. Zero-sum timed games played on timed automata (defined by [1]) have been introduced in [27] as a formal model for the synthesis of reactive systems with *timed specifications*. A practical algorithm for the problem was first presented in [17] and implemented in the tool UPPAAL-TIGA [5].

Timed games, as defined in [27] and in almost all subsequent works, see e.g. [2, 15–17], are zero-sum games. In zero-sum games, the environment is considered as *fully antagonist*. The zero-sum game abstraction is often used because it is *simple* and *sound*: a winning strategy against an antagonistic environment is winning against any environment including obviously those that strive to secure their own objective. But, in general the zero-sum hypothesis is a bold abstraction of reality: most often the environment has its own objective which, in general, does not correspond to that of falsifying the specification of the controller. Then, it should be clear that the zero-sum approach may fail to find a winning strategy even if solutions exist when the objective of the environment is taken into account, or it may produce sub-optimal solutions because those solutions are overcautious in order to be able to face with all possible behaviors of the environment, even if they are in contradiction with the environment's objectives. Recently, several new solution concepts for synthesis of reactive systems that take the objectives of the environment into account, and so relax the fully adversarial assumption, have been introduced [10]. One approach that is particularly promising is based on the notion of admissible strategies [7,11–13,23].

Assume Admissible Synthesis. In [12], we have introduced a new synthesis rule based on *admissibility* in the general case of n-player multiplayer games. This synthesis rule can be summarized as follows. For a player with objective ϕ, a strategy σ is dominated by σ' if σ' does as well as σ w.r.t. ϕ against all strategies of the other players, and better for some of those strategies. A strategy σ is *admissible* if it is not dominated by another strategy. Starting from the fact that only admissible strategies should be played by rational players (dominated strategies being clearly sub-optimal options), when synthesizing a controller, we search for an admissible strategy that is winning *against all admissible strategies* of the environment. Assume admissible synthesis is sound: if all players choose admissible strategies that are winning against all admissible strategies of the other players, the objectives of all players is guaranteed to be satisfied.

Assume Admissible Timed Synthesis. In the classical setting of game graphs with ω-regular objectives, admissibility is well behaved: admissible strategies always exist in perfect information n-player game graphs with ω-regular objectives, both for turn-based games [7,13,23] and for concurrent games [4]. By contrast, in this paper, we show that, in the *continuous time* semantics, players in a timed game are not guaranteed to have admissible strategies. This is because in some timed games there may not exist an optimal time to play. This is the case for example if a player has to play as soon as possible but strictly after a given deadline. We exhibit concrete games with this property. We also show that those problems are an artefact of the continuous time semantics. In contrast, in the discrete-time semantics of timed games, admissible strategies always exist.

To obtain our results in the discrete-time semantics we provide a reduction to finite concurrent games with an additional player that arbitrates situations in which several players propose to play at the exact same time. While the reduction to finite concurrent games is adequate to obtain theoretical results, it is not practical. This is why we define symbolic algorithms based on zones to solve the model-checking under admissible strategies and the assume admissible synthesis problem for safety objectives. To obtain those symbolic algorithms, we show how to use (continuous) timed zones to represent efficiently sets of discrete time valuations. We believe that those results are also interesting on their own. Note that it is possible to solve discrete-time games by enumerative techniques [25]; however, our algorithms require representing complex sets of states, so being able to solve a given game is not sufficient, and we do need some form of succinct representation.

Other Related Works. Related works on zero-sum timed games have been given above. To the best of our knowledge, our work is the first to deal with admissibility for timed games. In this paragraph we discuss several works related to admissibility in (untimed) games.

Other works in the literature propose the use of Nash equilibria (NE) in n-players non-zero sum games to model variants of the reactive synthesis problem. Most notably, assume-guarantee synthesis, based on secure equilibria [19] (refining Nash equilibria), has been proposed in [18], while cooperative rational synthesis has been proposed in [24], and non-cooperative rational synthesis in [26]. In the context of infinite duration games played on graphs, one well known limitation of Nash equilibria is the existence of non-credible threats. Refinements of the notion of NE, like sub-game perfect equilibria (SPE), have been proposed to overcome this limitation. SPE for games played on graphs have been studied in e.g. [14,29]. Admissibility does not suffer from this limitation. In [23], Faella proposes several alternatives to the notion of winning strategy including the notion of admissible strategy. His work is for two-players but only the objective of one player is taken into account, the objective of the other player is left unspecified. In that work, the notion of admissibility is used to define a notion of best-effort in synthesis. The notion of admissible strategy is definable in strategy logics [20,28] and decision problems related to the assume-admissible rule can be reduced to satisfiability queries in such logics. This reduction does not lead to worst-case optimal algorithms; we presented worst-case optimal algorithms in [21] based on our previous work [13].

The only works that we are aware of and that consider non-zero sum timed games are the following two papers [8,9] that study decision problems related to the concept of Nash equilibria and not to the concept of admissibility.

2   Admissibility in Concurrent Games

Let $P = \{1, 2, \ldots n\}$ denote a set of players. A *concurrent game* played by players P is a tuple $\mathcal{G} = (S, s_{\text{init}}, \Sigma, (\mathsf{M}_i)_{i \in P}, \delta)$ where,

- S is a set of *states*, and $s_{\text{init}} \in S$ the *initial state*;
- Σ is a set of *moves*;
- For all $i \in P, \mathsf{M}_i : S \to 2^\Sigma \setminus \{\emptyset\}$ assigns to every state $s \in S$ and player i the set of *available moves* from state s.
- $\delta : S \times \Sigma \times \ldots \times \Sigma \to S$ is the *transition function*.

The game is called *finite* if S and Σ are finite. We write $\mathsf{M}(s) = \mathsf{M}_1(s) \times \ldots \times \mathsf{M}_n(s)$ for every $s \in S$. A *history* is a finite path $h = s_1 s_2 \ldots s_N \in S^*$ such that (i) $N \in \mathbb{N}$; (ii) $s_1 = s_{\text{init}}$; and (iii) for every $2 \leq k \leq N$, there exists $(a_1, \ldots, a_n) \in \mathsf{M}(s_{k-1})$ with $s_k = \delta(s_{k-1}, a_1, \ldots, a_n)$. A *run* is defined similarly as a history except that its length is infinite. For a history or a run ρ, let us denote its i-th state by ρ_i. The game is played from the initial state s_{init} for an infinite number of rounds, producing a run. At each round $k \geq 1$, with current state s_k, all players i select simultaneously moves $a_i \in \mathsf{M}_i(s_k)$, and the state $\delta(s_k, a_1, \ldots, a_n)$ is appended to the current history.

It is often convenient to consider a player i separately and see the set of other players $P \setminus \{i\}$ as a single player denoted $-i$. Hence, the set of moves of $-i$ in state s is $\mathsf{M}_{-i}(s) = \prod_{j \in P \setminus \{i\}} \mathsf{M}_j(s)$.

An *objective* ϕ is a subset of runs of the game. We assume that concurrent games are equipped with a function Φ mapping all players $i \in P$ to an objective $\Phi(i)$. Thus, a run ρ is winning for player i iff $\rho \in \Phi(i)$. An objective $\phi \subseteq S^\omega$ is a *simple safety* objective if there exists $B \subseteq S$ such that $\rho \in \phi$ if, and only if $\forall j, \rho_j \notin B$; and for all $s \in B$ and $m \in \mathsf{M}(s), \delta(s, m) \in B$. In other terms, once B is reached, the play never leaves B. The set B is informally called *bad states* for the objective ϕ. Note that contrary to general safety objectives, simple safety objectives are prefix independent. Also, any safety objective can be turned into a simple safety objective by modifying the underlying concurrent game. Games equipped with simple safety objectives are called *simple safety games*.

A *strategy* for player i is a function σ from histories to moves of player i such that for all histories h: $\sigma(h) \in \mathsf{M}_i(s)$ where s is the last state of h. We denote by $\Gamma_i(\mathcal{G})$ the set of player i's strategies in the game; we might omit $\mathcal{G}$ if it is clear from context. A *strategy profile* $\boldsymbol{\sigma}$ for a subset $A \subseteq P$ of players is a tuple $(\sigma_i)_{i \in A}$ with $\sigma_i \in \Gamma_i$ for all $i \in A$. When the set of players A is omitted, we assume $A = P$. Let $\boldsymbol{\sigma} = (\sigma_i)_{i \in P}$ be a strategy profile. Then, for all players i, we let $\boldsymbol{\sigma}_{-i}$ denote the restriction of $\boldsymbol{\sigma}$ to $P \setminus \{i\}$ (hence, $\boldsymbol{\sigma}_{-i}$ can be regarded as a strategy of player $-i$ that returns, for all histories h, a move from $\mathsf{M}_{-i}(s)$ where s is the last state of h). We denote by Γ_{-i} the set $\{\boldsymbol{\sigma}_{-i} \mid \boldsymbol{\sigma} \in \Gamma\}$. We sometimes denote by $\boldsymbol{\sigma}$ the pair $(\sigma_i, \boldsymbol{\sigma}_{-i})$. For any history h, let $\boldsymbol{\sigma}(h) = (\sigma_i(h))_{i \in A}$ and be the tuple of choices made by all players (when they play from h according to $\boldsymbol{\sigma}$) and the resulting state, respectively. We let $\mathtt{Out}(\boldsymbol{\sigma})$ be the *outcome* of $\boldsymbol{\sigma}$, i.e. the unique run $\rho = s_1 s_2 \cdots$ such that $s_k = \delta(s_{k-1}, \boldsymbol{\sigma}(s_1 \cdots s_{k-1}))$.

Assume the game we consider has winning condition Φ. Then, we say that σ *is winning for i, from h*, written $\sigma \models_h \Phi(i)$, if h is a prefix of $\mathrm{Out}(\sigma)$ and $\mathrm{Out}(\sigma) \in \Phi(i)$. We write $\sigma \models_h \Phi(i)$, if for every $\tau \in \Gamma_{-i}$ such that h is a prefix of $\mathrm{Out}((\sigma, \tau))$ it holds that $\mathrm{Out}((\sigma, \tau)) \in \Phi(i)$.

Dominance and Admissibility. Fix a game $\mathcal{G}$ and a player i. Given two strategies $\sigma, \sigma' \in \Gamma_i$, we say that σ is *weakly dominated* by σ', denoted $\sigma \preccurlyeq \sigma'$ if for all $\sigma_{-i} \in \Gamma_{-i}, (\sigma, \sigma_{-i}) \models \Phi(i)$ implies $(\sigma', \sigma_{-i}) \models \Phi(i)$. Intuitively, this means that σ' is *not worse* than σ, because it yields a winning outcome (for i) every time σ does. When $\sigma \preccurlyeq \sigma'$ but $\sigma' \not\preccurlyeq \sigma$ we say that σ is *dominated* by σ'. Note that $\sigma \prec \sigma'$ if and only if $\sigma \preccurlyeq \sigma'$ and there exists at least one $\sigma_{-i} \in \Gamma_{-i}$, such that $(\sigma, \sigma_{-i}) \not\models \Phi(i)$ and $(\sigma', \sigma_{-i}) \models \Phi(i)$. That is, σ' is now *strictly better* than σ because it yields a winning outcome for i every time σ does; but i secures a winning outcome against at least one strategy of the other players by playing σ' instead of σ. A strategy is called *admissible* if it is not dominated.

Theorem 1 [4]. *For every finite concurrent game, for all objectives, the set of admissible strategies of each player is non-empty.*

Now that we have defined a notion of dominance on *strategies*, let us turn our attention to a more local definition of dominance on *moves*. Let h be a history. We say that a move $a \in M_i$ is *h-dominated* by another move $a' \in M_i$ iff for all $\sigma \in \Gamma_i$ s.t. $\sigma(h) = a$, there exists $\sigma' \in \Gamma_i$ s.t. $\sigma'(h) = a'$ and $\sigma \prec_h \sigma'$. We denote this by $a <_h a'$. If a move a is not h-dominated by any move, we say that a is *h-admissible*. This allows us to define a more local notion of dominated strategy: a strategy σ of player i is called *locally-admissible* (LA for short) if for every $h, \sigma(h)$ is an h-admissible move. By definition, all admissible strategies are also LA, but the converse only holds for simple safety games.

Theorem 2 [4]. *In concurrent finite simple safety games, a strategy is locally admissible if, and only if it is admissible.*

We close these preliminaries by explaining how to associate *values* to histories and moves. First, the value of history h for player i is defined as follows. $\chi_h^i = 1$ if $\exists \sigma \in \Gamma_i \; \forall \sigma_{-i} \in \Gamma_{-i}, (\sigma_i, \sigma_{-i}) \models_h \Phi(i)$; $\chi_h^i = -1$ if $\forall \sigma \in \Gamma, \sigma \not\models_h \Phi(i)$; and $\chi_h^i = 0$ otherwise.

So the intuition is that: (i) $\chi_h^i = 1$ iff i has a winning strategy from h; (ii) $\chi_h^i = -1$ iff *no outcome* is winning for i from h; and (iii) $\chi_h^i = 0$ when i has no winning strategy from h but can still win with the help of other players. Thus, $\chi_h^i = -1$ is stronger than saying that i has no winning strategy from h, since, in this case, i can never win, even with the help of other players. When the other players can help, we have rather $\chi_h^i = 0$, which means that there is some strategy σ of i such that there is a profile σ with $\sigma_i = \sigma$ and $\sigma \models_h \Phi(i)$.

Lemma 1 [4]. *In finite concurrent games, for any player i, history h that ends in a state s, and moves $a, b \in M_i(s)$, we have $a <_h b$ if, and only if the conjunction of the following conditions holds:*

(i) $\chi^i_{h\delta(s,a,c)} \leq \chi^i_{h\delta(s,b,c)}$ *for every* $c \in \mathsf{M}_{-i}(s)$;

(ii) $\chi^i_{h\delta(s,a,c)} < \chi^i_{h\delta(s,b,c)}$ *for at least one* $c \in \mathsf{M}_{-i}(s)$;

(iii) *if* $\chi^i_{h\delta(s,a,c)} = \chi^i_{h\delta(s,b,c)} = 0$ *then* $\delta(s,a,c) = \delta(s,b,c)$, *for every* $c \in \mathsf{M}_{-i}(s)$.

3   Multi-player Timed Games

In this section, we define multiplayer timed games and apply previously defined admissibility notions to this setting.

Given a finite set of clocks X, we call the elements of $\mathbb{R}^X_{\geq 0}$ *valuations*, and those of $\mathbb{N}^X$ *discrete valuations*. Let $\mathbb{N}^X_{\leq M}$ denote the subset of $\mathbb{N}^X$ in which all components are bounded by M. For a subset $R \subseteq X$ and a valuation ν, $\nu[R \leftarrow 0]$ is the valuation defined by $\nu[R \leftarrow 0](x) = \nu(x)$ for $x \in X \setminus R$ and $\nu[R \leftarrow 0](x) = 0$ for $x \in R$. Given $d \in \mathbb{R}_{\geq 0}$ and a valuation ν, the valuation $\nu + d$ is defined by $(\nu + d)(x) = \nu(x) + d$ for all $x \in X$. We extend these operations to sets of valuations in the obvious way. We write $\mathbf{0}$ for the valuation that assigns 0 to every clock.

An *atomic clock constraint* over X is a formula of the form $k \leq x \leq l$ or $k \leq x - y \leq l$ where $x, y \in X, k, l \in \mathbb{Z} \cup \{-\infty, \infty\}$. A *guard* is a conjunction of atomic clock constraints. A valuation ν satisfies a guard g, denoted $\nu \models g$, if all constraints are satisfied when each $x \in X$ is replaced with $\nu(x)$. We write Φ_X for the set of guards built on X.

Let P be a finite a set of players. A *multi-player timed game* between players P is a tuple $\mathcal{G} = (\mathcal{L}, \iota, \mathcal{I}, X, (\Delta_i)_{i \in P})$ where (i) $\mathcal{L}$ is a finite set of *locations*, (ii) ι is the *initial location*, (iii) X is a finite set of *clocks*, (iv) $\mathcal{I} : \mathcal{L} \to \Phi(X)$ is the *invariant* associated to each location; we assume that invariants only contain upper bounds on clocks, (v) $\Delta_i \subseteq \mathcal{L} \times \Phi(X) \times 2^X \times \mathcal{L}$, the set of *Player-i edges*: in each tuple (ℓ, g, R, ℓ'), ℓ is the *source location*, g is the *guard*, R the *reset set*, and ℓ' the *target location*. For any edge $e \in \Delta_i$, let us denote by $(\ell_e, g_e, R_e, \ell'_e)$ the tuple associated to it.

The Discrete-Time Semantics. In this paper, timed games are equipped with a discrete time semantics described now. We explain later why problems happen when a continuous time semantics is considered instead.

In the *discrete-time* semantics, not only are all delays restricted to be discrete, but we also assume that each clock tick is globally observable by all players. Thus, at each clock tick, all players simultaneously decide either to wait another clock tick, or to take an enabled edge. The non-determinism between suggested edges is resolved by an additional player called *scheduler*.

Given state (ℓ, ν) and an edge $e = (\ell, g, R, \ell')$ such that $\nu \models g$, and $\nu[R \leftarrow 0] \models \mathcal{I}(\ell')$, let us write $(\ell', \nu') = \mathsf{Succ}_e((\ell, \nu))$ where $\nu' = \nu[R \leftarrow 0]$.

Consider a bound $M > 0$ larger than all constants that appear in the guards and define the operation $+_M$ by $a +_M b = \min(M, a + b)$ for every $a, b \in \mathbb{R}$. We define the semantics of a timed game $\mathcal{G} = (\mathcal{L}, \iota, \mathcal{I}, X, (\Delta_i)_{i \in P})$ as a concurrent game $\mathcal{D}_M(\mathcal{G}) = (S, s_{\mathsf{init}}, \Sigma, (\mathsf{M}_i)_{i \in P'}, \delta)$ where $P' = P \cup \{\mathsf{sched}\}$. Let $\mathfrak{S}(n)$ denote the set of permutations over $\{1, 2, \ldots, n\}$. We have $S = \{(\ell, \nu) \in \mathcal{L} \times \mathbb{N}^X_{\leq M} \mid \nu \models$

$\mathcal{I}(\ell)\}$, $\Sigma = \cup_{i\in P}\Delta_i \cup \{\bot\}\cup \mathfrak{S}(n)$ where $\bot$ is a fresh symbol. For every $(\ell,\nu)\in S$, and $i\in P$, we have $\mathsf{M}_i(\ell,\nu) = \{e\in\Delta_i \mid \nu \models g_e \wedge \mathcal{I}(\ell), \nu[R_e \leftarrow 0] \models \mathcal{I}(\ell'_e)\}\cup\{\bot \mid \nu+_M 1 \models \mathcal{I}(\ell)\}$. For player $\mathtt{sched}$, we have $\mathsf{M}_{\mathtt{sched}}(\ell,\nu) = \mathfrak{S}(|P|)$. Note that $\mathcal{D}_M(\mathcal{G})$ is a finite concurrent game due to the bound M.

The transition function δ is defined from the current state (ℓ,ν) given moves $m_1,\dots,m_n$ chosen by the players of P and a permutation π chosen by the scheduler as follows:

$$\delta((\ell,\nu),m_1,\dots,m_n,\pi) = \begin{cases} (\ell,\nu+_M 1) & \text{if } \forall i\in P, m_i = \bot, \\ (\ell',\nu') & \text{if } i = \arg\min_{j\in P:m_j\in\Delta_j}\pi(j), \\ & m_i = (\ell,g,R,\ell'), \nu' = \nu[R\leftarrow 0]. \end{cases}$$

The intuition of the game is that at each discrete time step, each player can choose either to wait, or to switch state by picking an edge. If several players pick edges, then the player $\mathtt{sched}$ determines, by the permutation it has chosen, which edge is to be taken. In general, one add fairness constraints for the scheduler by specifying an objective for this player. However, we consider safety objectives in the present work, for which fairness is not useful.

In the rest of the paper, we only consider timed games with non-strict guards, since any strict constraint can be converted into a non-strict one when working in discrete time.

We denote by $\Delta_i(s) = \mathsf{M}_i(s)\backslash\{\bot\}$ the set of edges of player i available in s and by $\Delta_{-i}(s) = \cup_{j\in P\backslash\{i\}}\mathsf{M}_j(s)\backslash\{\bot\}$ the other edges available in s.

Non-existence of Admissible Strategy in Continuous-Time Semantics. We now show that admissible strategies are not guaranteed to exist if one considers a continuous-time semantics instead of the discrete time semantics.

In the *continuous-time* semantics, all players simultaneously suggest moves that are pairs of delay and edges to be taken, and a move with the least delay is taken. The precise choice of the edge with the least delay is determined by an additional player, named *scheduler*, which determines a priority order between players.

Given a timed game $\mathcal{G} = (\mathcal{L},\iota,\mathcal{I},X,(\Delta_i)_{i\in P})$ we define an infinite-state concurrent game $\mathcal{C}(\mathcal{G}) = (S^c,\Sigma^c,s^c_{\mathsf{init}},(\mathsf{M}^c_i)_{i\in P'},\delta^c)$ where $P' = P\cup\{\mathtt{sched}\}$. We have $S^c = \{(\ell,\nu)\in\mathcal{L}\times\mathbb{R}^X_{\geq 0} \mid \nu\models\mathcal{I}(\ell)\}$. The moves are $\Sigma^c = \{(d,e)\mid d\in \mathbb{R}_{\geq 0}, e\in\cup_i\Delta_i\}\cup\mathfrak{S}(|P|)$, and $\mathsf{M}^c_i((\ell,\nu)) = \{(d,e)\mid d\geq 0, e\in\Delta_i, \nu+d\models g_e\cap\mathcal{I}(\ell)\wedge\nu[R_e\leftarrow 0]\models\mathcal{I}(\ell'_e)\}$. For player $\mathtt{sched}$, we have $\Sigma_{\mathtt{sched}}(\ell,\nu) = \mathfrak{S}(|P|)$. The initial state is $s^c_{\mathsf{init}} = (\iota,\mathbf{0})$. The transitions are defined as follows. Intuitively, each player in P suggests a pair (d,e) of delay and an edge, and player $\mathtt{sched}$'s choice determines which player's move is to be taken among those that have suggested the least delay. Formally, we have $\delta((\ell,\nu),(d_1,e_1),\dots,(d_n,e_n),\pi) = \mathsf{Succ}_{e_{i_0}}((\ell,\nu+d_{i_0}))$ where $i_0 = \arg\min_{i\in P:d_i=\min_{j\in P}d_j}\pi(i)$.

Consider the game on the left in Fig. 1 where the safety objective of player P1 is to avoid location $\mathtt{BAD}_1$. Consider any move (t,e) of P1, the move $(t/2,e)$ dominates (t,e) because any strategy of P2 that plays (t',e') either makes both moves winning if $t' > t$ (or $t = t'$ and P1 is scheduled); either makes both moves

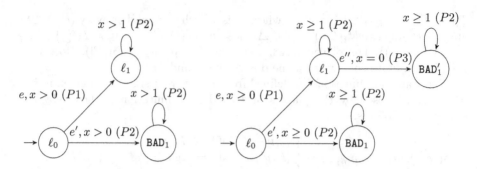

Fig. 1. Two timed games. Invariants are $x \leq 2$ everywhere.

losing if $t' < t/2$ (or $t = t'/2$ and P2 is scheduled); either makes $(t/2, e)$ wins and (t, e) loses otherwise. However, it can be seen that $(t/2, e)$ is also dominated by $(t/4, e)$, which is itself dominated, and so on. Thus, there is no admissible strategy in this game.

Here the non-existence of admissible strategy in the continuous time semantics is partly due to the presence of *open guards* (that is, involving strict inequalities only). With these guards, there is no minimal delay that players can choose. Unfortunately problems also occurs in games with *closed guards*. Consider the game on the right in Fig. 1. The same discussion holds for moves of P1 with positive delays, each such move is dominated by any move with strictly smaller but positive delays. This time there is a unique admissible strategy, the one that plays $(0, e)$. However, the move $(0, e)$ leads to the state $(\ell_1, 0)$ where player P3 can make P1 lose by going to the right, so the unique admissible strategy does not dominate the other strategies. Further, there exist safety conditions for P2 and P3 such that $(0, e)$ is arguably the worst possible move for P1 (e.g. P2 wants to avoid $\mathtt{BAD}_1 \wedge x = 0$ so does not play $(0, e')$ and P3 wants to avoid $\ell_1 \wedge x > 0$ so plays $(0, e'')$ in $(\ell_1, 0)$).

4   Admissible Strategies in Discrete Timed Games

Consider a game $\mathcal{D}_M(\mathcal{G})$ for some constant M, and simple safety objectives $(\phi_i)_{i \in P}$. We will only consider simple safety objectives, which are prefix-independent. Therefore, the value of a history only depends on its last state. For each player i, let us partition the state space S of $\mathcal{D}_M$ into $\mathtt{Win}_i = \{s \in S \mid \chi_s^i = 1\}$, $\mathtt{Maybe}_i = \{s \in S \mid \chi_s^i = 0\}$, $\mathtt{Lose}_i = \{s \in S \mid \chi_s^i = -1\}$.

For each player i and history h ending in a state s, a move $m \in \mathsf{M}_i(s)$ is said to be a *winning move* from h if there exists a winning strategy σ for Player i such that h is compatible with σ, and $\sigma(h) = m$.

We introduce the following notations. For any edge $e = (\ell, g, R, \ell')$, and set of states Z, let $\mathtt{Succ}_e(Z) = \{(\ell', \nu') \mid \exists (\ell, \nu) \in Z, \nu \models \mathcal{I}(\ell) \wedge g_e, \nu[R \leftarrow 0] = \nu', \nu' \models \mathcal{I}(\ell')\}$, which is the *immediate successors of Z through edge e*. We define the *immediate predecessors through e* as $\mathtt{Pred}_e(Z) = \{(\ell, \nu) \mid \nu \models g_e \wedge \mathcal{I}(\ell), \exists (\ell', \nu') \in$

$Z, \nu' \models \mathcal{I}(\ell'), \nu[R \leftarrow 0] = \nu'\}$, and *immediate predecessors for Players $I \subseteq P$* as $\mathtt{Pred}_I(Z) = \bigcup_{i \in I, e \in \Delta_i} \mathtt{Pred}_e(Z)$.

Lemma 1 applied to discrete-time semantics of Sect. 3 gives the following characterisation of dominance of moves in terms of values obtained in case the prescribed move is selected.

Theorem 3. *Consider any player i and state q of $\mathcal{D}_M(\mathcal{G})$. If $q \in \mathtt{Win}_i$, then exactly all winning moves from q are locally admissible. If $q \in \mathtt{Lose}_i$ then all available moves are locally admissible. Assume now that $q \in \mathtt{Maybe}_i$. A move $e \in \Delta_i(q)$ is locally admissible from q if, and only if either $\mathtt{Succ}_e(q) \in \mathtt{Win}_i$ or the following conditions hold*

- $\forall e' \in \mathsf{M}_i(q), \mathtt{Succ}_{e'}(q) \notin \mathtt{Win}_i,$
- $\mathtt{Succ}_e(q) \in \mathtt{Maybe}_i$, *or* $\perp \notin \mathsf{M}_i(q) \wedge \forall e' \in \Delta_i(q), \mathtt{Succ}_{e'} \in \mathtt{Lose}_i,$
- $q +_M 1 \in \mathtt{Win}_i \Rightarrow \exists e' \in \Delta_{-i}(q), \mathtt{Succ}_{e'}(q) \notin \mathtt{Win}_i \wedge \mathtt{Succ}_e(q) \neq \mathtt{Succ}_{e'}(q).$

Moreover, $\perp$ is locally admissible if, and only if, $\perp \in \mathsf{M}_i(q), \forall e \in \Delta_i(q), \mathtt{Succ}_e(q) \notin \mathtt{Win}_i$ and one of the following conditions holds.

1. $q +_M 1 \in \mathtt{Maybe}_i \cup \mathtt{Win}_i$, *and if $\exists e \in \Delta_i(q), \mathtt{Succ}_e(q) = q$ and $q +_M 1 = q$, then $\exists e' \in \Delta_{-i}(q), \mathtt{Succ}_{e'}(q) \notin \mathtt{Lose}_i$, and $\mathtt{Succ}_{e'}(q) \neq q$.*
2. $\forall e \in \Delta_i(q)$ *such that $\mathtt{Succ}_e(q) \in \mathtt{Maybe}_i$, we have that $\exists e' \in \Delta_{-i}(q)$, with $\mathtt{Succ}_{e'}(q) \notin \mathtt{Lose}_i$ and $\mathtt{Succ}_{e'}(q) \neq \mathtt{Succ}_e(q).$*

Proof. Let us show that moves satisfying the above properties are locally admissible. We consider history h ending in some state $q \in \mathtt{Maybe}_i$ which is the only non-trivial case.

Let us start with the following simple but useful remark.

Remark 1. Consider any state $q, c \in \mathsf{M}_{-i}(q), e, e' \in \Delta_i(q)$. Then, either $\delta(q, e, c) = \mathtt{Succ}_e(q)$ and $\delta(q, e', c) = \mathtt{Succ}_{e'}(q)$ or $\delta(q, e, c) = \delta(q, e', c)$.

- Consider $e \in \mathsf{M}_i(q)$ where $\mathtt{Succ}_e(q) \in \mathtt{Win}_i$. If $e <_h e'$, by Remark 1 and Lemma 1 item (i), we must have $\mathtt{Succ}_{e'}(q) \in \mathtt{Win}_i$ too. But by the same remark, item (ii) of Lemma 1 cannot hold, which shows $e \not<_h e'$.
- Consider $e \in \mathsf{M}_i(q)$ with $\mathtt{Succ}_e(q) \in \mathtt{Maybe}_i$, and assume $\forall e' \in \mathsf{M}_i(q), \mathtt{Succ}_{e'}(q) \notin \mathtt{Win}_i$.
  - Assume $e <_h e'$. If $\mathtt{Succ}_e(q) = \mathtt{Succ}_{e'}(q)$, then e' cannot dominate e by Remark 1 and Lemma 1 item (ii). Otherwise, by assumption, $\mathtt{Succ}_{e'}(q) \notin \mathtt{Win}_i$. If $\mathtt{Succ}_{e'}(q) \in \mathtt{Lose}_i$, then $e \not<_h e'$ by Lemma 1 item (i). If $\mathtt{Succ}_{e'}(q) \in \mathtt{Maybe}_i$, since $\mathtt{Succ}_e(q) \neq \mathtt{Succ}_{e'}(q)$, we have $e \not<_h e'$ by Lemma 1, item (iii).
  - Assume $\perp \in \mathsf{M}_i(q)$ and $e <_h \perp$.
    - Consider the case $q +_M 1 \notin \mathtt{Win}_i$. Let $c \in \mathsf{M}_{-i}(q)$ be such that all players wait. Then, $\delta(q, \perp, c) = q +_M 1 \notin \mathtt{Win}_i$, while $\delta(q, e, c) = \mathtt{Succ}_e(q) \in \mathtt{Maybe}_i$. Assume $q +_M 1 \neq q$. Then, we also have $q +_M 1 \neq \mathtt{Succ}_e(q)$, so $e \not<_h \perp$ by Lemma 1, item (iii).

Assume $q +_M 1 = q$. If $\mathsf{Succ}_e(q) \neq q$, then we conclude similarly as above since $\mathsf{Succ}_e(q) \in \mathsf{Maybe}_i$. Assume $\mathsf{Succ}_e(q) = q$. Since $q \notin \mathsf{Win}_i$, there must be an edge $e' \in \Delta_{-i}(q)$, such that $q \neq \mathsf{Succ}_{e'}(q) \notin \mathsf{Win}_i$. If $c \in \mathsf{M}_{-i}(q)$ denotes the profile which gives Player i priority, and otherwise chooses e', we have $\delta(q, e, c) = q$, and $\delta(q, \perp, c) = \mathsf{Succ}_{e'}(q) \neq q$. This shows that $e \not<_h \perp$: if $\mathsf{Succ}_{e'}(q) \in \mathsf{Lose}_i$, this follows by item (i) of Lemma 1, and if $\mathsf{Succ}_{e'}(q) \in \mathsf{Maybe}_i$, by item (iii).

- Consider now the case $q +_M 1 \in \mathsf{Win}_i$, and let $e' \in \Delta_{-i}(q)$ such that $\mathsf{Succ}_{e'}(q) \notin \mathsf{Win}_i \wedge \mathsf{Succ}_e(q) \neq \mathsf{Succ}_{e'}(q)$. Let $c \in \mathsf{M}_{-i}(q)$ which gives priority to Player i, and otherwise picks e'. We thus have $\delta(q, e, c) \neq \delta(q, \perp, c)$ and neither of them are winning, while $\delta(q, e, c) \in \mathsf{Maybe}_i$. So, by Lemma 1, $e \not<_h \perp$.

Consider the delays. Assume that $\perp \in \mathsf{M}_i(q)$, and $\forall e \in \mathsf{M}_i(q), \mathsf{Succ}_e(q) \notin \mathsf{Win}_i$.

- Assume $q +_M 1 \in \mathsf{Maybe}_i \cup \mathsf{Win}_i$ and fix $e \in \Delta_i(q)$. If $q +_M 1 \in \mathsf{Win}_i$ or $\mathsf{Succ}_e(q) \in \mathsf{Lose}_i$, then, we cannot have $\perp <_h e$ by case (i) of Lemma 1. Assume that both belong to Maybe_i. Whenever $q +_M 1 \neq q$ or $\mathsf{Succ}_e(q) \neq q$, we have $q +_M 1 \neq \mathsf{Succ}_e(q)$ for any target location and reset set e might have, which entails $\perp \not<_h e$ by Lemma 1, item (iii). Assume now that $q +_M 1 = q$ and $\mathsf{Succ}_e(q) = q$. In this case, there is $e' \in \Delta_{-i}(q), \mathsf{Succ}_{e'}(q) \in \mathsf{Maybe}_i \cup \mathsf{Win}_i, \mathsf{Succ}_{e'}(q) \neq q$. For $c \in \mathsf{M}_{-i}(q)$ which gives priority to Player i, and otherwise chooses e', we have $\delta(q, \perp, c) = \mathsf{Succ}_{e'}(q)$ and $\delta(q, e, c) = q$. If $\delta(q, \perp, c)$ has value 1, then $\perp \not<_h e$ by Lemma 1 item (i); and if it has value $0, \perp \not<_h e$ follows from Lemma 1, item (iii) since $\mathsf{Succ}_{e'}(q) \neq q$.

- Assume that $\forall e \in \Delta_i(q)$ such that $\mathsf{Succ}_e(q) \in \mathsf{Maybe}_i$, we have that $\exists e' \in \Delta_{-i}(q)$, with $\mathsf{Succ}_{e'}(q) \notin \mathsf{Lose}_i$ and $\mathsf{Succ}_{e'}(q) \neq \mathsf{Succ}_e(q)$.

  Assume that $\perp <_h e$. If $\mathsf{Succ}_e(q) \in \mathsf{Lose}_i$, then item (ii) of Lemma 1 cannot be satisfied which contradicts $\perp <_h e$. Suppose that $\mathsf{Succ}_e(q) \in \mathsf{Maybe}_i$, and let $e' \in \Delta_{-i}(q)$ given by the above property. Let $c \in \mathsf{M}_{-i}(q)$ which gives Priority to i, and otherwise chooses e'. We have that $\delta(q, \perp, c) = \mathsf{Succ}_{e'}(q) \in \mathsf{Maybe}_i \cup \mathsf{Win}_i$ while $\delta(q, e, c) = \mathsf{Succ}_e(q) \in \mathsf{Maybe}_i$. If $\mathsf{Succ}_e(q) \in \mathsf{Lose}_i$ or $\mathsf{Succ}_{e'}(q) \in \mathsf{Win}_i$, this contradicts $\perp <_h e$ by item (i) of Lemma 1; and if $\mathsf{Succ}_e(q) \in \mathsf{Maybe}_i$, by item (iii) since $\mathsf{Succ}_e(q) \neq \mathsf{Succ}_{e'}(q)$.

We now show the other direction. We prove that any move that does not satisfy the conditions is locally dominated. Consider any history h ending in q, and $e \in \Delta_i(q)$ that satisfies $\mathsf{Succ}_e(q) \notin \mathsf{Win}_i$ and

$$\exists e' \in \Delta_i(q), \mathsf{Succ}_{e'}(q) \in \mathsf{Win}_i$$
$$\vee$$
$$\mathsf{Succ}_e(q) \notin \mathsf{Maybe}_i \wedge (\perp \in \mathsf{M}_i(q) \vee \exists e' \in \Delta_i(q), \mathsf{Succ}_{e'}(q) \in \mathsf{Maybe}_i)$$
$$\vee$$
$$q +_M 1 \in \mathsf{Win}_i \wedge \forall e' \in \Delta_{-i}(q), (\mathsf{Succ}_{e'}(q) \in \mathsf{Win}_i \vee \mathsf{Succ}_e(q) = \mathsf{Succ}_{e'}(q)).$$

- Case $\exists e' \in \mathsf{M}_i(q), \mathsf{Succ}_{e'}(q) \in \mathsf{Win}_i$. We have $e <_h e'$ by Remark 1. In fact, if Player i's move is selected given some $c \in \mathsf{M}_{-i}(q)$, from $\delta(q, e, c)$, he can continue with a winning strategy, although from $\delta(q, e', c)$ he can lose. If another player's move is selected, then the successors are identical.

- Case $\mathrm{Succ}_e(q) \notin \mathrm{Maybe}_i \wedge (\bot \in M_i(q) \vee \exists e' \in \Delta_i(q), \mathrm{Succ}_{e'}(q) \in \mathrm{Maybe}_i)$. This means that $\mathrm{Succ}_e(q) \in \mathrm{Lose}_i$. We distinguish two cases. If such an e' exists, then it is clear that $e <_h e'$ by Remark 1. Let us assume that no such e' exists and $\bot \in M_i(q)$.

  Define a move $c \in M_{-i}(q)$ as follows. If there exists $e' \in \Delta_j$ for some $j \in P$ such that $\mathrm{Succ}_{e'}(q) \in \mathrm{Maybe}_i \cup \mathrm{Win}_i$, then $c_j = e', c_k = \bot$ for all $k \neq i, j$; and sched gives priority to i, and then to j. Notice that all players k can wait since $\bot \in M_i(q)$. Otherwise, let $\forall k \in P, c_k = \bot$, and sched is arbitrary. Since $q \in \mathrm{Maybe}_i$, we have $\delta(q, \bot, c) \in \mathrm{Maybe}_i \cup \mathrm{Win}_i$ in all cases. We show that $e <_h \bot$ using Lemma 1. Notice that $\chi^i_{\delta(h,e,c)} < \chi^i_{\delta(h,\bot,c)}$ since e moves to Lose_i, and $\chi^i_{\delta(h,\bot,c)} \geq 0$ by the previous remark. This shows (ii). Furthermore, for all $c \in M_{-i}(q), \chi^i_{h\delta(h,e,c)} \leq \chi^i_{h\delta(h,\bot,c)}$ since either Player i's edge is picked and the inequality is strict, or another move is picked and the successor states are identical in both cases (Remark 1). This shows (i) and (iii), proving $e <_h \bot$.

- Case $q +_M 1 \in \mathrm{Win}_i$ and for all $e' \in \Delta_{-i}(q)$, either $\mathrm{Succ}_{e'}(q) \in \mathrm{Win}_i$ or $\mathrm{Succ}_e(q) = \mathrm{Succ}_{e'}(q)$. Here, we show that $e <_h \bot$. Note that $q +_M 1 \in \mathrm{Win}_i$ means $\bot \in M_i(q)$. Item (i) of Lemma 1 is satisfied since for all $c \in M_{-i}(q)$, either $\delta(q, e, c) = \delta(q, \bot, c)$ or $\delta(q, \bot, c) \in \mathrm{Win}_i$. Item (iii) follows from this remark. Moreover, $q +_M 1$ is a possible successor under $\bot$, which shows item (ii).

Consider the move $\bot$ from history h ending in q with $\bot \in M_i(q)$, such that either $\exists e \in \Delta_i(q), \mathrm{Succ}_e(q) \in \mathrm{Win}_i$ or we have the conjunction of the following:

(a) $q +_M 1 \in \mathrm{Lose}_i$, or $q +_M 1 = q$ and $\exists e \in \Delta_i(q), \mathrm{Succ}_e(q) = q$ and $\forall e' \in \Delta_{-i}(q), \mathrm{Succ}_{e'}(q) \in \mathrm{Lose}_i \vee \mathrm{Succ}_{e'}(q) = q$.

(b) $\exists e \in \Delta_i(q)$ with $\mathrm{Succ}_e(q) \in \mathrm{Maybe}_i$ and $\forall e' \in M_{-i}(q), \mathrm{Succ}_{e'}(q) \in \mathrm{Lose}_i \vee \mathrm{Succ}_{e'}(q) = \mathrm{Succ}_e(q)$.

  - If $\exists e \in \Delta_i, \mathrm{Succ}_e(q) \in \mathrm{Win}_i$, then $\bot <_h e$. In fact, whenever Player i has priority, the move e yields to a winning state; while if Player i waits, then either a delay or another edge $e' \in \Delta_{-i}(q)$ must yield to a state in $\mathrm{Maybe}_i \cup \mathrm{Lose}_i$ since $q \in \mathrm{Maybe}_i$.

  - Consider first the case $q +_M 1 \in \mathrm{Lose}_i$ and (b). We show that $\bot <_h e$. For all $c \in M_{-i}(q)$, by hypothesis, $\delta(q, \bot, c)$ is losing if $\delta(q, \bot, c) = q +_M 1$ or $\delta(q, \bot, c) = \mathrm{Succ}_{e'}(q) \in \mathrm{Lose}_i$ for some $e' \in \Delta_{-i}(q)$. Otherwise, if $\delta(q, \bot, c) = \mathrm{Succ}_{e'}(q) \notin \mathrm{Lose}_i$ then, we must have $\mathrm{Succ}_e(q) = \mathrm{Succ}_{e'}(q)$. This shows items (i) and (iii) of Lemma 1. Moreover, we have item (ii) since when all other players wait, $\delta(q, \bot, c) = q +_M 1 \in \mathrm{Lose}_i$ while $\delta(q, e, c) \in \mathrm{Maybe}_i$.

    Last, assume that $q +_M 1 = q$ and $\exists e \in \Delta_i(q), \mathrm{Succ}_e(q) = q$, and $\forall e' \in \Delta_{-i}(q), \mathrm{Succ}_{e'}(q) \in \mathrm{Lose}_i \vee \mathrm{Succ}_{e'}(q) = q$, and (b). This means that $\forall e' \in \Delta_{-i}(q), \mathrm{Succ}_{e'}(q) \in \mathrm{Lose}_i$ or $\mathrm{Succ}_{e'}(q) = q$. Observe also that since $q \in \mathrm{Maybe}_i$, and $q +_M 1 = q$, there must exist $e_0 \in \Delta_{-i}(q)$

with $q \neq \mathtt{Succ}_{e_0}(q) \in \mathtt{Lose}_i \cup \mathtt{Maybe}_i$ since otherwise q would be a winning state. It follows that $\mathtt{Succ}_{e_0}(q) \in \mathtt{Lose}_i$. Let us show $\bot <_h e$. Let $c \in \mathsf{M}_{-i}(q)$. If $\delta(q, \bot, c) \notin \mathtt{Lose}_i$, then $\delta(q, \bot, c) = q$, that is, either $\delta(q, \bot, c) \in \mathtt{Lose}_i$, or $\delta(q, \bot, c) = \delta(q, e, c)$. This shows item (i) and (iii) of Lemma 1. Moreover, if c gives Priority to i, and otherwise chooses e_0, we have $\delta(q, \bot, c) = \mathtt{Succ}_{e_0}(q) \in \mathtt{Lose}_i$ and $\delta(q, e, c) = q \in \mathtt{Maybe}_i$, which shows item (ii).   □

5   Computation Using Zones

We assume that clocks are bounded in all locations by an invariant:

Assumption 4. In all considered timed games, the invariant at each location implies $\bigcap_{x \in X} x < M$.

5.1   Zones and Difference-Bound Matrices

Formally, a *zone* Z is a convex subset of $\mathbb{R}_{\geq 0}^X$ definable by a conjunction of constraints of the form $x \bowtie k, l \bowtie x$, or $x - y \bowtie m$ where $x, y \in X, k, l \in \mathbb{N}_{\geq 0}, m \in \mathbb{Z}$, and $\bowtie \in \{<, \leq\}$.

We recall a few basic operations defined on zones. Let $Z{\uparrow}$ denote the time-successors of Z, i.e., $Z{\uparrow} = \{\nu \in \mathbb{R}_{\geq 0}^X \mid \exists \nu' \in Z, \exists t \geq 0, \nu = \nu' + t\}$; and similarly the time-predecessors are $Z{\downarrow} = \{\nu \in \mathbb{R}_{\geq 0}^X \mid \exists t \geq 0, \nu + t \in Z\}$. For $R \subseteq X$, we define $Z[R \leftarrow 0] = \{\nu \in \mathbb{R}_{\geq 0}^X \mid \exists \nu' \in Z, \nu = \nu'[R \leftarrow 0]\}$, and $\mathtt{Free}_R(Z) = \{\nu \in \mathbb{R}_{\geq 0}^X \mid \nu[R \leftarrow 0] \in Z\}$. Intersection is denoted $Z \cap Z'$. It is well known that zones are closed under all these operations [6].

Zones can be represented by *difference-bound matrices (DBM)* which are $|X_0| \times |X_0|$-matrices with values in $\mathbb{Z} \times \{<, \leq\}$ [22], where $X_0 = X \cup \{0\}$. Here 0 is seen as a clock whose value is always 0. Intuitively, each component $(x, y) \in X_0 \times X_0$ of a DBM stores a bound on the difference $x - y$. We use the following notations to access to components of a DBM D. For $x, y \in X_0$, let the component (x, y) be written as $(D_{x,y}, \prec_{x,y}^D)$. For any DBM D, let $[\![D]\!]$ denote the zone it defines. The DBM D is *reduced* if no constraint can be made tighter without changing the defined zone. This is true when the following inequalities are satisfied: for all $x, y, z \in X_0, (D_{x,y}, \prec_{x,y}^D) < (D_{x,z}, \prec_{x,z}^D) + (D_{z,y}, \prec_{z,y}^D)$ where we define $(a, \prec) + (b, \prec') = (a + b, \prec'')$ with $\prec'' = <$ if, and only if $\prec = <$ or $\prec' = <$; while $(a, \prec) < (b, \prec')$ if $a < b$ or $a = b$ and either $\prec = \prec'$ or $\prec = <$ and $\prec' = \leq$. Every DBM can be made reduced using shortest path algorithms. We refer the reader to [6] for details on operations on DBMs.

We define an *extended DBM* as a pair (ℓ, Z) where ℓ is a location and Z a zone. Let $[\![(\ell, Z)]\!]$ denote the set $\{\ell\} \times [\![Z]\!]$. By a slight abuse of notation, we will use the same operations for DBMs as for zones, for instance, we will write $D' = D{\uparrow}$ where D and D' are DBMs such that $[\![D']\!] = [\![D]\!]{\uparrow}$. In this case, D' can be computed using algorithms described in [6]. Successors and predecessors of zones are zones as well, and can be computed efficiently using DBMs. Let us consider an extended state (ℓ, Z) and an edge $e = (\ell, g, R, \ell')$. We define $\text{Succ}_e((\ell, Z)) = \cup_{q \in [\![(\ell, Z)]\!]} \text{Succ}_e(q)$, and $\text{Pred}_e((\ell', Z)) = \{\ell\} \times \{\nu \mid \nu \models g, \nu[R \leftarrow 0] \in [\![Z]\!]\}$. A DBM (resp. a zone) is closed if the set it defines is topologically closed. Equivalently, a closed DBM can be defined using a conjunction of non-strict constraints.

A *federation* is a list of DBMs $F = \cup_i D_i$, and defines the set $[\![F]\!] = \cup_i [\![D_i]\!]$. We define the complement of a zone Z in $\mathbb{R}^X_{\geq 0}$ as $\overline{Z}$. If a zone is represented as a DBM D, its complement can be computed as a federation, denoted $\overline{D}$; that is, $[\![\overline{D}]\!] = \overline{[\![D]\!]}$. By extension, we also call an *extended federation* a union of extended zones. Given an extended federation F and location ℓ, we denote by $\ell \cap F$ the set $\{\ell\} \times \mathbb{R}^X_{\geq 0} \cap F$; thus, each location ℓ denotes an extended zone at that location with no constraint on clocks. A *closed federation* is a federation whose DBMs are closed. We extend all operations on DBMs to federations by applying them on all elements of the federation. For instance, $F\downarrow = \cup_i D_i \downarrow$; while intersection is defined by $(\cup_i D_i) \cap (\cup_j D'_j) = \cup_{i,j} D_i \cap D'_j$. For the complement, we set $\overline{F} = \cap_i \overline{D_i}$.

In order to consider the discrete-time semantics, let us define $[\![Z]\!]_d = \{\nu \in \mathbb{N}^{X_0} \mid \nu \models Z\}$. In other terms, $[\![Z]\!]_d = \mathbb{N}^{X_0} \cap [\![Z]\!]$. Given any DBM D, let $\text{closed}(D)$ denote the largest closed zone contained in D. Formally, we have $D' = \text{closed}(D)$ where for all i, j, $D_{i,j} = D'_{i,j}$ if the latter is a non-strict constraint, and $D_{i,j} = (a - 1, \leq)$ if $D'_{i,j} = (a, <)$. Intuitively, the $\text{closed}(D)$ returns a closed DBM whose discrete valuations are identical to those of D. Notice that $\text{closed}(D)$ can be empy although D is not. For any zone Z, let $\overline{Z}^d = \mathbb{N}^X \setminus Z$; and we extend this notation to DBMs and federations. We also define discrete time-successors as $Z\uparrow^d = \{\nu + d \mid d \in \mathbb{N}, \nu \in Z\}$, and $Z\downarrow^d = \{\nu \mid \exists d \in \mathbb{N}, \nu + d \in Z\}$. Similarly, let $\text{Free}^d_R(Z) = \{\nu \in \mathbb{N}^X \mid \nu[R \leftarrow 0] \in Z\}$.

Lemma 2. *Let Z, Z' be DBMs and $R \subseteq X$. The following properties hold.*

- $[\![\text{closed}(Z)]\!]_d = [\![Z]\!]_d,$
- $\overline{[\![Z]\!]_d}^d = [\![\text{closed}(\overline{Z})]\!]_d,$
- $[\![Z]\!]_d \cap [\![Z']\!]_d = [\![Z \cap Z']\!]_d,$
- $\text{Free}^d_R([\![Z]\!]_d) = [\![\text{Free}_R(Z)]\!]_d,$
- *if Z is closed,* $[\![Z]\!]_d[R \leftarrow 0] = [\![Z[R \leftarrow 0]]\!]_d,$
- *if Z is closed,* $[\![Z]\!]_d\downarrow^d = [\![Z\downarrow]\!]_d,$
- *if Z is closed,* $[\![Z]\!]_d\uparrow^d = [\![Z\uparrow]\!]_d.$

Closed federations are closed under all above operations.

Thanks to the above lemma, we will represent sets of discrete states using DBMs. Intuitively, we let a closed zone represent the set of discrete valuations it contains, while the lemma ensures that basic operations applied on the zone corresponds to the corresponding operations in the discrete semantics.

Note that all operations but complementation are continuous, thus preserve closedness. Since all guards are closed in the discrete-time setting, the successor and predecessor operators are defined identically to the continuous case, without using the $\texttt{closed}$ operator. That is, given extended zone (ℓ, Z) where Z is represented by closed DBM D, and edge $e = (\ell, g, R, \ell')$, $[\![\texttt{Succ}_e((\ell, Z))]\!]_\mathsf{d} = \{(\ell', \nu') \in \mathcal{L} \times \mathbb{N}^X \mid \nu \models g \wedge \mathcal{I}(\ell), \nu[R_e \leftarrow 0] = \nu' \models \mathcal{I}(\ell')\}$, while this set can be computed by $(((D \cap g_e) \cap \texttt{Inv}(\ell))[R \leftarrow 0]) \cap \texttt{Inv}(\ell'))\!\uparrow \cap \texttt{Inv}(\ell')$, where $\texttt{Inv}$ is the extended federation defining for each ℓ the invariant $\texttt{Inv}(\ell)$ at location ℓ. The predecessors are computed similarly by $(\texttt{Free}_R(Z \cap \texttt{Inv}(\ell') \cap (R = 0)) \cap g_e \cap \texttt{Inv}(\ell))\!\downarrow \cap \texttt{Inv}(\ell)$.

5.2 Computing State Values

We show how to use a zone-based exploration to compute state values for each player. As in the previous section, we consider the extended federation $\texttt{Inv}$ which defines the set $\mathcal{I}$ of states that satisfy their locations' invariants, that is, $\mathcal{I} = [\![\texttt{Inv}]\!] = \cup_{\ell \in \mathcal{L}} \ell \times [\![\texttt{Inv}(\ell)]\!]$.

Given $B, G \subseteq S$. Let $\texttt{TPred}_i^\mathsf{d}(G, B) = \{q \in S \mid \exists d \in \mathbb{N}, q + d \in G, q + [0, d] \cap B = \emptyset\}$. This is the set of states which, by a discrete delay, can reach G while avoiding B in during the delay. One could also define $\texttt{TPred}_i^\mathsf{d}$ by fixing a unit delay $d = 1$, and repeating it. However, quantifying over $d \in \mathbb{N}$ will allow us to use DBMs to compute this operator efficiently.

We define $\pi_i^\mathsf{d}(Z) = \texttt{TPred}_i^\mathsf{d}(\texttt{Pred}_i(Z), \texttt{Pred}_{-i}(\overline{Z}^\mathsf{d}))$. Let us thus first state the set theoretic fixpoint defining the winning region in the discrete semantics. Below, ν is the greatest fixpoint operator; we will also use the least fixpoint operator μ.

Lemma 3. *For any timed game $\mathcal{G}$, player i, bad states B_i, we have* $\texttt{Win}_i = \nu Z. \overline{B_i}^\mathsf{d} \cap S \cap \pi_i^\mathsf{d}(Z)$.

When G and B are federations, we write $\texttt{TPred}_i^\mathsf{d}(G, B) = \texttt{TPred}_i^\mathsf{d}([\![G]\!]_\mathsf{d}, [\![B]\!]_\mathsf{d})$, and $\pi_i^\mathsf{d}(G) = \pi_i^\mathsf{d}([\![G]\!]_\mathsf{d})$. The following lemma is adapted from [17, Lemma 4].

Lemma 4. *Consider any timed game $\mathcal{G}$, player i, bad states B. Given closed federations $G = \cup_k G_k$ and $B = \cup_j B_j$ both contained in $\texttt{Inv}, \texttt{TPred}(G, B)$ can be computed as follows. $\texttt{TPred}^\mathsf{d}(G, B) = \bigcup_k \bigcap_j \texttt{TPred}^\mathsf{d}(G_k, B_j)$, where*

$$\texttt{TPred}^\mathsf{d}(G_k, B_j) = [\![\texttt{Inv} \cap \left((G_k\!\downarrow \cap \overline{B_j\!\downarrow}^\mathsf{d}) \cup \left(G_k \cap (B_j\!\downarrow) \cap \overline{B_j}^\mathsf{d} \right)\!\downarrow \right)]\!]_\mathsf{d}.$$

It follows from Lemmas 2 and 4 that given a closed federation $F, \pi_i^\mathsf{d}(F)$ can be computed as a closed federation. Thus, $\texttt{Win}_i$ can be computed as an extended closed federation. The next lemma will show that $\texttt{Maybe}_i$ can also be computed as an extended closed federation.

We define the discrete variant of $\texttt{Pred}$ by $\texttt{Pred}_I^\mathsf{d}(Z) = \cup_{i \in I, e \in \Delta_i} \texttt{Pred}_e^\mathsf{d}(Z)$, where $\texttt{Pred}_e^\mathsf{d}(Z) = \{q \in S \mid \texttt{Succ}_e(q) \in Z\}$.

Lemma 5. *For any timed game $\mathcal{G}$, player i, bad states B_i, we have* $\texttt{Maybe}_i = \nu Z. \overline{B_i}^\mathsf{d} \cap S \cap \texttt{Pred}_P^\mathsf{d}(Z)\!\downarrow^\mathsf{d}$.

Last, the set $\texttt{Lose}_i$ can be computed as the complement of $\texttt{Win}_i \cup \texttt{Maybe}_i$.

We thus showed, in this section, that sets of states with a given value can be computed using federations.

6   Model Checking Under Admissibility

In this section, we show how to check whether all states reachable under admissible strategy profiles satisfy a given invariance property. Formally, the problem is stated as follows.

Problem 1 (Model Checking Under Admissibility). Given a timed game $\mathcal{G}$, simple safety objectives $(\phi_i)_{i\in P}$, and (arbitrary) safety property ϕ, check

$$\forall \sigma \in \prod_{i\in P} \mathrm{Adm}_i(\mathcal{D}_M(\mathcal{G})), \forall \sigma_{\mathsf{sched}} \in \Gamma_{\mathsf{sched}}, \mathrm{Out}(\mathcal{D}_M, \sigma, \sigma_{\mathsf{sched}}) \models \phi.$$

We describe a forward exploration algorithm using federations similar to the usual reachability algorithm except that both discrete transitions and time delays are modified so that only locally admissible moves are considered by players.

For $I \subseteq P$, let $\mathrm{Trap}_I(Z) = \cap_{i\in I}\mathrm{Pred}_i(\overline{Z}^{\mathsf{d}})$, that is, the set of states from which no player in I can avoid the set Z by choosing a move.

For a reduced DBM D, and $a, b \in \mathbb{N}$, define $\mathrm{Shift}_{a,b}(D) = D'$ as $D'_{i,j} = D_{i,j}$ for all $i, j \neq 0$; $D'_{i,0} = D_{i,0} + b$ and $D'_{0,i} = D_{0,i} - a$ for all $i \neq 0$. Notice that the resulting DBM D' may no more be reduced, so it must be made reduced.

Lemma 6. *Let D be a reduced DBM.*

- $[\![\mathrm{Shift}_{-1,-1}(D)]\!]_{\mathsf{d}} = \{\nu \in \mathbb{N}^X \mid \nu + 1 \in [\![D]\!]_{\mathsf{d}}\}$,
- $[\![\mathrm{Shift}_{0,-1}(D)]\!]_{\mathsf{d}} = \{\nu \in [\![D]\!]_{\mathsf{d}} \mid \nu + 1 \in [\![D]\!]_{\mathsf{d}}\}$,
- $[\![\mathrm{Shift}_{-1,0}(D)]\!]_{\mathsf{d}} = \{\nu \in \mathbb{N}^X \mid \nu \in [\![D]\!]_{\mathsf{d}} \vee \nu + 1 \in [\![D]\!]_{\mathsf{d}}\}$,
- $[\![\mathrm{Shift}_{0,1}(D)]\!]_{\mathsf{d}} = \{\nu \mid \nu \in [\![D]\!]_{\mathsf{d}} \vee \nu - 1 \in [\![D]\!]_{\mathsf{d}}\}$.

Constrained Guards. For any location ℓ and edge $e \in \Delta_i(\ell)$, let us define

$$W_e = \{(\ell, \nu) \in \mathrm{Win}_i \mid \nu \models g_e, \mathrm{Succ}_e((\ell, \nu)) \in \mathrm{Win}_i, \mathrm{Succ}_{-i}((\ell, \nu)) \in \mathrm{Win}_i\}.$$

In other terms, W_e is the set of states from which Player i can pick the transition $e \in \Delta_i$ which guarantees staying in Win_i.

Given two edges $e_i = (\ell_i, g_i, R_i, \ell'_i)$ for $i = 1, 2$, let us define the expression $\mathrm{Eq}(e_1, e_2) \equiv (\wedge_{x\in X}((x \in R_1 \cap R_2) \vee x = 0)) \wedge \ell'_1 = \ell'_2$. In other terms, $\mathrm{Eq}(e_1, e_2)$ are the set of states from which the successors through these edges are identical. Let us define

$$g'_e = g_e \wedge (\mathrm{Win}_i \Rightarrow W_e) \wedge (\mathrm{Maybe}_i \Rightarrow \mathrm{Pred}_e(\mathrm{Win}_i) \vee g''_e), \tag{1}$$

where

$$g''_e = \mathrm{Trap}_i(\mathrm{Lose}_i \cup \mathrm{Maybe}_i) \wedge \left(\mathrm{Pred}_e(\mathrm{Maybe}_i) \cup \overline{\mathrm{Shift}_{0,-1}(\mathrm{Inv})}^{\mathsf{d}} \wedge \mathrm{Trap}_i(\mathrm{Lose}_i)\right) \wedge$$
$$(\mathrm{Shift}_{-1,-1}(\mathrm{Win}_i) \Rightarrow (\vee_{e'\in\Delta_{-i}}\neg\mathrm{Eq}(e, e') \wedge \overline{\mathrm{Pred}_{e'}(\mathrm{Win}_i)})).$$

Lemma 7. *For any player $i \in P$, an edge $e = (\ell, g, R, \ell') \in \Delta_i$ is locally admissible at (ℓ, ν) if, and only if $\nu \models g'_e$.*

The proof follows immediately from Theorem 3.

Constrained Time Successors. For each location ℓ, and edge $e \in \Delta_i(\ell)$, define $G_e = \ell \wedge g_e$. For each player i, we define A^i, as the set of states from which waiting is locally admissible, as follows.

$$A^i = \mathtt{Shift}_{0,-1}(\mathtt{Inv}) \cap \left(\mathtt{Lose}_i \cup \mathtt{Shift}_{0,-1}(\mathtt{Win}_i) \cup \left(\mathtt{Maybe}_i \cap \overline{\mathtt{Pred}_i(\mathtt{Win}_i)} \cap (B^i \cup C^i) \right) \right), \quad (2)$$

where $B^i = \mathtt{Shift}_{-1,-1}(\mathtt{Win}_i \cup \mathtt{Maybe}_i)$ and

$$C^i = \bigcap_{e \in \Delta_i} \left(G_e \cap \mathtt{Pred}_e(\mathtt{Maybe}_i) \Rightarrow \bigcup_{e' \in \Delta_{-i}} G_{e'} \cap \overline{\mathtt{Pred}_{e'}(\mathtt{Lose}_i)} \cap \neg \mathtt{Eq}(e, e') \right).$$

Lemma 8. *Consider state q, and player $i \in P$. Move $\perp$ is locally admissible at q for player i if, and only if $q \in [\![A^i]\!]_\mathtt{d}$.*

Let $A = \cap_{i \in P} A^i$. Given set F, let $F \uparrow_A^d = \{ q \in S \mid \exists q' \in F, d \in \mathbb{N}, q' + d = q, q' + [0, d-1] \subseteq A \}$. Hence, this is the set of time successors of F which are reachable by staying inside A (except that the last state can be outside of A). Notice that all states of $F \uparrow_A^d$ satisfy the invariants.

Lemma 9. *For any set F, $F \uparrow_A^d = \mu Z.F \cup \mathcal{I} \cap \mathtt{Shift}_{0,1}(Z \cap A)$.*

Algorithm 1. Model checking under admissibility algorithm for safety properties

1: **Input:** Game $\mathcal{G}$, simple safety objectives $(\phi_i)_{i \in P}$, $M \in \mathbb{N}$, safety property ϕ
2: Let $\mathtt{Win}_i = \nu Z.\phi_i \cap \pi_i^d(Z)$, $\mathtt{Maybe}_i = \nu Z.\phi_i \cap \pi_P^d(Z)$, $\mathtt{Lose}_i = \overline{\mathtt{Win}_i \cup \mathtt{Maybe}_i}$
3: For all $i \in P$, let $\Delta_i' = \{ (\ell, g', R, \ell') \mid (\ell, g, R, \ell') \in \Delta_i \}$ where g' is defined (1).
4: Define A as in (2)
5: $\mathtt{Waiting} = \{ (\ell_0, \mathbf{0}) \}$
6: $\mathtt{Passed} = \emptyset$
7: **while** $\mathtt{Waiting} \neq \emptyset$ **do**
8:     Let $Z = \mathtt{Pop}(\mathtt{Waiting})$
9:     **if** $Z \not\models \phi$ **then**
10:         **return** False
11:     $\mathtt{Passed} = \mathtt{Passed} \cup \{Z\}$
12:     **for all** $i \in P, e \in \Delta_i'$ **do**
13:         $Z' = \mathtt{Succ}_{e'}(Z) \uparrow_A^d$
14:         **if** $\neg \exists Z'' \in \mathtt{Passed} \cup \mathtt{Waiting}, Z' \subseteq Z''$ **then**
15:             $\mathtt{Waiting} = \mathtt{Waiting} \cup \{Z'\}$
16: **return** True

Exploration. Now during the exploration, given any federation F in the waiting list, and edge e, we expand the search by $\mathtt{Succ}_{e'}(F)$ where e' is the edge e whose guard g_e is replaced by g_e'. We then compute its constrained time successors by restricting the delays to those states A where all players can indeed wait. The algorithm is summarized in Algorithm 1 Notice that Assumption 4 allows us to ensure the termination of the algorithm without using extrapolation operators.

7   Assume-Admissible Synthesis

We now show how to solve the assume-admissible synthesis problem.

Problem 2 (Assume-Admissible Synthesis). Given a timed game $\mathcal{G}$, simple safety objectives $(\phi_i)_{i \in P}$, check if for each player i,

$$\exists \sigma_i \in \text{Adm}_i(\mathcal{D}_M(\mathcal{G})), \forall \sigma_{-i} \in \text{Adm}_{-i}(\mathcal{D}_M(\mathcal{G})), \forall \sigma_{\text{sched}} \in \Gamma_{\text{sched}}, \text{Out}(\mathcal{D}_M, \sigma, \sigma_{\text{sched}}) \models \phi_i.$$

If for each player i, we manage to find an admissible strategy that is winning against all admissible strategy profiles of $-i$, then the combination of these strategies is a profile that satisfies all objectives. Note that players can choose their strategies arbitrarily among these winning ones without coordination with other players as long as other players choose admissible strategies. Let us call σ_i *assume-admissible-winning (AA-winning)* if it witnesses the above condition for Player i.

We are going to solve this problem by using the results of the previous section. In fact, we showed how to strengthen the guards of the edges of the timed automaton so that they are only taken by respective players if the corresponding move is locally admissible. We also characterized those states from which a delay is locally admissible for all players. It remains to show how to solve the game where all players are restricted to behave admissibly.

Given a timed game $\mathcal{G}$, let $\mathcal{G}'$ be obtained by strengthening the guards of all edges as in the previous section. Let A be the set from which waiting is locally admissible for all players, as defined in the previous section. For any set F of states, let us define the A -*constrained time-predecessors* as $F\!\downarrow_A^{\mathsf{d}} = \{q \in S \mid \exists d \in \mathbb{N}, q + d \in F, q + [0, d-1] \subseteq A\}$. Intuitively, this is precisely the set of states which can reach F by time delays while staying in A (except at the last state). This operator can be computed as follows.

Lemma 10. *For all sets* $F \subseteq \mathbb{R}_{\geq 0}^X$, $F\!\downarrow_A^{\mathsf{d}} = \mu Z.F \cup (A \cap \text{Shift}_{-1,0}(Z \cap \mathcal{I}))$.

We define $\text{TPred}_{A,i}^{\mathsf{d}}(G, B) = \{q \in S \mid \exists d \in \mathbb{N}, q + d \in G, q + [0, d] \cap B = \emptyset, q + [0, d-1] \subseteq A\}$. This defines the set of states from it is admissible for players to wait until reaching G while avoiding B.

Lemma 11. *Consider any timed game* $\mathcal{G}$, *player* i, *bad states* B. *Given closed federations* $G = \cup_k G_k$ *and* $B = \cup_j B_j$ *both implying* Inv, $\text{TPred}_{A,i}^{\mathsf{d}}(G, B)$ *can be computed as follows.* $\text{TPred}_{A,i}^{\mathsf{d}}(G, B) = \bigcup_k \bigcap_j \text{TPred}_{A,i}^{\mathsf{d}}(G_k, B_j)$, *where*

$$\text{TPred}_{A,i}^{\mathsf{d}}(G_k, B_j) = [\![\text{Inv} \cap \left((G_k\!\downarrow_A^{\mathsf{d}} \cap \overline{B_j\!\downarrow_A^{\mathsf{d}}}) \cup \left(G_k \cap (B_j\!\downarrow_A^{\mathsf{d}}) \cap \overline{B_j}^{\mathsf{d}} \right) \downarrow_A \right)]\!]^{\mathsf{d}}.$$

Let $\pi_{i,A}^{\mathsf{d}}(Z) = \text{TPred}_{A,i}^{\mathsf{d}}(\text{Pred}_i(Z), \text{Pred}_{-i}(\bar{Z}))$.

Theorem 5. *Let* $\mathcal{G}$ *be a game with simple safety objectives* $(\phi_i)_{i \in P}$. *Let* $\mathcal{G}'$ *be obtained by replacing each guard* g_e *by* g_e' *as defined in* (1). *Let* $W_i = \nu Z.\phi_i \cap S \cap \pi_{i,A}^{\mathsf{d}}(Z)$ *computed in* $\mathcal{G}'$. *Then, Player* i *has a AA-winning strategy in* $\mathcal{G}$ *if, and only if, the initial state belongs to* W_i.

8 Example: Synthesis of Train Controllers

We consider a one-way circular train network with n segments, and K trains. Each segment models either a station, or a part of the line between two stations. For safety reasons, each segment can accomodate at most one train. In order to optimize performance criteria, trains are allowed to independently regulate their travel time at each segment as long as they meet this safety critical requirement.

Model. We describe the system as a network of timed automata defining a discrete timed game with Boolean variables. Each segment j is modeled as in Fig. 2: it can be "occupied" by a train upon receiving event m_j, after which it is "freed" by the occupation of the next segment, by event m_{j+1}. The clock y_j stores the time elapsed since the latest train leaving.

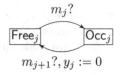

Fig. 2. Component for segment j

Each train i is modeled as a separate player, and its moves are defined by the component in Fig. 3. If the current state of the component is $s_{i,j}$ or $s'_{i,j}$, this means that the train i is at segment j. The train can attempt to move to segment $j+1$ by sending event m_{j+1} if it has spent at least 10 s in the current segment. This lower bound corresponds to the minimum travel time (with maximal speed) of a train over a segment. If 30 s have elapsed in a given segment, the train either has to move to the next segment, or enters state $s'_{i,j}$ from which at least one unit of time will elapse and the variable $\mathbf{err}_i$ will be set. In our model, the segments are passive, and they only react to actions received by trains.

For better readability, we use a particular synchronization semantics: we assume that an event m_i is only possible if three components synchronize on the action. That is, if a train enters from segment j to segment $j+1$, then the train sends $m_{j+1}!$, upon which the first segment is freed by $m_{j+1}?$, and the second one is occupied by $m_{j+1}?$

Each train controls the edges of its automaton, and the edges of the segments are only taken in synchronization with trains' edges. Thus, each transition in the overall system is controlled by a unique player (i.e. train).

We define the initial state by assigning each train i to an arbitrary segment j while respecting mutual exclusion: no pair of trains can be at the same segment. Moreover, the segment j is at state Occ_j if, and only if some train is in state s_j. All clocks are initially 0.

Specification. Our overall objective $\varPhi$ is that each segment is served at least once every 150 s; in other words, the clocks y_j never exceed 150. Let us thus write $\varPhi = \wedge_j \mathsf{G}(y_j \leq 150)$. It is clear that this is not the case in general: if a train stops moving, the following segment is never served. However, we also know that trains do not behave arbitrarily. In fact, to guarantee acceptable passenger experience, each train is also required not to stay for more than 30 s at each segment. Let us define $\phi_i = \mathsf{G}(\neg\mathbf{err}_i \wedge x_i \leq 30)$, which is the local specification of train i, that is, its objective. Notice that ϕ_i is a simple safety objective: once $\mathbf{err}_i$ is set to 1, it remains so. Moreover, if x_i exceeds 30, the

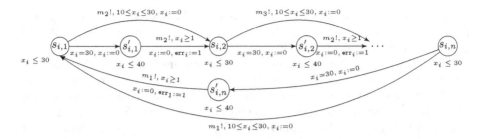

Fig. 3. Component for train i whose edges are controlled by Player i. In addition to the transitions shown in the figure, we add the self-loops with no resets at each state $s_{i,j}$ and $s'_{i,j}$, with the following guard: $\bigvee_{j,k}(s_{j,k} \wedge x_j = 30 \vee s'_{j,k} \wedge x_j = 40)$. In fact, if some train j reaches the upper bound of its invariant, then train i can still choose this self-loop to remain in the current segment.

train is necessarily at some state $s'_{i,j}$ at which the variable err_i will be set to 1 simultaneously when x_i is reset.

We assume that each train regulates its travel time with the restriction of behaving admissibly with respect to its objective ϕ_i. Now, assuming each train i is admissible for objective ϕ_i, does the global objective Φ hold under all induced executions? This is precisely a model checking under admissibility problem.

Admissible Strategies. We have $\text{Win}_i = \emptyset, \text{Lose}_i = \text{err}_i \vee (\vee_j s'_{i,j})$, and Maybe_i is the rest of the states, that is, $\neg\text{err}_i \wedge (\vee_j s_{i,j})$. We have already explained why there are no winning states in the system. To see that all states satisfying $\neg\text{err}_i \wedge x_i \leq 30$ have value 0, consider such a state where train i is at segment j. If station $j+1$ is free, then train i can move as soon as $x_i \geq 10$. Otherwise, if $i+1$ is the index of the train at segment $j+1$, then $x_i \leq x_{i+1}$ since train $i+1$ must have entered segment $j+1$ before train i has entered segment j. In this case, all segments and $n-1$ trains in the network, all trains that are blocking the way to train i can wait until their clocks reach 10, and simultaneously move one after the other to free segment $j+1$. At this point, train i can (wait and) move to segment $j+1$. By repeating this argument, one can construct a run in which train i satisfies its specification.

Let us now apply Theorem 3 to describe locally admissible moves from states of Maybe_i. Notice that the successor of any state of Maybe_i through edges of type $s_{i,j} \to s_{i,j+1}$ leads to Maybe_i. Since there is no winning states, all these edges are locally admissible according to the theorem. On the other hand, an edge $s_{i,j} \to s'_{i,j}$ is only locally admissible if $x_i = 30$ and no other edge is available. Moreover, any delay at states $s_{i,j}$ is locally admissible as long as the delay is allowed (that is, $\forall i, x_i \leq 29$). Last, from Lose_i, any move is locally admissible.

Model Checking Under Admissibility. At any moment, the trains form several blocks of consecutive occupied segments. By the previous description of the locally admissible moves, it follows that the train at the head of each block must eventually move to the next segment before its clock exceeds 30, thus allowing the previous train to move as well. One shows by induction on n that all trains move before their clocks exceed 30, thus along all runs with locally admissible moves, all objectives ϕ_i are satisfied.

Now, the satisfaction of Φ depends on the parameters n and K. One can see that Φ is satisfied as long as $K \geq n - 4$. In fact, if there are four consecutive segments at any time, each segment will be entered and left by a train within 150 time units. The specification fails however, when $K < n - 4$. This can also be determined by Algorithm 1 applied to the game described above with specifications $(\phi_i)_i$ for the trains, and the global safety property Φ.

Assume-Admissible Synthesis. Rather than checking whether *all* executions under admissible strategies satisfy the specification, let us now apply assume-admissible synthesize to synthesize an admissible strategy for each train satisfying its objective against all admissible strategies. One solution to the AA-synthesis is to let trains move to the next segment *as soon as possible*, that is, whenever the following segment is free, and the guards allow them to move. Let σ_i^{ASAP} denote this strategy. According to the previous paragraph, σ_i^{ASAP} is admissible since it only chooses locally admissible moves. Moreover, it ensures ϕ_i against all admissible strategies of the other trains since we saw that all executions under admissible strategy profiles satisfy ϕ_i.

Thus, for each i, the particular strategy σ_i^{ASAP} is admissible and ensures ϕ_i. What are possible outcomes under the profile $(\sigma_1^{\text{ASAP}}, \ldots, \sigma_n^{\text{ASAP}})$? Observe that all trains move to the next segment whenever their clocks reach 10 (in fact, this is true for the train at the head of its block, and this shows that other trains will also move at the same time). Thus, each train moves to the next segment every 10 time units under this profile. This means that the specification Φ actually holds when $K \geq n - 14$. In fact, given any block of at most 14 unoccupied consecutive segments, each of them will be served by a train in at most $(14 + 1) \times 10$ time units. Hence, we have synthesized a particular admissible strategy profile in which, not only, each train ensures its own specification against *all* admissible strategy profiles of other trains, but moreover, together, the strategy profile satisfies the specification Φ for a larger choice of parameters K and n.

Discussion. We showed that all admissible strategies satisfy the minimal performance requirement Φ in our system (given constraints on the parameters K, n). Thus, an admissible strategy for each train can be chosen separately according to other given performance criteria if desired, and Φ will hold regardless of the precise choice.

We thus suggest a two-step synthesis methodology where we separate minimal performance requirement Φ from further optimization criteria. We ensure this first step formally using admissibility, while the further steps can be done using other methods: above, we used assume-admissible synthesis, but other methods can be used as well such as statistical learning with the only requirement of being compatible with locally admissible moves. Thus, one is able to formally ensure strong guarantees for Φ, and use other methods with relaxed guarantees for further optimization.

We kept the model extremely simple in order to make it human-readable. Several details can be added to approach a more realistic model. First, the topology of the network can be made arbitrary, and two-way traffic can be incorporated with possible shared (thus, mutually exclusive) portions between different lines. Most importantly, perturbations in travel times can be added by introducing a player which adds a bounded amount of error to each travel time.

9   Conclusion

We studied admissible strategies in non-zero sum multiplayer timed games. As we showed that admissible strategies do not always exist in the continuous semantics, so we concentrated here on the discrete-time setting. By a reduction to finite concurrent games, we showed the existence of admissible strategies, and gave a characterization of admissible strategies. We gave algorithms to compute the set of admissible outcomes using zone federations, yielding algorithms for model checking under admissibility and assume-admissible synthesis. As future work, we would like to study these symbolic algorithms without the assumption of bounded clocks, thus, using extrapolation operators. We will also implement a prototype tool to test the feasability of our methods.

References

1. Alur, R., Dill, D.L.: A theory of timed automata. Theoret. Comput. Sci. **126**(2), 183–235 (1994)
2. Asarin, E., Maler, O.: As soon as possible: time optimal control for timed automata. In: Vaandrager, F.W., Schuppen, J.H. (eds.) HSCC 1999. LNCS, vol. 1569, pp. 19–30. Springer, Heidelberg (1999). doi:10.1007/3-540-48983-5_6
3. Baier, C., Katoen, J.: Principles of Model Checking. MIT Press, Cambridge (2008)
4. Basset, N., Geeraerts, G., Raskin, J., Sankur, O.: Admissibility in concurrent games. CoRR, abs/1702.06439 (2017)
5. Behrmann, G., Cougnard, A., David, A., Fleury, E., Larsen, K.G., Lime, D.: UPPAAL-tiga: time for playing games!. In: Damm, W., Hermanns, H. (eds.) CAV 2007. LNCS, vol. 4590, pp. 121–125. Springer, Heidelberg (2007). doi:10.1007/978-3-540-73368-3_14
6. Bengtsson, J., Yi, W.: Timed automata: semantics, algorithms and tools. In: Desel, J., Reisig, W., Rozenberg, G. (eds.) ACPN 2003. LNCS, vol. 3098, pp. 87–124. Springer, Heidelberg (2004). doi:10.1007/978-3-540-27755-2_3
7. Berwanger, D.: Admissibility in infinite games. In: Thomas, W., Weil, P. (eds.) STACS 2007. LNCS, vol. 4393, pp. 188–199. Springer, Heidelberg (2007). doi:10.1007/978-3-540-70918-3_17
8. Bouyer, P., Brenguier, R., Markey, N.: Computing equilibria in two-player timed games *via* turn-based finite games. In: Chatterjee, K., Henzinger, T.A. (eds.) FORMATS 2010. LNCS, vol. 6246, pp. 62–76. Springer, Heidelberg (2010). doi:10.1007/978-3-642-15297-9_7
9. Bouyer, P., Brenguier, R., Markey, N.: Nash equilibria for reachability objectives in multi-player timed games. In: Gastin, P., Laroussinie, F. (eds.) CONCUR 2010. LNCS, vol. 6269, pp. 192–206. Springer, Heidelberg (2010). doi:10.1007/978-3-642-15375-4_14

10. Brenguier, R., Clemente, L., Hunter, P., Pérez, G.A., Randour, M., Raskin, J.-F., Sankur, O., Sassolas, M.: Non-zero sum games for reactive synthesis. In: Dediu, A.-H., Janoušek, J., Martín-Vide, C., Truthe, B. (eds.) LATA 2016. LNCS, vol. 9618, pp. 3–23. Springer, Cham (2016). doi:10.1007/978-3-319-30000-9_1

11. Brenguier, R., Pérez, G.A., Raskin, J., Sankur, O.: Admissibility in quantitative graph games. In: 36th IARCS Annual Conference on Foundations of Software Technology and Theoretical Computer Science, FSTTCS 2016, Chennai, India, 13–15 December 2016. LIPIcs, vol. 65, pp. 42:1–42:14. Schloss Dagstuhl - Leibniz-Zentrum fuer Informatik (2016)

12. Brenguier, R., Raskin, J.-F., Sankur, O.: Assume-admissible synthesis. In: Proceedings of the CONCUR. LIPIcs, vol. 42, pp. 100–113. Schloss Dagstuhl-LZI (2015)

13. Brenguier, R., Raskin, J.-F., Sassolas, M.: The complexity of admissibility in omega-regular games. In: Proceedings of the CSL-LICS, pp. 23:1–23:10. ACM (2014)

14. Brihaye, T., Bruyere, V., Meunier, N., Raskin, J.-F.: Weak subgame perfect equilibria and their application to quantitative reachability. In: Kreutzer, S. (ed.) 24th EACSL Annual Conference on Computer Science Logic (CSL 2015), Leibniz International Proceedings in Informatics (LIPIcs), vol. 41, pp. 504–518. Schloss Dagstuhl-Leibniz-Zentrum fuer Informatik, Dagstuhl (2015)

15. Brihaye, T., Bruyère, V., Raskin, J.-F.: On optimal timed strategies. In: Pettersson, P., Yi, W. (eds.) FORMATS 2005. LNCS, vol. 3829, pp. 49–64. Springer, Heidelberg (2005). doi:10.1007/11603009_5

16. Brihaye, T., Henzinger, T.A., Prabhu, V.S., Raskin, J.-F.: Minimum-time reachability in timed games. In: Arge, L., Cachin, C., Jurdziński, T., Tarlecki, A. (eds.) ICALP 2007. LNCS, vol. 4596, pp. 825–837. Springer, Heidelberg (2007). doi:10.1007/978-3-540-73420-8_71

17. Cassez, F., David, A., Fleury, E., Larsen, K.G., Lime, D.: Efficient on-the-fly algorithms for the analysis of timed games. In: Abadi, M., Alfaro, L. (eds.) CONCUR 2005. LNCS, vol. 3653, pp. 66–80. Springer, Heidelberg (2005). doi:10.1007/11539452_9

18. Chatterjee, K., Henzinger, T.A.: Assume-guarantee synthesis. In: Grumberg, O., Huth, M. (eds.) TACAS 2007. LNCS, vol. 4424, pp. 261–275. Springer, Heidelberg (2007). doi:10.1007/978-3-540-71209-1_21

19. Chatterjee, K., Henzinger, T.A., Jurdziński, M.: Games with secure equilibria. Theoret. Comput. Sci. 365(1), 67–82 (2006)

20. Chatterjee, K., Henzinger, T.A., Piterman, N.: Strategy logic. Inf. Comput. 208(6), 677–693 (2010)

21. Condurache, R., Filiot, E., Gentilini, R., Raskin, J.: The complexity of rational synthesis. In: 43rd International Colloquium on Automata, Languages, Programming, ICALP 2016, 11–15 July 2016, Rome, Italy. LIPIcs, vol. 55, pp. 121:1–121:15. Schloss Dagstuhl - Leibniz-Zentrum fuer Informatik (2016)

22. Dill, D.L.: Timing assumptions and verification of finite-state concurrent systems. In: Sifakis, J. (ed.) CAV 1989. LNCS, vol. 407, pp. 197–212. Springer, Heidelberg (1990). doi:10.1007/3-540-52148-8_17

23. Faella, M.: Admissible strategies in infinite games over graphs. In: Královič, R., Niwiński, D. (eds.) MFCS 2009. LNCS, vol. 5734, pp. 307–318. Springer, Heidelberg (2009). doi:10.1007/978-3-642-03816-7_27

24. Fisman, D., Kupferman, O., Lustig, Y.: Rational synthesis. In: Esparza, J., Majumdar, R. (eds.) TACAS 2010. LNCS, vol. 6015, pp. 190–204. Springer, Heidelberg (2010). doi:10.1007/978-3-642-12002-2_16

25. Jensen, P.G., Larsen, K.G., Srba, J.: Real-time strategy synthesis for timed-arc petri net games via discretization. In: Bošnački, D., Wijs, A. (eds.) SPIN 2016. LNCS, vol. 9641, pp. 129–146. Springer, Cham (2016). doi:10.1007/978-3-319-32582-8_9

26. Kupferman, O., Perelli, G., Vardi, M.Y.: Synthesis with rational environments. In: Bulling, N. (ed.) EUMAS 2014. LNCS (LNAI), vol. 8953, pp. 219–235. Springer, Cham (2015). doi:10.1007/978-3-319-17130-2_15

27. Maler, O., Pnueli, A., Sifakis, J.: On the synthesis of discrete controllers for timed systems. In: Mayr, E.W., Puech, C. (eds.) STACS 1995. LNCS, vol. 900, pp. 229–242. Springer, Heidelberg (1995). doi:10.1007/3-540-59042-0_76

28. Mogavero, F., Murano, A., Vardi, M.Y.: Reasoning about strategies. In: Proceedings of the FSTTCS. LIPIcs, vol. 8, pp. 133–144. Schloss Dagstuhl - LZI (2010)

29. Ummels, M.: Rational behaviour and strategy construction in infinite multiplayer games. In: Arun-Kumar, S., Garg, N. (eds.) FSTTCS 2006. LNCS, vol. 4337, pp. 212–223. Springer, Heidelberg (2006). doi:10.1007/11944836_21

Modal Stochastic Games
Abstraction-Refinement of Probabilistic Automata

Joost-Pieter Katoen[1] and Falak Sher[2]([⊠])

[1] RWTH Aachen University, Aachen, Germany
[2] Information Technology University, Lahore, Punjab, Pakistan
chfalak@gmail.com

Abstract. This paper presents an abstraction-refinement framework for Segala's probabilistic automata (PA), a slight variant of Markov decision processes. We use Condon and Ladner's two-player probabilistic game automata extended with *possible* and *required* transitions—as in Larsen and Thomsen's modal transition systems—as abstract models. The key idea is to refine player-one and player-two states separately resulting in a nested abstract-refine loop. We show the adequacy of this approach for obtaining tight bounds on extremal reachability probabilities.

1 Introduction

Probabilistic automata (PAs) [1] extend Markov decision processes (MDPs) by allowing for states having more than one choice labeled with the same action. This extension is needed for parallel composition. Whereas in an MDP, each distribution (over states) is unique, this no longer holds for PA. PAs have been used as operational model for probabilistic process algebras, the PIOA language, and have served to reason about randomized distributed algorithms, see [2]. Segala [1] has studied several behavioral relations on PAs such as (weak and strong) bisimulation and simulation pre-orders, as well as trace inclusions. These relations form the basis for obtaining abstractions of PAs, i.e., smaller models that then can be used for further analysis. This includes for instance, determining extremal (minimal and maximal) reachability probabilities.

To obtain coarser abstractions, more aggressive abstraction schemes have been proposed in the literature. These include finite-state approximations [3], abstract probabilistic automata [4], game-based abstractions [5], abstractions that are based on distribution-based simulation pre-orders [6], and compositional abstraction [7]. This paper is a continuation of this line of research that is aimed at obtaining an automated abstraction-refinement framework for PAs that yields tight bounds on extremal reachability probabilities.

The first key ingredient of this paper is to use Condon and Ladner's two-player probabilistic game automata (PGAs) [8] and extend them with possible and required transitions as known from modal transition systems [9,10]. There

This work has been partially funded by the Excellence Initiative of the German federal and state government and the CDZ project CAP (GZ 1023).

L. Aceto et al. (Eds.): Larsen Festschrift, LNCS 10460, pp. 426–445, 2017.
DOI: 10.1007/978-3-319-63121-9_21

are two main differences with existing works on game-based abstraction of PAs: *(1) both players are fully symmetric (and randomized), and (2) transitions have modalities.* We define satisfaction and refinement relations—much in the style of modal transition systems—on these models, define (alternating) simulation relations, and prove the special role of two specific implementations that provide (upper and lower) bounds on extremal reachability probabilities for competing and collaborating players.

The second key ingredient, and the major contribution of this paper, is an (nested) abstraction-refinement scheme. The main idea is separate refining player-one and player-two states. We formally define the notion of stable abstraction from the perspective of each player, prove that each refinement loop indeed yields a refinement, and that the iterative abstraction-refinement terminates for every PA with a finite bisimulation quotient.

Put shortly, the major contributions of this paper are: (1) generalizing two-player probabilistic game automata (by annotating transitions with modalities) and proposing them as abstractions of PAs, (2) showing that our abstractions yield *at most* as tight bounds on extremal reachability probabilities as game-based abstractions, however, they are *at most* the sizes of game-based abstractions, and (3) proposing an abstraction-refinement framework consisting of a nested loop – the inner-loop (outer-loop) refines player-one (player-two) states.

This paper is organized as follows. Section 2 sets the ground for this work. Sections 3 and 4 introduce abstract PGAs and the abstraction technique based on it, respectively. Section 5 proposes our abstraction-refinement framework for PAs. Section 6 discusses related work. Section 7 concludes the paper. Proofs of theorems can be found in the Ph.D. thesis [18].

2   Preliminaries

A *distribution* μ is a function on a countable set S iff $\mu : S \to [0,1]$ and $0 < \sum_{s \in S} \mu(s) \leq 1$; its support set is $\mathrm{supp}(\mu) = \{s \in S \mid \mu(s) > 0\}$; and its mass w.r.t. set $S' \subseteq S$ is given as $\mu(S') = \sum_{s \in S'} \mu(s)$. A distribution μ is a *full-distribution* iff $\mu(S) = 1$, otherwise, it is a *sub-distribution*. Let $\mathrm{Dist}(S)$ denote the set of full-distributions over S. Let $\iota_s \in \mathrm{Dist}(S)$ denote the *Dirac* distribution for $s \in S$, i.e., $\iota_s(s) = 1$.

2.1   Probabilistic Game Automata

PGAs are used for modeling systems in which players, behaving probabilistically, compete for certain objectives, i.e., some players maximize whereas the others minimize the probability of reaching a set of goal states. In this paper, we deal with PGAs having only two players that make their moves alternatively. Intuitively, it is a game of chance played between two players, say, player one and player two. The game arena is a bipartite graph—having, say, S_1 and S_2 as sets of vertices—in which each player owns a specific set of vertices; say, the players one and two own S_1 and S_2 respectively. The game is started by player one and evolves in a turn-based fashion. Starting from the initial state in S_1, player one non-deterministically chooses an action-distribution pair. Based on the selected distribution, a state in S_2, say s_2, is randomly selected and the control is passed to player two; who then behaves in the same way as player one and the control passes back to player one. This goes on until some goal is achieved either by player one or player two. Let UAct be a countable universe of actions including the internal action τ.

Definition 1 (Probabilistic game automaton [8]). *A PGA is a tuple* $\mathcal{G} = (S, \{S_1, S_2\}, A, \Delta, s_0)$ *where S is a non-empty, countable set of states, partitioned into S_1 and S_2, with $s_0 \in S_1$; $A \subseteq$ UAct, and $\Delta \subseteq (S_1 \times A \times \mathrm{Dist}(S_2)) \cup (S_2 \times A \times \mathrm{Dist}(S_1))$ is a set of transitions.*

We denote $(s, a, \mu) \in \Delta$ by $s \xrightarrow{a} \mu$; $\mathrm{Act}(s) = \{a \in A \mid s \xrightarrow{a} \mu\}$ as the set of enabled actions from state s; $\mathrm{succ}(s) = \{u \in S \mid \exists (s, a, \mu) \in \Delta : \mu(u) > 0\}$ as the set of successor states of s; and $\Delta(s) = \{(s, a, \mu) \mid s \xrightarrow{a} \mu\}$ as the set of transitions emanating from s. PGAs are thus a generalization of SGs [11] in which both players are random; in SGs only one player is random. In the sequel, let $\mathcal{G} = (S, \{S_1, S_2\}, A, \Delta, s_0)$ be a finitely branching – each state has a finite number of transitions and each distribution has a finite support – PGA. To depict PGAs we represent states in S_1 and S_2 as rectangles and

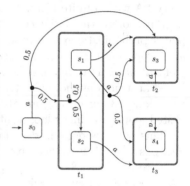

Fig. 1. A sample PGA $\mathcal{G}$

double rectangles respectively. Moreover, if a player-one state s has a unique predecessor t, we show s inside t for simplicity. Figure 1 illustrates a sample PGA with $S_1 = \{s_0, \ldots, s_4\}$, $S_2 = \{t_1, t_2, t_3\}$ and transitions $t_1 \xrightarrow{a} \mu$ with $\mu(s_1) = \mu(s_2) = \frac{1}{2}$. In order to analyze reachability properties on PGA $\mathcal{G}$, at each state non-determinism is resolved by means of a scheduler for each player, resulting in a Markov chain with a countable state space. The induced chain further reduces to a path once probabilistic choices are resolved. A set of paths obtained thus is measurable, see e.g., [12, Ch. 10]. Let $\mathrm{Pr}_{\kappa_2}^{\kappa_1}(T)$ be the probability of the set of paths from the initial state s_0 in $\mathcal{G}$ that reach some set of states $T \subseteq S$ under schedulers (κ_1, κ_2) for players one and two respectively. Let

$$\mathrm{Pr}^{+-}(T) = \sup_{\kappa_1} \inf_{\kappa_2} \mathrm{Pr}_{\kappa_2}^{\kappa_1}(T)$$
$$\mathrm{Pr}^{++}(T) = \sup_{\kappa_1} \sup_{\kappa_2} \mathrm{Pr}_{\kappa_2}^{\kappa_1}(T)$$
$$\mathrm{Pr}^{--}(T) = \inf_{\kappa_1} \inf_{\kappa_2} \mathrm{Pr}_{\kappa_2}^{\kappa_1}(T)$$
$$\mathrm{Pr}^{-+}(T) = \inf_{\kappa_1} \sup_{\kappa_2} \mathrm{Pr}_{\kappa_2}^{\kappa_1}(T)$$

be the *optimal* (i.e., maximum and minimum) probabilities for reaching states in T. They can be achieved by *deterministic memoryless* schedulers [8], and computed through value iteration, policy iteration or by linear programming for games with finite state spaces.

Let $w_T : S \to [0,1]$ be a *probability valuation function* mapping a state s to the probability of reaching $T \subseteq S$ from s under a given pair of deterministic memoryless schedulers. We omit the subscript T whenever T is clear from the context. The probability valuation functions $W_T = \{w \mid w : S \to [0,1]\}$ form a complete lattice $(W_T, \leq, \bot, \top)$ with order $\leq\subseteq W_T \times W_T$, bottom element $\bot \in W_T$ and top element $\top \in W_T$. We write $w \leq w'$ iff $\forall s \in S : w(s) \leq w'(s)$; $\bot(s) = 0$ and $\top(s) = 1$ for $s \in S$. For a set $M \subseteq W_T$, the least upper bound is given as $\bigsqcup M(s) = \sup_{w \in M} w(s)$, and the greatest lower bound as $\bigsqcap M(s) = \inf_{w \in M} w(s)$ for $s \in S$. Let $w(\mu) = \sum_{s \in S} \mu(s) \cdot w(s)$ for $\mu \in \mathrm{Dist}(S)$. For PGA $\mathcal{G}$, let $\tau(\mathcal{G})$ be the closed PGA, a PGA $\mathcal{G}$ in which all actions of $\mathcal{G}$ are changed into τ.[1]

Definition 2 (Probability valuation transformer [8]). *Let $T \subseteq S$ be the set of goal states in PGA $\tau(\mathcal{G})$. For reachability objectives $\mathbf{1}, \mathbf{2} \in \{\min, \max\}$ for players one and two respectively, the* probability valuation transformer $\mathrm{Prt}_\mathbf{2}^\mathbf{1} : W_T \to W_T$ *is defined for $w \in W_T$ and $s \in S$ as:*

$$\mathrm{Prt}_\mathbf{2}^\mathbf{1}(w)(s) = \begin{cases} 1 & \text{if } s \in T \\ \mathbf{1} = \max? \, 0 : 1 & \text{if } s \in S_1 \cap T_0 \\ \mathbf{2} = \max? \, 0 : 1 & \text{if } s \in S_2 \cap T_0 \\ \mathbf{1}\{w(\mu) \mid s \xrightarrow{\tau} \mu\} & \text{if } s \in S_1 \setminus (T \cup T_0) \\ \mathbf{2}\{w(\mu) \mid s \xrightarrow{\tau} \mu\} & \text{if } s \in S_2 \setminus (T \cup T_0) \end{cases}$$

where $T_0 \subseteq S$ is the set of all states without outgoing transitions.

$\mathrm{Prt}_\mathbf{2}^\mathbf{1}$ is a monotonic function over the complete lattice W. By Tarski's theorem [14], it has a least **Fix** $\mathrm{Prt}_\mathbf{2}^\mathbf{1}(\bot)$ and a greatest **Fix** $\mathrm{Prt}_\mathbf{2}^\mathbf{1}(\top)$ fixed point. For finite-state PGA, they can be computed through e.g., value iteration [13].

2.2 Probabilistic Automata

PAs [1] extend labeled transition systems (LTSs) in which the target of any action-labeled transition is a distribution over states instead of a single state. A *probabilistic automaton* (PA) is a quadruple $\mathcal{M} = (S, A, \Delta, s_0)$ where S, A, and s_0 are as before, and $\Delta \subseteq S \times A \times \mathrm{Dist}(S)$ is a set of transitions. A PA can be embedded into a PGA (where player-two states have one emanating transition) in a straightforward manner. Figure 2 depicts a sample PA. Its embedding as PGA is provided in Fig. 4 (left, page 8).

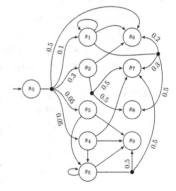

Fig. 2. A sample PA $\mathcal{M}$

---

[1] As this paper does not cover parallel composition all PGAs are closed. For modeling PGAs in a compositonal manner though, the distinction between internal and other actions is important, see [7].

Definition 3 (Embedding a PA into an PGA [6]**).** *PA* $\mathcal{M} = (S, A, \Delta, s_0)$ *induces the PGA* $\alpha_{\mathrm{PA}}(\mathcal{M}) = (S', \{S_1', S_2'\}, A, \Delta', (s_0, 1))$ *with* $S_1' = S \times \{1\}$, $S_2' = S \times \{2\}$ *and for every* $s \in S$:

1. $(s, 1) \overset{a}{\to} \mu'$ *iff* $s \overset{a}{\to} \mu$ *and* $\mu'(u, 2) = \mu(u)$, *and*
2. $(s, 2) \overset{a}{\to} \mu'$ *with* $\mu'(s, 1) = 1$ *iff for some* $u \in S$ *with* $u \overset{a}{\to} \mu$ *and* $s \in \mathrm{supp}(\mu)$.

2.3   Simulation Relations

Simulation relations for probabilistic systems are pre–orders requiring that whenever state u simulates state s, then u can at least mimic the stepwise behaviour of s. They can be computed for finite models by reducing them to network max-flow problems [15]. They are lifted to distributions over states as follows:

Definition 4 (Simulation relation [16]**).** *Let* S *be a countable, non-empty set of states, and let* $\mu, \mu' \in \mathrm{Dist}(S)$. *For* $R \subseteq S \times S$, μ' *simulates* μ *w.r.t.* R, *denoted* $\mu R \mu'$, *iff there exists a function* $\delta : S \times S \to [0, 1]$ *such that for all* $u, v \in S$: *(1)* $\delta(u, v) > 0 \Rightarrow u R v$, *(2)* $\sum_{s \in S} \delta(u, s) = \mu(u)$, *and (3)* $\sum_{s \in S} \delta(s, v) = \mu'(v)$.

We define two simulation relations on PGAs: *simulation* and *alternating simulation*. Simulation relations compare reachability probabilities in case of collaborating players (i.e., both players want to maximize/minimize reachability probabilities), whereas alternating simulation relations do so in case of competing players.

Definition 5 (Simulation on PGAs [6]**).** $R \subseteq \bigcup_{j \in \{1,2\}} S_j \times S_j$ *is a simulation relation on PGA* $\mathcal{G}$ *iff for every* $s R s'$, $s \overset{a}{\to} \mu$ *implies* $s' \overset{a}{\to} \mu'$ *with* $\mu R \mu'$. *Let* $\prec$ *be the largest simulation relation.*

Definition 6 (Alternating simulation on PGAs [6]**).** $R \subseteq \bigcup_{j \in \{1,2\}} S_j \times S_j$ *is an* alternating simulation *relation on PGA* $\mathcal{G}$ *iff for every* $s R s'$ *the following holds: (1) if* $s, s' \in S_1$, *then* $s' \overset{a}{\to} \mu'$ *implies* $s \overset{a}{\to} \mu$ *such that* $\mu R \mu'$, *(2) if* $s, s' \in S_2$, *then* $s \overset{a}{\to} \mu$ *implies* $s' \overset{a}{\to} \mu'$ *such that* $\mu R \mu'$. *Let* $\preccurlyeq$ *be the largest alternating simulation relation. We write "s' alt-simulates s" iff* $s \preccurlyeq s'$.

Intuitively, in case of player-one states, the behaviour of s' is mimicked by that of s; whereas in case of player-two states, it is the other way round.

We write $\mathcal{G} \prec \mathcal{G}'$ ($\mathcal{G} \preccurlyeq \mathcal{G}'$) if $s_0 \prec s_0'$ ($s \preccurlyeq s_0'$), where $\prec$ ($\preccurlyeq$) is taken on the disjoint union of $\mathcal{G}$ and $\mathcal{G}'$. By the following theorem, $\mathcal{G} \prec \mathcal{G}'$ ($\mathcal{G} \preccurlyeq \mathcal{G}'$) implies that $\mathcal{G}'$ bounds Pr^{++} (Pr^{+-}) and Pr^{--} (Pr^{-+}) values of $\mathcal{G}$ from above (below) and below (above) in case of collaborating (competing) players.

Theorem 1. *For PGA* $\mathcal{G}$ *and* $\mathcal{G}'$, *and* $T \subseteq S$. *Then:*

1. $\mathcal{G} \prec \mathcal{G}'$ *implies* $\mathrm{Pr}^{--}(T') \leq \mathrm{Pr}^{--}(T)$ *and* $\mathrm{Pr}^{++}(T) \leq \mathrm{Pr}^{++}(T')$, *and*
2. $\mathcal{G} \preccurlyeq \mathcal{G}'$ *implies* $\mathrm{Pr}^{-+}(T'') \geq \mathrm{Pr}^{-+}(T)$ *and* $\mathrm{Pr}^{+-}(T) \geq \mathrm{Pr}^{+-}(T'')$

where $T' = \{s' \in S' \mid \exists s \in T : s \prec s'\}$ *and* $T'' = \{s' \in S' \mid \exists s \in T : s \preccurlyeq s'\}$.

3   Modal Stochastic Games

This section presents an extension of PGAs by annotating their transitions with *required* (must) and *possible* (may) modalities as in modal transition systems [9,10]. This results in *abstract* probabilistic game automata (APGAs, for short). The semantics of an APGA is a *set* of PGAs, namely all PGAs that have at least all required transitions and zero or more possible transitions. These games are called *implementations* of APGA.

Definition 7 (Abstract PGA). *An* abstract PGA *(APGA) is a tuple* $\mathcal{H} = (S, \{S_1, S_2\}, A, \Delta_r, \Delta_p, s_0)$ *with* S, S_1, S_2, A, *and* s_0 *as in PGA,* $\Delta_p \subseteq S_{1+x} \times A \times \mathrm{Dist}(S_{2-x})$ *is a set of* possible *transitions and* $\Delta_r \subseteq S_{1+x} \times A \times \mathrm{Dist}(S_{2-x})$ *is a set of* required *transitions with* $\Delta_r \subseteq \Delta_p$, *where* $x \in \{0,1\}$.

We denote $(s, a, \mu) \in \Delta_y$ by $s \xrightarrow{a}_y \mu$, and transitions emanating from a state s as $\Delta_y(s) = \{(s, a, \mu) \mid s \xrightarrow{a}_y \mu\}$ for $y \in \{p, r\}$. Every PGA is an APGA with $\Delta_r = \Delta_p$. We depict required transitions as solid lines, and others as dotted lines (see Fig. 3). Let closed APGA be defined in a similar way as closed PA (page 4). In the sequel, let $\mathcal{H} = (S, \{S_1, S_2\}, A, \Delta_r, \Delta_p, s_0)$ be a finitely branching APGA.

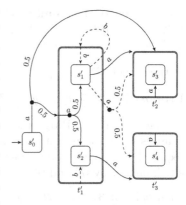

APGAs are compared using *refinement relations*. Intuitively, when a state s refines a state s', then s' mimics at least the step-wise *possible* behaviour of s, whereas s mimics at least the step-wise *required* behaviour of s'. A special class of refinement relations, called *satisfaction*

Fig. 3. A sample APGA $\mathcal{H}$

relations, relates implementations (concrete models, i.e., PGAs) with APGA (specifications). In the sequel, let S_j be the set of states of player i in PGA $\mathcal{G}$ (APGA $\mathcal{H}$), and S'_j be its set of states in the APGA $\mathcal{H}'$.

Definition 8 (Satisfaction relation). $R \subseteq \bigcup_{j\in\{1,2\}} S_j \times S'_j$ *is a satisfaction relation between PGA $\mathcal{G}$ and APGA $\mathcal{H}'$ iff for sRs', (1) $s \xrightarrow{a} \mu$ implies $s' \xrightarrow{a}_p \mu'$ such that $\mu R \mu'$, and (2) $s' \xrightarrow{a}_r \mu'$ implies $s \xrightarrow{a} \mu$ such that $\mu R \mu'$. Let $\models$ be the largest satisfaction relation.*

The set of implementations of APGA $\mathcal{H}$ is defined by $\llbracket \mathcal{H} \rrbracket = \{\mathcal{G} \mid \mathcal{G} \models \mathcal{H}\}$.

Definition 9 (Refinement relation). $R \subseteq \bigcup_{j\in\{1,2\}} S_j \times S'_j$ *is a refinement relation between APGA $\mathcal{H}$ and $\mathcal{H}'$ iff for sRs', (1) $s \xrightarrow{a}_p \mu$ implies $s' \xrightarrow{a}_p \mu'$ such that $\mu R \mu'$, and (2) $s' \xrightarrow{a}_r \mu'$ implies $s \xrightarrow{a}_r \mu$ such that $\mu R \mu'$. Let $\preceq$ be the largest refinement relation.*

The conditions (1) and (2) are the same as in Definition 8 except that in (1) the transition from s is a *possible* transition, whereas in (2) the transition from s is a *required* transition.

Example 1. $R = \bigcup_{i=1...3}(t_i, t_i') \cup \bigcup_{i=0...4}(s_i, s_i')$ is a refinement (in fact, a satisfaction) relation between PGA $\mathcal{G}$ (Fig. 1) and APGA H (Fig. 3).

Proposition 1. $\preceq$ *is a pre–order.*

Extremal Implementations. We focus on two special implementations of APGA $\mathcal{H}$, denoted $\mathcal{G}^p$ and $\mathcal{G}^r$, and show that they bound the optimal reachability probabilities of every implementation of $\mathcal{H}$. We call $\mathcal{G}^p$ and $\mathcal{G}^r$ *extreme* PGAs (EPGAs, for short). Both $\mathcal{G}^p$ and $\mathcal{G}^r$ inherit the player-two transitions from its possible transitions in $\mathcal{H}$. They differ for player one, though. EPGA $\mathcal{G}^p$ inherits its player-one transitions (denoted by the superscript) from the possible transitions of player one in $\mathcal{H}$, whereas $\mathcal{G}^r$ inherits its player-one transitions from the required transitions in $\mathcal{H}$.

Definition 10 (Extremal PGAs implementations). *For* $y \in \{p, r\}$*,* $\mathcal{G}^y$ *is an EPGA of* $\mathcal{H}$ *iff* S, S_1, S_2, A *and* s_0 *in* $\mathcal{G}^y$ *are as in* $\mathcal{H}$*,* $\Delta(s) = \Delta_p(s)$ *for* $s \in S_2$*, and* $\Delta(s) = \Delta_y(s)$ *for* $s \in S_1$*.*

In the sequel, $\mathcal{G}^y = (S, \{S_1, S_2\}, A, \Delta, s_0)$ is an EPGA of $\mathcal{H}$ for $y \in \{p, r\}$.

Proposition 2. *For every* $\mathcal{G} \in \{H\}$*, it holds* $\mathcal{G} \prec \mathcal{G}^p$ *and* $\mathcal{G} \precapprox \mathcal{G}^r$*.*

By Theorem 1 and Proposition 2, EPGAs suffice for the optimal reachability analysis of $\mathcal{H}$. Note that the two extreme implementations by considering the required (as opposed to the possible) transitions of player two are simulated and alt-simulated by $\mathcal{G}^p$ and $\mathcal{G}^r$ respectively.).

Proposition 3. $\mathcal{H}_1 \preceq \mathcal{H}_2$ *implies (1)* $\mathcal{G}_1^p \prec \mathcal{G}_2^p$ *and (2)* $\mathcal{G}_1^r \precapprox \mathcal{G}_2^r$*.*

It follows from Propositions 2, 3 and Theorem 1 that if $\mathcal{H}_1 \preceq \mathcal{H}_2$, then $\mathcal{H}_2$ bounds the extremal reachability probabilities in $\mathcal{H}_1$.

4   Abstraction

This section presents our abstraction technique, a combination of abstraction of PA using modalities [7] and game-based abstraction [5]. It is based on partitioning the state space such that player-one and player-two states are kept separate. The key principle is that player-one states that have the same set of transitions (after abstraction) must at least be assigned to the same abstract state. Every transition from a concrete state, either belonging to player-one or two, becomes a *possible* transition from its corresponding abstract state. For player-one states we additionally apply the following approach. An abstract player-one state is equipped with a required a-transition to distribution μ' iff every of its concrete states has a required a-transition to μ such that μ' is the abstract counterpart of μ. Required transitions for player-two states are not detailed further, as they play no role in the analysis of optimal reachability probabilities (see Proposition 2).

Let $\alpha : S \twoheadrightarrow S'$ be an abstraction (a surjective function) and $\gamma : S' \to 2^S$ be the corresponding concretization function. That is, $\alpha(s)$ is the abstract state of

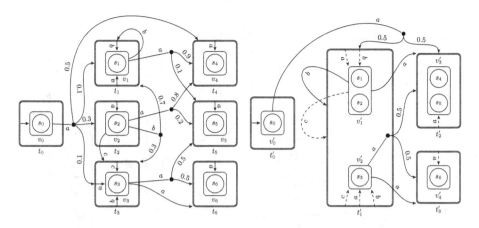

Fig. 4. The embedding $\mathcal{H}$ (left) of the PA in Fig. 2, and its abstraction $\mathcal{H}' = \alpha(\mathcal{H})$ (right)

s whereas $\gamma(s')$ is the set of concrete states abstracted by s'. The abstraction of distribution μ is given as $\alpha(\mu)(s') = \mu(\gamma(s'))$. The functions α and γ are lifted to sets of states or sets of distributions in a point-wise manner.

Definition 11 (Abstraction). *For APGA $\mathcal{H}$, the* abstraction function α : $S \rightarrow S'$ *induces the APGA $\mathcal{H}' = \alpha(\mathcal{H})$ if the following conditions are satisfied: $A' = A$; $S'_i = \alpha(S_i)$ for $i \in \{1, 2\}$; $\forall s, u \in S_1 : \alpha(\Delta_y(s)) = \alpha(\Delta_y(u))$ for $y \in \{\mathrm{p}, \mathrm{r}\}$ implies $\alpha(s) = \alpha(u)$; and for every $s' \in S'$:*

1. $s' \in S'_1$ *implies* $s' \xrightarrow{a}_r \mu'$ *iff* $\forall s \in \gamma(s') : s \xrightarrow{a}_r \mu$ *such that* $\alpha(\mu) = \mu'$,
2. $\exists s \in \gamma(s') : s \xrightarrow{a}_p \mu$ *implies* $s' \xrightarrow{a}_p \mu'$ *such that* $\alpha(\mu) = \mu'$, *and*
3. $s' \xrightarrow{a}_p \mu'$ *implies* $\exists s \in \gamma(s') : s \xrightarrow{a}_p \mu$ *such that* $\alpha(\mu) = \mu'$.

In the sequel, α denotes an *abstraction* function. Our framework considers abstractions of APGAs. For simplicity, all examples consider the abstractions of PAs.

Example 2. Let $\mathcal{H}' = \alpha(\mathcal{H})$ in Fig. 4 (right) be the induced abstract model of APGA $\mathcal{H}$ (left) with $\gamma(t'_0) = \{t_0\}$, $\gamma(t'_1) = \{t_1, t_2, t_3\}$, $\gamma(t'_2) = \{t_4, t_5\}$ and $\gamma(t'_3) = \{t_6\}$ as well as $\gamma(v'_0) = \{v_0\}$, $\gamma(v'_1) = \{v_1, v_2\}$, $\gamma(v'_2) = \{v_3\}$, $\gamma(v'_3) = \{v_4, v_5\}$ and $\gamma(v'_4) = \{v_6\}$. Let us consider the abstract state v'_1, it has a *required* a-transition to t'_2 because both of its concrete states (v_1 and v_2) have *required* a-transitions with target distributions over t_4 and t_5 (the concrete states of t'_2). By a similar reason there exists a *required* b-transition from v'_1 to t'_1. However, only v_2 has a *required* c-transition to t_3, therefore, v'_1 has a *possible* c-transition to t'_1 (the abstract state of t_3). Note that the incoming transition of state v_0 indicates that v_0 is initial; there is no transition from t_0 to v_0. The rest of the example is self-explanatory.

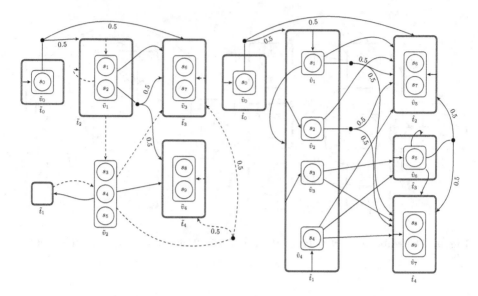

Fig. 5. For PA $\mathcal{M}$ (Fig. 2), APGA-based abstraction $\tilde{\mathcal{H}} = \alpha(\alpha_{\mathrm{PA}}(\mathcal{M}))$ (left) with $|\tilde{\Delta}| = 17$, $|\tilde{S}_1| = 5$ and $|\tilde{S}_2| = 5$; and game-based abstraction $\hat{\mathcal{H}} = \alpha(\alpha_{\mathrm{PA}}(\mathcal{M}))$ (right) with $|\hat{\Delta}| = 26$, $|\hat{S}_1| = 8$ and $|\hat{S}_2| = 5$.

The proposition below establishes that concrete models refine their abstractions; therefore, by Theorem 1 and Proposition 3, their reachability probabilities are bounded by those of their abstractions.

Proposition 4. $\mathcal{H} \preceq \alpha(\mathcal{H})$.

Proposition 4 and the corollary below (that follows from Definition 11) prove that APGA-based abstractions yield *at most as tight bounds* as SG-based abstractions, whereas they are *at most* the sizes of SG-based abstractions. (Note that in order to compare concrete with abstract models (in terms of their sizes), we take the sizes of probabilistic transitions equal to the cardinality of the support sets of their target distributions, e.g., the size of a transition $s \xrightarrow{a} \mu$ is equal to $|\mathrm{supp}(\mu)|$.)

Corollary 1. *Let $\mathcal{H}_{sg}$ be an SG-based abstraction and $\mathcal{H}_{apga}$ be an APGA-based abstraction of PA $\mathcal{M}$ with $S_2^{sg} = S_2^{apga}$. Then: (1) $|S_1^{sg}| \geq |S_1^{apga}|$, and (2) $\mathcal{H}_{sg} \preceq \mathcal{H}_{apga}$.*

Example 3. Consider the game-based abstraction $\hat{\mathcal{H}}$ (Fig. 5 right) of PA $\mathcal{M}$ (Fig. 2). The maximum probability to reach states $\{s_6, s_7\}$ lies in $[0.75, 1]$ in $\hat{\mathcal{H}}$ whereas in APGA-based abstraction $\tilde{\mathcal{H}}$ (Fig. 5 left), it lies in $[0.5, 1]$. Note that both $\tilde{S}_2$ and $\hat{S}_2$ represent the same partitioning of the concrete state space, the reachability probability bounds of $\tilde{S}_2$ states contain that of $\hat{S}_2$ states, and $\tilde{\mathcal{H}}$ is smaller than $\hat{\mathcal{H}}$.

Sher [18] defines a composition operator in a TCSP-like manner for the class of APGAs representing abstract models of PAs, and shows that our abstraction technique is compositional.

5   Iterative Abstraction-Refinement

The key idea of our abstract-refine framework (see Fig. 6) is to separate the *iterative* refinement of player-one and player-two states. It *automatically* generates APGA-based abstractions of (closed) PAs with a finite bisimulation quotient in which the bounds on probabilities for reaching a set of goal states are within the allowed range.

The input is a closed PA, a reachability property (max/min probability to goal states) and an error bound $\epsilon \in \mathbb{R}_{(0,1)}$. Starting from an initial abstraction (obtained by partitioning S_1 and S_2 states in the embedding of PA), we incrementally refine player-one states (yielding a new partitioning for the player-one state space) until the reachability probability bounds of player-two states stabilize. Next, we check whether the probability bounds of a set of player-two states (that are of interest) are within the allowed range ϵ. If not, some of the player-two states are refined yielding a new partitioning of the concrete state space—recall that S_1 states having the same set of transitions under a given partitioning of S_2 states are at least assigned to the same abstract state (see Definition 11). The first step is then repeated for the new abstract model. The

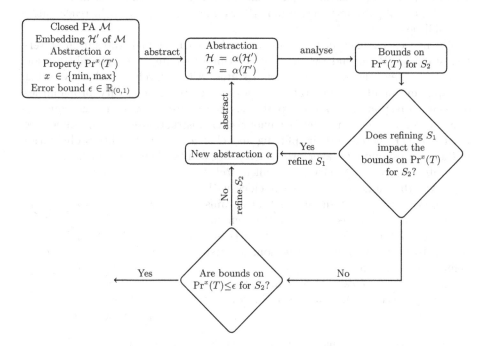

Fig. 6. Abstraction-refinement framework for closed PAs

above two steps form the inner and the outer loop, that refine player-one and player-two states respectively, of our abstract-refine framework.

Our *refinement strategy* is based on optimal probability valuation functions. It induces a strictly finer partition in each iteration, and thus makes the nested loop eventually terminate for PA having a finite bisimulation quotient.

Let $\mathcal{M}$ be a closed finite PA, having a finite bisimulation quotient, with its embedding $\mathcal{H}' = \alpha_{PA}(\mathcal{M})$ and set of goal states $T' \subseteq S_2'$. Let $\Pr^x(T')$ be the probability for reaching states in T' from the initial state s_0, where $x \in \{\min, \max\}$. Let $Abst(\mathcal{H}')$ be the set of abstraction functions defined on $\mathcal{H}'$ such that $\gamma(\alpha(T')) = T'$ for all $\alpha \in Abst(\mathcal{H}')$, i.e., α does not merge T' states with $S_2' \backslash T'$ states. Let $\mathcal{H} = \alpha(\mathcal{H}')$ and $T = \alpha(T')$ for $\alpha \in Abst(\mathcal{H}')$.

Depending on the property $\Pr^x(T')$, let $\mathbf{1}, \mathbf{2} \in \{\min, \max\}$ with $\mathbf{1} \neq \mathbf{2}$[2]. Let $w_{11}, w_{12} \in W$ be the probability valuation functions (see Definition 2) such that $w_{12} = \mathbf{Fix}\ \mathrm{Prt}_2^1(\bot)$ and $w_{11} = \mathbf{Fix}\ \mathrm{Prt}_1^1(\bot)$ (both players have the same objective, i.e., $\mathbf{1}$) are defined on EPGA $\mathcal{G}^p$ of $\mathcal{H}$ for the set of goal states T. Thus, w_{12}/w_{11} maps a state $s \in S$ to the probability of reaching T in case of competing/collaborating players; and therefore define bounds on $\Pr^x(T')$ for the initial state in $\mathcal{H}'$. In the sequel, we assume (α, γ), $\mathcal{H}'$, $\mathcal{H}$, $\mathbf{1}$, $\mathbf{2}$, w_{11} and w_{12} are given; unless stated otherwise. Moreover, let $\Delta_y(s) = \{\mu \mid s \xrightarrow{\tau}_y \mu\}$ for $y \in \{\mathrm{p}, \mathrm{r}\}$.

5.1   Stable Abstractions

We now explain our abstract-refine framework (Fig. 6). We only consider states s with $\Delta_p(s) \neq \emptyset$ for refinement, as only their refinement can affect the reachability probabilities.

We first check whether the probabilities for reaching goal states from player-two states in $\mathcal{H}$ depend on the non-determinism induced by the abstraction process in their successor (player-one) states. Alternatively, we check whether the splitting of player-one states (alone) affects the reachability probabilities of their corresponding player-two states. (Recall we allow to merge concrete player-one states even if their behaviour after abstraction is not the same (see Definition 11), therefore their splitting may change the reachability probabilities of their corresponding player-two states.). Let us first define some notions.

State $t \in S_2$ in APGA $\mathcal{H}$ is called *stable* whenever the value $w_{12}(t)$ (a) coincides with that of one of its direct successors that obtains it via a *required* transition, and (b) remains unchanged after splitting its direct successor states. To formally define this notion, we first define the notion of a *stable* player-one state. A state $s \in S_1$ is *stable* if its reachability probability $w_{12}(s)$ is obtained via some of its *required* transitions.

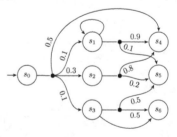

Fig. 7. A PA $\mathcal{M}$.

---

[2] For example, let $x = \max$ in $\Pr^x(T')$ then $\mathbf{1} = \max$ and $\mathbf{2} = \min$ (player-one maximizes whereas the player-two minimizes the probability) or vice versa.

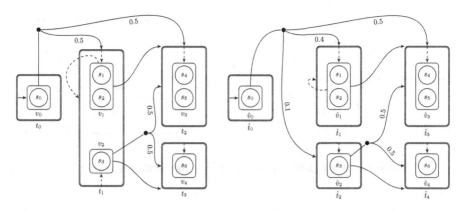

Fig. 8. For $\mathbf{1} = \min$ and $\mathbf{2} = \max$, APGA $\mathcal{H}$ (left) is a stable abstraction of PA $\mathcal{M}$ (Fig. 7) w.r.t. $T = \{t_3\}$; and APGA $\hat{\mathcal{H}}$ (right) is a bounded abstraction w.r.t. $T = \{\hat{t}_4\}$ and $\epsilon = 0.4$.

Definition 12 (Stable player-one states). *State $s \in S_1$ is stable iff $w_{\mathbf{12}}(s) = w_{\mathbf{12}}(\mu)$ for some $\mu \in \Delta_\mathrm{r}(s)$. States that are not stable are unstable.*

Example 4. APGA $\mathcal{H}$ (Fig. 8 left) is an abstraction of PA $\mathcal{M}$ (Fig. 7). Let $\mathbf{1} = \min$, $\mathbf{2} = \max$, $T = \{t_3\}$ with $w = \mathbf{Fix}\ \mathrm{Prt}_{\mathbf{2}}^{\mathbf{1}}(\bot)$ where $w(v_0) = 0.25$, $w(v_1) = 0$, $w(v_2) = 0.5$, $w(v_3) = 0$, $w(v_4) = 0$, $w(t_0) = 0$, $w(t_1) = 0.5$, $w(t_2) = 0$ and $w(t_3) = 1$. Note that $\Delta_\mathrm{r}(v_1) \neq \emptyset$ and $\Delta_\mathrm{p}(v_1) \neq \emptyset$. As $w(v_1) = w(\iota_{t_2}) = 0$, and $\iota_{t_2} \in \Delta_\mathrm{r}(v_1)$, v_1 is stable.

Proposition 5. *Refining stable player-one states preserves reachability probabilities.*

Intuitively, if the reachability probability (w.r.t. $w_{\mathbf{12}}$) of a player-two state, say t, depends on one of its stable successors, it remains unchanged if any of them is split. This is because a stable (player-one) state, say s, obtains its reachability probability via a *required* transition. And if s is split, then the partitions of s inherit the *required* transitions of s; as a result the reachability probabilities of partitions of s remain unchanged – because they obtain them via the same *required* transition as s. Thus, in the refined model the reachability probability of t again depends on one of its stable successors, and remains unchanged. This is not ensured if an unstable successor, say u, of t is split. Because in this case different partitions of u might have different sets of *required* and *possible* transitions, possibly resulting in different reachability probabilities in the refined model. Now if the reachability probability of t depends on one of them, it might be different from that in the abstract model.

In the following definition, we state conditions that guarantee the preservation of reachability probability w.r.t. $w_{\mathbf{12}}$ of a player-two state irrespective of whether its stable or unstable successor is refined.

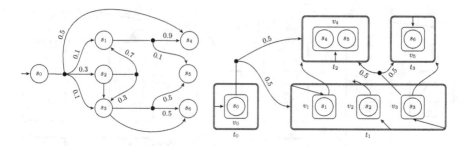

Fig. 9. PA $\mathcal{M}$ (left) with its SG-based abstraction $\mathcal{H}$ (right).

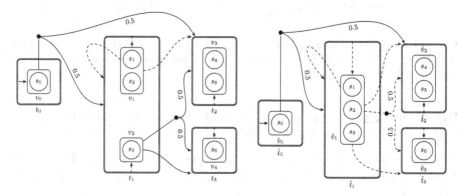

Fig. 10. $\mathcal{H}$ (left) and $\hat{\mathcal{H}}$ (right) are abstract models of PA $\mathcal{M}$ in Fig. 9 with $\mathcal{H} \preceq \hat{\mathcal{H}}$.

Definition 13 (Stable player-two states). *State $t \in S_2$ is stable iff (1) $w_{12}(t) = w_{12}(v)$ for a stable $v \in \mathrm{succ}(t)$, and (2) $\forall u \in \mathrm{succ}(t)$: $w_{12}(t) = \mathbf{2}\{w_{12}(v), w_{12}(\eta)\}$ for every $\eta \in \Delta_p(u)$. States that are not stable are unstable.*

Condition (1) assures that the reachability probability of t depends on a stable successor. Condition (2) assures that $w_{12}(t)$ will remain unchanged even if the successor states of t are split into their constituent states.

Example 5. Let $\mathbf{1} = \min$ and $\mathbf{2} = \max$ for APGA $\mathcal{H}$ (left in Fig. 10) with $w = \mathbf{Fix} \, \mathrm{Prt}_2^1(\bot)$ for $T = \{t_3\}$, where $w(v_0) = 0.25$, $w(v_1) = 0$, $w(v_2) = 0.5$, $w(v_3) = 0$, $w(v_4) = 0$, $w(t_0) = 0$, $w(t_1) = 0.5$, $w(t_2) = 0$ and $w(t_3) = 1$. (Note that this APGA is a copy of Fig. 8 left, except that $v_1 \to t_2$ is now a *possible* transition.) The reachability probability of t_1 depends on a stable successor v_2, i.e., $w(t_1) = 0.5 = \max\{w(v_1) = 0, w(v_2) = 0.5\}$ (fulfilling condition (1) of Definition 13). Moreover, as $w(v_2) = 0.5 = \max\{w(\iota_{t_1}) = 0.5, w(\iota_{t_2}) = 0, w(v_2) = 0.5\}$ (fulfilling condition (2) of Definition 13), therefore the *possible* transitions of unstable state v_1 have no impact on the reachability probability of t_1 in any refinement of v_1. Thus, t_1 is stable. Note that in APGA $\hat{\mathcal{H}}$ (right in Fig. 10), the state $\hat{t}_1$ is not stable w.r.t. the above objectives as the reachability probability of $\hat{t}_1$ does not depend on a stable successor.

Proposition 6. *The reachability probabilities of stable player-two states are invariant to the refinement of their direct successors.*

An APGA $\mathcal{H} = \alpha(\mathcal{H}')$ is *stable* if all player-two states t with $\Delta_p(t) \neq \emptyset$ are stable; we call α a *stable abstraction function*. Any refinement of a stable abstraction, with the same player-two state space, preserves reachability probabilities. Therefore, if further tightening of probability bounds is required, we should consider refining player-two states (see Fig. 6). First we discuss the refinement of player-one states.

5.2   Refining Player-One States

We consider unstable successors of unstable player-two states for refinement.

Definition 14 (Effective unstable). *State $s \in S_1$ is effectively unstable iff (1) s is unstable, and (2) there exists an unstable $t \in S_2$ with $s \in \mathrm{succ}(t)$.*

Let $\mathrm{eus}(\mathcal{H})$ be the set of effectively unstable states. We define how to split an effectively unstable state in $\mathcal{H}$ into two blocks yielding a new partitioning of the state space of $\mathcal{H}'$. (Recall $\mathcal{H}' = \alpha_{\mathrm{PA}}(\mathcal{M})$, and $\mathcal{H} = \alpha(\mathcal{H}')$).

Definition 15. *For $s \in \mathrm{eus}(\mathcal{H})$, let $\mu \in \Delta_p(s) : w_{12}(s) = w_{12}(\mu)$. Then, $\mathrm{B}_1(s) = \{s' \in \gamma(s) \mid \exists \rho' \in \Delta'(s') : \alpha(\rho') = \mu\}$ and $\mathrm{B}_2(s) = \gamma(s) \backslash \mathrm{B}_1(s)$.*

This is the basis for the inner-loop of our abstract-refine framework (Fig. 6).

Definition 16 (Inner abstraction). *The* inner abstraction transformer *function* IAT : *Abst* $(\mathcal{H}') \to Abst(\mathcal{H}')$ *is defined for $\alpha \in Abst(\mathcal{H}')$ with $\mathcal{H} = \alpha(\mathcal{H}')$ and $s' \in S'$ as:*

$$\mathrm{IAT}(\alpha)(s') = \begin{cases} \alpha(s') & \text{if } \alpha(s') \in S_2, \text{ or } \alpha(s') \in S_1 \backslash \mathrm{eus}(\mathcal{H}) \\ \mathrm{B}_1(\alpha(s')) & \text{if } \alpha(s') \in \mathrm{eus}(\mathcal{H}) \text{ and } s' \in \mathrm{B}_1(\alpha(s')) \\ \mathrm{B}_2(\alpha(s')) & \text{if } \alpha(s') \in \mathrm{eus}(\mathcal{H}) \text{ and } s' \in \mathrm{B}_2(\alpha(s')) \end{cases}$$

Note that $\mathrm{IAT}(\alpha)$ maps s' to the same partition block as α does if either $\alpha(s')$ is a player-two or a stable player-one state. In case $\alpha(s') = s$ is an effectively unstable state, it is either mapped to the partition block $\mathrm{B}_1(s)$ or $\mathrm{B}_2(s)$.

Example 6. APGA $\hat{\mathcal{H}}$ (right Fig. 10) is an abstraction of PA $\mathcal{M}$ (left in Fig. 9). Let $\mathbf{1} = \min$ and $\mathbf{2} = \max$ for $\hat{\mathcal{H}}$ with $\hat{w} = \mathbf{Fix}\ \mathrm{Prt}_2^1(\bot)$ for $\hat{T} = \{\hat{t}_2\}$, where $\hat{w}(\hat{v}_0) = 0.5$, $\hat{w}(\hat{v}_1) = 0$, $\hat{w}(\hat{v}_2) = 0$, $\hat{w}(\hat{v}_3) = 0$, $\hat{w}(\hat{t}_0) = 0$, $\hat{w}(\hat{t}_1) = 0$, $\hat{w}(\hat{t}_2) = 1$ and $\hat{w}(\hat{t}_3) = 0$. Note that $\hat{t}_1$ has only one successor, i.e. $\hat{v}_1$, having only *possible* transitions. Therefore, $\hat{\mathcal{H}}$ is not a stable abstraction of PA $\mathcal{M}$.

Let us refine $\hat{\mathcal{H}}$, and let $\mathcal{H}' = \alpha_{\mathrm{PA}}(\mathcal{M})$. For the successor state $\hat{v}_1$ of $\hat{t}_1$, we have $\hat{v}_1 \to \iota_{\hat{t}_3}$ with $\hat{w}(\iota_{\hat{t}_3}) = \hat{w}(\hat{v}_1) = 0$. We separate the concrete states of $\hat{v}_1$ that have a transition (after abstraction) to $\iota_{\hat{t}_3}$, which is v'_3. Therefore, $\hat{v}_1$ is partitioned into two blocks $v_1 = \{v'_1, v'_2\}$ and $v_2 = \{v'_3\}$; and $\mathcal{H}$ (left in Fig. 10) is the APGA induced by the new partitioning of the state space of $\mathcal{H}'$. Note that $\mathcal{H}$ is a stable abstraction w.r.t. objectives $\mathbf{1}$, $\mathbf{2}$ and $T = \{t_2\}$; and moreover $\mathcal{H} \preceq \hat{\mathcal{H}}$.

Instead of refining all states in eus($\mathcal{H}$) in one step, one may pick some of them. In this way, unnecessary refinements of some states in eus($\mathcal{H}$) in the next iteration may be avoided (because of splitting of states in the current step).

Proposition 7. IAT(α) $\preceq \alpha$ for $\alpha \in Abst(\mathcal{H}')$.

The fixpoint of the function IAT is guaranteed to exist for abstraction functions defined (on the embedding of) PAs with finite bisimulation quotient. Intuitively, because of the finite number of player-one states and transitions, the refinement process (in the worst case) will eventually result in a model having only *required* transitions from player-one states. At that point, all player-one states will be stable, thus, making their further partitioning impossible (see Definition 16). This provides the basis to iteratively refine player-one states in $\alpha(\mathcal{H}')$ resulting in a stable abstraction **Fix** IAT(α)($\mathcal{H}'$) of $\mathcal{H}'$.

Theorem 2. Fix IAT(α)($\mathcal{H}'$) *is a stable abstraction.*

The following corollary follows from Theorem 2, and shows that for a given partitioning of states of PA $\mathcal{M}$, the SG-based abstraction [5] is as precise as the APGA-based abstraction when refined to a stable abstraction. However, the size of the latter is at most that of the former.

Corollary 2. *Let* $\mathcal{H}_{sg}$ *be an SG-based abstraction and* $\alpha(\mathcal{H}') = \hat{\mathcal{H}}_{apga}$ *be an APGA-based abstraction of APGA* $\mathcal{H}'$ *with* $S_2^{sg} = \hat{S}_2^{apga}$. *Let* w_{12}^{sg} *and* w_{12}^{apga} *be defined on* $\mathcal{H}_{sg}$ *and* $\mathcal{H}_{apga} = $ **Fix** IAT(α)($\mathcal{H}'$) *respectively. Then, (1)* $\forall t \in S_2^{sg}, u \in S_2^{apga} : w_{12}^{sg}(t) = w_{12}^{apga}(u)$, *and (2)* $|S_1^{sg}| \geq |S_1^{apga}| \geq |\hat{S}_1^{apga}|$.

Example 7. APGA $\mathcal{H}$ (right) is an SG-based abstraction [5] of PA $\mathcal{M}$ (left) in Fig. 9; whereas the left APGA in Fig. 10, say $\mathcal{H}''$, is a stable abstraction of $\mathcal{M}$ w.r.t. the objectives $\mathbf{1} = \min$, $\mathbf{2} = \max$ and $T = \{t_3\}$. Note that both models have the same reachability probabilities to t_3 (i.e., 0.25) from the initial states. Moreover, $|S_1| = 6$ and $|S_1''| = 5$, and $|\Delta| = 12$ and $|\Delta''| = 11$.

5.3   Refining Player-Two States

We now discuss the outermost loop refining player-two states. This is, in principle, similar to *strategy-based refinement* in [5]. Let $\mathcal{H}$ be a *stable* abstraction of APGA $\mathcal{H}'$. If the reachability probabilities – w.r.t w_{12} and w_{11} – of S_2 states (that are of interest) are at most ϵ-apart, we are done. Otherwise, we refine some of the player-two states.

Definition 17 (ϵ-boundedness). *State* $s \in S$ *is* ϵ-bounded *for* $\epsilon \in \mathbb{R}_{(0,1)}$ *iff* $|w_{12}(s) - w_{11}(s)| \leq \epsilon$. *Distribution* $\mu \in Dist(S)$ *is* ϵ-bounded *iff* $|w_{12}(\mu) - w_{11}(\mu)| \leq \epsilon$. *APGA* $\mathcal{H}$ *is* ϵ-bounded *iff all its states are bounded.*

Lemma 1. *In an unbounded APGA, the reachability probabilities of some player-two state—w.r.t* w_{11} *and* w_{12}—*depend on two different successors.*

The lemma follows from the fact that if the reachability probabilities of each player-two state in an APGA depends on one of its successors, then the APGA represents the embedding of a PA that is 0-bounded—upper and lower bounds of reachability probabilites coincide for each player-two state.

The above lemma helps finding player-two states that can be refined. Let $\mathrm{ub}(\mathcal{H}) = \{t \in S_2 \mid \exists u, v \in \mathrm{succ}(t) : u \neq v \wedge w_{12}(t) = w_{12}(u) \wedge w_{11}(t) = w_{11}(v)\}$ be the set of player-two states in $\mathcal{H}$ whose reachability probability bounds depend on two different successors. A state in $\mathrm{ub}(\mathcal{H})$ can be refined as:

Definition 18. *State $t \in \mathrm{ub}(\mathcal{H})$ can be partitioned into* $\mathrm{P}_1(t) = \{t' \in \gamma(t) \mid \exists \iota_{u'} \in \Delta'(t') : w_{12}(t) = w_{12}(\alpha(u'))\}$, *and* $\mathrm{P}_2(t) = \gamma(t) \backslash \mathrm{P}_1(t)$.

Intuitively, concrete states (of t) whose player-one abstract states' reachability probabilities (w.r.t. w_{12}) coincide with $w_{12}(t)$ are separated from other concrete states. This is the basis for the outer-loop of our abstract-refine framework (Fig. 6).

Definition 19 (Outer abstraction). *The* outer abstraction transformer *function* $\mathrm{OAT} : Abst\ (\mathcal{H}') \to Abst(\mathcal{H}')$ *is defined for* $\hat{\alpha} \in Abst(\mathcal{H}')$ *with* $\mathcal{H} = \mathbf{Fix}\ \mathrm{IAT}(\hat{\alpha})(\mathcal{H}')$ *and* $s' \in S'$ *as:*

$$\mathrm{OAT}(\alpha = \mathbf{Fix}\ \mathrm{IAT}(\hat{\alpha}))(s') = \begin{cases} \alpha(s') & \text{if } \alpha(s') \in S_1\ or \alpha(s') \in S_2 \backslash \mathrm{ub}(\mathcal{H}) \\ \mathrm{P}_1(\alpha(s')) & \text{if } \alpha(s') \in \mathrm{ub}(\mathcal{H})\ and\ s' \in \mathrm{P}_1(\alpha(s')) \\ \mathrm{P}_2(\alpha(s')) & \text{if } \alpha(s') \in \mathrm{ub}(\mathcal{H})\ and\ s' \in \mathrm{P}_2(\alpha(s')) \end{cases}$$

Note that $\mathrm{OAT}(\alpha)$ maps s' to the same partition block as α does if $\alpha(s')$ is a player-one state or a *bounded*-player-two state. Otherwise, it maps s' either to $\mathrm{P}_1(s)$ or $\mathrm{P}_2(s)$.

Example 8. For $\epsilon = 0.4$, $\mathbf{1} = \min$, $\mathbf{2} = \max$ and $T = \{t_3\}$, the APGA $\mathcal{H}$ in Fig. 8 (left) is not an ϵ-bounded abstraction of PA $\mathcal{M}$ in Fig. 7, as $|w_{12}(t_1) - w_{11}(t_1)| = |0.5 - 0| > \epsilon$ (0 is the reachability probability with $\mathbf{1} = \min$ and $\mathbf{2} = \min$). It is possible to refine $\mathcal{H}$ in order to have reachability probability bounds of t_1 at most ϵ-apart. $\hat{\mathcal{H}}$ (Fig. 8 right) is an ϵ-bounded abstraction of $\mathcal{M}$ obtained by partitioning the concrete states of t_1 in $\mathcal{H}$ into two blocks, i.e., $\mathrm{P}_1 = \{s_3\} = v_2'$ and $\mathrm{P}_2 = \{s_1, s_2\} = v_1'$. Note that $0 = |0 - 0| < \epsilon$ and $0 = |0.5 - 0.5| < \epsilon$ for $\hat{t}_1$ and $\hat{t}_2$ respectively.

The following theorem asserts that for $\tilde{\alpha} \in Abst(\mathcal{H}')$ with $\alpha = \mathbf{Fix}\ \mathrm{IAT}(\tilde{\alpha})$, the model induced by $\mathbf{Fix}\ \mathrm{IAT}(\mathrm{OAT}(\alpha))$ has at least as tight bounds on the reachability probabilities of player two states as the model induced by α.

Theorem 3. *For* $\tilde{\alpha} \in Abst(\mathcal{H}')$ *with* $\alpha = \mathbf{Fix}\ \mathrm{IAT}(\tilde{\alpha})$, $\mathbf{Fix}\ \mathrm{IAT}(\mathrm{OAT}(\alpha))(\mathcal{H}')$ *has at least as tight bounds on the reachability probabilities of player-two states as* $\alpha(\mathcal{H}')$.

Like IAT, the fixpoint of the function OAT is guaranteed to exist for abstraction functions defined on the embedding of PAs with finite bisimulation quotient.

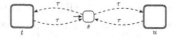

Fig. 11. $\alpha_\top(\mathcal{H}')$ for APGA $\mathcal{H}'$.

Because in the worst case, the refinement of player-two states will eventually result in the embedding of PA that is 0-bounded, i.e., upper and lower bounds of reachability probabilites coincide for each player-two state. This therefore provides the basis to iteratively compute the partitioning of the state space of the model induced by $\alpha \in Abst(\mathcal{H}')$ such that the model induced by **Fix** OAT(α) is an ϵ-bounded abstraction.

Theorem 4. *For fixed $\epsilon \in \mathbb{R}_{(0,1)}$, **Fix** OAT($\alpha$)($\mathcal{H}'$) is an ϵ-bounded abstraction.*

In order to have an ϵ-bounded abstraction, one can start with a coarsest abstraction $\mathcal{H}'$ given as $\alpha_\top(\mathcal{H}') = (\{s = \alpha(S_1'), t = \alpha_\top(T'), u = \alpha_\top(S_2' \backslash T')\},$ $\{\{s\}, \{t, u\}\}, \{\tau\}, \emptyset, \{s \to_\text{p} t, s \to_\text{p} u, t \to_\text{p} s, u \to_\text{p} s\}, s)$—recall that T' is a set of goal states in $\mathcal{H}'$—(see Fig. 11), and then refine it iteratively by Definition 19.

Corollary 3. **Fix** OAT($\alpha_\top$)($\mathcal{H}'$) *is an ϵ-bounded abstraction.*

6   Related Work

Abstraction of probabilistic automata (PAs) and the strongly related MDPs has received considerable attention. Starting from initial work by D'Argenio et al. [19] in 2001, techniques such as three-valued abstraction [20], counterexample-guided abstraction refinement (CEGAR) [21], and game-based abstraction [5] have been tailored to these probabilistic models. For a recent overview of abstraction techniques of probabilistic models, see [22].

Abstraction. Our abstraction is closely related to game-based abstraction. We separate the non-determinism in the concrete model and the non-determinism introduced by the abstraction. For each source of non-determinism, one player is used. Whereas [5] uses Shapley's stochastic games [11] as abstract models, we use (1) a variant in which both players are symmetric, and (2) extend this with modal transitions. Our abstract models are thus a *modal variant of probabilistic game automata* [8]. Whereas [5] uses the principle "states *must* have the same step-wise behaviour after abstraction to be merged together [5]"; in our setting states having the same step-wise behaviour after abstraction are *at least* merged together. SG-abstractions are thus a special case of our abstractions.

Modal Games and Probabilistic Models. Modal extensions of two-player games have been studied in [23]. De Alfaro *et al.* show that modal game abstraction preserves alternating μ-calculus, and provide (amongst others) a completeness results for a safety fragment of that logic. Our abstract stochastic games can be considered as lifting their model to the stochastic setting. Modal transitions for probabilistic models have been advocated in our earlier work [4,7].

Tighter Abstractions. All aforementioned abstraction techniques (including the one in this paper) for probabilistic models are state-based. That is, the relation between the concrete and abstract model is given by a simulation relation that relates groups of concrete states to an abstract state. This has been casted in a general abstract interpretation setting in [24]. The abstraction in [5] is optimal in the sense of abstract interpretation [25] when relating states. Our earlier work [6] showed that using simulation and refinement relations that relate probability distributions rather than states has the potential to provide more precise abstractions. Relating distributions has also been applied [26] so as to obtain a distribution-based variant of Larsen and Skou's notion of probabilistic bisimulation [27]. Applying this principle to our abstraction-refinement framework has been briefly described in [18].

Refinement. Depending on whether the two players join forces so as to maximize or minimize the reachability probability or they act as opponents, analyzing the abstract game yields a lower or upper bound on the minimal or maximal reachability probability. If these bounds are sufficiently precise, the satisfaction or refutation of the property on the original PA can be concluded. Otherwise, the abstraction is refined. The resulting game then yields more precise results and, similarly to CEGAR, the procedure may be iterated until the obtained bounds are precise enough. In contrast to other refinement techniques, the crux of our technique is to separate the refinement of the various players, resulting in a *nested* abstraction-refinement loop. Player-two refinement is a mild variant of that in [5] in which states are always split in two parts[3]. Player-one refinement heavily relies on exploiting the modal transitions in the abstract model, a concept that is absent in [5].

7 Conclusion

This paper presented a *nested abstraction-refinement framework* for Segala's probabilistic automata (PAs). It is complete in the sense that termination is guaranteed for every PA with a finite bisimulation quotient. The key to our technique is to use a *modal variant* of Condon and Ladner's two-player probabilistic game automata. Abstraction using this model yields (tight) upper and lower bounds on extremal reachability probabilities. We believe that modal stochastic games are of interest as such and deserve further investigation. This paper focused on the theoretical underpinnings of our abstraction-refinement technique. An implementation and experimental comparison to game-based abstraction [5] is needed to check its practical feasibility and performance.

---

[3] This may converge slower than allowing for coarser splittings (as in [5]), but yields smaller state spaces.

Acknowledgements. This work is strongly inspired by and heavily builds upon the work of Kim G. Larsen. The idea of using possible (may) and required (must) transitions goes back to his seminal work with Thomsen [28]. Simulation and refinement relations for probabilistic models originated in his work with Jonsson [16]. Kim developed one of the first, if not the very first, abstraction-refinement technique for MDPs [19]. His work on constraint Markov chains [29] provided the basis for our joint work on abstract PAs [4]. The uncertainty of the non-deterministic choices in APA is modeled by modal transitions while uncertainty of the stochastic behavior is expressed—as in constraint Markov chains—by (underspecified) stochastic constraints. Besides the influence of all these work, Kim has always been extremely inspiring. This started in 1996 at the conference FTRTFT in Uppsala, when he stimulated us to use Uppaal—at those days in its very early stage of development [30]—to take up the challenge of modeling and verifying Philips' bounded retransmission protocol [31]. This relationship has continued over the years and has led to several joint EU projects. It has been a great pleasure and enormous honor to work with Kim. This paper is a salute to his 60th birthday.

References

1. Segala, R., Lynch, N.A.: Probabilistic simulations for probabilistic processes. Nordic J. Comput. **2**(2), 250–273 (1995)
2. Norman, G.: Analysing randomized distributed algorithms. In: Baier, C., Haverkort, B.R., Hermanns, H., Katoen, J.-P., Siegle, M. (eds.) Validation of Stochastic Systems. LNCS, vol. 2925, pp. 384–418. Springer, Heidelberg (2004). doi:10.1007/978-3-540-24611-4_11
3. Huth, M.: On finite-state approximants for probabilistic computation tree logic. Theoret. Comput. Sci. **346**(1), 113–134 (2005)
4. Delahaye, B., Katoen, J.P., Larsen, K.G., Legay, A., Pedersen, M.L., Sher, F., Wasowski, A.: Abstract probabilistic automata. Inf. Comput. **232**, 66–116 (2013)
5. Kattenbelt, M., Kwiatkowska, M.Z., Norman, G., Parker, D.: A game-based abstraction-refinement framework for Markov decision processes. Formal Methods Syst. Des. **36**(3), 246–280 (2010)
6. Vira, F.S., Katoen, J.-P.: Tight game abstractions of probabilistic automata. In: Baldan, P., Gorla, D. (eds.) CONCUR 2014. LNCS, vol. 8704, pp. 576–591. Springer, Heidelberg (2014). doi:10.1007/978-3-662-44584-6_39
7. Sher, F., Katoen, J.-P.: Compositional abstraction techniques for probabilistic automata. In: Baeten, J.C.M., Ball, T., Boer, F.S. (eds.) TCS 2012. LNCS, vol. 7604, pp. 325–341. Springer, Heidelberg (2012). doi:10.1007/978-3-642-33475-7_23
8. Condon, A., Ladner, R.E.: Probabilistic game automata. J. Comput. Syst. Sci. **36**(3), 452–489 (1988)
9. Antonik, A., Huth, M., Larsen, K.G., Nyman, U., Wasowski, A.: 20 years of modal and mixed specifications. Bull. EATCS **95**, 94–129 (2008)
10. Huth, M., Jagadeesan, R., Schmidt, D.: Modal transition systems: a foundation for three-valued program analysis. In: Sands, D. (ed.) ESOP 2001. LNCS, vol. 2028, pp. 155–169. Springer, Heidelberg (2001). doi:10.1007/3-540-45309-1_11
11. Shapley, L.S.: Stochastic games. Proc. Natl. Acad. Sci. USA **39**(10), 1095–1100 (1953)
12. Baier, C., Katoen, J.P.: Principles of Model Checking. MIT Press, Cambridge (2008)
13. Bertsekas, D.P., Tsitsiklis, J.N.: An analysis of stochastic shortest path problems. Math. Oper. Res. **16**, 580–595 (1991)

14. Tarski, A.: A lattice-theoretical fixpoint theorem and its applications. Pacific J. of Math. **5**(2), 285–309 (1955)
15. Baier, C., Engelen, B., Majster-Cederbaum, M.E.: Deciding bisimilarity and similarity for probabilistic processes. J. Comput. Syst. Sci. **60**(1), 187–231 (2000)
16. Jonsson, B., Larsen, K.G.: Specification and refinement of probabilistic processes. In: LICS, pp. 266–277. IEEE Computer Society (1991)
17. Larsen, K.G., Thomsen, B.: Compositional proofs by partial specification of processes. In: Chytil, M.P., Koubek, V., Janiga, L. (eds.) MFCS 1988. LNCS, vol. 324, pp. 414–423. Springer, Heidelberg (1988). doi:10.1007/BFb0017164
18. Sher, F.: Abstraction and refinement of probabilistic automata using modal stochastic games. Ph.D. thesis, RWTH Aachen University Aachener Informatik-Berichte AIB-2015-10 (2015)
19. D'Argenio, P.R., Jeannet, B., Jensen, H.E., Larsen, K.G.: Reachability analysis of probabilistic systems by successive refinements. In: Alfaro, L., Gilmore, S. (eds.) PAPM-PROBMIV 2001. LNCS, vol. 2165, pp. 39–56. Springer, Heidelberg (2001). doi:10.1007/3-540-44804-7_3
20. Katoen, J.P., Klink, D., Leucker, M., Wolf, V.: Three-valued abstraction for probabilistic systems. J. Log. Algebr. Program. **81**(4), 356–389 (2012)
21. Hermanns, H., Wachter, B., Zhang, L.: Probabilistic CEGAR. In: Gupta, A., Malik, S. (eds.) CAV 2008. LNCS, vol. 5123, pp. 162–175. Springer, Heidelberg (2008). doi:10.1007/978-3-540-70545-1_16
22. Dehnert, C., Gebler, D., Volpato, M., Jansen, D.N.: On abstraction of probabilistic systems. In: Remke, A., Stoelinga, M. (eds.) Stochastic Model Checking. Rigorous Dependability Analysis Using Model Checking Techniques for Stochastic Systems. LNCS, vol. 8453, pp. 87–116. Springer, Heidelberg (2014). doi:10.1007/978-3-662-45489-3_4
23. de Alfaro, L., Godefroid, P., Jagadeesan, R.: Three-valued abstractions of games: uncertainty, but with precision. In: LICS, pp. 170–179. IEEE Computer Society (2004)
24. Cousot, P., Monerau, M.: Probabilistic abstract interpretation. In: Seidl, H. (ed.) ESOP 2012. LNCS, vol. 7211, pp. 169–193. Springer, Heidelberg (2012). doi:10.1007/978-3-642-28869-2_9
25. Wachter, B., Zhang, L.: Best probabilistic transformers. In: Barthe, G., Hermenegildo, M. (eds.) VMCAI 2010. LNCS, vol. 5944, pp. 362–379. Springer, Heidelberg (2010). doi:10.1007/978-3-642-11319-2_26
26. Hermanns, H., Krčál, J., Křetínský, J.: Probabilistic bisimulation: naturally on distributions. In: Baldan, P., Gorla, D. (eds.) CONCUR 2014. LNCS, vol. 8704, pp. 249–265. Springer, Heidelberg (2014). doi:10.1007/978-3-662-44584-6_18
27. Larsen, K.G., Skou, A.: Bisimulation through probabilistic testing. Inf. Comput. **94**(1), 1–28 (1991)
28. Larsen, K.G., Thomsen, B.: A modal process logic. In: LICS, pp. 203–210. IEEE Computer Society (1988)
29. Caillaud, B., Delahaye, B., Larsen, K.G., Legay, A., Pedersen, M.L., Wasowski, A.: Constraint Markov chains. Theoret. Comput. Sci. **412**(34), 4373–4404 (2011)
30. Bengtsson, J., Larsen, K.G., Larsson, F., Pettersson, P., Yi, W.: UPPAAL in 1995. In: Margaria, T., Steffen, B. (eds.) TACAS 1996. LNCS, vol. 1055, pp. 431–434. Springer, Heidelberg (1996). doi:10.1007/3-540-61042-1_66
31. D'Argenio, P.R., Katoen, J.-P., Ruys, T.C., Tretmans, J.: The bounded retransmission protocol must be on time!. In: Brinksma, E. (ed.) TACAS 1997. LNCS, vol. 1217, pp. 416–431. Springer, Heidelberg (1997). doi:10.1007/BFb0035403

Semantics and Reasoning

A Coinductive Equational Characterisation of Trace Inclusion for Regular Processes

Matthew Hennessy[✉]

Trinity College Dublin, Dublin, Ireland
matthew.hennessy@cs.tcd.ie

Abstract. In 1966 Arto Salomaa gave a complete axiomatisation of regular expressions. It can be viewed as a sound and complete proof system for regular processes with respect to the behavioural equivalence called *language equivalence*. This proof system consists of a finite set of axioms together with one inductive proof rule.

We show that the behavioural preorder called *language containment* or *trace inclusion* can be characterised in a similar manner, but using a coinductive rather than an inductive proof rule.

1 Introduction

In 1966 Arto Salomaa gave two complete axiomatisations for regular expressions; see [8,13]. We concentrate on the first one where the key idea is the uniqueness of the solution of certain regular expression equations. This is recalled in Sect. 2 within the framework of *regular processes*, from [9]. We use a language for defining recursive processes of the form RECx.t where the body t can be defined using *prefixing*, $a.u$, nondeterministic choice, $u_1 + u_2$, or a termination event 0; of course the body t may also contain further regular processes.

This language, referred to as rCCS, can be given various semantic interpretations, which can be expressed in terms of *behavioural equivalences* between processes. One such behavioural equivalence is called *language equivalence*, where each process p in rCCS is interpreted as a (regular) set of sequences of actions $\mathcal{L}(p)$, intuitively the sequences of actions it can perform. Then two processes are deemed to be *language equivalent*, written $p \equiv_{\mathcal{L}} q$ whenever $\mathcal{L}(p) = \mathcal{L}(q)$. This corresponds to *may equivalence* from [6] or *trace equivalence* from [7].

In this framework Salomaa's result, as formulated for example in [12], is a sound and complete proof system for determining when $p \equiv_{\mathcal{L}} q$. The proof system consists of

- simple proof rules for embodying the principle of *substitution of equals for equals*

This work was supported with the financial support of the Science Foundation Ireland grant 13/RC/2094 and co-funded under the European Regional Development Fund through the Southern & Eastern Regional Operational Programme to Lero – the Irish Software Research Centre.

© Springer International Publishing AG 2017
L. Aceto et al. (Eds.): Larsen Festschrift, LNCS 10460, pp. 449–465, 2017.
DOI: 10.1007/978-3-319-63121-9_22

- a set of equations (or axiom schemas)
- an inductive proof rule for $\equiv_{\mathcal{L}}$ for regular processes, called *unique fixpoint induction*

Unique fixpoint induction is very intuitive:[1]

$$\frac{t\{x \mapsto q\} = q}{\text{REC}x.t = q} \; (\text{UFI})$$

It states that if a process q satisfies (semantically) the body of a recursive process then it is semantically equal to the recursive process itself.

Many other behavioural equivalences for regular processes can be captured in the same manner, simply by varying the equations. For example *strong bisimulation equivalence* and *weak bisimulation equivalence* are captured in this manner in [10,11].

However many behavioural theories of processes are expressed in terms of behavioural preorders rather than equivalences. Typical examples include *refusals* [7], *must testing* [6], or the various contract preorders considered in [2]. It is unclear how Salomaa's proof system can be adapted for such behavioural preorders. In particular there is no known complete induction principle to replace unique fixpoint induction.

Here we consider a simple behavioural preorder, *language* or *trace inclusion*. Let $p \leq_{\mathcal{L}} q$ if $\mathcal{L}(p) \subseteq \mathcal{L}(q)$. Of course it is straightforward to establish for a particular pair of processes p, q whether or not $p \leq_{\mathcal{L}} q$ using Salomaa's proof system; it is sufficient to try to establish $p + q =_{\mathcal{L}} q$. But this does not in itself give a sound and complete proof system for the behavioural preorder $\leq_{\mathcal{L}}$ based on the ideas outlined above, namely

- simple proof rules for embodying the principle of *substitution of equals for equals*
- a set of inequations
- some inductive proof rule for $\leq_{\mathcal{L}}$ over regular processes.

This is the purpose of the current short paper. We show that by using a simple *coinductive* proof rule we can give such a sound and complete proof system for regular processes.

We now outline the remainder of the paper. In the next section we define formally the language of regular processes, and their semantics. We then outline the sound and complete proof system for language equivalence, based on an inductive proof rule. In Sect. 4 we outline our novel proof system, based on a set of standard inequations, together with one coinductive proof rule. Proving the soundness of the proof system is non-trivial, and is given in Sect. 5. The following section is devoted to completeness. The proof here depends on the fact that the set of *reachable states* of processes, in a novel interpretation as a labeled transition system, is finite. This topic is isolated in the independent Sect. 7. The paper ends with a short conclusion.

---

[1] For soundness the variable x in body t should be *guarded*.

$$\frac{}{\mu.p \xrightarrow{\mu} p} \text{ (A-Pre)} \qquad\qquad \frac{}{\text{REC}x.t \xrightarrow{\tau} t\{x \mapsto \text{REC}x.t\}} \text{ (Rec)}$$

$$\frac{p \xrightarrow{\mu} p'}{p + q \xrightarrow{\mu} p'} \text{ (Ext-L)} \qquad\qquad \frac{q \xrightarrow{\mu} q'}{p + q \xrightarrow{\mu} q'} \text{ (Ext-R)}$$

Fig. 1. Operational semantics

2 Regular Processes and Language Equivalence

The language of recursive terms is given by the following grammar:

$$\text{rCCS}: \qquad t ::= 0 \mid \mu.t, \; \mu \in \text{Act}_\tau \mid t_1 + t_2$$
$$\mid x \in \text{Var} \mid \text{REC}x.t$$

where Act is a set of actions, ranged over by a, and Act_τ represents Act $\uplus \{\tau\}$, where τ is a special symbol for an internal action. All occurrences of the variable x in t are *bound* in the term $\text{REC}x.t$, and this leads to the standard notion of *free* and *bound* variables. We are only interested in *closed terms*, those not containing any free variables, which we refer to as *processes*. For the sake of simplicity we will also assume that all terms of the form $\text{REC}x.t$ are *guarded*; that is every occurence of x in the body of the recursion t appears underneath an external prefix $a.-$.

The (standard) operational semantics of processes is given in Fig. 1, with judgements for transitions of the form $p \xrightarrow{\mu} q$, where μ ranges over Act_τ. The rule (Rec) uses the standard notion of substitution: in general $t\{x \mapsto p\}$ represents the result of substituting all free occurrences of the variable x in the term t by the closed term p. This may be defined by structural induction on t.

The transitions in Fig. 1 are generalised to *weak transitions* of the form $p \overset{s}{\Longrightarrow} q$, where s ranges over Act^* as follows:

- $p \overset{\varepsilon}{\Longrightarrow} p$
- $p \xrightarrow{a} p'$, $p' \overset{s}{\Longrightarrow} q$ imply $p \overset{as}{\Longrightarrow} q$
- $p \xrightarrow{\tau} p'$, $p' \overset{s}{\Longrightarrow} q$ imply $p \overset{s}{\Longrightarrow} q$

We use $p \overset{s}{\Longrightarrow}$ to indicate that for some q, $p \overset{s}{\Longrightarrow} q$.

Definition 1 (Language of a process). *For every $k \geq 0$ let $\mathcal{L}^k(p) = \{ s \in \text{Act}^* \mid p \overset{s}{\Longrightarrow}, |s| \leq k \}$, and let $\mathcal{L}(p) = \cup_{k \geq 0} \mathcal{L}^k(p)$. $\mathcal{L}(p)$ is refered to as the language of the process p, or it's set of traces.*

We write $p \leq_{\mathcal{L}} q$ if $\mathcal{L}(p) \subseteq \mathcal{L}(q)$, and $p \equiv_{\mathcal{L}} q$ if $\mathcal{L}(p) \subseteq \mathcal{L}(q)$ and $\mathcal{L}(q) \subseteq \mathcal{L}(p)$. $\square$

3 The Proof System for Language Equivalence

The proof system for language equivalence is given in Fig. 2, with judgements are of the form $\vdash p = q$ where p, q are processes. A simple side-condition would be required on the rule (UFI), if we did not have our simplifying assumption that all recursive processes are guarded.

$$\frac{}{\vdash p = p} \; (\text{ID})$$

$$\frac{\vdash p_1 = p_2, \; \vdash p_2 = p_3}{\vdash p_1 = p_3} \; (\text{TR})$$

$$\frac{\vdash p = p'}{\vdash p' = p} \; (\text{SYM})$$

$$\frac{\langle p, p' \rangle \in \text{Ins}(\textbf{Eq})}{\vdash p = p'} \; (\text{EQ})$$

$$\frac{\vdash p = p'}{\vdash p + q = p' + q} \; (\text{PL})$$

$$\frac{\vdash p = p'}{\vdash a.p = a.p'} \; (\text{PRE})$$

$$\frac{}{\vdash \text{REC}x.t = t\{x \mapsto \text{REC}x.t\}} \; (\text{REC})$$

$$\frac{\vdash t\{x \mapsto q\} = q}{\vdash \text{REC}x.t = q} \; (\text{UFI})$$

Fig. 2. The proof system for language equivalence

$$X + X = X \qquad\qquad X + Y = Y + X \qquad\qquad\qquad \tau.X = X$$
$$X + (Y + Z) = (X + Y) + Z \qquad X + 0 = X \qquad\qquad a.(X + Y) = a.X + a.Y$$

Fig. 3. The equations for language equivalence

The rule (EQ) presupposes a set of equations **Eq** such as those in Fig. 3. In general axioms take the form $T = U$ where T, U are words formed from the alphabet $\{\, 0, \mu.-, \; -+- \,\}$ using axiom-variables $X, Y, \ldots$ taken from a set AVar. We say the pair $\langle p, p' \rangle$ is an instance of an equation, written $\langle p, p' \rangle \in \text{Ins}(\textbf{Eq})$, if there exists some axiom $T = U$ in **Eq** such that $p = \sigma(T)$, $p' = \sigma(U)$ where σ is an instantiation, that is a mapping from AVar to processes.

Let us write $\vdash_{eq} p = q$ if there is a proof of $\vdash p = q$ in the proof system using the equations in Fig. 3. Those on the left hand side determine an idempotent commutative monoid; on the right hand side there is an axiom which says that τ transitions are essentially invisible, together with the distribution of prefixing over nondeterministic choice.

This proof system is both sound and complete with respect to language equivalence:

Theorem 1 (Salomaa, Rabinovich). *For all processes,* $\vdash_{eq} p = q$ *if and only if* $p \equiv_{\mathcal{L}} q$.

Proof. The proof for a corresponding property for regular expressions was given in [13]. This was adapted in [12] for a slight variation on our regular processes, using a proof technique from [10]. ☐

One could attempt to adapt this proof system to deal with language inclusion, with judgements of the form $\vdash p \leq q$; for example the set of equations could be replaced by *inequations*. However the major issue would be the replacement of the fixpoint rule (UFI) with a fixpoint rule for inequations which is sufficiently powerful to attain completeness.

In the next section we suggest an alternative approach.

$$\frac{}{\vdash p \leq p} \text{ (ID)}$$

$$\frac{A \vdash p_1 \leq p_2, \ A \vdash p_2 \leq p_3}{A \vdash p_1 \leq p_3} \text{ (TR)}$$

$$\frac{\langle p, p' \rangle \in \mathsf{Ins(\mathbf{InEq})}}{A \vdash p \leq p'} \text{ (INEQ)}$$

$$\frac{A \vdash p \leq p'}{A \vdash p + q \leq p' + q} \text{ (PL)}$$

$$\frac{A, a.p \leq a.p' \vdash p \leq p'}{A \vdash a.p \leq a.p'} \text{ (COREC)}$$

$$\frac{}{\vdash \text{REC}x.t \leq t\{x \mapsto \text{REC}x.t\}} \text{ (UFD)}$$

$$\frac{}{\vdash t\{x \mapsto \text{REC}x.t\} \leq \text{REC}x.t} \text{ (FLD)}$$

$$\frac{}{p \leq p' \vdash p \leq p'} \text{ (HYP)}$$

$$\frac{B \vdash p \leq p', \ A \subseteq B}{AS \vdash p \leq p'} \text{ (W)}$$

Fig. 4. The proof system

4   The Proof System for Trace Inclusion

This proof system has judgements of the form

$$A \vdash p \leq p'$$

where p, p' are processes and A is a *finite set* of assumptions, each of which takes the form $p_1 \leq p_2$. The rules for forming proof trees are given in Fig. 4, many of which are straightforward adaptations of corresponding rules from Fig. 2. We have (INEQ) for instantiating inequations and the rule (REC) from Fig. 2 has been split into two rules, one for unfolding and the other for folding. There are also two obvious rules for managing assumptions, (HYP) and (W). The major change is the replacement of the structural rule for prefixing, (PRE) in Fig. 2, with the rule (COREC). Note that this can be viewed as a generalisation as in the new proof system the rule (PRE) can be derived:

$$\frac{\dfrac{A \vdash p \leq p'}{A, a.p \leq a.p' \vdash p \leq p'} \text{ W}}{A \vdash a.p \leq a.p'} \text{ CoRec}$$

We call this a *coinductive* rule because the conclusion of the rule is one of it's hypotheses. This of course makes it's soundness problematic; see the discussion in the next section.

Each equation in Fig. 3 can be interpreted as two inequations. For example in place of idempotency $X + X = X$ we have the two inequations $X + X \leq X$ and $X \leq X + X$. In addition we need one new inequation:

$$X \leq X + Y \tag{1}$$

Let us write $\vdash_{leq} A \vdash p \leq p'$ to mean that there is a valid proof tree with conclusion $A \vdash p \leq p'$; that is a proof tree constructed using the rules in Fig. 4, using the set of inequations just outlined. We abbreviate $\vdash_{leq} \emptyset \vdash p \leq p'$ to $\vdash_{leq} p \leq p'$. We also use $p \leq_{ineq} p'$ to mean that p may be rewritten to p' using this set of inequations. More specifically, in the rewriting all the rules in Fig. 4 may be used, except (HYP), (W) and (COREC).

Example 1. Let r_1, r_2 denote $\text{REC}x.a.x$, $\text{REC}x.a.a.x$ respectively. The following is a valid proof tree:

$$
\cfrac{
  \cfrac{
    \cfrac{
      \cfrac{a.r_1 \leq a.a.r_2,\ a.r_1 \leq a.r_2 \vdash a.r_1 \leq a.a.r_2}{a.r_1 \leq a.a.r_2,\ a.r_1 \leq a.r_2 \vdash r_1 \leq r_2} \text{ (TR,FLD,UFD)}
    }{a.r_1 \leq a.a.r_2 \vdash a.r_1 \leq a.r_2} \text{ (COREC)} \quad \cfrac{}{\vdash r_1 \leq a.r_1} \text{(UFD)}
  }{
    \cfrac{a.r_1 \leq a.a.r_2 \vdash r_1 \leq r_2}{\vdash a.r_1 \leq a.a.r_2} \text{ (COREC)} \quad \cfrac{}{\vdash r_1 \leq a.r_1} \text{(UFD)} \quad \cfrac{}{\vdash a.a.r_2 \leq r_2} \text{(UFD)}
  } \text{ (TR)}
}{\vdash r_1 \leq r_2} \text{Tr}
$$

(HYP,W)

This means that $\vdash_{leq} \text{REC}x.a.x \leq \text{REC}x.a.a.x$. □

5 Soundness

To prove soundness of the proof system we need a semantic interpretation of the judgements $A \vdash p \leq p'$ which is preserved by all instances of the proof rules. There is an obvious choice, which is however unsound.

Example 2. Let us write

$$p_1 \leq p_1', \ldots p_k \leq p_k' \vDash^w p \leq p', \text{ for } k \geq 0,$$

if $p_1 \leq_{\mathcal{L}} p_1', \ldots p_k \leq_{\mathcal{L}} p_k'$ implies $p \leq_{\mathcal{L}} p'$.

Unfortunately this is not preserved by the rule (COREC). An instance of this rule is

$$\frac{a.b.0 \leq a.0 \vdash b.0 \leq 0}{\vdash a.b.0 \leq a.0}$$

Note that the premise is (vacuously) semantically valid, $a.b.0 \leq a.0 \vDash^w b.0 \leq 0$, because $a.b.0 \not\leq_{\mathcal{L}} a.0$. However the conclusion is not semantically valid, $\not\vDash^w a.b.0 \leq a.0$, because $a.b.0 \not\leq_{\mathcal{L}} a.0$. □

Instead, as in [3], we base our semantic interpretation on a *stratified* characterisation of language inclusion.

Definition 2 (Semantic interpretation). *For $n \geq 0$ write*

$$p_1 \leq p_1', \ldots, p_k \leq p_k' \vDash_n p \leq p'$$

if $\mathcal{L}^n(p_1) \subseteq \mathcal{L}^n(p_1'), \ldots, \mathcal{L}^n(p_k) \subseteq \mathcal{L}^n(p_k')$ implies $\mathcal{L}^n(p) \subseteq \mathcal{L}^n(p')$.
We use $A \vDash p \leq p'$ to mean that $A \vDash_n p \leq p'$ for every $n \geq 0$. □

The counterexample given above no longer works for this stratified semantic interpretation. This is because

$$a.b.\,0 \leq a.\,0 \;\not\models\; b.\,0 \leq 0$$

In particular $a.b.\,0 \leq a.\,0 \;\not\models_1\; b.\,0 \leq 0$ because $\mathcal{L}^1(a.b.\,0) \subseteq \mathcal{L}^1(a.\,0)$ but $\mathcal{L}^1(b.\,0)$ is not a subset of $\mathcal{L}^1(0)$.

Theorem 2 (Soundness). $\vdash_{leq} A \vdash p \leq p'$ implies $A \models p \leq p'$.

Proof. It suffices to show that each of the proof rules in Fig. 4 preserves the semantics. The only non-trivial case is the rule (COREC).

So suppose $A, a.p \leq a.p' \models p \leq p'$; that is

$$A, a.p \leq a.p' \models_k p \leq p' \qquad \text{for all } k \geq 0 \tag{2}$$

We have to show that from this hypothesis, which we refer to as the *outer hypothesis*, the conclusion $A \models a.p \leq a.p'$ follows. In particular we show that $A \models_n a.p \leq a.p'$, for every $n \geq 0$, by induction on n.

The base case, when $n = 0$, is straightforward, as $\mathcal{L}^0(r) = \{\varepsilon\}$ for any process r.

In the inductive case we let $n = (m+1)$, and we can assume

$$A \models_m a.p \leq a.p' \tag{3}$$

which we refer to as the *inner hypothesis*. We have to deduce $A \models_{(m+1)} a.p \leq a.p'$.

To this end suppose $\mathcal{L}^{(m+1)}(q) \subseteq \mathcal{L}^{(m+1)}(q')$ for every $q \leq q' \in A$. We have to show $\mathcal{L}^{(m+1)}(a.p) \subseteq \mathcal{L}^{(m+1)}(a.p')$.

First we apply the inner hypothesis (3): this is possible since $\mathcal{L}^{(m+1)}(q) \subseteq \mathcal{L}^{(m+1)}(q')$ implies $\mathcal{L}^m(q) \subseteq \mathcal{L}^m(q')$. So we obtain $\mathcal{L}^m(a.p) \subseteq \mathcal{L}^m(a.p')$.

With this we can apply the outer hypothesis (2) with $k = m$. We obtain $\mathcal{L}^m(p) \subseteq \mathcal{L}^m(p')$, from which the required $\mathcal{L}^{(m+1)}(a.p) \subseteq \mathcal{L}^{(m+1)}(a.p')$ follows. □

In particular this soundness result means that if we can construct a valid proof tree for the judgement $\vdash p \leq p'$ then $p \leq_{\mathcal{L}} p'$:

Corollary 1. $\vdash_{leq} p \leq p'$ implies $p \leq_{\mathcal{L}} p'$.

Proof. Suppose $\vdash_{leq} p \leq q$, that is $\emptyset \vdash p \leq q$. By Theorem 2 we have that $\mathcal{L}^n(p) \subseteq \mathcal{L}^n(q)$ for all $n \geq 0$. This means that $\mathcal{L}(p) \subseteq \mathcal{L}(q)$ and therefore by definition $p \leq_{\mathcal{L}} q$. □

6 Completeness

The proof of completeness is constructive; we design an algorithm for constructing valid proof trees. To describe the algorithm we need to introduce some notation.

Definition 3 (Head normal forms). *A process of the form* $\sum_{a \in A} a.p_a$, *where A is a finite subset of* Act *is said to be a* head normal form, *abbreviated to* hnf. □

Proposition 1. *For every process p there exists some head normal form,* HNF(p), *such that $p =_{ineq}$ HNF(p).*

Proof. See the appendix. The proof relies on the fact that all proceses are *guarded.* □

It will also be convenient at some point to work with processes up to the equivalence generated by three axioms from Fig. 3; that is the commutativity and associativity of + together with idempotency. Let $[p]$ denote the equivalence class of all processes equivalent to p. However rather than manipulating these sets of processes we will use particular representatives. We use $(p)_r$ to refer to any actual process in the set $[p]$, for which the idempotency axiom $X + X = X$ cannot be applied to it from left to right. Thus it will take the form $s_1 + s_2 \ldots + s_n$ where each of the processes s_i are syntactically different. We call such processes *reduced.*

The algorithm also uses the three following derived proof rules:

$$\frac{A \vdash p_1 \leq q, \ A \vdash p_2 \leq q}{A \vdash p_1 + p_2 \leq q} \ (\textsc{PlusL}) \qquad\qquad \frac{A \vdash p \leq q_1}{A \vdash p \leq q_1 + q} \ (\textsc{PlusR}q)$$

$$\frac{}{A \vdash 0 \leq q} \ (\textsc{Zero}q)$$

We leave the reader to show that these can be derived from the rules in Fig. 4. All use the transitivity rule (TR). The derivation of (PLUSL) uses two applications of (PL), and an application of the inequation $X + X \leq X$. That of (PLUSq) uses an application of the new inequation (1) above; this is also required in the derivation of (ZEROq), in addition to the inequation $0 \leq 0 + X$.

The pseudo-code for the algorithm $C(A, p, q)$ is given in Fig. 5. It takes as parameters A, a finite set of premises of the form $p_i \leq q_i$, and a pair of processes p, q. It returns with

- **FAIL**, indicating that $p \not\leq_{\mathcal{L}} q$,
- or a proof tree T, which is a valid proof tree for the judgement $A \vdash p \leq q$.

The code is executed by matching the actual parameters sequentially against the patterns on the left hand side in Fig. 5; each of the possible five patterns may be considered as *rules* for matching the actual parameters. The first call transforms the parameters p, q into head normal forms. The remainder can be considered as a case analysis on the structure of p, which when line 6 is reached is guaranteed to be in head normal form. Note that if the final rule, on line 16, is ever fired then we know that q, which is a hnf, does not have an a transition, and therefore we can conclude the $a.p \not\leq_{\mathcal{L}} q$.

The non-trivial rule is on line 11. Here both the processes being analysed have a transitions. Moreover because they are hnfs we know r does not have

```
 1 C(A,p,q) ⇒ if (p or q not in hnf)
 2                then
 3                    let T =  C(A, hnf(p), hnf(q))
 4                    in return   (T;(HNF))
 5                else
 6 C(A,0,q) ⇒ return Zeroq
 7 C(A,  p_1 + p_2,q) ⇒ let T_1 = C(A,p_1,q)
 8                                let T_2   = C(A,p_2,q)
 9                    in
10                        return  (T_1,T_2);(PLUSL)
11 C(A,a.p,  a.q + r)  ⇒ if a.p ≤a.q in A then return  (HYP;PLUSRR)
12                        else let B = {A, a.p<a.q}
13 corec                    let T = C(B,(p)_r,(q)_r)
14                        in
15                            T;(COREC);(PLUSRR)
16 S(A,a.p,q)             ⇒ return FAIL
```

Fig. 5. The algorithm

an a transition. If the assumption $a.p \leq a.q$ is already available in A then the required proof tree is readily constructed. Otherwise this assumption is added to A to get the set of assumptions B, and a proof tree T is constructed for the judgement $B \vdash (p)_r \leq (q)_r$. The returned proof tree for the judgement $A \vdash p \leq q$ is then constructed using T, with an instance of the coinductive rule (COREC), together with the derived rule (PLUSRR) We elide the transformation of $(p)_r, (q)_r$ into the original parameters p, q respectively, but the use of these reduced processes will be important in showing that the algorithm terminates. For the purposes of later discussions we label this recursive call which constructs the proof tree T with *corec*.

Note that in order to simplify the pseudo-code we have assumed that occurrences of **FAIL** are percolated upwards through the code. For example on line 8 if the innner call to $C(A, p_2, q)$ returns **FAIL** then **FAIL** is also returned by the outer call $C(A, p_1 + p_2, q)$.

Execution of the code for given parameters, $C(A, p, q)$ consists of a sequence of recursive calls $C(A_i, p_i, q_i)$ until at some point a base case, such as on lines 6, or 11, or 16, is reached. In order to analyse the behaviour of the algorithm we introduce some notation for describing these sequences.

Definition 4 (Call trees). *Let us write*

$$C(A, p, q) \mapsto C(A', p', q')$$

if executing $C(A, p, q)$ leads directly to a recursive call to $C(A', p', q')$. The call tree of $C(A, p, q)$ is defined to be the tree with root labelled by $C(A, p, q)$ with sub-trees consisting of all the call trees of the recursive calls $C(A', p', q')$ such that $C(A, p, q) \mapsto C(A', p', q')$. Note that in these trees the out-degree of each node is at most 2. A recursive call matching line 7 generates two sub-nodes; all other recursive calls generates at most one.

A call path for $C(A, p, q)$ is a path (finite or infinite) in the call tree of $C(A, p, q)$ starting with the root. □

$$\frac{}{\mu.t \xrightarrow{\mu} t} \text{ (A-Pre)} \qquad\qquad \frac{}{\text{REC}x.t \xrightarrow{\tau} t\{x \mapsto \text{REC}x.t\}} \text{ (REC)}$$

$$\frac{t \xrightarrow{\tau} t'}{t + u \xrightarrow{\tau} t' + u} \text{ (TAU-L)} \qquad\qquad \frac{u \xrightarrow{\tau} u'}{t + u \xrightarrow{\tau} t + u'} \text{ (TAU-R)}$$

$$\frac{t \xrightarrow{a} t', \ u \xrightarrow{a}\!\!\!\!\not\;, \ u \xrightarrow{\tau}\!\!\!\!\not\;}{t + u \xrightarrow{a} t'} \text{ (EXT-L)} \qquad\qquad \frac{u \xrightarrow{a} u', \ t \xrightarrow{a}\!\!\!\!\not\;, \ t \xrightarrow{\tau}\!\!\!\!\not\;}{t + u \xrightarrow{a} u'} \text{ (EXT-R)}$$

$$\frac{t \xrightarrow{a} t', \ u \xrightarrow{a} u'}{t + u \xrightarrow{a} t' + u'} \text{ (EXT)}$$

Fig. 6. Towards hnfs

Proposition 2 (Algorithmic correctness). *Suppose $C(A, p, q)$ terminates.*

(i) If it returns **FAIL** *then $p \not\leq_{\mathcal{L}} q$.*

(ii) If it returns a proof tree, then this is a valid proof tree for the judgement $A \vdash p \leq q$.

Proof. In each case the proof is by induction on the number of recursive calls to $C(-, -, -)$.

(i) **FAIL** can be returned on any one of the lines 3,7,8,13, or 16.

If it is the last then p has the form $a.p'$ and moreover, because there was no match on line 11, we also know that q, which is a hnf, does not have an a derivative. Consequently $a.p' \not\leq_{\mathcal{L}} q$.

Suppose it is on line 13, because the recursive call $C(B, (p')_r, (q')_r)$ returns **FAIL**, in which case p, q have the form $a.p', a.q' + r$. By induction we know that $(p')_r \not\leq_{\mathcal{L}} (q')_r$, that is $p' \not\leq_{\mathcal{L}} q'$. Since $a.q' + r$ is a hnf we know that r does not have an a derivative, and therefore it follows that $a.p' \not\leq_{\mathcal{L}} a.q' + r$. The other cases are handled in a similar manner.

(ii) A proof schema can be returned on any of the lines 4, 6, 10, 11, or 15. In each case the proof consists in checking that the returned schema is indeed a valid proof of the judgement $A \vdash p \leq q$, if necessary by invoking induction. □

The main difficulty in proving that the algorithm always terminates is to characterise the parameters which can be used in a call path from $C(A, p, q)$. This characterisation is complicated by the use of head normal forms in the code. We can capture their use via a relation $t \xrightarrow{\mu} t'$ defined by the rules in Fig. 6. Note that for reasons which will be come apparent presently this relation is defined over arbitrary process terms, rather than simply closed terms, as used in Fig. 1. So in the rule (REC) we assume the standard notion of general substitution of (open) terms for variables, which may involve applications of α-conversion in order to avoid free variables being captured.

$$\frac{\dfrac{\dfrac{\dfrac{\dfrac{a.r_1 \leq a.(r_2 + a.r_2) \vdash a.r_1 \leq a.(\mathbf{r_2} + \mathbf{a.r_2})}{a.r_1 \leq a.(r_2 + a.r_2) \vdash a.r_1 \leq a.(\mathbf{r_2} + \mathbf{a.r_2} + \mathbf{r_2})}\text{(Ax,Tr)}}{a.r_1 \leq a.(r_2 + a.r_2) \vdash a.r_1 \leq a.(r_2 + a.r_2) + a.r_2}\text{(Ax,Tr)}}{a.r_1 \leq a.(r_2 + a.r_2) \vdash r_1 \leq r_2 + a.r_2}\text{(Fld/Ufld)}}{\dfrac{\vdash a.r_1 \leq a.(r_2 + a.r_2)}{\vdash a.r_1 \leq r_2}\text{(coREC)} \quad \dfrac{a.(r_2 + a.r_2) \leq r_2}{}\text{(Fld)}}{\vdash a.r_1 \leq r_2}\text{(Tr)} \quad \dfrac{}{\vdash r_1 \leq a.r_1}\text{(Ufld)}}{\vdash r_1 \leq r_2}\text{(Tr)}$$

Fig. 7. $r_1 = \text{REC}x.a.x$, $r_2 = \text{REC}x.a.(x + a.x)$

Proposition 3. *Suppose* $\text{HNF}(p) \xrightarrow{a} q$. *Then* $p \xrightarrow{\tau}{}^* \xrightarrow{a} q$.

Proof. See the appendix. □

Let $\text{Reach}(t) = \{\, u \mid t \xrightarrow{s}\!\!\twoheadrightarrow u, \ s \in \text{Act}^* \,\}$. In general $\text{Reach}(t)$ is not finite.

Example 3. Consider $r_2 = \text{REC}x.a.(x + a.x)$. Then $\text{Reach}(r_2)$ contains all processes of the form $r_2 + \sum_{1 \leq i \leq n} u_i$ where each u_i is the process $r_2 + a.r_2$; therefore $\text{Reach}(r_2)$ is infinite.

This explains the use of the function $(-)_r$ in line 13 of the algorithm in Fig. 5. Without the application of this function one can check that a call to $C(\emptyset, r_1, r_2)$, where r_1 denotes $\text{REC}x.a.x$, would not terminate. However with the use of $(-)_r$ one can check that $C(\emptyset, r_1, r_2)$ terminates after six recursive calls.

Moreover in Fig. 7 we have constructed a valid proof tree for the judgement $\vdash r_1 \leq r_2$, although some abbreviations are used. We have indicated in bold font an essential use of the idempotency axiom $X = X + X$. □

Definition 5. *Let* $t \xrightarrow{\mu}\!\!\twoheadrightarrow u$ *if* $t \xrightarrow{\mu}\!\!\twoheadrightarrow u'$ *for some* u' *such that* $u = (u')_r$. *Thus if* $t \xrightarrow{\mu}\!\!\twoheadrightarrow u$ *the rules in Fig. 6 are used to find a* u' *such that* $t \xrightarrow{\mu}\!\!\twoheadrightarrow u'$, *and then* u' *is reduced to* u. *Let* $\text{rReach}(t) = \{\, u \mid t \xrightarrow{s}\!\!\twoheadrightarrow u, \ s \in \text{Act}^* \,\}$. □

It is easy to check that $\text{rReach}(r_2)$, where r_2 is defined in Example 3, is the finite set $\{\, r_2, \ r_2 + a.r_2, \ a(r_2 + a.r_2), \ a.(r_2 + a.r_2) + a.r_2 \,\}$. This is a particular instance of a general phenomenon:

Theorem 3. *For every term* t, *the set* $\text{rReach}(t)$ *is finite.*

Proof. See the next section. □

In the sequel we use $\text{Act}(p)$ to denote the (finite) set of actions from Act which appear in the process p.

Proposition 4. *Suppose*

$$C(A_0, p_0, q_0) \mapsto C(A_1, p_1, q_1) \mapsto \ldots \mapsto C(A_k, p_k, q_k), k \geq 0$$

is an arbitrary call path. Then

(1) $A_i \subseteq A_{i+1}$, $\mathsf{Act}(p_n) \subseteq \mathsf{Act}(p_0)$
(2) If none of the recursive calls $C(A_k, p_k, q_k)$ triggers the rule labelled corec, on line 13 in Fig. 5, then there exists some bound K such that $k \leq K$.
(3) If $p \leq q \in A_k$ then either $p \leq q \in A_0$ or p, q have the form $a.p', a.q'$ respectively, where $a \in \mathsf{Act}(p)$ and $p' \in \mathsf{rReach}(p_0)$, $q' \in \mathsf{rReach}(q_0)$.

Proof. The statement (1) follows by an analysis of the pseudo-code in Fig. 5. First note that nowhere is the set of assumptions A_k decreased. Only in one place, line 12, is it changed; it is augmented. Secondly note that $\mathsf{Act}(\mathrm{HNF}(p)) = \mathsf{Act}(p)$, and therefore by code one can check that $\mathsf{Act}(p_{n+1}) \subseteq \mathsf{Act}(p_n)$.

Similarly (2) follows by an analysis of the code.

Part (3) is proved by induction on the number of i, $0 \leq i \leq k$ such that $A_{i+1} \neq A_i$. We look at the first step, the least i such that $C(A_{i-1}, p_{i-1}, q_{i-1}) \mapsto C(A_i, p_1, q_1)$ where $A_i \neq A_0$.

This call must be as a result of matching the rule labelled *corec* on line 13 in Fig. 5. So p_{i-1}, q_{i-1} must have the form $a.p'$, $a.q' + r$, and p_i, q_i the form p', q', and A_i must be $A_0 \uplus \{ a.p' \leq a.q' \}$.

From part (1) we immediately have that $a \in \mathsf{Act}(p_0)$. Moreover all preceeding recursive calls must have either matched line 3, transforming p_0, q_0 to hnfs, or successive matches to line 7. Therefore $hnf(p)$ has the form $a.p' + \ldots$ and $hnf(q)$ has the form $a.q' + r$. It now follows from Proposition 3 that $p' \in \mathsf{rReach}(p_0)$ and $q' \in \mathsf{rReach}(q_0)$, as required. $\qquad\square$

Theorem 4 (Termination). *The recursive procedure $C(A, p, q)$ terminates for all parameters A, p, q.*

Proof. Suppose

$$C(A, p, q) = C(A_0, p_0, q_0) \mapsto \ldots \mapsto C(A_k, p_k, q_k) \mapsto \ldots \qquad (4)$$

is an arbitrary call path, finite or infinite.

First consider any step $C(A_n, p_n, q_n) \mapsto C(A_{n+1}, p_{n+1}, q_{n+1})$ resulting from a successful match to line 13 in the algorithm, which we have labelled *corec*. We know that p_n, q_n have the form $a.p'$, $a.q' + r$ respectively and p_{n+1}, q_{n+1} are p', q'. Because the test on line 11 failed we have that $A_{n+1} = A_n \uplus \{ a.p' \leq a.q' \}$. By Proposition 4(3) $p' \in \mathsf{rReach}(p_0)$, $q' \in \mathsf{rReach}(q_0)$ and $a \in \mathsf{Act}(p)$. Obviously $\mathsf{Act}(p)$ is a finite set, as are $\mathsf{rReach}(p_0)$, $\mathsf{rReach}(q_0)$ from Theorem 3. Therefore there exists some k such that for all $i \geq k$ $A_i = A_k$.

It follows that in the sequence (4) above the rule labelled *corec* on line 13 can only be called a finite number of times. By part (2) of Proposition 4 we have that the sequence (4) can only be finite. $\qquad\square$

We can now conclude with the main result of the paper:

Corollary 2 (Soundness and Completeness). $\vdash_{leq} p \leq q$ *if and only if* $p \leq_{\mathcal{L}} q$.

Proof. One direction, Soundness, follows from Corollary 1.

Conversely suppose $p \leq_{\mathcal{L}} q$. We know from Theorem 4 that the algorithm $C(\emptyset, p, q)$ terminates. By design this algorithm either returns **FAIL** or a proof tree. By algorithmic correctness, Proposition 2, the former is not possible; the same proposition ensures that the returned proof tree is a valid proof tree for $\emptyset \vdash p \leq q$. That is $\vdash_{leq} p \leq q$. $\qquad\qquad$ $\square$

7 Finite Reachability

We prove Theorem 3 by giving an over-approximation to the set of terms reachable from an arbitrary term t. The definition is by structural induction on t, and by construction the resulting set is obviously finite.

Definition 6 (Over-approximation). *For every term t the set of approximants $t^\star$ is defined as follows:*

(i) $0^\star = \{ 0 \}$, $x^\star = \{ x \}$
(ii) $(\mu.t)^\star = \{ \mu.t \} \cup \{ \mu.t' \mid t' \in t'^\star \}$
(iii) $(t_1 + t_2)^\star = t_1^\star \cup t_2^\star \cup \{ t_1' + t_2' \mid t_i \in t_i^\star \}$
(iv) $(\text{REC}x.t')^\star = \{ \text{REC}x.t' \} \cup \{ \Sigma(S) \mid S \subseteq T \}$,
$\quad$ *where* $T = \{ t''\{x \mapsto \text{REC}x.t'\} \mid t'' \in t'^\star \text{ or } t'' + x \in t'^\star \}$ *and for any set of*
$\quad$ *terms* $S = \{ s_1, s_2, \ldots s_n \}$, $\Sigma(S)$ *denotes the term* $s_1 + s_2 + \ldots + s_n$. $\quad\square$

Lemma 1. *For every t, the set $t^\star$ is finite.*

Proof. By structural induction on t. $\qquad\qquad\qquad\qquad\qquad\qquad\qquad$ $\square$

The proof that $\mathsf{rReach}(t) \subseteq t^\star$ is also by structural induction on t and most of the cases are straightforward. For example the case when t has the form $t_1 + t_2$ is handled by the following lemma. Here, and in subsequent proofs we ignore the sequence of actions performed by terms, writing $t \twoheadrightarrow^* t'$ in place of $t \overset{s}{\twoheadrightarrow} t'$, or sometimes $t \twoheadrightarrow^k t'$ when we know that there are k steps in the derivation. We also use some standard notion of the size of such a derivation.

Lemma 2. *Suppose $t_1 + t_2 \twoheadrightarrow^* u$, with a derivation of size n. Then*

1. $t_1 \twoheadrightarrow^* u$, with a derivation of size less then n
2. $t_2 \twoheadrightarrow^* u$, with a derivation of size less then n
3. or $u = u_1 + u_2$ where $t_i \twoheadrightarrow^* u_i$, each also having a derivation size less than n.

Proof. A straightforward induction on the length of the derivation $t_1 + t_2 \twoheadrightarrow^* u$ and a case analysis of why $t_1 + t_2 \twoheadrightarrow u$. $\qquad\qquad\qquad\qquad\qquad$ $\square$

The most difficult case of $\mathsf{rReach}(t) \subseteq t^\star$ to treat is when t has the form $\text{REC}x.u$. In general a sequence of transitions takes the form

$$\text{REC}x.u \twoheadrightarrow u\{x \mapsto \text{REC}x.u\} \twoheadrightarrow \ldots \twoheadrightarrow t'$$

Therefore in order to understand the forms that t' can take we need to characterise the derivatives of $u\{x \mapsto r\}$ in terms of those of u and r.

Definition 7. *We define the predicate $t \downarrow x$ by structural induction on t, as follows:*

> (i) RECy.u $\downarrow x$, *for all x and y*
> (ii) $t_1 \downarrow x$, $t_2 \downarrow x$ *implies $t_1 + t_2 \downarrow x$*
> (iii) $\mu.u \downarrow x$ *for every $\mu \in \mathsf{Act}_\tau$.*

We use $t \uparrow$ to mean that $t \downarrow$ is not true.   □

Intuitively $t \downarrow x$ means that r does not play any role in any transition from $t\{x \mapsto r\}$. This is captured in the first part of the following proposition.

Proposition 5. *Suppose $t\{x \mapsto r\} \xrightarrow{\mu} u$, where t is reduced. Then if t is different from x, one of the following holds:*

> (i) $t \downarrow x$ *and $u = t'\{x \mapsto r\}$ where $t \xrightarrow{\mu} t'$*
> (ii) $t \uparrow x$, $t = t_1 + x$, t_1 *is reduced, and*
> > (a) $u = t_1\{x \mapsto r\} + r'$ *where $r \xrightarrow{\mu} r'$*
> > (b) $u = t_1'\{x \mapsto r\} + r$ *where $t_1 \xrightarrow{\mu} t_1'$*
> > (c) $u = t_1'\{x \mapsto r\} + r'$ *where $t_1 \xrightarrow{\mu} t_1'$, $r \xrightarrow{\mu} r'$*

Proof. By structural induction on t, with an intricate case analysis.   □

Proposition 6. *Suppose $t\{x \mapsto r\} \twoheadrightarrow^* (u)_r$, with a derivation of size k. Then u has one of the following forms:*

> (i) $t'\{x \mapsto r\}$, *where $t \twoheadrightarrow^* t'$ has a derivation of size less then k*
> (ii) $\sum_{1 \le i \le n} r_i'$, *where each $r \twoheadrightarrow^* r_1'$ has a derivation of size less than k*
> (iii) $t'\{x \mapsto r\} + \sum_{1 \le i \le n} r_i'$, *where the derivations $t \twoheadrightarrow^* t' + x$ and $r \twoheadrightarrow^* r_i'$ again have smaller size.*

Proof. By induction on the size of the derivation k. In the general case the transitions have the form

$$t\{x \mapsto r\} \twoheadrightarrow^* u' \xrightarrow{\mu} (u)_r$$

where u' is reduced. Induction can be applied to the derivation $t\{x \mapsto r\} \twoheadrightarrow^* u''$, to give three possibilities for the structure of u'', (i), (ii), (iii) above. In case (i) we apply Proposition 5 to the transition $u' \xrightarrow{\mu} u$. The case (ii) is a straightforward argument, while (iii) is a combination of the first two cases.   □

Theorem 5. *For every term t, rReach$(t) \subseteq t^*$.*

Proof. By structural induction on t. We show that if $t \twoheadrightarrow^* u$ then $u \in t^*$.

The cases when t has one of the forms x, 0 are trivial, while when it is of the form $\mu.t'$ a very simple inductive argument suffices. When it has the form $t_1 + t_2$ an inductive argument is also used, supported by Lemma 2. We look briefly at the final and most difficult, case when it has the form RECx.t_1.

Here we use an inner induction on the size of the derivation $\mathrm{REC}x.t_1 \longrightarrow\!\!\!\to^\star u$. If u is $\mathrm{REC}x.t_1$, that is the length of the derivation is zero, then the result is immediate as by definition $\mathrm{REC}x.t_1 \in (\mathrm{REC}x.t_1)^\star$. Otherwise we have

$$\mathrm{REC}x.t_1 \xrightarrow{\tau} t_1\{x \mapsto r\} \longrightarrow\!\!\!\to^\star u$$

where r denotes $\mathrm{REC}x.t_1$, and we can read off the possible structure of u from Proposition 6. There are three possibilities, and we examine the third when u has the form

$$t'\{x \mapsto r\} + \sum_{1 \leq i \leq n} r'_i$$

where $t \longrightarrow\!\!\!\to^\star t' + x$, $r \longrightarrow\!\!\!\to^\star r'_i$, and each of these derivations being smaller in size than the original one.

Using the inner induction we have $r_i \in (\mathrm{REC}x.t_1)^\star$ for each $1 \leq i \leq n$. Using the other (structural) induction we have $t' + x \in t_1^\star$, and therefore by definition $t'\{x \mapsto r\} \in (\mathrm{REC}x.t_1)^\star$.

It follows that $u \in (\mathrm{REC}x.t_1)^\star$, since this is defined so that $u_i \in (\mathrm{REC}x.t_1)^\star$, $1 \leq i \leq n$, implies $u_1 + \ldots + u_n \in (\mathrm{REC}x.t_1)^\star$.   □

8   Conclusions

We have given a novel sound and complete proof system for trace inclusion of regular processes. The novel rule of the proof system is co-inductive in nature, in that the conclusion of the rule is already one of it's hypotheses. Proof of soundness is based on a technique used in [3] for a proof system for recursive types, while completeness is demonstrated constructively; an algorithm is given which constructs a proof for every semantically valid judgement. Intuitively the algorithm works by *on the fly* determinising the processes, and systematically comparing their a-derivatives, for each action a from Act. The proof that the algorithm actually terminates is conceptually straightforward, but syntactically intricate. It relies on the fact the set of reachable states from a given process is finite, modulo a structural equivalence. A similar result is proved in [5] for the language of regular expressions, where the equivalence used, between regular expressions, is *semantic identity*. An alternative approach to proving termination of our algorithm might be based on defining a relation between our semantics for regular processes, and the derivatives of regular expressions given in [5].

We believe that our proof system can be adapted to a range of semantic preorders between regular processes, such as the testing preorders of [6]. Of particular interest are the contract preorders from [2,4], and variations thereof. Such preorders often have alternative characterisations, often expressed in terms of intricate behavioural properties of processes; as an example see Definition 6 of [1]. It would be instructive to instead characterise these preorders over regular processes using variations on our proof system; the rules, including (COREC), would remain but the set of inequations used would depend on the particular contact preorder in mind.

Acknowledgements. The author would like to thank the anonymous referees, and Giovanni Bernardi, for their useful comments on a previous draft.

A   Some Proofs

Guarded Terms: A variable x is *guarded* in the term t if each free occurrence of x in t occurs underneath a prefix $a.-$. A recursion $\text{REC}x.t$ is *guarded* if x is guarded in t. Finally a term u is a *guarded term* if every sub-term of the form $\text{REC}x.t$ is guarded.

It will be convenient to have an inductive principle for guarded processes, that is closed terms which are guarded.

Definition 8. *Let $\Downarrow$ be the least predicate over processes which satisfies the following rules:*

(a) $0 \Downarrow, a.p \Downarrow$
(b) $p \Downarrow, q \Downarrow$ *implies* $\tau.p \Downarrow$ *and* $(p + q) \Downarrow$
(c) $t\{x \mapsto \text{REC}x.t\} \Downarrow$ *implies* $\text{REC}x.t \Downarrow$.

Lemma 3. *Suppose x is guarded in t for every $x \in \text{FV}(t)$. Then $t\rho \Downarrow$, for any substitution ρ such that $\text{DOM}(\rho) \subseteq \text{FV}(t)$.*

Proof. By structural induction on t.   □

Proposition 7. *If p is guarded then $p \Downarrow$.*

Proof. By structural induction on p. The only non-trivial case is when it has the form $\text{REC}x.t$, where we know that x is guarded in t. By the previous lemma this means that $t\{x \mapsto \text{REC}x.t\} \Downarrow$, and therefore employing rule (c) from Definition 8 we can conclude that $\text{REC}x.t \Downarrow$.   □

In the remainder of this appendix we will assume that all processes are guarded; this assumption is also used throughout the paper.

Proposition 8 (Proposition 1). *For every process p there exists a head normal form* $\text{HNF}(p)$ *such that* $p =_{ineq} \text{HNF}(p)$.

Proof. By induction on $p \Downarrow$. We proceed by an analysis of the structure of p.

- If p has the form $a.q$, or 0 then it is already a hnf.
- If p is $\text{REC}x.t$ then by induction on $\Downarrow$ we know that there is some hnf h such that $t\{x \mapsto \text{REC}x.t\} =_{ineq} h$. Using the (UFD) and (FLD) rules we obtain $\text{REC}x.t =_{ineq} h$.
- If p is $\tau.q$ again the result follows by induction, using the axiom $\tau.X = X$.
- Finally suppose p has the form $p_1 + p_2$. By induction $p_i =_{ineq} h_i$ for some hnfs h_1, h_2. Suppose these have the form $\sum_{a \in A_i} a.p_a^i$, for $i = 1, 2$. Then one can show that

$$p =_{ineq} \sum_{a \in (A_1 - A_2)} a.p_a^1 + \sum_{a \in (A_2 - A_1)} a.p_a^2 + \sum_{a \in (A_2 \cap A_1)} a.(p_a^1 + p_a^2)$$

which is in hnf.   □

Corollary 3 (Proposition 3). *If* $\text{HNF}(p) \xrightarrow{a} q$ *then* $p \xrightarrow{\tau}_{\twoheadrightarrow}^{\star} \xrightarrow{a}_{\twoheadrightarrow} q$.

Proof. The proof proceeds by induction on $p \Downarrow$ and a case analysis on the construction of $\text{HNF}(p)$ as outlined in the previous proposition. $\square$

References

1. Bernardi, G., Francalanza, A.: Full-abstraction for must testing preorders (extended abstract). In: Jacquet, J.-M., Massink, M. (eds.) COORDINATION 2017. LNCS, vol. 10319, pp. 237–255. Springer, Cham (2017). doi:10.1007/978-3-319-59746-1_13
2. Bernardi, G., Hennessy, M.: Mutually testing processes. Log. Methods Comput. Sci. **11**(2), 1–43 (2015)
3. Brandt, M., Henglein, F.: Coinductive axiomatization of recursive type equality and subtyping. Fundam. Inform. **33**(4), 309–338 (1998)
4. Bravetti, M., Zavattaro, G.: A foundational theory of contracts for multi-party service composition. Fundam. Inform. **89**(4), 451–478 (2008)
5. Brzozowski, J.A.: Derivatives of regular expressions. J. ACM **11**(4), 481–494 (1964)
6. De Nicola, R., Hennessy, M.: Testing equivalences for processes. Theoret. Comput. Sci. **34**, 83–133 (1984)
7. Hoare, C.A.R.: Communicating sequential processes (reprint). Commun. ACM **26**(1), 100–106 (1983)
8. Kozen, D.: A completeness theorem for Kleene algebras and the algebra of regular events. Inf. Comput. **110**(2), 366–390 (1994)
9. Milner, R.: A Calculus of Communicating Systems. Springer, Heidelberg (1982)
10. Milner, R.: A complete inference system for a class of regular behaviours. J. Comput. Syst. Sci. **28**(3), 439–466 (1984)
11. Milner, R.: A complete axiomatisation for observational congruence of finite-state behaviors. Inf. Comput. **81**(2), 227–247 (1989)
12. Rabinovich, A.: A complete axiomatisation for trace congruence of finite state behaviors. In: Brookes, S., Main, M., Melton, A., Mislove, M., Schmidt, D. (eds.) MFPS 1993. LNCS, vol. 802, pp. 530–543. Springer, Heidelberg (1994). doi:10.1007/3-540-58027-1_25
13. Salomaa, A.: Two complete axiom systems for the algebra of regular events. J. ACM **13**(1), 158–169 (1966)

Syntactic Markovian Bisimulation for Chemical Reaction Networks

Luca Cardelli[1], Mirco Tribastone[2], Max Tschaikowski[2],
and Andrea Vandin[2(✉)]

[1] Microsoft Research and University of Oxford, Oxford, UK
[2] IMT School for Advanced Studies Lucca, Lucca, Italy
{andrea.vandin,mirco.tribastone}@imtlucca.it

Abstract. In chemical reaction networks (CRNs) with stochastic semantics based on continuous-time Markov chains (CTMCs), the typically large populations of species cause combinatorially large state spaces. This makes the analysis very difficult in practice and represents the major bottleneck for the applicability of minimization techniques based, for instance, on lumpability. In this paper we present syntactic Markovian bisimulation (SMB), a notion of bisimulation developed in the Larsen-Skou style of probabilistic bisimulation, defined over the structure of a CRN rather than over its underlying CTMC. SMB identifies a lumpable partition of the CTMC state space a priori, in the sense that it is an equivalence relation over species implying that two CTMC states are lumpable when they are invariant with respect to the total population of species within the same equivalence class. We develop an efficient partition-refinement algorithm which computes the largest SMB of a CRN in polynomial time in the number of species and reactions. We also provide an algorithm for obtaining a quotient network from an SMB that induces the lumped CTMC directly, thus avoiding the generation of the state space of the original CRN altogether. In practice, we show that SMB allows significant reductions in a number of models from the literature. Finally, we study SMB with respect to the deterministic semantics of CRNs based on ordinary differential equations (ODEs), where each equation gives the time-course evolution of the concentration of a species. SMB implies forward CRN bisimulation, a recently developed behavioral notion of equivalence for the ODE semantics, in an analogous sense: it yields a smaller ODE system that keeps track of the sums of the solutions for equivalent species.

1 Introduction

Chemical reaction networks (CRNs) are a powerful model of interaction at the basis of many branches of science such as organic and inorganic chemistry, ecology, epidemiology and systems biology. In computer science, the interpretation of biological systems as computing devices has stimulated a vigorous line of research ranging from the understanding of the computational power of such

© Springer International Publishing AG 2017
L. Aceto et al. (Eds.): Larsen Festschrift, LNCS 10460, pp. 466–483, 2017.
DOI: 10.1007/978-3-319-63121-9_23

models (e.g., [13, 40, 48]) to the development of formal techniques for their specification, analysis, and verification (e.g., [15, 17, 29, 46]).

Traditionally, CRNs have been equipped with the well-known quantitative semantics based on a system of ordinary differential equations (ODEs), where an ODE relates to the time-course deterministic evolution of the concentration of each species. It is well-known, however, that such semantics may not always accurately reflect the observed behavior, for example when some species are present in low copies [22]. The alternative stochastic semantics based on continuous-time Markov chains (CTMCs) may provide more accurate estimates, but at an increased computational expense. Indeed, since each CTMC state is a population vector giving the number of copies of each species, there is a combinatorial explosion of the CTMC state space as a function of the initial population of species. In order to cope with this, it would be highly desirable to be able to perform CTMC aggregation, e.g., based on lumpability [5, 20]. However, its applicability in practice is fundamentally hampered by the fact that available methods require to explicitly enumerate the state space. This is typically infeasible for realistic CRNs sizes, or even impossible because CRNs may give rise to infinite state spaces.

Inspired from the seminal work of Larsen and Skou on probabilistic bisimulation [36], in this paper we propose a reduction technique that avoids the generation of the original state space. Instead of reasoning at the semantic level, we identify conditions on the *CRN syntax*. More precisely, we provide a new notion of equivalence over CRN species, called *syntactic Markovian bisimulation* (SMB), based on properties that can be checked by inspecting the set of reactions only, but it induces a partition on states of the underlying CTMC: two CTMC states are related if they are invariant with respect to the total population of species in the same SMB equivalence class. To clarify this, suppose we have a CRN with species A, B, and C, and the SMB that gives the partition $\{\{A, B\}, \{C\}\}$. Then the CTMC state $(n_A = 1, n_B = 2, n_C = 1)$ belongs to the same block as state $(n_A = 2, n_B = 1, n_C = 1)$ because they have equal sums within the equivalence classes. The resulting CTMC partition is an ordinarily lumpable one [5]: in the lumped CTMC each macro-state represents the sum of the probabilities of the original states of a partition block.

Importantly, the lumped CTMC can be obtained avoiding the generation of the original state space altogether, owing to an algorithm that constructs a quotient CRN for an SMB. The possibility of such a CRN-to-CRN transformation is useful not only for model *minimization*, but also for using bisimulation as a technique for model *comparison*. This has received increased attention, largely motivated by applications to evolutionary biology [7–9, 11, 14, 25, 41, 47].

SMB turns out to be a natural extension of the ordinary lumpability condition (defined on the underlying CTMC semantics) to the CRN syntax. Ordinary lumpability relates two CTMC states whenever they have the same cumulative transition rates toward any partition block. Analogously, SMB relates two species when, roughly speaking, the cumulative kinetic parameters of the reactions where they are involved as reagents are the same for every *lifted equivalence class* of products. This lifting is defined by relating two products that are invariant up to the SMB equivalence classes, as above. An important consequence of this definition style is that it allows us to also extend the aforementioned CTMC minimization algorithms to SMB. In particular, we present an algorithm for computing the largest SMB that refines a given input partition of species in polynomial time and space.

Being syntactically driven, it is perhaps not surprising that SMB is only a sufficient condition for CTMC lumpability. As a consequence, it is important to understand to what extent it can be effectively applied in practice. On CRN models of biological systems taken from the literature we show that SMB can achieve substantial compressions, yielding reduced CRNs with significantly fewer species and reactions in some cases. We measure the impact of SMB on the analysis of the CRN when this is done by means of stochastic simulation [27], the method of choice in realistic systems due to the large state spaces involved (e.g., [18]). We report noticeable runtime speed-ups in many cases, up to two orders of magnitude, even allowing the execution of benchmark models that would otherwise generate out of memory errors if not reduced. These numerical tests also reveal an interesting connection between SMB and the deterministic semantics of CRNs: the equivalence classes of species found in all the analyzed models coincide with those recently reported in [8] for *forward CRN bisimulation* (FB), an equivalence relation over species that aggregates related ODEs in an analogous way, exactly preserving their total concentration trajectories at all time points. We explain this fact by showing that SMB implies an FB, however the converse is not true in general. Nevertheless, in our tests FB was not able to aggregate more than SMB.

Further Related Work. The closest approach to ours is by Feret et al. [24] who identify *stochastic fragments* on the rule-based language κ [19]. These represent syntactic criteria that yield a sufficient condition for *weak* lumpability (see, e.g., [5]) on the CTMC. The advantage is that the rule-based model is often combinatorially smaller than its underlying CRN description; however, the approach is domain specific in that it can be applied to systems, e.g., protein-protein interaction networks, which can be conveniently expressed as rule-based systems. On the contrary, since SMB works at the level of the CRN it is more general, at the expense of a more expensive syntactic analysis in this application domain.

For process algebra with quantitative semantics based on CTMCs, several approaches have been proposed for *on-the-fly* computations of lumped chain that avoid the generation of the original state space. These are based on deriving transitions of the lumped chain from a canonical representative of an equivalence class (e.g., [28,30,35,43]). Here considerable state-space compressions are owed to *symmetry reduction*, whereby identical copies of a process in parallel composition can be collapsed through a lumpable partition that contains all processes that are equal up to a permutation of the composed sub-terms. Symmetry reduction could be useful in the case that the CRN is described at the individual molecular level, as for instance in Cardelli's Chemical Ground Form [6]. However, we remark that a CRN gives a CTMC that tracks the population sizes of each species, implicitly accounting already for symmetry due to the assumption that two molecules of the same species are identical. SMB, instead, captures structural relations, see [8] for a physical interpretation of some equivalence classes. In this sense, SMB is closer in spirit to the idea of *place bisimulation* for Petri nets, which establishes a relation over places that induces a bisimulation in the classical, non-quantitative strong sense [2].

Paper Structure. Section 2 introduces the notion of CRN and defines its semantics. SMB is introduced in Sect. 3, while in Sect. 4 it is shown that SMB induces a reduced CRN whose CTMC is related via ordinary lumpability to the CTMC of the original CRN. Section 5 presents the algorithm for computing the largest SMB. Applicability and efficiency of the algorithm are demonstrated on biological models from the literature in Sect. 6. A formal comparison of SMB with FB complements the experiments. Conclusions are drawn in Sect. 7.

2 Chemical Reaction Networks

In this paper we consider *mass-action* CRNs, where each reaction is labeled with a constant, the reaction rate. The speed of the reaction will be proportional with this rate to the product of the abundances of the reactants. In particular, we focus on basic chemistry where only *elementary reactions* are considered: *unary reactions*, involving a single reactant performing a spontaneous reaction, and *binary reactions*, where two reactants interact; we call a binary reaction a *homeoreaction* if the two reactants are of the same species. Elementary reactions pose no restrictions on products. Several models found in the literature (including those discussed in Sect. 6) belong to this class. Also, this is consistent with the physical considerations which stipulate that reactions with more than two reactants are very unlikely to occur in nature [26]. In the rest of the paper we will refer to such *elementary mass-action CRNs* as just CRNs.

Formally, a CRN (S, R) is a set of species S and a set of chemical reactions R. Each reaction is a triple written in the form $\rho \xrightarrow{\alpha} \pi$, where ρ and π are the multi-sets of species representing the *reactants* and *products*, respectively, and $\alpha \geq 0$ is the reaction rate. We denote by $\rho(X)$ the multiplicity of species X in the multi-set ρ, and by $\mathcal{MS}(S)$ the set of finite multi-sets of species in S. To adhere to standard chemical notation, we shall also use the operator $+$ to denote multi-set union, e.g., $X + Y + Y$ (or just $X + 2Y$) denotes the multi-set of species $\{\!|X, Y, Y|\!\}$; similarly $\rho - X$ denotes multi-set difference $\rho \setminus \{\!|X|\!\}$. We also use X to denote either the species X or the singleton $\{\!|X|\!\}$.

Example 1. We now provide a simple CRN, (S_e, R_e), with $S_e = \{A, B, C, D, E\}$ and

$$R_e = \{A \xrightarrow{6} D, A \xrightarrow{2} 3C, C{+}D \xrightarrow{5} 2C{+}D, B \xrightarrow{6} C,$$
$$B \xrightarrow{2} 3D, E{+}D \xrightarrow{5} 2C{+}D, 2D \xrightarrow{3} C\},$$

which will be used as a running example throughout the paper.

We next recall the well-known CTMC semantics of CRNs (see, e.g., [6,27]), which allows us to associate a population-based CTMC to a given CRN and an initial population of its species. Here the state descriptor gives the number of elements for each species, hence it is formally represented as a multi-set of species. The CTMC specification is mediated by a multi-transition system (MTS), to record multiplicity of transitions. This is needed to account for two or more reactions contributing to the same CTMC transition, e.g., $A + B \xrightarrow{\alpha_1} B + C$ and $A \xrightarrow{\alpha_2} C$. The whole state space is defined by enumerating states, starting from some initial state.

Definition 1 (Multi-transition system of a CRN). *Let* (S, R) *be a CRN. The multiset of outgoing transitions from state* $\sigma \in \mathcal{MS}(S)$ *is obtained as*

$$out(\sigma) = \{\!\!\{\sigma \xrightarrow{\alpha \cdot \sigma(X)} \sigma - X + \pi \mid (X \xrightarrow{\alpha} \pi) \in R \}\!\!\}$$
$$\uplus \{\!\!\{\sigma \xrightarrow{\alpha \cdot \sigma(X) \cdot \sigma(Y)} ((\sigma - X) - Y) + \pi \mid X \neq Y \wedge (X + Y \xrightarrow{\alpha} \pi) \in R \}\!\!\}$$
$$\uplus \{\!\!\{\sigma \xrightarrow{\frac{\alpha}{2} \cdot \sigma(X) \cdot (\sigma(X) - 1)} ((\sigma - X) - X) + \pi \mid (X + X \xrightarrow{\alpha} \pi) \in R \}\!\!\}$$

The set of reachable states from σ, *denoted by* $reach(\sigma)$, *is the smallest set such that: (i)* $\sigma \in reach(\sigma)$; *and (ii) if* $\sigma' \in reach(\sigma)$, *then the target states of* $out(\sigma')$ *belong to* $reach(\sigma)$. *Finally, for an initial state* $\sigma_0 \in \mathcal{MS}(S)$, *the MTS for* (S, R) *and* σ_0 *is the union of the multi-sets of transitions outgoing from any reachable state, i.e.* $MTS(\sigma_0) = \uplus_{\theta \in reach(\sigma_0)} out(\theta)$.

We note that each reaction $\rho \xrightarrow{\alpha} \pi$ can be applied to source states σ containing ρ, i.e. $\sigma = \sigma' + \rho$ for some multi-set σ'. The corresponding target state is $\sigma' + \pi$. The rate for unary reactions $X \xrightarrow{\alpha} \pi$ is $\alpha \cdot \sigma(X)$ and accounts for the fact that each instance of the reagent can perform the reaction independently. For binary reactions $X + Y \xrightarrow{\alpha} \pi$ with $X \neq Y$, instead, the transition rate is proportional to the product of the populations of the species involved, i.e. $\alpha \cdot \sigma(X) \cdot \sigma(Y)$. This corresponds to the number of possible interactions between molecules, proportionally to the reaction propensity α [27,34]. For a homeoreaction involving X, the number of distinct interactions is given by $\binom{\sigma(X)}{2} = \frac{1}{2} \cdot \sigma(X) \cdot (\sigma(X) - 1)$.

Example 2. Consider the initial population $\sigma_{0e} = 2A + C + D$ for (S_e, R_e). Then we have $out(\sigma_{0e}) = \{\!\!\{\sigma_{0e} \xrightarrow{6 \cdot 2} A + C + 2D, \sigma_{0e} \xrightarrow{2 \cdot 2} A + 4C + D, \sigma_{0e} \xrightarrow{5} 2A + 2C + D \}\!\!\}$. The three transitions are due, respectively, to the first, second and third reaction of R_e.

We wish to stress the difference between a CRN and its MTS. While both are collections of triples in $\mathcal{MS}(S) \times \mathbb{R} \times \mathcal{MS}(S)$, the elements of the former are *syntactic*. Instead, the nature of the latter is *semantic* because it induces the underlying CTMC. In particular, given an MTS the CTMC is obtained by collapsing all transitions between the same source and target into a single CTMC transition and summing their rates.

Definition 2 (CTMC semantics). *Let (S, R) be a CRN, and σ_0 an initial population. The CTMC of (S, R) for σ_0 has states reach(σ_0) and its transitions are given by*

$$MC(\sigma_0) = \{\sigma \xrightarrow{r} \theta \mid \sigma, \theta \in reach(\sigma_0) \wedge \sigma \neq \theta \wedge r = \sum_{\sigma \xrightarrow{r'} \theta \in MTS(\sigma_0)} r'\}.$$

For any two states $\sigma, \theta \in \mathcal{MS}(S)$ the element of the infinitesimal generator matrix of $MC(\sigma_0)$ from σ to θ is defined as:

$$q(\sigma, \theta) = \begin{cases} r & \text{if } \sigma \neq \theta \wedge \sigma \xrightarrow{r} \theta \in MC(\nu_0) \\ -\sum_{\theta' \in \mathcal{MS}(S) \text{ s.t. } \theta' \neq \sigma} q(\sigma, \theta') & \text{if } \sigma = \theta \\ 0 & \text{otherwise} \end{cases}$$

For any $\mathcal{M} \subseteq \mathcal{MS}(S)$, we define $q[\sigma, \mathcal{M}] = \sum_{\theta \in \mathcal{M}} q(\sigma, \theta)$ and $q[\mathcal{M}, \theta] = \sum_{\sigma \in \mathcal{M}} q(\sigma, \theta)$.

3   Syntactic Markovian Bisimulation

This section introduces Syntactic Markovian Bisimulation (SMB) as a sufficient condition for CTMC ordinary lumpability. We first recast this latter notion to our notation.

Definition 3. *Let (S, R) be a CRN, σ_0 an initial population, $MC(\sigma_0)$ the underlying CTMC and $\mathcal{H}$ a partition of $\mathcal{MS}(S)$. Then, $MC(\sigma_0)$ is ordinarily lumpable with respect to $\mathcal{H}$ iff for any σ_1, σ_2 in the same block of $\mathcal{H}$ we have $q[\sigma_1, \mathcal{M}] = q[\sigma_2, \mathcal{M}]$ for all $\mathcal{M} \in \mathcal{H}$.*

Lumpability is given in terms of an equivalence relation among the states of a CTMC. Instead, SMB is an equivalence over the species of a CRN. Note that there is no one-to-one correspondence between species and the state space of the CTMC underlying a CRN. Indeed, the species define the state descriptor, but the cardinality of the state space is typically much larger since it depends on all the possible configurations of populations that are reachable from a given initial population. Thus we need to lift a relation over species to one over CTMC states. We do so by providing the notion of *multi-set lifting*: given a CRN (S, R) and an equivalence relation $\mathcal{R}$ over S, the lifting of $\mathcal{R}$ relates multi-sets with same number of $\mathcal{R}$-equivalent species.

Definition 4 (Multi-set Lifting). *Let (S, R) be a CRN, $\mathcal{R} \subseteq S \times S$ be an equivalence relation over S, and $\mathcal{H}$ be the partition induced by $\mathcal{R}$ over S. We define the* multi-set lifting *of $\mathcal{R}$ on $\mathcal{MS}(S)$, denoted by $\mathcal{R}^\uparrow \subseteq \mathcal{MS}(S) \times \mathcal{MS}(S)$, as*

$$\mathcal{R}^\uparrow \triangleq \big\{(\sigma_1, \sigma_2) \mid \sigma_1, \sigma_2 \in \mathcal{MS}(S) \wedge \forall H \in \mathcal{H} : \sum_{X \in H} \sigma_1(X) = \sum_{X \in H} \sigma_2(X)\big\}$$

The multi-set lifting of $\mathcal{R}$ can be readily seen to be an equivalence relation over $\mathcal{MS}(S)$.

Example 3. Consider the equivalence relation $\mathcal{R}_m$ over S_e inducing $\mathcal{H}_m = \{\{A\}, \{B\}, \{C, E\}, \{D\}\}$. Examples of multi-sets related by $\mathcal{R}_m^\uparrow$ are C and E, $2C$ and $2E$, and $C + E$ and $2E$, while $(A + C, B + C) \notin \mathcal{R}_m^\uparrow$.

The syntactic checks of SMB are performed via the notion of *reaction rate* given below. It computes, in essence, the cumulative rate that transforms a given reagent ρ into a certain product π.

Definition 5 (Reaction rate). *Let (S, R) be a CRN, and $\rho, \pi \in \mathcal{MS}(S)$. The reaction rate from ρ to π is defined as $\mathbf{rr}(\rho, \pi) = \sum_{\rho \xrightarrow{\alpha} \pi \,\in\, R} \alpha$. For any $\mathcal{M} \subseteq \mathcal{MS}(S)$, we define $\mathbf{rr}[\rho, \mathcal{M}] = \sum_{\pi \in \mathcal{M}} \mathbf{rr}(\rho, \pi)$.*

We can now define SMB.

Definition 6 (Syntactic Markovian Bisimulation). *Let (S, R) be a CRN, $\mathcal{R}$ an equivalence relation over S, $\mathcal{R}^\uparrow$ the multi-set lifting of $\mathcal{R}$ and $\mathcal{H}^\uparrow = \mathcal{MS}(S)/\mathcal{R}^\uparrow$. We say that $\mathcal{R}$ is a syntactic Markovian bisimulation (SMB) for (S, R) if and only if*

$$\mathbf{rr}[X + \rho, \mathcal{M}] = \mathbf{rr}[Y + \rho, \mathcal{M}], \text{ for all } (X, Y) \in \mathcal{R}, \rho \in \mathcal{MS}(S), \text{ and } \mathcal{M} \in \mathcal{H}^\uparrow.$$

We define the syntactic Markovian bisimilarity of (S, R) as the union of all SMBs of (S, R).

Remark 1. Note that the multi-sets $X + \rho$ and $Y + \rho$ differ only in one species (X and Y), thus projecting comparisons involving multisets (i.e., $X + \rho$ and $Y + \rho$) onto species (i.e., X and Y). In this view, ρ plays a role similar to an action type in traditional bisimulations, since it restricts interactions with a given reagent partner (or $\emptyset$ in case of unary reactions). Furthermore, Definition 6 entails a finite number of checks because all evaluations of $\mathbf{rr}$ are equal to zero for multisets that are not products in the CRN, see the algorithm of Sect. 5.

Example 4. Consider again $\mathcal{R}_m$ and $\mathcal{H}_m$. From $\mathbf{rr}(C + D, 2C + D) = \mathbf{rr}(E + D, 2C + D)$ can be inferred that $\mathcal{R}_m$ is an SMB.

As usual, we are interested in the largest bisimulation. The next result ensures that syntactic Markovian bisimilarity is an SMB, thus showing that it is also the largest one. Following the approach of [31], we show this by proving that the transitive closure of a union of SMBs is an SMB.[1]

Proposition 1. *Let (S, R) be a CRN, I a set of indices, and $\mathcal{R}_i$ an SMB for (S, R), for all $i \in I$. The transitive closure of their union $\mathcal{R} = (\bigcup_{i \in I} \mathcal{R}_i)^*$ is an SMB for (S, R).*

We now provide our first major result.

---

[1] The proofs of all statements are provided in the technical report available at http://sysma.imtlucca.it/tools/erode/.

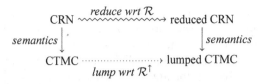

Fig. 1. The relation among ($\mathcal{R}$-reduced) CRNs and ($\mathcal{R}^\uparrow$-lumped) semantics, with $\mathcal{R}$ an SMB.

Theorem 1. *Let $\mathcal{R}$ be an SMB for the CRN (S, R). Then, its multi-set lifting $\mathcal{R}^\uparrow$ induces the ordinarily lumpable partition $\mathcal{H}^\uparrow$ on $MC(\sigma_0)$ for any initial state σ_0.*

Three remarks are in order. First, we stress that a single SMB induces infinitely many ordinarily lumpable partitions because there are no constraints on σ_0. Second, Theorem 1 makes no assumption on the cardinality of the CTMC state space underlying the CRN. In particular, it can also be applied to infinite state spaces; indeed Example 1 is an instance of such a situation because, e.g., of the reaction $C+D \xrightarrow{5} 2C+D$, which may generate infinitely many copies of C whenever the initial state has at least one copy of species D and one of species C. The original result of ordinary lumpability applies to finite CTMCs. However, using concepts from functional analysis and the theory of linear ODEs on Banach spaces, this statement can be extended, under certain assumptions, to CTMCs with countably infinite state spaces [38]. A sufficient condition for the theory to apply is to assume that the state space of the CTMC is partitioned in blocks of finite size. Indeed, the multi-set lifting ensures that any CTMC partition stemming from SMB enjoys this property. Third, as anticipated in Sect. 1, SMB is only a sufficient condition for CTMC ordinary lumpability.

Example 5. Consider the CRN $(\{F, G\}, \{F \xrightarrow{\alpha_1} G, G \xrightarrow{\alpha_2} F\})$ with $\alpha_1 \neq \alpha_2$ and $\sigma_0 = F$. The underlying CTMC has the state space $\{F, G\}$ and it readily follows that $\{\{F, G\}\}$ is an ordinarily lumpable partition, while it is not an SMB.

At the same time, however, SMB can be computed efficiently and induces significant reductions to biological models from literature, as discussed in Sect. 6.

4   Reduced CRN

Given a CRN (S, R) and an SMB $\mathcal{R}$, we next provide an algorithm that efficiently computes a $\mathcal{R}$-*reduced CRN* that induces directly the CTMC aggregated according to $\mathcal{R}^\uparrow$, without exploring the state space of the original CTMC. This is visualized in Fig. 1.

We wish to point out that this reduction algorithm happens to coincide with the *forward reduction* of [8], which has been applied to obtain a quotient CRN up to an FB, mentioned in Sect. 1, defined for the ODE semantics of CRNs. For the sake of completeness we state the notion of reduced CRN according to this paper's notation. To this end, we introduce the following notions. Given a partition $\mathcal{H}$ of S such that $\mathcal{H} = S/\mathcal{R}$, let X^H denote the canonical representative of a block $H \in \mathcal{H}$. Moreover, for any $\rho \in \mathcal{MS}(S)$, set $\rho^{\mathcal{R}} = \sum_{X \in \rho} X^H$ for the multiset obtained replacing each species with its canonical representative. Also, for any $\mathcal{M} \in \mathcal{H}^\uparrow$ we use $\mathcal{M}^{\mathcal{R}}$ for $\rho^{\mathcal{R}}$, with ρ any multi-set in $\mathcal{M}$.

Definition 7 (Reduced CRN). *Let (S, R) be a CRN, $\mathcal{R}$ an equivalence relation on S and $\mathcal{H} = S/\mathcal{R}$. The $\mathcal{R}$-reduction of (S, R) is defined as $(S, R)^{\mathcal{R}} = (S^{\mathcal{R}}, R^{\mathcal{R}})$, where $S^{\mathcal{R}} = \{X^H \mid H \in \mathcal{H}\}$ and $R^{\mathcal{R}}$ is computed as follows: (F1) Discard all reactions $\rho \xrightarrow{\alpha} \pi$ such that $\rho \neq \rho^{\mathcal{R}}$, i.e. whose reagents have species that are not representatives; (F2) Replace the species in the products of the remaining reactions with their canonical representatives; (F3) Fuse all reactions that have the same reactants and products by summing their rates.*

In the case of our running example, the above definition yields the following.

Example 6. Consider the SMB $\mathcal{R}_m$ of Example 3 and the underlying partition $\mathcal{H}_m = \{\{A\}, \{B\}, \{C, E\}, \{D\}\}$. With C being the representative of its block, the $\mathcal{R}_m$-reduction of (S_e, R_e) is $S_e^{\mathcal{R}_m} = \{A, B, C, D\}$, $R_e^{\mathcal{R}_m} = \{A \xrightarrow{6} D, A \xrightarrow{2} 3C, B \xrightarrow{6} C, B \xrightarrow{2} 3D, C+D \xrightarrow{5} 2C+D, 2D \xrightarrow{3} C\}$. Note that the reaction $E + D \xrightarrow{5} 2C + D$ is discarded.

Theorem 2. *Let (S, R) be a CRN, $\mathcal{R}$ denote an SMB and $\mathcal{H} = S/\mathcal{R}$. Further, let $\mathcal{H}^\uparrow$ denote the partition induced by $\mathcal{R}^\uparrow$ on $\mathcal{MS}(S)$. Then, for any initial population σ_0 of (S, R), the underlying CTMC is such that for all $\sigma \in \mathcal{MS}(S)$ it holds that $q_{(S,R)}[\sigma, \mathcal{M}] = q_{(S^R, R^R)}(\sigma^{\mathcal{R}}, \mathcal{M}^{\mathcal{R}})$ for any $\mathcal{M} \in \mathcal{H}^\uparrow$.*

If we assume that each block of an SMB partition stores a pointer to its representative, the reduced CRN can be computed in $O(r \cdot s \cdot \log s)$ steps [8], where $s := |S|$ and $r := |R|$.

5   Computing Syntactic Markovian Bisimilarities

Syntactic Markovian bisimilarity can be encoded as a partition refinement problem [37], analogously to well-known algorithms for quantitative extensions of labeled transition systems [3, 10, 32]. Hence, we only detail the conceptually novel parts, i.e., the computation of the quantities in Definition 6 and the notion of multi-set lifting.

Notation and Data Structures. Our algorithm for syntactic Markovian bisimilarity, SMBisimilarity, is given in Fig. 2, where (S, R) is the input CRN, and $\mathcal{H}$ the initial partition to be refined up to SMB. We use $s := |S|$, $r := |R|$, and $\mathcal{L}(R)$ for the set of all *labels*, i.e., all species multi-sets ρ to

```
1  SMBisimilarity(S, R, H)  :=          1  Split(S, R, ρ, M_spl, H,spls) :=
2    H↑ = lift(H, Π(R))                  2    forall (X ∈ S)
3    spls = L(R) × H↑                    3      X.rr0
4    while (spls ≠ ∅)                    4    forall (π ∈ M_spl)
5      (ρ, M_spl) = pop(spls)            5      forall (X + ρ --r--> π ∈ π.inc)
6      Split(S, R, ρ, M_spl, H,spls)     6        X.rr = X.rr + r
                                         7    updatePartitionAndSplitters(S, R, H, spls)
```

Fig. 2. Syntactic Markovian bisimilarity

be considered according to Definition 6 in the computation of **rr**. That is,
$\mathcal{L}(R) = \{\{|X|\} \mid X \in S \wedge \exists Y \in S, \exists X + Y \xrightarrow{r} \pi \in R\} \cup \{\emptyset\}$. We use $\{|\emptyset|\}$
to account for unary reactions, and $\{|X|\} \in \mathcal{L}(R)$ for each reagent X occurring
in at least one binary reaction in the CRN. We set $l := |\mathcal{L}(\mathcal{R})|$, which is bounded
by $\min(s + 1, 2 \cdot r)$.

In this pseudo-code we assume that species and reactions are stored in data
structures via pointers. Species are stored in a list, while a block of $\mathcal{H}$ is a list
of its species, each species in turn having a pointer to its block, requiring $O(s)$
space. Also R is stored in a list. Each reaction has two fields for the reagents, and
a list of pairs in the form (species,multiplicity) for the products, sorted according
to a total ordering on species. Thus, R requires $O(s \cdot r)$ space. Finally, $\mathcal{L}(\mathcal{R})$ is
stored in a list too, for an overall $O(s \cdot r)$ space complexity.

Overview. SMBisimilarity is based on Paige and Tarjan's classical solution to
the *relational coarsest partition problem* [37] and quantitative extensions thereof
(e.g., [3,20]). A given initial partition is iteratively refined (i.e., its blocks are
split), until a partition satisfying the required conditions is found. Refinements
are based on the notion of *splitter*, here given by $(\rho, \mathcal{M}_{spl})$, with $\rho \in \mathcal{L}(R)$ and
$\mathcal{M}_{spl} \in \mathcal{H}^{\uparrow}$: a block of $\mathcal{H}$ is *split* in sub-blocks of species with same ρ-reaction
rate towards a block $\mathcal{M}_{spl}$ of *equivalent* multi-sets of species. We stress that,
differently from classic bisimulations, in SMB splitters are blocks of products
obtained via the multi-set lifting from a species partition $\mathcal{H}$, rather than blocks
of $\mathcal{H}$ itself. Note that the set $\mathcal{MS}(S)$ of all possible multi-sets of species in S
is infinite. However, we can restrict to the set $\Pi(R) = \{\pi \mid (\rho \xrightarrow{\alpha} \pi) \in R\}$
only, collecting the multi-sets of species appearing as products in the reactions
of the considered CRN. This is because any multi-set in $\mathcal{MS}(S) \setminus \Pi(R)$ will
not contribute to the reaction rates. We store $\Pi(R)$ as a list, requiring $O(r)$
space, while a partition of $\Pi(R)$ is encoded by representing a block with a list
of pointers to its products.

The SMBisimilarity Procedure (Lines 1–6). The procedure starts (Line 2)
by creating the partition $\mathcal{H}^{\uparrow}$ of $\Pi(R)$ according to the multi-set lifting of $\mathcal{H}$. This
requires $O(s \cdot r \cdot \log r)$ time; this is because $O(s \cdot r)$ is required to count the number
of species of each block of $\mathcal{H}$, for each product, while $O(s \cdot r \cdot \log r)$ is required to
partition the products. This is done by iteratively sorting the products according
to the number of H-species they have, for each $H \in \mathcal{H}$. It requires $O(r \cdot \log r)$
per block of $\mathcal{H}$. Then, a set spls of initial candidate splitters is generated for
each $\rho \in \mathcal{L}(R)$ and $\mathcal{M} \in \mathcal{H}^{\uparrow}$. In order to bound the size of spls to $O(s)$ we

do not explicitly store each pair $(\rho, \mathcal{M}_{spl})$ for all ρ. Instead we store only one, initialized with a reference to the first position of $\mathcal{L}(R)$, and then update the pointer to the next position when necessary.

Lines 4–6 iterate until there are candidate splitters to be considered. One is selected and removed from spls, and the procedure Split is invoked to refine each block of $\mathcal{H}$ according to that splitter, and to generate new candidate ones.

The Split Procedure (Lines 1–7). Each species X has associated a real-valued field X.rr, initialized to 0 in Lines 2–3 in $O(s)$ time. Also, we assume that each product $\pi \in \Pi(R)$ is provided with a list, inc, which points to all the reactions that have that product. Each list inc has size $O(r)$, while exactly r entries appear in all inc. The inc list allows to compute the reaction rates by iterating all reactions at most only once. In fact, given an input splitter $(\rho, \mathcal{M}_{spl})$, Lines 4–6 store $\mathbf{rr}[X + \rho, \mathcal{M}_{spl}]$ in X.rr, for each species X, by iterating once the inc list of each product multi-set $\pi \in \mathcal{M}_{spl}$. In particular, we can have two cases: either $\rho = \emptyset$, when only unary reactions are considered (as $X + \emptyset = X$), or $\rho = Z$, with $Z \in S$, when only binary reactions having Z in their reagents are considered. In both cases, checking for the presence of ρ in the reagents of each reaction takes constant time. The computation has $O(r)$ time complexity, since each reaction appears in π.inc for one π only.

The Actual Splitting (Line 7). Using the computed rates, Line 7 then performs the actual splitting. We do not detail this part, as it is inspired by the usual approach, e.g., [3,20], consisting of the following three steps: (i) Each block is split using an associated balanced binary search tree (BST) in which each species X of the block is inserted providing $\mathbf{rr}[X + \rho, \mathcal{M}_{spl}]$ as key, and a new block is added to $\mathcal{H}$ for each leaf of the BST; this requires $O(s \cdot \log s)$ time, as there are at most s insertions in the BSTs, each having size at most s; (ii) If at least one block has been split, all candidate splitters must be discarded; this takes $O(r)$ time, as spls contains at most an entry per product $\pi \in \Pi(R)$, [2] while deletion from spls takes constant time assuming that it is implemented as a linked list; (iii) If at least a block has been split, all splitters have to be recomputed. This is because another multi-set lifting must be considered from the new partition. It takes $O(s \cdot r \cdot \log r)$ to do so. Thus, overall Split has time complexity $O(s \cdot (\log s + r \cdot \log r))$. Also, note that the BSTs do not worsen the space complexity, as only one for a block is built at a time.

Complexity. We observe that Split is invoked $O(l \cdot s \cdot r)$ times. This is because, initially, $l \cdot r$ candidate splitters have to be considered. At every step where some blocks of $\mathcal{H}$ get split (which happens at most s times), all splitters are removed, and at most $l \cdot r$ new candidate splitters are added to spls. In conclusion, syntactic Markovian bisimilarity takes $O(l \cdot s^2 \cdot r \cdot (\log s + r \cdot \log r))$ time and $O(s \cdot r)$ space.

---

[2] Recall that, given a block $\mathcal{M}_{spl}$, only one entry is stored to represent all pairs $(\rho, \mathcal{M}_{spl})$.

Table 1. SMB reductions and corresponding speed-ups in CTMC simulation.

Id	Int.	Original model				SMB reduction			
		$|R|$	$|S|$	CTMC (s)	SMB (s)	Red. (s)	$|R|$	$|S|$	CTMC (s)
M1	50	3538944	262146	—	2.68E+5	2.04E+1	990	222	1.77E+1
M2	50	786432	65538	—	6.67E+3	4.09E+0	720	167	1.15E+1
M3	50	172032	16386	—	1.95E+2	3.4E-1	504	122	7.96E+0
S1	50	36864	4098	9.12E+2	9.38E+0	1.01E-1	336	86	5.28E+0
S2	50	7680	1026	1.03E+2	7.33E-1	3.00E-2	210	58	3.69E+0
M5	3600	194054	14531	3.54E+5	5.88E+2	1.20E+0	142165	10855	3.29E+5
M6	3840	187468	10734	1.79E+4	1.96E+2	5.68E-1	57508	3744	1.47E+3
M7	3840	32776	2506	1.34E+3	8.80E+0	2.68E-1	16481	1281	4.88E+2
S3	500000	284	143	4.13E+2	3.30E-2	1.40E-2	142	72	1.39E+2

Remark 2. We wish to stress that step (iii) of the actual splitting phase is not necessary in classic partition refinement algorithms [3, 10, 20]. This is because only blocks of the current partition are used as splitters in those algorithms. Hence, splitters are computed and maintained at no additional cost. It is exactly due to this reason that the time complexity of our algorithm exceeds those from [3, 10, 20].

6 Evaluation

In this section we experimentally evaluate SMB studying its effectiveness to reduce a number of biochemical models from the literature. All experiments were performed on a 2.6 GHz Intel Core i5 with 4 GB of RAM, and are replicable using a prototypal tool available at http://sysma.imtlucca.it/tools/erode/samba/. The tool takes in input CRNs specified in the .net format of BioNetGen [4], version 2.2.5-stable. The CRN reduced by SMB is then converted back to the BioNetGen format to perform stochastic simulations using Gillespie's stochastic simulation algorithm [27].

SMB was tested in terms of model reduction capabilities and corresponding CTMC analysis speed-ups on the collection of models listed in Table 1. Models with labels starting with "M" are the largest models also considered in [8]. Additionally, in this paper we analyze models S1–S3; M1–M3 and S1–S2 belong to the same family of synthetic benchmarks that are generated by varying the number of phosphorylation sites in a complex described in BioNetGen's rule-based format [39]. S3 arises by studying ultrasensitivity in multisite proteins [21]. In all cases we applied our reduction technique starting from the trivial partition with one block only (i.e., $\{S\}$ for every CRN (S, R)).

Column "*Int.*" shows the units of time used for the simulation, taken from the respective papers. This information was missing for M1–M3 and S1–S2, for which we used an estimate of their steady states. Initial populations for the simulations were taken as well from the respective papers. Under *"Original model"* are listed the number of reactions ($|R|$) and species ($|S|$) of the CRN, and the overall time to perform 10 simulations. The same information is given in the columns under *"SMB reduction"* for the corresponding CRNs reduced up to SMB, providing in addition the time necessary to compute the SMB partition (*SMB (s)*) and to perform the reduction (*Red. (s)*).

The results indicate that SMB can find equivalences in a significant number of models concerning different biological mechanisms. In the three largest models, M1–M3, SMB was able to provide a compact aggregated CRN which could be straightforwardly analyzed, while the simulations of the original models did not terminate due to out-of-memory errors in our experimental set-up. This is consistent with [39], where the same issue was reported for model M1. Models with more sensible reductions in the number of reactions gave better speed-ups. For example, for S1–S2 and M6–M7, the reduced CRN could be analyzed in about one tenth of the time necessary for the original one. We attribute this to the fact that at every simulation step, Gillespie's algorithm scans all reactions (in the worst case) to decide which one to fire next. Also, we note that typically many simulations, often in the order of hundreds or thousands, are necessary to satisfy a given confidence interval (or precision); hence, even small speed-ups per single run may turn into consistent gains in the overall simulation runtimes. Finally, as can be expected from their respective computational complexities, the runtimes to reduce a CRN by SMB according to Definition 7 are considerably smaller compared to the runtimes for computing the largest SMB.

Comparison with κ-Based Reduction Techniques. SMB and stochastic fragmentation can be experimentally compared in rule-based biochemical models with finite underlying CRNs, like those in Table 1, where both techniques can be applied. In [8] we have shown that FB and *differential fragmentation*, a variant of fragmentation defined for the ODE semantics of κ, are not comparable. The same holds for SMB and stochastic fragmentation. For example, SMB reduces M12 from [8] to 56 species, while fragmentation does not. Conversely, the κ model of cross-talk between a model of the early events of the EGF pathway and the insulin receptor of [16] can be reduced by stochastic fragmentation, but not by SMB.

Comparison with Forward Bisimulation. We now relate SMB with FB, introduced in [8] for the ODE semantics of CRNs. For this, it is convenient to recall such semantics. The ODE system $\dot{V} = F(V)$ underlying a CRN (S, R) (where the dot notation indicates derivative with respect to time) is given by $F : \mathbb{R}_{\geq 0}^S \to \mathbb{R}^S$, where each component F_X, with $X \in S$ is defined by the expression

$$F_X(V) := \sum_{\rho \xrightarrow{\alpha} \pi \in R} (\pi(X) - \rho(X)) \cdot \alpha \cdot \prod_{Y \in S} V_Y^{\rho(Y)}. \tag{1}$$

This provides the well-known *mass-action* kinetics, where the reaction rate is proportional to the concentrations of the reactants involved.

Example 7. The ODE system associated to our running example is as follows.

$$\dot{V}_A = -8\,V_A \quad \dot{V}_C = 6\,V_A + 5\,V_C\,V_D + 6\,V_B + 10\,V_D\,V_E + 3\,V_D^2 \quad \dot{V}_E = -5\,V_D\,V_E$$
$$\dot{V}_B = -8\,V_B \quad \dot{V}_D = 6\,V_A + 6\,V_B - 6\,V_D^2$$

As for SMB, FB is an equivalence over the species of a CRN computed by looking at the reactions only. Also, FB induces a notion of lumpability similar in spirit to that of Definition 3, as it allows to rewrite the ODEs underlying a CRN in terms of macro-variables that govern the evolution of the cumulative concentrations of the species of each block.

Example 8. Consider the partition $\{\{A, B\}, \{C, E\}, \{D\}\}$ for our running example. This can be shown to be an FB. Indeed, the ODEs of (S, R) can be rewritten, under the variable renaming $V_{AB} = V_A + V_B$, $V_{CE} = V_C + V_E$, as

$$\dot{V}_{AB} = -8\,V_{AB} \quad \dot{V}_{CE} = 6\,V_{AB} + 5\,V_{CE}\,V_D + 3\,V_D^2 \quad \dot{V}_D = 6\,V_{AB} - 6\,V_D^2$$

Although SMB and FB work on different semantics, the fact that they are both equivalences over species that induce analogous aggregations at the semantic level calls for the question of establishing a formal relation between the two equivalences.

Theorem 3. *Let (S, R) be a CRN, and $\mathcal{R}$ an equivalence relation over S. Then, if $\mathcal{R}$ is an SMB for (S, R), it also is an FB for (S, R'), with*

$$R' = \{X \xrightarrow{\alpha} \pi \mid (X \xrightarrow{\alpha} \pi) \in R\} \cup$$
$$\{X + Y \xrightarrow{\alpha} \pi \mid (X + Y \xrightarrow{\alpha} \pi) \in R \wedge X \neq Y\} \cup$$
$$\{X + X \xrightarrow{\alpha/2} \pi \mid (X + X \xrightarrow{\alpha} \pi) \in R\}$$

When R has singleton products only, then $\mathcal{R}$ is an SMB for (S, R) iff it is an FB for (S, R').

An important remark to be made regarding this result is that it requires to halve the rates of homeoreactions. This is due to an inherent, well-known inconsistency existing between the CTMC and ODE semantics of CRNs. While, as discussed in Sect. 2, homeoreactions are treated specially in the CTMC semantics in order to capture the combinatorial nature of the discrete molecular interactions, the ODE semantics does not make such difference, e.g., [23], see also (1). We refer to [6] for a more in depth discussion on this. It is interesting to note that a *different* ODE semantics would be possible, grounded on a limit result by Kurtz which establishes the ODE solution as the asymptotic behavior of a sequence of infinitely large CTMCs induced by the same CRN with increasing volumes of a solution having given initial concentrations of species. This interpretation would lead to a $1/2$ coefficient in the rates of homeoreactions also in the ODE case [34]. We leave it for future work to understand if, by appropriately adapting FB to this different ODE semantics, Theorem 3 can be stated so as to relate SMB and FB *on the same CRN* also in presence of homeoreactions.

We also remark that the converse of the theorem does not hold in general for CRNs with non-singleton products: in our running example $\{\{A, B\}, \{C, E\}, \{D\}\}$ has been discussed to be an FB. However, given that $\mathbf{rr}(A + \emptyset, D) = 6$ and $\mathbf{rr}(B + \emptyset, D) = 0$, it is not an SMB.

FB has been applied to the models of Table 1 in [8], where a biological interpretation of the obtained aggregations was also provided. Interestingly, the largest SMBs of Table 1 correspond to the largest FBs of [8] on these models. Since none of these models have homeoreactions, we conclude that for these CRNs FB has the same discriminating power as SMB. Since S3 has unary products only, in that case this is guaranteed by Theorem 3.

7   Conclusion

Syntactic Markovian bisimulation (SMB) is an equivalence relation operating at the syntactic level of a chemical reaction network that induces a reduced one in the sense of the theory of Markov chain lumpability. A numerical evaluation has demonstrated its usefulness in practice by showing significant reductions in a number of models available in the literature, even if SMB is only a sufficient condition for aggregation. A partition-refinement algorithm computes the largest SMB that refines a given input partition. The freedom in choosing such input may be exploited to single out certain *observable species*. Thus, SMB may give a reduced model that exactly preserves the dynamics of interest. Since the CRN syntax is often combinatorially smaller than the underlying CTMC, we envisage SMB to be used as a pre-processing stage for CTMC analyses or for further reduction techniques on the semantics, either in exact or approximate form (e.g., [1]). Indeed, it would be interesting to conduct further experiments in order to understand how tight the lumping is with respect to the coarsest one obtained by applying Markov chain minimization algorithms on the fully enumerated state space; for this, we plan to develop fully integrated support for SMB into our software tool for model reduction techniques, *ERODE* [12] (http://sysma.imtlucca.it/tools/erode/). We have shown that SMB is stricter than forward bisimulation (FB), a recently introduced bisimulation for the ODE semantics of CRNs. In related line of research, we have developed behavioural equivalences for the ODE semantics of process algebra [33,42,44,45]. In the future, we plan to investigate variants which imply lumpability for the CTMC semantics underlying stochastic process algebra.

Acknowledgments. This work was partially supported by the EU project QUANTI-COL, 600708. L. Cardelli is partially funded by a Royal Society Research Professorship.

References

1. Abate, A., Brim, L., Češka, M., Kwiatkowska, M.: Adaptive aggregation of Markov chains: quantitative analysis of chemical reaction networks. In: Kroening, D., Păsăreanu, C.S. (eds.) CAV 2015. LNCS, vol. 9206, pp. 195–213. Springer, Cham (2015). doi:10.1007/978-3-319-21690-4_12

2. Autant, C., Schnoebelen, P.: Place bisimulations in Petri nets. In: Jensen, K. (ed.) ICATPN 1992. LNCS, vol. 616, pp. 45–61. Springer, Heidelberg (1992). doi:10. 1007/3-540-55676-1_3

3. Baier, C., Engelen, B., Majster-Cederbaum, M.E.: Deciding bisimilarity and similarity for probabilistic processes. J. Comput. Syst. Sci. **60**(1), 187–231 (2000)

4. Blinov, M.L., Faeder, J.R., Goldstein, B., Hlavacek, W.S.: BioNetGen: software for rule-based modeling of signal transduction based on the interactions of molecular domains. Bioinformatics **20**(17), 3289–3291 (2004)

5. Buchholz, P.: Exact and ordinary lumpability in finite Markov chains. J. Appl. Probab. **31**(1), 59–75 (1994)

6. Cardelli, L.: On process rate semantics. Theoret. Comput. Sci. **391**(3), 190–215 (2008)

7. Cardelli, L.: Morphisms of reaction networks that couple structure to function. BMC Syst. Biol. **8**(1), 84 (2014)

8. Cardelli, L., Tribastone, M., Tschaikowski, M., Vandin, A.: Forward and backward bisimulations for chemical reaction networks. In: CONCUR, pp. 226–239 (2015)

9. Cardelli, L., Tribastone, M., Tschaikowski, M., Vandin, A.: Comparing chemical reaction networks: a categorical and algorithmic perspective. In: LICS, pp. 485–494 (2016)

10. Cardelli, L., Tribastone, M., Tschaikowski, M., Vandin, A.: Efficient syntax-driven lumping of differential equations. In: Chechik, M., Raskin, J.-F. (eds.) TACAS 2016. LNCS, vol. 9636, pp. 93–111. Springer, Heidelberg (2016). doi:10.1007/ 978-3-662-49674-9_6

11. Cardelli, L., Tribastone, M., Tschaikowski, M., Vandin, A.: Symbolic computation of differential equivalences. In: POPL, pp. 137–150 (2016)

12. Cardelli, L., Tribastone, M., Tschaikowski, M., Vandin, A.: ERODE: a tool for the evaluation and reduction of ordinary differential equations. In: Legay, A., Margaria, T. (eds.) TACAS 2017. LNCS, vol. 10206, pp. 310–328. Springer, Heidelberg (2017). doi:10.1007/978-3-662-54580-5_19

13. Cardelli, L., Zavattaro, G.: Turing universality of the biochemical ground form. Math. Struct. Comput. Sci. **20**(1), 45–73 (2010)

14. Cardelli, L., Csikász-Nagy, A., Dalchau, N., Tribastone, M., Tschaikowski, M.: Noise reduction in complex biological switches. Sci. Rep. **6**, 20214 (2016)

15. Ciocchetta, F., Hillston, J.: Bio-PEPA: a framework for the modelling and analysis of biological systems. Theoret. Comput. Sci. **410**(33–34), 3065–3084 (2009)

16. Conzelmann, H., Fey, D., Gilles, E.D.: Exact model reduction of combinatorial reaction networks. BMC Syst. Biol. **2**, 78 (2008)

17. Danos, V., Feret, J., Fontana, W., Harmer, R., Krivine, J.: Abstracting the differential semantics of rule-based models: exact and automated model reduction. In: LICS (2010)

18. Danos, V., Feret, J., Fontana, W., Krivine, J.: Scalable simulation of cellular signaling networks. In: Shao, Z. (ed.) APLAS 2007. LNCS, vol. 4807, pp. 139–157. Springer, Heidelberg (2007). doi:10.1007/978-3-540-76637-7_10

19. Danos, V., Laneve, C.: Formal molecular biology. TCS **325**(1), 69–110 (2004)

20. Derisavi, S., Hermanns, H., Sanders, W.H.: Optimal state-space lumping in Markov chains. Inf. Process. Lett. **87**(6), 309–315 (2003)

21. Dushek, O., van der Merwe, P.A., Shahrezaei, V.: Ultrasensitivity in multisite phosphorylation of membrane-anchored proteins. Biophys. J. **100**(5), 1189–1197 (2011)

22. Elowitz, M.B., Levine, A.J., Siggia, E.D., Swain, P.S.: Stochastic gene expression in a single cell. Science **297**(5584), 1183–1186 (2002)

23. Feinberg, M.: Lectures on chemical reaction networks. Technical report, University of Wisconsin (1979)
24. Feret, J., Henzinger, T., Koeppl, H., Petrov, T.: Lumpability abstractions of rule-based systems. TCS **431**, 137–164 (2012)
25. Gay, S., Soliman, S., Fages, F.: A graphical method for reducing and relating models in systems biology. Bioinformatics **26**(18), i575–i581 (2010)
26. Gillespie, D.: The chemical Langevin equation. J. Chem. Phys. **113**(1), 297–306 (2000)
27. Gillespie, D.T.: Exact stochastic simulation of coupled chemical reactions. J. Phys. Chem. **81**(25), 2340–2361 (1977)
28. Gilmore, S., Hillston, J., Ribaudo, M.: An efficient algorithm for aggregating PEPA models. IEEE Trans. Softw. Eng. **27**(5), 449–464 (2001)
29. Heath, J., Kwiatkowska, M., Norman, G., Parker, D., Tymchyshyn, O.: Probabilistic model checking of complex biological pathways. TCS **391**(3), 239–257 (2008)
30. Hermanns, H., Ribaudo, M.: Exploiting symmetries in stochastic process algebras. In: European Simulation Multiconference, Manchester, UK, pp. 763–770, June 1998
31. Hillston, J.: A Compositional Approach to Performance Modelling. CUP, Cambridge (1996)
32. Huynh, D.T., Tian, L.: On some equivalence relations for probabilistic processes. Fundam. Inform. **17**(3), 211–234 (1992)
33. Iacobelli, G., Tribastone, M., Vandin, A.: Differential bisimulation for a Markovian process algebra. In: Italiano, G.F., Pighizzini, G., Sannella, D.T. (eds.) MFCS 2015. LNCS, vol. 9234, pp. 293–306. Springer, Heidelberg (2015). doi:10.1007/978-3-662-48057-1_23
34. Kurtz, T.G.: The relationship between stochastic and deterministic models for chemical reactions. J. Chem. Phys. **57**(7), 2976–2978 (1972)
35. Kwiatkowska, M., Norman, G., Parker, D.: Symmetry reduction for probabilistic model checking. In: Ball, T., Jones, R.B. (eds.) CAV 2006. LNCS, vol. 4144, pp. 234–248. Springer, Heidelberg (2006). doi:10.1007/11817963_23
36. Larsen, K.G., Skou, A.: Bisimulation through probabilistic testing. Inf. Comput. **94**(1), 1–28 (1991)
37. Paige, R., Tarjan, R.: Three partition refinement algorithms. SIAM J. Comput. **16**(6), 973–989 (1987)
38. Rózsa, Z., Tóth, J.: Exact linear lumping in abstract spaces. Electron. J. Qual. Theory Differ. Eqn. **21**(7), 1–20 (2004). Proceedings of the Colloquium on the Qualitative Theory of Differential Equations
39. Sneddon, M.W., Faeder, J.R., Emonet, T.: Efficient modeling, simulation and coarse-graining of biological complexity with NFsim. Nat. Methods **8**(2), 177–183 (2011)
40. Soloveichik, D., Cook, M., Winfree, E., Bruck, J.: Computation with finite stochastic chemical reaction networks. Nat. Comput. **7**(4), 615–633 (2008)
41. Tognazzi, S., Tribastone, M., Tschaikowski, M., Vandin, A.: EGAC: a genetic algorithm to compare chemical reaction networks. In: The Genetic and Evolutionary Computation Conference (GECCO) (2017, to appear)
42. Tschaikowski, M., Tribastone, M.: Exact fluid lumpability for Markovian process algebra. In: Koutny, M., Ulidowski, I. (eds.) CONCUR 2012. LNCS, vol. 7454, pp. 380–394. Springer, Heidelberg (2012). doi:10.1007/978-3-642-32940-1_27
43. Tschaikowski, M., Tribastone, M.: Generalised communication for interacting agents. In: QEST, pp. 178–188, September 2012
44. Tschaikowski, M., Tribastone, M.: Tackling continuous state-space explosion in a markovian process algebra. Theoret. Comput. Sci. **517**, 1–33 (2014)

45. Tschaikowski, M., Tribastone, M.: A unified framework for differential aggregations in Markovian process algebra. JLAMP **84**(2), 238–258 (2015)

46. Tschaikowski, M., Tribastone, M.: Approximate reduction of heterogenous nonlinear models with differential hulls. IEEE Trans. Automat. Contr. **61**(4), 1099–1104 (2016)

47. Vandin, A., Tribastone, M.: Quantitative abstractions for collective adaptive systems. In: Bernardo, M., Nicola, R., Hillston, J. (eds.) SFM 2016. LNCS, vol. 9700, pp. 202–232. Springer, Cham (2016). doi:10.1007/978-3-319-34096-8_7

48. Zavattaro, G., Cardelli, L.: Termination problems in chemical kinetics. In: Breugel, F., Chechik, M. (eds.) CONCUR 2008. LNCS, vol. 5201, pp. 477–491. Springer, Heidelberg (2008). doi:10.1007/978-3-540-85361-9_37

Assertion-Based Reasoning Method for Calculus of Wireless System

Luyao Wang[✉], Wanling Xie, and Huibiao Zhu

Shanghai Key Laboratory of Trustworthy Computing,
School of Computer Science and Software Engineering,
East China Normal University, Shanghai, China
{lywang,wlxie}@ecnu.cn, hbzhu@sei.ecnu.edu.cn

Abstract. Wireless technology has been widely used in various wireless network scenarios and applications. To model and analyze wireless systems, a calculus of wireless system called CWS has been introduced. In this paper, we put forward an assertion-based reasoning method for this calculus in order to support the verification of the correctness and some interesting properties of wireless system. To simplify the complexity of verification, we first present the assertion-based verification rules for processes separately. Due to the features of wireless system (e.g., broadcast, synchrony, interference), cooperation rules are introduced to combine the processes into a complete system. Finally, there is a case study about using our method to analyze and prove the correctness of Stop-and-Wait ARQ Protocol as well as some properties.

1   Introduction

With the rapid development of wireless technology, wireless networks and applications are playing an increasing role in the lives of people throughout the world. Wireless applications range from user applications for Personal Communication Services (PCS) to industrial applications for commerce, including personal area network, ambient intelligence, cellular network, sensor network, wireless local network, etc. [1,2]. There are several important features in wireless system including broadcast, synchrony and interference. Broadcast means the wireless device can transmit message to many other devices without waiting the feedback at the same time [3]. Interference is an essential aspect of wireless systems, which gives rise to complex situations on communications in wireless network. When there is an interference, the wireless device cannot receive the data correctly. Therefore, a number of formal languages and methods have been proposed in order to analyze and model the wireless system, including CWS [4], CMAN [5], CMN [6], CBS# [7], etc.

Among all these formal languages and methods, CWS is a calculus of wireless systems used to specify the behaviors of wireless systems combined with features of local broadcast, interference and synchrony [4]. Each wireless device named as node has a unique location, a valid transmission radius and transmission channel. Every single transmission is divided into two boundary events to

© Springer International Publishing AG 2017
L. Aceto et al. (Eds.): Larsen Festschrift, LNCS 10460, pp. 484–502, 2017.
DOI: 10.1007/978-3-319-63121-9_24

distinguish the beginning and end of a transmission in this language. Instead of treating broadcast as an atomic action in other calculi, this calculus can simulate a wireless system at the lower level. In particular, it can describe the forms of interference among the activities of processes in accordance with the physical aspect of wireless devices.

In this paper, we put forward an assertion-based reasoning method for CWS in order to support the verification of the correctness of wireless systems. We verify the wireless system by verification rules from the perspective of logic. The correctness in this context means that the systems enjoy certain desirable properties, such as interference-free [8]. Due to the features of wireless systems, the properties of interference freedom, fair behavior and data transmission security are also taken into account. In our method, a wireless system is considered as a distributed system enjoying the properties of broadcast, synchrony and interference. Here, synchrony means in a single time unit multiple events can happen in a wireless system, such as message transmission. There are two models for message transmitting from one node to another. The first approach is via communication by a channel. The second approach is via shared-variable mechanism in rely-guarantee techniques [9]. Here, we use the first approach to formalise the message passing between two nodes. To make verification more straightforward, we first investigate each process considered in isolation and provide verification rules separately. However, some communication commands such as $out\langle e\rangle.P$ and $in(x).P$ are meaningful only in the context of parallel composition or distributed system. Hence we then deduce properties of complete system by comparing the proof rules for the component processes and present cooperation proof rules for the whole system.

The remainder of this paper is organized as follows. Section 2 introduces the core language of the calculus for wireless systems and lists some assumptions about wireless system used in this paper. In Sect. 3, we provide the assertion-based reasoning rules, including the rules for dealing with communication commands, sequential composition and the whole system composition. Furthermore, the Subsect. 3.3 mainly provides the cooperation verification rules for the whole system and a few simple examples are given to illustrate the rules. In the last subsection of Sect. 3, we discuss the soundness of our assertion-based reasoning rules [10]. Sect. 4 gives a case study of correctness proofs by applying our method. We show the verification of the Stop-and-Wait ARQ protocol as well as the property that can be formalized in this framework. Sect. 5 concludes the paper.

2 Calculus for Wireless System

The Calculus for Wireless Systems (CWS), first put forward by Mezzetti and Sangiorgi, is a calculus for specifying the behavior of wireless communication [11]. It is applied to formalization of the wireless system at the lower level with several interesting features, including local broadcasting, half-duplex channel and transmission interference. In this section, we give a brief recapitulation of CWS.

The core language consists of two parts, including the process part as P and the network part as N. P represents a sequence of processes in a single wireless device considered as node. Thus, each node is the basic network element which cannot be created or destroyed. In addition, the wireless system can be modeled by a number of nodes which work independently and also communicate from time to time by message passing.

The syntax of core language, which models the basic communication mechanism in wireless systems, is given in Table 1. The full version of CWS language is contained in [4,11], including other sequential program commands.

Table 1. The syntax of CWS

$P ::= out\langle e\rangle.P$	output
$\mid \langle v\rangle.P$	active output
$\mid in(x).P$	input
$\mid (x).P$	active input
$\mid \mathbf{0}$	inactive process
$N ::= n[P]^c_{l,r}$	node (or device)
$\mid N \mid N$	parallel composition
$\mid \mathbf{0}$	empty network

For process P, there are five key processes listed for describing the communication in this calculus, including begin and end of a broadcast transmission action, begin and end of a reception action and empty process.

- $out\langle e\rangle.P$ represents a begin transmission process. If the transmission can be initiated, it broadcasts the value of expression e and evolves to $\langle v\rangle.P$. Note that v is the value of expression e defined as $[|e|] = v$.
- $\langle v\rangle.P$ is an end transmission process, which means that the value v is currently being transmitted. The number of nodes which can receive the data ranges from zero to many. After the process is terminated, it becomes P.
- $in(x).P$ is a begin reception process. If there is only one begin transmission process, the reception process can be initiated and process $(x).P$ is active.
- $(x).P$ describes that the process is currently receiving the data. If the process can be terminated successfully, the data is stored into the variable x. Otherwise, x is assigned with a notation $\bot$.
- 0 is an inactive process used to stand for the terminated process.

In the syntax for networks, N denotes the whole wireless network system, which consists of three constructs including a single network node, parallel composition of nodes and empty network.

- $n[P]^c_{l,r}$ indicates the node which is addressed as n, located at l, with a transmission radius r, and using channel c for communication. Here, P is the process executed in node n. Note that two different nodes cannot share the same location. Thus, each node identifier is unique and can be defined by the location l.

- $N \mid N$ denotes two network nodes that execute in parallel. When we model the network system, we can add more nodes and each node can communicate with others by message passing.
- 0 means there is no active node in a network.

Next, we provide some assumptions and list some notations which will be used in our work. We put forward our method based on the well-formed network definition in [4]. Each node status can be expressed as a triple $s =_{df} (l, r, c)$ with a unique location l, transmission radius r and communication channel c. Besides, both of the end transmission process $\langle v \rangle.P$ and the end reception process $(x).P$ cannot be considered as the initial state in a system.

Distance function is presented for the purpose of describing the network topology. $d(l_1, l_2)$ returns the distance between two locations named as l_1 and l_2.

Active sets T and R are two sets of nodes. Each node in the active transmission set T is currently transmitting the data. Likewise, each node in active reception set R is currently receiving the data.

Active neighbor node of node $n[P]_{l,r}^c$ is a subset of T, denoted as $T|(l, r, c)$. As the name implies, the nodes in this set are transmitting the data to the node $n[P]_{l,r}^c$ at that moment. The formal definition is as below.

$$T|(l, r, c) =_{df} \{(l', r', c') \mid (l', r', c') \in T \ \wedge \ d(l', l) \leq r' \ \wedge \ c' = c\}$$

Example 2.1. We model a network with an interference

$$Network = N_1 \mid N_2 \mid N_3 \mid N_4$$

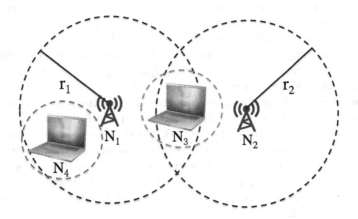

Fig. 1. The network topology for example 2.1

where the node N_1 sends the data to the nodes N_3 and N_4, while the node N_2 also sends the data to the node N_3 at the same time via channel c. The nodes of this network can be defined as follows:

$$\text{Let } N_1 =_{df} n_1[out\langle e_1\rangle.P_1]^c_{l_1,r_1} \quad N_2 =_{df} n_2[out\langle e_2\rangle.P_2]^c_{l_2,r_2}$$
$$N_3 =_{df} n_3[in(x_3).P_3]^c_{l_3,r_3} \quad N_4 =_{df} n_4[in(x_4).P_4]^c_{l_4,r_4}$$

where, we have $d(l_1,l_3) \leq r_1$, $d(l_2,l_3) \leq r_2$ and $d(l_1,l_4) \leq r_1$.

Moreover, the network topology is illustrated in Fig. 1. We can see that the node N_3 is in the transmission range of both N_1 and N_2. However, N_1 and N_2 cannot transmit to each other. As a result, there is an interference when N_1 and N_2 are both sending data to N_3. In contrast, the node N_4 is only in the transmission range of N_1, so it can get the data from N_1. Hence, the transition can be displayed as below.

$$n_1[out\langle e_1\rangle.P_1]^c_{l_1,r_1} \mid n_2[out\langle e_2\rangle.P_2]^c_{l_2,r_2} \mid n_3[in(x_3).P_3]^c_{l_3,r_3} \mid n_4[in(x_4).P_4]^c_{l_4,r_4}$$
$$\rightarrow n_1[\langle(\lfloor e_1\rfloor)\rangle.P_1]^c_{l_1,r_1} \mid n_2[out\langle e_2\rangle.P_2]^c_{l_2,r_2} \mid n_3[(x_3).P_3]^c_{l_3,r_3} \mid n_4[(x_4).P_4]^c_{l_4,r_4}$$
$$\rightarrow n_1[\langle(\lfloor e_1\rfloor)\rangle.P_1]^c_{l_1,r_1} \mid n_2[\langle(\lfloor e_2\rfloor)\rangle.P_2]^c_{l_2,r_2} \mid n_3[(x_3).P_3]^c_{l_3,r_3} \mid n_4[(x_4).P_4]^c_{l_4,r_4}$$
$$\rightarrow n_1[P_1]^c_{l_1,r_1} \mid n_2[\langle(\lfloor e_2\rfloor)\rangle.P_2]^c_{l_2,r_2} \mid n_3[P_3\{\perp/x_3\}]^c_{l_3,r_3} \mid n_4[P_4\{\lfloor e_1\rfloor/x_4\}]^c_{l_4,r_4}$$

where, e_i represents the message transmitted by node N_i and x_i is the variable in node N_i used to receive the message from other node. Note that $\lfloor e\rfloor$ is the value of expression e which can be computed by the program in the node.

3 Assertion-Based Reasoning Rules

We present an assertion-based reasoning method for Calculus of Wireless Systems in order to prove the correctness of wireless systems formalized in CWS. Due to the features of wireless system, the properties of interference freedom, fair behavior and data transmission security are very important.

Firstly, we consider each process in isolation and provide the verification rules separately. However, some communication commands such as $out\langle e\rangle.P$ and $in(x).P$ are meaningful only in the context of parallel composition or distributed system. Consequently, we then deduce the properties of complete system by comparing the verification rules for the component processes and put forward some cooperation verification rules.

Here we show the form of our assertion-based reasoning rules. To put it most simply, our assertion-based reasoning rules are in the form of a Hoare triple $\{p\} N \{q\}$, where N stands for the network system, while p and q stand for the precondition and the postcondition respectively. Essentially, the network system consists of program commands, while p and q are assertions. It describes how the execution of programs changes the state of the computation. When the network system starts in a state that satisfies p, after the execution, postcondition q should be satisfied [12].

3.1 Communication Command Rules

In this subsection we give the verification rules for the core part of the language viewed in isolation as follows.

In order to model the interference of communication in distributed system, the action of output is divided into two parts: the output command which is used to check whether a node can start to output data or not and the active output command which is used to transmit v.

Rule 1. Output

$$\{T|_{l,c} = \emptyset\} \; n[out\langle e \rangle]_{l,r}^c \; \{(l,r,c) \in T\}$$

This rule describes the changes of the state when the output command is executed. Here, $T|_{l,c}$ is short for active neighbor node set $T|(l,r,c)$. The nodes in this set are those who can reach a node located in l and synchronized on channel c. In other words, the node in $T|_{l,c}$ is transmitting the data to the node with location l and channel c. In addition, only when $T|_{l,c}$ is empty can the output command be executed. After the execution of output command, the node with location l and channel c is in the set of active transmitter T.

Rule 2. Active Output

$$\{(l,r,c) \in T\} \; n[\langle v \rangle]_{l,r}^c \; \{(l,r,c) \notin T\}$$

The meaning of this rule is that before the active output command is executed, the node should be in the active transmitter set T. After the transmission, the node is no longer in set T.

Similarly, the input action also consists of two parts: input command and active input command. Before input command, the node will check if it can receive data from other nodes. Once the input action begins, the input command will be executed and the interference may occur between input command and active input command.

Rule 3. Input

$$\{T|_{l,c} = \emptyset\} \; n[in(x)]_{l,r}^c \; \{(l,r,c) \in R\}$$

This rule gives the precondition and postcondition of the input command. Note that $T|_{l,c}$ is a set of neighbor active transmitter nodes whose transmissions reach a node with location l and channel c. When the node starts to receive the data, it will detect whether there is a node transmitting the data or not. If the set $T|_{l,c}$ is empty, the process can execute and become the active input process. Thus, the node is in the active receive set R.

Rule 4. Active Input

$$\{(l,r,c) \in R \; \wedge \; T|_{l,c} \neq \emptyset\} \; n[(x)]_{l,r}^c \; \{(l,r,c) \notin R\}$$

Note that the set $T|_{l,c}$ should not be empty before the active input can be executed. That is to say, only when there is a node currently transmitting data to node $n[(x)]_{l,r}^c$ can the receiver get the data. Also, R is the active receiver set.

Rule 5. Empty

$$\{p\} \; n[0]_{l,r}^c \; \{p\}$$

In the context of process, 0 represents an inactive process. In the context of network, 0 represents an empty network. Therefore, this empty rule has no side effect, which is a terminated signal.

3.2 Sequential Program Rules

The sequential node programs constitute the whole distributed network system. We define the behavior of the sequential node program in a manner analogous to the while system in [8]. The following verification rules establish a sequential node program proof system.

Rule 6. Skip

$$\{p\}\ n[Skip]^c_{l,r}\ \{p\}$$

Rule 7. Assignment

$$\{p[u := t]\}\ n[u := t]^c_{l,r}\ \{p\}$$

Note that the u is a variable and t is an expression.

Rule 8. Composition

$$\frac{\{p\}\ n[S_1]^c_{l,r}\ \{r\}, \{r\}\ n[S_2]^c_{l,r}\ \{q\}}{\{p\}\ n[S_1.S_2]^c_{l,r}\ \{q\}}$$

The rule states that the processes are connected by the notation . in our system.

Rule 9. Conditional

$$\frac{\{p \wedge B\}\ n[S_1]^c_{l,r}\ \{q\}, \{p \wedge \neg B\}\ n[S_2]^c_{l,r}\ \{q\}}{\{p\}\ n[\textbf{if } B \textbf{ then } S_1 \textbf{ else } S_2 \textbf{ fi}]^c_{l,r}\ \{q\}}$$

Rule 10. Loop

$$\frac{\{p \wedge B\}\ n[S]^c_{l,r}\ \{p\}}{\{p\}\ n[\textbf{while } B \textbf{ do } S \textbf{ od}]^c_{l,r}\ \{p \wedge \neg B\}}$$

Rule 11. Consequence

$$\frac{p \rightarrow p_1, \{p_1\}\ n[S]^c_{l,r}\ \{q_1\}, q_1 \rightarrow q}{\{p\}\ n[S]^c_{l,r}\ \{q\}}$$

Rule 12. Conjunction

$$\frac{\{p\}\ n[S]^c_{l,r}\ \{q\}, \{p\}\ n[S]^c_{l,r}\ \{r\}}{\{p\}\ n[S]^c_{l,r}\ \{q \wedge r\}}$$

Since communication rules and sequential rules have been introduced, we here give a simple example to show how it works.

Example 3.1. Let $N = n_1[S_1]_{l_1,r_1}^c$, where

$$S_1 =_{df} flag := 1. \text{ if } flag = 1 \text{ then } out\langle open\rangle$$
$$\text{else } out\langle close\rangle$$
$$\textbf{fi.}$$

We prove the correctness formula: $\{T|_{l_1,c} = \emptyset\} \, N \, \{flag = 1\}$.
To this end, we apply the composition rule, then we have

$$\frac{\{T|_{l_1,c} = \emptyset\} \, n_1[flag := 1]_{l_1,r_1}^c \, \{T|_{l_1,c} = \emptyset \, \wedge \, flag = 1\},}{\{T|_{l_1,c} = \emptyset\} \, n_1[flag := 1.S_1']_{l_1,r_1}^c \, \{q\}}$$

where

$$S_1' =_{df} \text{ if } flag = 1 \text{ then } out\langle open\rangle$$
$$\text{else } out\langle close\rangle$$
$$\textbf{fi.}$$

Now we should prove that the assertion q in the correctness formula $\{T|_{l_1,c} = \emptyset \, \wedge \, flag = 1\} \, n_1[S_1'] \, \{q\}$ equals to or implies the desired assertion $\{flag = 1\}$. To this end we apply the conditional rule, the output rule, the active output rule and empty rule, then we have

$\{T|_{l_1,c} = \emptyset \wedge flag = 1\}$
$n_1[out\langle open\rangle]_{l_1,r_1}^c$
$\{flag = 1 \wedge (l_1, r_1, c) \in T\}$
$n_1[\langle open\rangle]_{l_1,r_1}^c$
$\{flag = 1 \, \wedge \, (l_1, r_1, c) \notin T\}$
$n_1[0]_{l_1,r_1}^c$
$\{flag = 1 \, \wedge \, (l_1, r_1, c) \notin T\}$

Since $flag = 1 \, \wedge \, (l_1, r_1, c) \notin T \to flag = 1$, by the consequence rule, we get the desired result.

3.3 Wireless System Composition Rules

Wireless network system is a kind of distributed system, which consists of a number of physically wireless network nodes. On the one hand, these nodes work independently using their own private storage. On the other hand, these nodes communicate with each other from time to time by message passing. However, the way of message passing in wireless system is different from the way it works in concurrent system. In the wireless system, if there are no transmission or reception tasks, one node can start a broadcast transmission process at any time and finish the transmission regardless of whether there is a reception node or not. Moreover, a node can start a reception process at any time, but only can finish the reception when there is a node which is currently transmitting the data. We assume there are no internal conditions (e.g., timeouts, interrupts, exceptions) in order to focus on the feature of interference.

For the verification of correctness in wireless system, we here introduce wireless system composition rules. First of all, we give some definitions and notations in our rules. Let N stands for a wireless network system which is of the form:

$$N = [N_1 \mid .... \mid N_m],$$

where there is no nested parallelism in N_i and processes $N_1, ..., N_m$ are pairwise disjoint. In addition, each node N_i for $i \in \{1, ..., m\}$ can be formalized as below:

$$N_i = n_i[S_{i,0}]_{l_i,r_i}^{c_i}; \mathbf{do} \ \square_{j=1}^{M_i} B_{i,j}; n_i[\alpha_{i,j}]_{l_i,r_i}^{c_i} \rightarrow n_i[S_{i,j}]_{l_i,r_i}^{c_i} \ \mathbf{od},$$

where $n[.]$ means process in a network program and $S_{i,0}$ denotes the initial process in the sequential node program N_i. The loop body between do and od is the main loop of N_i which may be further do loops inside N_i. Note that when $M = 0$, the loop is considered as $skip$. Besides, any nondeterministic program is a process. Here, $\alpha_{i,j}$ represents the communication command such as output or input command which is listed in Subsect. 3.2. Moreover, $\alpha_{i,j}$ can be executed when the boolean guard B is true. Finally, if all guards evaluate to false, the main loop terminates.

Definition 3.1 (Disjoint). For process N, let $change(N)$ indicate the set of all variables in N on the left-hand side of an assignment or in an input command. Let $var(N)$ denote the set of all variables appearing in N. Furthermore, let $channel(N)$ denote the set of channels in N. Nodes N_1 and N_2 are called **disjoint** if they satisfy:

$$change(N_1) \cap var(N_2) = var(N_1) \cap change(N_2) = \varnothing.$$

We say that a channel c connects two node N_i and N_j if

$$c \in channel(N_i) \cap channel(N_j).$$

Definition 3.2 (Match). We consider output and input commands in node $n_i[P]_{l_i,r_i}^c (i \in \{1, ..., m\})$ **match**, if the following conditions hold:

(i) The same channel connects these nodes.
(ii) The distance between input and output nodes is in the range of output node transmission radius, i.e. $d(l_1, l_2) \leq r_1$, where r_1 is an output node transmission radius.
(iii) If there are more than two input and output commands satisfying (i) and (ii), link every two commands which can communicate with each other. The topology of the graph should be all connected.

Once there are input and output commands matched and the Boolean guards before them are true, the communication takes place. Formally, we use the notation below to stand for the match among the different components:

$$match(n[\alpha_1]_{l_1,r_1}^c \mid ... \mid n[\alpha_m]_{l_m,r_m}^c);$$

Table 2. The relationship between rules and cases

Rule number	Relationship between receiver and sender	Example
Match Cooperate Rule I	every receiver in one sender	
Match Cooperate Rule II	one receiver in multiple senders and senders can transmit to each other	
Match Cooperate Rule III	one receiver in multiple senders and not all senders can transmit to others	
Match Cooperate Rule IV	one receiver in multiple senders and none of senders can transmit to others	

The match part of the wireless network system can be verified by the following Match Rule.

Match Rule

$$\frac{\{p_i\}n_i[\alpha]^c_{l_i,r_i}\{q_i\}, \ i = 1...m, \ cooperate}{\{p_1 \wedge ... \wedge p_m\} \ n_1[\alpha]^c_{l_1,r_1}|...|n_m[\alpha]^c_{l_m,r_m} \ \{q_1 \wedge ... \wedge q_m\}}$$

where, cooperate means other four match cooperate rules should be used in verification. There are four match cooperate rules corresponding to different communication cases. We list the corresponding relations between match cooperate rules and communication cases in Table 2. In addition, four network topology examples are shown after each communication case, where the computer icon represents the receiver node and base station icon represents the sender node.

Match Cooperate Rule I

$$\{true\}n_j[out\langle e\rangle.P_j]^c_{l_j,r_j} \mid \prod_{i\in I} n_i[(x_i).P_i]^c_{l_i,r_i}\{\bigwedge_{i\in I} x_i = [\![e]\!]\}$$
$$\{true\}n_j[\langle v\rangle.P_j]^c_{l_j,r_j} \mid \prod_{i\in I} n_i[(x_i).P_i]^c_{l_i,r_i}\{\bigwedge_{i\in I} x_i = v\}$$

where, the notation $\prod_{i\in I} n_i[(x_i)]^c_{l_i,r_i}$ stands for the parallel composition for all processes $n_i[(x_i)]^c_{l_i,r_i}$ which communicate with $n_j[out\langle e\rangle]^c_{l_j,r_j}$. P_i and P_j represent the remainder of the process in n_i and n_j respectively.

For match cooperate rule III, we assume every receiving node is only in the sending range of just one transmitting node. Formally, this rule can be used when the following formula holds:

$$\forall_{i\in I}(n_i[in(x)]^c_{l_i,r_i} \quad (\exists n_a[out\langle v\rangle.P]^c_{l_a,r_a}(d(l_i,l_a) \leq r_a) \wedge$$
$$\exists n_b[out\langle v\rangle]^c_{l_b,r_b}(d(l_i,l_b) \leq r_b) \to r_a = r_b))$$

Match Cooperate Rule II

$$\{true\}n_i[(x).P_i]^c_{l_i,r_i} \mid \prod_{j\in J} n_j[out\langle e_j\rangle.P_j]^c_{l_j,r_j}\{\bigvee_{j\in J} x_i = [\![e_j]\!]\}$$
$$\{true\}n_i[(x).P_i]^c_{l_i,r_i} \mid \prod_{j\in J} n_j[\langle v_j\rangle.P_j]^c_{l_j,r_j}\{\bigvee_{j\in J} x_i = v_j\}.$$

For match cooperate rule II, we assume every receiver is in more than one transmission range of the transmitting nodes. Besides, the transmitting nodes are also in the transmission range of each other.

Match Cooperate Rule III

$$\{true\}n_i[(x).P_i]^c_{l_i,r_i} \mid \prod_{j\in J} n_j[out\langle e_j\rangle.P_j]^c_{l_j,r_j}\{x_i = \bot \vee x_i = [\![e_{max}]\!]\}$$
$$\{true\}n_i[(x).P_i]^c_{l_i,r_i} \mid \prod_{j\in J} n_j[v\langle e_j\rangle.P_j]^c_{l_j,r_j}\{x_i = \bot \vee x_i = v_{max}\}$$

where, max is the maximum value of r among the nodes $n_j[out\langle e_j\rangle]^c_{l_j,r_j}$. In addition, notation $\bot$ indicates there is an interference in communication and input node has not received the correct value.

For match cooperate rule III, we assume every receiver is in more than one transmission range of the transmitting nodes. Besides, not all transmitting nodes are in the transmission range of each other.

Match Cooperate Rule IV

$$\{true\}n_i[(x).P_i]^c_{l_i,r_i} \mid \prod_{j\in J} n_j[out\langle e_j\rangle.P_j]^c_{l_j,r_j}\{x_i = \bot\}$$
$$\{true\}n_i[(x).P_i]^c_{l_i,r_i} \mid \prod_{j\in J} n_j[\langle v_j\rangle.P_j]^c_{l_j,r_j}\{x_i = \bot\}$$

For match cooperate rule IV, we assume every receiver is in more than one transmission range of the transmitting nodes. Besides, all of transmitting nodes are not in the transmission range of each other.

Rule 13. Wireless System Composition

$$\frac{\begin{array}{c} \{p\}\ n_1[S_{1,0}]^{c_1}_{l_1,r_1}; ...; n_m[S_{n,0}]^{c_m}_{l_m,l_m}\ \{I\} \\ \{I \wedge B_{i,j} \wedge ... \wedge B_{i_x,j_y}\}\ match(n_i[\alpha_{i,j}]^{c_i}_{l_i,r_i}\ |\ ...\ |\ n_x[\alpha_{i_x,j_y}]^{c_x}_{l_x,r_x}); \\ n_i[S_{i,j}]^{c_i}_{l_i,r_i}; ...; n_x[S_{i_x,j_y}]^{c_x}_{l_x,r_x}\ \{I\}, \\ for\ all(i_1,i_2,...,i_x,j_1,j_2,...,j_y) \in Network \end{array}}{\{p\}\ N\ \{I \wedge TERM\}}$$

where I is a global invariant variable. $Network$ is a set defined as $\{(i_1,i_2,...,i_x,\ j_1,j_2,...,j_y)|n_{i_1,j_1}, n_{i_2,j_2},..., n_{i_x,j_y}\ match\}$. The signal $TERM = \bigwedge_{i=1}^{m} \bigwedge_{j=1}^{m_i} \neg B_{i,j}$. m is the number of the total nodes in network. m_i means the number of all the input/output commands in node i. As for the processes in $match(...)$, it should be verified by match rule as below.

Example 3.2. Let $N = n_1[S_1]^c_{l_1,r_1}\ |\ n_2[S_2]^c_{l_2,r_2}$, where $d(l_1,l_2) \le r_1$, $S_2 =_{df}$ $in(x).(x)$ and S_1 has been defined in Example 3.1. This example describes a communication between a sender and a receiver which also can be extended to multiple senders and receivers. At the very beginning, there is no communication happening in nodes N_1 and N_2. Hence the precondition can be described as: $\{T|_{l_1,c} = \emptyset\ \wedge\ T|_{l_2,c} = \emptyset\}$. After execution, we should verify that the receiver has successfully accepted the value $open$ from sender which can be defined as: $\{x = open\}$. Here, the verification is given as below:

$$\{T|_{l_1,c} = \emptyset\ \wedge\ T|_{l_2,c} = \emptyset\}$$
$$n_1[S_1]^c_{l_1,r_1}|\ n_2[S_2]^c_{l_2,r_2}$$

We notice that only $out\langle open\rangle$ and $in(x)$ match in this case. From Example 3.1, we can obtain some assertions as below:

$$\{T|_{l_1,c} = \emptyset\ \wedge\ flag = 1\ \wedge\ T|_{l_2,c} = \emptyset\}$$
$$n_1[out\langle open\rangle.S_1']^c_{l_1,r_1}\ |\ n_2[in(x).S_2']^c_{l_2,r_2}$$
$$\{(l_1,r_1,c) \in T\ \wedge\ (l_2,r_2,c) \in R\ \wedge\ flag = 1\}$$

Here, we get rid of the assertion $\{flag = 1\}$ by consequence rule:

$$\{(l_1,r_1,c) \in T\ \wedge\ (l_2,r_2,c) \in R\}$$
$$n_1[\langle open\rangle.S_1']^c_{l_1,r_1}\ |\ n_2[(x).S_2']^c_{l_2,r_2}$$

The communication meets the condition of match case I, so we can use match cooperate rule I to get the key assertion:

$$\{x = open\ \wedge\ (l_1,r_1,c) \notin T\ \wedge\ (l_2,r_2,c) \notin R\}$$
$$n_1[0]\ |\ n_2[0]$$
$$\{x = open\}.$$

Finally, we verify that the program satisfies the postcondition. This indicates that the second node in wireless system has received the value from the first node and the data transmission has finished successfully.

3.4   Soundness

In this subsection we discuss the soundness of our approach. Firstly, we define the meaning of soundness based on the operational semantics described in [4]. In order to prove our reasoning system is sound, we should show every verification rule in the reasoning system is indeed valid [13]. For most verification rules, soundness follows directly from the definition of the semantics and part of rules in subsect. 3.2 has been proved in [8]. Therefore, we take a typical match cooperate rule III as an example to give the proof process. Here is the definition of soundness.

Definition 3.3. Let N be a network system and σ a proper state.

(i) a configuration C is a pair $\langle N, \sigma \rangle$.

(ii) a transition $\langle N, \sigma \rangle \to \langle N', \tau \rangle$ means when the first command in N with the state σ is executed, it will lead to the state τ. N' is the remainder of N. The transition should abide by the operational semantics.

(iii) the correctness semantics is a mapping

$$M[N] : \Sigma \to P(\Sigma)$$

with $M[N](\sigma) = \{\tau | \langle N, \sigma \rangle \to^* \langle E, \tau \rangle\}$
where Σ is a set of output states, E means empty program and the system terminates in state τ.

(iv) $\models \{p\}\ N\ \{q\}$ means the verification rule $\{p\}\ N\ \{q\}$ is true, which meets if and only if $M[N]([p]) \subseteq [q]$ holds.

Definition 3.4 (Soundness). Let G be a reasoning system which can be used to prove the correctness of the wireless system defined in CWS. $\vdash_G \{p\}\ N\ \{q\}$ means $\{p\}\ N\ \{q\}$ is provable in G. We say that G is **sound** for correctness of the wireless system defined in CWS if for all verification rules $\{p\}\ N\ \{q\}$, we have:

$$\vdash_G \{p\}\ N\ \{q\}\ \text{implies} \models \{p\}\ N\ \{q\}$$

Proof for Match Cooperate Rule III

$$\{true\}n_i[(x).P_i]^c_{l_i,r_i} \mid \prod_{j \in J} n_j[out\langle e_j \rangle.P_j]^c_{l_j,r_j}\{x_i = \perp \vee x_i = [|e_{max}|]\}$$

$$\{true\}n_i[(x).P_i]^c_{l_i,r_i} \mid \prod_{j \in J} n_j[v\langle e_j \rangle.P_j]^c_{l_j,r_j}\{x_i = \perp \vee x_i = v_{max}\}$$

Let $N = n_i[(x).P_i]^c_{l_i,r_i} \mid \prod_{j \in J} n_j[out\langle e_j \rangle.P_j]^c_{l_j,r_j}$. According to the proof system, to prove this rule is sound is to prove: $M[N](\{true\}) \subseteq (\{x_i = \perp \vee x_i = [|e_{max}|]\})$.

For the first rule, since $M[N](\{true\}) = \{\tau | \langle N, \{true\} \rangle \to^* \langle E, \tau \rangle\}$, we should find the transition sequence of the command in N. There are two kinds of transition sequences in this case.

In the first case, from the operational semantics I in [4]:

$$\frac{T|_{l,c} = \phi\ \forall h \in I \cup J \cup K.d(l, l_h) \le r \forall i \in I.T|_{l_i,c} = \phi\ \forall j \in J.T|_{l_j,c} \neq \phi}{T \triangleright n[out\langle e \rangle.P]^c_{l,r} \mid \prod_{h \in I \cup J} n_h[in(x_h).P_h]^c_{l_h,r_h} \mid \prod_{k \in K} n_k[(x_k).P_k]^c_{l_k,r_k} \hookrightarrow^c_{l,r}}$$

$$n[\langle |e| \rangle.P]^c_{l,r} \mid \prod_{i \in I} n_i[(x_i).P_i]^c_{l_i,r_i} \mid$$

$$\prod_{j \in J} n_j[in(x_j).P_j]^c_{l_j,c_j} \mid \prod_{k \in K} n_k[P_k\{\perp/x_k\}]^c_{l_k,r_k}$$

we can deduce that one situation is same as the node $n[out\langle e\rangle.P]^c_{l,r}$ and $n_k[(x_k).P_k]^c_{l_k,r_k}$, the transition is as followed.

$$seq_1 =< N, \{true\} >\rightarrow< n_i[P_i\{\bot/x_i\}]^c_{l_i,r_i}|\prod_{j\in J} n_j[\langle\langle|e|\rangle.P]^c_{l_j,r_j}, \{x_i = \bot\} >$$

The second situation is according to the operation semantics I and II in [4]:

$$\frac{\forall i \in I, d(l,l_i) \leq r}{T \triangleright n[\langle v\rangle.P]^c l, r \mid \prod_{i\in I} n_i[(x_i).P_i]^c l_i, r_i| \prod_{j\in J} n_j[in(x_j).P_j]^c l_j, r_j \hookrightarrow}$$
$$n[P]^c l, r \mid \prod_{i\in I} n_i[P_i\{v/x_i\}]^c l_i, r_i \mid \prod_{j\in J} n_j[in(x_j).P_j]^c l_j, r_j$$

We can deduce that other situation is like the sender with the max value of transition radius can send to the receiver and other senders can not. So the transition is as followed and m means the node with the max value of transition radius.

$$seq_2 =< N, \{true\} >\rightarrow< n_i[P_i\{\langle|e_{max}|\rangle/x_i\}]^c_{l_i,r_i}|\prod_{j\in(J-max)} n_j[out\langle e\rangle.P]^c_{l_j,r_j}|$$
$$n_{max}[out\langle e\rangle.P]^c_{l_{max},r_{max}}, \{x_i = \langle|e_{max}|\rangle\} >$$

In conclusion, the $M[N](\{true\}) = \{x_i = \bot \vee x_i = \langle|e_{max}|\rangle\}$.

Therefore, $M[N](\{true\}) \subseteq (\{x_i = \bot \vee x_i = [|e_{max}|]\})$, the first rule is sound. The proof process is similar to the second rule. Thus, the whole rule is sound. $\square$

4 Case Study: Stop-and-Wait ARQ Protocol

In this section we study an example about Stop-and-Wait ARQ (automatic repeat-request) protocol operating at the data link layer. Additionaly, we show how to apply our method to prove the correctness and a few properties of this protocol.

Stop-and-Wait ARQ protocol is one of automatic repeat request protocols widely used to ensure reliability for transmitted data [14]. It can retransmit lost or corrupted messages and restrict the order of messages to ensure receivers get messages in turn.

The working idea of this kind of protocol is as follows. The sender A has to send a sequence of messages to receiver B. Each message is in a packet consisting of information bits and a one-bits sequence number s. The one-bits sequence number s can either be 0 or 1. When A sends a message packet, it waits for an acknowledgment (ACK) before sending a new packet. If the acknowledgment from B contains the same sequence number, it means that the message packet has been successfully received by B and A starts transmitting the next packet. On the contrary, if the acknowledgment is not expected or a timeout expires, it means that the message packet is received in error and A should resend the message packet with the same sequence number. Retransmissions continue until an ACK is received.

On the other hand, when B receives a message packet with a sequence number 0, it will send back an acknowledgment ACK0 with a sequence number 0 and keep sending until it receives a valid message with sequence number 1. Note that

Table 3. An example for Stop-and-Wait ARQ in CWS

$Sender[q, s] =_{def}$ **while** $\neg empty(q)$
$\qquad\qquad$ **do**
$\qquad\qquad\qquad$ **if** $empty(q)$ **then** $out\langle(l_1, End, s)\rangle.in(x).$
$\qquad\qquad\qquad\qquad$ **if** $x = (l_2, Ack, s)$ **then** $Skip$ **fi**
$\qquad\qquad\qquad$ **else**
$\qquad\qquad\qquad\qquad$ $out\langle(l_1, front(q), s)\rangle.in(x).$
$\qquad\qquad\qquad\qquad$ **if** $x = (l_2, Ack, s)$ **then**
$\qquad\qquad\qquad\qquad\qquad$ $pop(q).s := \neg s.$
$\qquad\qquad\qquad\qquad$ **fi**
$\qquad\qquad\qquad$ **fi**
$\qquad\qquad$ **od**

$Receiver[q, s] =_{def}$ $in(x).$
$\qquad\qquad\qquad$ **while** $snd(x) \neq End$
$\qquad\qquad\qquad\qquad$ **do if** $fst(x) = l_1 \ \wedge \ trd(x) = s$ **then**
$\qquad\qquad\qquad\qquad\qquad$ $out\langle l_1, Ack, s\rangle.push(q, snd(x)).s := \neg s.$
$\qquad\qquad\qquad\qquad$ **else**
$\qquad\qquad\qquad\qquad\qquad$ $out\langle l_1, Ack, \neg s\rangle.$
$\qquad\qquad\qquad\qquad$ **fi**
$\qquad\qquad\qquad\qquad$ $in(x).$
$\qquad\qquad\qquad$ **od**
$\qquad\qquad\qquad$ $push(q, End)$

---

in our model, we assume that all the messages have been transmitted correctly so that we can focus on other simultaneous transmissions. That is to say, failure is due to interference in this model. Table 3 displays the model of this protocol.

Sender A and receiver B are modeled in CWS and defined above. We assume that the sender is located at l_1 and the receiver is located at l_2, while $d(l_1, l_2) \leq r_1, r_2$. The parameter q in sender represents a queue with a sequence of messages to be sent. In the very beginning, sequence number s is initialized as 0. There are several operations about the queue which are similar to C++ STL (Standard Template Library). $Front(q)$ returns the first element; $back(q)$ returns the last element; $empty(q)$ returns true when q is empty; $pop(q)$ drops the first element of q; $push(q, element)$ can push the element in the end of q. Moreover, $fst(x)$, $snd(x)$ and $trd(x)$ return the first, second and third element in x respectively.

In this case study, we should prove the correctness of protocol by verifying that the receiver can accept the message of q_s successfully. On the purpose of this, we first construct the program in CWS and then give the precondition. Finally, we apply our method to deduce that whether the program meet the postcondition or not.

Let $N = n_s[Sender[q_s, s]]^c_{l_s, r_s} \mid n_r[Receiver[q_r, s]]^c_{l_r, s_r} \mid M.$

where, M is the network environment and there is no malicious process in it, while $d(l_s, l_r) \leq r_s, r_r$ indicates the topology of these two nodes.

At the very beginning, there is no transmission in the network and node sender has the message in queue q_s. Besides, the queue q_r in node receiver is empty. Therefore, the precondition can be defined below:

$$\{T|_{l_s,c} = \emptyset \;\wedge\; T|_{l_r,c} = \emptyset \;\wedge\; q_s \neq \emptyset \;\wedge\; q_r = \emptyset\}.$$

Likewise, when the transmission has finished, the queue q_r has received the value from the queue q_s. Therefore, the value of the last element in the queue q_r is equal to that in the queue q_s. Hence, the postcondition is described below:

$$\{back(q_r) = End\}.$$

Proof Process

In this case, due to the features of ARQ protocol, once the transmission fails, the transmission will repeat again and again. Therefore, we assume the system can terminate and focus on the correctness of this system. For N, we apply the wireless system composition rule in order to get the postcondition $\{back(q_r) = End\}$. Firstly, we assume the p in wireless system composition rule is equal to the precondition we have given in the beginning and set the global invariant variable I as the assertion $T|_{l_s,c} = \emptyset \;\wedge\; T|_{l_r,c} = \emptyset$. Then, we can obtain:

$$\{T|_{l_s,c} = \emptyset \;\wedge\; T|_{l_r,c} = \emptyset \;\wedge\; q_s \neq \emptyset \;\wedge\; q_r = \emptyset\}$$

$$N$$

$$\{T|_{l_s,c} = \emptyset \;\wedge\; T|_{l_r,c} = \emptyset \;\wedge\; TERM\}$$

Note that the $TERM$ is $\bigwedge_{i=1}^{n} \bigwedge_{j=1}^{m_i} \neg B_{i,j}$ and n means the number of nodes in N which are match, while m is the number of transmissions among match pairs. Also, we find that the $n[B]$ in receiver node is about the first and third elements of message, so we cannot get our postcondition in $TERM$. Thus, we continue to consider other parts in details. Firstly, we consider the sender and receiver nodes separately.

Sender Part. For sender node, before the $empty(q)$ becomes true, the loop part in the node sender is like:

$$out\langle(l_1, front(q), s)\rangle.in(x).\textbf{if } x = (l_2, Ack, s) \textbf{ then } pop(q).s := \neg s.\textbf{ fi}$$

It sends the message with location, the front element of q_s and the sequence number s. Then, it waits for an Ack. If the Ack is true, it will send the next element of q_s, otherwise it repeats the transmission.

For $n_s[Sender[q_s, s]]_{l_s,r_s}^c$, we use the loop rule 10, if the process can terminate then we have:

$$\{T|_{l_s,c} = \emptyset \;\wedge\; q_s \neq \emptyset\}$$
$$n_s[\textbf{Sender}[q_s, s]]_{l_s,r_s}^c$$
$$\{T|_{l_s,c} = \emptyset \;\wedge\; q_s = \emptyset\}.$$

Receiver Part. As for the node receiver, the main loop is described as:

if $fst(x) = l_1 \wedge trd(x) = s$ **then** $out\langle l_1, Ack, s\rangle.push(q, snd(x)).s := \neg s.$
else $out\langle l_1, Ack, \neg s\rangle.$ **fi** $in(x).$

It will check whether the location and sequence number are right or not and send the Ack back to node sender and push the element in the q_r. Then it waits for other messages. In addition, the postcondition is similar to node sender.

Match Part. Next, we consider the match part in the system. If we can get the postcondition in match part, then the result can be verified by using conjunction rule.

There are four kinds of match situation in this case and all of them can satisfy the match cooperation rule I. We list them as below:

$$n_s[out\langle(l_1, front(q), s)\rangle.P'_s]^c_{l_s,r_s} \mid n_r[in(x).P'_r]^c_{l_r,r_r}$$
$$n_s[in(x).P'_s]^c_{l_s,r_s} \mid n_r[out\langle l_1, Ack, s\rangle.P'_r]^c_{l_r,r_r}$$
$$n_s[in(x).P'_s]^c_{l_s,r_s} \mid n_r[out\langle l_1, Ack, \neg s\rangle.P'_r]^c_{l_r,r_r}$$
$$n_s[out\langle(l_1, End, s)\rangle.P'_s]^c_{l_s,r_s} \mid n_r[in(x).P'_r]^c_{l_r,r_r}$$

Take the first situation as example:

$$\{T|_{l_s,c} = \emptyset \wedge T|_{l_r,c} = \emptyset \wedge q_s = \emptyset\}$$
$$n_s[out\langle(l_1, End, s)\rangle.P'_s]^c_{l_s,r_s} \mid n_r[in(x).P'_r]^c_{l_r,r_r}$$
$$\{(l_s, r_s, c) \in T \wedge (l_r, r_r, c) \in R \wedge q_s = \emptyset\}$$
$$n_s[\langle(l_1, End, s)\rangle.P'_s]^c_{l_s,r_s} \mid n_r[(x).P'_r]^c_{l_r,r_r}$$
$$\{x = (l, End, s) \wedge (l_s, r_s, c) \notin T \wedge (l_r, r_r, c) \notin R\}$$

From the assertion above, we can deduce the assertion that

$$\{x = (l, End, s) \wedge T|_{l_s,c} = \emptyset \wedge T|_{l_r,c} = \emptyset\}.$$

Moreover, because $x = (l, End, s)$, so $snd(x) = End$. The final command in the node receiver can be executed and we finally get the target postcondition.

$$\{snd(x) \neq End\}$$
$$\boldsymbol{Push(q, End)}$$
$$\{back(q_r) = End\}$$

Therefore, when there is no malicious process, the program can receive the message successfully.

5   Conclusion

In this paper, we have presented an assertion-based reasoning method for Calculus of Wireless Systems in order to prove the correctness of wireless systems formalized in CWS. Our approach firstly introduces the assertion in the form of Hoare triple to verify the wireless system combined with the features of local broadcast, asynchrony and synchrony. In order to make the verification more straightforward, we first provide the verification rules for each process viewed in isolation. Then we give a set of composition rules which can be used for making every process meaningful in a complete system. The key contribution we have made is the cooperation rules which can be applied in verification of various broadcast situations in wireless systems. In addition, our method also can be used to describe the interference in transmission of wireless system, which is an essential feature of this kind of systems.

For the future, we are continuing to explore the assertion-based reasoning method for wireless systems. On one hand, the mobility feature in wireless system is very important [15]. We can introduce some specific assertions used to describe this feature and verify some properties related to mobility. On the other hand, it is also challenging to investigate the linking theories between our deduction approach and the semantics (operational, denotational and algebraic) for wireless systems [4,16,17]. Furthermore, this reasoning system can be implemented in a tool so that it can be automated and become usable for verifying larger programs.

Acknowledgment. This work was partly supported by the Danish National Research Foundation and the National Natural Science Foundation of China (Grant No. 61361136002) for the Danish-Chinese Center for Cyber Physical Systems. It was also supported by Shanghai Collaborative Innovation Center of Trustworthy Software for Internet of Things (No. ZF1213).

References

1. Willig, A., Matheus, K., Wolisz, A.: Wireless technology in industrial networks. Proc. IEEE **93**(6), 1130–1151 (2005)
2. Fratu, O., Pejanovic-Djurisic, M., Poulkov, V., Gavrilovska, L.: Introduction to special issue "current trends in information and communications technology". Wireless Pers. Commun. **87**(3), 615–617 (2016)
3. Prasad, K.V.S.: A calculus of broadcasting systems. Sci. Comput. Program. **25**(2–3), 285–327 (1995)
4. Lanese, I., Sangiorgi, D.: An operational semantics for a calculus for wireless systems. Theor. Comput. Sci. **411**(19), 1928–1948 (2010)
5. Godskesen, J.C.: A calculus for mobile ad hoc networks. In: Murphy, A.L., Vitek, J. (eds.) COORDINATION 2007. LNCS, vol. 4467, pp. 132–150. Springer, Heidelberg (2007). doi:10.1007/978-3-540-72794-1_8
6. Merro, M.: An observational theory for mobile ad hoc networks (full version). Inf. Comput. **207**(2), 194–208 (2009)
7. Nanz, S., Hankin, C.: Formal security analysis for ad-hoc networks. Electr. Notes Theor. Comput. Sci. **142**, 195–213 (2006)
8. Apt, K.R., de Boer, F.S., Olderog, E.: Verification of sequential and concurrent programs. In: Apt, K.R., de Boer, F.S., Olderog, E. (eds.) Texts in Computer Science. Springer, Heidelberg (2009)
9. Xu, Q., de Roever, W.P., He, J.: The rely-guarantee method for verifying shared variable concurrent programs. Formal Asp. Comput. **9**(2), 149–174 (1997)
10. Goguen, H.: Soundness of the logical framework for its typed operational semantic. In: Girard, J.-Y. (ed.) TLCA 1999. LNCS, vol. 1581, pp. 177–197. Springer, Heidelberg (1999). doi:10.1007/3-540-48959-2_14

11. Mezzetti, N., Sangiorgi, D.: Towards a calculus for wireless systems. Electr. Notes Theor. Comput. Sci. **158**, 331–353 (2006)
12. Hoare, C.A.R.: An axiomatic basis for computer programming. Commun. ACM **12**(10), 576–580 (1969)
13. Gallier, J.: Mathematical reasoning, proof principles, and logic. In: Gallier, J. (ed.) Discrete Mathematics. Springer, New York (2011)
14. De Vuyst, S., Tworus, K., Wittevrongel, S., Bruneel, H.: Analysis of stop-and-wait ARQ for a wireless channel. 4OR **7**(1), 61–78 (2008)
15. Wu, J., Fan, P.: A survey on high mobility wireless communications: challenges, opportunities and solutions. IEEE Access **4**, 450–476 (2016)
16. Wu, X., Zhu, H., Wu, X.: Observation-oriented semantics for calculus of wireless systems. In: Naumann, D. (ed.) UTP 2014. LNCS, vol. 8963, pp. 105–124. Springer, Cham (2015). doi:10.1007/978-3-319-14806-9_6
17. Hoare, C.A.R.: Algebra of concurrent programming. In: Meeting 52 of WG 2.3. (2011)

Taming Living Logic Using Formal Methods

Hasan Baig and Jan Madsen[✉]

Department of Applied Mathematics and Computer Science,
Technical University of Denmark, 2800 Kongens Lyngby, Denmark
{haba, jama}@dtu.dk

Abstract. One of the goals of synthetic biology is to build genetic circuits to control the behavior of a cell for different application domains, such as medical, environmental, and biotech. During the design process of genetic circuits, biologists are often interested in the probability of a system to work under different conditions. Since genetic circuits are noisy and stochastic in nature, the verification process becomes very complicated. The state space of stochastic genetic circuit models is usually too large to be handled by classical model checking techniques. Therefore, the verification of genetic circuit models is usually performed by the statistical approach of model checking. In this work, we present a workflow for checking genetic circuit models using a stochastic model checker (Uppaal) and a stochastic simulator (D-VASim). We demonstrate with experimentations that the proposed workflow is not only sufficient for the model checking of genetic circuits, but can also be used to design the genetic circuits with desired timings.

1 Introduction

Synthetic biology has emerged as an important discipline in which the synthetic digital [1, 2] and analog [2] computations in living cells have been implemented. Computation in living cells will revolutionize the fields of medicine and biotechnology. The aim of biological computation is to develop genetic devices to address the real-world problems including tumor destruction [4], bio-fuels [5], consuming toxic wastes [6], pharmaceuticals [7], etc. These biological devices are constructed from genetic circuits. A genetic circuit represents a gene regulatory network (GRN), which is composed of small genetic components, e.g., promoter, operator, ribosome binding site, protein coding site, and terminator. These components interact with the external signals (like temperature, light, etc.) to control the behavior of a living cell. Similar to electronic engineers who develop circuits using electronic logic gates (such as AND, NAND, and NOT gates), genetic network engineers use biological equivalents of these components to control the function of a cell [1, 8].

Figure 1(a) shows an example of a genetic implementation of a NAND gate represented in SBOL [9] notation. P_1 and P_2 are promoters, which are the regions of DNA that initiates the process of transcription (or production) of a gene. In this case, when two proteins, LacI and TetR, are present in sufficient amount within the cell, they inhibit promoters P_1 and P_2 to produce the output protein i.e. green fluorescent protein (GFP). This type of gene regulatory networks is based on the "central dogma" of

© Springer International Publishing AG 2017
L. Aceto et al. (Eds.): Larsen Festschrift, LNCS 10460, pp. 503–515, 2017.
DOI: 10.1007/978-3-319-63121-9_25

molecular biology, which states that genes in the DNA specify the sequence of mes-
senger RNA (the transcription process by RNA polymerase), which in turn specify the
sequence of proteins (the translation process by ribosomes). Regulatory proteins can
control gene expression by either preventing transcription (repression), which is the
case for LacI and TetR in the NAND gate, or by promoting RNA polymerase binding
to the promoter (activation). A careful selection and balance of the genetic components,
as expressed in the NAND gate in Fig. 1, can provide a functional gene regulatory
network. To make genetic circuits work, it is not enough to be able to control the
production of certain proteins, i.e. increasing the concentration, but also to be able to
reduce concentrations of proteins. This happens by natural degradation of proteins, i.e.
a protein has a certain lifetime, before it is dissolved into the amino acids from which it
was constructed.

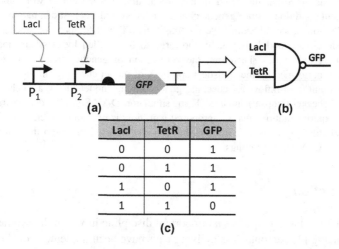

LacI	TetR	GFP
0	0	1
0	1	1
1	0	1
1	1	0

(c)

Fig. 1. Genetic NAND gate [55]. (a) Genetic implementation in SBOL notation. (b) Circuit
schematic (c) Truth table.

Signals in electronic logic gates propagate in separate electrical wires which do not
interfere with each other, if designed correctly. However, in genetic circuits, signals are
proteins drifting in the same volume of the cell, in order to establish a connection (a
biological "wire"), compatibility between input- and output-proteins must be ensured
and crosstalk with other signals from neighboring components, has to be avoided. This
makes it challenging to work with genetic circuits, and thus requires a library of genetic
components that can be used to develop complex circuits without causing crosstalk.
The standard part libraries and toolboxes of well-characterized genetic components
have been constructed through numerous laboratory experiments over the last decade
[10–18]. These components have been extensively used to develop genetic circuits with
different functionalities including oscillators [3], amplifiers [19, 20], linearizer gene
circuit [21], memory devices [22, 23], switches [1, 12, 24], time-delay circuits [25, 26],
genetic logic gates [27–30] etc.

The field of synthetic biology is still in its infancy, and the process of design and implementation of genetic circuits remains very slow. Similar to the electronic design automation (EDA) process which dramatically enhanced the design, verification, validation and production of electronic circuits, researchers have started to work on the development of genetic design automation (GDA) tools to automate the design, test and verification processes of genetic circuits prior to their validation in laboratory. Several computational tools [31–34] have been developed to assist users in the model construction and design [35–37], simulation [35, 36, 38–40], logic and timing analysis of genetic circuits [40], and model checking [36, 41–44]. Model checking of biological systems is getting popular as it is an effective means of analyzing the dynamics of complex biological systems [45–53]. The dynamics of genetic circuits, and hence their correct functioning, are dependent on a large set of parameters (such as reaction and degradation rates) which in general are very difficult to predict and control. Hence, biologists are usually interested in determining the sensitivity of their circuits for fluctuations in these parameters. For instance, it might be a question of interest to find out, if the circuit behaves as expected when the values of certain parameters are varied within a specified range. Such sensitivity analysis is well suited for explorations using statistical model checking (SMC) and the aim of this work is to show how Uppaal SMC can be used to address the problem, effectively taming living logic.

In this work, we propose a flow of statistical model checking for genetic circuits using Uppaal [41] and D-VASim [39]. In particular, we performed experimentations on genetic circuit models and explored their design parameter sensitivity using Uppaal SMC [42]. There are a certain number of tasks which cannot be performed in Uppaal [41]. We therefore used D-VASim [39] to address those, which will be detailed in the experimentation section. The paper is organized as follows; Sect. 2 describes the digital abstraction and a brief introduction to D-VASim and Uppaal SMC. Section 3 contains the experimentation on genetic circuit models and Sect. 4 concludes the results.

2   Methodology

To determine the range of parameter values for which the genetic circuit would work, it is first important to know the threshold concentration levels of the inputs of those circuits. The threshold level of a genetic circuit can be defined as *the minimum concentration of input protein(s), which causes the average concentration of output protein to cross the level of input protein(s) concentration* [40]. D-VASim [39] is a simulation tool which supports the capability of analyzing the threshold value and timings of genetic circuits through an automated process. It further allows the user to perform runtime interactive simulations. For example, Fig. 2(d) shows the stochastic simulation traces of a genetic NOT gate obtained from D-VASim. The input is TetR protein and the output is GFP protein. When the input concentration of TetR goes high, the output concentration of GFP goes low.

In Fig. 2(d), the initial output concentration is about 100 molecules when the input concentration of TetR protein is low. When the concentration of TetR is triggered to 4 molecules, the concentration of output protein starts to degrade, but stays above the

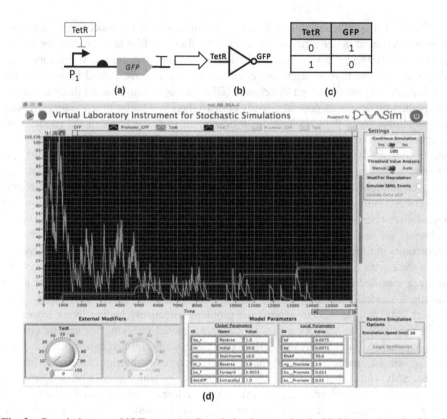

Fig. 2. Genetic inverter (NOT) gate. (a) Genetic implementation in SBOL notation. (b) Circuit schematic. (c) Truth table. (d) Stochastic simulation traces in D-VASim.

input concentration level. Increasing the input concentration further up (10 molecules) causes the output concentration to oscillate around the input concentration level. When we increase the input concentration level further (21 molecules), the output concentration stops oscillating around the input concentration level and settles down to zero. Here, the first input concentration level (up to 4 molecules) can be considered as low-threshold level as it does not cause the output concentration level to fall below it. Similarly, the third input concentration level (21 or more molecules) can be considered as high-threshold level as it causes the output concentration level to be in a clear logic-low state. The region between these two levels is considered as a transition region. This behavior is analogous to electronic circuits where the logic levels are well characterized. For example, the logic-1 of a 3.3 V CMOS-based electronic device is at least 2.4 V, which means that a minimum of 2.4 V is required to turn the circuit on. Similarly, the circuit is considered off, when the output voltage is below 0.8 V. The region between 0.8 V and 2.4 V is considered as a transition region, where the output is considered invalid.

Once the correct threshold levels are found, the inputs are triggered to that level and the circuit parameters can be varied to determine if the circuit still behaves correctly.

As shown in Fig. 2(d), the threshold value and the logic of a circuit can be determined by varying the input concentration level and check if it significantly effects the concentration level of output. The case discussed above is a very simple case in which the genetic circuit has only one input and one output. However, this analysis could be very time consuming for large genetic circuit models with more inputs. For large-scale circuits, it is difficult to determine or verify the expected logic of a circuit without careful analysis. To determine or verify the logic of a genetic circuit, it is important to know the correct input combination with the correct threshold levels which trigger the output of the circuit. This may apparently become a tedious task to check different input concentration levels for each input combination.

The search process of threshold value can be automated by the use of statistical model checking in Uppaal. Uppaal is an integrated tool environment for modeling, verification and validation of real-time systems modeled as networks of timed automata.

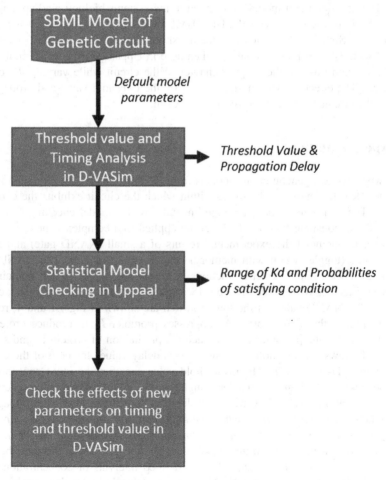

Fig. 3. Experimental flow of genetic circuit model checking and verification.

Uppaal SMC is an extended plug-in tool to Uppaal which allows the user to check the expected behavior of models in the form of probability distributions. In Uppaal SMC, it is possible to let the tool arbitrarily select any input concentration value, within a specified range, and see if the chosen value significantly effects the output concentration level. This can, however, only be achieved when the correct input combinations triggering the output of the circuit are known. As Uppaal does not have the capability to automatically detect the input combination which triggers the output of the circuit, the threshold value analysis of a genetic circuit cannot be performed *automatically* in Uppaal. D-VASim [39] is the only tool which allow users to perform threshold value and propagation delay analysis of genetic circuits through an automated process [40]. However, D-VASim is not capable of performing the automated statistical model checking. Thus, we used D-VASim for threshold value analysis and then perform the statistical model checking in Uppaal to determine the range of circuit parameters within which the circuit satisfy the desired behavior.

The proposed experimental flow of checking genetic circuit models is shown in Fig. 3. The genetic circuit models developed in the systems biology markup language (SBML) [54] are used in this work. The SBML model of a genetic circuit is used as input to D-VASim. D-VASim analyses the threshold and propagation delay (details are given in Sect. 3). The threshold value is then used in Uppaal to trigger the input levels to this value and observe the output behavior of the circuit while varying the circuit parameters. The effects of varying parameters on the threshold value and propagation delay of the circuit are then analyzed in D-VASim.

3 Experimentation

In this work, we test genetic circuit models from [55], by varying the degradation rate parameter (Kd) to determine the range within which the circuit exhibits the expected behavior. The aim is to propose an experimental flow for model checking of genetic circuits. To demonstrate that this flow can be applied to a complex genetic circuit as well, we have included the experimental results of a small (NAND gate) and a reasonably large (toggle switch with memory) genetic circuit models. The NAND gate contains 5 species and 5 kinetic reactions, whereas the toggle switch contains 20 species and its behavior is defined by 18 kinetic reactions. The schematic circuit models of the NAND gate and the toggle switch are shown in Figs. 1 and 4, respectively. In Fig. 4, the input protein A suppresses promoter P_1 to produce protein D, which in turn inhibits promoter P_4 to reduce the production of protein F, and so on.

Table 1 shows the threshold and propagation delay values for both of the circuits obtained from D-VASim. The high threshold value specifies the input concentration level above which the logic is considered high, and the low threshold value specify the input concentration level below which the logic is considered low. The propagation delay is defined as *the time from when the input concentration reaches its threshold value until the corresponding output concentration crosses the same threshold value* [40]. The confidence intervals of threshold values are not specified in this table because D-VASim analyzes threshold values for pre-defined intervals of concentrations. For example, in the case of genetic NAND gate, the threshold level is analyzed for

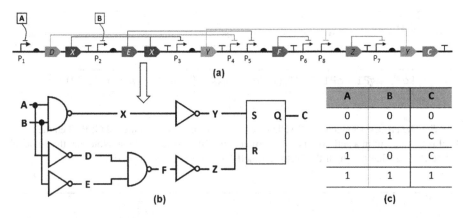

Fig. 4. Genetic toggle switch with memory [55]. (a) Genetic implementation in SBOL notation. (b) Circuit schematic. (c) Truth table.

predefined concentration intervals each of which have a difference of 5 molecules. Therefore, D-VASim gradually increases the concentration from 0 → 5 → 10 → 15 and so on, to determine the lower and upper threshold levels of a NAND gate. For more accurate results, the concentration intervals for these analyses can be minimized in D-VASim.

Table 1. Threshold and propagation delay values obtained in D-VASim prior to SMC in Uppaal.

Circuit name	Threshold value (High)	Threshold value (low)	Propagation delay value
NAND	15	5	324 (±51.61)
Toggle switch	10	5	1108 (±272.89)

These models are then checked in Uppaal by randomly choosing the value of Kd within a certain interval and checking if the output of the circuit satisfy the expected behavior for all possible input combinations. Uppaal uses a continuous time markov chain model (CTMC) for model checking, therefore the SBML models were first converted into CTMC models using the simple conversion utility in Uppaal. It creates a separate automaton for each of the reaction kinetics defined in the SBML file. For instance, Fig. 5(a) shows one of the processes, in the genetic NAND gate circuit, which represents the kinetic reaction (Fig. 5(b)) to produce the 10 molecules of GFP when the input protein LacI is not sufficiently present in the cell.

Figures 6 and 7 shows the Uppaal SMC simulation results of the genetic NAND and the toggle switch circuits, respectively. These figures show all the simulation traces for 100 iterations. All possible input combinations are applied and the correct operation is verified within a defined range of Kd. Due to the stochastic nature of a model, the probability of an expected behavior cannot be 100% satisfied when the value of Kd is

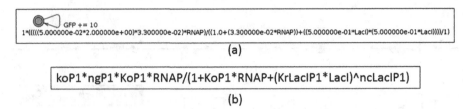

(a)

$$koP1*ngP1*KoP1*RNAP/(1+KoP1*RNAP+(KrLacIP1*LacI)^{ncLacIP1})$$

(b)

Fig. 5. The process of a genetic NAND gate to produce the 10 molecules of GFP when the input LacI is not present in a cell (a) Uppaal interpretation. (b) Kinetic Reaction. Note that the value of ncLacIP1 is 2, due to which the factor KrLacIP1 is multiplied twice in (a).

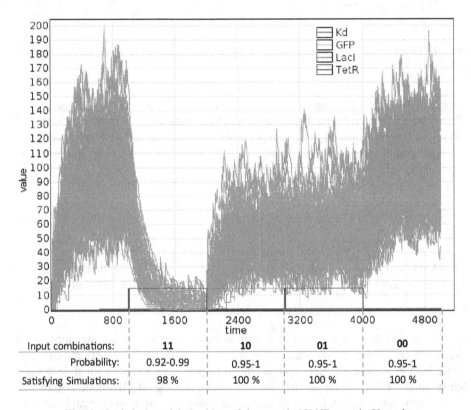

Input combinations:	11	10	01	00
Probability:	0.92-0.99	0.95-1	0.95-1	0.95-1
Satisfying Simulations:	98 %	100 %	100 %	100 %

Fig. 6. Statistical model checking of the genetic NAND gate in Uppaal.

randomly chosen from a defined range. We, therefore, set the probability of the expected behavior to be greater than at least 90% as the acceptance criteria. Inputs correspond to the applied combination of input proteins over the course of simulation time. The logic-1 for the NAND gate corresponds to 15 or more molecules and logic-0 corresponds to 5 or less molecules. For the toggle switch, the logic-1 corresponds to 20 or more molecules and logic-0 corresponds to 10 or less molecules, as obtained from D-VASim.

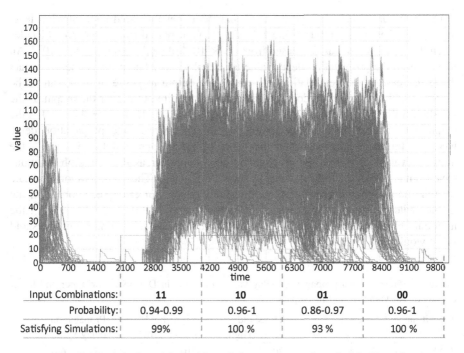

Input Combinations:	11	10	01	00
Probability:	0.94-0.99	0.96-1	0.86-0.97	0.96-1
Satisfying Simulations:	99%	100 %	93 %	100 %

Fig. 7. Statistical model checking of the genetic toggle switch in Uppaal.

Probability values at the bottom of both figures signifies the probability of the expected behavior of a circuit for all possible input combinations, where each input combination is applied for 1000 time units for the NAND gate and 2000 time units for the toggle switch. These values are chosen sufficiently larger than their respective propagation delay values, estimated from D-VASim, to ensure that the appropriate amount of delay is provided to observe the effects of applied input combinations on the output of the circuit.

Satisfying Simulations indicates the percentage of simulations which satisfy the defined condition for specific input combination. These conditions are set according to the truth tables of respective circuits. For example, for the NAND gate, the condition to be checked for when the input combination is 11, is to see if the concentration of output protein, GFP, falls below its lower threshold level i.e. 5 molecules. The NAND gate circuit exhibits the probability of greater than 98% to work correctly when the value of Kd varies between 45×10^{-4} and 85×10^{-4}. Similarly, the toggle switch is at least 93% probable to work correctly when the value of Kd varies between 60×10^{-4} and 85×10^{-4}. Outside, these ranges of Kd, the expected behavior do not satisfy the acceptance criteria mentioned above. In a similar manner, other circuit parameters can be varied to check the output response of genetic circuits.

Finally, we used D-VASim to observe how the changes of Kd values impact the threshold value and the output of a circuit. In Table 2, we show the effects of the boundary values of Kd for both circuits. For example, in the case of the NAND gate, the effects of lower and higher-bound values of a Kd, 45×10^{-4} and 85×10^{-4}, respectively, are checked. It is observed that the upper threshold concentration level required to trigger the output of the NAND gate is increased from 15 to 20 molecules when the value of Kd was decreased from 75×10^{-4} (default value) to 45×10^{-4}. An increment in the propagation delay value is also observed. The latter is due to the fact that a decrease in the degradation rate causes the output response of the circuit to be slower, and thus more input concentration may be required to trigger the output. If the threshold value of a circuit is kept to its previous value, i.e., 15 at Kd = 45×10^{-4}, the output may appear after a very long time; in other words, the propagation delay increases further. Likewise, when the value of Kd is increased to 85×10^{-4}, the threshold values as well as the propagation delays are decreased. Similar observations have been made for the toggle switch as shown in Table 2. These observations indicate the minimum-high and maximum-low threshold values. For example, in order for the toggle switch to work within a range of Kd between 60×10^{-4} and 85×10^{-4}, the minimum-high threshold value would be 20 molecules and a maximum-low threshold value would be 10 molecules.

Table 2. Threshold and propagation delay values obtained in D-VASim for upper and lower bounds of Kd values found in Uppaal.

Circuit name	Kd ($\times 10^{-4}$)	Threshold value (High)	Threshold value (low)	Propagation delay value
NAND	45	20	10	554 (± 56.07)
	85	15	0	274 (± 91.78)
Toggle switch	60	20	10	1228 (± 135.11)
	85	10	5	833(± 97.41)

4 Conclusion

In this paper, we propose a workflow for checking genetic circuit models using statistical model checking and stochastic simulation. We performed experimentations on two different-sized genetic circuit models to demonstrate that the proposed workflow can be applied for the timing and threshold values analysis of any genetic circuit model. We varied the design parameters of the genetic circuits and checked their probabilities of working correctly. Furthermore, we analyzed the effects of changing design parameters on the behavior of a given circuit. The proposed work flow can be used to check any other property of a genetic circuit; such as the probability of a circuit to reach a certain state within a specific amount of time. Future work includes using the work flow to experiment with models of recently published genetic circuits [37] and to verify those results directly in the laboratory.

Acknowledgment. We would like to thank Marius Mikucionis (Aalborg University) for providing us an extensive support and help on using Uppaal. We would further like to thank Prof. Chris Myers (University of Utah) for providing us the SBML models of the genetic circuits, and Associate Prof. Michael Reichhardt Hansen (Technical University of Denmark) for fruitful discussions on model checking and for giving constructive feedback.

References

1. Gardner, T.S., Cantor, C.R., Collins, J.J.: Construction of a genetic toggle switch in Escherichia coli. Nature **403**, 339–342 (2000)
2. Weiss, R., Basu, S.: The device physics of cellular logic gates. In: The First Workshop on Non-Silicon Computing, pp. 54–61 (2002)
3. Elowitz, M.B., Leibler, S.: A synthetic oscillatory network of transcriptional regulators. Nature **403**, 335–338 (2000)
4. Anderson, J.C., et al.: Environmentally controlled invasion of cancer cells by engineering bacteria. J. Mol. Biol. **355**, 619–627 (2006)
5. Atsumi, S., Liao, J.C.: Metabolic engineering for advanced biofuels production from Escherichia coli. Curr. Opin. Biotech. **19**(5), 414–419 (2008)
6. Cases, I., De Lorenzo, V.: Genetically modified organisms for the environment: stories of success and failure and what we have learned from them. Int. Microbiol. **8**, 213–222 (2005)
7. Ro, D.-K., et al.: Production of the antimalarial drug precursor artemisinic acid in engineered yeast. Nature **440**, 940–943 (2006)
8. McAdams, H.H., Shapiro, L.: Circuit simulation of genetic networks. Science **269**, 650–656 (1995)
9. Bartley, B., et al.: Synthetic biology open language (SBOL) version 2.0.0. J. Integr. Bioinform. **12**(2) (2015)
10. Ellis, T., et al.: Diversity-based, model-guided construction of synthetic gene networks with predicted functions. Nat. Biotech. **27**, 465–471 (2009)
11. Sydney, R., et al.: Programming gene expression with combinatorial promoters. Mol. Syst. Biol. **3**, 145 (2007)
12. Canton, B., et al.: Refinement and standardization of synthetic biological parts and devices. Nat. Biotech. **26**, 788–793 (2008)
13. Kaern, M., et al.: The engineering of genetic regulatory networks. Annu. Rev. Biomed. Eng. **5**, 179–206 (2003)
14. Knight, T.: Idempotent vector design for standard assembly of biobricks. MIT Artificial Intelligence Laboratory (2003). http://hdl.handle.net/1721.1/21168
15. Salis, H.M., Mirsky, E.A., Voigt, C.A.: Automated design of synthetic ribosome binding sites to control protein expression. Nat. Biotechnol. **27**, 946–950 (2009)
16. Mutalik, V.K., et al.: Precise and reliable gene expression via standard transcription and translation initiation elements. Nat. Methods **10**, 354–360 (2013)
17. Cambray, G., et al.: Measurement and modeling of intrinsic transcription terminators. Nucleic Acids Res. **41**, 5139–5148 (2013)
18. Rodrigo, G., Jaramillo, A.: AutoBioCAD: Full biodesign automation of genetic circuits. ACS Synth. Biol. **2**, 230–236 (2013)
19. Krig, D., Weiss, R.: Signal-amplifying genetic circuit enables in vivo observation of weak promoter activation in the Rhl quorum sensing system. Biotechnol. Bioeng. **89**(6), 709–718 (2005)
20. Nistala, G.J., et al.: A modular positive feedback-based gene amplifier. J. Biol. Eng. **4**(1), 4 (2010)
21. Nevozhay, D., et al.: Negative autoregulation linearizes the dose-response and supresses the heterogeneity of gene expression. Proc. Natl. Acad. Sci. USA **106**(13), 5123–5128 (2009)
22. Ajo-Franklin, C.M., et al.: Rational design of memory in eukaryotic cells. Genes Dev. **21**(18), 2271–2276 (2007)
23. Fritz, G., Buchler, N., Hwa, T., Gerland, U.: Designing sequential transcription logic: a simple genetic circuit for conditional memory. Syst. Synth. Biol. **1**, 89–98 (2007)

24. Cherry, J.L., Adler, F.R.: How to make a biological switch. J. Theor. Biol. **203**(2), 117–133 (2000)
25. Weber, W., et al.: A genetic time-delay circuitry in mammalian cell. Biotechnol. Bioeng. **98**(4), 894–902 (2007)
26. Bashor, C.J., et al.: Using engineered scaffold interactions to reshape MAP kinase pathway signalling dynamics. Science **319**(5869), 1539–1543 (2008)
27. Guet, C.C., Elowitz, M.B., Hsing, W., Leibler, S.: Combinatorial synthesis of genetic networks. Science **296**, 1466–1470 (2002)
28. Dueber, J.E., Yeh, B.J., Chak, K.: LimWA: reprogramming control of an allosteric signaling switch through modular recombination. Science **301**, 1904–1908 (2003)
29. Anderson, J.C., Voigt, C.A., Arkin, A.P.: Environmental signal integration by a modular AND gate. Mol. Syst. Biol. **3**, 133 (2007)
30. Win, M.N., Smolke, C.D.: Higher-order cellular information processing with synthetic RNA devices. Science **322**, 456–460 (2008)
31. MacDonald, J.T., Barnes, C., Kitney, R.I., Freemont, P.S., Stan, G.-B.V.: Computational design approaches and tools for synthetic biology. Integr. Biol. **3**, 97–108 (2011)
32. Chandran, D., Bergmann, F.T., Sauro, H.M., Densmore, D.: Computer-aided design for synthetic biology. In: Koeppl, H., Setti, G., di Bernardo, M., Densmore, D. (eds.) Design and Analysis of Biomolecular Circuits, pp. 203–224. Springer, New York (2011). doi:10.1007/978-1-4419-6766-4_10
33. Beal, J., Lu, T., Weiss, R.: Automatic compilation from high-level biologically-oriented programming language to genetic regulatory networks. PLoS ONE **6**, e22490 (2011)
34. http://sbml.org/SBML_Software_Guide/SBML_Software_Matrix
35. Funahashi, A., et al.: Cell designer 3.5: a versatile modeling tool for biochemical networks. Proc. IEEE **96**, 1254–1265 (2008)
36. Myers, C.J., et al.: iBioSim: a tool for the analysis and design of genetic circuits. Bioinformatics **25**, 2848–2849 (2009)
37. Nielsen, A.A., et al.: Genetic circuit design automation. Science, **352**(6281) 2016
38. Stefan, H., et al.: COPASI – a COmplex PAthway SImulator. Bioinformatics **22**, 3067–3074 (2006)
39. Baig, H., Madsen, J.: D-VASim – an interactive virtual laboratory environment for the simulation and analysis of genetic circuits. Bioinformatics **32**(20), 1–3 (2016)
40. Baig, H., Madsen, J.: Logic and timing analysis of genetic logic circuits using D-VASim. In: 8th IWBDA 2016, pp. 77–78 (2016)
41. Bengtsson, J., Larsen, K., Larsson, F., Pettersson, P., Yi, W.: UPPAAL — a tool suite for automatic verification of real-time systems. In: Alur, R., Henzinger, Thomas A., Sontag, E. D. (eds.) HS 1995. LNCS, vol. 1066, pp. 232–243. Springer, Heidelberg (1996). doi:10.1007/BFb0020949
42. Bulychev, P., David, A., Larsen, K.G., Legay, A., Mikučionis, M., Poulsen, D.B.: Checking and Distributing Statistical Model Checking. In: Goodloe, A.E., Person, S. (eds.) NFM 2012. LNCS, vol. 7226, pp. 449–463. Springer, Heidelberg (2012). doi:10.1007/978-3-642-28891-3_39
43. Jha, S.K., Clarke, E.M., Langmead, C.J., Legay, A., Platzer, A., Zuliani, P.: A Bayesian approach to model checking biological systems. In: Degano, P., Gorrieri, R. (eds.) CMSB 2009. LNCS, vol. 5688, pp. 218–234. Springer, Heidelberg (2009). doi:10.1007/978-3-642-03845-7_15
44. Clarke, E.M., Faeder, J.R., Langmead, C.J., Harris, L.A., Jha, S.K., Legay, A.: Statistical model checking in *BioLab*: applications to the automated analysis of T-Cell receptor signaling pathway. In: Heiner, M., Uhrmacher, Adelinde M. (eds.) CMSB 2008. LNCS, vol. 5307, pp. 231–250. Springer, Heidelberg (2008). doi:10.1007/978-3-540-88562-7_18

45. Calder, M., Gilmore, S., Hillston, J.: Modelling the influence of RKIP on the ERK signaling pathway using the stochastic process algebra PEPA. Trans. Comput. Syst. Biol. VII **4230**, 1–23 (2006)
46. Calder, M., Vyshemirsky, V., Gilbert, D., Orton, R.: Analysis of signaling pathways using the PRISM model checker. In: Proceedings of Computational Methods in Systems Biology (CMSB), pp. 179–190 (2005)
47. Cardelli, L.: Abstract machines of systems biology. In: Priami, C., Merelli, E., Gonzalez, P., Omicini, A. (eds.) Transactions on Computational Systems Biology III. LNCS, vol. 3737, pp. 145–168. Springer, Heidelberg (2005). doi:10.1007/11599128_10
48. Fisher, J., Piterman, N., Hubbard, E.J., Stern, M.J., Harel, D.: Computational insights into caenorhabditis elegans vulval development. Proc. Natl. Acad. Sci. USA **102**(6), 1951–1956 (2005)
49. Calzone, L., Chabrier-Rivier, N., Fages, F., Soliman, S.: Machine learning biochemical networks from temporal logic properties. In: Priami, C., Plotkin, G. (eds.) Transactions on Computational Systems Biology VI. LNCS, vol. 4220, pp. 68–94. Springer, Heidelberg (2006). doi:10.1007/11880646_4
50. Chabrier, N., Fages, F.: Symbolic model checking of biochemical networks. In: Priami, C. (ed.) CMSB 2003. LNCS, vol. 2602, pp. 149–162. Springer, Heidelberg (2003). doi:10.1007/3-540-36481-1_13
51. Kwiatkowska, M., Norman, G., Parker, D., Tymchyshyn, O., Heath, J., Gaffney, E.: Simulation and verification for computational modelling of signaling pathways. In: WSC 2006: Proceedings of the 38th Conference on Winter simulation, pp. 1666–1674 (2006)
52. Langmead, C.J., Jha, S.K.: Predicting Protein Folding Kinetics Via Temporal Logic Model Checking. In: Giancarlo, R., Hannenhalli, S. (eds.) WABI 2007. LNCS, vol. 4645, pp. 252–264. Springer, Heidelberg (2007). doi:10.1007/978-3-540-74126-8_24
53. Langmead, C., Jha, S.K.: Symbolic approaches to finding control strategies in boolean networks. In: Proceedings of the Sixth Asia-Pacific Bioinformatics Conference, (APBC), pp. 307–319 (2008)
54. The Systems Biology Markup Language (SBML): Language Specification for Level 3 Version 1 Core, 06 October 2010
55. Myers, C.J.: Engineering Genetic Circuits. Chapman & Hall/CRC Press, Boca Raton (2009)

Comparing Source Sets and Persistent Sets for Partial Order Reduction

Parosh Abdulla, Stavros Aronis, Bengt Jonsson$^{(\boxtimes)}$, and Konstantinos Sagonas

Department of Information Technology, Uppsala University, Uppsala, Sweden
{parosh,stavros.aronis,bengt,kostis}@it.uu.se

Abstract. Partial order reduction has traditionally been based on persistent sets, ample sets, stubborn sets, or variants thereof. Recently, we have presented a strengthening of this foundation, using source sets instead of persistent/ample/stubborn sets. Source sets subsume persistent sets and are often smaller than persistent sets. We introduced source sets as a basis for Dynamic Partial Order Reduction (DPOR), in a framework which assumes that processes are deterministic and that all program executions are finite. In this paper, show how to use source sets for partial order reduction in a framework which does not impose these restrictions. We also compare source sets with persistent sets, providing some insights into conditions under which source sets and persistent sets do or do not differ.

1 Introduction

Verification and systematic testing of concurrent programs are difficult, since they must consider all the different ways in which processes/threads can interact. *Model checking* [6,19] addresses this problem by systematically exploring the state space of a given program and verifying that each reachable state satisfies a given property. A serious hindrance to the applicability of model checking is the *state-space explosion* problem, i.e., that the number of possible interleavings grows exponentially with the length of program execution. There are several approaches that limit the number of explored interleavings. Among them, *Partial Order Reduction* (POR) [7,9,18,27] stands out, as it provides full coverage of all behaviours that can occur in *any* interleaving, even though it explores only a representative subset. POR is based on the observation that two interleavings can be regarded as equivalent if one can be obtained from the other by swapping adjacent, non-conflicting (independent) execution steps. POR exploits this observation by guaranteeing that for each possible interleaving, it explores one that is equivalent to it. This is sufficient for checking many interesting safety properties, including race freedom, absence of global deadlocks, and absence of assertion violations [7,9,27].

This work was carried out within the Linnaeus centre of excellence UPMARC (Uppsala Programming for Multicore Architectures Research Center), partly supported by the Swedish Research Council.

L. Aceto et al. (Eds.): Larsen Festschrift, LNCS 10460, pp. 516–536, 2017.
DOI: 10.1007/978-3-319-63121-9_26

Partial order reduction approaches are based on reducing the set of process steps that are explored at each scheduling point. This set of process steps has been given different names, including *stubborn sets* [27], *persistent sets* [9], and *ample sets* [7]. These approaches are rather similar: their differences are mainly due to the considered model of computation and the class of properties to be checked. In the following, we will consider the approach based on persistent sets. Recently, we have proposed an improvement over the persistent set technique, which is based on a new class of sets called *source sets* [2]. Source sets subsume persistent sets (i.e., any persistent set is also a source set), and source sets are often smaller than persistent sets. Moreover, source sets are provably minimal, in the sense that the set of explored processes from some scheduling point must be a source set in order to guarantee exploration of all equivalence classes. This implies that techniques based on source sets have the potential to produce better reduction than techniques based on persistent sets.

In our previous work [2], we introduced source sets in the context of stateless model checking, as a basis for *Dynamic Partial Order Reduction* (DPOR). We used a framework, which assumes as restrictions on analyzed programs that processes (or threads) are deterministic and that all program executions are finite. We demonstrated the power of source sets by using them as the basis for two DPOR algorithms: (i) *Source-DPOR*, which minimally adapts the original DPOR algorithm due to Flanagan and Godefroid [8] to use source sets instead of persistent sets, leading to notably better reduction, and (ii) *Optimal-DPOR*, which is provably optimal in the sense that it explores exactly one representative execution in each equivalence class.

In this paper, we consider how to use source sets for partial order reduction in a framework which does not impose the restrictions of deterministic processes and terminating computations. We therefore consider a framework of arbitrary finite-state concurrent programs, in which processes can be non-terminating and exhibit control non-determinism. This is essentially the class of programs that is considered in classical works [7,9,18,27] on POR that employ ample/persistent/stubborn sets, and is used, e.g., in the Promela language of the widely used SPIN model checker [11]. For this model, we show in this paper how source sets can be used as a basis for POR in enumerative state-space exploration. We also show how the theory of POR can equally well be based on source sets, and that the underlying theory is at least as simple as when using persistent sets.

We first consider the basic principles for partial order reductions, as they have been formulated for non-deterministic finite-state concurrent programs in standard texts, e.g., the survey by Clarke *et al.* [7] or the textbook by Baier and Katoen [3, Chap. 8]. For simplicity, we limit the exposition to the detection of local assertion violations and deadlocks. We show that the use of ample/persistent/stubborn sets can be replaced by source sets.

We thereafter consider the framework of stateless model checking for terminating programs, but allowing control non-determinism, thereby generalizing the standardly used restriction to deterministic processes [2,8]. We present a generalization of the Source-DPOR algorithm to this setting.

Finally, we make a direct comparison between source sets and persistent sets, with the purpose to characterize under which conditions source sets provide a strict advantage over persistent sets. We provide examples of situations in which sources sets are guaranteed to be strictly smaller than corresponding persistent sets, and also situations in which this is not the case.

To keep the presentation simple, we do not include complementary techniques, most notably sleep sets [10]. Sleep sets are complementary to persistent sets and source sets; especially in stateless model checking they are essential for reduction. Including sleep sets, as we did in our prior paper [2], makes the algorithms, and particularly their correctness proofs, more complex. For simplicity, we have omitted them from this paper, but the observed differences between source sets and persistent sets remain essentially the same also in the presence of sleep sets.

Related Work. Early persistent set techniques [7,9,27] relied on static analysis to compute persistent sets. Sleep set techniques [10] were also used to dynamically prevent explorations that would be redundant. The DPOR algorithm of Flanagan and Godefroid [8] showed how to construct persistent sets on-the-fly "by need", leading to better reduction. Similar techniques have been combined with dynamic symbolic execution, which is also known as *concolic testing*, where new test runs are initiated in response to detected races by flipping these races using postponed sets [24]. Since then, several variants, improvements, and adaptations of DPOR for stateless model checking [14,26] and concolic testing [21,23] have appeared, all based on persistent sets. In 2014, we introduced source sets, which are provably more succinct than persistent sets, as a basis for two DPOR algorithms [2]. We subsequently applied one of them, namely the Source-DPOR algorithm, to programs executing under the TSO and PSO memory model [1].

Other techniques for reducing state-space explosion in model checking include, unfoldings [16], which can in principle achieve better reduction than POR in number of interleavings. However, such techniques [13,20] have larger cost per explored execution than techniques based on POR, and one of them [13] also needs an additional post-processing step for checking non-local properties such as races and deadlocks. Another line of work exploits a weaker form of equivalence, the *maximal causal model* for a concurrent computation from a given execution trace, a notion defined by Serbanuta *et al.* [25]. This was used recently [12] for a stateless model checking algorithm, which also explores fewer traces than classical DPOR techniques. The corresponding algorithm, called Maximal Causality Reduction, relies on an offline constraint analyzer to formulate constraints that are then solved using an SMT solver.

For the analyses of timed systems, such as those performed by the UPPAAL model checker [5], partial order reduction techniques have been developed [4,22], but they have not achieved reductions that are comparable in magnitued to those observed for untimed concurrent programs.

Organization. In the next section, we introduce our computational model. In Sect. 3 we formulate a partial-order view of program executions, the partial-order framework, along with the definition of source sets. In Sect. 4 we show that source sets can be used as a basis for POR in state-space exploration. In Sect. 5 we consider how to actually construct source sets, and consider two settings: static computation of source sets, as performed in model checkers such as SPIN, and dynamic computation, as performed in DPOR. We present algorithms for constructing source sets in both these settings. In Sect. 6 we recall the definition of persistent sets, and show how, under various conditions, source sets are strictly smaller than persistent sets, but that the strictness may disappear in some settings. Finally, in Sect. 7 we summarize the findings of the paper.

2   Framework

Let us introduce the technical background material. First, we present our model of concurrent programs, and thereafter the concepts of independence, races, and the happens-before relation. To keep the exposition simple, we assume a simple model of concurrent programs as composed of a finite set of processes, each of which is finite-state, can be non-terminating, and exhibit control non-determinism. Processes communicate by reading from and writing to a set of shared variables. Locks can be seen as shared variables that are manipulated in a certain way.

2.1   Computation Model

We model a concurrent program as a transition system $TS = \langle \mathcal{P}, \mathcal{X}, S, s_0, T \rangle$, where $\mathcal{P}$ is a finite set of *processes* (or *threads*), $\mathcal{X}$ is a finite set of shared variables, S is a finite set of *global states*, each of which consists of a valuation of the shared variables and a local state of each process, $s_0 \in S$ is the *initial global state*, and T is a finite set of transitions. Each transition t belongs to a unique process, denoted $\hat{t}$. We assume that each transition can be represented as a guarded command over the shared variables and the local state of its processes. If the guard of transition t evaluates to true in s, we say that t is *enabled* in s; we denote this by $s \vdash t$ and write $t(s)$ for the unique state that results after t is executed from state s. We let $enabled(s)$ be the set of transitions that are enabled in s. A process is said to be *blocked* in some state s if none of its transitions is enabled in s. Often, the local state of a process will include a control location, which is updated by transitions in the usual way.

For a sequence $w = t_1 \ldots t_k$ of transitions, we write $s \vdash w$ to denote that the sequence w can be executed from s, i.e., that there are states $s_1 \ldots s_k$ such that with $s_0 = s$ we have $s_{i-1} \vdash t_i$ and $s_i = t_i(s_{i-1})$ for $i = 1, \ldots, k$, and write $w(s)$ for s_k. If $s \vdash w$ we say that w is an *execution sequence from s*. An *execution sequence of TS* is an execution sequence from its initial state. We will use w and v with sub- and superscripts for execution sequences from some state, and E with sub- and superscripts for execution sequences from the initial state. Since transitions are deterministic, an execution sequence w from s takes the program to a unique state $w(s)$. When s is the initial state, we will use $s_{[E]}$ to denote

$E(s_0)$. We sometimes use execution sequences instead of states in concepts and notations; e.g., we sometimes write $E \vdash w$ to denote $s_{[E]} \vdash w$. For a sequence of transitions w, we let $w \backslash t$ denote w with the first occurrence of t removed; if $t \notin w$, then $w \backslash t$ is w.

For a set of sequences of transitions W, we write $s \vdash W$ to denote that $s \vdash w$ for each $w \in W$. We write $\mathcal{E}(s)$ for the set of execution sequences w with $s \vdash w$.

2.2   Partial Order Representation

The basic idea in partial order reduction is to consider executions as partial orders on transitions. Executions that are represented by the same partial order are considered equivalent. We therefore formalize how to view executions as partially ordered sets of events.

Let E be an execution sequence. An *event* of E is a particular occurrence of a transition in E. More precisely, an event is a pair $\langle t, i \rangle$, representing the ith occurrence of transition t in the execution sequence. We use $e, e', \ldots$ to range over events. We let $[e]$ denote the transition of e, and $\hat{e}$ denote the process of $[e]$. We let $dom(E)$ denote the set of events $\langle t, i \rangle$ which are in E (i.e., $\langle t, i \rangle \in dom(E)$ iff E contains at least i occurrences of t). We use $<_E$ to denote the total order between events in E, i.e., $e <_E e'$ denotes that e occurs before e' in E. We use $next_{[E]}(t)$ to denote the event that transition t represents when executed immediately after E.

The partial order view of an execution sequence is obtained by defining a *happens-before relation* on its events. Intuitively, the happens-before relation captures the causal ordering between events in an execution sequence. More precisely, it captures the orderings that are important for the result of the execution sequence. For each execution sequence E, the happens-before relation $\rightarrow_E$ is defined on $dom(E)$ as the transitive closure of the relation $\leadsto_E$ defined by letting $e \leadsto_E e'$ if $e <_E e'$ (i.e., e occurs before e' in E) and either

(i) e and e' are performed by the same process, or
(ii) some shared variable is accessed by both e and e', and at least one of e or
     e' performs a write access.

Note that two events that are different occurrences of the same transition can access different sets of variables, e.g., if the accesses are conditional on some test. It follows that $\rightarrow_E$ is a partial order on $dom(E)$. Any linearization E' of $\rightarrow_E$ on $dom(E)$ is an execution sequence that has exactly the same events as E (i.e., $dom(E') = dom(E)$) and the same happens-before relation $\rightarrow_{E'}$ as $\rightarrow_E$. This means that the relation $\rightarrow_E$ induces a set of equivalent execution sequences, all with the same happens-before relation. We will sometimes refer to such equivalence classes as *Mazurkiewicz traces* [15]. We use $E \simeq E'$ to denote that E and E' are linearizations of the same happens-before relation, and $[E]_\simeq$ to denote the equivalence class of E. If $E \simeq E'$, then all variables are modified by the same sequence of statements, implying that $s_{[E]} = s_{[E']}$.

```
p:                q:                r:
    write x;          read y;           read z;
                      read x;           read x;
```

Fig. 1. Writer-readers code excerpt.

Example 1. In Fig. 1, the three processes p, q, and r perform dependent accesses to a shared variable x. In this example, let us consider two accesses as dependent if they concern the same variable and one of them is a write. Since there are no writes to y and z here, accesses to y and z are not dependent with anything else. For this program, there are four Mazurkiewicz traces (i.e., equivalence classes of executions), each characterized by its sequence of accesses to x (three accesses can be ordered in six ways, but two pairs of orderings are equivalent since they differ only in the ordering of adjacent reads, which are not dependent). An execution sequence and its corresponding happens-before relation is shown in Fig. 2.

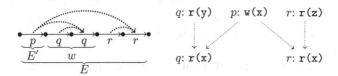

Fig. 2. A sample execution sequence of the program in Fig. 1 is shown to the left. This execution sequence is annotated by a happens-before relation (the dotted arrows). To the right, the happens-before relation is shown as a partial order.

Partial order reduction reduces the effort for analyzing a concurrent system by analyzing only a representative subset of all execution sequences. The idea is that for each execution sequence E of TS, it is sufficient to analyze a sequence E' which is equivalent to E. In fact, it is sufficient to analyze a sequence E' which is equivalent to some extension of E, i.e., such that $E' \simeq E.v$ for some v. Any local assertion violation or global deadlock in E is then also visible in E'. This relation between E' and E is important, so we will introduce some additional notation that will make the subsequent exposition more convenient.

Definition 1. *Let E and E' be execution sequences.*

- *Let $E \sqsubseteq E'$ denote that there is a sequence w such that $E.w$ is an execution sequence with $E.w \simeq E'$.*
- *Let $E \sim E'$ denote that there are sequences w and w' such that $E.w$ and $E'.w'$ are execution sequences with $E.w \simeq E'.w'$.*

Intuitively, $E \sqsubseteq E'$ denotes that the sequence E is a possible way to start an execution that is equivalent to E'; thus E can be thought of a "partial order prefix" of E', in the sense that the events in E are a downward-closed subset of the events in E', with the same happens-before relation as in E'. Analogously, $E \sim E'$ denotes that the sequence E is a possible way to start an execution that is equivalent to an execution sequence of the form $E'.w'$; thus E and E' are "consistent" in the sense that they can be extended to produce two equivalent sequences.

We also introduce relativized versions of these definitions:

Definition 2. *Let E be an execution sequence. Then*

- $v \sqsubseteq_{[E]} w$ *denotes that $E.v \sqsubseteq E.w$.*
- $v \sim_{[E]} w$ *denotes that $E.v \sim E.w$.*
- $v \simeq_{[E]} w$ *denotes that $E.v \simeq E.w$.*

We will sometimes use $\sqsubseteq_{[s]}$ for $\sqsubseteq_{[E]}$, where E is such that s is $s_{[E]}$, and analogously for $\sim_{[s]}$ and $\simeq_{[s]}$ (note that $\sqsubseteq_{[E]}$ and $\sim_{[E]}$ and $\simeq_{[E]}$ are uniquely determined by $s_{[E]}$). An important property is that

- $v \sqsubseteq_{[E]} w$ and $w \sim_{[E]} w'$ implies $v \sim_{[E]} w'$.

Note that $v \sqsubseteq_{[E]} w$ and $w \sim_{[E]} w'$ does not in general imply $v \sqsubseteq_{[E]} w'$. As a simple counterexample, let v and w be p and let w' be the empty sequence $\langle \rangle$, and observe that $v' \sim_{[E]} \langle \rangle$ for any sequence v'. From this observation, it also follows that $\sim_{[E]}$ is not transitive.

Finally, we introduce special notation and terminology for the case that w consists of a single transition:

Definition 3 (Initials and Weak Initials). *For an execution sequence w from s, the set $I_{[s]}(w)$ of initials and the set $WI_{[s]}(w)$ of weak initials are sets of transitions defined as follows:*

- $t \in I_{[s]}(w)$ *iff $t \sqsubseteq_{[s]} w$, and*
- $t \in WI_{[s]}(w)$ *iff $t \sim_{[s]} w$.*

We let $s \vdash t\Diamond w$ denote that $s \vdash t.w$ and $next_{[E.t]}(t) \not\to_{E.t.w} e$ for each $e \in dom_{[E.t]}(w)$ (i.e., the event of t does not "happen before" any event in w), where E is such that s is $s_{[E]}$. Intuitively, $s \vdash t\Diamond w$ means that t and w are independent after the state s. If $s \vdash t\Diamond w$ and s is $s_{[E]}$, then $E.t.w \simeq E.w.t$, which implies $s_{[E.t.w]} = s_{[E.w.t]}$, i.e., t and w can be swapped without changing the resulting state. In the special case when w contains only one transition t', then $s \vdash t\Diamond t'$ denotes that the transitions t and t' are independent after s. We use $s \not\vdash t\Diamond w$ to denote that $s \vdash t$ and $s \vdash w$, but that $s \vdash t\Diamond w$ does not hold.

As examples, in Fig. 2, we have $q.r \sqsubseteq_{[E']} q.q.r.r$ but $q.q \not\sqsubseteq_{[E']} r.r$. We also have $q.q \sim_{[E']} r.r$ since $E'.q.q.r.r \simeq E'.r.r.q.q$. In Fig. 2, we further have $E' \vdash q\Diamond r$ since q and r are not happens-before related in $E'.r.q$. We also observe that $I_{[E']}(w) = \{q\}$, as q is the only process occurring in w and its first occurrence has no predecessor in the dotted relation in w. Furthermore, $WI_{[E']}(w) = \{q, r\}$, since r is not happens-before related to any event in w.

3   Principles of Partial Order Reduction

The purpose of partial order reduction is to reduce the state-space explosion that arises from the many possible interleavings of transitions of concurrent processes. Instead of generating and analyzing all executions of a concurrent system, POR generates and analyzes only a representative subset.

Following other works [7,9], we can consider partial order reduction as constructing a *reduced state graph*. A transition system $\langle \mathcal{P}, \mathcal{X}, S, s_0, T \rangle$ induces a labeled state-transition graph A_G, whose nodes are the states in S, with labeled edges of the form $s \xrightarrow{t} s'$ whenever $t(s) = s'$. Each execution sequence of the concurrent system corresponds to a path from the initial node of A_G. One can explain POR as constructing a *reduced* state-transition graph A_R, whose nodes are a subset S_R of S, and whose edges are a subset of the edges of A_G. The reduced graph A_R must still cover all behaviors of A_G in the sense that for any execution sequence E of A_G, there is an execution sequence E' in A_R with $E \sqsubseteq E'$. Note that the above principle of constructing a reduced state-transition graph represents the situation both in stateful model checking, with an arbitrary A_G, as well as in stateless model checking, where A_G is tree-shaped.

In enumerative state-space exploration, A_G is constructed by a recursive exploration of all enabled transitions from global states already found to be reachable, starting from the initial global state. When applying partial-order reduction, only a subset of the enabled transitions are explored from any global state, thereby constructing a reduced state-transition graph A_R. Let us consider what are the restrictions on this subset. Consider a global state s. The above requirement that A_R must cover all behaviors of A_G can be satisfied by requiring that for any execution sequence w from s in A_G, there is an execution sequence w' from s in A_R with $w \sqsubseteq_{[s]} w'$. Let now w' be of the form $t.w''$, i.e., let t be the first transition in w'. From $w \sqsubseteq_{[s]} t.w''$ it follows that $w \sim_{[s]} t$, i.e., $t \in WI_{[s]}(w)$. Since w is an arbitrary execution sequence from s, we conclude that the set of transitions explored from s must include some transition in $WI_{[s]}(w)$ for each execution sequence from w. Thus, in the reduced state graph, it is is *necessary* to explore at least one transition in $WI_{[s]}(w)$ for each execution w from s. We therefore give a name to such sets.

Definition 4 (Source Sets). *Let s be a state, and let W be a set of execution sequences from s. A set T of transitions is a* source set *for W after s if for each $w \in W$ we have $WI_{[s]}(w) \cap T \neq \emptyset$.*

We say that T is a source set after s to denote that T is a source set for $\mathcal{E}(s)$. For an execution sequence E, we say that T is a source set (for W) after E if T is a source set (for W) after $s_{[E]}$.

The key property is that if T is a source set after s, then for each execution sequence $w \in W$, there is a transition $t \in T$ and an execution sequence w' such that $E.t.w' \simeq E.w.v$ for some sequence v. In particular, if $E.w$ is maximal, then $E.t.w' \simeq E.v$. Therefore, when an exploration algorithm intends to cover all of $\mathcal{E}(s)$, the set of transitions that are chosen for exploration from s *must* be a source set after s. We formulate this observation as a theorem.

Theorem 1 (Key Property of Source Sets). *Let s be a state, and let W' be a subset of $\mathcal{E}(s)$ such that for each $w \in \mathcal{E}(s)$ there is a $w' \in W'$ with $w \sqsubseteq_{[s]} w'$. Then the set of first transitions of sequences in W' is a source set after E.*

This theorem implies that a necessary condition for the correctness of POR is that the set of explored transitions is a source set. As we will show in the next section, this condition is actually sufficient if A_G is acyclic. If A_G may contain cycles, one more condition will be needed.

4   Partial Order Reduction in State-Space Exploration

In this section, we show how source sets can be used for partial order reduction in enumerative model checking. This section has borrowed inspiration from the presentation by Clarke et al. [7, Sect. 4], that shows how to use ample sets (which for the purposes of this paper are essentially the same as persistent sets) in POR. We show that source sets can be used instead of ample sets or persistent sets to obtain reduction. Since, as we show in Sect. 6, source sets are at least as powerful as persistent sets of ample sets, the obtained reduction will be at least as good and sometimes better.

Let us consider the conditions for producing a reduced state transition graph A_R by restricting the set of enabled transitions that are explored from each state. We have the following main theorem.

Theorem 2. *Assume a concurrent system with global state graph A_G. Let A_R be a reduced state transition graph obtained from A_G by restricting the set of transitions that are explored from each state. If the following two conditions are satisfied:*

1. *for each state s in A_R, the set of explored transitions is a source set after s, and*
2. *for each cycle in A_R, if a transition t is enabled in all states of the cycle, then t must be explored from some state of the cycle,*

then for each execution E in A_G, there is an execution E' in A_R with $E \sqsubseteq E'$.

Proof. We will prove the following stronger property:

for each state $s \in A_R$ and execution sequence w from s in A_G, there is an execution w' in A_R with $w \sqsubseteq_{[s]} w'$

by induction on the length of w. The base case is trivial. For the inductive step, by condition (1), A_R explores some transition t in $WI_{[s]}(w)$ from s. We have two cases.

- $t \in w$. From $t \in WI_{[s]}(w)$ we infer $t.(w \backslash t) \simeq w$. By the induction hypothesis applied to the state $t(s)$ and execution sequence $w \backslash t$ from $t(s)$, the reduced state graph A_R contains a sequence w'' with $(w \backslash t) \sqsubseteq_{[t(s)]} w''$, implying that A_R contains the sequence $t.w''$ from s. We furthermore have that $t.(w \backslash t) \sqsubseteq_{[s]} t.w''$, i.e., since $t.(w \backslash t) \simeq_{[s]} w$ we have $w \sqsubseteq_{[s]} t.w''$, meaning that we can take $t.w''$ as w'.

– $t \notin w$. Let us use t_1 to denote t. Then $t_1 \in WI_{[s]}(w)$ and $t_1 \notin w$ imply $s \vdash t_1 \Diamond w$, which implies that w is an execution sequence also from $t_1(s)$. Therefore, again by condition (1), A_R explores some transition t_2 in $WI_{[t(s)]}(w)$ from $t(s)$. Continuing in this way, we have two cases:

  (i) there is a sequence $t_1 t_2 \ldots t_k$ such that for $i = 1, \ldots, k$, the sequence w is an execution from $(t_1 \ldots t_{i-1})(s)$ and $(t_1 \ldots t_{i-1})(s) \vdash t_i \Diamond w$ but $t_k \in I_{[(t_1 \ldots t_{k-1})(s)]}(w)$. By extending the reasoning from the first case, we have that A_R contains a sequence $t_1 \ldots t_k . w''$ from s such that $t_k . (w \setminus t_k) \sqsubseteq_{[s]} t_1 \ldots t_{k-1} w''$. Since $t_k . (w \setminus t_k) \simeq_{[s]} w$, we have $w \sqsubseteq_{[s]} t_1 t_2 \ldots t_{k-1} w''$, meaning that we can take $t_1 t_2 \ldots t_{k-1} w''$ as w'.

  (ii) there is an unbounded sequence $t_1 t_2 \ldots$ such that for $i = 1, 2, \ldots$, the sequence w is an execution from $t_1 \ldots t_{i-1}(s)$ and $t_1 t_2 \ldots t_{i-1}(s) \vdash t_i \Diamond w$. It follows that the sequence of states $t_1 \ldots t_{i-1}(s)$ must form a loop somewhere, and furthermore that the first transition of w is enabled in all states of that loop. By condition (2), the first transition must then be executed from some state of the loop, and we are back to the previous case.   □

5   Computing Source Sets

In the previous section, we showed how source sets can be used for partial order reduction in model checking. In this section, we consider the problem of how to actually compute source sets, given some transition system model. The definition of source sets can not be used directly for this purpose, since it is formulated in terms of all possible sequences that should be analyzed, and we do not want to explore all of them in the first place. For the case of persistent sets, a variety of techniques for computing them have been proposed. One broad classification of techniques is into *static* techniques, which compute source sets by analyzing the program source, and *dynamic* techniques, which compute persistent sets incrementally by analyzing already performed exploration. We will present algorithms for computing source sets in both these settings. We first present a technique for static computation of source sets, and thereafter a dynamic one.

5.1   Static Computation of Source Sets

Early approaches to partial order reduction [9,18,27] computed persistent sets statically, by analyzing the program text. Various static algorithms were proposed for computing persistent sets, ample sets, or stubborn sets; these algorithms are not so different from each other, and are related to an earlier algorithm by Overman [17]. Below, we present an analogous technique for static computation of source sets.

We say that a transition t is *may-enabled* in a state s if it is enabled in s or can become enabled after a sequence of transitions from processes other than

$\widehat{t}$. An *access* is defined to be a read or a write to some shared variable. Two accesses *conflict* if they access the same shared variable and at least one of them is a write.

For the computation of source sets, we assume that for each state we can compute an over-approximation of the set of *may-enabled* transitions in that state. Define a *may-set* in a state s to be a set of transitions which contains exactly one may-enabled transition of each process that has a may-enabled transition in s; for this definition, we use the computed over-approximation of the set of may-enabled transitions. We further assume that we can compute the following, possibly overapproximating, sets. This can be done, e.g., by static analysis of the control flow of the code of each process.

- $init\_accesses_{[s]}(t)$, for an enabled transition t, contains the set of accesses t can perform when t is executed as the first transition of process $\widehat{t}$ from s.
- $future\_accesses_{[s]}(t)$, for a may-enabled transition t, contains the set of accesses that can be performed by $\widehat{t}$ in any execution sequence from s, in which t is the first transition of $\widehat{t}$.

We expect that $init\_accesses_{[s]}(t) \subseteq future\_accesses_{[s]}(t)$.

The following theorem provides a sufficient characterization of source sets.

Theorem 3. *Let s be a global state, A set $T \subseteq enabled(s)$ of transitions is a source set after s if each may-set T' in s contains a non-empty subset T'' such that*

- *for each $t'' \in T''$ and each $t' \in (T' \setminus T'')$, no access in $init\_accesses_{[s]}(t'')$ conflicts with any access in $future\_accesses_{[s]}(t')$.*

Proof. We use the definition of source sets (Definition 4). Consider a sequence $w \in \mathcal{E}(s)$. Define a may-set T' in s which for each process p that has a transition in w contains the transition of p that occurs first; if p has no transition in w then T' can contain any may-enabled transition of p. By the condition in the theorem, the set T' has a subset $T'' \subseteq T$ such that for each $t'' \in T''$ and each $t' \in (T' \setminus T'')$, no access in $init\_accesses_{[s]}(t'')$ conflicts with any access in $future\_accesses_{[s]}(t')$. We split the proof into two cases.

1. w contains no transition in T''. We then claim that $s \vdash t'' \Diamond w$ for each $t'' \in T''$. This follows by establishing that no access by t'', when performed in s, conflicts with any access by any transition in w. To see this, consider an arbitrary transition t''' in w. Let t' be the first transition of process $\widehat{t'''}$ in w. The condition in the theorem then implies that no access in $init\_accesses_{[s]}(t'')$ conflicts with any access in $future\_accesses_{[s]}(t')$, in particular not with any access by t'''.

2. w contains a transition in T''. Then let t'' be the first of these. Then w has a prefix of the form $v.t''$, and by using the condition in the theorem in the same way as in the previous case, we infer that $s \vdash t'' \Diamond v$, which implies that $t'' \in I_{[s]}(w)$, i.e., $t'' \in WI_{[s]}(w)$. $\square$

p:
    write x; (t_1)
      or
    write y; (t_2)

q:
    write y; (t_3)

Fig. 3. Non-deterministic program.

Let us illustrate a use of Theorem 3, and also contrast it with persistent sets. Consider the simple program with two processes in Fig. 3. Here, the set $\{t_2, t_3\}$ is a source set, which satisfies the conditions in Theorem 3. If we choose T' as $\{t_1, t_3\}$ in the theorem, then we can choose T'' as $\{t_3\}$. Note that $\{t_2, t_3\}$ is *not* a persistent set: any persistent set must include all transitions.

5.2 Dynamic Computation of Source Sets

Let us next consider how source sets can be computed dynamically, i.e., by actually exploring execution sequences from a state. The motivation for the dynamic approach is that static analysis often over-approximates possible conflicts between transitions, thereby limiting the achievable reduction. Dynamic approaches improve the precision by recording actually occurring conflicts during the exploration and using this information to construct source sets on-the-fly, "by need". The dynamic approach has been particularly successful in stateless model checking, under the name *Dynamic Partial Order Reduction* (DPOR), first presented by Flanagan and Godefroid [8]. DPOR requires that the state space is acyclic and finite. This means that executions must terminate by themselves within a bounded number of steps. Then the state space is a finite tree, built from execution sequences E. Each execution sequence E leads to a unique $s_{[E]}$. From the point of view of the exploration, two different execution sequences E and E' are considered to be different states, even if $s_{[E]} = s_{[E']}$.

Let us consider how to compute source sets dynamically. A naïve approach may consume a significant effort in exploring sequences from $s_{[E]}$ only for the purpose of computing source sets, exploration which is otherwise wasted. A key idea of DPOR is to compute source sets, not by separate exploration, but by analyzing the execution sequences that are anyway explored for analyzing the transition system. More precisely, if E is an explored execution sequence, then the set of transitions which will be explored from $s_{[E]}$ is constructed incrementally by the DPOR algorithm. Following [8], we use $backtrack(E)$ to denote this set of transitions. When initiating the exploration from $s_{[E]}$, the set $backtrack(E)$ is initialized with the enabled transitions of an arbitrary process. During the exploration from $s_{[E]}$, the algorithm explores sequences of the form $t.w$ from $s_{[E]}$, for each $t \in backtrack(E)$. These sequences are analyzed and, if needed, transitions are added to $backtrack(E)$, which will then induce exploration of additional sequences, etc. The key idea is that whenever a sequence of form $t.w'.t'$ is explored from $s_{[E]}$, in which the events corresponding to t and t' are in a race, then the DPOR algorithm must ensure that $backtrack(E)$ contains a transition which begins some execution sequence in which this race is reversed. At the end of the exploration, the set $backtrack(E)$ should be a source set after $s_{[E]}$.

Let us now make this idea more precise in our context. We first introduce some notation. For an execution sequence E and an event $e \in dom(E)$, let:

- $pre(E, e)$ denote the prefix of E up to, but not including, the event e.
- $notdep(e, E)$ denote the sub-sequence of E consisting of the events that occur after e but do not "happen after" e (i.e., the events e' that occur after e such that $e \not\rightarrow_E e'$).

Let E be an execution sequence, and let e and e' be two events in $dom(E)$, with $e <_E e'$. We say that e and e' are in a *reversible race*, denoted $e \precsim_E e'$, if

- $\widehat{e} \neq \widehat{e'}$ and $e \rightarrow_E e'$ and there is no event $e'' \in dom(E)$, different from e' and e, such that $e \rightarrow_E e'' \rightarrow_E e'$, i.e., e and e' are in a race, and
- $pre(E, e) \vdash notdep(e, E).[e']$, i.e., e' can be executed even if e is not, i.e., it is not the case that e' is enabled by e.

Intuitively, $e \precsim_E e'$ denotes that there is an equivalent execution sequence $E' \simeq E$ in which e and e' are adjacent, and that e does not enable e'. Therefore, the order of e and e' can be reversed.

Example 2. In Fig. 2, there are two pairs of events e and e' that are in a race, namely $\langle p, 1 \rangle, \langle q, 2 \rangle$ and $\langle p, 1 \rangle, \langle r, 2 \rangle$. It also holds for both these pairs that $e \precsim_E e'$ since both q and r are enabled before $\langle p, 1 \rangle$. In other words, both the races in the program are reversible.

We will now derive sufficient conditions for adding transitions to $backtrack(E)$. For this derivation, we assume, as inductive hypothesis, that whenever $t \in backtrack(E)$, our algorithm explores all sequences in $\mathcal{E}(E.t)$ in the sense that for each $w \in \mathcal{E}(E.t)$ it explores a sequence w' with $w \sqsubseteq_{[E.t]} w'$. This inductive hypothesis can also be used to build a proof of correctness the resulting DPOR algorithm (see [2,8]).

The requirement that $backtrack(E)$ be a source set after $s_{[E]}$ upon finishing the exploration implies that upon finishing the exploration from $s_{[E]}$, there should be no execution sequence w from $s_{[E]}$ with $WI_{[E]}(w) \cap backtrack(E) = \emptyset$. Assume, to derive a contradiction, that such a sequence w anyway exists. W.l.o.g. we can assume that w does not have any proper prefix with this property. It then follows from Definition 4 that w is of form $w'.t'$ such that $E \vdash t \Diamond w'$ for some $t \in backtrack(E)$. To see this, note that by the assumption that w is shortest there is a transition t in $WI_{[E]}(w') \cap backtrack(E)$, and since we cannot have $t \in I_{[E]}(w')$ (this would imply $t \in I_{[E]}(w)$), we must have $E \vdash t \Diamond w'$. Since $t \in backtrack(E)$, it could be hoped that the exploration will explore a sequence of the form $t.w'.t'$ from $s_{[E]}$. However, in spite of the fact that $E \vdash (w'.t')$, it is not certain that $E \vdash (t.w'.t')$, since t' may be disabled by t (note that $E.t.w' \simeq E.w'.t$ since $E \vdash t \Diamond w'$). We must therefore consider two cases.

1. $E \vdash (t.w'.t')$, i.e., t' is not disabled by t after $E.w'$. Let the events in $E.t.w'.t'$ corresponding to t and t' be e and e', respectively. Then $e \precsim_{E.t.w'.t'} e'$, i.e., e and e' are in a reversible race, since e depends with e' but not with any event in w'. In this case, since t is already in $backtrack(E)$, by the above inductive hypothesis, some sequence of the form w'' with $w'.t' \sqsubseteq_{[E.t]} w''$ is explored from $s_{[E.t]}$. Since the sequence $w'.t'$ is a partial-order prefix of w'', the race between e and e' will occur also in $E.t.w''$, i.e., w'' has a prefix $w'''.t'$ where t' corresponds to e', such that $e \precsim_{E.t.w'''.t'} e'$. Now let u be $notdep(e, E.t.w''')$, i.e., u consists of the events of w''' that do not happen-after e (note that e corresponds to t in $E.t.w'''$). It follows that $u \sqsubseteq_{[E.t]} w'''$, hence that $u \sqsubseteq_{[E.t]} w''$, which together with $w'.t' \sqsubseteq_{[E.t]} w''$ implies $w' \sim_{[E.t]} u$. Noting that no events in w' nor in u happen-after e, we derive $w' \sim_{[E]} u$. Moreover, since w' and u contain the same events that happen-before e' after E, we infer $w'.t' \sim_{[E]} u.t'$. Let us now impose the requirement that $backtrack(E)$ must contain some transition t'' in $I_{[E]}(u.t')$: if $backtrack(E)$ does not already contain such a transition, then one is added. Then $w'.t' \sim_{[E]} u.t'$ and t'' in $I_{[E]}(u.t')$ implies $t'' \in WI_{[E]}(w'.t')$, i.e., $t'' \in WI_{[E]}(w)$. This violates the assumption $WI_{[E]}(w) \cap backtrack(E) = \emptyset$, and we have derived our contradiction.

   The conclusion in this case is that the dynamic computation of source works if it has the property that whenever a race of the form $e \precsim_{E.t.w'''.t'} e'$ is encountered during exploration, then $backtrack(E)$ must contain some transition in $I_{[E]}(u.t')$, where $u.t'$ is as above.

2. $E \nvdash (t.w'.t')$, i.e., t' is disabled by t after w'. In this case, we can only rely on the fact that $E \vdash (t.w')$. As in the previous case, it is guaranteed that a sequence of the form w'' such that $w' \sqsubseteq_{[E.t]} w''$ will be explored from $s_{[E.t]}$ We would now like to find some prefix of w'' which plays the same role as w''' in the preceding case, i.e., such that thereafter t' could be executed but has been disabled by t. If so, we could detect a "race" between the (blocked) execution of t' and e (corresponding to t), and proceed as in case 1. The problem is that, in general, there may not be such a prefix. Namely, it may be the case that w'' contains other transitions of $\widehat{t'}$ that are independent from the events in w', and change the control location of $\widehat{t'}$ so that t' cannot be performed even if it had not been disabled by t. This can be solved by requiring that the race detection in the construction of source sets consider the possible subsequences u of w'' that may be equivalent with w', for which $w' \simeq_{[E]} u$ could be possible. Since the race detection does not know the sequence w''', it must consider any subsequence u with $u \sqsubseteq_{[E]} w''$. For any such subsequence, we let u play the same role as in the previous case, and continue as in the previous case.

In conclusion, we have derived requirements on how to add transitions to the set $backtrack(E)$, which guarantee that $backtrack(E)$ is a source set when the exploration from $s_{[E]}$ has completed. The above inductive hypothesis can then be used to prove that the resulting DPOR algorithm explores all equivalence classes of executions, in the same way as in Theorem 2.

Algorithm 1. Source-DPOR algorithm.

    Initial call : $Explore(\langle\rangle)$

---

1 $Explore(E)$
2   **foreach** $e \in dom(E)$ **do**
3   let $E' = pre(E, e)$;
4   let $w = notdep(e, E)$;
5   **foreach** subsequence u *of* w **such that** $u \sqsubseteq_{[E']} w$ **do**
6   **foreach** transition t that is blocked in $s_{[E]}$ **do**
7   **if** $[e]$ *disables* t *after* $E.u$ **then**
8   let $v = u.t$;
9   **if** $I_{[E']}(v) \cap backtrack(E') = \emptyset$ **then**
10   add some $t' \in I_{[E']}(v)$ to $backtrack(E')$;

11   **if** there is some enabled process p at $s_{[E]}$ **then**
12         $backtrack(E) :=$ all enabled transitions of p;
13   **while** $\exists t \in backtrack(E)$ **do**
14   **foreach** $e \in dom(E)$ **such that** $(e \precsim_{E.t} next_{[E]}(t))$ **do**
15   let $E' = pre(E, e)$;
16   let $v = notdep(e, E).t$;
17   **if** $I_{[E']}(v) \cap backtrack(E') = \emptyset$ **then**
18   add some $t' \in I_{[E']}(v)$ to $backtrack(E')$;

19             $Explore(E.t)$;

Let us now collect this reasoning into an algorithm. Algorithm 1 shows an adaptation of the Source-DPOR algorithm [2, Algorithm 5] to our setting, without the use of sleep sets.

Source-DPOR uses the recursive procedure $Explore(E)$ to perform a depth-first search, where E can be interpreted as the stack of the search, i.e. the past execution sequence explored so far. The algorithm maintains, for each $E'E$, a set $backtrack(E')$ of transitions that will eventually be explored from E'. Each set $backtrack(E)$ is a set of transitions that are enabled from $s_{[E]}$. It will be gradually expanded during the exploration; at the end it will be a source set after E. $Explore(E)$ initializes $backtrack(E)$ to consist of all enabled transitions of some arbitrary process (line 12). Thereafter, for each transition t in $backtrack(E)$ the algorithm performs two phases: race detection (lines 14–18) and state exploration (line 19). In addition, for each explored execution E, it performs a race detection for disabled transitions (lines 2–10).

In the race detection phase, which corresponds to case 1 above and starts at line 14, the algorithm finds the events $e \in dom(E)$ that are in a reversible race with the next step of t. This next step of t corresponds to event e' in the above case 1. For each such event $e \in dom(E)$, the algorithm must explore execution sequences in which the race is reversed. This is done as explained in case 1 above, where E' in the algorithm corresponds to E in case 1, where E in the algorithm corresponds to $E.t.w'''$ in case 1, where t in the algorithm corresponds to t' in case 1, and where v in the algorithm corresponds to $u.t'$ in case 1.

The race detection for disabled transitions, corresponding to case 2 above, is at lines 2–10. It is done for each execution sequence E, as explained in the text in case 2, where E' in the algorithm corresponds to E in case 2, where E in the algorithm corresponds to $E.t.w''$ in case 2, where u in the algorithm corresponds to u in case 2, and where t in the algorithm corresponds to t' in case 2.

6 Relating Source Sets and Persistent Sets

In this section, we provide some comparisons between source sets and persistent sets. We first define persistent sets. Thereafter, we show some properties of source sets and persistent sets that distinguish them from each other, followed by theorems that provide conditions under which source sets can be strictly smaller than persistent sets.

6.1 Persistent Sets

Let us first define persistent sets in our framework. Adapted to our context, a set T of transitions is a persistent set for W after s if for each sequence in W, the first step that is dependent with the first step of some transition in T must be taken by some transition in T. A formalization could go as follows.

Definition 5. (Persistent Sets). *Let s be a state, and let $W \subseteq \mathcal{E}(s)$ be a set of execution sequences from s. A set T of transitions is a persistent set for W after s if for each prefix w of some sequence in W, which contains no occurrence of a transition in T, we have $E \vdash t \Diamond w$ for each $t \in T$.* ·

We say that T is a *persistent set after s* to mean that T is a *persistent set for $\mathcal{E}(s)$ after s*. We note that the definition of persistent sets is slightly more complex than the definition of source sets. In particular, since its definition involves universal quantification over all elements of the persistent set, the elements of a persistent set are not independent of each other. This is noted in the following theorem.

Theorem 4. *If T is a source set after s and $T \subseteq T'$, then T' is a source set after s. This property does not hold for persistent sets, i.e., it is possible that T is a persistent set after s, but T' is not.*

In other words, persistent sets have the unpleasant property that adding a process may disturb the persistent set so that even more process may have to be added. This property is relevant in the context of DPOR, where the first member of the persistent set is often chosen rather arbitrarily (it is the next process in the first exploration after E), and where the persistent set is expanded by need.

For source sets, Theorem 4 follows directly from Definition 4. For persistent sets, a counter-example is provided by the program in Fig. 1, where $\{q\}$ is a persistent set, but $\{p, q\}$ is not.

Continuing the comparison between source sets and persistent sets, we first note some rather direct properties, including the following.

- *Any persistent set is a source set.*
- *Any one-process source set is a persistent set.*

An interesting question is then whether there are situations where any persistent set contains a strictly smaller source set. We note that the program in Fig. 1 does not illustrate such a situation, since the smallest persistent sets and the smallest source sets coincide: they are either $\{q\}$ or $\{r\}$. Nevertheless, the answer to this question is yes, and we formulate this as a theorem.

Theorem 5. *There are programs for which any persistent set from the initial state contains a strictly smaller source set.*

Proof. We give an example. In Fig. 4, the three processes p, q, and r perform dependent accesses to the shared variables x, y, and z. Two accesses are dependent if they access the same variable and at least one is a write. For this program, there are 75 possible execution sequences, partitioned over 7 Mazurkiewicz traces (there are 8 ways to direct the three races in the program, but it is not possible to let the read precede the write in all of them).

$$\boxed{\text{Initially: x = y = z = 0}}$$

p:		q:		r:	
m := x;	$(p1)$	n := y;	$(q1)$	o := z;	$(r1)$
if (m = 0) then		if (n = 0) then		if (o = 0) then	
z := 1;	$(p2)$	x := 1;	$(q2)$	y := 1;	$(r2)$

Fig. 4. Program with non-minimal persistent sets.

In Fig. 4, it is obvious that a single transition cannot be a source set. For instance, the set $\{p1\}$ does not contain the initials of execution $q1.q2.p1.r1.r2$, since $q2$ and $p1$ perform conflicting accesses. On the other hand, any subset containing two enabled transitions is a source set. To see this, let us choose $\{p1, q1\}$ as the source set. Obviously, $\{p1, q1\}$ contains an initial of any execution that starts with either $p1$ or $q1$. Any execution sequence which starts with $r1$ is equivalent to an execution obtained by moving the first step of either $p1$ or $q1$ to the beginning:

- If $q1$ occurs before $r2$, then $q1$ is an initial, since it does not conflict with any other transition.
- If $q1$ occurs after $r2$, then $p1$ is independent of all steps, so $p1$ is an initial.

We claim that $\{p1, q1\}$ cannot be a persistent set. The reason is that the execution sequence $r1.r2$ does not contain any transition in the persistent set, but its second step is dependent with $q1$. By symmetry, it follows that no other two-transition set can be a persistent set. $\qquad\square$

6.2   Fine-Grained Source Sets

It follows rather directly from the definition that for persistent sets we have the following property:

> *If some enabled transition of process p is in the persistent set at s, then all enabled transitions of process p are in the persistent set at s.*

The property follows by observing that if transition t of process p is in the persistent set, and t' is some other enabled transition of p, then the execution sequence t' is dependent with t, and therefore t' must be in the persistent set.

Initially: x = y = flg = 0

p:
await (flg = 0) then flg := 1; $(p1)$
   or
x := 1; $(p2)$

q:
await (flg = 0) then flg := 1; $(q1)$
   or
y := 1; $(q2)$

Fig. 5. Program with fine-grained source set.

For source sets, however, this property need not hold. Consider the program in Fig. 5. Here the transitions $(p1)$ and $(q1)$ should be interpreted as guarded commands that are enabled only when `flg = 0`. (It is possible to make example programs also without disabling transitions, but merely changing their effect depending on some test.) We claim that the set $\{(p2), (q2)\}$ is a source set from the initial state. For instance, if an execution sequence E begins with $(p1)$, then $(q1)$ is disabled, so $(q2)$ is a weak initial of E.

6.3   Excluding Conditionals

We note that the example in Fig. 4 uses conditionally executed statements. This is not a coincidence. In fact, it turns out that if the code of the processes does not contain any branches or conditionals, i.e., all executions of a process access the same variables in the same order, then Theorem 5 does not hold as long as processes are deterministic. Still recall however, that non-minimal source sets need not be persistent sets.

If we allow non-determinism, then it was shown in Fig. 3 that there are simple programs whose minimal source sets are strictly included in any persistent sets. In the absence of both conditionals and non-determinism, minimal source sets and persistent sets are the same, as shown in the following theorem.

Theorem 6. *For programs, in which each process performs a single sequence of unconditional reads and writes, minimal source sets coincide with minimal persistent sets.*

Proof. To see this, consider a program consisting of a set of processes, in which each process executes a deterministic straight-line program without conditionals. We can uniquely identify a transition by the process that executes it. Let us consider the program in its initial state. For processes p, q, let $p \triangleright q$ denote that the first step of p is dependent with *some* step of q. It can easily be seen that persistent sets satisfy the following property:

P is a persistent set iff $p \in P$ and $p \triangleright q$ implies $q \in P$.

This follows rather naturally from the definition of persistent sets: if $p \in P$ and $p \triangleright q$ and $q \notin P$, then consider the sequence of steps of q up to and including the step that is dependent with the first step of p. This sequence is outside P, but is dependent with the first step of some process in P, hence P is not a persistent set. The above property implies that each minimal persistent set is a terminal strongly connected component (SCC) in the direct graph whose nodes are processes, and whose directed edges are defined by the relation $\triangleright$. Conversely, a terminal SCC P is a persistent set, since any execution sequence that does not contain steps of processes in P is by definition independent of the first steps ot processes in P.

For source sets, it also holds that a source set must include a terminal SCC in the direct graph defined by the relation $\triangleright$. Namely, suppose some set T does not include a terminal SCC. This means that for each $p_1 \in T$ there is a sequence of processes $p_1 \, p_2 \ldots p_n$ with $p_i \in T$ and $p_i \triangleright p_{i+1}$ for $i = 1, \ldots, n-1$, but $p_n \notin T$. Consider a longest such sequence. We first assume that it includes all processes in T. Let the execution sequence E consist of all the steps of process p_n, thereafter the steps of process p_{n-1} and so on, until finally all steps of p_1. It is obvious that no process in T can be a weak initial of E. This argument can also be extended to the case where there is no sequence that includes all processes in T. Conversely, any set which includes a terminal SCC is a source set, since for any execution sequence E we can take as initial the first occurring process of that SCC.   □

7 Concluding Remarks

In this paper, we have shown that source sets are suitable as a general foundation for partial order reduction. We have shown that source sets can be used both in enumerative model checking, as performed by SPIN, and in stateless model checking for possibly non-deterministic terminating programs. We have also highlighted some differences between source sets and persistent sets, thereby providing some insights into conditions under which source sets and persistent sets do or do not differ.

Since source sets are more succinct, and often strictly more succinct than corresponding persistent sets, it means that source sets can replace persistent sets as a foundation for partial order reduction.

Acknowledgments. We would like to thank the anonymous reviewers for comments and suggestions that have improved the presentation.

References

1. Abdulla, P.A., Aronis, S., Atig, M.F., Jonsson, B., Leonardsson, C., Sagonas, K.: Stateless model checking for TSO and PSO. In: Baier, C., Tinelli, C. (eds.) TACAS 2015. LNCS, vol. 9035, pp. 353–367. Springer, Heidelberg (2015). doi:10.1007/978-3-662-46681-0_28
2. Abdulla, P., Aronis, S., Jonsson, B., Sagonas, K.: Optimal dynamic partial order reduction. In: Proceeedings of the 41st Annual ACM SIGPLAN-SIGACT Symposium on Principles of Programming Languages, POPL 2014, pp. 373–384. ACM, New York (2014)
3. Baier, C., Katoen, J.P.: Principles of Model Checking. MIT Press, Cambridge (2008)
4. Bengtsson, J., Jonsson, B., Lilius, J., Yi, W.: Partial order reductions for timed systems. In: Sangiorgi, D., Simone, R. (eds.) CONCUR 1998. LNCS, vol. 1466, pp. 485–500. Springer, Heidelberg (1998). doi:10.1007/BFb0055643
5. Bengtsson, J., Larsen, K., Larsson, F., Pettersson, P., Yi, W.: UPPAAL — a tool suite for automatic verification of real-time systems. In: Alur, R., Henzinger, T.A., Sontag, E.D. (eds.) HS 1995. LNCS, vol. 1066, pp. 232–243. Springer, Heidelberg (1996). doi:10.1007/BFb0020949
6. Clarke, E.M., Emerson, E.A., Sistla, A.P.: Automatic verification of finite-state concurrent systems using temporal logics specification: a practical approach. In: Conference Record of the Tenth Annual ACM Symposium on Principles of Programming Languages, pp. 117–126. ACM Press (1983). http://doi.acm.org/10.1145/567067.567080
7. Clarke, E.M., Grumberg, O., Minea, M., Peled, D.: State space reduction using partial order techniques. Int. J. Softw. Tools Technol. Transf. 2(3), 279–287 (1999). http://dx.doi.org/10.1007/s100090050035
8. Flanagan, C., Godefroid, P.: Dynamic partial-order reduction for model checking software. In: Proceedings of the 32nd ACM SIGPLAN-SIGACT Symposium on Principles of Programming Languages, POPL 2005, pp. 110–121 (2005). http://doi.acm.org/10.1145/1040305.1040315
9. Godefroid, P.: Partial-order methods for the verification of concurrent systems: an approach to the state-explosion problem. Ph.D. thesis, University of Liège (1996). Also, vol. 1032 of LNCS, Springer
10. Godefroid, P., Wolper, P.: Using partial orders for the efficient verification of deadlock freedom and safety properties. In: Larsen, K.G., Skou, A. (eds.) CAV 1991. LNCS, vol. 575, pp. 332–342. Springer, Heidelberg (1992). doi:10.1007/3-540-55179-4_32
11. Holzmann, G.: The model checker SPIN. IEEE Trans. Softw. Eng. **SE-23**(5), 279–295 (1997)
12. Huang, J.: Stateless model checking concurrent programs with maximal causality reduction. In: Proceedings of the 36th ACM SIGPLAN Conference on Programming Language Design and Implementation, PLDI 2015, pp. 165–174. ACM, New York (2015). http://doi.acm.org/10.1145/2737924.2737975
13. Kähkönen, K., Saarikivi, O., Heljanko, K.: Unfolding based automated testing of multithreaded programs. Autom. Softw. Eng. **22**(4), 475–515 (2015). http://dx.doi.org/10.1007/s10515-014-0150-6
14. Lauterburg, S., Karmani, R.K., Marinov, D., Agha, G.: Evaluating ordering heuristics for dynamic partial-order reduction techniques. In: Rosenblum, D.S., Taentzer, G. (eds.) FASE 2010. LNCS, vol. 6013, pp. 308–322. Springer, Heidelberg (2010). doi:10.1007/978-3-642-12029-9_22

15. Mazurkiewicz, A.: Trace theory. In: Brauer, W., Reisig, W., Rozenberg, G. (eds.) ACPN 1986. LNCS, vol. 255, pp. 278–324. Springer, Heidelberg (1987). doi:10. 1007/3-540-17906-2_30

16. McMillan, K.L., Probst, D.K.: A technique of a state space search based on unfolding. Form. Methods Syst. Des. **6**(1), 45–65 (1995)

17. Overman, W.: Verification of concurrent systems: function and timing. Ph.D. thesis, UCLA, August 1981

18. Peled, D.: All from one, one for all: on model checking using representatives. In: Courcoubetis, C. (ed.) CAV 1993. LNCS, vol. 697, pp. 409–423. Springer, Heidelberg (1993). doi:10.1007/3-540-56922-7_34

19. Queille, J.P., Sifakis, J.: Specification and verification of concurrent systems in CESAR. In: Dezani-Ciancaglini, M., Montanari, U. (eds.) Programming 1982. LNCS, vol. 137, pp. 337–351. Springer, Heidelberg (1982). doi:10.1007/3-540-11494-7_22

20. Rodríguez, C., Sousa, M., Sharma, S., Kroening, D.: Unfolding-based partial order reduction. In: 26th International Conference on Concurrency Theory, CONCUR 2015. LIPIcs, vol. 42, pp. 456–469. Schloss Dagstuhl - Leibniz-Zentrum fuer Informatik (2015). http://dx.doi.org/10.4230/LIPIcs.CONCUR.2015.456

21. Saarikivi, O., Kähkönen, K., Heljanko, K.: Improving dynamic partial order reductions for concolic testing. In: 12th International Conference on Application of Concurrency to System Design (ACSD), pp. 132–141. IEEE, Los Alamitos, June 2012

22. Salah, R.B., Bozga, M., Maler, O.: On interleaving in timed automata. In: Baier, C., Hermanns, H. (eds.) CONCUR 2006. LNCS, vol. 4137, pp. 465–476. Springer, Heidelberg (2006). doi:10.1007/11817949_31

23. Sen, K., Agha, G.: Automated systematic testing of open distributed programs. In: Baresi, L., Heckel, R. (eds.) FASE 2006. LNCS, vol. 3922, pp. 339–356. Springer, Heidelberg (2006). doi:10.1007/11693017_25

24. Sen, K., Agha, G.: A race-detection and flipping algorithm for automated testing of multi-threaded programs. In: Bin, E., Ziv, A., Ur, S. (eds.) HVC 2006. LNCS, vol. 4383, pp. 166–182. Springer, Heidelberg (2007). doi:10.1007/978-3-540-70889-6_13

25. Şerbănuţă, T.F., Chen, F., Roşu, G.: Maximal Causal Models for Sequentially Consistent Systems. In: Qadeer, S., Tasiran, S. (eds.) RV 2012. LNCS, vol. 7687, pp. 136–150. Springer, Heidelberg (2013). doi:10.1007/978-3-642-35632-2_16

26. Tasharofi, S., Karmani, R.K., Lauterburg, S., Legay, A., Marinov, D., Agha, G.: TransDPOR: a novel dynamic partial-order reduction technique for testing actor programs. In: Giese, H., Rosu, G. (eds.) FMOODS/FORTE -2012. LNCS, vol. 7273, pp. 219–234. Springer, Heidelberg (2012). doi:10.1007/978-3-642-30793-5_14

27. Valmari, A.: Stubborn sets for reduced state space generation. In: Rozenberg, G. (ed.) ICATPN 1989. LNCS, vol. 483, pp. 491–515. Springer, Heidelberg (1991). doi:10.1007/3-540-53863-1_36

Real-Time and Distributed Systems

A Framework for Evaluating Schedulability Analysis Tools

Lijun Shan[1,2(✉)], Susanne Graf[1], Sophie Quinton[2], and Loïc Fejoz[3]

[1] Verimag, Saint-Martin-d'Hères, France
`lijun.shan@imag.fr`
[2] Inria Grenoble – Rhône-Alpes, Montbonnot-Saint-Martin, France
[3] RealTime-at-Work (RTaW), Villers-lés-Nancy, France

Abstract. There exists a large variety of schedulability analysis tools based on different, often incomparable timing models. This variety makes it difficult to choose the best fit for analyzing a given real-time system. To help the research community to better evaluate analysis tools and their underlying methods, we are developing a framework which consists of (1) a simple language called *RTSpec* for specifying real-time systems, (2) a tool chain which translates a system specification in RTSpec into an input for various analysis tools, and (3) a set of benchmarks. Our goal is to enable users and developers of schedulability analysis tools to compare such tools systematically, automatically and rigorously.

Keywords: Real-time systems · Schedulability analysis · Formal semantics

1 Introduction

Schedulability analysis is an offline approach to evaluating the temporal correctness of real-time (RT) systems in terms of whether all software tasks meet their deadlines at runtime. Numerous timing models and corresponding schedulability tests have been proposed since the 1970s; see [10,24] for surveys. Some of them have been implemented in tools, called *analyzers* in the sequel, e.g. MAST [15], TIMES [5], Cheddar [26], SymTA/S [16], SchedMCore [8], pyCPA [12], etc.

This variety of analyzers makes it difficult to choose the best fit for a given real-time system under study. Indeed, the timing models underlying analyzers are often incomparable, mainly because they make incomparable choices on the precision with which one can express the timing-relevant aspects of an RT system. Such choices mainly concern the models describing (1) the activation of tasks, (2) their resource requirements and (3) the scheduling policies used to arbitrate between them. Also, schedulability is only one possible type of timing requirement: other options include e.g. weakly-hard properties (no more than m deadline misses out of k task executions).

To compare the expressivity of the models used by analyzers as well as the precision of the analysis results that they produce, we need a common set of

© Springer International Publishing AG 2017
L. Aceto et al. (Eds.): Larsen Festschrift, LNCS 10460, pp. 539–559, 2017.
DOI: 10.1007/978-3-319-63121-9_27

test cases provided in a *common input format*. Several formalisms exist (e.g. MARTE [20] and Amalthea [1]) whose goal is to be as expressive as possible. Unfortunately they are not suitable for our purpose as they do not provide a formal semantics. In contrast, timed automata [3] provide a formal model which can be used to represent real-time systems at an arbitrary level of precision, and can thus express the operational semantics of any RT system model. This expressivity comes at a price: there is currently no generic way of specifying real-time systems in a timed automata based tool such as UPPAAL [17].

In this paper we propose *RTSpec*, a formalism for real-time system specification with flexible syntax and rigorous semantics. A modular library of UPPAAL models provides the operational semantics of RTSpec. Based on this library, the timing model of various analyzers can be formalized, and mappings between their respective input formats can be rigorously defined. Our overall target is a framework which comprises the RTSpec formalism, a tool chain for automatically translating RTSpec into the input of various analysis tools, and a set of benchmarks which are synthetic or derived from industrial case studies. Such a framework would provide a systematic, automated and rigorous methodology for evaluating analyzers.

The paper is structured as follows. Section 2 discusses related work. Section 3 sets the background of our work with a brief introduction to RT systems and timed automata. Section 4 overviews the automata library RTLib. Section 5 presents the syntax of RTSpec. Section 6 presents the methodology our framework provides for different types of users. Section 7 concludes the paper and discusses the future work.

2   Related Work

Our contribution relates to the research in three areas: specification languages for real-time systems, formal models for real-time system specification and comparison of real-time analyzers.

2.1   Specification Languages for Real-Time Systems

Let us first note that, in principle, the input format of any existing analyzer could be a candidate for the role of common input format. But these specification languages can only express, quite understandably, the system features that their analyzer can handle. For example, only a few tools such as pyCPA [12] propose an expressive activation model which specifies the maximum number of activations in a given time window. Using an input format which does not encompass such functions would be unfair towards the corresponding family of tools and analysis methods. The same goes for input formats which do not allow specifying offsets, or dependent tasks etc. Note that some simulation tools, e.g. ARTISST [11], provide much more expressive specification languages. In that case however, the semantics of the input format is not formally given and can only be clarified through simulation. We therefore restrict ourselves for the moment to static analyzers. RTSpec could be a good starting point to providing a common input format for simulation tools as well.

There exist a few *high-level* specification languages aiming at generality. For example, MARTE [20] is a UML profile for embedded and real-time aspects of systems that has been defined with the aim of putting together all the concepts used in some existing framework or tool. This generality, however, is mainly meant at the level of vocabulary. No formal semantics is given for the different concepts in the vocabulary, and this is done on purpose, in order to leave room for semantic variations. Note that there exists a semantic framework but it would only allow to define a declarative semantics — defined by a set of constraints on timed event streams. Amalthea [1] is an open source framework for specifying real-time embedded systems maintained by an industrial consortium. It aims to be comprehensive with respect of the real-time features captured by its language. It additionally provides connections to simulation and analysis. Unfortunately, there is no explicit effort to formally define a semantics for the Amalthea language. Instead, the semantics is implicitly defined by the connections with these external tools, and hopefully in a non-contradictory manner.

Another related work is the on-going project Waruna[1], which aims to integrate tools at different development stages so as to automate the analysis of timing properties on design models of real-time systems. Seeing that architecture design models in AADL [13], SysML [28] or MARTE [21] may contain timing properties, Waruna intends to extract timing related information from design models and input them to analysis tools, e.g. Cheddar, MAST, RTaW-Pegase[2], etc. In contrast to RTSpec, the model transformations in Waruna are defined at the metamodel level and lacking of a formal semantics.

We view our RTSpec contribution as complementary to initiatives such as MARTE, Amalthea or Waruna. Indeed, our effort is less focused on having an exhaustive set of timing features. Instead, we provide a well-founded semantic background for those features that can currently be handled by at least one schedulability verification tool.

2.2 Formal Models for Real-Time System Specifications

We aim to provide a unified semantic framework for specifying real-time systems. Let us here review existing formalisms which could provide such a framework and show their limitations.

The UPPAAL [17] model checker can be used for the verification of real-time systems. TIMES [5] is a front-end for UPPAAL dedicated to schedulability analysis. TIMES however deals with a restricted set of concepts (uniprocessor systems with sporadic tasks). Another tool which uses UPPAAL is SchedMCore [8], a multiprocessor schedulability analyzer. But the task model supported by SchedMCore is restricted to periodic tasks.

---

[1] http://www.waruna-projet.fr/, https://www.polarsys.org/projects/polarsys.time4sys.

[2] http://www.realtimeatwork.com/software/rtaw-pegase/.

UPPAAL has also been used directly for the timing analysis of industrial case studies, e.g. [19,25]. The model proposed in [19] and extended in [25] allows describing uniprocessor systems of periodic tasks with a preemptive fixed-priority scheduler and shared memory. Synchronization protocols for shared memory access are implemented, including priority-inheritance and priority-ceiling.

Even more relevant to us are two UPPAAL-based modeling frameworks: [9] comprises 5 Timed Automata (TA) templates to specify sporadic tasks and partitioned schedulers on multiprocessor systems, and a sub-template for job enqueuing for each scheduling policy. [7] proposes a framework, which consists of templates for specifying sporadic tasks, schedulers and processing units, for hierarchical scheduling systems.

All the above-mentioned approaches are of rather limited expressivity. They do not support, for example, weakly-hard real-time systems. To fit our purpose, they would therefore need to be easily extendable. This is unfortunately not the case because they have not been designed with modularity and reusability in mind. For example, the Task template in all these frameworks captures not only the task activation and task execution pattern, but also its worst-case response-time computation and deadline-miss analysis. As a result, one cannot define independently variants of, e.g., the activation pattern and of the execution pattern. Instead, one would need to define a specific template for all possible combinations of variants of the aspects handled in Task.

In comparison, the primary focus of our formal library is on modularity. Our work builds on top of the TA-based representation of real-time systems — in particular tasks and schedulers — of [19]. Our representation of task activation patterns is inspired by task automata [14], which is a variant of TA for expressing task activation patterns.

2.3   Comparison of Analyzers

To our knowledge, the work presented in [22,23] is the only effort on systematic evaluation of schedulability analyzers. Four tools for performance analysis of distributed embedded systems are evaluated, namely MAST, SymTA/S, Real-Time Calculus [29] and UPPAAL. A formalism in SystemC is proposed for specifying the benchmarks which are then manually translated into an input for each analyzer under study. By observing the output of each tool for the chosen benchmarks, their underlying analysis algorithms are compared in terms of precision and efficiency.

This work sets a good starting point for further investigation in two directions. First, this evaluation of analyzers is restricted to their common functionality. In practice however, given a complex system, various analyzers allow to characterize the system with different abstractions, such that the result obtained using one tool depends both on its timing model and its underlying analysis algorithm. The effect of the composition of these two factors cannot be inferred from the conclusion of [22]. Secondly, a manual construction of the inputs for various tools is impractical for evaluating analyzers on more complex benchmarks than the ones of [22, 23]. We aim to provide a tool chain which automates the translation of a system specification into the input of several tools, so that a system can be specified once in RTSpec and analyzed with multiple tools.

3 Preliminaries

To set the background of our work, this section will first introduce the terminology on real-time systems with some typical examples. Then we will briefly present the timed automata formalism and the UPPAAL model checker.

3.1 Terminology on Real-Time Systems

A real-time system usually comprises three parts: a hardware platform which provides computation and communication resources; a set of software tasks which require access to the resources; a set of schedulers which manage the allocation of resources to tasks.

Platform. The hardware resources of an RT system include processing units, i.e. processors and cores, and possibly shared resources e.g. memory and communication network. For example, a distributed RT system consists of a number of nodes, where each node contains a number of processors. For simplifying schedulability analysis, the communication network which connects the distributed nodes can also be regarded as a node, and messages transmitted over the network can be considered as tasks on this network node.

Task Set. The software in an RT system is usually a task set, where each task is a piece of code. An execution of a task is also called a *job*. One task may have a number of jobs running in parallel.

A task is characterized by a set of parameters on its timing features, including its *arrival pattern* i.e. the time of the task's first arrival and recurrence, its *resource requirement* e.g. the CPU time it needs for execution, and its *timing requirement* e.g. a relative deadline. In their seminal paper [18], Liu and Layland proposed to characterize a task with two parameters: *period* for both the arrival interval and the deadline, and *WCET* for (an upper bound on) the worst-case execution time. This abstraction is called the *periodic task model*. A period task set consists of periodic, synchronous and independent tasks with implicit deadlines. To describe tasks with more diverse features, researchers have extended the Liu and Layland task model with different additional parameters, which lead to variations in the tractability and precision of feasibility and schedulability analysis [27].

Scheduler Set. Scheduling policies can be static (also called offline) or dynamic (also called online). The former group provides a scheduling table for all tasks before the system's execution, hence only applies to periodic task sets. The latter group is applicable to any task sets. Our work focuses on the more challenging class of dynamic schedulers. Relevant properties of dynamic scheduling policies include preemptiveness (a scheduler can interrupt the execution of a job to allocate the resource to another job), job migration, etc. Additionally a scheduler may take decisions according to fixed priorities assigned to tasks, as for e.g. the Deadline Monotonic (DM) policy, or to dynamic priorities (priorities are assigned at the job level), e.g. Earliest Deadline First (EDF), or without any notion of priority, e.g. First-In-First-Out (FIFO).

Timing Model. A set of parameters which characterize the timing properties of a platform, a task set and a scheduler set of an RT system compose a timing model. A system can be captured by diverse timing models. With a more expressive timing model, the schedulability analysis is more precise at the cost of a higher computational complexity.

Many timing models have been used for specifying and analyzing RT systems. But they lack a common formal background. Even more problematic, different schedulability analysis methods and tools may interpret one parameter differently, which brings difficulty for their users to understand and compare them. In order to clarify the existing terminology and to facilitate rigorous definition of diverse extensions on it, we propose to formally define the semantics of timing models using timed automata.

3.2   Timed Automata

Timed automata [6] has been widely adopted as the language for formal representation and analysis of RT systems, because it allows to specify RT systems at an arbitrary level of precision, meaning that it can express the semantics of any concept proposed by a timing model. Therefore, we chose timed automata as the language for building RTLib, which is the library of TA templates providing a formal semantics for RTSpec.

A timed automaton is a finite automaton consisting of a finite set of nodes denoted *locations* and a finite set of labeled edges denoted *transitions*, extended with real-valued variables [6]. Time progress and time-dependent behavior are expressed using a set of *clocks* that can be started, reset, halted and read. A location can be assigned with an invariant, which is a clock constraint. A transition can be labeled with a *guard* i.e. the condition for enabling the transition, a *channel* with which an automaton synchronizes with another automaton and moves simultaneously, and an *update* which may contain actions and reset of clocks. UPPAAL supports *stopwatch automata* [4], an extension of timed automata where clocks may be stopped occasionally. Syntactically, a stopwatch expression is an invariant in the form of $x' == c$, where x is a clock and c is an integer expression which evaluates to either 0 or 1 [19].

As an example, Fig. 1 shows a timed automaton representing a task execution process in a preemptive environment, assuming that a task has at most one live job at any moment. A clock *resTime* tracks the task's response time, i.e., the time span between its activation and finish. Another clock *exeTime* tracks its execution time. On the location *Scheduled*, the invariant *exeTime* $<= WCET$

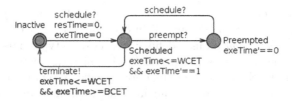

Fig. 1. An example of timed automata: task's execution process

ensures that the duration of the task's execution is at most *WCET*. The invariant $exeTime' == 1$ ensures that the clock $exeTime$ progresses when the task is executing on a processor. The invariant $exeTime' == 0$ on the location *Preempted* stops the clock $exeTime$ when the task is preempted. A job finishes execution when the CPU time it consumes is between BCET (best case execution time) and WCET. This automaton exhibits the operational semantics of the two task parameters BCET and WCET.

3.3 UPPAAL

UPPAAL is the standard tool for editing, executing and analyzing timed automata. UPPAAL supports the specification of timed automata as well as *automata templates*, i.e., parameterized timed automata. In a valid UPPAAL model, automata templates have to be instantiated into automata. As a result, UPPAAL models consist of three parts (the keywords given by UPPAAL are denoted in **bold** font):

- **Declarations.** Elements used by the model templates, which can be:
  - *Generic*: user-defined data types (e.g. bounded integers, structs, arrays); (parameterized) synchronization channels; global variables; functions used within the templates.
  - *Specific* to a system: global variables instantiated with actual parameters.
- **Templates.** Parameterized timed automata.
- **System declarations.** Elements which are specific to an instance system:
  - *Instantiation statements*: statements which instantiate templates into automata by assigning values to the template parameters.
  - **System**: declaration of a system as a set of automata.

Logically, such a UPPAAL input file is composed of two levels:

1. a *system type* made of the *generic* part in **Declarations** and the **Templates**;
2. an *instantiation* into a specific system which consists of the *specific* part in **Declarations** and the **System declarations**.

Since UPPAAL was designed for formalizing specific systems rather than system types, it does not provide sufficient support for defining system types on a higher abstraction level. For example, data type definitions, which are logically a part of *system type*, may depend on instance systems, as we explain now.

UPPAAL provides two basic data types: bool and (bounded) integer — to reduce the state space of a system, all integer variables must be bounded. In particular, this means that all user-defined integer data types must be bounded. As an example, defining a data type for WCET of tasks requires to provide a bound for them, which can only be done for specific system instances. In other words, the system type definition and instance definition are interleaved and mutually dependent, which brings difficulty for users to understand and extend a system type. Note that the limitations of UPPAAL with respect to system type definitions have pushed us to develop a front-end tool called *RTLibEx* to help with the formalization of timing models.

4   The RTLib Library

In this section, we introduce RTLib, a library of UPPAAL templates formalizing concepts which are commonly utilized in real-time system analysis. RTLib provides the basis for a formal semantics of RTSpec, our formalism for specifying real-time systems. The key advantages of RTLib are: (1) its formal basis, (2) its expressivity, which can be easily increased if needed; (3) its modularity, which makes it much easier to compare different models by allowing the user to focus on the concepts that differ. The RTLib library is structured around a core of *basic* concepts that exist in most frameworks. Thanks to its modular structure, one can easily enrich RTLib with *extensions*, i.e., variants of one or more templates of the basic library. Two extensions that can be meaningfully combined at the conceptual level can be combined directly at the library level.

RTLib can be used for specifying concrete real-time systems on which the UPPAAL model checker can conduct exact or statistical schedulability analysis. This can help evaluating the correctness and accuracy of other analyzers on small systems. The main objective of RTLib is however at a higher abstraction level: RTLib is meant to provide a common, formal basis to describe the semantics of the timing models used by analyzers. This will help proposing rigorous transformations between the timing models.

RTLib defines a set of *system types* for real-time systems, i.e. timing models. As discussed in Sect. 3, a *system type* in UPPAAL consists of several parts, among which the most complicated are data types and automata templates. This section overviews these two parts in RTLib before describing how RTLib can be extended.

4.1   Automata Templates

As discussed in Sect. 3, a timing model defines a set of parameters which characterizes the three parts of a real-time system: platform, task set and scheduler. Following this compositional view, we organize RTLib as a hierarchy of templates. The UML class diagram in Fig. 2 shows the structure of the RTLib Basic library, where each concrete class denotes an automata template, and an abstract class denotes a concept which is implemented by a number of automata

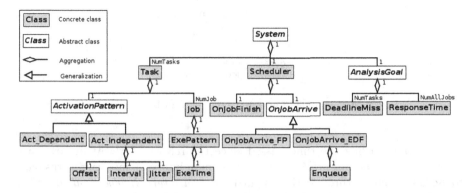

Fig. 2. Structure of the library RTLib Basic

templates. Note that RTLib explicitly specifies analysis goals, but does not have templates related to the platform, as we explain now.

For the moment RTLib only captures multiprocessor/distributed systems. The platform information, i.e. the number of processors in each node, is thus represented by a parameter of schedulers. We leave to future work the extension of RTLib with templates for more complicated platforms. Besides, we have chosen to explicitly specify analysis goals in RTLib, e.g. absence of deadline misses for hard real-time systems, to cover more system-level timing requirements than just schedulability.

In RTLib, an automata template may call its *sub-templates* through synchronization channels. In Fig. 2, an aggregation relation connects a template with its sub-template, and a generalization relation connects a concept with its special case[3]. For instance, the Task template has two sub-templates: ActivationPattern which characterizes the activation pattern of a task, and Job which represents the lifecycle of a task's instance. ActivationPattern has two special cases: Act_Dependent and Act_Independent, for dependent tasks and independent tasks, respectively. The activation pattern of an independent task may have three constraints: Offset, Interval and Jitter, each denoted by a parameter of a task model. The operational semantics of the parameters are represented by separate automata templates.

For example, Interval constrains the separation between job arrivals. Once an independent task τ releases a job τ^i, the automaton Task immediately calls its sub-automaton Act_Independent, which in turns calls its sub-automaton Interval through the channel *Independent_call_Interval*. As shown in Fig. 3, a transition is triggered from the location *Start* to *WaitInterval*, and the clock x is reset

---

[3] We use the following conventions. Template A_B is a specialization of template A for extension B. Synchronization channels are named as follows:

- A_e_B: automaton A sends a message to B on event e;
- A_call_B: automaton A calls its sub-automaton B;
- A_return_B: automaton A, a sub-automaton of B, returns.

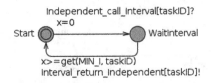

Fig. 3. An example of automata template in RTLib: interval

to zero for recording the time passed since the release of τ^i. At an arbitrary moment after x reaches MIN_I (i.e. the minimum interval), Interval returns back to Act_Independent through the channel *Interval_return_Independent*, meaning that the arrival constraint of job τ^{i+1} has been satisfied.

4.2 Data Types

User-defined data types determine the data structure processed by automata. The structure of data type definition in RTLib resembles the structure of the templates in the library.

We classify the data types in RTLib into two groups according to their roles: *parameter types* whose variables represent the parameters of RT systems, hence determined by a timing model; *state types* whose variables represent the dynamic state of RT systems during their execution, hence common to any timing model. Therefore, to formalize a new timing model based on RTLib Basic, *state types* can be reused, while *parameter types* need to be extended.

Parameter Types. According to their structural relations, the parameter types can be further classified onto three levels: elementary types, composite types and collective types, as shown in Fig. 4.

- Elementary type: a bounded integer, representing the data type of some parameters, e.g. *time_t* as the data type of tasks' timing parameters including period, deadline, WCET, etc.
- Composite type: a struct built upon elementary types, e.g. *task_t* which consists of a set of task parameters.
- Collective type: an array whose elements belong to some composite type, e.g. *taskSet_t* as an array of *task_t* representing the taskset in a system.

Each task model which characterizes a task with a set of parameters is mapped to a definition of *task_t*, and any task characterized by the task model can be expressed as a variable of the type *task_t*. Similarly, elementary types, composite types and collective types are defined to represent scheduler parameters, schedulers and scheduler sets, respectively. Such data types form a hierarchy following the compositional view of a real-time system. The leaves of this hierarchy represent the data types of the parameters defined by a timing model, hence may vary from one timing model to another. The non-leaf part of the hierarchy are reusable for various timing models. This stable hierarchy of data types,

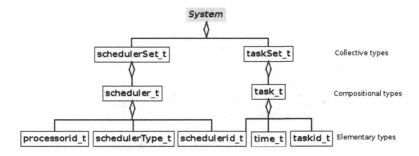

Fig. 4. Hierarchy of parameter data types

together with the stable hierarchy of automata templates, reveals the reusability and extensibility of RTLib. By extending the data types and the automata templates, RTLib can be adapted to formalize a wide range of timing models.

State Types. A RT system formalized as an automata network simulates the timing-related behavior of the system. To track the dynamic state of a system during its execution, the following data types are defined for all timing models:

– For representing the state of tasks:
  • *job_t*: a composite data type with two fields *taskID* and *jobID*, altogether denoting the identifier of a job;
  • *jobQ_t*: an array of *job_t*, denoting the ready job queue.
– For representing the state of a node under the management of a scheduler:
  • *nodeState_t*: a composite data type, whose fields denote the current jobs upon each processor, new arrived job, just finished job, etc.;
  • *nodeStateSet_t*: an array of *nodeState_t*, denoting all nodes in a system.

4.3   Extension of RTLib

Let us now show the extension capabilities of RTLib. By extension, we understand either the introduction of an entirely new concept or a new variant of an existing one. To define an extension, one proceeds in two steps:

1. possibly extend the data type definitions to express the new concepts;
2. add or replace the relevant templates.

To argue that the chosen structure of RTLib achieves sufficient modularity, we illustrate this process with an example.

The *event stream model* [2] is a generalization of the sporadic task model which constrains not only the minimal time distance between any two consecutive activations of task τ, but may for any k impose a stronger constraint for the minimal time interval that may contain k activations. In practice, it is sufficient to consider a strictly increasing constraint sequence only for some first N values for k. Thus, such a *minimum distance* function can be specified by a

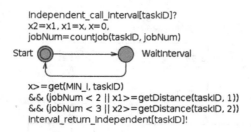

Fig. 5. Interval_MinDistance for 3 distances

vector $[D_0, D_1, \ldots, D_{N-1}]$ of minimal distances D_i between the activation of job τ^k and τ^{k+i+1}, $\forall k$. Note that the minimum interval of the sporadic task model is a minimum distance vector with a single element D_0.

Extending the basic activation pattern of the sporadic task model to handle minimum distance functions only requires to modify the Interval template (see Fig. 3). To represent a vector of N minimum distances requires N clocks. Figure 5 shows the template for $N = 3$. It extends the Interval template with two additional clocks: $x1$ records the distance between τ^k and τ^{k+2}, and $x2$ records the distance between τ^k and τ^{k+3}. Function $countJob()$ counts the job arrivals up to $N - 1$.

4.4   RTLibEx: A GUI Tool for RTLib Extensions

As already discussed, RTLib is intended both for:

1. defining timing models i.e. system types of RT systems;
2. specifying actual systems i.e. instances of some system types.

It is however not possible to distinguish properly these two activities, which may concern different users, in UPPAAL, as the system type definitions and instance definitions are interleaved and mutually dependent (see Sect. 3).

RTLibEx is a front-end tool for UPPAAL intended to address this issue. It provides two distinct editors (implemented in the same GUI): a *timing model editor* and an *instance editor*. The timing model editor mainly supports the extension and specialization of data types. The instance editor is then automatically generated by our tool from the data type definitions, which allows users to define an actual system by just filling an array of parameters. In the rest of this section, we briefly describe these two editors.

The Instance Editor. As shown in Fig. 6, an instance editor is a GUI for defining an actual system. RTLib Basic defines an RT system as a set of schedulers and tasks whose parameters are defined by the data types *scheduler_t*, resp. *task_t*. Thus, defining a scheduler or a task means providing values for its parameters. The generated instance editor therefore provides two tables for schedulers and tasks, where the system designer inputs the actual parameters

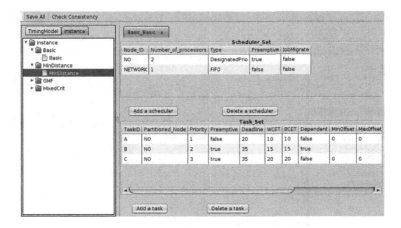

Fig. 6. Snapshot of RTLibEx: instance editor

of a real-time system. The tables look similar to the GUI of existing analyzers, e.g. TIMES [5] and Cheddar [26]. The significant difference is that RTLibEx automatically generates the GUI from the relevant user-defined data types for any user-defined timing model, while the existing timing analysis tools hard-wire specific timing models hence cannot be extended by the user.

Once the system actual parameters are given, RTLibEx checks its consistency and reports diagnostic information. For a consistent definition, it generates the representation of the system as an input file for UPPAAL.

The Timing Model Editor. As stated in Sect. 3.3, a UPPAAL file contains three parts: Declarations, Templates and System declarations. In most cases, to define a new timing model implies extending the data types of RTLib Basic and adding or replacing existing templates. RTLibEx facilitates the extension of the Declarations part and then automatically generates the System declarations part. In parallel, the user should modify Templates with UPPAAL.

Declarations include two subsets: the *generic* subset for a system type, and the *specific* subset for a specific system. The instance editor of RTLibEx allows users to input the parameters of a system, which becomes the *specific* declarations of the system. The timing model editor of RTLibEx provides a GUI for users to specify the *generic* subset of declarations for defining a system type.

The *generic* declarations consist of data type definitions, synchronization channels, global variables and functions used within the templates. Among them, data type definitions is the major part to be modified when defining a new timing model based on RTLib Basic. As we stated in Sect. 4.2, we classify data types into *parameter types* and *state types*.

RTLibEx enables users to reuse RTLib Basic as much as possible when defining a new timing model. On the left side of Fig. 7 is a tree of loaded Timing Models, where each one is a tree with five main nodes. The first four nodes, *parameter types*, *state types*, *functions* and *channels* represent the respective parts

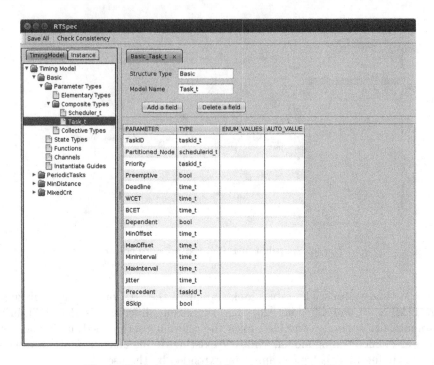

Fig. 7. Snapshot of RTLibEx: timing model editor

of a UPPAAL system type. The last one, *instantiation guides*, specifies a set
of rules generating instantiation statements. Given the instantiation statements,
UPPAAL can instantiate a set of automata templates into a system instance.

The right side of Fig. 7 is a table of parameters of a composite type, i.e. *task_t*
and *scheduler_t* presented in Sect. 4.2. To extend the parameter list of Task or
Scheduler, the user adds items into the respective table. Each table comprises 4
columns:

- PARAMETER: name of a parameter.
- TYPE: data type of the parameter.
- ENUM_VALUE: enumerated values of the data type of the parameter. This
  field is useful only when the parameter has a enumeration data type.
- AUTO_VALUE: default value of the parameter.

To build a new timing model, the user first builds a copy of the Basic library
by right-clicking on the node Basic, and then fills in the sub-nodes of the new
timing model. When all the nodes of a timing model tree are completed, the
timing model editor stores this model and generates the tables *Scheduler_Set* and
Task_Set in the instance editor. Thus, RTLibEx enables a logical and procedural
separation of timing model definition from instance system declaration.

5   The RTSpec Format

Based on the formal library RTLib, we define RTSpec, a human-readable textual format for specifying a wide scope of real-time systems. Following the structure of RTLib, a real-time system specification in RTSpec declares a platform, a task set and a scheduler set. An entity, e.g. a processor or a task or a scheduler, is characterized by a set of attributes, where each attribute has its operational semantics defined in RTLib.

As an intermediate textual format, RTSpec aims to cover not only the features shared by all timing models underlying existing analyzers, but also attributes which are characteristic of some existing analyzers, such that comparison between different tools is fair. For that reason, and following the two-layer structure of RTLib, RTSpec provides language constructs at two levels: the *basic* elements represent the concepts defined in RTLib Basic, and the *extension* elements characterize concepts which may be handled only by some analyzers. A simple system specification that conforms to the basic timing model can be translated into the input of different analyzers through syntactical mapping, which enables to compare their common subset. A more complex system specification that is beyond the basic model can be translated into the input of different analyzers through semantic mapping, i.e., abstraction and approximation.

5.1   The RTSpec Basic Syntax

We have designed the RTSpec basic syntax with three concerns in mind: conciseness, flexibility and extensibility, as we briefly discuss now.

Conciseness. In RTSpec, default values for parameters allow systems to be specified in a concise manner. For example, if a task has no jitter, instead of declaring `jitter = 0`, the jitter attribute can simply be omitted. As a result, even in presence of language extensions, it is still possible to define a simple entity, e.g. a classic periodic task, using a small set of attributes.

Flexibility. As a unified specification format, RTSpec represents a synthesis not only of the timing models of various analyzers, but also of the style of their input formats. The concrete syntax of RTSpec provides 3 representation styles:

- Positional style: An entity is characterized by a set of parameters, where the position of each parameter indicates its meaning. This style is similar to the input format of the SchedMCore [8] tool. This style can be used to specify simple systems which only need this limited set of attributes.
- Canonical style: An entity is characterized by a set of attributes, where each attribute is declared as a name-value pair and the attributes of an entity can be declared with an arbitrary order.
- Record style: An entity is characterized as a record, where each field represents an attribute such that attributes of an entity can be declared in any order. This style is similar to the input format of pyCPA [12]. It allows interleaving task declarations and referring to attributes declared before.

All task declarations are automatically translated into the canonical style before further processing. The flexibility of the syntax style enables a user to choose a preferred representation according to her/his habits or the complexity of the system to be analyzed. The flexibility in the order of attribute declarations facilitates extensions and modifications of attribute lists when incorporating new timing models. The following listing shows an example of a task set declared using the three representation styles.

```
-- Positional style:
-- Task(name,period, wcet, deadline, offset):
Task("task1", 20, 3, 15, 2)

-- Canonical style:
Task{name="task2", period=23, wcet=4, deadline=8}

-- Record style:
Task("task3")
task3.wcet = 5
task3.period = 23
task3.deadline = 13
task3.offset = 5
Task("task4")
task4.wcet = 9
task4.period = task3.period
task4.deadline = 2 * task3.deadline
task4.offset = 7
```

Extensibility. We are currently extending RTSpec with constructs which are characteristic of some analyzers, e.g. minimum distance functions for pyCPA. It is our intention to have specific keywords identifying extensions in a specification. Such constructs must correspond to extensions of the RTLib UPPAAL library and whenever possible semantic mappings must be provided to transform an extension-dependent specification into a coarser grained basic specification.

5.2 Current Status of the RTSpec-based Tool Chain

So far, we have: (1) defined the basic part of RTSpec based on a subset of the RTLib basic library, (2) implemented a translator which takes any RTSpec input and translates it into an equivalent canonical form, (3) implemented translators which transform an RTSpec (canonical) specification into a number of formats, including the CPAL Language[4], MAST PTE file[5], pyCPA[6], SchedMCore[7] and

---

[4] http://www.designcps.com/.

[5] http://mast.unican.es/.

[6] http://pycpa.readthedocs.io/en/latest/.

[7] https://forge.onera.fr/projects/schedmcore.

Times[8]. Note that these tools do not provide a formal semantics for their input format. As a consequence it is not possible to prove the correctness of our translations in any formal way. Instead we rely on a tight collaboration with the researchers involved in the development of the targeted analyzers. Another way to look at this issue is then to consider RTSpec and RTLib as the reference semantics for these input formats.

6   Methodology

Our framework is targeted at developers but also users of timing analysis tools. This section describes the methodology that our framework supports for these two categories of people.

6.1   For System Architects

With a variety of available tools, it can be difficult for the architect of a real-time system to select the best fit to analyze his/her particular system. Our framework enables her/him to compare tools by taking the following steps:

1. System specification: specify the system in RTSpec and apply automatic translations to generate an input for some existing tools.
2. Comparative experiment: analyze the system with several tools and compare their analysis results.

6.2   For Developers of Analyzers

With the advance of research on schedulability analysis, researchers propose new methods and implement new tools. Such new methods often incorporate new concepts for characterizing real-time systems more faithfully than existing models, so as to obtain more precise analysis results. The incompatibility and incomparability between the timing models underlying all these tools lead to difficulties for the developer of a new analyzer to argue about the advantages of their new tool over existing analyzers.

Our framework enables tool developers to formally relate their timing models to existing ones and to conduct comparative experiments. More specifically, let T denote a new tool, and M_T the timing model underlying tool T. The workflow for the developer of T is as follows:

1. Semantics definition: Formalize M_T by extending RTLib, i.e. providing an operational semantics for the new concepts in M_T by refining or modifying the related concepts in RTLib. The extension of automata templates can be conducted with the UPPAAL model checker. Our tool RTLibEx helps to extend the data types in RTLib.

---

[8] http://www.timestool.com/.

2. Syntax definition: Extend the syntax of RTSpec so as to represent the new concepts in M_T. In principle this could be automated in RTLibEx but the process is manual at the moment.

3. Translator development: Develop a translator between RTSpec and the input format of T. Additionally, whenever possible a semantic mapping of RTSpec extensions for T to basic elements must be provided to enable comparison with tools which cannot handle such features.

4. Benchmark specification: Design some benchmarks in RTSpec, or in the input format of T if a translator from T to RTSpec is implemented.

5. Comparative experiment: Conduct an analysis of the benchmarks with various tools, and compare their analysis results.

7   Conclusion

This paper presents our ongoing work on a framework for evaluating schedulability analysis tools. We propose RTSpec as a common format for specifying real-time systems. The formal semantics of RTSpec is represented by a modular and extensible UPPAAL model library, which covers a wide range of terminology in schedulability analysis. We are developing a tool chain which translates RTSpec files into an input for diverse tools, such that a system only has to be specified once to be analyzed by several tools.

Compared to more general formalisms such as Amalthea [1] or MARTE [20], the expressiveness of RTSpec is constrained to only support features that are useful for rigorous timing analysis, i.e. supported by static analyzers. This principle allows us to formalize all concepts used in RTSpec, and hence enables rigorous mappings between various timing models.

For evaluating various timing analysis tools, researchers have developed tool-neutral languages and implemented their mappings to different tools, e.g. in [22] and Waruna. However, this approach has two defects: (1) it cannot ensure the correctness of the mappings; (2) a special feature which can be expressed by one tool may have no direct mapping in other tools. With our approach, the semantics of the terminology is defined independent from the translations between tools. The semantics of the formalism of each tool helps users to understand the concepts and the assumptions underlying the tool. With the explicit semantics, different but related concepts can be mapped to each other through approximation/abstraction.

RTSpec serves as an extensible framework for connecting different formalisms. Currently, the expressivity of RTSpec Basic is the common subset of the existing formalisms. Next, we will extend RTSpec, in collaboration with the tool developers, to incorporate the special features of their formalisms. The aim is to incorporate the important features of existing tools, so that the tools can be evaluated with a comprehensive set of benchmarks. We are still developing the benchmarks, and will present them later.

Note that in this paper the primary usage of UPPAAL models is as the operational semantics of the terminology concerning real-time systems. Given specific RT systems, the UPPAAL model checker can be used for exact timing analysis, if the complexity of the model does not exceed the capability of the model checker.

Ongoing and Future Work. Let us summarize here the topics on which we are currently working or plan to work in the near future.

- *Extension of RTLib.* To encompass the key elements of the pyCPA and MAST timing models, RTLib is currently being extended in two directions: the platform model, to take shared resources into account, and the task model, to handle more complex dependencies between tasks.
- *Semantic mappings.* We want to investigate mappings from timing model extensions to the basic timing model. In particular we need to rigorously define mappings between timing models based on their formal semantics, and prove their correctness in the sense that schedulability analysis on the approximated system specification is possibly pessimistic but still correct.
- *Extension of RTSpec and its associated tool chain.* The current RTSpec is based on the basic timing model defined by RTLib Basic, which is the common subset of the timing models of various analyzers. Further, we will extend RTSpec with typical special features supported by some of the existing analyzers and extend the corresponding translators.
- *Comparative experiments and benchmarks.* Finally, we will develop a set of benchmarks derived from synthetic and industrial cases, and conduct a comparative evaluation of existing analyzers. The analysis results thus obtained with these benchmarks will show the relative strengths of the analyzers on different types of systems, and help users to choose tools according to the features of their systems.

Acknowledgment. The authors would like to thank Claire Pagetti and Eric Noulard from Onera, Olivier Cros from ECE Paris, and Jean-François Monin from Verimag for the fruitful and inspiring discussions.

References

1. The Amalthea project. http://www.amalthea-project.org/
2. Albers, K., Slomka, F.: An event stream driven approximation for the analysis of real-time systems. In: Proceedings of the 16th Euromicro Conference on Real-Time Systems, ECRTS 2004, pp. 187–195. IEEE (2004)
3. Alur, R.: Timed automata. In: Halbwachs, N., Peled, D. (eds.) CAV 1999. LNCS, vol. 1633, pp. 8–22. Springer, Heidelberg (1999). doi:10.1007/3-540-48683-6_3
4. Amnell, T., et al.: UPPAAL - now, next, and future. In: Cassez, F., Jard, C., Rozoy, B., Ryan, M.D. (eds.) MOVEP 2000. LNCS, vol. 2067, pp. 99–124. Springer, Heidelberg (2001). doi:10.1007/3-540-45510-8_4
5. Amnell, T., Fersman, E., Mokrushin, L., Pettersson, P., Yi, W.: TIMES: a tool for schedulability analysis and code generation of real-time systems. In: Larsen, K.G., Niebert, P. (eds.) FORMATS 2003. LNCS, vol. 2791, pp. 60–72. Springer, Heidelberg (2004). doi:10.1007/978-3-540-40903-8_6

6. Bengtsson, J., Yi, W.: Timed automata: semantics, algorithms and tools. In: Desel, J., Reisig, W., Rozenberg, G. (eds.) ACPN 2003. LNCS, vol. 3098, pp. 87–124. Springer, Heidelberg (2004). doi:10.1007/978-3-540-27755-2_3

7. Boudjadar, A., David, A., Kim, J.H., Larsen, K.G., Mikučionis, M., Nyman, U., Skou, A.: Statistical and exact schedulability analysis of hierarchical scheduling systems. Sci. Comput. Program. **127**, 103–130 (2016)

8. Cordovilla, M., Boniol, F., Forget, J., Noulard, E., Pagetti, C.: Developing critical embedded systems on multicore architectures: the Prelude-SchedMCore toolset. In: 19th International Conference on Real-Time and Network Systems (2011)

9. David, A., Illum, J., Larsen, K.G., Skou, A.: Model-based framework for schedulability analysis using UPPAAL 4.1. Model-Based Des. Embed. Syst. **1**(1), 93–119 (2009)

10. Davis, R.I., Burns, A.: A survey of hard real-time scheduling for multiprocessor systems. ACM Comput. Surv. (CSUR) **43**(4), 35 (2011)

11. Decotigny, D., Puaut, I.: Artisst: an extensible and modular simulation tool for real-time systems. In: Proceedings of the Fifth IEEE International Symposium on Object-Oriented Real-Time Distributed Computing, (ISORC 2002), pp. 365–372. IEEE (2002)

12. Diemer, J., Axer, P., Ernst, R.: Compositional performance analysis in python with pyCPA. In: Proceedings of WATERS (2012)

13. Feiler, H., Lewis, B., Vestal, S.: The SAE architecture analysis and design language (AADL) standard. In: IEEE RTAS Workshop (2003)

14. Fersman, E., Krcal, P., Pettersson, P., Yi, W.: Task automata: schedulability, decidability and undecidability. Inf. Comput. **205**(8), 1149–1172 (2007)

15. Harbour, M.G., García, J.G., Gutiérrez, J.P., Moyano, J.D.: MAST: Modeling and analysis suite for real time applications. In: 13th Euromicro Conference on Real-Time Systems, pp. 125–134. IEEE (2001)

16. Henia, R., Hamann, A., Jersak, M., Racu, R., Richter, K., Ernst, R.: System level performance analysis - the SymTA/S approach. IEE Proc.-Comput. Digit. Tech. **152**(2), 148–166 (2005)

17. Larsen, K.G., Pettersson, P., Yi, W.: UPPAAL in a nutshell. Int. J. Softw. Tools Technol. Transf. (STTT) **1**(1), 134–152 (1997)

18. Liu, C.L., Layland, J.W.: Scheduling algorithms for multiprogramming in a hard-real-time environment. J. ACM (JACM) **20**(1), 46–61 (1973)

19. Mikučionis, M., Larsen, K.G., Rasmussen, J.I., Nielsen, B., Skou, A., Palm, S.U., Pedersen, J.S., Hougaard, P.: Schedulability analysis using UPPAAL: Herschel-Planck case study. In: Margaria, T., Steffen, B. (eds.) ISoLA 2010. LNCS, vol. 6416, pp. 175–190. Springer, Heidelberg (2010). doi:10.1007/978-3-642-16561-0_21

20. OMG: UML profile for MARTE: Modeling and analysis of real-time embedded systems (2011). http://www.omg.org/spec/MARTE/1.1/PDF/

21. OMG: Modeling and analysis of real-time and embedded systems. Object Management Group (2008)

22. Perathoner, S., Wandeler, E., Thiele, L.: Evaluation and comparison of performance analysis methods for distributed embedded systems. Master's thesis, Swiss Federal Institute of Technology, Zürich (2006)

23. Perathoner, S., Wandeler, E., Thiele, L., Hamann, A., Schliecker, S., Henia, R., Racu, R., Ernst, R., González Harbour, M.: Influence of different abstractions on the performance analysis of distributed hard real-time systems. Des. Autom. Embed. Syst. **13**(1), 27–49 (2009)

24. Sha, L., Abdelzaher, T., Årzén, K.E., Cervin, A., Baker, T., Burns, A., Buttazzo, G., Caccamo, M., Lehoczky, J., Mok, A.K.: Real time scheduling theory: a historical perspective. Real-Time Syst. **28**(2–3), 101–155 (2004)

25. Shan, L., Wang, Y., Fu, N., Zhou, X., Zhao, L., Wan, L., Qiao, L., Chen, J.: Formal verification of lunar rover control software using UPPAAL. In: Jones, C., Pihlajasaari, P., Sun, J. (eds.) FM 2014. LNCS, vol. 8442, pp. 718–732. Springer, Cham (2014). doi:10.1007/978-3-319-06410-9_48

26. Singhoff, F., Legrand, J., Nana, L., Marcé, L.: Cheddar: a flexible real time scheduling framework. In: ACM SIGAda Ada Letters, vol. 24, pp. 1–8. ACM (2004)

27. Stigge, M., Yi, W.: Graph-based models for real-time workload: a survey. Real-Time Syst. **51**(5), 602–636 (2015)

28. Team, SysML Merge: Systems modeling language (SysML) specification. OMG document: ad/2006-03-01 (2006)

29. Thiele, L., Chakraborty, S., Naedele, M.: Real-time calculus for scheduling hard real-time systems. In: Proceedings of the 2000 IEEE International Symposium on Circuits and Systems, ISCAS 2000 Geneva, vol. 4, pp. 101–104. IEEE (2000)

WUPPAAL: Computation of Worst-Case Execution-Time for Binary Programs with UPPAAL

Franck Cassez[1]([⊠]), Pablo Gonzalez de Aledo[1,3], and Peter Gjøl Jensen[1,2]

[1] Macquarie University, Sydney, Australia
franck.cassez@mq.edu.au
[2] Aalborg University, Aalborg, Denmark
[3] University of Cantabria, Santander, Spain

Abstract. We address the problem of computing the worst-case execution-time (WCET) of binary programs using a real-time model-checker. In our previous work, we introduced a fully automated and modular methodology to build a model (network of timed automata) that combined a binary program and the hardware to run the program on. Computing the WCET amounts to finding the longest path time-wise in this model, which can be done using a real-time model checker like UPPAAL.

In this work, we generalise the previous approach and we define a generic framework to support arbitrary binary language and hardware.

We have implemented our new approach in an extended version of UPPAAL, called WUPPAAL. Experimental results using some standard benchmarks suite for WCET computation (from Mälardalen University) show that our technique is practical and promising.

Keywords: Binary program · Control flow graph · Worst-case execution-time

1 Introduction

Embedded real-time systems (ERTS) are composed of a set of periodic tasks (software) to run on a given architecture (hardware). The tasks are usually released at periodic time intervals. For safety-critical ERTS, each task must be completed by a deadline (relative to the release time). Checking whether a set of periodic tasks can be scheduled on a processor such that they always complete before their deadline is a *schedulability analysis*.

Tests for schedulability are based on the tasks' parameters, among them an upper bound for the *execution time* of each task. Over-estimating the execution time of a task may be safe but can also result in a set of tasks being declared non schedulable. This may lead to a choice of over-powered and over-expensive hardware.

P.G. Jensen—Part of this work was done while this author visited Macquarie University.

L. Aceto et al. (Eds.): Larsen Festschrift, LNCS 10460, pp. 560–577, 2017.
DOI: 10.1007/978-3-319-63121-9_28

With the ever increasing connectivity of many devices, ERTS are also subject to malicious attacks. Some of them can make use of time measurements to establish communication channels (*timing covert channel*): private information can be communicated or leaked to attackers by controlling/observing the time intervals between events (e.g., how long a computation takes).

It follows that tight bounds for the execution time of the tasks are instrumental to designing safe (schedulable), efficient and secure ERTS. Each task in an ERTS executes a program. The execution time of the program may depend on the input. The worst-case execution-time (WCET) of the program is the supremum of the execution times of the program over all the input. Computing the WCET for binary programs is a non-trivial task for at least two reasons:

- the set of input data may be very big and simulating the program over a subset of the input data only provides a lower bound of the worst-case execution-time;
- the hardware that runs the program is complex (pipelined architecture, caches) and it is effectively a *timed concurrent system* (e.g., the pipeline runs in parallel with the caches and they both have timing specifications.)

The WCET Problem. Given a binary program P, some input data d and the hardware H, the *execution time* of P for the input d on H, denoted Xtime (P, d, H), is measured as the number of processor cycles between the beginning and end of P's computation for d (we assume P always terminates.) The *worst-case execution time (WCET)* of program P on hardware H, denoted $\mathsf{WCET}(P, H)$, is the supremum of the $\mathsf{Xtime}(P, d, H)$ for d ranging over the input data domain $\mathcal{D}$:

$$\mathsf{WCET}(P, H) = \sup_{d \in \mathcal{D}} \mathsf{Xtime}(P, d, H). \tag{1}$$

The WCET problem asks the following:

"Given P and H, compute $\mathsf{WCET}(P, H)$".

In general, the WCET problem is undecidable because otherwise we could solve the halting problem. However, for programs that always terminate and have a bounded number of paths, it is computable. Indeed the possible runs of the program can be represented by a finite tree (and there is a finite number states for the program and the hardware). This does not mean that the problem is tractable though: the (values of the) input data (e.g., an fixed-size array to be sorted) are usually unknown and the number of program paths to be explored may grow exponentially in the size of the program.

As mentioned before, programs run on increasingly complex architectures featuring multi-stage *pipelines* and fast memory components like *caches*: they both influence the WCET in a complicated manner. It is then a challenging problem to determine a precise WCET even for relatively small programs running on complex single-core architectures.

Computing a precise WCET for a given program is very hard and the WCET problem is usually re-stated as:

"Given P and H, compute a *tight upper bound* of $\mathsf{WCET}(P, H)$".

Tightness can be measured (see [9]) by comparing actual WCET to the ones computed using a particular method. In the sequel we use WCET(P, H) to denote an upper bound of the WCET for a given program.

Standard Methods and Tools for Computing WCET. The survey article [23] provides an exhaustive presentation of WCET computation techniques and tools. A first set of methods based on simulations [5, 18, 19] are not suitable for safety-critical ERTS as they only provide lower bounds for the WCET.

A second set of methods rely on the construction of a Control Flow Graph (CFG) for the binary program to analyse, and the determination of *loop bounds*. The CFG is then annotated with some timing information about the cache misses/hits (some may/must analysis using abstract interpretation based techniques) and pipeline stalls to build a finite model of the system. A final paths analysis is carried out on this model e.g., using Integer Linear Programming (ILP). There are many implementations of this technique, the most prominent one is probably aiT [1, 13] which combines static analysis tools and ILP for computing WCET.

Real-Time Model-Checking Based Methods for Computing WCET. Considering that (*i*) modern architectures are composed of *concurrent* components (the units of the different stages of the pipeline, the caches) and (*ii*) the *synchronisation* of these components depends on *timing constraints* (time to execute in one stage of the pipeline, time to fetch data from the cache), formal models like *timed automata* [2] and state-of-the-art *real-time model-checkers* like UPPAAL [3, 16] appear well-suited to address the WCET problem.

The use of network of timed automata (NTA) and the model-checker UPPAAL for computing WCET on pipelined processors with caches was first reported in [11, 12] where the METAMOC method is described. METAMOC consists in: (1) computing the CFG of a program, (2) composing this CFG with a (network of timed automata) model of the processor and the caches. Computing the WCET is then reduced to computing the longest path (time-wise) in a NTA.

The previous framework is very elegant yet has some shortcomings: (1) METAMOC relies on a *value analysis* phase to compute the CFG but this may not terminate, (2) some programs cannot be analysed (if they contain register-indirect jumps), (3) manual annotations (loop bounds) is required on the binary program, and (4) the *unrolling* of loops is not safe for some cache replacement policies (FIFO). In our previous work [7, 9] we have reported some results on the computation of WCET using NTA that overcome the limitations of METAMOC: (1) we introduced an automatic method to compute a CFG and a reduced abstract program equivalent WCET-wise to the original program; (2) we designed detailed hardware formal models and (3) we evaluated the accuracy of our technique (comparison of measured execution times and the results of our analysis).

The technique we introduced in [7, 9] still has some drawbacks:

- the UPPAAL model (NTA) contains the CFG of the program and the machinery that is needed to simulate some instructions (written as functions in

UPPAAL); some instructions (e.g., setting the overflow flag) are partially modelled because of the restricted expressiveness of the C-like operators supported by UPPAAL;

- the UPPAAL model (NTA) also contains components to explicitly model the caches as large arrays (of cache lines) which contributes a big part of the state of the system;
- as a result, we rely on UPPAAL to perform a lot of discrete computations which is not effective; moreover, the discrete state of the UPPAAL model contains a large amount of information (e.g., the full state of the caches) which also impacts the efficiency of the UPPAAL analysis engine.

Our Contribution. Based on our previous work [7,9], we propose three new contributions: (1) a generic framework for computing WCET which is language agnostic; (2) a new implementation of our framework based on an extended version UPPAAL and (3) a tool chain that combines our extended UPPAAL and an off-the-shelf binary program simulator (based on *gdb* [22]).

Outline of the Paper. In Sect. 2 we recall how the WCET can be computed via model-checking. The material in this section is based on [7,9]. In Sect. 3, we introduce our new generic technique to compute the WCET of arbitrary programs. Examples are provided for an mono-processor pipelined ARM architecture. Section 4 provides details of the implementation of our technique, a tool chain architecture and some experimental results.

2   Computation of WCET via Real-Time Model-Checking

In this section we introduce the basic concepts of program runs together with an abstract model of the hardware in order to compute the execution time of a sequence of program instructions.

Hardware. The hardware usually consists of a finite set $\mathcal{R}$ of registers, a multi-stage execution pipeline and caches (e.g., instruction and data caches). It typically supports a finite set of instructions, $\mathcal{I}$, e.g., `mov r1,r2` is an instruction that copies the contents of register r_2 into register r_1. The main memory component is a table of words of a given width 32-bit or 64-bit words. $\mathcal{M}$ is the (finite) set of main memory cells and we denote $\mathcal{D}$ the memory domain (e.g., 32-bit or 64-bit words). A memory state is thus a map from $\mathcal{M}$ to $\mathcal{D}$. The caches and the pipeline are essential components of the hardware performance-wise but they are not necessary to define the semantics of the instructions. We omit them for now and will account for them later in this section. A *state* of the hardware is fully determined by the contents of the registers, the contents of the memory and the contents of the pipelines and caches. The hardware has a designated register, the *program counter* that points to the next instruction to process. An example of such an architecture, the ARM920T, is given in Fig. 1. The orange blocks are the blocks we need to model to compute the execution time of program runs.

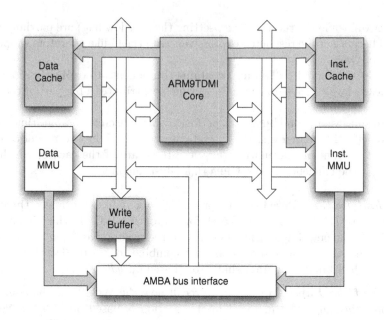

Fig. 1. Simplified ARM920T architecture (Color figure online)

Program Runs. A binary program is a map $P : \mathbb{P} \to \mathcal{I}$, with $\mathbb{P} \subseteq \mathcal{M}$, that associates with some memory locations $\ell \in \mathbb{P}$ an instruction. $P(\ell)$ is the instruction to be processed when the program counter of the hardware is at ℓ.

Given a program P, we let $\mathcal{L}_H(P) \subseteq \mathbb{P}^*$ be the set of *valid* executions of P on H. Actually we only require $\mathcal{L}_H(P)$ to over-approximate the set of feasible executions of the program P. To define this set we need to take into account the semantics of each instruction in $\mathcal{I}$, and the values of the registers of H and the memory state: this state is given by a valuation $\nu : \mathcal{R} \cup \mathcal{M} \to \mathcal{D}$. There are usually many different possible initial states of the hardware (e.g., a sorting

```
1   int c_entry(int a, int b){
2       int c=1,i;
3       for (i = 0; i < 10; i++) {
4           if(a < b){
5               c *= 10;
6           } else {
7               c += 10;
8           }
9       }
10      return c;
11  }
```

Listing 1.1. Prog1

program that sorts an array of k arbitrary elements, there are $\mathcal{D}^k$ initial possible input data).

An example of a binary program compiled for the ARM920T is provided in Fig. 2a. This program can be obtained by compiling the C program Prog1 (Listing 1.1). The Control Flow Graph (CFG) is given in Fig. 2b. The semantics of the program does not depend on the pipeline architecture nor on the caches: these components only impact the execution time of the program runs. However, to ensure that the WCET of each program is well-defined, we may assume that $\mathcal{L}_H(P)$ is finite. Otherwise it contains arbitrary long sequences (the alphabet $\mathbb{P}$ is finite) and the set of execution times is unbounded and the WCET is $+\infty$.

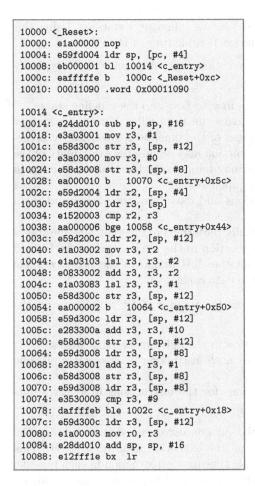

```
10000 <_Reset>:
10000: e1a00000 nop
10004: e59fd004 ldr sp, [pc, #4]
10008: eb000001 bl    10014 <c_entry>
1000c: eafffffe b     1000c <_Reset+0xc>
10010: 00011090 .word 0x00011090

10014 <c_entry>:
10014: e24dd010 sub sp, sp, #16
10018: e3a03001 mov r3, #1
1001c: e58d300c str r3, [sp, #12]
10020: e3a03000 mov r3, #0
10024: e58d3008 str r3, [sp, #8]
10028: ea000010 b     10070 <c_entry+0x5c>
1002c: e59d2004 ldr r2, [sp, #4]
10030: e59d3000 ldr r3, [sp]
10034: e1520003 cmp r2, r3
10038: aa000006 bge 10058 <c_entry+0x44>
1003c: e59d200c ldr r2, [sp, #12]
10040: e1a03002 mov r3, r2
10044: e1a03103 lsl r3, r3, #2
10048: e0833002 add r3, r3, r2
1004c: e1a03083 lsl r3, r3, #1
10050: e58d300c str r3, [sp, #12]
10054: ea000002 b     10064 <c_entry+0x50>
10058: e59d300c ldr r3, [sp, #12]
1005c: e283300a add r3, r3, #10
10060: e58d300c str r3, [sp, #12]
10064: e59d3008 ldr r3, [sp, #8]
10068: e2833001 add r3, r3, #1
1006c: e58d3008 str r3, [sp, #8]
10070: e59d3008 ldr r3, [sp, #8]
10074: e3530009 cmp r3, #9
10078: daffffeb ble 1002c <c_entry+0x18>
1007c: e59d300c ldr r3, [sp, #12]
10080: e1a00003 mov r0, r3
10084: e28dd010 add sp, sp, #16
10088: e12fff1e bx  lr
```

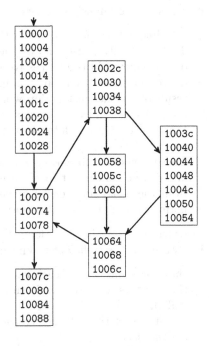

(b) CFG of the binary program

(a) ARM binary for Prog1

Fig. 2. ARM binary and corresponding CFG for Prog1

The set $\mathcal{L}_H(P)$ of program runs is finite but may contain more than one trace even if the program is deterministic. For instance in Prog1 (Listing 1.1), the values of a, b are arbitrary at the beginning of the program because they are parameters of the function c_entry. This makes the test at line 4 a non-deterministic choice in our program over-approximation because the values of a and b are arbitrary (there are input parameters of the c_entry function). We can over-approximate the set of runs of this program by assuming that each time the test at line 4 is performed, the outcome is either true or false and both cases should be taken into account to compute the WCET. Notice that this is an over-approximation if $a < b$ evaluates to TRUE (resp. FALSE) the first time it must evaluate to TRUE (resp. FALSE) in the following iterations. Using this strategy we generate a super set of the set feasible runs of Prog1.

Execution Time of a Run. The execution time of a run $\sigma \in \mathbb{P}^*$ typically depends on the following factors:

- the time it takes for the instructions in σ to flow into the pipeline stages. This is usually non-trivial as the stages run in parallel. Moreover, the flow of instructions in the successive stages of the pipeline is governed by precedence rules: the execution of an instruction may require the availability of the result of another instruction which may temporarily block an instruction in a pipeline stage: this is known as a pipeline *stall*.
- the time it takes to fetch instructions and data from the caches and main memory.
  These memory transactions are usually performed in different pipeline stages and can be concurrent (e.g., an instruction in the *fetch* stage can be fetched from the instruction cache while another instruction in the *memory* stage performs some transactions with the data cache.)

In order to determine how long it takes for a run $\sigma \in \mathbb{P}^*$ to execute on the hardware H, it is sufficient to know:

- the processing time of each instruction in the different pipeline stages,
- the registers read from/written to by each instruction (to determine pipeline stalls),
- the status of the memory transactions for the instructions in σ: cache *hits* and *misses*.

Given a run $\rho \in \mathcal{L}_H(P)$, we can build an *annotated run* $\tilde{\rho}$ that contains the information required to fully determine the execution time of ρ on H. This extended run may capture the processing time of the instruction in each pipeline stage, the registers read from/written and the cache hits and misses. We let $\mathcal{L}_H^a(P)$ be the set of annotated runs associated with $\mathcal{L}_H(P)$.

For example, the following run $\rho = 10000.10004.10008.10014.10018$ in $\mathcal{L}_H(P)$ can be annotated with the time it takes to process each corresponding instruction in Prog1 (Fig. 2b), and whether fetching the instruction (from the instruction cache) will result in cache Hit or a cache Miss. Hence $\mathcal{L}_H^a(P)$ can be defined as sequences of pairs $(k, b) \in \mathbb{N} \times \mathbb{B}$ with the following meaning: k is the time it takes to process the instruction at p in the execution stage (E stage) of the pipeline; if b is true, fetching the instruction from the instruction cache results in a Hit otherise it is a Miss. This transformation will give an annotated run $\tilde{\rho} = (2, \text{TRUE}).(1, \text{FALSE}).(2, \text{TRUE}).(2, \text{FALSE}).(1, \text{FALSE})$.

As mentioned earlier, it is noticeable that the hardware model needed to compute the execution time of a run is much simpler than the actual concrete hardware model: there is no need to model the actual processing unit (e.g., registers, memory) nor to perform actual computations (e.g., execute instructions).

Formal Hardware Model. As a sequence $\tilde{\rho} \in \mathcal{L}_H^a(P)$ contains enough information to compute the execution time of a program run $\rho \in \mathcal{L}_H(P)$ we can define an abstract model of the hardware as a timed automaton *transducer*, $Aut(H)$, that maps each $\tilde{\rho} \in \mathcal{L}_H^a(P)$ to a positive natural number $Aut(H)(\rho)$, which is the execution time of ρ on H. Hence the WCET of a program P on the hardware H is defined by:

$$\text{WCET}(P, H) = \max_{\sigma \in \mathcal{L}_H^a(P)} Aut(H)(\sigma). \qquad (2)$$

As $\mathcal{L}_H^a(P)$ over-approximates the set of program runs, we ensure that the value of the WCET we compute (Eq. (2)) is an upper bound of the actual WCET (this assumes that the hardware model $Aut(H)$ correctly models the timing behaviour of the hardware).

Modular Computation of the WCET of a Program. In practice to compute $\text{WCET}(P, H)$ we need to provide a generator for $\mathcal{L}_H^a(P)$ and the model of the hardware $Aut(H)$. $\mathcal{L}_H^a(P)$ can be generated by a finite state automaton $Aut(P)$ (see [7,9]). In general $\mathcal{L}_H^a(P)$ is a finite set of runs and can be defined by a finite computation tree.

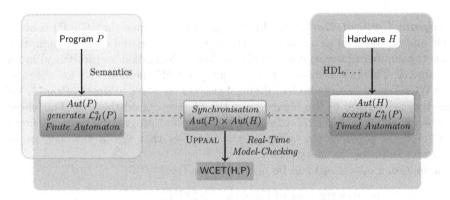

Fig. 3. Modular computation of WCET

In [7,9] the modular computation of the WCET depicted in Fig. 3 is fully implemented in UPPAAL as follows:

- a UPPAAL automaton, $Aut(P)$, that generates $\mathcal{L}_H^a(P)$ is computed based on the control flow graph of a program (for an ARM architecture.)
- the hardware model is provided for a given architecture (ARM920T). It comprises of a model of the pipeline and a model for the caches (complete model with the current state of the caches.) Notice that our method is robust against the so-called *timing anomalies* [10].
- the WCET can be computed either using a binary search or using UPPAAL *sup* operator.

This implementation has several drawbacks:

- the automaton $Aut(P)$ that generates $\mathcal{L}_H^a(P)$ is implemented using a limited C-like language. This is sometimes cumbersome and the semantics of some instructions had to be partially modelled (e.g., some bit-wise operations on registers). The result is that the UPPAAL model of the program which is a finite automaton, is hard to encode using UPPAAL restricted set of C supported operations. This set was sufficient to model a large set of instructions of the ARM920T processor but may be too limited to model the semantics of more complex processors.

– the FIFO caches (instruction and data) are modelled precisely using an array to model the lines in the caches. The hardware model $Aut(H)$ contains the full state of the caches. This makes the discrete part of the state of the system $Aut(P) \times Aut(H)$ very large and impacts the efficiency of the model-checking algorithm.

In the next section we describe how to overcome the previous limitations by having $\mathcal{L}_H^a(P)$ generated by a C-library outside UPPAAL.

3   WUPPAAL

Program Computation Tree. In this section we assume that $\mathcal{L}_H^a(P)$ is available and represented as a finite tree $\mathsf{Tree}_H^a(P)$. This is based on the assumption that the number of iterations in the loops do not depend on an (arbitrary) input parameter. This is a usual assumption[1] in the WCET methods [23] as otherwise the WCET may be unbounded. Figure 4 shows a sub-tree of $\mathsf{Tree}_H^a(Prog1)$. We use a *sliced* version of the binary program when we build the tree. This sliced version is equivalent WCET-wise [6,9] to the actual program. The components $\mathcal{M}^i$ in Fig. 4 provides the values of the variables that are in the slice (some registers and other memory cells).

The following operations can be performed on $\mathsf{Tree}_H^a(P)$:

– $get\_init()$ returns the root of the tree $\mathsf{Tree}_H^a(P)$.
– $get\_next(n)$ returns the list of children of the node n (empty if n is a leaf).
– $hit\_ins(n)$ is a Boolean that indicates whether the instruction to be executed at n will result in a hit or a miss in the instruction cache.
– $get\_exec(n)$ returns the execution (in cycles) in the E stage of the pipeline for the instruction at n.

We refer to these operations as the *tree-API* in the sequel. The implementations of the Tree-API operations live outside UPPAAL in the library libgdb2uppaal (see Sect. 4 for the WUPPAAL architecture). The UPPAAL template in Fig. 5 implements a full search on $\mathsf{Tree}_H^a(P)$ given the $get\_init()$ and $get\_next(n)$ functions; we assume each node of the tree has at most 2 children for the sake of simplicity. The UPPAAL version of $get\_init()$ is get_init(succ) and fills in the vector succ with the pair $(get\_init(), \perp)$ ($\perp$ denotes the absence of node). Similarly $get\_next(n)$ is implemented by the function get_next(n,succ) and fills in the vector of integers succ with the children of n where succ[0] (resp. succ[1]) is the first (resp. second) child of n; the $\perp$ value is represented by

---

[1] An exact test for this assumption does not exist as this problem is undecidable.

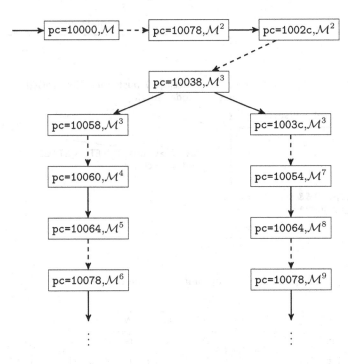

Fig. 4. Subtree of $\mathsf{Tree}_H^a(Prog1)$ where we let $\mathcal{M}$ be the memory tracked, and $r3 = 10$ in $\mathcal{M}^2$. Dashed arrows indicate sequences of deterministic instructions omitted for brevity.

a negative integer. The non-deterministic guarded choices in the template Program Automaton (Fig. 5) push the children nodes to be processed to the first stage of the pipeline (see hardware model below). Each path through the template Program Automaton from the initial location (double circle) to the END location represents an annotated trace of $\mathcal{L}_H^a(P)$. When we model-check a safety property on this model, UPPAAL generates all the traces in $\mathcal{L}_H^a(P)$.

Hardware Specification. The hardware consists of a multi-stage execution pipeline and the caches (e.g., instruction and data caches). As a case-study we model an ARM920T 5-stage *execution pipeline*, the instruction cache and main memory components. The pipeline can execute concurrently the different stages (Fetch, Decode, Execute, Memory, Writeback) needed to fully process an instruction. An instruction is fetched (from the instruction cache) in stage F, decoding and operand register accesses occur in D, execution in E and if there are load/store instructions the memory accesses happen in M. The results are written back to registers in W. The (normal) flow of instructions in the pipeline is shown in Fig. 6. This optimal flow may be slowed down when pipeline *stalls* occur: if the instruction $i + 1$ needs a register written to by instruction i there will be a one cycle stall at cycle $j + 3$ for instruction $i + 1$; when the W stage is finished for instruction i, the E stage can begin for instruction $i + 1$.

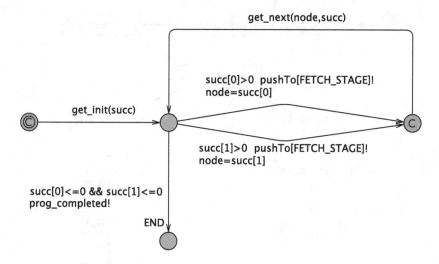

Fig. 5. Program automaton to enumerate $\mathcal{L}_H^a(P)$.

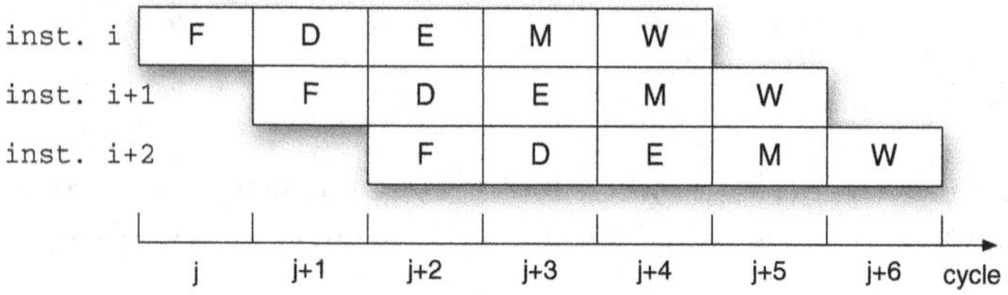

Fig. 6. Pipeline of the ARM920T

Hardware Abstract Model. A formal model of the hardware for the ARM920T can be specified by a network of timed automata [9]. We provide here simpler models of the hardware because we factor out the actual state of the caches: to compute the execution time of a sequence of instructions we only need to know whether a transaction with a cache is a hit or a miss. This information is provided by each node in $\mathrm{Tree}_H^a(P)$ ($\mathcal{L}_H^a(P)$) for a given program P. It can be computed by monitoring the addresses that are used on a given trace and using a model of the caches (e.g., number of lines, ways and FIFO replacement policy). In [8] we also proposed an abstraction/refinement scheme to model the caches. For instance the 5-stage pipeline of the ARM920T can be specified by a network of 5 timed automata (see Fig. 7) each of them modelling a single stage of the execution pipeline.

Each stage automaton has a unique identifier **me** (an integer). The values of this identifier for the templates (F, D, E, M, W) are respectively (0, 1, 2, 3, 4). This encodes the fact that the stages F, D, E, M, W are ordered: each node of $\mathrm{Tree}_H^a(P)$ flows from one stage k to the next $k+1$ when the pushTo[k] channels synchronise. For instance, the F-Stage template automaton is idle until

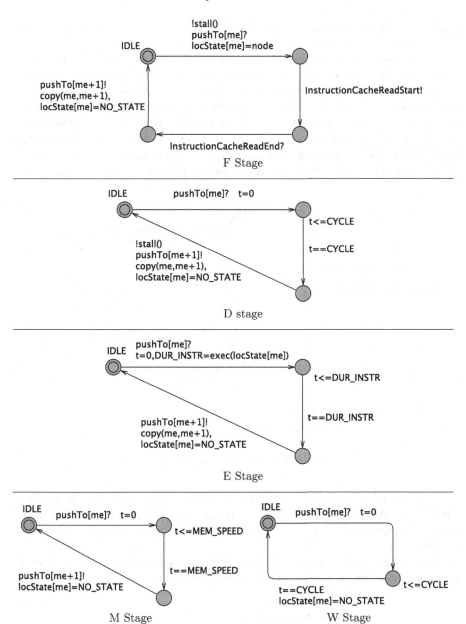

Fig. 7. Timed automata for F, D, E, M and W stages (pipeline ARM920T).

the Program Automaton (Fig. 5) pushes a node via the pushTo[0]? transition. It updates the local *state* of this stage 0 (locState[0]=node) where node is a (meta) variable used to retrieve the value sent by the Program Automaton that issues the pushTo[0]! command. The F stage template automaton then synchronises with the instruction cache (see Fig. 7) to simulate the time it takes to fetch the instruction from the instruction cache.

The memory stage (M stage) assumes a constant time to read data from the data cache: each transaction takes MEM_SPEED cycles. We can easily model the data cache but for the sake of simplicity we use a simple version here. The other stages (D, E, M, W) are based on the same logic: they are idle until the previous stage pushes some information to them. The copy(me,me+1) commands transfers the information from stage me to stage me+1. When going back to the IDLE (initial) location, the local information of the templates are reset to the default value NO_STATE which indicates that the pipeline state is empty.

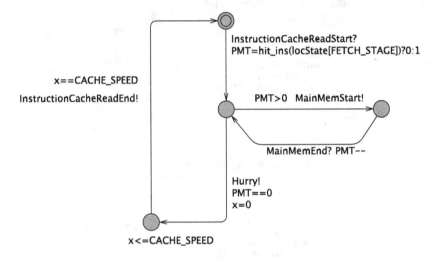

Fig. 8. Instruction cache template.

The instruction cache is specified by the template timed automaton in Fig. 8. The PMT variable holds the number of Pending Memory Transactions. This number is determined by the hit_ins function that can be retrieved from the annotated node in the tree.

Finally the main memory template simply simulates how long it takes to perform a transaction (read or write) with the main memory.

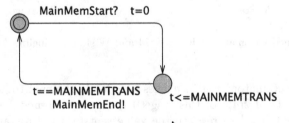

Fig. 9. Main memory template.

4   Implementation and Experimental Results

Tool Chain. Let us dwell on the tool chain we have constructed to demonstrate our methodology described in Sect. 3. The tool-chain, visualized in Fig. 10, is composed of five components:

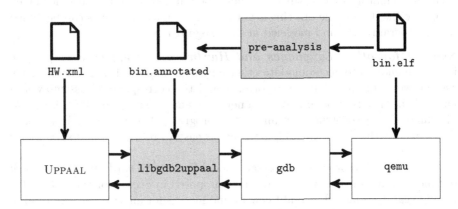

Fig. 10. The tool chain of WUPPAAL. Orange blocks are the modules we implemented. Other blocks are existing modules. (Color figure online)

- a **pre-analysis** module for constructing an annotated program that can be used to generate the program traces $\mathcal{L}_H(P)$; this step is developed in SCALA and uses some powerful Grammar and Language Processing packages KIAMA [20] and SBT-RATS! [21].
- **qemu** [4] to emulate the chosen hardware and enables us to compute the next state after executing a program instruction. As an example of usage, we set up the hardware to a given initial state (program counter and values of registers and stack), and with **qemu** we can compute the effect of an instruction. What is communicated back (using **gdb**) is the next program counter and the next state of the registers and stack.
- **gdb** [22] for inspecting **qemu**,
- **libgdb2uppaal** to implement the tree-API given at the beginning of Sect. 3.
- a Timed Automaton model of the hardware **HW.xml** (an example is provided on Fig. 7, page 13 for the pipelines and Fig. 8, page 14 and Fig. 9, page 14 for the main memory and instruction cache.)
- UPPAAL for computing the worst-case execution time given a sequence of nodes using the Program Automaton template Fig. 5, page 11, The UPPAAL model uses an integer counter to identify the current state of the program. The **libgdb2uppaal** maintains a table that maps integers to actual program states (program counter, values of the registers and the stack). The **get_next** function in the Tree-API returns all the possible successors of a state as integers and updates the table that maps integers to program state (when a new state is encountered). The Program Automaton (Fig. 5) will explore all the successor states.

Computing the WCET for a given binary program `bin.elf` using our framework is a two-stage process. In the first stage we compute an annotated program (e.g., a CFG and the set of variables needed to generate the annotated language $\mathcal{L}_H^a(P)$) by using `pre-analysis`. In the second stage we use UPPAAL to drive a search through the state space, interfacing (by proxy of `gdb` and `libgdb2uppaal`) with the emulator of the hardware as described in Sect. 3. In the current model, we ignore the data cache but this is not a restriction as the caches can be added to the program state and modeled in the `libgdb2uppaal` library.

Support for other Languages and Hardware. The approach we propose is general enough to accommodate other languages and hardware. For instance, assume we want to use an x86 processor and the corresponding assembly language. What needs to be provided is a new `pre-analysis` module for this assembly language to construct the annotated program. The pre-analysis we have developed for the ARM assembly language is easy to re-use to build support for other languages.

We also need to provide an abstract model for the x86 hardware as a network of timed automata. The widgets we have proposed in Sect. 2 for the ARM920T pipeline can be adapted to build new formal models for an x86 platform (and of course new pipeline stages can be added if the architecture requires it).

Finally we need `qemu` (or an equivalent program) to support the emulation of the hardware. The general architecture we introduced in Fig. 10 can be re-used as well as the modular method depicted in Fig. 3 to compute the WCET for programs running on the x86.

Results. We have experimented our technique using some of the standard benchmarks [17] from Mälardalen University, for computing WCET. As we can see in Table 1, we are achieving a reasonable computation time (less than 5 s for all experiments), demonstrating the feasibility of our approach. We can also see that for all of the test-cases, the constructed trees are fairly small in size. In this paper we do not provide a thorough comparison with the actual measured execution times because we use simple models for the caches. The models used in [9] may be used in the future. The results in [9] demonstrated that our approach provides very accurate WCET and the new implementation should give similar results when precise models of the caches are used.

Table 1. The experimental results, time is given in seconds and includes startup overhead from initializing `gdb` and `qemu`. The *loc* measure is the number of lines of assembly. Note that more experiments will be added by the final submission.

Program	Loc	$|\mathsf{Tree}_H^a(P)|$	Time	WCET
duff	145	1750	4.51	61215
fibcall	48	553	2.91	19320
insertsort	84	7	2.09	210
janne_complex	67	360	3.21	12565
lcdnum	100	250	2.52	8715

5   Conclusion

We have presented a method, based on timed automata and real-time model-checking with UPPAAL, to compute the WCET of binary programs. The method we designed is generic and can accommodate arbitrary hardware. The proposed tool chain allows us to achieve a modular approach to WCET-computation, reducing the overhead needed to support new binaries, and new architectures. To support different binaries we only have to provide pre-analysis with a different input. To support different processors, it is sufficient to provide a new hardware-model (HW.xml) and emulator (qemu).

Moreover, our technique does not rely on the computation of *loop bounds* or the assumption that the hardware is free of *timing anomalies*: this is one of the strengths of the model-checking method. Another strength is that it generates a witness program trace that produces the WCET. Other interesting features of this approach includes its generality: we do not need to assume that the initial state of the caches is known. The only requirement is that the annotated language $\mathcal{L}_H^a(P)$ over-approximates the program behaviours.

Our technique is also general enough to be paired with *program refinement* techniques. As mentioned in Sect. 3 for Prog1, some traces in $\mathcal{L}_H(P)$ may not be feasible: if the first choice for the test $a < b$ is TRUE (resp. FALSE), the following test of the same condition must be TRUE (resp. FALSE). In that case we compute a refinement $R_1 \subseteq \mathcal{L}_H^a(P)$ of the annotated program to rule the spurious traces and analyse the refinement R_1. This can de done using the *trace abstraction approach* of [14,15]. This enables us to define an *iterative* method to compute better and better over-approximations of the WCET and ensure that one witness trace exists.

Notice that this refinement also applies to the hardware model: we can start with a very simple model of the caches where every transaction is either a Hit or a Miss. Once a WCET is computed with UPPAAL, we can check whether the witness trace is feasible in the program *and* in the caches. If the cache behaviour that is in the witness is spurious (infeasible) we can refine it as well. We have implemented a cache refinement technique in [8]. This enables us to get some control on the accuracy of the computation via model-checking.

On another note, we can use our technique as a simulation based technique: the bin.annotated component in the tool chain Fig. 10 can be replaced by a generator of traces. In this case we can only compute a lower bound for the WCET but we get access to the *statistical model-checking* engine of UPPAAL. This opens a new avenue to compute some probabilistic distributions of the WCET.

In addition, outsourcing the semantics of a binary program to a trusted emulation tool (qemu) eliminates errors that occurs when semantically translating binary programs into timed automata. As such a translation necessitates a very high level of detail, it can easily result in a state-space explosion – even for simple architectures and programs. With our construction, knowledge of the hardware and static-analysis and abstraction refinement methods can be used to reduce the size of explored state space.

References

1. AbsInt Angewandte Informatik: aiT Worst-Case Execution Time Analyzers. http://www.absint.com/ait/
2. Alur, R., Dill, D.: A theory of timed automata. TCS **126**(2), 183–235 (1994)
3. Behrmann, G., David, A., Larsen, K.G., Håkansson, J., Pettersson, P., Yi, W., Hendriks, M.: Uppaal 4.0. In: QEST, pp. 125–126. IEEE Computer Society (2006)
4. Bellard, F.: QEMU, a fast and portable dynamic translator. In: Proceedings of the Annual Conference on USENIX Annual Technical Conference, ATEC 2005, p. 41. USENIX Association, Berkeley (2005). http://dl.acm.org/citation. cfm?id=1247360.1247401
5. Bernat, G., Colin, A., Petters, S.M.: pWCET a toolset for automatic worst-case execution time analysis of real-time embedded programs. In: Proceedings of the 3rd International Workshop on WCET Analysis, Workshop of the Euromicro Conference on Real-Time Systems, Porto, Portugal (2003)
6. Cassez, F.: Timed games for computing worst-case execution-times. Research report, National ICT Australia, 31 p., June 2010. http://arxiv.org/abs/1006.1951
7. Cassez, F.: Timed games for computing WCET for pipelined processors with caches. In: ACSD 2011, pp. 195–204. IEEE Computer Society, June 2011
8. Cassez, F., de Aledo Marugán, P.G.: Timed automata for modelling caches and pipelines. In: van Glabbeek, R.J., Groote, J.F., Höfner, P. (eds.) Proceedings Workshop on Models for Formal Analysis of Real Systems, MARS 2015, Suva, Fiji, 23 November 2015. EPTCS, vol. 196, pp. 37–45 (2015)
9. Cassez, F., Béchennec, J.: Timing analysis of binary programs with UPPAAL. In: 13th International Conference on Application of Concurrency to System Design, ACSD 2013, pp. 41–50. IEEE Computer Society, July 2013
10. Cassez, F., Hansen, R.R., Olesen, M.C.: What is a timing anomaly? In: 12th International Workshop on Worst-Case Execution Time Analysis, WCET 2012, 10 July 2012, Pisa, Italy. OASICS, vol. 23, pp. 1–12. Schloss Dagstuhl - Leibniz-Zentrum fuer Informatik, July 2012
11. Dalsgaard, A.E., Olesen, M.C., Toft, M., Hansen, R.R., Larsen, K.G.: Metamoc: modular execution time analysis using model checking. In: Lisper, B. (ed.) WCET. OASICS, vol. 15, pp. 113–123. Schloss Dagstuhl - Leibniz-Zentrum fuer Informatik, Germany (2010)
12. Dalsgaard, A.E., Olesen, M.C., Toft, M.: Modular execution time analysis using model checking. Master's thesis, Department of Computer Science, Aalborg University, Denmark (2009)
13. Ferdinand, C., Heckmann, R., Wilhelm, R.: Analyzing the worst-case execution time by abstract interpretation of executable code. In: Broy, M., Krüger, I.H., Meisinger, M. (eds.) ASWSD 2004. LNCS, vol. 4147, pp. 1–14. Springer, Heidelberg (2006). doi:10.1007/11823063_1
14. Heizmann, M., Hoenicke, J., Podelski, A.: Refinement of trace abstraction. In: Palsberg, J., Su, Z. (eds.) SAS 2009. LNCS, vol. 5673, pp. 69–85. Springer, Heidelberg (2009). doi:10.1007/978-3-642-03237-0_7
15. Heizmann, M., Hoenicke, J., Podelski, A.: Software model checking for people who love automata. In: Sharygina, N., Veith, H. (eds.) CAV 2013. LNCS, vol. 8044, pp. 36–52. Springer, Heidelberg (2013). doi:10.1007/978-3-642-39799-8_2
16. Larsen, K.G., Pettersson, P., Yi, W.: Uppaal in a nutshell. J. Softw. Tools Technol. Transf. (STTT) **1**(1–2), 134–152 (1997)

17. Mälardalen WCET Research Group: WCET Project - Benchmarks. http://www.
    mrtc.mdh.se/projects/wcet/benchmarks.html
18. Rapita Systems Ltd. Rapita Systems for timing analysis of real-time embedded
    systems. http://www.rapitasystems.com/
19. Rieder, B., Puschner, P., Wenzel, I.: Using model checking to derive loop bounds
    of general loops within ANSI-C applications for measurement based WCET analy-
    sis. In: 6th International Workshop on Intelligent Solutions in Embedded Systems
    (WISES 2008), Regensburg, Germany (2008)
20. Sloane, A.M.: Lightweight language processing in Kiama. In: Fernandes, J.M.,
    Lämmel, R., Visser, J., Saraiva, J. (eds.) GTTSE 2009. LNCS, vol. 6491, pp. 408–
    425. Springer, Heidelberg (2011). doi:10.1007/978-3-642-18023-1_12
21. Sloane, A., Cassez, F., Buckley, S.: The sbt-rats parser generator plugin for Scala
    (tool paper). In: Proceedings of the 2016 7th ACM SIGPLAN Symposium on Scala,
    SCALA 2016, pp. 110–113. ACM, New York (2016). http://doi.acm.org/10.1145/
    2998392.3001580
22. Stallman, R., Pesch, R., Shebs, S., et al.: Debugging with GDB. Free Software
    Foundation 51, 02110–1301 (2002)
23. Wilhelm, R., Engblom, J., Ermedahl, A., Holsti, N., Thesing, S., Whalley, D.B.,
    Bernat, G., Ferdinand, C., Heckmann, R., Mitra, T., Mueller, F., Puaut, I.,
    Puschner, P.P., Staschulat, J., Stenström, P.: The worst-case execution-time prob-
    lem - overview of methods and survey of tools. ACM Trans. Embed. Comput. Syst.
    7(3) (2008). Article no. 36

Centrally Governed Blockchains: Optimizing Security, Cost, and Availability

Leif-Nissen Lundbæk, Andrea Callia D'Iddio, and Michael Huth[✉]

Department of Computing, Imperial College London, London SW7 2AZ, UK
{leif.lundbaek,a.callia-diddio14,m.huth}@imperial.ac.uk

Abstract. We propose the formal study of blockchains that are owned and controlled by organizations and that neither create cryptocurrencies nor provide incentives to solvers of cryptographic puzzles. We view such approaches as frameworks in which system parts, such as the cryptographic puzzle, may be instantiated with different technology. Owners of such a blockchain procure puzzle solvers as resources they control, and use a mathematical model to compute optimal parameters for the cryptographic puzzle mechanism or other parts of the blockchain. We illustrate this approach with a use case in which blockchains record hashes of financial process transactions to increase their trustworthiness and that of their audits. For Proof of Work as cryptographic puzzle, we develop a detailed mathematical model to derive MINLP optimization problems for computing optimal Proof of Work configuration parameters that trade off potentially conflicting aspects such as availability, resiliency, security, and cost in this governed setting. We demonstrate the utility of such a *mining calculus* by applying it on some instances of this problem. We hope that our work may facilitate the creation of *domain-specific* blockchains for a wide range of applications such as trustworthy information in Internet of Things systems and bespoke improvements of legacy financial services.

1 Introduction

There is little doubt that modern accounting systems have benefitted, ever since the advent of commercial computing machines, from the digitization of the processing and recording of financial transactions. The automated processing of payroll information in the 1950ies was perhaps one of the earliest examples of such benefits: IBM introduced its *702 Data Processing System* for businesses in 1953. And the use of RFID technology or smart phones for contactless payment of small items such as coffees is a more recent example thereof.

It is then striking that the mechanisms used for managing the integrity of accounts are, in essence, those developed at least a thousand years ago. What we call the modern *double-entry bookkeeping* was already used by Florentine merchants in the 13th century, for example. Without going into great detail, the key idea is in simplified terms that each account has an associated *dual* account and that each credit in one account is recorded as a debit in that dual account. This allows for the formulation and verification of an important *financial invariant*:

© Springer International Publishing AG 2017
L. Aceto et al. (Eds.): Larsen Festschrift, LNCS 10460, pp. 578–599, 2017.
DOI: 10.1007/978-3-319-63121-9_29

no matter how complex financial transactions may be, or how many transactions may occur, it must always be the case that over the totality of accounts

"Assets equal liabilities plus capital."

Modern realizations of this method may enrich account entries with time stamps and other contextual data so that the flow of assets can be better understood, for example to support an audit. The above invariant may be quite simple to verify, and its verification may give us reassurance that every debit has an associated credit. But it does not prevent the recording of transactions that may be unauthorized, fraudulent, or that may be incorrect due to human error. For example, transaction records within accounting books may be manipulated to commit fraud whilst these manipulations still satisfy the above invariant.

One may say that processing of transactions is governed by a form of *legal code* that is informed by policy on fraud prevention and detection, regulation, compliance, risk, and so forth. But the enforcement of such legal code within the *technical code* that operationalizes modern financial processes has been difficult at best, and too costly or impossible at worst.

Digitized financial processes can utilize cryptographic primitives to help with narrowing this gap between legal and technical code: digital signatures can be associated to transactions (for example embedded within transaction objects), and commitment schemes can be used to realize consistent distributed storage whose consistency is resilient to adversarial manipulation; see for example the discussion of Byzantine Agreement Protocols in [19]. But the advent of decentralized, *eventual consistency* storage protocols, as pioneered in the cryptocurrency Bitcoin [13], opened up a new way of thinking about the processing of financial transactions, even of creating and managing a currency as a unit of account.

In the Bitcoin network, a randomized race of solving a cryptographic puzzle, *Proof of Work*, is used to elect a leader whose block will be added to the blockchain. The leader election is done for each new block, and a consensus protocol ensures that the majority of network nodes have a consistent copy of the blockchain. There is little doubt that cryptocurrencies are one of the most important innovations [1,14], along with the invention and introduction of central banks, in financial services since the advent of the double-entry bookkeeping.

In this paper, we investigate how governed, closed blockchains can be designed so that they can support the resilient, distributed, and *trustworthy* storage of authentication of transactions within conventional financial processes. Such governed systems restrict access, notably to the definition and solving of cryptographic puzzles. Therefore, they give us better control on balancing the use of energy for puzzle solving with the security of the Proof of Work algorithm when compared with open systems that rely on Proof of Work, such as Bitcoin. Specifically, we propose that transactions (in the sense of Bitcoin) within blocks are hashes of transactions (in the sense of conventional financial processes). We then define mathematical models that describe the design space of such a blockchain in terms of the cryptographic puzzle used – in this paper Proof of Work, in terms of expected availability, resiliency, security, and cost, and in terms that reflect that the system is centrally governed. We stress that our approach is also consistent with transactions within blockchains that encode transaction history, which we don't consider in the use case of this paper.

Outline of Paper. In Sect. 2 we present our use case. Our mathematical model for governed Proof of Work is subject of Sect. 3. The derivation of optimization problems for these is done in Sect. 4 and shown to support robust design security in Sect. 5. An algorithm for solving such optimization problems and experimental results are reported in Sect. 6. The wider context of our work and related work are discussed in Sect. 7, and the paper concludes in Sect. 8.

2   Use Case

Our use case is one of a financial process that creates financial transactions. We would like to enhance the trustworthiness of this process through a blockchain that records hash-based authentications of transactions, see Fig. 1, where the interaction between the legacy process and the blockchain is conceptually simple – and consistent with the use of double-entry bookkeeping if desired.

Our assumption is that the event streams of such transactions are not linearizable and so we cannot rely on techniques such as hash chains [7] to obtain immutability of transactions. A hash chain could also be recomputed by an attacker with partial control of the system. Alternatively a blockchain created through consensus protocols such as BFT [10,19] would also be subject to manipulation after consensus protocols have been executed and blocks added to the chain. A blockchain based on cryptographic puzzles is thus much more resilient to such manipulation attacks, since it takes considerable effort to solve the number of cryptographic puzzles needed for rewriting parts or all of a blockchain.

Our data model represents a transaction as a string *input*, authenticated with a hash *hash(input)*. String *input* may be a serialization of a transaction object that contains relevant information such as a time stamp of the transaction, a digital signature of the core transaction data and so forth. The trustworthiness of transaction *input* is represented outside of the blockchain by the triple

$$(input, hash(input), location) \tag{1}$$

where *location* is either the block height (≥ 0) of a block b in the blockchain such that *hash(input)* occurs in block b or *location* is NULL, indicating that the transaction is not yet confirmed on the blockchain.

The hashes *hash(input)* of transactions that still need to be confirmed are propagated on the blockchain network, where they are picked up by miners and integrated into blocks for Proof of Work. We assume a suitable mechanism by which nodes that manage legacy accounts learn the blockheights of their transactions that have been successfully added to the blockchain. Such nodes may have a full copy of the blockchain and update *location* values in accounts if the hash of the corresponding transaction occurs in a block that was just added.

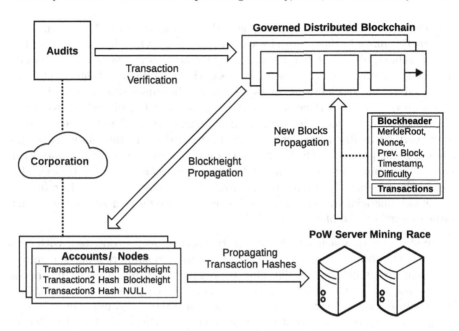

Fig. 1. Governed blockchain for financial process authentications: note that **Transactions** recorded in blocks on the left are mere hashes of transactions conducted in the legacy system. The latter are listed in **Accounts/Nodes** on the left

A transaction is unverified if its *location* value is NULL or if its hash does not equal the one stored externally as in (1); it is trustworthy if $0 \leq location$ and $location + k \leq currentBlockHeight$ where $k \geq 0$ is a suitable constant and *currentBlockHeight* denotes the number of blocks added to the blockchain so far. The value of k may be a function of how fast blocks are added to the chain on average, to ensure sufficient resiliency of trustworthiness. An auditor could then inspect any transaction by examining its triple stored as in (1). If *location* equals NULL or if $location + k > currentBlockHeight$, the transaction is considered neither valid nor trustworthy by the auditor. Otherwise, we have $0 \leq location$ and $location + k \leq currentBlockHeight$ and the auditor uses the Merkle tree hash in block *location* to verify that $hash(input)$ is in the block of height b. If that is the case, the auditor considers the transaction to be verified; otherwise, the auditor considers the transaction not to be trustworthy.

Note that this use case does not require transaction scripts to be stored, nor any run-time system for verifying such transactions. But the mathematical modelling approach we present in this paper is consistent with use cases that have such script generation and verification support.

System Architecture. A system architecture that could support such a use case is shown in Fig. 1. Unverified transactions have their hashes propagated on the network. Miners pick up those hashes and integrate them into blocks for Proof of Work. We abstract away how miners manage their pools of hashes and how Proof of Work blocks are propagated and added to the blockchain; this gives us flexibility in the use of blockchain technology. Once blocks are added to the blockchain, blockheights are propagated to the legacy account. As mentioned above, these accounts could have full copies of the blockchain and thus implement their own update mechanisms for value *location* in triples stored as in (1).

Auditors would interface with both accounts and the blockchain to verify, in a trustworthy manner, the authenticity of transactions. Any transaction that is not verified as discussed above would be flagged up in this audit. Any pre-existing audit process – which may focus on compliance, regulations and other aspects – is consistent with such *trustworthiness checking*; and the trustworthiness of the pre-existing audit process would be increased as it would refuse to certify any financial transaction histories that involved a transaction that is not authenticated on the blockchain.

Analysis. The approach we advocate in this section seems consistent with consensus mechanisms as used in Bitcoin but it may also support 2-phase commitment schemes as proposed in [5]. Our system architecture allows for full nodes to be associated with accounts, sets of accounts or corporate boundaries. Our blockchain does not create any currency, and so there is no inherent incentive to mine. But there is an incentive for the owners of this blockchain to allocate mining resources in a manner that establishes trustworthiness of transactions as recorded in this blockchain. We deem elimination of incentives for miners and their game-theoretic implications to be a benefit, as well as the simple ways of propagating trust through hashes of transactions. Such a blockchain may also be consulted by legacy systems to inform the authorization of further financial transactions.

Our blockchain does not spend any funds and so has no problem of *double spending*, and double spending in the legacy system would be detectable with existing mechanisms such as audits. Our approach does allow for *double authentication* though: a transaction hash may occur more than once in a blockchain, be it in the same block or in different blocks. We deem this to be unproblematic as audits would only need to establish *some*, sufficiently old, authentication of the transaction in the blockchain to establish its trustworthiness – noting that hash-based authentication is deterministic.

One expectation is that blocks would only be added to the blockchain if signed by one of the miners that is resourced for this Proof of Work service. This requires that the public keys of such miners are securely stored and available within the system. Over time, some of these miners may be removed from such a list (e.g. decommissioned) and new ones may be added (e.g. system upgrade).

3   Mathematics for Centrally Governed Proof of Work

Our model assumes a cryptographic hash function

$$h\colon \{0,1\}^p \to \{0,1\}^n$$

where $p \geq n > 0$ such that h has *puzzle friendliness* [14]. The *level of difficulty* d is an integer satisfying $0 < d < n$: Proof of Work has to produce some x where $h(x)$ has at least d many leftmost 0 bits. We write $T > 0$ for the time to compute a sole hash $h(x)$ and to decide whether it has at least d leftmost zeros. Since the range of d will be relatively small, we make T a device-dependent constant.

Our probabilistic modeling will treat h in the *Random Oracle Model* (ROM): function h is chosen uniformly at random from all functions of type $\{0,1\}^p \rightarrow \{0,1\}^n$; that is to say, h is a deterministic function such that any x for which h has not yet been queried will have the property that $h(x)$ is governed by a truly random probability distribution over $\{0,1\}^n$.

We may assume that x consists of a block header which contains some random data field – a nonce *nonce* of bitlength r, that this nonce is initialized, and that the nonce is then increased by 1 each time the hash of x does not obtain Proof of Work. In particular, this yields that $\{0,1\}^p \cong \{0,1\}^{p-r} \times \{0,1\}^r$ where $0 < r < p$: the input to h will be of form $x = data \parallel nonce$ where $data$ and $nonce$ have $p-r$ and r bits, respectively. Our use of ROM will rely on the following assumption:

Assumption 1 (Invariant). *The mining of a block with one or more miners will use an input to h at most once, be it within or across miners' input spaces.*

This assumption and ROM give us that hash values are always uniformly distributed in the output space during a mining race. Now consider having $s > 1$ many miners that run in parallel to find Proof of Work, engaging thus in a *mining race*. We assume these miners run with the same configurations and hardware. As already discussed, in our approach miners do not get rewarded:

Assumption 2 (Miners). *Miners are a resource controlled by the governing organization or consortium, and have identical hardware. In particular, miners are not rewarded nor have the need for incentive structures.*

But miners may be corrupted and misbehave, for example they may refuse to mine. To simplify our analysis, we assume miners begin the computation of hashes in approximate synchrony:

Assumption 3 (Approximate Synchrony). *Miners start a mining race at approximately the same time.*

For many application domains, this is a realistic assumption as communication delays to miners would have a known upper bound that our models could additionally reflect if needed.

Next, we want to model the *race* of getting a Proof of Work where each miner j has some data $data_j$. To realize Assumption 1, it suffices that each miner j has a nonce $nonce_j$ in a value space of size

$$\lambda = \lfloor 2^r / s \rfloor$$

such that these nonce spaces are mutually disjoint across miners.

Our probability space has $(data_j)_{1 \le j \le s}$ and d as implicit parameters. For each miner j, the set of basic events E^j is

$$E^j = \{\otimes^k \cdot \checkmark \mid 0 \le k \le \lambda\} \cup \{\text{failure}\} \tag{2}$$

Basic event failure denotes the event that all λ nonce values $nonce_j$ from $\{(j-1) \cdot \lambda, \ldots, j \cdot \lambda - 1\}$ for miner j failed to obtain Proof of Work for $data_j$ at level of difficulty d. Basic event $\otimes^k \cdot \checkmark$ models the event in which the first k such nonce values failed to obtain Proof of Work for $data_j$ at level d but the $k+1$th value of $nonce_j$ did render such Proof of Work for $data_j$.

To model this mining race between s miners for $(data_1, data_2, \ldots, data_s)$ and d as implicit parameters, we take the product $\prod_{j=1}^{s} E^j$ of s copies E^j and quotient it via an equivalence relation $\equiv$ on that product $\prod_{j=1}^{s} E^j$, which we now define formally.

Definition 1

1. *The s-tuple* (failure, $\ldots$, failure) *models failure of this mining race, and it is $\equiv$ equivalent only to itself.*
2. *All s-tuples* $a = (a_j)_{1 \le j \le s}$ *other than tuple* (failure, $\ldots$, failure) *model that the mining race succeeded for at least one miner. For such an s-tuple a, the set of natural numbers k such that $\otimes^k \cdot \checkmark$ is a coordinate in a is non-empty and therefore has a minimum $\min(a)$. Given two s-tuples $a = (a_j)_{1 \le j \le s}$ and $b = (b_j)_{1 \le j \le s}$ both different from* (failure, $\ldots$, failure), *we can then define*

$$a \equiv b \text{ iff } \min(a) = \min(b)$$

So two non-failing tuples are equivalent if they determine a first (and so final) Proof of Work at the same round of the race. This defines an equivalence relation $\equiv$ and adequately models a synchronized mining race between s miners.

The interpretation of events $\otimes^k \cdot \checkmark$ in the mining race is then the equivalence class of all those tuples a for which $\min(a)$ is well defined and equals k: all mining races that succeed first at round k. The meaning of failure is still overall failure of the mining race, the equivalence class containing only tuple (failure, $\ldots$, failure). The set of events for the Proof of Work race of s miners is therefore

$$E^s = \{\otimes^k \cdot \checkmark \mid 0 \le k \le \lambda\} \cup \{\text{failure}\} \tag{3}$$

In (3), expression $\otimes^k \cdot \checkmark$ denotes an element of the quotient

$$\left(\prod_{j=1}^{s} E^j\right)/\equiv$$

namely the equivalence class of tuple $(\otimes^k \cdot \checkmark, \text{failure}, \text{failure}, \ldots, \text{failure})$. Next, we define a probability distribution $prob^s$ over E^s. To derive the probability $prob^s(\otimes^k \cdot \checkmark)$, recall

$$\tilde{p}(\otimes^k) = (1 - 2^{-d})^k$$

as the probability that a given miner does not obtain Proof of Work at level d in the first k rounds. By Assumption 1, these miners work independently and over disjoint input spaces. By ROM, the expression

$$\left[(1 - 2^{-d})^k\right]^s = (1 - 2^{-d})^{k \cdot s}$$

therefore models the probability that none of the s miners obtains Proof of Work in the first k rounds. Appealing again to ROM and Assumption 1, the behavior at round $k + 1$ is independent of that of the first k rounds. Therefore, we need to multiply the above probability with the one for which at least one of the s miners will obtain a Proof of Work in a single round. The latter probability is the complementary one of the probability that none of the s miners will get a Proof of Work in a sole round, which is $(1 - 2^{-d})^s$ due to the ROM independence. Therefore, we get

$$prob^s(\otimes^k \cdot \checkmark) = (1 - 2^{-d})^{k \cdot s} \cdot [1 - (1 - 2^{-d})^s] \tag{4}$$

This defines a probability distribution with a non-zero probability of failure. Firstly,

$$\sum_{k=0}^{\lambda}(1 - 2^{-d})^{k \cdot s} \cdot [1 - (1 - 2^{-d})^s]$$

is in $(0, 1)$: to see this, note that this sum equals

$$[1 - (1 - 2^{-d})^s] \cdot \frac{1 - [(1 - 2^{-d})^s]^{\lambda+1}}{1 - (1 - 2^{-d})^s} = 1 - (1 - 2^{-d})^{s \cdot (\lambda+1)}$$

Since $0 < d, s$, the real $1 - 2^{-d}$ is in $(0, 1)$, and the same is true of any integral power thereof. Secondly, $prob^s$ becomes a probability distribution with the non-zero probability $prob^s(\text{failure})$ being $1 - prob^e(E^s \backslash \{\text{failure}\})$, that is

$$prob^s(\text{failure}) = (1 - 2^{-d})^{s \cdot (\lambda+1)} \tag{5}$$

That this failure probability is almost identical to that for $s = 1$ is an artefact of our modeling: if each miner has 64 bits of nonce space, e.g., then our model would have $r = 64 \cdot s$, so failure probabilities do decrease as s increases.

4   Mathematical Optimization in Mining Design Space

Generality of Approach. We want to optimize the use of $s > 1$ miners using a level of difficulty d, and a bit size r of the global nonce space with respect to an objective function. The latter may be a cost function, if containing cost is the paramount objective or if a first cost estimate is sought that can then be transformed into a constraint to optimize for a security objective – for example to maximize the level of difficulty d, as seen further below. Higher values of d add more security: it takes more effort to mine a block and so more effort to manipulate the mining process and used consensus mechanism. But lower values of d may be needed, for example, in high-frequency trading where performance can become a real issue. We want to understand such trade-offs. Moreover, we want to explore how corruption of some miners or inherent uncertainty in the number of deployed miners or in the level of difficulty across the lifetime of a system may influence the above tradeoffs.

Optimizing Cost and Security. The flexibility of our approach includes the choice of an objective function for optimization. Let us first consider an objective function

$$\text{Cost}(s, r, d) = \text{TVC} \cdot E^s(noR) \cdot s + \text{TFC} \cdot s \qquad (6)$$

that models cost as a function of the number of miners s, the bit size of the nonce r – implicit in random variable $E^s(noR)$, and the level of difficulty d; where we want to *minimize* cost.

The real variable TVC models the *variable* cost of computing *one* hash for *one* miner, reflecting the device-dependent speed of hashes and the price of energy. The real variable TFC models the *fixed* costs of *having one miner*; this can be seen as modeling procurement and depreciations. Variables s, r, and d are integral, making this a *mixed integer* optimization problem [8]. The expression $E^s(noR)$ denotes the *expected number of rounds* (of approximately synchronous hash attempts) needed to mine a block in a mining race that uses s miners, level of difficulty d, and nonce bitsize r. The derivation of this expression below shows that it is non-linear, making this a MINLP optimization problem [8,16].

We may of course use other objective functions. One of these is simply the expression d, which we would seek to *maximize*, the intuition being that higher values of d give us more trust into the veracity of a mined block and the blockchains generated in the system. Figure 2 shows an example of a set of constraints and optimizations of security and cost for this.

$$0 < s_l \leq s \leq s_u \qquad 0 < d_l \leq d \leq d_u \qquad 0 < r_l \leq r \leq r_u \qquad \epsilon \geq prob^s(\text{failure})$$
$$\tau_u \geq T \cdot E^s(noR) \geq \tau_l \qquad\qquad \delta_2 \geq prob^s(\textit{disputes within } \mu)$$
$$\delta \geq prob^s(PoWTime > th) \qquad \delta_1 \geq prob^s(PoWTime < th')$$

Fig. 2. Constraint set $\mathcal{C}$ for two optimization problems: (a) *minimize* $\text{Cost}(s, r, d)$ as in (6) subject to constraints in $\mathcal{C}$; and (b) *maximize* d subject to $\mathcal{C} \cup \{\text{Cost}(s, r, d) \leq budget\}$ for cost bound $budget$. This is parameterized by constants $0 \leq \delta, \delta_1, \delta_2, \epsilon, th, th', \tau_l, \text{TVC}, \text{TFC}$ and $0 < T, s_l, r_l, d_l$. Variables or constants $s_l, s_u, s, d_l, d_u, d, r_l, r_u, r$ are integral

Integer constants s_l and s_u provide bounds for variable s, and similar integer bounds are used to constrain integer variables r and d. The constraint for ϵ uses it as upper bound for the probability of a mining race failing to mine a block. The next two inequalities stipulate that the expected time for mining a block is within a given time interval, specified by real constants τ_l and τ_u.

The real constant δ_2 is an upper bound for

$$prob^s(disputes\ within\ \mu)$$

the probability that more than one miner finds PoW within μ seconds in the same, approximately synchronous, mining race. The constraint for real constant δ says that the probability

$$prob^s(PoWTime > th)$$

of the *actual* time for mining a block being above a real constant th is bounded above by δ. This constraint is of independent interest: knowing that the expected time to mine a block is within specified bounds may not suffice in systems that need to assure that blocks are *almost always* (with probability at least $1 - \delta$) mined within a specified time limit. Some systems may also need assurance that blocks are almost always mined in time *exceeding* a specified time limit th'. We write

$$prob^s(PoWTime < th')$$

to denote that probability, and add a dual constraint, that the actual time for mining a block has a sufficiently small probability $\leq \delta_1$ of being faster than threshold th'.

Constraints as Analytical Expressions. We derive analytical expressions for random variables occurring in Fig. 2. Beginning with $E^s(noR)$, we have

$$E^s(noR) = \sum_{0 \leq k \leq \lambda} prob^s(\otimes^k \cdot \checkmark) \cdot (k+1) \tag{7}$$

which we know to be equal to

$$\sum_{0 \leq k \leq \lambda} (1 - 2^{-d})^{k \cdot s} \cdot [1 - (1 - 2^{-d})^s] \cdot (k+1)$$

We may rewrite the latter expression so that summations are eliminated and reduced to exponentiations: concretely, we rewrite $\sum_{0 \leq k \leq \lambda} prob(\otimes^k \cdot \checkmark) \cdot (k+1)$, the righthand side of (7), to $\lambda + 1$ summations, each one starting at a value between 0 and λ, where we exploit the familiar formula

$$\sum_{k=a}^{b} x^k = \frac{x^a - x^{b+1}}{1 - x}$$

This renders

$$E^s(noR) = \frac{1 - y^{\lambda+1} - (\lambda + 1) \cdot (1 - y) \cdot y^{\lambda+1}}{1 - y} \tag{8}$$

where we use the abbreviation

$$y = (1 - 2^{-d})^s \tag{9}$$

The expected time needed to get a proof of work for input *data* is then given by

$$E^s(poW) = T \cdot E^s(noR) \tag{10}$$

We derive an analytical expression for the probability $prob^s(PoWTime > th)$ next. Note that $(th/T) - 1 < k$ models that the actual time taken for $k+1$ hash rounds is larger than th. Therefore, we capture $prob^s(PoWTime > th)$ as

$$\sum_{\lceil (th/T)-1 \rceil < k \leq \lambda} prob^s(\otimes^k \cdot \checkmark) = y^{\lceil (th/T)-1 \rceil +1} - y^{\lambda+1} \tag{11}$$

assuming that $\lceil (th/T) - 1 \rceil < \lambda$, the latter therefore becoming a constraint that we need to add to our optimization problem. One may be tempted to choose the value of δ based on the Markov inequality, which gives us

$$prob^s(PoWTime \geq th) \leq T \cdot E^s(noR)/th$$

But we should keep in mind that upper bound $T \cdot E^s(noR)/th$ depends on the parameters s, r, and d; for example, the analytical expression for $E^s(noR)$ in (8) is dependent on λ and so dependent on r as well. The representation in (11) also maintains that expression $y^{\lceil (th/T)-1 \rceil +1} - y^{\lambda+1}$ is in $[0, 1]$, i.e. a proper probability. Since $y = (1 - 2^{-d})^s$ is in $(0, 1)$, this is already guaranteed if $\lceil (th/T) - 1 \rceil + 1 \leq \lambda + 1$, i.e. if $\lceil (th/T) - 1 \rceil \leq \lambda$. But we already added that constraint to our model. Similarly to our analysis of $prob^s(PoWTime > th)$, we get

$$prob^s(PowTime < th') = 1 - (1 - 2^{-d})^{s \cdot (\lfloor (th'/T)-1 \rfloor +1)} = 1 - y^{\lfloor (th'/T)-1 \rfloor +1} \tag{12}$$

which needs $0 < \lfloor (th'/T) - 1 \rfloor$ as additional constraint.

To derive an analytical expression for $prob^s(disputes \ within \ \mu)$, each miner can perform $\lfloor \mu/T \rfloor$ hashes within μ seconds. Let us set

$$w = (1 - 2^{-d})^{\lfloor \mu/T \rfloor +1} \tag{13}$$

The probability that a given miner finds PoW within μ seconds is

$$\sum_{k=0}^{\lfloor \mu/T \rfloor} (1 - 2^{-d})^k \cdot 2^{-d} = 2^{-d} \cdot \frac{1 - (1 - 2^{-d})^{\lfloor \mu/T \rfloor +1}}{1 - (1 - 2^{-d})} = 1 - w \tag{14}$$

Therefore, the probability that no miner finds PoW within μ seconds is

$$prob^s(0 \ PoW \ within \ \mu) = (1 - (1 - w))^s = w^s \tag{15}$$

The probability that exactly one miner finds PoW within μ seconds is

$$prob^s(1 \ PoW \ within \ \mu) = s \cdot w^{s-1} \cdot (1 - w) \tag{16}$$

Thus, the probability that more than one miner finds PoW within μ seconds is

$$prob^s(disputes\ within\ \mu) = 1 - prob^s(0\ PoW\ within\ \mu) - prob^s(1\ PoW\ within\ \mu)$$
$$= 1 - w^s - s \cdot w^{s-1} \cdot (1 - w)$$
$$= 1 - w^s - s \cdot w^{s-1} + s \cdot w^{s-1} \cdot w$$
$$= 1 + (s - 1) \cdot w^s - s \cdot w^{s-1} \tag{17}$$

Figure 3 shows the set of constraints $\mathcal{C}$ from Fig. 2 with analytical expressions and their additional constraints, we add constraint $0 \leq \lfloor \mu/T \rfloor$ to get consistency for the analytical representation of $prob^s(disputes\ within\ \mu)$.

$$s_l \leq s \leq s_u \qquad d_l \leq d \leq d_u \qquad r_l \leq r \leq r_u \qquad \lambda = \lfloor 2^r/s \rfloor$$
$$y = (1 - 2^{-d})^s \qquad w = (1 - 2^{-d})^{\lfloor \mu/T \rfloor + 1} \qquad 0 \leq \lfloor \mu/T \rfloor$$
$$\epsilon \geq y^{\lambda+1} \qquad \lceil (th/T) - 1 \rceil < \lambda \qquad 0 < \lfloor (th'/T) - 1 \rfloor$$
$$E^s(noR) = \frac{1 - y^{\lambda+1} - (\lambda + 1) \cdot (1 - y) \cdot y^{\lambda+1}}{1 - y}$$
$$\tau_u \geq T \cdot E^s(noR) \geq \tau_l \qquad \delta_1 \geq 1 - y^{\lfloor (th'/T) - 1 \rfloor + 1}$$
$$\delta \geq y^{\lceil (th/T) - 1 \rceil + 1} - y^{\lambda+1} \tag{18}$$
$$\delta_2 \geq 1 + (s - 1) \cdot w^s - s \cdot w^{s-1}$$

Fig. 3. Arithmetic version of set of constraints $\mathcal{C}$ from Fig. 2, with additional soundness constraints for this representation. Feasibility of (s, r, d) and $r_u \geq r' > r$ won't generally imply feasibility of (s, r', d) due to the constraint in (18)

5   Robust Design Security

Our model above captures design requirements or design decisions as a set of constraints, to optimize or trade off measures of interest subject to such constraints. We can extend this model to also *manage uncertainty* via robust optimization [2]. Such uncertainty may arise during the lifetime of a system through the possibility of having corrupted miners, needed flexibility in adjusting the level of difficulty, and so forth. For example, corrupted miners may refuse to mine, deny their service by returning invalid block headers, pool their mining power to get more mining influence or they may simply break down. Robust optimization treats such uncertainty as non-deterministic choice and refers to it as *strict* or *Knightian* uncertainty.

Consider $1 \leq l < s$ corrupted miners. We can model their *pool power* by appeal to ROM and the fact that the mining race is approximately synchronized: the probability that these l miners win $c > 0$ many subsequent mining races is then seen to be $(l/s)^c$. We can therefore bound this with a constant δ_3 as in Fig. 3.

We model uncertainty in the number of miners available by an integer constant u_s as follows: if s miners are deployed, then we assume that at least $s - u_s$

and at most s many miners participate reliably in the mining of legitimate blocks: they will not mine blocks that won't verify and only submit mined blocks that do verify to the network. Constant u_s can model aspects such as denial of service attacks or a combination of such attacks with faults: $u_s = 3$, e.g., subsumes the scenario in which one miner fails and two miners mine invalid blocks.

Integer constant u_d models the uncertainty in the deployed level of difficulty d: intuitively, our analysis should give us results that are robust in that they hedge against the fact that any of the values d' satisfying

$$|d - d'| \leq u_d$$

may be the actually running level of difficulty. This enables us to understand a design if we are unsure about which level of difficulty will be deployed or if we want some flexibility in dynamically adjusting the value of d in the running system.

The corresponding robust optimization problem for cost minimization is seen in Fig. 4. It adds to the constraints we already consider further requirements on constants l, c, and δ_3 as well as the constraint

$$l^c \leq \delta_3 \cdot s^c$$

The robustness of analysis is achieved by a change of the objective function from $\text{Cost}(s, r, d)$ to

$$\text{Cost}_{u_d}^{u_s}(s, r, d) = \max_{s - u_s \leq s' \leq s, |d - d'| \leq u_d} \text{Cost}(s', r, d') \tag{19}$$

The latter computes a worst-case cost for triple (s, r, d) where s and d may vary independently subject to the strict uncertainties u_s and u_d, respectively. We call a triple (s, r, d) *feasible* if it satisfies all constraints of its optimization problem. Costs such as the one in (19) for a triple (s, r, d) are only considered for optimization if all triples (s', r, d') used in (19) are feasible – realized with predicate *feasible*$_{u_d}^{u_s}$: robust optimization guarantees [2] that the feasibility of solutions is invariant under the specified strict uncertainty (here u_s and u_d).

6   Experiments and Validation

We submitted simple instances of the optimization problem in Fig. 4 to state of the art MINLP solvers. All these solvers reported, erroneously, in their pre-processing stage that the problem is infeasible. These solvers were not designed to deal with problems that combine such small numbers and large powers, and rely on standard floating point implementations. Therefore, we wrote a bespoke solver in Haskell that exploits the fact that we have only few integral variables within limited ranges so that we can explore their combinatorial space completely to determine feasibility and therefore optimality as well.

Experimental Setup. We solve the robust optimization problem for the analytical expressions we derived above with the algorithm depicted in Fig. 5. This

$$\min\{\mathrm{Cost}^{u_s}_{u_d}(s,r,d) \mid \mathit{feasible}^{u_s}_{u_d}(s,r,d)\}$$

subject to the set of constraints $\mathcal{C}$ from Figure 3 together with

$$4 = l < s \qquad\qquad c = 6 \qquad\qquad 0.001 = \delta_3$$

$$l^c \leq s^c \cdot \delta_3 \qquad\qquad u_s = 5 \qquad\qquad u_d = 3$$

Fig. 4. Robust cost optimization for the set of constraints from Fig. 3, where up to $u_s = 5$ miners may be non-functioning, refusing to mine or mining invalid blocks; where the level of difficulty may vary by up to $+/-3$; and where the probability of any mining *pool* of size $l = 4$ winning $c = 6$ consecutive mining races is sufficiently small (here $\delta_3 = 0.001$). Predicate $\mathit{feasible}^{u_s}_{u_d}(s,r,d)$ characterizes *robustly feasible* triples and is true iff all triples (s',r,d') with $s - u_s \leq s' \leq s$ and $|d - d'| \leq u_d$ are feasible

---

input : p, α, and values for all constants in Figure 4
invariant: *list* lists tuples $(s,r,d,cost)$ in descending order for d

```
 1  begin
 2  │   define all constants for constraints in Figure 4;
 3  │   list = [(s, r, d, cost) | cost = Cost(s, r, d), feasibleFloat(s, r, d) is true];
 4  │   list = [(s, r, d, cost) ∈ list | feasibleFloat^{u_s}_{u_d}(s, r, d) is true];
 5  │   while (∃(s, r, d, cost) ≠ (s', r', d, cost') ∈ list) do
 6  │   │   case (cost' < cost) ∨ (r' < r) remove (s, r, d, cost) from list);
 7  │   │   case (cost < cost') ∨ (r < r') remove (s', r', d, cost') from list);
 8  │   end while
 9  │   c_m = min{c | ∃(s, r, d, cost) ∈ list};
10  │   while (∃(s, r, d, cost) ∈ list: cost > α · c_m) do
11  │   │   remove (s, r, d, cost) from list;
12  │   end while
13  │   results = list of first p tuples from list;
14  │   results = [(s, r, d, cost) ∈ results | feasibleBigFloat^{u_s}_{u_d}(s, r, d) is true];
15  │   return results;
16  end
```

Fig. 5. Algorithm, written in imperative style of list processing, for reporting the best p robustly feasible tuples $(d,r,s,cost)$ such that d is maximal subject to the cost $cost = Cost(s,r,d)$ satisfying $cost \leq \alpha \cdot c_m$ where c_m is the minimal cost for all robustly feasible tuples (s,r,d) and $\alpha \geq 1$ is a tolerance factor for increasing cost beyond c_m. Predicate $\mathit{feasibleFloat}(s,r,d)$ is true iff all constraints in Fig. 3 are true for this choice of s, r, and d under normal precision floats. Predicates $\mathit{feasibleBigFloat}$ and $\mathit{feasibleBigFloat}^{u_s}_{u_d}$ are true iff their mathematical definition is true under arbitrary-precision floating points (applying package `Data.BigFloat` version 2.13.2).

algorithm has as input the set of constraints, a parameter p and a parameter α. It will output at most p robustly feasible tuples $(s,r,d,cost)$ from a list of all robustly feasible such tuples as follows: it will identify the maximal values of d for which such tuples are robustly feasible, and it will report exactly one such tuple for each value of d where r is minimal, and $cost$ is minimal whilst also bounded above by $\alpha \cdot c_m$ where c_m is the globally minimal cost. This also determines the values of s in these tuples and so the algorithm terminates.

Now, having defined the required analytical expressions and the algorithm to report the best p robustly feasible tuples in Fig. 5, we also want to validate these expressions and the algorithm experimentally. Our setup for this is based on pure Haskell code, as functional – and in particular – Haskell programs offer the advantages of being modular in the dimension of functionality, being strongly typed as well as supporting an easy deconstruction of data structures, particularly lists [3]. Furthermore, the arbitrary-precision verification is handled by the external `Data.BigFloat` package, which is also written in Haskell. Further verification and validation of the received results are pursued by unit testing using an arbitrary precision calculator. Moreover, our experiments ran on a machine with the following specifications: Intel(R) Xeon(R) CPU E5-4650 with 64 cores and 2.70 GHz and 500 GB total RAM. Our machines required between 322.12 and 261.425 s to compute the respective optimizations. The entire experiment took 10,457.58 s.

Table 1. Constants for our experiments. This does not specify the values of τ_u which will vary in experiments. Some experiments will also vary the values of δ, δ_2 or δ_3

$s_l = 4$	$s_u = 80$	$r_l = 24$	$r_u = 64$
$d_l = 4$	$d_u = 64$	$\text{TVC} = 2 \cdot 10^{-12}$	$\text{TFC} = 3000$
$\alpha = 1.5$	$T = 0.002 \cdot 10^{-9}$	$th = 300$	$th' = 300$
$\delta = 10^{-9}$	$\delta_1 = 1$	$\delta_2 = 0.001$	$\delta_3 = 0.001$
$\tau_l = 0$	$\mu = 1/10000$	$\epsilon = 2^{-64}$	$k = 5$
$u_d = 3$	$u_s = 5$	$c = 6$	$l = 4$

We instantiate the model in Fig. 4 with the constants shown in Table 1. We choose T to be $1/(50 \cdot 10^9) = 0.02 \cdot 10^{-9}$ for a mining ASIC from early 2016 with an estimated cost of 2700 USD at that time, so a fixed cost of TFC = 3000 USD seems reasonable. Let us now explain the value $2 \cdot 10^{-12}$, which models the energy cost of a sole hash (we can ignore other costs on that time scale). A conservative estimate for the power consumption of an ASIC is 10 W per Gigahashes per second, i.e. 10 W per Gh/s. We estimate the cost of one kilowatt hour kWh to be about 10 cents. A kWh is 3600 s times kW and one kW is 1000 W. So 10 W per Gh/s equals $10 \cdot 3600$ W, which amounts to 36 kWh. So the cost for this is $36 \cdot 10$ cents per hour, i.e. 360 cents per hour. But then this costs $360/3600 = 0.1$ cents per second. The price for a sole hash is therefore 0.1 divided by $50 \cdot 10^9$, which equals TVC $= 2 \cdot 10^{-12}$.

We insist on having at least 4 miners and cap this at 80 miners. The *shared* nonce space for miners is assumed to be between 24 and 64 bits. The level of difficulty is constrained to be between 4 and 64. We list optimal tuples that are within a factor of $\alpha = 1.5$ of the optimal cost. We make the value th' irrelevant by setting $\delta_1 = 1$ which makes the constraint for th' vacuously true. The probability for mining failure is not allowed to exceed $\epsilon = 2^{-64}$. Setting

$\tau_l = 0$ means that we don't insist on the average mining time to be above any particular positive time. The probability that mining a block takes more than $th = 300\,\text{s}$ is bounded by 10^{-9}. And the probability that more than one miner finds PoW within $\mu = 1/10000\,\text{s}$ is bounded by 0.001, which we also use as bound for winning 6 consecutive mining races. The algorithm reports the top $k = 5$ optimal tuples – and reports fewer if there are no 5 feasible tuples. The remaining constants for robustness are as given in Fig. 4.

Let us now specify some values of τ_u of interest. As reported in [5], Bitcoin is believed to handle up to 7 transactions per second (although this can be improved [6]), Paypal at least 100 transactions per second (which we take as an average here), and Visa anywhere between 2000 and 7000 transactions per second on average. By *transactions per second* we mean that blocks are mined within a period of time consistent with this. Of course, this depends on how many transactions are included in a block. For sake of concreteness and illustration, we take an average number of transactions in a Bitcoin block, as reported for the beginning of April 2016, that is 1454 transactions.

For a Bitcoin style rate, but in our *governed* setting, this means that a block is mined in about $1454/7 \sim 207.71\,\text{s}$. Since $T \cdot E^s(noR)$ is the expected (average) time to mine a block, we can model that we have 7 transactions per second on average by setting $\tau_u^{Bitcoin}$ to be $1454/7$. Similarly, we may compute τ_u^{PayPal} and τ_u^{Visa} based on respective 100 and 7000 transactions per second:

$$\tau_u^{Bitcoin} = 1454/7 \qquad \tau_u^{PayPal} = 1454/100 \qquad \tau_u^{Visa} = 1454/7000 \qquad (20)$$

Experimental Results. We now discuss the results of our experiments. Each experiment is conducted in three different configurations:

C1 constants in as Table 1, i.e. $\delta = 10^{-9}$, $\delta_2 = \delta_3 = 0.001$
C2 smaller δ, that is $\delta = 2^{-64}$, $\delta_2 = \delta_3 = 0.001$
C3 smaller δ and δ_3, that is $\delta = 2^{-64}$, $\delta_2 = 0.001$, and $\delta_3 = 0.0001$.

Transactions per Second as in Bitcoin, PayPal, and Visa. We show in Table 2 output for the top 5 optimal robustly feasible tuples for the various values of τ_u in (20) for configuration C1. We see that all three transaction rates can be realized with 18 miners and a 48-bit shared nonce space in our governed setting, and this gives each miner a nonce space of about 43 bits. The achievable level of difficulty (within the uncertainty in u_s and u_d) ranges from 37 to 41 for both the Bitcoin style rate and the PayPal style rate. For the Visa style rate, the feasible levels of difficulty are 34 and 35. For the optimal tuples reported in Table 2, the value of r remains feasible whenever $48 \le r \le 64$. Note that these results also imply that, for all three rate styles, feasibility requires at least 18 miners.

Let us run this experiment in configuration C2. This models that the probability of mining to take more than $300\,\text{s}$ is very small. We now only report the changes to the results shown in Table 2 for the top rated, optimal tuple. For $\tau_u^{Bitcoin}$, the level of difficulty drops from 41 to 40 but there are still 18 miners and a shared nonce space of 48 bits. This tuple $(s, r, d) = (18, 48, 40)$ is also

Table 2. Output for top 5 optimal tuples for our robust optimization problem run in configuration C1 and with values τ_u as listed in (20): 5 optimal tuples are found for $\tau_u^{Bitcoin}$ and τ_u^{PayPal}, i.e. at least 5 values of d are feasible. The problem has two feasible levels of difficulty for τ_u^{Visa}. Costs are rounded up for three decimal places

$\tau_u^{Bitcoin}(s, r, d, cost)$	$\tau_u^{PayPal}(s, r, d, cost)$	$\tau_u^{Visa}(s, r, d, cost)$
(18, 48, 41, 54004.4)	(18, 48, 41, 54004.4)	(18, 48, 35, 54000.07)
(18, 48, 40, 54002.2)	(18, 48, 40, 54002.2)	(18, 48, 34, 54000.035)
(18, 48, 39, 54001.1)	(18, 48, 39, 54001.1)	
(18, 48, 38, 54000.55)	(18, 48, 38, 54000.55)	
(18, 48, 37, 54000.27)	(18, 48, 37, 54000.27)	

optimal for τ_u^{PayPal} now, whereas the optimal tuple $(s, r, d) = (18, 48, 35)$ for τ_u^{Visa} from configuration C1 remains to be optimal for C2.

Next, we run this experiment for configuration C3, also decreasing the probability that corrupt miners can win 6 consecutive mining races. For $\tau_u^{Bitcoin}$ and for τ_u^{PayPal}, the top 5 optimal tuples are $(s, r, d) = (24, 49, d)$ where $36 \leq d \leq 40$. In particular, this requires at least one more bit for the nonce space and at least 6 more miners. For τ_u^{Visa}, only tuples $(24, 49, 35)$ and $(24, 49, 34)$ are reported, so this also requires at least 24 miners and a 49-bit nonce space, where 35 and 34 are the feasible levels of difficulty.

We may explore the *feasibility boundary* for τ_u for configuration C2. The robust optimization problem is infeasible for $\tau_u = 0.06871$ but becomes feasible when τ_u equals 0.06872. In that case, the only feasible tuples are $(s, r, d) = (18, r, 34, 54000.03)$ where $48 \leq r \leq 64$.

Larger Transaction Rates per Second. Next, we want to vary the average number of transactions *ant* in a block from *ant* = 1454 to larger values. This is sensible for our use case as transactions only record a hash, which may be 8 bytes each. These results are seen in Table 3 for 50000 transactions on average in a block, running in the configuration C1. Let us discuss the impact of changing the *ant* in a block from 1454 to 50000. This has no impact when 7 or 100 transactions per second are desired. For 7000 transactions per second, this robust optimization problem still has the same s and r values in optimal tuples but the level of difficulty (which was 35 or 34) can now be between 36 and 40. This quantifies the security and availability benefits from packing more transactions into a block for mining throughput.

Let us now see how these results change when we run the experiment in configuration C2. Now, all three rate styles report the same optimal 5 tuples which are equal to the tuples listed in the rightmost column in Table 3: $(s, r, d) = (18, 48, d)$ where $36 \leq d \leq 40$. The results for configuration C3 are also idential for all three rate styles, they equal $(s, r, d) = (24, 49, d)$ where $36 \leq d \leq 40$. So this requires one more bit in the nonce space and at least 6 more miners.

Table 3. Output for top 5 optimal tuples for our robust optimization problem running in configuration C1 and with values τ_u given as 50000/7, 50000/100, and 50000/7000 (respectively). Results for the first two columns are identical with those in the first two columns of Table 2. The first 4 optimal tuples for $\tau_u = 50000/7000$ equal that last 4 of the 5 optimal tuples for 50000/7. Costs are rounded up for three decimal places

$Bitcoin \equiv 7(s, r, d, cost)$	$PayPal \equiv 100(s, r, d, cost)$	$Visa \equiv 7000(s, r, d, cost)$
(18, 48, 41, 54004.4)	(18, 48, 41, 54004.4)	(18, 48, 40, 54002.2)
(18, 48, 40, 54002.2)	(18, 48, 40, 54002.2)	(18, 48, 39, 54001.1)
(18, 48, 39, 54001.1)	(18, 48, 39, 54001.1)	(18, 48, 38, 54000.55)
(18, 48, 38, 54000.55)	(18, 48, 38, 54000.55)	(18, 48, 37, 54000.27)
(18, 48, 37, 54000.27)	(18, 48, 37, 54000.27)	(18, 48, 36, 54000.138)

Feasibility Boundary for Transaction Rates per Second. We repeat the last experiment by varying the *ant* from 50000 to half a million, in increments of 50000. We summarize these results as follows:

- *Configuration C1:* For all three rate styles and all transaction values in increments of 50000 up to 500000, the optimal tuples are the same: $(s, r, d) = (18, 48, d)$ where $37 \leq d \leq 41$.
- *Configuration C2:* For all three rate styles and all transaction values in increments of 50000 from 100000 up to 500000, the optimal tuples are the same: $(s, r, d) = (18, 48, d)$ where $36 \leq d \leq 40$. In contrast, for 50000/x where x is 7, 100 or 7000, we need at least a 49-bit nonce space and at least 24 miners.
- *Configuration C3:* For all three rate styles and all transaction values in increments of 50000 up to 500000, the optimal tuples are the same: $(s, r, d) = (24, 49, d)$ where $36 \leq d \leq 40$.

Range of Feasible Sizes for Nonce Space. We can compute and validate whether a robustly feasible tuple $(s, r, d, cost)$ has any other values r' for which $(s, r', d, cost)$ is robustly feasible. For example, for all the optimal tuples $(s, r, d, cost)$ we computed above, we conclude that we may change r to any r' satisfying $r < r' \leq 64$.

7   Discussion and Related Work

We made Assumption 1 only for appeal to the ROM model of the hash function used for mining. Implementations may violate this assumption, without compromising the predictive value of our models. Our Assumption 2 is at odds with Proof of Work as used in Bitcoin. But it does simplify the reasoning about mining behavior, and makes that more akin to reasoning about Byzantine fault tolerant consensus protocols [19]: for BFT protocols, network nodes are either honest (and so comply with protocol rules without incentives) or malicious (and so may behave in an arbitrary manner). Assumption 3 is related to the assumption that a communication network be *weakly synchronous*.

The mathematical model we proposed for Proof of Work did not specify details of the communication environment in which Proof of Work would operate. It would be of interest to extend our mathematical model with suitable abstractions of such a network environment, for example to reflect on upper bound on the communication delay between any two network points. This value could then be used to reflect Assumption 3 in finer detail in our model. Such an extension would also allow us to investigate whether consensus protocols can be simplified by providing Proof of Work as a service with specific behavioral guarantees.

Let us discuss related work next. In [6], a quantitative framework is developed for studying the security and performance of blockchains based on Proof of Work. This framework reflects a range of parameter values such as block size and those pertaining to network propagation, and allows to determine implications of such choices on security (double-spending and selfish mining in particular) and performance. It concludes that Bitcoin could well operate at a higher transaction rate while still offering its current level of security.

In [18], the quest for the "ultimate" blockchain fabric is discussed: getting secure blockchains that can process high transaction volumes (performance) but do this with thousands of nodes (security). Bitcoin offers good scalability of nodes, but its transaction rate does not scale. Dually, BFT protocols [4,10,19] can offer high transaction throughput rates but their communication complexity makes use of thousands of nodes impractical. The BFT state-machine replication protocol PBFT reported in [4] is designed to survive Byzantine faults in asynchronous networks – a proven impossibility that is circumvented with the aforementioned weak synchrony assumption in [4]. For a fixed number of $3f + 1$ nodes, this resiliency to faults can be realized if at most f nodes are faulty. A current leader proposes a new record to be added to the database, and three phases of communication arrive at final consensus of that addition. Views manage the transition of leadership, for example when timeouts suggest that the leader is not complying or not able to cooperate.

The cryptocurrency ByzCoin [9] combines ingredients from PBFT, from Bitcoin-NG (which separates leadership election and transaction verification aspects in the blockchain), and from Proof of Work to devise a hybrid blockchain: its *keyblock chain* uses Proof of Work to elect the next leader, whereas the *microblock* chain uses PBFT style consensus to add transactions during the current leadership. The network is open (nodes may join or leave), and the current consensus group is determined by stakes in mining that occurred within a current window of time. It uses a collective signing mechanism to reduce the communication complexity within the prepare and commit phases of the PBFT protocol.

A growing body of work uses blockchains for transactions that are not financial as such. In [20], e.g., a blockchain is used as a manager for access control such that this mechanism does not require trust in a third party. The architecture of our use case can also support transactions that are not financial.

The paper [11] discusses the work we reported in this paper in more detail. In particular, it includes a statistical validation of the random variables used in our mathematical model. In future work, we would like to support instances of our robust optimization problems in which not only d, s, and r are non-constant but also other parameters of interest – for example the time to compute a hash T or the period of time μ during which we want to avoid a conflict in the mining race. Current MINLP tools don't support such capabilities at present.

8   Conclusions

In this paper we considered blockchains as a well known mechanism for the creation of trustworthiness in transactions, as pioneered in the Bitcoin system [13]. We studied how blockchains, and the choice and operation of cryptographic puzzles that drive the creation of new blocks, could be controlled and owned by one or more organizations. Our proposal for such governed and more central control is that puzzle solvers are mere resources procured by those who control or own the blockchain, and that the solution of puzzles does not provide any monetary or other reward. In particular, solved blocks will not create units of some cryptocurrency and there is therefore no inherent incentive in solving puzzles.

We illustrated this idea with a use case in which financial transactions recorded within conventional accounts would be recorded as hashes within a governed blockchain and where it would be impractical to use hash chains, due to non-linearizability of transaction flows, and due to the lack of resiliency that such a solution would give to tampering with the blockchain.

We developed mathematical foundations for specifying and validating a crucial part of a governed blockchain system, the solving of cryptographic puzzles – where we focussed on Proof of Work. In our approach, owners of a blockchain system can specify allowed ranges for the size of the shared nonce space, the desired level of difficulty, and the number of miners used; and they can add mathematical constraints that specify requirements on availability, security, resiliency, and cost containment. This gives rise to MINLP optimization problems that we were able to express in analytical form, by appeal to the ROM model of cryptographic hash functions used for cryptographic puzzles.

We gave an algorithm for solving such MINLP problems for sizes of practical relevance and used it on some MINLP instances to demonstrate our capability of computing optimal design decisions for a governed Proof of Work system, where robust optimization models resiliency. This *mining calculus* also supports change management, such as an increase in mining capacity or mining resiliency.

Our approach and mathematical model are consistent with the consideration of several organizations controlling and procuring heterogeneous system resources, with each such organization having its bespoke blockchain, and with the provision of puzzle solving as an outsourced service. We leave the refinement of our mathematical models to such settings as future work. It will also be of interest to develop mathematical techniques for the real-time analysis of such blockchains, for example, to assess statistically whether the observed history of cryptographic puzzle solutions is consistent with the design specifications.

We hope our work will provoke more thinking about the design, implementation, and validation of blockchains that are centrally – or in a federated manner – owned and controlled and that may fulfil domain-specific needs for the creation of trustworthiness. We believe that many domains have such needs that the approach advocated in this paper might well be able to meet: existing financial processes and payment workflows, but also systems that have governed blockchains at the heart of their initial design.

Open Access of Research Data: The main algorithms needed for reproducing the experimental results reported in this paper were mere prototypes and not optimized very well. We make these algorithms available in a public repository bitbucket.org/lundbaek/haskell-governed-blockchain-optimiser.

Acknowledgements. This work was supported by the UK EPSRC with a Doctoral Training Fees Award for the first and second author and with projects [grant numbers EP/N020030/1 and EP/N023242/1]. We expressly thank Ruth Misener for having run some of our models on state-of-the-art global MINLP solvers – the tools ANTIGONE [12], BARON [15], and SCIP [17].

References

1. Ali, R., Barrdear, J., Clews, R., Southgate, J.: Innovations in payment technologies and the emergence of digital currencies. Q. Bull. (2014). Published by the Bank of England
2. Ben-Tal, A., Ghaoui, L.E., Nemirovski, A.: Robust Optimization. Princeton University Press, Princeton (2009)
3. Bird, R.: Thinking Functionally with Haskell. Cambridge University Press, Cambridge (2015)
4. Castro, M., Liskov, B.: Practical Byzantine fault tolerance. In: Proceedings of OSDI 1999, pp. 173–186 (1999)
5. Danezis, G., Meiklejohn, S.: Centrally banked cryptocurrencies. CoRR abs/1505.06895 (2015)
6. Gervais, A., Karame, G.O., Wüst, K., Glykantzis, V., Ritzdorf, H., Capkun, S.: On the security and performance of proof of work blockchains. In: Proceedings of the ACM CCS 2016, pp. 3–16 (2016)
7. Horne, D.: Hash chain. In: van Tilborg, H.C.A., Jajodia, S. (eds.) Encyclopedia of Cryptography and Security, 2nd edn, pp. 542–543. Springer, Heidelberg (2011). doi:10.1007/978-1-4419-5906-5_780
8. Jünger, M., Liebling, T.M., Naddef, D., Nemhauser, G.L., Pulleyblank, W.R., Reinelt, G., Rinaldi, G., Wolsey, L.A. (eds.): 50 Years of Integer Programming 1958–2008 - From the Early Years to the State-of-the-Art. Springer, Heidelberg (2010)
9. Kokoris-Kogias, E., Jovanovic, P., Gailly, N., Khoffi, I., Gasser, L., Ford, B.: Enhancing bitcoin security and performance with strong consistency via collective signing. In: Proceedings of the USENIX Security 2016, pp. 279–296 (2016)
10. Lamport, L.: Paxos made simple. ACM SIGACT News **32**(4), 18–25 (2001)
11. Lundbaek, L., D'Iddio, A.C., Huth, M.: Optimizing governed blockchains for financial process authentications. CoRR abs/1612.00407 (2016)

12. Misener, R., Floudas, C.A.: ANTIGONE: algorithms for continuous integer global optimization of nonlinear equations. J. Glob. Optim. **59**(2–3), 503–526 (2014)
13. Nakamoto, S.: Bitcoin : A Peer-to-Peer Electronic Cash System. Published under Pseudonym, May 2008
14. Narayanan, A., Bonneau, J., Felten, E., Miller, A., Goldfeder, S.: Bitcoin and Cryptocurrency Technologies: A Comprehensive Introduction. Princeton University Press, Princeton (2016)
15. Tawarmalani, M., Sahinidis, N.V.: A polyhedral branch-and-cut approach to global optimization. Math. Program. **103**, 225–249 (2005)
16. Vigerske, S.: MINLP Library 2. http://www.gamsworld.org/minlp/minlplib2/html/
17. Vigerske, S.: Decomposition in multistage stochastic programming and a constraint integer programming approach to mixed-integer nonlinear programming. Ph.D. in Mathematics, Humboldt-University Berlin (2012)
18. Vukolić, M.: The quest for scalable blockchain fabric: proof-of-work vs. BFT Replication. In: Camenisch, J., Kesdoğan, D. (eds.) iNetSec 2015. LNCS, vol. 9591, pp. 112–125. Springer, Cham (2016). doi:10.1007/978-3-319-39028-4_9
19. Wattenhofer, R.: The Science of the Blockchain. Inverted Forest Publishing (2016)
20. Zyskind, G., Nathan, O., Pentland, A.: Decentralizing privacy: using blockchain to protect personal data. In: Proceedings of the SPW 2015, pp. 180–184 (2015)

Modeling and Simulation

Energy Consumption Forecast of Photo-Voltaic Comfort Cooling Using UPPAAL Stratego

Mads Kronborg Agesen, Søren Enevoldsen, Thibaut Le Guilly,
Anders Mariegaard$^{(\boxtimes)}$, Petur Olsen, and Arne Skou

Department of Computer Science, Aalborg University,
Selma Lagerlöfs Vej 300, 9220 Aalborg, Denmark
{kronborg,senevoldsen,thibaut,am,petur,ask}@cs.aau.dk

Abstract. To balance the fluctuations of renewable energies, greater flexibility on the consumption side is required. Moreover, solutions are required to handle the uncertainty related to both production and consumption. In this paper, we propose a probabilistic extension to FlexOffers to capture both the interval in which a given energy resource can be operated and the uncertainty that surrounds it. Probabilistic FlexOffers serve as a support for a method to forecast energy production and consumption of stochastic hybrid systems. We then show how to generate a consumption strategy to match a given consumption assignment within a given flexibility interval. The method is illustrated on a building equipped with solar cells, a heat pump and an ice bank used to feed the air conditioning system.

1 Introduction

The use of renewable energies is an essential component to reduce the carbon footprint and moving our modern society towards more sustainability. A major inconvenience of renewables, such as solar cells or wind turbines, is that their production cannot be controlled. Therefore, forecasts on the production from renewable sources are often provided with some uncertainty. This is in particular problematic during peak consumption times, where the high demand for energy might not be matched by production from renewables. In practice, conventional production methods using fossil energies are used to palliate the potential mismatch. At the opposite, there may sometimes be excess of production during off-peak hours, for example during nighttime. A solution is thus to shift part of the consumption loads from the peak hours to the off-peak hours. If this is not possible for all loads, it is possible for some of them. Examples include Heating Ventilation and Air Conditioning Systems (HVAC), charging of electric vehicles and some industrial processes. In order to make use of these *flexible* loads, it is necessary to encode their energy profile to facilitate their manipulation. The European project MIRABEL[1] proposed such a representation, called *FlexOffers* [4]. A limitation of FlexOffers is that they do not provide information about

---

[1] www.mirabel-project.eu.

© Springer International Publishing AG 2017
L. Aceto et al. (Eds.): Larsen Festschrift, LNCS 10460, pp. 603–622, 2017.
DOI: 10.1007/978-3-319-63121-9_30

the uncertainty of the flexibility interval. This means that either the estimation of flexibility has to be very conservative, ensuring that any consumption trajectory within the flexible interval can be followed, or errors must be tolerated when a resource is unable to follow an assigned trajectory. An alternative, proposed in this paper, is to quantify the uncertainty on the flexibility using probability distributions on the bounds of a FlexOffer slice. The notion of FlexOffer and its proposed extension to Probabilistic FlexOffers are detailed in Sect. 2.

Having a satisfactory representation of flexible loads with quantifiable uncertainty, the next step is to be able to estimate both the flexibility interval and the uncertainty on its bounds for a given system. The difficulty is that the dynamics of flexible systems such as those previously mentioned tend to be non-linear. Moreover, taking into account their stochasticity as well as potential environmental or user constraints, render the problem particularly challenging. In this paper, we propose to take advantage of the recent advances in controller synthesis and statistical model checking as a way to forecast flexibility with explicit uncertainty. The approach is described in Sect. 3. To illustrate it, we describe its application on a concrete use case, with an office building equipped with solar panels, a heat pump and an ice bank used to feed the HVAC system. The details of this use case and the application of the proposed approach are presented in Sect. 4. Section 5 discusses related work and Sect. 6 concludes the paper and gives directions for future work.

2   FlexOffers and Probabilistic FlexOffers

This section introduces first the context of FlexOffers in the virtual market of energy, then the basic notion of FlexOffers and its extension to probabilistic FlexOffer.

2.1   Virtual Market of Energy

The Virtual Market of Energy (VME) is a market for trading flexibility in energy consumption (when we mention energy consumption we mean consumption and/or production, where production is represented as negative consumption). The VME does not trade in energy, only in promises of flexibility in energy consumption. Energy is still bought from the normal channels.

The flexibility expressed in a FlexOffer is intended to be sold on the market to the highest bidder. The sellers on the market are entities flexible about its consumption of energy (referred to as a *flexible resource*). The buyers are Balance Responsible Parties (BRP) or Distribution System Operators (DSO) among others (hereafter named buyers). The buyers do forecasts on the load on the grid. If the forecasts show potential issues, such as a grid overload, the buyers can buy flexibility on the VME to move consumption away from the grid overload.

Given a FlexOffer, the buyers can buy an amount of flexibility. This amount is called the schedule, and represents a request for the resource to consume (or produce) a given amount of energy within the flexible interval. In case a Flex-Offer is sold but the resource does not follow the assigned schedule, a penalty must be paid.

The benefit of FlexOffers is that loads can be shifted out of potential grid overloads by the market buyers while normally also providing economic compensation to the flexible resource provider. The cost is used by the buyer to evaluate how much they are willing to pay. Once a schedule is assigned, the buyer will compensate the flexible resource for the amount of energy that has been shifted.

The process for the flexible resource is to first do local energy planning, resulting in an optimal profile for energy consumption. This profile is called the default schedule, and will be used if the FlexOffer is not sold. Second, the flexible resource calculates how much it can deviate from the optimal schedule, and what costs it will incur. This deviation represents the flexibility of the resource. If buyers on the VME are willing to pay more for the flexibility than the cost of deviating from the optimal schedule, then it is beneficial for the flexible resource to follow a suboptimal schedule and be compensated.

2.2 FlexOffer

The notion of FlexOffer was introduced in the MIRABEL project [4]. It is currently used in the Arrowhead[2] and TotalFlex[3] projects [8]. The benefits of flexible loads have also been quantified in previous research [14]. Note that other models for representing energy flexibility exist, as for example the notion of control space proposed in the Energy Flexibility Platform and Interface (EFPi) from the PowerMatcher[4] suite [15].

An example of a FlexOffer is shown in Fig. 1. It is composed of a number of slices, each slice corresponding to a time interval (here one hour). A FlexOffer encodes two types of flexibility. The first one is time flexibility, illustrated by the possibility to move the block of slices within a given timed interval. The second type of flexibility is energy flexibility, and is the one of interest in the context of this paper. The lower area of a slice represents the non-flexible energy load of a flexible resource. The upper area represents the energy interval in which it can operate while delivering correct service. The upper and lower bound on the upper green area represents the maximum and minimum amount of energy the resource can consume, respectively. As illustrated by the second slice, the energy amounts can be negative for entities producing energy. Each FlexOffer contains a default schedule. This schedule represents the optimal energy consumption for the resource. Along with the default schedule can be assigned some pricing information, detailing the cost of deviating from the default schedule.

2.3 Probabilistic FlexOffer

A limitation of the FlexOffer model is that it does not capture uncertainties about the bounds of the flexible interval. However, there are many cases where

---

[2] www.arrowhead.eu.

[3] www.totalflex.dk.

[4] https://flexiblepower.github.io/.

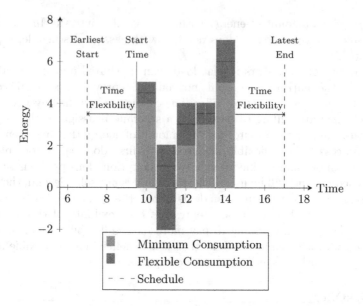

Fig. 1. Example of a FlexOffer. (Color figure online)

it is difficult to provide strong guarantees about these bounds. Solar cells or wind turbines are good examples on the production side, while an office building could deviate from its expected consumption pattern based on unexpected variations of its occupancy. Dealing with such uncertainties necessitates either making conservative estimates, reducing the likelihood of prediction errors, or tolerating a certain number of them. On the other hand, making probabilities explicit can provide valuable information on the likelihood of prediction errors, enabling to increase or reduce the flexibility interval based on desired confidence. Figure 2 shows an example of the representation of a slice of a probabilistic FlexOffer. The minimum and maximum bounds of the slice are expressed by probability distributions, normal distributions in this example.

Let the minimum/maximum consumption distributions be referred to as `min` and `max`, respectively. Then, for each energy input x, the schedule success function `succ` is given by

$$\text{succ}(x) = \text{min}_{\text{CDF}}(x) - \text{max}_{\text{CDF}}(x)$$

where CDF refers to the associated cumulative distribution function[5]. The function describes the probability that the system is able to follow a given schedule. At the mean of the minimum consumption density function ($x = -1$), the probability that the actual minimum consumption is greater than -1 is exactly 50%. Thus, there is a 50% probability that a schedule assigning a consumption of -1 cannot be executed properly by the system i.e. the rate of success is 50%,

---

[5] Note that the Y-axis on Fig. 2 only shows relative values. The scale should not be compared between the success function and the distribution functions.

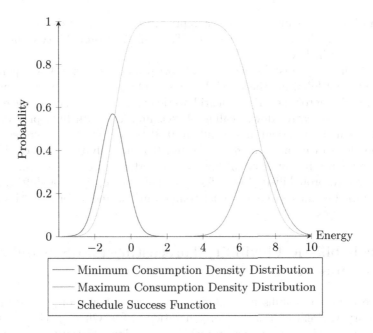

Fig. 2. Example of a slice of a probabilistic FlexOffer.

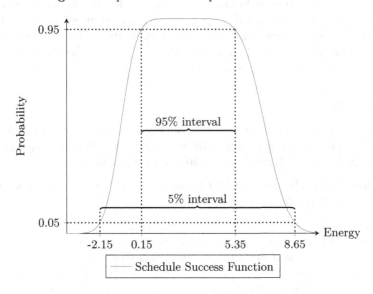

Fig. 3. 95% and 5% success intervals for the schedule success function.

as witnessed by the graph of succ. Similarly, there is a 50% probability that a schedule of $x = 7$ can be followed. Conservative schedules in the interval $[2, 3]$ would have a rate of success of approximately 100%, as it is almost certain that the system is able to operate within this energy interval. Figure 3 depicts the

95% and 5% success intervals. These represent energy intervals $[0.15, 5.35]$ and $[-2.15, 8.65]$ in which there is at least 95% (resp. 5%) probability of being able to follow the schedule.

If the buyer assigns a schedule with low probability, then lower penalty is incurred for not following the schedule. This can be used by the buyer to evaluate if they are willing to take a risk, if a grid overload is severe enough. In the example in Fig. 2 a conservative down-scaling of consumption, with high probability of success, might be to assign a schedule of 0. If the overload is severe enough, a schedule of -1 or even -2 might be better. It is unlikely that the schedule will be followed entirely, but it might give better performance for the grid.

In this way, probabilistic FlexOffers can offer more options for shifting energy loads for the buyers, as well as higher compensations and lower penalties for the flexible resources.

3   Probabilistic Flexibility Forecasting and Schedule Assignment

To make use of probabilistic FlexOffers, a convenient way of generating them is necessary. Current approaches for generation of FlexOffers, such as described in [12], use model based prediction technique. An issue however is that popular models such as available in Simulink do not enable the explicit specification of stochastic parameters. In this paper, we propose an approach based on the recent advances in synthesis and optimization of strategies for stochastic hybrid games [5], available in the UPPAAL-STRATEGO[6] tool [6]. The different steps of the approach are described in this section.

3.1   Modeling

The objective of the modeling step is to obtain a realistic representation of the system for which to generate probabilistic FlexOffers. The modeling formalism employed is Stochastic Hybrid Game [10], defined as follows:

Definition 1 (Stochastic Hybrid Game). *A stochastic hybrid game $\mathcal{G}$ is a tuple $(\mathcal{C}, \mathcal{U}, X, \mathcal{F}, \delta)$ where:*

1. *$\mathcal{C}$ is a controller with a finite set of (controllable) modes C,*
2. *$\mathcal{U}$ is the environment with a set of (uncontrollable) modes U,*
3. *$X = \{x_1, \cdots, x_n\}$ is a finite set of continuous (real-valued) variables,*
4. *for each $c \in C$ and $u \in U, \mathcal{F}_{c,u} : \mathbb{R}_{>0} \times \mathbb{R}^X \to \mathbb{R}^X$ is the flow function that describes the evolution of the continuous variables over time in the combined mode (c, u), and*
5. *δ is a family of density functions, $\delta_\gamma : \mathbb{R}_{\geq 0} \times U \to \mathbb{R}_{\geq 0}$, where $\gamma = (c, u, v) \in C \times U \times \mathbb{R}^X$. More precisely, $\delta_\gamma(\tau, u')$ is the density that $\mathcal{U}$ in the global configuration $\gamma = (c, u, v)$ will change to the uncontrollable mode u' after a delay of τ.*

---
[6] Available at www.uppaal.org.

The controller encodes different configurations of components of the underlying system such as the state of a heater, AC system or heat pump and is one of the players of the game. The opponent player is the environment, encoded as a set of uncontrollable modes. These can represent inhabitants of the building, the temperature, humidity, sun irradiance or other completely uncontrollable aspects. The continuous variables model the system parameters of interest, such as temperature or energy. The dynamics of the continuous variables as flow functions may be described by ordinary differential equations (ODEs) for each combined mode of the system. Finally, the density functions enable specifying a distribution that describes the change of uncontrollable modes over time. These probabilities can be determined based on historical information or external information such as weather forecast. The proper modeling of the system can be determined using simulations to compare the results with actual system behavior. We assume that the controller $\mathcal{C}$ can only change mode periodically, with time period P.

3.2   Estimating Probabilistic Bounds

Having a satisfactory model of the system, the next step is to use it to generate a probabilistic FlexOffer for a given time horizon H. It is assumed that the model includes two continuous variables kWh and $time$ representing the total energy balance of the system and the global time respectively. The optimization capabilities of UPPAAL-STRATEGO are then used to generate two (memoryless) strategies σ_{min}^{H} and σ_{max}^{H}, that minimize (resp. maximize) the expected value of kWh for the horizon H. In this setting, a strategy for a controller $\mathcal{C}$ is a function $\sigma : \mathbb{C} \rightarrow C$ from the set of global configurations $\mathbb{C} = C \times U \times \mathbb{R}^X$ to a new control mode. For a given configuration $\gamma = (c, u, v), \sigma(\gamma)$ thus gives the controllable mode to be used in the next period. A run according to the strategy σ is then a sequence of configurations (γ_i) and delays (τ_i), $\gamma_1 \tau_1 \gamma_2 \tau_2 \ldots$ such that each τ_i respects the period and each γ_i respects the decision made by the controller in a given configuration (see [10] for details). Under a strategy σ, the game $\mathcal{G}$ becomes a stochastic process $\mathcal{G} \upharpoonright \sigma$, implying the existence of a (unique) well-defined probability measure on sets of runs. Given a time horizon $H \in \mathbb{N}$ and a random variable $D, \mathbb{E}_{\sigma,H}^{\mathcal{G},\gamma}(D) \in \mathbb{R}_{\geq 0}$ is the expected value of D with respect to random runs of $\mathcal{G} \upharpoonright \sigma$ of length H, starting in configuration γ.

For generation of flex-offers, the random variable is the energy consumption kWh. Thus, $\sigma_{min}^{H} = \arg\min_{\sigma} \mathbb{E}_{\sigma,H}^{\mathcal{G},\gamma}(kWh)$ and $\sigma_{max}^{H} = \arg\max_{\sigma} \mathbb{E}_{\sigma,H}^{\mathcal{G},\gamma}(kWh)$. Assuming the existence of a reasonable UPPAAL-STRATEGO encoding of the game $\mathcal{G}$, the computation of the two strategies is done by the execution of the following two queries[7]:

```
strategy minkWh = minE (kWh) [<=H]: <> time == H
strategy maxkWh = maxE (kWh) [<=H]: <> time == H
```

---

[7] Syntax for UPPAAL-STRATEGO commands can be seen in [6].

Under these two strategies, the expected value of the minimum and maximum energy balance for a given number of runs N are obtained using the following queries[8]:

```
E[<=H;N] (min:kWh) under minkWh
E[<=H;N] (max:kWh) under maxkWh
```

The resulting probability distributions constitute the bounds of a probabilistic FlexOffer slice of duration H.

3.3   Scheduling

Once a schedule is assigned to a FlexOffer, the associated system is required to follow it as closely as possible. A schedule corresponds to an amount of energy $schEnd$ to be consumed (or produced if negative) within the horizon H. The optimization method used to generate the bounds of a FlexOffer slice can also be applied to generate a strategy that leads the system to approach an assigned consumption amount. To do so, a variable $sch = (schEnd/H) * time$ is defined. This variable represents the ideal consumption pattern to be followed by the system to fulfill the assigned schedule. The error $error$ is then defined as $error = (kWh - sch)^2$, representing the (squared) distance between the expected and actual consumption. In this way, the accumulated error function is monotone w.r.t. time and outliers are punished harder. The objective is then to minimize the error to obtain a strategy σ_H^{sch} that matches the expected consumption pattern as closely as possible. The following query is used to obtain this strategy:

```
strategy schedule = minE (error) [<=H]: <> time == H
```

Assigning a schedule within the probabilistic bound of a FlexOffer can lead to uncertainties about whether the system can follow it. To quantify this uncertainty, a first possibility is to compute it from the probability distribution of the FlexOffer. Another possibility is to estimate, under the strategy σ_H^{sch}, the probability of the consumption falling outside a given interval around the assigned schedule. This is done using the following query:

```
Pr[<=H] (<> (kWh < schEnd - delta || kWh > schEnd + delta)) under schedule
```

where $delta$ corresponds to an acceptable error value.

A buyer on the flexibility market can use this approach to assign a schedule to a FlexOffer, generate a strategy for satisfying it, and then check that the probability of the system deviating from it is within an acceptable range. In case the uncertainty is too high, a different schedule can be assigned.

---

[8] Note that in the case that the evolution of energy is not monotonous, modeling tricks are required, that will be described in Sect. 4.

4   Use Case

To illustrate the proposed methodology, we apply it on a concrete use case. The case concerns comfort cooling for a bank building located in the northern part of Denmark. With a facade composed mainly of glass, the large office space tends to become hot during the summer. To improve the comfort, an innovative cooling system was installed, using solar panels to utilize energy generated from the sun. An overview of the system is shown in Fig. 4.

The system is based around thermal energy storage in the form of an ice bank. The ice bank is a large tank of water with coils running through it. As the liquid inside the coils is cooled down, the water in the tank freezes. During a sunny day, the energy generated by the solar panels is used to power a grid-coupled heat pump for heat exchange between the ice bank and the outside environment. During this process, the ice bank is being "charged" i.e. ice is forming. Finally, a heat exchanger provides an interface between the ice bank and a ventilation system, allowing the ventilation system to "discharge" the ice bank while providing cooling to the building. The ventilation system is configured with a set point T_{set} and automatically turns on if the room temperature, T_r, exceeds the desired set point, T_{set}, by a specified allowed margin of deviation, T_Δ; $T_r > T_{set} + T_\Delta$. Cooling is turned off when the temperate is T_Δ degrees below T_{set}; $T_r < T_{set} - T_\Delta$. Furthermore, if the level of the ice bank falls below a lower limit, the system is hardwired to automatically turn on the heat pump at the maximum setting to quickly "re-charge" the ice bank. In this case, the energy generated from the solar panels may be insufficient, implying a purchase of energy from the grid. Note that, although the ventilation system cannot directly be controlled, the output is completely determined for any time point by T_r, T_{set} and T_Δ.

The control unit computes input settings to the heat pump in order to indirectly adjust the level of the ice bank according to the desired objective. As

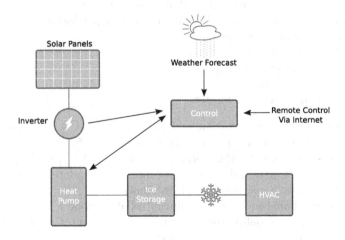

Fig. 4. System component overview.

indicated in Fig. 4, the concrete strategy is influenced by a weather forecast. The default schedule is given by a control strategy that computes heat pump input settings to maximize the use of produced energy from the solar panels. Thus, under the default schedule the goal is to keep the energy balance at zero.

One way of generating a FlexOffer for this use case would be to simply use the lowest possible heat pump setting (off) for the minimum consumption and the maximum possible setting for the upper bound on the flexible interval. This approach has several drawbacks. If the heat pump is always off, the ice bank level might violate the lower bound and therefore automatically turn on the heat pump, for some time, with the maximum input setting. If this happens when the sun is not shining, a purchase of energy from the grid is the only option. In addition, this approach is only viable in the simple case where no pricing information is available. If pricing information is available, the controller should not only optimize for energy consumption, but also take into account the different pricing structures for buying/selling energy from/to the grid.

4.1   Stochastic Hybrid Game Encoding

To encode the system as a stochastic hybrid game, we identify variables describing the important characteristics of the system as well as the (un)controllable modes. As the building is mainly a large open office space, we model it as a single room. We thus consider the stochastic hybrid game $\mathcal{G} = (\mathcal{C}, \mathcal{U}, X, \mathcal{F}, \delta)$ where controller $\mathcal{C}$ has a finite set of controllable modes S corresponding to input settings to the heat pump. The environment $\mathcal{U}$ has modes I, encoding all possible values of the irradiance from the sun, hence $I = \mathbb{R}$. We assume $0 \in S$ to be the lowest setting (turn off) and $100 \in S$ the highest setting available to the controller.

In addition to kWh and *time*, the variables included in X are:

- HP: heat exchange between HP and ice bank (charge).
- $HVAC$: heat exchange between HVAC and ice bank (discharge).
- T_r: temperature of the room.
- IB: level of the ice bank.
- T_{env}: outside temperature.
- Irr: irradiance from the sun.
- $IrrStd$: standard deviation for Irr.

For a given global configuration $\gamma = (s, i, v) \in S \times I \times \mathbb{R}^X$ with $v(Irr) = i_\gamma, v(IrrStd) = IrrStd_\gamma$ we assume that $\mathcal{U}$, given density function δ_γ, can switch among modes according to the normal distribution $\mathcal{N}(i_\gamma, IrrStd_\gamma)$ at every period P. Thus, each period defines an uncontrollable update to the irradiance forecast, according to a specific normal distribution.

For any controllable mode $s \in S$, uncontrollable mode $i \in I$, variable $x \in X$ and time-delay τ we define the flow function $\mathcal{F}_{s,i}(\tau, x)$. Concrete values for constants mentioned can be found in Appendix A.

The flow function $\mathcal{F}_{s,i}(\tau, HP)$ computes the output of the heat pump after a delay of τ:

$$\mathcal{F}_{s,i}(\tau, HP) = \begin{cases} 0 & \text{if } \mathcal{F}_{s,i}(\tau, IB) \geq IB_{full} \\ (A_s \cdot 100 + B_s) \cdot COP_s & \text{if } \mathcal{F}_{s,i}(\tau, IB) \leq IB_{empty} \\ (A_s \cdot s + B_s) \cdot COP_s & \text{o.w} \end{cases}$$

where IB_{full}, IB_{empty} are the bounds on the level of the ice bank, indicating if the ice bank is full or empty. If the ice bank is full, the chosen setting is disregarded and the output of the heat pump is set to 0. If it is empty, the current system automatically turns on the heat pump with the highest setting (100). Otherwise, the chosen setting, s, is applied. The first term of the product converts the setting s to power consumption of the heat pump, which is multiplied by the coefficient of performance (COP) of the heat pump at the given setting, s.

Flow function $\mathcal{F}_{s,i}(\tau, HVAC)$ is given by

$$\mathcal{F}_{s,i}(\tau, HVAC) = \begin{cases} 0 & \text{if } \mathcal{F}_{s,i}(\tau, T_r) < T_{set} - T_\Delta \\ (\mathcal{F}_{s,i}(\tau, T_r) - T_{HVAC}) \cdot H_{HVAC} & \text{if } \mathcal{F}_{s,i}(\tau, T_r) > T_{set} + T_\Delta \\ HVAC & \text{o.w} \end{cases}$$

where T_{set} is the set temperature, T_Δ the allowed temperature deviation, T_{HVAC} the temperature of the cooling air and H_{HVAC} the heat exchange coefficient.

The flow function $\mathcal{F}_{s,i}(\tau, T_r)$ computes the room temperature T_r' after τ time units have passed. It is given by the solution to the following differential equation, where the initial condition is the current temperature T_r:

$$\frac{d}{dt}T_r(t) = D \cdot ((HVAC(t) + i \cdot A_{eff} + P_{free}) - (T_r(t) - T_{env}(t) \cdot H_{env})).$$

P_{free} denotes "free" heat produced by people, electronics, lighting etc. in the room and A_{eff} is the effective area of the windows through which the sun irradiance heats up the room. H_{env} is the heat exchange coefficient for the walls of the building and the environment. Finally $HVAC(t), T_r(t)$ and $T_{env}(t)$ are values for the HVAC cooling power, room temperature and outside temperature at time t, respectively. Hence, the temperature depends on whether or not the ventilation system is turned on or off, the irradiance from the sun heating up the building, free heat and the heat exchange with the environment.

Finally the flow function $\mathcal{F}_{s,i}(\tau, IB)$ for the ice bank level is given by the solution to the following equation:

$$\frac{d}{dt}IB(t) = HP(t) + HVAC(t).$$

The initial condition is given by the current ice bank level IB. This gives a perfect linear model of the ice bank with no heat exchange between the ice bank and the surrounding air. This is not expected to be a correct model, but seems to give reasonable results on short timescales. It is planned to do regression learning on measured data to get a better representation of the actual behavior of the ice bank.

Note that, in addition to the infinite number of uncontrollable modes, the flow functions are recursively defined. Although this may be problematic when seeking an analytical solution, simulation is possible as long as each successor state is well defined. To this end, we impose an ordering on the computation of the recursively defined flow functions. This ordering is the same as the one used above in the list of variables in X: $HP, HVAC, T_r, IB$.

4.2 Experimental Results

The stochastic hybrid game described in the previous section was implemented in UPPAAL-STRATEGO. Concrete details of the model can be found in Appendix B.

The experiments are made by varying the values of some of the variables in the model. Then a FlexOffer can be generated based on the values. The variables are:

- Level of the ice bank.
- A forecast of the irradiance.
- A standard deviation of the irradiance forecast.

The experiments are separated into three sections. First experiments are made at different levels of the ice bank and different forecast scenarios to see how the ice bank performs, and what types of FlexOffers we can expect. Second we show how the standard deviation can be used to make probabilistic FlexOffers and how schedules can be assigned. And finally we discuss the benefits from probabilistic FlexOffers.

Generating FlexOffers. FlexOffers can be generated with UPPAAL-STRATEGO using the queries from Sect. 3.3. Due to technicalities in UPPAAL-STRATEGO, the queries are slightly different than previously shown.

```
E[<=H;N] (min:final_kWh) under minkWh
E[<=H;N] (min:final_kWh) under maxkWh
```

Here `final_kWh` is a new variable which is set to a high number at the beginning and updated to be equal to `kWh` after `H` time units. This is because this type of query returns the minimum value along the trace, but we need the final value at the end of the trace. Running this for different scenarios, we get an idea of the FlexOffers that can be generated.

For the experiments, the ice bank level is varied in three levels: Empty, Mid and Full, with values 0, 25, 55, respectively. The forecast is varied with High, Average, and None (values 600, 200, 0). The standard deviation is set to be 10% of the current forecast. Currently uncertainty is not available from irradiance forecast services, but it is expected to be available in the near future [9].

Table 1 shows results for 9 scenarios with varying amount of solar radiation and varying levels in the ice bank. Each result is an average of 10 runs, where each run took an average of 200 ms on a standard modern laptop. The scenarios are run with time horizon H = 15 (fifteen minutes). For each scenario, the maximum is shown in the top row and the minimum in the bottom row. Six of the scenarios are visualized in Fig. 5. These will be explain left-to-right, top-to-bottom.

Table 1. FlexOffers generated for different scenarios.

		Full	Mid	Empty
High irradiance	Max	$\mathcal{N}(-0.97, 0.03)$	$\mathcal{N}(1.37, 0.03)$	$\mathcal{N}(1.47, 0.03)$
	Min	$\mathcal{N}(-1.17, 0.03)$	$\mathcal{N}(-1.17, 0.03)$	$\mathcal{N}(-0.98, 0.03)$
Average irradiance	Max	$\mathcal{N}(-0.18, 0.01)$	$\mathcal{N}(2.26, 0.01)$	$\mathcal{N}(2.24, 0.01)$
	Min	$\mathcal{N}(-0.39, 0.01)$	$\mathcal{N}(-0.26, 0.01)$	$\mathcal{N}(-0.16, 0.01)$
No irradiance	Max	$\mathcal{N}(0.23, 0.00)$	$\mathcal{N}(2.50, 0.00)$	$\mathcal{N}(2.64, 0.00)$
	Min	$\mathcal{N}(0.04, 0.00)$	$\mathcal{N}(0.06, 0.00)$	$\mathcal{N}(0.28, 0.00)$

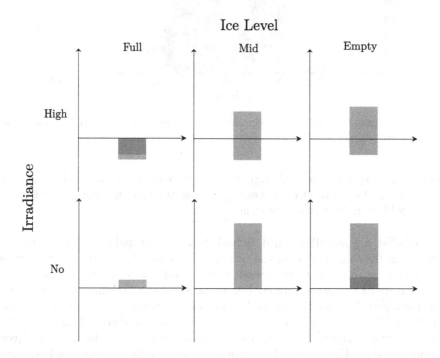

Fig. 5. FlexOffers generated for different scenarios.

First, we have a full ice bank and high irradiance, giving a lot of produced energy. We can see on the FlexOffer that both maximum and minimum are below zero. This means we have excess production we are unable to store in the ice bank, and are forced to sell some to the grid. Second, we have medium level in the bank and high irradiance. This scenario gives us high flexibility. We can choose to buy extra energy from the grid or we can choose to sell production to the grid. Third, we have an empty ice bank and no irradiance. Here we are unable to sell much to the grid, since we need it to charge the ice bank. However, we are able to buy extra energy to charge the bank faster.

For the bottom row in Fig. 5, we can see in all cases that we are unable to sell energy since we have no production. First we have almost no flexibility at all, since we cannot buy more energy for a full bank (the little we can buy is the

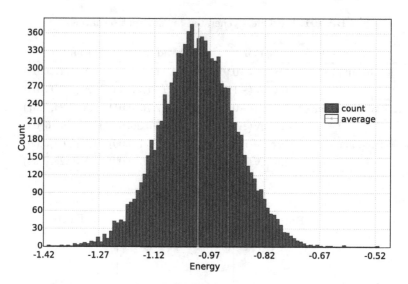

Fig. 6. Histogram showing estimated minimum consumption, with high irradiance and mid ice level.

amount used to cool the building). Second, we have flexibility in buying and, finally, we are forced to buy some energy in case the bank is empty. Here we still have flexibility in how much we want to buy.

Probabilistic FlexOffers and Schedules. The probabilities in the results come from the uncertainty on the irradiance forecast. Currently uncertainty is only added for the irradiance forecast, but it could also be added for the outside temperature or the amount of cooling required by the building. Since the only uncertainty in the model is sampled according to a normal distribution, the output from UPPAAL-STRATEGO will also follow a normal distribution. When we query UPPAAL-STRATEGO for the minimum and maximum values, we are given the mean value. The standard deviation can be calculated from the frequency histogram from UPPAAL-STRATEGO. Figure 6 show an example histogram generated for the case with high irradiance and mid ice bank level.

Probabilistic FlexOffers can be generated using the standard deviation together with the minimum and maximum. Schedules can now be assigned according to this FlexOffer using the query:

```
strategy schedule = minE (error) [<=H]: <> time == H
```

This creates a strategy, which minimizes the error between the schedule and the actual energy used.

The probability of being able to follow a schedule is given by the normal distributions formed by using the minimum and maximum values as mean and their respective standard deviations. A strategy for following the schedule can be generated using UPPAAL-STRATEGO. The probability of being able to follow

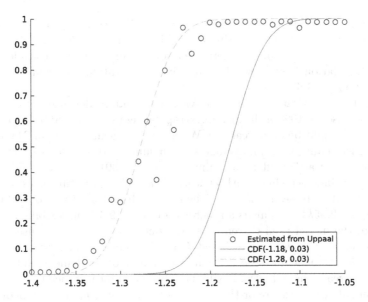

Fig. 7. Probability of being able to follow an assigned schedule. (Color figure online)

a schedule can be estimated by trying to assign schedules in incremental steps using the query:

```
Pr[<=H] (<> (kWh < schEnd - delta || kWh > schEnd + delta)) under schedule
```

We set `delta = 0.1`. Here `schEnd` is the assigned schedule. By varying this in incremental steps from below the mean to above the mean, we can estimate the probability of following different schedules.

Figure 7 shows this estimate for an example minimum value of -1.18 and standard deviation of 0.03. The blue circles are values estimated in steps of 0.01, while the red line is the cumulative distribution function. Each blue circle shows an average of 10 runs, each run an average of took 150 ms. Since the delta is 0.1 all estimates from UPPAAL-STRATEGO are left-shifted by 0.1, due to overestimation. The dashed yellow line shows the CDF shifted by 0.1. The estimates from UPPAAL-STRATEGO follow the CDF quite closely. The reason for the deviation from the CDF is that the models are made to only allow 10 different speed settings on the heat pump, while the actual heat pump supports 100 speed steps. This is done to reduce the state space such that strategies and estimates can be generated faster.

Discussion. The amount of flexibility offered by a FlexOffer depends on the desired accuracy. For a normal FlexOffer we can simply subtract the minimum from the maximum to get the available flexibility. For probabilistic FlexOffers we need to take the desired certainty and the standard deviations into account. If we want a certainty of 95% the flexibility is decreased at both ends. Conversely, if we want 5% the flexibility interval is expanded. For the shown FlexOffer the difference in flexibility offered when requiring a 95% certainty of being able to follow the schedule versus requiring 5% is about $0.1974kWh$ or $197.4Wh$. This might not seem like much, but there are a few circumstances to consider. First, this is a simulation done over a fifteen minute interval, for one hour this would average almost $0.8kWh$.

Second, the simulations are made with the standard deviation of the irradiance forecast set to 10% of the mean. Extrapolating from the graphs in [9] a deviation of 30% might be more realistic. When running a simulation of 24 h using a measured irradiance from an average Danish summer day as forecast with 30% deviation, we get a FlexOffer with min: $\mathcal{N}(-16.41, 0.30)$ and max: $\mathcal{N}(5.55, 0.30)$. If we only include schedules with at least 95% probability, this gives a flexibility of $20.97kWh$. If we include the schedules with at least 5% probability, this increases to $22.95kWh$. This is an increase of about 9.4% in flexibility.

Third, the model used currently is very deterministic in the sense that not many stochastic elements are included. Only the forecast on the solar irradiance is stochastic. If we include stochastic information on other elements in the model we could increase the potential flexibility. This could for instance be uncertainty on the outside temperature or the amount of free heat generated by people and electronics in the building.

Finally, these FlexOffers are intended to be used together with an aggregator [8], which collects a large amount of FlexOffers from several flexible resources. When joining all these, the difference will likely become significant from the buyers perspective.

5   Related Work

The methodology presented in this paper is inspired by several applications of control synthesis and optimization such as presented in [6,11]. In particular, the application of these techniques to synthesize a floor heating controller in [10] has provided good basis for developing and optimizing the model as well as performing the synthesis and optimization. Here however, the objective differs in that the synthesis aims at obtaining the energy bounds in which a system can be operated, not only in optimizing the consumption. The experimental setting described is also similar to the one employed in [1]. An addition to the setting is the inclusion into the flexibility energy framework supported by the Arrowhead framework described in [8,12].

The use case used to illustrate the proposed methodology was previously presented in [2]. The main difference is that the control strategy aimed at maximizing the use of the solar energy while here the objective is to obtain the control interval in which the system can be operated. The model of the system used is derived from the one that was previously presented, with the addition of stochasticity on the irradiance forecast.

The idea of using stochastics in the modelling of flexible loads is not new: In [3] uncertainty about flexible loads is modelled via a single global probability on deviating from expectations. This is used to calculate an overall probability of overload. In [13] more refined stochastic models of households are defined and used to calculate an overall stochastic model of the their aggregated consumption profile. In [7] parameters for price-response stochastic household models are updated and broadcast on a daily basis in order to balance the flexible loads. Our work on probabilistic FlexOffers extends this work by allowing storage, consumption and generation in a single model, and also by allowing model and parameter updates on a frequent basis.

6   Conclusion and Future Work

In this work, we have proposed a probabilistic extension of FlexOffers to model the uncertainty of behaviour caused by an environment consisting of human activities as well as weather conditions like e.g. sun radiation. Also, we have demonstrated how to generate probabilistic FlexOffers from a stochastic model of an office building containing both consumption, storage and generation devices using the UPPAAL-STRATEGO tool. Simulations done on the case study show that probabilistic FlexOffers can increase the flexibility available to the market by about 9.4%.

As next steps, we plan work in two directions: First, we will experiment on how probabilistic FlexOffers interact with the aggregators and markets as developed in other projects [4,8]. Here it will be interesting to observe how the more optimistic constraints affect the schedules received from the market. Secondly, we will investigate how generated FlexOffers can be exploited to optimize the electricity costs by combining them with information on the spot price market.

A   Thermodynamics

Constants from Sect. 4.

$$A_s = \begin{cases} 80 & \text{if } s \leq 25 \\ (s-25) \cdot 120 & \text{o.w} \end{cases}$$

$$B_s = \begin{cases} 0 \cdot s & \text{if } s \leq 25 \\ 2000 & \text{o.w} \end{cases}$$

$$COP_s = \begin{cases} 0.16 \cdot s & \text{if } s \leq 25 \\ 4 & \text{o.w} \end{cases}$$

$$H_{HVAC} = \dot{M}_{air} \cdot C_{air}$$

$$T_{HVAC} = 18\,^{\circ}C$$

$$D = \frac{1}{M_{air} \cdot C_{air}}$$

$$A_{eff} = \frac{6\,\text{m}^2}{10}$$

$$H_{env} = \frac{1}{0.0093}$$

$$IB_{full} = 55$$

$$IB_{empty} = 0$$

where

- $\dot{M}_{air} = 1\frac{kg}{s}$ is the HVAC air flow rate.
- $C_{air} = 1005.4\frac{J}{kg \cdot K}$ is the specific heat capacity of air.
- $M_{air} = 7113.5$ kg is the mass of air in the building.
- $M_{ice} = 1500$ kg is the total mass of ice within ice bank.
- $C_{ice} = 2108\frac{J}{kg \cdot K}$ is the specific heat capacity of ice.

B   Model Specifics

Figure 8 depicts the UPPAAL-STRATEGO model used for on-line controller synthesis. It consists of two location Choose_speed and Wait. The solid edge from Choose_speed to Wait encodes a non-deterministic choice between the available heat pump settings i.e. the controllable modes in the stochastic hybrid game. When the next controllable mode is set, update_irr() computes the next uncontrollable mode, i.e. the irradiance forecast. apply_flow() then updates each variable according to the flow functions of the corresponding stochastic hybrid game, as seen in Listing 1.1. To this end, numeric integration using the Euler method is implemented in each update_X() function call, for numSteps number of steps. Finally, update_kWh() updates the energy consumption/production for this period. Invariant $x \leq 1$ in the Wait location and guard $x == 1$ on the clock x together encode the period. The dotted edge encodes a reset to a new period and is considered uncontrollable by UPPAAL-STRATEGO for control strategy synthesis.

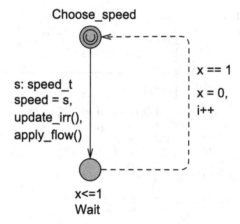

Fig. 8. UPPAAL-STRATEGO model for on-line controller synthesis.

```
void apply_flow () {
    // Manuel integration  for  numSteps steps
    int j;
    for (j = 0; j < numSteps; j++) {
        update_heatpump();
        update_cooler();
        update_temperature();
        update_icebankk();
        update_kWh();
    }
}
```

Listing 1.1. Function to update variables according to flow functions.

References

1. Agesen, M.K., Larsen, K.G., Mikučionis, M., Muñiz, M., Olsen, P., Pedersen, T., Srba, J., Skou, A.: Toolchain for user-centered intelligent floor heating control. In: Industrial Electronics Society, IECON 2016-42nd Annual Conference of the IEEE, pp. 5296–5301. IEEE (2016)
2. Agesen, M., Skou, A., Pedersen, K.: Preliminary report: controller prototyping and validation for photo-voltaic comfort cooling (2016)
3. Bai, J., Gooi, H., Xia, L., Strbac, G., Venkatesh, B.: A probabilistic reserve market incorporating interruptible load. IEEE Trans. Power Syst. **21**(3), 1079–1087 (2006)
4. Boehm, M., Dannecker, L., Doms, A., Dovgan, E., Filipič, B., Fischer, U., Lehner, W., Pedersen, T.B., Pitarch, Y., Šikšnys, L., Tušar, T.: Data management in the MIRABEL smart grid system. In: Proceedings of the 2012 Joint EDBT/ICDT Workshops, EDBT-ICDT 2012, pp. 95–102. ACM, New York (2012)
5. David, A., Jensen, P.G., Larsen, K.G., Legay, A., Lime, D., Sørensen, M.G., Taankvist, J.H.: On time with minimal expected cost!. In: Cassez, F., Raskin, J.-F. (eds.) ATVA 2014. LNCS, vol. 8837, pp. 129–145. Springer, Cham (2014). doi:10.1007/978-3-319-11936-6_10
6. David, A., Jensen, P.G., Larsen, K.G., Mikučionis, M., Taankvist, J.H.: UPPAAL STRATEGO. In: Baier, C., Tinelli, C. (eds.) TACAS 2015. LNCS, vol. 9035, pp. 206–211. Springer, Heidelberg (2015). doi:10.1007/978-3-662-46681-0_16
7. Dorini, G., Pinson, P., Madsen, H.: Chance-constrained optimization of demand response to price signals. IEEE Trans. Smart Grid **4**(4), 2072–2080 (2013)
8. Ferreira, L.L., Siksnys, L., Pedersen, P., Stluka, P., Chrysoulas, C., le Guilly, T., Albano, M., Skou, A., Teixeira, C., Pedersen, T.: Arrowhead compliant virtual market of energy. In: Proceedings of the 2014 IEEE Emerging Technology and Factory Automation (ETFA), pp. 1–8, September 2014
9. Kreutzkamp, P., Gammoh, O., De Brabandere, K., Rekinger, M.: PV forecasting confidence intervals for reserve planning and system operation. In: Proceedings of the 28th European Photovoltaic Solar Energy Conference and Exhibition, EU PVSEC 2013, pp. 4527–4534 (2013). doi:10.4229/28thEUPVSEC2013-6CO.14.6
10. Larsen, K.G., Mikučionis, M., Muñiz, M., Srba, J., Taankvist, J.H.: Online and compositional learning of controllers with application to floor heating. In: Chechik, M., Raskin, J.-F. (eds.) TACAS 2016. LNCS, vol. 9636, pp. 244–259. Springer, Heidelberg (2016). doi:10.1007/978-3-662-49674-9_14

11. Larsen, K.G., Mikučionis, M., Taankvist, J.H.: Safe and optimal adaptive cruise control. In: Meyer, R., Platzer, A., Wehrheim, H. (eds.) Correct System Design. LNCS, vol. 9360, pp. 260–277. Springer, Cham (2015). doi:10.1007/978-3-319-23506-6_17

12. Le Guilly, T., Siksnys, L., Stluka, P., Pedersen, T.B., Olsen, P., Pedersen, P.D., Skou, A., Ferreira, L.L., Albano, M.: An energy flexibility framework on the internet of things. In: The Success of European Projects using New Information and Communication Technologies, pp. 17–37 (2015). doi:10.5220/0006163400170037

13. Molina-Garcia, A., Kessler, M., Fuentes, J.A., Gomez-Lazaro, E.: Probabilistic characterization of thermostatically controlled loads to model the impact of demand response programs. IEEE Trans. Power Syst. **26**(1), 241–251 (2011)

14. Neupane, B., Pedersen, T.B., Thiesson, B.: Evaluating the value of flexibility in energy regulation markets. In: Proceedings of the 2015 ACM Sixth International Conference on Future Energy Systems, e-Energy 2015, pp. 131–140. ACM, New York (2015). https://doi.org/10.1145/2768510.2768540

15. van der Waaij, B., Wilco Wijbrandi, M.K.: White paper energy flexibility platform and interface (EF-PI). Technical report, TNO, June 2015

Towards a Tool: TIMES-Pro for Modeling, Analysis, Simulation and Implementation of Cyber-Physical Systems

Jakaria Abdullah[1]([✉]), Gaoyang Dai[1], Nan Guan[2], Morteza Mohaqeqi[1], and Wang Yi[1]

[1] Uppsala University, Uppsala, Sweden
{jakaria.abdullah,gaoyang.dai,morteza.mohaqeqi,yi}@it.uu.se
[2] Northeastern University, Shenyang, China

Abstract. We consider a Cyber-Physical System (CPS) as a network of components that are either physical plants with continuous behaviors or discrete controllers. To build CPS's in a systematic manner, the TIMES-Pro tool is designed to support modeling, analysis and code generation for real-time simulation and final deployment. In this paper, we present our decisions in designing the modeling language, the tool architecture and features of TIMES-Pro, and also a case study to demonstrate its applicability.

Keywords: Cyber-Physical System · Timing analysis · Real-time simulation · Automated code generation

1 Introduction

Cyber-Physical Systems are systems that contain both discrete components such as digital controllers that generate and react to discrete events according to control laws and continuous components such as physical plants whose behaviors change continuously according to natural laws. Existing design tools for designing such hybrid systems such as Simulink [1] and Modelica [2] have inherent limitation due to the lack of expressiveness in their underlying modeling language and ability for analysis. In this paper, we present an integrated system design tool TIMES-Pro which adopts an expressive yet analytically tractable modeling language based on the Digraph Real-Time (DRT) task model [3–5] to model discrete components and conditional differential equations to model continuous physical components (differential equations with mode switches). For analysis, the continuous components of a system will be abstracted according to a set of predicates of interests, controlling the interaction with the discrete components of the system. DRT models will be used to approximate the continuous components for automated analysis. Our goal is to develop a toolbox supporting modeling and abstraction of both discrete and continuous components, timing

© Springer International Publishing AG 2017
L. Aceto et al. (Eds.): Larsen Festschrift, LNCS 10460, pp. 623–639, 2017.
DOI: 10.1007/978-3-319-63121-9_31

analysis and code generation for real-time simulation as well as final deployment on a given execution platform for the discrete components. The rest of the paper is organized as such, first we present different design decisions related to our system design tool. Next, we briefly introduce our modeling language and its existing analysis and code generation supports. Then we present the status of our tool implementation. Finally, we present an intended case study involving a pacemaker and a random heart model.

2   Design Decisions

In this section we summarize design decisions concerning mainly the design of the modeling language as well as the architecture and the features of TIMES-Pro.

Trade-Off Between Expressiveness and Analysis Efficiency. Ideally, the modeling language of a tool should be as expressive as possible to enable faithful modeling of complex system behaviors such as dynamic branching and looping. As the expressiveness of models grows, so grows the complexity of their analysis. For example, timed automata have been found to be the most expressive model for real-time workload [6], but its analysis suffers from state-space explosion problem which makes it impractical to be used in large system design. To study the trade-off, different real-time models have been developed to compromise the expressiveness and analysis efficiency [7].

The DRT task model [3] is a rather expressive model allowing large flexibility to express release patterns accurately by representing each computation task as a directed graph. It generalizes most existing models in real-time scheduling theory [7]. It is shown that the feasibility problem of DRT can be solved in pseudo-polynomial time [3]. Additionally, efficient techniques of exact response-time analysis for DRT task models, for both static-priority and EDF scheduling have been developed using over-approximation of workload abstraction and refinement methods [5]. Finally, DRT model is extended to support rendezvous-style synchronizations with efficient analysis using over-approximation and under-approximation of workload abstractions [8]. Based on availability of these efficient analysis methods we choose DRT as the core modeling language of our design tool.

Separation of Communication and Computation Concerns. The two major aspects of computer systems embedded in a CPS are computation and communication. Computational elements of a system should be independently designed without adherence to any specific communication mechanism. This allows not only, separation of concerns, in system design but also efficient analysis. From our previous work on task automata and scheduling analysis [9], it is known that many decision problems are computationally hard (even undecidable) for systems where feedback is allowed. Allowing communication to occur during the execution of a computation task may easily bring the feedback effects and change the workload of the system dynamically [9]. Obviously, making communication independent of computation may also allow modularity in system design, and flexible and portable design.

We impose this principle by allowing communication to occur only on the release of computational jobs. This means that the released computation job involves no blocking or non-blocking communication primitives and thus communication can not happen during the execution of the job, which makes it easier to analyse the timing properties of a computation job and also the global timing properties of a system when scheduling is involved.

Functional Correctness Independent of Non-functional Behavior. The functional correctness of a system should be maintained during design-space exploration for satisfying the non-functional requirements. For example, changing the execution time of a task should not change its output or its logical correctness. This sounds a simple principle to implement if only the functional correctness of a task is concerned. On the system level, this is a challenging problem. For example, a functionality of a system is implemented by the execution of a number of tasks. The system designer should make sure that the execution order of tasks by the scheduler will not change the functionality. Technically, this requires that the scheduling policies adopted by the scheduler should ensure the functional correctness implied by system-level global invariants.

System Development in a Simulated Environment. A popular engineering technique to validate or certify CPS is emulation. Emulation, popularly known as hardware-in-the-loop simulation, is used to validate controllers by running them in closed-loop with the actual plant. However, in many cases the actual plant is not available for emulation. Firstly, the plant may be a hardware which is developed at the same time. Secondly, actual plant may be too sensitive and can not tolerate an error during simulation (such as human organs). Finally, construction of the actual plant may be too expensive for the test of a prototype of concept. To encounter these deficiencies, we decide that our system design tool should provide simulated environment using realistic but approximated model of the actual plant.

Here the challenge lies in modeling the continuous semantics of a physical process using discrete software so that all important plant behavior necessary for the simulation can be generated. Current practice of using numerical solvers for evaluating continuous state is either too slow or too complex for any real-time simulation. To counter this, we tend to explore computationally efficient approximation techniques for solving differential equations which we can model using only software components. Our final goal in this regard is to generate code of plant to allow real-time co-simulation.

Analysis Based on Abstraction Refinement Techniques. Analysis of complex system behavior is computationally challenging as possible combinations of concurrent component behaviors grow exponentially with the number of active system components. However, for analysis of many properties such as non-functional properties (e.g. schedulability) partial orders may be derived for the search space, preserving the properties of interests. Thus a hierarchy of abstractions may be generated and systematically evaluated using different levels of the abstractions until an acceptable solution is found. This is the fundamental behind combinatorial abstraction refinement approach [5] which is generalized in [10,11]. We intend to use this abstraction refinement framework for different analysis problems of our design tool.

3   Modeling Language

This section introduces the modeling language of our tool. In particular, we describe the model used to represent independent real-time tasks and its extension with inter-task synchronization.

3.1   Task Model

The core of our modeling language is the Digraph Real-Time (DRT) task model [3]. A DRT task T is represented by a *directed graph* $G(T)$ with vertex and edge labels. Each vertex $v \in G(T)$ represents a type of real-time job that T can release. Here a real-time job is a piece of recurrent sequential code. A vertex v is labeled with worst-case execution time $e(v)$ and relative deadline $d(v)$ of the corresponding job. Both values are assumed to be positive integers.

The graph structure of $G(T)$ denotes the order in which jobs generated by T is released. Each edge (u, v) is labeled with a positive integer $p(u, v)$ denoting the minimum job inter-release separation time. We assume a job deadline $d(u)$ is bounded by the minimal of $p(u, v)$ for all outgoing edges (u, v). Finally, we describe a system with a DRT task set $\tau = \{T_1, \ldots, T_N\}$.

We assume the execution of each DRT task to be independent of each other. While DRT tasks can generate independent real-time jobs of a system, in reality many systems contain jobs with inter-task dependencies. To support such inter-task synchronization requirements we extend DRT task model to Synchronous Digraph Real-Time (SDRT) task model [8]. An SDRT task has the same syntax as a DRT task, except that an edge (u, v) may be labeled with an action $a(u, v)$. The actions are used to model synchronization among tasks. Two SDRT tasks T_1 and T_2 are said to have a synchronization on action s if there exist some edges $(u, v) \in G(T_1)$ and $(u', v') \in G(T_2)$ such that $a(u, v) = s$ and $a(u', v') = s$. To model these actions as rendezvous synchronization primitives of programming language we define two types of valid actions. We use $s?$ ending with ? to represent a get/accept action in a pairwise rendezvous. At the same time, we use $s!$ ending with ! to denote the corresponding send/call action of $s?$. $a(u, v) = []$ means that an edge (u, v) is not associated with any synchronization.

In a synchronous execution, the jobs of two SDRT tasks associated to a common synchronization action must be released at the same time. If one of the synchronizing jobs is ready to be released while the other one is not, the former one will be blocked until the latter one becomes ready. This synchronization behavior is a special case of rendezvous synchronization where synchronization only happens when two synchronous jobs release together.

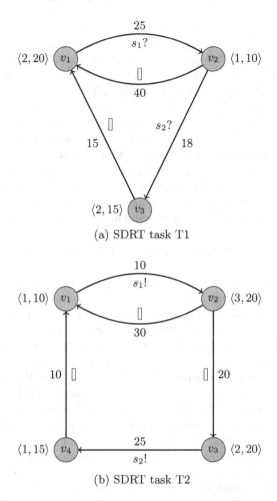

Fig. 1. Two SDRT tasks with two synchronizations on actions s_1 and s_2.

Example 1. Figure 1 shows two SDRT tasks which have two synchronizations on actions s_1 and s_2. Here, the release of job v_3 of task $T1$ is synchronized with the release of job v_4 of task $T2$ on action s_2. As a result, v_3 and v_4 must be released at the same time after satisfying their respective minimum job inter-release separation times. The jobs that have no synchronization such as v_1 of task $T1$ can be released without considering release of any jobs of $T2$.

3.2   System Model

A CPS system model contains components which model software, hardware and the surrounding physical environment. A software or hardware component may be modeled with a set of discrete states and corresponding transitions among them. Continuous states of a physical component is usually expressed using differential equations. A simple way to model such physical component is to adopt a discrete time-step based approach where the continuous behavior is sampled every time-step of length δ. The granularity of such time-step δ is chosen according to the nature of modeled system and the differential equations involved.

A major challenge in CPS simulation is to integrate hardware, software, and physical components so that their combined system behavior conforms to the reality. The heterogeneity of their behaviors makes this integration difficult as a discrete-time component may need to communicate with a continuous-time component. A way to tackle this problem is to use assertions in component interfaces that confirm certain component behaviors. These types of assertions establish a clear interface of the component with precise obligations for caller, callee and environment. This idea is similar to Design-by-contract [12] which is a software engineering technique that exploits runtime assertions to define precise verifiable interface specifications with so-called invariants and pre- and post-conditions.

A system model S in TIMES-Pro is a set of interacting components $C_1, C_2, \ldots, C_N$. Each component C_i is described by SDRT tasks with timing and synchronization constraints. Tasks in two different components can be connected/glued by a common synchronization action. Direction of communication between two connected components is defined based on the type of inter-component synchronization actions. This direction is from the component with "send" action to the components with "accept" actions. We allow two types of inter-component connections using synchronization in TIMES-Pro. In a *conditional* (or *branching*) connection, a component connects with several other components using the same synchronization action. As a result, communication can only happen with one component at a time, among those are ready to communicate. This means different components can share a communication channel to receive from/send to the same component. In *multi-way* connection, a component connects with different components using different synchronization actions. As a result, different components use different communication channels to receive from/send to the same component.

For the purpose of analysis and simulation, a CPS system model needs all types of components (software, hardware and physical environment). However, only software components are required for code generation.

4   Analysis and Synthesis

In TIMES-Pro, a system design is represented by a DRT or SDRT task set. Currently the tool offers two main functions: timing analysis of design models and generation of executable code from the models. In this section, first we describe the analysis techniques implemented in TIMES-Pro. Then we show the code generation approach used in the tool to generate Ada code.

4.1 Analysis

DRT/SDRT is supported by a rich theoretical foundation for timing analysis. Efficient feasibility and schedulability analysis algorithms have been developed, even for those problems that are generally intractable (from the computational complexity point of view). The following analysis algorithms are currently implemented as Python scripts in our tool:

1. Feasibility analysis (or EDF schedulability analysis) of DRT tasks in uniprocessor. It is based on an iterative graph exploration procedure based on a novel path abstraction technique [3].
2. Static priority (SP) schedulability analysis of DRT/SDRT tasks using combinatorial abstraction refinement techniques [5,8].
3. Exact response-time calculation of DRT tasks under SP and EDF scheduling. It is also based on the combinatorial abstraction refinement framework to achieve exact results from initial overapproximations [13].
4. DRT workload partitioning on multiprocessors for Partitioned SP and EDF scheduling algorithm. The partitioning algorithms are based on bin-packing algorithms for sporadic task in multiprocessors [14] but extended to support DRT tasks. These algorithms must determine two criteria:

    Task ordering criteria: Different measures can be used to determine the order by which the tasks are selected to be assigned to a core. These ordering criteria can be considered as either "increasing" or "decreasing". Currently, two ordering metrics have been used in TIMES-Pro:

    Utilization: The utilization of each cycle in the DRT graph is defined as the ratio between WCET sum of nodes in that cycle, and sum of their inter-release times. The utilization of a task is defined as the maximum utilization among all the (simple) cycles in the graph.

    Density: The density of a job is obtained by dividing its execution time by its relative deadline. Intuitively, the density of a job shows that how stringent the deadline of a job is with respect to its execution demand. The density of a task is the maximum density among all of its jobs.

    Core selection criteria: Different bin-packing heuristics can be used to select a core to test for the possibility to accommodate the selected task. Currently TIMES-Pro supports two bin-packing heuristics Best-Fit and Worst-Fit [14]. In Best-Fit packing, cores are sorted according to the decreasing utilization order while in Worst-Fit cores are sorted in the increasing utilization order. Uniprocessor schedulability tests of DRT for SP and EDF are used to decide where the selected task can be assigned to that core. In case of SP, the priorities are assumed to be unspecified. Thus, the partitioning algorithm is free to assign suitable priorities to the tasks for better schedulability.

4.2 Code Generation

The goal of code generation is to transform a design model to executable code while preserving the execution behavior of the model. We use the Ada programming language [15] for code generation, as it provides a run-time system suitable for executing real-time tasks. The following important behaviors of the DRT/SDRT task model need to be handled carefully for code generation:

Synchronization in Job Release: In SDRT, release of jobs from two different tasks can be synchronized based on an action. In Ada, rendezvous is a similar mechanism for controlled synchronization between two tasks. Ada's rendezvous is based on a *client-server* model. A client task requests a rendezvous with a server task by making *entry calls* just as if the server is a protected object. Server tasks indicate willingness to accept a rendezvous on an entry by executing an *accept* statement. For the rendezvous to take place, both the server and the client task must have issued their requests. A task issuing a rendezvous request is blocked until the rendezvous happens. As described earlier, we defined two types of actions in SDRT. The send/call action $s!$ directly maps to Ada rendezvous entry calls. Similarly, the get/accept action $s?$ of SDRT matches the Ada rendezvous accept statement. However, in SDRT semantics, a rendezvous is only allowed during a job release. If an SDRT job release has both timing and synchronization constraints, then the timing one must be satisfied first. This can be implemented in Ada code by first waiting for a delay and then executing the respective rendezvous operation. For the purpose of simplicity, we only use simple rendezvous (without exchange of parameters) of Ada to implement this behavior. As we see next, rendezvous behaviors can be combined with branching in job releases.

Branching in Job Release: A DRT/SDRT task can release jobs sporadically, i.e., after the release of a job, the next job can only arrive after waiting for the minimal inter-release separation time. This sporadic behavior may be combined with the branching of jobs in the sense that different types of jobs can be released if their respective inter-release times after the predecessor job are satisfied. To generate code for this behavior, we have two options.

In *branching based on condition*, the next job to be released is determined according to the satisfaction of some conditions. It is assumed that the conditions are checked in an if-then-else structure which, at run-time, deterministically determines which path the program should follow. For example, in Fig. 1(b) the job v_2 has two successors v_1 and v_3. We illustrate corresponding Ada branching code in Listing 1.1. However, this interpretation of branching can not handle job release constrained by a synchronization action where blocking is needed. Therefore this type of branching is only preferable in DRT tasks.

```
1  case Current_job is
2      when v2 =>
3          v2_code;
4          if Branch_condition then
5              Current_job := v1;
6              Next := Next + v2_v1_del;
7              delay until Next;
8          else
9              Current_job := v3;
10             Next := Next + v2_v3_del;
11             delay until Next;
12         end if;
13         .........
```

Listing 1.1. Branching Ada code for job v_2 of Fig. 1(b).

In *branching based on synchronization*, the next job to be released is decided non-deterministically based on satisfaction of both timing and synchronization constraints. Here we observe three cases: (a) releases of all branch jobs that have both timing and synchronization constraints, (b) some of the branch jobs have release constrained by synchronization constraints but not the rest and (c) releases of branch jobs that are only constrained by timing constraints. Case (c) can be implemented using branching based on condition as described earlier. An example of situation (b) is depicted for job v_2 in Fig. 1(a). Here v_2 has two successors v_1 and v_3. The release of v_3 has to be synchronized with action s_2 while v_1 can be released upon expiration of minimum inter-release separation.

To implement this behavior, we use *selective accept* feature of Ada. As mentioned earlier, we allow a synchronization action to be either a call or an accept action. In *selective accept* of Ada, branching of code is only allowed using *accept* action of rendezvous. For the case of entry call synchronization action, we assume it to be executed once the timing requirement of the job is satisfied. This behavior is implemented in the following steps: first, we sort all outgoing transitions or edges from a job in increasing order of their inter-release times. After observing the smallest possible delay, we insert a selective accept (which means now we can accept an synchronization action and release the branch with the smallest inter-release time) with a delay alternative until the time point when it is also possible to release the next branch. These selective accept blocks are iteratively generated until there is a branch which can be immediately released. The immediate release of a job satisfying both its timing and synchronization constraints is similar to an urgent transition in timed automata. We illustrate Ada branching code for job v_2 in Fig. 1(a) using selective accept in the code segment in Listing 1.2.

```
1  case Current_job is
2      when v2 =>
3          v2_code;
4          Next := Next + v2_v3_del;
5          delay until Next;
6          Next := Next + v2_v1_del;
7          select
8              accept s2;
9              Current_job := v3;
10             Next := Clock;
11             goto end_of_case;
12         or
13             delay until Next;
14         end select;
15         . . . . . . . . . . . . .
```

Listing 1.2. Branching Ada code for job v_2 of Fig. 1(a).

5 Tool Overview

In this section, we present the main features of TIMES-Pro, the tool architecture and the main components in the implementation. Architecture of our tool is shown in Fig. 2.

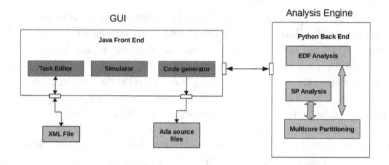

Fig. 2. Tool architecture of TIMES-Pro.

5.1   Features

– **Editor** (see Fig. 3) to graphically model a system and its associated timing, execution resource and synchronization requirements. A system description consists of either a DRT or SDRT task set. The list of all tasks with their assigned priorities is shown in the left side of the main graphical editor. Timing properties of the jobs of a selected task is presented in a table below the task set. All the properties (including the names) of both the task set and jobs properties table are editable.

   In the main graphical editor, a task is described by its directed cyclic graph structure. User can define a jobtype by assigning its WCET, relative deadline and associated execution code segment. Different job types are connected by edges where the user can specify the minimum inter-release time between the two jobs. As an incoming edge denotes release constraints of the job, a synchronization action relevant to this job is also specified as the edge property. In the first option, the system designer explicitly states the branching condition variable together with the job code. Branching conditions are also allowed inside a job.

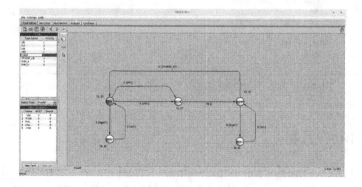

Fig. 3. System modeling using SDRT tasks in TIMES-Pro editor.

- **Simulator** (see Fig. 4) to dynamically visualise the execution behavior and the resource utilization of a system model. The simulator generates possible execution traces with zero or random initial phase. This trace is displayed either stepwise or continuously up to the first deadline miss. It is possible to configure the speed of visual simulation within a scale of 1 to 10. System utilization is dynamically displayed below the main simulation. Currently the simulator supports fixed priority and EDF scheduling simulation on a uniprocessor.

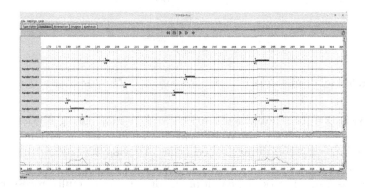

Fig. 4. Visualization of job execution simulation in TIMES-Pro simulator.

- **Analyzer** to check that the tasks associated to a system model satisfy their timing requirements. The analysis suite includes schedulability analysis of tasks under Fixed Priority and EDF scheduling, computation of worst-case response times of tasks and partitioning of workload into multiprocessors. To help testing the algorithms, analyzer has a configurable random task generator which can generate task sets of different size and utilization. Additionally, analyzer provides visualization data of different abstractions used for analysis like request functions.
- **Code Generator** to generate executable Ada code from task sets. The code generator realises a subset of the behavior specified in the DRT/SDRT task model and assumes Ada runtime system will ensure proper execution of the generated code.

5.2   Implementation

Current implementation of the tool is logically divided into three parts:

- **Graphical User Interface** consists of the editor, simulator, visualization of analysis and code generator. It also includes an abstraction visualization tab to visualize workload abstractions to be used in analysis (see Fig. 5). It is possible to check syntax of the model before analysis and the whole system model can be load from or save to an XML file. Currently, the complete GUI has been implemented using JAVA.

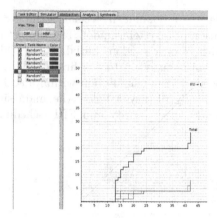

Fig. 5. Workload abstraction visualization in TIMES-Pro abstraction tab.

- **Analysis Engine** implements analysis algorithms using Python scripts.
  Schedulability analysis and WCRT calculation algorithms for DRT tasks are
  included in a Python library called *libdrt*. All these algorithms are available
  for both preemptive Fixed Priority and EDF scheduling algorithms. Analysis
  engine has a set of workload partitioning algorithms for multiprocessors. Currently implemented algorithms include Best-Fit and Worst-Fit bin-packing
  algorithms [14] using density or utilization criterion for both partitioned Fixed
  priority and EDF scheduling. Figure 6 shows different options available in current implementation of the analyzer integrated with GUI. A random task set
  generator is implemented for creating task sets with different utilizations, size
  and timing constraints (see Fig. 7).

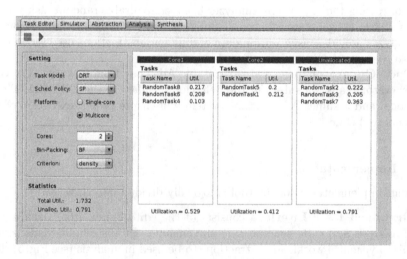

Fig. 6. A sample analysis scenario in TIMES-Pro analyzer using Best-Fit bin-packing
in dual core multiprocessor.

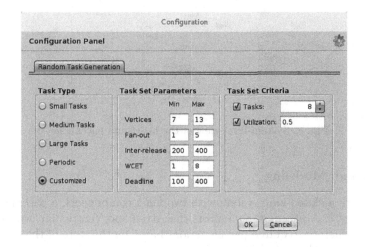

Fig. 7. Configurations for random task generation in TIMES-Pro.

- **Code Generation** is currently implemented with a separate editor. The code generator translates the graphical model of a task set loaded in the editor into a single Ada implementation file (with .adb extension). It allows editing and syntax checking of auto-generated Ada code. The generated code can be compiled to run on top of generic Ada runtime system.

5.3   Ongoing and Future Extensions

Currently we are working on following feature extensions for TIMES-Pro:

- We are developing novel timing analysis techniques to precisely model the controller software driven by physical system behavior. As a first step, we study an engine control application and present an exact timing analysis by partitioning the state space of the engine behaviors [17]. In future, we intend to generalize this result for any control software driven by physical process and integrate the method to TIMES-Pro.
- We are extending the Code Generator for C code generation that can run using the FreeRTOS [18] real-time operating system. In future, we will generate executable code for multicore platforms based on partitioned multiprocessor scheduling [14].

6   Case Study

We use the heart and dual chamber DDD pacemaker model used in [16] as a case study to illustrate CPS system modeling with our tool.

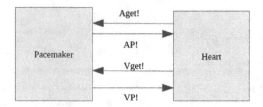

Fig. 8. System-level view of the heart and pacemaker.

6.1   System Modeling

We deal with a closed-loop system with two main components, a pacemaker and a human heart. A pacemaker monitors the Atrial and Ventricular events in the heart and generates required pacing actions based on the state of the heart. The system model is shown in Fig. 8.

The pacemaker receives Aget and Vget events from the heart. These are internally recognized as the signals AS (Atrial Sense) and VS (Ventricular Sense) which are used to synchronize different states of the different tasks of the pacemaker. There is another internal signal called AR (Atrial refractory) which is used for the monitoring purpose. The pacemaker generates AP (Atrial pacing) and VP (Ventricular pacing) action signals to the heart model.

6.2   Component Modeling

The pacemaker has five main tasks capturing different timing requirements based on inputs from the heart. Here we describe each of these tasks using SDRT models:

- PVARP: Post Ventricular Atrial Refractory Period (PVARP) task receives Atrial events (Agets) and detects them as AS for synchronizing the other tasks. With each Ventricular event (VP or VS) there will be a period of t_PVAB + t_PVARP when Agets are not recognized as AS. During the period of t_PVAB all Agets will be ignored. However during the period of t_PVARP the incoming Agets are recorded as AR signals.
- VRP (Ventricular Refractory Period): This task receives Vget events from the heart and recognize them as VS. After each Ventricular event (VS or VP) the task should wait for a period of t_TVRP to generate next Ventricular event.
- LRI (Lower Rate Interval): This task keeps the heart rate above desired minimum value. If no AS is received after t_TLRI − t_TAVI time period following a Ventricular event then AP is delivered.
- AVI (Atrio-Ventricular Interval): This task maintains the delay between the Atrial and the Ventricular activations. If no VS has been sensed within t_TAVI after an Atrial event (AS, AP), the task will generate VP. The task should maintain an interval of t_TURI between two Ventricular events (VP, VS).

– URI (Upper Rate Interval): This task works as a timer to limit Ventricular
pacing events. Two consecutive VPs should be separated by an interval of
t_TURI.

The simple version of the random heart model has two tasks, one for generating the Atrial events and another for generating the Ventricular events. Both
of these components can randomly generate an intrinsic heart event within a
range of valid intervals.

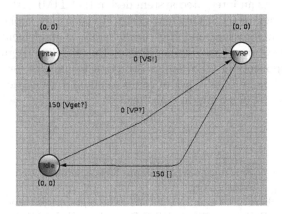

Fig. 9. SDRT model of the VRP component in TIMES-Pro.

```
 1  when Init =>
 2      Init_code;
 3      Next := Next + Init_to_temp_delay;
 4      delay until Next;
 5      Next := Next + Init_to_VRP_delay;
 6   select
 7      accept Vget;
 8      Current_State := temp;
 9      Next := Clock;
10      goto end_of_case;
11   or
12      delay until Next;
13   end select;
14   select
15      accept Vget;
16      Current_State := temp;
17      Next := Clock;
18      goto end_of_case;
19   or
20      accept VP;
21      Current_State := VRP;
22      Next := Clock;
23      goto end_of_case;
24   end select;
25      .........
```

Listing 1.3. Partial view of the code generated for the component VRP by TIMES-
Pro.

Currently we have modeled these pacemaker and heart components in our tool using SDRT tasks. We generated Ada executable code from the model. For example, Fig. 9 shows the VRP component of pacemaker in TIMES-Pro and Listing 1.3 partially shows the generated code. In future we would like to use more complex heart models and visualize the simulation.

7   Conclusions and Future Work

This paper presents an integrated system design tool TIMES-Pro for the design and implementation of CPS. Different design decisions are explained and motivated; the tool architecture and the current state of implementation are presented. As future work, we will further develop the modeling language to support continuous components of CPS, and abstraction techniques for the analysis of combined behaviors by both types of components and generation of executable code to simulate the behaviors in real-time.

References

1. Simulink. http://www.mathworks.com/products/simulink/
2. Modelica. http://modelica.org
3. Stigge, M., Ekberg, P., Guan, N., Yi, W.: The digraph real-time task model. In: Proceedings of RTAS, pp. 71–80. IEEE Press, New York (2011)
4. Stigge, M., Yi, W.: Hardness results for static priority real-time scheduling. In: Proceedings of ECRTS, pp. 189–198 (2012)
5. Stigge, M., Yi, W.: Combinatorial abstraction refinement for feasibility analysis. In: Proceedings of RTSS, pp. 340–349. IEEE Press, New York (2013)
6. Amnell, T., Fersman, E., Mokrushin, L., Pettersson, P., Yi, W.: TIMES — a tool for modelling and implementation of embedded systems. In: Katoen, J.-P., Stevens, P. (eds.) TACAS 2002. LNCS, vol. 2280, pp. 460–464. Springer, Heidelberg (2002). doi:10.1007/3-540-46002-0_32
7. Stigge, M., Yi, W.: Models of real-time workload: a survey. In: Audsley, N., Baruah, S. (eds.) Real-Time Systems: The Past, the Present, and the Future, pp. 133–160 (2013)
8. Mohaqeqi, M., Abdullah, J., Guan, N., Yi, W.: Schedulability analysis of synchronous digraph real-time task. In: Proceedings of ECRTS 2016, pp. 176–186 (2016)
9. Fersman, E., Krcal, P., Pettersson, P., Yi, W.: Task automata: schedulability, decidability and undecidability. Inf. Comput. **205**(8), 1149–1172 (2007)
10. Stigge, M.: Real-time workload models: expressiveness vs. analysis efficiency. Ph.D. dissertation, Uppsala University (2014)
11. Guan, N., Tang, Y., Abdullah, J., Stigge, M., Yi, W.: Scalable timing analysis with refinement. In: Baier, C., Tinelli, C. (eds.) TACAS 2015. LNCS, vol. 9035, pp. 3–18. Springer, Heidelberg (2015). doi:10.1007/978-3-662-46681-0_1
12. Meyer, B.: Applying "design by contract". Computer **25**(10), 40–51 (1992). http://dx.doi.org/10.1109/2.161279
13. Stigge, M., Guan, N., Yi, W.: Refinement-based exact response-time analysis. In: Proceedings of ECRTS, pp. 143–152 (2014)

14. Davis, R.I., Burns, A.: A survey of hard real-time scheduling for multiprocessor systems. ACM Comput. Surv. **43**(4), 35:1–35:44 (2011)
15. Ada programming language. http://www.adacore.com/
16. Jiang, Z., Pajic, M., Moarref, S., Alur, R., Mangharam, R.: Modeling and verification of a dual chamber implantable pacemaker. In: Flanagan, C., König, B. (eds.) TACAS 2012. LNCS, vol. 7214, pp. 188–203. Springer, Heidelberg (2012). doi:10.1007/978-3-642-28756-5_14
17. Mohaqeqi, M., Abdullah, J., Ekberg, P., Yi, W.: Refinement of workload models for engine controllers by state space partitioning. In: Proceedings of ECRTS (2017, to appear)
18. FreeRTOS Real-time Operating System. http://www.freertos.org

Formalising a Hazard Warning Communication Protocol with Timed Automata

Ernst-Rüdiger Olderog$^{(\boxtimes)}$ and Maike Schwammberger$^{(\boxtimes)}$

Department of Computing Science, University of Oldenburg, Oldenburg, Germany
{olderog,schwammberger}@informatik.uni-oldenburg.de

Abstract. In previous work, we used an extended version of timed automata to build safe controllers for autonomous car manoeuvres like changing lanes or crossing an intersection. These automata use formulae of Multi-lane Spatial Logic as guards and invariants and have special controller actions for car manoeuvres. As a case study, we now adapt our approach to formalise a multi-hop communication protocol for hazard warning for highway traffic scenarios. We prove that, if a car detects a hazard, this information timely reaches all cars for which it is relevant via a communication chain so that they can avoid colliding with the hazard.

Keywords: Timed automata · Multi-hop communication protocols · Hazard warning · Autonomous cars · Multi-dimensional spatial logic

1 Introduction

During the last years, autonomously driving cars are a topic of increasing interest for society and research. In this connection, a wide range of *intelligent transportation systems* were introduced to increase safety, security and comfort of autonomous driving [1].

In this paper, we focus on the approach of Müllner et al. [2], where the authors analyse a communication protocol which is used to send a timely traffic-hazard warning to other traffic participants. The authors use simulation techniques to estimate the probability that the hazard warning message is received in time. Their simulation framework works with discrete time steps, where a decentralised environmental notification message is sent at intervals of one time step.

Our contributions in this paper are as follows. We formalise the timing aspects of the simulation-based analysis of the communication protocol studied in [2] by using extended timed automata, called automotive-controlling timed automata (ACTA) [3]. ACTA communicate via broadcast channels using data structures. Using this formalisation we prove the timely warning property, partly supported by the model checker UPPAAL [4]. Note that with extended timed automata, we will also use a continuous time dimension instead of discrete time steps.

This research was partially supported by the German Research Council (DFG) in the Research Training Group GRK 1765 SCARE.

L. Aceto et al. (Eds.): Larsen Festschrift, LNCS 10460, pp. 640–660, 2017.
DOI: 10.1007/978-3-319-63121-9_32

Also, we link the timely warning property with spatial reasoning to prove avoidance of hazard collision using a new extension of the *Multi-lane Spatial Logic* MLSL [5] to cope with stationary hazards, called HMLSL. Formulae of this logic appear in the guards and invariants of ACTA to establish the desired spatial safety properties. Using (H)MLSL we abstract from the underlying car dynamics [6].

In the remainder of this section, we introduce the traffic scenario and goal of our case study. In Sect. 2, we define the adjusted abstract model and the *Hazard Warning Multi-lane Spatial Logic* (HMLSL). We then explain in Sect. 3 how to derive a communication chain and define our broadcast communication with data structures. In Sect. 4, we introduce two controllers to formalise the proposed hazard warning communication protocol, and in Sect. 5, we describe the adaption of these controllers for the use of UPPAAL [4]. In Sect. 6, we show the timely hazard warning message delivery with an inductive proof assisted by UPPAAL and further on prove spatial hazard safety. We conclude with some ideas for future work in Sect. 7.

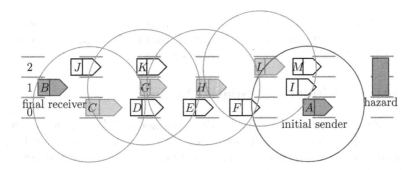

Fig. 1. The initial sender, car A, detects a hazard on lanes $L_{\xi} = \{1, 2\}$ and sends a timely warning message via the communication chain $\vec{c} = \langle A, L, H, G, C, B \rangle$ with intermediate cars L, H, G, C to the final receiver, which is car B.

Case Study. We adopt the basic scenario for our case study from [2]. Therefore, we consider highway traffic scenarios where all traffic drives in one driving direction. This paper focuses on stationary traffic hazards, like traffic jams, collisions, slippery street parts (ice, aquaplaning), and limited sight (e.g. due to fog). We assume a hazard to stretch over an arbitrary amount of lanes and to have a positive extension along the lanes. For now, we restrict the number of occurring hazards to one at a time.

The first car to approach and perceive such a hazardous situation, we call *initial sender* A (cf. Fig. 1). The overall safety goal is that A transmits a hazard warning as fast as possible to a specific *final receiver* B driving behind A. We assume that car B is about to reach the hazard in t time units. The safety goal is missed if B reaches the hazard without receiving a hazard warning before t time units after it has occurred. It that case B may not be able to initiate braking or another emergency manoeuvre preventing it from colliding with the hazard (e.g., leaving the highway or changing to a lane without a hazardous situation). In this paper, we do not consider how such an emergency manoeuvre is conducted, but concentrate on sending timely warnings. Note that initial sender A sends the warning even if itself is not affected by it because it is driving on a non-hazardous lane, cf. Fig. 1.

The hazard warning is communicated via a broadcast channel *hazard* through a *communication chain* comprising other traffic participants (cf. Fig. 1). Following the approach from [2], we presume every car to have the same communication antenna and thus the same communication radius r. With this, we can determine the minimal amount of cars needed to build a communication chain and send the hazard warning from initial sender A to final receiver B. In the following, we assume that a communication chain between initial sender and final receiver can always be established. Additionally, we assume that the cars in the communication chain $\overrightarrow{c}$ drive spatially behind one another. We do not communicate the warning message forwards, because a car in front of an arbitrary car C can not communicate further behind C itself (coherent communication radius r for all cars).

We furthermore assume that all cars are autonomous and equipped with the lane change and distance controllers introduced in [5] to guarantee collision freedom while the hazard warning message is propagated.

2   Abstract Model and Spatial Logic

In this section, we summarise and modify the model of [5]. In this model, a multi-lane highway has an infinite extension with positions represented by real numbers in $\mathbb{R}$ and with lanes represented by a finite set of natural numbers, $\mathbb{L} = \{0, \ldots, N\}$. We assume that all traffic proceeds in one direction, with increasing position values, in pictures shown from left to right. The highway is populated by cars with unique identities denoted by capital letters $\mathbb{I} = \{A, B, C, D, E, \ldots\}$.

At each moment in time, we represent the traffic on the highway by a *traffic snapshot*. It records for each car its current position *pos* (at the rear end of the car), its speed *spd*, and on which lanes it *reserves* space. For safety, we have to show that reserved spaces of different cars are mutually exclusive. In [5] we considered also *claimed* spaces for lane change manoeuvres, but these are not in the focus of this paper.

Here we consider a new feature in the abstract model of road traffic: a *hazard*. Intuitively, we think of a hazard as a space of rectangular shape on a multi-lane road that, from a certain moment on, blocks several adjacent lanes. To this end, we modify the notion of traffic snapshot introduced in [5] by a component *haz* with three attributes:

- a Boolean attribute *haz.on* ranging over $\{0, 1\}$ and indicating whether the hazard is present (*haz.on* $= 1$) or not,
- an attribute *haz.lanes* representing the set of lanes affected by the hazard, which is a contiguous subset of $\mathbb{L}$,

- an attribute *haz.ext* representing a fixed horizontal extension of the hazard, which is an interval $[haz.start, haz.end] \subseteq \mathbb{R}$ with $haz.start < haz.end$.

A *traffic snapshot* is thus a structure $\mathcal{TS} = (pos, spd, res, haz)$ which besides *haz* comprises the functions *pos*, *spd*, *res*:

- $pos : \mathbb{I} \to \mathbb{R}$ such that $pos(C)$ is the position of car C along the lanes,
- $spd : \mathbb{I} \to \mathbb{R}$ such that $spd(C)$ is the current speed of the car C,
- $res : \mathbb{I} \to \mathcal{P}(\mathbb{L})$ such that $res(C)$ is the set of lanes C reserves.

In [5], traffic snapshots also comprise functions *clm* and *acc* for specifying the claimed lanes and the acceleration of cars, respectively, but we omit them here because we do not consider lane changes and overtaking in this paper.

The length of reserved spaces is given by the *safety distance*, which is the length of the car plus a safe estimate of the (speed-dependent) braking distance that the car will need to come to a complete standstill. It is not specified in $\mathcal{TS}$, but given by an uninterpreted function *se* for *safety envelope*. For a given traffic snapshot $\mathcal{TS}$, the *safety envelope* $se_{\mathcal{TS}}(C)$ of a car C is the interval $se_{\mathcal{TS}}(C) = [pos(C), pos(C) + d(C)]$ starting at the current position $pos(C)$ of the car and of some uninterpreted length $d(C) > 0$, which is intended to be the safety distance of car C dependent on its current speed $spd(C)$. The exact value of $d(C)$ is not known in the abstract model, but will be determined in the underlying dynamic model [6].

2.1   View

For reasoning about safety, we need to consider only finite parts of a traffic snapshot $\mathcal{TS}$ called *views*. A *view* $V = (L, X, E)$ consists of an interval of lanes visible in the view, $L = [l, n] = \{\ell \in \mathbb{L} \mid l \le \ell \le n\}$ for some $l, n \in \mathbb{L}$, and the extension visible in the view, $X = [r, t] = \{x \in \mathbb{R} \mid r \le x \le t\}$ for some $r, t \in \mathbb{R}$, and $E \in \mathbb{I}$, the identifier of the car under consideration.

A *subview* of V is obtained by restricting the lanes and extension we observe. For this we use sub- and superscript notation: $V^{L'} = (L', X, E)$ and $V_{X'} = (L, X', E)$, where L' and X' are subintervals of L and X, respectively.

The *standard view* of a car E in a traffic snapshot $\mathcal{TS} = (pos, spd, res, haz)$ is defined as

$$V_s(E, \mathcal{TS}) = (\mathbb{L}, [pos(E) - ho, pos(E) + ho], E),$$

where the *horizon ho* is chosen such that a car driving at maximum speed can, with lowest deceleration, come to a standstill within the horizon.

2.2   Transitions

A traffic snapshot is an instant picture of the highway traffic. *Transitions* describe how it may change. Time may pass or a car may perform actions of a traffic manoeuvre. In this paper, we consider only time-passing transitions between traffic snapshots. In such a transition a hazard may occur (by switching $haz.on$ from 0 to 1) and remain present, i.e., $haz.on = 1$ is a stable predicate. Further on, the car will move, i.e., its position will increase, and it may change its speed. For a traffic snapshot $\mathcal{TS} = (pos, spd, res, haz)$ and time $t \in \mathbb{R}_{\geq 0}$, a *time transition* is thus defined as follows:

$$\mathcal{TS} \xrightarrow{t} \mathcal{TS}' \Leftrightarrow \mathcal{TS}' = (pos', spd', res', haz') \text{ and}$$
$$\forall C \in \mathbb{I}\colon pos'(C) > pos(C) \text{ and } res' = res \text{ and } haz' \geq haz,$$

where $haz' \geq haz$ abbreviates $haz'.on \geq haz.on$, $haz'.lanes = haz.lanes$ and $haz'.ext = haz.ext$, i.e., a hazard that is present in haz remains present in haz', but it does not change its position and size when time is passing.

During a time transition, each car C continues to move, formalised by its increasing position ($pos'(C) > pos(C)$), but it does not change its reserved lanes ($res' = res$). Note that the speed may change in an unconstrained manner. However, for safety a distance controller will have to adapt the speed so that a sufficient distance is kept to the cars ahead and thus the reserved spaces remain disjoint.

2.3   Spatial Logic

To specify properties of traffic snapshots within a given view in an intuitive and yet precise way, we use a two-dimensional spatial interval logic, MLSL (Multi-lane Spatial Logic) [5]. In this logic, the horizontal dimension is continuous, representing positions on a highway, and the vertical dimension is discrete, representing the number of a lane on a highway. In the syntax, variables ranging over car identifiers are denoted by small letters c, d, u and v. To refer to the car owning the current view, we use a special variable ego. By Var we denote the set of all these variables.

In this paper, we extend the logic Multi-lane Spatial Logic MLSL by a new atom hz representing a hazard at the logical level.

Definition 1 (Syntax). *The syntax of* Hazard Warning Multi-lane Spatial Logic HMLSL *is defined as follows.*

$$\phi ::= true \mid u = v \mid free \mid re(c) \mid hz \mid \neg\phi \mid \phi_1 \wedge \phi_2 \mid \exists c \bullet \phi_1 \mid \phi_1 \frown \phi_2 \mid \begin{smallmatrix} \phi_2 \\ \phi_1 \end{smallmatrix},$$

where $c, u, v \in$ Var. *We denote the set of all HMLSL formulas by* $\Phi_{\mathbb{H}}$.

Formulae of HMLSL express the spatial status of neighbouring lanes on a multi-lane highway. For a lane, the spatial status describes whether parts of it are completely free or reserved by a car or endangered by a hazard. To this end, the logic has atoms $free, re(c)$, and hz (expressing that the considered space is not occupied by any car, that it is reserved by a car denoted by the variable c, and that it is occupied by a hazard, respectively), propositional connectives and quantifiers over car variables, and two chop operators: the horizontal chop $\phi_1 \frown \phi_2$ expresses that a space can be divided into two horizontally adjacent parts such that ϕ_1 holds in the left part and ϕ_2 in the right part, and the vertical chop $\frac{\phi_2}{\phi_1}$ expresses that a space can be divided into two vertically adjacent parts where ϕ_1 holds on the lower part and ϕ_2 on the upper part. We use juxtaposition for the vertical chop to have a correspondence to the visual layout in traffic snapshots.

The logic is given a semantics that defines when traffic snapshots satisfy a given formula, as detailed in [5]. We focus here on the new atom hz:

Definition 2 (Semantics of hz). *The satisfaction of the atom hz with respect to a traffic snapshot $\mathcal{TS}$, a view $V = (L, X, E)$, and a valuation ν of the variables with $\nu(ego) = E$ is defined as follows:*

$$\mathcal{TS}, V, \nu \models hz \;\Leftrightarrow\; |L| = 1 \text{ and } \|X\| > 0 \text{ and}$$
$$hz.on = 1 \text{ and } L \subseteq hz.lanes \text{ and } X \subseteq hz.ext.$$

Note that the atom hz holds only in one lane. To express that a hazard holds in several lanes, the vertical chop operator can be used. Often, we want to express that there is *no* hazard in the considered space. To this end, we use the derived two-dimensional modality *somewhere* ϕ, denoted by $\langle \phi \rangle$ and defined by

$$\langle \phi \rangle \equiv true \frown \begin{pmatrix} true \\ \phi \\ true \end{pmatrix} \frown true.$$

Informally, $\langle \phi \rangle$ states that *somewhere* in the considered space the property ϕ holds. Now, safety in the presence of hazards can be specified as follows:

$$Safe\text{-}hz \equiv \neg \exists c : \langle re(c) \wedge hz \rangle,$$

i.e., no car has some overlap of its reserved space with a hazard. The hazard detection controller introduced in Sect. 4 will use the following formula as a transition guard:

$$\langle re(ego) \rangle \frown \langle hz \rangle.$$

It specifies that to the right of the car *ego* (more precisely, of the car that the variable *ego* currently evaluates to in the considered valuation ν) there is hazard. By the semantics of the two somewhere operators, the hazard need not be on the same lane that *ego* is driving on. This is e.g. the case for car A in Fig. 1.

3   Communication

In our abstract model, the autonomous cars can be understood as nodes in a *Vehicular ad hoc network* (VANET), without a fixed wireless infrastructure and without taking roadside units into account. Following the approach in [2], an instantaneous transitive bridge relay between the initial sender node A and the final receiver node B is required, once a hazard is detected. This bridge relay we call *communication chain* and formalise it as a finite sequence $\overrightarrow{c}$ of cars, the first one being the initial sender and the last one being the final receiver (cf. Fig. 1).

The warning message is distributed via a broadcast channel *hazard*, where only cars contained in the communication chain actively forward the message. This approach avoids flooding the message by all traffic participants and thus avoids network overload. Note that due to the use of broadcast channels, all the other cars – even while not involved in the communication chain – receive the hazard warning, but they need not react to it. With this, all cars between initial sender and final receiver will be warned and can react to the hazard by e.g. (emergency) braking or changing to a non-hazardous lane. However, in this paper we focus on safety of the cars in communication chain $\overrightarrow{c}$, particularly final receiver B.

Communication Chain. There are several results on how to calculate an optimal communication chain. We refer to the approach of Claypool and Kannan [7], where the authors introduce the concept of *Selective Flooding* for improved *Quality-of-Service Routing*. This approach precomputes routes between all communication nodes, based on static "snapshots" of the topology, which resemble our traffic snapshots $\mathcal{TS}$. These precomputed routes are then stored in a routing table. Whenever one node requests a transitive communication link to another node, the optimal route between those nodes is estimated by flooding control packages through the precomputed routes. The authors furthermore propose a combination of Selective Flooding and *Source Routing* to cope with network topology changes, like moving cars in our case.

In our approach, we assume that whenever one car forwards the warning message, it listens on channel *hazard* if the next car in the communication chain really forwards the message in some time bound t_w. Therefore, the cars have to stay in communication range until the message is successfully forwarded. In [8], Satyajeet et al. present several methods for *Cluster-based Routing Protocols* in VANETs. In these hierarchical protocols, a *cluster head* is obligated to communicate with the other nodes in his cluster to maintain the cluster formation. Additionally, the authors describe how routes from a source to a destination node can be established via Cluster-based Routing Protocols, which again is interesting for generating our communication chain $\overrightarrow{c}$.

Broadcast Communication with Data Constraints. In Sect. 4, we present controllers for our hazard warning protocol modelled as extended timed automata [9]. One extension is the use of data variables and data constraints in guards, invariants and updates, as described by Behrmann et al. in [4] for UPPAAL. We broaden this use of data constraints in timed automata even more by sending data via our broadcast channel *hazard*.

Alrahman et al. propose a *Calculus for Attribute-based Communication* in [10]. The authors consider systems with a large amount of dynamically adjusting components that interact via broadcast channels. Components broadcast valuations of data variables u via an attribute-based output $(u)@\Pi$ to all processes whose attributes satisfy the predicate Π. By using updates $a := u$ of local attributes a, the received data u can be used locally by these processes, e.g. to determine if a predicate Π is satisfied. Other components only then synchronise with an output $(u)@\Pi$ when they have an input $\Pi(x)$ and their local attributes a, together with the received message x, satisfy the predicate Π. We use this concept of attribute-based broadcast synchronisation for the following definition of input and output actions for our later introduced controller.

For data types on our broadcast channels, we use the Z notation [11] of sequences: $seq\ X$ denotes the set of all finite sequences of elements from a given set X. A sequence s consisting of elements A, B, C is written as $s = \langle A, B, C\rangle$. It stands for a function $s = \{1 \mapsto A, 2 \mapsto B, 3 \mapsto C\}$ from indices $1, 2, 3$ to elements A, B, C. Thus the ith element of s is denoted by function application $s(i)$, e.g., $s(2) = B$. The *length* of s is denoted by $\#s$, here $\#s = 3$. For the empty sequence $\langle\rangle$ the length is 0.

Definition 3 (Input and Output actions). *For a finite list of data variables $d = \langle d_1, \ldots, d_n\rangle$ and a HMLSL formula φ we define an* output action OUT *on a broadcast channel a by $OUT := a!d$ and a related* input action IN *by $IN := a?d : \varphi$. The set of data variables $d_i \in \mathbb{D}$ ranges over the set of all car identifiers $\mathbb{I}$, the power set $\mathcal{P}(\mathbb{L})$ of the set of all lanes $\mathbb{L}$, and finite sequences from the sets $seq\ \mathbb{I}$ and $seq\ \mathbb{L}$.*

In Z notation, the function $head\ s$ returns the first element of a non-empty sequence s while the function $tail\ s$ returns the part that follows the first element of s, such that $s = \langle head\ s\rangle \frown tail\ s$. We add to this notation the function $second\ s$, which returns the second element of s for $|s| > 1$. With $s' := tail\ s$ and $second\ s = head\ s'$, this leads to $s = \langle head\ s\rangle \frown \langle second\ s\rangle \frown tail\ s'$.

Example. In the hazard warning controller later introduced, a warning message is sent via broadcast channel $hazard$. The corresponding output action is $hazard!\langle L_{\xi}, \overrightarrow{c}\rangle$, where L_{ξ} is the set of lanes affected by the hazard and $\overrightarrow{c}$ is the communication chain, comprising of unique car identifiers. With this output action the current values $\nu(L_{\xi})$ resp. $\nu(\overrightarrow{c})$ of these two data variables are sent over broadcast channel $hazard$.

For synchronisation with this output, consider a corresponding input action $hazard?\langle L, \overrightarrow{d}\rangle : head\ \overrightarrow{d} = ego$ in another automaton. There, we first store the received values in local variables L and $\overrightarrow{d}$, such that $\nu(L) = \nu(L_{\xi})$ and $\nu(\overrightarrow{d}) = \nu(\overrightarrow{c})$. This input action synchronises with the given output action only if the HMLSL formula $head\ \overrightarrow{d} = ego$ evaluates to true, that is, if the first element of the communicated chain $\nu(\overrightarrow{d}) = \nu(\overrightarrow{c})$ agrees with the value of ego.

4   Controller for Hazard Warning Protocol

In previous work [5] we showed that if every car on a highway is equipped with a distance and a lane change controller, safety in the sense of disjointedness of reservations is preserved under all time and action transitions. To express this property we use the somewhere operator:

$$Safe\text{-}re \;\equiv\; \neg \exists c, d : c \neq d \wedge \langle re(c) \wedge re(d) \rangle \,,$$

i.e., there is never any spatial overlap of the reservations of any two different cars. Here we focus on safety in the sense that there is never any spatial overlap of a reservation with a hazard. Formally,

$$Safe\text{-}hz \;\equiv\; \neg \exists c : \langle re(c) \wedge hz \rangle \,.$$

To check such properties while a car is driving, we need variants of these formulae from the viewpoint of a car *ego* in which such a controller is deployed. To maintain *Safe-re* under time transitions, each car has a *distance controller*. According to [6], such a controller keeps for each car *ego* the property

$$Safe\text{-}re(ego) \;\equiv\; \neg \exists c : c \neq ego \wedge \langle re(ego) \wedge re(c) \rangle$$

invariant under time transitions. Note that by demanding the disjointedness of (the speed-dependent) reserved spaces, *Safe-re(ego)* indirectly requires that car *ego* lowers its speed (to shorten its reserved space) when a car c ahead of *ego* starts breaking. This link between spatial and dynamic reasoning is formalised in [6].

In the hazard warning controllers proposed below we need the following variant of *Safe-hz* from the viewpoint of a car *ego*:

$$Safe\text{-}hz(ego) \;\equiv\; \neg \langle re(ego) \wedge hz \rangle \,,$$

i.e., there is never any spatial overlap of the reservation of car *ego* with a hazard. In the states of the controllers, we employ the invariant

$$\mathcal{I} \;\equiv\; b \rightarrow Safe\text{-}hz(ego),$$

where b is a Boolean variable that is set to the value true if the controller detects a hazard or receives a hazard warning message from another car. Informally, this means that whenever a car has knowledge about a hazard, it avoids colliding with it. Thus a kind of distance controller sensitive to hazards is part of the controllers. We prove in Sect. 6 with the assistance of UPPAAL that the hazard warning will arrive in time so that the car can react to it.

In [3], we introduced extended time automata, called *automotive-controlling timed automata* (ACTA), to formalise the mentioned lane change and distance controllers from [5]. Here, we formalise a *multi-hop communication protocol* by using ACTA to construct our hazard warning controllers. As variables, these controllers use both clock and data variables. For clock variables $x, y \in \mathbb{X}$ and clock updates we refer to the classical definition of timed automata from Alur and Dill [9] and for the use of data variables $d_i \in \mathbb{D}$ and data updates we refer to the extension of timed automata proposed for UPPAAL by Behrmann et al. [4]. These clock and data updates ν_{act} are allowed on transitions of the automata. Note that we allow for the same set of data variables $\mathbb{D}$ we introduced in Definition 3 for input and output actions.

Further on, the controllers use HMLSL formulae φ_ϕ as well as clock and data constraints φ_X resp. $\varphi_{\mathbb{D}}$ as guards φ on transitions and as invariants $I(q)$ in states q, such that the set Φ of all guards and invariants is defined by

$$\varphi \equiv \varphi_\phi \mid \varphi_X \mid \varphi_{\mathbb{D}} \mid \varphi_1 \wedge \varphi_2 \mid \mathit{true}.$$

Additionally, we use the broadcast communication with data structures as defined in previous Sect. 3. Remember that we consider output actions OUT which can synchronise with appropriate input actions IN in another controller. In related work [3, 5, 12], we also use *controller actions* c_{act} to commit lane change manoeuvres and turning manoeuvres at crossings. As our hazard warning controller focuses on timely message delivery, these manoeuvres and actions are not needed here, but we mention them here for completeness. A transition in an ACTA comprises the elements depicted in Fig. 2. The guard $\varphi \wedge IN$ shown before the separator / has to hold in the current traffic snapshot $\mathcal{TS}$, the standard view $V_S(E, \mathcal{TS})$ of car E under consideration and the valuation ν in order to execute the output, controller and update actions shown after the separator /, yielding a sucessor state q' and a valuation ν'. The invariant $I(q')$ has to hold in ν'.

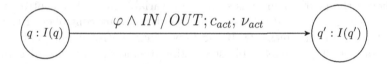

Fig. 2. Transition in an ACTA with communication

For the implementation of the multi-hop communication protocol, we assume every car to be equipped with two controllers. The first one is a *hazard detection controller* that detects the hazard, determines the communication chain, and sends the initial hazard warning message. The second controller is a *forwarding controller* that is used to forward the message to all cars in reach of its communication antenna. In order to send a hazard warning message, we use the broadcast channel *hazard* to send and receive hazard warnings as described in Sect. 3. In the following, we will refer to the initial sender as car A and to the final receiver as car B.

In timed automata, transitions are taken immediately if guards and invariants allow it. For the sake of reality, we assume a communication not to happen immediately, but to take some positive upper time bound $t_c > 0$ to take hardware limitations into account. We assume all cars are equipped with the same communication technology and therefore use the same time bound t_c for all cars.

Hazard Detection Controller. If the HMLSL formula $\langle re(ego) \rangle \frown \langle hz \rangle$ evaluates to *true*, the *hazard detection controller of initial sender* A initiates the sending of the hazard warning message by changing from its initial state q_0 to q_1. While doing so, A determines the set of affected lanes using the function *affected_lanes*() and stores them in a set named L_{ℓ}. By definition of our abstract model, we have *affected_lanes*() = *haz.lanes* (cf. Sect. 2). On the same transition, an optimal communication chain is calculated with the function *comm_chain*() and stored in $\vec{c}$. For details about deriving the communication chain we again refer to Sect. 3. The derived communication chain contains the car identifier A of initial sender as first entry and the car identifier B of final receiver as last entry. If we cannot establish a communication chain, *comm_chain*() returns $\vec{c} = \langle A \rangle$ and the controller changes back to its initial state, because there is no car to warn in reach ($\#\vec{c} \leq 1$).

We remember whether a warning message was already sent, by setting the value of a Boolean control variable b to *true*. With this we avoid unlimited resending of the warning message and thus unnecessary flooding of channel *hazard*. As soon as the hazard is detected, until the next car in the communication chain forwards the warning message, initial sender A is obligated to maintain the communication link to the next car in chain $\vec{c}$.

After t_c time units, the hazard detection controller sends the initial warning message to the next car in $\vec{c}$ over broadcast channel *hazard*, along with the affected lanes L_{ℓ} and the communication chain $\vec{c}$ and changes to state q_2. The identifier of the next car in $\vec{c}$ is stored in a variable *next*. The controller then listens on channel *hazard* to ensure that the forwarding controller of the next car really resends the message. If the forwarding controller does not forward the message within a (reasonable short) time bound t_w, the hazard detection controller changes back to state q_1 and repeats the warning message. Note that one could implement a continuous warning message sending – as proposed for common *decentralised environmental notification messages* – by assuming a time bound $t_w = 0$ (cf. ETSI standard 102 637-3 [13]).

If the controller receives the forwarded message from the next car in $\vec{c}$, the warning was successful and it changes back to its initial state q_0. The constructed hazard detection controller $\mathcal{A}_{det}$ is depicted in Fig. 3.

Forwarding Controller. The forwarding controller copies part of the behaviour of the hazard detection controller. The main difference is the transition from r_0 to r_1, where the forwarding controller does not detect a hazard, but listens on channel *hazard* whether a hazard warning message is forwarded. If a warning message is received, the forwarding controller of a car synchronises with the sender only if its car identifier is the second entry in the communication chain. With this behaviour we prevent that every car that listens on channel *hazard* resends the warning message.

If a car is second in the communication chain $\vec{c}$, the forwarding controller synchronises with the sender. Furthermore, we remove the first element of the communication chain $\vec{c}$, so that the car identifier of the active forwarding controller now is the first element of the resulting shortened communication chain

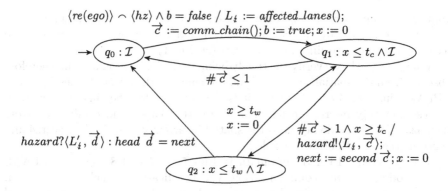

Fig. 3. Hazard detection controller $\mathcal{A}_{det}$.

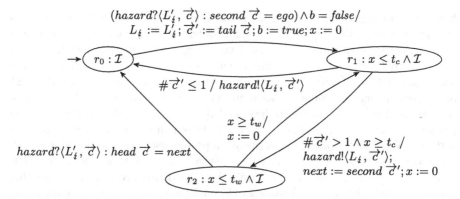

Fig. 4. Forwarding controller $\mathcal{A}_{for}$.

$\overrightarrow{c}' = tail\ \overrightarrow{c}$. If $\overrightarrow{c}'$ contains more than one element, the forwarding controller sends the new communication chain via channel *hazard*. The following behaviour is the same as that from the hazard detection controller; the forwarding controller listens whether the next car in chain again forwards the warning. The constructed forwarding controller $\mathcal{A}_{for}$ is depicted in Fig. 4.

Provided in the newly derived communication chain only contains the identifier of the current car ($\#\overrightarrow{c}' \leq 1$), the controller confirms that the message was delivered and changes back to the initial state. Note that this is only the case if the current car is the final receiver.

5   Implementation in UPPAAL

For our implementation in UPPAAL we conduct the following two adaptions of our hazard detection controller $\mathcal{A}_{det}$ and forwarding controller $\mathcal{A}_{for}$ to the type of extended timed automata UPPAAL uses. We distinguish these adapted automata from the controllers introduced in Sect. 4 by writing Detection

Controller and **Forwarding Controller**. As before, we name the first car to perceive the hazard by the car identifier A and the car which is supposed to receive the timely warning message by B (cf. Fig. 1).

With UPPAAL, we verify the timely behaviour of our automata and therefore abstract from the spatial aspects. We do not consider the affected lanes $L_{\dot{\ell}}$ in our UPPAAL implementation because it is not relevant for the timely forwarding process and only interesting for manoeuvres that cars could conduct to avoid the hazard. Also, we do not need the spatial invariant $\mathcal{I}$ described in Sect. 4 and hence neither the Boolean variable b.

The depicted UPPAAL automata in Figs. 5, 6, 7 and 8 use the UPPAAL colour coding, where communication via broadcast channels is shown in turquoise, guards are depicted in green, updates in blue, and state names and invariants in purple.

Setting and Results. In our implementation, we successfully performed several system executions with N cars for different values for N ranging over $2 \leq N \leq 100$. Following [2] our goal was that a warning message from A is delivered to B in at most t time units, where $t = 100$, as proposed there. In the simulation with UPPAAL each car i owns a Detection Controller **Detection(i)** and a Forwarding Controller **Forwarding(i)**. Additionally, we introduce an environment and two observer controllers needed for the verification in the following paragraphs. The overall number of UPPAAL timed automata for every execution is thus $2 \cdot N + 3$. Every one of the verification properties later introduced was each checked in less than 0.1 s with a memory usage peak each time less than 85 KB on a normal work station. Note that only those automata are actively interacting with each other the through broadcast channel $hazard$ that are neighbouring in the communication chain $\overrightarrow{c}$ (e.g., the fourteenth car in $\overrightarrow{c}$ is only answering a forwarding request from the thirteenth car). In the following paragraphs, we explain the adaptions of our controllers to UPPAAL and the additional controllers needed for the verification as well as the verification properties.

HMLSL Formulae. The hazard detection controller (cf. Fig. 3) is using the HMLSL formula $\langle re(ego) \rangle \frown \langle hz \rangle$ as a guard at the transition from q_0 to q_1. Instead of using an HMLSL formula – which is not available in UPPAAL – for hazard detection, we introduce an additional automaton **Environment** that places and removes hazards. On placing a hazard, the Environment informs controllers via a broadcast channel att(ention) about the existence of a hazard and additionally sets **init_id** $= A$. Initially, all Detection Controllers are in state q_0 and listen on channel att. As every of those Controllers additionally checks the guard **id == init_id**, only the **Detection Controller** of initial sender A synchronises with this output. The resulting **Detection Controller** for the implementation in UPPAAL is depicted in Fig. 5.

Sending Data over Channels. Sending data over channels is not provided by UPPAAL, therefore we cannot pass our communication chain from car to car. But a distinction between local variables, only accessible and changeable by

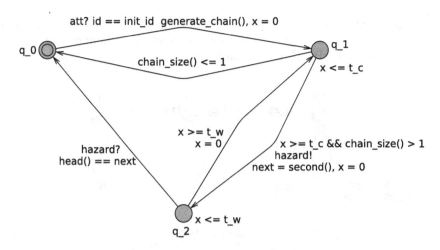

Fig. 5. Adapted `Detection Controller` for implementation in UPPAAL. (Color figure online)

one specific automaton, and global variables, accessible and changeable by all automata in the system, is available. However, by using a global variable for the communication chain $\vec{c}$, we have to restrict access to it.

Consider again the forwarding controller from Fig. 4. On sending a hazard warning (transition from state r_1 to r_2), the controller remembers the second element of $\vec{c}$ in a local variable $next$. The controller in the next car in $\vec{c}$ synchronises with this output (transition from its state r_0 to r_1), and removes the head of $\vec{c}$ on the same transition with the function $tail\ \vec{c}$. This is consistent with our definition of data sending, because only a local version $\vec{c}'$ of $\vec{c}$ is shortened and sent later. With a global communication chain $next$ would be probably valuated with the wrong element, because write and read access for $\vec{c}$ is uncontrolled.

We overcome this problem in our `Forwarding Controller` by simply separating the use of the function $tail\ \vec{c}$ from the transition from r_0 to r_1 and introducing a new intermediate state r_{im} between r_0 and r_1. The state r_{im} is committed, so no interleaving transitions from any other automata is allowed until r_{im} was left. On the transition from r_{im} to r_1, the global communication chain is shortened. Since no synchronisation happens on this transition, there is no read access on the global communication chain at the same time.

Note that besides the initial generation of $\vec{c}$ in the first Detection Controller through function $generate\_chain()$, only the function $tail()$ manipulates the communication chain, by removing its first element. The functions $head()$, $second()$ and $chain\_size()$ only return the respective elements or the current size of $\vec{c}$.

Because of the committed state r_{im}, the special case where the current forwarding controller is located in final receiver B, and thus $\#\vec{c} \leq 1$, is handled slightly differently in our UPPAAL implementation. Particularly no transition from r_1 to r_0 exists, but the behaviour of that transition is implemented within the internal data structure of $\overrightarrow{c}$. The adapted Forwarding Controller for the implementation in UPPAAL is given in Fig. 6.

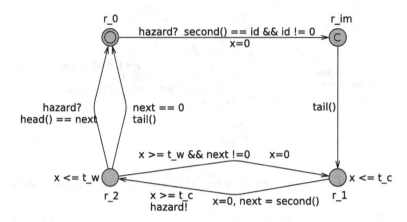

Fig. 6. Adapted Forwarding Controller with additional committed state r_{im}. (Color figure online)

Verification. We pursue two verification goals with UPPAAL. For each of them we introduce automata Observer1 resp. Observer2. Remember that the overall goal of our approach is a hazard warning message delivery before the final receiver B reaches the hazard after t time units and that we assume one single communication to take t_c time units.

Following [2], we set $t := 100$ and assume one communication to take $t_c := 1$ time units due to hardware restrictions (cf. Sect. 4). With these assumptions, the hazard warning is supposed to be timely delivered if at most $N = 100$ cars are considered for the communication chain and the warning delivery is finished before t time units. This fits the maximal amount of cars that were used in the simulation in [2].

Observer1. This Observer checks the end-to-end latency of the warning delivery between the first and the last car in the communication chain. The time bound t introduced in Sect. 1 we use as a failure time bound in Observer1. If t is exceeded, Observer1 changes to a distinct bad state Observer1.fail and our timely message delivery verification goal is missed. Observer1 monitors the following three events in the given order:

1. The environment places a hazard (change to state Observer1.hz_on).
2. The detection controller of the initial sender (first element in $\overrightarrow{c}$) sends the initial warning message (change to state Observer1.warning_sent).
3. The forwarding controller of the final receiver (last element in $\overrightarrow{c}$) confirms that it received the warning message (change to state Observer1.warning_received).

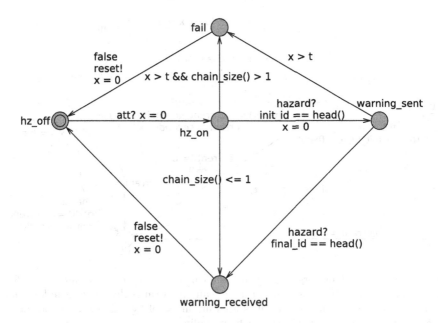

Fig. 7. Observer1 monitors that when initial sender A forwards the hazard warning, car B finally receives the message in less than t time units, where t is the time in which car B would arrive at the hazard and our timely warning goal would be missed. (Color figure online)

Observer1 enters Observer1.fail if either 2. does not occur in less than t time units, or if 2. occurred timely, but 3. was not reached in less than t time units. This would be the case if final receiver reaches the hazard without receiving a warning. Observer1 is depicted in Fig. 7. For Observer1 we verified the following requirements with UPPAAL for $N \leq 100$, where -> is the leads-to operator in the logic of UPPAAL.

Unreachability of fail I: A[] not Observer1.fail
Liveness I: Observer1.hz_on ->
  (Observer1.warning_sent or chain_size <= 1))
Liveness II: Observer1.warning_sent ->
  (Observer1.warning_received and Observer1.x <= t)

Observer2. This Observer checks the timely forwarding of the hazard warning between two consecutive cars in the communication chain. In Observer2 we use the time bound t_c for one single communication as failure time bound. If a communication is not resent in less than t_c time units, the bad state Observer2.fail is entered. The automaton monitors the following three events in the given order:

1. Wait for a hazard warning (by idling in state Observer2.wait).
2. A hazard warning of an arbitrary forwarding controller n is received (change to state Observer2.listening).
3. Forwarding controller $n + 1$ forwarded the warning (change to state Observer2.success).

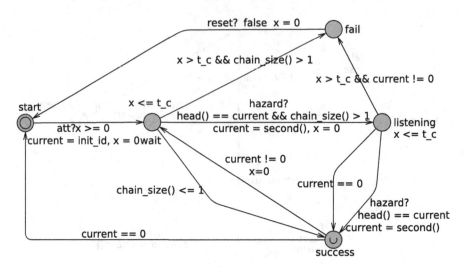

Fig. 8. Observer 2 monitors that whenever a car in the communication chain $\overrightarrow{c}$ forwards a warning message, the next car in $\overrightarrow{c}$ really reforwards this message in less than t_c time units. This verification result is used in our proof by induction for the timely hazard warning safety property. (Color figure online)

Note that Observer2 monitors not only one hazard warning, but listens if every single warning itself is resent timely by the next automaton in communication chain $\overrightarrow{c}$. We use this timed liveness property later in our inductive proof in Sect. 6.1. The fail state Observer2.fail is entered, if a single communication is not forwarded in less than t_c time units.

We consider the last forwarding as a special case: If forwarding controller $n + 1$ belongs to the last car B in $\overrightarrow{c}$, Observer2 does not change back to Observer2.wait, because not further forwarding messages will occur. Observer2 is depicted in Fig. 8. For Observer2 we verified the following requirements with UPPAAL for $N \leq 100$:

Unreachability of fail II: A[] not Observer2.fail
Liveness III: Observer2.wait -> Observer2.success

We use the verification results of our implementation in UPPAAL to prove the timely message propagation in the following Section.

6 Hazard Safety

In this section we stipulate that every car is equipped with a hazard detection controller $\mathcal{A}_{det}$ and a forwarding controller $\mathcal{A}_{for}$ as introduced in Sect. 4. We now prove that warned cars do not collide with the hazard. We divide the safety proof into two steps.

First, we show a timing property: whenever a hazard is detected by a car A, the final receiver B in a communication chain from A to B is warned within some time bound depending on the length of the chain. This proof is supported by the model checker UPPAAL. Second, we link the timing property to a spatial property: when the established time bound is below the time it takes car B to reach the hazard then we can guarantee hazard safety of B in the sense that it satisfies the spatial property

$$Safe\text{-}hz(ego) \equiv \neg \langle re(ego) \wedge hz \rangle,$$

i.e., the reserved space of B does not overlap with the hazard.

6.1   Timely Hazard Warning Message Propagation

We begin with the timing property.

Theorem 1 (Timely warning). *Suppose a communication chain $\vec{c} = \langle A, \ldots, B \rangle$ of length $N \geq 2$ is built up after a hazard detection by the initial car $\vec{c}(1) = A$ in the chain. Then a hazard warning is received by the final car $\vec{c}(N) = B$ in the chain within $(N-1) \cdot t_c$ time after it has occurred.*

Proof. We show by induction over i that

(∗) for every $i \in \{1, \ldots, N\}$ a hazard warning is detected or received by car $\vec{c}(i)$ within $(i-1) \cdot t_c$ time after it has occurred, and if $i < N$ holds, the hazard warning is forwarded to car $\vec{c}(i+1)$ at most t_c time later.

Induction basis: $i = 1$. By construction of $\mathcal{A}_{det}$, the initial car $\vec{c}(1) = A$ senses the hazard immediately, i.e., within 0 time after it has occurred, and forwards it to $\vec{c}(2)$ at most t_c time later.

Induction step: $i \to i+1$, where $i+1 \leq N$. By induction hypothesis, the hazard warning is received by car $\vec{c}(i)$ within $(i-1) \cdot t_c$ time after it has occurred, and car $\vec{c}(i)$ forwards it at most t_c time later. This communication is instantaneously received by the next car $\vec{c}(i+1)$ in the chain. Thus altogether the hazard warning is received by car $\vec{c}(i+1)$ within $i \cdot t_c$ time after it has occurred. By construction of $\mathcal{A}_{for}$, if $i+1 < N$ holds, car $\vec{c}(i+1)$ forwards the hazard warning at most t_c time later.

We checked the induction step for fixed values in our implementation of the controllers with UPPAAL. We refer to Observer2 which monitors the properties **Unreachability of fail II** and **Liveness III** (cf. Sect. 5). There we showed for a communication chain $\vec{c}$ with $N = 100$ and a fixed constant t_c that if an arbitrary car $\vec{c}(i)$ with $i < N$ receives a warning message, this message is really resent to the next car $\vec{c}(i+1)$ and that this communication takes less than t_c time units: The state Observer2.fail is entered, iff one single communication exceeds t_c time units. Unreachability of Observer2.fail proves that indeed no single communication exceeds t_c time units. The property **Liveness III** verifies that whenever an arbitrary element $\vec{c}(i)$ receives a warning, it is successfully forwarded to $\vec{c}(i+1)$.

As we can only verify our properties in UPPAAL for a fixed and finite amount of cars N, a forwarding exception is the special case $\vec{c}(N) = B$, where B is the final receiver and therefore last element in $\overrightarrow{c}$. In this case, the message is not forwarded, because the communication goal is reached. From $(*)$ the statement of the theorem follows. $\square$

As described, for the induction step we used the properties monitored by Observer2, which observes if one single timely message forwarding process from an arbitrary car $\overrightarrow{c}(i)$ to the next car $\overrightarrow{c}(i+1)$ is successful. Additionally to that, we derived interesting verification results from Observer1, which monitors the overall timely message sending from initial sender A to final receiver B. In several iterations, we showed for various values of N with $2 \le N \le 100$ that a warning message from A indeed is delivered to B in at most t time units, where again $t = 100$, as proposed in [2]. With Observer1, the property **Liveness I** verifies that if A has knowledge of the hazard, it actually sends the initial warning and **Liveness II** verifies that message is finally received by B. **Unreachability of fail I** shows that the overall message sending happens in at most t time units.

6.2   Avoidance of Hazard Collisions

We now turn to the spatial property. For the following safety theorem, we state the following assumptions:

A1. $\mathcal{TS}_0$ is the traffic snapshot where the hazard first occurred. In $\mathcal{TS}_0$ all cars satisfy the property *Safe-hz*.

A2. Car A is closest to the hazard and detects it in $\mathcal{TS}_0$, thereby building up a communication chain $\overrightarrow{c} = \langle A, \dots, B \rangle$ of length $N \ge 2$ to car B.

A3. Car B needs t time to reach the hazard and during this time it satisfies the property *Safe-hz*.

A4. For the time bound t_c used in the controllers $\mathcal{A}_{det}$ and $\mathcal{A}_{for}$ the inequality $(N-1) \cdot t_c \le t$ holds.

Theorem 2 (Hazard safety). *Suppose the assumptions* **A1–A4** *hold. Then in every traffic snapshot* $\mathcal{TS}^*$ *that is reachable from* $\mathcal{TS}_0$ *via time transitions car B satisfies the property Safe-hz(ego) (under the valuation $\nu(ego) = B$).*

Proof. Note that by **A2**, Theorem 1 is applicable. Let $\mathcal{TS}^*$ be reachable from $\mathcal{TS}_0$ via time transitions. Then $\mathcal{TS}_0 \xrightarrow{t^*} \mathcal{TS}^*$ for some time $t^* \in \mathbb{R}_{\ge 0}$. If in $\mathcal{TS}^*$ car B has not yet received the hazard warning sent by car A via the communication chain $\overrightarrow{c}$, we know by Theorem 1 and **A4** that $t^* < (N-1) \cdot t_c \le t$ holds. Thus by **A3**, car B satisfies *Safe-hz(ego)* in $\mathcal{TS}^*$.

If in $\mathcal{TS}^*$ car B has received the hazard warning via its controller $\mathcal{A}_{for}$, this controller guarantees *Safe-hz(ego)* from the moment on that the hazard warning has first been received by B, say in the traffic snapshot $\mathcal{TS}_1$. Thus we can split the time t^* into $t^* = t_1 + t_2$ such that

$$\mathcal{TS}_0 \xrightarrow{t_1} \mathcal{TS}_1 \xrightarrow{t_2} \mathcal{TS}^*,$$

where $t_1 \le (N-1) \cdot t_c \le t$ due to Theorem 1 and **A4**. Then car B satisfies *Safe-hz(ego)* in $\mathcal{TS}^*$ by the invariant of its controller $\mathcal{A}_{for}$. $\square$

By a similar argument, we can extend the above theorem and show that every car in the communication chain $\overrightarrow{c}$ satisfies the property $Safe\text{-}hz(ego)$.

7   Conclusion

In this paper, we formalised the timing aspects of the simulation-based analysis of a communication protocol for timely traffic hazard warning to other traffic participants in [2] by using extended timed automata, called automotive-controlling timed automata (ACTA) [3]. Using this formalisation we prove the timely warning property, partly supported by the model checker UPPAAL [4].

Also, we linked the timely warning property with spatial reasoning to prove avoidance of hazard collision using a new extension of the Multi-lane Spatial Logic MLSL [5] dealing with hazards, called HMLSL. Formulae of this logic appear in the guards and invariants of ACTA to establish the desired spatial safety properties. Using (H)MLSL we abstract from the underlying car dynamics [6].

Future Work. So far, we only prove hazard safety for the cars in communication chain $\overrightarrow{c}$, because only those synchronise with a hazard warning (cf. transition in $\mathcal{A}_{for}$ from r_0 to r_1). However, with our broadcast communication we can also reach all other cars not involved in the communication chain.

We therefore assume the communication radius r to stretch over all lanes $\mathbb{L}$ and to have a positive extension along the lanes. For formalisation, we refer to the definition of a view from Sect. 2.1, as the communication radius of a car can be considered to be a *communication view*. Only cars inside the communication view of a warning car C can synchronise with C.

For cars outside $\overrightarrow{c}$ to synchronise with a warning in their communication view, we add a transition in the forwarding controller $\mathcal{A}_{for}$. The new transition leads from initial state r_0 to a new state r_4, where the invariant $\mathcal{I}$ is required to hold (cf. Sect. 4). The new transition gets the guard

$$(hazard?\langle L_4, \overrightarrow{c}\rangle : not\text{-}element(\overrightarrow{c}, ego) \wedge b = false$$

and the variable update $b := true$. The function $not\text{-}element(\overrightarrow{c}, ego)$ evaluates to true if the car identifier that ego evaluate to is not included in $\overrightarrow{c}$.

In this paper, we consider timely hazard warnings for highway traffic scenarios. In [3,12], we considered traffic safety on country roads with oncoming traffic and in urban traffic scenarios at intersections. A linkage of our hazard warning approach with these scenarios is highly possible for future work.

Acknowledgements. We thank two anonymous reviewers for their helpful comments.

References

1. Figueiredo, L., Jesus, I., Machado, J., Ferreira, J., de Carvalho, J.M.: Towards the development of intelligent transportation systems. Intell. Transp. Syst. **88**, 1206–1211 (2001)

2. Müllner, N., Fränzle, M., Fröschle, S.: Estimating the probability of a timely traffic-hazard warning via simulation. In: Proceedings of the 48th Annual Simulation Symposium (ANSS), pp. 130–137. Society for Computer Simulation International, San Diego (2015)

3. Hilscher, M., Schwammberger, M.: An abstract model for proving safety of autonomous urban traffic. In: Sampaio, A., Wang, F. (eds.) ICTAC 2016. LNCS, vol. 9965, pp. 274–292. Springer, Cham (2016). doi:10.1007/978-3-319-46750-4_16

4. Behrmann, G., David, A., Larsen, K.G.: A tutorial on UPPAAL. In: Bernardo, M., Corradini, F. (eds.) SFM-RT 2004. LNCS, vol. 3185, pp. 200–236. Springer, Heidelberg (2004). doi:10.1007/978-3-540-30080-9_7

5. Hilscher, M., Linker, S., Olderog, E.-R., Ravn, A.P.: An abstract model for proving safety of multi-lane traffic manoeuvres. In: Qin, S., Qiu, Z. (eds.) ICFEM 2011. LNCS, vol. 6991, pp. 404–419. Springer, Heidelberg (2011). doi:10.1007/978-3-642-24559-6_28

6. Olderog, E.-R., Ravn, A.P., Wisniewski, R.: Linking discrete and continuous models, applied to traffic manoeuvrers. In: Hinchey, M.G., Bowen, J.P., Olderog, E.-R. (eds.) Provably Correct Systems. NMSSE, pp. 95–120. Springer, Cham (2017). doi:10.1007/978-3-319-48628-4_5

7. Claypool, M., Kannan, G.: Selective flooding for improved quality-of-service routing. In: ITCom 2001: International Symposium on the Convergence of IT and Communications, pp. 33–44. International Society for Optics and Photonics (2001)

8. Satyajeet, D., Deshmukh, A.R., Dorle, S.S.: Article: heterogeneous approaches for cluster based routing protocol in vehicular ad hoc network (VANET). Int. J. Comput. Appl. **134**, 1–8 (2016)

9. Alur, R., Dill, D.: A theory of timed automata. TCS **126**, 183–235 (1994)

10. Alrahman, Y.A., De Nicola, R., Loreti, M., Tiezzi, F., Vigo, R.: A calculus for attribute-based communication. In: Proceedings of the 30th Annual ACM Symposium on Applied Computing (SAC), pp. 1840–1845. ACM (2015)

11. Woodcock, J., Davies, J.: Using Z - Specification, Refinement, and Proof. Prentice Hall, Upper Saddle River (1996)

12. Hilscher, M., Linker, S., Olderog, E.-R.: Proving safety of traffic manoeuvres on country roads. In: Liu, Z., Woodcock, J., Zhu, H. (eds.) Theories of Programming and Formal Methods. LNCS, vol. 8051, pp. 196–212. Springer, Heidelberg (2013). doi:10.1007/978-3-642-39698-4_12

13. ETSI: Intelligent Transport Systems (ITS); Vehicular Communications; Basic Set of Applications; Part 3: Specifications of Decentralized Environmental Notification Basic Service (ETSI TS 102 637-3 V1.1.1) (2010)

Author Index

Printed in the United States
By Bookmasters